By the same author

A Secret Between Gentlemen: Suspects, Strays And Guests. (Vol II)

A Secret Between Gentlemen: Faith & Desire. (Vol III)

As editor

The Dead Past by Sir Edmund Trelawny Backhouse.

A Secret Between Gentlemen

Volume I

Lord Battersea's hidden scandal
and the lives it changed forever.

Peter Jordaan

ΔLCHEMIE

For my mother, brothers, and friends, for their love and support.

And to the memory of Damien Luke Lorrain.

CONTENTS

Acknowledgements 7
Preface 13
Prologue 17

I. The Realm That Was 27

1 The New Reign 29
2 The Way Of The World 59
3 Noble Decadence 79
4 The Other World 110
5 Them And Us 161
6 The Age Of Blackmail 182
7 Naples 1897 191

Images

II. Hidden Scandal 205

8 Careless Passion 207
9 A Serious Question Of Public Policy 220
10 Fearsome Charges 225
11 The Worst Offences Known To Law 230
12 A Most Painful Case 239
13 The Air Is Electric 252

Images

III. This Strange Journey Called Life 285

14 The Most Handsome Man In Parliament 287
15 The Elusive Mister W 460
16 A Swordsman Of His Holiness 491
17 An Ideal English Gentleman 504
18 A Laird Most Rich And Powerful 573
19 Jewels 634
Envoi 671

Appendices 703

Battersea Case Timeline 705
Select Bibliography 706
Image Credits 709
Sources 711
Index 797

Truth will out.

– *The Merchant Of Venice* (1596), William Shakespeare.

ACKNOWLEDGEMENTS

Researching and writing *A Secret Between Gentlemen* was an engrossing adventure. Yet writing any book, particularly one such as this, can occasionally be a lonely and doubting business, so I am enormously grateful for the uplifting kindness, assistance, understanding, encouragement, good humour, and not least — trust, which came my way. I am indebted to the following people:

Australia: First and foremost, I wish to thank John H. Day A.M., former Headmaster of The Southport School, for his invaluable thesis on Charles Thorold; his generous sharing of additional information, and his encouragement and support, without which this book would be so much the lesser. I also thank Ruth Dunn, née Thorold (a grand-daughter of Charles Thorold) for her sharing of family memories, and coming to the rescue in identifying the young Charles within a vast group photo; the unstintingly helpful Debbie Turner of The Southport School Archives; Morwenna Pearce, Barker College Archives; Peter Newton, Mentone Grammar Archives, and Suzanne Ashley, Alumni Manager, for permission to use the photograph of Jeffery Thorold; Caitlin McConnel; Cameron Hazlehurst; Melanie Oppenheimer; Andrea Hurt, Baillieu Library; Martyn Smith; Barbara Petersen; the ever-patient Judy Ingram for her design assistance; Sherri McIver and my brother Kim, for their reading of the manuscript and suggestions; and not least, George Collings, for the gift of his friendship and support.

Austria: Erwin Strouhal and Eva Smekal, Musik und Kunst Privatuniversität der Stadt Wien; Martin Feurstein, Gemeindeamt, Au; Birgitt Humpeler, Vorarlberger Landesbibliothek; Thomas

7

Klagian, Stadtarchiv der Landeshauptstadt Bregenz.

Canada: Kate Barlow, Michael H. Kater, Simon Stern.

France: Elizabeth Cauchois, Saïd Bellakhdar, Hubert Cottin, Etienne de Kergariou, Goulven de Kergariou; Sylvain Manville, Mission des Archives de France, Ministère de l'Intérieur; Laëtitia Picand, Centre de Documentation de la Musique Contemporaine; Louis Absil, Conseil International de la Musique; Y. Grondin, Archives de la Préfecture de Police, Paris; Serge Drouot, Commission Mémoire-Histoire Guerre d'Algérie; Emilie Charrier, le département Justice et Intérieur des Archives Nationales; Sylvain Manville, Conservateur de patrimoine, Chef de la Mission des Archives de France, Ministère de l'Intérior.

Germany: James Conway, Jean-Claude Kuner, Beatrix van Ooyen, Barbara Hauck; Michael Schelter, Bundesarchiv; Christina Kunkel, Institut für Zeitgeschichte, Munich.

Ireland: Desmond McCabe.

Italy: Rosario Lentini, Giovanna Fiume; Beatrice Palmigiano Gozzo, Arianna Cona, Fondazione Salvare Palermo.

Norway: Nils Axel Nissen.

Sweden: Göran Mörner, Riddarhuset, Stockholm.

Switzerland: The Duke of Bronte the Viscount Bridport and the Hon. Peregrine Hood, including for sharing the unpublished memoirs of Sir Alexander Hood.

United Kingdom: I am especially indebted to Sara Flower (a great-grand-daughter of Lord Battersea's brother Arthur Flower), who shared family memories and the Visitors Book of The Pleasaunce, which proved invaluable; Charles Flower (a great-grandson of Arthur Flower) for family photographs; the late Susan Boag, née Fraser (a great-grand-daughter of Colonel Henry Francis Fraser), and her husband David Boag who drove 150 miles to meet with me, and who shared family photographs and information; Valerie Hart, formerly of the Guildhall Library, whose Sherlockian skills uncovered crucial information; Glenn Chandler for his insights, encouragement, research on my behalf, for pointing me in the right direction with Commander Hutchinson, and for his book *The Sins Of Jack Saul*; and Timothy d'Arch Smith for his peerless knowledge of fin de siècle byways. I also thank Jill Hares of The Pleasaunce, and also manager Jillian Orme, who treated me to a private tour on a glorious autumn day.

I am also very grateful to Sir Oliver Thorold, Bart., and John and Elizabeth Thorold, for family information and photographs; Sir Julian Seymour and his late godmother Virginia Johnstone (a granddaughter of Arthur Flower); Martin Spychal for his research on Lord Ronald Gower and scholarly generosity; Emma Goodrum, Archivist, Worcester College, Oxford, for helping further unravel the mysteries of Arthur Thorold's university career; Mark Bainbridge, Librarian, Worcester College for unearthing a photo; Nicolas Bell for assistance with barely decipherable handwriting; the Duke of Argyll and Alison Diamond, Argyll Estates Archives; the Duke of Devonshire and James Towe, Chatsworth Archives; the Duke of Fife; the Earl of Sandwich; the Earl of Portsmouth and Viscount Lymington; the Hon. Robert Montagu, and Pippa Wright; the late 4th Earl of Selborne; Earl Spencer and Annie Kemkaran-Smith; Lord Carrington; Lord Hollenden; Lord Latymer; Lord Lexden; Lord Suffield and Sam Harbord-Hamond; the Hon. Matthew Brett; Julie Crocker and Bill Stockting, Royal Archives; Samantha Blake, BBC Archives; Marcus Budgen, Spink & Son; Kathryn Adamson, Amy Foster, Ilse Woloszko, Royal Academy of Music; Ann Martin and colleagues, Guildhall Library; Peter Horton, Royal College of Music; Heather Roberts, Royal Northern College of Music; Janet Portman, Adrian Shindler, Jeff Kattenhorn, Zoe Stansell, and Karen Waddell, The British Library; Erik Lundberg, Wardlaw Mausoleum Trust; George Smith, Norton College (Worcester); Julie Thompson, Norton College (Yorkshire); Tracey McKay, BBC Enquiries Team; Angie Mew, Southampton City Council; Alice Walsh, National Museum of the Royal Navy; Andrew Tullis, Martin Salmon, National Maritime Museum; Hugh Turner, Friends of H.M. Trincomalee; Amy Bruce, The Crown Prosecution Service; Florence Rees, A.M. Heath; Paul Holden and Ginnie Clotworthy, Lanhydrock House; Sarah Davis and Alison Mussell, Shropshire Archives; Alistair Murphy, Cromer Museum; Saraid Jones, Attingham Park; David Thomas, Cornwall Records Office; Flora Chatt, Oxford University Archives; Amy

Boylan, Balliol College Library; Isabel Robinson, Archives & Special Collections, Exeter College, Oxford; Adrienne Sharpe-Weseman, Beinecke Rare Book and Manuscript Library; Chris Nathan, Archivist, St. Edward's School; Siân Mogridge, Royal Artillery Museum; Lucy and Jonathan Chenevix-Trench, and Helen Vose, Madresfield Court; Martin Deacon, Bedfordshire Archives; Steven Gunn, Merton College, Oxford; Verity Parkinson and Julian Reid, Merton College Library; Judith Curthoys, Christ Church College, Oxford; Richard Ward, Parliamentary Archives; Amy Todman, Archives & Manuscript Collections, National Library of Scotland; Hannah Williams, Suffolk Archives; Gemma Pardue, Ipswich Archives; Nicholas Robinson, Fitzwilliam Museum; Joyce Field, Leigh & District Historical Society; Molly Archer-Zeff for her research assistance with the Rev. R.C. Fillingham's diaries; the ever-helpful William P. Cross; Amber K. Regis; Rictor Norton; Tessa Murdoch (great-granddaughter of Sir Carl Meyer) and Sir Ashley Meyer; Colin Harris, Weston Library; Martin Brayne & Katharine Solomon, Parson Woodforde Society; Robin Harcourt Williams, Archives, Hatfield House; Edward Wortley, Archives, Euston Hall; Sophie Bridges, Heidi Egginton, Churchill Archives Centre; Sarah Hepworth, University of Glasgow Library; Emily Hicks, Martin Grier, Bridport Museum Trust; Jonathan Smith, Adam Green, Trinity College Library, Cambridge; Patricia McGuire, Kings College, Cambridge; Michelle Barnes, Cambridge University Library; Philip Ward-Jackson; Lauren Alderton, Royal Institute of British Architects; Adam Waterton, Royal Academy; Gil Newman, Hastings Library; Oliver House, Sophie Littlewood, Collections, Welbeck Abbey; Charlotte Berry, Magdalen College; Mogg Morgan of Mandrake Of Oxford; Darryl Lundy of ThePeerage.com; Carl Buck of International Autograph Auctions; Martin Levy, Special Collections, University of Bradford; Richard Temple, Senate House Library, University of London; Tony Trowles, Head of the Abbey Collection and Librarian, Westminster Abbey; Lesley Edwards, Archives, Lancing College; David Roper-Curzon; Allan Downend and Keith Cavers, E.F. Benson Society; Glenn Mitchell, Peter Harrington Ltd; Oliver Hawkins, Simon J Roberts, Michael Meadowcroft, National Liberal Club; Steve Cattell, Hougham and Marston Local History Group; James Stevens Curl, Rev. Stuart Hadley, Liz Naeem, Peter Straker-Smith; Tricia Whiteaway, Dawlish History Group; Jane Ridley, including for her biography of Edward VII; Laurel, Lady Walpole; Clive Emsley; Frank Bowles, Cambridge University Library; Terry

Thomas, Leeds Beckett University; Sally Bate, The Gardens Trust; Jehanne Wake, Benjamin Chubb, Richard Barton, Harry Cocks, the late John Russell Vincent and Nicolette Vincent, Andrew Lownie, Paul Attinello, Grevel Lindop, Janet Howarth, Patrick Kearney, Alan Montefiore, Trevor Marriott, Leo McKinstry, Harland Walshaw, Ben Roberts, Andrew Roberts, Malcolm Shifrin, Peter Bance, Matthew Sturgis, James Yorke, Antony Lentin, Christopher Stray, Michael Bloch, Ann Read, Mark Richards, Ronald Hyam, Matthew Sturgis, Derek Wilson, Michael Hall, Sophie Dupré, Jill Pellew, Sir Roy Strong, Ronald Munro Ferguson, Jonathan Tennyson, Helen Rappaport, Paul Frecker, Sophie Hawkins, Kim Stevenson, Richard Davenport-Hines, David Churchill, Jane Winter, Kay Crosby, Tim Knight, Joy Field of the Leigh & District Historical Society, and Kenneth D. Brown.

I am also grateful to the Royal Collection Trust for permission to use the image of Princess Louise and party; the Duke of Argyll to quote from the letters of the 9th Duke of Argyll; the Marquess of Salisbury to quote from the letters of Lady Gwendolen Cecil; Viscount Dalmeny for permission to quote from the letters of the 5th Earl of Rosebery; William Gascoigne for permission to quote from the letters of the 1st Viscount Harcourt; the late Cecil Woolf for permission to quote from *The Venice Letters*; the heirs of the Attingham Collection for permission to quote Harold Boulton's letters to Teresa, Lady Berwick; the Syndics of the Fitzwilliam Museum for permission to quote from the diary of Wilfrid Blunt; the Master and Fellows of Trinity College Cambridge to quote from the Frederic Myers Papers; the Warden and Fellows of Merton College, Oxford, to quote from the diaries of the Rev. R. C. Fillingham; the Bodleian Library, Oxford for permission to quote Cyril Flower's letters from the Harcourt Papers; the Provost and Fellows of Kings College, Cambridge for permission to quote from the Oscar Browning papers; the Provost and Fellows of Worcester College, Oxford for permission to quote from the alumni file of A.C.C. Thorold and for the use of a photo; the University of Southampton for permission to quote from a letter of E.F. Benson; Peter Higgins & Associates representing the Estate of John Lehmann for permission to quote from *In The Purely Pagan Sense*; Princeton University Library for permission to quote from *The Princess Au Revoir* by Edward Sutton; and the Royal Museum for Central Africa, Belgium, for permission to quote from the Henry Morton Stanley Archive. Every effort has been made to identify and

11

trace copyright holders, and the author apologises for any errors or omissions.

U.S.A.: Brian Lewis for his scholarly generosity in sharing transcripts from the George Ives diaries, and additional information; James Jope for Latin translations and assistance with identifying quotes; Jonathan Glasser, Ethan B. Katz, Richard A. Cosgrove, Edmund White, the late William A. Percy, the late Ned Rorem, Carolyn Burke, Robert Rotberg, Janet Martinez, Erik Mitchell, Gavan Tredoux; David Deiss, Elysium Press; Michael DiRuggiero, Manhattan Rare Book Company; Kate Carlin, Cornell University Library; Jana H. Zevnik, Harry Ransom Center, University of Texas at Austin; Sandra Bossert and Squirrel Walsh, Firestone Library, Princeton; Paula Dempsey, University of Illinois at Chicago; Kirsten Clark, University of Minnesota Libraries; Larry Scott, Stanford University; Lyndsi Barnes and Carolyn Vega, New York Public Library; Amanda Faehnel, Kent State University; Erin Weinman, New York Historical Society; Robin Cookson, National Archives; Allyson Hayward; and Todd S. Gernes.

There are three Algerian sources to whom I am also very grateful, but whose identities must remain anonymous due to ethnic and wartime sensitivities.

This book would also not have been possible without the help of the National Archives UK, Bibliothèque Nationale de France, Find My Past, Ancestry.com; the digitalised newspapers of Fulton History created by the heroic Tom Tryniski; the British Newspaper Archive, Gale Cengage British Library Newspapers, UK Press Online, Papers Past of New Zealand, Trove of Australia, Chronicling America, Austrian Newspapers Online; the Historical Directories of England & Wales at the University of Leicester's Special Collections Online; and lastly, the *Chicago Tribune*, which sparked this journey by making access to its archive temporarily free, thereby encouraging exploration and discovery. All conclusions are my own.

PREFACE

This is a story of hidden history. Commencing at the dawn of the Edwardian era, it concerns little-known names and great ones, and stretches from Great Britain to France, to Africa and Australia. It has never been told, and until recently could not be told. It involves an extraordinary high-stakes government cover-up, rank injustice, and re-invented lives.

What unfolded serves to remind that the powerful protect their own; that the tides and undercurrents of sexual desire shape history; that human beings can manifest remarkable powers to recover from the very worst possible circumstances; and not least — that truth can be stranger than any fiction.

I feel privileged to have had the good fortune of being able to tell one of the great untold stories. Its skeleton was serendipitously stumbled upon in an American newspaper archive. Besides the misdeeds of entitlement, another of the themes of the book is the discretion of the British press in serving its masters. I would not have been able to tell the story, to the extent I've been able to, were it not for the more democratic spirit that infused a small group of radical British, American, and Australian journalists and editors. As each eye-opening fact unfolded, my curiosity became ever greater. The author Toni Morrison once said: "If there's a book that you want to read, but it hasn't been written yet, then you must write it." So I have.

I make no apologies for the book's length, and not merely because this epic tale demanded it. When a friend comes to me with a secret, invariably my response is — "Tell me *everything*". Therefore, what lies within the pages ahead is that everything I wanted to know. Who were these people? What was their reality? How could this happen?

Halfway through this quest I realised that to fully answer those questions would require a much wider historical and social perspective than I had initially envisaged, and a far deeper trek into that vanished place and time. Part I of the book is therefore devoted to taking the pulse of the Edwardian Age, and presenting a panorama of both the social landscape, and the parallel world of hidden desire. It explores the influences that shaped the minds of the characters, and the motivations and machinations of the British elite when, then as now, 'hushing up' was not merely the default setting of its response to scandal: smothering the misdemeanours of the privileged was unofficial government policy. Part II reveals the scandal at the heart of the story, while Part III details the lives it changed forever. More impatient readers may wish to turn to the second part immediately, but I urge not. Because everything in life is inter-connected, context is everything.

Besides being personal, *A Secret Between Gentlemen* is idiosyncratic. I don't just wish to read a saga of a lost world — I want to go there. The narrative path is therefore not tight and linear, lit with the occasional glow-worm of anecdote, but something more exploratory and lush. Should you wonder 'Why am I being taken here?', be assured: all will become clear. In short: you're about to be smuggled down a surreal Edwardian rabbit hole.

Amongst the characters you'll meet, who seized life and ran with it, is that explorer of the deepest Congo, Henry Morton Stanley. Of *How I Found Livingstone*, his own published account of a journey into a different darkness, Stanley wrote in a simple, empire-winning manner to defend its broad focus:

> A great many people complained that the book was bulky; that, in fact, there was too much of it. So are newspapers too large, and contain a great deal more reading matter than any man cares to read. In a book of travels some readers prefer the adventures, the incidents of the chase; others prefer what relates to the ethnography of the country; others geography; others dip into it for matters concerning philology. The person who reads the

whole book through is one interested in the subject, or is attracted to it by its style.

There is not much philology ahead, but in whatever way you approach this account of my own quest, I hope you find something of interest. It is not the history that its protagonists might have wished. Or their admirers, or descendants. However, every life is a strange unforeseen journey. I have tried my best to tell what really happened, and hope I have done everyone justice.

PJ
February, 2022

Third Edition Note

This edition incorporates fresh information, corrections and other improvements. It was completed shortly after the coronation of King Charles III, which feels apt for a story that opens at the beginning of a reign and new era. Even in the brief interregnum since the appearance of the first edition, what change the world has witnessed. Artificial intelligence suddenly leapt to the fore, generating concern over its ability to add to what seems increasing confusion over what constitutes truth and reality.

Just as today, the Edwardian era became gripped by the notion of powerful hidden forces shaping events, and the suppression of public dialogue at odds with those who ruled. However, Victorian certainties still lingered. Retreating to that 'golden afternoon', and the company of these gentlemen, felt a refreshing scholarly pleasure. I'm delighted to share the outcome, and once again, thank everyone who helped me.

PJ
June, 2023

PROLOGUE

It seemed like a lost place. The more local people he asked about it, the less they appeared to know.

It was May 1987. Road touring then still relied upon directions from strangers, and paper maps that bent begrudgingly into concertina folds. What he did know was that the village lay just a few miles from Grantham. The previous afternoon he and his wife had arrived in that Lincolnshire town. Once known as the birthplace of Sir Isaac Newton, it was now more recognised for spawning Margaret Thatcher, who by then had been Prime Minister for so long, she seemed a permanent national fixture.

The following morning, leaving his wife to spend the day sightseeing in Grantham, he set off in their hire car, travelling north along the A1. Here the motorway follows the route of the original Great North Road, along which mail coaches once travelled from London to Edinburgh. It took him across Gonerby Moor, where Oliver Cromwell first defeated the Royalist forces, and where the flat landscape of Lincolnshire fully opens out.

It was only a short while before he spotted what he'd been told to look out for. It was just as described. A lonely garage, next to an easy-to-miss side road. There was a sign: 'Marston 1½'.

The name of the byway, Tollbar Road, alluded to its past as the site of a Georgian turnpike gate. Here a toll was once imposed for those wishing to proceed north or south. Behind the garage, though much

17

altered, the original toll house still survived.

He turned the car into the byway, and the roar of the A1 and the modern world quickly receded. Tall lush hedgerows flanked the roadside, intermittently hiding the view and altering the light to a soft viridescence. A few minutes on, and their green curtain suddenly vanished, revealing like a magician's cloak a smattering of substantial red-brick Victorian cottages. A few of their gables bore crests with dates from the 1860s, and the initials 'JHT'. These he guessed stood for a previous squire, Sir John Henry Thorold. It was probably the last time the village had been truly prosperous, before the flood of grain from America had brought agricultural depression and the slow collapse of the old order. "Marston – a place seldom patronised," a foxhunting account of the 1870s had observed. It could well have been the village motto.

At a fork in the road a public house appeared, the Thorold Arms. Here he halted. In the near distance, a church steeple speared above the trees. He knew that if he continued on the main road, it would take him on to the neighbouring village of Hougham: the two villages were so close they'd been combined into one parish, Hougham-cum-Marston. He turned the car into the side lane. Barely a hundred yards on lay his goal, marked by a pair of stone entrance piers with ball finials. Beyond them, in a deep pastoral hush, stood a low rambling stone manor. This was Marston Hall, held by the Thorold family since the fourteenth century.

If the village had disappointed, the sight of the Hall compensated. Like a painting on a cake tin, it was almost too picturesque, and not quite real, as if a Hollywood art director had been asked to conjure up a vision of Olde England. To the left there was a low stone wall, behind which gardens slumbered in florescent splendour. On the right, stretching behind the manor, lay an idyllic view across a spring-green field with a narrow winding stream, to distant hills.

The Hall was home to the Reverend Henry Croyland Thorold.[*] Unlike the rest of the family, he pronounced his surname with noble

---

[*] Rev. Henry Croyland Thorold (1921–2000). High Tory Anglican, naval chaplain, schoolmaster, architectural and topographical author; son of the Rev. Dr. Ernest Hayford Thorold, who was chaplain to Kings George V, Edward VIII and George VI, and a cousin of the 14th Thorold baronet.

idiosyncrasy as 'thorough'. He was sixty-six years old, but looked older. Graced with "a profile like George III's and a stomach like George IV's," as one acquaintance put it, he knew "Lincolnshire backwards and all the families that ever were, they being to a man his relations." He presented "an amazing spectacle...walking not on the soles of his shoes but the sides." Then there was the voice: "resounding, melodic and perfectly modulated – once heard...never forgotten."

A newspaper profile would describe him as "a splendid, indeed unrivalled example of that now-vanished country type, the bachelor antiquarian squire, imbued with a deep love and knowledge of architecture, ecclesiology, heraldry and the classics." Like something out of a Victorian novel, reputation had it that he was the squarson – that is, the squire who was also the parson. If there was anywhere such anachronisms could linger on, Hougham-cum-Marston was certainly such a place.

Opening village fetes with a lordly flourish, as Henry did, it was easy to assume this was so. However, the last true squire of the parish had been his cousin, the 13th Thorold baronet,* who'd sold up the estate shortly after the Second World War. Long before then, Marston Hall had become a mere dower house and estate office for the baronets, who in the mid-eighteenth century had moved to grander quarters at Syston several miles off. Marston Hall only belonged to Henry because his father had purchased it in the great sell-off.

Once, at a fete opening, a stranger had the temerity to question Henry about the latest Anglican controversies. "Don't you ask me about the Church, my man," he had boomed. "I may be in holy orders, but I have absolutely nothing, absolutely nothing, to do with the Church." This was despite the fact, that in addition to an elaborate floral buttonhole, Henry was then sporting a dog collar.

Henry did occasionally preach in remote churches. As *The Times* put it, he had a "declamatory style of preaching, often involving long pauses which kept the congregation on the edge of their pews". Depending on one's point of view, reserves of patience, and tone of

---

* A baronetcy is a British hereditary knighthood that also bestows the prefix 'Sir'. A baronet ranks above a knight, but below a baron and other gradings of the aristocracy, and unlike the latter, is legally a commoner (albeit, of the gentry), rather than a member of the peerage.

rump, this sermonising was either reverently dignified or exhaustingly camp.

However, as Henry made plain to another enquirer: "I don't *like* duties." The truth was, he much preferred *stones* to parishioners, or indeed, prelates. As a friend wrote: "He believed you could learn far more about Christianity by pottering around old churches and abbeys than by heeding what contemporary clerics had to say." Henry was a doughty campaigner for the preservation of old churches, and writing in longhand in his armchair, diligently produced several definitive books on ecclesiastical buildings and their ruins, another volume on Lincolnshire houses, and was co-author of five of the renowned Shell county guidebooks.* His co-authors and friends included John Piper, John Betjeman, and Peter Burton.†

In his earlier life, Henry had served as a chaplain and school housemaster, including at Lancing, from which he'd been dismissed, due to a spat with another chaplain over liturgical revision. Change was one of Henry's pet hates. Nonetheless, the school had presented him with an avenue of Lombardy poplars. His herbaceous borders, rose garden, vegetable garden, hedges, and lawns with their essential 'Gothick' gazebo, were tended by a full-time gardener who lived in the former stables.

Henry was also the self-appointed family historian. Amongst his celebrated relations was a long-deceased nephew, Arthur Charles Campbell Thorold. It was with the hope that Henry might shed light upon the mystery of Arthur's life in Lincolnshire that his visitor had now come, all the way from Australia.

Thirty years afterwards, the memories of that day for the visitor had faded to a series of overlapping impressions. His footsteps crunching on the gravel. The great Tudor door of the manor. Henry's English upper class dishevelled appearance, which suggested long acquaintance with stodge and port.

---

* Now keenly sought collectors' items, they were published by the Shell oil company between 1934 and 1987.
† John Egerton Christmas Piper (1903–1992) painter, printmaker and designer; Sir John Betjeman (1906–1984), Poet Laureate, writer, and broadcaster; Peter Burton (1927–2014), schoolmaster and author, including of: *Six Inches of Bath Water: 100 Years of Scarborough College* (1998). Not to be confused with gay journalism pioneer Peter William Burton (1945–2011), publisher, editor and author of *Parallel Lives* (1985), *Amongst the Aliens* (1995), etc.

Inside the house it was at least ten to fifteen degrees colder than the air outside, the damp cold of centuries. Those who braved overnighting at Marston Hall believed it held strong claim to be the coldest house in Europe; a condition to which Henry was impervious. Fine portraits of ancestors, including some by Reynolds and Lely, lined the walls. There was even a Poussin. Above the fireplace, carved in relief in darkened oak, the Thorold coat-of-arms staked its claim.

Compared to the palatial country house of Henry's close friend Sir Giles Isham,* Marston Hall was small beer. However, with the help of another friend, classical architect Francis Johnson,† elaborations had been undertaken, including the insertion of an extravagant 17th century plaster ceiling rescued from another Thorold house.

It all spoke of feudal privilege, and money so old it was mildewed. The heavily embossed wallpaper in the drawing room was draped with cobwebs, and in places damp had broken through in brown stains. The visitor noted there appeared to be no television or radio in the house: in fact, Henry did not even take a newspaper. Here time was kept at bay. It was wholly in keeping that Henry dedicated his guidebook for ruined abbeys to a series of abbesses, Dames Eugenia, Christina, and Catherine Thorold of Pontoise, and Sister Catherine Thorold of Ghent, the most recent of whom had last drawn breath in 1699.

Henry beckoned his guest to the staircase: "Arthur Thorold would

---

* Sir Gyles Isham (1903–76), 12th baronet, of Lamport Hall, Northamptonshire. A homosexual bachelor, and romantically handsome golden youth of 1920s Oxford, he became an actor (including opposite Greta Garbo), before serving in the Eighth Army, and MI6. In later life he was a scholar squire, hospital governor and trustee of the National Portrait Gallery. For Cecil Beaton, Isham's celebrated Hamlet provided "the most beautiful back view I'd ever seen". [Adrian Woodhouse, *Angus McBean: Face-maker*, Alma Books, London 2006, p185; Stephen Dorril, *MI6: Inside the Covert World of Her Majesty's Secret Intelligence Service*, Fourth Estate Limited, London 2000, p544, Sir Roy Strong, *Splendours and Miseries: The Roy Strong Diaries, 1967-87*, Weidenfeld & Nicolson, London 1977, p38.]
† Francis Frederick Johnson (1911–1995), neoclassical architect. He lived with his partner Edward Ingram, a touchy schoolmaster and local historian, at Reighton Hall, North Yorkshire, where they were looked after by Edward's sister, whose singing and indifferent food were their daily sufferance. Clients of Francis included Armatrude, Lady Waechter de Grimston, "a somewhat Gothic figure who radiated an aura of fantasy and saw herself as the last of the ancient East Riding family of Grimston of Grimston Garth," and who was always improving her various residences: "The best music," she once pronounced, "is the sound of workmen's trowels." [John Martin Robinson, David Neave, *Francis Johnson Architect: A Classical Statement*, Oblong Creative Ltd, Leeds 2001, *passim*.]

have walked up these very stairs!" he declaimed. The visitor endeavoured to look impressed. His host next suggested that they repair to the Thorold Arms, to which the visitor readily agreed. He could do with a whisky and soda, and it would enable him to meet some of the villagers, and perhaps tap the more elderly amongst them for memories of Arthur.

In what seemed like a seigneurial gesture, Henry insisted they take his ancient silver-grey Bentley, despite the public house being a short walk away. When they eventually entered the portal of the Arms, the visitor was nonplussed by the reception: Henry was greeted by the staff "as if God himself had arrived." There was another surprise: apart from the staff, they were the only persons there.

A single dining table had been laid out with silver for lunch – or luncheon, as Henry phrased it, beckoning him to a chair. It looked like a set piece. It *was* a set piece. Wherever the villagers were, they weren't here. The thought crossed the visitor's mind that they'd been banished, and he was being carefully quarantined.

However, when the food arrived, it was excellent traditional English country fare. The visitor now took the opportunity to broach the subject of his enquiries. Two generations previously, Arthur Thorold's father had been the rector of Hougham-cum-Marston.

"We are not the oldest family in the district, or in England," replied Henry, "but we have been about for a long time." Arthur had been "very much a member of the family – a family used to living in the public eye; a family steeped in the history of the area."

Like the son of gentry he was, Arthur had received the finest of educations, including going up to Oxford in 1892. Yet all had not gone smoothly. According to the visitor's research, it had taken Arthur seven years to achieve a simple Bachelor of Arts degree. In a letter, Henry had written that Arthur might have achieved honours, but took a pass degree because he had "spent most of his undergraduate life acting and enjoying the social life… entirely in keeping with his delightful character!"

Now when the visitor again pressed the topic, a cloud had passed over Henry's face. He admitted that, within the family, Arthur was used "as a cautionary tale…a sorry story of what happens to a talented young man who dissipates his time and energy in the pursuit of pleasure."

To help ferret out information about Arthur, the visitor had enlisted a local historian. In the archives of the Diocese of Lincoln she'd struck paydirt. It took the form of several letters in the Bishop's correspondence. These revealed that in the summer of 1902, a crisis of some kind had struck Arthur's family. From that time onwards, his father began taking extended leaves of absence from the parish. In 1905, he petitioned the Bishop for permission to move from his benefice, the letter pleading:

> on account of certain great family troubles which have happened to the Petitioner and which are well known to your Lordship and on account of which the wife of the said Petitioner cannot at present live in the Petitioner's parish.

The ink of the copperplate script had faded to sepia. Yet the anguish behind the words was as clear as when they'd been written.

There was also an earlier letter. Penned by a visiting clergyman to the Bishop, it contained a sentence with underlinings that would have stopped any reader in their tracks:

> Since I came to Grantham this morning I learnt that the 'bride' I married the other day was the sister of the boy with whom Mr. Thorold's son committed so grievous a Sin.

Although eighty-five years had passed since the letter was first read, Henry's manner suggested little progression, and the visitor didn't feel he could broach that particular correspondence with him. However, he did delicately raise the matter of Arthur's emigration to Australia. The research had uncovered the fact he was assisted during this time by a charitable organisation, the Church Army. Why would someone like Arthur, a gentleman from a family of substance, need their help?

Henry skated around this with polite condescension. Three decades later, the visitor couldn't recall the evasive reply. Perhaps it was something about the Thorolds being intimately connected with the Church, and that its blessings, particularly in those far off days, reached across all life.

If the visitor felt he'd stepped into a novel, it would have been the ideal moment for its author to have Henry muse that, in England, there were all sorts of things that seemed to make no sense – to the casual visitor. However, they had their own logic. Of which time had proved the worth. Perchance the mystery in Arthur Thorold's life was testament to this anomaly? Such a reflection, if voiced, would surely form a perfect prelude to the improbable narrative now to be told.

Possibly Henry had then deftly changed the subject by asking: "How was the lamb? Perhaps a drop more of the excellent wine?" He was certainly a generous host, and charming conversationalist, with a fund of stories for those of whom he approved. Just as in the pulpit, he laid a sonorous balm over the room.

Lunch concluded, Henry had taken his guest on a short village tour in the Bentley, waving airily to a few passing villagers like the lord of his domain. The first stop was All Saints church at Hougham; a typical parish church with its ancient arches and darkened oak pews. "Here Arthur would have sat every Sabbath," Henry reverently intoned. For the final tour item, the Bentley was paused in front of the Georgian rectory, the size of which startled the visitor. Henry wasn't boasting when he spoke of Arthur being of the gentry. This was no vicar's cottage. It looked positively manorial.

With a gracious farewell wave, Henry sent his inquiring visitor back to Grantham. Job done. "There is no need for you to go any further than the house," Henry had written to him, referring to Marston Hall. He realised this had been no casual instruction. Henry was clearly hiding something. But what? Could it be connected with the family crisis the Bishop's letters had revealed?

It was mid-afternoon by the time he met up with his wife in their hotel in Grantham. "I've just had the strangest experience," he told her. "The meeting with Henry…it felt completely stage-managed!" This forgotten parish in the middle of nowhere, this Hougham-cum-Marston, suddenly seemed a place of secrets.

The following day he had another appointment, which he hoped would prove more rewarding. This was at the offices of the local newspaper, *The Grantham Journal.* Its original Victorian masthead had proclaimed it as *The Grantham Journal of Useful, Instructive and Entertaining Knowledge and Monthly Advertiser.* As it also reported events in Hougham-cum-Marston, he hoped its bold promise would prove true.

An overseas visitor seeking historical information was then still something of an unusual occurrence. When he arrived at the offices of the *Journal,* he found that back copies of the paper dating from Arthur Thorold's time were laid out ready for his perusal.

Several hours later, he would admit defeat. Apart from coming across a few scattered reports of Arthur being best man at his brother's wedding, and assisting his father raising money for the Church Fund, the record appeared silent. If something significant had occurred in this branch of the Thorold family, the local newspaper had studiously avoided mentioning it.

He was stymied. Yet when he returned to Australia, the more his conviction grew that there was mystery at the heart of Arthur Thorold's life he had not been able to crack.

Back in England, the Reverend Henry would continue to preach, and motor the shires in his Bentley, seeking ancient churches, country houses, and ruins to admire, until the turn of the Millennium, when he expired at his beloved Marston Hall at the age of seventy-eight.

It's likely he went to his grave at peace with the knowledge that, as his family's historical custodian, the confidences he held, and one in particular, would be buried with him. By then it had been hidden for almost a century. This was despite the fact it was far more than just the petty secret of a proud provincial family.

It was a national secret.

It would be another thirty years until the visitor learnt the truth, and how breathtakingly close he'd come to uncovering it. What he had chanced upon were the echoes of a great convulsive drama.

At the offices of *The Grantham Journal* he'd stared in vain at the fragile yellowed pages. Turning them to the year Arthur's family troubles

25

began, from the month of August he read:

> In the face of cold north-easterly winds, and almost incessant rain, the decorations at Grantham have made but tardy progress...Only fine weather is needed to witness a general blossoming of bunting such as never before has been seen in Grantham.

That summer of 1902 had been no ordinary one. It was a Coronation year.

PART I.

The Realm That Was

1. THE NEW REIGN

On the 9th of August 1902, in Westminster Abbey, the Archbishop of Canterbury lowered St. Edward's Crown onto the head of Edward VII. From high up in the cathedral's gallery, trumpet volleys broke the silence of held breaths, as peers and peeresses donned their coronets, and great shouts of *God Save The King!* rang out above the heads of the assembled great and good.

In the same breathless moment, the new electric lights of the Abbey were turned on for the first time, flooding out the darkness in what must have seemed the golden dawn of a new era – "the jewels, almost lost in the afternoon gloom, flashed with sudden splendour."

"There was a somewhat theatrical touch in this incident," noted one spectator, "but it added much to the brilliancy of a magnificent scene." Indeed, it was a wholly appropriate gesture for the new Edwardian Age: artificial, showy, and artfully thrilling.

Edward was sixty and had waited a lifetime for this day, including two months' postponement of the ceremony while he recovered from an operation to drain an abscess on his appendix. The nationwide relief at his recovery, and the decisive British victory that ended the Second Boer War in May, had added to the swell of patriotism and optimism. As King and Emperor, Edward reigned over a third of the peoples of the earth.

At his side was his wife and consort, Queen Alexandra. Celebrated for her beauty, the death from pneumonia ten years previously of her eldest son Prince Albert Victor,* had aged her, and a photograph that escaped the retoucher's hand reveals she fully looked her fifty-seven years. She was also labouring under severe deafness, a gammy leg, and a large wig. Into the latter a discreet hole had been cut to allow the holy oil during the Anointing to reach her scalp, the Archbishop of York, or someone on his behalf, having explained it would be quite impossible he should sanctify a mound of false hair. Despite such earthly shortcomings, in the hallowed half-light of the Abbey, discreetly made up, gowned in golden silk gauze, and with all the jewels her slender shoulders could carry, one of her Ladies in Waiting, the Countess of Antrim, described her as a vision that "made one rub one's eyes and think of fairy stories – & even then the half is not said".

Alexandra was loving, sympathetic, lighthearted and beguiling, but also girlish and deeply selfish. Edward's philandering had resulted in a slew of scandals that would have endangered the throne in a less phlegmatic nation.

The success the new King was to eventually make of his reign was far from assured. Like many, the author Henry James† considered him little more than "an arch-vulgarian". With a waistline that would balloon to 48 inches, as a recent historian wryly observed: "Like a sort of cement-mixer in a top hat, he risked apoplexy on a daily basis."

Also unimpressed was William Marcus Thompson,‡ an Irish barrister who was editor of the popular *Reynolds's Newspaper*. Founded by a leader of the Chartist§ movement, the Sunday paper championed what it termed 'radical democracy'. It claimed to be, aside from *The Times*, "the most extensively quoted of any English newspaper abroad," which was very likely true – the reason being, Thompson thumbed his nose at wealth and power, and printed what most of the English press didn't. In the opinion of a newspaper directory of the time: "but for its violent politics, it might be characterised as a good

---

* Prince Albert Victor, Duke of Clarence and Avondale, aka 'Prince Eddy' (1864–1892).
† Henry James (1843–1916), Anglo-American author. He latterly lived at Rye, Sussex.
‡ William Marcus Thompson (1857–1907).
§ Chartism was a movement for political reform, most active between 1838 and 1848, which sought political rights and influence for the working class. It gained its name from the formal petition, or People's Charter, that listed its principal aims: the vote for all men over 21, secret ballot, no property qualification to become an M.P., payment for M.P.s, electoral districts of equal size, and annual elections for Parliament. Three petitions were presented to Parliament in 1839, 1842 and 1848, and all were rejected.

family paper." Despite headlines such as 'The Parasite Of Royalty', ironically, one of the paper's keenest readers, and of newspapers generally, was the King. Given Edward had been regularly the subject of scandal in his earlier years, this was perhaps not surprising.*

W.M. Thompson wrote compellingly in plain English. In 1902, he would make the timeless complaint: "The Rich Men's Government is so busy spending our money on the slaughter of weaker peoples that they have no time to attend to the most urgent domestic questions." Thompson was described as "the very incarnation of advanced Radicalism – a good hater of ecclesiastics, aristocrats, and Courts." For him, the House of Lords was "The House of Landlords...So here's a toast to Lickspittle, the Englishman's god." He also denounced:

> the loathsome snobs and toadies who are constantly placing upon a pedestal the very ordinary individuals who compose the royal house; prostrating themselves before this shoddy shrine; and setting a demoralising example of rank-worship to the youth of the nation.

As for the man who was now monarch:

> He is affable, good-natured, kind-hearted...there are many of our acquaintance who have all these qualities; yet we never think of establishing palaces and pensions for them.

However, the King's popularity was immense, and by sheer force of personality he would stamp the new era as his own. As one writer put it, he was "the universal uncle with his smile and his cigar":

> the King, if he stood for the best time that money could buy, stood also for the social stability that made such a time possible...the supreme symbol, for his subjects, of the two things of which they felt themselves to stand most in need, enjoyment and security.

---

* Thirty years previously, the paper had cruelly printed: "We have much satisfaction in announcing that the newly born child of the Prince and Princess of Wales died shortly after its birth, thus relieving the working men of England from having to support hereafter another addition to the long roll of State beggars they at present maintain." [A Happy Release, *Reynolds's Newspaper*, 16 April 1871, p1.]

In matters of state, Edward possessed a sound head, shrewd judgement, and a sense of tact that warmed people to him. "I'm not sure that he could do the rule of three," wrote Admiral of the Fleet, John Fisher, "but he had the heavenly gift of Proportion and Perspective!" Prime Minister William Gladstone* considered him far more fitted to the role of a constitutional monarch than Queen Victoria: "He would see both sides. He would always be open to argument. He would never domineer or dictate." Longtime courtiers Lord Esher† and Sir Frederick Ponsonby‡ found him considerate and human, and a born organiser; Ponsonby believed that had he not been king he would have been a successful businessman.

Edward's possession of organisational skills was fortunate, because suppressing his romantic contretemps involved the expenditure of vast effort. In 1928, almost two decades after his death, royal advisers were still panicking over the memoirs of the most rogue of his mistresses, the socialist countess, Daisy, Lady Warwick.§

Amongst the glittering assembly in Westminster Abbey for Edward's crowning were his 'special female friends', including his then mistress Alice Keppel. For the Countess of Antrim it was "the one discordant note in the Abbey – for to see the row of lady friends in full magnificence did rather put my teeth on edge."

When the barely-recovered King and his consort retired to the vestry while the choir sang the *Te Deum*, a reporter observed:

> For now the suspense was over – the suspense that had seemed to brood over the whole assembly from first to last – the half-ashamed, the half-superstitious dread that something might happen to stop the crowning, the anxious fear of calamity, born of a previous shock. That suspense, unreasoning, but always present, now gave way to a burst of almost hilarious joy.

---

* William Ewart Gladstone (1809–1898), four times Liberal Prime Minister between 1868 and 1894. Married Catherine Glynne, and had issue.
† Reginald Baliol Brett, 2nd Viscount Esher (1852–1930), Liberal politician, administrator, courtier, historian. Married Eleanor van der Weyer, and had issue.
‡ Frederick Edward Grey Ponsonby, 1st Baron Sysonby, (1867–1935), soldier and courtier.
§ Frances 'Daisy' Evelyn Maynard Greville, Countess of Warwick (1861–1938), philanthropist and social activist. Her memoirs were published as *Life's Ebb And Flow* (1929).

Yet unknown to all but one person in that noble assembly, a dramatic intervention almost *had* occurred. Seated in the Abbey that day was a son of the Duke of Beaufort, Lord Henry Somerset,* known to his family, friends and lovers as 'Penna'. He was a former Tory M.P., Privy Counsellor, Comptroller of Her Majesty's Household, and not least, a song composer, whose works were popular both in England and the colonies. Twenty-three years previously, Lord Henry's wife Isabel† had discovered a passionate love letter to him, wrapped around a personal photograph from Harry Smith,‡ the seventeen-year-old son of a shipping magnate. "Mille Baisers" – 'a thousand kisses' the letter had concluded.

Lord Henry had married Isabel purely for her money; subsequently taking up with other gentlemen and treating her with callous contempt. Spurred on by her domineering mother, Isabel gained a legal separation and custody of their child, while her parents printed and circulated the judgement, ruining Lord Henry's political career, and hounding him into exile on the Continent, from where he published *Songs of Adieu*, a maudlin collection of poems expressing his desperate love for Harry:

> Oh, Thou, who on my empty life didst shine,
> Turning my night to one short, glorious day…
> life is death without thee – oh, come back!

After decades of pining for Harry in Monaco and Florence, and having been fed a false story of his death, Lord Henry deemed it safe to return to England to attend the Coronation – his right as a former

---

* Lord Henry Richard Charles Somerset (1849–1932), second son of the 8th Duke of Beaufort. Married Lady Isabella Somers-Cocks, with whom he had one son. Lord Henry established a convalescent home in Bournemouth for poor young men suffering tuberculosis, and became one of Florence's most notable expatriates. Of his villa, a magazine rhapsodised: "Even in such a beautiful city as Florence, where so much that is beautiful is to be found, it would, indeed, be difficult to discover a more exquisite interior." [A New Home For Consumptives, *Hampshire Advertiser*, 26 January 1884, p7; The Retreat Of A Famous Songwriter, *The Bystander*, 4 September 1907.]

† Lady Henry Somerset, née Lady Isabella Caroline Somers-Cocks (1851–1921).

‡ William Henry 'Harry' Smith (1856–1922), eldest son of shipbuilding magnate, art collector and M.P., Thomas Eustace Smith. Harry's mother, a worldly heiress in her own right, had an affair with M.P. Charles Dilke, who then embarked on an affair with one of her married daughters, whose husband subsequently sought a divorce. The resulting scandal led to the Smiths spending fifteen years in self-imposed exile in Spain. [Philip Ward-Jackson, 'Lord Ronald Gower, Gustave Doré and the Genesis of the Shakespeare Memorial at Stratford-on-Avon', *Journal of the Warburg and Courtauld Institutes*, Vol. 50 (1987), p164, n22.]

Privy Counsellor. Unfortunately, he hadn't reckoned on the continuing rage of "those she-devils, my wife and mother in law," who had private detectives shadow him.

In her husband's absence, Isabel's frustrations had found an outlet in women's rights and the temperance movement. She was President of the British Women's Temperance Association and Woman's Christian Temperance Union; she also ran a home for inebriated women at Duxhurst, and according to E.F. Benson,[*] "found humour in everything." Well, not quite everything. The intoxicating nectar of illicit love had met its match. Isabel threatened to create a public disturbance if her husband turned up at the ceremony.

Lord Henry's fear that *Vivat Regina!* might not be the only thing shouted in the Abbey that day was very real. As he wrote later to a friend, to his immense relief, "her heart failed her and her seat, next to mine, was vacant! She contented herself with sending a more than usually beastly anonymous letter…The woman is mad as well as bad!" Isabel wasn't yet done. She alerted Scotland Yard to her husband's presence in the country, and Lord Henry was forced to hurriedly return to his Florentine retreat.

Much more than an estranged wife could have spoiled the Coronation. A quarter of London was then living in poverty. Only a short walk from Buckingham Palace were some of the foulest and overcrowded rookies in the metropolis. In 1890, the founder of The Salvation Army, William Booth, published *In Darkest England And The Way Out*, which nodded to Henry Morton Stanley's *In Darkest Africa*, but surveyed the lost continent of his own nation's enslaved destitute. Booth estimated they amounted to one-in-ten citizens – what he termed 'The Submerged Tenth', and equivalent to the entire population of Scotland. An official figure was even more telling: out of every thousand persons, 939 died without any property worth recording.

Throughout Victoria's reign and into Edward's, fear of the rise of what was termed 'The Mob' – the vast alien underclass, haunted the patrician id. There was further concern that unrest was being churned by destitute immigrants, particularly intemperate Irish bearing

---

[*] Edward Frederic Benson (1867–1940), author.

generational grudges against English rule, and Polish and Russian Jews fleeing pogroms.

With great wealth and deepest poverty separated often by a mere few streets, the truce between order and chaos was, in some minds, an uneasy one, secured only by Anglo-Saxon reserve, common sense, good cheer, and respect for Government and Crown. However, this respect for the ruling class rested solely on a thin crust of aristocratic mythology and social prestige. Any erosion of the esteem and deference accorded it, including from exposures of high-placed immorality, threatened its hegemony.

This was no idle fear. Angry crowds of the poor had occasionally invaded the precincts of the rich. The scale and violence of the Gordon Riots* in London in 1780 had shocked Europe. In a June week of utter chaos, official buildings, prisons, churches and homes were pillaged, and sometimes literally demolished. The rioting was triggered by anti-Catholicism, but embraced a litany of grievances stoked by the unemployment and poverty of a struggling economy. In a familiar situation, more orderly protesters were infiltrated by, as a handbill put it: "a set of miscreants, whose purpose is to burn this City, and plunder its Inhabitants."

By royal proclamation of George III, London and Westminster were placed under martial law and fifteen thousand troops sent in. Amongst the scores of homes destroyed was that of the Earl of Mansfield in Bloomsbury Square: he and his wife fled through a backdoor as the mob broke in, throwing their furniture into the street, and setting fire to a library said to hold, "the choicest manuscripts ever known in the possession of an individual." The Bank of England was only saved from sacking by a battalion, who themselves were fired upon. "History cannot parallel a convulsion of the State like the present," lamented one newspaper, "into what a despicable situation this country is falling."†

---

* Named after Lord George Gordon (1751–1793), head of the Protestant Association.
† The same paper pleaded: "it is earnestly to be wished that every individual who has from fatal experience learnt the difference between the comforts of a civil government, as established by the British constitution, and the savage tyranny of democratical fury, will keep his servants at home of an evening, and advise them to shun joining any crowd." However, it also noted: "The public spirit of the monied men has not sunk under the horrid disorders that have prevailed for some days past: at the Stock Exchange yesterday the buyers were in proportion of two to one of the sellers, the consequence of which was, that the stocks rose

Hundreds of rioters were shot by the military before the tumult was finally suppressed, but it could well have tipped into revolution. The official death count of 385 was considered a gross underestimate. Troops remained quartered in London's parks for a decade, while permanent barracks were constructed in succession throughout the city. More profoundly, the riots instigated a greater centralisation of government, and the building of an administration that would manage and police the nation more effectively, as well as its expanding Empire.

A decade later during the French Revolution there was a succession of more or less orderly processions of ruffians through London's West End protesting various causes, including oppressive legislation. The end of the Napoleonic Wars in 1815 also witnessed chronic unemployment, and famine that was exacerbated by tariffs on imported grain (the so-called Corn Laws). These were imposed to keep grain prices high, so favouring domestic producers, and thereby – at the expense of 90 per cent of the British public – shoring up upper class incomes from land ownership and the political power it brought. This resulted in protests and calls for reform, culminating in the Peterloo Massacre in Manchester in 1819, when cavalry charged into a large crowd, killing a dozen and injuring hundreds.

In October 1831, in the wake of the rejection by the House Of Lords of the 2nd Reform Bill, which sought to widen the right to vote, London was spared insurrection, but rioting broke out in several counties. Nottingham Castle, home of the Duke of the Newcastle,* who had prominently opposed the bill, was burned to a shell, while Bristol was in the hands of the mob for three days.

Potato blight resulted in the decade known as 'The Hungry Forties', with widespread starvation in Ireland and Scotland, and across Europe, stirring political upheaval. In March 1848, following a cruel winter and economic depression, there were two Chartist marches in London, leading to an immense gathering in April, before which the

---

one half per cent." [Saturday's Post, *Jackson's Oxford Journal*, 10 June 1780, p3.]
* Henry Pelham Fiennes Pelham-Clinton, 4th Duke of Newcastle-under-Lyne. Deeply evangelical, in 1823, his valet and two others were sent to the gallows for sodomy following the interception of an incriminating letter by His Grace, or one of his secretaries. [Harry Cocks, 'Horrid Crimes, Unnatural Offences', *East Midlands History and Heritage*, Issue 2, December 2015.]

young Queen Victoria and Prince Albert retreated to the safety of Osborne on the Isle of Wight. The Duke of Wellington was put in charge of defence of the city, with 10,000 troops at the ready, and 170,000 citizens were sworn in as special constables. The demonstration petered out in driving rain, but disturbances had continued into June. One crowd, described as "of the lowest and most abandoned class," voiced the diffuse simmering anger:

> The Queen, her progeny, the present Government, with that of the late Premier's, the constitution of the country, the representatives of Parliament, the Lords Spiritual and Temporal, were all denounced as accursed, and loud complaints were made of the necessity for a complete social revolution by the equal distribution of the wealth of the country.

In July 1866, the Reform League, an organisation headed by a barrister, Edmond Beales,* which rapidly grew into a force for agitation to expand the franchise, announced a late afternoon rally to take place in Hyde Park. Fearing violence, the Commissioner of Metropolitan Police forbade it. Faced with police lines and closed Park gates, the marchers moved on to Trafalgar Square, but a subsidiary crowd of what *The Morning Post* termed "the vilest scum of the metropolis" succeeded in entering the Park and a riot ensued: "never, in the memory of the oldest inhabitant of London," said the paper, "has such a disgraceful and violent scene been witnessed." Given what had occurred during the Gordon Riots this was Fleet Street hyperbole, but the evening would nevertheless be memorable.

Prior to the mayhem, a quintessentially English incident occurred when, as *The Morning Post* detailed, "a gentleman of strikingly handsome appearance, apparently between sixty and seventy years of age, drove up in a hansom cab." He turned out to be the Honourable Charles Clifford,† a magistrate and ardent reformer. Addressing the crowd, he informed them:

> He was the son of a peer, his son-in-law was a peer, and all his family belonged to the aristocratic classes. With their thousands

---

* Edmond Beales (1803–1881); President of the Reform League and a central figure in the 19th century reform movement.
† Hon. Charles Thomas Clifford (1797–1870), son of the 6th Baron Clifford of Chudleigh. A Deputy-Lieutenant, and magistrate of Lincolnshire; High Sheriff in 1844.

upon thousands a year, were they afraid of the working intelligent classes of England? No! On the contrary, he was prepared to grant them all the political and social privileges they could desire.

To a background of cheering he added that the Tory newspapers would no doubt abuse him the following morning, but having been the brunt of them before, he despised their insinuations: "three cheers for the Queen were proposed by the hon. gentleman, and enthusiastically given, after which he drove off amid renewed applause."

A telling account of what happened next was shared by an anonymous lady who had been returning home from a garden party. Despite the Park's gates being closed, as her letter to a newspaper detailed, like others of her class she encountered no problem in her cab being allowed through:

> I presume the police had instructions to keep back working people only, which must have raised a very unpleasant feeling in the minds of those who were denied admission...It was not the crowd of Trafalgar Square, which also by chance I had seen and mingled with. The men that streamed past my cab window were resolute-looking fellows in working clothes. They were not 'roughs', who are easily distinguished in a London mob. There were 'roughs' there plenty; but it would be a bad lookout for London if they could muster the resolution and strength which carried Hyde Park in the teeth of the police last night...What is more, they had the sympathy of a large proportion of the lookers-on from cabs and omnibuses. Men in broadcloth were clapping their hands heartily. More than one 'Quite right' reached my ears when the determination to make good their entrance was made apparent to the mob.

"I dearly loved what is called 'a row' – who does not, at twenty at any rate?" So later wrote the young Lord Ronald (Ronnie) Gower,[*] the artistic son of the 2nd Duke of Sutherland. "Meeting with a congenial spirit in Francis Knollys,[†] we saw what we could of the riot." The twenty-nine-year-old Knollys was then Treasurer to the Prince of

---

[*] Lord Ronald Charles Sutherland-Leveson-Gower (1845-1916), Scottish Liberal politician, sculptor, and writer.
[†] Sir Francis Knollys, later Baron Knollys, and Viscount Knollys (1837–1924).

Wales, and would later become his Private Secretary, including as monarch. Gower recalled the scene:

> On reaching the Marble Arch we found the place surrounded by a yelling mob of several hundreds, who were pulling down the iron rails on either side of the Arch. In a short time they had got about three hundred yards of this railing down, and then the mob poured into the Park like a dirty torrent...There was some sharpish fighting going on...Sir Richard Mayne [Commissioner of Police] kept riding about, and was much groaned at and hooted by the mob...The most amusing part of the affair was when the mounted police charged the crowd. This they did rather indiscriminately, and our party had to fly before them along with tag, rag, and bobtail. The mob was of the very lowest sort, demonstrative but cowardly. 'Gladstone and Reform!' 'Gladstone for ever!' and such cries were roared *ad libitum*.

Gladstone and Lord Ronald Gower's mother were the very closest friends – "Nobody makes me feel more the happiness of knowledge," she told her son. Ronnie would be elected to Parliament the following year as the Liberal member for Sutherland – which was almost a family sinecure. Divorced from worldly cares by wealth, aristocratic and youthful insouciance, and family connections to the mob's hero, Ronnie was able to look upon the riot as a diverting evening's entertainment. Given his connections, perhaps it's not surprising that the following year he took up with William Mayne,* the bachelor youngest son of the Commissioner.

The Prime Minister's son was also untroubled by the events of the evening, writing that "there was more mischief than malice in the affair, and much more of mere larking than either." The Prime Minister, Lord Derby, and his successor, Benjamin Disraeli,† were similarly unperturbed, and like the majority of citizens, had the utmost disdain for those who stooped to violence. Reform was already on the political agenda, and neither the riot, or a larger peaceful rally the

---

* William Mayne (1845–1902). Gower told his diary: "he is 22 & quite beautiful; Spanishy; lived a good deal in Paris and has the most charming manners." However, what appears to have been a summer romance didn't last beyond the Season of 1867. Mayne died unmarried and 'without profession' at Ostend. [Lord Ronald Gower diary, 27 July 1867: D6578/15/21, Staffordshire Record Office.]
† Benjamin Disraeli, 1st Earl of Beaconsfield, (1804–1881); Prime Minister 1874–1880, and 1868.

following year, played any meaningful part in bringing about *The Representation of the People Act* (1867) – The Second Reform Act.

Yet the riot occurred literally across the road from some of the grandest private palaces in the capital. In the stone-throwing mayhem at the peak of it, and on the following evening, 265 policemen were injured (including the Commissioner, who was struck twice), and between forty and fifty policemen permanently disabled. What it did do, or rather, the press reports of it, including of a subsequent parliamentary inquiry into the actions of the police, was reinforce the lingering concern of what lay out there. The anonymous lady observer concluded her published letter on an ominous note:

> I do not think Mr. Beales and his followers are very wise; but those who opposed their harmless, if useless 'demonstration' were still less so. A little more of the same kind of thing, and a spirit might be roused from the vasty deep beneath us here,* not quite so easy to lay.

Indeed, throughout the 1870s working class militancy increased. In July of 1884, an immense but good-humoured march took place in London in support of the Third Reform Bill, which when passed, widened the vote to two-thirds of the male population. By the close of the demonstration an estimated two hundred thousand people had entered Hyde Park, watched by aristocratic observers from their balconies and windows. Amongst them were the Prince and Princess of Wales and their daughters. Edward had opposed reform in 1866, but now older and wiser, he welcomed it – and indeed, had to be dissuaded from voting for the Bill in the House of Lords. Recognised by the marchers he received one of the greatest ovations of his life. When a group of processionists carrying a banner with the motto "Will the Lords defy the labourers?" passed his residence Marlborough House, their band struck up the tune 'God Bless The Prince of Wales'.

That was the balmy days of summer. However, a distant and remarkable event was making its force felt. The previous year in East Java, Krakatoa had exploded in a series of eruptions. The apocalyptic ash cloud that entered the atmosphere wrought a succession of hard

---

* A paraphrase of Glendower from Shakespeare's *Henry IV*: "I can call spirits from the vasty deep."

European winters and economic distress. Global weather patterns would not return to normal for five years. In February 1886, during the coldest winter for 30 years, a meeting of 20,000 unemployed men in Trafalgar Square devolved into rioting. "In a word, the West-end was for a couple of hours in the hands of the mob," reported *The Times*. Shops were looted, gentlemen's clubs damaged, and in Hyde Park, carriages were stopped and "jewels ripped from the necks of the ladies wearing them, who were then turned out of their vehicles." In Grosvenor Square, volleys of stones smashed the windows of its palatial homes: one ducal family, the Percys, peered out at the rioters while holding pillows to their heads. For two more days, as the capital was gripped in a freezing fog, there was fear of further invasions. Shops and banks lay shuttered under a massive police presence. The tensions continued into Queen Victoria's Golden Jubilee year of 1887, with encampments of the unemployed in Trafalgar Square and St James Park. In November, they would finally be cleared by police and troops, on what was termed 'Bloody Sunday'.

In the 1880s, a brief fad arose for what was called 'slumming' – poverty tourism for the sheer thrill of it.* One who did so in 1884, but with far better intentions, was the future king, then Prince of Wales, in preparation for his role as head of a Royal Commission on working class housing. Dressed in rough clothes, and accompanied by another member of the Commission and a detective, Edward inspected some of the most blighted courts in St Pancras and Holborn. In one room they came across a half-starved mother with three children lying naked in a heap of rags, with another child gone missing.

---

* It was partly sparked by a popular novel *All Sorts and Conditions of Men*, first serialised in 1882. In its preface the author, Walter Besant (1836–1901), wrote of his wanderings in the East End. His story featured two young philanthropists: an heiress and a gentleman who'd been adopted, who undertake "voluntary descent and eclipse," in Stepney to acquaint themselves with its way of life. This infuses them with a determination to lift up the downtrodden, and they end up creating a utopian Palace of Delight in the precinct that offers education and culture. Although Besant was criticised for painting too joyless a picture of East Enders, the "impossible story," as he called it, inspired the creation of The People's Palace in Mile-End Road, opened in 1887 by Queen Victoria. Enabled by the trust fund of philanthropist John Thomas Barber Beaumont (1774–1841), and an energetic businessman, administrator, and fund-raiser Sir Edmund Hay Currie (1834–1913), the visionary complex possessed a library, wintergarden, dining and recreation rooms, gymnasia, and classrooms offering instruction for adults and children in science, art, languages and technical subjects. There was even a swimming pool funded by Lord Rosebery. [Walter Besant, *All Sorts and Conditions of Men*, Chatto & Windus, London 1882, Vol II, p20; Walter Besant And East London, *Aberdeen Evening Express*,12 May 1883, p2; The Ceremony At The People's Palace, *Morning Post*, 16 May 1887, p5; Lord Rosebery At The People's Palace, *London Daily News*, 16 May 1888, p6.]

Ignorance of the plight of 'The Submerged Tenth' remained widespread. Montagu Williams,* a celebrated barrister and magistrate working in the police courts in the East End, was stunned by what he encountered. The destitution extended far beyond the unemployed. As he wrote of Deptford:

> My experience of the way in which even the industrial classes were living in this neighbourhood was certainly most astounding…Whole families lived in one room…The majority of the rooms had no furniture at all, not even a bedstead. There would be an old sack in the corner, and upon that the whole family, consisting of sometimes six, seven, and even eight persons would lie at night.†

Armies of working-class children of school-age, many half-starved from over-crowded homes, also worked before and after school up to 50 hours a week, and even more; one study finding a schoolboy who measured corpses for an undertaker for a shilling a week.

While the average lifespan in 1902 among the upper and professional middle classes was a constrained fifty-five years; amongst the artisan classes of Lambeth it amounted to just twenty-nine years – a twenty-six year difference.

Alice Keppel once pointedly asked Lord Alington, one of her lovers, to drive her through Hoxton. As her daughter Sonia recalled:

> Hoxton was a poor slum in East London where Lord Alington owned a lot of property. Hitherto, he had not visited it…Altogether the drive took three hours, and at the end of it,

* Montagu Stephen Williams (1835–1892), barrister, magistrate, army officer, playwright and actor.
† Another author who explored these precincts was the then young American Jack London, who spent the Coronation summer living in disguise in the East End; the following year publishing a portrait of its poverty, titled *The People of the Abyss*. However, many reviews were critical, and not just of the author's over-egged, jejune style: "he tells no new story. Nor does he suggest a remedy"; "a very pleasant and absurd book of the type we expect from the more violent journalists who visit our Abyss seeking sensation…Mr. London might perhaps be invited to explore portions of New York and Chicago." [The People Of The Abyss, *The Daily Telegraph*, 18 November 1903, p12; The Abyss, *The Daily News*, 4 November 1903, p6. For the same newspaper's sympathetic earlier coverage of the problems of urban poverty in America, see: The City Abyss, *The Daily News*, 10 March 1903, p8.]

Lord Alington was speechless and miserable. As he dropped her home, Mamma thanked him enthusiastically. "I do think it was charming of you to let me see Hoxton as it is now," she said. "Next time I go there I shan't recognise it."

Another new fad, that of bicycling, brought visits in the opposite direction. Princess Mary Adelaide* felt compelled to write to the Home Secretary, asking him to deal with the 'evil' of bicyclists, who were besieging Richmond Park in which her residence White Lodge was situated:

> especially on Saturdays and Sundays, when their number is legion…[their bicycles resting] against our palings…and refreshing the inner man leaving sad traces in the way of orange peel and greasy paper! To add to this their…Conversation is not edifying and they can hear all we say in the garden.

More seriously, Edward, again when Prince of Wales, had experienced the terror of angry mobs at first hand. On a state tour of Ireland in 1885, he and Princess Alexandra's cortege was confronted by nationalist crowds simmering with insurrection. An equerry wrote to Queen Victoria:

> The streets were filled with sullen faces – hideous, dirty, cruel countenances, hissing and grimacing into one's very face, waving black flags and black kerchiefs…No one who went through this day will ever forget it…It was like a bad dream. The Prince and Princess showed the greatest calmness and courage.

Although Edward later made light of the event, it would have impressed upon him anew how fragile the social contract could be, and how central his role was in maintaining it. His intense aversion to corrosive high life scandal entering the public sphere was surely borne

---

* Princess Mary Adelaide of Cambridge, Duchess of Teck (1833-1897), granddaughter of George III. Charming and immensely popular, her alarming girth earned her the nickname 'Fat Mary'. Her engagement to the handsome Francis, Duke of Teck, was considered nothing short of miraculous. There was a logical reason: being impecunious, he required an advantageous marriage. (He actually preferred the company of young officers and other fetching gentlemen.) Their daughter became Queen Mary, consort of George V. [James Pope-Hennessy, *Queen Mary*, George Allen & Unwin, London 1959, pp24, 37, 62; James Pope-Hennessy, Hugo Vickers (ed), *The Quest for Queen Mary*, Zuleika, London 2018, p20.]

of his cross-class experiences and encounters with The Mob. His mother's unpopularity in the mid-1870s had also shadowed him, so he was fully alive to the fickleness of public approval.

Beginning in 1901, and continuing into the Coronation Year and beyond, London was again unsettled by processions of the unemployed, organised by Britain's first socialist political party, the Social Democratic Federation. Wrote a spectator of one such winter march:

> Seldom has West London had so startling a living picture of misery...One afternoon alone I counted over four thousand men marching in the ranks...Many were lads, and some were very old men. Stunted beings barely five feet high, with white faces and pigeon breasts, marched by burly porters...Their garments had nearly all assumed that greyish brown hue which is the last stage of dilapidation...Hands in pockets, heads down to shelter themselves against the wind, they formed as mournful a procession as imagination could conjure...Judged from the point of view of those who desire permanently to uplift the poor, the unemployed processions were a great mistake. It was impossible in them to sift out the idlers from the genuinely needy...but they were also a menace and a warning.

For what was loftily termed The Upper Ten Thousand, which included the gentlemen of government, it was yet another grim reminder that for all their civilisation, Britain's great metropolises were cauldrons of unknowable millions. The dread of what festered in the shadows of their slums would remain a native fear. As a deep diver in both high and low London, Montagu Williams, was under no illusions:

> there exists, side by side with our modern wealth, an amount of destitution and misery probably unequalled in any former age, and the equivalent of which is perhaps not to be met with in any other country of the world.

Barely three months after the Coronation, *Reynolds's Newspaper* bluntly stated: "Not for many a long year has so much poverty and real destitution been witnessed in the streets of London as is to be seen today."

Yet despite this, for a great many, life had never been so blessed; its more privileged spectators would recall the era in terms of a splendid pageant. As one wrote: "The spacious days of King Edward and Queen Alexandra were without doubt the gayest and pleasantest England had ever known."

Only a few decades previously, privileged Society had been a feudal club consisting of a few hundred families. "Riches were still respectable, the rise of a millionaire was yet a romance," and the journalist Walter Bagehot could confidently write: "every day it is proved that money alone…will not buy 'London Society'." Now an ocean of cash from commerce and speculation was flooding into the capital, accelerating the transition from landed wealth, and undermining the old social sureties. The parvenu and social climber, who once could not force an entrance, now found freshly minted bank notes opened any number of doors. With ancestral agricultural estates having collapsed in value, resulting in a flight to investment markets, as Osbert Sitwell* recalled: "the Stock Exchange was in full swing. The institution now set every standard." Like the musical of the age, *The Merry Widow*, "Mammon underlay the smudgy softness and superficial prettiness of the whole thing." Barely a week passed without the exposure of dodgy get-rich-quick share offerings and flim-flam men. Bemoaned a Society columnist: "Many drawing rooms in the West End are little else now than auxiliary stock-exchanges."

The small circle of aristocracy and landed gentry ballooned into a new elite that included the *nouveau riche*, celebrities, and many foreigners. The parade of the *beau monde* during The Season in Hyde Park, where they gathered each afternoon to take the air, and to see and be seen, formed a brilliant spectacle.

For the Old Guard, and those concerned by the worship of mere wealth over rank and virtue, it was exceedingly troubling. Aged relics such as the Dowager Lady Cardigan considered "it was the duty of the old aristocracy to brighten the life of the populace by a display of pomp and circumstance," but England had never seen anything like the new plutocracy. Bemoaned songwriter Cotsford Dick,† "Where

---

* Sir Francis Osbert Sacheverell Sitwell, 5th baronet, (1892–1969), writer.
† Charles George Cotsford Dick (1846–1911), popular songwriter, including of comic operas, and author. "I am an Englishman…and was born with an ineradicable reverence for any rank

are the manners of yester-year? Swagger and swindle now domineer."
For greying social swans like Hamilton Aïdé,* The Season had
become an uphill swim: "I hate London at this time!" he wrote to a
friend. "Such a scramble – such turmoil – such unrest! The scene at
[Joseph] Chamberlain's the other night beggars description."

Anecdotes of the new social buccaneers were relished. Before her
husband's financial collapse, an arriviste was heard to say "she
intended to have her portrait painted by one of the old masters."
When a new merchant prince and his wife purchased a Park Lane
palace, the departing housekeeper left an advisory note on the
characters of the staff for her successor. Appended was her withering
observation of the couple upstairs: "they behave as well as they know
how."

Whereas, only a generation previously, gentlemen had turned their
noses up at the taint of trade, now a quarter of the peerage held
company directorships. The surge of money also came from finance
itself: as the capital of the greatest empire in history, London was the
world's banker. To the horror of the Old Guard, King Edward
welcomed the company of the new tycoons, including the Jewish
nouveau riche, and the compliment was more than repaid.

It was not just a *quid pro quo*, cash-for-social-recognition transaction.
Cosmopolitan to his fingertips, Edward was devoid of Society's
ingrained antisemitism. As one biographer has written, "The King's
mind moved fast beneath that monolithic exterior." The quick-
wittedness, sagacity, sophistication, and even brashness of his Jewish
friends appealed to him, as much as their business capabilities and
bank accounts.

This money-chasing by the monarch was as unseemly then as it would

---

above my own," he wrote in a satirical work. However, in his case it was more than a half-
truth. In 1893 he was bankrupted due to "unjustifiable extravagance", and would later be the
victim of homosexual blackmail. In his latter years poor health rendered him an invalid.
[Cotsford Dick, *Society Snapshots: Taken at Random on a Trip Through the World*, George Allen,
London 1901, p211; Law Report, *The Times*, 11 October 1893; Cotsford Dick's Bankruptcy,
Sheffield Evening Telegraph, 11 January 1894, p3; Cliburn, Robert, Theft, Receiving March 7 1898.
Proceedings of the Old Bailey: oldbaileyonline.org; The Embankment Robbery, *Illustrated Police
News*, 27 February, 1897, p2; Blackmailing Gangs, *Reynolds's Newspaper*, 13 March 1898, p5;
The West-End Blackmailing Affair, *The Illustrated Police News*, 29 January 1898, p2.]
* Charles Hamilton Aïdé (1826–1906), playwright, novelist, musician, watercolour painter, and
maiden aunt socialite. Although deeply conventional, he was exceptionally kind.

be now, but the good times were rolling. Edward was unable to live even on the massive income from the Duchy of Cornwall (which was his as heir apparent), and which was topped up by an annuity granted by Parliament. By the 1880s, he had been in desperate financial straits, and was rescued successively by a Scottish millionaire James Mackenzie,* Lord Rothschild,† and Baron Hirsch,‡ a prickly and relentless social mountaineer, who became his financial advisor. As a social columnist recorded in 1890:

> The most sensational figure in society at this moment is Baron Hirsch, the foreign Hebrew financier, whom the Prince delighteth to honour. Society is very discontented, or pretends to be very discontented, at having to follow suit. Loud are the lamentations which have followed the startling announcement that her parents permitted or directed the Princess Maud of Wales to dance with the financier at the Montagu House ball.

Society might have been even more discontented had it learnt that before Hirsch stepped up with the cash, Edward had been in loan negotiations with a French moneylender and newspaper proprietor, Collard: the sum was to be advanced by a champagne merchant in exchange for royal endorsement of his product.

When Hirsch died in 1896, his alleged instructions to his executor Sir Ernest Cassel§ were that Edward's enormous £300,000 debt to him should be written off. Cassel also succeeded Hirsch as Edward's financial advisor and friend. When a lady asked Cassel's opinion of her lapis lazuli necklace, she received the reply: "Very pretty stuff. I've got a room made of it." Edward's friendship with the world-weary Cassel was the greatest pleasure of them both. However, the King's social approval of the Jewish financiers added to their increased visibility, helping fuel popular perceptions of their power and influence. Following in the rolling footsteps of Randlord and folk

---

* Sir James Thompson Mackenzie, 1st Baronet of Glenmuick (1818-1890).

† Nathaniel 'Natty' Mayer de Rothschild, 1st (UK) Baron Rothschild (1840-1915). Married a cousin, Emma Louisa von Rothschild, and had issue.

‡ Baron Maurice de Hirsch (1831–1896). He devoted a significant proportion of his fortune to sponsoring Jewish immigration and charities. Married Clara Bischoffsheim, and had issue. Following the early deaths of their children, the Hirschs adopted two of Maurice's illegitimate sons, one of whom became Baron de Forest. [Samuel J. Lee, *Moses Of The New World; The Work Of Baron de Hirsch*, Thomas Yoseloff, Cranbery, New Jersey 1970, p197.]

§ Sir Ernest Joseph Cassel (1852–1921), banker. Married Annette Mary Maud Maxwell, and had issue.

figure Barney Barnato,* a few became household names.

For the man on the street and in the clubs, the swell of fast and flashy fortunes appeared to have come out of nowhere, and seemed – in the manner of Russian oligarchs – unearned, shady, and worst of all – 'un-English'. It just wasn't cricket. "Fair play is the pith and fibre of the Empire," proclaimed the baronet Sir Shane Leslie:† "Anti-Semitic feeling is as degrading and out of date as the pillory, but social discrimination can be an ethical necessity." In his view, the new "society-seeking swarm" were "out of place, as is shown by their total lack of sporting sense, except in the occasional guise of magnificent patrons." It was typical of the polite prejudice that found voice.

Yet due to a dramatic decline in agricultural rents, traditional aristocratic patronage and charity was suffering. It was this gulf that the King now bridged. From the 1870s onwards, as Prince of Wales, he reinvented himself to become (like the later King Charles III, when Prince of Wales) the Nation's most important charity advocate and enabler. His friendships with financiers and businessmen would give birth to a new age of unprecedented plutocratic philanthropy.‡

This was given greater focus in the 1890s by a statistician and hospital administrator, Sir Henry Burdett,§ who provided royal philanthropic advice. It was possibly further advanced by the pressings of Edward's then mistress, the socialist Daisy, Countess of Warwick, who in turn, was urged on by her Svengali, the social activist and editor W.T. Stead.**

---

* Barney Barnato (1851–1897), born Barnet Isaacs.
† Sir 'Shane' John Randolph Leslie, 3rd baronet (1885–1971), eccentric Anglo-Irish diplomat and author and translator, including under the pseudonym Ion Ionicos, of *Strato's Boyish Muse* (Fortune Press, 1932). [See: Otto Rauchbauer, *Shane Leslie: Sublime Failure*, Lilliput Press, Dublin 2009; W. J. McCormack, *Roger Casement in Death: Or, Haunting the Free State*, University College Dublin Press, 2002.]
‡ For an overview of this beneficence, see: Frank Prochaska, 'King Edward VII: The Impresario of the Plutocracy', in *Great Philanthropists: Wealth and Charity in the Modern World 1815-1945*, Peter Mandler, David Cesarani (eds.) Vallentine Mitchell, Elstree 2016.
§ Sir Henry Charles Burdett (1847–1920). Author of the treatise of the philanthropy of the Prince and Princess of Wales, *Prince, Princess And People* (1889).
** William Thomas Stead (1849–1912) English newspaper editor, social reformer, and pioneer of investigative journalism. "Stead was the most tender-hearted of men; but the most blood-curdling in his denunciations of the prevailing weakness of mankind," wrote H.J. Thaddeus who painted his portrait. "I sometimes feared he would explode and go up like a rocket to heaven." Stead died aboard the Titanic; he was seen standing alone at the edge of the deck in a "prayerful attitude of profound meditation" – an equanimity perhaps explained by his deep belief in spiritualism and the afterlife. [H. Jones Thaddeus, *Recollections Of A Court Painter*, John

Edward had a keen interest in medicine, and by 1900 was patron of seventy-five hospitals. One example of his practical efforts was the King Edward VII Sanatorium for Consumption at Midhurst. It was inspired by a leading sanatorium he had seen at Falkenstein in Germany, when visiting his dying sister the Empress Frederick. Exasperated at the tardiness of hospital administrations to exercise their funds, he used what became known as King Edward's Hospital Fund to expedite its construction.

Those on the Fund's committee included not only the Bishop of London, but the Chief Rabbi, as well as Lord Rothschild and Sir Ernest Cassel. It was Cassel who furnished the then unheard-of donation of £200,000 for the Midhurst sanatorium,* and by the end of his life had given away £2 million pounds (several billion today) to causes ranging from the Red Cross to adult education.

This new scale of giving constituted a handsome response to those of Sir Shane Leslie's ilk, but it didn't silence the carping. Some of Cassel's gifts were targeted to garner influence, such as the oak-lined library and American stocks given to Winston Churchill, but much else was given with no other motive but a desire to relieve the distress of others; Cassel once remarking: "I have had everything in the world that I did not want, and nothing that I did." Having no interests outside of finance, and an inner barrenness, his enjoyment of life's pleasures was blunted.

Others were not so satiated. Observed Society stalwart Lady Greville: "the race for amusement and the forces of toil and play increase in speed and complexity daily." The symbol of it, and of flashy expenditure beyond the pockets of humble folk, was the motor car. The days of the leisurely horse-drawn hansom cab were numbered. "London's gondola" Disraeli had called them: a few even sported striped awnings and drivers with boutonnières. "Quite a lot of my 'pals' have emigrated to Canada," a hansom driver told a newspaper in 1907, "while others are learning to be motormen." The silk hat, which signalled respectability, and had once been worn by "Every male above the age and status of an office boy or a labouring man,"

Lane, London 1912, p171; Frederic Whyte, *The Life Of W. T. Stead*, Vol II, Jonathan Cape, London 1925, p314.]
* Cassel's beloved only child, Maude, died of tuberculosis in 1911.

would be sported a while longer.

"Everybody rushes now. London has no more time to spare than New York does." The new restlessness, loss of grace and repose, and decline in decorum and politeness, was keenly felt by older generations. Signs of the pace of change were all around. "Are you working here, mate" queried a friendly policeman at the Houses of Parliament to the plainly dressed working class M.P. Keir Hardie. "Yes I am," he replied. "On the roof?" asked the policemen. "No, on the floor," replied Hardie.* The changes in status were also in the opposite direction. Although not without precedent, the admittance to a workhouse of a destitute baronet, Sir William Gordon McGregor, made headlines. Nonetheless, social distinctions remained deeply entrenched.

While some viewed the new era as one of fresh prosperity, greater personal liberty, and widening horizons, others looked upon its trumpeting feverish zest with a more jaundiced eye, and even concern, seeing signs of growing decadence, and what the more ardent proclaimed was a generalised decay in the empire-building virtues of the noble English race. When 11,000 men volunteered in Manchester for the Second Boer War, 8,000 were found upon examination to be unfit for service. "What a comment is that single fact on the increasing degeneracy of our city-bred populations!" exclaimed the *Illustrated London News*.

This line of rhetoric was inspired by Max Nordau,† a German Jewish physician and writer living in Paris, who in 1892 had published the book *Entartung* (Degeneration). Nordau claimed:

> The inhabitant of a large town, even the richest, who is surrounded by the greatest luxury, is continually exposed to unfavourable influences which diminish his vital powers far more than what is inevitable.

Nordau was not only fascistic, but a censorious prude of the first

* Admiral Fisher once angered King Edward VII after he questioned why he was inquiring after the health of the republican Hardie: "You don't understand me!" he roared, "I am king of ALL the people!" [Jane Ridley, *Bertie: A Life Of Edward VII*, Chatto & Windus, London 2012, p476.]
† Max Simon Nordau, born Simon Maximilian Südfeld (1849–1923), Zionist leader, physician, author, and social critic.

water. Those he believed manifested this degeneracy were conclusively damned. They included not only the obvious targets for decadence alarmists, like Charles Baudelaire and Oscar Wilde, but Walt Whitman too: "one of the deities to whom the degenerate and hysterical of both hemispheres have for some time been raising altars." Two months before Wilde's jailing, Nordau's book appeared in an English translation, and quickly ran into seven editions. Chock full of choice phrases like "a pathological aberration of a racial instinct," its quack medicalised sociology chimed with those seeking answers to the believed social decline.*

Another social anatomist – and one who was even more reassuringly home-bred – was the polemical journalist and eugenicist Arnold White.† A disciple of philosopher Herbert Spencer,‡ who coined 'survival of the fittest', White's concerns included unrestricted Jewish immigration (Herr Doktor Nordau possibly exempted), and organised charity. The latter he argued was a public evil as it preserved the unfit, thereby becoming a potent means of racial degeneration, and the decay of the moral health of the nation. As White saw it, the rise of plutocratic smart society and financial speculators who acted in their own interests – 'kakocrats', had also led to the corruption of wholesome nation-building values upheld by the traditional aristocracy of gentlefolk:

> aristocracy is nothing more than the most efficient people in the nation, whose efficiency has been graded up by generations of training…When efficiency goes out at the door, it is inevitable that Empire will fly out at the window.

---

* Nordau's critics included writer and social philosopher Alfred Egmont Hake (1849–1916), who anonymously-published an analysis stating that Nordau's racial bias had "warped his perceptions, his reasoning, and his conclusions…The anti-semitism in Germany, which Max Nordau ascribes to degeneration…springs from causes so patent, that no man who aspires to be considered an acute observer of his time should ignore them." [Anon, *Regeneration: A Reply To Max Nordau*, Archibald Constable, London 1895, pp20, 190.]

† Arnold Henry White (1848–1925). Like Nordau, White also believed decadence and sodomy were allied. During World War I he was to become concerned about homosexual Hun: "Of the vices of the Cities of the Plain, Palestine taught nothing to Potsdam…When the blond beast is an urning he commands the urnings of other lands. They are moles. They burrow. They plot. They are hardest at work when they are most silent. Britain is only safe when her statesmen are family men…" [Arnold White, Efficiency and Vice, *The English Review*, May 1916, pp446-452.]

‡ Herbert Spencer (1820–1903), the famous philosopher of his time.

51

One of the most cynical observers of the age was Henry Labouchère,[*] popularly known as 'Labby'. A wealthy Liberal M.P. for Northampton, and journalist and theatre owner, Labouchère would later retire to Florence, and leave an estate of two million pounds. Despite his social position, Labby was always an outsider. Of French origin, he was a remarkable figure on the national stage: a brazen posturer and poseur; unscrupulous in business; an impish hypocrite, and a sceptic of most things. Sniped one columnist: "Labby's mind long ago became so distorted that he can believe no story until it is proved to be false." Wilfrid Blunt[†] considered him to be, after Oscar Wilde, "the most brilliant talker in England."[‡] A biographer observed:

> As far as a man can be, he was without inhibitions; he was fearless; and he wrote and spoke what he thought. He delighted in the comedy of life and was amused by the enthusiasms, rages, contradictions and imbecilities of his fellow-creatures...He certainly believed in social reform, but he had little faith that human beings would be much improved thereby...A born free-thinker and free-speaker, he had no respect of principles or persons and could never be depended upon to toe the party line or give deference to the mighty or even lip-service to the Almighty.

Besides having "absolutely no reverence for men or their creeds," and chronic mischief-maker, Labby was as eccentric as any character of Dickens. It was said, "he used to go about London looking like a dilapidated bagman," and was once glimpsed smashing his troublesome false teeth with a hammer. As a Member of Parliament, he was coldly detached, and was caught vote-buying. This was par for the course: as a young man he'd been suspended from Cambridge for suspected cheating. Labby used his position as the publisher and editor of *Truth*, a gossipy 'radical' social and political weekly, to advance his personal and business interests, including share-rigging. Yet he also delighted in using it to expose fraudsters and sanctimonious hypocrites.

The motto of the sixpence *Truth* was taken from Cicero: *'Cultores*

---

[*] Henry Du Pré Labouchère (1831–1912). See: George W.E. Russell, *Portraits Of The Seventies*, T. Fisher Unwin, London 1916, pp137-153.
[†] Wilfrid Scawen Blunt (1840-1922), poet and writer.
[‡] He had little time for bores: to one who informed him, "Mr. Labouchère, I believe I had the happiness to know your mother very well in old days," he replied, "Indeed, then perhaps you are my father." [Stephen Coleridge, *Memories*, John Lane, London 1913, pp122-123.]

Veritatis Fraudis Inimici' – 'Worshippers of Truth, Enemies of Fraud'. Its pages were imbued with Labby's distinctive voice. He could churn out biting and brilliant copy effortlessly by the yard: a fellow journalist describing its production as, "one of the most extraordinary things I have seen...never pausing for a word, never correcting a word," leaving it to the paper's shadow-editor, Horace Voules, to do what he liked with it.*

Being a contrarian pragmatist, Labby's radicalism only went so far. In 'Entres Nous',† his (endless) column in *Truth*, he didn't hesitate to attack the Royal Family's allowances. Yet week after week he also let Voules serve up, in tones of deepest gravity, reams of inconsequential tripe about even its most minor members. An admiration for King Edward is also apparent, which was mutual. This is not surprising given Labby shared much in common with him: both were insiders who were also outsiders: rebels who were their own men. As *Truth* printed of Edward, he was: "a man of the world...his wide experience of all sorts and conditions of men has broadened his views."

Labouchère believed the nation was monarchical by sentiment, but he loathed flunkeyism. Like W.M. Thompson at *Reynolds's Newspaper*, he despaired of the state of the nation. In the summer of 1902, in an editorial titled 'Neurotic Degeneration In Politics,' he wrote: "The policy of the party now in power is to convert us into a vast military empire." Certainly, pride in the British Empire and the 'divine mission to redeem the world,' infused everything. Some newspapers even headlined the daily record of parliamentary proceedings: 'Imperial Parliament'. Of these 'jingo' papers Labby spluttered:

> the Imperialism inculcated by the Press is the raving of lunatics...London dailies which live by exaggeration, political cant, sensation, perversion of facts, and appeals to the passions rather than reason.

In his view, the crowds lining the streets to cheer the new King were merely due to the fact "the desire for shows, festivals and rejoicings has become a positive mania with us. It has been fostered by the war

---

* After he entered Parliament, Labouchère's contributions to *Truth* were mostly political copy, with the remainder of the paper being written by staff. [Anon (Robert Augustus Bennett), The Real Labouchère, *Truth*, 24 & 31 January 1912.]
† Between Ourselves.

and its maffickings."

The Boer War had indeed been popular with the British working people, who were angered by the disenfranchisement of British immigrants in the Dutch Transvaal, as retailed by the popular press. Seizing the moment, the *Daily Mail* instituted a 'war express', employing the blackest coal and 'the most famous living engine driver' to deliver copies of the paper to the north of England for breakfast. Patriots even took to sporting khaki ties. An observer at Waterloo station noted at a send-off of troops: "There was scarcely a single 'well-dressed' man or woman in the crowd...neither the upper nor the middle classes were present – only the lower classes, shouting like mad."

It was music to the ears of imperialists like J. Astley Cooper,* editor of the jingo magazine *King And Country*. One of his contributors, a Mr. Stanley Little, admitted he held the very lowest opinion of the morals of the English, but extending their sovereignty over other races was an urgently needed blessing:

> Our very crassness of blood, our very coarseness, which exceeds the coarseness and crassness of many Africans – and certainly the Zulu is far more refined – is the very quality which, in an Imperial race, is most to be prized...The Briton is neither subtle, nor aesthetic, nor intellectual, but he has an unerring instinct for the best things of the earth.

In southern Africa, the links between imperialism and finance were particularly naked. The War had been a criminal enterprise from its beginning, resulting in the slaughter of not only British soldiers, but those of colonial contingents. A great swathe of liberals and socialists,

---

* John Astley Cooper (1858–1930), propagandist for British imperialism and athleticism. Consistently mischaracterised as a clergyman, he was the eldest son of the Rev. Astley Cooper. He worked as a commercial agent, travelling extensively throughout the world, before becoming a journalist, and editor and part-owner of the short-lived imperialist magazines *Greater Britain* and *King And Country*. Due to their losses, he was twice bankrupted. His proposals for a pan-Britannic festival of the Anglo-Saxon race, involving an athletic gathering and scholarships, influenced the eventual Rhodes Scholarships and Empire Games. He married and had issue. It has been claimed he was homosexual, but no evidence has been presented. [Ramsgate Journalist And Company Director, *Dover Express*, 28 August 1925, p13; Pan-Britannic Movement, *London Evening Standard*, 2 June 1908, p10; Buckminster, *The Grantham Journal*, 8 May 1915, p4; Robert I. Rotberg; Miles F. Shore, *The Founder: Cecil Rhodes And The Pursuit Of Power*, Oxford University Press, 1988, p664.]

including radical editors such as Labby, were convinced that, at the very least, the British Government had been duped into it by the Randlords, the entrepreneurs and speculators who controlled its diamond and gold mining. As they were predominately Jewish, and often German-born, the untrammelled group capitalism* became looked upon as an alien tribal conspiracy – "the Anglo-Jewish financiers who are the masters of the existing disreputable Government," as W.M. Thompson put it. "We have no objection to seeing Jews in Parliament, but we think that, for their numbers in this country, they have more than a fair share of representatives there already."†

Cecil Rhodes‡ was seen as their South African facilitator. In a speech he delivered in 1899, Rhodes had summed up his belief why British imperialism was vital:

> The practical reason for the further acquisition of territory was that every Power in the world, including their kinsman the Americans, as soon as they took new territory placed hostile tariffs against British goods...Great Britain's position depended on her trade, and if they did not take and open the portions of the world which were at present devoted to barbarism they would be shut out from the world's trade....The politics of the next hundred years were going to be tariffs and nothing else. They were not going to war for the amusement of Royal families as in the past, but they meant practical business.

---

* The homogenous opportunism was similar to that which enabled the rise of the predominately Jewish oligarchs of Russia. [Luke Harding, 'The Richer They Come...', The Guardian, 2 July 2000.]

† Despite this, *Reynolds's Newspaper* would denounce the Aliens Act of 1905, which introduced immigration controls, stating it "is really an attempt to get a little show of popularity for the Government by playing the anti-Semitic game. It would be impossible to conceive any more disgraceful trick, for, of course, it is easy, and it has always been found easy in every country to arouse hatred against the Jews." [The Talking Shop, *Reynolds's Newspaper*, 7 May 1905, p4.]

‡ Cecil John Rhodes (1853–1902), leading imperialist, mining magnate, Prime Minister of the Cape Colony, and founder of Rhodesia (currently Zimbabwe and Zambia). Throughout his life he surrounded himself with attractive young men, who were known as his 'lambs' and 'apostles'. They included Neville Ernest Pickering, a young Englishman who was secretary, and the likely love of his life. Until Pickering's premature death after falling from a horse, he was sole beneficiary of Rhodes' will. "His dislike of English female company and servants was notorious; his high-pitched, effeminate voice did not help matters, nor did his openly displayed collection of phallic cult carvings." [Robert I. Rotberg, *The Founder: Cecil Rhodes And The Pursuit of Power*, Oxford University Press, 1988, pp147-148, 407, 589; Ronald Hyam, *Empire And Sexuality: The British Experience*, Manchester University Press, 1990, p39.]

With its implication Rhodes only viewed war as a means to commercial ends, the speech was seized on by his opponents. They believed the 'practical business' to hand was less about tariffs, and more about British annexation of the Transvaal enabling the Randlords to reduce labour costs, thereby increasing their shareholder profits. Indeed, the consulting engineer of the Consolidated Gold Fields company had blithely stated he hoped the reduction in wages under the new regime would amount to half. The President of the Witwatersrand miners union, who also happened to be a member of the Johannesburg stock exchange, was equally blunt: "'Imperialism' is only another name for speculation, stock-jobbing, and financial operations on a stupendous scale."

Back in London, W.M. Thompson was also under no illusions of what he termed "our Corrupt Oligarchy".

> Plenty of honest people supported the late war, innocently believing the great campaign of lies, engineered by the classes out of the money provided by the Anglo-Jewish syndicates, for whom British lives were laid down, and British capital expended…500,000 men confronted a little band of 50,000 determined peasants fighting for their country.

In an editorial delicately titled 'The New Enemies Of Mankind', he wrote: "Getting the Transvaal under English rule meant the war which cost us 30,000 lives and more than £200,000,000 in money. But that is what the South African millionaire would call a matter of detail."

A few believed a reckoning was coming. That Coronation Year, the most popular novelist of the day, Marie Corelli,* published *Temporal Power: A Study In Supremacy*, a novel about a king who, suddenly aware he is not doing his duty by his people, joins a society of socialists. Its first edition alone sold a record 120,000 copies. In her own time, Corelli would be dismissed as an "ignorant, affected, tinselled sentimentalist," but her concerns and prejudices reflected those of her vast readership. As one of her obituaries put it, she was "the prophet of all the simple souls of the world, and for the simple reason that she

---

* Marie Corelli, pen name of Mary Mackay (1855–1924). She inspired the socially-thrusting character of Emmeline Lucas in E.F. Benson's series of comic Lucia novels. Her life companion was Bertha van der Vyver, who is buried with her.

was one of them." In a preface written four years later for an American edition of the novel, she had looked back on King Edward's first year:

> Everywhere strong signs of discontent were manifest...Snobism and Flunkey-ism were the ruling influences of the time. Jew financiers and plutocrats generally were, as they still are, the favourites of Court and society – and the actual Workers of the nation – they who toil unremittingly for no other reward than poverty, slow starvation and death – went apparently without notice or consideration of their needs...I felt sure of a speedily coming revolt of the People against 'upper class' effeminacy, laziness and luxury.

How much more Corelli would have feared an approaching storm had she known of the great aristocratic scandal then secretly unfolding. At the very heart of the British Establishment a deep rift of homosexual procurement had been exposed. So gilded were the names involved, and so shocking and socially dangerous was the story considered, that under no circumstances would it be allowed to come to the knowledge of the public.

Some of the persons of consequence it touched were in the Abbey that Coronation Day. They included, berobed in velvet and ermine, the nobleman at the very centre of the drama – Cyril Flower, Lord Battersea. Or to quote his title in full: 1st Baron Battersea of Battersea in the County of London, and of Overstrand in the County of Norfolk.

Once considered the most handsome man in Parliament, Lord Battersea was stupendously rich and immensely well-connected: husband to a Rothschild heiress, and future chairman of one of the most prominent Randlord mining and financial corporations. For those like Corelli, easily swayed by rumours of conspiracy arising from base yearnings, this would have been the very stuff of high corruption and social decay. Had the public been made aware of it, the affront to morality could have led to widespread discontent. And those who held the reins of power well knew it.

However, on that day of days, such roiling temporal concerns were briefly suspended. For when Westminster Abbey's great organ, and a full orchestra and choir sounded the first soaring notes of the Coronation anthem *I Was Glad*, the spirits of those present – including perhaps even those of the plutocratic amongst the congregation, were elevated. For a few brief hours, the shimmering, spine-tingling religious spectacle like no other induced a collective state of being – scrabbling mortal selves temporarily forgotten in a rapture of national oneness. They were all in it together.

Cyril Flower's wife, Constance, Lady Battersea,[*] confided to her diary:

> It was touching & stirring. Everyone present seemed to take part in it, people & throne closely united. It was feudal, medieval, English yet Imperial. It held one enthralled thro' eye, ear & heart. It was religious & yet of this world...It represented all that has made England great.

---

[*] Constance Flower, Baroness Battersea; née de Rothschild (1843–1931).

2. THE WAY OF THE WORLD

London was both 'the heart of Empire' and a world within itself. And at its very centre existed yet another realm – The Great World, as it was sometimes knowingly termed. This was London Society, great only in its influence, for it was small and intensely artificial; full of pomps and vanities, as it had ever been, but for all its lordly rigidities, also a living, breathing, protean thing.

From Buckingham Place and St James's to the corridors of Whitehall, onwards to the drawing rooms of Mayfair and Belgravia, and the gentlemen's clubs of Pall Mall, the elect and those who administered their governments, wealth and justice existed in a sequestered environment where everyone knew everyone, or knew someone who did. The tight-knit connections of intermarriage, public schools,* Oxbridge, the civil service, clubs, Parliament, Society and Court, ensured it was so. The Society paper *The Sketch* noted that during the Season of 1901:

> Never was the Lobby of the House of Commons gayer than it is these June afternoons. Ladies dressed in the brightest fashions flutter through the corridors about five o'clock and peep into the House through the window at the inner door before going to tea on the Terrace. Smart Society takes pleasure in the Lobby, and members ambitious of a place in Society gladly pay attention to these visitors.

Another writer observed:

---

* i.e. the leading *private* schools, such as Eton, Harrow and Rugby.

the outsider who happens upon a gathering of Ministerial personages, and finds them all cousins, and brothers-in-law, and all more or less intricately related, or at any rate on such terms of intimacy that the wives are calling each other by their Christian names, and the younger men are 'Bobby', and 'Jack', and 'Dolly' all round, is apt to entertain the idea that English politics is still controlled by a sort of Family Compact. Of course, the outsider does get in…but he has to be an outsider of unusual ability and force of character, and even then he does not, as a rule, win his chance till he has either married into the proper set or acquired sufficient wealth and social prestige to be assimilated by it.

Most importantly, everyone knew the behavioural codes and obligations, including those of class loyalty. No less than the Prime Minister, Lord Salisbury,* had written that telling white lies in order to help "a fugitive who is in danger, or a friend who is in trouble," was sometimes acceptable. It was a minor foible amongst chums, and everyone amongst the Upper Ten Thousand was, in one way or another, a chum.

"English morality is inscrutable and illogical," wrote Sir Shane Leslie:

> The most bankrupt and disreputable peer passes as a decayed gentleman, but a nobleman who has cheated at cards enters the class that Orientals call 'the untouchables'.…A man may live with whom he will, provided only England never knows.

The aristocracy were extremely conscious of being an elite who believed they carried the torch of *areté* – the spirit of excellence in all things. Their earliest school lessons in Greek instilled the fact they embodied *áristos* (best) and *kratos* (power). Besmirching the honour of peers by defamatory words had once been considered an especially grave offence: *scandalum magnatum*. Although obsolete by the close of the 18th century, it was only finally repealed in 1887. Rare was an aristocrat like the 8th Viscount Strangford, who dismissed his peerage as "a tin kettle tied to a dog's tail".

One individual who was perfectly placed to observe the workings of

---

* Robert Arthur Talbot Gascoyne-Cecil, 3rd Marquess of Salisbury (1830–1903); three times Prime Minister between 1885 and 1902.

the Great World as an inside-outsider was American actress Eleanor Calhoun,* who later married a Serbian aristocrat. A keen admirer of the writings of John Stuart Mill and other utopians, she was taken up by Edwardian Society, dining with King Edward, and spending time in country houses with Arthur Balfour† and other luminaries of the period.

"Deeply embedded in English nature is the sense of hierarchy," she wrote in her memoirs. "This is observable any afternoon at Hyde Park Corner," where Society gathered. She noted how, in the promenade of carriages, there was "tacit recognition" of the right-of-way of the grander equipages, the coachmen of such vehicles not hesitating to put the others in their places. In contrast, "the royal carriage is the great leveler, putting for the moment one and all, great and small, into the same class as they make their way for it to pass."

Of her daily travels across Edwardian London, she wrote, "It seemed to me that I was wading through vast tides of human woe." Of the great homes she visited, she remarked that: "ideas of reform were in some manner considered or discussed in every house."

A halo of assumed superiority suffused the entire upper class, who commanded and expected not only respect, but deference. At every moment of the day their social position was demarcated by speech, accent, dress and manner: it is impossible to overstate the defining power of this. As landlords and legislators, between 1760 and 1880 they passed The Enclosure Acts, which served to consolidate over 10 million acres of common land in their hands, to the exclusion of small-holding peasant farmers. The intention had been to make agriculture more efficient and productive, which it did. However, many of the land transfers were manipulated by the wealthy to their further advantage: a phenomenon the social activist Edward Carpenter‡ lambasted as "petty robbery".§

---

* Princess Lazarovich-Hrebelianovich, born Eleanor Hulda Calhoun (1862-1957).
† Arthur James Balfour, 1st Earl of Balfour, (1848–1930), Conservative politician, Prime Minister from 1902 to 1905.
‡ Edward Carpenter (1844–1929), socialist, poet, philosopher, and activist for homosexual emancipation.
§ Common land had been under the control of local lords of the manor, who leased it out. Unused land, generally the least fertile and most challenging, was able to be farmed by anyone – usually the poorest. When farmed fields and waste land were consolidated under the Acts, only existing tenants were financially compensated.

Simply due to their status a huge number of the upper class also benefited from sinecures, pensions, and other emoluments and opportunities that were walled off from the rest of society.* The greatest of these iniquities subsidised by ordinary working people were a series of semi-secret hereditary annuities that benefited a number of privileged families. Labelled 'perpetual pensions', they included continuing payments to the descendants of the bastards of Charles II. As late as 1890, the radical parliamentarian Charles Bradlaugh,† who campaigned for their abolition, informed the public that the 6th Duke of Richmond was in receipt of an astonishing £19,000 a year‡ from the Government, simply due to the fact the 1st Duke, born 1672, had been a son of Charles's mistress Louise de Kérouaille!§

The myth and status of the upper class was also buttressed by the noble proportions and siting of their residences; their flattering portrayals in gilded portraits; the subservience of tenants, servants, and almost all others; and their glorious and respectful histories within the story of the Nation itself.

This superiority was consecrated by their continued grip on power both in the House of Commons, and the House of Lords, whose very name, like their noble titles, reflected their godly status.** As with the monarchy that bestowed their honours, it was a right to rule "divinely instituted for the good of the people," as Queen Victoria neatly put

---

* The oligarchical abuses by the vested interest groups that controlled the British state, including the aristocracy and the Church, were fully exposed in 1823 by a remarkable radical journalist, John Wade (1788–1875). Funded by philosopher Jeremy Bentham, and printed and supported by Bentham's publisher, Effingham Wilson, a man of "great moral courage," he compiled and published *The Black Book*, which detailed lists of all those who benefited from taxpayers' money and other privileges. The degree of preposterous payments almost defies belief. The book created a sensation, and contributed to the spirit that carried forward the Reform Bill of 1832. Wade ultimately benefited from a small State pension himself of £50 p.a., but died in great poverty. [Anon (John Wade), *The Black Book or Corruption Unmasked*, John Fairburn, London 1823; The Late Mr John Wade, *The Acton Gazette*, 6 November 1875, p3.]
† Charles Bradlaugh (1833 –1891), radical Liberal M.P. for Northampton, Republican, atheist, and political activist. Married Susannah Lamb Hooper, and had issue. Following his death, shamed by his exposure of hereditary annuities, successive Governments gradually and quietly extinguished them with payments of the capital value to their recipients.
‡ In excess of £2,220,000 per annum in 2021 values. [Measuringworth.com]
§ Louise de Kérouaille (occasionally rendered Querouaille), Duchess of Portsmouth (1649–1734).
** Ironically, amongst the Upper Ten Thousand, schoolyard nicknames reigned supreme: Sloper, Jumbo, Muffins, Bimbash, Wiggy, and Bunny were the monikers of some of the grandest men of the day: Lord Saltoun answered to Satan; Lord Lonsdale to Mollie. [Nicknames of Well Known Men, *New Zealand Herald*, 12 January 1903.]

it. The merciless barb of writer A.A. Gill* – "Sifting an unearned social advantage out of the ossuary is ridiculous and demeaning" – seems pertly apt in a modern world where all is shifting sand, and every construct is up for grabs, but reverencing hereditary rank met deep collective desires for rootedness, meaning and generational identity. Even if the reality of the chinless duffer lord too often diverged from the ideal, unlike the classes below them, whose crabbed lives were consumed by unending toil for their daily bread, the ruling class believed that their privileges bestowed virtues.

"The office of an order of nobility is to impose on the common people...on their quiescent imaginations what would not otherwise be there," Walter Bagehot had written with Olympian condescension in 1866:

> Nobility is the symbol of mind...In reverencing wealth we reverence not a man, but an appendix of a man; in reverencing inherited nobility, we reverence the probable possession of a great faculty – the faculty of bringing out what is in one. The unconscious grace of life *may* be in the middle classes; finely-mannered persons are born everywhere, but it *ought* to be in an aristocracy; and a man must be born with a hitch in his nerves if he has not some of it.

When not slaughtering wildlife, or seducing anything else that moved, the breadth and richness of aristocratic lives, and their abundant leisure, certainly encouraged a few peers, like the ancient patricians, to cultivate higher learning and philosophy, and sophisticated tastes. In its best representatives, this blessed existence bestowed a grand and measured perspective – with the corresponding benefits to the progression of the great British nation itself.

Of course, there was the greater lumpen mass of the peerage, but for Bagehot, even they had their virtues:

> A great part of the 'best' English society keep their mind in a state of decorous dullness...they have no notion of *play* of mind...they think cleverness an antic, and have a constant though needless horror of being thought to have any of it...But

---

* Adrian Anthony Gill (1954–2016), British writer and critic.

63

a good government is worth a great deal of social dullness. The dignified torpor of English society is inevitable if we give precedence – not to the cleverest classes, but to the oldest classes – and we have seen how useful that is.

Such narratives, touched with truth but wreathed with hypocrisy, were sustained by the 'respectable' organs of the national press, which would, in almost every instance, chronicle and refer to members of the upper class on bended knee – an automatic respect and obsequiousness that would remain until the 1960s.

Indicative of the romance and powerful allure of this national myth, which protected and sustained the generational entitlements of what was simply a mass of rich people holding the remainder of the populous economically hostage, is the fact that homage to it lingers on in reduced form today. Its endurance is also due to an often grudging recognition of the sundry benefits (as plentiful as the drawbacks) that rule by this elite rendered.* This included its institutions, such as the great public schools and universities, that today cower under ideological assault. A remarkable, but rarely considered aspect of the Britain of the time, was that a vast amount of the work undertaken by upper class administrators, in all tiers of government, was unremunerated.†

Typical of aristocrats who embodied the spirit of *noblesse oblige* were the 12th Earl and Countess of Meath.‡ He was an ardent Tory imperialist who founded Empire Day. Together the couple devoted their energies to innovative philanthropy. Their work included creating open spaces and gardens in poorer districts for children to play in, and the purchase of a large country house for female epileptics. In her drawing room, Lady Meath founded the Ministering Children's League. Its goal was to instil unselfishness in children – by implanting the seed of a desire to take an active interest in their parish, and help others in need. It was a simple but powerful idea, and the League spread across the globe, including establishing homes and hospitals for destitute infants. Its motto, "No day without a deed to

---

* An unplanned benefit of incalculable national worth was that, by default, the great estates preserved much of the British countryside from the blight of small parcel development.
† See: Algernon West, *One City And Many Men*, Smith Elder & Co, London 1908, pp242-258.
‡ Reginald Brabazon, 12th Earl of Meath (1841–1929); Mary Jane Brabazon, née Maitland, Countess of Meath (1847–1918).

crown it," reflected the personal ideals of the couple.

In 1916, in an article titled 'The Sacrifice Of The Peerage', *The Times* catalogued the forty-five aristocratic eldest sons and heirs so far lost in the Great War. Another paper called it:

> the noblest possible answer to those political agitators who, in the interest of partisanship, have been wont to traduce the ennobled class as selfish idlers, degenerate and unworthy of their honours.*

In the worst representatives of the upper class, privilege merely produced pomposity, suffocating the expression of humanity. A notable exemplar was the Liberal M.P. Montague Guest:† "'Monty Guest' was *persona gratissima* wherever he went," stated *The Athenaeum*. "No man was better known in London society, especially in Court and dilettante circles." He was the bachelor son of a baronet who owned the world's largest iron foundry. An American journalist called Guest:

> the most imposing specimen of *dégagé* swelldom…'You be d___dness'…shows itself in every facial expression, social mannerism, or casual movement…[He did] embody, in its highest perfection, the easy and superb insolence which the titled aristocracy sends its sons to Eton, into the Guards, or into diplomacy to acquire.

Guest's homes at the Albany in London, and at Brighton, were jammed with expensive *bric-à-brac*. It was a taste acquired from his formidable polymath mother Lady Charlotte, of whom it was said, "she gave to *bric-à-brac* what was meant for mankind." The Irish dramatist Lady Gregory equally labelled Guest "a selfish creature". However, to many of his station, like the English colonel's daughter Princess Daisy of Pless, he was "dear old Monty". To those unfortunate enough to exist below it, whom he looked down upon through the heavy-rimmed pince-nez he affected, he must have

---

* Barely three months into the War even the Royal Family lost a member, when Prince Maurice of Battenberg (son of Princess Beatrice, and grandson of Queen Victoria), who was fighting in the King's Royal Rifle Corps, died on a Flanders battlefield.

† Montague John Guest (1839–1909), third son of Sir John Josiah Guest, 1st baronet.

seemed like one of the more peevish incarnations of Vesta Tilley,* the male impersonator of the music halls.

Yet for upholders of caste condescension like Guest, swatting down those who didn't know 'their place' was becoming a losing battle. Given the increasing degree of permeability between classes, and their upward-thrust, it was sometimes said that the caution and reserve exercised by Englishmen was due to the fact they were never entirely sure of the social position of their companions, or indeed, of their own.

Although the liberality of Edwardian social entrée was something very new, the British aristocracy had always been open to those of new money and vaulting ambition who were prepared to play by the rules, and exercise patience – given ennoblement had more usually required a wait of several generations. This fresh blood had served to invigorate the aristocracy, and ensure it never entirely ossified. As late as 1895, a reviewer could confidently observe:

> the Government of Britain is still an aristocratic oligarchy, largely tempered by plutocracy…The system is not a bad one, and it has worked on the whole extremely well. But it is an admirable piece of satire to call it Democratic.

The trouble was, it wasn't working well. As the journal of the Liberal party, *The Speaker*, noted in 1892, it was mostly a Tory party club:

> Only those who have come into contact with the masses in times of political excitement can realise the hatred of the 'Upper House' which prevails amongst them…They have learned that the House of Lords never initiates any useful reform; cares for nothing except the privileges of its own class, and resists every Liberal measure until reduced to surrender by fear of consequences.

As far back as 1848, the Year of Revolutions, and even further, the House of Commons had accepted petitions to abolish the House of Lords. Successive bills for its reform, including for the creation of life peers, had been put forward unsuccessfully, including by Lord

---

* Matilda Alice (née Powles), Lady de Frece: stage name Vesta Tilley (1864–1952), popular Edwardian male impersonator. Her hits included *Burlington Bertie*.

Salisbury in 1888. In 1893, a National League for the Abolition of the House of Lords was established, with the pithy motto 'Worth, not birth'. Labouchère was its President. The following year it mounted a demonstration with the support of trade unions, in Hyde Park. According to one press report the good-humoured crowd amounted to 60,000, but the majority of the press dismissed the numbers as 10,000 or less, the *Illustrated London News* stating:

> Mr. Henry Labouchère, who is at Carlsbad, will probably regard the failure of the Hyde Park demonstration against the Lords as an excellent joke...It came into being under Mr. Labouchère's special guardianship, but that will not prevent him from laughing at it. A smaller display of popular enthusiasm was never seen.

By 1895 the League had fallen apart, with even the Metropolitan Radical Federation declaring it to be "rotten to the core". There was besides a belief amongst its members that, given the matter had been placed on the agenda of the Liberals, abolition or reform would soon succeed. Even Lord Rosebery* had attacked "the indiscriminate and untempered heredity" of the House of Lords.

However, the aristocracy's pedestal would be slowly eroded by rising affluence across all society, as well as socialism,† and a growing cynicism. The First World War particularly exposed its failings. Even arch jingoist J. Astley Cooper was dismayed, writing in 1917:

> One of the chief causes of our catastrophes in this war is the social and moral anarchy which has existed for so long in the upper and plutocratic circles. What is called 'influence' is a euphemistic term for social blackmail, and when people get honours, billets, and are promoted, not on their merits, because they know so much about one another that they can't be refused, you cannot expect proficiency or discipline.

---

* Archibald Philip Primrose, 5th Earl of Rosebery (1847–1949), Prime Minister 1894–95.
† Two of the richest and most socially prominent socialists were the aforementioned Daisy, Countess of Warwick, and her half-sister, Millicent, Duchess of Sutherland, who recalled: "As far as a miserable Duchess could be an agitator, I strove to be one." [The Amazing Duchess, *The Tatler*, 7 August 1912]

He believed it had led to "lions being directed by asses in high command", and "concealed from the people by a tissue of official and Parliamentary lies."

Amongst the upper class, Victorian certainties succumbed to creeping doubt, and most especially self-doubt. Bowing to what seemed inevitable – if not equality, at least a greater fairness – it acceded a large measure of power.

In addition to the power wielded by aristocracy and gentry through their close associations, was another force, much subtler, but no less forceful and effective. This was royal influence, and its patronage. It required secrecy to operate, not least because its limits were so vaguely defined by legislation. As Walter Bagehot wrote in his work *The English Constitution*:

> A secret prerogative is an anomaly – perhaps the greatest of all anomalies. That secrecy is, however, essential to the utility of English royalty as it now is. Above all things our royalty is to be reverenced, and if you begin to poke about it you cannot reverence it…as to the magnitude of royal influence…It is…an accepted secret doctrine that the Crown does more than it seems.

The most influential of courtiers at the Edwardian court, Lord Esher, addressed how King Edward's distinct personality shaped the way this secret prerogative was wielded:

> Our Constitution withholds power from the Sovereign, but it clothes him with an influence which in the hand of King Edward was highly potent…the King's love and knowledge of his fellow-men, his genial temper, consummate tact, and complete freedom from rancour and sustained resentment, clothed him with an undisputed authority greater, because far more subtle, than autocratic power would have given him. The pre-eminent men, politicians, religious and social leaders, foreign statesmen, and the most distinguished of his Colonial subjects, who came into contact with him, never left his presence without a desire, in so far as in them lay, to meet his wishes.

Esher added:

Personal charm is indefinable. It is also a most potent weapon, and a dangerous one in the hands of the unscrupulous. King Edward's charm was invincible.

For the republican politician Sir Charles Dilke,* the cost to the nation was "chiefly not waste but mischief." For courtiers like Esher with an inside view, royal interventions in the form of dispassionate criticism, even when reactionary, were for the good, staying ministers' hands in sometimes too hasty actions.

One example of a high-level action taken by the King that critics like Dilke were not privy to occurred in 1907. A conference at the Hague failed to produce any agreement on arms limitation. At Edward's instigation, his close friend the financier Sir Ernest Cassel negotiated continually with the German shipping magnate Albert Ballin, a fellow Jew who had some influence with the Kaiser, in an unsuccessful attempt to limit Anglo-Germany naval rivalry. The secret negotiation was well-meaning, but arguably not the remit of a constitutional monarch.

Royal patronage ensured the press discretion surrounding matters royal was maintained. In 1908, the *Daily Mail* newspaper tycoon Lord Northcliffe† wrote to the King's private secretary Lord Knollys:

> The editors of newspapers are really very glad to receive any hint as to what or what not to publish. Sometimes, when His Majesty is at Marienbad or Biarritz, we shall be very glad to be told what to print and what to omit.

Northcliffe was well aware of where the power lay, writing in an office memo: "The power of the press is very great, but not so great as the power of suppress." Such unctuousness did not go unrewarded. The King now stepped over the line into corruption, pressing for a peerage for Northcliffe; the favour greased by a massive cash payment to Edward's mistress, Alice Keppel. Its unconscionable acceptance was a rare failure of Edward's good sense, but the acquisitive Alice dominated him by charm, and as the proverb goes – a stiff prick

---

* Sir Charles Wentworth Dilke, 2nd baronet (1843–1911), Liberal and Radical politician. Married Emilia Francis Strong, author, art historian, feminist and trade unionist.
† Alfred Charles William Harmsworth, 1st Viscount Northcliffe (1865–1922), newspaper magnate.

knows no conscience.* Keeping the florid show going in their hothouse world, including the King's gambling habit, required the constant stoking of buckets of money, and the hunger of both for it was as much out of necessity as greed.

Garnering honours for his friends and favourites was, to employ the very softest term, one of Edward VII's foibles. Yet it also brought public benefits: "The millionaire's quickest and surest route to royal favour," wrote one Society observer, "is a big cheque for a necessitous hospital."

Twice in his life Edward, when Prince of Wales, was to find himself in an ordinary courtroom. In 1869 an M.P., Sir Charles Mordaunt, filed for divorce after his wife confessed to infidelity with several gentlemen, including Edward, who had regularly enjoyed private afternoon visits. Some of his ostensibly innocuous letters to her were leaked to *The Times* which published them. Edward decided to testify to clear his name. In this he was encouraged by the Lord Chief Justice,

---

* From the Latin: *Penis erectus non habet conscientiam*. According to the British politician and brewery heir George, Viscount Younger, Northcliffe paid £200,000 for his barony; £100,000 each for the King and Keppel. However, Northcliffe's baronet nephew Sir Geoffrey Harmsworth (like many gay persons, their family's historian), claimed the payment was half that amount, made in one hundred £1,000 notes. Keppel, as avaricious as her royal lover, was experiencing financial difficulties at the time. She spent part of the 'bequest' on a Mayfair mansion, and later a villa in Florence. That may not have been the end of it. A surviving letter from the King to Balfour confirms he requested both Northcliffe's peerage, and that banker Herbert Stern, 1st Baron Michelham (1851-1919), who also tendered financial advice to Keppel. A recent biographer of Northcliffe has suggested the payment allegations were mere gossip, but there was no other compelling reason for the King's ask, except Northcliffe's possible suppression of scandalous stories about his private life. Northcliffe was raised to a viscount in 1918. Royal biographers have always claimed Alice Keppel's wealth and hard spending were principally enabled by the investment advice of Sir Ernest Cassel. However, given the scale of it, and the brief investment timeframe, this seems financially naive. At Keppel's death in 1947, her gross estate was £177,637 in the UK alone, which didn't include her North American assets or Italian estate. It has been claimed King Edward presented Keppel with shares in a rubber company, which over time, earned her some £50,000. If so, it was most likely Pneumatic Tyre, which financial fraudster Ernest Terah Hooley acquired, renamed as the Dunlop Pneumatic Tyre Company, and resold at enormous profit. [George Allardice Riddell, Baron Riddell; J.M. McEwen (ed.), *The Riddell Diaries 1908-1923*, Athlong Press, London, 1986, p371; Cecil Harmsworth King, *The Cecil King Diary: 1970-1974*, Jonathan Cape, London 1972, p345; G.R. Searle, *Corruption In British Politics*, Clarendon Press, Oxford 1987, p92-93; Barry McGill, 'Glittering Prizes and Party Funds in Perspective, 1882–1931', *Bulletin of the Institute of Historical Research*, Longmans Green, London 1982, Vol 55, p91; Andrew Roberts, *The Chief: The Life Of Lord Northcliffe*, Simon & Schuster, London 2022; Raymond Lamont-Brown, *Edward VII's Last Loves: Alice Keppel & Agnes Keyser*, The History Press, London 2013, pp164, 167; Diana Souhami, *Mrs Keppel And Her Daughters*, HarperCollins, London 1996, pp52-62; Leslie Carroll, *Royal Affairs*, Berkley, New York 2008, p389.]

Sir Alexander Cockburn, who wrote to him:

> I am sure that the country would be more ready to look with
> indulgence on what might be thought only a youthful
> transgression, especially with a lady apparently of such fragile
> virtue, than on a supposed disregard for truth in one who will
> one day be the fountain of justice and in whose name the law
> will be administered. It must not be forgotten that a man, no
> matter what his station, comes forward on such an occasion
> under very disadvantageous circumstances, arising out of the
> notion that one to whom a woman has given herself up, is
> bound, even at the cost of committing perjury, to protect her
> honour.

Edward was hardly disadvantaged, and had first endeavoured to have
the case suppressed. Lady Mordaunt had always been high strung, and
the royal doctor William Gull declared her mentally incapable of
giving testimony. Given she had taken up finger-painting with
excrement and eating carpet, this seems a not unreasonable
assessment, but her husband believed she was feigning. Ultimately,
the jury decided her confession was the ravings of a madwoman, and
Sir Charles was not granted his divorce until several years afterwards.
Lady Mordaunt was committed to an asylum. Edward's Private
Secretary Lord Knollys later privately wrote:

> Mr. Gladstone, who was the Prime Minister, took all the indirect
> means in his power (and successfully) to prevent anything being
> brought out in the court of the trial that could prove to be
> injurious to the Prince or the crown.

Like Gladstone, subsequent prime ministers, including Salisbury and
Balfour, needed no reminding of their duty to protect the 'fountain
of justice' from scandal – even if it meant discreetly defiling justice
itself.

In 1891, the Prince of Wales was again in court due to what was
known as the Tranby-Croft case. A society figure, Sir William
Gordon-Cumming had been accused of cheating at baccarat during a
country house party at Tranby Croft, home of the Wilson family. He
was pressured into signing an agreement never to play cards again, in
exchange for the silence of the guests. However, the secret leaked,

and he demanded a retraction from the Wilsons, whom he blamed for it. They refused, and he filed a writ for slander. The Prince, who'd been one the guests, was summoned to testify, and Gordon-Cumming lost. Edward's involvement in such a petty squalid affair damaged his public reputation for several years. Looking back in 1937, Sir Shane Leslie wrote that at the time it had been compared:

> to the famous affair of the Diamond Necklace which precipitated the French Revolution. It is difficult to recall the emotional horror which swept the British nation when the heir to the Throne was discovered playing baccarat!...The nation shook, but the Throne remained.

In his summing up for the court, the barrister Sir Edward Clarke,* who cross-examined Edward, addressed the issue of the negative aspects of undefined royal power:

> There is a strong and subtle influence of royalty – a personal influence – which has adorned our history with chivalrous deeds; and has perplexed the historian with unknightly and dishonouring deeds done by men of character, and done by them because they gave their honour as freely as they would have given their lives to save the interests of a dynasty or to conceal the foibles of a prince.

The speech incensed Edward, who considered it effrontery. However, the course of events suggests that at least three times he used his royal clout, in conjunction with the Prime Ministers of the day and other officials, to encourage men of character to pervert the course of justice, for what was viewed as a higher purpose. These incidents, ironically all of a homosexual character, were the Cleveland Street Scandal of 1889, the Irish Crown Jewels theft of 1907, and the case this book reveals. The first two interventions were undertaken to protect the stature of the Royal Family, and thereby the Crown. The third intervention may also have been made to shield a royal party, but was certainly undertaken to protect the reputation of the ruling class.†

---

* Sir Edward George Clarke (1841–1931), barrister and politician, considered one of the leading advocates of his era.
† Another criminal case that may have involved the perversion of justice due to a royal association occurred in 1923. An icy-hearted former courtesan, Marie Marguerite Fahmy

In addition to the influence of position and privilege on public policy, lay another hidden code. In the late nineteenth and early twentieth centuries, freemasonry ran through royalty, aristocracy, government, the civil service, armed forces and the police like a cool, silent stream. In Britain, loyalty to the Crown was an essential principle of it; the traditional masonic loyal toast being 'To The King/Queen and the Craft'.

Masonic membership ranged down from the King (who before becoming monarch had been Grand Master of the Freemasons of England), to the Lord Chancellor (the head of the judiciary in England and Wales), Lord Halsbury; the Commissioner of Police Sir Charles Warren; and in the Parliament of 1889, to at least 338 members. Freemasonry was said to appeal to King Edward's "fraternal and philanthropic instincts". And of course, to the boyish thrill of belonging to a secret society with pantomime dress-up and ritual.

Freemasonry was consequently a power in the land. Like any other Old Boys network, it naturally encouraged cronyism. This partiality made freemasonry inimical to good policing.* The asking and granting of 'just and lawful' favours at an individual level amongst masonic 'brothers' was a fact of life. When not restrained by moral sense, this could lead to corruption.

Yet the suggestion, pushed by conspiracy theorists, that masonic lodges in Britain sanctioned amorality for the sake of fraternity, is absurd. In 1912, for example, the trial of Frederick Seddon for arsenic poisoning ended sensationally when the accused made an eloquent appeal and, raising his hand, gave a masonic sign to the judge.

(1890–1971), shot dead her young aristocratic Egyptian husband, Ali Kamel Fahmy Bey, in the Savoy Hotel. Her defence counsel sought to imply he was bisexual: he certainly preferred to bugger his wife, who had previously been a lover of the then Prince of Wales (the future Edward VIII; later Duke of Windsor). She was acquitted of the murder. It has been speculated the surprising verdict involved more than just good lawyering, and that Fahmy, who possessed compromising letters from the Prince, blackmailed him to have those managing the case leaned upon. Evidence suggests that some form of agreement with Fahmy was struck to avoid her mentioning the Prince's name. [See: Andrew Rose, *The Prince, The Princess And The Perfect Murder*, Coronet, London 2013.]

* Which is why, in recent years, successive Metropolitan Police Commissioners have attempted to break masonic connections. As recently as 2017, freemasons were accused of blocking police reform. [Police Reform 'Thwarted By Masons', *The Times*, 1 January 2018]

Nonetheless, his Honour delivered the death sentence, saying: "We both belong to one brotherhood, and it is very painful for me to say what I am saying. But our Brotherhood does not encourage crime, on the contrary it condemns it."*

The fraternity was also of no use to Oscar Wilde in his troubles, despite him having risen to the rank of Master Mason. That said, due to the Marquess of Queensberry† conducting a vendetta not only against Wilde, but also against the then Prime Minister Lord Rosebery for his association with another of his sons, the stakes for the Government were simply too high not to prosecute Wilde's case.

All this said, the remarkable lenience of the authorities towards a few of those in the upper reaches of the Craft who found themselves in legal strife, such as Alexander Meyrick Broadley,‡ is more easily explained by masonic-aproned connections and clout.

In the early months of King Edward's reign, the Marquess of Salisbury was still Prime Minister. Deeply religious, Lord Salisbury was committed to maintaining the status quo: the privileges of his class, limited democracy, and a firmly subjugated Empire – including Ireland. As a schoolboy at Eton, he had been mercilessly bullied,

---

* One recent Jack The Ripper study quotes a masonic oath that demands the inductee: "charitably hide and conceal and cover all the sins, frailties and errors of every Brother to the utmost of my power". As the author rightly says of this permit for criminal conspiracy: "It doesn't come clearer than that". His source is *England's Masonic Pioneers* by Dudley Wright (1925, pp62-3). The oath originates from a fragment of 'masonic formulae' transcribed by freemason Robert Samber (1682-1745). Yet according to another masonic scholar, the manuscript's erasures and additions give it the appearance of "a suggestion or rough draft," and there is "no means of ascertaining whether it was ever in actual use." [Bruce Robinson, *They All Love Jack*, HarperCollins 2015, p57; Bro. Edward Armitage, 'Samber's Masonic Formulae', *Ars Quatuor Coronatorum: being the transactions of the Lodge Quatuor Coronati, no. 2076, London*, Vol XI, Keble's Gazette Office, Margate, 1898, p109.]
† John Sholto Douglas, 9th Marquess of Queensberry (1844–1900), pugnacious and erratic Scottish nobleman noted for his outspoken views; for lending his name to the Queensberry Rules that form the basis of modern boxing, and for his role in the downfall of Oscar Wilde.
‡ Alexander Meyrick Broadley (1847–1916), barrister, journalist, and crook. As a magistrate in India he upset the colonial government by publicly criticising policy. Subsequently charged with homosexuality, he absconded. Following his legal defence of the Egyptian nationalist Arabi Pasha, he deemed it safe to return to England, where he reinvented himself as a magazine editor and high-profile society figure. In 1889, at the height of the Cleveland Street Scandal, and at the instigation of the Prince of Wales, he was ordered to leave the country. Five years later, through some form of official absolution, he again returned, and became the right-hand man of financial fraudster Ernest Terah Hooley. When Hooley was made bankrupt, Broadley used his ill-gotten wealth to retire to the country in splendour.

which imbued him with a pessimistic view of human nature.* Democracy he considered merely Mob Rule.

Salisbury eschewed initiatives, especially reform he saw as ego-driven. In this he was simply following Sir Robert Walpole,† whose favourite motto was *quieta non movere* – 'do not move settled things'. It was a reminder to heed the law of unintended consequences – that actions almost always have effects that are unanticipated. Doing nothing, was almost always best. As Salisbury put it: "Whatever happens will be for the worse, and therefore it is in our interest that as little should happen as possible." Why risk stirring up a hell-broth? In his youth in the 1850s, politicians from both sides of the House had believed there were actually *too many* laws.

In 1877, Salisbury wrote to Lord Lytton, then Viceroy of India: "English policy is to float lazily downstream, occasionally putting out a diplomatic boat-hook to avoid collisions." It was government by inertia. As an historian has eloquently expressed it: "The gusts of mass suggestion, that swayed democracy like reeds, moved them not at all...These elder statesmen were, in fact, slightly bored with life, and particularly with modern life."

That said, some direct measures to address inequality were taken. It was Salisbury who initiated the Royal Commission into working class housing, and *The Housing of the Working Classes Act (1885)* helped to improve it. Seeking to kill the desire for Irish Home Rule with kindness, Salisbury's government also initiated a land reform programme that helped hundreds of thousands of Irish peasants gain land ownership. However, the Tories believed the most effective means of raising up the poor was an indirect one – that of economic growth. In ensuring the national stability which fostered this, Salisbury's government was immensely successful.

A month before the Coronation, feeling ill and out of step with the changing world,‡ Lord Salisbury resigned as Prime Minister to be

---

* There was a grain of truth in the observation: "Salisbury was not a very lovable personage. He despised everybody, and perhaps the Tory hounds among whom he moved more than others." [The Secret History Of To-Day, *Reynolds's Newspaper*, 23 August 1903, p1.]
† Sir Robert Walpole, later 1st Earl of Orford (1676–1745), first Prime Minister of Great Britain.
‡ There were reports Lord Salisbury, in addition to believing "the reign of the landed autocracy" was over, had quarrelled the King and refused to approve the ennoblement of his

replaced by his nephew Arthur Balfour. Heir to 180,000 Scottish acres, Balfour was one of the richest young men in Britain. Like so many other scions of the aristocracy and gentry who treated politics as a diverting pastime, his parliamentary career had begun languidly. *The Pall Mall Gazette* recalled him then as:

> A lounging, rather effeminate-mannered young man, who toyed with a scented handkerchief as he sprawled supine over the Treasury Bench…He was christened as schoolboys christen a mollycoddle – 'Miss Balfour' and 'Nancy' and 'Lucy.'

Another paper noted: "as a bored semi-invalid, he sat in the House of Commons, sucking a thermometer and taking it out now and then to note his temperature."

Then his uncle had appointed him Irish Secretary. "That Lord Salisbury should assign so delicate a piece of china to so rude a service seemed inexplicable." However, as the Irish members were soon to discover, Balfour not only possessed a grandee's "supercilious indifference to abuse and invective," but an interior of cold steel. He gave orders to shoot down rioters without hesitation. Given he considered the Irish little more than barely-governable rabble, the decision was effortless. Behind his façade of serene affability, he discovered a taste for political intrigue, and his career took off. Yet he would remain what had always been: a detached, pessimistic, preening dilettante, who was only truly at home with The Souls – the small coterie of high-brow aristocrats of the Nineties: the press dubbed him their 'high priest'.

Correspondence suggests Balfour conducted a tepid relationship spiced by sadomasochistic birchings with Lady Elcho, wife of the heir to the earldom of Wemyss. Like many of his ilk hailing from distant parents and cold dormitories, desire and consolation lay in substitute mothers and strict matrons. However, his true passion may have been golf.* As *The Pall Mall Gazette* recorded:

---

financially-enabling friends Thomas Lipton and Ernest Cassel. [G.R. Searle, *Corruption In British Politics*, Clarendon Press, Oxford 1987, pp93-94; The Secret History Of To-Day, *Reynolds's Newspaper*, 22 June 1902 & 23 August 1903, p1.]
* For a recent discussion of Balfour's narcissism and sexuality, see: Michael Bloch, *Closet Queens: Some 20th Century British Politicians*, Little Brown, London 2015.

His conversation is noted for its facile and urbane charm...His circle is the cream of London culture. His figure is never missed at the best galleries, the best concerts...From the noise and babble of the Commons Mr. Balfour goes home to the great, spacious house – gloomy without, and austere on first entering, but stored in its inner penetralia with the treasures of all the arts and half the sciences. Here is the key to much distinction, dignity, aloofness, half-contemptuous good-humour.

Roffe Thompson,* an editor of the popular magazine *John Bull,* surmised that:

Mr. Balfour's lack of sympathy with democratic ideals is, in fact, based on something less robust than the Cecilian arrogance. It is rather the shrinking of a provincial blue-stocking from what she considers the 'vulgar'.

First and foremost, the new Prime Minister viewed himself as a philosopher, once saying: "I would rather be known as having added something to our knowledge of truth and nature than for anything else I can imagine." His best-known book was *Defence of Philosophic Doubt,* and he was later noted for the dictum "Nothing matters very much, and few things matter at all," which while true, is more akin to a deathbed reflection than a trumpet call for legislative vigour. Winston Churchill would be led to quip: "If you wanted nothing done, A.J.B. was undoubtedly the best man for the task." Unfortunately, the times were now against those who considered the aim of statesmanship was maintaining the status quo.

Balfour's government reflected its leader: "in many matters his administration seemed essentially a Society affair. Too often its ministers looked indifferent or listless, the political equivalent of drawingroom loungers." To most of the British people, Arthur Balfour remained an abstraction, and an ineffectual one at that, failing to deal satisfactorily with the most pressing issues, including unemployment. Even by the standards of the day, the people of Britain deserved better.

---

* (Edward) Roffe Thompson (1891–1973), author and journalist. His pen names were E.T. Raymond and Edward Raymond Thompson. He wrote a number of biographies of British political figures and celebrities, and an early self-help book, *The Human Machine: Secrets of Success* (1925).

The people thought so too. The introduction of punitive taxation on generational fortunes – the very lifeblood of the traditional upper class, and which ensured their power and status, could not have happened otherwise. This was eventually brought to fruition in 1909-10 by the Liberal Government with 'The People's Budget', the measure ostensibly instituted to fund new social welfare programmes. Equally, *The Parliament Act 1911*, which assured the dominance of the House of Commons over the Lords, marked the twilight of noble rule. It was the final ascent of those whom Lord Sherbrooke* had termed, following the passing of the Second Reform Act, "our new masters".

The peerage was still a pillar on which Crown and Government rested: the semi-divine embodiment of all the virtues believed worthy of veneration. As always, its fraying ranks could be bolstered by new money. But esteem for the aristocracy as an institution was dissipating. And it was now under assault from a force even more potent than the taxman – the popular press.

To the despair of those who represented nobility in its best sense, an increasing succession of exposures of high-placed immorality were, in consequence, serving to mock it. More than just showing up a few black sheep, the subtext of the prevailing daily narrative had become one of a gilded nest of venal, fornicating hypocrites. While the Nation's bounteous good humour and curiosity would be tickled by the high comedy of some of these exposures, even the English people's love of a lord has its limits. Nothing captures the popular imagination quite like sex and money. And nothing undermines authority faster than ridicule. The risk to respect and fortune was the least of it. The threat to power was alarming.

---

* Robert Lowe, 1st Viscount Sherbrooke (1811–1892), an opponent of the development of electoral democracy: "It is the principle of numbers as against wealth and intellect." [*Hansard*, House of Lords, 15 July 1867, vol 188, c1540.]

3. NOBLE DECADENCE

How comes it that the people of today are filled with nothing but sex, sex, sex? Influenza is not the only new disease which has come to reside amongst us. Another more terrible and potent plague has grabbed hold of the nation – sex-mania.

The alarm was raised in 1895 by the editor of *Reynolds's Newspaper*, William Marcus Thompson. While the reign of Queen Victoria had been marked by "an overshadowing inhibition, an incarnate 'Thou Shalt Not'," Thompson now believed this injunction was being swept away by a wave of sensuality. "Our society is honeycombed with corruption as a decaying cheese is with maggots," he wrote. "In every street we meet grave-looking débauchees of either sex." Thomson had drunk deep at the bubbling font of Max Nordau, and through his editorials, would bring those moral worriments to a wider audience.

Dismay over a belief in national moral breakdown had actually been building for a long time. It was encouraged by a grassroots groundswell of moral campaigning that came to be known as the Social Purity Movement. This had been spurred by the Contagious Diseases Acts – legislation introduced in 1864 to reduce the level of venereal disease, with a focus on the British military.* It mandated that in a number of districts surrounding naval towns any woman suspected of prostitution by the police was required to undergo a medical examination, and if found infected, confined to a hospital for

---

* As an indication of the criticality of the situation, in 1869, one in twenty children admitted to the Children's Hospital in Newcastle were suffering from a 'contagious disease' acquired from their parents. [The Extension Of The Contagious Diseases Act, *The Newcastle Daily Journal*, 25 May 1869, p3.]

a number of months to be treated. The Acts affected the very dregs of the population – the lowest kind of prostitutes, such as those known as Bushrangers, who lived like rabbits in holes on the sandbanks outside Aldershot military camp: "filthy, covered in vermin, like idiots in their manner, very badly diseased."

Given that no consequences fell upon infectious men, The Acts were inherently unfair; but any idea that such legislation should be applied equally was a premise for a future age. With input from doctors, police and civil servants, the legislation was modified in 1866, and in 1869 its coverage expanded. This gave it greater prominence, and spurred critics, for whom it constituted a mere licensing of prostitution, and thereby the regulation of vice rather than its desired suppression. Opponents even alleged it was 'state patronage of vice'. The most high-profile campaigner for repeal of the legislation was Josephine Butler,* who proclaimed it had created: "a slave class of women for the supposed benefit of licentious men." A high-strung charismatic beauty, and highly conscious of her looks, Butler was an admirable charity worker, and feminist ahead of her time. However, she was also a dogmatic Puritan. As Gladstone put it:

I wish she would keep to her welfare work, and not enter politics. She has a tendency to confuse the issues. I am, however, conscious that a great many people have strong emotional impulses on this subject which blind them to realities.

Speaking from his experience as a former Secretary to the Admiralty, Lord Henry Lennox† informed Parliament that the only problem with

---

* Josephine Elizabeth Butler (1828–1906), campaigner for women's rights and moral reform.
† Lord Henry Charles George Gordon-Lennox (1821–1886), a Conservative M.P. who was the third son of the 5th Duke of Richmond. Considered an amiable eccentric, "a dilettantist of the dilettantists", he was nicknamed 'Miss Lennox', and survived on an allowance from his ducal brother. When the Duke died it ceased, forcing him into marriage with a wealthy widow many years his junior. Despite this, he was bankrupted three years later with liabilities of over £11,000, and died soon after. Punch caricatured him as an effete strolling player, while another paper recorded: "His thin hair was carefully dyed; he most always wore patent leather shoes; his trousers were nearly always too short, and this, coupled with the habit of walking on tip-toe, gave him a curiously effeminate air. People used occasionally to speak of him as 'Mr Mantalini.'" This was a reference to the gigolo fop in Charles Dickens's *Nicholas Nickleby* who depends on his older wife to supply his extravagant tastes. In a statement indicative of its time, another paper wrote: "Lord Henry Lennox was not a statesman, nor even a conspicuously successful administrator. But he was the...son of a duke...the House of Commons...recognised in him a man of honest and generous impulses, who meant well and did his faltering best. With his mincing manners, his quaint curtsey in saluting an acquaintance, his trousers carefully turned up amidst the dust of a summer day, his juvenility of dress which

80

the legislation was its poor implementation. Where properly applied, as at the major naval port of Sheerness in Kent, venereal disease had been eradicated. Contrary to the accusation of purity campaigners that prostitutes had been driven into Devonport Hospital, he stated they had flocked there, anxious to enjoy its benefits; and that during their cure, they had benefited from instruction in morality and household work. Official statistics also indicated the Acts wrought significant reductions in both disease and prostitution. For the suffragists and the purity movement, the legislation's efficacy was an inconvenient truth. Even if the statistics could be questioned, doing something was surely better than doing nothing.

However, raw data is rarely a match for raw emotion. In effect, repealers preferred prostitutes and their children be hollowed out by disease rather than subject to legislatively-imposed medical treatment which they deemed immoral and patriarchal. Although the M.P. for Devonport, John Puleston,* could tell Parliament, "Not only in Plymouth, but in kindred constituencies, there was a unanimity in deploring the repeal of those Acts," all over the country societies sprang up to advocate for their abolition. At the head of the push was the Salvation Army and the churches – with the exception of the Church of England, which remained aloof, although many figures within it were staunch abolitionists. With the support of sympathetic M.P.s, repeal was placed on the Liberal Party agenda, and eventuated in 1886.

The Purity Movement was further galvanised by agitation for greater legislative protection of young girls and children, including raising the age of consent from twelve. This was given greater impetus in the 1880s, when two Quaker gentlemen, Alfred Dyer† and George

---

three score years could not depress, his real simplicity, his kindly heart, and his striving after the highest type of British statesmanship, Lord Henry Lennox was one of the personal favourites of the House of Commons." It will cause no stupefaction that he "exercised an untiring vigilance over all that concerned the navy. He was seen to best advantage, perhaps, in the Committee on Naval Estimates." [The Death Of Lord Henry Lennox, *Portsmouth Evening News*, 1 September 1886, p2; Poor Henry Lennox, *The Pall Mall Gazette*, 31 August 1886, p4; London Letter, *Western Daily Press*, 31 August 1886, p3; Master Slender, *Punch*, Vol. 84, 14 April 1883, p.178; London Letter, *Cardiff Times*, 4 September 1886, p5; Political Nicknames, *Southend Standard and Essex Weekly Advertiser*, 29 July 1886, p6; Edward Legge, *Fifty Years Of London Society*, 1870-1920, Brentano's, New York 1920, p130.]

* Sir John Henry Puleston (1830–1908) Welsh entrepreneur, broker and journalist, in the United States), and later, Conservative M.P.

† Alfred Stace Dyer (1849–1926), Quaker moral reformer, editor and publisher.

Gillett,* uncovered a small white slave traffic (including in what was termed 'unripe fruit' – girls as young as ten years of age) that was running between England and brothels on the Continent – particularly, but not surprisingly, from Belgium. Dyer and another social reformist Benjamin Scott,† who was Chamberlain for the City of London,‡ established the London Committee for Suppressing the Traffic in British Girls for Purposes of Continental Prostitution, which became another strong force for change. With the assistance of Lord Granville,§ in 1881 they succeeded in having the House of Lords establish a Select Committee to investigate the matter.

Everyone knew that London and other British metropolises were heaving with prostitution: as far back as 1857 the medical journal *The Lancet* had estimated that one house in every sixty in the capital was a brothel, and one in sixteen women a whore. Even so, it must have been sobering for the peers to be informed by the director of Scotland Yard's Criminal Investigation Department that: "From three o'clock in the afternoon, it is impossible for any respectable woman to walk from the top of the Haymarket to Wellington Street, Strand." That was the best part of a mile through London's West End. More concerning still was testimony of an increasing demand for young girls. However, even ten years previously a *Royal Commission into Contagious Diseases* reported: "The traffic in children for infamous purposes is notoriously considerable." The London Society for the Protection of Young Females recorded 2,700 cases of venereal disease amongst girls aged eleven to sixteen in eight years in three London hospitals alone.

The recommendations of the Select Committee formed the basis of the *Criminal Law Amendment Act*, which sought to protect women and girls from procurement, prostitution and sexual abuse. Due to opposition and apathy, its passage through Parliament became bogged down.

After the Bill had been delayed four years, in early 1885 a thoroughly

---

* George Gillett, (1837–1893) Quaker banker and moral reformer.
† Benjamin Scott (1814–1892) social activist and Chamberlain of the City of London from 1858 until his death.
‡ The finance director of the City of London Corporation. One of England's ancient offices, dating to at least 1237.
§ Granville George Leveson-Gower, 2nd Earl Granville (1815–1891), leader of the Liberal Party in the House of Lords for almost 30 years.

fed-up Benjamin Scott and Alfred Dyer decided that, for the purposes of publicity, and as an example, the London Committee would take on the prosecution of Mary Jeffries,* whom they dubbed 'an Empress of Vice'. Jeffries was London's leading brothel madam, maintaining a string of houses in Chelsea, but the police had hitherto declined to prosecute. She informed a new police inspector to the district, Jeremiah Minahan,† that it was pointless for her houses to be watched as she "did business with persons in the highest ranks of life".

When Jeffries offered Minahan gold, he refused the bribe. In a subsequent investigative report he characterised her Chelsea houses as "brothels for the nobility" – an imputation which the Assistant-Commissioner of the Metropolitan Police considered "highly improper". Minahan was demoted, and resigned from the Force. A stubborn Irishman, he was incensed, and assisted the Committee as a paid investigator, and witness at Jeffries' trial.

When the Committee first applied for a warrant for Jeffries' arrest, it was refused by the stipendiary magistrates, and it was only when they reapplied under an Act of Parliament, which gave the sitting magistrate no option but to issue a warrant, that it was granted.

The authorities were particularly concerned that no great names should be aired in the courtroom. Despite the magistrate at a preliminary hearing of Jeffries' case forbidding any mention of client names, her coachman let drop on the witness stand that Jeffries was paid a retainer of eight hundred pounds a month by King Leopold of Belgium.‡ The leading periodical of the Purity Movement was *The Sentinel,* published by Alfred Dyer and his brother. It now thundered:

The inferences from the evidence (we are in possession of

---

* Mary Frances Jeffries (1819–1891). She began her career as a prostitute in a high-end Mayfair brothel, Berthe's, and was set up in business by a client following a trip to Paris, where allegedly she recognised a gap in the London market in catering for kink. [Michael Pearson, *The Age Of Consent: Victorian prostitution and its enemies,* David and Charles, Newton Abbot 1972, pp105-106.]

† Jeremiah Minahan (1842–1897) His later life was unfortunate. He became insane and was committed to an asylum, but escaped, and stabbed his wife to death. [Murder By An Ex-Inspector Of Police, *Nottingham Evening Post,* 5 April 1895, p5.]

‡ Leopold II (1835–1909), King of the Belgians, and sole owner of the Congo Free State, which he plundered in a genocidal manner for personal gain, until forced to cede it to Belgium.

something more tangible than inferences) point to a state of moral corruption, heartless cruelty, and prostitution of authority, almost sufficient, even in this law-abiding country, to goad the industrial classes into revolution.

Regrettably for the Committee, when the Jeffries trial took place in the middle of May, there were higher powers at work who held very different, more worldly views.

Mrs. Jeffries was defended by barrister Montagu Williams – the very same Montagu Williams who would write so eloquently in his memoirs of East End poverty. *The Sentinel,* mused:

> one could not help pondering upon how far a person's character becomes assimilated to his occupation. A near approach to the manner of Mr. Montagu Williams can be found in the hired bullies that hang about the licensed dens of infamy in Brussels.

Williams had been one of the leading bucks of London's high Bohemia. His own dissipations had led to a large moral blindspot: behind his urbane facade lay an unscrupulous character who was happy to accept payment to defend those who trafficked women and girls as mere goods. The previous year he'd defended a dressmaker who'd white-slaved a ten-year-old servant girl to a Brussels brothel: his fee was paid by her facilitators. Tellingly, this case and the even more celebrated one of Mrs. Jeffries, were absent from the pages of his two volumes of memoirs.

A former servant of Jeffries made a statement alleging the rape of a thirteen-year-old girl in one of her brothels, and was in line to give evidence for the prosecution. Oddly, she was not called to give evidence – possibly because the alleged abuse had occurred eleven years previously, and the Committee's counsel considered her an unreliable witness. However, *The Sentinel* alleged that Williams conspired to defeat justice by sending the servant on an extended holiday during the prosecution.

The public were barred from the courtroom of Jeffries' trial. Despite sentences of hard labour being usual for lesser offenders of her type, Jeffries and her clients were of a different order. Before commencement of the proceedings, the judge summoned the counsels for both prosecution and defence to a private meeting. On re-entering the courtroom, Montagu Williams told Jeffries to plead Guilty, which she accordingly did. The Committee's counsel then astonished them by delivering a speech so mollifying it sounded like it was for Jeffries' defence, and which only needed Montagu Williams to further add a wreath of agreement to. Jeffries was then fined a token sum of £200, which was at once paid, and was ordered to give up just two of her brothels. It was a farce of justice. However, it's possible Jeffries' only serious crime was that of being too successful in the upmarket brothel trade.*

That same month, the *Criminal Amendment Act*, which had been four years in the making, was talked out in its second reading by the Conservative M.P. George Cavendish-Bentinck,† who had vigorously objected to it from the first. A father of four, he was described by the reformist politician A.J. Mundella‡ as "a little, mean, drunken aristocrat without the slightest capacity for business." More particularly, he would be named in the police statement of a rentboy John Saul§ as being a regular client – information that was never made public.

Another prominent objector of the legislation was the then Home Secretary, Sir William Harcourt.** Like Cavendish-Bentinck and other parliamentary colleagues, he was suspicious and contemptuous of *petit bourgeois* reformers and fanatical moralists, whom he considered killjoys.

While the Committee and its supporters had long realised what they were up against, the filibustering of the bill and cossetting of Jeffries

---

* Jeffries was finally jailed (without hard labour) for six months in 1887. Contrary to popular belief of her wealth, her estate amounted to only £445, which was swallowed by debts. [Occasional Notes, *The Pall Mall Gazette*, 22 November 1887, p4; Jeffries, Mary Frances, 1891, UK Probate; The Late Mrs Jeffries Estate, *Lloyds Weekly Newspaper*, 21 June 1891, p4.]
† George Augustus Frederick Cavendish-Bentinck (1821–1891); grandson of Prime Minister the 3rd Duke of Portland. A barrister and Tory politician; owner of Branksea (Brownsea) Castle and island. His wife, who cultivated celebrities, was a queen of London Society. Some of his objections were legitimate concerns. [What Mr. Cavendish Bentinck Wants, *The Pall Mall Gazette*, 28 May 1885, p2.]
‡ Anthony John Mundella (1825–1897), Liberal Party politician and manufacturer.
§ John 'Jack' Saul, christened Johannes Saul (1857–1904).
** Sir William George Granville Venables Vernon Harcourt, (1827–1904); a lawyer, journalist and Liberal statesman, and father of Lewis Harcourt. Of his pugnacious reputation, it was said he "had never opened his mouth without making an enemy." [Sir William Harcourt, *The Review of Reviews*, Volume 30, 1904, p619.]

hardened their determination to raise the stakes in their fight. One woman's published letter to a parliamentarian called it:

> a just and holy vengeance – a vengeance which is been waiting, kept back, and gathering strength from year to year...the time has now come when no more mercy should be shown to licentious gentlemen of high position than they themselves have shown to the women of the poor, both by their personal acts and by their support of legislation, calculated to bind down those who have once fallen to a public life of infamy, carried on under official supervision.

At a packed meeting at Luton, James Wookey,* a handsome, charismatic, and hot-headed young Welsh churchman, who was Secretary of the Gospel Purity Association, delivered an impassioned speech that echoed the sentiments of the anonymous woman's letter. He proclaimed that in England there were "nearly 150,000 fallen girls" who earned their living from prostitution:

> Where they come from or to what place they are going few want to know...yet the male traitors, but for whom these girls might still have been in the bright sunshine of those summer days when not a cloud passed by to darken them, are allowed to walk in and out amongst the pure as if there was nothing in their soul-and-body murdering life of which they need be ashamed. Nay more, they are ofttimes found sitting in Parliament making laws by which we have to abide. They have occupied the chief places in the Courts of Justice...Working men, it is your daughters that are sacrificed, and it's time you rose up in all your strength and looked these rich scoundrels in the face.

This was hardly the end of his speech. Having been given access to the evidence the Committee had assembled for the Jeffries case, Wookey then proceeded to name some of her clients, including King Leopold, and to what was described as "immense sensation" in the

---

* James Benjamin Wookey (1857–1929), evangelist. A former Salvation Army captain, in his earlier life he had battled alcoholism.

crowd, the Prince of Wales, his friend Lord Aylesford,* Lord Fife† – who four years later would marry one of the Prince's daughters; and one the Prince's equerries, the Hon. Harry Tyrwhitt-Wilson.‡ Also named was Lord Henry Lennox, the opponent of repeal of the Contagious Diseases Acts. Given Lord Henry was noted for his effeminacy, his brothel patronage may have been of another kind entirely. However, it may have been the false slander of an enemy, and if so, not Wookey's only lie.§ He and other purity agitators spread fabricated allegations about the harshness of the implementation of the Contagious Diseases Acts.

The vast majority of the British public remained blissfully ignorant of Wookey's roll call of brothel patrons, and may not have wished to know. Most newspapers never reported his speech. Even *Reynolds's Newspaper* only referred to it mentioning "a reigning sovereign, four noblemen, one baronet, colonels, captains, consuls, and that of a conspicuous member of the English royal family." However, it directed readers to *The Sentinel* where, with the bravery of white-hot anger, Alfred Dyer had printed the names. (Distributors W.H. Smith promptly banned it.) In Australia, a newspaper observed:

> If the statements made are true – and they appear to be founded on the depositions of witnesses who would have been examined, had not the woman [Jeffries] pleaded guilty – we can well understand the eager anxiety to bring the case to a sudden end.

In May 1885, Benjamin Scott approached the campaigning editor W.T. Stead of *The Pall Mall Gazette* and implored his help to publicise their cause. Scott could not have found a more willing audience. Stead was the son of a poor Northumberland Congregational minister, and

---

* Heneage Finch, 7th Earl of Aylesford (1849–1885). Married Edith Peers-Williams: her infidelity led to an ugly divorce-separation case in 1878, while his own resulted in syphilis. *Reynolds's Newspaper* minced no words, labelling him: "a sot, a spendthrift, an adulterer, and pretty well all that is foul and filthy". [Charles Higham, *Dark Lady*, Da Capo Press, Cambridge, Mass. 2006, p54; Another Aristocratic Scandal, *Reynolds's Newspaper*, 7 July 1878, p5.]

† Alexander William George Duff, 1st Duke of Fife, (1849–1912); known as Earl Fife, 1879-1889; he married Princess Louise, eldest daughter of King Edward VII.

‡ The Hon. Harry Tyrwhitt-Wilson (1854–1891), eldest son of Sir Henry Thomas Tyrwhitt, 3rd baronet, and Emma Harriet Wilson, 13th Baroness Berners. He acted as the Prince of Wales's unofficial procurer. His early death was due to tuberculosis. [John Juxon, *Lewis And Lewis*, Collins, London 1983, p92; Death Of The Hon. Harry Tyrwhitt-Wilson, *The St James's Gazette*, 10 August 1891, p11.]

§ His pamphlet *Human Wrecks!* (1887), part of the Purity Movement's anti-masturbation crusade, featured lurid accounts of the death-bed agonies of practitioners.

"Like many journalists, he was a curious mixture of conviction, opportunism and sheer humbug." Stead's austere upbringing shaped him for life. He never stepped foot in a theatre, remembering his father's injunction that they were 'The Devil's Chapel'. In the view of *Reynolds's Newspaper*: "That may account for his numerous fads and follies. He has seen the world from an attic window: been a journalist monk."

Like many moral vigilantes, Stead was sexually obsessed. While acknowledging his probity, Lynn Linton,* a woman journalist who later worked with him, mordantly remarked: "he exudes semen through the skin". He was also highly credulous, including as a keen believer in spiritualism.

Lord Esher, who admired Stead's flair (they had bonded over their mutual admiration of General Gordon),† wrote of him: "Nothing has happened to Britain since 1880 which has not been influenced by the personality of this extraordinary fanatic, visionary and philanthropist." However, after lunching with Stead in 1889, he told his son:

> He is wild and odd as ever, and thinks he has inherited the spirit of Charles II, who – through him – is making amends for his previous life on earth! Pretty good loony! All his female friends he endows with the attributes of Charles' mistresses! If he wasn't so sane in other matters he would have to be shut up.

Following Benjamin Scott's appeal for help, Stead got to work immediately. With the assistance of the Committee, as well as Josephine Butler and the Chief of Staff of The Salvation Army, Bramwell Booth‡ – who together with his wife was also convinced the soliciting of girls had become systematic – Stead began compiling a press report. Titled 'The Maiden Tribute Of Modern Babylon', and published in *The Pall Mall Gazette* as a series throughout July, it was a remarkable example of pioneering investigative journalism – albeit, a seriously flawed one. In Stead's words, he promised to detail:

---

* Eliza Lynn Linton (1822–1898), the first female salaried journalist in Britain, and author of over 20 novels.
† Major-General Charles George Gordon (1833–1885), the 'Hero of Khartoum'. His pederastic desires may have played a part in his martyrdom.
‡ (William) Bramwell Booth (1856–1929), son of William Booth, and later second General of The Salvation Army. Married Florence Eleanor Soper, and had issue.

I. The sale and purchase and violation of children.
II. The procuration of virgins.
III. The entrapping and ruin of women.
IV. The international slave trade in girls.
V. Atrocities, brutalities, and unnatural crimes.

The fifth part, which included homosexuality, would be abandoned for the sake of public morality following Government pressure.

In an ominous preamble headlined 'We Bid You Be Of Hope', Stead wrote:

> in dealing with this subject, the forces upon which we rely in dealing with other evils are almost all paralysed. The Home, the School, the Church, the Press are silent. The law is actually accessory to crime... If Chivalry is extinct, and Christianity is effete, there is another great enthusiasm to which we may with confidence appeal. The future belongs to the combined forces of Democracy and Socialism, which when united are irresistible. Divided on many points they will combine in protesting against the continued immolation of the daughters of the people as a sacrifice to the vices of the rich... in all the annals of crime can there be found a more shameful abuse of the power of wealth than that by which in this nineteenth century of Christian civilisation princes and dukes, and ministers and judges, and the rich of all classes, are purchasing for damnation, temporal if not eternal, the as yet uncorrupted daughters of the poor?

Stead revealed how country girls arriving in London for employment were entrapped at railway stations. To demonstrate the ease of procurement of young virgins, he personally oversaw the purchase for prostitution of a thirteen-year-old girl, Eliza Armstrong, from her mother for five pounds, and also made purchases of older virgins, whose authenticity was confirmed by his doctor. The exposé published incendiary remarks such as:

> "In my house," said a most respectable lady, who keeps a villa in the west of London, "you can enjoy the screams of the girl with the certainty that no one else hears them but yourself."

The British press and public had never seen anything like it. With the exception of the 'penny dreadful' newspapers, the reporting of vice had hitherto been circumscribed. It had also rested on deep apathy and hypocrisy. In a section subtitled 'Liberty For Vice, Repression For Crime', Stead was careful to distinguish between the two, arguing that:

> sexual immorality, however evil it may be in itself or its consequences, must be dealt with not by the policeman but by the teacher, so long as the persons contracting are of full age, are perfectly free agents, and in their sin are guilty of no outrage on public morals. Let us by all means apply the sacred principles of free trade to trade in vice and regulate the relations of the sexes by the haggling of the market and liberty of private contract.*

The authorities and conservative press were appalled at the *Gazette*'s "gross violation of public decency". Like the quasi-military Salvation Army with its motto 'Blood And Fire', the articles were considered by a great many as the action of a pack of half-crazed, puritanical zealots aided by a sensation-monger.

Police were ordered to arrest vendors selling copies of the *Gazette* (eleven news-boys were charged), but its presses kept rolling. "We knew we had forged a thunderbolt," wrote Stead, "but even we were hardly prepared for the overwhelming impression which it has produced on the public mind." Indeed, while most of the press remained circumspect regarding the contents of the articles, they provoked a moral panic and firestorm of public debate. The Archbishops of Canterbury and York and the Bishop of London condoned the exposure, but for press such as *John Bull* it amounted to nothing less than a "carnival of filth". In a letter to *The Times*, the influential Rev. Llewelyn Davies† termed it a "new apocalypse of evil". *The St James's Gazette*, a staunchly Conservative paper, printed:

---

* Such a sentiment would not have gone down well with some of Stead's supporters. Reginald Brett confided to his journal: "[Stead] gave me two letters from Josephine Butler to read. They show that craze for chastity which in the XIXth century is a Fetish whatever uses it may have had in the XIth century." [Esher diary, 3 April 1891, quoted in Morris B. Kaplan, *Sodom On The Thames: Sex, Love & Scandal In Wilde Times*, Cornell University Press, Ithaca & London 2005, p175.]

† Rev. John Llewelyn Davies (1826–1916), Liberal churchman and translator of Plato.

our distinct opinion is that four-fifths of his [Stead's] narrative is mere imposture. That, however, is not the point. The man who invented the 'sensation' might have worked it out with some little regard to decency. This shameless creature has flung all decency aside, openly dealing with the worst abominations in the plainest and foulest language.

When two hundred women, some of them very prominent, presented an address in support of Stead, *The Spectator* magazine was horrified, printing: "these good women, in the depth of their zeal for purity, are not aware of the mischief that will be done."

More than a little drunk on his own messianic vision and daring, Stead delightedly reprinted the response of the Press, including his critics. Proclaimed *The Standard*:

> We venture to say that no other capital in Europe would tolerate for an hour the spectacle presented in the main thoroughfares of London at the present moment of men, women, and children offering to men, women, and children copies of a newspaper containing the most offensive, highly-coloured, and disgusting details concerning the vicious ways of a small section of the population.

However, *The Methodist Times* was thrilled to its core:

> The battle is already won. In vain did the London daily papers enter into a conspiracy of silence. In vain did Messrs. W. H. Smith & Son [newsagents] refuse to sell *The Pall Mall Gazette* last week. In vain did the Prince of Wales stop his copy. In vain did the West-end clubs vote the paper out of their sacred buildings. In vain did the city solicitor hurry and persecute the poor men who sold the paper in the streets…In vain did Mr. Cavendish Bentinck pose before the astonished and indignant public as a great champion of propriety, decency, and purity…Even now the agitation is only beginning.

It was true. Throughout the land there were meetings and proposals. In July 1885, a monster petition demanding better legal protection of girls, endorsed with three hundred and ninety-three thousand signatures collected by the Salvation Army, was borne in procession through the streets of London to Parliament.

As a result of this brouhaha, Parliament could no longer ignore its responsibilities. After years of dilatoriness over the *Criminal Law Amendment Act*, the legislation was promptly passed in August, raising the age of consent for girls from thirteen to sixteen. (For boys, the age of criminal responsibility, which was fourteen, functioned as the age of consent.)

A last-minute addition to the bill, but one that would have profound consequences for tens of thousands of lives, was Section 11, introduced by Henry Labouchère. Stead had sent him a report on the prevalence of homosexuality. Despite his worldliness, Labby loathed such amatory expression, and was determined to have it quashed. Employing the vague term of 'gross indecency' between male persons, Section 11 further criminalised homosexual acts, whether committed publicly or in private.

However, the Government now acted upon its fury against Stead. He and the others involved in the virgin-purchasing stunt were prosecuted on charges related to abduction. The evidence presented in court established that Stead had been deceived by a key witness, but also suggested he had exaggerated the evidence. As detailed to the court, the circumstances surrounding the pseudo-purchase of the girl Eliza Armstrong had been appalling: she had been taken without her father's consent, her vagina inspected twice to confirm her virginity – once by a brothel madam; she had twice been chloroformed, sent to France, her letters to her mother suppressed, and her restitution refused. In the words of the Judge: "An irreparable injury had been done." He considered Stead had acted recklessly for motives he believed good, and denounced the affair as "a disgrace to journalism," sentencing him to three months imprisonment. There had never been a more willing martyr.

Fortunately, Queen Victoria was an admirer of Stead's intentions, if not his methods, and after one day as an ordinary prisoner, by Royal Command, Stead was able to serve the remainder of his sentence as a 'first class misdemeanant', which provided his own furnished room with fireplace. However, with the revelation that the Armstrong purchase had been a put-up job, his reputation was forever tarnished.

Yet some of the horrors Stead wrote of unquestionably existed. In 1862, the Goncourt brothers* of French literary fame had been shocked by Frederick Hankey,† an exquisitely polite English sadist, who informed them he'd whipped girls as young as thirteen in a London brothel run by a Mrs. Jenkins – "the little ones, oh! not too hard but the big ones quite hard," as well as pushing short pins into them: "Yes, we wanted blood!"

The demand for virgins was also inevitably catered to, and the Belgium trafficking case that provoked Dyer and Gillett likely had substance. However, as the court found, Stead's belief in the existence of a massive virgin slave trade for a debased nobility had led to a lurid beat-up. A distinguished physician, Dr James Edmunds,‡ who'd worked in the East End on behalf of the Metropolitan Police, and also in St James's, told the press he had investigated many assaults upon girls:

> Probably I have had to give evidence in our higher criminal courts in London with regard to fifty charges of this kind, in some of which very long terms of penal servitude had to be awarded. But all the cases that I remember were apart entirely from any systematic villainy of procuration such as that pictured so ostentatiously by *The Pall Mall Gazette*; nor do I remember a single case the incidents of which would in the least bear out the attack made by *The Pall Mall Gazette* upon our aristocracy.

Unfortunately, the damage to the reputation of the nobility had been done. Reginald Brett was particularly concerned over the potential for the articles to "set class against class". While the investigation had shown "the offenders were nearly all obscure persons," The Maiden Tribute left the impression that "that these crimes were peculiar to 'Princes of the Blood and prominent public men'".

---

* Edmond de Goncourt (1822–1896), Jules de Goncourt (1830–1870).
† Frederick 'Jack' Hankey (1821–1882), bibliomaniac sadist. [See: Patrick J. Kearney, *Frederick Hankey 1821–1882: A Biographical Sketch*, Scissors & Paste Bibliographies, Santa Rosa CA 2019: www.scissors-and-paste.net].
‡ James Edmunds M.D. (1832–1911). For seven years, surgeon to H Division (Whitechapel) of the Metropolitan Police; one of the founders of, and senior physician to, the London Temperance Hospital. An early advocate of the admission of women to the practice of medicine, he also founded the Female Medical College. [Obituary, The *British Medical Journal*, 25 February 1911, pp470-471; Dr James Edmunds, *The Times*, 17 February 1911, p11.]

While virgin trafficking may not have been endemic, there were other troubling social developments. And again, in his long editorial 'Sex-Mania', W.M. Thompson of *Reynolds's Newspaper* was ready to point the finger:

> The 'New Woman' is, to a certain extent, a development of sex-mania: the male decadent is its victim...what shall we say to a woman like Lady Henry Somerset screaming in an American magazine, *The Arena*, against what she calls 'compulsory motherhood'?

Lord Henry's wife had indeed been vocal. She had already roused members of the Women's Christian Temperance Union by proclaiming:

> All that we ask of the average woman is that she be an earnest woman, all that we hope of the aroused woman is that she shall become an enfranchised woman; all that we hope for the New Woman is that she shall be a true woman.

One London journalist snarked: "there is nobody now except Lady Henry Somerset to instal as universal female pan-sexual potentate and spirit empress of both hemispheres." W.M. Thompson too was unimpressed:

> It is time that a healthier blast was blown through the ranks of our Society...It is not necessary that woman should confine herself to making jam; but if there was a little more of that kind of domestic industry, not only would it add immeasurably to the comfort and convenience of our homes, but it would provide a useful occupation for persons like Lady Henry Somerset, who – excellent woman as she is – is one of those depressing Cassandras who, in ever-increasing numbers, are inflicting themselves upon our age and nation.

Some claimed the advent of the New Woman was encouraging woman-haters. Although such bachelors had a strong aversion to the 'fair sex', they were not generally perceived as Oscar Wildean in their inclinations. Indeed, the press readily discussed the fact that the leading woman haters of the day* were those pillars of Empire, Cecil Rhodes and Lord Kitchener.† As one report enumerated:

> Lord Kitchener is supposed to be an avowed woman-hater. The rumour once reached the late Queen Victoria, and it is said that the first time he went to Windsor she taxed him on the point. 'I have heard that you dislike women. Is that so?' she asked. 'All except one,' he replied. 'And who is that?' 'Your Majesty', he replied, with one of his delightful smiles.

It was also reported of him that:

> The 'man of ice and iron' has been getting into trouble for his frank declaration of his preference for bachelor over married officers as his comrades and subordinates… Lord Kitchener is… loud in his praise of the bachelor state.‡

Another newspaper warned: "the woman-hater is generally dyspeptic, and if a woman marries a dyspeptic man then Lord help her!" An anonymous writer in *The Cornhill Magazine* furnished the helpful advice that "Morocco is a paradise for the woman-hater."

---

* Earlier holders of that once semi-respectable title included the 5th Duke of Portland (1800–1879), and his Tory M.P. brothers Lord George Bentinck (1802–1848), and Lord Henry Bentinck (1804–1870). The latter laid down "the stipulation was that he was never to see a female servant. One morning, rising earlier than usual, he found a female cleaning the stairs, and he at once left the place." [Sporting Notes, *The Sporting Times*, 14 December 1907, p1.]

† Field Marshal (Horatio) Herbert Kitchener, 1st Earl Kitchener, (1850–1916), British Army officer, colonial administrator, and national icon. His critics included Major-General Sir Hamilton St Clair Bower (1858–1940), who served in India and China, and who considered him "a windbag, a poltroon…His schemes are paper schemes that appear good on paper but are impracticable." Major Albert Ernest Wearne (1871–1954), an Australian veteran of the Boer War who also served in Egypt during the First World War, before becoming a Reuters correspondent and chief, held "the utmost contempt for Kitchener as a commander in the field," further stating: "he drinks and has the other failing acquired by most of the Egyptian officers, a taste for buggery." [Cyril Pearl, *Morrison of Peking*, Angus & Robertson, Sydney 1967, pp175-176, 200.] During the War, Kitchener sought relief from stress by visiting (sometimes directly from Cabinet meetings) the Chiswick studio of artists John Houghton Bonnor, and his wife Annie Susan. Using a young son of the couple as a model, here he sculpted a series of playful cupids. One pair dance together; another are about to kiss. A further grouping is of two slightly older boys in a tackle: one is bent forward, while the other, who holds him from behind, has his head thrown back and mouth open in an expression of release. [Kitchener's "War Babies" For The Ideal Home, *The Sketch*, 8 March 1933, p419; Lord Kitchener As Modeller, *The Civil & Miltiary Gazette* (Lahore), 30 May 1923, p10.]

‡ The bevy of brisk young colonels he surrounded himself with, known as the 'Band of Boys', included his secretary Hubert Hamilton – nicknamed 'Handsome Hammy'. [Peter King, *The Viceroy's Fall: how Kitchener destroyed Curzon*, Sidgwick & Jackson, London 1986, p124.]

There were, of course, other men disinclined to seek comfort in the rising bosom of womanhood. Perhaps thinking of Lady Henry Somerset's husband, W.M. Thompson observed:

> A feature of a low state of morals amongst the patrician class always has been that the most conspicuous devotees of unnatural offences have been persons already married. The inference is obvious. They have led their unloved or wooden spouses to the altar from motives other than affection – position, money, influence. They have gone into the marriage mart, and bought a female for commercial reasons. What the female may be in other ways does not enter into their consideration.

In 1889 a novel, *A Marriage Below Zero,* created a minor sensation by addressing this very subject. Published in America, but written by an English émigré,[*] it was the story of a young woman who discovers her husband is conducting an affair with a long-time male friend. It established a tradition of the homosexual character committing suicide. In the words of one American reviewer: "The sins of Sodom and Gomorrah have been used for the first time by the novelist, and the result is horrible, but readable," adding, "The book is selling like hot cakes."[*]

However, it was another work, first published in America the following year by another Englishman, that created a true ruckus. The July 1890 issue of the magazine *Lippincott's Monthly* carried the text of

---

[*] *A Marriage Below Zero* by Alan Dale. (G.W. Dillingham & Co, New York.) Written under a pseudonym, the author was a twenty-seven-year-old music and drama critic, and later a Hollywood silent film director and actor, Alfred J. Cohen, (1861–1928), whose other works included *Familiar Chats With Queens Of The Stage.* One of his caustic theatre reviews resulted in a front-page incident in 1910 when Sir Henry Irving's actor son, Laurence Irving, denounced him from the New York stage as "a blot of scum" (according to some accounts "a blob of scum") for a review which said Irving's legs were too thin, and his actress-wife Mabel "ought to be running a typewriter, or handing out ribbons over the counter." The scum epithet was particularly unfortunate, as four years later Laurence and Mabel drowned in the sinking of *RMS Empress of Ireland.* [Irving On Stage Raps Alan Dale, *New York Press,* 7 January 1910.]

[*] An 1875 German novel *Fridolin's Heimliche Ehe,* published in translation in 1885 in America as *Fridolin's Mystical Marriage,* had also addressed the topic of "beings with masculine intellect and womanly feelings, or womanly gifts and masculine character, or a medley," with a story of a professor who finds his life's fulfilment in a young male student who moves in with him. However, their relationship was carefully presented as hazily intellectual; leading to happy reviews: "fanciful, quaint, sentimental, and thoroughly German" (*The Syracuse Standard*); "very bright and unfatiguing reading for a dull summer's day." (*The Gazette,* Boston) [Adolf Wilbrandt, Clara Bell (trans.) *Fridolin's Mystical Marriage,* William S. Gottsberger, New York 1888, p54.]

Oscar Wilde's *The Picture of Dorian Gray*. With pursued lips, *The Pall Mall Gazette* informed readers:

> Dorian Gray with his "finely-curved scarlet lips, his frank blue eyes and his crisp gold hair," is of the same sex as his admirers; but that does not make their worship of him, and the forms of its expression, seem any the less nauseous. The air does not freshen as the story proceeds...

Oscar Wilde replied: "it is poisonous if you like, but you cannot deny that it is also perfect." While *The Graphic* admitted, "The plot is the most powerful and original that has been written for some time," it also took issue with "The twaddle of his emasculate men." Other reviewers were more blunt: "Pleasure there is none. The subject is revolting, and the people in the story are offensive." The 'people in the story' were more of those decadent upper class. While sales of the magazine had soared, its British distributor, W.H. Smith, pulled the issue from railway station news-stands. Before the novel was published in book form, a chastened Wilde cut the most blatant of the homosexual references. In 1895, in his libel case against Lord Queensberry, the defence would read to the court passages from the *Lippincott's* text to devastating effect.

A dissenting voice that vice was on the increase was the highly popular journalist Augustus Sala.* Having been born in 1828, Sala had known elderly Georgian rakes and roysterers. In his opinion, compared to their "madcap dissipation" and "The riot, the turmoil, the inebriety, the pugnaciousness of which you obtain inklings in the literature and the newspaper files of fifty years ago," all was now tameness:

> I incline to the impression that what little 'fast' life we have left among us in the upper ranks of society has had its roughness materially modified by the habit of donning evening dress on the slightest provocation; of smoking cigarettes; of wearing gardenias in the button-hole, and of drinking lemon squashes, or at least modicums of ardent spirits largely diluted with aerated waters.

---

* (George) Augustus Henry Fairfield Sala (1828–1895). Married Harriett Elizabeth, née Hollingsworth, and after her death, a divorcée, Bessie Caralampi, née Stannard.

That said, Sala was writing from a distinct vantage point: while happily married, he was an enthusiastic pornographer. Obsessed by flagellation, he was co-author with James Campbell Reddie* of a tale set in a girls' boarding school *The Mysteries of Verbena House* (1882), in which the headmistress memorably remarks of a comely pupil, "I'll flog her till the blood runs down the whole school." Sala had also penned the rollicking unperformed play *The New And Gorgeous Pantomime Harlequin Prince Cherrytop And The Good Fairy Fairfuck* (1879) in which a bishop declares to a prince, "Not for years, ere I met you, had I come/in aught less genial than a schoolboy's bum."

A significant factor encouraging a belief in social decay, was the cascade of scandals, *exposés*, and *cause célèbres* embroiling the elite. As W.M. Thompson observed, "The English aristocracy is cutting a contemptible figure in the world. Scarcely a day passes that some one or other of its members does not appear in a disreputable light." These delinquencies, printed in ever-larger headlines, were prime sales fuel for the increasingly vigorous popular press. New halfpenny evening papers retailing scandal and sensation became such a phenomenon, at least one theatre manager expressed the fear they were reducing the need for people to leave their firesides to seek further entertainment.

The falling away of the Victorian discretion that had protected the upper class now made it appear, in the eyes of some, a sink of corruption. Lamented another observer: "An eminent author once wrote of the glory of Britain's aristocracy. Had he been alive today he might very reasonably have asked leave to withdraw his words." Thompson certainly had an opinion on the matter:

> For a body so limited in numbers, the amount and gravity of their offences against public and private morals are astounding. By what is revealed we may guess at what is concealed. Every effort is made to hush up aristocratic scandals...Humbug and cant are the prevailing notes of our time.

In the view of Lord Randolph Churchill, the aristocracy and working

---

* James Campbell Reddie (1807–1878), homosexual pornography author. n.b. Five letters purportedly written by Reddie to Henry Spencer Ashbee, allegedly found in an attic in 2007, are actually a scholarly prank that scissors and pastes true events from Reddie's life. [Information from Patrick Kearney.]

class were "united in the indissoluble bands of a common immorality." As always, the public appetite for scandal amongst the privileged was insatiable, but now there was a far greater eagerness to feed it. When the eccentric Dowager Countess of Cardigan published her indiscreet memoirs in 1909, they became a runaway bestseller.* In the opinion of one reviewer: "Lady Cardigan oversteps not only the modest limits of propriety, for she is seldom within them, but even those bounds which are permitted in the relaxed atmosphere of the smoking room." The famous courtesan Skittles* took a more worldly view, quipping: "Let us drink to the health of the head of my profession, the Countess of Cardigan."

Bachelor political salonist George Russell believed the moral slide of the 'Upper Ten' was due to the collapse of the Old Order:

> more and more the landed gentry of England desert the 'sweet, sincere surroundings of country life'; they increasingly ignore the patriarchal and feudal elements which have played so great a part in the formation of our national polity, and increasingly they develop those vulgar and worldly characteristics which seem to be inseparable from the ostentatious and artificial life of an over-luxurious town.

As the leading English mouthpiece of Max Nordau, W.M. Thompson believed the idleness that encouraged upper class decadence was spreading, due to:

> the increasing luxury of the age and the ever-growing population who live on the labours of others...Luxury, more cruel than war,

---

* Adeline Louisa Maria Brudenell, née de Horsey, Countess of Cardigan and Lancastre (1824–1915), second wife of the 7th Earl of Cardigan. Her habit of organising steeplechases through the local graveyard, smoking in public, and cycling clad in her first husband's regimental trousers, were considered the least of her social transgressions. The Countess's ghostwriter, Maude ffoulkes, consciously modelled the memoirs on those of the Regency courtesan Harriet Wilson, as she considered both women "fearless souls who had the absolute courage of their convictions." However, even the broad-minded ffoulkes had been at times shocked by her subject, and "the blue pencil had to be exercised very freely". Even so, for newspapers like the *Daily Telegraph*, "Never was there such a book...it held nothing sacred, it respected nobody". Considered especially beyond the pale was an anecdote concerning William Ward, 1st Earl of Dudley, who had prised open the mouth of his wife's corpse in order to show one of her male admirers her bad teeth. [Maude M.C. ffoulkes, *My Own Past*, Cassell And Company, London 1915, pp236, 222; William Le Queux, *Things I Know about Kings, Celebrities, and Crooks*, E. Nash and Grayson, London 1923, p134.]
* Catherine Walters (1839–1920).

is descending from the patrician cast: its example is demoralising all grades of Society.

It was The Fall Of Rome all over again:

> History teaches us that moral corruption has always been the forerunner of the downfall of nations…So we may take it that the shocking depravity of the English idle classes at this moment is a symptom of our approaching dissolution.

Echoing Thompson, in early 1902 a journalist on a magazine *The Week-End*, reflected:

> It sounds very sweeping, but there is no doubt that society as it exists to-day, in the year of the Coronation of His Majesty, is not a little rotten. It is the age of advertisement, of publicity, and of luxury; and luxury has always heralded the downfall of an Empire from time immemorial.

These words, slightly paraphrased, were then repurposed the following year for the opening of a novel, *Souls: A Comedy Of Intentions*. Its popular authoress was Mrs. Desmond Humphreys,** who voraciously scribbled under the pen name of 'Rita'. Her novel was pitched as a satire on jaded high society, but unlike E.F. Benson and others who mined the same territory for humour, Rita was deadly serious – her Preface more a sermon that channelled Thompson:

> Scarcely a week passes but some high name is dragged into the mire of public opprobrium…They choose to be a law unto themselves, but they appear to forget the obligations of position. To live solely for amusement or excitement appears to be their sole idea of existence. An existence that denotes a total lack of responsibility…

Within a few months, *Souls* had gone into five editions. More than this, Rita had opened her war on noble decadence on two fronts. The previous year, for *The Gentlewoman* magazine, she'd churned out a ten-part series of denunciations, *The Sin & Scandal Of The Smart Set*: "Their

---

** Eliza Margaret Jane Humphreys, née Gollan (1850–1938). Her first marriage to German aristocratic composer (Karl Edmund) Otto von Booth ended in divorce; she married, secondly, Irishman Desmond Humphreys.

hypocrisies of friendship, their slang and vulgarity, their extravagances, their drugging and drinking, their gambling, their marriages and intrigues." Such was reader demand, ten thousand copies of the series were also snapped up in booklet form at the price of a shilling.*

Rita was not without her critics. A reviewer in *The Graphic* blithely observed she was "neither a Juvenal nor a Swift," while fellow author and 'New Woman' Ella Hepworth Dixon† in the *Daily Mirror* more crushingly suggested that Rita, who resided at 'The Bungalow, Swanage, Dorset,' was not exactly in the front ranks of the social swim, having "retired from the polluting contact of the world of fashion...one cannot escape the suspicion that she takes her data about modish women chiefly from the newspaper reports of divorce cases." Sporting paper *The Referee* was equally snorting, labelling *Souls*:

> absurdly exaggerated, highly coloured, and indifferently written...Rita had her success of curiosity. Now she wants a success of morality. She is scolding the people whom she invented and described for our amusement. Remember, "Scandal is gossip made tedious by morality."‡ A solemn and censorious air is assumed to disguise a rampant snobbishness. The 'smart set' as described by 'Rita' is a feverish figment of a journalist's brain...The 'upper classes' have always desired freedom, having more convention forced on them even now than they care about.

This was close to the bone, as Rita was not merely gloriously snobbish, but not quite whole either, renting herself out in advertisements as an advocate for a patent tonic containing phosphoric acid:

> I have great pleasure in stating that I have derived great benefit

---

* Rita's concerns included "the loss of dignity and delicacy", for which she pointed an accusing finger at the American women who'd invaded London Society. These Amazons exhibited "a 'brainy' effervescence that is apt to get on one's nerves" –"with them advertisement is an absolute craze, the first law of *their* nature." More damningly, they had introduced The Cake Walk: "a common nigger dance...A moving panorama of unbridled levity and unlicensed vulgarity." [The Sin & Scandal Of The Smart Set, *The Gentlewoman*, 28 November 1903, p732 (p42); 5 December 1903, p788 (p30).]
† Ella Hepworth Dixon (1857–1932), pen name, Margaret Wynman. Her best-known work is *The Story of a Modern Woman.*
‡ Oscar Wilde: *Lady Windermere's Fan.*

from the use of Phosferine, especially when fagged or exhausted after a long spell of brain work...I have also found it excellent for attacks of neuralgia.

Nonetheless, moral panic had set in. By December 1902, it was reported a missionary intervention consisting of:

men and women drawn from the humbler ranks of society have devoted themselves to the moral upraising of that section of society known as the smart set... Several thousand copies of Wordsworth's *Ode to Duty** have been printed, and will be distributed at club and theatre doors. Special meetings will be held during the Henley, Ascot, Cowes, and other Society gatherings...

Careful thought had been expended on how to attract the vice-wracked jades of upper class society to lectures on "early rising, regular labour, and simple foods":

weekly meetings will be held in the West-end, and every inducement will be tried to attract the people. The women will be provided with cigarettes and coffee, and at the close of the meetings each man will be presented with a copy of *The Tailor And Cutter.*

Not to be left out, a celebrity Jesuit priest, the Rev. Bernard Vaughan,† of the Church of the Immaculate Conception in Mayfair, launched his own series of doorbusting sermons denouncing the gilt-edged sinners of the 'Smart Set'. Again, *The Refeee* took issue; this time not denying high life dissipations existed, but that there was:

very little British blood, or British bullion, at the bottom of the movement, which is the canned horror order of importation. The Shocking Set vagaries to which Father Vaughan takes exception would not be dreamed of by the sane, true-born

---

* "Oh, let my weakness have an end!/Give unto me, made lowly wise, /The spirit of self-sacrifice; etc."

† Rev. Bernard Vaughan (1847–1922). He achieved happy notoriety through attacks on luxury, socialism, 'Mayfair Magdalens', and what was termed 'Race Suicide' – contraception. An opposer of premature peace in World War I, he further boosted his public profile with the rousing call: "Keep on killing Germans". [Death of Father Bernard Vaughan, *Western Morning News*, 1 November 1922, p5; Race Suicide, *The Globe*, 3 April 1911, p1.]

British aristocrat, or the men and women of the British Upper Middle Classes.

Rita begged to differ. Amongst her over-heated effusions were thinly-veiled personal attacks on Anglo-Saxon personages born to the purple:

> What of the titled youth who turns his castle into an imitation Drury Lane on Boxing night; whose highest ambition is the display of family jewels on his own person as a Prince of pantomime? What of the illustrious peer who roams from the Old World to the New with no higher ambition than to wear the skirts of a ballet girl, and pass for one? What of the effete Boudoir Boys who give smoking parties to each other in order to display the latest thing in satin corsets, and lace-frilled tea coats?

What indeed. The first such youth under Rita's withering gaze was the harmless (except to his family fortune) Henry Cyril Paget, known to intimate friends as 'Toppy'. Tall, elegant, perfumed and bejewelled, he was nonetheless a lieutenant of the Royal Welsh Fusiliers. In 1898, at the age of 23, he'd succeeded to the title of 5th Marquess of Anglesey, and an annual income of £120,000 (equivalent to £11 million per year in 2018). A mere six years later he'd bankrupted the estate. When a reporter asked how he had achieved the remarkable feat, his lordship was refreshingly frank:

> Just how I could not tell you. It cost me £3,000 a year for underwear...I had braces (suspenders) woven of threads of gold instead of the usual elastic webbing that other men rely upon to support their trousers. The buckles were of gold too. Imagine one's manner of living carried me [*sic*] out of that scale, and it is not hard to see where a good deal of my money went.

It also went on jewels, furs, costumes, cars, perfumes, horses, and a theatrical touring company. As one report noted:

> The Marquess of Anglesey has throughout the week been entertaining large parties at Anglesey Castle, his seat on the banks of the Menai Straights. Nightly there were tableaux of 'Romeo and Juliet', to quote the bills, to which the public were freely

admitted, his Lordship posing as Romeo.

Finally reduced to the mere pittance of £3,000 a year, there were rumours he intended to join a monastic order. At Monte Carlo (a locale conducive to ascetic philosophers) he informed the press he was "sick of world and its vanities". He died in 1905 of pneumonia, his estranged wife by his bedside. Their marriage had remained unconsummated. News of death caused "much regret" in Bangor, where blinds were drawn in mourning.

Beyond extravagance and carnality, the righteous also despaired of the shameless pursuit of money, which had previously been more discreetly practised. Its flag-wavers were the battalion of peers who chased American heiresses. The most ruthless was the second young peer in Rita's sights: the Earl of Yarmouth,* the bankrupt heir of the Marquess of Hertford. After assiduously heiress-hunting in America, in 1903, Yarmouth contracted a marriage with Alice Cornelia Thaw of Pittsburg. Moments before the wedding, in the vestry of the church, and in the company of his solicitor, he demanded the bride's parents sign a revised dowry, or he would walk out. Amongst other clauses, it doubled his annual allowance to $10,000. With the organ already playing, the Thaws caved in and signed. Five years later the marriage was annulled due to non-consummation. There then followed a legal battle in which he sought to retain Miss Thaw's property portfolio of half a million dollars, rather than only the interest from it, as the marriage settlement stipulated. He lost, and the following year was bankrupted again.

Although Lord Yarmouth was described as "the hope and the despair of the mothers of eligible daughters," he was something far more incandescent. Despite holding a lieutenancy in the Black Watch, in 1894 his family had packed him off to the antipodes, "for the good of his health and his country". What resulted was the unbridled flowering of his theatrical predilections.

On a spring evening in 1894, at the Theatre Royal in Hobart, Tasmania, there took place what *The Australian Star* newspaper termed: "Probably the most remarkable theatrical entertainment ever seen in the southern hemisphere." It was most likely so for the

---

* George Francis Alexander Seymour, 7th Marquess of Hertford (1871–1940).

distinguished audience, which included the State governor and his wife, members of Parliament, and "the officers from H.M.S.s Katoomba and Goldfinch, now lying in the harbour." As the *Star* reported:

> when the Earl of Yarmouth appeared in a loose white wrapper, with blue ribbons, and a flowing wig of soft brown hair falling over his shoulders, there was something like a gasp from the dress-circle. The next act saw his lordship appear in "abbreviated skirts reaching just below his knees, black stockings, dainty shoes, and a large white sun-bonnet...He threw himself into his part with a thorough obliteration of self, which, from an artistic point of view, was admirable, and kicked as high as the most exacting ballet mistress could desire.

The evening's highlight was the Serpentine Dance, performed under his lordship's 'nom-de-ballet' (as printed on the playbills) 'Mademoiselle Roze':

> whirling his drapery in each hand in the most approved fashion, he gyrated before the astonished throng in one whirling blaze of kaleidoscopic colours, and danced with unabated vigour in aid of the funds of the Girl's Industrial School and the Dorcas Society.

In a breathless climax challenging fellow skirt-dancer Loie Fuller, the limelight man projected onto his skirt Millais's painting 'Bubbles,' which graced every wrapper of Pears Soap, followed by portraits of the Prince and Princess of Wales, the Duke and Duchess of York, and the Governor of Tasmania and his wife. *The Star* reported that "thunders of applause greeted him, and several large bouquets were thrown." As a house-shaking encore the Earl gyrated once more, and the curtain was brought down as his whirling skirt displayed the projected face of Her Majesty Queen Victoria herself.

From the castellated Government House in Hobart, where his lordship was a guest of the vice-regal couple, he moved on to Melbourne, repeating the performance on behalf of the Old Colonialists Association and other charities. There his dance 'The Moth And The Candle' was considered "perhaps the most effective item on the programme," another report noting: "At the close of the performance Lord Yarmouth acknowledged the applause by throwing his hands above his head in the manner peculiar to drowning men." A less-forgiving theatrical reviewer wrote that, "his general appearance suggested a scraggy, hard-featured woman disguised as a pantomime prince," before adding, "Melbourne sassiety will continue to hug the delusion that a lantern slide reflected on an earl's apparel is a terpsichorean triumph."

Lord Yarmouth settled in Mackay in subtropical Queensland where he attempted to farm, but harvested little more than animosity, displaying the heartless greed that had chilled even the Thaws. A Japanese labourer was forced to sue him for wages, and he boasted of tricking the Pacific Islanders who bought his chickens that gold sovereigns were less valuable than silver half-crowns. Appropriately, he also made an appearance in a local performance of the comic operetta *Morocco Bound*. It was said the locals were more interested in his departure than his arrival. As one newspaper characterised him: "Empty pockets and a supreme contempt for the Petty Debts Court as an institution, are not a happy combination." He left in 1897, remembered for his local theatrics, a sequinned outfit with butterfly wings, and men-only parties at his isolated property 'The Rocks.'

Back in London, Yarmouth was rescued from bankruptcy by inheriting the marquessate, Ragley Hall, and 11,000 acres. It didn't stop his heiress hunting: in 1913, he attempted to marry the improbably named Rita Mosscockle,* a rich older widow and poetess, who sported a marmalade wig and twenty-four Pekingese. However, soon after the announcement of the Marquess's engagement, it fell through, or as *The Sporting Times* put it, "he gathers no Mosscockle". Society laughed, but perhaps a snarking paragraph in *Truth* that for Yarmouth's creditors "the wedding day should be a joyful one," plus more scathing references in the American press to the 'Purse Hunting Marquis'[*sic*], reached Rita's love-struck eyes.

In addition to such noble butterflies, the contretemps of peers and chorus girls was to become a meme of the age. Typical of such affairs was the unsuccessful attempt by Viscount Dunlo, the eldest son of the 4th Earl of Clancarty, to divorce his wife, a music hall artiste by the name of Maude 'Belle' Bilton. Accused of adultery with a Jewish

---

* Harriet 'Rita' Francis Mosscockle, née Sparrow (1858–1943), authoress of *Fantasias, The Golden Quest and Other Poems*, etc.

gentleman, Isador Wertheimer,* the son of a Bond Street bric-a-brac dealer, it was alleged in court that she had also been liberal in her affections with at least two other gentlemen, one a son of the Duke of Leeds. However, as a colonial newspaper reported, "the lady…means to fight for her title to the last gasp." The defence counsel of the Countess was coolly honest about her motives: "She was ambitious of the title, and having married, did they think that she would be likely to jeopardise it by committing adultery?"

The pre-war zenith of these mercenary marital trainwrecks occurred in 1913, when 'Bim', the 6th Marquess of Northampton,† who was appropriately blessed with matinee idol looks, offered to settle the astounding sum of £50,000 pounds‡ on a thirty-year-old divorced actress, Daisy Markham, after she brought a breach of promise suit. The scale of the payment, which required the Northampton estate to undertake land sales to meet, left the nation dumbfounded.

Given its expense, divorce was almost solely a ruling class privilege. By 1887, the endless unsavoury details of evidence printed by the popular press – what was termed 'divorce muck' – had become of such concern to the authorities that the Home Secretary, Henry Matthews,§ put pressure on the President of the Divorce Court to limit its publication; a desire heartily endorsed by *The Times*. In 1910, a *Royal Commission On Divorce Law,* as part of its remit, investigated the possibility of restricting press access to the divorce courts. Again, W.M. Thompson in *Reynolds's Newspaper* pulled no punches:

> The Divorce Court has so laid bare the horrible profligacy and filthy instincts of the aristocracy, that the general public is annoyed at these disclosures of the most abominable vice in the highest ranks of society. And, on the other hand, the members of the privileged orders are themselves terrified at the impression these revolting revelations create on the public mind. Hence it is that they would willingly have all the facts in such

---

* He had a reputation for appearing in bedclothes with his face painted to imitate smallpox or scarlet fever whenever debtors called. [Arthur M. Binstead, Ernest Wells, *A Pink 'Un And A Pelican*, Bliss Sands & Co., London 1898, p164.]

† William Bingham Compton, 6th Marquess of Northampton, (1885–1978). Awarded the Distinguished Service Order for bravery in World War I.

‡ At the very minimum, over £5 million in today's money. [measuringworth.com]

§ Henry Matthews, 1st Viscount Llandaff (1826–1913) lawyer and Tory politician.

cases...suppressed.*

In what seemed a darkening situation, an American paper gravely observed:

> There are newspapers of enormous circulation in Great Britain, supported by the humbler class, whose pages are filled with every story, true or false, discreditable to royalty or aristocracy. And this glaring show of immorality among the so-called great is dangerous...it offends the religious and moral sense of the English middle class, which is as virtuous, if sometimes narrow and prejudiced, as pure in morals and manners as any class in any people on earth. This class will one day repudiate an aristocracy that is not clean.

A broad swath of British society had supported the idea that the aristocratic principle enabled a stable foundation for the social structure. The prevailing belief was that those who provided the leadership of the nation had the ear of good society.

Yet no small number of the aristocracy, like the King Emperor himself, looked upon a measured hedonism as their birthright. Unlike the 'dull and worthy masses', they considered it integral to the cultivation of the senses. Indeed, many of their own family histories suggested to them that this was so.

In any case, self-denial was never the aristocracy's strong suit, and when desire presented itself, it was usually leaned into. If the homosexuality tapped during their school days happened to linger on, so be it. Not answerable to others, and not caring much what they thought, they were naturally spoilt, and used to doing what they liked, and having what they wanted. Like a recent Marquess of Anglesey, who at a dinner party loftily stated, "One doesn't care what the press say," and then when asked by the hostess whether he'd prefer the moussaka or cold turkey, replied "I'd like both," a lifetime of privilege made the socially high-risk decision to sexually enjoy the best of both

---

* Public morals, and the reputation of the upper class who could afford divorce, were finally protected in 1926 by the passage of the *Judicial Proceedings (Regulation of Reports) Act* which prohibited the press from reporting divorce court testimony. [See: Gail Savage 'Erotic Stories And Public Decency: Newspaper Reports Of Divorce Proceedings In England', *The Historical Journal*, 41, 2, 1998, pp511-528.]

genders, or simply one's own, an easier one. The only rule, as with adultery, was the 11th Commandment: "Thou shalt not get caught."

The carnal pleasures of the upper class had hitherto been discreetly enjoyed, and their missteps generally hidden. However, now the pervasive scandals trumpeted by the popular press, following on as they did in the wake of Stead's 'Maiden Tribute' exposé and the campaigns of the Purity Movement, were leaving an impression upon the public that, rather than the ruling class having just a few black sheep, the most un-English, Continental-style decadence ran rife throughout it. It even became the stuff of drawing-room comedy. In the 1902 smash hit *The Marriage Of Kitty*, a butler observed: "I 'ave always lived with the best families of the British aristocracy, and that makes a man's thoughts run rather on the seamy side of life."

For the British people, the implicit daily news message that their 'betters' were more worthy of mockery than respect, constituted nothing less than a betrayal of their trust. This breach of the social contract contributed to the loss of faith in the aristocracy's right to rule. And the profound political consequences would alter the very land itself.

4. THE OTHER WORLD

"There is no doubt that of late years a certain offence – I will not give it a name – has become more rife than it ever was before."

In 1890, when Henry Labouchère addressed Parliament on this matter, he was not alone in his opinion that a telling symptom in the perceived rise in degeneracy was 'the unmentionable vice'. Considered to be an aberration of the natural order, and an affront to God (rather than an expression of the biological exuberance that is intrinsic and essential to Nature), it had been further isolated with a freshly coined term – 'homosexuality'.* Following in the bootsteps of Max Nordau, it was theorised that what appeared to some to be a ballooning number of 'inverts' was due to the growth of metropolises, and civilisation's "nervous collapse in the face of the feverish activity of modern life".

Homosexual desire was then – as it had been throughout history – much of a soup, with little demarcation between men and youths. The public celebration of childhood beauty, the honouring and deep familiarity with the Classics, gender segregation, the unfettered world of the forbidden, plus sheer opportunity, encouraged a breadth of

---

* The word 'homosexual' entered the British public consciousness in 1907 from Germany. The modern movement for homosexual emancipation arose in that country in the late nineteenth century, where it created a public discourse that included use of the word, which had been coined in 1868 by one of the movement's activists, Karl-Maria Kertbeny. (Karl-Maria Kertbeny or Károly Mária Kertbeny, born Karl-Maria Benkert (1824–1882) Austrian-born Hungarian journalist, memoirist, and human rights campaigner.) While it was picked up by a few overseas sexologists, it was journalists and news bureaus interpreting German newspaper reports of the Eulenburg Scandal amongst the Kaiser's camarilla that began its global adoption.

passions which marked the lives of many figures of the period. As exemplified by the much-loved statue of Lord Shaftesbury's memorial* in the heart of Piccadilly, then a landmark for homosexual soliciting, the adolescent was widely considered an ideal of transcendent beauty.

In England, as previously noted, the age of criminal responsibility for males, which was fourteen, acted as the age of consent. However, given those attracted to their own gender constituted, by their very existence, legal outlaws and abominations, a prescribed consenting age was a social nicety that was irrelevant to them. Man proclaims, but Nature reigns. (Only since the 1980s, when homosexuals were legislatively accepted by society as ostensible equals in most Western nations, have intergenerational passions become as strictly circumscribed as they are today, by law, custom, peer and societal pressure, and personal resolve.†)

The last men executed for buggery in Britain had been John Smith and James Pratt in 1835. Their prosecution arose when, in a characteristically English act, a landlord and his wife had peered through a bedroom keyhole. In sentencing the prisoners to death the judge declared:

> Without offending the ears of the audience by dilating upon the enormity of the offence, he would implore them to seek mercy from God, as they stood on the brink of eternity, guilty of offences which could hardly excite a tear of pity for their fate, and in consideration of which in a British country mercy ever had been a stranger.

It was also reported: "The prisoners wept very much during the address." Had the judge been completely frank, he would have reminded the prisoners that mercy was dependent upon status. Though the younger man Pratt had a wife and children, both men were mere poor labourers, so they could hardly expect the indulgence extended to those of higher station.

---

* By Sir Alfred Gilbert, it depicts the god Anteros, the god of selfless love, but is commonly misconstrued to be Eros.
† In Italy and France, where homosexuality was decriminalised in the nineteenth century, the age of consent for boys was thirteen until the 1920s. [Helmet Graupner, 'Sexual Consent: The Criminal Law In Europe And Overseas,' *Archives Of Sexual Behaviour*, 29 No5 (2000).]

While capital punishment for sodomy was repealed in 1861, brutal sentences, and revulsion and concern over homosexuality remained. Yet despite this, contradictory ironies lay everywhere, and most especially at the heart of Government. The supreme paradox was that the Established Church, under whose spiritual authority homosexual acts were morally damned, and which thereby legitimised the legal and social persecution of a swathe of the population, was from parish vicars, to embroidered archbishops, to scrapping theologians, widely represented by those it condemned.

At a dinner in London in 1897, the imaginative Conan Doyle* related an anecdote concerning an alleged friend who, having been told that every person, however respectable, harboured a skeleton in their closet, decided to put this opinion to practical test. Selecting a venerable archdeacon, they sent him a telegram stating "All is discovered. Fly at once." After which, so Doyle told his bemused audience, the gentleman had disappeared.

Doyle's fictions were rooted in reality. "I thought so much of my darling little Georgie." So wrote Canon John Neale Dalton of Windsor, chaplain to Queen Victoria, about his former pupil, the future George V, then eighteen years old and serving in the navy. Dalton's effusions weren't simply the usual sentimental dotings that litter Victorian letters: after his death, his son discovered a hoard of correspondence with young men that reflected even deeper feelings. Dalton also tutored Prince George's brother, Prince Albert Victor, struggling in vain with what he termed the young man's "abnormally dormant condition of his mental powers."

Upon reaching middle age, Dalton had married the sister of a naval cadet he'd taken a fancy to. Although she was half his age, he proposed three days after meeting her. Dalton's closest friend was the social campaigner and homosexual rights advocate Edward Carpenter.

For gentlemen of such leanings, and particularly if financially constrained, a career in the Church offered an amenable lifestyle.†

---

* Sir Arthur Ignatius Conan Doyle (1859–1930), writer and creator of the character Sherlock Holmes.
† Compared to lay persons, clergy involved in homosexual incidents often found a comforting

While most tended their parish flocks with quiet diligence, inevitably the ecclesiastical and criminal courts also played host to a small trickle of dog-collared delinquents: mostly obscure parsons of no consequence.

However, this would not be the case when, on an autumn evening in 1884, a police constable arrested two men in Hyde Park who'd been in the throes of committing a misdemeanour with each other. The younger was a nineteen-year-old unemployed working class lad, Charles Telfer. His fifty-nine-year-old partner for the occasion turned out to be a widower with two daughters – the Very Reverend George Herbert,* who was not only Dean of Hereford, but a son of the Earl of Powis. Officials undertook the usual jobbery to conceal the charge from the public, but this time unsuccessfully, and Herbert was released on £300 bail. The unfortunate Telfer was unable to meet his own bail, and with no one willing to offer it, remained in prison. Herbert employed the most eminent defence counsel, and the case was sent to a grand jury who dismissed it, although not unanimously. Most papers suggested their decision came "after long investigation", but *Reynolds's Newspaper* had no time for sycophant tosh, and printed that the deliberation had been brief. The Dean and English Church Union issued "an indignant protest against the atrocious insult," and a scribbler at the Society paper *Life* reassured its gentle readers he had:

> been at some pains to ascertain the truth…I can safely say that a more scandalous and unfounded charge was never brought even by a policeman. The dean was walking in the park, met a boy who looked hungry and tired, asked him, out of pure kindness a few questions, eventually gave him half-a-crown, and walked off. For this act of benevolence he was hailed by an officious policeman before the magistrate.

The Reverend's acts of benevolence were indeed extensive: political insider Lewis Harcourt† told his diary: "It is said of the Dean of Hereford…that he always paid dearer for his women than any other

---

latitude extended to them by the Establishment. See: William T. Gibson, 'Homosexuality, Class and the Church in Nineteenth Century England: Two Case Studies', *Journal of Homosexuality*, 1991, Vol 21, No4; Matthew Parris, *The Great Unfrocked: Two Thousand Years of Church Scandal*, Robson Books, London, 1999.

* The Very Rev. the Hon. George Herbert (1825–1894), third son of the 2nd Earl of Powis, and brother of the 3rd Earl. His wife Beatrice was the daughter of Sir Tatton Sykes.

† Lewis Vernon Harcourt, 1st Viscount Harcourt, (1863–1922), Liberal M.P.

man in London because he insisted on having them young and high church!"

The Dean travelled back to Hereford, where he was presented with an illuminated address of sympathy by the Mayor and Alderman of Hereford in a grand ceremony before an audience of a thousand. No such sympathies are recorded as being offered to young Telfer.

Beyond Hyde Park's bushery, the ritualism of Anglo-Catholicism, as espoused by the Oxford Movement,* held especial appeal for clerics of romantic and theatrical bent. With its clouds of incense, candlelight, mysticism, and if one was lucky – pretty young priests shimmering in gold-embroidered vestments – it promised rapture.†
However, for 'muscular Christians,' High Churchism was the work of Beelzebub. As its arch-foe Charles Kingsley wrote:

> In all that school, there is an element of foppery – even in dress and manner; a fastidious, maundering, die-away effeminacy, which is mistaken for purity and refinement; and I confess myself unable to cope with it, so alluring is it to the minds of an effeminate and luxurious aristocracy.

Critics also dismissed its congregations as being women of the wealthier classes and shop-boys. Writing of St. Alban's in Holborn, a notorious High Church sanctum, *The Times* observed: "foremost, perhaps, among the devotees are young men of 19 or 20 years of age, who seem to have the intricacies of ritualism at their fingers' ends." One such young man drawn to ritualism in 1870 was a military cadet of slender physique, striking looks, and impulsive nature: so obsessed was the young Horatio Kitchener, that in his spare time as a cadet at the Royal Military Academy, he studied Hebrew with his then friend Claude Conder.‡

---

* The Anglican movement that arose in the mid-nineteenth century at Oxford University that sought to reinstate some Catholic thought and practice. Some of its leaders, including Cardinal John Henry Newman, are presumed to have been homosexual. [See: Frederick S. Roden, *Same-Sex Desire In Victorian Religious Culture*, Palgrave Macmillan, Basingstoke 2002, pp11-22.]
† As envisioned by Simeon Solomon's luminous 1870 watercolour *The Mystery of Faith*, with its beautiful young priest cloaked in gold-embroidered white silk. See also: Dominic Janes, 'Seeing and Tasting the Divine: Simeon Solomon's Homoerotic Sacrament', in Gabriel Koureas (ed.), *Art, History and the Senses: 1830 to the Present*, Taylor & Francis, London 2017.
‡ Colonel Claude Reignier Conder (1848–1910), soldier, explorer, antiquarian, author, and bachelor. As young officers, he and Kitchener carried out survey work in Palestine. They later fell out.

The tug of war between sober, muscular Protestantism and heady High Churchism raged throughout the latter half of the nineteenth century.* The Anglo-Catholic otherworld threw up a succession of brotherhoods and guilds that attracted young men seeking its woo-woo ecstasies and alternative homosocial families. The histories of these orders were punctuated with quarrels and scandals. At their very heart lay the homoerotic desire to revive English monasticism.†

Possibly the most exclusive and placid of these establishments was St Austin's Priory in South London. It was founded in 1867 by the Rev. George Nugée,‡ a wealthy Anglican clergyman and "Ritualist of the most advanced order." Nugée devoted his life and fortune to doing good, including providing breakfasts for the poor; co-founding a home for 'fallen women'; establishing the Work Girls Protection Society – which offered city and seaside homes for shop and factory girls; and undertaking endless mission work in London's worst slums. "There were many sides to Fr Nugée's versatile character," a clerical chronicler has observed, "He was just as happy running clubs for men and boys."

However, the Rev. Nugée's heart lay in St. Austin's. The small gilded order was, as one of its lay brothers, Richard C. Jackson§ aka Brother à Becket, phrased it: "a 'Monkery' of rich men." The deluxe interiors, with their thick carpets, serious furniture, statues, and precious books, offered an appropriate background for its brethren of taste and discernment. "The services at St Austin's were of a most ornate description...Its chapel – the talk of London – became one of those exclusive places that everybody wished to see." Fortunately too, Nugée's good works and private wealth enabled him to keep the Church of England's more austere administrators at bay.

---

* To a degree, it was a clash between heterosexual and homosexual sensibilities, although there were representatives of each on both sides. For illuminating histories, see: David Hilliard, 'Unenglish and Unmanly: Anglo-Catholicism and Homosexuality', *Victorian Studies*, University of Indiana, Winter 1982; Dominic Janes, *Visions of Queer Martyrdom from John Henry Newman to Derek Jarman*, University of Chicago Press, 2015.
† See: Peter F. Anson; A.W. Campbell (ed.) *The Call of the Cloister: Religious Communities and Kindred Bodies in the Anglican Communion*, S. P. C. K., London 1964.
‡ Rev. George Nugée (1819–1892).
§ Richard Charles Jackson (1851–1923), wealthy collector, scholar and eccentric. Author of many works, including *Love Poems* (1902), which has been called "the sinless Catullus". See: G.E. Bentley, Jr, Richard C. Jackson, 'Collector Of Treasures And Wishes', *Blake: An Illustrated Quarterly*, Vol 36, Iss 3, (Winter 2002/03), University of North Carolina.

One gentleman whom Nugée desired to bring into the fold was the High Priest of the Aesthetic Movement, Walter Pater.* It was not to be. The appeal of religion for Pater was less of the spirit than of the senses – beginning with "high altars banked with flowers – the arum, the narcissus, the jonquil," and ending with young priests and disciples equally dewy and fragrant. He bluntly told Nugée: "I am interested in the Christian religion only from the fact of my being Page-in-Waiting upon your Professor of Church History." This being the fetchingly-faced, comfortingly rich, and twelve years younger Brother à Becket, whose book and art stuffed home in then-rural Camberwell had by this time become Pater's second home.†

As well as painting the illuminations of the chapel of St Austin's, Brother à Becket also authored its choicer hymns, such as the gently erotic 'Nearer To Me', whose verses included:

Come, gentle Saviour come,
That I may see
Thy more than Sacred Form!
Closer to be
Drawn still by Thee
Nearer to me
Come kindest Friend, and best;

---

* Walter Horatio Pater (1839–1894), Oxford don and highly influential essayist, and art and literary critic. His *Studies in the History of the Renaissance* (1873) was the bible of sensitive young men; his novel, *Marius the Epicurean* (1885), embodied its spirit in an Ancient Roman setting. A romance with the Balliol undergraduate and future novelist William Money Hardinge damaged Pater's career.

† When published in 1907, the first edition of Thomas Wright's two-volume *The Life Of Water Pater* sold out in three days. Not all critics were seduced: *The Morning Post* responded with an amusingly bitchy review that surely provoked many a drawing room snicker:

> The author of this rather pretentious work writes in the preface: "In short, my ambition is that the critics and the public should say of this book: 'It tells the truth, though only just as much as the public should know, and tells it in the most delicate manner conceivable.'... The author's principal aim appears to be to write about a gentleman called Mr. Richard Jackson [Becket] on every possible occasion. There are four photographs of him and five photographs of his house in the second volume. "To omit Mr. Jackson is to tell the story of David and leave out Jonathan." By way of carrying out this analogy he prints (Vol II, page 22) the following verse addressed by Mr. Jackson to Pater:
>
> > "Your darling soul I say is enflamed with love for me;
> > Your very eyes do move I cry with sympathy:
> > Your darling feet and hands are blessings ruled by
> > As forth was sent from out the Ark a turtle dove!"

[The Life Of Walter Pater, *The Morning Post*, 25 March 1907, p2.]

Still yearningly,
Pants my sin-burden'd heart
With Thee to be
In Unity.

Following the death of Nugée in 1892, St. Austin's closed, but not before it witnessed the induction of Benjamin Carlyle,* a wildly eccentric dreamer who took Nugée's monastical vision, and ran with it. A former medical student, he dubbed himself Abbot Aelred, and would go on to build the spectacular abbey on Caldey Island – the first Benedictine monastery in the Church of England since the Reformation. It reduced the Anglo-Catholic ecumenicalist Lord Halifax to rhapsodies: writing to his son he called it "a paradise…If Caldey did not belong to the monks I would give anything to have it myself." Writer Rose Macauley called it a "fabulous and gorgeous dream, in which medieval monastic splendour was outsoared."

Carlyle lived long enough to not only enjoy "a smart private yacht lying in the slips", but also "a handsome Daimler to take him to and fro." He favoured, as he put it, "religious life without starch." And how! His monks were permitted embraces and kisses, and he made their nude bathing on the Island's beaches compulsory. Carlyle also sought succour with the noviciate intake, as a member of the community recalled:

> he was inclined to favouritism and the joys of spiritual friendship with charming young men…Our Abbot, like his patron, generally had his 'Simon', 'Hugh', 'Ivo', or 'Little Ralph'. It was not only the twelfth-century Cistercerian abbot [Aelred of Rievaulx] who chose a young monk who soothed him, when he was worried, and refreshed his leisure…

Another Anglican figure with monastical dreams was the more rackety Rev. J.L. Lyne. Better known in his self-styled persona as Father Ignatius,† for decades he furnished newspapers throughout the land with colourful copy. In 1880, Labouchère's *Truth* wrote of him

---

* Rev. Benjamin Fearnley Carlyle, Abbot Aelred. (1874–1955).
† The Rev. Joseph Leycester Lyne, aka Father Ignatius (1837–1908); Anglican curate, zealous heresy hunter, and eccentric, who sought to revive English monasticism. He adopted a son, the ruby-lipped William Leycester Lyne, né Pritchard ('Brother David'), who married and had issue.

in mid-career. The sardonic profile began:

> Elizabeth, Queen of Bohemia…once declared she would rather reign over a barren plain than not reign at all…many who have never had the chance of becoming autocratic monarchs, may well have embraced the pedagogic career from a feeling that it would be pleasant to command, if only boys.

Lyne's command of lads was no second-best option. After, or perhaps even before the worship of God, it was the *raison d'etre*. Beginning as a humble curate, he exercised his desire for such sovereignty with the establishment of a guild for men and boys, the Society of the Love of Jesus. In 1863, with no official sanction, he then founded a monastery at Norwich. As a report put it, here he:

> performed religious rites of a highly original character, and on religious anniversaries got up processions of a Wild West originality in conception and execution which, in the absence of a circus were the delight of the good people of the town.

Life at the monastery was also a circus. A well-publicised scandal involving a love letter from Lyne's second-in-command to a boy chorister exposed Lyne's own favouritisms. Insurrection amongst the brotherhood followed. In 1869 he began afresh, relocating to the Black Mountains in Wales, and building there New Llanthony Abbey. This offered more of the same, including monastic kisses, and floggings to leaven the icy climate, with the added attraction of heavenly vistas.

In addition to the drama he produced, Lyne helped birth an even more sensational ecclesiastical creation. His name was Francis Widdows.* Beginning in 1863 as a thirteen-year-old apostle at Lyne's Norwich monastery, six years later Widdows made his press debut, after being taken to court by an older former monk from the monastery, James Barrett Hughes, aka Brother Stanislaus, whom he'd hit over the head with a bottle in a lover's spat. "If I may say so," Widdows informed the Judge, "we are bound together as married; in fact, I am his wife." He further claimed it was Lyne who'd conducted their wedding vows.

---

* Francis George Widdows, born George Nobbs (1850–1936).

By any measure, it was an extraordinary performance for an English court-of-law, where a mere eight years previously buggery had mandated death. But then, living on his wits, Widdows was from the hard-scrabble end of the working class, where personal loyalty mattered for more than bourgeois propriety.

Bringing limitless powers of florid expression to the task, Lyne's official biographer, the fragrant Baroness de Bertouch,* rose to new rhetorical heights in addressing Widdows' claims – allegations "almost too monstrous to be touched by a woman's pen." She considered Lyne's name "had been invoked to pillar up and give realistic plausibility to an otherwise intangible chaos of unclean suggestion." For his part, Lyne attempted to deflect the allegation by pointing an accusatory finger at other parties:

> If Brother Osmund [Widdows] was really as bad as he has been represented, how is it that the late Dr. Jowett† of Baliol, Oxford, and his admiring friend Dean Fremantle,‡ should have been allowed to go 'scot free' in their applause of Plato and the translation (by Jowett) of his *Dialogues?* Jowett said his happiest hours had been spent in translating Plato's abominations for the benefit of the people of England. In this book of Jowett's – to be had at any library I believe – sins of the kind alluded to in this chapter are held up, not as crimes, but as ideals to be admired and emulated by the youth-student of the day.

When Widdows' trial again came to court, his partner Hughes never turned up to continue the prosecution, having possibly finally realised his teenage boyfriend was capable of saying and doing anything. After leaving Norwich, Hughes pulled a living as an itinerant preacher, but following in his footsteps, Widdows would soon far eclipse him in Bible-thumping eloquence and dramatic power: he became a

---

* Baroness Beatrice de Bertouch (1859–1931), a Society journalist and high strung Irish-born romantic with a fascination for the occult; wife of Baron Montagu de Bertouch, the King of Denmark's hunt master. Her hagiography of Lyne, *The Life Of Father Ignatius, O.S.B., the Monk of Llanthony* (1904), was penned under his supervision. [Personal Pars., *Irish Society And Social Review*, 15 July 1922, p504.]

† Benjamin Jowett (1817–1893) influential Oxford tutor, administrative reformer, and translator (and bowdleriser) of Plato.

‡ The Very Reverend William Henry Fremantle (1831–1916), Dean of Ripon. A prominent liberal Anglican (Benjamin Jowett was his Oxford tutor and a mentor), whose reformist theology Lyne (and Baroness de Bertouch) considered heresy.

phenomenon.

Born illegitimate, and raised in a Norwich workhouse, Widdows' scarred childhood had left him with a bottomless craving for recognition of his worth, and like Carlyle and Lyne, for power over others. It had also imbued him with a wilfulness of psychotic intensity, that made him forge the seemingly impossible into reality. Presenting himself as a champion of Protestantism, while peddling anti-Catholic bigotry, he was able to gather multitudes before him, ever seeking "those localities where fanaticism was most rampant."

Referring to Widdows' life work, a newspaper called it: "a peculiar and incongruous combination, keeping out of prison on infamous charges and denouncing Romanism." As to what was termed "his preferred crime," this involved offences with adolescent boys, which brought him to court no less than five times, and saw him jailed thrice – all of which he denounced as vengeful Catholic plotting against an innocent. His rabble-rousing also caused his name to be raised three times in Parliament; the last being in 1902, when the Home Secretary informed the Chamber that, "Widdows' true history and infamous character are well known at the Home Office." And not only there. Throughout Britain and Canada, 'Ex-Monk Widdows' became a well-worn headline.

Burlesques of the Catholic Mass were a colourful part of Widdows' routine. The climax of his career, which stretched over half a century, came early at Dundee in 1879. There at one of his lectures he challenged an Irish Catholic interjector: "I will show you your God." Holding up a Eucharist wafer, he munched down on it, and in the subsequent uproar, pounded out *God Save Ireland* on a harmonium. It was reported: "In a few days he converted that peaceful city into a first-class Bedlam."

To maintain order, two companies of troops had to be sent from London, and hundreds of special constables were sworn in. After another of Widdows' lectures was cancelled due to a mob of thousands of Irish Catholics, for his supporters, and possibly a sizeable proportion of the Protestant citizenry of the city, the issue turned to one of liberty – a fight for the right of public assembly and free speech, against its suppression by an alien minority – "the priests of the Church of Rome, acting on the more ignorant and fanatical of their followers." From being an iconoclast, Widdows "now took on the high rank of martyr," a role he would relish to the last breath.

When John Leng,* the sceptical editor of a local newspaper, *The Dundee Advertiser*, caught rumours about a previous stay of Widdows in Canada, he telegraphed the editor of *The Globe*, a Toronto newspaper, to enquire whether he'd been convicted there. The Atlantic cable soon furnished a reply: "SODOMY; FIVE MONTHS; CENTRAL PRISON, TORONTO."

The Dundee paper reprinted this verbatim in caps, and it was picked up by other newspapers.† "There is no doubt the terrible charge against Mr. Widdows has fallen like a bombshell amongst the ultra-Protestants of Glasgow," affirmed one report.

Such damning exposure would have crushed lesser mortals: for Widdows, claiming Popish conspiracy, it was merely fuel to further his evangelical advancement. On the following evening in Dundee, before an audience of 1,600, his lecture became a vindication of himself. Given his career was based on instilling belief, this was second nature to him, and he misled in a very modern way: by ardently presenting a rigorous exposure of the truth – his truth. This included reading a letter, purportedly written by a Catholic noviciate in Toronto, James Rogers, renouncing his testimony on which Widdows had been convicted. Widdows then read out the entire report from *The Globe* of his trial – for the attempted buggery of Rogers in the crypt of a Toronto cathedral.

That Widdows declared all this for the edification of a mass audience, in a respectable venue, was barely conceivable, yet not unprecedented: he'd perpetrated the same at lectures in Canada. It was all the more shocking for the period because, as was reported, "A large proportion

---

* Sir John Leng (1828–1906) proprietor and editor of *The Dundee Advertiser* and other publications; Liberal M.P. for Dundee from 1889; knighted 1893.
† Leng also wrote to Archbishop Lynch in Toronto, who replied in ruthless detail: "He [Widdows] began his hellish work of the corruption of the boys almost at once." Canadian newspaper reports indicate Widdows was highly popular with the pupils, and assisted Lynch with ceremonies, so his dismissal obviously occurred quietly. [Seraphim Newman-Norton, *The Terrible Tale Of Ex-Monk Widdows*, The Seraphic Press, London 2015, p33. (John Leng's name is misstated as John Long.)]

of the audience was women" – who constituted the bulk of his followers. The bare-knuckle moral grifter who at nineteen was prepared to sacrifice all to score a point in argument, had not changed.

Such was the success of this exculpation, Widdows would repeat the show for audiences across Britain, and again in Canada. Whatever else might be said of sodomy – it filled seats.

"I write this in bed with a lovely acolyte holding the ink." So began a letter Widdows penned in 1888. Unfortunately for him, these cosy words were read out for the jury at another of his trials for indecent assault. In 1896, he finally came to the attention of Labouchère, who informed his readers the sainted preacher had been: "recommended to me for a place in my gallery of pious knaves. He is thoroughly worthy of it." Yet due to Widdows' contumacious character, just as at Dundee, his exposure by Labby, and the rest of the national press, proved mostly futile. In 1910, after Labouchère had again labelled him "unspeakable" and "a disreputable scoundrel," Labby was the recipient of a postcard:

> Thank you for your notice. I sent you the handbills, etc., to let you see what I was doing. Keep me before the public. Don't care what you say or print so long as you notice me. F.G.Widdows, Ex-Monk.

Nonetheless, Widdows' glory days were now behind him. Under further assault from the police and press for his molestations, the church collections thinned, despite him complaining to an interviewer: "I tell them, they've got to pay; and why shouldn't they?" Insulated by cast-iron self-belief, Widdows ranted on to a dwindling congregation in Hackney – with the occasional intermissions of prison – until released by senility and death in 1936.

So much for the more colourful elements of the clergy. Yet, even the most revered verses of the Poet Laureate of Great Britain and Ireland, Lord Tennyson,* extolled love between men. From Queen Victoria downwards, Tennyson's *In Memoriam A.H.H.*, his great elegy of

---

* Alfred Tennyson, 1st Baron Tennyson (1809–1892). Considered 'startling handsome' as a young man, he married Emily Sarah née Sellwood, with whom he had two sons, Hallam (2nd Baron Tennyson), and Lionel.

spiritualised passion for Arthur Hallam,* was a consolation to those suffering due to love and loss. By giving voice to a love that otherwise dared not be spoken, the poem was both a validation and talisman for those attracted to their own gender, and Tennyson, like Lord Byron a generation before him, became a shining herald for them. Although *In Memoriam* received extremely laudatory reviews on its appearance, and was a best-seller, the Queen wrote in her journal after her last meeting with Tennyson: "he said I could not believe the number of shameful letters of abuse he had received about it. Incredible!"†

Circulated privately were other verses, such as *Don Leon*, an anonymously authored lyrical defence of homosexuality penned in the 1830s, which affected to be Lord Byron's confessions. Its lines include:

> To this conclusion we must come at last:
> Wise men have lived in generations past,
> Whose deeds and sayings history records,
> To whom the palm of virtue she awards,
> Who, tempted, ate of that forbidden tree,

---

* Arthur Henry Hallam (1811–1833). Possessed of a fine mind, he was also something of a minx. Before Tennyson, he was the Eton crush of William Gladstone. (Sixty years after Hallam's death, Tennyson and Gladstone were still jealous of his place in each other's affections.) Hallam confessed to a friend that, "the basest passions have roused themselves in the deep caverns of my nature & swept like storm-winds over me." In an essay which affected Tennyson deeply, Hallam wrote: "erotic feeling is particularly divine, and raises the soul to heights of existence, which no other passion is permitted to attain." And so it was that Hallam came to live on in his verses:

> "Known and unknown; human, divine;
> Sweet human hand and lips and eye;
> Dear heavenly friend that canst not die
> Mine, mine, for ever, ever mine;
>
> Strange friend, past, present and to be;
> Loved deeplier, darklier, understood,
> Behold I dream a dream of good,
> And mingle all the world with thee."

[Robert Bernard Martin, *Tennyson: The Unquiet Heart*, Faber and Faber, London 2009, pp70-71, 74; Arthur Henry Hallam, Jack Kolb (ed.) *The Letters Of Arthur Henry Hallam*, Ohio State University Press 1981, p312; Thomas Hubbard Vail Motter (ed.) *The Writings of Arthur Hallam*, Modern Language Association, New York 1943, p203; Alfred Tennyson, *In Memoriam*, CXXIX.]

† Reflecting the anxiety the poem created for a few readers, a review attributed to Manley Hopkins (father of the poet Gerald Manley Hopkins), which was published in *The Times*, considered its tone of 'amatory tenderness' to be a defect. [The Poetry Of Sorrow, *The Times*, 28 November 1851, p8.]

Which prejudice denies to you and me.

Then be consistent; and, at once confess,
If man's pursuit through life is happiness,
The great, the wise, the pious, and the good,
Have what they sought not rightly understood;
Or deem not else that aberration crime,
Which reigns in every caste and every clime.

Another talisman within the small circles of gilded youth was *Ionica*, published in 1858. It was the first poetic anthology of William Johnson (Cory),* a handsome near-sighted man with a high-pitched voice, who was considered "the most brilliant Eton tutor of his day." A favoured pupil, Reginald Brett, (the future Lord Esher) later wrote: "William Cory...was a sower":

> His love of literature, his knowledge of history and politics, his catholic handling of the Classics, his emotional approach to science, his reverential treatment of England's past, present, and future, left an indelible impression upon every boy who came into contact with him...Unconsciously the boys recognised in him a kindred soul.

In the footsteps of Plato and Socrates, Cory advocated for the character-building possibilities of an erotic, but hazily chaste, mentoring pederasty.† He treated his pupils – many later to be leaders and luminaries – as his equals, which inspirited them. His philosophy and teaching derived from a deep reading of the Classics, which he stripped of their bowdlerism. Given the great Greek thinkers believed sensuality essential for the happiness of cultivated men, it naturally infused his ethos. In what was already an adolescent hothouse of yearning, he took a voyeuristic delight in encouraging the romances of his pupils, writing in 1864:

I have seen young lovers interlacing like honeysuckle, rose and

---

jessamine, romantic chivalrous friendships forming under my eye, to which I am almost admitted as a partner.

"I envy you being kissed by him" he wrote to the young Reginald Brett about a fellow student, "If I were dying like Nelson I would ask him to kiss me. I kissed his dear foot last Thursday on the grass at Ankerwyke."

Johnson had a propensity for making favourites, but his youngest pupils were said to feel in him "a wondrous sympathy for their 'vernal joy', and adored him because of it." His tutorage was an overwhelming intellectual and sensory experience that coloured the rest of their lives. As one wrote: he possessed "the art of awakening enthusiasm, of investing all he touched with a mysterious charm, the charm of wide and accurate knowledge illuminated by feeling and emotion." Most of all, he believed in their potential, with all his heart and soul.*

Johnson chose to open *Ionica* with 'Desiderato', a poem both romantic and erotic:

> Oh, lost and unforgotten friend,
> Whose presence change and chance deny;
> If angels turn your soft proud eye
> To lines your cynic playmate penned,
>
> Look on them, as you looked on me,
> When both were young; when, as we went
> Through crowds or forest ferns, you leant
> On him who loved your staff to be…
>
> Seek for his heart within his book…
> Its murmurs mean: "I yearn for thee".

---

* As he was to write in the book *Eton Reform*, Johnson defined a great education not with regard to any specific knowledge it supplied, but for the arts and habits it inculcated: "for the habit of attention, for the art of expression, for the art of assuming at a moment's notice, a new intellectual position, for the art of entering quickly into another person's thoughts, for the habit of submitting to censure and refutation, for the art of indicating assent or dissent in graduated terms, for the habit of regarding minute points of accuracy, for the art of working out what is possible in a given time, for taste, for discrimination, for mental courage, and for mental soberness. Above all, you go to a great school for self-knowledge." [William (Cory) Johnson *Eton Reform*, Volume II, Longman, Green, Longman & Roberts, London 1861, p7.]

The poem was inspired by a love of his youth, and later priest, John Morland Rice, born in 1823, the same year as he. However, its sentiment is addressed to all Johnson's favoured former pupils, who would have recognised themselves within it.

In 1872, after decades of service to Eton, Johnson was suddenly dismissed, allegedly after an 'indiscreet letter' he'd written to a pupil was intercepted by the boy's parents, but also likely due to concern over the nature of his mentoring, distrust over his reformist approach to teaching, and academic jealousies. He changed his surname to Cory, and never returned to Eton.*

One of the tributes paid to Johnson was a privately printed collection of his letters and journals issued in 1897. Arthur Benson† wrote that it "reveals the extraordinary quality of his mind, its delicacy, its beauty, its wistfulness, its charm." The volume's 23 subscribers – former pupils – were a roll call of not only the great and good, but leaders of the nation. They included the Lords Rosebery, Esher, Halifax, Pembroke, and Northcote, as well as Howard Sturgis,‡ Arthur Benson, and the Eton masters Arthur Campbell Ainger (a mentor to Lord Esher throughout his life), Eton master Henry Elford Luxmoore, and gentleman publisher Edward Chenevix Austen-Leigh. In 1923, Esher further published *Ionicus*, a memoir of Johnson with letters. It was dedicated to three Prime Ministers – Rosebery, Balfour, and Asquith§ – the first two "who at Eton learnt the elements of high politics" from him, and the latter who, as a Hampstead neighbour and intimate friend, "showed him kindness in his old age". In their long correspondence, Johnson had counselled the young Brett: "Be unworldly; don't worship celebrities; like simple people, honest

---

* Reginald Brett, then a Cambridge undergraduate, took a term off to console him. For an illuminating study of Johnson and his favoured pupils, and what he meant to them in their lives, see: Morris B. Kaplan, *Sodom On The Thames*, Cornell University Press, Ithaca & London 2005, pp102-165.]

† Arthur Christopher Benson (1862–1925), essayist, poet, author, and master at Cambridge. Brother of author E.F. Benson.

‡ Howard Overing Sturgis (1855–1920), a wealthy and witty American-born novelist and host, who lived with his partner, William Haynes-Smith, aka 'The Babe', at their mansion Queen's Acre, Windsor. A treasured friend of many, including Edith Wharton, Henry James, and Lord Esher.

§ Herbert Henry Asquith, 1st Earl of Oxford and Asquith, (1852–1928); Home Secretary from 1892 to 1895; Liberal Prime Minister of the United Kingdom from 1908–1916. Married Helen Melland and was widowed; and secondly, Margot Tennant, and had issue.

people."

For most upper class men, adolescent homosexual experiences at the great public schools were the norm, rather than exception. Were it not for Biblical injunctions of its 'unnaturalness', the public and legal abhorrence of homosexuality would have seemed not merely peculiar, but schizophrenic. From childhood, until they left Oxford and Cambridge at the age of twenty-one, the youth of aristocracy and gentry existed in exclusively male worlds for three-quarters of the year. Passionate friendships were celebrated and honoured, and student days looked back upon with misted eyes.*

At Harrow, as John Addington Symonds† recalled, "Every boy of good looks had a female name, and was recognised as either a public prostitute or as some fellow's 'bitch'." At Eton, the prettiest boy was traditionally 'Pop bitch' – available to the prefects who constituted 'Pop', the Eton Society. Raymond Asquith,‡ son of future Prime Minister Herbert Asquith, described how his headmaster at Winchester, standing before the assembled pupils, "harangued us for twenty minutes in a tearful voice on the disadvantages of unconventional forms of vice…of whom eighty five p.c. – by the lowest estimate – were legally liable to incarceration on that charge."§

From mid-century onwards, Oxford had been the centre of a reform movement, led by Benjamin Jowett and other liberals. Seeking to instil transcendent values via the study of Greek history, literature and philosophy, they overhauled the curriculum. The result served to act as an alternative to Christian theology, which had underpinned

---

* For a fuller discussion of sex in the public school system, see: Alisdare Hickson, *The Poisoned Bowl: Sex, Repression and the Public School System*, Constable, London 1995, and Jonathan Gathorne-Hardy, *The Old School Tie: The Phenomenon of the English Public School*, Viking, New York 1977. As for university, Compton Mackenzie had one of his fictional heroes forthrightly state: "The great point of Oxford, in fact the whole point of Oxford, is that there are no girls." [Compton Mackenzie, *Sinister Street, Vol II*, Martin Secker, London 1914, p811.]
† John Addington Symonds (1840–1893), author, literary critic, cultural historian, and activist for homosexual emancipation. After being gifted a copy of *Ionica* by a friend, Symonds wrote a fan letter to Johnson, and received a reply, which was, in his own words: "a long epistle on paiderastia in modern times, defending it…Under Johnson's frank exposition of this unconventional morality there lay a wistful yearning sadness – the note of disappointment and forced abstention." [John Addington Symonds, *The Memoirs of John Addington Symonds: A Critical Edition*, Amber K. Regis (ed.), Palgrave Macmillan, London 2016, p.170.]
‡ Raymond Asquith (1878–1916), barrister. Eldest son of Herbert Asquith.
§ One love letter penned to him by a fellow pupil evocatively states: "Your soul, my dear Raymond, would be such an adornment to my ideal land." [Colin Clifford, *The Asquiths*, John Murray, London 2002, p75n.]

Oxford since the Middle Ages. It was a transformation that would profoundly impact the lives of England's elite for generations. This Hellenism washed over Cambridge as well, and the drawing out of its homosexual aspects by writers like Walter Pater and John Addington Symonds, created an environment further conducive to homoeroticism.

It is perhaps not to be wondered that the anonymous authors of two works that circulated in the 1880s, *Boy-Worship** and *Paederastias Apologia*,† were Oxford students. Before its suppression, the former publication sparked an unprecedented public discourse in the *Oxford And Cambridge Undergraduate's Journal* that alarmed the University administration. The magazine printed letters readily admitting the phenomenon was rife within the University precincts, and that the appearance of the pamphlet was regrettable. One correspondent evocatively protested:

> The mind of the average schoolboy is quite sufficiently disposed to pruriency already, without having "wells of passionate love," etc., forced down his throat.

Other writers expressed dismay that platonic friendships had been tarred: "On many a man boys exercise a very powerful influence for good." Another who signed himself 'Common Sense' admitted:

> There is no doubt that a boy (say, from 14 to 19) is sometimes as beautiful as a woman. Indeed, I have seen beauty in boys far surpassing, in my opinion, anything I have ever seen in women. This being so, all of us except the most pure-minded, require to guard ourselves very carefully in our intercourse with boys... My solution of the very difficult question, how men ought to treat boys is this, – *keep them at a distance*... Ugly boys need not be kept a distance. Where there is no temptation, no self-control is

---

* The author was the future (ordained 1890) Rev. Charles Edward Hutchinson (1855–1926), curate of St Andrews, Montpelier, and vicar of Alderton 1899–1910. Hutchinson reassured his readers: "It is often alleged that boys dislike to be caressed,—a statement, by the way, which is utterly without foundation, experience indeed showing the exact reverse." [Anon, *Boy-Worship*, 1880, p13.]

† The booklet was a defence of platonic pederasty. Schoolmaster Norman Moor (a former lover of J.A. Symonds) recalled that the student author had been "sent down from Balliol, and sent on a voyage round the world, much as one sends an invalid round the world to get rid of a disease." [J.A. Symonds, *The Memoirs of John Addington Symonds: A Critical Edition*, Amber K. Regis, (ed.) Palgrave Macmillan, London 2016, p540.]

required, and no scandal can arise.

In the opinion of this advocate of apartheid, boys with whom friendships could be formed without fear of risk included those with: "red hair, a snub nose, thick lips, goggle eyes, and repulsive features."

In an editorial, the *Journal* remarked: "It is acknowledged by all that the evil begins at school." Yet a copious literature market existed to cater for and capitalise on the romantic longings of school and university days. The floodgates had been opened in 1857 with *Tom Brown's Schooldays* by Thomas Hughes, the story of a boy from his time as a fag to becoming a fagmaster.[*] It includes the passage:

> The youth…was one of the miserable little pretty white-handed curly-headed boys, petted and pampered by some of the big fellows who…spoil them for everything in this world and the next.

In the 1889 edition, Hughes included a frank footnote which concluded: "I can't strike out the passage; many boys will know why it is left in."

There were also underground works like *The Memoirs of a Voluptuary: The Secret Life Of An English Boarding School,* which in three volumes detailed the amatory adventures of the thirteen-year-old Charles Powerscourt:

> You know how to do it properly, Charlie, and no mistake. I felt as if I were going to pieces, and all the little atoms were whirling round and round in all kinds of beautiful sensations.

Throughout the 1890s and onwards, the Continent would witness a minor cascade of writings on homosexuality.[†] At the same time, England was graced by a gentle shower of slender volumes of 'Uranian' poetry, which venerated (to paraphrase Oscar Wilde) 'fair slim boys not made for this world's pain.'[‡] None were more popular

---

[*] A senior student who has a junior student as his fag, i.e. servant.
[†] e.g. the works of poet and wealthy gentleman-scholar Marc-André Raffalovich (1864–1934), including his 1896 treatise *Uranism and Unisexuality.* (English edition: Philip Healy, Frederick S. Roden (eds.) Palgrave Macmillan, Basingstoke 2016.)
[‡] See: Timothy D'arch Smith, *Love In Earnest: some notes on the lives and writings of English 'Uranian' poets from 1889 to 1930,* Routledge & Kegan Paul, London 1970.

than the eleven anthologies of the rollicking versifier, the Rev. Dr. Edwin Emmanuel Bradford,* who urged:

Turn away from the wench, with her powder and paint
And follow the Boy, who is as fair as a saint.

However, Bradford was careful to state his boundaries:

Desire itself is no more bad or good
Than thirst or hunger, rightly understood.
But oh! my blood boils when, on every side
I see low passion swept in, like the tide,
O'erwhelming friendship, honour, love and all.

On the streets, noble sentiment gave way to grittier realities, such as the ditty sung to 'La Donna è mobile' from Verdi's *Rigoletto*:

---

* The Rev. Edwin Emmanuel Bradford (1860–1944), poet and beloved vicar of Nordelph, Norfolk; formerly of St.Petersburg and Paris. Author of such anthologies as *Boyhood* and *The True Aristocracy*. Reviews were gently admiring: "He is alive to the beauty of unsullied youth as was Plato" (*The Westminster Gazette*). Bradford's move to the Church was perhaps shaped by a tragic childhood: his mother died when he was thirteen, and his father suicided by cutting his throat soon after. Bradford held ecclesiastical appointments in several English counties, and in St.Petersburg and Paris, where he was a co-chaplain with fellow Oxford graduate and uranian poet the Rev. Samuel Elsworth Cottam (1863–1943), to whom he wrote the lines: "Friendship grounded upon Truth/Is even sweeter than the loves of youth." In his private life, Bradford employed a cipher that is yet to be broken. John Betjeman who visited him in 1935 recorded: "A modernist, but likes ritual. Last boyfriend called Edmund. Not had a boyfriend for 30 years. V happy with Nordelph. A Saint & thinks laws against sexuality wicked cruel and out of date. Said the Queen asked for one of his books. Obviously a joke played on him poor old thing…Children get a penny for coming, kept in little boxes in a draw of his desk…Felt the better for seeing such a saintly and sweet little man…Surely never did a bad thing in his life." A swimming pond which Bradford had dug next to his vicarage in order to enjoy the sporting of the local lads unfortunately caused its subsidence. A letter from Bradford pasted in a copy of *The True Aristocracy* (1923) states: "When Mr. Betjeman came to see me the old Vicarage was tumbling down: now it has gone altogether, and for the present I live in a small cottage close to the Church, with one old servant." Despite his humble fenland church drawing occasional poetic pilgrims, or perhaps because of this, the Diocese of Ely demolished it in 2010. A jape perpetrated by John Betjman was writing false presentation inscriptions in copies of Bradford's books. Lord Baden-Powell was one target, and A.F. Winnington Ingram, Bishop of London, another – the latter volume inscribed "Because he will understand." [A Terrible Tragedy, *Torquay Times and South Devon Advertiser*, 23 May 1874; Cottam marginal note under 'August: To A Friend' in *The Romance Of Youth: And Other Poems*, Burwood Books, Abebooks.com; Bradford Collection, Timothy d'Arch Smith; Betjeman diary, 9 December 1935; Bradford insert letter, Ebay item no. 224161556176; Holy Trinity, Nordelph: norfolkchurches.co.uk/nordelph/nordelph.htm; Timothy d'Arch Smith, 'The Poetry of E.E. Bradford: The Author's Own Copies', *The Book Collector*, Vol 66, No2, 2017; E.E.Bradford, *The Kingdom Within You*, eBay item number: 224161638753.]

Arseholes are cheap today
Cheaper than yesterday
Little boys are half-a-crown
Standing up or lying down
Bigger boys are three-and-six
They are meant for bigger pricks.

A more quietly popular poet was the schoolmaster and amateur footballer John Gambril Nicholson,[*] author of such privately-issued anthologies as *A Garland Of Ladslove*:

Hot as summer
And subtle as the rain
Hast though that power.

In a poem of 1892, 'Your City Cousins', he captured the streets and offices that were then teeming with working adolescents:

As I go down the street
A hundred boys a day I meet,
And gazing from my window high
I like to watch them passing by.

I like the boy that earns his bread;
The boy that holds my horse's head,
The boy that tidies up the bar,
The boy that hawks the Globe and Star.

Smart looking lads are in my line;
The lad that gives my boots a shine,
The lad that works the lift below,
The lad that's lettered G.P.O.

I like the boy of business air
That guards the loaded van with care,
Or cycles through the city crowd,
Or adds the ledger up aloud.

---

[*] John Gambril (Francis) Nicholson (1866–1931), schoolmaster, Uranian poet, amateur photographer and footballer. His works include *Love in Earnest: Sonnets, Ballades, and Lyrics* (1892), *A Garland of Ladslove* (1911), and *Opals And Pebbles* (1928). A few of his poems were acrostics, spelling out the names of his boy muses.

I like the boy that's fond of play:
The office-boy cracks jokes all day,
The barber's 'prentice makes me laugh,
The bookstall-boy gives back my chaff.

When travelling home by tram or train
I meet a hundred boys again,
Behind them on the 'bus I ride
Or pace the platform by their side.

And though I never see you there
All boys your name and nature share,
And almost every day I make
Some new acquaintance for your sake.*

It wasn't simply the streets that presented erotic and moral challenges for some gentlemen. In 1907, Lytton Strachey† wrote to Leonard Woolf about a large West End restaurant:

> Have you ever been to the Trocadero? It's filled with little messenger boys, who do their best to play the catamite, but it hardly comes off. The nearest one of them got was to put his arm round [Maynard] Keynes' neck as he was helping him on with his coat! Remarkable? The truth is that sodomy is becoming generally recognised in England – but of such a degraded sort! Little boys of 13 are what the British Public love. There are choruses of them at most Comic Operas, and they flood all but the most distinguished of the Restaurants.

Amongst other respectable authors who struggled with desire was the previously mentioned Arthur Benson, a son of the Archbishop of Canterbury who became a master at both Eton and Cambridge, and

---

* Across the Atlantic, Walt Whitman expressed the sentiment more explicitly in a story 'The Child's Companion' published at the age of twenty-two, in which he mused of a twelve-year-old boy: "O, it is passing wondrous, how in the hurried walks of life and business, we meet with young beings, strangers, who seem to touch the fountains of our love, and draw forth their swelling waters." [Walter Whitman, 'The Child's Companion', *The New World*, 20 November 1841, p322.]

† (Giles) Lytton Strachey (1880–1932), Bloombury Group writer and critic. Leonard Sidney Woolf (1880 – 1969), political theorist, author, publisher and civil servant; husband of author Virginia Woolf.

went on to edit Queen Victoria's letters. In 1888, under a pen name, he published *Memoirs of Arthur Hamilton, B.A., Of Trinity College, Cambridge*. A tale of passionate friendship, repentance of desire, and transcendent chastity, it included such observations as:

> Edward Bruce was a boy of extraordinary beauty…his eyelids dropped languidly, but when he opened his eyes and looked full at you! — I felt relieved to think I should not have to conduct his education; I could not have denied him anything.

The novel ran to several editions. In 1905, Benson confided to his diary:

> if we give boys Greek books to read + hold up the Greek spirit + the Greek life as a marvel, it is very difficult to slice out one portion, which was a perfectly normal part of Greek life, and to say that it is abominable, etc. etc. A strongly sensuous nature – such as Pater or Symonds – with a strong instinct for beauty + brought up at an English public school, will almost certainly go wrong, in thought, if not in act.

John Addington Symonds had indeed been one so illumined. At seventeen, he'd opened a translation of Plato's *Dialogues* and, as he put it: "discovered the true *liber amoris** at last, the revelation I had been waiting for, the consecration of a long-cherished idealism."[†] Despite this, he married at twenty-four, going on to have four daughters, but was tortured by his homosexual longings. As he recalled:

> Being physically below the average in health and strength, my development proceeded more upon the intellectual than the athletic side…What was more, my constitution in the year 1865 seemed to have broken down, and no career in life lay open to

---

* Free love.

† Ironically, Symonds would later be concerned that study of the classics by boys might be 'harmful', and sought Oscar Browning's views. Browning declined, but another master, Norman Moor, whom Symonds had loved as a youth, told him that – contrary to the opinion of Arthur Benson – the classics boys read at school did not as a rule contain allusions to pederasty, and he believed it would not occur to boys to think there was anything between, say, Achilles and Patroclus. (Norman Moor credited Symonds and John Percival, headmaster of Clifton College, for helping him overcome his pederastic desires.) The popular bowdlerised translations of the classics by Benjamin Jowett – himself riveted by male beauty – ensured the ruse was maintained. [John Addington Symonds, *The Memoirs of John Addington Symonds: A Critical Edition*, Amber K. Regis (ed.) Palgrave Macmillan, London 2016, pp540-541.]

me.

The chance sighting of a graffito "'Prick to prick, so sweet'; with an emphatic diagram of phallic meeting, glued together, gushing" proved an epiphany. And then came another life-changing moment.

> In the autumn of that year, my friend Frederic Myers* read me aloud a poem from *Leaves of Grass*. We were together in his rooms at Trinity College, Cambridge, and I can well remember the effect of his sonorous voice rolling out sentence after sentence, sending electric thrills through the very marrow of my mind.

It was the verse from the 1860 edition that begins: "Long I thought that knowledge alone would suffice me," and which closes:

> I will go with him I love,
> It is to be enough for us that we are together – We never separate again.

Plato, and the heartache of Michelangelo and Tennyson, had enabled Symonds to see himself. Walt Whitman was a revelation of the spirit:

> I will make divine magnetic lands,
> With the love of comrades,
> With the life-long love of comrades.

To hear from a contemporary man the open expression of such a utopian ideal – a world healed and made whole through manly love, imbued Symonds with a rush of hope like the force of life itself. In a kingdom which looked down upon 'the passion of comrades' with the full force of the Church and the Law, Whitman's ennobling portrayal of it was both a solace and an inspiration.†

Like a latter-day Jesus, Whitman lifted up the consciousness of those daily damned as villainous, filthy lepers. They read and they recognised: here, like themselves, was a loving brother. In life-affirming prose, Whitman bathed their bruised and battered souls,

---

* Frederic William Henry Myers (1843–1901), English poet, classicist, and psychical researcher.
† In both America and England many critics condemned *Leaves of Grass* as obscene, one suggesting its author deserved "nothing so richly as the public executioner's whip." [Leaves of Grass, *The Critic*, 1 April 1856, pp170-171.]

and proclaimed their desires as natural and as pure as sunlight:

> I mind how once we lay such a transparent summer morning
> How you settled your head athwart my hips and gently turn'd
> over upon me
> And parted the shirt from my bosom-bone, and plunged your
> tongue to my bare-stript heart
> And reach'd till you felt my beard, and reach'd till you held my
> feet.

Whitman's open depiction of sexual ecstasy, and transcendence of self, wrapped in free verse that was both romantic and mystical, yet also street-fresh and direct, seized and shook imaginations: it was like a vast gust of liberating air from the Rockies carrying the voice of American freedom. (Yet it had actually evolved out of Whitman's voracious sexual cruising in the streets, parks, and bohemian bars of New York.) What left Symonds and others particularly breathless wasn't the trumpeting and occasionally corny poetical voice Whitman used to declaim democracy; it was the low intimate one that voiced love between men:

> Of a crowd of workmen and drivers in a bar-room around the
> stove, late of a winter night – And I unremarked seated in a
> corner,
> Of a youth who loves me, and whom I love, silently approaching,
> and seating himself near, that he may hold me by the hand.*

As an article in the *Westminster Review* of 1871 forthrightly put it: "If the strong, full grown working man wants a lover and comrade, he will think Walt Whitman especially made for him."

Admiration for the sturdy working man, sexual candour, comradeship, physical union and transcendence, universal democracy

---

* The poem mirrors Peter Doyle's recollection of his fated pickup of Whitman on his trolleycar when he was nineteen: "We were familiar at once – I put my hand on his knee – we understood. He did not get out at the end of the trip – in fact went all the way back with me." However, the poem actually refers to an earlier love who inspired the Calamus poems: Fred Vaughan, a young man Whitman lived with; the bar-room most likely being the bohemian and gay-friendly Pfaff's, their regular hangout in Greenwich Village. [Richard Maurice Bucke (ed.) *Calamus: A Series Of Letters Written During the Years 1868-1880 By Walt Whitman To A Young Friend* (Peter Doyle), Laurens Maynard, Boston 1897, p23; Charley Shively, *Calamus Lovers*, Gay Sunshine Press, San Francisco 1987, pp38-40.]

– what was there not to like? In a fervent white heat, Symonds wrote to a friend:

> It is quite indispensable that you should have this book…It is not a book…it is a man, miraculous in his vigour & love & ingenuousness & omniscience & animalism & omnivorous humanity.

Leaves Of Grass became Symonds' touchstone. More than that, it was the key that released him from the torture of his sexual denial, and into the soul-deep embrace of the masculine love he craved. By 1870, still married but in the midst of an affair with a handsome sixth former, Norman Moor, he wrote: "Ah, but the fragrance of his body! Who hath spoken of that scent undefinable, which only love can seize, and makes love wild mad and suicidal?" In 1893, Symonds published *Walt Whitman: A Study*, which has the tone of an adorative dance around a guru; its tangled interpretations an almost comic contrast to its plain-speaking subject.

Whitman liked Symonds, saying of him:

> Symonds is as tall as a mountain peak – and gentle: always gentle…I am always strangely moved by a letter from Symonds: it makes the day, it makes many days, sacred.

However, Symonds also irritated the poet, pestering him to be explicit, writing to him:

> I have pored for continuous hours over the pages of Calamus (as I used to pore over the pages of Plato), longing to hear you speak, <u>burning</u> for a revelation of your more developed meaning, panting to ask – is this what you would indicate?…Most of all did I desire to hear from your own lips – or from your pen – some story of athletic friendship from which to learn the truth.

With his verse already attacked for indecency, Whitman ignored the fevered appeals. Symonds confessed to Edward Carpenter: "I think [Whitman] was afraid of being used to lend his influence to 'Sods'. Did not quite trust me perhaps." To the calmer Carpenter, Whitman would be more frank, telling him that he had "concealed, studiously concealed…I think there are truths which it is necessary to envelop or wrap up."*

Carpenter had studied for the priesthood at Cambridge. Of those days, he later wrote:

> How well I remember going down, as I so frequently did, alone to the riverside at night, amid the hushed reserve and quiet grace of the old College gardens, and pouring my little soul out to the silent trees and clouds and waters! I don't know what kind of longing it was – something partly sexual, partly religious, and both.†

Life had also changed for him when, in the summer of 1868, "one of the Fellows of Trinity Hall…came into my room with a blue-covered book in his hands (William Rossetti's edition of Whitman's poems)‡ only lately published, and said: – 'Carpenter, what do you think of this?'"

---

* Whitman's reticence contrasts markedly with the street pickups of men and youths listed in his notebooks, as well as letters from teenage Civil War soldier friends, such as Alonzo Bush, who wrote to him in a horny state in 1863: "I am glad to Know that you are once more in that hotbed City of Washington So that you can go often and see that friend of ours at Armory Square L.[ewis] K.[irk]B.[rown]. The fellow that went down on your BK [possibly 'buck', then slang for penis], both so often with me. I wished that I could see him this evening and go in the Ward Master's Room and have some fun for he is a gay boy." However, as a young school teacher on Southold, Long Island in 1841, Whitman had been denounced from the pulpit and tarred and feathered by a mob for having sexual relations with one or more of his pupils, and his schoolhouse referred to locally for decades afterwards as 'the Sodom School'. [Charley Shively (ed.) *Calamus Lovers: Walt Whitman's Working Class Camerados*, Gay Sunshine Press, San Francisco 1987, pp81-82; Gary Schmidgall, *Walt Whitman: A Gay Life*, Dutton, New York 1997, p103.]

† In his poem *The Lake Of Beauty*, Carpenter would write:
"All that you have within you, all that your heart desires, all that your Nature so specially fits you for…
It will surely come to you…
Do not recklessly spill the waters of your mind…
But draw them together into a little compass, and hold them still, so still;
And let them become clear, so clear – so limpid, so mirror-like;
At last the mountains and the sky shall glass themselves in peaceful beauty…
And Love himself shall come and bend over, and catch his own likeness in you."
[Carpenter, Edward *Towards Democracy*, George Allen & Unwin, London 1915, p372.]

‡ Unlike Frederic Myers, who had obtained the 1865 edition of *Leaves of Grass*, this was a neutered version. In 1868, another fan of Whitman's, William Michael Rossetti, brother of Dante and Christina, and a force in the pre-Raphaelite movement, broke the self-enforced censorship of British publishers by issuing *Poems by Walt Whitman*. However, as Rossetti stated in its Preface, it did: "omit entirely every poem which could with any tolerable fairness be deemed offensive to the feelings of morals or propriety in this peculiarly nervous age." That amounted to half the original poems!

Yearning for body and spirit to be united and elevated, Carpenter was yet another young man in whom Whitman lit a fire. As he wrote: "From that time forward a profound change set in within me."

Carpenter was ordained in 1870, but experiencing "the insuperable feeling of falsity and dislocation," by 1874 he'd resigned from the priesthood.* Despite this, Carpenter was more at ease with his sexuality than Symonds, and Whitman fuelled his interest in liberty, justice and spirituality. He wrote to Whitman: "Because you have, as it were, given me a ground for the love of men I thank you continually in my heart... For you have made men to be not ashamed of the noblest instinct of their nature." More simply, he wrote to him: "I am yours."

Carpenter would go on to become perhaps the greatest embodiment of Whitman's ethos. Like an English mirror of *Leaves of Grass*, in 1883 Carpenter published the first edition of his prose poem *Towards Democracy*, which also equated, but in a veiled manner, homosexual freedom with the utopian promise of universal comradeship. In heady lines, Carpenter imagined being spiritually united with the working people, such as "The thick-thighed hot coarse-fleshed young bricklayer with the strap round his waist":

> I will be the ground underfoot and the common clay; The ploughman shall turn me up with his plough-share among the roots of the twitch in the sweet-smelling furrow; The potter shall mould me, running his finger along my whirling edge (we will be faithful to one another, he and I); The bricklayer shall lay me: he shall tap me into place with the handle of his trowel; And to him I will the utter the word which with my lips I have not spoken.

For many young socialists, *Towards Democracy* became their bible. George Ives† wrote in his diaries of Carpenter: "An Eastern saint: he

---

* The following year he was offered the position of tutor to Prince Albert Victor and his brother Prince George (later King George V), but respectfully declined. [Chushichi Tsuzuki, *Edward Carpenter, 1844-1929: Prophet of Human Fellowship*, Cambridge University Press, 2005, p77.]

† George Cecil Ives (1867-1950). The bastard son of an Anglo-Spanish baroness, Ives devoted his life to homosexual & penal law reform; to that end founding a secret society for homosexuals, the Order of Chaeronea, and co-founding the British Society for the Study of Sex Pyschology. Lord Alfred Douglas was one of his conquests. From the family home, Benworth Hall in Hampshire, he told his diary: "I would like to go for one long midnight walk, or ride, with Bosie, through the black, deep woods. He would learn the Kingdom of the Night,

gave one the sense of calm. Like a mountain he seemed to rest over the wide earth and to be founded on the archaic rocks."

Other homosexual Cambridge scholars stirred by Whitman included C.R. Ashbee* and Goldsworthy Lowes Dickinson.† Equally overwhelmed, and desperate to meet the poet, were Oscar Wilde and his friend Bram Stoker,‡ the deeply sexually repressed future author of *Dracula*. In 1872, Stoker penned a long and searing psychosexual confession to Whitman, which began:

> If you are the man I take you to be you will like to get this letter…I have read your poems with my door locked late at night, and I have read them on the seashore where I could look all round me and see no more sign of human life than the ships out at sea: and here I often found myself waking up from a reverie with the book lying open before me.

Emboldened by Whitman's poetry, in 1883, John Addington Symonds printed ten copies of *A Problem in Greek Ethics*, a treatise on pederasty as a social institution in Classical Greece, which he'd written ten years previously. In 1891, he further printed 50 copies of *A Problem in Modern Ethics*, one of the first examinations of homosexuality in historical, medical, and legal contexts, and which also outlined proposals for legislative change. These booklets were only privately circulated. Theories about homosexuality, particularly

---

and the beautiful wild soul would understand." [Diary of George Ives, 25 October 1893, quoted in John Stokes, *Oscar Wilde: Myths, Miracles and Imitations*, Cambridge University Press, 1996, pp71-72. See: Matt Cook, 'Sex Lives and Diary Writing: The Journals of George Ives' in David Amigoni (ed.), *Life Writing And Victorian Culture*, Routledge, Abingdon 2017.]

* Charles Robert Ashbee (1863–1942); architect and designer, and prime mover of the Arts and Crafts movement. Inspired by John Ruskin, William Morris, Walt Whitman, and Edward Carpenter, Ashbee established an Arts and Crafts cooperative community in the Cotswolds. (A distinguished client was Ernst, Grand Duke of Hesse.) Ashbee is believed to have been a member of George Ives' Order of Chaeronea. He wrote to his future wife, Janet Elizabeth Forbes, the daughter of a wealthy London stockbroker: "Comradeship to me so far,– an intensely close and all absorbing personal attachment, 'love' if you prefer the word, – for my men and boy friends, has been the one guiding principle of my life, and has inspired anything I may have vouchsafed to accomplish…you are the first and only woman to whom I have felt I could offer the same loyal reverence of affection." Although the marriage was rocky, it produced four children. [Alan Crawford, *C.R. Ashbee, Architect, Designer, and Romantic Socialist*, Yale University Press, New Haven, 2005, p75.]

† Goldsworthy Lowes Dickinson (1862–1932) humanist, pacifist and author; he played an important role in the establishment of the League of Nations. His popular book *The Greek View of Life* (1896) brought Greek philosophy, including that concerning male friendship and love, to a wider audience.

‡ Abraham 'Bram' Stoker (1847–1912), Irish author.

when propounded by those perceived to be its defenders, were looked upon by the authorities with the sternest eye.

Concern over homosexuality had increased alongside the issue of age difference and consent. Now there was public worry not only for the welfare of girls, but for boys as well. Debates about the influence of the Classics on young readers, and a succession of prominent scandals, would heighten it further. Symonds was all too aware of social anxieties over the corruption of youth, and having overcome his pederastic desires, or at least suppressed them, sought to emphasise age-consistent desire in his advocacy.*

He suggested to the sexologist Havelock Ellis† that they should collaborate on a book addressing the subject in greater depth; Symonds particularly desiring to see Section 11 of the *Criminal Law Amendment Act* of 1885, which targeted homosexuals, rescinded.

As it happened, in 1893 Symonds died of influenza in Rome, and Ellis was forced to complete the book, by then titled *Sexual Inversion*, with the help of Edward Carpenter, who furnished case studies and assisted with its editing. Amongst the sexual case histories, the book contained was Symonds' own: "he seeks strong fellows between 18 and 25 years of age who have full members, are sexually potent and always below his social station."‡ However, a single sentence affectingly explained his heroic stand: "No pleasure he has enjoyed, he declares, can equal a thousandth part of the pain caused by the internal consciousness of Pariahdom."

Blessed with a private income, Edward Carpenter had settled far away from feverish London, in the peaceful rural village of Millthorpe in Derbyshire. Here theories of neurotic modern life generating outlawed passion evaporated like the morning dew. Carpenter believed happiness lay in living close to mother earth, and in personally fulfilling work. As *The Australian Worker* newspaper later put it:

---

* See: Jana Funke, "'We Cannot Be Greek Now'": Age Difference, Corruption of Youth and the Making of Sexual Inversion' in *English Studies*, Volume 94, 2013, Issue 2.
† Henry Havelock Ellis, (1859–1939), English physician, writer, sexologist, and progressive intellectual and social reformer.
‡ The passage only appeared in the German edition.

He was not merely a democrat from conviction; he was a democrat from instinct. He liked simple living, simple people, and simple ways…He did his utmost to appear like a British artisan, and on the whole his disguise was fairly successful. But one thing always gave him away, he had the refined accent of the born aristocrat. As long as he remained silent he was a man of the people. As soon as he opened his mouth he became a member of the ruling classes.

While so, he was a wholly transgressive one. A neighbour recalled:

Carpenter's personal charm was the result, I think of his peculiar strength of character, his clarity of thought, his simplicity of life, and above all his catholicity of spirit. I have never met any other man who seemed to me to embody so much of the Christ-like spirit.

For at least one acolyte: "His head and features were of extraordinary beauty…there was refinement in his every movement and in the tone of his voice. One admired and loved him at once."

In 1891, Carpenter met his life partner, the working class labourer, George Merrill* – drawn by Merrill's wistful countenance and the individualism of his dress. Said Carpenter: "We exchanged a few words and a look of recognition." By the following year, he was publishing poetry of the deepest passion:

All night long in love, in the darkness, passing through your lips, my love –
Breathing the same breath, being folded in the same sleep, losing sense of Me and Thee.
Into empyreal regions, beloved of the gods, united, we ascend together.

The anchor of this relationship, and the emotional enrichment it brought, imbued Carpenter with greater confidence to address homosexual emancipation: a desire undoubtedly further spurred by Symonds's untimely death, and the wish to build upon his legacy.

---

* George Merrill (1866–1928).

In 1894, Carpenter wrote a series of four pamphlets addressing sex, marriage, the role of women, and not least, *Homogenic Love, and Its Place in a Free Society*. Writing such a general series on sex and social topics was part of Carpenter's tendency to seek broad alliances, but also provided him with the cover of not being viewed as simply a defender of homosexuals, or worse, one of that tribe. Even so, while the four pamphlets were printed by the Manchester-based 'Labour Press', the fourth was for private circulation only. The love declared elsewhere as unnatural was, in *Homogenic Love*, reverenced by Carpenter not only as an integral part of nature, but its highest evolutionary form. Taking a leaf from Plato, and from Ulrichs,* Whitman, and Symonds, he idealised it as more spiritual, intellectual, beautiful and pure:

> as the ordinary love has a special function in the propagation of the race, so the other has its special function in social and heroic work, and in the generation – not of bodily children – but of those children of the mind, the philosophical conceptions and ideals which transform our lives and those of society.

Walking in socialist sandals, *Homogenic Love* was an overstatement of what are now truisms: the inextricable link between homosexuality and creativity, and that natural variance drives social progression. In short: homogenic love was a necessity for the advancement of humanity. Rather than earthly baby-making, it looked outwards to the stars. Carpenter himself fulfilled the patrician ideal of boundless vision: as well as good food and conversation, peering through his telescope was one of the pleasures for Millthorpe guests. When the wife of C.R. Ashbee asked George Merrill why the young labourers at Millthorpe were so fine to look at, he replied it was because they had learned to be kissed. In 1902, Carpenter published the first English collection of historic homoerotic verse, *Ioläus: An Anthology of Friendship*; more prosaically known in the book-trade as 'The Bugger's Bible'.

Like others, Carpenter also believed 'sexual inversion' was accompanied by a more acute perception: it explained the association of inversion with shamans, priests, and enlightened others throughout the ages. To further his spiritual studies, Carpenter travelled to India and Ceylon, and in 1911 published a paper *On the Connection Between*

---

* Karl Heinrich Ulrichs (1825–1895), pioneering German homosexual rights activist.

Homosexuality And Divination. Walt Whitman's personal physician, Dr Maurice Bucke,* who was passionately devoted to his famous patient, also theorised on higher states of awareness – Cosmic Consciousness, a term he borrowed from Carpenter. In 1891, he visited England and met with Carpenter and other homosexual Whitman disciples, who embraced these beliefs like a new generation of Illuminati.

On the more earthly level, in 1894 an overtly homosexual literary magazine, *The Chameleon*, suddenly made a furtive appearance in an edition of one hundred copies. Billing itself 'A Bazaar of Dangerous and Smiling Chances', the editor was a young Oxford high churchman, Jack Bloxam.† Inspired by his friend Lord Alfred Douglas, who with contributions from Oscar Wilde and others had transformed a student magazine into an organ of insinuated decadence, Bloxam created a print sensation beyond his wildest dreams – just not in the way he had hoped.

The first issue of *The Chameleon* featured 'Phrases and Philosophies for the Use of the Young' – a collection of aphorisms by Wilde, plus two overtly homosexual poems by Douglas, another by John Gambril Nicholson, and not least, 'The Priest And The Acolyte': a short story pseudonymously authored by Bloxam, in which a clergyman and youth commit a lover's suicide.

It was not long before the magazine's scent of dying lilies wafted to the offices of the tuppenny weekly *To-Day*, whose founder-editor was the urbane Jerome K. Jerome. *The Chameleon* caused him to quite lose his usual drollery:

---

* Dr Richard Maurice Bucke (1837–1902): Whitman's physician, executor, and first biographer. Author of *Cosmic Consciousness: A Study in the Evolution of the Human Mind.*
† The Rev. John 'Jack' Francis Bloxam (1873–1928). Described by Wilde as "an undergraduate of strange beauty," he was ordained in 1897, and was a curate and later vicar at churches in London and Worthing, also serving as a chaplain to British forces during World War I. "Shy and reticent, he was well loved in his various parishes, and his friends have described him as a remarkable influence on any boy with whom he came into contact. Being wealthy, Father Bloxam put many of them on the road to good careers." Remembered a clerical colleague: "it would be hard to say whether he was more remarkable for his power of winning affection or for his lavishness in bestowing it." Anglo-Catholic leader and former Cory pupil, the Earl of Halifax, and his son, were amongst his congregationalists. [Wilde to Ada Leverson, December 1894: Rupert Hart-Davis (ed.) *The Letters of Oscar Wilde*, Hart-Davis, London, 1962, p379; J.Z. Eglinton (Walter Breen), The Later Career of John Francis Bloxam, *International Journal Of Greek Love*, Oliver Layton Press, New York 1966, Vol1, No2, pp40-42; *Church Times*, 27 April 1928; David Hilliard, 'Unenglish and Unmanly: Anglo-Catholicism and Homosexuality', *Victorian Studies*, University of Indiana, Winter 1982.]

About vice I never care to argue…but the passions stirred, and intended to be stirred up by the literature of this precious periodical are not the passions of man, woman, or beast…That young men are here and there cursed with these unnatural cravings, no one acquainted with our public school life can deny…This magazine, which is to be issued three times a year, is an insult to the animal creation…It can serve no purpose but that of evil.

And on his rant went. But not *The Chameleon*. The first issue became its last. However, with the prosecution of Oscar Wilde in 1895, its notoriety soared. This resulted in a hand-wringing letter from the publisher's solicitor to the *Daily Telegraph* claiming that printing had been stopped once its contents had become known. As it had always been a limited edition, this was perhaps a sweaty half-truth.

The same year *The Chameleon* went to its early grave, another magazine, *The Artist and Journal of Home Culture,* also found its content being called into question. The anonymous editor was a London solicitor, Charles Kains Jackson.* Since assuming the editor's chair in 1888, he'd been quietly infusing the magazine's pages with articles and poetry of particular interest to certain gentleman readers. This influx included Theodore Wratislaw's* ode 'To A Sicilian Boy', which featured the stanza:

> Between thine arms I find my only bliss;
> Ah let me in thy bosom still enjoy
> Oblivion of the past, divinest boy,
> And the dull ennui of a woman's kiss!

However, Kains Jackson wanted more. Gazing out from the coal-smut stained window of his London office, he envisioned a natural aristocracy of men embodying the Greek ideal of *areté* – which embraced physical, intellectual, and moral virtue.

---

* Charles Philip Castle Kains Jackson (1857–1933), Uranian poet, editor, solicitor. He was a keen social host for George Ives' Order of Chaeronia group. [Matt Smith, 'A Bend In The River: queer home and heritage in a house in Hammersmith' in Brent Pilkey (ed.), and others, *Sexuality And Gender at Home*, Bloomsbury Academic, London 2017, p124.]
* Theodore William Graf Wratislaw (1871–1933), poet and civil servant. Thrice married.

In 1894, the influential magazine *The Fortnightly* Review published an article titled 'The New Hedonism'. Authored by a science writer and novelist Grant Allen,* it championed the secular pursuit of beauty and self-development, "to the highest point, freely, in every direction." This tract spurred Kains Jackson to put his own dream into words, with an article in *The Artist* titled 'The New Chivalry'. It argued that overpopulation had made love between men the natural erotic choice of the future. Whereas the chivalry of old exalted the feminine ideal, the new chivalry would turn its melting glance upon the masculine. Rather than procreation, the New Chivalry:

> will rest content with beauty – God's outward clue to the inward Paradise...The gain in human happiness will be direct and immediate...The New Chivalry then is also the new necessity.

The owners of the magazine were less convinced, and Kains Jackson was sacked. However, there was a warmer response in other quarters, not least in the distant fens of Norfolk, whence lay the happy parish of that unstoppable versifier, the Reverend E.E. Bradford. Thrilled to the marrow by Kains Jackson's article, he borrowed its title for one of his anthologies, and was inspired to pen:

> ...for women we have ceased to sigh
> Passion must be refined, but need not die.
> The cult of youth ideal will tend to be
> For more and more, the source of poetry,
> Romance and chivalry.†

---

* (Charles) Grant Blairfindie Allen (1848–1899). In a small-circulation humanist magazine he later repudiated the suggestion his argument was an endorsement of homosexuality. It prompted George Ives to pen his own response to the magazine, in which he championed Greek Love: "It could have been no mean and unworthy ideal of love which was followed by so many master minds... If they ask our judgement upon acts, I say all logical Hedonists can have but one reply: If they add to the sorrow of living things, then those acts are evil, but if they conduce to the world's happiness they must be accounted good." [George Ives, 'The New Hedonism Controversy', *The Humanitarian*, Vol 5, No4, October 1894, pp292-297.]
† In 1914, Rev. Bradford would also make clear his opinion of the New Woman, whose "charms and virtues" were as "vanishing as summer snow":
"So, sisters, if we now contend
On equal terms for equal prize,
What wonder I prefer my friend
Till you become as strong and wise."
['The New Woman', in Rev. E. E. Bradford, *In Quest Of Love And Other Poems*, Kegan Paul, Trench, Trübner & Company, London 1914, p42.]

The New Chivalry was in for a shock. In 1895, the Wilde trials produced a global firestorm of hysteria over homosexuality. Confirmed bachelors would never be looked upon with such an innocent eye again; the scandal forging a heightened level of suspicion everywhere. In an article titled 'The Oscar Wilde Episode', one colonial paper observed:

> We are within measurable distance of the time when some young men's clubs in Australia will have to be placed under the strict surveillance of reliable police officers...in Australia even business is immorally affected by the degraded...However, it would be useless for the Press, no matter how zealous it may be in the interests of public morality to expose anybody in 'good' society. Indeed, there is very little chance just now for the law to be enforced in connection with anybody who has plenty of money or social influence.

Like the New Woman, references to a new kind of male also became a meme. As one lyric put it: "A cheap spick-and-spandy, twopenny dandy, effeminate modern man." The year after the Wilde trials, Cotsford Dick published *An Alphabet For Adults*, which featured the verse: "Y is the Youth who, so drolly affects, The ways and wiles of the opposite sex." Another of its poems snarked:

> Behold him mincing o'er the social stage,
> The New Narcissus, *mignon* of his age!
> How weird his ways, how willowy his talk!
> How tight his waist, how loose appears his eye,
> A rose his cheek, a butterfly his tie!
> His room's a show of photographs and flowers,
> Greek nudities, French novels, Roman 'Hours'...
> Well dressed, well fed, lapped in luxurious ease,
> His one anxiety – himself to please,
> He asks what most in life is worth his care,
> Looks in the glass, and finds the answer there.

More seriously, in 1896, Havelock Ellis finally published *Sexual Inversion* under his own and Symonds name in Berlin, where it caused no particular stir. After great difficulty in finding an English publisher brave enough to undertake the task, the following year it was printed London, via a press with anarchist links. However, Symonds's widow

146

was distressed by its appearance. She sought the advice of friends, including future Prime Minister Herbert Asquith. They all counselled that the book would damage Symonds reputation, and also that of his family and descendants. Consequently, Symonds executor Horatio Brown* bought up all the existing copies and destroyed them.* Havelock Ellis then rewrote and republished the book solely under his own name.

Again Ellis was challenged in finding a printing house that would commit themselves to such potentially illegal material, but finally persuaded an outfit which also published *The Adult*, the journal of the British Legitimation League. Founded in 1893, the League advocated for property rights for the children of the unmarried. George Bernard Shaw was a member, but the authorities looked upon it as a nest of freelovers, anarchists and other ne'er-do-wells.**

Sexual Inversion was sold under the counter, but in 1898 a Scotland Yard detective managed to purchase a copy, and the League member and bookseller, George Bedborough, who had sold it to him, was sent to trial. The married son of a retired clergyman, Bedborough suddenly found himself charged as being, in the words of the indictment:

> a person of a wicked and depraved mind and disposition…wickedly devising, contriving and intending to vitiate and corrupt the morals of the liege subjects of our said Lady the Queen…and to raise and create within them disordered and lustful desires.

---

* Horatio Robert Forbes Brown (1854–1926), Scottish historian of Venice, where he lived and played host to Anglo-Venetian society, and an international homosocial circle. Slender and handsome when young, he was also a keen alpinist. Author of *Life On The Lagoons* (1895), *Drift: verses* (1900), *Letters and Papers of John Addington Symonds* (1923), etc.

* This was ironic given that Brown was an especially gratified reader of *Homogenic Love*, writing to Carpenter: "I should like to tell you with what admiration, sympathy, and enthusiasm I have read it. It is in this cool, quiet, convincing, scientific way that I think this difficult &, at present, obscure problem should be brought to the notice of an ignorant and hostile society." [Bart Schultz, *Henry Sidgwick – Eye of the Universe: An Intellectual Biography*, Cambridge University Press, 2004, p709]

** In 1929, the League's chairman and owner of the publishing house, a German swindler who ran a sideline as a pornography wholesaler was arrested. Two tons of his merchandise was discovered hidden at his residence, but he dropped dead of a heart attack at the police station before he could be charged. In the view of the authorities, it would have simply been another case of 'perversion' loving company, and further justification for its suppression. [Jonathon Green, Nicholas J. Karolides, *Encyclopedia of Censorship*, Facts on File Inc., New York, 2005, p508.]

Labelled obscene, the book was banned. Eight years later, in 1906, the exceedingly brave Edward Carpenter republished a revised version of *Homogenic Love* in his book *Love's Coming Of Age*. All seemed well until 1909, when he suddenly found himself under attack from M.D. O'Brien,* an unhinged stalker, and member of the right-wing Liberty And Property Defence League.†

O'Brien distributed his own pamphlet titled *Socialism and Infamy: The Homogenic or Comrade Love Exposed*, and threatened to hire a public hall and read every word of *Homogenic Love* to an audience, challenging Carpenter to explain it away if he could. In the letters-to-the-editor columns of the *Sheffield Daily Telegraph*, O'Brien threw down his gauntlet:

> If this thing called 'comrade love' is such a glorious and splendid thing, why should it not be proclaimed openly to the whole world? Why should it be sent through the country in privately circulated pamphlets? Why should the 'comrades' have all of it to themselves?

Seriously rattled, but determined not to become a martyr, Carpenter calmly responded with his own letters to the paper, suggesting less than truthfully that he'd printed the booklet solely for "a few scientific friends, for the purpose of comparing notes and obtaining more information on a subject then new to me."

Carpenter's partner, George Merrill, was less composed, telling a friend: "It would be a pleasure to just twist such vermons [*sic*] necks." Fortunately for the couple, O'Brien made the mistake of proclaiming Carpenter's village the Sodom of Derbyshire and suggesting the vicar was in collusion. The outraged parishioners united in support of Carpenter, and O'Brien's campaign imploded.

Not to be put off, he continued to heckle Carpenter over *Homogenic Love* at public meetings, and petitioned the Metropolitan Police to have it banned for indecency, and Carpenter and Merrill prosecuted for homosexual offences. The Derbyshire Police advised they would

---

* Manuel Donatus O'Brien (1862–1938), a travelling salesman.
† One newspaper dryly observed: "it may safely be predicted that it is composed of members who care very little for liberty and a great deal for property." [Liberty And Property Defence League, *Sunderland Daily Echo*, 28 June 1883, p2.]

be keep a "discreet watch" on Carpenter. Although Merrill was an incorrigible seducer, O'Brien was again thwarted by the refusal of the local men to give police statements. This was due to the couple being embedded in the community, as well as a gruff working class tolerance, and distrust of middle class and state involvement in private lives.*

The view of homosexuality as an upper class degeneracy caused by idleness was very prevalent.† As another colonial newspaper put it in 1902:

> Dealing with the more refined phases of this evil – if so disgusting a thing can be said to have anything refined about it – it is to be remarked that primarily sodomy is aristocratic. It is a sin considered venial in a *blasé*, blue-blooded *roué*, but cardinal in a commoner.

The streets and parks of London and other major cities were one great cruising ground, including soldiers up for fun, and eager to supplement their miserable pay.‡ Since the Gordon Riots they'd been quartered in the capital in huge numbers, and their gorgeous uniforms added swagger and colour to the city. As one citizen recalled:

> They were dandies too…and they filled the eye. Their saucy scarlet, short waisted jackets, their jaunty fatigue caps, their tight trousers with broad stripes, on shapely legs which seemed

---

* O'Brien was eventually jailed in 1913 for distributing the pamphlets, *An Infernal Scoundrel*, and *An Unnatural Mother*, that libelled his own family. In court, one of his daughters admitted that, at least on one occasion, she had gone about the village dressed in male attire, sporting a pipe. Labelling his wife "a bold and shameless wanton," O'Brien accused the family of treating him "as a blank, a cypher, a nonentity." If so, they had excellent judgement. [In The Police And County Courts, *Derbyshire Courier*, 2 August 1913, p4.]

† There is certainly a long history of noblesse oblige in that direction. William Courtenay, 9th Earl of Devon (1768–1835), once paid a butcher's boy £250 pounds for the privilege of kissing his arse. Ironically, the 18th Earl (1942–2015) lost his wedding license after refusing to host same-sex unions at the family seat, Powderham Castle, a prohibition that his son, the 19th Earl, happily rescinded. [James Lees-Milne, *Prophesying Peace*, Chatto & Windus, London 1977, p239; Henry Mance, 'How UK heritage is coming to terms with its links to slavery', *Financial Times*, 25 September 2020.

‡ Soldiers hired themselves out as walkers to women at a regular fixed tariff, which ranged from half-a-crown and beer for a member of the Household Cavalry, to two shillings for the Royal Horse Artillery. Other services were available for a shilling. A newspaperman observed: "The fact that there is a big demand is shown by the large number of females at barrack gates early in the afternoon and evening waiting to engage escorts." [R.D. Blumenfeld, *R. D. B.'s Diary, 1887-1914*, William Heinemann Ltd., London 1930, p18.]

tremendous in length, were at once the admiration of nursemaids and the envy of small boys...

And not just maids and boys. So notorious was the soliciting, in 1903 the army issued an order forbidding uniformed soldiers from loitering "without lawful purpose in the parks after dusk." As for the streets, six years later a periodical stated:

Lord Roberts and General Baden-Powell have done much to advertise the Army and make it popular. Obviously they have its welfare at heart. We invite them to walk down Piccadilly any night at 12.30 and to keep their eyes open. They will find there a traffic among men...

An anonymously-authored fictionalised memoir, *The Sins Of The City Of The Plain*, published in 1881, stated there were six male brothels in London:

The best known is now closed. It was the tobacconist's shop next door to Albany Street Barracks, Regent's Park, and was kept by a Mrs. Truman. The old lady would receive orders from gentlemen, and then let us know.

This was likely the establishment at which, in 1877, John Addington Symonds paid for an assignation with "a brawny young soldier". Symonds recalled:

He was a very nice fellow, as it turned out: comradely and natural, regarding the affair which brought us together in that place from a business-like and reasonable point of view. From him at all events it involved nothing unusual, nothing shameful; and his simple attitude, the not displeasing vanity with which he viewed his physical attractions, and the genial sympathy with which he met the passion they aroused, taught me something I had never before conceived about illicit sexual relations.

Of the prostitution of the soldiery, a Londoner, Gifford Skinner,* stated: "They were more than willing because it was the only bit of

---

* Clifford 'Gifford' Skinner (1911–1990?), warehouseman and housing welfare officer. See: Clifford Skinner, 'Cocktails In The Bath', *Gay News*, Issue 135, 1978; *Gay Life*, London Weekend Television, 1981.

sexual pleasure it was possible for them to have…If they were sent abroad, they'd sell their address book to their mate, and he'd take over where they left off." The publisher John Lehmann,* ex-Eton and Cambridge, wrote a *roman-à-clef* detailing his pursuit of working class men and boys in the first-decades of the twentieth century: "The straightforward, pagan coarseness of these boys was a constant delight to me." Writing of the Brigade of Guards, he added:

> They went with men like myself because, partly because of the ancient and accepted tradition that they were there in the capital to do so, partly because they liked exploring a world strange to them – in a way they were anxious to better themselves; and partly because they wanted a protector who would provide a sexual outlet of what they considered a completely innocent sort…*

Gifford Skinner recalled that pulling rank through class could sometimes prevent one's arrest:

> Police could be intimidated actually if you got into trouble with them; it was largely done by the way one spoke. I…learnt that one should address them as c*u*nstable with a 'u', rather than c*a*nstable, which was a little bit common, you see. And they *knew* the difference. So if you said c*u*nstable they'd [think] "Oh my God, I've got hold of somebody here." And they'd well [say]: "I just wanted to tell you sir, it's rather dangerous to linger here, so if I were you I'd go home, you've had a drop too much, haven't you", something like that – very, very fatherly, and very *charming*.

However, some officers were not so accommodating. In his 1890 novel *The Picture Of Dorian Gray*, Oscar Wilde captured the paranoia of shame and damnation that attended the discovery of homosexuality in a gentleman:

> Why is your friendship so fatal to young men?…What about Lord Kent's only son, and his career? I met his father yesterday

---

* Rudolf John Frederick Lehmann (1907–1987).
* As late as the 1970s, the film director Brian Desmond Hurst could tell a friend: "Exciting news…The corporal-major of the Household Cavalry telephoned to say that the colonel has just opened a new box of recruits." As Hurst once outlined: "I like a man to have either three children or three convictions". [Christopher Robbins, *The Empress Of Ireland: Chronicle Of An Unusual Friendship*, Scribner, New York 2004, pp21,30.]

in St James's Street. He seemed broken with shame and sorrow. What about the young Duke of Perth? What sort of life has he got now? What gentleman would associate with him?

A bestseller of far lower quality was the anonymously authored *Shams*,* published in 1889, which similarly dealt with a young man of 'marvellous beauty' who falls under the influence of an aristocratic aesthete. Despite being boycotted by booksellers and newsagents, the novel ran to several editions. In a Preface, its author wrote: "The word 'Immorality' is one of wide meaning. It gilds the crown of the monarch and 'becomes' the sceptre of censorship."

The hypocrisy did indeed run right to the top. Someone who knew the truth of this was the wistful-faced George Merrill, Edward Carpenter's partner. Born into a family of nine children in the slums of Sheffield, Merrill had known deadly poverty and despair. At times in his childhood home, everything available had been pawned. Carpenter paid tribute to him, writing:

> Knowing as I do, thousands of people, of all classes – and many very intimately – I still doubt whether I find anyone more natively human, loving, affectionate, and withal endowed with more general good sense and tact than he.

Fascinated by the class gulf, Carpenter wrote down Merrill's recollections. They provide a remarkable window into working class life and fraternity of the time. Like most men of his station in life, Merrill had commenced work at thirteen. Later unemployed, one day he walked 23 miles in search of a job, and out of pity, was taken in for the night by an unemployed plumber and wife – she sleeping with a neighbour so that Merrill might have a bed. Merrill drifted from job to job, meeting lovers randomly. As a young man, he found himself in York, and recalled:

---

* The novel has been ascribed to the prolific novelist and journalist Cyril Arthur Edward Ranger Gull (1875-1923). [See: David Wilkinson, *Guy Thorne: C. Ranger Gull: Edwardian Tabloid Novelist and His Unseemly Brotherhood*, Rivendale Press, High Wycombe, 2012.] However, contemporary critics believed the author was a woman, due to several mistakes regarding matters a gentleman should have known. Margaret Raine Hunt (Mrs Alfred W. Hunt), whose daughter Violet had been courted by Oscar Wilde, employs the name of one of the novel's characters, Lord Edensor, in her 1892 novel *Mrs Juliet*.

one day I was at the station there, and the Prince of Wales…was in the station just going off to Tranby Croft on a visit, with some of his suite.

Of course they were all very smart with frock coats and tall hats and flowers in their buttonholes: but one of them was such a good-looking fellow – real nice and kind looking – and only about twenty-six or seven. And he got into the last carriage, just where I was standing on the platform outside, and as soon as he got in he put his head out of the window and made a movement to me to speak to him; and directly I went up he said quite sharp and business like, "Where will you be this evening at nine o'clock?" And I said, "Here," and he said, "All right! Mind you come" – And the train went off.

And in the evening he came all right – only in a tweed suit and cap. Oh! He was nice – such a real gentleman and such a sweet voice. And we walked along by the river, and sat on the seat under the trees, and he had brought some lovely grapes with him to eat.

For Merrill the grapes represented a rare luxury, as did the bunches of violets that the gentleman later left for him with notes of when to meet. The courtier told Merrill he lived:

in a big country house…and if I was ever in that part to let him know. And I said, "Nay, I couldn't come and call upon such as you." But he said, "Oh! I'll manage it. Don't be afraid."

However, out of work and miserable, and with troubles at home, Merrill mislaid the address.

"Eros is a great leveller," Carpenter would later write, "Perhaps the true Democracy rests, more firmly than anywhere else, on a sentiment which easily passes the bounds of class and caste, and unites in the closest affection the most estranged ranks of society."

A poem, 'Bored: at a London Music' by Horatio Brown, a close friend of Lord Rosebery, delicately captured the social levelling that desire could kindle:

153

Two rows of foolish faces blent
In two blurred lines; the compliment,
The formal smile, the cultural air,
The sense of falseness everywhere.
Her ladyship superbly dressed—
I liked their footman, John, the best.
The tired musicians' ruffled mien,
Their whispered talk behind the screen,

Remote I sat with shaded eyes,
Supreme attention in my guise,
And heard the whole laborious din,
Piano, 'cello, violin;
And so, perhaps, they hardly guessed
I liked their footman, John, the best.

George Merrill's courtier was hardly alone in his desires. Then as now, a small but significant proportion of the government and civil service were homosexual.[*] The family-unfriendly three months 'in waiting' duties for courtiers also made them better suited to confirmed bachelors, as did the late hours of ministerial secretaryships. So for example, the Hon. Spencer Lyttelton[†] and Lord Drumlanrig,[‡] Private Secretaries to Prime Ministers Gladstone and Rosebery, were almost certainly homosexual, as were a string of courtiers, including Sir Alexander 'Alec' Hood,[§] Sir Harry Stonor,[**] and Alexander 'Alick'

---

[*] An early-Victorian representative was Edward Leeves (1788–1871). Born Edward Fowler, he was a dilettante from the gentry who divided his time between London and Venice, and became private-secretary and later biographer of M.P. William Huskisson (Leeves' brother was his agent). Although Leeves only performed the role for five years, on Huskisson's recommendation he was granted a government pension of £200; the thin justification being that he'd left his profession of solicitor to accept the position. (Huskisson died in 1830 when the famous 'Rocket' locomotive ran over one of his legs after a fall.) A diary survives detailing Leeves patronage of guardsmen – "He is a bold, audacious blackguard, such as I like," and love for one in particular. [FindMyPast.com; William Berry, *County Genealogies: Pedigrees of the Families in the County of Sussex*, Sherwood, Gilbert & Piper, London 1830, p104; Anon (John Wade), *The Black Book of England*, C Mitchell, London 1847, p204, 202; Deaths, *Morning Advertiser*, 16 August 1871, p8; Edward Leeves, John Sparrow (ed.) *Leaves From A Victorian Diary*, Secker & Warburg, London 1985, p64.

[†] (George William) Spencer Lyttelton (1847–1913); fourth son of George Lyttelton, 4th Baron Lyttelton.

[‡] Francis Archibald Douglas, Viscount Drumlanrig (1867–1894), later, 1st Baron Kelhead; eldest son of the 9th Marquess of Queensberry, and brother of Lord Alfred Douglas.

[§] Sir Alexander Nelson Hood, 5th Duke of Bronte (1854–1937); longtime bachelor courtier.

[**] Sir Henry 'Harry' Julian Stonor (1859–1939), bachelor son of the 3rd Baron Camoys. Courtier to five monarchs, he was an excellent shot, which led to a close friendship with grouse nemesis George V. Icily handsome, "over six feet tall of rigid elegant slimness," he was

Yorke.* And hovering above them all, was Lord Esher, Edward VII's closest adviser. Edward Carpenter would further write:

> It is noticeable how often Uranians of good position and breeding are drawn to rougher types, as of manual workers, and frequently very permanent alliances grow up in this way, which although not publicly acknowledged have a decided influence on social institutions, customs and political tendencies.

While Carpenter, Whitman, and others championed the democracy of their desires, for upholders of rank, fortune, and order, the thought that homosexuality might be a kind of universal libertarian solvent, would have been a troubling one. For the British Government, it constituted more than a sin – it was a noxious risk to the status quo.

The Establishment had been spooked in 1883-85, when a rabble-rousing Irish nationalist newspaper editor, William O'Brien, stirred up what was to be known as the Dublin Castle Scandal. Weaponising homosexuality for his own ends, he used it to suggest moral corruption in Ireland's British administration: "Providentially the cowardice of persons thus diseased is commonly as abject as their depravity." Three male brothels close to military barracks were exposed, as well as a network of cross-class homosocial connections that included senior officials. In melodramatic, self-serving prose O'Brien called it:

> a criminal confederacy which, for its extent and atrocity, almost staggered belief. It included men of all ranks, classes, professions, and outlawries, from aristocrats of the highest fashion to outcasts in the most loathsome dens.

It also resulted in a flurry of court cases and ruined lives.† At the first

---

haughty as he was facile. According to a daughter of the 6th Baron Camoys, in old age he feared that her mother Jeanne – supposedly an ardent Nazi who blackmailed homosexuals (and was possibly responsible for the suicide of Cecil Beaton's brother), would do the same to him. [Simon Heffer (ed.), *The Diaries Of Henry 'Chips' Channon*, Vol 1, Hutchinson, London 2021; Jeffrey Amherst, *Wandering Abroad*, Secker & Warburg, London 1976, p59; Julia Camoys Stonor, *Sherman's Wife*, Stonor Lodge Press, London 2012.]

* The Hon. Alexander Grantham Yorke (1847–1911).

† A likely apocryphal story circulated that Lady Spencer, the wife of the Lord Lieutenant, "asked her husband why so many people had suddenly disappeared from Dublin society: & he ἐν ἀπορίᾳ [at a loss] told her they had been charged with 'tampering with Her Majesty's mails.'" [Rev. R.C. Fillingham diary, 5 February 1886, p114; Merton College Library.]

trial, the grand jury had sent an extraordinary appeal to the presiding judge, which asked:

> In the interest of public morality, we most respectfully suggest that Your Lordship should prevent and forbid the publication of any part of the evidence in the felony cases which have just come before us, and if possible make a ruling that any such publication would be a contempt of court.

In reply, His Honour stated: "I commend the resolution to the discretion and Christian forbearance of the Press, and will do all consistent with law to carry out your wishes." Reporting this, *The Times* pronounced: "In doing so he will have the hearty approval of the public." The paper further warned that if the local press failed to exercise discretion and regard for public decency and morals:

> imaginative reports will be furnished by unprincipled persons which will find their way into papers of the lowest class, which will feed on scandals, and that the object of the Court will be defeated, and possibly greater mischief done by their circulation.

The Times need not have worried. Given the details were considered by Irish Catholic propriety to be so unsavoury, as well as politically sensitive, reportage in both Irish and British newspapers was minimal. However, the scandal was a political victory for the Irish Nationalists, who succeeded in implanting in many Irish minds the belief that Dublin Castle and its administration was a bastion of perverts preying on wholesome Irish youth.

On its own turf, *The Times* exercised a rigorous censorship: between 1872 and 1885 it reported but a single homosexual prosecution. The exception, which occurred in 1881, was due to the case involving a diplomatic impasse. A corporal of the Scots Guards and a secretary at the German Embassy, Count zu Lynar,* had been found conducting intimate international relations in a Chelsea coffee house, and Lynar claimed diplomatic immunity.

However, in July 1895, a homosexual case arose with all the ingredients that gave the authorities migraines: social prominence,

---

* Count Guido zu Lynar (1849–1915).

cross-class association, and representatives of the State. Even worse, it involved personages who were supposed to uphold the very law they were charged under. It was a nervous time: Oscar Wilde had been sent to prison only two months before, and suspicion over homosexuality was poisoning private lives everywhere. At a county police station in Hampshire, the improbably named Superintendent Sillence* entertained concerns of his own about the orientation of a new recruit, the twenty-six-year-old Constable Walter Stocks.

Sillence was a born-for-the-job nosey parker, and it was reported: "his suspicions being aroused, he put a detective on the watch to see who it was that Stocks went to meet when he had leave." The detective soon reported back of seeing Stocks with another gentleman on a rainy day at Winchester walking "arm in arm together down the street under an umbrella…and shadowing them until he saw them go into the Market Hotel."

For Sillence, this was enough. He demanded to inspect Stocks' locker at the police station. It was found to hold a mass of letters from a gentleman Sillence actually knew. Indeed, he'd received letters from him as well, one of which "was enclosed with a book of prayer." However, the letters to Stocks were of a very different character.

Their author was the same esteemed gentleman who'd recommended Stocks for the Force – the esteemed Richard Stephens,† who was not only a magistrate, but chairman of the Bournemouth Magisterial Bench, and Deputy-Lieutenant of the county. Seventy years old, with a wife and family, Stephens was also prominent member of the Conservative Party, and his spouse a leading light of its Primrose League. He'd also helped found a cottage hospital and dispensary for the relief of the poor, and was president of its managing committee, whose meetings were held in his home. Stocks had become acquainted with him the previous year while working as a groom.

Confronted with the letters, Stocks caved in, admitting to indecent acts with Stephens, and saying: "It means over the wall for me" – an allusion to the adjoining prison. Superintendent Sillence informed a

---

* Julius Sillence (1848–1930). See: Leaves From A Notebook Of Crime, *Hampshire Observer*, 5 May 1906, p7.
† Richard Stephens (1824–1898). Married baronet's daughter Henrietta Maria Pottinger (1829–1905), and had issue.

magistrate that the trainee constable had also begged to him:

> Good God, Sir, have mercy on me. I should not have done it, but I went to him as a poor ward without a friend. I thought he was a gentleman. I am a poor man, and this is how he took advantage of my position. I wish to God I had told you of it, as I meant to do before...

This seems barely a half-truth born of terror. Richard Stephens was arrested at his hilltop mansion Eastington House, Bournemouth, while in the middle of dinner. (However, radicals in the borough were soon grumbling that, due to his social position, there had been a deliberate delay in the police response.) More damning letters from Stocks to Stephens were found in fragments in a wastepaper basket in the latter's study.

The two men were charged with buggery and gross indecency. Given Stephens' social prominence, and Stocks hailing from a family well known in Romsey, the hearing of their case at Winchester was a spectacle, as a newspaper recorded:

> Early there was a crowd round the Guildhall, anxious to get a sight of the prisoners...Those who knew Mr. Stephens in his best days were shocked at the change which has come over him. At times he appeared to be bent nearly double. He leaned upon the rails of the dock, and appeared every now and again to faint or to want to vomit. He was constantly supplied with water, which he drunk copiously, and applied a handkerchief, on which was his monogram, vigorously to his head. His overcoat was thrown over the dock rail, and occasionally he would lay his head upon it and shut his eyes, sighing very audibly..."I cannot hear," he would occasionally say in a distressed tone, and this was principally the case when Superintendent Sillence was telling his story...A remarkable feature of the case was the production in evidence of a book of prayers, composed by Mr. Stephens and a copy sent out, amongst others to Mr. Sillence, with an explanatory letter, and, strange to say, this very letter was used in evidence against the writer, as proof of his handwriting. The book of prayers was of an exceedingly devotional character, and "breathed a simple Christian faith throughout." Mr. White [for the Prosecution] had a whole bundle of letters to quote from,

and some he read. Probably in no court in the world has such a mixture of religion, filth, and poetry been read together. There were written the finest maxims which could guide a man through life; divinely inspired passages were quoted and then some of the noblest verses which have enriched the English language. Then, as if by a sudden and unaccountable drop, the writer would descend to indecencies over which a veil may well be drawn.

The case was sent to court, where the presiding judge Sir Alfred Wills,[*] who'd earlier sentenced Oscar Wilde, again made his revulsion plain, terming the case: "this hideous conspiracy of foulness and filth." He informed the Grand Jury that he'd dutifully read "every fragment of the correspondence", and it was:

> absolutely incredible...The wealth of detail, rejoicing and revelling in the degradation...There was a sandwiching of sentiment; filth, piety, gratitude to God for creating opportunities to these persons to misbehave...filth of the most disgusting description...invocations to God, and appeals [to Stocks] never to neglect his prayers.

Nonetheless, the Jury threw out the charges of buggery, leaving Wills to pronounce judgement on the lesser charges. He told the court: "A cruel wrong had been done to Stocks, who had been debauched and ruined by Stephens, whose creature he was," and whose 'corruption' he'd enabled "by offers of assistance, by presents, and by kindnesses of a sort." Stephens pleaded an outbreak of "senile madness," with two doctors testifying on his behalf that they had "no doubt his mind was in a disordered condition...and judging from his letters his whole being was centred in a gross sort of immorality." However, Wills dismissed this as nonsensical, stating:

> I cannot believe for an instant a decent-minded man would suddenly break out in his old age into filthiness of an indescribable character such as this has been. It would add a new terror to the fact of growing old...From the perusal of the terrible correspondence I have had to read I cannot doubt that things of the same sort have been familiar to you for years.

---

[*] Sir Alfred Wills (1828–1912).

Stephens was handed a sentence of two years hard labour. He'd already been on remand for three months; the prison medical officer finding him "in a very feeble condition," with a collapsed left lung, and weak pulse. Stephens' defence counsel protested that the sentence would kill him, but Wills replied that this was for the Prison Authorities to deal with: "it is a matter with which I have no concern." When his sentence was pronounced, Stephens was unable to hear, and Wills had to repeat it, which produced the reply, "Oh my God," before he was assisted from the dock.

Addressing Stocks, Wills told him: "you are a man apparently of good character." And yet paradoxically, he was supposedly the opposite:

> I think you must have been a nasty-minded man or you could not have yielded even to the temptations which were so lavishly placed before you, but I cannot help remembering that they were placed before you by a man immeasurably your superior in social position.

Wills believed Stocks deserved a sentence of at least nine months, but given his time on remand, handed down five months.

The attitude of the press towards the former magistrate and constable ranged from anger ("Disgusting Hypocrisy" – *Reynolds's Newspaper*) to bewilderment ("Strange And Serious Charge" – *The Weekly Dispatch*). The respectability of the accused, the marked discrepancy in age and status, and the nature of letters, further described as containing "most beautiful poetry and expressions, and dated from the Carlton Club, London, and from Stephens's house at Bournemouth," threw up before the eyes of the public a troubling narrative that served to reinforce all the Government's reservations about airing such prominent cases. And not simply because of their 'immorality'. The normalcy of the accused, their very humanity, constituted a transgressive narrative that inherently cast doubt on the validity of the holy war being waged against them. Up and down the country, quieter lives were being destroyed for the same reason.

For some newspaper readers, it surely prompted the thought that perhaps these monsters were not so alien after all. If they could be anyone... they could even be us.

5. THEM AND US

On a Saturday afternoon in London in late May 1889, an immense crowd gathered at Horse Guards Parade to witness a royal review of the Metropolitan Fire Brigade. It was a good-natured multitude, but the numbers were far in excess of what had been anticipated. The event soon turned into a fiasco. There were a series of dangerous crowd surges that almost overwhelmed the Prince and Princess of Wales.

While Edward and Alexandra managed to remain calm, this was not the case with the elderly and choleric Duke of Cambridge,* a grandson of George III, who was caught in an onrush. Possibly believing The Mob had come for him at last, His Royal Highness throttled the first hapless spectator pushed against him that he could lay his Hanoverian sausage fingers on. As the comedy of fate would have it, this happened to be a Sunday newspaper reporter, who'd only just recovered from an illness.

Left bruised and shaken, the pressman wished to have a summons taken out against the Duke. The magistrate responsible for the case declined, believing the intemperate old duffer had acted in misguided

---

* Prince George, Duke of Cambridge (1819–1904). Commander-In-Chief of the British Army until 1895, and notorious for his opposition to army reform. In the words of a London correspondent for a colonial newspaper: "one of the most stupid persons in England…I have never heard that he had intellectual gifts or moral graces even approaching mediocrity." However in the manner of 'characters' he was popular with the public; a phenomenon the journalist elucidated for his distant readers: "The English are a great nation with an uncontrollable liking for fourth-rate or fifth-rate men. Occasionally they are not satisfied unless they can get a sixth-rate or seventh-rate man; and when they can lay their brawny clutches on a demigod of this description, their bliss is extreme." [Home Topics, *The Age*, (Melbourne, Australia) 21 October 1856, p4.]

self-defence, and the reporter hadn't been seriously hurt. The reporter persisted with his grievance, but the superior courts had no power to compel a magistrate to issue a summons. It was all a bit of a beat-up in more ways than one, but for the radical press it provided another high-profile hook on which to hang its charge of unequal justice in Britain's courts.

That same month a number of upper class gentlemen, including the Earl of Dudley* and Lord Lurgan,† were arrested in a raid on an illegal gaming house. When, thirteen years later, Dudley was appointed Lord Lieutenant of Ireland, and Lurgan's post as State Steward was renewed, W.M. Thompson of *Reynolds's Newspaper* legitimately asked: "When will a law be passed embodying the principle that law breakers shall not be permitted to be law makers?"

Scandal was blossoming everywhere that spring of 1889. Also in May, it was reported that an official who held "a high position under the War Office", and "had been mentioned in despatches for his personal bravery" and honoured by the Queen, had absconded due to – as one account flatulently phrased it – "a charge which cannot here be particularised." It was further reported that "the affair is not one which can be hushed up" and that those privy to it predicted that "when the whole matter is made public it will create a sensation such as has not been equalled for a long time past." Yet, successfully hushed up it was.

A few months later, papers like *Reynolds's Newspaper*, and the *North London Press*, which had a far smaller circulation but was the more radical for it, had turned their attention to a fresh, but already festering criminal case. They were incensed at the delay in bringing to trial another nobleman, the Earl of Galloway.‡

Lord Galloway had been indicted for the sexual assault of a ten-year-old girl, which had occurred while she was sitting on a wall on a public

---

* William Humble Ward, 2nd Earl of Dudley, (1867–1932), military officer and Tory M.P. As Governor-General of Australia he was unpopular due to his extravagance and political interference. Despite marrying twice, during the Cleveland Street Scandal he was reported as having fled to the Continent. [Swindling The Emigrants, *The New York Times*, 17 November 1889.]

† William Brownlow, 3rd Baron Lurgan (1858–1937), Anglo-Irish aristocrat, landowner, hotel proprietor and sportsman. Married Lady Emily Julia Cadogan.

‡ Alan Plantagenet Stewart, 10th Earl of Galloway (1835–1901).

road after gathering blackberries. There were several witnesses to his lordship's hand being under the girl's dress, and also to his inebriated condition, but in court Galloway claimed he'd only put his hand on her knee. When a woman had come to the girl's aid, Galloway reportedly said: "What are you to do with it?" and attempted to pull rank, demanding of her, as she told the court, "if I knew who he was".

His lordship was, amongst other things, a former M.P., an ex-Lord High Commissioner of the General Assembly of the Church of Scotland, a Knight of the Thistle, a magistrate, and not least, brother-in-law of the Prime Minister, Lord Salisbury. While Galloway had been self-governed and handsome in his youth, he'd evolved into a red-faced alcoholic.

The police handed the case to a public prosecutor, who quietly sat on it for weeks until a Liberal newspaper, the *Scottish Leader*, published the details. One reader was Ernest Parke,* the twenty-nine-year-old editor of a radical weekly, the *North London Press*. Infuriated, he thundered his anger in its columns:

> We are constantly assured that in this country all are equal before the law. There is no distinction of persons, rich and poor are treated alike, equal measure is meted out to peer and peasant, millionaire and pauper. No statement could be wider of the truth, and these incidents serve to demonstrate the absurdity of the contention; serve to show that there is one law for the rich and another for the poor.

Parke also pointed his finger at the press as culpable:

> There is another fallacy common amongst us, and that is that the great London newspapers are independent; that they, too, like the representatives of the law, are above all considerations of the rank and station of the culprit when ill-doing ought to be exposed. As a matter of fact, and we do not speak without knowledge, the friends of the Earl of Galloway have succeeded in muzzling the London press.

The editor of *Reynolds's Newspaper*, W.M. Thompson, would also

---

* Ernest Parke (1860–1944). Also sub-editor of *The Star*.

lament:

> It is only to be regretted that there are so many servile journalists in this country – men without independence of spirit, breadth of view, or feeling themselves intellectually strong enough not to be afraid to write the truth – who by their utterances in the Press tend to foster the natural inclination of the English people to toady to rank.

In court, Lord Galloway was represented by the former Solicitor General for Scotland and Privy Counsellor, J.B. Balfour.[*] The defence argued that it was merely a case of misinterpreted playfulness, Galloway's brother stating that he was "very fond of children, and had a way of playing with them." Despite the testimony of witnesses, and the girl being described as "severely shaken" following the incident, a jury of 15 unanimously acquitted Galloway.[†] The Society magazine *Vanity Fair* pompously blustered that:

> A more ridiculous accusation was never brought against any man, and the Sheriff Substitute could not help saying that, in all his experience, he had never known such a charge based on 'circumstances' – he could not call them evidence – so slight. In no country but Scotland would such a groundless charge have received any attention at all.

With such lickspittle deference, the common man had little hope of justice when up against those of a higher class and their lawyers. The following year, Galloway was again in court for stalking and harassing a sixteen-year-old girl and others in the street. Despite several witnesses, he was again acquitted. The *Edinburgh Evening News* noted, "The Earl of Galloway, who has made two unenviable appearances in public is somewhat tall, with a red face, close whiskers and moustache, and shaven chin." If libel had not been a concern, it might have added he was also a molesting pest.

By the mid-summer of 1889, what *The Times* and its ilk termed 'the

---

[*] John Blair Balfour, 1st Baron Kinross (1837–1905), lawyer and Liberal M.P.
[†] In 1890, an Australian journalist observed: "an English jury is a peculiar thing. It can be only too easily brow-beaten...by a resolute judge on a point of law...he can often use the immemorial subserviency of the poor frightened, little British shopman-juror to effect his own purpose." [In Moral And Merrie England, *The Bulletin* (Sydney), 25 January 1890, p5.]

radical press' was simmering at the entrenchment of class-riven injustice being cosily meted out by the courts. As *Reynolds's Newspaper* voiced it: "People are fast losing faith in the justice and impartiality of all men and things connected with what we call our judicial system." That anger would explode in a cataclysmic scandal.

At the same time as the first Galloway case had been wending its way to court, an even greater miscarriage of justice was quietly unfolding. In early July 1889, a routine investigation into theft at London's General Post Office turned up a fifteen-year-old telegraph boy* who admitted to having fourteen shillings on his person, a sum greater than could be accounted for by his salary. He soon confessed that he and other G.P.O. boys were supplementing their wages with prostitution. This was occurring at a house in central London, No.19 Cleveland Street, that was solely patronised by gentlemen of the higher classes, and which operated as both a brothel, and a safe house for assignations.

Those fourteen shillings in a lad's pocket would fission like a handful of plutonium. Knowing something of the background of the Cleveland Street Scandal is important to understanding what was to unfold twelve years later with Lord Battersea's case.

Amongst the clients named by the boys in the Cleveland Street Scandal were the sons of two dukes – the Earl of Euston,† and Lord Arthur Somerset,‡ who was a major in the Royal Horse Guards, and superintendent of the stables of the Prince of Wales, as well as his extra equerry. He was also the younger brother of the self-exiled Lord Henry Somerset.

Attempts by officials to suppress the case fuelled a scandal that filled London with toxic gossip for months, and shook both the Government and Crown. For a few nervous weeks, it even appeared to threaten them.

---

* A deliverer of telegrams.
† Henry James FitzRoy, Earl of Euston (1848–1912), eldest son of the 7th Duke of Grafton. Married music hall artiste and courtesan Kate Walsh, whom he unsuccessfully attempted to divorce. No issue.
‡ Major Lord Henry 'Podge' Arthur George Somerset (1851–1926), third son of the 8th Duke of Beaufort. A bachelor, he later lived at Hyères with an English companion, James Andrew Neale.

The Cleveland Street Scandal generated three stage-managed trials. The first, for gross indecency, was undertaken by the Government to imprison two minor procurers for the House, and remove them beyond the reach of reporters. The second trial, for criminal libel, was initiated by Lord Euston against newspaper editor Ernest Parke, who publicly named him and Lord Arthur as clients of the House. While the Government didn't wholly game this case, official obstruction and the incompetence of the defence ensured Parke lost, and he too was imprisoned. The third trial, for conspiracy to defeat the course of justice, was to prosecute Lord Arthur's solicitor, Arthur Newton,* for attempting to smuggle some of the telegraph boy witnesses out of the country.

Unlike the hapless Lord Arthur, the authorities never considered prosecuting Lord Euston. As clear as day it signalled he was protected. While Euston was prominent in freemasonry, being Provincial Grand Master of Northamptonshire and Huntingdonshire, a far more important factor was that of primogeniture. Unlike Lord Arthur, who was a relatively poor younger son and theoretically disposable, Euston was the eldest son and heir of his father, the 7th Duke of Grafton.

It mattered not a jot that the ducal title had been created by Charles II merely to bestow respectability on a bastard son he'd spawned with Barbara Villiers,† one of his string of mistresses. Together with the title had come vast wealth. The ducal estates that Euston was in line to be custodian of amounted to 31,198 acres stretching across England and Scotland. They included the mansions of Euston Hall in Suffolk, and Wakefield Lodge in Northamptonshire. Topping up the enormous rent roll these lands generated was an hereditary Government annuity – one of those iniquitous 'perpetual pensions'. It then amounted to £5,870 per year.

---

* Arthur Newton (1860–1930), one of London's most famous solicitors. He defended and acted on behalf of several figures in Cleveland Street Scandal, both named and unnamed, and assisted the flight of Charles Hammond, the brothel's proprietor, for which he served a sentence of six weeks for the obstruction of justice. He also acted for Oscar Wilde's co-defendant Alfred Taylor. In 1913 he was sentenced to three years for fraud, and struck off the Rolls. When the lighting in Hyde Park was improved in the late 1880s, Newton claimed to have lost £2,000 a year in fees, due to the reduction in arrests for soliciting. [Hyde, H. Montgomery *The Cleveland Street Scandal*, W.H. Allen, 1976, p45.]
† Barbara Palmer, 1st Duchess of Cleveland (née Barbara Villiers (1640–1709), married Roger Palmer, later 1st Duke of Castlemaine, and had issue with Charles II.

As with most great British landowning, came great responsibility. Hundreds of estate workers and their dependants relied upon the Graftons for their livelihoods. Across villages and parishes, it was still the order of things. Whatever Lord Euston's behaviour in private, if the police of Scotland Yard dreamt for a moment that the gentlemen of Government would consent to the ready prosecution of the heir of such a ducal family, with the attendant disruption across four counties at the least, they were very much mistaken.

A prostitute, John Saul,[*] gave sensational testimony against Lord Euston at the libel trial, but the judge was incensed by Saul's effeminate and brazen manner, and dismissed his allegations. The Attorney-General,[†] then Sir Richard Webster,[‡] also declined to prosecute Saul for prostitution, or perjury. The danger was too great. Saul was no naïve GPO telegraph boy, but rather, a streetwise, thirty-two-year-old Irishman who had done jail time. He'd been connected with the 1884 homosexual scandal at Dublin Castle, and was so notorious he'd been the subject of two pornographic fictionalised autobiographies.[§] Saul also harboured a strong sense of injustice, and agreed to give evidence on Parke's behalf, even though he didn't know him. As he put it, "I thought he was acted very unfair with." Like Mrs. Jeffries, had Saul been backed into a corner on the witness stand, there was no telling what else he might have said, or whom he may have implicated. And the Attorney-General well knew it.

There was worse. Much worse. Arthur Newton could play dirty. He discreetly warned the Government that if prosecutions proceeded, they risked exposing another client of the house – the eldest son of the Prince of Wales, and heir-presumptive to the throne, Prince Albert Victor.

Behind the scenes, this radiant titbit went down like a nuclear trigger. "I wonder if it is really a fact or only an invention of that arch ruffian H[ammond]'s,"[**] Lord Arthur wrote to Reginald Brett, referring to

---

[*] John 'Jack' Saul, christened Johannes Saul (1857–1904).
[†] The chief legal adviser to the Crown and Government in England and Wales.
[‡] Sir Richard Everard Webster, later 1st Viscount Alverstone (1842–1915); barrister, politician and judge.
[§] The anonymously-authored *The Sins of the Cities of the Plain or Recollections of a Mary-Ann, With Short Essays on Sodomy and Tribadism* (1881), and its sequel, *Letters from Laura and Eveline, Giving an Account of Their Mock-Marriage, Wedding Trip, etc.* (1883).
[**] Charles Hammond (1854–?), brothel keeper, prostitute, and blackmailer. Married to a

the House's proprietor. Nobody was sure, least of all the Government. Anything was possible. While a vacuous slow developer, the Prince had managed to rack up several mistresses, intractable gonorrhoea, and possibly syphilis as well. Most of the British press maintained a cowered silence over the allegation, but when, on its front page, *The New York Times* named the Prince as being involved in the scandal, matters spiralled into crisis.

Before an arrest warrant was issued for him, Lord Arthur Somerset fled to the Continent on a night steamer. Earlier that same evening, the Prime Minister, Lord Salisbury, had met with Sir Dighton Probyn,* Comptroller and Treasurer to the Prince of Wales. When Labouchère learned of this, it gave him a convenient lynching post on which to hoist before the public the Government's conniving in the case, with the inflammatory allegation that the Prime Minister had tipped off Lord Arthur, via Probyn. Given Somerset's immediate flight, the logical conclusion is that Probyn did indeed pass on the grave news to him.

In the House of Lords, Lord Salisbury firmly denied he was responsible. He claimed he'd only informed Probyn that Somerset was a person of interest in the investigation. Yet as Labby told the press, "he said quite enough to induce Lord Arthur Somerset to leave the country if the facts were conveyed to him, and that is whole point." Even then, Salisbury was telling a half-truth: what he evaded saying was that he'd been meddling in the case to stall proceedings.†

In late November 1889 another liberal newspaper, *The Star*,

French prostitute 'Madame Caroline', by whom he had two sons.
* General Sir Dighton MacNaghten Probyn (1833–1924), awarded the Victoria Cross for valour at the Battle of Agra. According to one of the King's mistresses, Lady Warwick, Probyn was "a Liberal, in politics and also in everything else". [Daisy, Countess Warwick, *Discretions*, Charles Scribner's Sons, New York, 1931, p55.]
† Indicative of the byzantine machinations of those involved, Sir Dighton Probyn actually learnt of impending warrant against Lord Arthur Somerset from the Assistant Commissioner of Police – a fact that never became publicly known. When Lord Salisbury's Private Secretary told him of it, he memoed back: "Probyn played me an ugly trick – for he did his best to make me consent to a letter, which would have implied that he had obtained his information from my conversation. He told me that he had no communication with Somerset for several weeks before the flight." Salisbury was understandably upset, because he believed Probyn had attempted to frame him, to deflect public blame from himself, but more importantly, from the Prince of Wales, on whose behalf he'd been acting. Salisbury would already have felt undermined, as Labouchère alleged his informant of the meeting at the train station had been the Prince's Private Secretary, Sir Francis Knollys! [Jane Ridley, Bertie: *A Life of Edward VII*, Chatto Windus, London 2012, p539n84; p539n82.]

announced in a front page editorial (reprinted by W.M. Thompson), that it had also doffed its gloves:

> The Convention of Silence – to which we ourselves confess to have been partners – has been broken, and the whole situation is revolutionised. Now that the exposure has come it must go on to the end without pause, without veil, without mercy…There is – nobody can doubt it – in the hands of the authorities documentary evidence that lays bare the whole foul conspiracy in everything – in its inception, its operations, in its leaders and its subordinates, its wealthy maintainers and its vile hirelings…if the whole story be not told in the criminal courts of the country – then our lips, which have hitherto been dumb, will join in the tempest-wrath of all England that vice, if only rich and exalted enough, can protect itself…

On an extraordinary night in Parliament in February 1890, the scandal reached its climax when, to a packed House of Commons, Labouchère accused the Prime Minister of lying, and, with the aid of other officials, of conspiring to defeat the course of justice. Labouchère was expelled from the chamber for incivility, and in the hour and a half that followed, the Attorney-General, Sir Richard Webster, succeeded in dismissing his accusations by a skilled performance in obfuscation.

Fully conscious of the momentousness of the proceedings, Webster told the chamber:

> Of all the occasions on which I have spoken in the House and of all the questions I have heard raised since I have had the honour of being a Member of the House, nothing in my opinion has approached the importance of the occasion on the charge made by the hon. Member for Northampton [Labouchère] to-night.

It is something of a tribute to patrician shrewdness, Anglo-Saxon reserve, and the self-censorship and fear of libel of the mainstream British press, that tumult did not result. Given the Cleveland Street Scandal embodied the spectre of a sodomitical and dissipated heir to the throne, a debased aristocracy, a lying Prime Minister, a conniving civil service, and the wholesale compromising of justice, it truly was, as Ernest Parke wrote, "moral dynamite sufficient to wreck the good name of the nation." While its eventual smothering prevented it from becoming Victorian Britain's most sensational scandal, it was certainly its gravest one.

Yet the Cleveland Street Scandal would never have broken into the public domain had it not been for the small cadre of radical newspaper editors who championed its exposure – Ernest Parke, Henry Labouchère, W.M. Thompson, W.T. Stead, and T.P. O'Connor* – the latter, like Labouchère, also an M.P. and newspaper proprietor and editor.

The Scandal is also a primer on how British Government cover-ups are undertaken: silence the weak, protect the powerful, deny the truth, and erect in its place a simulacrum of it – or as a parliamentary writer once put it, "a British standard of graceful untruth." Yet not everyone in officialdom acted in lockstep. Within the civil service and police, equivocation, dissent and disgust at the miscarriage of justice being commanded from above was very real.

Lord Salisbury, who was both immensely overweight and wearily urbane, maintained a lugubrious, semi-somnolent exterior. It was therefore easy for him to feign an insouciant disinterest in the affair as a trifling matter to him, when in fact it was of the greatest importance. He was a long-standing friend of Somerset's parents, and the record shows he was involved from the get go. However, the prime mover in the conspiracy of suppression was the Prince of Wales, who gave it his unofficial imprimatur.

Acting as their facilitators in the cover-up were the Lord Chancellor, Lord Halsbury,† the highest law officer in England and Wales; the Attorney-General, Sir Richard Webster, the principal legal adviser to the Crown in England and Wales, responsible for prosecutions; and

---

* Thomas Power O'Connor (1848–1929), known as T. P. O'Connor and Tay Pay. Irish Nationalist M.P., journalist, and sometime-editor and part-owner of *The Star* newspaper, and others.
† Hardinge Stanley Giffard, 1st Earl of Halsbury (1823–1921), barrister, politician and government minister. He served thrice as Lord Chancellor of Great Britain. The Lord Chancellor is head of the judiciary, and also presiding officer ('The Speaker') of the House of Lords, and a member of the Cabinet. Once designated 'Keeper of the Royal Conscience', they were (and continue to be) custodian of The Great Seal of the Realm, the tangible representation of the will of the monarch, which is affixed to important state documents to indicate the sovereign's approval.

the Home Secretary, Henry Matthews, responsible for the police handling of criminal cases.

Hardinge Giffard, Lord Halsbury, was to spend longer in the post of Lord Chancellor than anyone in the previous century. A man of tireless energy who would live to ninety-eight (he was a non-smoker), his appearance on his daily walks to Parliament in glossy silk top hat would cause strangers to turn round in the street, so struck were they by his "sprightly aspect" and "look of such lively force of character in the face":

> His cheeks were as round and as ruddy as those of a farmer, his eyes shone with health and the joy of life, and, stick in hand, he bowled doggedly along looking as cheerfully determined and as happy as any farmer's boy.

One of the first things to be glimpsed was his necktie of royal blue:

> the 'true blue' of the Old Tories. No one could pass that bright blue tie without taking notice of it...Lord Halsbury's blue tie is the bluest tie in London, just as Lord Halsbury is the 'bluest' Tory in the House of Lords.

Not only a deep political and social conservative, Lord Halsbury was also well-versed in doing favours: in appointing magistrates for political ends, he'd earned "a deathless reputation for pitchforking relatives and friends into positions for which they were quite unfitted." As Labouchère later put it: "If the Attorney-General had had to select a thick-skinned partisan to aid him, it would have been impossible for him to have made a better choice."

To his friends, Halsbury was "a perennial spring of jests and genial sallies," and he and Salisbury, the last Prime Minister to lead a government from the House of Lords, were very close. *The Pall Mall Gazette* noted:

> As long as the Marquess of Salisbury attended the sittings others had little chance of hobnobbing with the Lord Halsbury, for the two were special cronies, and spent much time shoulder to shoulder on the woolsack.

Both gentlemen were vigorous upholders of the rights of the aristocracy. In the constitutional crisis of 1909-11, when the Liberal Government pushed forward a bill to dramatically increase taxes to fund welfare reform and redistribute wealth, but which also curbed the power of the House of Lords to veto legislation, Halsbury would become the nominal leader in the House of a group of die-hards (or 'Dine-hards' as their critics nicknamed them) opposing the move.*

In his role as Lord Chancellor, Halsbury was also in regular contact with the Prince of Wales, furnishing advice on matters of state. Not least, the Prince had been made an honorary member of Halsbury's masonic lodge of Chancery Bar, membership of which was otherwise restricted to the legal profession.

Then there was the Attorney-General, Sir Richard Webster: kindly but austere, and a staunch churchman – *Reynolds's Newspaper* snarked that he "really ought to have been a female evangelist, instead of a lawyer." Webster took the very dimmest view of unsavoury matters entering the public sphere, and championed the movement to ban the publication of divorce proceedings, denouncing their circulation by the press as "a popular evil".

Lastly, there was the Home Secretary, Henry Matthews. A wealthy Catholic of some charm, like Webster he altered his opinion on prosecuting the case as the desires of his superiors became known.

These gentlemen had the strongest reasons for wishing the suppression of the Scandal. The first, and least defensible reason, and consequently the one most open to public anger, lay in self-serving familial associations and class loyalty. Lord Salisbury was a close friend of Lord Arthur Somerset's ducal parents, and the Prince of Wales had a personal affection for Lord Arthur. There were also other prominent figures implicated who were known to them, and an understandable desire to spare them and their families further distress – and a shame beyond voicing.

---

* The 3rd Lord Salisbury having by then died, in this endeavour he was joined by Salisbury's like-minded son, the 4th Marquess. Both feared the further radical legislation that the Liberals and emerging Labour Party would champion.

The second reason was the very nature of the scandal. The requirements of evidence in homosexual prosecutions were stringent, and they were normally the preserve of the Police. Officials were leery of the Government taking on such cases, not only due to the risk of failure and embarrassment, but because it gave additional publicity to criminal narratives that were considered to be morally and socially corrosive. Time and time again this concern manifests itself in official communications.

At two meetings in 1880 and 1884 (the latter at the height of the Dublin Castle scandals), the Director of Public Prosecutions (DPP) and Treasury Solicitor,* Sir Augustus Stephenson,† had, urged "on grounds of public policy, the expediency of not giving unnecessary publicity to cases of this character." In Parliament, the Attorney-General Sir Richard Webster would also state of the Senior Treasury Counsel:

> Mr. Poland‡ is of opinion, an opinion which I entirely share, that no good is done by reporting cases of this description, and it is greatly to the credit of the reporters of the Press that they almost invariably refrain from reporting them.

It was not enough to punish homosexuals: it was considered prudent that they be broken in secret.§ Thanks to the discretion of the mainstream English press, such was usually the case. However, so troubled was Lord Halsbury by the reporting of the Cleveland Street Scandal and subsequent Wilde trials, that in March 1896 he attempted to introduce the *Indecent Evidence Bill*. This would have criminalised the publication of specified evidence in more sordid divorce proceedings

---

* Difficult and important criminal cases in England and Wales were referred by the police to the Director of Public Prosecutions (DPP), who had to conduct prosecutions when ordered by the Home Secretary or the Attorney-General, under whose direction they were. The role and its office are part of the Home Office, the ministerial department responsible for the administration of the police, judicial and penal systems. Its head is the Home Secretary. Typical of the paradoxical structure of British public institutions, at the time of the Scandal the DPP was also Solicitor to the Treasury, and had his office in the Treasury building in Whitehall. Consequently, prosecutions by the Crown (i.e. the British Government) were then commonly referred to as being undertaken by the Treasury.
† Sir Augustus Frederick William Keppel Stephenson, (1827–1904).
‡ Sir Harry Bodkin Poland (1829–1928), barrister, Counsel to the Treasury and adviser to the Home Office. A bachelor, he was knighted in 1895.
§ Webster was also the keenest proponent of restricting publication of unsavoury divorce testimony. [Ex-Attaché (Frederick Cunliffe-Owen): Movement To Suppress Publication Of Divorce Muck, *New York Daily-Tribune*, 13 February 1910.]

and prosecutions of homosexuality. As he put it to the House of Lords:

> within the last two or three years, cases had been published in the newspapers containing details of the most grossly indecent character. The publications containing those details had been spread through the country, causing, he believed, infinite mischief.

In this endeavour, he had the total support of Prime Minister Salisbury, who told Parliament:

> The reason why the publication of that class of cases is so much to be deprecated is not merely because it offends our taste, and makes the reading of the newspapers disgusting, but because it is a well-ascertained fact that the publication of details in cases of that kind has a horrible, though undoubtedly direct, action in producing an imitation of the crime by other people...a kind of epidemic in consequence of the case published.

The bill never became law; it was opposed by the Lord Chief Justice,* the Master of the Rolls† and the Liberal opposition, on the grounds of press freedom, the freedom of judges, and the fact that "great discrimination was shown by the press in the publication of cases involving indecency." In his argument against the bill, the Liberal leader Lord Rosebery told the House: "You are going to legislate with respect to a corner, a fragment of an evil which is not itself great and which has a tendency to become less and less every day," which was received with shouts of "hear, hear!" However, he agreed with Lord Salisbury that publication of evidence in such cases was "likely to provoke the imitation" of the behaviour. Given Rosebery was one of the nation's foremost collectors of pornography, including homosexual erotica, this was patrician hypocrisy at its richest.

The third and most important reason for suppression of the Cleveland Street Scandal, and which made quashing it not simply a wish, but an imperative matter of state, was the alleged involvement

---

* The second-highest judge in England and Wales, then Lord Russell of Killowen.
† The judge who presides over the Court of Appeal (Civil Division), and who was formerly in charge of the Public Record Office. Then the 1st Lord Esher (the father of Reginald Brett, the 2nd Lord Esher.)

of Prince Albert Victor.

The Prince of Wales, Lord Salisbury, Lord Halsbury, Sir Richard Webster, and Henry Matthews had an unswerving loyalty to the Crown, which they, together with a large portion of citizens, believed was the glue that bound the Nation together. Consequently, the dignity of the Crown needed to be upheld and protected: a task which included shielding its living embodiments, and those who served them, from unsavoury rumour. Matthews is alleged to have replied to someone who pressed him to prosecute the Cleveland Street Scandal's high-born guilty: "Do you think I'm going to shake the Constitution to its foundations for a lot of wretched boys?"

Equal justice was a fine ideal, but not when a sordid case risked compromising the Crown, ruling class, or social cohesion. During the Scandal, the civil service, police, and those further down the line would chafe at the judgements of their superiors, but as the five prevailing gentlemen would have seen it, they had a far higher responsibility: the preservation of national unity and order. Superficially their actions had all the markings of a seedy conspiracy resting on generational entitlement, but the end goal was to do God's duty. As the motto of the Crown daily reminded: *Dieu et mon droit* – literally 'God and my right': the Sovereign had been empowered by the grace of God. Yes, it was pure religious superstition, but without some degree of faith, the edifice would fall apart.

And so, having been badgered by the Prince of Wales, Lord Salisbury colluded with Lord Halsbury, and together they leaned on Henry Matthews and Sir Richard Webster. The result was a succession of instructions to the Director of Public Prosecutions which were evasive, delaying, or straight refusals, and drove him, and those under him, to despair. However, the stakes for Government and Crown in suppressing the accusations were so sky high, it was a case of whatever it takes. In the end, what they desired was accomplished, but it left a public stench of wrongdoing. Britain's international reputation was bruised. As W.M. Thompson editorialised in *Reynolds's Newspaper,* following the conviction of Ernest Parke:

> The whole nation is upbraided for tolerating such an awful miscarriage of justice. The newspapers abroad, in the colonies, and elsewhere are shocked at what has already transpired in

reference to these fearful crimes. One thus expresses itself: – "It is incidents such as these which presage revolutions."

Never again would colonial newspapers be quite as complacent as the *Timaru Herald* of New Zealand, which four years before had printed:

> We are so accustomed to speak of the purity of justice in the English Courts – so habituated to take it for granted that whatever else may be said against the judicial system, it is perfect as regards the absolute impartiality of its administrators – that it comes with a rude shock of surprise to hear even a doubt expressed on the subject.

Despite all the newspaper column inches it generated, the Cleveland Street Scandal was soon dropped by the Press. It was considered too repugnant for words, and morally and legally, a national embarrassment. Yet, time and again the authorities found it necessary to suppress scandalous cases – two of the occasions concerned the very devout Lord Salisbury's own domestic chaplains at his Hertfordshire seat of Hatfield house.

The first was the Rev. Huth Walters,* who was then also chaplain to Oxford's Christ Church college, home to its cathedral and famous choir. Walters was also a staunch supporter of the Tory party. In 1884, as a result of complaints by a theological student at Christ Church over the associations of some university men with boys of the college choirs, an inquiry was instituted. It lead to a number of undergraduates being expelled, and the removal of Walters. As a consequence, he was turfed out of Hatfield as well. None of this came to the attention of the press.† Neither was Walters charged or required to flee to the Continent, although he never held an appointment in the Church of England again.

The second chaplain was the Rev. Edward John Edwards.‡ In 1883 while on a visit to Oxford, Lord Salisbury met Edwards, who was curate of St. Mary's. When Walters departed, Edwards accepted

---

* Rev. Edmund Huth Walters (1846–1926).
† It is only known through the handwritten memo of a Bodleian librarian, Falconer Madan, that exists in a surviving copy of the booklet of pederastic advocacy, *Boy-Worship*.
‡ The Rev. Edward John Edwards (1851–?), third son of John Barber Edwards, of solicitors Mercer & Edwards, Deal, Kent.

Salisbury's offer to be his replacement. In 1892, a report published in American and Canadian papers detailed the subsequent events:

> In this position he [Edwards] acquired an ascendancy over the ladies of the family to such an extent that both Lord Salisbury and his son, Lord Carnbrook, [*sic*: Cranborne] thought it advisable to protest. Some dissensions in the family resulted, but finally the matter was ended by the appointment of Edwards as rector of Essendon, about three miles from Hatfield house, of which living Lord Salisbury is patron. Edwards, who is a bachelor, occupied the rectory house, and according to village gossip frequent orgies took place there. The scandal that resulted from these doings gradually grew worse until a crisis was reached last May, and formal charges of criminal immorality were made against Edwards before the local magistrates. These officials, who were friends and beneficiaries of Lord Salisbury, and incidentally friendly to Edwards, took no action. The persons who were bent on exposing the scandal did not cease their activity, however, and the police were kept advised of what was going on. On June 11th, the day of the great Primrose [League] demonstration in Hatfield park, Rev. Lord William Cecil, son of Lord Salisbury, and rector at Hatfield, was seen in earnest conversation with Rev. Mr. Edwards in the park. It is supposed that Cecil warned Edwards that he was in danger, as that same night, when the police suddenly descended upon the Essendon rectory, they found that Edwards had fled. The next day (Sunday) Rev. Lord Cecil conducted the service at Essendon. On Monday a warrant was issued for Edwards' arrest, the visit of the officers to the rectory on the previous Saturday having been made in the hope of capturing the accused parties in flagrante delicto...Edwards has not been seen since. The police were unable to get any information when they arrived at Hatfield and Essendon. It is believed, however, that Edwards is now in New York, and the police of that city have been warned to look out for him.

Not a word of the scandal appeared in the English press until *The Police Gazette* printed the following bulletin:

> Hertford (County). For committing acts of gross indecency...at Ossendon, [*sic*: Essendon] Edward John Edwards, a clergyman

of the Church of England, age 42, height 5 feet 9. or 5ft 10in., stout, complexion pale, hair (cut short) black, no whiskers or moustache, eyes dark grey, thick colourless lips, good set of teeth, broad shoulders, a native of Deal, Kent. Warrant issued. Information to Supt. Parish, Hertford.

While a moral incident involving a clergyman always created a minor stir, there the matter might have rested, but for *The Star*. This previously mentioned newspaper, founded by the Irish Nationalist T.P. O'Connor, and mostly edited by fellow radical H.W. Massingham,* had been a success from the day of its launch in 1888, and enjoyed an enormous circulation that had been boosted by its coverage of the Jack the Ripper murders. In its first issue, O'Connor had laid out his aims: "The rich, the privileged, the prosperous need no guardian or advocate; the poor, the weak, the beaten require the work and word of every humane man and woman to stand between them and the world."

The Star reprinted *The Police Gazette*'s report, but illumined readers as to Edwards' connection with Lord Salisbury, and his removal from Hatfield "to another parish in the Premier's gift":

> Mr. Edwards...became exceedingly popular in the village. A jovial, pleasant man he is said to be, a man of culture, and good taste in art, and an eloquent preacher. He had not been long in Essendon, however, before rumour again assailed him, and for 15 or 18 months unsavoury stories were current in the village...The police heard the rumours, and, it is said, they watched the clergyman secretly.

The Star then provided a four point diary of events, which like the overseas reports, also implied Edwards was tipped off about the police warrant by one of Salisbury's sons, and allowed to escape.

Overseas, this breach of editorial discretion was noted: "*The Star* is the only paper that has done more than hint blindly at the affair. This paper is being approached with a view to induce its silence in the future." However, a few English papers dared to reprint or quote from *The Star*'s report. Across the Atlantic, the press also observed:

---

* William Henry Massingham (1860–1924).

The horrible scandal which has just been mentioned publicly for the first time in the newspapers regarding the immoral conduct of Rev. John Edwards has been known and commented upon privately for weeks. The difference between English and American election methods could hardly be better illustrated than by this fact. Though the family of Lord Salisbury, the Conservative leader, is unpleasantly involved in the affair in respect of conspiring to defeat justice even if in no more lamentable way, not a hint of the scandal has crept into print or been used for political purposes by the opponents of the Premier...Owing to the severity of the English libel laws, only the most distant hints as to what developments are in the background are indulged in.

In contrast, foreign reports sought to make sense of the affair:

It transpires that Lord Salisbury acted in the interest mainly of the Church in the matter...Lord Salisbury compelled Edwards to resign under pain of arrest...Edwards has ample private means, and will probably be able to take himself to some remote part of the globe until the scandal in which he was the chief figure is forgotten. It is not likely that a serious attempt will be made to bring him back and prosecute him. Even the new Liberal Home Secretary will probably be willing to cooperate in sparing Lord Salisbury the annoyance that would be involved in following up the case...The theory of the authorities in such cases seems to be that it is better to allow the culprit to escape than to have the scandal of a public prosecution.

Unfortunately for Edwards, he no longer had "ample private means": the previous year the firm of Kent solicitors in which his seventy-four-year-old father was co-partner collapsed with enormous liabilities. His father was not only bankrupted, but jailed for eight years after it was discovered that, as a trustee, he'd been defrauding clients of huge sums for over a decade.

Nothing more would be heard of the Rev. Edwards until 1906 when, in a bizarre case, Lord Salisbury's daughter Lady Gwendolen Cecil*

---

* Lady Gwendolen Gascoyne-Cecil (1860–1945); philanthropist and biographer of her father.

brought a libel suit against a Mrs. Lavinia Stanley,* formerly the chapel organist at Hatfield, who was the wife of a curate. Stanley had alleged that, in 1890, Gwendolen gave birth to an illegitimate child by Edwards, and to save her reputation, scapegoated her as its mother. To get the word out, Stanley had printed up thousands of pamphlets and leaflets detailing her grievance, distributing them on a carriage decorated with banners. "The probability is," the judge helpfully informed the jury prior to the proceedings, "that the woman is insane." Stanley presented no evidence to support her claim, and was jailed for six months. Lady Gwendolen considered the trial "a perfect farce," writing to her sister: "the ludicrous absurdity of it all became one's dominant impression. Even pity for her was lessened by her evident indifference to her position – which was another sign of madness," adding of Stanley's supporters: "I have no doubt they all genuinely believe her to be the victim of aristocratic persecution. What stupendous fools there are in the world!"†

Lord Salisbury again helped ensure silence was maintained when, in 1899, one of the most high profile dignitaries of the Church of England, the Rev. Robert Eyton,‡ Canon of Westminster, rector of St. Margaret's, and Sub-Almoner to the Queen§ was forced to resign for molesting choirboys.

Salisbury was personally informed of the circumstances, and provided with one of Eyton's resignation letters. As for the English press: it merely restated the official line that Eyton's resignation was for reasons of health. It was left to foreign newspapers to detail the true state of affairs. The New York paper *The World* was one of several happy to step into the breach:

> In such cases, where the evidence is positive, as it is in this, the Home department offers the offender an opportunity to flee the country to obviate a public scandal. The dean of Westminster received not long ago notification from the Home office that information had been given to the police which would involve

---

* (Matilda) Lavinia Stanley, née Sheehan, (1864–1934); wife of the Rev. William Hubert Stanley.
† With the exception of entries for early 1888, Lady Gwendolen's diaries were destroyed.
‡ Rev. Robert Eyton (1845–1908.)
§ The Sub-Almoner assists the Lord High Almoner of the Royal Almonry, one of the ancient offices of the Royal Household, in managing the Sovereign's charities, and the mummery of the annual Maundy Money ceremony.

Canon Eyton's arrest within thirty-six hours. Eyton was informed of it and took the next train to the continent.

Given that the exposure of moral falls of the high-born and notable was believed to damage the common weal, forewarning such privileged persons of impending arrest warrants for 'unnatural offences' was considered by British governments to be a pragmatic win: the hasty emigration of the indicted placed them beyond the reach of not only its courts, but also journalists and gossips. The priority was that horrid truths should be aborted, rather than scandal birthed.

When, three years later, a new homosexual scandal in the highest reaches of the Establishment threatened to darken the dawn of Edward VII's reign, those in authority would know what had to be done — at any cost.

6. THE AGE OF BLACKMAIL

> There is no security now but in obscurity. Shot or scandal is the portion of all who attain prominence. Blackmailing is the most flourishing industry of the moment.

So lamented a writer in *Truth* in 1907. For those seeking proscribed pleasure, it was an ever-present threat.

In 1915, the former Chief of the Criminal Investigation Department of Scotland Yard, Sir Melville Macnaghten, wrote in his memoirs: "A journalist friend of mine once cynically remarked that everyone in London was either a blackmailer or a blackmailee." Macnaghten admitted, "the amount of blackmail levied in the Metropolis is stupendous, and the unsuspected cause of many a suicide and voluntary banishment from the country."

There were said to be twenty or thirty blackmailers in Piccadilly who drank to the health of 'Good old Lab' – Henry Labouchère. This was due to his addition to the 1885 *Criminal Law Amendment Act* – sometimes called 'The Blackmailer's Charter'. One convicted blackmailer, whose assumed name was William Allen, gave a full statement to the Sunday *Reynolds's Newspaper* in 1898. It must have made illuminating Sabbath reading for the good British public. According to Allen, each blackmailer generally kept a gang of some half-dozen well-dressed youths as lures. They were to be found:

> at Drawing Rooms, Levées, &c., Regent-street, Burlington Arcade, Piccadilly, all the West-end buffets, &c., in fact,

wherever there is likely to be a congregation of gentlemen…Let anyone look in at the Piccadilly bars, or along the tables of certain well known West-end restaurants, at the time I have mentioned [late Saturday evening], and it will be palpable to him. I may add that a great many of H.M. Guards go to make up the number. The majority of these people, independent of the 'renter', as the male prostitute is called, are what are known as 'love-birds', and are at constant war with the 'renter' who obtains his living by these means.

As to their clients, *Reynolds's* added:

The writer of the above article gives a list of names which would astonish the public were we at liberty to publish them. He also made a written statement to the police, which they have not acted upon.

Like a Fagan, one blackmailer even maintained a training seminary: a pamphlet of the time dubbed his students the 'Guild Of Wandering Nephews'.

One of the most proficient blackmailers, and a working partner of Allen's, was Robert Cliburn.* In his early life, Cliburn had been employed in a number of positions, including as a butcher's boy and telegraph messenger, but found extortion more to his taste. Tall with dark brown hair, an olive complexion and hazel eyes, he was described as "a beautiful but dangerous youth," and "a bold, scheming, enchanting…panther." George Ives considered he possessed "a beautiful but mad face, the face of a tiger though very handsome."

One of his victims was Oscar Wilde, who actually treated him and an accomplice to dinner. In *De Profundis,* Wilde recalled: "Clibborn [*sic*]

---

* Robert Henry Cliburn (1873–1934), convicted blackmailer who employed a number of aliases; married Elizabeth Pittock, née Iverson. He was first incarcerated for blackmailing at fifteen. After release from prison for his blackmail of Cliburn, he migrated to Canada, becoming a successful billiard table salesman for the firm of Burroughes & Watts, which is still existent. [Adam Wood, *Donald Swanson: The Life And Times Of A Victorian Detective*, Mango Books, London 2020, pp444-445; Joseph Bristow, 'Homosexual Blackmail in the 1890s: The Fitzroy Street Raid, the Oscar Wilde Trials, and the Case of Cotsford Dick', *Australasian Journal Of Victorian Studies*, 2018, Vol. 22, No. 1.]

and Atkins* were wonderful in their infamous war against life. To entertain them was an astounding adventure." Another victim was the Earl of Euston, who'd bluffed his way out of the Cleveland Street Scandal. Wilde quipped that Cliburn deserved the Victoria Cross for the tenacity of his blackmailing of Euston.

As a newspaper report put it, Cliburn's gang "wrought most terrible havoc in the West End," responsible for untold misery, and at least one death. Finally, one of Cliburn's victims risked their reputation and sought police protection. That gentleman was the popular songwriter Cotsford Dick.

It resulted in Cliburn being put on trial in 1898, and jailed for seven years. In the courtroom, a solicitor revealed that he paid Cliburn an annuity of £100 pounds a year on behalf of one client, and that the money came through "Mr. Wallis, late partner of Mr. Arthur Newton." The source may well have been Lord Euston. It was a small, enfolded world.

Perhaps it was Cotsford Dick's longings for Cliburn, or an associate, which helped forge the lyrics of his popular song *Forget, Forgive*:

> Ah! wherefore must I stand alone
> Beyond the sunshine of your smile,
> Ah! wherefore with regretful tears,
> Must I the weary hours beguile
> Come back, sweetheart, forget, forgive,
> And bid me love again, and live…
> Ah! gain, and live.

It wasn't merely Cliburn whose brazen tenacity was extraordinary. A law tutor, Maitland Francis Morland, described as "a venerable looking personage," supplemented his income writing letters to noblemen that appeared to have come from a young widow 'Ruth Morland', demanding money for having had sexual relations with her. If the victims didn't respond to the first extortion attempt, Morland dramatically escalated his tactics. One of his victims was the bisexual Lord Russell.† After Russell ignored the first letter, Morland sent

---

* Frederick 'Fred' Atkins (1875–?), rentboy, blackmailer, music hall comedian. Alias Fred Denny.
† John Francis 'Frank' Stanley Russell, 2nd Earl Russell (1865-1931). Thrice married, his

letters to Russell's fiancée and her mother. When that didn't work, Morland commenced an action in the High Court! Only when, at considerable expense, Russell briefed counsel, did Morland drop his bluff. Morland perpetrated his terror for seven years before being apprehended and jailed for a decade.

Another gentleman who fell foul of the merciless trade was a guest at the 1902 Coronation, Prince Francis Joseph of Braganza.* A twenty-two-year-old sprig of the royal house of Portugal, he was an army lieutenant in a regiment of the Austrian hussars, and grand nephew of the Emperor. Accompanying his elder brother Prince Miguel, he had arrived in London on the 24th of June, two days before the originally scheduled date of the Coronation, and wasted no time in partaking of the delights of the capital. As his brother later recounted in court, on his first evening Prince Francis visited The Empire Theatre musical hall in Leicester Square. What he didn't say was that its balcony promenade was an infamous cruising ground for prostitutes and homosexuals.†

His Royal Highness ended the evening fast asleep in a bed in rented rooms in working class Lambeth, in the company of two teenage labourers, Henry Chandler and Charles Sherman, who were in league with a bookmaker's clerk, William Gerry. The Prince paid Chandler and Sherman a pound each for their services.

Unfortunately, the royal slumber was to be interrupted. In this lower world, where prying eyes behind net curtains was a fact of life, the landlord's wife had seen the lads walking up and down the street with a 'toff' in a silk hat, which immediately raised her suspicions. The landlord peered through the keyhole of the bedroom door, and cut a further peephole. Having witnessed the royal party, he had held Gerry, and summoned the police. When a constable arrived and told the Prince, "Come on, get up," he protested: "I've paid £2 for this room."

---

sexuality was exposed during a series of sensational court battles with his first wife and mother-in-law.
* Prince Francis Joseph of Braganza, Infante of Portugal aka Francisco José Gerardo Maria Jorge Humberto Antonio Henrique Miguel Rafael Gabriel de Bragança, (1879–1919).
† One obvious homosexual patron who requested a ticket was informed at the box office, "Yes, but unfortunately sitting-room only." [Timothy d'Arch Smith, 'Retrieving Our Past', *Gay Times*, Issue 250, 30 Sept-13 Oct 1982, p55.]

The lads, their pimp, and the Prince, were taken to a police station. On the way there, Gerry said: "I will take the blame for this. I don't want to see the boys get into trouble. I put them on the game, and told them what to do." They were all charged with gross indecency, and remanded in custody, the Prince confessing: "I cannot help it."

On the following day at Southwark Police Courts, a journalist noted:

> The names of the prisoners and the prosecutor did not appear on the ordinary charge-sheet of the court, to which reporters have access...All requests for these names were refused by officials of the court, acting, of course, on higher instructions, and it was very evident that a determined attempt would be made to try the case in secret.

Before the prisoners were brought in, reporters and public were told they must leave the courtroom, and the initial evidence was heard in-camera.

When the case again came to court the following week, there was a different magistrate who, according to a press report:

> did not interfere with the press or public, but permitted the proceedings, so far as they went, to be conducted without the names of parties or the nature of the charge being mentioned. Four prisoners were brought into the Court. The first, who was not placed in the dock, but allowed to stand beside it, was a faultlessly dressed young gentleman of twenty-two, clean shaven, dark of complexion, with fair hair. Nothing was said to identify him...The other prisoners, who were placed in the dock, were two youths of 15 and 17, roughly dressed, and of untidy, unwashed appearance, and a man of 24 of the same class. The charge against all the prisoners is understood to be one of a repulsive and unreportable character and to have arisen in a squalid neighbourhood.

The press succeeded in learning the identity of the distinguished young gentleman, and it was reported: "The Prince was dressed in a frock coat and wore lavender gloves. He was accommodated with a chair at the side of the dock."

By now he'd also concocted the alibi that he'd gone to the house under the impression there would be a woman waiting for him, suggesting it was not uncommon on the Continent for men and boys to go about touting to take men to brothels.

The case was sent to trial; the Prince and Chandler charged with committing an act of gross indecency, and Chandler, Sherman and Gerry having been parties to, and conspired for the same.* In his address to the jury, the counsel for the prosecution bravely suggested that:

> although the four defendants were of different class – one being of the highest birth and the other three men of quite a low order – he felt certain they would treat them all exactly on the same footing.

He further added:

> The offence with which they have been charged was far too common in the metropolis, and therefore, so far as the charge was concerned, the case was quite an ordinary one.

The landlord's testimony was contradicted by the police who said that it was only possible to see nine inches of the bed through the hole in the door. Judge and jury agreed that there was no evidence on which to support the accusation. To loud applause in the courtroom the Prince was discharged. Chandler and Sherman received ten and eight months respectively. Gerry, whom the Judge was convinced had intended blackmail, received two years hard labour.

While Prince Francis Joseph had been exonerated by a British court, his regiment and family made their own judgement. His commission in the Austrian hussars was withdrawn, and in early 1903 he departed for, or was packed off to the never-never land of ne'er-do-wells, Australia, where under the discreet guise of 'Count de Nieva' – a secondary title of his father's, he shot pigeons, attended balls, and cooled his heels. Summoned back to Europe that September, he was

---

* Observing the case from a distance, an unworldly American commentator thought royal intermarriage was the problem: "I cannot help thinking that their minds might be improved, as well as their bodies, if only they would imitate their aristocracy and marry sound American girls." [*The Pittsburg Press*, 12 October 1902, p14.]

placed under curatel, which reduced his legal status to that of a minor or lunatic, with the administration of his affairs vested in a trustee. Nonetheless, by 1909 he succeeded in being the victim of a swindler who passed himself off as a member of the wealthy Vanderbilt family, and encouraged him to unsuccessfully woo an American heiress. At the commencement of the First World War, the Prince's commission was restored. While a prisoner of war on the Italian island of Ischia, he died at the age of forty, allegedly of heart failure.

As the Braganza case shows, even royalty wasn't safe from the risk of extortion. During the hearings there had been a telling incident, as one reporter captured:

> a respectably-dressed man standing at the back of the Court suddenly interrupted the magistrate's remarks by shouting at the top of his voice "It's blackmail. Blackmail." With the judge calling for his removal, the gentleman went on: "I shall not go until I have said all I have got to say. I tell you it is blackmail. I have been through it all myself, and I know all about it."

Not every blackmailer hailed from the lowest strata. In 1927, the periodical *John Bull* informed its readers that almost forty years before, a then "very popular young man about town" had:

> in the exuberance of youth...penned a letter full of airy banter in which he touched upon certain subjects which are generally missing from the compositions of the polite letter-writer, explaining his reasons for not being able to accept an invitation to Cleveland Street...

– this being the house at No.19, which was at the centre of the notorious 1889 scandal.

Following the flight of its occupants, and the dispersal of the contents to the four winds, the "extremely silly" letter, with its signature, eventually fell into the hands of "the younger son of a once-notorious nobleman." Allegedly, this scion of the aristocracy was being hounded in his middle-age by creditors, and viewed the letter as an answer to his predicament, for its author had "attained a great and distinguished position in Parliament."

The aristocrat first wrote to the politician to test the waters:

> asking if he would 'lend' him £5,000 'to buy a literary paper'. The request, coming from one who was practically a stranger, elicited a curt refusal in the handwriting of a secretary.

He had then telephoned the M.P. and made his demand known. The £5,000 was swiftly handed over and the letter returned, but when the money was spent, the extortionist informed his victim that he possessed a photographic facsimile. *John Bull* alleged:

> No semi-savage bred in the gutter of the criminal underworld ever acted with such heartless cruelty or behaved so meanly and contemptibly...As his victim rose higher in public estimation so did he grade the amount of his hush-money until it was as much as the statesman could do to keep out of debt, although the income from his estates was a considerable one. Year after year the blackmailer lived in luxury and actually gave dinner parties at fashionable hotels to which near relations of his victim were invited.

Supposedly, only the M.P.'s death at a comparatively young age from heart disease released him from the grip of his persecutor. According to *John Bull*, when the politician was given the fatal diagnosis of his condition, he murmured to his doctor, "Thank God, at any rate it means no more of ———."

John Bull's then editor, Edward Roffe Thompson, vouched for the truth of the story, claiming that when the blackmailer's annuity ceased:

> The loss of income sent him to the Continent to avoid his creditors, but he is now living in a cheap flat in suburban London...we cannot identify him further...unless the grave intervenes he will one day decorate the dock at the Old Bailey before we hear the last of him.

Given the hints to the blackmailer's identity, including mention of a literary magazine, one obvious candidate would be Lord Alfred Douglas. In 1893, when Oscar Wilde was being blackmailed by a rent

boy, Alfred Wood, Douglas wrote to his friend Maurice Schwabe:*
"That boy is the worst blackguard of all the renters in London." It
would be damning if, in an hour of desperate need, the erratic and
spendthrift Douglas had stooped to become the same. With heart
disease claiming an impressive number of M.P.s in the 1920s, the
identity of the victim presently remains obscure.

For prominent and respected gentlemen there had to be a better way
of having an illicit sex life. While the *John Bull* report underlined the
grim reality that potential blackmailers lurked everywhere, putting
oneself into the hands of low-life procurers was an infinitely greater
risk. How much safer then, if the introductions could be arranged by
persons of one's own class. It was this very thought that occurred to
the esteemed Cyril Flower, Lord Battersea. Only he would make it a
reality.

---

* Maurice Salis Schwabe, later Maurice Shaw (1871–1915). As well as his affair with Douglas
for whom he was "My darling Pretty," he'd been bedded by Wilde. He was sent to Sydney by
his parents to avoid scandal, and died fighting in France in World War I.

7. NAPLES 1897

The past eight years have witnessed such sweeping changes, that Naples is a different city materially if not morally.

So observed the British Consul for South Italy, Eustace Neville-Rolfe* in 1897. Despite the civic improvements, its social eternities remained. As a guidebook by Augustus Hare† reminded readers:

Naples has been truly described as 'a paradise inhabited by devils'; but they are lively and amusing devils…always laughing, except if thwarted, when they will stab their best friends without a pang…Almost everybody in Naples cheats, but they cheat in as lively and pleasant a manner as is compatible with possibilities.

Hare also warned of "the horrible condiment called *Pizza*" which was "esteemed a feast".

Another popular guidebook, *Mediterranean Winter Resorts*, whose English author was another hyphenated Eustace – Eustace Reynolds-

---

* Eustace Neville-Rolfe (1845–1908), later Consul-General. A highly cultured Norfolk squire who was married with three daughters, Rolfe settled permanently at Naples allegedly due to his dislike of England's climate and its politics. He authored popular guide books, and also ran an iron foundry which manufactured replicas of famous bronzes from Naples and Pompeii. For the Neapolitan upper class, such trade constituted his social death warrant. The autobiography of Norman Douglas, who was a friend, suggests he was well-known in expatriate homosexual circles, although his official role naturally led to wide acquaintance. [Douglas Sladen, *Twenty Years Of My Life*, Constable, London 1915, p207; Arthur Lambton *My Story*, Hurst & Blackett, London 1925, p79; Norman Douglas, *Looking Back: An Autobiographical Excursion*, Harcourt, Brace and Company, New York 1933, p364.]
† Augustus John Cuthbert Hare (1834–1903), travel guidebook author and memorialist.

Ball,* considered it prudent to devote one and a half pages to cautioning his genteel readership regarding Neapolitan 'Sharks'. These he identified as:

> (1) boatmen, (2) cab-drivers (3) guides, porters, hotel touts, etc. Of these the boatmen are the most truculent and rapacious…Usually for foreigners a great theatrical show is made, the money handed back, or thrown on the ground; but simple indifference, in this and all such demonstrations will command respect.

By 1908 the advisory had vanished from the guidebook: perhaps British *froideur* had chilled the more mercenary of the populous. The other Eustace – Neville-Rolfe, was optimistic: "the time is coming when a Neapolitan will answer a letter, keep an appointment, have some little regard for the truth." More regretfully he noted: "so much of the local colour has faded away…Things move quickly in these days, but much of the picturesqueness must last our time."

'See Naples and die' stated the proverb, and for many, the old sentiment still rang true: "the most beautiful shore not only of Italy but of all the globe of earth." With half-a-million densely housed inhabitants, and a lively theatre, opera, concert season, Naples was, as another guidebook enthused: "a delightful winter residence for those fond of pleasure and gaiety." Reynolds-Ball agreed: "A few weeks stay in this lively city is a good cure for ennui." Even so, the turmoil of Neapolitan streets, where life was fully lived, could come as a shock: "I thought London noisy, but compared to Naples, it is tranquillity itself," wrote an Irishman, Hamilton Geale:

> the vast and motley crowds of Naples whirl about in groups like eddies…in their wild enjoyment of the present hour, the most reckless and abandoned population in the world.

The worldly Lord Ronald Gower agreed; however the city's inhabitants were too much for even his broad tastes. Visiting in 1879, he damned it as: "the most over-rated place in Christendom. A dirty, unhealthy town, with a ruffianly population of filthy beggars, insolent cabmen, and dissolute upper crust." Visiting again fifteen years later,

---

* Eustace Alfred Reynolds-Ball (1858–1925), prolific travel guidebook author.

his opinion hadn't improved: "A more deformed, bestial-looking lot of men and women than the Neapolitans it would be hard to match." Naples certainly carried a reputation. There was also its surrounds. Even Ronnie confessed that next to an Italian sunset:

> the prettiest thing at Sorrento was a concert of peasant boys and girls, given in the hotel; one of the latter was really beautiful, with a profile like a cameo; and two of the boys might have sat for angels to Raffaelle.

While Dr. Johnson declared "almost all that sets us above savages, has come from the shores of the Mediterranean," his biographer James Boswell was led to confess:

> During my stay in Naples I was truly libertine. I ran after girls without restraint. My blood was inflamed by the burning climate, and my passions were violent. I indulged them. My mind had almost nothing to do with it.

Another admirer of Italian shores was the soldier Kenneth Searight*, who opined: "we are all of us God and brute beast." Southern Italy was where one went to self-realise both.

Fornication on the Grand Tour had been considered a rite of passage, and a hundred years on, the Vesuvian delights of the Bay of Naples were undiminished. Together with Capri, Taormina and Venice it was also heavily pencilled on the *Belle Époque* itineraries of those seeking the embrace of Greek Love. The abundance of beautiful willing youths, Italian tolerance of homosexuality, the cheap cost of living, and the presence of like-minded expatriates, made it a mecca in that respect. There was a belief that the further south one travelled, the warmer the reception. Writing to Havelock Ellis in 1892, John Addington Symonds confided:

---

* Arthur Kenneth Searight (1883–1957), British Army officer in India and the Middle East; lover of Italy; and creator of the international language Sona. Described as possessing "a romantic Bryonic temperament" and "perpetually in love with some boy or other," he was the author of six manuscript volumes of erotica, of which one volume, *Paidikion: An Anthology or The Book Of Hyakinthos And Narkissos*, (unpublished: The Carl A. Kroch Library), survives. [Ronald Hyam, *Understanding the British Empire*, Cambridge University Press, 2010, p454; Timothy D'Arch Smith, 'Enumerating The Enfer', *The Times Literary Supplement*, 29 May 1981, p601.]

A male prostitute whom I once saw at Naples told me he was Venetian, but he had come to Naples because at Venice he only found custom with Englishmen, Swedes and Russians, whereas at Naples he could live in excellent Italian society and be abundantly supported.

Over sixty years before, Count von Platen* had noted in his diary, "here in Naples love between men is so common that one cannot choose to refuse the most daring demands." The daring went both ways. The twenty-nine-year-old Norman Douglas,† who purchased a villa at nearly Posillipo in 1896, attempted to seduce a Neapolitan girl, but ended up with her prettier young brother:

the boy fell in love with me desperately, as only a southern boy of his age can do; so blindly that at a hint from myself he would have abandoned his work and family and everything else. It came in a flash, and he did not care who knew it. And the queer thing is (queer, at least, to our English way of thinking) that his mother and sister were not in the least surprised; they thought it the most natural thing in the world. *"L'avete svegliato,"* the mother said; you have woken him up.

In southern Italy, adolescent homosexual experience was traditionally

---

* Karl August Georg Maximilian, Count von Platen-Hallermünde (1796–1835), German poet and dramatist.

† (George) Norman Douglas (1868–1952) British author, including of *Old Calabria* (1915) and *South Wind* (1917), honorary citizen of Capri, whom by his sixties "could endure the society of fewer and fewer people over the age of fourteen". A dispassionate observer, the man-of-letters Sir Peter Quennell, recalled: "'Uncle Norman' loved the young, both platonically and passionately, and the young were drawn to him…his natural cynicism had simplified his view of life, and made him infinitely tolerant…When I knew him he was a cheerful old Garden-God, staunch, resolute and undismayed…I doubt if he had ever felt a regret, remorse or repentance …*angst*…would have been far beyond his comprehension." Typically, in 1911 he took Eric Wolton, a twelve-year-old East End boy he'd met the previous year, to Calabria with him, with parental approval. Wolton later married and became a police officer in East Africa, writing to Douglas: "They were happy times too Doug were'nt [*sic*] they, I have no evil thoughts about them although I am different today than I was then…I want you to understand Doug that you are more to me than ever you were. The difference is now that I am old enough to realise it." [Paul Fussell, *Abroad: British Literary Traveling Between the Wars*, Oxford University Press, 1982, p130; Peter Quennell, *The Wanton Chase*, Atheneum, New York 1980, pp52-53; Michael Allan (ed.), *Dear Doug! Letters to Norman Douglas from Eric Wolton, René Mari, Marcel Mercier and Ettore Masciandaro and A Selection of Letters from Emilio Papa.*, W. Neugebauer Verlag, Graz, 2008, pp18-19. See also: Rachel Hope Cleves, *Unspeakable: A Life Beyond Sexual Morality*, University of Chicago Press, 2020, and also its review by the William A. Percy Foundation: https://web.archive.org/web/20230313053629/https://wapercyfoundation.org/?page_id=1056]

tolerated as a channel for the sexual energy of its youths, in order to preserve the virginity of unmarried girls, in which family honour resided. Such experience was viewed not as an anomaly, but as an expression of virility, and preparatory and complementary to future heterosexual relations. Casual prostitution at all ages also thrived. There was an ambivalent attitude to foreign men associating with boys, but provided the relations were temporary, pragmatism generally prevailed. Sex was a prime commodity in Naples.* As well as prostitutes generally, the city was notorious for the number of boys offering themselves for a few coins.†

In 1897, another Englishman arrived in Naples seeking rest and pleasure. However, this was someone infinitely grander. After the failure of his prime ministership, and an almost psychological collapse, the Earl of Rosebery had semi-retired from politics, and would spend late January and February in the city he'd loved since his youth. "I certainly do not feel to care about the North of Italy so much as the south," he wrote, "The people are so lifeless in comparison, and the scenery round Florence is so comparatively tame."

Lord Rosebery was an international celebrity. Margot Asquith‡ quipped that "when the Prince of Wales went up the aisle, he was a nobody compared to Rosebery." Handsome, immensely aristocratic, eloquent of speech, rich beyond imagining, he was the man who had it all. Frederick Rolfe,§ who cadged money from Rosebery, observed him closely at the Venetian home of his good friend Horatio Brown.** In his novel *The Desire And Pursuit Of The Whole* he portrayed him as

---

* Over half-a-century later, the visiting Alfred Kinsey could still write: "I don't suppose we spoke to any person of any age, male or female, in the city who didn't promptly offer to find sexual relations for us." [Wardell Baxter Pomeroy, C. A. Tripp, *Dr. Kinsey and the Institute for Sex Research*, Harper & Row, New York, 1972, p425.]
† So intense was the poverty and competition, when some Italian village boys began trailing Norman Douglas and a friend, one of the boys with them stoned the smallest of their pursuers to drive them away. [Rachel Hope Cleves, *Unspeakable: A Life Beyond Sexual Morality*, The University Of Chicago Press, 2020, p209.]
‡ Emma Alice Margaret 'Margot' Asquith, Countess of Oxford and Asquith, née Tennant, (1864–1945), socialite, author, and wit; wife of H. H. Asquith, Prime Minister 1908–1916.
§ Frederick William Rolfe, (1860–1913), aka 'Baron Corvo': English writer, artist, photographer, eccentric, and literary cult figure. He claimed his false title was gifted to him by an Italian duchess.
** One of the reasons for Horatio Brown's regular return visits to Scotland, accompanied by his servant-companion, ex-gondolier Antonio Salin, was to visit Rosebery. [Leo McKinstry, *Rosebery: Statesman In Turmoil*, John Murray, London 2005, p407.]

Lord Hippis:

> firm, grave, sleek, plump as a church cat…marvellously clean and clear and straight of eye, the very finest flower and quintessence of the last and best which mighty unconquerable England can make of a man.

Yet Rosebery was also neurotic: a highly-strung, lonely insomniac, and deeply secretive, as he had reason to be. Despite being a widower and father of four, rumour stalked him. Following the death in October 1894 of his young private secretary, Francis, Viscount Drumlanrig (Lord Alfred Douglas's brother) in a likely suicide, he was stalked by their father, the unstable Marquess of Queensberry, who believed Rosebery was one of a cabal of, as he put it, "Snob Queers" who'd corrupted his sons. It was rumoured Queensberry had threatened that if Oscar Wilde was not prosecuted, and a verdict of guilty handed down, he would publicly expose senior members of the Liberal Government as homosexuals, including Rosebery. Not least, letters from Queensberry that included insults against Rosebery were submitted as evidence for the defence in Wilde's libel trial against the Marquess. The fact Rosebery's name was mentioned leaked into the public sphere, resulting in further concern for the Government, and crippling stress to Rosebery in the last months of his premiership.

Insomnia may not have been the only reason for the long late night strolls and carriage rides Rosebery indulged in. George Ives recorded in his journal:

> I saw him once at Lord Rothschild's. He was very small but very good looking. He is said by almost everyone to have been a homosexual. I was told by a deputy coroner, that one of the chiefs of the C.I.D., Dr McNaughton,*[sic] told him that the Hyde Park Police had orders never to arrest Lord R. on the principle that too big a fish often breaks the line.

The 7th Earl Spencer,† who came of age before the First World War, found on joining Rosebery's club, the Turf, that its members spoke of the ex-P.M.'s homosexuality "as if it were a well-known fact."

---

* Sir Melville Leslie Macnaghten (1853–1921), Chief Constable (1890), and Assistant Commissioner of Police (1903-1913). Author of the memoir *Days Of My Years* (1915).
† Albert Edward John Spencer, 7th Earl Spencer (1892–1975).

Eustace Neville-Rolfe had been Rosebery's fag-master at Eton, and it was Rosebery who recommended him for the role of Consul following his private appeal to him. Now they renewed their friendship, and being the master of his time, Rosebery enjoyed playing the role of "the flâneur resident" as he put it. In a succession of droll notes, he invited Neville-Rolfe to accompany him on his daily peregrinations:

> "I breakfast at noon now which may be a little early for you."

> "Descend from your heights when you have sufficiently represented the Empire and let us celebrate this glorious day at Camaldoli or elsewhere."

> "Shall we take a prowl this afternoon? Pepe, Museum, Duke della Regina* or what not?"

The succession of moneyed visitors seeking Neapolitan warmth in that winter of 1897 included Rothschild relations of Rosebery's late wife Hannah. Rosebery lunched with Natty, Lord Rothschild who arrived on his steam yacht, the Veglia, whose lavish appointments were said, "to surpass even Vanderbilt annals of floating fairy palaces." Another yacht, the Rona, owned by the effete Ferdinand de Rothschild,† who was hopelessly infatuated with Rosebery, was also expected. On the 11th of February, Rosebery wrote:

> "My dear Rolfe, Ought we not, if the Rona has not arrived, to try and let Rendel's launch today. The weather is divine."

---

* Carlo Capece-Galeota, Duke della Regina (1824–1908); the premier Neapolitan noble.
† Baron Ferdinand 'Ferdy' James Anselm de Rothschild (1839–1898); Liberal M.P. Second son of the Viennese Baron Anselm Salomon von Rothschild, head of the Austrian branch of the banking family, and his English wife Charlotte von Rothschild née Rothschild. He became a British subject and married his second cousin Evelina de Rothschild, who died in childbirth. His older bachelor brother, Nathaniel Mayer 'Puggy' von Rothschild (1836–1905), was also homosexual, and maintained a long friendship with Philipp, Prince zu Eulenburg-Hertefeld (later to be involved in the famous homosexual scandal of the German Court), despite the latter's anti-Semitism, and bequeathed him a fortune. The Prince wrote to him: "God be praised we have an awareness of our souls locked together in solidarity, that we can think back to our similarly formed, sensitive natures and console each other." [Norman Domeier, Deborah Lucas Schneider (trans.), *The Eulenburg Affair*, Camden House, New York 2015, pp176-177; John C.G. Röhl; Terence F. Cole (trans.) *The Kaiser And His Court*, Cambridge University Press 1994, p55.]

Rendel was George Rendel,* the millionaire son of a celebrated engineer and industrialist. Having spent his earlier life designing gunboats for the British Navy, ill-health prompted his move to a warmer climate. As his second wife was Italian, Italy was an obvious choice, and he accepted an offer from his former business partner, the armaments supplier and naval shipbuilder Armstrongs, to be co-director of their Naples works. While continuing to spend part of every year in England and Switzerland, Rendel lived with his young family at Posillipo in a spectacular castellated residence, the Villa Maraval,† that jutted out into the Bay of Naples. It possessed its own harbour, and an "army of retainers."

Also then resident at the Villa Maraval was another Englishman: a temporary secretary for Rendel who was also acting as tutor to his eight-year-old son. The gentleman's name was Arthur Thorold.‡ A twenty-three-year-old Oxford undergraduate, he was the son of a Lincolnshire rector. Almost six foot tall, with dark brown hair and brown eyes, Arthur had an imposing presence: a passion for rowing had made him very well built. Impressive rather than classically handsome, he possessed a distinctive self-assurance. Though his face had a serious cast, which reflected his upbringing, this was somewhat of a mask, for he possessed a ready smile. At a corner of his lower lip there was also a red birthmark. Like the stain of a trickle of wine, it gave him an almost rakish appearance that seemed to hint at – if not reckless abandon, definitely something more. And there *was* more. A surviving photograph of a seated Arthur in bulging trousers suggests he was blessed with a teacup-rattling endowment. Such a legacy goes some way to explaining his brazen self-confidence. It can also create its own discreet notoriety. Like not a few of his fellow Oxonians, Arthur Thorold was ardently bisexual.

He was also keenly interested in singing and acting, and the theatre generally. It was these temptations, and other social distractions of university life amidst the sons of privilege under the 'dreaming spires', that had gone to his head, leading to him not completing his degree. Given he'd failed to exercise self-control at Oxford, Naples was the least likely place for him to regain it. "No country so much as Italy inspires one with the sense of the infinite *potentialities of life*," another

---

* George Wightwick Rendel (1833–1902), engineer, and naval architect.
† Today known as the Villa Rocca Matilde and Villa Lauro. The estate has been subdivided.
‡ Arthur Charles Campbell Thorold (1873–1939).

Victorian bachelor would write: "Intensity of life and exquisite beauty are the two chief messages of Italy." Adding to this euphoria, the Villa Maraval's breathtaking panoramas of endless azure sea and sky promised a world of limitless possibilities.

"I had a divine expedition with Rendel yesterday," Rosebery informed Rolfe in a note dated the 20th of February. George Rendel was "the most stately and courteous of men," and it would have been characteristic of him to introduce his gentleman secretary to Lord Rosebery. Given Rosebery was the subject of endless gossip and conjecture, not least for the homosexual demi-monde, Arthur Thorold would have been doubly keen to make the acquaintance.

As Rosebery's string of private secretaries over the years proved, he had an eye for "amiable young men with good looks." Charming, courteous, ever so correct, and ever so well built, young Arthur Thorold would have made an impression. As his later actions were to show, when opportunities for social advancement presented themselves, he was also a young man with plenty of front in every respect. Thrusting even.

During his Naples stay, Rosebery may also have been introduced to another gentleman who was also wintering in the south – a tall, lean, dark-haired and moustachioed thirty-one-year-old Scotsman with ice-blue eyes named Bernard Fraser.* A rich worldly homosexual, Fraser was a regular figure in London Society. As such, Rosebery may already have known him. Whatever the case, it was during these months that Fraser befriended Arthur Thorold. The young Oxford undergraduate was about to get an even richer schooling in the high life he'd set his sights on.

A further wealthy gentleman of homosexual leaning arrived in Naples that February – William Lygon, the Earl Beauchamp.† Only twenty-five years old, Byronically handsome, and known to family and friends as 'Boom', deference had already bestowed him the role of Mayor of Worcestor, while his charm, conviviality and splendid inheritance

---

* (John) Bernard Fraser-Ross (1866–1929).
† William 'Boom' Lygon, 7th Earl Beauchamp (1872–1938), Governor of New South Wales 1899–1901, Liberal politician, including leader of the Liberal Party in the House of Lords; Lord Warden of the Cinque Ports. Married Lady Lettice Grosvenor, with whom he had seven children. In 1931, in lieu of arrest for homosexuality, he was forced into self-exile until 1937.

made him a cynosure of all circles, not least bachelor ones. Accompanied by his sister, he was on his way to Rome, where like the old-family Catholics the Lygons were, an audience with the Pope was on the cards. Also on the cards may have been a catch-up with Bernard Fraser and Lord Rosebery.

During his own sojourn, Rosebery looked to purchase a villa, finally managing to secure for a £16,000 fortune the spectacular Villa Delahante, which as he confided to a friend, "has been the dream of my life." He'd visited it as a child, and in 1882 had shown it to Hannah, whom he wrote, "was amazed and stupefied at the beauty of the place." Once loaned by its owner to the Empress Eugénie, it stood in an immense garden of groves of evergreen oaks, olives, and arbutus that sloped down to a curve in the Bay of Naples. Maintained by thirty gardeners, it was a secluded world within itself. Besides the main residence, there were two smaller guest houses, plus a pavilion, and private harbour. 'Hebe', an anonymous scribe for *The Gentlewoman and Modern Life* magazine, was driven to exclaim: "The view from the windows of Versuvius, Castellamare, and Sorrento is alone worth a journey to see!"

At the beginning of March, Rosebery returned to England, but in his absence, Neville-Rolfe assisted with getting the villa's gardens, drainage, and decoration in order. As Rosebery's letters show, Neville-Rolfe devoted himself to the task with a fagmaster's attention to detail. The villa would eventually become a treasure house. On this matter, 'Hebe' had an equally firm opinion: "There are many 'house-proud' women, but very few house-proud men. Lord Rosebery is one of the few":

> With an inborn talent for acquiring as well as appreciating rare *objects d'art*, Lord Rosebery has collected together a wondrous array of brocades, enamels, tapestries, statuary, wherewith to beautify his villa. For old *Capo di Monte* he has a special weakness.

In November 1897, in one of his letters to Neville-Rolfe, Rosebery informed him – leaving it to the last as a teasing revelation: "P.S. Thorold (late of Villa Maraval) has written to suggest himself as agent for the Villa!"

The postscript with its exclamation mark indicates a very mutual awareness of the young man. By this time Arthur Thorold had also returned to England to complete his Oxford degree. Rosebery's news apparently flustered Rolfe.* In a subsequent letter, Rosebery reassured him: "I only told you of Thorold's application as a joke. But I am seriously concerned at the trouble I am giving you."

The exchange is certainly intriguing, and the knowingness may be a wry nod to something beyond gentlemanly surfaces. However, as dapper and cocky as Arthur Thorold may have looked, particularly in a light summer suit draping his young and slung rower's body, Rosebery wasn't buying – or hiring. He already had a Neapolitan agent, and the offer clearly wasn't appealing enough for him to consider a replacement.

Rosebery was a shrewd man-of-the-world: a sun-king whose life was lived surrounded by those seeking favours. Like Arthur Thorold, he also maintained a false façade. It's very possible he saw the ambitious young man for exactly who he was, and held reservations. He may also have recalled Plato's account of Socrates, when momentarily overcome by a glimpse of what lay beneath the cloak of the handsome young Charmides, and the philosopher's resolution not to become a youth's trophy.†

A few weeks later Rosebery would be more concerned over another interloper, when the Prince of Wales informed him that Oscar Wilde had become his near-neighbour at Posillipo. In one of Rosebery's diva moods, he wrote to Neville-Rolfe that it "makes me fear that the villa will be uninhabitable." Replying in a letter marked 'Very Secret', Rolfe reassured him that:

> He and Lord Alfred Douglas have definitely parted and Wilde lives a completely secluded life…He looks thoroughly abashed, much like a whipped hound…I really cannot think he will be any trouble to you, and after all the poor devil must live somewhere.

---

* Rolfe's reply is not with the Rosebery Papers in the National Library of Scotland, but may survive amongst the inaccessible Rosebery papers at Dalmeny.
† "I saw inside his cloak and caught fire, and could possess myself no longer; and I thought none was so wise in love-matters as Cydias, who in speaking of a beautiful boy recommends someone to 'beware of coming as a fawn before the lion, and being seized as his portion of flesh'; for I too felt I had fallen prey to some such creature." – *Charmides*: Plato [H. N. Fowler, W.R.M. Lamb (trans.), *Plato*, Vol 8, Heinemann, London 1927, p17.]

Adding to the circus, Rolfe enlightened Rosebery about another local incident. Norman Douglas (known to them as 'the bombardier'), and a diplomat friend of his, had been misidentified by the press:

> The papers a little while ago had a paragraph saying that the 'bombardier' was Lord A.D. and a Spanish diplomat (who had been chief Secretary for years to the Spanish Ambassador at the Vatican and was staying with him was O.W.!!) You can realise the bombardier's wrath!

Despite his pariah status, Oscar Wilde was still able to enjoy the Neapolitan scenery, writing to a friend: "It is not for pleasure that I come here, though pleasure, I am glad to say, walks all round."

It was for these reasons and more that Rosebery's purchase of the Villa Delahante only served to further fuel rumours about his proclivities. *Reynolds's Newspaper* had begun featuring a regular column of high-life gossip and insinuation titled 'The Secret History Of To-Day'. It was penned by the paper's radical editor W.M. Thompson, and later, the pseudonymous 'Frou Frou'.* In May 1902 it printed: "Lord Rosebery has a villa at Naples," slyly adding for readers who'd never ventured further than Margate: "'Sir Richard Calmundy' gives a striking picture of life at Naples."

The reference was to the sensational novel of the hour, *The History of Sir Richard Calmady: A Romance*,† in which the city was described as: "unrivalled all the western world over for natural beauty, for spiritual and moral grossness!" In 1908, the Rosebery gossip found its way into a history of homosexuality *The Intersexes*, which was pseudonymously published in an edition of just 125 copies, probably at Naples, by an expatriate American, Edward Prime-Stevenson:‡

---

* Possibly a pseudonym of (Robert) Wherry Anderson (1864–1937), who was responsible for the paper's 'Personal' column, and a member of the Committee of the National Liberal Club. He also wrote under the pen name 'Gracchus'. The writer, poet, politician and teacher, Allen Upward (1863–1926) would borrow the column's title for a novel: *Secret History Of To-Day: Being Revelations Of A Diplomatic Spy* (Chapman & Hall, 1904). [New Year's Greetings, *Reynolds's Newspaper*, 1 January 1905, p1.]

† By Lucas Malet, the pseudonym of Mary St. Leger Harrison. After becoming a Catholic she removed some chapters that had drawn criticism.

‡ Edward Irenaeus Prime-Stevenson (1858–1942), expatriate American author and music critic. For a biography, see the introduction and appendices of the 2003 Broadview Press edition of his novel *Imre: A Memorandum*, edited by James J. Gifford.

One eminent personage of British political life, who once reached the highest honours in a career that has appeared to be taken up or thrown by with curious capriciousness or hesitancy, is a constant absentee in his beautiful homeland in Southern Europe, where only gentle rumours of his racial homosexuality reach his birth-land.

Just one year later, Rosebery's Italian dream was over. Exhibiting his curious capriciousness, in 1909 he gave the Villa Delahante, which he'd so longed for, to the British Government as a summer residence for its Italian ambassador.* Whatever he'd hoped its possession would fulfil within him, like so much else he'd desired and gained, 'the dream of his life' had only delivered a lonely emptiness.

As for Arthur Thorold: following his time in Naples, he would bear "a love for Italy and for all things Italian" for the remainder of his life. Bernard Fraser returned to Italy four years later. However, the meeting of he and Thorold in Naples that year of 1897 would alter both their lives, and those of others, forever.

---

* In the lean post-War years, the estate, now named Villa Rosebery, was considered an extravagance by the British Government, and was returned to the Primrose family, who attempted to sell it, before the 6th Earl presented it to the Italian state in 1932.

FLORES · CVRAT · DEVS ·

CYRIL FLOWER.

Bookplate of Cyril Flower.
Flores Curat Deus: God Cares for the Flowers

Furze Down House, Streatham, 1872.

A very aesthetic young man.
Cyril Flower in costume as Victor Hugo's Ruy Blas.

Cyril Flower as Mrs. Sebright, Cambridge A.D.C.

Lord Ronald as Mrs. Rabbits, Cambridge A.D.C.

The great world in Rotten Row, Hyde Park.

Cyril Flower by Frederick Sandys, 1872.

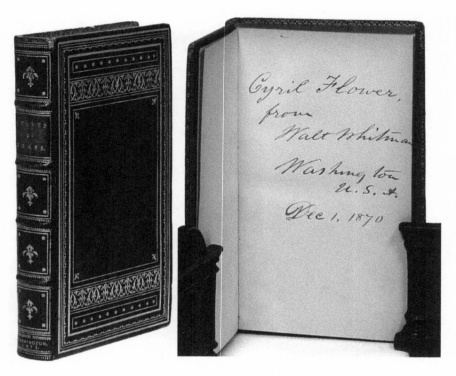

Cyril Flower's copy of Leaves of Grass.

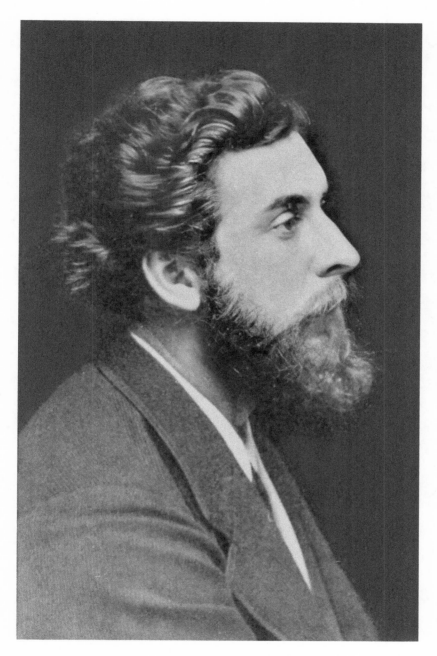

Cyril Flower.

Constance Flower photographed by Cyril Flower.

Lord Battersea as Lord Hunsdon.
The Duchess of Devonshire's Ball, 1897.

Lord & Lady Battersea in later life.

The Pleasaunce.

The Pleasaunce, aerial view.

A snuggery, The Pleasaunce.

The Grass Walk and Dovecote, The Pleasaunce.

Pergola Walk, The Pleasaunce.

The Cloisters, The Pleasaunce today.

Lord Battersea's bedroom by Carlo Bugatti, Surrey House.
Photo by James H.L. Hyatt.

First Floor Corridor, Surrey House.
Photo by James H.L. Hyatt.

A wonderful statuary marble figure, with marble base, of **KING SARDANAPALUS**, by the late distinguished American sculptor, William Wetmore Story.

Size, 5 ft. 6 in. wide by 5 ft. high by 3 ft. 3 in. deep

King Sardanapalus was a luxurious monarch who lived 817 B.C. This magnificent piece was in the possession of the late Lord Battersea

To view and for price apply:

J. & A. CREW

34, CUMBERLAND MARKET, LONDON, N.W.1

Telephone No.: Museum 2337

A 1930 advertisement for Lord Battersea's doppelgänger statue of Sardanapalus. J. & A. Crew were a firm of masonry contractors and stone merchants.

William (Cory) Johnson

Frederic Myers, 1873.

The Marquess of Lorne, later Duke of Argyll.

Reginald Brett, later Lord Esher, photographed by Cyril Flower.

Lord Rosebery, 1890s

Alfred de Rothschild as Henri III,
the Duchess of Devonshire's Ball, 1897.

Lord Euston.

Lord Harcourt.

Lord Beauchamp, 1902.

Lord Ronald Gower.

Frank Shackleton.

Arthur Brown on his Gordon Bennett Napier.

Princess Louise in Canada, 1880. Left to right, standing: Dr Royle; Princess Louise, Marchioness of Lorne; Captain (later Lieut-Colonel) Arthur Collins, Robert Hawthorn Collins. Seated: Hon. Mrs. Langham, Prince Leopold, Sir J. McNeill, Lady Pelly, Hon. Alexander 'Alick' Yorke.

PART II.

Hidden Scandal

8. CARELESS PASSION

The Battersea Scandal began, as scandals often did, with the discovery of letters. Like the fourteen shillings of the Cleveland Street telegraph boy, this small event was to have unimagined consequences.

This time the setting was not the heaving metropolis of London, but far away on England's southern coast at Plymouth. Here in 1902 at the Royal Navy's Devonport base were berthed two training ships for boys. Two perfect petri dishes in which the seed of sodomy could easily take root.

The minimum entrance age for the Navy then was fifteen – although privately operated training-ships (working under a Treasury grant scheme) accepted lads as young as twelve, and until the 1890s, even eleven-year-olds. Upon recruitment the boys were called – or 'rated' as it was termed, 'Second Class boys'. After a year they became 'First Class boys', and at eighteen were rated ordinary seamen. The pay was miserably low: a Second Class boy earned 6d a day; £9 2s 6d a year. Like all Royal Navy seamen, trainees also had to pay for any replacement uniforms from their salary. When they became First Class boys the pay rose to 7d a day, plus a potential shilling a month for special good conduct, and a £2 10s annual allowance for clothing. The social reformer Lord Shaftesbury considered the ships of "unspeakable value" for preparing "the most destitute lads" for a marine life.

The social difference between such boys, and those who trained elsewhere to become officers, was vast. The fifteen-month training of a naval cadet cost £200 pounds in combined fees and expenses, plus £50 pounds a year for five years until they became a lieutenant – sums far beyond the means of working class families, or even lower middle class ones.

The two Devonport training ships were the H.M.S. Impregnable, and the H.M.S. Lion. On board the Impregnable alone there were 950 boys, and at one stage in the 1890s, over 1,500. With the race of the British Government against Germany to build its fleet in the 1890s, the Navy's demand for manpower was insatiable. This had led to shocking overcrowding and bad sanitation on the training ships. So tight was space that hammocks had needed to be slung underneath one another, and even in the schoolrooms. Epidemics of fever and mumps spread from hammock to hammock, leading to alarming rates of death that became a scandal. By the turn of the century, some improvements in conditions had been made, but in November 1902 the Navy announced that the training ships were to be eventually scrapped.

Discipline on the ships was extremely strict: canings were considered a light punishment by the authorities, and took place in front of all the crew for maximum humiliation. Although the Government denied it, the Humanitarian League alleged that floggings also took place – i.e. the birch rod was steeped in brine before being applied to bare flesh. On H.M.S. Lion, boys who failed to achieve proficiency in swimming were caned by default: the punishment being considered better than their drowning. In one month alone, 126 boys went under the rod. The zealous Commander of the Lion who instituted this regime was John de Mestre Hutchinson.

Zeal. That is the word, and its adjective, which repeatedly appears on Commander Hutchinson's service record. "Great zeal, tact and ability." "Very zealous and correct in his duties and takes a great interest in his men." "A most zealous, loyal and capable officer with very high abilities." And not least: "A thorough seaman." He was certainly that. When Hutchinson died as an Admiral in 1932, as requested in his will he was buried at sea.

In early 1902, Hutchinson would have been especially on his mettle. That March was a momentous one at the naval base. On the afternoon of the 8th, the new King Edward VII, accompanied by

Queen Alexandra and their daughter Princess Victoria, arrived at Devonport for the first part of a royal tour of the district.

"Soon after four o'clock the crowds that lined the route from the Park steps to the Dockyard gates settled down to await the arrival of the Royal visitors," reported a local paper:

> The bluejackets stood at their posts resting on their rifles with fixed bayonets, and the police patrolled the road on each side. The beautiful effect of the decorations had been enhanced by more garlands and flags…The sailor boys in the Dockyard were provided with lamps, but these were not required, for the King and Queen reached their yacht before sunset…All the ships in the harbour were dressed in rainbow fashion…

On the deck of the royal yacht, the Victoria and Albert, officers of the base were waiting to greet the genial royal party. Amongst them was Commander Hutchinson.

Royal tours have forever served as an excellent excuse to clean, repair and tidy every facility in the general locale, however unlikely that it may be inspected or even glimpsed. For the armed services this is especially the case. The weeks preceding the royal tour would have plunged the naval base into a flurry of preparations and general alertness. The boys of H.M.S. Lion would have been put to ensuring its surfaces were cleaned and polished till they gleamed. Their personal 'kit' would have received an equal thorough going over and inspection.

It may have been during this time of febrile alertness that Hutchinson's attention was first drawn to a series of envelopes containing remittances that were being received by one of his trainees, a sixteen-year-old named Albert Collins.

Collins's service record states that he held the rank of First Class boy, having joined the Navy the previous June. It also details he was born in March 1886, was five foot one inch in height, had brown hair, grey eyes, and possessed a 'fresh complexion'.

A part of Hutchinson's zealous care for the welfare of his young charges was ensuring that their contacts with the civilian world were as correct and above board as both the Navy and their parents would have wished. This included at least a cursory review of the mail they received and sent. Like the Internet today, the potential dangers lurking in postal communications for vulnerable youth was something their guardians were particularly conscious of. Epistolary flirtations, improprieties, and blackmails were the very stuff of novels and scandals of the period. As a result of Hutchinson's suspicions, one of the letters was opened and read. Its contents were perturbing: indicative of an illicit relationship with an adult male. The clear grey eyes of young Albert Collins had seen something of life.

While some worldly observers have suggested 'rum, bum and baccy' could have been the Royal Navy's unofficial motto,* it officially viewed homosexuality in the gravest possible terms: not only as contradictory to the laws of God and Nature, but a dire threat to the discipline vital for its functioning. Homosexuality was a court-martial offence that resulted in immediate dismissal, and the Royal Navy punished those who engaged in it with a ferocity beyond even that of civil society.

Nonetheless, in the Navy's exclusively male world, where boys and men lived cheek by jowl, bathed together in communal bathrooms, and slept in adjoining swaying hammocks, eros was as ever-present as ozone. The awareness of the desire that floated below the surface of naval life, and the ambiguous attitude to it, is indicated by the jokes, lingo, and lore. The expression 'chuff for duff' referred to the carryings-on bartered for extra pudding, while The Golden Rivet – the mythical final rivet hammered into a ship, allegedly of gold, and which naive new recruits were invited into the vessel's bowels to bend over to inspect – with predictable results, was a source of amusement for generations of sailors. The ambivalent attitude is well-conveyed in the lyrics of one ribald sailor song:

> Backside rules the navy.
> Backside rules the sea.
> If you wanna get some bum,
> better get it from your chum,

---

* When the Royal Navy experienced a moral panic over homosexuality in the 1960s, its senior legal officer privately wrote: "Senior naval officers have warned me that they reckon that at least 50 per cent of the fleet have sinned homosexually." [Michael Smith, "Sacking all gay sailors 'would have scuppered the fleet'", *The Daily Telegraph*, 31 October 2002, p9.]

'cause you'll get no bum from me.

For boys and men, the very allure of heading to sea was the promise of adventure and freedom – escape from stifling convention and social mores. It was considered tradition for older crew members to pair up and mentor young chums – termed 'wingers', because they were taken under the wing of another. While these friendships could be innocent, it was often because, as one recruit recalled, "they were after your cherry". Strong evidence suggests that so long as the encounters were between consenting adult sailors, a blind eye was regularly turned by shipmates and those in authority. There was reluctance to bring shipmates up on such a grave and often difficult-to-prove charge that would immediately destroy their careers, and possibly, their lives. However, the lower deck staunchly disapproved of any coercion of boys by those older than them.

The thoughts of Commander Hutchinson, as he read the letter to Albert Collins, are easy to imagine. He would have viewed it in the first instance as a threat to the virtue of a vulnerable youth, and secondly, as a threat to the internal discipline and honour of his ship.

Letters were discovered in the same hand to another boy sailor by the name of Crawley, but of him, nothing else is known. Hutchinson passed the correspondence on to his superiors at Devonport. The content was more than just a matter of endearments to a lad: it was indicative of a wider soliciting, and was considered so serious that the matter was escalated to the top of the Admiralty, the organisation then responsible for the management of the Royal Navy. At the head of its command sat the Sea Lords – a clutch of admirals and civilian grandees, usually politicians, officially known as Lords of the Admiralty. In 1902, the First Lord of the Admiralty was a respected statesman and colonial administrator, the Earl of Selborne.

After reviewing the matter, the collective decision of these distinguished gentlemen was to call in Scotland Yard. There the case was placed into the hands of Detective-Inspector Charles Arrow. Energetic but sanguine, Arrow was already on his way to becoming famous in his profession. When the young Albert Collins next stepped ashore, it was under police watch, and he was followed.

The personal history of Albert Collins bears echoes of the Cleveland

Street Scandal, and its telegraph boys. Before joining the Navy at fifteen, Collins had worked as a groom, and as a messenger boy for a new London enterprise that would soon become famed: The District Messenger Company.* Providing express delivery of messages and parcels, and other concierge services, just like the General Post Office with its telegraph boys, who were held to the highest standards of trust and propriety, the company employed spritely lads as the means of delivery. Clients paid one guinea a year for an electric callbox that could summon a boy messenger, or a cab, policeman, or the fire brigade. The Gaiety Theatre even mounted a musical farce, *The Messenger Boy*, that proved a smash hit. Its hero, Tommy Bang, enabled the line "Go Bang!"

Teenage messenger boys were then a common sight in the metropolis. Like G.P.O. lads, those of The District Messenger Company were also outfitted in blue serge uniforms with silver-plate buttons. Rather than circular hard caps bearing the silvered letters G.P.O. surmounted by the Crown, they sported equally eye-catching pillbox hats worn chicly on the angle. These featured a silver-plate medallion also polished to flashing brightness. Across their chests lay a diagonal leather strap bearing a hip purse. A few of the boys were even equipped with 'Street Skates' (also called 'Road Rollers'). These were an early version of inline skates, each boot featuring two five-inch high spoked wheels, placed one behind the other.

A reporter was entranced by the sight of one of the modern Mercurys of the District Messenger Company gliding on them, "merrily dodging along the Strand, cutting across the noses of bus horses, and occasionally aiding his progress by clinging on to a friendly hansom." According to a Company representative, the boys "seem to think that

---

* Its full name was The District Messenger and Theatre Ticket Company. Founded in 1890 in emulation of similar successful services in America, until 1898 it was known as The District Messenger Service and News Company. By 1897 it was employing 750 boys, and had 13,000 installed call boxes. In that year, in heavy rain, the Duke of Cambridge reviewed a parade of its young corps in Hyde Park. The service, which at its peak was highly renowned, lasted until the Second World War. By 1940, with boys being evacuated to the country, or filling the jobs of young men gone into the Army, a reporter noted: "A call for a district messenger boy nowadays often results, I find, in the appearance of a middle-aged man." The service finally closed in 1943, its managing director stating melancholically: "You will see no more of those lads in the smart blue uniforms with their little caps set at a jaunty angle." [The District Messengers' Parade, *London Evening Standard*, 26 July 1897, p4; London Notes And Comment, *Yorkshire Post and Leeds Intelligencer*, 7 March 1940, p6.; The Messenger Boy Has Taken His Last Message, *Daily Mirror*, 17 September 1943, p5.]

skating through the streets of the metropolis is about as near to Elysium as they have ever dreamed." Nonetheless the days were long – ten hours, eight on Sundays, with regular all-night shifts, and all for the miserable remuneration of six to ten shillings per week.

The District Messenger Company delivered not only across the metropolis, but internationally, which for an elite group of lads offered the even greater thrill of foreign travel. The boys could also be summoned to act as valets, to accompany children travelling, to shop for the elderly, deliver cheques, and carry luggage – including on bicycling tours. Occasionally the requests verged on the bizarre, and included minding a corpse, looking after a lunatic, and delivering a pedigree dog to the Sultan in Constantinople. As a Company spokesman observed:

> In consequence of the infinite variety of duties that fall their lot, the London messenger boys are among the smartest youthful workers in the country. Entering all manner of households, from the duke's downwards, and seeing so much of the practical side of life, they become amazingly sharp and resourceful.

Just as the prospect of a fleet-footed G.P.O. boy on the doorstep was appealing and convenient for the general public, so the District Messenger Company's premium service was well-patronised by those of means.* For more than a few gentlemen, its smartly turned out lads would have represented an equally as spiffing object of desire. "Few men, indeed, are proof against the fresh young voice and pretty petulance of a boy of fourteen or fifteen," the author of *Boy-Worship* firmly pronounced. How much more irresistible then, when they were spruce, quick-witted, affable, and trustworthy.

Thanks to the tailing of Albert Collins, it was not long before it became clear to the police that the author of the incriminating letters was a thirty-five-year-old London society gentleman whom we have previously met – Bernard Fraser, a scion of Scottish gentry.

---

* Unsurprisingly, Montague Guest was a keen early subscriber. "I have had one of the machines in my house now three weeks," he informed *The Times*, "and it enables me to get a boy within two minutes to carry a note to any part of the town, and I have called cabs, both hansoms and four-wheelers, at all hours." [The Post Office And Private Enterprise, *The Times*, 20 March 1891, p3. See also the photo of Company chairman Sir George Manners with a contingent of tykes, August 1916: K997/101/5, Suffolk Record Office.]

Fraser was a keen patron of the District Messenger Company. After Collins became one of its boys, Fraser wrote to the office requesting that he be sent to wait on him, and look after his guns. The lad subsequently travelled with Fraser to Scotland, and also to Canterbury, Henley, and the Norfolk Broads.

When in London, Bernard Fraser lived with his widowed mother and family in a Belgravia terrace. Consequently, youthful assignations required discreet snuggeries; preferably far away from the all-seeing net-curtained windows of the metropolis. Bernard had a friend in the similar situation of libido compromised by lack of privacy. This was his Naples chum Arthur Thorold. Now twenty eight years old, Arthur was finally completing his degree at Oxford. A yachting holiday would provide the answer to their needs.

As with naval recruits, the lure of the water as a realm of absolute escape – an autonomous zone – was a particularly compelling fantasy for those whose desires were socially constrained. It coloured the canvases of Henry Scott Tuke,* the iconic *plein air* maritime painter of naked youths, and it glimmered, shimmered and lulled in the verses of Uranian poets. John Gambril Nicholson's poem 'The Boy In The Boat' conveys the erotic seaborne drowse in which the forbidden becomes possible:

> The sunny afternoon, so gaily beaming
> Across the opalescent sea
> The distant ship, the far-off headland gleaming
> Are not so fair as he.

At Wroxham† in Norfolk the men found what they were looking for, renting a vessel from a gentleman appropriately named, given their purposes, Mr. Loynes. Here in August 1899, Bernard brought Albert Collins, who was then just thirteen.

---

* Henry Scott Tuke (1858–1929). Cornish marine painter famed for his glorification of adolescent male beauty, and the play of sunlight on naked flesh. His extensive friendships included a wide homosocial circle. A man of great charm, his long-term lover, according to a former model, was another of his models. The informant was likely John Alfred 'Jack' Hone (1895–1978), a stockbroker, and former subject of Tuke's, who was one of his executors. Hone was also recalled as "a charming man," and lived in a Tuke-lined London flat with an Irish working class male partner. [Jonathan Gathorne-Hardy, *The Old School Tie: the phenomenon of the English public school,* Viking Press, New York 1977, p214; information from Timothy D'Arch Smith who visited Hone.]

† A village situated within the Norfolk Broads – a network of rivers and lakes.

Arthur Thorold brought another lad, Benjamin Brumfield, one of the eleven children of his village's railway signalman. The family lived in the railway Station House at Hougham, which also housed the family of the porter. A later resident recalled that even in the late 1940s the building was still lit with oil lamps, and water was pumped from an outside well. Born in 1887, Brumfield had just turned twelve, but two years later was working as a farm labourer in the broad flat fields of the parish.

Any holiday, let alone the adventure of a yachting trip with worldly older gentlemen, would have been an immense enticement for any working class lad. Their existences were usually ones of provincial or metropolitan tedium, dismal and cramped living conditions, and dawn-to-dusk labour. Life was hard for the majority, who were thrown into an often harsh adult working existence at puberty. A sheltered adolescence was a middle-class luxury. Both the minimum school leaving age and the minimum age of employment had been raised to twelve in 1901, and probably by necessity as much as expectation, Brumfield and Collins commenced work as soon as possible.

Another Uranian poem, by Charles Kains Jackson, which was inspired by a painting of Tuke's, expresses the fleeting freedom such a holiday would have meant in these cramped lives:

> Of living light that laughs along the sea
> And freshness of kind winds...
> The kisses that make red each honest face
> Are of the breeze and salt and tingling spray
> So, may these boys know never of a place
> Wherein, to desk or factory a prey,
> That colour blanches slowly, nature's grace
> Made pale with life's incipient decay.

While the age difference between the men and boys was significant, the difference in class would have felt the far greater transgression. It's difficult to over-emphasise what the gulf between two sprigs of the gentry and two poor working lads would have felt to them. At the turn of the century, the difference between rich and poor was still as marked as when Benjamin Disraeli had written, over half a century before, that it was like:

> Two nations between whom there is no intercourse and no sympathy; who are as ignorant of each other's habits, thoughts, and feelings, as if they were dwellers in different zones, or inhabitants of different planets.

Desire can create bridges, but for the men at least, the anomaly of the situation and its risk would have provided as much a sexual thrill as Oscar Wilde's dining with working class rentboys, of which he wrote: "It was like feasting with panthers; the danger was half the excitement."

Few stratagems for cornering human prey are more perfect than luring them onto a boat. However, the record of later criminal charges shows Arthur Thorold had already had sexual relations with Brumfield as early as May that year, and the same probably applied to Bernard Fraser and Collins. The fact the boys repeated the adventure suggests they enjoyed yachting, the men's company, and more than a stiff sailing breeze too.

In September the group yachted at Hunstanton,* and the following summer again at Wroxham. On that occasion Albert Collins was unable to join them, having by then joined the Navy. Bernard sought out fresh company, forming a friendship with a lad who bore the nickname of 'Boss'. It suggests a cocksure character, typical of the streetwise cockney lads who lived on their wits.

Fraser and Thorold were also complicit in facilitating youthful seductions for others – crimes that would never be brought to court. And so things continued until July 1902, when Detective-Inspector Arrow began his enquiries.

His investigation, at least at the start, was textbook simple. As the recipient of Bernard's letters, Albert Collins was interviewed at the Treasury building in Whitehall around the middle of July. It would have been an intimidating circumstance for anyone, and the lad plainly confessed all, because Arrow then boarded a train and journeyed into the depths of Lincolnshire to take a statement from

---

* A Norfolk coastal town; home to the Le Strange family, who hold the ancient hereditary office of Lord High Admiral Of The Wash.

Brumfield.

The information the lads supplied was more than enough for arrests to be made. Collins was discharged from the Navy on the 22nd of July. Given his youth and cooperation, and because the police investigation was still underway, he was not dishonourably discharged – indeed, his service record notes his character as "V.G." – Very Good. The official reason listed for his discharge, after a mere thirteen months of service, was recorded as "no longer required". Given that the Navy was aggressively recruiting, it was a thin excuse. In readiness for the boys to act as prosecution witnesses, arrangements were made for keeping them in London, but separate from each other.

Bernard Fraser was also interviewed about his correspondence with Collins. He claimed to have taken an interest in the lad after reading in the press that he had attempted to take his life. (No such newspaper reports have been found: it was possibly a false claim.) In any case, if Bernard had been motivated by charitable concerns for the young Albert, his interests soon stretched beyond the philanthropic.

Following his police interview, Bernard panicked. He now penned another letter to the H.M.S. Lion, but this time addressed to Commander Hutchinson. It was described as 'lengthy', and was a desperate attempt to absolve himself. In it, he again attempted to explain what he knew of Collins – or rather, of what he thought he could convince the Commander.

On July 26th, Detective-Inspector Arrow submitted his findings for execution of the arrest warrants for Bernard and Arthur, which were issued. Two days later, accompanied by Detective-Sergeant Lynn of the Norfolk Constabulary, Arrow walked up the steps of the Belgravia home of Bernard's mother Susan and her family. Just as today, the great barren streets and anonymous facades of the suburb resembled a dystopian internment camp for the rich; the sour-cream cliffs of its grand terraces coldly exuding wealth and power. The two phlegmatic officers may have felt slightly intimidated as they stood before the pillared entrance of the Fraser residence. On being admitted by a servant, they were informed that Bernard Fraser was not at home.

Near midnight on the evening of that same day, at a dock in distant Southampton, a distinguished looking gentleman stood on the deck of the steamship Alma. Mr. Clarke – for that was the name he'd given when booking the tickets, could at last relax a little. It had been a long, all-too-worrying day. One that included a journey from London in the South Western Railway's boat train, which for all its speed, must have seemed tryingly slow. But now, as the Alma prepared to cast off at the stroke of twelve, he was at last safe.

There was a cool fresh breeze which promised a swell in the English Channel, but nothing too rough. In his jacket were two First Class tickets from Le Havre to Paris. Two tickets, because standing on the deck with Mr. Clarke was a lad, a possibly cocky-looking lad, who may not have much resembled a gentleman's nephew. Bernard Fraser had wisely decided to cut his losses and flee with Boss. Unfortunately, he'd left his escape mere heartbeats too late.

Informed at Chester Street of Bernard's whereabouts, or having a strong hunch, the two detectives had rushed to Southampton – possibly by the same train. And now, in the very last minutes before the Alma was due to sail, they boarded and spotted their quarry. Snaking through the mingling passengers, they moved in. Whether Detective-Inspector Arrow had met Bernard at his interrogation, or this was to be their first encounter, it was certainly with some confidence that he now confronted him. Arrow recalled on the witness stand that he said:

> "I believe you are Mr. Bernard Fraser."
> Bernard replied: "Yes, but you have the advantage of me."
> "I am a police officer," announced Arrow, "and I arrest you on warrants."
> "Impossible," Fraser stated.

Arrow informed him it was his duty to execute the warrants. Bernard Fraser would not have been a man desirous of making a scene. He was indeed cornered. In the custody of Arrow and Lynn he reluctantly walked off the ship. Before the end of that long, soul-raking night, Bernard would find himself in a police holding cell. His carefree, champagne life was over.

And what of Boss? On that evening at least, he was not arrested. Whether Boss thought it foolish to waste a First Class ticket to the City of Light when things were getting so hot, is not recorded.

However, as Bernard would have informed him, by 8 a.m. the Alma would be at Le Havre, and by late morning, summery Paris would be all his. That said, even without the attentions of Scotland Yard, the journey was not without some risk. Earlier that year, on the foggy night of April 1st, the Alma had been badly damaged when she collided in the English Channel with a merchant ship, the Cambrian Princess. The latter had immediately sunk, the icy water drowning eleven of her seamen, some of them mere teenagers like Boss. Yet now, just four months later, the Alma was fully repaired and repainted, and as its advertisements promised, 'sumptuously appointed'; her First Class saloon and 34 cabins described as 'splendid'. Possibly quite what the Boss thought he deserved. And life, like the lives of the quickly-forgotten young ghosts of the Cambrian Princess – amongst them Percival, Pedro, Thomas, and a Norwegian lad, Fahne – can be so terribly, unexpectedly short. It is best seized while breath remains.

Bernard Fraser was not so comfortably accommodated that long night, and on the 30th of July he was received into custody at Norwich Prison. Arthur Thorold was arrested immediately afterwards at Oxford, where he'd begun teaching at a boys' school, St. Edward's. Whether Bernard had telegraphed him a warning, and he chose to see things out, or he'd been hung out to dry, is unknown. Arthur was received into custody at Norwich Prison on August 1st.

However, the real investigation had just begun. Because this wasn't simply a case of two men of privilege and their boys. The correspondence showed that Bernard Fraser had been engaged in a regular campaign of procuring youths throughout the country. In this undertaking he'd been aided not only by Arthur Thorold, but by two other gentlemen as well.

The police investigation was about to get very hot indeed.

9. A SERIOUS QUESTION OF PUBLIC POLICY

No sooner had Bernard Fraser and Arthur Thorold been arrested, then the other two procurers vanished. Or did the police let them escape? A new London press upstart, the *Daily Express*, dared publish what other papers well knew, but did not print: "it is asserted that their arrest would mean the besmirching of the names of more than one high personage."

As Detective-Inspector Arrow's investigation progressed, what became clear was that the four men had been acting as procurers for a group of richer, grander, socially powerful gentlemen, at least thirty in number. Given that the owner of Cleveland Street's boy brothel had been an illiterate blackmailer, it would have been reassuring to these clients that this time the pimping was being managed by persons of their own class.

The investigative trail led detectives to what was described as "well known country houses, private yachts, and other quarters of the most wealthy and aristocratic circles," revealing "a regular campaign to deprave the morals of youths all over the country."

The police became alarmed at what they were uncovering. An American newspaper printed that the case "involves names of wider than English reputation," and that for the police, "it became a serious question of public policy as to how far they should proceed in their inquiries."

The leader of the group, whose name was to remain unpublished, was the aforementioned Cyril Flower, Lord Battersea. Hugely rich in his own right, and married to Constance de Rothschild of the plutocratic banking family, he was a popular and highly prominent member of Parliament.

More than this, the same American press report alleged the involvement of "Another still greater name, which must not be indicated." Given that American newspapers had readily published the allegation of Prince Albert Victor's patronage of 19 Cleveland Street, this was heady stuff indeed. Any suspicion that more naval trainees may have been involved would, for a government directly responsible for their welfare, have also been a grave concern. The possible headlines of an exposure didn't bear thinking about.

As with the Cleveland Street Scandal, management of the case would quickly have escalated to the highest levels of the Government. Some form of prosecution was necessary to quell what was viewed as a social cancer, but exactly whom to prosecute, and to what degree? Prosecuting the most guilty risked a host of dangers.

If the Dublin Castle and Cleveland Street Scandals had taught anything to those in authority, it was that in a nation of strong class divisions, homosexuality respected none; that big cities were small homosexual towns where, like the aristocracy, many knew each other – including intimately; and that a criminal scab of lavender hue could, if not handled carefully, quickly haemorrhage in public, with potentially catastrophic consequences for the Government of the day, its institutions, and most especially, persons of consequence.* As late

---

* The danger was again demonstrated in an 1891 case, when a Frenchman employing the surname Van Delba was arrested for sexual misdemeanours with a seventeen-year-old London clerk. He was described as a sallow complexioned man of about twenty-six, with a small waxed moustache: "He wears his black hair *en brosse*, and is exceedingly well dressed in clothes of obviously French manufacture...When he was taken into custody the police found money and property of considerable value, including a 1,000f. note (£40), a diamond pin, a gold watch and chain, a revolver, and some cartridges, and a visiting card bearing the name 'Le Prince Georges de Grece' surmounted by a crown." For the press, the card became the signature aspect of the case, although nothing more of the royal association was learnt. He was jailed for eighteen months with hard labour. However, the card may have been evidence of an attempt at extortion: Prince George (1869–1957) conducted a life-long love affair with his uncle Prince Valdemar of Denmark (1858–1939), despite both their marriages. In 1893, the offender, now using the name Paul Joly, was again sentenced, this time to twenty years, for homosexual blackmail (undertaken with the help of a young cousin), of an elderly Hove gentleman, (William) Thomas Pardoe. Released from prison in 1910, and employing the name Victor Siellet Roger, he gained employment as a hotel manager. In 1915, he was arrested a third time, with another man, for procuring boys for sex. Absconding on £1,000 bail, he was

as 1923, an informant in *John Bull* would write:

> Since the Cleveland Street scandal of long ago, the police have been very chary of taking action against mass depravity; and although isolated cases come up to the Assizes and Old Bailey with monotonous regularity at every session, the police prefer that these horrible charges should be few and far between.

That the lesson had been learnt was shown in the Oscar Wilde trials of 1895. In a decision taken at the highest levels, Lord Alfred Douglas was not charged. Instead, he was treated as a victim, despite clear evidence he was an accomplice. However, Douglas would surely have been as worryingly mouthy on the witness stand as John Saul, and because of his high status, and his father's vendetta against Lord Rosebery, twice as dangerous. The very last thing the Government desired would have been to antagonise either the father or the son.

In 1902, Lord Halsbury's opinion, as Lord Chancellor, regarding the dangers of prosecuting such cases when prominent individuals were involved, remained unchanged – the resulting publicity would encourage imitative behaviour in those of lower station. (Presumably due to it being endorsed by their betters.) There was also the risk of it tainting the entire ruling class by association. And Balfour's government, like all those before it, remained deeply aristocratic.

Then as now, important criminal cases were referred by the police to the Director of Public Prosecutions (DPP), whose jurisdiction was part of the Home Office. With the Battersea case, this occurred on the 23rd of June 1902. The Director was then an Irish peer and able barrister, Hamilton Cuffe, Earl of Desart,* who bore the amusing nickname of 'Hand Cuff'. Perhaps appropriately for this case, in his

---

re-arrested and sentenced to two years hard labour for gross indecency, but was not tried on the more serious additional charge of buggery. [Charge Of Unnatural Assault Against A Foreigner, *Reynolds's Newspaper*, 20 September 1891, p6; Abominable West End Scandal, *Reynolds's Newspaper*, 4 October 1891, p1; Eighteen Months Hard Labour For An Abominable Offence, *Reynolds's Newspaper*, 1 November 1891, p4; Shocking West-End Scandal, *The People*, 11 October 1891, p1; Celia Bertin, *Marie Bonaparte: A Life*, Harcourt Brace Jovanovich, New York 1982, pp85-86, 96-98; Extraordinary Case Of Blackmailing At Hove, *Sussex Agricultural Express*, 2 December 1893, p9; £1,000 Bail Required, *Marylebone Mercury*, 13 March 1915, p6; Absconded To Bail In £1,000, *Western Mail*, 14 June 1915, p9; Van Delba, alias Paul Joly, alias Victor Siellet Roger, 1891, 1893, 1915: Calendar of Prisons, FindMyPast.com]

* Hamilton John Agmondesham Cuffe, 5th Earl of Desart (1848 –1934), Irish peer and barrister.

early life, Cuffe had been a Royal Navy midshipman. He also brought considerable experience in prosecuting cases of this nature, both the Cleveland Street Scandal and Oscar Wilde case having earlier fallen under his remit as Assistant Director, and then Director. It was Cuffe who alerted his superiors to Arthur Newton's threat that Prince Eddy's name would be raised if the investigation proceeded. And while the Wilde case had appeared a straightforward prosecution to the public, behind the scenes it had been anything but.

London's justice system was a very small circle in which everyone knew each other, and the most prominent of those they represented. Even more so than today, this led to a collective knowledge of cases and personalities that was far deeper than what was brought before the courts.

The DPP was under the direction of the chief legal adviser of the Crown, the Attorney General, then Sir Robert Finlay,* a Scottish lawyer and M.P.. However, given the prominence of the persons involved in this case, it is unthinkable that the Home Secretary and Prime Minister were not consulted. These gentlemen were respectively, a Kentish parson's son with the wonderfully rhythmic name of Aretas Akers-Douglas†, and the steely aesthete Arthur Balfour, who'd succeeded Lord Salisbury as Prime Minister in July. Akers-Douglas was also a member of Chancery Bar Lodge, the same masonic lodge as Lord Halsbury, and of which the Prince of Wales was an honorary member. Balfour's associations were, as will be later detailed, even more intriguing.

To ensure the case didn't bleed endlessly like that of Cleveland Street, it was decided the strictest of tourniquets would be applied. Only the two procurers, Thorold and Fraser would be charged. The thirty-some elite clients, plus the ringleader Lord Battersea, would ultimately be granted complete immunity, and their anonymity protected with a profound official silence. Like the Government's handling of Lord Arthur Somerset's case, this high-level decision undoubtedly rankled with the police, and those lower down in the Home Department.

---

* Sir Robert Finlay, later 1st Viscount Finlay (1842–1929), solicitor, doctor and Liberal & Liberal Unionist M.P.; Lord Chancellor 1916-1919.
† Aretas Akers-Douglas, later 1st Viscount Chilston (1851–1926), Conservative M.P.

In 1925, Harry Butler Simpson,* who'd been Assistant Secretary of the Home Office during these events, retired. Simpson had joined the Office in 1884, and when his successor went through the papers in his office with a colleague, they discovered, "tucked away in the drawers of his desk many long-lost files which he had found inconvenient, and had put quietly to sleep." Perhaps the now missing criminal file of Lord Battersea was one of them.

Arthur Thorold's file has also vanished, but against all odds, Bernard Fraser's dossier in part survives. Originally held at the Home Office, and closed until 2009, at the fifty-year mark in 1952 it was reviewed, as two ink stamps on the cover, 'Seen By Researcher' and '23 May 1952', indicate. The official weeder also left notations in red ink on the cover and final page: '2-10 Destroyed', '13-17 Destroyed'. It's apparent there were further extractions. One sheet bears a page number in pencil: 64. Yet the existing file amounts to only 26 pages. Fifty years on from the scandal, it was still diligently being covered up. It would be 107 years before the file was released.

---

* Henry 'Harry' Butler Simpson (1861–1940).

10. FEARSOME CHARGES

Whatever Bernard Fraser and Arthur Thorold had claimed under interrogation, the confessions of the boys are likely to have been damning. The police also held Bernard's letters, and had obtained his diary.

The existing legislation under which the charges were laid was overlapping, and in part, troublingly vague. Some charges could have been made under *The Assault of Young Persons Act* of 1880. However, at the time, prosecutions for homosexuality in Britain were almost always undertaken under two other pieces of legislation.

The first was the *Offences Against the Person Act* of 1861. As well as detailing punishments for murder, abortion, and other crimes against the corporeal body, the Act included a section 'Unnatural Offences'. Buggery it classed as a felony – that is, a crime considered so serious it was, or had been at one time, a capital offence. The Act had repealed the death penalty for buggery, mandating instead a sentence of penal servitude (i.e. hard labour as a convict) of ten years to Life. This included whether it was committed "with Mankind or with any Animal".

As for attempted buggery, including assault with the intention of committing it, or "any indecent assault upon a male person" which didn't include the act of penetration (i.e. oral, manual, and intercrural* sex), these were classed by the Act as misdemeanours, and mandated three to ten years of penal servitude, or a maximum of two years of

---

* Insertion of the penis between the partner's legs.

225

simple imprisonment, with or without hard labour.

The second piece of relevant legislation was Section 11 of the 1885 *Criminal Law Amendment Act* – the so-called Labouchère Amendment. This had introduced the new offence of 'gross indecency with another male person'. It rated the crime as a misdemeanour, and mandated terms not exceeding two years, with or without hard labour. What exactly constituted 'gross indecency' the *Amendment* left conveniently undefined, enabling a broad application. While homosexual acts committed by either assault or consent had been prosecuted in Britain since 1533, the charge of 'gross indecency' was increasingly used to prosecute consensual acts. (The prohibition would remain until 1967, by which time it had been used to convict, and fracture the lives, of well over 50,000 men.)

Buggery was difficult for the courts to prove when it was consensual and had occurred in private. While 'emission of seed' in the rectum wasn't necessary to bring down a guilty verdict, penetration had to be proved. Consequently, the Crown often resorted to gaining guilty verdicts on charges that were easier to confirm: attempted buggery, or conspiracy to incite or commit buggery, and as a fallback option, the conveniently broad and vague charge of gross indecency.

It was not uncommon for indictments for homosexuality to include a variation of these charges, in the expectation that some would stick; depending on what happened in court, the Crown wouldn't necessarily waste the court's time proceeding with all charges.

The indictment of Fraser and Thorold similarly featured two sets of charges. Those that constituted misdemeanours were for gross indecency, indecent assault, and conspiring, aiding, abetting, and procuring to commit buggery. The graver charges were for the felony of buggery itself. The only other persons named on the indictment, but not charged, were the two lads Albert Collins (mistranscribed in one instance as 'Arthur'), and Benjamin Brumfield (mistranscribed as 'Bromfield'), whom in the eyes of the law were victims.

Even today, the indictment is a sobering thing to read. The string of charges is couched in several hundred words of the most fearful and convoluted legalese. The phrasing was a matter of convention, but if Fraser and Thorold weren't already numbed to the bone, each charge would have hammered home the unutterable grimness of the fate that awaited them.

The indictment read:

- Conspiring together that the said Bernard Fraser should commit the abominable crime of buggery with persons unknown, and

- that the said Arthur Thorold should aid and abet him in the commission of the said crime, and

- that the said Arthur Thorold should commit the said abominable crime, and that the said Bernard Fraser should aid and abet him therein, and

- conspiring that they being male persons should unlawfully procure the commission by divers* persons unknown of acts of gross indecency with them, and

- conspiring together that the said Bernard Fraser should commit the said abominable crime with Arthur [sic] Collins, and

- that the said Arthur Thorold should aid and abet him, and

- that the said Bernard Fraser should commit acts of gross indecency with Albert Collins and

- that they should procure the commission by Albert Collins of acts of gross indecency with the said Bernard Fraser, and

- conspiring together that the said Arthur Thorold should commit the said abominable crime and acts of gross indecency with Benjamin Bromfield, [sic] and

- that the said Bernard Fraser should aid and abet him therein, and

---

* Various.

227

- that they should procure the commission by the said Benjamin Bromfield of acts of gross indecency with the said Arthur Thorold on divers days between the 1st May 1899 and the month of August 1900, and

- the said Bernard Fraser committing acts of gross indecency with Albert Collins at Wroxham on the 2nd August 1899, and

- the said Bernard Fraser and Arthur Thorold procuring the commission of an act of gross indecency with the said Bernard Fraser, and

- the said Arthur Thorold attempting to commit the said abominable crime of buggery with Benjamin Bromfield on the 2nd August 1899 at Wroxham, and

- indecently assaulting the said Benjamin Bromfield a male person, and

- committing acts of gross indecency with him on the 2nd August and 5th September 1899 and 10th August 1900, and

- the said Bernard Fraser and Arthur Thorold procuring the commission by the said Benjamin Bromfield of acts of gross indecency with the said Arthur Thorold at Wroxham on the 2nd August 1899 and 2nd August 1900, and at Hunstanton on the 5th September 1899 and

- the said Bernard Fraser attempting to commit the abominable crime of buggery with Albert Collins at Wroxham on the 2nd August 1899.

- The said Bernard Fraser, feloniously and against the order of nature committing and perpetrating the abominable crime of buggery with Albert Collins at Wroxham, on the 2nd of August 1899, and

- the said Arthur Thorold, feloniously being present, aiding, abetting and assisting the said Bernard Fraser in committing the said felony.

- The said Arthur Thorold, feloniously and against the order of nature committing and perpetrating the abominable crime of buggery with Benjamin Bromfield at Wroxham, on the 2nd of August 1899, and

- the Bernard Fraser, feloniously being present, aiding, abetting and assisting the said Arthur Thorold in committing the said felony.

Lurking in the string of charges was the true reason for the prosecution: "conspiring that they being male persons should unlawfully procure the commission by divers persons unknown of acts of gross indecency with them," including "the abominable crime of buggery with persons unknown". The identities of those "divers persons unknown" *were* known to the Crown – or at least by mid-August mostly would be. However, the Government had zero intention of pursuing the dangerous matter of procurement, with its risk of raising names. Fraser and Thorold represented an appalling embarrassment that could be removed from the public sphere purely on the basis of their own crimes, without tainting other gentlemen.

This narrow focus of the prosecution enabled more legal sleight of hand. While the press later reported, "Fraser had for a long while been engaged in this sort of crime all over the country" (including presumably London), the two men's offences with Brumfield and Collins had occurred in Norfolk. This enabled the Government to proceed with the prosecution in that county at Norwich. The regional location was inconvenient for the journalists of London's scandal-hungry popular press – and therefore perfect. Just as in the case of Cleveland Street they might have raised troubling questions, including about those 'divers persons'.

So suavely was the prosecution set up, the authorities might have congratulated themselves. The lessons in silencing these matters had not only been learnt, but learnt well. With both prisoners held in custody at Norwich, a committal hearing was swiftly scheduled for August 2nd. The news was surely spreading like wildfire through London and county Society.

229

11. THE WORST OFFENCES KNOWN TO LAW

In a committal or preliminary hearing, a magistrate decides whether the prosecution has enough evidence for a case to be committed for trial or sentence. While committal hearings had long been an aspect of English law, their modern form dates only from 1848. It was then codified in law that the accused had the right to be present when all witnesses were examined, and that their evidence should be taken down in the form of a deposition. This enabled the accused to know exactly what case they needed to defend.

The preliminary proceedings for Bernard Fraser and Arthur Thorold involved four hearings spread across a fortnight at the Norwich Shirehall. Constructed in the 1820s, the Shirehall is a low castellated building of brown brick and stone which complements the nearby stone keep of Norwich Castle. It contained two courtrooms: one for civil cases, the other for criminal. A tunnel from the keep enabled the easy transfer of prisoners to a holding cell next to the latter courtroom. In 1887 the old prison was shuttered, giving way to the new and larger H.M. Prison Norwich on Mousehold Heath, overlooking the town.

On Saturday the 2nd of August 1902, Bernard and Arthur found themselves in the grim, low-ceilinged holding cell adjoining the criminal courtroom. The walls and stalls of the courtroom itself were painted a buff colour appropriately known as 'drab'. Yet the courtroom's high windows ensured it was surprisingly light, and despite being a large space, it retained an intimate atmosphere. The seating for newspaper reporters was to the immediate right of the criminal dock, while prisoners faced the judge and witness stand, with their backs to their families and the general public. This was perhaps a blessing: every flicker of shame, regret and pain on the faces of the accused was as near as the flick of a whip.

Today it's difficult to conceive the almost inexpressible repugnance the average upstanding British man and woman held for what the two men were about to be accused of, although the language of the law gives some sense of it. Buggery was 'the abominable crime'. It was almost beyond the bounds of reason that those who practised it could be, like Thorold and Fraser, the sons of rectors, or the flower of Scottish gentry. They might as well have been creatures from Hell's underworld. For at least one court reporter, these were the "worst offences known to law". Standing in that provincial dock, how very far the two men would have felt from the racy, raffish existence of the Edwardian *beau monde*, which barely a few days prior, had seemed a ticket to anything-goes freedom.

The hearings took place before local magistrate Gilbert Hardinge Stracey, Frederick William Magnay, J.P., and magistrate and fellow pillar of the Norfolk gentry, Major Frank Astley Cubitt, a veteran of the Indian Mutiny at Lucknow.

Prosecuting on behalf of the Crown, i.e. the Government, was the highly exacting Archibald Henry Bodkin,[*] a future Director of Public Prosecutions, who was being instructed by solicitor Francis Sims. Further underlining the gravity of the situation was the presence of the Chief Constable of the county, Sir Paynton Pigott.[†] For their defence, Bernard and Arthur had hurriedly called upon that ubiquitous defender of homosexuals in legal strife, solicitor Arthur Newton. While Newton had a reputation for being able to secure acquittals in cases regarded as hopeless, in this matter the Government had no intention of letting him have his way.

The hearing was opened by Bodkin specifying the roll-call of charges. He was noted for his meticulous indictments, but both prisoners

---

[*] Sir Archibald Henry Bodkin (1862–1957), lawyer and Director of Public Prosecutions from 1920 to 1930. Prosecuting counsel at Roger Casement's trial for treason. Bodkin was known for his strong grasp of legal principle, shrewdness, and pugnacity: as one observer put it, he was a 'bonny fighter'. [Devon's Debt To Sir Archibald Bodkin In Administration Of Justice, *The Western Morning News*, 15 September 1950, p4.]
[†] Sir Paynton Pigott (1840–1915), barrister; Chief Constable Of Norfolk 1880–1909.

pleaded Not Guilty. After this interlude, which must have scarred the souls of those members of Bernard and Arthur's families who were present, he outlined how the case had come to the Director of Public Prosecutions. Bodkin then sketched for the court the privileged backgrounds of Bernard and Arthur, and the very different lives of Albert Collins and Benjamin Brumfield. He detailed the discovery of the letters, and the subsequent investigation, or rather, the part of it the DPP deemed safe to share. Bodkin told how young Collins had accompanied Bernard to Scotland, to the Norfolk Broads, to Henley, and to Canterbury, and of the rented yacht with Arthur and Benjamin. It would have painted a deepening impression of the corruption of innocent youths by an idle *roué* and his accomplice.

Bodkin read to the court some of the correspondence between the parties, which indicated the procurement engaged upon. This would have only further darkened the mood in the courtroom. He then detailed Bernard's claim of concern for Albert Collins's welfare following his alleged suicide attempt. Bodkin also spoke of the letter that Bernard had written, following his police interview, to Commander Hutchinson. Lastly, Bodkin told the court of Bernard's attempt to flee justice, and of his last-minute arrest. Evidence was then called, but none of the press reports of the first hearing published any further details. An application for bail was refused, and Bernard and Arthur were returned to their cells at Norwich Prison.

The second hearing at the Norwich Shirehall took place six days later on Friday, the 8th of August, Coronation Eve. The centre of Norwich was gaily decorated, although it was noted that the bunting was not as profuse as it had been in June went the crowning was originally scheduled. Nonetheless, a sense of expectation and celebration was in the air.

None of this festivity penetrated the courtroom, where the hearing was again held before Gilbert Stracey, Frederick Magnay, and Major Cubitt. Archibald Bodkin, instructed by Francis Sims, again prosecuted on behalf of the Treasury. While Arthur Newton again defended Arthur Thorold, Bernard Fraser had now obtained a different legal representation, turning to the *ne plus ultra* of solicitors, Lewis & Lewis. The most prominent legal firm in London, it had been founded by Sir George Lewis,* who'd just been granted a baronetcy in the Coronation Honours – a remarkable achievement at the time for a solicitor, let alone a Jewish one. It was an honour well-earned: Sir George's leading client was the King, whom he'd extricated from a succession of scrapes over the years.

At his London home on Portland Place, Sir George and his wife Lady Lewis maintained a popular salon where the Establishment and Bohemia embraced. Another of his clients, Oscar Wilde, greatly admired the couple, gifting Lady Lewis a feather fan, and saying of Sir George: "Brilliant. Formidable. Concerned in every great case in England. Oh, he knows all about us, and he forgives us all."† Bernard Fraser may have met Lewis in his socialising. However, another of Sir George's clients was Lord Battersea, from whence the recommendation may have come – and even possibly the briefing.

Unfortunately, and likely due to the suddenness of the case, Sir George wasn't personally representing Fraser. Instead, Lewis & Lewis had instructed the future chief magistrate of the Metropolitan Police Courts, Henry Chartres Biron.‡ Biron was perhaps not the ideal choice. A lifelong bachelor, Chartres Biron (he used his grander second name) appears to have preferred books to people (his published reminiscences were graced with a photograph of a corner of his library), but only the right kind of books. In 1928, he was to preside over the trial of Radclyffe Hall's lesbian novel, *The Well of Loneliness*. The work was judged obscene, Biron informing the court that it contained:

> not one word which suggested that anyone with the horrible

---

* Sir George Henry Lewis, 1st Baronet (1833–1911). Married Elizabeth Eberstadt.

† The sympathy of Sir George for homosexual clients may have been due to an appreciation of their mutual social otherness; similar, for example, to the friendships that the star portraitist of the day, the homosexual John Singer Sargent, maintained with his Jewish clients. Sargent was also a friend of the Lewises, as was E.F. Benson, who praised Sir George's "shrewdness, kindness and amazing common sense...His clients were his friends". On Wilde's behalf, in 1893 Lewis silenced the blackmailing rentboy Alfred Wood. Nonetheless, it cost him Lewis's esteem. [Patricia Failing, 'The Hidden Sargent', *Art News*, May 2001, pp170-71; Trevor J. Fairbrother, 'The Complications of being Sargent' in Norman L. Kleeblatt (ed.) *John Singer Sargent: Portraits of the Wertheimer Family*, The Jewish Museum, New York 1999; E.F. Benson, *Final Edition: Informal Autobiography*, Longmans Green And Co, London 1940, pp55,59; Letter from Lord Alfred Douglas to Maurice Schwabe, 5&9 March 1893, Safe 1/2c, State Library Of New South Wales.]

‡ Sir Henry Chartres Biron (1863–1940) barrister; chief magistrate of the Metropolitan Police Courts from 1920.

tendencies described was in the least degree blameworthy. All the characters in the book were presented as attractive people and put forward with admiration. What was even more serious was that certain acts were described in the most alluring terms.

The speech suggests that representing a pederast in a criminal case was not something Biron might approach with natural conviction.

There was further legal representation. Instructed by Arthur Newton, William Wilson Grantham, a solicitor, and son of the famous judge Sir William Grantham, held a watching brief for the unnamed and unprosecuted other parties. While possibly not present in body, they most certainly formed an invisible herd of elephants in the courtroom.

When the hearing opened, both Bernard Fraser and Arthur Thorold again pleaded Not Guilty. Benjamin Brumfield was called to the witness stand and sworn in, and gave evidence against Arthur. As was to be the situation throughout the hearings and trial, the press studiously refrained from quoting any of the boys' testimony.

After an adjournment for lunch, Mr. Loynes of Wroxham gave testimony as to the letting of boats to Arthur, and of seeing Bernard on board. Next to give evidence was the superintendent of the District Messenger Company, William Holman. He confirmed that Albert Collins had been in the employ of the company, and produced letters from Bernard requesting that Collins be sent to wait on him, including looking after his guns.

Detective-Inspector Arrow was then called and gave evidence on the taking of statements from Albert Collins and Benjamin Brumfield in the middle of July. He spoke of the arrests, and of Bernard's attempted flight.

Lastly, the boy sailor Albert Collins was called to the stand, and cross-examined by Arthur Newton, on behalf of Arthur Thorold. Chartres Biron, acting for Bernard Fraser, reserved his cross-examination.

At five o'clock the Bench adjourned the case. Biron applied for bail for Fraser, and Newton for Thorold, stating that the younger man's case was entirely different. (As was to be later revealed, Reverend

Thorold wrongly blamed Bernard for corrupting his son, and had pleaded his case with Newton.)

Archibald Bodkin for the prosecution rose to oppose these requests, making the intriguing statement that "he hoped his friend Biron would not press him to state in public the further reasons, which had come to light since last week, why bail ought not to be granted." Detective-Inspector Arrow's investigation was still progressing, and more of the troublingly grand names involved had evidently been discovered.

Gilbert Stracey, as Chairman, announced that the Bench were unanimous in the view that bail could not be granted to either defendant. The second hearing had taken five hours. Once again, Bernard and Arthur were returned to Norwich Prison.

The following day, Coronation Day, was celebrated loyally in Norwich. In the morning there was a special thanksgiving church service attended by the alderman, town councillors and magistrates, followed by a pealing of bells. A mayoral reception was held at the Guildhall for county worthies, while a water carnival and gymkhana were staged for the general public. For the patients of the town's two hospitals, and those dependent on charity, there were also religious services, at the conclusion of which they were gifted a pint bottle of ale or stout, or the equivalent in ginger ale. Not least, inmates of the workhouse enjoyed a special breakfast at which each received a coronation handkerchief – ever useful for drying the tears of poverty, and the children a commemorative mug. Salutes were fired from the local Britannia Barracks, and there was a fireworks display in the evening.

Despite the thickness of the walls of Norwich Prison, the sounds of the church bells, volleys, fireworks and cheers would have penetrated the cells, providing a melancholy accompaniment to the prisoners' solitude. Bernard and Arthur may well have imagined how they would have been celebrating with London's 'swells' had things been different. Throughout that day and night, the near-yet-distant hubbub of the happy world outside would have reinforced the ache of their isolation. Never would they have felt so alone.

On the following Thursday, the 14th of August, the case was

resumed. The legal teams of prosecution and defence were as before, and for a third time, Bernard and Arthur pleaded Not Guilty. In the morning, Detective-Inspector Arrow was recalled to the witness stand and gave evidence as to recognising some letters of Albert Collins. He was followed on the stand by Arthur Harry Matsell, at whose house in Hunstanton Arthur and Benjamin Brumfield had stayed, and who testified of speaking to them.

Next to give evidence, regarding the letters sent by Bernard to boy sailors, were Commander Hutchinson, plus a lieutenant, and the Master of Arms of the H.M.S. Lion. Albert Collins was then recalled for cross-examination, and also the boy sailor Crawley. The case was then further adjourned.

Two days later, on Saturday the 16th of August, the last of the gruelling hearings took place in the Shirehall's criminal court. For a fourth time, the prisoners pleaded Not Guilty.

Among the witnesses called were the brother and mother of Albert Collins. For Bernard, it must have been especially confronting testimony. In the end, Archibald Bodkin for the prosecution requested that the Bench commit the prisoners for trial on charges of misdemeanour under the *Criminal Law Amendment Act*, and upon the more grave felonious charges of buggery, alleged to have taken place on Wroxham Broad in August 1899.

Addressing the Bench on behalf of Fraser, Chartres Biron submitted that:

> as regards the charge of felony, there was no evidence which would justify them in committing him for trial upon so serious a charge. There was not an atom of evidence before the Court of that offence save that adduced by the two lads, in support of whose serious allegations there was not a scrap of corroboration. He need not tell the Bench that the evidence of an accomplice, unless corroborated, should not be acted upon, and that it was equally a principle of law that the evidence of one accomplice could not be corroborated by the evidence of another. He submitted that with regard to the felony charge, evidence was lacking, whilst with regard to the other charges although there might be evidence, looking on its character, the Bench would he

was sure, consider very carefully before feeling themselves justified in placing any man upon trial in respect of them.

In his address to the Bench on behalf of Thorold, Arthur Newton submitted that there was no evidence whatsoever of his alleged commission of the felonious charge of buggery with Brumfield.

Gilbert Stracey, Frederick Magnay, and Major Cubitt of the Bench retired for a few minutes. On their return to the court, Stracey announced that they had given the case their very careful consideration, and had come to the decision that both Bernard and Arthur must be committed for trial on all counts asked for by the prosecution. Given the evidence, it would have been the expected outcome.

Lastly, Stracey stated that if bail was requested on behalf of Bernard Fraser, the Bench would refuse it. In respect of Arthur Thorold, bail would be granted – the prisoner himself of £3000, plus two sureties of £2000 each.

Arthur's father the Reverend Algernon Thorold, who was likely present in the courtroom, must have reeled. These were huge sums which surely drew gasps from the spectators. At his death twenty years later, the Reverend's estate amounted to what then would have been considered a substantial inheritance: £6,489. What the Bench was now demanding in bail was more than his entire estate!

How exceptional these sums were is indicated by another criminal case a few months later involving a Worcester brewer, who was charged with gross indecency with an eight-year-old boy, which had occurred in the company of two other boys. He was granted bail at £20, plus two sureties of £10 each.

As clearly as one of Bernard's sailor boys waving signal flags, the huge bail demand semaphored that there was far more to this case than a pair of piffling toffs and their bumboys. The Government had obviously shared its concerns with these provincial magistrates. It wanted a lid screwed down on the affair – the very tightest of lids. As they filed out of the Shirehall, the small group of spectators and reporters would have been buzzing with speculation.

237

The record is silent as to whether the bail money was raised, but it seems highly unlikely. Aside from the sheer scale of the sums, the Reverend Thorold was then experiencing financial difficulties. Given the immense shame surrounding the crime, it's equally unlikely the proud rector went begging to his rich relatives for the cash. While believing that his son had been corrupted, he may also have felt that prison would allow him time for proper reflection and atonement.

In Arthur Thorold's home county in Lincolnshire, the idiosyncratic life of the shires went on without him. In October, Montague George Thorold, the second son of the 11th Thorold baronet, held a ball at his be-towered seat of Honington Hall. It was in celebration of the safe return from active service in South Africa of a popular neighbour who bore the most English of names: Reginald Bastard. It was an entertainment that Arthur would normally have attended, as a relation and eligible bachelor. The local newspaper noted that "the ball was kept merrily rolling until four o'clock," but that "to the great regret of all, Lieutenant Bastard was prevented by illness from being present." His was not the only absence.

12. A MOST PAINFUL CASE

The courts of assize, or assizes, were periodic courts that took place throughout the counties of England and Wales until 1972. They were usually scheduled twice a year. Until the mid-twentieth century, their proceedings were of intense interest to the public: the local press reporting them in the detail once accorded to royal tours.

On the evening of Wednesday the 29th of October 1902, Sir William Grantham* (referred to, per the style of the high judiciary when in office, as Mr. Justice Grantham), stepped off the train from London at Norwich Thorpe Station. As the *Norwich Mercury* reported, the time was 7.52pm. The nemesis of Bernard Fraser and Arthur Thorold had arrived.

Befitting the importance of his station as a judge for the Norfolk assizes circuit, Grantham was greeted on the platform by a bevy of local grandees. First and foremost was the magnificently named Sir Thomas Foxwell Buxton, who was temporarily discharging the social duties of the recently deceased High Sheriff of Norfolk. Also present was the Under-Sheriff; the late High Sheriff's Chaplain, the Vicar of Sprowston; the Sheriff of Norwich; and the Under-Sheriff for the City. Then, as the *Norwich Mercury* breathlessly informed its readers, "His Lordship was at once driven to his lodgings in the Close."

As *The Times* would diplomatically phrase it in his obituary, Justice Grantham "did not pose as a profound lawyer". A Sussex landowner

---

* Sir William Grantham (1835–1911); Conservative M.P., barrister and judge; knighted 1886.

239

and solid churchgoer, when in London he was notable for riding up to Royal Courts each morning on his iron-grey horse:

> the picture of an English squire, keen-visaged, with a friendly look and kindly speech…booted and spurred, and with hunting crop in hand…He was indifferent to the opinion of people, with a big 'p' or a little 'p', provided he had the esteem of those whose good opinion he prized…It was a simple, robust character, with its foibles, but with many loveable qualities.

Depending on where one sat in court, Justice Grantham's loveable qualities may have included his 'cheery audacity', a tendency to hastiness in judgement, and not least, his forthright opinions:

> the public were warned "never to take a cheque from a bookmaker"…husbands appeared to be advised in certain circumstances to box their wives' ears; and prisoners ordered to be whipped were told that they were "weak scoundrels" who cried "directly their dirty hides were touched."

Grantham had little hesitancy in haranguing juries, once saying of a flamboyant bookmaker in his summing up: "Her Majesty would rather give up her throne than be addressed by such a man."

"He was never much of a lawyer," opined *Reynolds's Newspaper*, "as everyone knows who is aware of the vast number of his decisions which have been reversed by the Court of Appeal. When in the House of Commons he was one of its most shallow windbags."

Still vigorous at seventy-two, but increasingly deaf, Grantham's time on the bench was beginning to be marked by hints from the press that the public interest would best be served by his retirement. As *The Times* damningly put it with patrician understatement: "with him, as with some others, practice did not make perfect." A socialist newspaper, *Justice*, labelled him "a notorious Tory political wirepuller, as ignorant of law as a parish beadle, who was pitchforked onto the bench for services rendered and 'services to be rendered'." The sometime editor of *John Bull*, Edward Roffe Thompson, wittily recalled:

> Mr. Justice Grantham, like necessity, knew no law…[he]…could

not, without severe mental discomfort, listen to more than one side of a case. His ordinary course was to take a glance at both litigants; that was generally sufficient, but if both seemed equally objectionable he might be impelled to take sides according as he liked or disliked counsel. Taking a side was quite necessary to him.

This cavalier approach he also brought to steeplechases, where he acted as a judge, once saying: "I know which was the winner, but I could not see his number." As for his deafness, a veteran of his courts wrote: "This may account for everything – or anything…what the ear does not hear the brain does not trouble about." Yet for the Government, Grantham's simplicity made him the perfect stooge to dispose of a problematic case.

On Thursday morning, Grantham met with and empowered the two Grand Juries who would be sitting. He was pleased to inform the jury trying municipal cases for Norwich that there were not many to deal with. He then spoke with the jury trying cases for the remainder of Norfolk. Unlike the previous group of gentlemen who consisted of plain 'misters', this was a shire jury with bells on. The twenty-two men included a viscount, three baronets, a knight, a rear-admiral, a major with the Victoria Cross, and two colonels. Grantham was also able to reassure them that there was also nothing on the court calendar indicative of any serious crime in the county – with one singular exception: "the series of charges against Fraser and Thorold – two gentlemen as he believed they were or supposed to be." However, he informed the assembled worthies that, "if they believed the statements of the two lads, [they] would not need to go into all the unpleasant details."

His Honour had likely been well apprised of the suppressed facts of the case, very possibly by his own son, but also by officials. The separation of powers between judiciary and government was, in theory, the same as today, where a judge trying a criminal case would not be briefed by anybody. However, in those intensely clubbable days, prosecutions which were perturbing to the Government, such as that of Cleveland Street, were subject to hazier gentleman's rules: the demarcation looked upon as a nicety, rather than necessity.

The trials for minor crimes were then proceeded with. First came the shire cases. For setting fire to a stack of barley straw, a repeat arsonist was sentenced to five years. A bigamist who'd found his first wife 'intolerable', and had attempted suicide after his crime was discovered, was given twelve months with hard labour. In the third case, a thirteen-year-old girl give evidence against her brother-in-law, who was charged with committing 'an offence' against her. However, she now denied the truth of her earlier statement. The jury found the prisoner Not Guilty, and he was discharged, but not before Grantham told him that there could be no doubt he and his wife had induced the girl to alter her claim, and that there was now a greater stigma upon him than if he'd fought the case on proper grounds and been convicted. Lastly, a man who had accidentally set fire to some stacks of corn was acquitted.

Rounding out the day were two city cases. A pair of thieves who'd broken into the warehouse of a shoe manufacturer were sentenced to terms of 18 months hard labour, and one month hard labour, respectively. Finally, a petty thief who'd stolen property to the value of £1 3s., and who was described as "a worthless scamp," was handed five years penal servitude. "Thank you, your Honour," he replied to Grantham, "I have a good heart and will do that." The Court then adjoined for the day. Friday was to be given over to the matter of Fraser and Thorold.

The next morning, Friday the 31st of October 1902, Bernard and Arthur once again found themselves in the holding cell outside the door of the Shirehall's criminal courtroom: a cell from which so many other men had gone before, to be sentenced to severe terms, and to their death.

If Justice Grantham was a striking figure, the legal support was equally impressive. Appearing for the prosecution was Horace Avory* K.C.,† assisted by Archibald Bodkin who'd prosecuted the hearings. Avory was also a character: an austere little man who, later as a judge, became renowned for the severity of his sentencing, sending more individuals to death than any other judge on the Kings Bench division. Although no great lawyer, he was conscientious and courteous, but his

---

* Sir Horace Avory (1851–1935) judge of the King's Bench Division of the High Court; knighted 1910.
† A King's Counsel is an eminent lawyer; also called a Queen's Counsel if the reigning monarch is a woman. Commensurate with the position, their fees are usually premium.

forbidding appearance radiated lack of sympathy for those he tried. A critic remarked: "Like most judges he was at his best in cases not involving personal relations, particularly sexual relations."

Appearing for Bernard Fraser was Charles Gill* K.C., a kindly but hard-headed Irishman who was considered one of the greatest advocates of his generation; he was supported in the court by Chartres Biron. Like Hamilton Cuffe, both Avory and Gill had appeared for the prosecution in the Cleveland Street and Wilde trials. George Elliott,† later also to be a K.C., appeared for Arthur Thorold. Grantham's son, William Wilson Grantham again held a watching brief for the unnamed and uncharged other parties.‡

When the charges were read out, Bernard and Arthur again pleaded Not Guilty to the felonious charges of buggery, but surprisingly, now pleaded Guilty to most of the misdemeanour charges, namely committing and inciting to commit gross indecency.§

It was perhaps more than the Crown had hoped for. Some of the press would speculate that their guilty pleas were made in an attempt to gain lighter sentences. In Norwich, the rumours were otherwise. There was a strong feeling that Bernard and Arthur had been pressured to hold their tongues and fall on their swords, as gentlemen, in order to protect more eminent persons from being engulfed by moral and social catastrophe.

Horace Avory for the prosecution now stated that, as the prisoners had pleaded guilty to the charges of misdemeanour, unless the Judge thought otherwise, he considered it unnecessary to proceed with the felony indictment. In coming to this decision he said that he was:

---

* Sir Charles Frederick Gill (1851–1923), Senior Counsel to the Treasury at the Old Bailey; knighted in 1921.

† George Elliott (1860–1916), a noted barrister.

‡ While such a close association with the sitting judge might be thought inappropriate, in practice it was not considered an impediment to him doing the job, which was simply observing what happened in court on behalf of his clients.

§ The Home Office Calendar of Prisons entry for Bernard Fraser states he pleaded Guilty to all charges. [HO140-219-158/HO140-219-159, National Archives] However, both local newspapers, the *Norwich Mercury* and *The Eastern Daily Press*, and an Ipswich paper, *The Evening Star*, whose account also appears to be eye-witness, reported that, like Thorold, Fraser pleaded Not Guilty to the charges of felony. Given the subsequent trial proceedings, these reports seem the correct version. The Calendar also lists the Date of Warrant for Fraser and Thorold as August 16th, which was actually the date of the 4th hearing, when they were committed for trial.

influenced by the fact that the Judge had certain powers under Section 62 of the Offences Against The Person Act, 1861, under which some of the counts in the misdemeanour indictment were framed. Under that Act the Judge would be able to deal with the cases.

"I think you have exercised a wise discretion," replied Justice Grantham unctuously to this piece of stage management. Gill and Elliot for the defence also consented to the proposed course. The prisoners' confessions of guilt having rendered the services of the jury redundant, the facts behind the charges needed only to be circumspectly sketched for Grantham to determine sentencing.

Horace Avory then opened the case. Nicknamed 'Slim', Avory's thin body, elongated neck and small head made him resemble a very serious bird: such was the gravity of his demeanour, even as a baby, his nurse had pronounced that his career lay in the courtroom. Standing before the court he declaimed that the case was:

> one of the very worst of the kind that had ever come before a Court.* Both prisoners were men of education and of good social position. Fraser was a man of independent means, who was living in London at a good address, was a member of one of the best clubs in London; and Thorold was a schoolmaster by profession, the son of a clergyman, and living at the time of the commencement of these offences with his father at the vicarage.

Avory went on to tell the court that:

> The shocking story began in May 1889...the correspondence which had been found showed that Fraser had been engaged in a regular campaign of this sort of crime throughout the country, in conjunction with a man named Bolton [sic: Boulton], who had absconded, and another named Wiley.

In the flow of Avory's oratory, these last facts gave pause. Who were these men, Boulton and Wiley, and why were their names not on the indictment? The fleeting statement had fallen from Avory's lips like

---

* Phrased in another report as: "the cases were the worst description that could be brought under the Statute."[Norfolk And Norwich Assizes, *Norwich Mercury*, 1 November 1902]

something meaningful tossed into a dark well. It would have left the lingering impression on those who heard or read it, including other journalists, that things were disturbingly amiss in this prosecution, which was surrounded by a miasma of rumour. Judge Grantham did not question this point (and given his probable full knowledge of the case, nor did he need to), and the proceedings glided on.

The solid form of Charles Gill now rose to speak for the defence of Fraser. Gill had a quiet convincing style of advocacy. His only mannerism, as *The Times* once noted, was:

> his habit of removing his eye-glasses to emphasise the particular emotion – surprise, doubt, indignation, encouragement, or incredulity – which he desired to convey. The expressiveness which he could impart into that trivial action cannot be adequately described.

This may have been such an eye-glasses moment, because Mr. Gill – and more specifically, those above him, had very grave doubts indeed. After what was probably a dramatic pause, he told the court that: "having considered the documents in this case" he had "come to the conclusion that it was quite impossible to put Fraser in the witness-box." And therefore, he:

> thought it right that the scandal of a trial of such a matter should not take place, and that the time of the court and of the jury should not be wasted in trying a case, the result of which could only be a verdict of guilty, so far as the misdemeanours were concerned.

He asked Justice Grantham to "take into consideration the fact the accused had pleaded guilty, and so had saved much unpleasantness," and which was "a fact which carried its own punishment." Like Avory, "He suggested it was a case which his Lordship might deal with under the special section in the *Criminal Law Amendment Act.*"

The unpleasantness spared was less talk of buggery, than the challenge of having to skate around the names of the uncharged guilty. It is glaringly obvious the trial had been an all too neat and tidy stitch-up from the start: a smooth smothering of the truth on behalf of 'British justice'.

George Elliott then rose to address the Court on behalf of Thorold. Elliott, who was to die at the relatively young age of fifty-six, had a suave courtroom manner marked by a clear and precise enunciation. He was considered an astute rather than brilliant advocate, with a fund of common sense.

His defence was mounted on the claim that there was "a material distinction between the offences" of the provincial God-fearing rector's son Arthur Thorold, and that of the cosmopolitan Society figure Bernard Fraser. "Until 1897, when he [Thorold] became a tutor at Naples, there was nothing whatsoever against his character. It was there he met Fraser and fell under his influence." It was implied that Arthur's natural manly innocence had been corrupted by the older libertine, and he had been entirely led into depravity by him: "it was impossible to deny that from that association Thorold had been brought into his present position."

It was definitely an every-man-for-himself strategy, and until this moment, one that Arthur was unaware would be adopted. Unbeknownst to him, the evening before the trial his father, the Reverend Algernon, had visited Elliott, and convinced him of the truth of this version of events.

All that was left was for the Judge's summing up and sentencing. The legal counsel may have braced themselves: Justice Grantham's speeches were prone to throw off 'showers of sparks' in the form of remarks which, at the very least, could levitate eye-brows. Echoing the opening remarks of Avory, Grantham commenced by stating:

> it was one of the most painful cases that had ever fallen to his lot or to the lot of any other judge, in finding two men bearing honoured names – names that had been honoured in the field and in the forum, and in every branch of life – pleading guilty to one of the most discreditable offences known to our law.

> He had heard everything said on their behalf, but was very sorry to say he had been able to agree with very little that had been said as a reason why they should be dealt with leniently.

Grantham then when on to speak of why he had no intention of being softhearted:

It had been said that in cases of this sort, the crime was its own punishment. When people of the position of the prisoners were found guilty of such offences, they were removed from the sphere in which they had previously moved, from their homes and from their friends, and the punishment, therefore, whatever might be inflicted, was very severe He was aware that it was so, but there was another aspect of such cases to be looked at — example.

The Judge of Assize generally had to deal with uneducated people, with ignorant people, who had not had the benefit of either education, or of social influence, such as the men of the prisoners' station had had. Too many criminals, unfortunately, had not had the benefit of the soothing and restraining influence of religion; and yet judges had to deal with them, and to punish them, sometimes most severely, for the crimes they committed.

How could it be said, when dealing with educated men, who had had every advantage life could give them, that they should be punished less severely than those who had been brought up without the benefits the prisoners had enjoyed?

Painful as it was, he must deal with them in a way which, he hoped, would have the effect not only of punishing them, but of preventing other men from falling from the high positions they occupied, and from committing crimes such as had evidently been perpetrated by the prisoners for many years.

Given other men were being saved 'from falling from the high positions they occupied' by the government's adamantine suppression of the facts, it was a somewhat spurious argument. However, Justice Grantham pressed on:

It had been said that there was more of such crime going on than the public were aware of. He sincerely hoped the suggestion was not true. In any case, it was impossible to imagine a worse case than the present one before him. The correspondence which had been referred to, and Fraser's diary, showed that for many years, he had been doing his best to contaminate the minds of honest and respectable boys – boys who would otherwise have grown up honest men, men worthy of their country, instead of being reduced to the condition of those of whom they read in ancient history.

Following that zinger, Grantham reiterated that he "had listened with great patience," to all the arguments of the defence, and "had anxiously considered what punishment should be inflicted." He then reflected on the punishing of homosexual offences:

When he first had the honour of being called to the Bar, the least sentence that could possibly have been passed on anyone found guilty of the full offence – however much might be said on his behalf, however young and ignorant he might be, and however much he might have been tempted, was ten years penal servitude, and from that up to penal servitude for life.

A change came over the spirit of the judicial life, and it was thought that there were some cases which might be dealt with less severely...He had been asked to deal with the prisoners under that section of legislation which limited the term of imprisonment to two years.

This was the more recent *Criminal Law Amendment Act* of 1885, which enabled judges to limit the punishment to two years' imprisonment for cases of gross indecency. However, as he told the court, he knew that Act:

was never intended to apply to such a case as this. Therefore, he must fall back upon what would have been considered proper punishment for this offence under the old law of 1861.

It was true that judges rarely gave the full sentence, and nearly always took off something, because, in most cases there is something to be said in favour of criminals. With regard to the prisoner Fraser, he was sorry to say that, as far as he could read through the case, there was nothing to be said in his favour.

Fraser's case was, without exception, the worst that he had ever heard of. Numbers of people had been contaminated by him. While moving in high society, among respectable people, it was evident he had been living a double life, and not only had he himself become depraved, but, what made the crime more serious, he had depraved others. It was, therefore, his painful duty to inflict the full punishment, and send him to penal servitude for ten years.

Turning to address Thorold, Grantham stated that:

> he saw no reason to doubt what had been said about him; that it was through his unfortunate introduction to Fraser that the prisoner was first led astray from the path of uprightness. He felt justified in dealing differently with him, but at the same time could not help remarking that it was a very bad case indeed. The prisoner would go to penal servitude for five years.

The prisoners were removed from the courtroom, and taken down. In the gulf that followed, Grantham then addressed the courtroom once more, to praise the naval officers involved in the case, saying:

> he could not help feeling that the country was very much indebted for the way in which those holding high and official positions at Devonport – Captain Hutchinson in particular – had acted in the matter. Captain Hutchinson was to be commended for the discretion and intelligence he had shown in bringing this matter to light, and if it had not been for him, this thing might have gone on for years without being discovered, and many other boys brought under the influence of the prisoners.

One local newspaper reported Grantham's closing sentence slightly differently. Instead of referring to the corruption of boys, it rendered his statement as: "and a great many people might have been ruined." While this may have been a transcription error, or a matter of discretion, one thing is certain: a great many adults involved in the case were missing from that courtroom.

As they departed in police custody to begin their sentences, Bernard Fraser and Arthur Thorold might have counted their luck that the 1861 Act had repealed the death sentence for buggery, so it was beyond Grantham's grasp to wield it in their case. In the months and years that followed, as they lay at night in their frigid cells, and woke to icy grim dawns, they no doubt bitterly contemplated what English justice had dealt them, and worse, the injustice of having been the scapegoats for richer, more powerful men who lived free.

Given the opprobrium still meted out to those who consort with the underaged, had they been tried today, like Oscar Wilde who also feted teenagers, their sentences (while not served in conditions as harsh) are likely to have been as long, if not longer.

Twelve days following Fraser and Thorold's trial, and despite a recommendation of mercy from the jury, Justice Grantham would don the black cap to sentence a twenty-year-old unemployed servant girl to death for drowning her baby, and a month after that, a twenty-eight-year-old woman for the same crime. (Both sentences were reprieved by the Home Secretary.) As an observer of Grantham later wrote:

> He shrank from such innovations as a Court of Criminal Appeal; it was, he thought, an attempt to abolish by a side wind capital punishment. He was confident that English law was nearly as perfect as it could be made.

On a cold late November afternoon in 1911, at his home in Eaton Square, a pneumonia-wracked Sir William Grantham found his own rest at the age of seventy-seven. The editor of *John Bull* memorialised:

> Personally he was an extraordinarily good-hearted man, and those who had least respect for his judicial qualities were among his warmest friends. There was not a dry eye in the Law Courts when it became known that he had been called before the highest of all tribunals.*

---

* In 1906, Grantham was finally accused in parliament of being politically partisan in his judicial decisions. In a speech in 1911, a few months before his death, he rebuked the charge, stating he'd intended to wait until he retired before attempting to clear his name, but "life was uncertain". The speech drew a scathing rebuke from Prime Minister Herbert Asquith, who said Grantham had violated the reciprocal obligation of parliament and the judiciary to refrain from censure or comment of each other. In the 1906 parliamentary debate on the matter, Arthur Balfour as a fellow Tory had come to his defense, telling the Commons, "a more transparently natural candid man than Mr. Justice Grantham never exercised judicial functions". However, closer to the mark was the Society magazine which eulogised he was, "too ardent a partisan to be a perfect judge. But find him away from his wig and robe and one could not have wished for more congenial company." [Mr Justice Grantham, *Birmingham Mail*, 8 February 1911; Hansard, House of Commons, 6 July 1906, vol 160 c406; Pink and Silk: A Good Man Gone, *The Tatler*, 13 December 1911.]

In 1902, the DPP prosecuted 454 cases. The procedural costs to the Government for the majority of these was under £20 or £30 each. That of Fraser and Thorold, listed in a Parliamentary accounting as case No. 223 – "Attempt to commit sodomy and conspiracy," incurred charges of £200. That made it the fourth most expensive case of the year – only the prosecution of two cases of forgery and an attempt to defraud creditors in a case of bankruptcy exceeded it. For the Government, it was no doubt considered money well spent. It had been far and away the most dangerous trial of the year.

13. THE AIR IS ELECTRIC

On the first day of November 1902, an American newspaper in Virginia published in its regular feature *Religious Truths*:

> Do not fear circumstances. They cannot hurt us if we hold fast by God and use them as the voices and ministries of His Will.

The author of the homily was the late and renowned Anglican Bishop of Winchester, Anthony Thorold.* Someone who may have found comfort in this sentiment was the good bishop's close relation, Arthur Thorold. Especially when, a few days later, the paper joined others in publishing scarifying revelations about him.

While press coverage of the prosecution of Fraser and Thorold was global, given its sordid nature it was also constrained – especially in England. When it came to Society scandal, there was a constant smorgasbord of more palatable cases to feature.†

The most detailed accounts of the hearings and trial were published by three Norwich-based newspapers, the *Norwich Mercury*, *Eastern Daily Express*, and the *Norfolk News*, the reports of the latter being edited versions of those of the *Express*. *The Evening Star*, a paper based

---

* The Rt. Rev. Anthony Wilson Thorold (1825–1895), a grandson of the 9th baronet.

† At the time of Fraser and Thorold's sentencing, the story of the day was that of Lady Violet Beauchamp, who was being sued for libel by the wife of her ship-owner lover. Violet would later succeed in marrying him, while he would attempt to have his ex-wife murdered. During several years of subsequent litigation, and relishing her scarlet woman status, Violet would turn up in court, a "small vehement figure wrapped in an astonishing mantle of strawberry coloured velvet reaching to the heels." [Anthony Louis Ellis, *Prisoner At The Bar*, Heath Cranton Ltd, London 1943, p69.]

at Ipswich, neglected the hearings, but covered the trial at length.

While not stooping to the word 'buggery', the reports plainly stated that Bernard and Arthur were charged with "a series of felonies and misdemeanours in association with two lads," including "committing and inciting to commit gross cases of indecency." Reporting of the prisoners' associations with others was mentioned in vague terms, but salacious evidence was rigorously omitted. The court proceedings were otherwise well-sketched, including Judge Grantham's scorching summary speech. Only one newspaper followed up on the flight of Boulton. Investigative reporting was uncommon, and it certainly wasn't the remit of court reporters.

While *The Times* covered the assizes courts, true to form, it didn't pick up the story, although its editor George Buckle* would have been well aware of the case. However, three days after Fraser and Thorold's sentencing, in London, the *Daily Mail*, *London Evening News* and *Evening Mail* featured brief reports, and the following day *The Daily Telegraph* published a three-paragraph article titled 'A Scandalous Case', which was a cut-down of the *Eastern Daily Press* report. It detailed Fraser and Thorold's genteel backgrounds, and that they had been charged with felony and misdemeanour, but the nature of the offences was only alluded to: "one of the most discreditable offences known to our law...Fraser had been living a double life and debauching others." Any mention of the involvement of youths was omitted.

Throughout the first week of November, a small smattering of provincial papers throughout the British Isles printed the *Eastern Daily Press* or *The Daily Telegraph* reports in various forms under titles such as 'A Scandalous Case' (*Gloucester Citizen*), and 'Scandalous Offences' (*Worcestershire Chronicle*). Reference was made to "abominable felonies and misdemeanours with a number of lads," but accompanied by that well-worn phrase, "the details of the case are unfit for publication." One of the most bowdlerised reports appeared in Cyril's own county in *The Norfolk Chronicle*. It merely referred to "a shocking offence", and paraphrasing Horace Avory, printed that "Fraser had been engaged in a regular system which he had practiced throughout the

---

* George Earle Buckle (1854–1935), editor of *The Times*, 1884–1911. Married Alicia Isobel and had issue; and secondly, Beatrice Anne Earle.

country, in conjunction with a man named Boulton, who had absconded." As to what the offence and 'system' might be, there was not a single word!

Adhering to their ingrained habit of discretion, most British newspapers also rigorously downplayed the significance of the case, withholding the fact that other prominent names were involved. However, in this widespread suppression, there were notable exceptions.

Reynolds's Newspaper had excellent informants. On the 3rd of August, the Sunday immediately following Fraser and Thorold's arrest, and six days before the Coronation, a brief paragraph had appeared on the back page of the paper in its aptly titled column 'The Secret History Of To-Day'. The blind item stated:

> I understand that a serious matter is being investigated in the shape of a charge against a gentleman moving in aristocratic circles. The suspicions, out of which the affair has arisen, were originally excited by the opening of letters addressed to a boy on one of His Majesty's ships in the South of England. We understand that people in Norwich will soon be startled with details of the case.

While intriguing, the unseemly item wasn't picked up by other papers. Immediately following the case hearings, the paper featured another item: "A week or two ago we intimated in our 'Secret History' that a case would shortly be heard at Norwich which would cause considerable sensation. The brief details of the case are appended." There then followed a bare-bones report of the hearings, but nothing hinting at its grander connections or graver scale.

However, on November 2nd, following Fraser and Thorold's trial, The Secret History of To-Day featured a riveting paragraph:

HEREDITARY LEGISLATORS.
ASTOUNDING RUMOUR.

> An ugly rumour was in circulation in the City yesterday afternoon that a peer well known in financial and philanthropic circles had fled the country in consequence of the issue of a warrant

254

charging him with an offence under the Criminal Law Amendment Act. On inquiry at his lordship's London residence last evening our representative could ascertain no information as to the noble lord's location.

That same day, the allegation was also published by *The Sunday Special*, which billed itself as "London's Best High-class Sunday Morning Paper". The report was picked up by a handful of newspapers across the Kingdom, and as one paper stated, "has set everyone talking". This version read:

> There are persistent rumours in society circles that a well-known Peer has been compelled to leave the country in order to escape prosecution on a criminal charge of a most serious character. Sensational developments may be expected.

The *Edinburgh Evening News* was more explicit:

> Speculation is rife as to the strange disappearance from society haunts of a peer whose name is well known. All sorts of rumours are about, and it is hinted that he has fled the country to avoid standing in the dock where Oscar Wilde had to answer the charge that closed his career.

The following day, in the north-east of England, the *Sunderland Daily Echo and Shipping Gazette* elaborated:

> A most sensational story, writes a London correspondent, is current in London. I can only mention it as rumour, although the source of the tale seems to demand for some credence; and, personally, I may say that I find it difficult to believe the entire tale. As goes, a Peer, whose name is well known all over the country, has, within the last two days, been arrested, released on very large bail, and has fled the country. If this should prove to be true the case will create an enormous sensation, although every endeavour will be made to hush up the facts, and especially to suppress names.

Indicative of the new speed of telegraphed syndicated news, the story was already breaking out in newspapers across America. One report, headlined "Another Scandal Agitates London," read:

A tremendous sensation was caused here today by statements that another scandal of the Oscar Wilde type was about to become public property. It is asserted that the man whose name is connected with the affair, and who is a peer, has fled the country, but there is every reason to believe that he is at present lying ill at an English watering place. A report of this affair found its way into print, in guarded language this morning, but every effort will be exerted to prevent further publicity.

A New York newspaper printed: "According to one account, he was arrested a few days ago and held in £5,000 bail, which was furnished, after which he has disappeared." It also stated: "The name of the same nobleman has been previously mentioned, notably a few months ago, in connection with such offences." This was Yankee hyperbole: there had only been the blind item in *Reynolds's Newspaper* in August. However, by the Monday following the trial, a syndicated report had been made America aware that the case of the peer and the court case in Norwich were linked. In Washington D.C. it appeared as 'London Wrought Up,' on the front page of *The Evening Star.*

The excitement yesterday over the reported flight of a peer to the continent was heightened to-day by the announcement that a well-known London society man, Bernard Fraser, had been sentenced, at the Norwich assizes, to ten years' penal servitude. With him was also sentenced Arthur Thorold, the son of a clergyman connected, as is Fraser, with one of the oldest and proudest families in the United Kingdom. The prisoners were charged with carrying on a regular campaign to deprave the morals of youths all over the country.

By Tuesday, *The New York Times*, and newspapers as remote as *The Waxahachie Daily Light* in Texas were carrying versions of it.

In England, the connection between the two cases was also made by the weekly journal *To-Day* – the same publication that had stomped on *The Chameleon* when it reared its colourful head. By 1902, *To-Day* was owned by Horatio Bottomley,* a journalist, M.P. and swindler,

---

* Horatio William Bottomley (1860–1933). In 1922 he was expelled from Parliament, and sentenced to seven years prison for fraud. He was described as "small fat and gross, with a thick bilious skin and small habits which were far from pleasant…but he seemed to win every

who would find fame as owner-editor of the magazine *John Bull*. The report in *To-Day* stated:

> Another of those painful scandals which have been unpleasantly frequent of late is agitating London society. Three or four men moving in leading circles, and members of the best clubs, are implicated, and the information in the hands of the police shows that a revolting system procuration had been carried on. Two of the men, both bearing honoured names, have been laid by the heels, and at the Norfolk Assizes on Saturday were sentenced to penal servitude for ten and five years respectively, but a third, who is one of the wealthiest members of the peerage, and a well-known politician, managed to get out the country before the warrant issued for his arrest could be made effective.

The brief item was picked up by at least one regional newspaper. That same Tuesday, the new populist London paper the *Daily Express* published a report that not only confirmed this was far more than just a simple matter of a couple of miscreants from the gentry, but also provided background on the handling of the case, which would have alarmed the Government:

SOCIETY SENSATION
Well-Connected Criminal Gets Ten Years

> Considerable feeling has been aroused in social circles throughout Norfolk by the extremely painful case dealt with by Mr. Justice Grantham at Norfolk Assizes on Friday last.

> The prisoners were Bernard Fraser, a well-known man in the county circle, who, as the judge remarked, "had been moving in high society," and Arthur Thorold, a schoolmaster. They were charged with offences under the Criminal Law Amendment Act, and, pleading guilty, were sentenced, Fraser to ten years' penal servitude, and Thorold to five years.

> Fraser, it was stated, had been engaged in a regular campaign of

---

heart by his strange silvery accents, by a caressing language, by a familiarity that was almost vulgar." He was indifferent to public opinion, once observing of Jesus: "Made rather a mess of his life, didn't he?" [Anon (Herbert Vivian), *Myself Not Least*, Henry Holt And Company, New York 1928, pp123-124.]

crime in conjunction with a man named Bolton[*sic*], who had absconded, and another named Willey[*sic*].

The entire evidence for the prosecution was collected by Inspector Arrow, who arrested Fraser at Dover as he was about to cross to France, and the prisoner Thorold at a school in Essex, where he was engaged as head master.

There was a strong feeling in Norwich that social influence was brought to bear on the two prisoners to persuade them to plead guilty to the misdemeanour in order to shield others of high rank who would have been involved if the case had been thoroughly gone into.

The two men, Bolton and Willey, whose identity is known to the Scotland-yard authorities, were not named in the indictment, but it is probable that the public prosecutor would have been forced to take action if the witnesses had been heard.

The idea is prevalent that there are a number of men of position implicated with Fraser and Thorold.

Both Fraser and Thorold appeared prepared to receive their sentences, and took them most nonchalantly.

In speaking of the case everyone in Norwich expresses the opinion that the thing should be thoroughly thrashed out, and if there are more guilty parties they should be equally punished, no matter how high their position may be.

The following day the paper further dared express editorial dissatisfaction with the justice that had been meted out:

A PUBLIC SCANDAL
Rumours Which Besmirch Honoured Names

The case of the men Fraser and Thorold, who were sent to penal servitude by Mr. Justice Grantham at Norwich for an offence the seriousness of which cannot be over-estimated, has given rise to rumours which bid fair to become a public scandal.

It is hinted, and in some cases strongly affirmed, that the man Fraser, who, it will be remembered, was spoken of as having 'moved for years in high society', had as accomplices in his crimes persons of high rank.

At the trial of Fraser and Thorold the names of two men, 'Wiley' and 'Boulton', were mentioned as having been concerned with the prisoners in their offences. These men were, however, not included in the indictment, and it is asserted that their arrest would mean the besmirching of the names of more than one high personage.

The matter is becoming a grave public scandal. If the rumours have a foundation in fact, then justice demands that the parties should be put upon their trial.

On the other hand, if the rumours have no foundation, some decisive step should be taken by the authorities to deny them. As it is, names which have hitherto been held in the highest honour in England are being bandied about from mouth to mouth in connection with the disgraceful affair...

This was open press dissent to be sure. Yet while at least one provincial paper reprinted the story, and five days later *The Weekly Dispatch* of London printed the sentence "social influence was brought to bear on the two prisoners... to shield others of high rank," it was hardly a chorus. The fact the *Daily Express* wasn't sure about the veracity of the rumours, indicates how tight a lid the Government was keeping on the case. Nonetheless, the paper attempted to keep up the heat. The next day it published a further item headlined:

WHO ARE THEY?
Rumour Still Busy With Society Scandal

The recent notorious case at Norwich has caused considerable excitement in West End Clubs, and social circles generally, as to the identity of the men of high position who are rumoured to be implicated in the correspondence of the two prisoners, Fraser and Thorold...On inquiry being made yesterday in police circles, it was learned that the man named Boulton had escaped to the Continent, and was last seen at Brussels.

Of fellow procurer 'Wiley', who also got away – or was allowed to get away, there was not a word.

"It would be idle to attempt disregard the rumour which is circulating in society," proclaimed the London correspondent of the *Wigan Observer* on the 5th of November:

> It is averred that a great nobleman – great in his wealth, great in his popularity, great in his family associations – has been compelled to fly the land. The alleged offence for which it is asserted he is sought is a terrible one. Handsome, debonair, graceful in talk, happy in wit, the possessor of two of the most redolently beautiful palaces in England, a veritable Croesus in wealth, this noble is said to be sought by the police.

Flagging their virtue vigorously, they added:

> I would not give the story any circulation had it not already appeared in print. As it is I add not a line to it beyond to pray that it be but the mouthings of the garbage-hunters.

That same day, George Ives, the well-connected and discreet campaigner against the oppression of homosexuals, confided to his diary:

> The last few days it has been said in several papers that a certain peer well known in financial circles has been charged with offences against morality and held to bail in 5,000. Rumour of information from several people said it was Lord B[attersea],* and that he was safe across the water.

> But now I notice that my Lord B is reported to be ill at his country place, of this is profound silence: I wonder what it means?

True enough, on the 3rd of November – the day after the news broke of a nobleman's arrest and flight, reports of Lord Battersea's indisposition were published. For what was a case of flu, the large

---

* The full name is a later annotation in Ives' hand.

scale of the headlines employed to announce it by a Norfolk newspaper, the *Eastern Daily News*, suggests a hidden agenda to draw special attention to the story. Given the paper was quartered in Norwich where the trial occurred, and where gossip concerning the case was rampant, this is very likely. The report stated:

LORD BATTERSEA'S ILLNESS.
TODAY'S BULLETIN

We regret that Lord Battersea is lying ill at the Pleasaunce, Overstrand, suffering from bronchitis, following an attack of influenza. This morning's bulletin states: 'Fairly good night; strength maintained; bronchial condition better.

Another wire received at two o'clock says: 'Better night; fever less.'

Four days later the *Daily Express* was able to report:

Lord Battersea is very much better, and it is hoped he will soon be convalescent, although his brother's death* proved a terrible shock to him in his weak condition. It is probable that his medical advisers will insist upon his wintering out of England.

Scenting the zeitgeist, on 13th of November, Arnold White cautioned readers of the *Daily Dispatch*: "Sodomism in London is an allied and friendly Power with all foreigners that hate us."

If there was any hope at The Pleasaunce, the Norfolk seat of Lord Battersea, that gossip of his arrest might be quelled by issuing health bulletins to the press with the assiduity of an illness in the Royal Family, it was in vain. On the 15th of November, the raffish but widely-read paper of the turf, *The Sporting Times* (or 'The Pink 'Un', as it was known), which dished up scraps of tittle-tattle, published in its front page gossip column 'Sporting Notes' a two-line item pregnant with insinuation:

These riddles again.
"What did Battersea?"†

---

* Lewis Flower.
† A play on the riddle: "What did Battersea?" Answer: "Cheyne Walk across the river.

Two days later another sporting paper, *The Scottish Referee*, printed:

> They are cackling a great deal, are the Cockneys, about a certain 'scandal' that has been hushed up by the police. A lord is in it. Nothing like a full-flavoured, disgusting scandal as a lever for Cockney conversation... They do not argue about Education Bill, or hinterlands, or Somaliland, or the Parliamentary guillotine, or the widening of the Strand, or what the Bishop of Ripen said or said he did not say about miracles. Not they!

The rumour continued to sweep London, high and low. On the 22nd of November, it reached the ears of the writer Wilfrid Blunt through his friend the publisher Wilfrid Meynell.[*] Blunt recorded in his diary:

> Meynell was full of a new scandal in which Cyril Flower, Lord Battersea, is involved. Accusations have been made against him by the police & he has been committed for trial but released on a £500 bail[†] with a private hint that he should leave the country. This has been done. At the Clubs they are repeating the following rhyme:
>> It is time the Lords should understand
>> They can't do all they please
>> Since Battersea of Overstrand
>> Is stranded over seas.

A week later George Ives made another diary entry on the matter:

> The air is electric with scandal that Lord Battersea has had to flee and forfeit his bail – love affair – but Lord Euston? has dared face it & escaped the storm, perhaps because he's so near the crown. What with hypocrisy of unjust laws we are in a pretty mess but homogenic nature will not be ignored.

The further rumour of Lord Euston, the veteran of the Cleveland Street Scandal, would certainly have added to the electricity. Had lightning struck in the same place twice? The question mark Ives inserted after his name indicates he wasn't sure. With the scarcity of information, anything seemed possible.

---

[*] Wilfrid Meynell (1852-1948), a British newspaper publisher and editor. Meynell and his wife Alice rescued the poet and mystic Francis Thompson from destitution.
[†] Given the scale of Thorold's bail, the reports of £5,000 seem the more likely figure.

In late October, Ives had visited Oscar Browning,* noting in his diary: "he's looking very robust but somewhat troubled as to many little things, as usual." Two letters survive from Ives to Browning that concern a crisis. Written in haste and undated, they are assumed to be from sometime between 1901 and 1903. In the first letter, Ives writes:

> My dear OB, <u>Friday Late</u>
>
> I am engaged in cricket fixtures. Much troubled about the news or rather want of news; what can I do? can you not come up here, or send F [Fred, Browning's secretary of the time] or some person you can trust.
>
> I hope nothing has gone wrong with anybody whom I know, but life is so uncertain. I am scribbling this to catch the post. <u>might</u> come down [to Cambridge] Sunday or Monday for a few hours if you think it reasonable... I am at least thankful nothing is wrong with <u>you</u>. G

In the second letter of two days later, Ives writes of his intention to train down to Cambridge for the day:

> I cannot imagine what good I can do in this matter whatever it may be, but you know my feelings upon many things & I would go very far to help wherever I could.

While these troubles may refer to another affair, at some later date Ives added a postscript to his first diary entry on the Battersea scandal:

> "It probably was [Lord Battersea]. King Edward is said to have squashed the whole thing tho it was quite well known."

Throughout November, *Reynolds's Newspaper* in its column 'The Secret History Of To-Day', published further titbits:

> Two fashionable individuals moving in what is called the best Society have just been sentenced to ten and five years respectively for an odious offence. But the remarkable thing

---

* Oscar Browning (1837–1923); a beloved and eccentric pederastic schoolmaster, education advocate, historian, radical Liberal, and *bon viveur.*

about these offences is the easy way in which several suspected persons have escaped in recent years. The list of those who have avoided prosecution includes two bishops, a dean, a canon, and the son of a duke.

A gentleman who has occupied a position of great responsibility in the East-end for many years has, we hear, resigned under peculiar circumstances. His interest in London politics is likely to be eclipsed for a time.

It is not generally known that in a certain class of criminal cases the accused receive twenty-four hours' warning to give them an opportunity of leaving the country, it being felt that the publication of such charges does more harm than the punishment of the offenders.*

November 22nd was Lord and Lady Battersea's Silver Wedding Anniversary. At Aston Clinton, their country estate in Buckinghamshire, the villagers had been hoping to present their subscribed gifts of a silver vase and picture frame in person, but as Lord Battersea was still recovering at Overstrand, this was not possible. However, a newspaper report stated: "We are glad to be able to announce that his Lordship is now progressing most satisfactorily."

However, on the 11th of December the *Birmingham Daily Gazette* also printed the rumour of the absconding peer, with its London correspondent providing an additional hint as to his identity:

A highly unpleasant story is coupled in a report which reaches me with the name certain peer who occupied a prominent position in politics a few years ago and whose wife belongs to one of the wealthiest families in the country. The report is to the effect that he was about month ago brought before the magistrates on an exceedingly grave charge. He was liberated on heavy bail, and steps were taken to prevent the matter coming to the knowledge of the press. Instead of appearing in court on the

---

* The dispensation, although only for the privileged, was better known than *Reynolds's* imagined. At the time of the Cleveland Street Scandal, the diary of a clergyman records: "There is much indignation because the Government & the police have given warnings to people & allowed them to escape." [25 November 1889, Rev. R.C. Fillingham diary, p406; Merton College Library.]

date fixed for the further hearing of the case, however, he left the country. Searching inquiries have been instituted, but so far his whereabouts remain a secret. It is hardly possible that the matter can be concealed much longer...

The story was reprinted the very same day by the *Lancashire Evening Post*, with the exception of the words: "but so far his whereabouts remain a secret," suggesting the editor knew exactly where Lord Battersea was. He also slapped a triple headline on the story, which expressed strong dissatisfaction with the proceedings:

GRAVE SOCIETY SCANDAL
PEER ALLEGED TO HAVE BROKEN BAIL
A SUBJECT FOR PARLIAMENTARY INQUIRY.

Two days later, with its editor apparently still simmering, the *Lancashire Evening Post* precipitately reported:

Lord Battersea, it is said, will take no further part in Liberal politics. Indeed, it is more than likely that he has gone out of public life altogether. As a Whip he was exceedingly popular. His wealth, handsome figure, and skill in the hunting-field – he won the House of Commons' Steeplechase,* once made him a social favourite.

As for any hope of a parliamentary inquiry and sensational developments, the steps taken "to prevent the matter coming to the knowledge of the press" clearly did the trick: apart from reports on his health, as George Ives wrote, there was only a profound silence.

If it had ever been puzzled, *The Sporting Times* soon unravelled the Battersea riddle. In January its 'Sporting Notes' column offered the sly dig:

Motor car was the feature of the Newmarket election, and automobiles lent to Mr. Rose [the Liberal candidate Charles

---

* In 1889. It became part of his personal legend. However, he was later disqualified. He'd originally planned on riding a horse he'd provocatively named 'Home Rule', but due to it being restive, rode another called 'Sultan' that had previously won a steeplechase, which was against the rules, as was riding a different horse to the one registered. [Untitled items, *The Morning Post*, 9&13 April 1889, p5.]

Rose]* by Lord Battersea and others were to be seen even in such an out of the way place as Six Mile Bottom.

In the colonies, the press was almost as quiet on the matter. None of the newspapers in Australia picked up the story at all: an extremely fortunate circumstance for Arthur Thorold in the years ahead. In the most English of Britain's colonies, New Zealand, just two newspapers published brief items. However, they readily combined separate news stories to state that Fraser and Thorold's case was connected with that of 'a certain peer', and that other prominent names were involved. It shows that even at the bottom of the world newspaper editors were across the facts, supplied by submarine cable, that the majority of the press in the home country were keenly withholding.

Given this, and the fact it had even become the subject of doggerel in the London clubs, it begs the question why, unlike in the Cleveland Street Scandal, the radical press, with the exception of some blind-item snipes by W.M. Thompson in *Reynolds's Newspaper*, didn't pursue the story after the initial leaks.

As it happened, in the years since 1889, there had been significant changes within the radical press. W.T. Stead had stepped down as editor from *The Pall Mall Gazette*, and under its new owner William Waldorf Astor,† the paper had reverted to its conservative roots. The appointment diary of the Home Secretary, Aretas Akers-Douglas, indicates he was meeting regularly with the new editor, Sir Douglas Straight,‡ who would have also known of the scandal through club gossip. The versatile Straight was a former barrister and popular society figure, but unlike Stead, was not an editor interested in retailing sensation. It is therefore sobering to turn the pages of the *Gazette* – the supposed record of what mattered to persons of substance in the capital, and note that despite the reams of social trivia detailed during those weeks, there is a complete absence of even the slightest reference to the story then gripping Society.

---

* Sir Charles Day Rose, 1st Baronet (1847–1913), British-Canadian businessman, race horse breeder, yachtsman, and Liberal M.P. Married Eliza McClean and had five children. He may have been a model for Mr Toad of the children's novel *The Wind In The Willows* by Kenneth Grahame.
† William Waldorf Astor, 1st Viscount Astor (1848–1919) American-British attorney, politician, businessman and philanthropist. Married Mary Dahlgren Paul, and had issue.
‡ Sir Douglas Straight (1844–1914) lawyer, Conservative M.P., judge and journalist. A bachelor.

T.P. O'Connor had also left his high-circulation radical evening newspaper *The Star*, founding another paper *The Sun*, before selling it to embark on milder ventures. These were the founding and editing of *M.A.P.* ('Mainly about People'), a weekly magazine of 'pleasant' gossip, personal portraits, and social news, and the higher toned *T.P.'s Weekly*, which billed itself as 'A Journal of Life And Literature'. Neither publication was in the business of shocking revelations. The assistant but real editor of *The Star*, H.W. Massingham, who officially succeeded to the editor's chair in 1890, had gone on to the *Daily Chronicle*, where he was sacked for his disapproval of the Boer War.

While Henry Labouchère had handed over the running of *Truth* to editor Horace Voules, he still found time to fulminate in its columns against imperialists and swindlers. Yet not a word of the scandal found its way into that paper either, despite Labouchère's particular loathing for homosexuals and class injustice.* Three possible reasons assert themselves. Firstly, unlike Cleveland Street, where Labouchère had excellent sources of information from within the Post Office, it appears details of the Battersea scandal were confined to a much tighter police and official circle. While the bare bones of the story had leaked, even the well-connected insider George Ives was unaware of what was going on. Secondly, like Labouchère, Lord Battersea was a prominent Liberal who had hosted him at his London home.

While Labby publicly referred to Cyril as "An amiable but politically obscure gentleman," privately his opinion was even more dismissive. When, on behalf of Gladstone, Liberal whip Edward Marjoribanks had approached him in the early 1890s about donating to the Party, Labby sent back the reply that he had no money, but pointed out that Gladstone had just given peerage to Cyril Flower "who is a fool. He must have paid you a million for that.† So you don't need my modest offering."

Cyril was hardly alone in not being on Labby's dance card. He had a rich contempt for most of his political colleagues, once telling a

---

* Two years later, a Belfast court case involving conjugation between the ex-Lord Mayor's private secretary and a nineteen-year-old working-class youth, in which both secured a stage-managed acquittal due to alleged severe intoxication and no recollection, would see Labby label it a disgrace to the judge, jury and "superlatively moral City of Belfast". [*Truth*, 29 September 1904, p759 (p13)]

† A jesting exaggeration.

bemused Wilfrid Blunt over lunch that, "If you were to take them together…and boil them in a pot, Campbell Bannerman, Asquith, Morley, Rosebery, and Grey, you would not get the worth of a mouse out of them." However, the last thing he would have wished was to damage his own party, of which he was a leading light.

When Labouchère had made his stand in Parliament over suppression of the Cleveland Street Scandal, the conservative press subjected him to a bluster of attacks, characterising his interest in the affair being solely about what damage to the Tory government he could wring from it. One such newspaper, *The Globe*, scored a particularly sharp point. Mocking him as "the champion of Truth and the Rights of the People," it made a case for his partisan hypocrisy, claiming he'd made no such fuss when a similar scandal had touched a member of the Liberal party:

> Who was Prime Minister, who was Attorney-General, and what party was in power when the brother of a well-known Gladstonite nobleman was accused of the same crime as Lord Arthur Somerset? Who on that occasion gave the accused person three days' warning to quit the country, and told him that upon the expiry of that time a warrant would be issued for his arrest? And what use did that titled criminal make of the 'law' which he was thus given in place of the law by which he might justly have been condemned to penal servitude? If Mr. Labouchère does not know the answer to these questions Mr. Gladstone or Sir Charles Russell may be able to tell him.*

If, as is highly likely, the Battersea scandal involved prominent Liberal Party figures beyond Cyril Flower, the reticence of Labby, and W.M. Thompson, is even more understandable.

---

* The nobleman has not been identified. A week later the paper published a clarification stating that the event had not occurred when Russell was Attorney-General – his name had merely been raised because, being the highest legal adviser in the Liberal Party, he was someone whom Labouchère could question about the matter. [Three Questions For Mr Labouchere To Answer, *The Globe*, 10 March 1890, p4.] It should be noted that during the Cleveland Street Scandal, the Liberal M.P. Lord Edward Cavendish (1838–1891), the married youngest son of the 7th Duke of Devonshire, was named by overseas press as being involved. Like Lord Battersea, he also contracted a genuine life-threatening illness in his darkest hour; in his case, Scarlet Fever. His regular diaries suddenly break off with the entry: "I am afraid it looks rather like a change of weather." [The West-End Scandal, *The Press* (New Zealand) 20 November 1889, p5; Lord Edward Cavendish diary, 2 September 1889; Chatsworth Archive.]

The third reason why Labby may have held his fire was for a simple family consideration: his sister Emily was the widow of the Bishop of Winchester – the Rt. Rev. Anthony Thorold, whose homily opened this chapter. Protecting Emily, her three children, and the extended Thorold family from any associated taint may have exercised Labby's mind.*

Ernest Parke was now editing T.P. O'Connor's *The Star*. Like Labouchère, he possibly also had no inside information. During his time in prison, Parke's health had suffered severely. The thought of being subject to another libel action may well have stayed his hand – and that of others. Lord Euston's ducal family were rich, well-connected, and influential, but the Rothschilds, from whence hailed Lord Battersea's spouse, were another matter altogether. The fear of being subject to legal action from an innately mysterious family of almost limitless pan-European banking wealth was enough to pause any journalist's pen – especially if they were not in full possession of the facts.

Even the gossip magazine *Vanity Fair* had lost the sophisticated irreverence and pointed wit it had enjoyed under its founder Thomas Bowles: he'd sold out in 1889. Under the current owner-editor, an expatriate Tasmanian, Oliver Armstrong Fry,† it was in decline, and had become a mere clearinghouse for purring paragraphs on the sables of duchesses and whatnot: social news at its most overweeningly deferential and banal.

As for the mainstream press: typical was the organ of the middle class, *The Daily Telegraph*. Its owner and editor-in-chief was Sir Edward Lawson,‡ a socially ambitious first baronet who'd Anglicised his Jewish name, and so embedded himself into the Establishment that King Edward annually visited his country home, Hall Barn, for its shooting. Despite all the honeyed words for the Government and Empire in *The Daily Telegraph's* pages, Lawson had been "terribly

---

* When Labby died in 1912, he bequeathed £5,000 to Emily, and the same amount to one her sons, Algar Labouchère Thorold, who would write his authorised biography.
† Oliver Armstrong Fry (1855–1931); schoolmaster, tutor, classical professor, barrister, journalist, and eminent Freemason. Married Annie Zetherquist Rolfe, and had issue.
‡ Edward Levy-Lawson, 1st Baron Burnham (1833–1916), born Edward Levy. He inherited the paper from his father Joseph Moses Levy. Despite his deep conservatism, he held a reputation as one of London's wittiest conversationalists.

disappointed at not getting his peerage" in the Coronation honours.*
No secrets upsetting to the status quo would be issuing from that
quarter. The notable exception among the mainstream newspapers
besides *Reynolds's* was the new and enormously successful *Daily
Express*, published by the enterprising philanthropist Arthur Pearson.†
As noted, it printed three short items on the Battersea case, but then,
either from lack of verifiable information, fear of libel, or because it
was leaned on, abruptly dropped the matter.‡

The 1880s in Britain had witnessed the arrival of radical editors
venting opinionated anger – what was termed 'the new journalism'.
In an observation that has resonance today, critic Matthew Arnold§
called the phenomenon:

> full of ability, novelty, variety, sensation, sympathy, generous
> instincts; its one great fault is that it is *feather-brained*. It throws
> out assertions at a venture because it wishes them to be true;
> does not correct either them or itself, if they are false; and to get
> at the state of things as they truly are seems to feel no concern
> whatever.

The stodgy decorous papers had considered the New Journalism
merely disrespectful and insincere rowdyism. However, as happened
with the coverage of the Cleveland Street Scandal by the radical
papers, it sometimes served to kick them out of their complacency,
servility, and timidity.**

As the twentieth century dawned, the tone of the Press again changed.

---

* He attained it the following year.
† Sir (Cyril) Arthur Pearson, 1st baronet (1866–1921).
‡ Its editor in 1902 was (Bertram) Fletcher Robinson (1870–1907), a Liberal Unionist who
collaborated with Sir Arthur Conan Doyle on *The Hound Of The Baskervilles*.
§ Matthew Arnold (1822–1888); poet and cultural critic who worked as an inspector of schools.
** Perhaps the new journalism was not so very new. In the wake of criticisms of the press, a
periodical observed: "Anyone who reads the extracts from the 'Times' of 1802 which the great
newspaper of to-day is printing cannot but be struck by the breezy and robust style in which
the journalist of one hundred years ago discussed men and matters. We want more vigorous
plain-speaking comment in these days. There would be fewer scandals going unchecked if our
newspapers were free to tell all they knew. A thin-skinned nation is an unhealthy nation." [*The
Weekly Survey*, quoted in *The Cornish Echo and Falmouth & Penryn Times*, 5 December 1902, p5.]

Newspaper operations under owners like Lord Northcliffe became ever more industrialised. With the increased business-like footing came a greater standardisation of spirit, and a wider sobriety. Personal editorial passions and the upsetting of apple carts was not on the agenda. Rather than stories sparked by moral fervour, now they were more often calibrated by the need to boost circulation figures – topics of popular appeal like the Boer War, and surface emotions that were 'rubbed in'. The time of editors as preachers, prophets and crusaders was passing.

If in England there was little taste for spilt blue blood, in the breezy democratic air of the United States, the case of Fraser and Thorold chimed well with the always popular theme of the degeneracy of Olde England and its ruling class. As *Reynolds's Newspaper* later noted:

> So great is the tacit and ignorant boycott of certain kinds of news by the leading journals of this country that some of the more enterprising newspapers get a regular daily telegraphic supply from the American newspapers, whose London correspondents seem to know more about the inner history of politics and Society than do most English journalists.

Early transatlantic reports of the Battersea case occasionally misspelt Fraser as Frazer, but the headlines convey the vigour of the American press, and also what most of its British equivalent hadn't shared – that the scandal involved high life names, and all London – or rather, the London that mattered – was talking of it:

> 'Another Sensation In Modern Sodom' – *The Salt Lake Herald* (Utah, 3 November)

> 'Corruptors Of Youth In The Toils. Penal Servitude For Two Society Men Of London' – *New-York Tribune* (New York, 4 November.)

> 'London Society Men Sentenced: English Capital Agog Over Sensational Developments' – Another O. Wilde." – *The Butte Inter Mountain* (Montana, 4 November.)

> 'Deserve The Lash. Scions of Proudest Families in Great Britain Sentenced.' – *Williston Graphic* (North Dakota, 6 November.)

'It is Horrible. The Latest High Life English Scandal Becomes Public.' – *Belding Banner* (Michigan, 13 November.)

Allusions were made to the high stakes in the case: "An array of prominent King's Counsellors appeared for both sides." A number of reports, including in *The New York Times*, alleged there was an aristocrat on the run, linking the two cases. One report in *The Times* of Richmond Virginia comprehensively summarised the case in four brief paragraphs. It noted that the investigation:

> was begun at the instance of the officials of the Admiralty…the detectives working up the case quickly discovered a wide conspiracy of immorality. Fraser and Thorold were the tools of a band of rich eminent rogues, several of whom are men of titled eminence… some thirty men concerned, all wealthy and distinguished.

Only the third paragraph was wildly wrong: "The government determined to prosecute the case, no matter whom it implicated, so grave and widespread was the scandal." Other newspapers, including *The Intermountain Catholic* of Salt Lake City, and the *Iowa County Democrat*, had heard differently:

> A scandal involving peers of England is of such a disgraceful nature that the government has suppressed the evidence and issued an unofficial decree of banishment against one prominent lord.

A German-language newspaper, *Der Deutsche Correspondent* of Baltimore, called Fraser and Thorold the equivalent of 'posh dirty pigs' (vornehme Schweinigel), and in an editorial equated the scandal with Sodom and Gomorrah, observing:

> While such conditions prevail among the upper classes of Great Britain, the vices of drunkenness continue to spread among the women of the lower classes…drunken women are to be seen in large numbers every day on the streets of the cities of England and Scotland…In such circumstances, one might well wonder why England doesn't take a short break from its efforts to civilise savages in other parts of the world, to create a little more

civilisation at home.

In Minnesota, a Negro newspaper was driven to editorialise: "Last Sunday we picked up one of the local morning dailies and found it to contain such an array of immoralities etc., that we were startled..." These included, "a London scandal of a rank unmentionable nature, which involves many of England's aristocracy...and yet the 'superior race' prates about the crime and immorality among Afro-Americans as being characteristic. Let's hear no more of such bosh."

However, it was a report first published in the New York newspaper *The Sun,* and on the same day in the *Chicago Tribune*, which really blew the lid off the story. Its headline read:

LONDON SHOCKED BY SCANDAL.
POLICE CATCH OF DEGENERATES LED BY A
NOBLEMAN.
King Has Ordered Him Banished – Many Other Members Of
Aristocratic Families Involved, but Shielded – Two of the Least
Prominent Sentenced in Open Court – Clergyman's Discovery"

In the *Chicago Tribune*'s version, the headline was even more dramatic:

BRITAIN BOWS IN SHAME.
NATION STANDS AGHAST AT SCANDAL
DISCLOSURES.

Given that the British Government, aided by the discretion of the press, had placed a cap on the story, this was American sub-editor hyperbole. Beyond Whitehall, Belgravia and Mayfair the true facts were little known. However, the article deserves quoting in full:

It is impossible to entirely ignore the startling evidence of degeneracy in high places which today is the talk of all London. It is a matter blacker and more extensive than the Cleveland street scandal of fifteen years ago, and involves names of wider than English reputation.

So abhorrent is the story, so widespread are its ramifications, that it has been decided to 'Burke'* the full exposure, and so avoid, to some extent, a great national disgrace, and the pollution of the public mind. Justice will, therefore, only be partially executed, and in its place will be substituted a decree of banishment which will expatriate at least one prominent peer. Another still greater name, which must not be indicated, is, to use the expression employed by the police in the case, tinged by scandal.

Two Men Sent to Prison

No less than thirty persons have already been identified with this infamous coterie. They are nearly all men of advanced years, wealthy, and members of aristocratic families.

The only public action in the case which has been taken so far was the conviction of two men at the Norwich assizes this week. Bernard Fraser, a son of Gen. Fraser,[sic] a member of the Bachelors and other swell clubs, pleaded guilty on several counts, and was sentenced to ten years at penal servitude. Arthur Thorold, a nephew of the late Bishop Thorold, a tutor at Eton, made the same plea, and was sentenced to five years.

The magistrate, Justice Grantham, in passing sentence, said this was one of the most painful cases that he or any other judge had ever been called upon to try. Here were two men, bearing names that had been honoured in the field and the forum, and in every branch of life, who had pleaded guilty to one of the most discreditable offences known to the law.

Thanks Man Who Exposed Crimes

Fraser's case, the judge said, was the worst he ever had heard of. While moving in high society he had been leading a double life, and debauching others. It was, therefore, his honour's duty to inflict the full penalty of the law.

The judge thanked the British naval captain who furnished the evidence which led to the exposure by intercepting letters addressed to the members of the crew of his vessel.

---

* To quietly suppress. The word was changed in *The Sun*'s version to 'prevent'.

Investigations by the police led to the discovery of such appalling infamy that it became a serious question of public policy as to how far they should proceed in their enquiries, which had led them to well known country houses, private yachts, and other quarters of the most wealthy and aristocratic circles.

Nobleman Leads Criminal Gang

It was soon learned that the chief figure in this criminal band was a well known nobleman, who has already been referred to.

It should be said, in order to prevent confusion with a famous Earl whose name was connected by private gossip with the Cleveland street scandal, that the present individual is one of the peers created by Mr. Gladstone. He was formerly a member of parliament and at that time was regarded as the handsomest man in the House of Commons. He has held high office, and married the daughter of one of the wealthiest families in the world. He is also rich in his own right.

The report's dismissal of the ringleader being the Earl of Euston, and subsequent hints, would have made the identity of the figure obvious to cosmopolitan readers. Lord Battersea's personal wealth, Rothschild marriage, and recent ennoblement by Gladstone had been the subject of regular press comment, as had been his good looks when in the Commons.* The article continued:

King Banishes Peer

This matter assumed such ominous shape that, according to the current version in clubland, it was brought to the attention of the king. His Majesty's decision was that the offending peer, who is now ill, must leave England as soon as he is able to travel, never to return. It is notorious that this is not the first nobleman who has been banished from Great Britain for this cause.

Bernard Fraser wasn't, as the article claimed, the son of a general.

---

* e.g. "Mr Cyril Flower, as he was then, sat in the House of Commons for a dozen years or more, and was reputed to be the handsomest man in that assemblage." [Lord and Lady Battersea, *Bucks Herald*, 6 September 1902]; "Lord Battersea was regarded as the handsomest man in Parliament.", London Notes, *Daily Gazette for Middlesbrough*, 22 October 1892]

However, the gist of the anonymously authored article, which was obviously at least partially compiled from cablegram reports, appears well-informed. Who in New York City was privy to high levels of British Establishment gossip that could have penned it?

In fact, there were *two* highly connected expatriate journalists who were more than capable: Frederick 'Fritz' Cunliffe-Owen,* a former diplomat and holder of a string of honours, including a CBE and Legion of Honour, and his aristocratic wife Marguerite, a French countess.† Shortly after their arrival in America in 1885, the couple lost their European fortune in an investment collapse, but succeeded in pulling themselves up again through their wits, talent, and sheer hard work.

Marguerite's first marriage had been to a chamberlain of the Austrian royal court. She authored a string of 'insider' royal histories, novels and even an advice book for ladies,‡ which were published under her own name as well as under the couple's joint *nom de plume*, 'The Marquise de Fontenoy'. Under this name Marguerite wrote a highly-successful newspaper column devoted to European high life gossip; it appeared in the *New York Tribune* and was syndicated nationally. During an illness, she passed the writing of it over to her husband, who continued it for three decades.

Frederick was as remarkable a personality as his wife. He was a classic insider: the second Kaiser was his godfather, and newspaper magnate Lord Northcliffe a good friend. Frederick was a keen New York club man, but also maintained his connection with The Garrick Club of London all his life. He became foreign editor of the newspaper *The World*, and later the *New York Tribune*, and authored articles and editorials anonymously, and under the pen names 'Ex-Attaché' and 'Veteran Diplomat'. The tone of these and the Marquise de Fontenoy column was authoritative, but also snobbishly waspish: given the couple's impeccable connections, their sources were excellent. The illustrious backgrounds of the Cunliffe-Owens had given them a broad and deep life experience. They'd also known hardship, and

---

* Frederick Philip Lewis Cunliffe-Owen (1855-1926).
† Marguerite Isaure Anne-Marie Lucie Pierrette Cunliffe-Owen, née de Godart, Comtesse du Planty et de Sourdis (1859-1927).
‡ The Marquise de Fontenoy, *Eve's Glossary: The Guide-book Of A Mondaine*, Herbert S. Stone, New York 1897.

harboured a strong sense of justice. This confluence of factors sharpened their pens.

In his news collation Frederick was aided by a prodigious memory, immense clipping files, insider information, and brilliant deductive skills – "Straws showed him how the wind blew. The mention of a name would develop a Fontenoy paragraph," wrote a close friend. The result was remarkably well-informed articles which, due to the demands of newspaper deadlines, featured occasional errors, but whose substance was usually broadly accurate. In British newspaper offices his writings were followed appreciatively and filed.

The quoted article that appeared in *The Sun* on the 9th of November has all the hallmarks of Frederick's imperious style. There were specific reasons why he was likely to have been drawn to the Battersea story. His connections weren't solely diplomatic and high society: as well as the *haute monde* they included the *demi-monde*. He'd acted as secretary for his late father Sir Philip Cunliffe-Owen who, until shortly before his death in 1894, had been Director of the South Kensington Museum, and organised the British component of the great international exhibitions which marked the Victorian era. In 1874, Lord Ronald Gower had assisted in this task. At the unveiling of Gower's Shakespeare Memorial in Stratford-on-Avon in 1888, Sir Philip was, with Oscar Wilde, one of the speakers, and made mention of the fact he'd known Gower for 12 years. Sir Philip and Gower were also on the committee that established the Royal Windsor Tapestry Manufactory, an enterprise to manufacture fine tapestries in England that was under the patronage of Queen Victoria and her daughter Princess Louise,* wife of the Duke of Argyll.†

Any whispers that Gower may have been involved in the scandal, or more especially the Duke, known to intimates as 'Lorne', and the butt of rumour, would surely have galvanised Frederick. Gower was a lynchpin in upper class London homosexual society, and the Duke's uncle and closest friend.

Intriguingly, Princess Louise allegedly contributed articles to journals

---

* Princess Louise, Duchess of Argyll (1848–1939), sixth child of Queen Victoria and Prince Albert.
† John (Ian) George Edward Henry Douglas Sutherland Campbell, Marquess of Lorne; from 1900, 9th Duke of Argyll (1845–1914).

under the pseudonym 'Myra Fontenoy'. The similarity to Cunliffe-Owen's pen name is too striking to be mere coincidence, and was clearly a hat-tip. The Princess may have been aware of their work through Marguerite's popular 'royal revelations' books, or the syndicated newspaper column from her years spent in Canada when Lorne was Governor General. However, she may have been privy Cunliffe-Owens' pseudonym through Lord Ronald.

There was an addendum to the article in *The Sun* in the form of a seemingly unrelated story of further vice. However, this tale has an air of penny-dreadful artifice:

> Perhaps it is a mere coincidence that a sensational narrative should be published just at this time credited to a clergyman 'whose name is renowned throughout England, and who is a near relative of a member of the present government.'

> He was summoned one evening to Richmond, which is London's most aristocratic suburb, to the bedside of a dying girl. He was conducted by the back way of a large mansion, which was apparently dark and was situated on extensive grounds. The girl told a terrible story, the details of which have not been disclosed. The girl died before he left.

> He refused to accompany an attendant to the rear when descended, but went through the front rooms, where he found an orgy going on. Many men were being entertained by very young girls. Fully twenty men servants in gorgeous livery were scattered about.

> He paid no attention to these people at first, but presently he saw a drunken, decrepit man, at least 70 years of age, speak to a mere child. The girl shrank away. The master of the establishment, who has since been identified as a certain French Vicomte, signalled to a footman, who seized the girl and carried her from the room. The young woman screamed and struggled violently.

> Thereupon the clergyman stepped up to the manager and asked him what he meant by such brutality and what was the meaning of the whole conduct of the house. The reverend narrator continues his story thus:

"I have never seen such amazement as was depicted on the faces of all those present, and I am firmly convinced that I owe my life to the presence of two individuals, who, if they are depraved, are at least men; but each, I regret to say, is a member of one of the houses of parliament. I left the house, not only with the girl mentioned, but with two of her companions, who, rushing up to me, claimed my protection."

A respectable local newspaper, which prints the foregoing story, vouches for its truth.

The story of the vicomte had originally appeared in *Richmond News*, a local London newspaper. It was then picked up by *Reynolds's Newspaper*, which printed a brief paragraph about it in 'The Secret History Of To-Day' – immediately below the one that broke the Battersea story. However, it doubted its veracity, stating: "are the police of Richmond so stupid, or so corrupt, as not to have discovered this place? It is hard to believe." The inclusion of a decadent aristocrat who is not English, but French, might be assumed to be one more novelistic attempt to spice up, despite the assertion of truth, what already seems an over-egged tale.

That said, Bernard Fraser *did* have a friend who was a French vicomte. He was also his former business partner, and an executor to his will. The coincidence is certainly intriguing. The name of this aristocrat was Joseph de Kergariou.* While he certainly visited the capital, a search of London residential directories for the period has failed to uncover any listing for him. Until any real evidence turns up, linking that gentleman with a questionable account of murderous child abuse, is unwarranted.

However, the Cunliffe-Owens may have heard more about the Battersea case. Six days later, another syndicated article appeared in the *Tribune* and elsewhere:

SCANDAL STIRS BRITAIN.
DEVELOPMENTS IN DEGENERACY CASES
ASTOUND NATION.

---

* Vicomte Joseph Charles Marie Tugdual de Kergariou (1860–1936). Born at the Château de Lannuguy, Finistère, he married Henriette-Marie, née Lainé Darvel. No issue.

Charges Publicly Made by Writers, but Police Whitewash Crimes on Finding High Officials Involved – One Tells of Raid In Which Many Were Captured and Released Because of Their Prominence.

LONDON, Nov. 15. Evidence of the appalling degeneracy of certain circles of the British aristocracy continues to be printed. Arnold White, the author, has aroused much public comment this week by speaking plainly on the subject in two or three articles. The greatest sensation was caused, however, by astounding revelations furnished by the police.

The policy of 'burking' justice in the ordinary form of public prosecutions apparently has been coupled with that of private punishment of high placed offenders by the disclosure of infamy to friends. A police inspector, who has been engaged on these cases, told the following instance of something that happened this week.

Suspicion had been lately directed to a house in the Fulham district. The building stood alone on a large ground. The detectives surrounded it one evening, entered, and arrested the inmates, all men, numbering about forty, and took them to Scotland Yard. There it was found that the prisoners included a high court official and other prominent persons. On account of the magnitude of the scandal the police were compelled to turn the whole lot loose.

Five years earlier in 1897, under his other pen name of 'Ex-Attache', Frederick Cunliffe-Owen had penned a long article for the *New York Tribune* that addressed the manner in which high-level scandals were treated in England. Titled 'Hushing It Up', and reflecting upon what radical journalists like W.M. Thompson had railed against, it stated:

it may safely be taken for granted that not more than one-third, perhaps not even one-quarter of the scandals affecting prominent people in Great Britain ever reach the knowledge of the public. For, with all its faults, English society possesses an esprit de corps that is not to be found in that of New York. When one of its members happens to wander from the high road on honesty and honour – which is very broad and spacious in these modern times – into the byways of crime, all the members of his class, not alone in his interest, but also in their own, unite in an effort to hush the matter up...

Much diversity of opinion prevails in the policy of hushing up scandals, and whereas here in the United States, and particularly in New York, there appears to be an impression that publicity is the best safeguard of public morality, in the Old World, where there is so much more submissiveness and reverence on the part of the masses for the classes that anything calculated to impair the prestige of the latter in the eyes of the people is held to constitute a danger to society as a whole, concealment and oblivion are regarded as preferable. In Europe the people of the middle and lower grades of society show such a readiness and anxiety to follow blindly in the lead of those whom they regard as their superiors in rank, not alone in dress, manner and speech, but even in conduct, that it is argued even by criminologists exercising magisterial and judicial authority that any publicity accorded to the misdeeds of a person of rank and social position affects injuriously the moral tone of the masses and becomes not only a cause, but also an incitement to crime.

It is on the strength of these arguments that Sir George Lewis, and not only distinguished lawyers like himself, but likewise the officials entrusted with the administration of justice, and even the royal arbiters of the great world of London, unite in an endeavour to hush up crime to an extent of which the people of this country have little conception.

It is a member of the aristocracy, the Hon. Hamilton Cuffe, younger brother and heir to the Earl of Desart, who holds the important office of Crown Prosecutor. This functionary is charged with the duty of deciding which cases shall be prosecuted on behalf of the people...and it depends upon him to a great extent whether a criminal of high degree escapes or receives the punishment of his crime.

In a number of instances, both during the tenure of office of Mr. Cuffe, as well as under the regime of his predecessor, Sir Augustus Stephenson, no proceedings for prosecution have been instituted until the offender was well beyond the reach of the authorities and this practice is even carried to such a point that in some notable instances the police have actually warned titled criminals that warrants have been issued for their arrest, which would be held back for twenty-four hours in order to enable them to get out of the country. Many cases of this kind could be sited. But it is only fair to add that in acting thus, the judicial, the magisterial and the police officials concerned are prompted entirely by considerations of public weal and morality.

From a strictly legal point of view the Prince of Wales...and...George Lewis, as well as all those other distinguished Englishmen who have ever taken any part in an endeavour to hush up a crime in the interests of the good name of society and the moral welfare of the public may possibly be in the wrong. But it is difficult to withhold a feeling of warm sympathy and regard for those who, in their endeavours to rid their nest of undesirable birds, strive at the same time to prevent its being fouled by what they consider impolitic and unnecessary publicity.

Frederick Cunliffe-Owen's views were typical of an Englishman of his class and generation. Exactly ten years later during the Eulenburg scandals at the Kaiser's court,* Frederick recycled the article with some fresh material. Of the changes in society over the previous decade he noted:

whereas on this side of the Atlantic, the principle of equality is deeply rooted in the breast of every American citizen...in Europe, despite the spread of democracy and the phenomenal progress of socialism, much of the oldtime submissiveness and reverence on the part of the masses for the classes remains.

He also recalled the Cleveland Street Scandal, writing:

---

* A series of courts-martial and civil trials between 1907-09 involving a circle of prominent homosexual courtiers and officers. The sovereigns of the three most powerful courts in Europe – England, Germany, and Russia, were all in the thrall of homosexual courtiers: Lords Esher and Farquhar in England; Philipp, Prince zu Eulenburg-Hertefeld and his circle in Germany; and in Russia, Prince Vladimir 'Vovo' Meshchersky (1839–1914), a courtier, journalist, novelist, and publisher, who had homosexual cases against him quashed three times. [See: W. E. Mosse, 'Imperial Favourite: V. P. Meshchersky and the *Grazhdanin*', *The Slavonic and East European Review*, Vol.59, No.4; Oct. 1981 London, pp. 529-547.]

the incalculable harm resulting from the extraordinary publicity given to the unsavoury proceedings far outweighed any possible good that might have been derived by bringing some of the offenders to justice.

It dare not happen again. This time the cover-up would succeed.

In January 1903, Britain's first socialist political party, the Social Democratic Federation, celebrated its twenty-first birthday. Its founder, Henry Hyndman,* proclaimed that he saw all around him the signs of "last stage capitalism":

> Never before did peers and plutocrats strive so hard to suppress scandals; never before was it so clear to the people that they are governed by a crew of reprobates male and female, who have stripped themselves of the last vestiges of morality or decency.

With a touching faith in the purity of his own peer group, he added: "It is this break-down of the old society which makes us ready for the new."

---

*Henry Mayers Hyndman (1842 –1921) writer and socialist politician.

A District Messenger.

Detective Inspector Charles Arrow.

Sir George Lewis, 1903.

THE SOCIETY CARD SCANDAL.

MR. GEORGE LEWIS TO ILLUSTRIOUS CLIENT:—"COME ALONG, TEDDY; I'LL SEE THEY DON'T WORRY YOU!"

A cartoon published during the Tranby-Croft Scandal of 1891.

Sir William Grantham.

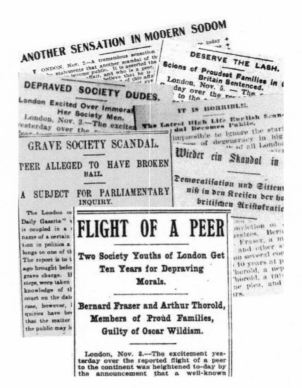

Battersea Scandal headlines.

Dartmoor Prison quarry.

Arthur Charles Thorold (top row, centre), Commemoration Ball, Oxford, 1895.

Charles Thorold (right) at Southport High School, 1907.

Charles Thorold's wedding to Kathleen Jeffery, Melbourne, 1913.

Charles and Kathleen with Jeffery, Southport, 1913.

Charles Thorold reviewing Hutchins School scouts with the Governor of Tasmania, Sir James O'Grady (right), 1920s.

Jeffery Thorold.

The Fraser family at their Edinburgh home.
Bernard stands at far right, next to Edmund.
Far left top: unknown (presumably a family friend or beau); Henry with dog.

The Fraser brothers: (left to right) Edmund, Henry and Bernard.

Bernard Fraser (detail of preceding photo).

Vicomte Joseph de Kergariou.

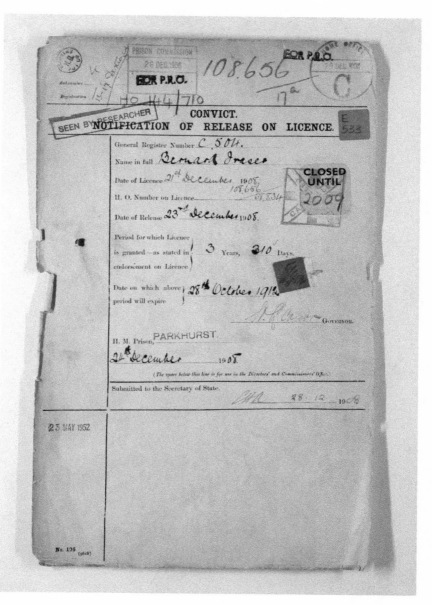

HO 144/710

17ª

E 533

CONVICT.
NOTIFICATION OF RELEASE ON LICENCE.

General Register Number C.504.

Name in full Bernard Fraser

Date of Licence 21ˢᵗ December 1908.

H. O. Number on Licence 108.656 / 68,534.

Date of Release 23ʳᵈ December 1908.

Period for which Licence is granted — as stated in endorsement on Licence } 3 Years, 310 Days.

Date on which above period will expire } 28ᵗʰ October 1912.

Governor.

H. M. Prison, PARKHURST.

24ᵗʰ December 1908.

(The space below this line is for use in the Directors' and Commissioners' Office.)

Submitted to the Secretary of State. 28·12·1908

No. 105 (0618)

Cover of Bernard Fraser's criminal file.

Bernard Fraser Ross in old age.

Mohamed Iguerbouchène, c.1931.

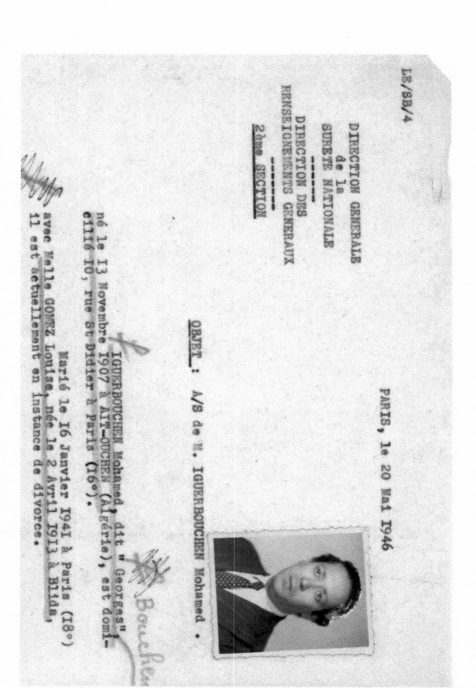

LE/SB/4

DIRECTION GENERALE
de la
SURETE NATIONALE

DIRECTION DES
RENSEIGNEMENTS GENERAUX

2ème SECTION

PARIS, le 20 Mai 1946

OBJET : A/S de M. IGUERBOUCHEN Mohamed .

IGUERBOUCHEN Mohamed, dit " Georges"
né le 13 Novembre 1907 à AIT—OUCHEN (Algérie), est domi-
cilié 10, rue St-Didier à Paris (16°).

Marié le 16 Janvier 1941 à Paris (18°)
avec Melle GOMEZ Louise, née le 2 Avril 1913 à Blida,
il est actuellement en instance de divorce.

Bouchen

A page from Mohamed Iguerbouchène's French intelligence service file.

DEATH OF LORD BATTERSEA.

FAMOUS LIBERAL WHIP DIES AT RYDE.

Lord Battersea, formerly Mr. Cyril Flower, who died yesterday in his sixty-fifth year, was Liberal member of Parliament for twelve years, and made his mark in the House as one of the most successful of Liberal Whips. Lord Battersea married, in 1877, the eldest daughter of the late Sir Anthony de Rothschild. There were no children of the marriage, and thus the peerage becomes extinct. Inset is Lady Battersea.—(Elliott and Fry.)

The last of Cyril. From *The Daily Mirror*.

Lord Battersea's bookplate.

PART III.

This Strange Journey Called Life

14. THE MOST HANDSOME MAN IN PARLIAMENT

Lord Battersea's love of bright colour is quite a passion with him. It extends to more than the decoration of his houses. At Overstrand, a gorgeous vision of pale blue, sea-green, or rose-coloured silk is constantly to be seen in the summer months, in the cricket field adjoining his grounds, or on the Cromer golf-links, which proves on nearer approach to be none other than the handsome and picturesque lord of The Pleasaunce himself. At the bathing hour in the morning he may be encountered 'clothed in white samite, mystic wonderful',[*] and in the evening he has been seen resplendent in a ruby velvet dinner suit. Few men have a greater variety of interests. Politician, enthusiastic art collector, golfer, cricketer, sportsman, whip, and photographer...

What the horny-handed workers of the industrial constituencies represented by Lord Battersea might have made of this tongue-in-cheek 1898 newspaper account, authored by T.P. O'Connor, one can only wonder. They may well have been amused and beguiled – as the very personable, very handsome, and immensely wealthy Cyril Flower, 1st Lord Battersea, had captivated people throughout his life.

The American social activist Maud Nathan[†] considered he possessed "the keenest sense of humour of any Englishman I ever met. His blue eyes twinkled over any expression of our American humour and he

---

[*] The apparel of The Lady of The Lake; this line from *Morte d'Arthur* by Lord Tennyson.
[†] Maud Nathan (1862–1946), American social worker, labour activist and suffragist.

showed his appreciation by his ever-ready and apt retort." Another friend, the artist Walter Crane,* found him "always very genial and good-natured."

If an interest in others, or at least the appearance of it, is one of the secrets of charm, Cyril possessed it. As a parliamentary profile put it:

> Mr. Cyril Flower is all smiles and bonhomie. To meet him you would imagine that to oblige and gratify you was an object to which he had always given his undivided attention; and though he is a smart person himself he is not less affable if you are a drab one. His responsibilities as Whip to the Liberal party sit lightly on him, and he is most 'at home' in all senses when he is entertaining the party leader, or the young men of the Eighty Club† in his house at the Marble Arch.

Another report observed:

> If you met Mr. Cyril Flower in the lobby and asked him a favour, he bowed his tall handsome head to yours, listened, and answered as if he was being the recipient of the greatest honour in the world.

Of course, not everyone is winnable. Thomas Gilmour,‡ a secretary to Lord Rosebery, told his diary that Cyril had "a touching belief in his powers of fascination." It may in part have been a showy act to woo and win in the theatre of life; yet despite the occasional cynic, Cyril was ever buoyant, energetic, and eloquent: as *Punch* would quip, "The Flower of the Flock."

Cyril Flower's roots were distinctly bourgeois; his money newly minted, which in the intense social stratification of the time, was the single strike against him. Born in 1843, he was the second son of a wool merchant Philip William Flower and his first wife Mary. Despite being remembered within the family as "a funny little man with terrible arthritis," Philip fathered at least eighteen children by two

---

* Walter Crane (1845 –1915); noted for his Arts & Craft book illustrations.
† A Liberal Party social club.
‡ Thomas Lennox Gilmour (1859–1936). As a young man he shared a flat with close friend and author (Sir) James Barrie, of Peter Pan fame. Like Barrie, he later married. [Piers Dudgeon, *The Real Peter Pan: The Tragic Life of Michael Llewelyn Davies*, Biteback Publishing, London 2015.]

wives. In 1838, he and his brother Horace sailed to Australia, and with two other merchants established the Sydney wool buying and exporting company of Flower, Salting & Co. It became the largest enterprise in the Australian wool trade.

Leaving Horace to manage the colonial side of the operation, Philip returned to London, where he founded P.W. Flower & Co. In addition to wool, he imported tallow and later gold, and branched out into property ownership and development. He created the Park Town estate, the second largest in Battersea. He also became a director of the London Joint-Stock Bank and Chartered Bank of Asia.

Cyril grew up in then-rural Streatham, on the family's estate of Furze Down.* After an education at Cheam, he was sent on to Harrow, where he was drawn to the schoolmaster Frederic Farrar,† later Dean of Canterbury, who was equally devoted to him – to say the least. This was perhaps fortunate as Farrar had a reputation for being addicted to flogging.

Taking time off from striping small buttocks, Farrar put pen to paper and authored the enormously popular mid-Victorian schoolboy novel *Eric; Or, Little By Little*, whose central character was inspired by Cyril. It was the account of a boy whom (as the preface put it) "in spite of the inherent nobility of his disposition, falls into all folly and wickedness, until he has learnt to seek help from above." The litany of sins amounted to drinking, smoking, cheating, and worst of all, masturbation:

> May every schoolboy who reads this page be warned by the waving of their wasted hands, from that burning marle of passion where they found nothing but shame and ruin, polluted affections, and an early grave.

The novel was soaked in sentimentality and piety. With a *frisson* of distaste, *The Saturday Review* observed that: "everything is served up with tear sauce. The boys quote hymns, and to the infinite indignation of all English readers, occasionally kiss each other." It accused the

---

* Furze Down House with its large conservatory survives within the grounds of Graveney School, at one end of Furzedown Drive, Tooting. At the Drive's other end the former gate lodge also survives.
† The Very Rev. Frederic William Farrar (1831–1903), Anglican cleric.

author of inculcating priggishness, conceit, and a morbid self-consciousness: "we can scarcely imagine a less healthy book to put into a boy's hands."

The public thought otherwise: it ran to 36 editions. Given Harrow's then reputation, discreet onanism after lights-out was the least of it. The granting of favours by pretty boys to older ones – occasionally encouraged by lollies or a sixpence, was English public school tradition at its most entrenched.

Farrar described the twelve-year-old Eric/Cyril in rapturous prose:

> his mind seemed cast in such a mould of stainless honour, that he avoided most of the weaknesses to which children are prone. But he was far from blameless. He was proud to a fault; he well knew that few of his fellows had gifts like his, either of mind or person, and his fair face often showed a clear impression of his own superiority.

The fair face was further sanctified when the Pre-Raphaelite artist William Holman Hunt* used Cyril as the model for the boy Jesus debating scripture with rabbis in a painting, 'Finding The Saviour In The Temple'. The holy Cyril, gazelle-eyed and ethnically coppery-toned for the occasion, is the focus of the picture, which caused a sensation when exhibited in 1860 in a travelling exhibition. For a subject hitherto idealised, Hunt's intense realism was striking, and drew criticism as well as praise, reducing many to ecstasies of adoration, not least for its small redeemer. "Christ is a healthy, beautiful boy of twelve, with a noble and almost royal countenance," sighed *The Athenaeum. The Daily News* was equally enraptured, asking: "How shall we describe the more than mortal radiance of those unfathomable eyes," while *Macmillans Magazine* could barely contain itself: "The eyes blue, clear, yet tender...the mouth, pure, sweet, small, yet pulpy and full."

From Harrow, Cyril went up to Trinity College, Cambridge, by which time, in the words of one Society chronicler:

> he was simply 'too handsome for anything', the sort of face

---

* William Holman Hunt (1827–1910). One of the founders of the Pre-Raphaelite Brotherhood.

dreamt of by poets, painters, and sculptors, and by young ladies who mentally illustrate the novels they read as they go along.

However, once again it was a man who sought to immortalise Cyril in art. Henry James, who was the same age and equally hypersensitive to beauty – especially when glimpsed in the male form, enjoyed with Cyril what he would term "our long and unclouded friendship". In his novel *The Tragic Muse*, the character of Nicholas Dormer, who vacillates between a political career and his desire to be a painter, contains recognisable aspects of Cyril, who is depicted as:

> a lean, strong, clear-faced youth, with a formed nose and thick light-brown hair which lay continuously and profusely back from his forehead, so that to smooth it from the brow to the neck but a single movement of the hand was required. I cannot describe him better than by saying that he was the sort of young Englishman who looks particularly well in strange lands and whose general aspect – his inches, his limbs, his friendly eyes, the modulation of his voice, the cleanness of his flesh-tints and the fashion of his garments – excites on the part of those who encounter him in far countries.

The scholar and politician Sir Richard Jebb,* then a fellow student at Cambridge, was so struck by Cyril's extraordinary popularity, he attempted to describe it in a letter to his mother:

> The more I see of Flower, the more interesting he becomes as a psychological study. He is the only instance with which I am acquainted of a man whom the whole world has agreed, with one consent, to pet, from Whewell (Master of Trinity) to the white-aproned men who carry the baked meats from the kitchens on their heads; nobody can resist him. The most dyspeptic and fastidious dons ask him to dinner. Professors write him notes and send him books...Artists are perpetually painting him. Bootmakers call to borrow his boots as models. I have constantly come into his rooms with him when he has found anonymous presents on his table. In short, he is an irresistible man.

Cyril had already created a minor flurry in London as well, where his

---

* Sir Richard Claverhouse Jebb (1841–1905), classical scholar and Conservative M.P. Married American widow Caroline Lane Reynolds. Cyril was one of his pallbearers.

nickname 'Flowery-Bowery' expressed the bounty of his beauty, and his cheerful open nature which cast its sunlight upon others. Cory wrote of him, "He is a nice fellow. Not an atom of malignity and unbounded aplomb." Jebb further added: "He is the only man I ever met who has some of the qualities of a charming woman also, and that without a shade of effeminacy!"

That said, it was in a cross-dressing role that Cyril created a minor-sensation. He had joined the Cambridge Amateur Dramatic Club, a menagerie of sensitive young men, and in 1866 they mounted Tom Taylor's comedy *The Overland Route*. As a volume on amateur theatrics breathlessly recorded:

> No doubt the most remarkable bit of acting in the play was Mr. Cyril Flower, now Lord Battersea, as Mrs. Sebright, the gay, flirtatious grass-widow.* The cast was a fine one all round, but this assumption stood out pre-eminently, and Mr. Flower's photograph, now hanging in the Club rooms, shows how wonderful he must have looked.

Also in the play, as 'Mrs. Rabbits', was another friend of Cyril's, Lord Ronald Gower, who later served as Oscar Wilde's inspiration for the urbane, witty and amoral Lord Henry Wotton in *The Picture of Dorian Gray*. A handsome blond young man of similar sensibilities who featured in the Club's cross-dressing roles, and who would become a lifelong friend was the 8th Duke of Argyll's heir, Lord Lorne. He and his brother Lord Archibald† nicknamed Cyril 'Flos'. A further fey performer in the troupe was Alfred de Rothschild,‡ who together with his younger brother Leopold,§ also became intimate friends of Cyril. They were the sons of Baron Lionel and Baroness Charlotte de Rothschild.** Letters indicate the closeness of Leo's friendship with the young man from Streatham disturbed Charlotte, who wrote of him: "He was far too beautiful – decked out in a wine coloured velvet coat – and several of his male friends were also endowed with an undesirable type of good looks..."

---

* A woman whose husband is away often or for a prolonged period.
† Lord Archibald Campbell (1846–1913).
‡ Alfred Charles de Rothschild (1842–1918), banker.
§ Leopold 'Leo' de Rothschild (1845–1917), banker. Married Marie Perugia, and had issue.
** Baron Lionel Nathan de Rothschild (1808–1879), banker, politician, and philanthropist, and Baroness Charlotte de Rothschild (1819–1884), German-born social figure. Lionel's father, Baron Nathan Mayer Rothschild (1777–1836), had established the British branch of the family.

It was an older Cambridge student, the son of a clergyman, who was to have the most profound effect on Cyril. This was Frederic Myers – he who had introduced John Addington Symonds to *Leaves Of Grass*. Myers confided to his diary:

> In 1863, just before my degree, Flower came up, – Flower, wreathed as it were, with roses, and scattering joy: – from that moment I was wholly given up to him, I lived mainly with his set, men junior to myself.

It was the beginning of another lifelong intimate friendship, a mentorship, and almost certainly, a love affair.

Strong, good-looking, and deeply intense, like many highly sexed individuals Myers was drawn to whatever gender was available: in Cambridge it was men, but after graduation, he was something of a womaniser. As his two-volume 1883 work *Essays Classical & Modern* was to reveal, he was also a most passionate, sensitive, and penetrating thinker.* For any young man, he would have been a remarkable mentor.

Prior to meeting Cyril, Myers had been part of a circle of yearningly metaphysical and homosexually-inclined young men who surrounded John Addington Symonds. However, the repressed Symonds was put off by what he considered was the coarseness of Myers's sensuality, writing, "I consider the tone of F Myers to be radically wrong in matters of passion." The young Myers that Cyril knew was a poet. He may even have used verse as a tool of seduction. It's doubtful Cyril would have needed much encouragement.

Then as now, 'the Backs' of Cambridge and adjoining pastures were a hushed idyll. In his *Collected Poems,* Myers wrote:

> I am he who long ago –
> (How well my heart recalls it yet!) –
> Beheld an early sun and low
> In fields I never shall forget…
> In pleasant paths my steps were set

---

* The essay topics include Virgil, Marcus Aurelius, George Sand, George Eliot, and Rossetti.

And life was young and love was new.

How changed is this from that estate!
How vexed with unfamiliar fears!...
But only sees the dark, and hears
A soundless echo of his sin.

In a letter to her younger son at the time of the Wilde trials, the social reformer Josephine Butler wrote:

> Yes, I have heard also as you have, that the Oscar Wilde madness is spread like a plague thro' London fashionable & artistic society...I long ago heard a dreadful account of Lord Battersea. It was Frederic Myers who first led him astray & many others*...A friend of Lady H[enry] Somerset came to see me (Lady H S's husband went that road.) She told me that London upper society is simply <u>rotten</u> with this vice. What fools people are who worship art & beauty & perfumes & poetry & nonsense in place of God.

Mrs. Butler sorely misunderstood. It was in literature and art that Cyril and his friends, like generations before them, sought understanding and validation of their passions, and for life itself. To appreciate the impact of Myers on Cyril in terms of mentorship, we must make a brief detour through their mental landscape. Like William (Cory) Johnson's *Ionica*, Plato's *Symposium*, and the poems of Shakespeare, Michelangelo and Byron were pored over. Myers later wrote of the classical authors: "They drew from me and fostered evil as well as good." While at Cambridge he also began corresponding with many of the leading figures of the day, including Gladstone, Ruskin,† George Eliot, and most especially, Tennyson.

That most febrile of Eton schoolmasters, Cory, would aptly describe the Victorian realm, filled with the smells of horses and leather, and smoke and violets, as "this upholsterous and hypnotic world." He observed: "The strange thing in this existing world is the coexistence

---

* According to Lady Battersea, Myers in his youth had been one of Josephine Butler's "most enthusiastic followers". [Constance Battersea, *Reminiscences*, Macmillan & Co, London 1923, p205.]
† John Ruskin (1819–1900), writer, philosopher, art critic and polymath. Married Euphemia 'Effie' Gray; the marriage was annulled unconsummated.

of wonderful power over 'nature' with a very rapid and wide-ranging increase in sensibility."

Undoubtedly the Cambridge of those years was a magical time to be young: there was an intellectual ferment, an opening up of culture and consciousness, and a sense of new possibilities in the air. It would have felt like another Enlightenment – or perhaps a Haight-Ashbury Summer of Love; albeit an immensely privileged and cossetted Victorian version, where golden youths could muse by the lingering hour, while college servants, called 'gyps' in Cambridge slang, brushed and laid out their clothes.

On the lips of hormonally flushed, privileged young gentlemen, especially those musing of forbidden love, there was now the name of another poet: one who was not only sensitive and profound, but revolutionary. An intensely modern man who boldly loved as they yearned to love, and who spoke of it in a clear assured voice that rang with freedom, and which lit up their consciousness like a skyrocket — Walt Whitman.

Edward Carpenter was then at Cambridge, but it was almost certainly Frederic Myers who introduced Cyril, as he had Symonds, to *Leaves Of Grass*. And just as Cyril followed in Myers's path to befriend Tennyson, so he too became one of the growing coterie of Whitman disciples.

Amongst those who made pilgrimages to meet the poet were Oscar Wilde and Bram Stoker. Edward Carpenter visited him in 1877, and again in 1884. However, Cyril got there even earlier, sailing to America with a small party of young aristocrats in 1870. After traversing the country, he met with Whitman in Washington.*

---

* The inscription in Cyril's presentation copy of *Leaves Of Grass* reads: "Cyril Flower from Walt Whitman. Washington U.S.A. Dec 1, 1870." Whitman was then still labouring as a clerk at the Attorney General's office in Washington. Unlike the lofty public persona he was carefully crafting, in private the Sage of Democracy was then a fraught mess. That summer the age difference between himself and Peter Doyle, and the latter's mood swings, had begun to cause strains in their relationship. Desperately trying to suppress his passion, Whitman's self-injunctions in his private notebook are – as self-denial often is – unintentionally comical: "TO GIVE UP ABSOLUTELY & for good from this present hour this FEVERISH, FLUCTUATING, useless, UNDIGNIFIED pursuit of 16.4 [Whitman's code for Peter Doyle's initials] – too long (much too long) persevered in – so humiliating...Outline sketch of a superb calm character...Depress the adhesive nature. It is in excess – making life a torment...Remember Fred Vaughan." However a fortnight later he was writing to Doyle: "I

295

Whitman had taken pains to market himself, via a smoldering, three-quarter length portrait that formed the frontispiece of *Leaves Of Grass,* as a cocky, sexy bohemian. In Charles Kains Jackson's copy, gifted to him by Henry Scott Tuke, one of Jackson's handwritten notes records someone's warning: "Whitman is a cowboy, a New York tough, a loafer, a frequenter of low places. Don't visit him." Just the thing to get a young man's blood coursing. A pilgrimage to Whitman wasn't just a literary quest: it was an erotic adventure.

While Whitman's taste in men and youths leaned more to what would now be termed 'rough trade', he is likely to have been taken with Cyril's looks and effortless charm. According to Carpenter, who confided to friends he'd shared Whitman's bed, the poet considered sex the best way to fully know another man. Whitman was then fifty-one years old, and three years away from his first stroke: according to his physician, no description could "give any idea of the extraordinary physical attractiveness of the man."

Cyril met the poet at his workplace in his dayjob as a clerk in the Treasury building: they went for a long walk and talk. Whitman gifted him a signed edition of *Leaves Of Grass*, plus some of his works to pass on to Tennyson, later also sending copies of his *Democratic Vistas* and *Passage to India.* The patrician Cyril was surely more relaxed than Symonds in his approach, but even he felt the pain of Whitman's tardiness as a correspondent. The following year, Cyril wrote to him:

> I have often wished, I may say even longed, to have from you a few, a very few, lines to tell me of your well being, a little of your doings and of your recollection (if it is not too much to ask) of one who is always your sincere friend and lover and who travelled many a mile to see and speak with you.

Like Bram Stoker and other disciples, Cyril opened his heart to him:

---

never dreamed that you made so much of having me with you, nor that you could feel so downcast at losing me. I thought it was all on the other side." [Cyril Flower's copy of Leaves Of Grass, Manhattan Rare Book Company, Inventory #2299, December 2019, Abebooks.com; Walt Whitman, Edward F. Grier (ed.), *The Collected Writings Of Walt Whitman: Notebooks And Unpublished Prose Manuscripts*, Vol2:, New York University Press, 1984, p888-890.]

I am indebted for the pamphlet I like it much: it strikes me as so simple, pure and powerful and reminds me as so much of your work does of all that is sweet and good and noble in the world. Somehow when I read you or think of you I feel once more the cool never to be forgotten breeze of a boundless prairie; my lungs seem to open and I respire more freely. I feel perhaps freer for the time and less material and then again I feel that I hold in my hand clasped strong and tight and for eternity the great hand of a friend – a simple good fellow, a man who loves me and who is beautiful because he loves – and with the consciousness of that I feel never alone, never sad – and much more I feel: but to what purpose do I write thus?

Having just returned from Paris, which was then under Prussian occupation, and knowing of Whitman's boundless admiration for young military men ("Many a soldier's kiss dwells on these bearded lips."), Cyril wrote to him of the conquerors, whose intimate acquaintance he appears to have made:

The Prussian soldiers are really splendid fellows. I think you would very much like them. They are so manly and simple – perhaps too warlike, but that is of course the fault of their education, for their temperament is it seems to me very domestic and affectionate.

He signed the letter "Forever Affectionately."* Domestic and affectionate are not terms normally bestowed upon an invading army, let alone a Prussian one, but Cyril's alluring vision of pliant military flesh did the trick, as Whitman finally responded:

You may think yourself neglected – perhaps forgotten – by your American Friend. Not at all the latter, believe me. Twenty times during the last year I have promised myself to write you… Dear Cyril Flower I send you my love and hope you will not think hard of me for not writing before.

---

* For gentlemen of leisure with a penchant for soldiers, following the forces – beyond loitering in the vicinity of city barracks – appears to have been, as it was for prostitutes, quite the thing. In the same conflict, Lord Ronald Gower followed the Prussian forces with the famous war correspondent William Howard Russell, Gower's status enabling that they did so, for part of the journey, in the company of the Crown Prince. [Lord Ronald Gower, *My Reminiscences*, Vol I, Kegan Paul, Trench & Co, 1883, pp239-380.]

As with Whitman's other disciples, it's impossible to underestimate the profound effect he had on Cyril, and what it meant for his life thereafter. It's likely Cyril's thoughts mirrored those of Oscar Wilde who said of Whitman, "I have an admiration for that man which I can hardly express," and after meeting him stated:

> He is the grandest man I have ever seen. The simplest, most natural, and strongest character I have ever met in my life. I regard him as one of those wonderful, large, entire, men who might have lived in any age and is not peculiar to any one people. Strong, true, and perfectly sane: the closest approach to the Greek we have yet had in modern times.*

While Cyril was blessed with the reassurance of looks and wealth, and all the self-confidence that an English public school education can instil, Whitman surely enabled him to be at peace with his sexuality. Whatever the world might declaim, he now knew that it made him no less a man, but rather, part of glorious Nature, and even perhaps of a brotherhood. As a golden youth, he would have accepted that the world was his to seize and make his own. But the uplifting assurance that his desires were true and right undoubtedly contributed to his happiness.

Whitman's glorification of life, his reinvention and shaping of self, and not least, his somewhat charlatan showmanship, undoubtedly also made a deep impression. Cyril was already becoming an accomplished showman himself, with a personality marked by a sense of grandeur and panache. However, his communing with Whitman in the flesh would have conveyed to him how fulfilling and thrilling it could be to not only possess a theatrical bravura, but to live a life imbued with a bold and brave transcendent vision.

Not least, as the archetypical American democrat, Whitman's poetical calls for freedom and equality likely further shaped Cyril's politics, and encouraged what was to be a lifetime of endless philanthropy on

---

* The impact of Whitman on Wilde was such that it may have further radicalised him, and also butched-him up. Certainly, after meeting Whitman, Wilde trimmed his long hair. One clued-in cartoon had Wilde's lily replaced with a calamus spathe, and suggested that if he continued his ways, prison would be the outcome. [Our Captious Critic, *The Illustrated Sporting & Dramatic News*, 21 July 1883, p493.]

behalf of the working class. While a well-bred English gentleman who was aesthetic to his fingertips, Cyril Flower was also a loving Whitman brother and comrade.*

Cyril's youthful self-identity and aesthetic tastes would have been further shaped by a confluence of publications. In 1873, there appeared Walter Pater's *Studies in the History of the Renaissance*. For Pater, the point of life was life itself: influenced by the view of the Greek philosopher Heraclitus that it was an ever-changing river, in his book's concluding chapter he beseeched readers to maintain a heightened perception and gather all the impressions and sensations they could in the time remaining to them on Earth:

> as Victor Hugo says: we are all under the sentence of death but with a sort of indefinite interval...our one chance lies in expanding that interval, in getting as many pulsations as possible into the given time.

Like a whispering opium dealer in Harris tweed, Pater added: "To burn always with this hard, gemlike flame, to maintain this ecstasy, is success in life."† The route to experiencing this "quickened, multiplied consciousness" could be through great passions, or absorbing activities, but he counselled, "Of this wisdom, the poetic passion, the desire of beauty, the love of art for art's sake, has most."

With its implicit endorsement of hedonism and amorality, wrapped up in that ever-appealing injunction to 'Live! Live! Live!', it was the literary equivalent of Isadora Duncan dancing at dawn at the pillars of the Parthenon. Yearning young men, and those who longed to be, clutched the book, and its sensuous, insinuating prose, to their hearts. Pater became a patron saint of the Aesthetic and Decadent Movements, but for those who believed "duty, responsibility and reason defined the Empire," it was like a gauntlet tossed in their face. *The Illustrated London News* was not alone when it chuntered: "We must

---

* A golfing partner of Cyril's, Dr. Denis Gratwicke Halsted, later wrote of his selfless generosity. Upon learning of the tuberculosis of an East End working man, Cyril immediately offered to pay for his rest cure. [D. G. Halsted, *Doctor in the Nineties*, Christopher Johnson, London 1959, pp89-90.]

† One scholar has suggested that, with his audience in his mind's eye being young men: "Pater is reacting here less to the shortness of life per se than to the unbearable briefness of *youth*. He is responding to the loss of masculine beauty with a sharp Hellenic grief." [Linda C. Dowling, *Hellenism and Homosexuality in Victorian Oxford*, Cornell University Press, Ithaca 1994, pp98-99.]

seriously dissent from his concluding remarks":

> If the moral and intellectual experience of Greek Italian and German art-epicures can teach any lesson for our instruction, it is a warning against this seductive tendency, which soothes and refines, but is also likely to enervate the mind that submits to its fascination.*

Such criticism as this caused Pater to omit the Conclusion in the book's second edition,† with the thin excuse he was concerned "it might possibly mislead some of those young men into whose hands it might fall." One young man who hardly needed Pater's sanction to pursue the richest, fullest life that money and privilege could buy – with "as many pulsations as possible," was Cyril Flower. But Pater also constituted welcome philosophical support.

Three other publications by John Addington Symonds would also have left their mark upon Cyril: the seven-volume *Renaissance In Italy*, which appeared between 1875 and 1886; *Studies of the Greek Poets*, in 1879; and his aforementioned treatise *A Problem In Greek Ethics*.‡ Together with Pater's writing they constituted a celebration of pagan aestheticism, and championing of the centrality of pederasty to Hellenistic thought, and the Western cultural tradition. The author of the more worldly *Boy-Worship* had very definite thoughts on the susceptibility of young men such as Cyril to arousal:

> in those of an artistic or aesthetic temperament, it is continually making itself felt. It will not suffer the mind to rest, but fills it with fevered longings...The ancient Greek knew well the power of this wondrous fascination. All beauty was to him a thing to be adored.

---

* *The Morning Post* reviewer witheringly agreed: "Pater's loitering and somewhat inconclusive contemplations are normal enough in a middle-aged gentleman of cultivated tastes and low physical vitality. But the activities of youth demand more than this, and are wont to stray into devious paths, if not directed to fairly definite aims." In contrast, Oscar Wilde called the work: "my golden book; I never travel anywhere without it, but it is the very flower of decadence: the last trumpet should have sounded the moment it was written." [The Life Of Walter Pater, *The Morning Post*, 25 March 1907, p2; W.B. Yeats, 'Four Years, 1887-1891', *The London Mercury*, Vol 4, Field Press Limited, 1921, p136.]

† He restored the chapter, with slight revision, in the third edition.

‡ Cyril may have read one of the ten copies Symonds printed for private circulation, or when it was republished in German in 1897. A pirated edition of 100 copies appeared in England in 1901.

In line with Whitman's liberalism, Cyril became a member of the Liberal Party, which in the latter half of the nineteenth century, together with the Conservatives (the Tories), formed the two major British political forces. Despite the admission of the middle classes to the franchise, both parties were still profoundly aristocratic, but the Liberals espoused a gently radical policy of reform, including improvements in labour conditions and public education, and eventually, Home Rule for Ireland. While there were a few genuinely radical voices in the Liberal Party, it still endorsed survival of the fittest, via laissez-faire unrestricted competition.

After completing a B.A. and M.A. at Cambridge, Cyril entered the legal profession, becoming a 'special pleader' – which were then persons who drafted 'pleadings', i.e. statements of case. However, the death of his father in 1872 required that he devote himself to the management of the family London estate in Battersea. Owners of more than 800 houses in the suburb, the Flowers were considered model landlords.

When Cyril's father first began laying out the Battersea estate in the 1860s, it had been planned for the middle classes, and substantial three-storey terraces constructed. By the 1890s the pleasantness of Battersea Park had been compromised by the railways. Added to this were the growing accommodation demands of what the newspapers termed "the superior class of workingmen," i.e. artisans. Cyril and his estate architect consequently revised the building strategy downwards to more modest two-storey half-houses. Cyril also built on his father's philanthropic reputation. As well as funding and fundraising, this included promoting 'Entertainments for the People'.

Despite these commitments, Cyril was generally more interested in living the life of a playboy, and could be glimpsed during in The Season riding his fine mare in Rotten Row with the rest of London's *jeunesse dorée*. His vague instructions to the estate office, issued from wherever he was staying, gave the administrators migraines, as did his spendthrift habits, particularly with regard to art.

He became an active patron of the technically brilliant, but incorrigibly bohemian and improvident artist Frederick Sandys,* who undertook several portraits of him. In one, showing Cyril at twenty-nine, he is embowered with honeysuckle and laurel: it is as delicately evocative as any Aesthetic Movement portrait of a femme fatale. In another, Sandys portrayed him as St. George. When not depleting the family fortune with lavish purchases, Cyril trained with the Buckinghamshire Yeomanry Cavalry. He was a fearless horseman, and rose to become a captain.

Amongst Cyril's most notable friends was the elderly Lord Houghton.† Born in the reign of George III, the ultra-sophisticated Houghton was one of the brightest intellects and wits of his time; a social power, and a man without illusions, writing of himself: "He hoped little and believed little, but he rarely despaired." Even his friends considered Houghton paradoxical. He inscribed in a Commonplace Book: "Yes, I live for Pleasure and for Power: for Pleasure that injures no one, and Power that benefits Mankind." It wasn't bombast. A fellow politician noted: "As years advanced he became not (as the manner of most men is) less Liberal, but more so; keener in sympathy with all popular causes; livelier in his indignation against monopoly and injustice." Houghton supported extension of the vote, the alleviation of poverty and improved education. Yet his character made him a manqué politician, as Cyril also would be.

Houghton was another admirer of Walt Whitman, and visited him while in America in 1875. Houghton also owned a legendary pornography collection, and added to it by pseudonymously authoring *The Rodiad*, an ode to schoolboy flagellation.‡ Its text was

---

* Frederick Sandys, born Antonio Frederic Augustus Sands, (1929–1904).
† Richard Monckton Milnes, 1st Baron Houghton (1809–1885); poet, patron of literature, politician, magistrate, and prominent social figure and wit. A founding member of the Cambridge Conversazione Society (The Apostles), and friend of Tennyson and Thackeray, his politics altered from Conservative to Liberal. He married a daughter of the 2nd Baron Crewe, with whom he had three children. His nicknames included 'The Cool Of The Evening', and from Swinburne: 'Baron Tattle of Scandal.' Milnes had taken London by storm in 1836, "having acquired through residence in Southern Europe a vivacity of manner which, by all accounts, took old stagers of the formal school considerably aback." When a grande dame informed him that, in her youth, "all the young men in London were at my feet," he asked her whether they were chiropodists. [T. Wemyss Reid, *Life, Letters, and Friendships of Richard Monckton Milnes, First Lord Houghton, Vol I,* Cassell & Company, London 1890, pp213-214; James Pope-Hennessy, *Monkton-Milnes: The Flight Of Youth,* Constable, London 1951, p108; Lloyd Sanders, *The Holland House Circle,* Methuen, London 1908, p374; W.H. Mallock, *Memoirs Of Life And Literature,* Chapman And Hall, London 1920, p45.]
‡ Its lines include:
I'm a schoolmaster of the good old school, –

302

hand-corrected for him by Richard Burton* no less, as well as by the aforementioned sadist Frederick Hankey, the supplier of erotica to them both. The fetish was also avidly shared by Houghton and his friend Algernon Swinburne† in letters to each other.

Little wonder Cyril was drawn to Houghton and his worldly milieu: like his sexuality, his curiosity, interests, and droll bonhomie mirrored Cyril's own. In the summer of 1868, at his Yorkshire seat of Fryston, Houghton's convivial guests included two of England's most devoted boy-worshippers: schoolmaster Oscar Browning and artist Simeon Solomon.‡ Together with Houghton, Swinburne, Hankey, Reddie, and other gentlemen, Solomon was a member of the Cannibal Club, a sexually libertarian dining society founded by Richard Burton in 1863. Its topics of discussion included pornography, Whitman's poetry, and phallic worship.§

By any measure, these friendships were transgressive. After leaving Yorkshire, Cyril joined the twenty-seven-year-old Solomon on a visit to the Lake District. The overt decadence of Solomon's art with its androgynous love-struck youths and angels had been noted by critics

---

One to whose ear no sound such music seems
As when a bold big boy for mercy screams –
Mercy, with which my will he will not get
Till his low beeches with his blood be wet…
Coarse birch, broad shoulders, and a rattling bum,
Are all you want from now to 'kingdom come'…
Delightful sport! whose never failing charm
Makes young blood tingle and keeps old blood warm.
[George Coleman (*sic*), *The Rodiad*, Cadell & Murray, London 1820 (actually 1870s), p8.]
* Sir Richard Francis Burton (1821–1890) explorer, translator, writer.
† Algernon Charles Swinburne (1837–1909), poet, playwright, novelist, and critic. Swinburne was obsessed with flagellation, and exchanged fantasies of the birchings of pretty boys with the equally keen Simeon Solomon. A photograph of the Eton flogging block inspired him to write 'An Heroic Poem', which begins:

> I sing the flogging block. Thou, red-cheek'd Muse,
> Whose Hand the Blood of smarting Boys imbrues,
> Scholastic Dame, revered of State & Church,
> Whose Lords to be have writhed beneath the Birch.

[Yopie Prins, *Metrical Discipline*, in: Stefano Evangelista, Catherine Maxwell (eds.), *Algernon Charles Swinburne: Unofficial Laureate*, Manchester University Press, 2013, pp101-103.]
‡ Simeon Solomon (1840–1905); Pre-Raphaelite painter of mystical androgynous beauties and Jewish life. His reputation and career never recovered following his arrest. [See: Carolyn Conroy, 'Mingling with the Ungodly: Simeon Solomon in Queer Victorian London', in: Simon Avery, Katherine M. Graham (eds.), *Sex, Time and Place: Queer Histories of London, c.1850 to the Present*, Bloomsbury, London 2018.]
§ See: Deborah Lutz, *Pleasure Bound: Victorian Rebels And The New Eroticism*, W.W. Norton, New York 2011.

from the first. Throughout the 1860s, Solomon was a crony of Swinburne. It was to him that in 1871 Solomon dedicated a privately printed prose poem, *A Vision of Love Revealed in Sleep*. Seeking to spiritualise his desires, Solomon had its narrator's soul visit him in the form of an angelic youth. When two years later Solomon was arrested in a London public lavatory for sodomy, Swinburne and other friends, distanced themselves: Solomon was too rogue, and the social risks of the association too high. However Cyril, who'd become a patron of Solomon, continued to purchase his works.

Besides Cyril's artistic confidants, there were his plutocratic ones. As well as Alfred and Leopold de Rothschild, another young close friend was Baron Ferdinand 'Ferdy' de Rothschild, the builder of the impressive and oppressive Buckinghamshire treasure house of Waddesdon. He was the son of the Viennese Baron Anselm von Rothschild, and his English wife, another Charlotte. A fussy febrile dilettante and hypochondriac, Ferdinand was enraptured with another of Cyril's friends, Archie Primrose, Lord Rosebery, to whom he poured out his loneliness and longing in a string of neurotic letters. This Rothschild circle was part of a heady gilded hothouse of worldly connoisseurs. Their wealth and position as the uncrowned Jewish royal family, reigning by the power of supranational debt, enabled them to write their own rules. In their sympathetic company, and the liberating atmosphere of their fantastical realms, Cyril thrived.

One day in 1864, Leo and Cyril had ridden over from Mentmore, that other great Rothschild palace in Buckinghamshire, to Aston Clinton, the country seat of Sir Anthony de Rothschild and his wife Louise.* Their daughter Constance, known as 'Connie', was there: a plump, jolly, but fundamentally serious young lady, who later wrote of the occasion:

> I can remember that we were much struck by the remarkably good looks of Leo's friend: his fine features, bright dancing eyes, mass of waving golden hair, vigorous health, and bright activity such as one seldom sees.

---

* Sir Anthony Nathan de Rothschild, 1st baronet (1810–1876); banker and philanthropist. His wife Louise de Rothschild (1821–1910) was widely admired, not only for her intellect, cultivation, and sense of fun, but as an appreciative listener, and her ability to bring out the best in people. In the words of Lord Rosebery, "no one was with her without being the better for it." [Lucy Cohen, *Lady de Rothschild And Her Daughters 1821-1931*, John Murray, London 1935, p291.]

In 1874, on a visit to Holland with her mother, Constance again encountered this vision of beauty, "buying everything he could lay hands on." As Lady de Rothschild explained to her younger daughter, Annie:[*]

> Mr. Flower is bitten with the Oriental blue and white china mania, and is as difficult to tear away from any shop containing those treasures as an American lady from Worth…Mr. Flower has just come back from a <u>blue</u> shop, much elated, having bought <u>ninety-three articles!</u>

This booty Cyril installed at his London flat in Victoria, in a suite of rooms he commissioned to showcase it: lined with leather that appeared gilded, their designer was probably Thomas Jeckyll,[†] of Peacock Room fame.

While Cyril was rich, the daughter of a Rothschild was something else again. Constance's ample form was a golden key that could open the door to almost any earthly dream, however grand – and her new suitor never thought small. A female guest at Aston Clinton, who witnessed him paying court to Constance, recalled: "Cyril Flower was a superb, golden-bearded Viking of a man whose wooing was impetuous and ardent." A very *aesthete* Viking. While the object of his affections embodied a means to an end, a voluptuous vision of limitless shopping can be both erotic, and provoke the tenderest of feelings. Even love. Or the self-delusion of it.

In 1874, Constance joined her cousins Leopold and Leonora who were holidaying with Cyril at St Moritz. Leo having informed Constance that Cyril loved her, on a "heavenly morning" she summoned him. They sat outside on the grass, and Cyril began to cry. Comforting him, as she later wrote, he "took me in his arms and kissed me and pressed me and loved me & I felt the passion of his love," adding, "I felt excited and half mad…I feel that Mamma is very much against it."

As for Constance: since adolescence, her diaries had expressed the

---

[*] Annie Henrietta Yorke, née de Rothschild, 1844–1926.
[†] Thomas Jeckyll (1827–1881), English architect, and leading figure of the Aesthetic Movement.

belief that almost every man she encountered was in love with her. In her teenage years there had been a series of infatuations with Rothschild cousins, and in her twenties she was tempestuously courted by the mincing middle-aged fortune-hunter Lord Henry Lennox. Flattered by his attentions, which included a proposal of marriage, Constance led him on, until lectured to by Ferdinand, who would have been all too aware of his true nature. She rejected a wealthy suitor, Alfred Seymour,* whom her parents approved of. On her birthday in 1872, she wrote: "I was a little fool some years ago and behaved like one. If it had not been so, I might have been married and comfortably settled."

The difference in Cyril and Constance's ancestry and faith would have represented an enormous obstacle to the alliance, but for time and circumstance. Several years previously, Constance and her younger sister Annie had become friendly with Victor Eliot,† a son of the 4th Earl of Hardwicke. In a surreal situation, during a visit to Aston Clinton in the Christmas of 1867, Victor suffered a fatal stroke in front of the girls while reading a poem by Tennyson – the belated result of a blow to the back of the head he'd sustained while serving in the Royal Artillery. The tragedy drew the Yorke and Rothschild families together. Constance developed a friendship with Victor's effeminate brother Alick, while Annie fell in love with another of the brothers, Eliot.‡ Constance had been their neurotic matchmaker, telling her diary, "I wish I could be a Christian. I love the faith and the worship." She also confessed:

> Eliot came, sat down, cried, took my hands, kissed them. I kissed his forehead. He raised his lips and touched mine. How I would go through fire and water for him. I love him so.

The eventual marriage of Annie and Eliot in 1873 was a minor sensation: while not the first of a Rothschild to a gentile, it anguished both families, and upset the Jewish community, who considered it a betrayal. Despite this, it was a happy union, until Eliot's untimely death five years later from pneumonia.

---

* Alfred Seymour (1824–1888), Liberal Party M.P. Married Isabella Leighton.
† Lieut. the Hon. Victor Alexander Yorke (1842–1867).
‡ The Hon. Eliot Constantine Yorke (1843–1878), M.P. and Equerry to the Duke of Edinburgh.

A further incentive to Cyril's wooing was that Lord Rosebery was courting Hannah, the daughter of Baron Mayer and Baroness Julia de Rothschild,[*] and the greatest heiress of her day.

Like Hannah, Constance was plain as well as stout, and also saddled with the awkwardness of being Jewish in a society that was politely antisemitic. However, she thought Cyril beyond wonderful. In 1876 Constance's father Sir Anthony died, leaving her £300,000,[†] in addition to the Rothschild trusts to which she was a beneficiary. His death also removed a further obstacle to the marriage. The following year, Constance's mother finally gave her assent to the union.

Immediately upon his engagement, Cyril wrote to Frederic Myers, who'd been privy to his plans:

> I am the happiest man in the world, BUT I beg you not to <u>say a single word to a human being</u> for no one knows (none of either her relations or my own) & she is very nervous.

Once the news was out, Cyril received a warm letter of congratulation from Sir Dighton Probyn, Comptroller and Treasurer to Edward VII:

> You are indeed a lucky man, the very luckiest in the whole of England I think, and I congratulate you most heartily – as also does my wife. You are marrying a person fit to be Queen of England…I know you will be – a very good husband.

Another luminary and friend whom Cyril was eager to inform was Lord Houghton. He wrote to him:

> I seem to know you so well & like you so much I do not wish you hear of my great happiness from anyone before this can reach you. I am going to be married to Constance Rothschild. Once upon a time you said to me words I am sure you have forgotten & which amused me immensely – "Why does not Constance R marry Lord Beaconsfield"? Now you know. I am very happy & all the family are so kind that it makes things much easier & pleasanter.

---

[*] Baron Mayer Amschel de Rothschild (1818–1874). Married Juliana Cohen.
[†] At the very least, £28 million in 2021 values. [measuringworth.com]

Houghton's droll jest that Constance should set her cap at the widowed Disraeli, forty years her senior, was wickedly apt. She was earnest by nature, and Dizzy, a dear friend of her mother, was, despite being baptised Anglican, the most famous Jew in the kingdom. Semitic to the point of caricature, he'd happily informed one of her cousins: "You and I belong to a race which can do everything but fail." Cyril's delight in Houghton's joke shows he took a bemused objective view of his future wife from the very beginning.

Houghton gifted Cyril a volume of his more respectable poetry – "the only present I can think of which you will not have from somebody else," to which Cyril replied, "You could not have sent me a present which I should more fully & deeply have valued." To top things off, the wedding ceremony was performed by Cyril's ever-loyal admirer Canon Farrar.

The couple were strikingly dissimilar: his primary interests artistic, hers religious, with only philanthropy in common. Yet for a time, Constance was content with being a peahen to a peacock, confiding to her diary: "I am radiantly happy. I love and am beloved. Oh God I thank thee." While *The Jewish Chronicle* expressed "the most poignant grief" over such nuptials, the couple attended services in each other's synagogue and church. Cyril loved the Bible, and could recite passages by heart, but institutional religion was another matter: as Constance learned to her dismay, churchgoing, even as irregularly as he undertook it, made him "intensely cross and irritable."

Had it not been for her fortune, undoubtedly Cyril would never have contracted the marriage, a fact that surely lingered on the fringe of her consciousness. She'd been rescued from the shelf of middle-aged spinsterhood. This was no jejune alliance: the couple were both thirty-four. Nonetheless, it's extremely unlikely Constance then realised the nature of her husband's sexuality.*

As with her sister Annie's marriage, the union dismayed some of the Rothschild relations, and not simply because Cyril was a gentile. They considered him unworthy of Constance, despite her obvious physical shortcomings. Just like Charlotte de Rothschild, who'd viewed Cyril

---

* Lady Henry Somerset had remained bewildered by her husband's blatant behaviour with men and cruel neglect of her, until confronted with the direct evidence. See: Olwen Claire Niessen, *Aristocracy, Temperance and Social Reform*, Tauris Academic Studies, London 2007, pp32-55.

and his coterie through narrowed eyes, his flamboyant beauty and friends made him appear a somewhat dubious character.

The Flowers were also likely less-than-thrilled by the match: years later when an Australian newspaper referred to Cyril as being "Hebrew himself," his uncle Horace was quick to pen a corrective to the paper's editor, stating that Cyril's father was "a 'true Briton', the lineal descendant of one of the oldest English families."

Constance possessed a keen intellect, vivaciousness, and a willingness to please. However, under the exuberance of what remained of her youth, she was remarkably straightlaced and deeply pious, "always interested by any form of religious emotion." Before her marriage she had often given lessons at the Jews' Free School in Spitalfields.

In 1870, the same year her future husband was making a pilgrimage to Walt Whitman on behalf of comradely love, Constance had published a 948 page, two-volume work she had authored with her sister Annie: *The History and Literature of the Israelites According To The Old Testament And the Apocrypha*. It ran into two editions.

This was not the end of Constance's literary work – the days of a Victorian upper class spinster lingered long. Inspired by a portrait of Nell Gwyn that hung at the Rothschild property of Tring Park, in 1875 she birthed a jejune but felicitously written novel starring the said royal mistress.* The following year then saw issue from her pen an over-ripe novelette about the need for self-sacrifice in marriage.† Not least, she authored a magazine article *The Hebrew Woman*. Of the ancient female Israelites, it boldly informed readers:

They resembled, indeed, in not a few respects the Teuton

---

* Anon, *A Buckinghamshire story of 1663*, Watson & Hazell, Aylesbury 1875.
† Anon, *Two days in Cadenabbia*, Hazell, Watson and Viney, Aylesbury 1876. It concerns "a stalwart young Englishman" Edgar, who is in love with 'Norah Graham', a moonlit pearl of self-denial. She wishes her sister Marion to live with them after their marriage, but Edgar will not hear of it. His friend Maxime, a worldly Frenchman, believes that marriage should be a short-term contract to be renewed at will with the consent of both parties. This prompts Edgar to have a nightmare in which he and Norah have made such a vow, and after years of marital bliss, she is casually considering leaving him, and compounding the horror, has contracted a deadly fever. Upon waking, Edgar realises that putting aside his selfishness, and permitting Marion to live with them, will make his love for Norah all the fervent. The end. The story was possibly inspired by equally wearisome conversations Constance may have held with suitors regarding her desire to remain close to her own sister Annie.

309

women, who, like them, were vigorous and high-spirited, renowned for their purity and courage…and who, we are told also, counted prophets and priests among their ranks…They did not shrink from life, with its stirring passions and awful tragedies, nor were they shut up in their own narrow grooves and petted as visions of fragile beauty, born to satisfy the caprice or whims of their lord.

Constance surely wished to identify with such Boadiceas. However, her prodigious publishing endeavours, while indicative of a fervent imaginative life, failed to impress Cyril. Gently nettled, in widowhood she confessed: "He never encouraged me to write, and thought very little of my literary capacities." Indeed, in Cyril's eyes, she did not measure up to her mother, Louise. As Constance modestly recalled:

> my husband…would often tell me, half in joke, half in earnest, that I was not a good a Liberal as she was, and that I had not her remarkable quickness of intellect or her penetration in character – which was quite true.

Given this, Lady de Rothschild's assessment of Cyril is worth consideration. She wrote:

> I trust that on the whole Constance has chosen the better and happier lot — and it ought to, and does make me happy to think that she will not be left alone in this cold world but that she will have the love and companionship of one, who I believe, is truly devoted to her, and who has a fine, kind and generous nature.

Being keenly aware of her deficiencies, Constance sought to make up for them by being infinitely amiable, which particularly explains why many of the political and social lions of the era enjoyed her attentions. The author E.F. Benson, one of Cyril's closest friends, wrote:

> She had a boundless fund of vague goodwill for the world in general, and for her husband an unbridled admiration. This fondly expressed itself in long enraptured glances, in calling him 'duckie' or 'luvie', in laying a caressing hand on his head as she passed his chair, and these little tributes sometimes exasperated him. He was coming up across the garden one morning from his early bathe, dressed in the bright colours he affected, a green

tam-o'-shanter, a blazer and pink shirt, and as he approached the loggia where we were breakfasting, she could not curb her fervour. "Does not dearest Cyril look too beautiful this morning?" she cried.

Constance clearly tried Benson's patience. In a telling scenario, he details how exhausting she could be:

> When he [Cyril] was present she had eyes and ears for no one else; and absently asked her neighbours at table ridiculous questions and did not listen to their answers. One night at dinner – he dined in a ruby-coloured velvet suit – he referred appositely but with Rabelaisian frankness to an unsavoury divorce case that was then in process. "I call it 'Love's Labour Lost'," he said. "Cyril, how could you?" exclaimed Lady Battersea from the other end of the table, and put up her hand to hide her blushes. But she could not maintain a disapproving attitude, and beamed at him. "Dearest Cyril, you are too brilliant!" she cried. " 'Love's Labour Lost!' Is that not clever? Did you hear what dearest Cyril said, Mr. Balfour?" And when her admiration had ceased to boil over, she asked Mr. Balfour if he was not very fond of reading.

Another guest of the couple, Violet Bonham Carter,[*] confirmed the comic play of adoration, artlessness, and self-delusion, writing to a friend in 1905 from Overstrand:

> He dines in pomegranate velvet & a perfumed beard. Connie shrieks amorously every night "Cyril you have a <u>very</u> good appearance, a very good appearance! Your nose is so straight to-night." She told me Bernard Shaw had been at Overstrand & said when she offered him tea "Don't give me tea Ly B. I implore you; it makes me tell lies." "Is it not strange that tea sh[ou]ld make him lie my dear?"

As the years rolled on, Constance's frustration with Cyril's off-hand treatment of her; his dismissal of her talents; their failure to have children; her likely envy of the more sympathetic marriages of others, and spiritual restlessness, bred a suppressed resentment that fuelled

---

[*] Helen Violet Bonham Carter; later Baroness Asquith of Yarnbury (1887–1969). Liberal politician and social activist. Daughter of Herbert Asquith and his first wife Helen Melland. Married Sir Maurice Bonham Carter.

within her what one of her Rothschild relations termed a "deep-seated streak of spitefulness".[*]

As early as 1881 cracks in the marriage were apparent. In March that year she told her diary: "Cyril brought two young men down" to Aston Clinton "who were a disturbing element." The next day, he took the unnamed gentlemen to a hunting meet. A few months later Constance described his treatment of her being "as usual rough & unkind." The following year she wrote of him behaving "in such a cold halfhearted way that at times it frightens me," concluding "He will never love me with passion that is not in him, but he might love goodness and holiness with passion." The excisions and blackings out in Constance's diaries, either by herself or an assiduous executor, are their own testament to the recurring heartache and soul-searching throughout her marriage. Philanthropic activism would increasing become her release, and compulsion.

Sounding like a naïve and prim heiress in an Oscar Wilde comedy, in her memoirs she recalled:

> At the beginning of my married life I was disappointed that we did not settle down in Battersea amongst the working classes. I suggested making a 'House Beautiful' in that region, allowing closer intercourse with and better knowledge of the men and women whose paths were so different from mine, and consequently so imperfectly understood by me.

Unlike the sheltered Constance, her aesthetic but worldly husband had long enjoyed intercourse with the working classes. Indeed, it had likely extended to that comradely 'adhesiveness' championed by Whitman in its most amatory sense. While Cyril fully shared her philanthropic attitude towards the lower orders, having them as

---

[*] One of Constance's surprising *bête noires* was her cousin Hannah de Rothschild. The genesis of the enmity may have been Hannah's siding with her parents against the marriage of Constance's sister Annie. Jealousy of Hannah's marriage may also have been a factor. "Hannah is a brute", Constance told her diary – "most selfish", and a "cold congenial hostess". As for Hannah's husband Lord Rosebery: "*He* is very pleasant." In 1889, Hannah had also circulated in Society a paper against women's suffrage: this would have offended Constance's burgeoning feminist views. However, at the time, there was a belief the enfranchisement of women would electorally benefit the Conservative Party more than the Liberals. [Richard Davis, *The English Rothschilds*, University of North Carolina Press, Chapel Hill 1983, p164; Peter Gordon (ed.) *The Journals Of Lady Knightly of Fawsley*, Routledge, London 2005, p172; Women's Suffrage, *Cambridge Daily News*, 27 March 1889, p3.]

neighbours was an entirely different matter from having them as lovers.

Constance had made it a condition of the marriage that when in the country they should live with her widowed mother on her splendid Buckinghamshire estate of Aston Clinton. A new wing was therefore added to the house, and its stables rebuilt. Awaiting an invitation to the house, Henry James joked to a friend:

> The Flowers seem to me aloft on Olympus like the 'Gods,' & I a struggling mortal, uncertain of divine decrees in the lower world. Cyril is Jove, & Mrs Cyril Juno.

For their London home, Cyril side-stepped Constance's desire for Battersea bijou, and instead paid a fortune for the lease of a mansion, Surrey House, at 7 Marble Arch West, directly opposite that monument. While grand, spacious, and commanding a fine view of Hyde Park from the upper rooms, the prominent site of the residence had disadvantages, as one magazine was keen to point out:

> it is a stopping-point for every omnibus that comes eastward from Bayswater or that descends the Edgware Road. As a result, the front door at Surrey House for three-quarters of the year is splashed over with mud, and so is the carriage of every caller. Happily, Lord Battersea is a good democrat, and he makes what music he can out of the clamorous cries of conductors that enter at each open window.

It wasn't just constantly cleaning off mud that would have kept the servants busy: there was a world of dusting too. Cyril transformed Surrey House into a palace of art. As one enraptured visitor recorded:

> Entering from the noisy thoroughfare leading from Oxford Street, into this lovely house, one seems as though transported from the world with all its anxieties, its bustle, its vehicles, to a century when Art in its highest capabilities was represented in the taste of its patrons. The "area" of present day London has been superseded by a fairy garden, whilst an early Italian fountain sprays its silver ripplets upon a marble pavement.... The suite of drawing rooms remind us not so much of a XIX century London home, but of an Italian palace of the period when the Borgias flourished and Italy was in its prime.

Cyril had the hall and dining room lined with marble that had once formed part of a side chapel of a church in Brescia, while another hall was lined with seventeenth-century carved oak shipped from Holland. Above the staircase, with its balustrade of gold bronze, was the painting 'The Golden Stairs', the magnum opus of Sir Edward Burne-Jones: its descending Aesthetic damsels in ethereal drapery, "like angelic visitants to this fairy palace." Through palm fronds could be glimpsed a golden bronze bust of a young Bacchus by Joseph Nollekens. On the walls hung works by da Vinci, Botticelli, Rubens, and Whistler. Underlining the fact this was also a seat of political power, in a prominent position in the dining room hung a photographic study of the owner's patron, Gladstone.

Cyril was only getting started. As Constance phrased it – with obviously gritted teeth:

> the space at the back of the house, unusual in a London building, allowed the necessary scope for many additions – not always improvements – which it gave my husband the most intense satisfaction to invent and construct. His ideas on architecture were always too big for the spaces where we made our homes...it proved a very expensive amusement.

Of Cyril's taste in interior decoration, the best that can be said is that it was eclectic. More was definitely more, and his rooms approached haute brickabrackmania. Unsurprisingly, like a moth to the moon, he was drawn to the schizophrenic mishmash of orientalia that was the furniture of Carlo Bugatti.* Pretty it wasn't, but it had the courage of its aesthetic convictions. For his bedroom at Surrey House, Cyril commissioned Bugatti to create a decorative scheme of retina-frying decadence worthy of a pharaoh's tomb, right down to the tiger skin rug. A further scenic acquisition was Abdul, an African servant.

It was a heady time for hedonists. A visitor to London in 1877 recalled:

> The cult for beauty was unlike anything I have ever known before or since. The aesthetic movement was at its height, and

---

* Carlo Bugatti (1856–1940), Italian decorator and designer whose works reflect Moorish, Islamic and Japanese influences.

the "short-haired women and long-haired men", familiar figures at all the great routs and public *fêtes*, waited to see the entrance of one of the 'beauties' as people wait to see Royalty pass.

Surrounded by artistic friends, Cyril was caught up in it. In their marriage, Constance would regularly have cause to bite her tongue, and suffer because of it. However, her adoration of Cyril sustained her: being married to him was a grand adventure. As she wrote, he opened up her life:

> Very different in character and pursuits were the guests we entertained. My husband was interested in variety, and I was deeply interested in human beings of all sorts and conditions.

One diarist records Cyril dining with a group of gentlemen who included Whistler and Tissot: their talk was of the novels of Balzac. The guests of Cyril and Constance also included his many homosexual friends, and their wives and partners. Studiously unmentioned in Constance's *Reminiscences* was one of their most famous guests – Oscar Wilde. Of other visitors, Constance recalled:

> Julian Sturgis*...entered with zest into the pencil games then in vogue. Together with Frederic Myers, Edmund Gurney† and others, we composed sonnets, wrote questions and answers in verse, tried our hand at essays or stories in the style of known authors, and indulged in a variety of such-like amusements.

Frederic Myers was by this time forging a career as Her Majesty's Inspector of Schools. As for Edmund Gurney, the heir to a Quaker fortune, Henry James' psychologist brother William considered him to be "one of the first-rate minds of the time...a magnificent Adonis, six feet four in height, with an extremely handsome face, voice, and general air of distinction about him," with not least, the "tenderest heart." Constance too "had been much struck with his very able and original mind and the beauty and charm of his young wife." However, according to James' sister Alice, Gurney was not in love with his wife;

---

* Julian Russell Sturgis, 1848–1904) novelist, poet, librettist and lyricist. Before his marriage, he shared a cottage during a summer vacation with Reginald Brett. It was conveniently only a few miles from Eton, prompting Cory to write to him that it was "indiscreet and muggery...and spoonery of the stalest kind." [James Lees-Milne, *The Enigmatic Edwardian*, Sidgwick & Jackson, London 1986, p42.]

† Edmund Gurney (1847–1888), psychologist and psychical researcher. Married Kate Sibley.

only marrying her due to Myers' persuasion, and an altruistic wish to raise her in status.

These guests of the Flowers were part of an interknit circle. Myers's close friendship with Edmund Gurney had, as with Cyril, possibly devolved from a love affair. They also shared another binding interest, the craze for which was sweeping Victorian society – spiritualism and all things psychical.

On an evening back in 1868, Frederic Myers had taken a walk under the stars with the Cambridge master Henry Sidgwick,* whom he'd studied with. Sidgwick was regarded by his students, who included Edmund Gurney and Arthur Balfour, as a kind of Socrates. Like Myers, Sidgwick also entertained severe religious doubt, and on the walk the two men speculated whether the answer to the riddle of the existence might lie in ghosts or spirits. That starlit walk became the impetus for the founding in 1882 of the Society for Psychical Research.

Like other esoteric followings of the time, including Theosophy, psychical research held an immense attraction for social outliers and sexual outsiders, as holding the keys to hidden realms and insights. As with their explorations in poetry and literature, for these young men and women it was inextricably bound up with their quest to fathom their own nature and its place in the cosmos. Given society had deemed them tainted due to their desires, and sought to disempower them, the idea of possessing arcane knowledge and special powers was compelling. As people forced to live secret lives, exploring the byways of the hidden was second nature.†

---

* Henry Sidgwick (1838–1900), philosopher and economist. Although homosexual by temperament, he married physics researcher Eleanor Mildred Balfour, the sister of his former student, Arthur Balfour. [Bart Schultz, *Henry Sidgwick: Eye of the Universe*, Cambridge University Press, 2009, *passim*.]

† Typical of such young men was the most celebrated medium of the nineteenth century, Scotsman Daniel Dunglas Home (1833–1886), who summoned spirits for the wealthy, including the crowned heads of Europe. An account of his séances conducted with Viscount Adare, *Experiences In Spiritualism With D.D. Home* (1870), which was privately published by Adare's father, the 3rd Earl of Dunraven, contains strong homosexual undertones. Rumours of Home's associations with young men circulated, and he and Viscount Adare lived together and shared a bed. A wholly discreditable character, Home enraptured a vulnerable wealthy widow, a Mrs Lyon, who was pining for her husband. She assigned £60,000 in bank stock over to him (at least £5 million in 2020), under the delusion, cultivated by Home, that it was what her late husband desired. She then came to her senses, and sought to revoke the gifts. The case came to court in 1868. The judge dismissed Home's claims that it was she who had

316

It was therefore inevitable that when the Society for Psychical Research was founded, a majority of its leaders and many of its membership were homosexual, or inclined to be. Some were also former Cambridge Apostles – members of the Cambridge Conversazione Society, a secretive intellectual society. Given devotion to a 'higher sodomy' was almost one of its precepts,* the Society for Psychical Research was somewhat an extension.

Founders and early members of the Society included Henry Sidgwick who became its first President); his wife Eleanor; Frederic Myers (who became its President in 1890); Edmund Gurney (Honorary Secretary); Frank Podmore,† who was also to be a founder of the Fabian Society; John Addington Symonds; and the educationist and classical scholar Arthur Sidgwick,‡ the brother of Henry.

An early Vice-President of the Society, and former Apostle, was Roden Noel,§ the poet son of the Earl of Gainsborough –

influence over him, rather than vice versa, and that she had only changed her mind when he had declined her wish for a physical relationship. Under the legal judgement, which pronounced that he'd exercised undue influence, Home was forced to return the investments. [Judgement In The 'Spiritual' Case: Lyon v. Home, *Cumberland and Westmorland Advertiser, and Penrith Literary Chronicle*, 26 May 1868; Untitled item, *The Morning Post*, 23 May 1868, p5.]

* Cambridge Apostle Henry Norton blithely wrote to a friend regarding a fellow Apostle, the future war poet and beauty Rupert Brooke (nicknamed the Rajah), who entered Cambridge in 1906: "It's astonishing, isn't it, how fond the Rajah is of being buggered, he feels, poor dear fellow, quite uncomfortable if one talks to him without an erection." [Henry 'Harry' Tertius James Norton to James Beaumont Strachey, c1906-1909: Lot 301, Fine Books, Manuscripts and Works on Paper, Forum Auctions, 30 May 2019; Lot Id: 55046.

[https://web.archive.org/web/20201216164931/https://www.forumauctions.co.uk/55046/Brooke-Rupert.-Mallory-George-Herbert-Leigh.-Norton-Henry-Tertius-James-35-Autograph-Letters-signed-some-initials-and-3-cards-from-Norton-to-James-Strachey-6-printed-invitation-cards-to-Cambridg?view=lot_detail&auction_no=1043] Previously: Lot 185, Fine Books and Manuscripts, Bonhams, 24 June 2015.

[https://web.archive.org/web/20191102075201/https://www.bonhams.com/auctions/22714/lot/185/]

† Frank Podmore (1856–1910), psychical researcher, author, socialist.

‡ Arthur Sidgwick (1840–1920), educationist and classical scholar, and father of five. He had an intense, possibly physical relationship with Frederic Myers while at university, and his reckless behaviour with a boy upset J.A. Symonds. In his diary, Sidgwick memorably described his wedding night, writing (in Greek) "lovingly with her lips she made holy my shame." [Trevor Hamilton, *Immortal Longings: F.W.H. Myers And The Victorian Search For Life After Death*, Imprint Academic, Exeter 2009, p50; Bart Schultz, *Henry Sidgwick - Eye of the Universe: An Intellectual Biography*, Cambridge University Press 2004, pp409-410; Emily Rutherford: Arthur Sidgwick's Greek Prose Composition: Gender, Affect, and Sociability in the Late-Victorian University, *Journal of British Studies*, Volume 56, Issue 1.]

§ Roden Berkeley Wriothesley Noel (1834–1894), poet, philosopher, philanthropist, and father of three. Henry Sidgwick wrote to Noel's widow: "I never knew any one more free from what

"handsome, feminine in manner and inordinately vain," and like his friends, Lord Ronald Gower and John Addington Symonds, an enthusiastic admirer of London's soldiery.

In 1894, the Society gained a new President in the form of another sensitive young man and ex-Apostle – the future Prime Minister, Arthur Balfour. Other distinguished members included Lord Houghton, and the Flowers, who were registered under Constance's name. Despite its pursuits, the Society was then considered a respectable endeavour, and honorary members included Gladstone, Ruskin, Lord Tennyson, and Henry Morton Stanley. Not a member, but also enraptured by the spirit world was Cyril's friend Lord Lorne.

A further associate of Frederic Myers and Cyril, as well as Constance, was the flamboyantly camp and kindly Alick Yorke, an equerry to Queen Victoria's youngest son Prince Leopold.* (Possibly finding him too dangerously effete after the Wilde scandal, Cyril's friendship with him cooled.) Yorke was an amateur medium, and together with Prince Leopold, arranged séances even within the royal household, including in the company of the Queen. The Prince's tutor and Comptroller, Sir Robert Collins,† was also a very close, sexually sympathetic friend of Myers.

Frederic Myers would go on to make significant contributions to the study of hypnosis and psychology. In 1886, with Gurney and Podmore, he authored *Phantasms of the Living*, which documented alleged sightings of apparitions. Further to this, between 1883 and

---

Goethe calls – '*was uns alle bändigt das Gemeine.*' [That which holds us all in bondage, the commonplace.] After conversing with him I always felt that the great realities of Life and Thought and Art, the true concerns of the human spirit, became more real and fresh and vivid to me." It was possibly Noel who introduced J.A. Symonds to a male brothel near Regent Park Barracks. [Arthur Sidgwick; Eleanor Mildred Sidgwick *Henry Sidgwick: A Memoir*, Macmillan and Co., London 1906, p531; Phyllis Grosskurth *The Woeful Victorian: a biography of John Addington Symonds*, Holt, Rinehart and Winston, New York 1965, p178.]

* HRH Prince Leopold, Duke of Albany (1853–1884), youngest son of Queen Victoria. Afflicted by both haemophilia and epilepsy, Leopold lived his life with an ever-present consciousness of early death, which came to him at 31. Despite this, two years prior to his death he married Princess Helena of Waldeck and Pyrmont, and fathered two children. Intellectual, with a love of the arts, he possessed a gentle sympathetic nature which created deep affection in those who knew him. He became friends with Frederic Myers, whose theories of an afterlife comforted him.

† Sir Robert Hawthorn Collins (1841–1908), tutor to Prince Leopold, Duke of Albany and later Comptroller to his Household. Collins' brother Arthur, Equerry and Comptroller for Queen Victoria's daughter Princess Louise, was a close friend of Cyril. Married May Elizabeth Wightwick.

1888, Edmund Gurney involved himself with experiments in mesmerism and telepathy, which took place at Brighton. The subjects were a group of working-class youths who lived in the town. Gurney was assisted by George Albert Smith,* a stage hypnotist and illusionist who became his paid private secretary. Smith would later pass off the lads as "Mr. Podmore's young men," but a rumour was later current in psychic research circles that the involvement of Gurney and other leaders of the Society with the Brighton lads had extended beyond chasing phantasms to more corporeal enthusiasms.

Whatever occurred, it's clear the Society for Psychical Research offered a comforting homosocial network of friends, sympathisers, and possibly even procurers. Eros and yearning, both spiritual and physical, were an inextricable aspect of the illumined and aroused Myers, and his tingly spiritualist circle.

For the ever-energetic Cyril Flower, the entertaining, town planning, collecting, photography, soldiering and spiritualism were not enough. Parliament was the natural forum for an ambitious young man hungry for access to influence, and the opportunity to elevate his social status. Cyril's good friend Archie, Lord Rosebery, had been encouraged to join the Liberal party by William Gladstone. As one newspaper noted, "Lord Rosebery, one of our most promising politicians, and Mr. Flower are greatly attached to each other." Rosebery possibly encouraged Cyril in his political desires, but the strongest push may have come from Constance, who was ever keen to curb Cyril's dilettantism. His political advancement was then aided by the bachelor Liberal powerbroker George Russell.†

As inevitably happens for those of means with political ambitions, a

---

* George Albert Smith (1864–1959), a colourful showman, and later an important figure in early British cinema.
† George William Erskine Russell (1853–1919), biographer, essayist, memoirist and radical Liberal politician; a grandson of the 6th Duke of Bedford. A spinal inflammation at twenty-one left him an invalid for life. Raised in an evangelical household where "the salvation of the individual soul was the constant concern of life", he was an ardent churchman, and a keen but somewhat aloof observer of his time. Like William Marcus Thompson, who quoted him, he despaired over Edwardian society, writing: "We are Romans of the worst period, given up to luxury and effeminacy, caring for nothing but money." However, one bachelor acquaintance (of which there were many) fondly recalled: "those rooms of his, where all kinds of people come and find rest and comfort (mental, physical, and spiritual) from his cheerful companionship." [Death of Mr G. W.E. Russell, *The Yorkshire Post and Leeds Intelligencer*, 18 March 1919; The Secret History Of To-Day, *Reynolds's Newspaper*, 18 May 1902, p1; Rev. James Adderley, *In Slums And Society*, T. Fisher Unwin, London 1916), p192.]

parliamentary seat for Cyril to contest was soon made available. It was Brecon in far-off South Wales: a bijou constituency with under a thousand eligible voters that was the perfect rich man's entry card to the Palace of Westminster club. It had hitherto been considered a safe Tory seat, being held by James 'Taffy' Gwynne-Holford, a genial local squire, but dissatisfaction with Disraeli's Conservative government was growing in both county and country.

Cyril and Constance would spend part of the years of 1878 and 1879 electioneering in Brecon. As she recalled:

> my first impression of the Brecon Borough...was not a very cheerful one, and my heart sank within me. The journey from London seemed endless, the weather was damp and cold; [the rain] would beat, for days together, against our windows!

Noting that "the moist atmosphere and prevalence of rain were known to produce a certain amount of mental depression that drove many to the dangerous exhilaration of intoxicants," Constance became a keen supporter of the temperance movement. In this endeavour she was encouraged by her sister Annie, who in the empty despair of her young widowhood, dedicated herself to it.

It's easy to assume that the vast means and social connections of the Flowers were the principal factor in Cyril's eventual win of the seat, but this dismisses his intelligence, personableness, and the indefatigable energy he brought to the task of electioneering. He claimed to have met everyone in the borough whilst campaigning, which given its size, was readily achievable. It was later said: "He came, he saw, he conquered." As Constance saw it:

> Cyril made way very quickly with the Welsh folk...His good looks, his joyous spirits, his delight in poetry, his dramatic rendering of the same, his quickness of repartee, his successful platform oratory, and above all his sympathy with the people and his real kindness of heart, were the chief factors of his undoubted popularity.

It was the simple truth. Public speaking came easily to him. He was glib, but the flow of oratory was apt, witty and winning for his provincial audiences. Said *The Cardiff Times*: "He is a first-rate canvasser, and a genial, frank, ready-witted young gentleman, to whom it will be a very hard matter to say 'No.' "

Overall, the press was friendly. Despite the stratospheric realm that Cyril and his Rothschild wife hailed from, they were portrayed as down-to-earth and dedicated to the welfare of working people, as indeed was the case. *The Cardiff Times* wrote:

> As a striking instance of the manner in which husband and wife work hand-in-hand for the common good, it may be mentioned that while Mr. Cyril Flower has a class of 40 or 50 young men, to whom he lectures on the beauties of Shakespeare and kindred subjects, Mrs. Flower gathers together, week by week, a school, consisting of some hundreds of girls, to whom she imparts information and advice that will assist them to make good wives and happy homes.

With an unmeant but perhaps appropriate double-entendre, Constance observed:

> Cyril took infinite trouble and pains to place young men in fitting situations...Welsh gardeners and Welsh carpenters were imported from Brecon to Aston Clinton, and were often most ill-suited to English ways, but Cyril thought them all most delightful.

In her assessment, Cyril found jobs for over a hundred Breconians, which was remarkable. The sunshine of the Flower's plutocratic philanthropy even healed the sick, with the couple enabling "orders of admission to the very best metropolitan hospitals" for the seriously afflicted.

Constance was an enormous asset to Cyril's campaigning: while somewhat scatterbrained, she was highly conscientious. Despite this, their canvassing was far from smooth sailing. Cyril received "anonymous and threatening letters by the score," and local Tory supporters resorted to bribes and intimidating thuggery, including an attempt to ambush Cyril's carriage one evening. However, the plot was discovered: Cyril sent his carriage on ahead, walking home in the company of his solicitor and a protective escort of supporters. *The Cardiff Times* reported:

the very attempt to intimidate the Liberal candidate only served to show the popularity with which he is regarded. The reason for the widely different opinions concerning the two candidates is not far to seek. Mr. Holford, who to do him justice does not forget old friends, was about to enter the house of an old supporter of his, when one of his intelligent supporters restrained him by saying 'Don't go there, she's only a widow,' and the unkind remark, though not intended to be overheard, was keenly felt by the one who was only a widow. As a contrast to this, it may be mentioned that when Mr. Flower first canvassed Brecon he called upon an old man, formerly a gentleman's servant, and delighted that worthy Conservative by a familiar gossip upon horses and hounds. The old man has died since that time, but this did not prevent Mr. Flower calling upon the widow.

In the summer of 1879, another more private problem manifested itself, Constance telling her diary: "Cyril felt very unwell, gout has declared itself, how strange." Indeed, he was only thirty-six.

Between 1878 and 1880, Lord Rosebery bankrolled and stage-managed a speechmaking tour by Gladstone (the famous Midlothian Campaign), which was an immense success. It unified the Liberal Party and gave it an impetus such that, after Disraeli called a Gèneral Election for April 1880, Gladstone and the Liberals were swept to power with a large majority. In the Brecon constituency, 822 persons voted. With 5 ballot papers spoiled, the result of the poll was Gwynne Holford 379, Cyril Flower 438. With a majority of just 59 votes, Cyril had made it to Westminster. A Welsh-language Liberal newspaper hailed him as "the enlightened Liberator".

The new Prime Minister could be an intimidating presence. As one report phrased it:

> Gladstone is very marked in his preferences; he is equally embarrassing in his aversions. Men who have spent a fortune in the interest of the party, and a matured lifetime in Parliament, have found themselves passed over in the hour of reward. On the other hand, the walking gentlemen of politics, thanks to a pretty face or academic manner, or the fact of them being their

father's sons, have been put into the Cabinet or otherwise honoured.

So it was with Cyril. "From his entry into the House of Commons Mr. Gladstone displayed a kindly interest in his handsome young supporter's welfare." This wasn't merely due to Cyril's looks and charm. Gladstone had long politically courted Nathaniel 'Natty' de Rothschild, whom he eventually made a peer.

Like many of the upper class, including the Prince of Wales through Sir Ernest Cassel, Gladstone privately held substantial investments in Egypt: 37% of his portfolio was in Ottoman Egyptian Tribute Loan bonds, which had been set up by the Rothschild bank. It was to protect the interests of English investors like himself that Britain went to war in 1882 to oust the rebel Egyptian nationalist Ahmad Arabi Pasha, who'd threatened the puppet ruler Khedive Tewfik, and the administration of Consul-General Sir Edward Baring, of Barings Royal Bank. British investment in Egyptian agriculture and infrastructure brought benefits to the country, but sending British soldiers to fight and die in the dust of Egypt on behalf of the wallets and purses of the rich was a moral obscenity; one that was papered over by pound notes and patriotism.

After Pasha was defeated, Gladstone's Tribute Loan bonds soared from £38 to £97, making him a rich man, and multiplying the fortunes of others. Cyril's wife was Natty's niece: keeping the Rothschilds onside meant it was prudent for Gladstone to ensure that Cyril basked in the sunshine of his approval. In 1889, when Gladstone was electioneering in the Westcountry, Cyril was even able to provide him with the use of the Garland, the steam yacht of his Rothschild sister-in-law, Annie; and the year following, Gladstone spent Easter at Aston Clinton.

Until his later financial involvement in South Africa indirectly made him so, Cyril was not an imperialist, believing Britain had no right to aggrandise itself by means of foreign wars. Like other Liberal politicians, he publicly criticised the interventions of Disraeli's government in Afghanistan and Zululand as "a blot in the history of England." This belief led him to be disloyal to his Party privately. Between 1880 and 1885 he secretly provided information to Lord Randolph Churchill, who was part of a splinter group of Conservative backbenchers nicknamed The Fourth Party,* which attacked both the Liberal government and the Conservative opposition. The Fourth Party opposed Gladstone's Anglo-Egyptian War, and supported Ahmad Arabi Pasha, including supplying funds for the defence at his trial.

With more fidelity, Cyril invested much time and money buttering up the leaders of the Liberal Party through his entertaining in the marbled splendours of Surrey House. He enjoyed doing it even more for the younger men of the Party's dining and socialising association, the Eighty Club. For older gentlemen seeking youthful company, and ambitious young men eager for powerful political mentoring, the Club was a hothouse. Its more colourful members and guests included Oscar Wilde, Oscar Browning, and St. George Lane Fox-Pitt,† a first cousin and eccentric friend of the aberrant Earl Russell; while its more decorative members included Ernlé Johnson,‡ a son of the Dean of Wells and former schoolboy passion of Lord Esher; and Charles Mendl,§ best known for his later marriage of convenience to interior decorator Elsie de Wolfe.

As the radical *Reynolds's Newspaper* suggested in a wry report, the Club was "now a power in the land":

---

* Other members were Henry Drummond Wolff, John Gorst, Arthur Balfour, Justin McCarthy, and Henry Labouchère.

† St. George Lane Fox-Pitt (1856–1932), electrical engineer, inventor, and early member of the Society for Psychical Research. Married Lady Edith Gertrude Douglas, a daughter of the 9th Marquess of Queensberry, and sister of Lord Alfred Douglas.

‡ Ernlé Sacheverell Wilberforce Johnson (1858–1939), poet, civil servant, and private secretary. Author of *Ilaria And Other Poems* (1884) and *A Day On The March* (1895). The former anthology includes the ode "Dear Bertram! child of the earth! faun of the field…That exquisite Praxitelean grace…The inly-stirred earth-heart will ne'er forget." Lord Esher met Ernlé at fifteen, and two years later committed to his diary: "I may record his sweet expression of gratitude when I sent him away with a gift of two bright sovereigns, a bottle of rose water for his eyes, and one of my Venetian photographs. His face lifted up with a look which you dream of upon the face of Raphael's violin player…Ernlé's fair hair haunts me." [Ernle S.W. Johnson, *Ilaria And Other Poems*, Kegan Paul, Trench & Company, London 1884, pp62–65; L.S. Milward, E.C. Bullock, The Malvern Register, 1865-1904, Malvern School, 1905, p66; James Lees-Milne, *The Enigmatic Edwardian: The Life Of Reginald 2nd Viscount Esher*, Sidgwick & Jackson, London 1986, p33.]

§ Sir Charles Ferdinand Simon Mendl (1871–1958), Press attaché and intelligence officer at the British Embassy at Paris. In an otherwise unexceptional career, he hired two ruffians to burgle the apartment of a blackmailing gigolo and retrieve compromising letters from Prince George, Duke of Kent. This was said to explain his otherwise unfathomable knighthood, awarded in 1924. He later made minor appearances in two Hollywood films, and married wealthy celebrity decorator and lesbian Ella Anderson 'Elsie' de Wolfe, and following her death, his reputed mistress, the twice previously married and divorced violinist Yvonne Riley. [Francis Henry King, *Yesterday Came Suddenly: An Autobiography*, Constable, London 1993, p278.]

the Eighty Club is entirely composed of 'superior' persons. They are all young-old men or old-young ones, and most of them are devoted to 'culchaw'...The club is largely recruited from the Oxford and Cambridge Debating Unions, where everyone knows 'superiority' is the order of the day...These 'superior' gentlemen are, in point of fact, 'politicians on the make.' Many of them have but the most jejune notion of politics, and some of them find a great difficulty in putting two consecutive sentences together; but they are so 'superior' that they contrive to elbow aside men who have been fighting the people's battles while they were being birched over their Latin verses (for they all do Latin verses)...its members are remarkably assiduous. But it has been discovered by observers that this assiduity is always proportioned to the prospects in store for the individual, which shows that the Eighty Club members are good men of business; for why fight forlorn hopes and do hard, unrecognised work when you can get a berth of £5,000 a year for a sonorous series of vague platitudes once or twice a year?

One such young man whom Cyril aided, and whose bright future he predicted, was the future Prime Minister Herbert Asquith.

Like many of their class, the Flowers usually spent part of the year abroad. To Constance's dread, the liberating air of the Continent spurred some of Cyril's most profligate off-leash behaviour. On a visit to Rome in 1881, they visited the studio of the American sculptor William Wetmore Story.* Constance's ears soon picked up some ominous chatter: "to my utter amazement, I heard Cyril ordering the Sardanapalus. I was fairly taken back." It was a £1,800 impulse purchase of a stupendous marble statue.

Sardanapalus was the last ruler of Assyria, whose downfall was attributed to luxurious living and sodomy, and whose memorial statue, according to Plutarch, had borne the inscription, "Eat, drink, indulge thy lust; all other things are nothing." With pursed lips, Story's bluestocking biographer noted: "The sculptor has represented this

---

* It was a visit Oscar Browning may have encouraged: Story and his wife were good friends of his, and he taught their sons at Eton. Story supplied Browning with casts of statuary, with which he decorated the halls of Eton in an effort to elevate its tone. [Ian Anstruther, *Oscar Browning: A Biography*, John Murray, London 1983, pp29, 39.]

effeminate monarch as sitting with every evidence of his royal tastes and uselessness." As an icon of voluptuous decadence, a Sardanapalus for Cyril was simply too irresistible.

He would also have savoured Lord Byron's blank verse play about Sardanapalus, in which the slavegirl Myrrha sets fire to his palace at Ninevah as a royal funeral pyre. Her evocative words, redolent with the promise of immortality, possibly echoed in Cyril's ears: "Lo! I've lit the lamp which lights us to the stars." As his senses soared to the heavens in an ecstasy of artistic acquisition, poor earth-bound Constance could only sigh, and await the bill. The statue was eventually placed in the large conservatory of Surrey House, where it sat enthroned amidst topiaried chrysanthemums, like a gleaming Ur-Cyril.

Long before he came into vogue, Cyril was also enraptured by the works of Whistler, who in a letter to him, dubbed Surrey House "the Hotel Flower," and Aston Clinton "your plantation". He wrote to Cyril beseechingly:

> Go round one morning to my place and look at a most lovely Nocturne in blue and silver…I want 300 gs [guineas] for it — but whether you go in for hanging it in your red room or not, never mind just go and look at it for I am delighted with it myself and want to show it…sky lovely and the sea of immense distance and gleaming in the soft light of the moon. This description is almost fit for the papers! But *faites pas attention, mon cher!* Go and see if ever you saw the sea painted like that!

A poem 'Ballade Of A Man Of The Period', which was probably authored by the editor of *The Studio* art magazine Gleeson White,[*] joked of "a species unknown to our dads" — the Aesthetic crew that frequented such places as the Café Royal, where Cyril was very much at home:

> All the men he 'don't know', he calls 'cads'
> Bets rarely, not liking to lose;
> Talks Jingo, yet thinks with the Rads;
> Takes life in its sordidest hues;

---

[*] Joseph William Gleeson White (1851–1898), writer and editor. His home at Christchurch, Hampshire was a haven for homosexual artists, writers, actors and intellectuals.

Paints his room in the greenest of blues,
At the play, looks the saddest of sads,
Dances little, but loves to refuse,
Raves a bit o'er a Japanese fan;
Yet would culture's sweet brightness diffuse,
The young nineteenth century man!

In marked contrast to this dizzy decadence, in 1882, Constance wrote in her diary:

> September 23rd. Fast Day. Spent it with dear Motherkins...With her, sunshine; without her, cold shade. Her love transforms me, her delicacy refreshes me. God be praised at having given me such a Mother!...All evening Cyril talked about servants, one of his favourite topics. I got heartily bored of it; for I do not believe in one class being so much better than the other.

Even their deep wealth couldn't insulate the couple from the bugbear of the age — servant problems. And the number on their payroll was not small. Constance's diary catalogued the domestic strife to which she was hostage:

> Have lost James from drink. Abdul thoroughly gone to the bad. Poor Milly Cambridge ruined by Cyril's second horseman. Pugh has resigned — a thorough drunkard. Disgraceful scene between him & Bell. A[ston] C[linton] in a perturbed & uncomfortable condition.

Constance may not have believed one class was better than the other, but she certainly recognised who had the whip hand. When one of her maids secretly married one of her footmen and bore a child, she sacked them both. "Of course it is secret and horrid of her," wrote architect Edwin Lutyens,* "I told her she would have to be godmother to the babe...I gave Lady B. fits." Benevolence to the working class when they were under one's own roof, rather than a distant mass, was obviously a different matter. "No home life can be perfect without sympathy," Constance would inform the National Union of Women Workers in 1898; four years later when addressing them again she added the codicil that ideals were "not always

---

* Sir Edwin Landseer Lutyens (1869–1944), premier architect of the period.

attainable in home life". Clearly.

As Constance's feminist interests increased and her confidence grew, so did her impatience with Cyril. In addition to her temperance work, she became active in the Association of Working Girls' Clubs, the Union of London School Teachers, the National Union of Women Workers, and improving conditions in women's prisons. In 1885, she was approached by a Christian missionary friend, who pleaded with her for help in assisting Jewish prostitutes who'd been rejected by their own community. It resulted in Constance overcoming community taboos and her own prudishness to co-found the Jewish Ladies Society for Preventive and Rescue Work, which sought to rehabilitate Jewish streetwalkers and assist Jewish immigrants. She told her diary:

> Have started a Home, furnished it, and engaged Superintendent and working Matron...Care less for society than I did formerly, far more for works which show some result.

This particular initiative, with Emma, Lady Rothschild* as its first President, grew to become a very large organisation, the Jewish Association for the Protection of Girls, Women and Children. Constance's other activities on behalf of the Jewish community included charitable visiting in the East End. Her high-mindedness had begun early under the influence of her mother, who was Lady Bountiful to her tenants and poorer friends. Travelling as a young woman in Ireland in 1865, Constance had also been impressed by the self-sacrificing Lady Bessborough: "She dresses herself as plainly as possible, to give away all she can." Journeying with Constance was her sister Annie, who wrote mockingly:

> To Connie's despair there is a melancholy scarcity of beggars, and she has only seen one till now who quite comes up to her beau ideal and has an unlimited number of rags.

Constance would write: "all my life long will I battle against human prejudice and intolerance, and will pray for charity among all men." She developed strong friendships with socially activist women such

---

* Emma Louisa, Lady Rothschild (née von Rothschild (1844-1935). Married her banker cousin Nathaniel Mayer de Rothschild, 1st Baron Rothschild.

as Frances Power Cobbe,* a full-hearted jolly Irishwoman who championed anti-vivisection and women's rights. Despite Cobbe having, in the words of George Moore,† "a tone of the trousers about her writings," Constance was puzzled why "dear precious Cobby" chose to live with sculptor Mary Lloyd, a Welsh Alice B. Toklas, whom Constance described as "devoted to Miss Cobbe & yet so unlike her. Pessimist, unsociable, gloomy," and worse, "with no belief in humanity, or I fear in God."‡

On Cyril's part, in 1885 two charities were established on which he sat as Chairman, and Lorne's wife, Princess Louise, as President. The first was The Gordon League, named in honour of national icon General Gordon. The endeavour was the idea of blowhard Arnold White. To his credit, and against his usual instincts – "Christian charity is invoked to canonise weakness" – White had organised free breakfasts for unemployed dockworkers of the East End, whose distress had gone unrecognised. He now suggested that halls be opened on Sunday evenings to provide moral improvement for the working classes, in the form of music, recitations, and addresses on interesting subjects. The result was the formation of the League at a meeting at Surrey House. Its aims expanded as the years went on, and it became a significant force for community support.

The second charity was the Recreative Evening Schools Association, which worked to further develop practical continuing education. It had been a dream of a Scottish Congregationalist minister and social activist, the Rev. John Paton.§ Being aware of his work, Princess

---

* Frances Power Cobbe (1822–1904), women's suffrage leader, anti-vivisection activist.
† George Augustus Moore (1852–1933), Irish author and critic.
‡ Given Constance's associations with progressive and independent women, there was inevitably a steady trickle of spinster guests through the Flower homes, mirroring to a lesser degree Cyril's bachelor flow, although it appears on Constance's part, with considerable more innocence. They included Irish novelist, historian and poet Emily Lawless (1845–1913), who set up house with Lady Sarah Spencer, a sister of the 5th Earl; the American social activist Louisa Lee Schuyler (1837–1926) and her equally unmarried sister Georgia; and Anna Molique (1838–1934), a jolly inhabitant of Aston Clinton Park who was "the intimate friend and companion" of Constance. The daughter of German musician Wilhelm Bernhard Molique, Anna was originally been hired by Constance's parents to teach her, and sister Annie, the piano. She stayed on for half-a-century, becoming a force of nature in the village: establishing a choral society, a profitable straw-mat enterprise, an evening school for boys, and sewing classes for girls; Constance noting: "she trained many little village girls for domestic service, at least one hundred must have passed through her hands." [Aston Clinton, *Bucks Herald*, 20 September 1924, p6; Death Of Miss Molique, In Memoriam, *Bucks Herald*, 2 February 1924, p10.]
§ Rev. Dr. John Brown Paton (1830–1911).

329

Louise introduced him to Cyril and Constance. Under the Princess's aegis, with Cyril acting as both Chairman and Treasurer, and Paton as Honorary Secretary, the Association came to fruition. National student numbers for its classes would grow to 500,000. It was a contribution to the betterment of working people's lives whose impact can't be underestimated.

That same year of 1885, the borough of Brecon was merged into the county, so losing Cyril his seat. For the people of Brecon it also constituted a huge loss. Upon his departure, Cyril was presented with an illuminated address of gratitude and esteem from the municipality, and also one from railway workers. This was due to his support of the *Employers' Liability Act (1880)* – the first legislation aimed at supporting working men who sustained onsite injury. In seeking to strengthen its clauses, during its passage Cyril had voted five times against his own Party. He'd also supported other bills that positively affected the lives of working people. Several years later *The Brecon County Times* would print:

> we do not believe in the whole Parliamentary history of our kingdom, can there be found another parallel case where the representative and the people were knit in closer bonds than those which united Mr. Cyril Flower...and the electors of Brecon. He won the good opinion of Liberals and Conservatives alike, and did a vast amount of genuine good for the town and its inhabitants during the five years he represented us. We have never seen his like since...

Cyril was now invited to be a candidate in the General Election of 1885 for the division of South Bedfordshire. Half its population resided in the industrial town of Luton, so it was predisposed to Liberalism. At a public meeting, the local chairman of the Liberal party introduced Cyril as candidate with a remark that brought laughter and cheers: "if his Liberal principles corresponded with his appearance he considered they had done well in their choice."

Cyril's own speech and witticisms were received with great enthusiasm. When the crowd demanded an interjector be removed, Cyril adroitly replied, "Let him stay and learn manners" – upon which it was reported, "A roar of laughter at once restored equanimity to the meeting." Cyril stated that the Gladstonian agenda had been clearly laid out, and suggested the Tories had been caught flatfooted in the face of the tide of social and industrial change, and were struggling to adjust their policies:

> One after another their ideals had been smashed, and now they came before the electors of the country not knowing…what to call themselves, and not knowing how to dress themselves. The Radical clothes were too large for them and the Conservative clothes were absolutely worn out.

With regard to land reform, Cyril said he believed: "The interests of the landlord, the interests of the tenant, and the interests of the labourer were all so united that they must be considered as one." He also wished entail and primogeniture to be abolished, and the positions of tenants and labourers to be made more secure. Reiterating his party's belief in Free Trade, he acknowledged "There was a great wave of depression and failure setting in," but considered it temporary.

Cyril further told the meeting that, due to the increase in population, he believed importation of grain was vital, but a tax on it to assist landowners would only hurt the poor, stating that "he had not the slightest objection to fill[ing] the pockets of the landlords, but he, as a landlord, did not want his pockets filled out of the mouths of the people." Lifting his audience up, he affirmed "that England was not on the wane, and that she was not going to rack and ruin," and quoted Tennyson's verses that had been penned at the time of the first Reform Bill:

> A land, where girt with friends or foes
> A man may speak the things he will;
>
> A land of settled government
> A land of just and old renown
> Where freedom slowly broadens down
> From precedent to precedent.

It was winning stuff. However, the prospect of Cyril as local M.P. was not embraced with wholesale enthusiasm by Alfred Atkins, the editor of the town's Conservative newspaper, the *Luton Times and Advertiser*. Atkins' obituary in the paper in 1894, eulogised him as a "genial, kindly soul," and that, "In a town like Luton it was no light matter formerly to hold up the banner of the Constitutional party."* When it came to dealing with Cyril, Atkins' banner pole was held at the sharp end. Cyril's swagger and brio clearly got under his skin, as did his good-humoured baiting of the paper in his speeches, which as Atkins noted on one occasion, "pleasantly tickled his supporters, the more so as the Editor was present."

Cyril also mocked the Tory candidate, Sydney Gedge, quoting some old doggerel to characterise him: "The Devil was dressed in his Sunday best, His coat was red, and his breeches blue, With a hole behind for his tail to go through." In response, Atkins published that Cyril's electioneering hopes in Bedfordshire would in hindsight be viewed as "the uneasy memory of a farcical interlude," and such comic lines could well be applied to himself. They were, Atkins considered:

> indicative of Mr. Flower's mingled aristocratic dawdledom and demagogic pandering...It was gratuitous vulgarity, without excuse... we do not believe the constituency will be satisfied with a candidate whose chief recommendation is a capacity for 'chaff', and that they will turn with satisfaction to one who makes fewer jokes but has better politics.

Cyril told an election crowd that the paper's jibes "had amused him more than he could say." However, this was surely only half true: as the election approached Atkins' attacks deepened. In March 1885, the *Luton Times* sketched the two principal candidates for its readers:

> Let us consider for a moment how they differ. Mr. Cyril Flower is one of the 'curled darlings' of the fashionable world, who 'toil not neither do they spin', and, in this particular instance, we may add, nor was 'Solomon, in all his glory, arrayed like' him. His first appearance in Luton was in the excruciating get-up of a 'Gaiety' walking gentleman,† with sealskin cape, and hat tucked under arm, in the latest manner of swelldom, an entourage of obsequious attendants emphasised his 'society' distinction, while his manner betokened contemptuous pity for his simple audience, and that the whole business was 'an awful bore don't-

---

* i.e. The Conservative Party.
† As in the noted London theatre The Gaiety.

cher-know.' Mr. Sydney Gedge [the Tory candidate] is of entirely different stamp. Attired in the black frock coat with stove-pipe hat which marks the professional man or City merchant, and carrying the conventional black bag which he clings to with curious pertinacity, he presents no mark whatever in regard to dress, but his appearance is nevertheless striking and attractive.

The article went on to paint Gedge as a busy practising lawyer associated with a large number of philanthropic institutions, while portraying Cyril as a languid "exquisite of aristocratic circles" and "lackadaisical politician" who even appeared to have a lack of respect for the Sabbath:

> Mr. Cyril Flower is a gaudy butterfly flitting here and there in the sunshine of wealth beyond the dreams of avarice, and having done nothing all the week, he devotes his Sundays (if rumour be true, but at present we give it with this qualification) to lawn tennis or croquet. We do not believe it is lawn tennis, at any rate, for that requires considerable skill and a good deal of exertion. It would not be that. Possibly croquet, for the gentle dullness of that exercise would even permit of his wearing a sealskin cape and would hardly put his hair out of curl.

It was not Atkins' first attempt to suggest Cyril's politicking was merely the droll novelty of a rich man desirous of staving off boredom. Earlier in the year, Atkins had worked himself into a paroxysm of loathing. Cyril, he claimed, indulged himself in embracing "every current craze" of radical politics:

> he attunes his utterances to the passing fancy of the crowd – although evidently it is all a great bore – while they…degrade their manhood wallowing before him.

Warming to this theme of emasculation, the tone became ever more vicious:

> By the influence of Mr. George Russell and through the selfish subserviency of the local managers to money bags and aristocratic connections, he has gained a foothold in Luton, while his glib tongue and la-di-da air have imposed on the credulous rank and file…their hearts have been ensnared by an effeminate

333

lisping dandy, the creature of numerous personal attendants...His speech was like the flow of the waterworks main, on the constant supply system...Everything he said betokened the immature politician, and mere Parliamentary butterfly...Mr. Flower has found this world an easy place to live in, to eat, drink, and make merry in, and maybe he has some genuine pity for the poor creatures to whom every day brings a struggle for existence, but it impossible that he can be in touch with the feelings and aspirations of the working classes of Luton. We believe it will be realised before long that his candidature is a huge mistake and that the revulsion of feeling which will ensue will prepare the way for the success of a Conservative candidate, one who is manly in all his ways, has definite views on the social problems of the age, and recognises that the greatest good of the greatest number does not consist in the destruction of any one class.

When one of the local papers referred to Cyril's 'brilliant career' at Cambridge, Sydney Gedge, who'd also attended the University, made enquiries. It was subsequently reported that he drew volleys of laughter with a speech in which he informed electors about "a distinguished body called 'The Amateur Dramatic Society'," and that:

Mr. Cyril Flower attained great fame by the 'brilliant' manner in which, gifted with a pretty feminine countenance, he performed the lady's part in the plays that society produced. So far as he (Mr. Gedge) could ascertain that constituted the 'brilliancy' of Mr. Cyril Flower's career.

Unfortunately for Sydney Gedge and Alfred Atkins, the 'effeminate lisping dandy' won the election with almost double the votes of his rival, a result fuelled by enthusiasm for Gladstone's reformist agenda, or as the *Luton Times* put it: "the labourer's revolt against the parson, the squire and the farmer. All the old influences have been scattered." The rapid growth of the urban working and middle classes was changing everything.

In the years 1885 and 1886, Cyril and Constance were indirectly affected by a scandal involving a friend of theirs, the Liberal member for Chelsea, Sir Charles Dilke. Dilke had become the lover of his brother's mother-in-law,* a situation which continued after his marriage. He also seduced her daughter, i.e. his sister-in-law. Most shockingly of all for the time, she alleged he'd persuaded a servant girl to join them in bed. Dilke's wife sued for divorce. The case became a long-running sensation, and ruined his career. Cyril remained loyal to Dilke, which caused Constance to fret that Cyril wasn't concerned with "whether he [Dilke] has done right or wrong. Oh the misery of sin." She further simmered in her diary:

> I believe him [Dilke] to be <u>guilty</u> [quadruple underlining]…Cyril of course takes his part violently, he seems to me to lose his proper judgement in such cases – makes it all the harder – more unpleasant for me, I as must stick to what I think <u>right</u> and <u>I will</u>. [triple underlining]

Oh to be a fly on the wall then at Surrey House, during an afternoon reception to which Constance had invited the cream of the aristocracy to meet Princess Louise: "All was going pleasantly…when like a thunderbolt of astonishment was heard announced Sir Charles and Lady Dilke." 'Beryl', the pert social columnist of *The Manchester Courier*, which reported the incident, mused: "Perhaps someone kindly fainted and created a diversion. It seems that Sir Charles and Lady Dilke were quite unaware of the party, and had merely gone to make an ordinary call."

The Dilke scandal exposed Cyril and Constance's differing moral standards: her upstanding morality, against his laissez-faire attitude to male sexual conduct – which was typical of men of his time generally.

That same year, Constance's mother told her diary: "Rather stormy discussions with Cyril about Women's Rights, Stead etc." Likely contributing to Cyril's impatience was Constance's deepening involvement in the temperance movement. Its most prominent leader was Lady Henry Somerset, the estranged wife of Lord Henry, and it was aligned with the social purity movement, which campaigned for the suppression of prostitution and other vice. A newspaper account of one temperance gathering soberingly states:

> Mrs. Cyril Flower then addressed the meeting, saying, in the

---

* Martha 'Ellen' Mary Smith, née Dalrymple, wife of shipowner Thomas Eustace Smith, and mother of Henry 'Harry' Smith, paramour of Lord Henry Somerset and Lord Ronald Gower.

course of a very practical speech, that if they, as members of the Society, wished to break through long established customs and fashions, they must be prepared to exercise self-control and practice self-denial, under many conditions and circumstances of social life.

While Cyril chaired temperance meetings for political purposes, and on behalf of Constance, self-denial in regard to anything wasn't part of his personal agenda.

In 1886, Gladstone made Cyril a parliamentary Whip. Named after the 'whipper in', the rider who keeps the hounds together in a fox hunt, Whips are aide-de-camps to their political leaders: they endeavour to ensure members of the party attend and vote as the leader desires, and also keep the leader informed of opinion within the party. The role was tailored to Cyril's diplomatic skills, and his convivial and urbane personality, and it was no surprise that he was very popular and successful in it. As it required collating and discreetly transmitting information, it also tapped that skill his forbidden sexuality had honed — a Machiavellian secrecy. The other Liberal Whips were Arnold Morley* (Chief Whip), Robert 'Bobby' Spencer,† Edward Marjoribanks,‡ and George Leveson Gower.§

As was common, in compensation for the additional work the role imposed, Gladstone rewarded him with a sinecure appointment – in this case as a Junior Lord of the Treasury, an ancient 'sparkler' post that carried a sweetener of £1,000 per annum. However, with the issue of Irish Home Rule, even Cyril's social talents would be taxed to the limit.

---

* Arnold Morley (1849–1916), wealthy barrister and Liberal M.P. A bachelor. (No relation to John Morley.)
† Charles Robert 'Bobby' Spencer, 6th Earl Spencer (1857–1922). An effeminate dandy who held the Spencer seat of Northamptonshire as a Liberal for twenty years. He married Margaret Baring of the banking family, with whom he fathered six children. Her death devastated him. Emotionally divorced from his offspring, a mental comfort in later life was his friendship with the equally elderly, repressed homosexual literary lion Sir Edmund Gosse.
‡ Edward Marjoribanks, 2nd Baron Tweedmouth (1849–1909), Liberal M.P. Married Lady Fanny Octavia Louise, a daughter of the 7th Duke of Marlborough, and had issue. During the Eulenburg scandal a German newspaper alleged he'd been accused of being homosexual. [Norman Domeier, Deborah Lucas Schneider (trans.), *The Eulenburg Affair: A Cultural History of Politics in the German Empire*, Camden House, Rochester N.Y, 2015, pp219, 351n76.]
§ Sir George Granville Leveson-Gower (1858–1951), and Liberal M.P. Married the Hon. Adelaide Violet Cicely Monson, and had issue.

Encouraged by Irish Nationalists, Gladstone introduced the Home Rule bill in April 1886. The issue was unpopular: Ireland was distant, and in the eyes of many English, the Irish were insolent, irrational, and ungovernable. In a much-quoted speech, Lord Salisbury compared them to 'Hottentots' – South African natives, saying:

> self-government, but which is really government by the majority, works admirably well when it is confided to people who are of the Teutonic race, but that it does not work so well when people of other races are called upon to join in it.

Across the Irish Sea, his lordship's droll reflections did not incite rejoicing. Closer to home, the issue split the Liberal party. Gladstone's bill was thrown out after its second reading, with a large breakaway faction of upper and upper-middle class Liberals who opposed Home Rule, led by Lord Hartington,* forming the new Liberal Unionist Party. In July there was another General Election, and the Liberals were trounced. The Conservative Party, led by Lord Salisbury, achieved a parliamentary majority via a pact with the Liberal Unionists. Cyril had remained with the Liberals, and again won his seat, but with a lowered majority. He'd previously declared his opposition to Home Rule, but after much prevarication, and loyal to Gladstone, ultimately announced his support, a policy flip-flop his critics pounced on. Given Society's almost overwhelming opposition to Home Rule, it was a bold stance.

That summer, Cyril graced the Royal Academy's exhibition in the form of a bust of himself he'd commissioned from sculptor Alfred Gilbert.† Critics considered it superb, except the magazine *John Bull*, which sniped that the artist had "cleverly contrived to make a heroic-looking bust from an original that is certainly wanting in that characteristic."

The following year of 1887, the Golden Jubilee of Queen Victoria, saw the streets of nighttime London ablaze with a light that not been seen since The Great Fire. The decorations in one West End block alone, that included the homes of the Duke of Northumberland and Graftan, featured 30,000 gas jets, while Cyril's arrangement of

---

* The future 8th Duke of Devonshire, who like others, was a Irish landholder.
† Currently lost, but possibly the bust visible in 'Overstrand, The Pleasaunce, The Reception Hall 1921': The Francis Frith Collection, photo ref: 70863 [https://www.francisfrith.com]

coloured lamps on the facade of Surrey House was also admired for its artistry. In Frederick Sargent's panoramic painting of the garden party at Buckingham Palace that June, Cyril stands noble and alone in the crowd.

In marked contrast, in February 1888, Cyril joined a group who made a deputation to Lord Salisbury seeking relief for the poor and unemployed. With the number of paupers in London exceeding 100,000, and hard winters still being suffered in the wake of Krakatoa's eruption, there was a level of distress in the Metropolis like never before. The petitioners, led by the Liberal politician Lord Herschell,[*] included Cardinal Manning,[†] Arnold White, and Cyril's political benefactor, George Russell. They were informed by Salisbury that he would give it his "most careful consideration". The problem was so overwhelming, it may have seemed to him beyond the remedy of any practical solution.

In June, a mysterious event occurred when Cyril's friend Edmund Gurney died at just 41. The cause was chloroform inhalation in a hotel in Brighton, to which he'd suddenly gone after receiving a letter. His death may have been accidental: Gurney used the compound to combat insomnia, and miscalculations in its use were not uncommon. The evening before his death he'd dined with Cyril and Arthur Balfour at the House of Commons, and had seemed in bright spirits. However, the mysterious circumstances led to speculation that it was a suicide prompted by blackmail, or depression over the failure of his career – including discovery that the psychical experiments conducted at Brighton were hoaxes perpetrated by George Albert Smith.

One person who was certain about the cause of his death was Josephine Butler. She blamed the influence of Frederic Myers, and would write at the time of the Wilde trials: "I hope Myers has got a fright. He quite deserves Oscar Wilde's fate. I am sorry for sensitive youths with some principle like Edmund Gurney, who died by his own hand, in despair because of having been so corrupted."

For Gurney's friends, it was a devastating loss. "Edmund Gurney was one of the elect, both in mind and character," remembered

[*] Farrer Herschell, 1st Baron Herschell (1837–1899).
[†] Henry Edward Manning (1808–1892), English Roman Catholic cardinal; from 1865, Archbishop of Westminster.

Constance. George Eliot simply called him the most beautiful person she had ever met.

That same year witnessed a happier event. Cyril adored Italy, and dreamt of a villa in the hills of Florence. Constance had on one occasion clipped his desire to take a lease on Palazzo Contarini Fasan, the legendary home of Desdemona in friendly, frisky, gondolieri-loving Venice. However, in 1888 she acquiesced to Cyril's hunger for a marine pleasuredome, provided it was on more sober home turf. A site near the Norfolk seaside village of Sheringham initially drew his attention, but a typhoid outbreak in the area, which highlighted its poor drainage, caused the plans to be cancelled.

It was near another Norfolk fishing hamlet, Overstrand, that Cyril found the place to create his Xanadu. In 1883 and 1884 a journalist and poet, Clement Scott,* had published a number of poems and articles extolling the quiet virtues of the area:

> It is difficult to convey an idea of the silence of the fields through which I passed, or the beauty of the prospect that surrounded me – a blue sky without a cloud across it; a sea sparkling under a haze of heat: wild flowers in profusion around me, poppies predominating everywhere...

In 1885, these reflections were collected in book form as *Poppy Land* – the area between Sheringham and Mundersley. Chiming with the universal dream of a seaside idyll and the Victorian wildflower mania, it ran into several editions, and together with the arrival of the railway in the locality, sparked a tourist boom. Capitalising on the demand, a range of Poppyland china appeared, and even a perfume, Poppyland Bouquet, which was marketed worldwide.

The clifftop site that captured Cyril's heart then featured two ugly semi-detached villas. However, it was blessed with a glorious, uninterrupted view of the sea. Following Constance's approval, adjoining land was purchased until it stretched to an estate of 60 acres, and was christened The Pleasaunce.

With the help of stellar architect Edwin Lutyens, the villas were

---

* Clement William Scott (1841–1904), English journalist, poet and critic.

absorbed into an ever-expanding, Edwardian country mansion. Red brick and gabled, with typical Lutyens touches of roughcast and tiles, like Cyril's collecting, it was a vast jumble of some beautiful parts that never came together as a scenic whole. "I do wish the Battersea house was better and not so spoiled by him," confided Lutyens to his wife. "He so murders and alters everything I design whilst it is being built." In the beginning, the house was only lived in from August to October, following the London Season.

While The Pleasaunce was a compromised architectural vision, the full force of Cyril's passion would be unleashed on its landscape – then just blustery fields. It was an unforgiving environment in which to create any kind of garden, but fortunately there was a model close to hand. On wind-swept dunes surrounding Cliff House at Cromer, a keen plantswoman, Lady Hoare,* had embedded blast defences of sea buckthorn and wattle fencing, before going on to plant myrtle, arbutus, holly, cypress, and bougainvillea, and within their shelter, notable gardens.

With the advice of one of Lady Hoare's under-gardeners, Cyril began his planning and planting, but would soon far outstrip anything botanical the district had ever seen. There were no elaborate hothouse ranges: Cyril laughingly told friends he was "all for outside show". With what E.F. Benson described as "dozens of gardeners to do his bidding," as one account put it:

> Lord Battersea set himself to make the gardens as perfect as an ideal Italian garden ever was, and he succeeded beyond his dreams. Once within the garden gates, the visitor wonders whether he is in Greece or Rome; there are suggestions of both; grand capitals that recall Corinth, and inset tanks amid pleasant lawns such as Vespasian might have envied.

The final result was a succession of fantasy vistas so immaculately tended the effect was hallucinatory. In her novel *Ten Degrees Backward*, Ellen Thornycroft Fowler, a friend of Constance, dubbed it "the Garden of Dreams...more like a garden out of the Arabian Nights which had been called into being in one night by some beneficent

---

* Katherine Louisa Hart, Lady Hoare, née Davis (1846-1931); wife of M.P. Sir Samuel Hoare, 1st Baronet; mother of Samuel John Gurney Hoare, 1st Viscount Templewood.

Djin."[*] Beyond the mansion's broad terrace lay a velvet lawn edged with flowering shrubs with the sea as a backdrop. Stretching out parallel to the house was a long cloister of twelve bays, draped with creepers in slumberous splendour. There was a sunken garden, "paved with coral and amethyst, as only pink and purple flowers were allowed to grow within…a Japanese garden of streams and pagodas and strange bright flowers…an ideal fruit garden, where the pear-trees and the apple trees were woven into walls and architraves of green and gold." There was also a summer house, a guest house, a loggia, a clock tower, a heather and conifer garden, and a rosary. Walking through a wrought-iron gate revealed more wonders:

> a cricket field surrounded by large trees: and beyond that again stretched the grassy alleys and shady paths of dreamland till they culminated in the very centre of the dream – a huge herbaceous border so glorious in its riot of colour that the dreamer's heart leaped up.[†]

It spoke of Edwardian plutocratic panache, but had the aura and tranquillity of immemorial aristocratic ways. To create this deception that added to Cyril's mythos, huge sums were spent transplanting fully grown trees and shrubs. Enveloping all was the invigorating East Coast air, that made the "weak grow strong and the old feel young again."

Edwin Lutyens considered Cyril a thwarted charming boy, but like Josephine Butler, it's unlikely he intuited his deeper motivation. Cyril's passion for a marine retreat set amidst a paradise garden wasn't simply due to his love of sea bathing. The vast walled estate and gardens, wrapped in the soothing background murmur of the sea and birdsong, and with its limitless clifftop sea view, provided the illusionary balm of a world away from the world – and its judgements.

The dream of an Arcadia far from 'the clank of the world', and more

---

[*] A spirit capable of assuming animal or human form. In *Ten Degrees Backward* the characters of Lord and Lady Carnaby also embody aspects of Cyril and Constance. Fowler describes Carnaby's calm resignation at not having fulfilled the political dreams of his youth: "those rose-tinted mountain-tops, which he had beheld in the light of dawn, and which he had then fondly imagined he was going to scale." [Ellen Thornycroft Fowler, *Ten Degrees Backward*, George H. Doran Co., New York 1915, p206.]
[†] For a horticulturalist's description, see: Frances Anne Bardswell, *Sea-Coast Gardens And Gardening*, Sherratt & Hughes, London 1908, pp109-114.

particularly, far from those who would deny freedom and love, pervaded the homosexual imagination as much as it did the Classics – somewhat the same thing. Even as a student, Cyril would have been familiar with the second of Virgil's *Ecologues*, with its pastoral vision of the unrequited love of the shepherd Corydon for the boy Alexis.*
In 1805, Queen Victoria's grandfather-in-law, Augustus, Duke of Saxe-Gotha-Altenburg,† had penned the novel *Ein Jahr in Arkadien*, a pastoral fable in which two handsome shepherds fall in love. The homoerotic dream of a pagan, pantheistic Eden was served up anew by Cory, Pater, and others, including Charles Kains Jackson proselytising for 'The New Chivalry', with its passages extolling: "The joys of the palaestra…and the exhilaration of the early-morning swim." Aided by an Everest of Rothschildian cash, on this stretch of blustery Norfolk coast, Cyril forged the fantasia into existence.

Emerging from his daily morning sea bath, he was described by author, friend, and guest George Moore‡ as "brinily radiant". In his own grand way, Cyril was the very embodiment of the Whitmanesque ideal of a masculine, well-rounded, homosexual man.§ It was a holistic vision that surely helped spur Cyril's enthusiastic support of not only continuing education for workers, but of athletic clubs, and the introduction, as in Germany, Scandinavia and Switzerland, of

---

* An 1810 leather-bound edition of the *Ecologues*, illustrated with botanical plates, and Lord Battersea's bookplate survives. His bookplate also appears in a copy of *Priapeia*, epigrams of divers poets on Priapus, translated by Sir Richard Burton and Leonard Smithers, and issued in 1890 by the Erotika Biblion Society, (the London imprint that also published the famous homosexual novel *Teleny*). One poem begins: "This grove I dedicate and consecrate to thee, Priapus". [P. Virgilii Maronis [Virgil], *Bucolica*, T. Bensley, 1810, Rooke Books, Bath UK, 2021, Abebooks.com; *Priapeia*, Auction Lot 407, Cheffins, Cambridge, 13 February 2002.]
† Emil Leopold August ('Augustus') von Sachsen-Gotha, Duke of Saxe-Gotha-Altenburg (1877–1822). A handsome gentleman of high culture, he married Princess Louise Charlotte of Mecklenburg-Schwerin, and secondly, Princess Karoline Amalie of Hesse-Kassel, from whom he was estranged. Occasionally wearing women's clothes, he preferred to be called 'Emilie' by his confidants.
‡ The sexually dubious George Moore shared Cyril's artistic interests, and Whitman's belief in personal liberation. As critic Adrian Fraser has noted: in a speech Moore gave in Dublin in 1904 at the Royal Hibernian Academy on Manet, he remarked that an artist "'must repudiate all conventions' and 'be ashamed of nothing but to be ashamed.' Over and over, he said it: unashamed, unashamed, unashamed! More than one person in the audience at the RHA was shocked by this menacing assault on respectability and decency…In the code-language of that era, *shame* was commonly associated with irregular sexuality." [Adrian Fraser, 'Napoleon in a Dress: Robert O'Byrne: Hugh Lane', *The Irish Review*, Cork University Press, No. 27 (Summer, 2001), p173.]
§ In 1858, under a pseudonym, Whitman had even authored a series of diet, exercise and eugenics articles, *Manly Health and Training*. [Zachery Turpin, Walt Whitman's 'Manly Health and Training', *Walt Whitman Quarterly Review*, Vol33, Number 3, 2016.]

gymnastics to schools. In 1899, he played host to Olof Rudbeck,[*] a Swedish baron who operated a gymnastics institute in London.

Another guest of The Pleasaunce who would have been wholly sympathetic to Cyril's vision, and perhaps helped shape it, was Alfred Parsons.[†] A landscape artist who became a landscape gardener, his signature appears in the Visitors Book in September 1898. Parsons was a confirmed bachelor who lived in London with two American artists: Frank Millet, who would die on the Titanic, and the diminutive but perfectly formed Edwin Austin Abbey. Henry James, who dined with them, referred to Parsons, in his Jamesian way, as the "fidus achates"[‡] of "dear little Abbey". Together with John Singer Sargent, in 1885 the group had rented a house for the summer in Worcestershire, where James visited as a guest. James wrote of Parsons' art for *Harper's Magazine,* and commissioned him to redesign the garden at Lamb House when he settled there in 1898. Cyril may have been introduced to Parsons through this coterie, or equally by Princess Louise, who was Parson's good friend, and commissioned him to design her own garden at Rosneath.

There were also the interiors of The Pleasaunce for Cyril to consider. According to an earlier visitor, unlike the florid style and daring colour effects to be seen in Surrey House, "At Overstrand, everything is as simple as it can be. The colouring is subdued, and nothing but the most delicate tints are to be seen." Like the exteriors, the calm restraint of Lutyens' interiors didn't survive Cyril's baroque tendencies. In 1887, Constance wrote from Granada: "Cyril has been buying lovely stuffs here. He still has the mania and always the taste and knowledge for such things." Cyril may not have had the collecting eye of his friend Archie, Lord Rosebery, but he was just as obsessive. For E.F. Benson, the result was:

> an extraordinary mixture of admirable and deplorable objects, but it was the possession of them rather than the beauty of them that he appreciated. "I've got such masses of things," he would say, "that I don't know where to put them."

---

[*] Baron Olof Reinhold Hugo Rudbeck, (1859–1934). Married Emily Frances Cutler, and had issue.
[†] Alfred William Parsons (1847–1920), illustrator, landscape painter and garden designer.
[‡] Faithful friend.

Defiantly out of place were a pair of gilded Venetian gondola lanterns that found their way to the main staircase, but which for their host possibly roused happy memories of gondolier *amore*. These were gazed upon by a portrait of Cyril by the Russian-American artist Prince Paolo Troubetzkoy, and a carved wooden statue of Apollo. In the words of one guest:

> The house is warm & dark & scented[,] with low wide yielding sofas & jars full of roseleaves & spikenard* & oriental curtains shutting off room from room. We play gambling games like sympathy & antipathy & 30 et quarante† after dinner & 'Connie' always loses.

Constance's large and airy Lutyenesque bedroom at The Pleasaunce was executed in cream and white, set off by a frieze of inspirational quotes picked out in gold – "Guard well thy thoughts. Our thoughts are heard in heaven," etc. Cyril's adjoining and smaller cream-panelled bedroom had the feel of a ship's cosy cabin.

Initially, Constance's like or dislike of The Pleasaunce depended on the weather: while delightful in high summer, Overstrand could also be grey, windswept, and 'stinging cold'. Her diary charted her moods. On her first visit in 1889, she was happy to write: "Little cottage quite lovely, like a Venetian Palace is very tiny. Beautifully and tastefully furnished, admiring it immensely." A year later, things were very different:

> Overstrand, August 28th: Came down with my Mother...the best companion I ever had. Little Cromer reached at last. Greeted by fierce storms of rain. Cyril at the station, with his rubicund, cheery, joyous face, seemed happy and pleased to see us. August 30th: Cyril's birthday. Very cheery and happy, but, oh, this is an odious place, cold, draughty, windy, bitter, bleak, almost ugly – I dislike it heartily. Why did we ever come here?

Pestered by his capricious patron, Lutyens' bills were as premium as his talent, and by 1891 Constance was writing:

---

* Muskroot (*Nardostachys jatamansi*). An aromatic plant with an earthy musky scent.
† From the family of French card games Vingt-Un (Twenty One).

Cyril tells me that we are spending too much – he has been drawing largely upon his capital – I have overdrawn my account – or rather what he pleases to call my account, for I never know how much he places to my credit. This makes me simply miserable. The fact that some of my heavy bills must remain unpaid for weeks nay months is a sickening prospect!…But at the end of this year we must come to some better arrangement, this drives me frantic. Neither S[urrey] H[ouse] nor O[verstrand] give me any real satisfaction! Why did we not begin modestly in a small house, with few servants – without a flourish of trumpets!

Construction of The Pleasaunce would eventually cost a princely £70,000. Economy was never Cyril's strong suit, and the financial crisis appears not to have weighed upon him. However, Lutyens and an army of workmen would conjure magic. As Constance recorded:

Overstrand, August 14th, 1891:…We came to our cottage — oh, what a transformation scene! I was simply astounded; I could not believe such a change possible. A large garden, a pretty drawing room, a comfortable sitting-room, no draughts, no cold anywhere. We sat outside until a late hour.

There was another work of literature likely close to Cyril's heart as he pursued this fantasy. In 1876 an Oxford graduate, William Mallock,[*] had anonymously published a series of satirical fictions in the London magazine *Belgravia*. They mocked leading figures at the university, and were developed into a novel, *The New Republic, or, Culture, Faith, And Philosophy In An English Country House*. It took the form of a philosophical discourse – "the wants of the soul" as one character put it, between a circle of friends at a villa overlooking the sea, that was owned by an epicure, 'Otho Laurence'.

Mallock believed the new curriculum of Classical secularism was undermining the Christian faith of English youth, and that they were being further corrupted by the aestheticism of public figures like Pater. In the novel, Pater was wickedly parodied as the effete 'Mr. Rose', who makes pronouncements such as:

---

[*] William Hurrell Mallock (1849–1923), novelist and journalist. An unprepossessing but dapper bachelor of the Devon gentry, he became a conservative political and religious polemicist, and critic of secular humanism, socialism and Marxism. His friendship circle included Lord Houghton, Sir Alexander Hood, and Hamilton Aïdé.

I rather look upon life as a chamber, which we decorate as we would decorate the chamber of the woman or youth that we love, tinting the walls of it with symphonies of subdued colour...

The splendid residence in the novel, stuffed with the beauties of the world, was elaborately and extensively described:

There above the sea, and overlooking it, with the everlasting seabreeze in its Parian porticoes, stood the villa, of which a Roman noble might have been proud...folly perhaps it was, but a splendid folly, and one which none but a patrician, whose blood beat blue from the heart to the taper finger-tips, could have been ever guilty.

Here Otho Laurence "seeks retirement from the caresses of the selectest circles in London, in a yet selecter circle of his own." This singular retreat is the creation of an uncle: a lettered pagan voluptuary who had squandered an immense fortune on it, that it might embody his tastes and character as far as possible. On his deathbed, the uncle shocks a parish clergyman by confessing: "my soul, if I have one, might perhaps be with Petronius, and with Seneca." He rejoices at the thought of seeing after death:

so many proud monarchs, so many fancied gods, groaning in the lowest abyss of darkness; so many magistrates who persecuted the name of the Lord, liquefying in a fiercer fire than ever they kindled against the Christians!

Mallock's novel was a *succès-de-scandale*, but for university students and gentlemen such as Cyril, it served to glamourise what it sought to criticise.* As an Overstrand celebrity, Cyril himself featured in a popular gossipy travel account, *Vera in Poppyland* by authoress Annie Berlyn,† which appeared in the *Lady's Pictorial*, and in book form. Attracted by the presence of the Flowers, Overstrand drew other wealthy residents, including the financial Midas Sir Edgar Speyer‡ and

---

* The work was reputedly edited by John Addington Symonds. For an extensive analysis, see: Linda C. Dowling, *Hellenism and Homosexuality in Victorian Oxford*, Cornell University Press, Ithica 1994.
† Ann 'Annie' Ambrosia Berlyn (1862–1943), journalist and author, including under the nom-de-plume 'Ambrosia'.
‡ Sir Edgar Speyer, 1st Baronet (1862–1932) Anglo-German Jewish financier and music

banker Lord Hillingdon.* It would briefly become known as 'The Village of Millionaires', and was less-charitably nicknamed, due to the Jewish contingent, 'Jerusalem-on-Sea'. The charms of the district also appealed to many lesser folk: Clement Scott lived to see his pristine rural haven become what he ruefully rechristened 'Bungalowland'. But not yet at Overstrand. While Cyril and Constance lived, they and the other principal landowners of the district – Lord Suffield and Richard Gurney of the Quaker banking family – ensured that, unlike at Cromer, speculative builders were held off, and the old picturesque farms, fields, and stretches of dark green pine were preserved.†

Cyril also opposed another development, but in London. It involved the requisition of Dane's Inn, "a picturesque former 'inn of court' in whose chambers journalists and other erratic persons lived cheaply and Bohemianly," and which the Flower brothers owned. One former resident described it as: "that queer, old-fashioned abode of bachelors situated off Wych Street – the oldest and quaintest thoroughfare in London." Here crooked timber-framed and gabled houses lurched charmingly over the street: at No.37 hung a golden crescent moon with a lugubrious face – reputedly the oldest shop sign in London. However, the civic authorities wished to widen and improve the Strand: their keenness sharpened by the area's reputation. Wych Street housed several brothels – some flagellation establishments, while adjoining Holywell Street, equally ancient and narrow, was the heart of London's pornographic book trade. To the dismay of those who loved Olde London, along with a swathe of other ancient byways and courts, including Dane's Inn, they were wiped from the map.

The Flowers and/or Rothschilds may also have had a financial involvement in the construction of a series of mansion apartment

---

patron, born in New York. Married violinist Leonora von Stosch. As well as building a new mansion in Grosvenor Street, London, in 1908 the Speyers commissioned Sea Marg, a mock-Tudor mansion at Overstrand. Following the outbreak of the First World War, Speyer was hounded out of Britain for alleged pro-German sympathies, and would later be stripped of his British citizenship, possibly unjustly, due to a series of unwise wartime transactions which, it was claimed, proved the allegation. The Speyers were satirised by E.F. Benson as Sir Herman and Lady Gurtner in his novel *Robin Linnet* (1919), but Benson attempted to make up for it with a sympathetic profile of them in *As We Are* (1932).

* Charles William Mills, 2nd Baron Hillingdon (1855–1919) banker and Conservative M.P. His home, Overstrand Hall, was also designed by Lutyens.

† At Sheringham, the glorious Sheringham Park estate, landscaped by Humphry Repton, remained protected in the hands of the Upcher family. Upon the deaths of the last squire (Henry) Thomas Simpson Upcher (1906-1985), and his partner Douglas Graham Persse Fitzpatrick (1908-1986), a majority of the estate was acquired by the National Trust.

blocks that were erected on Crown Land in the 1890s along Prince of Wales Drive in Battersea, by the property developer Charles Julius Knowles.* The blocks bore the names Overstrand, Sidestrand (now Park), Norfolk, Cyril, and Primrose.

Meanwhile, across the river in 1891, there were developments of a more lurid kind. Although Whitehall had only recently weathered the Cleveland Street Scandal, a number parliamentarians were issued with arrest warrants for sexual offences.† As one press report stated:

> no case has been so infinitely sad as that of Mr. Charles Alan Fyffe, the Liberal candidate for East Wilts, who is lying at his London house suffering from severe and self-inflicted wounds. Ten days ago Mr. Fyffe was made the subject of a terrible charge by a lad with whom he had travelled. Bursar of University College, a man of the highest mental achievement, a well-known literary man, the writer of a scholarly history of Europe during the last century, and a Parliamentary candidate of the highest promise, popular beyond measure with those who knew him as "Charlie Fyffe," the whole thing is heart-breaking.

A father of three, Fyffe had been charged with sexually harassing a sixteen-year-old cripple on a train – the youth was missing a foot. Fyffe attempted suicide by cutting his throat, which lead to the sensational scene of him being brought to the court hearing on a stretcher. The case was sent to trial, but was dismissed due to the charge being uncorroborated. Despite being devotedly nursed by his wife, Fyffe died the following year.

Earlier in the year, the Paris police had raided a men's bath house,

---

* Born Charles Julius Kino (c1839–1900), a Russian Jewish tailor.
† Captain Edmund Hope Verney (1838–1910), a Liberal M.P., who was a wealthy ex-naval Captain, baronet's heir, and noted for the zeal of his support in parliament for the Purity Movement, was jailed for a year for procuring a girl under the age of twenty-one for immoral purposes. Edward Samuel Wesley De Cobain (1840–1908), the Conservative member for East Belfast, and an evangelist and temperance movement leader, chose to flee: first to Spain, and then to New York, where he became a gospel preacher in Brooklyn. In 1893, he returned to Belfast, and was arrested. After eight young working class men detailed for the court how De Cobain had sexually assaulted them, he was imprisoned for a year, with hard labour. An Australian periodical printed: "De Cobain, M.P. wants to know why his alleged offences have excited so much attention from the authorities who tried to hush up the Cleveland-street scandal. Easy to answer. No member of the Royal Family was mixed up in Cobain's case." [Personal Items, *The Bulletin* (Sydney) 4 July 1891, p10.]

arresting nineteen men in its private *salons de repos*. A few were socially prominent, including a wealthy American,* but to the relief of the British Government, early reports that over half the accused were English proved false: there was only one. George Paston-Cooper,† a baronet's son who was also alleged to have been a client of the house in Cleveland Street, was imprisoned for four months.

The summer of 1892 witnessed another General Election. During his campaigning, Cyril even got into a brief public spat with Arnold White, who was then campaigning for the Tyneside division as a Unionist. In a speech, Cyril said he did not take White seriously as a politician – the same charge made against himself!

During the electioneering, Cyril shared a public stage with a flamboyant celebrity, the Rev. Robert Fillingham.‡ A radical Hertfordshire parson, he was considered "the most prominent, uncompromising Protestant clergyman within the gates of the Established Church." Across the kingdom, Fillingham upset squires, bishops, and the 'Jingo Press' alike with vigorous and eloquent speeches on behalf of the Liberal Party; his belief in disestablishment of the Church; and a visceral loathing High Churchism and its practices. As one paper put it, in an earlier time "he would have been hanged, drawn and quartered, or burnt at the stake".

Fillingham's admirers saw him as a "hero of religious and political freedom," and a supporter of "the weak and downtrodden" He possessed the conviction and courage of the zealot, but also their discontent and instability. While still a student at Oxford, he'd been

---

* Thomas J. MacPherson of Poughkeepsie, New York (1856–1908). A keen choirmaster who'd married a socially prominent wealthy widow, he was acquitted of the Paris charge. [Of Interest To Poughkeepsians, *Poughkeepsie Daily Eagle*, 30 April 1891, p8; The Paris Scandal – Sentences, *The Pall Mall Gazette*, 4 May 1891, p6.]

† Captain George Frederick Paston Paston-Cooper (1861–1895) of the Bedfordshire Regiment; eldest son of Sir Astley Paston Paston-Cooper, 3rd Baronet. He was described in court as "an effeminate young Englishman, with a fledgling moustache, a rosy complexion, large languid blue eyes, curly [hair] carefully curled with a curling-iron and displaying with affectation a girl's hands, with rings on every finger...He was, it seems, the big favourite. He wore around his neck a locket attached to a thin chain of gold, and which he threw to the eager crowd of his admirers like the Sultan of the Eastern Copts throw the handkerchief in the harem." Despite this, he'd been courting future garden designer Norah Lindsay. A mere four years later he died at Cape Town of pulmonary disease after a long illness. [Gazette Des Tribunaux, *Le Figaro*, 25 April 1891, p2; Allyson Hayward, *Norah Lindsay: the life and art of a garden*, Frances Lincoln Limited 2007, p30-32; George P. Cooper, Death Certificate, National Archives of South Africa, FamilySearch.org]

‡ The Rev. Robert Charles Fillingham (1861–1908).

placed on trial with an older married clergyman friend, the Rev. Henry Moffatt, who was charged with the seduction of two teenage lads, and sentenced to eighteen months hard labour. Fillingham, who'd been charged with aiding the commission of one of the offences was, with the help of a crack legal team, discharged due to lack of evidence. Although he unquestionably aided Moffatt, and was himself attracted to youths, his diary suggests he was nearly or entirely celibate.

There is no indication in Fillingham's diaries that he knew of Cyril's homosexuality, or of his later scandal, but his political support came at personal cost. When it was advertised he would speak on Cyril's behalf, the vicar of Luton, known as "a violent Tory," warned Fillingham that if he appeared at the Liberal meeting, his invitation to preach at a district church would be cancelled. Fillingham ignored the threat, which was carried out, resulting in Labouchère raging in the pages of *Truth* at the injustice, and lack of Christian charity.

The meeting at Luton, in June 1892, took place before at least 2,000 Liberal supporters, including Constance. To laughter and cheering, Cyril commenced the evening with a jab at the Conservative party support group, The Primrose League. With his characteristic sense of theatre, he snipped a large yellow bloom from a flower arrangement on the platform, and stuck it in his buttonhole.

He told the crowd that, in his opinion, Salisbury's government had been the worst of the century:

> six years of useless legislation, six years of wasted time, six years of keeping the peoples of England and Ireland waiting for the great reform which they wanted and which they would have before long.

He went on to joke about the cheap refreshments available at a recent meeting of the Primrose League: "when you can get tea and ices for a penny...I recommend everybody go." Cyril also offered his support for disestablishment of the Church of England, saying: "They didn't want to weaken the Church but to strengthen it...the parish priest should be there at the will of the people."

The Reverend Fillingham was introduced to an enthusiastic reception, and quipped that: "although he was a Radical parson they would see that he was allowed to take part in a 'flower service' in Luton – but it was a Cyril Flower service." In a spirited address, he promised the audience: "We will sweep this Government of sham and deceit into everlasting obscurity," and that if the Anglican Church "became the Church of one party and Conservatism became the test of orthodoxy, then over the portals of the Church 'Ichabod'* might be written for her glory would have departed."

A week later, Cyril and Fillingham addressed another Liberal meeting at Dunstable, at which wild disruptions by Tory and Liberal Unionist supporters required police intervention. Cyril's years of jousting on the hustlings had imbued him with the experience to deal with unruly crowds, and in his diary entry of the day, Fillingham wrote how:

> He was especially happy in his retorts...the uproar continuing, some Liberal cried: "They haven't got a vote, Sir!" "They haven't got half a vote," said Mr. Flower, "but they've got half a pint!" & again: "They won't care for the liberty of a public meeting, but they care for the licence of a public house." Presently, someone shouted that he was setting "class against class". He vociferated: "Your form is glass against glass"... Then the mob at the end of the room began to sing "Rule Britannia". Mr. Flower said to the chairman: "It's a gang of people sent by the Luton clergy against him," i.e. me...Presently there was another disturbance, lasting about 20 minutes: people getting up on the chairs & a free fight going on at the end of the room. Mr. Flower began to lose patience, & said: "If I have to stop here till 4 in the morning, I'll stop: if you think I'm going to be boo-ed out of speaking by a few Liberal Unionists, you've mistaken your man." The row got more violent...The chairs were seized & flung to the side, falling with a crash, so that there might be more room for fighting... Mrs. Flower turned faint, & I gave her water.

However, order was eventually restored, and the meeting ended on a triumphant note. On polling day, when the votes were finally counted, Cyril had increased his majority.

More than ever though, the electioneering had proved a hard slog. While Parliament was still overwhelmingly an aristocratic preserve,

---

* Hebrew: 'without glory'.

stuffed with figures who toyed with politics as a rich man's plaything, change was in the air. Foremost markers of it were Cyril's new fellow Liberal M.P.s elected that year, Keir Hardie, and John Burns.* Both were socialists who'd commenced work as children: Hardie at seven as a messenger boy for a steamship company, before becoming a miner; Burns at ten in a cotton factory, before graduating to ship work and activist rabble-rousing, for which he'd served prison time. *The Pall Mall Gazette* described Burns as:

> the *beau ideal* of the best kind of British artisan; strong in build, independent in character, hearty in manner, and intelligent in kind. His fists are as hard as his head, and his voice as strong as his opinions. Both of them have stood him in excellent stead in many an encounter on behalf of the 'rights of the people'.

Given Burns was the member for Battersea, and respected on both sides of the House for his moral and political conviction, Cyril was inevitably judged against him, and found wanting.

Despite Cyril's high public profile and popularity, his parliamentary career was largely undistinguished. While a winning candidate and invaluable party networker, he was a political lightweight who was never taken seriously by his betters because they sensed that behind the charm, he lacked conviction. When called upon to deliver a speech on any topic he could manage it with ease, but unlike his pursuit of blue and white china, the burning drive to institute social change against all odds was – at least after Brecon – mostly missing. Like many parliamentarians, what replaced it was eloquent bluster and wit. In a mocking speech, Colonel Duke, a Liberal Unionist candidate for South Bedfordshire, would state:

> as Mr. Cyril Flower...we none of us at any time ever took Lord Battersea's politics as serious...If we did not attach much weight to his arguments it was because we looked upon them rather as the tissue paper with which Christmas boxes are wrapped up than any serious political contribution to the politics of the day...we could not fail to recognise, whether for good or for evil, that he was the fancy man of the Radical party (laughter).

---

* John Elliot Burns (1858–1943), English trade unionist and radical Liberal M.P.

During Cyril's time in Parliament a significant amount of industrial legislation was passed that affected his constituents, and through his voting he would have played a part in placing it on the statute book. His commitment to seeing through improvements to the *Employers' Liability Act* had certainly been sustained. However, as member for Brecon, *Hansard* confirms that he made no other notable contributions to the parliamentary chamber whatsoever. Then again, neither had his predecessor, the affable squire Taffy Holford.* As the member for Luton, Cyril made just four contributions, in the form of questions: the first to enquire when a report on poverty in London was due; the second to enquire whether additional powers had been granted to Boards of Guardians to deal with poverty; the third to enquire whether the Government was aware of a report of sweatshop labour in the production of army uniforms; and the fourth to ask the vice president of an educational committee whether the existing cookery grant could be divided between laundry and cookery. Nonetheless, as a journalist observed:

> if the Member for Luton is not given to troubling the House with his oratory, there is no politician of note who does more for his cause outside of it. He has spoken on behalf of the Liberal candidate at nearly every by-election that has occurred...

However, there was one issue he was genuinely passionate about – educational improvement. On this he expended endless time and energy, and made enormous contributions. The Battersea Polytechnic Institute, which provided higher technical and physical education for men and women, and for which he and Constance were fundraisers, was tangible evidence of this commitment. He became one of its governors, quipping to a journalist that he was "great on polytechnics".

In addition to this, Cyril was overseeing the family estate in Battersea, and attending board meetings, both for companies in which he held investments, and for philanthropic purposes. These included the Metropolitan Hospital in Hackney, which treated the destitute and

---

* Due to the scrutiny that today's parliamentarians are subjected to, it would be almost impossible for a minister to sustain a similar scant record in the chamber without being penalised in some form. Particularly after World War II, the contributions of parliamentarians in the House, both in the chamber and in committee, gradually increased to the level of today, even when they sat in electoral safe seats.

local Jewish constituency. As usual, he was also holding large receptions at Surrey House; its interiors bedecked with an "immense quantity of beautiful orchids". Soon after the election there was one for the Eighty Club, and another for the Congress on Psychical Research. Rummaging amongst the antiques at Christie's in the hope of adding further finds to his booty also occupied his time. Not least, there were the distractions of Greek Love. He was nearing fifty. One social commentator dryly observed that Cyril had:

> grown rather stout, rubicund, and puffy, but is still a brilliant and magnificent person. The style with which he drapes his Inverness cape about his shoulders and allows his tawny beard and locks to float on the breeze is entirely incomparable.

However, even for someone so endlessly energetic, Parliament was beginning to feel both demoralising and exhausting. Before the election, Cyril had written to his friend Sir Charles Dilke:

> the next House will be as rum a kettle of fish as ever stewed since George III. The worst of it is, as the House gets more and more divided (like the French Chambers) into sets, it also becomes more and more incapable of getting through its business, and the littleness of the individual members becomes daily more apparent.

The divisive issue of Irish Home Rule, which tainted the political and social worlds for both himself and Constance, likely firmed his belief that he'd had enough of the Commons fray. Several months before the election, newspapers reported that:

> The Liberal Whips have recently come in for a large amount of money…Where the money comes from is not known, but there are a number of members who are very desirous of peerages, including Mr. Arnold Morley, Mr. Cyril Flower, Mr. Brunner, Mr. Colman, Baron Stern, Mr. Illingworth, and Mr. Stuart Rendel, and it is supposed that they have placed large sums down in the hope of becoming Barons of the United Kingdom.

This list of immensely wealthy gentlemen included a mustard manufacturer, a chemical industrialist, and a brother of George Rendel. Bartering political services for honours was a parliamentary pastime, and no less than a quarter of Gladstone's correspondence with Queen Victoria was consumed with matters regarding honours. The two elections of 1885 and 1886 had drained the Liberal Party's funds, and evidence indicates that, while likely done with the greatest reluctance, in return for large donations to the Party, Gladstone and his successor Lord Rosebery bowed to internal Party pressure and agreed to put forward for ennoblement some minor M.P.s.*

With his eye on such a prize, Cyril joined the queue to contribute to the Party's coffers in its time of need. Gladstone's Private Secretary Sir Algernon West† told his diary: "Cyril Flower wanted a Peerage, which surprised me." Whether he was due such an honour is questionable. His political legacy was slender. However, he'd worked hard on behalf of the Liberal cause as a parliamentary member, Whip, and born networker. He was popular with constituents and fellow parliamentarians, and was of prominent social and financial standing. Most importantly, he was looked upon fondly by Gladstone, especially due to his Rothschild alliance. It was enough for a knighthood, or at a push, a baronetcy. But Cyril secretly pined for the lordly embrace of ermine. As far back as 1886 the magazine *Vanity Fair* had included his name on a jokey list of candidates for the House of Lords, "because he married a Rothschild, has been in Parliament for five years, and has never done anything in his life except subordinate whipping for Mr. Gladstone." The gossip magazine *Figaro* considered it was an issue settled by established precedence:

> Mr. Cyril Flower mainly owes his peerage to the munificence with which he has contributed to the party funds. No complaint can, however, be made on this score, for successive Premiers have only too repeatedly rewarded their useful friends in the same manner.

While it became known in political and social circles that he was to be

---

* They were the bachelor Jewish banker Sydney Stern, and the varnish, oil cloth, and linoleum manufacturer James Williamson. Their elevation to the peerage occurred in 1895 as Lord Wandsworth and Lord Ashton respectively, and drew criticism as a signifier of the corruption of the honours system. Despite the graft which had enabled their ennoblement, both peers honoured the dictum of *noblesse oblige*, and bequeathed munificent public legacies. [H.J. Hanham, 'The Sale of Honours in Late Victorian England', *Victorian Studies*, Vol. 3, No. 3.]

† Sir Algernon Edward West (1832–1921), civil servant, Society favourite, ardent Liberal, and good friend of Cyril and Constance Flower, whose regular guest he was. A strict observer of outward form, he married Mary Barrington, and had three sons and a daughter. [Constance Battersea, *Reminiscences*, Macmillan & Co, London 1923, p212.]

given a peerage in the event of a Liberal win, its public announcement, particularly so soon after the election, came as an unpleasant and disillusioning shock to his constituents. The press had fun with it, reminding readers of his earlier "Mend 'em or End 'em" speeches demanding reform of the House of Lords. He was nicknamed 'Squirrel Flower'. One newspaper printed:

> Mr. Labouchère the sworn enemy of all hereditary legislators, wanted to know what Mr. Cyril Flower had done that his grandchildren should rule over Mr. Labouchère's grandchildren. Even his selection of a title gave offence. His claims to it rest upon some property he possesses in the constituency. There is but one peer in Battersea. His name is John Burns.

It was a stinging reference, and Labouchère's neat jest regarding inherited governance was much repeated. Yet Cyril's desire for a peerage should not have come as a surprise. If anyone was born to be an aristocrat, it was he. Being anointed 'Baron Battersea of Battersea in the County of London and of Overstrand in the County of Norfolk' was simply confirmation of the fact. Cyril would have been highly conscious that he constituted New Money. As one newspaper had previously snarked: "Mr. Flower's is a *bourgeois* beauty" The old nobility even smirked at the commonness of choosing Battersea as his title. Nonetheless, the House of Lords was his natural preserve.

Cyril had kept Constance in the dark over his machinations: she was in Antwerp when she heard the news. She had no desire to be a peeress –although the male Rothschilds courted honours keenly, as mental foreigners they looked upon them cynically as "part of the racket"– purely as a means to an end. She informed her diary:

> I was not pleased. It seemed to me almost ridiculous. I thought Cyril should have had real office work with all the dignity of responsibility.

However, 24 hours of reflection soothed Constance's irritation, as she wrote the next day:

> Letters from home. Mamma and Annie perfectly delighted with Cyril's appointment. I am getting accustomed to the idea, and, after all, it may be the best thing for Cyril.

Herbert Asquith wrote to her:

> I think Cyril is doing right. There is a considerable sphere for Liberal peers in these days, and not the least reason why he should regard himself or be regarded by others, as being on the shelf.

However, Cyril's desire for the peerage had less to do with politics than prestige. Upon receiving the news of the elevation, Constance had penned him a crushing letter, of which she later wrote:

> I feel that I was foolish to have written as I did on the spur of the moment...he was hurt or vexed by my letter & he will never quite forget it I fear.

While she wanted Cyril to be occupied in what she viewed as productive labour, she was not particularly sorry to see the end of his time in the Commons. In her published memoirs she gently damned his performance:

> I may here put into words what I often felt, namely, that although Cyril was deeply interested in the House of Commons, and although he was a most popular member there and in his constituency, his special talents did not lie in political work. His were not so much the attributes of the statesman as they were those of the man of artistic taste.

In her diary summary of the year, Constance wrote of the ennoblement: "I tried to be pleased, but could ill conceal my disappointment. Things grew worse as time went on. The constituents were disgusted; the speeches were odious and the new candidate was only returned by a majority of 250. I went through troubled waters for some time." Of her temperance work she noted: "Cyril minds it less. I pray for a real baptism of the spirit."

One paper reported: "Everyone in the clubs is laughing at Lord Battersea," calling him, "a rather dandified Gladstonian fossil...his special function seemed to be while in the House of Commons to fetch and carry Mr. Gladstone's overcoat."

Cyril's peerage didn't get him anywhere in one particular quarter: Queen Victoria vetoed him for two appointments to the Royal Household: as Master of the Buckhounds,* and later as a Lord-in-Waiting. Lord Carrington,† a fellow Liberal, told his diary that Cyril was "not very 'bien vu'"‡ and "he ought never have been proposed to her". The peerage might have been better received had not Cyril been so vocal in his denunciations of the Lords. In one speech, the Irish-born Conservative M.P. James Alexander Rentoul was reported as saying of him:

> Mr. Cyril Flower had a speech which he had delivered in the constituency for the last twelve or thirteen years (laughter), and the central point in that speech was that the House of Lords was a lot of old women upstairs who do some mangling; he meant that they mangled the bills the House of Commons passed. But the very moment that Mr. Cyril Flower got the chance he set up his mangle with the other old women (laughter).

More bitterly, a Scottish newspaper printed: "Lord Battersea is already beginning to shed his never-more-than-skin-deep Radicalism. He is now the apologist of the House of Lords, and he will soon become their defender."

While the carping gave Constance heartache, for Cyril, strolling by the seaside within his Overstrand realm, it may have seemed as vapourous

---

* A now-abolished post originally responsible for the royal hunting pack, but latterly the Royal Enclosure at Ascot.
† Charles Robert Wynn-Carington, 1st Marquess of Lincolnshire (1843–1928); 3rd Baron Carrington, from 1868 to 1895, 1st Earl Carrington from 1895 to 1912. A Liberal M.P., Governor of New South Wales from 1885 to 1890, Lord Chamberlain of the (Royal) Household 1892 to 1895, and joint hereditary Lord Great Chamberlain of England. Nicknamed 'Champagne Charlie', like many of the aristocracy, updating his stationery would have been a regular exercise. Born Robert Carrington, he changed his surname twice, first halving the double r, and later adding a double barrel. As a boy he was spanked for cheering the Chartists as they marched past his father's house in Whitehall, and in adulthood he became a political radical. Shrewd and tactful, he was a model landlord and progressive force on the London County Council, making real efforts to improve the living conditions of both city and rural workers. He married the Hon. Cecilia Margaret Harbord and had issue. However, his name is listed with that of other 'Sods' in a notebook of Scotland Yard detective Donald Swanson. Lord Rosebery, at whose wedding he was best man, was a cousin. [Richard Davenport-Hines, 'A Radical Lord Chamberlain at a Tory Court: Lord Carrington, 1892–95', *The Court Historian*, Volume 16, 2011, Issue 2; Rural Notes, *The Graphic*, 18 March 1882, p26; Adam Wood, *Swanson: The Life And Times Of A Victorian Detective*, Mango Books, London 2020, p440.]
‡ Well regarded.

and inconsequential as the evening breeze. In the upper house he would make no speeches at all, although at the time, blank or thin records were quite common for peers. Even so, it adds substance to the accusations that he was a dilettante for whom Parliament was just another gentleman's club — more than a hobby, less than a calling.

In August of that year, Oscar Wilde's wife rented a farmhouse for a family holiday in the village of Felbrigg, near Overstrand. Lord Alfred Douglas joined them in September, and the Wildes became regular visitors to The Pleasaunce. At one lunch, Wilde amusingly suggested that if he had to work for his living he would prefer to be a shepherd. To this, Constance suggested that he might "find looking after a lot of sheep rather trying". Wilde shot back, "Oh, I should not like to have more than one sheep." Amidst the laughter, Constance wryly remarked, "Well you've got one lamb already with a golden-fleece."

The flattering allusion to the blond Lord Alfred Douglas pleased both Wilde and Douglas, the latter of whom believed the remark was meant innocently, and that Constance considered him no more than a jejune admirer.* However, the anecdote was definitely not one Constance thought suitable for inclusion in her *Reminiscences*. In contrast, her husband had the issue of *Lippincott's* that carried *The Picture of Dorian Gray* bound in calf with his bookplate. While at Felbrigg, Wilde and Douglas became keen golfers on the links at Cromer; Douglas becoming enamoured with a boy caddy named Jack.

In January 1893, Cyril made another speech at Luton which got him into trouble. He referred to the city's high rate of infant mortality, and attributed it to child neglect due to "early, reckless, improvident, and therefore, wicked marriages…Many a man in Luton is living on the earnings of his wife." A Liberal-supporting local paper considered his remarks trenchant and "not a whit too strong." However, *Reynolds's Newspaper* quoted a local correspondent (very possibly Alfred Atkins of the *Luton Times*), who called it "a slander" on Luton workers, claiming the high death rate was due to "fierce competition in the straw trade which reduces industry to a fight for bare subsistence." The region was the centre of the straw plaiting industry (for hats, bonnets and other ornaments), in which a high proportion of women and children were employed in sweatshop conditions. "This lowers

---

* Constance later invited Douglas to a children's party at Surrey House!

the physical powers of the women, whose earnings, besides, are so small that proper nourishment cannot be given to the children." Mechanisation and foreign imports were further squeezing wages. *Reynolds's* added:

> My correspondent affirms that the assertion as to married men living on the earnings of their wives is equally untrue. Even were it true, he regards it as a most impudent criticism coming from a man who himself lives upon the earnings of others, and in whose social order the 'marriage of convenience' is the rule, not the exception.

It was a close jibe. More were to follow. In February 1893, Constance wrote:

> Cyril came home at 6.30 saying, I have good news for you. He flung himself into a chair, said: I have been offered the Governorship of NSW [New South Wales]. It struck me like a <u>knife</u>.

Given his father's early struggles in Sydney, for Cyril this would have been the ultimate achievement. Requiring diplomacy, sociability and showmanship, the post was tailor-made for him. In Sydney, always one of the most facile of cities, he would have been a star. For Constance, rescuing this southern sinkhole of inebriation would have offered limitless occupation. News of the offer soon leaked there; one local weekly printing with derisive delight:

> The Jewish half of Sydney society is literally on springs to know whether Lord Battersea is coming to Government House or not – for if he does the children of Israel will appear on the surface of society doings like so many corks in a pond. Lady Battersea is a daughter of Sir Anthony de Rothschild – and there never were such clannish people as the Chosen.

However, as Constance later wrote, the idea of leaving her elderly mother "for so long a term of years and going to the other end of the world appeared to me like committing a sin." Aware of this, Cyril suggested Lady de Rothschild accompany them. While Constance's sister Annie was in favour of Cyril accepting the appointment, Constance gave herself over to an emotional display that she was to later regret, telling her diary, "I went almost mad".

Cyril was utterly dismayed, but handed Constance two letters he'd written: one of acceptance of the offer, and one turning it down. He left the decision as to which to deliver to her. Constance went to her mother at Aston Clinton to break the news and choose. Lady de Rothschild being intensely possessive of her daughters, and a chronic hypochondriac, the result was a foregone conclusion of 'no'. Hoping to defuse Cyril's resentment, Annie wrote to him describing what had occurred:

> Constance behaved <u>splendidly</u>. She told all the arguments <u>in favour</u> quite impartially. You know the result, and you have earned our eternal gratitude for saving our Mother from a blow and a sorrow, which I honestly do not believe she <u>could</u> have borne. Of course you know how bound up she is in Constance; but, as I told you the other day, you little know how deeply attached she is to <u>you.</u> God bless you for making this <u>enormous</u> sacrifice for her sake.

"Cyril performed one of the greatest acts of renunciation, greater than my dear mother could ever have been aware of, for her sake, and for mine," Constance wrote in her autobiography. In her diary she added "had it been otherwise, it might have killed my mother". Yet Sydney's balmy climate and splendid harbour-side Government House might have done Lady de Rothschild a power of good: as it was, she lived another two decades. In a fraught letter, Constance pledged to Cyril:

> I am full of loving gratitude towards you <u>pray believe</u> [triple underlined] me, I know I am very far from being what I ought to be – but I promise most faithfully that you will never fear me wanting in deepest thankfulness towards you for what you have foregone.

Privately she feared she had "blighted my dear Cyril's career" and condemned them to "years of misery." Years later she would write:

> Were I to live again, I should act differently, for, to say the least, it is ill-judged, perhaps unpardonable, to stand in the way of a man's acceptance of an honourable and useful career.

The decision was a turning point for Cyril. Brutally disappointed, he lost much of his interest in politics and public life. According to E.F. Benson: "He was ambitious and it closed his career for him, forcing him into idleness when he should have been hardworked, and giving his native magnificence nothing to exercise itself on, except palatial projections of himself."

No longer needing to be in London, The Pleasaunce became Cyril's consolation, its beautification his keenest interest. Although hardly his only one. The expansive days at Overstrand, absent of Constance, would have been filled with diversions that stretched beyond gardening, golf, reading, and intimate conversation. If Whitman's vision of a democracy of loving comrades had always been an impossible Utopia, then this artificial Eden, peopled with sympathetic friends, was surely the next best thing. Here Cyril marshalled his army of manservants and gardeners – there were upwards of fifty male staff on the estate, including the Welsh lads – to the noble causes of beauty and pleasure. Writing to Constance's mother, Cyril confided that, when it was blessed by "a gentle Westerly breeze, brilliant sunshine, bright blue sky, dancing waves…This place conduces to a philosophic spirit."*

Cyril's playboy life at his marine paradise frustrated Constance. With comic exasperation she recalled in her memoirs:

> My husband was never tired of pursuing his botanical studies…he would sacrifice a whole year's work for some novel idea. Thus friends visiting the garden from time to time would

---

* One of Walt Whitman's Calamus poems, that Cyril would have been familiar with, gives expression to such a flight from conformity and the world's expectations, to an Arcadia where spiritual and physical yearnings can be met:

In paths untrodden,
In the growth by margins of pond-waters,
Escaped from the life that exhibits itself,
From all the standards hitherto publish'd—from the pleasures, profits, conformities,
Which too long I was offering to feed my Soul;
Clear to me, now, standards not yet publish'd—clear to me that my Soul,
That the Soul of the man I speak for, feeds, rejoices in comrades;
Here, by myself, away from the clank of the world,
Tallying and talk'd to here by tongues aromatic,
No longer abash'd—for in this secluded spot I can
respond as I would not dare elsewhere…
To celebrate the need of comrades.
[Walt Whitman, Calamus 1, *Leaves of Grass*, Thayer and Eldridge, Boston 1860, pp341-342.]

look for an accustomed feature, and would wonder where it could have strayed — or had their memories played them false? The watergarden took the place of the original tennis court, and was doubled in size after two years' existence, when a very promising rosary was sacrificed in its favour...Upon my yearly arrivals...I would expect to be greeted by some novelty, of which I was not always prepared to be an enthusiastic admirer; thus the first impression of the clock tower and the cloisters was an unfavourable one. Yet now I have become quite attached to the tower and the value of the cloisters for bazaars and fêtes is incontestable.

Nonetheless, when Lutyens and Cyril planned a feature too far that threatened her favourite view, Constance threw its bricks from a balcony. An enhancement to the garden that Constance possibly viewed in a similar light was when "a distant portion was made accessible by the construction of an underground passage".

This costly addition spawned family legends. As a descendant today recalls, those of her father's generation who'd visited 'Aunt Connie' for childhood holidays, "were amused by stories of secret passages from The Pleasaunce down which Uncle Cyril could go to assignations"; the principal story being "that a secret passage led to cottages where uncle's blond footmen lived."

While the subterranean passage was possibly employed for such trysts, as a sly means of escape from the more wearisome of Constance's guests, it would perhaps have offered even more priceless respite. Of his own visit to The Pleasaunce, Raymond Asquith wrote:

> I expected to find a handsome athletic comfortable amusing weekend party of the ordinary kind: nothing of the sort...he [Lord Battersea] suffers terribly from his wife, who is full of philanthropy and temperance and all that sort of nonsense, and while she is entertaining the good templars and prison matrons and heavens knows what horrors down in Buckinghamshire, he has been deputed to arrange a cricket match between the serfs on the Overstrand estate and the tenants of his Battersea shops...and here they are eating and drinking and exhaling a poisonous atmosphere of retail religion through one of the most

beautiful houses in Norfolkshire…And my host, hating them like death, but moving among them like a radiant god, the epitome of everything that is beautiful, luxurious, and refined, and treating them all with a cordiality that does infinite credit to his forbearance.

When Constance was in residence at Overstrand, Cyril was kept up to the mark. At such times The Pleasaunce was packed with guests and their children. As Constance wrote: "there are throngs of people all the summer. We are <u>never alone</u>. "

The Visitors Book of The Pleasaunce, "that precious possession," as Constance referred to it, survives. Its signatures include many glittering names, including Queen Alexandra, and her sister the Dowager Empress of Russia; Lord Curzon;* George Meredith;† social activist friends of Constance such as Lady Henry Somerset and Louise Creighton;‡ social stalwarts like Lady Dorothy Nevill,§ and Princess Louise and Lorne. While wearied by her petulance, Constance grew close to Louise: their wayward husbands and emotional starvation forging a mutual sympathy.

The Visitors book also recorded social comets, typified by Charles Glen Collins,** a military officer, and high-society adventurer and

---

* George Nathaniel Curzon, 1st Marquess Curzon of Kedleston 1859–1925, a Viceroy of India. Immortalised in the verse: "My name is George Nathaniel Curzon/I am a most superior person/My cheeks are pink, my hair is sleek/I dine at Blenheim once a week."
† George Meredith (1828–1909), novelist and poet. A radical Liberal, he married twice, with issue.
‡ Louise Hume Creighton, née von Glehn (1850–1936). Co-founder of the National Union of Women Workers; author of historical and sociopolitical works; and wife of Mandell Creighton, sometime Bishop of London.
§ Lady Dorothy Nevill (1826–1913). Writer, hostess, horticulturalist; an idiosyncratic and dauntingly snobbish *grande dame*. Daughter of 3rd Earl of Orford. Married Reginald Nevill.
** Charles Glen Collins (1880–1939). A Glasgow-born army officer, and keen golfer and cricketer, he married three times, twice to heiresses, and was bankrupted. In a prominent case, he was accused of obtaining jewellery by false cheques in India, and unsuccessfully fought extradition for six years, fleeing to New Orleans. "His war record and his family background gave him credibility before the jury, and he was acquitted." During World War I he worked in intelligence, travelling to Norway, Russia and China. He was immortalised by William Faulkner in his novel *Mosquitoes* as 'Major Ayers', in which he is portrayed as a florid gentleman with china-blue eyes. When a character in the novel states: "Freedom from the police is the greatest freedom man can demand or expect," Ayers retorts: "the only freedom is in wartime. Every one too busy fighting or getting ribbons or a snug berth to annoy you." [Col. Collins Admits To A Life Filled With Joy, *The Daily Leader* (Brookhaven, Mississippi), 16 June 2003; Collins' Journeys Lead Him To The French Quarter, *The Daily Leader*, 2 June 2003, Charles Glen Collins, Globe Trotter, Dies, *McComb Daily Journal* (Mississippi) 25 September 1939, p5;

rogue. Appearing too are strings of Asquiths and Rothschilds, as well as the ubiquitous bachelors Hamilton Aïdé and Augustus Hare. Names from high finance include Alfred Cole,* a director and future Governor of the Bank of England, who was a former pupil and friend of Oscar Browning. Amongst the regular appearing names is that of Frederic Myers; the signature of Myers' wife Eveleen also makes an occasional appearance.

There is another signature in the Visitors Book that appears year after year. It belongs to Gerald Balfour,† the younger brother of the Prime Minister. As self-absorbed, philosophical, golf-obsessed, and fascinated by the psychical world as his brother Arthur, he was married to a daughter of the 1st Earl of Lytton, and would father six children, including one with a mistress, the Liberal M.P. and spiritualist Winifred Coombe Tennant.‡

In her *Reminiscences*, Constance called Gerald and his wife, Lady Betty, "as original, interesting, and delightful a couple as one can ever hope to entertain." This recollection was discreetly veiled: behind closed doors they were as blithely libertarian and eccentric a pair as unlimited wealth and aristocracy can cast up.

Winifred Tennant informed her diary, "Lady Betty told me to make use of Gerald to the utmost," wishing them to enjoy "free and unfettered intercourse" – "She is a noble and great woman." Gerald and Winifred were convinced their bastard would be the Messiah, no less. Of Gerald, Constance added:

> He was extremely handsome as a young man, with delicate refined features and a graceful pose of the head...He loved flowers, and had made a study of them, appreciated the garden,

---

William Faulkner, *Mosquitoes*, Washington Square Press, New York, 1985, p55.]
* Alfred Clayton Cole (1854–1920). Governor of the Bank of England, 1911–1913. At the age of fifty-three he married a widow, Lilian Chamberlain.
† Gerald William Balfour, 2nd Earl Balfour (1853–1945). A Tory M.P. who served as Chief Secretary for Ireland and President of the Board of Trade, he purchased a villa in Florence and retreated there to study metaphysics. Like his older brother Arthur, he was a President of the Society of Psychical Research. He married Lady Elizabeth Bulwer-Lytton.
‡ Winifred Margaret Coombe Tennant, née Pearce-Serocold (1874–1956). Married Charles Coombe Tennant. [See: Peter Lord (ed.) *Between Two Worlds: The Diary of Winifred Coombe Tennant 1909-1924*, National Library of Wales, Aberystwyth 2011; Trevor Hamilton, *Arthur Balfour's Ghosts: An Edwardian Elite and the Riddle of the Cross-Correspondence Automatic Writings*, Imprint Academic, Exeter 2017.]

proved a devotee of golf, and used with pleasure our library of very readable books. More than all, Mr. Balfour was truly touched by Cyril's evident affection for him, and by the care he took to ensure the comfort and happiness of his guest. Humanity, as such, did not appeal to Mr. Balfour, so that some people who met him in our house thought him rather distant in manner, and found him difficult in conversation. His wife, with her pleasant, beaming face and kindly ways, was a less frequent guest than her husband, being greatly occupied with young and growing family of children.

As in other passages in Constance's memoirs touching on her husband's friendships, it seems very carefully worded. At Eton, Gerald had been one of the greatest infatuations of schoolmaster Oscar Browning, and at Cambridge, an Apostle. One of his private passions was embroidery. Whatever the nature of Cyril's relationship with the dreamy, indulged, and navel-gazing Gerald, either in the past or in that present, it was clearly highly important to at least one of them.

Far from being the superficial figure painted by his detractors, Cyril could be a deep thinker, whom Gerald and Arthur Balfour would have appreciated discussing philosophical matters with. In a letter to Cyril in 1891, Liberal Party colleague Richard Haldane* congratulated him on a speech he'd given, writing "I wish there were more earnest people in the world to talk like thou. For the majority it is only a game." Haldane then referred to the works of German theologian Otto Pfleiderer,† whom Cyril had plainly discussed with him.

Another regular and notable guest was John Morley,‡ a man of letters

---

* Richard Haldane, 1st Viscount Haldane (1856–1928), Scottish Liberal and later Labour imperialist politician, lawyer and philosopher.
† Otto Pfleiderer (1839–1908), influential German Protestant liberal theologian. Author of *Paulinism; a contribution to the history of primitive Christian theology* (1877), *The Philosophy of Religion: On the Basis of Its History* (1886–1894), etc.
‡ John Morley, 1st Viscount Morley of Blackburn, (1838–1923). His words and actions suggest a soul that was deeply repressed and conflicted. He contracted a highly unconventional and childless marriage with a shy unassuming widow, Rose Mary Ayling, with whom he lived before her abusive husband's death. She suffered bad health, enjoyed few of her husband's literary, political or social interests, and had two children of uncertain paternity. "I was not prudent", Morley confessed to a friend, "but in some respects life is too short for prudence". Writers Morley approved of were frequently accorded the status of 'manly' and 'wholesome'. Morley lambasted Swinburne for poetry of "nameless shameless abominations" and "unspeakable foulnesses," and denounced Richard Burton's translation of the Arabian Nights

and Liberal statesman, who became Chief Secretary for Ireland and Secretary of State for India, and was raised to the peerage in 1908. Constance records in her *Reminiscences* his confession that "the happiest days of my life were passed in the early times of The Pleasaunce, delightful days of friendship, gaiety, reading, and talks of serious things." He also gave the estate its name. Yet in Morley's own memoirs published ten years after Cyril's death, the only mention made of either of the Batterseas is a brief half-disguised reference: "Chat with Cyril F. and Tree* the actor." This was despite his autobiography stretching to two volumes. It could be seen as a snub, or expression of deep caution, were it not for the fact Morley was, like his friend Lord Rosebery, pathologically private. Of his memoirs, a friend wrote that while: "Autobiography is the literature of confession...there never was a book more reticent...It does not admit the reader to a single secret of the writer's heart."[†]

Cyril was President of the Overstrand Cricket Club, which operated on distinctly democratic lines: while its Vice-Presidents included such social luminaries as Sir George Lewis and Sir Edgar Speyer, the Club's Vice-Captain, and Assistant Secretary was Cyril's handsome valet John Compton, while its Secretary was The Pleasaunce's head gardener.

When what was termed 'The Golf Mania' swept England in the late 1880s, Cyril was also stricken. So much so that he quipped: "It is the people who don't play golf who are the maniacs." He would be

---

as not only "one of the grossest...books in the English language," but a threat to the national character by its attempt to import foreign vice under "the mask of scholarship and culture" until it reached the "unsullied British breakfast table." Given its celebrated Terminal Essay on pederasty was likely to have been one of Cyril's most fondly regarded texts, Morley's friendship with him was curious to say the least. Morley opposed the Boer War and condemned those who treated servants as dogs, yet he was outspoken against a bill that would have limited daily working hours to eight. One of his oddest friendships was with Lord Rosebery: they would walk London for hours together. [Patrick Jackson *Morley of Blackburn: A Literary and Political Biography of John Morley Patrick Jackson*, Fairleigh Dickinson University Press 2012, pp9-10, 13; Edward Alexander *John Morley*, Twayne, New York 1972, p142; *Saturday Review*, 4 August 1866; Colette Colligan *The Traffic in Obscenity From Byron to Beardsley*, Palgrave Macmillan, Basingstoke, 2006, p64-65; Robert Rhodes James, *Rosebery*, Weidenfeld & Nicholson, London 1964, p198.]
* Sir Herbert Beerbohm Tree (1852–1917), actor and theatre manager. Married Helen Maud Holt, and had issue, also fathering several illegitimate children. Lady Tree once exited their dining room, leaving him alone with the port and the cherubic-faced young actor Esmé Percy, while adding the caution: "Remember, Herbert, it's still adultery." [Neville Phillips, *Smack A Trifle: Odd Quirks In Prose And Rhyme*, Matador, Leicester 2009, p14.]
† Morley's diaries, discovered in 2003 and now at the Bodleian, are more frank, but only survive for the years 1882–1896.

profiled by the magazine *Golf Illustrated*, which glowingly recorded:

> Lord Battersea is a typical example of the *mens sana in corpore sano.*[*]
> Both in the political and social arena as well as on the field of
> sport he has been distinguished for a vigorous and healthy
> personality.

On the cliff-side links of the Royal Cromer Golf Club, of which he
was Vice-President, Cyril was a popular figure; fancifully accoutred he
was often to be seen teeing off with John Compton – "to show,
perhaps," sniffed one scribe, "that, though now a peer, he is still a
Radical." It was more likely he simply enjoyed Compton's company.
The Club boasted an illustrious membership, including Lord
Rosebery and the Duke of Fife.

Like gentlemen's clubs generally, golf provided a quiet masculine
refuge. For some players, like Lord Alfred Douglas, a particular
pleasure was its boy caddies. On the golf courses of the time they
were, as one player reflected, "as plentiful as blackberries in
September":

> They are so numerous that there is little hope of many of them
> getting a job; but, so far as my observation goes, they have
> acquired that peculiar and unprofitable philosophy that, whether
> they are employed or not, makes no matter. They turn up on the
> off-chance of making a shilling or so...they become happy-go-
> lucky and grow up anyhow.

Attempting to sketch a portrait of these self-effacing, mostly working-
class lads living on the edge of poverty, he wrote:

> That seemingly little shy fellow you meet on the links; the strip
> of a chap who looks on silently...He does not know why he is a
> bag carrier...his clothes fit him sack-like...The type I have in
> mind is strange and peculiar; he 'moons' about, an incorrigible
> dreamer about nothing...he is out and about to be picked up for
> a trifle. What becomes of him? Nobody can tell you in any
> definite sort of way; few care.

---

[*] A healthy mind in a healthy body.

The purlieus of The Pleasaunce were doubly blessed, one visitor noting, "Finer links are seldom to be met with than those which are so popular at Sheringham, Runton, and Cromer; and the caddies are a nicer set of boys than can be found in many places." Even so, when at a horticultural show held in the grounds of The Pleasaunce, a local M.P. blamed the lure of the links for drawing boys away from learning useful occupations, Cyril responded with a speech in which he remarked that golf:

> was no doubt a healthy and a manly game, but for boys to loaf around it as mere caddies would mean a demoralisation of the future generation, and he adjured their fathers to see that their interest in the most interesting of all pastimes – horticulture – was well developed.

With Cyril's fantasy garden expanding by the acre, such a desideratum was also essential for his outdoor staffing.*

In April 1893 came the news that John Addington Symonds had died at Rome. He'd just completed the drafts of his study on Walt Whitman, and a book of collected essays had appeared that March. One review tersely remarked: "The volume called *In The Key Of Blue* has a delicious cover – but that is its only delicious feature."

The cover – by Charles Ricketts† – of entwined bluebells and scattered laurel or mimosa blossom was indeed delicious, but the contents was even more so: in the last year of his life, Symonds had almost abandoned his previous reticence, and the text was suffused with homoeroticism and reflections on Greek Love. The essays included one titled 'Clifton And A Lad's Love' – "He made my life one living spring," while the essay of the title was a lyrical meditation on the graduations of Italian blue, and the beauty of Augusto: a Venetian whom Symonds had first encountered one hot June evening, as the then nineteen-year-old porter sat by the Grand Canal:

> Against the golden gaslight; grapes

---

* Here too his philanthropy further reached out, as a Vice-President of the Royal Gardeners Orphan Fund, which aided waifs with links to horticulture. [Royal Gardener's Orphan Fund, *The Morning Post*, 9 May 1900, p5.]
† Charles de Sousy Ricketts RA (1866 –1931), artist, illustrator, author and printer. His life companion was fellow artist Charles Haslewood Shannon (1863–1937).

Of dusky curls your brows embrace,
And round you all the vast night gapes...

Hushed was the night for friendly talk;
Under the dark arcades we walk,
Pace the wet pavement, where light steals
And swoons amid the huge abeles:
Then seek our chamber.

At Overstrand, the sensuous verses recalling Cyril's dream city would have been savoured like a fine wine. Yet in that spring of 1893, Cyril would be reminded that he lived in a very different land, and was perhaps better out of public politics. Foreshadowing the Oscar Wilde affair, it took the form of a malicious libel case. In the General Election the previous year, a Liberal candidate Charles Gatty* contested the seat of the sitting member for West Dorset, a thuggish squire named Henry Farquharson.† Having heard that Gatty had been expelled or compelled to leave Charterhouse school for 'an unnatural offence', Farquharson threatened to expose the story "in every club in London," and spread it in the House of Commons, and in placards and speeches. He also alleged that, more recently, Gatty was forced to leave Yeovil due to involvement with "printers boys".

Gatty sued for libel, but when the case finally came to court that June, a Charterhouse record book produced for the court upon subpoena, sensationally revealed that against Gatty's name was written: "Removed, Impudicitice Causa" – which broadly translated meant: "Removed for an offence against purity."

However, Gatty had been merely thirteen at the time, and it emerged that, likely after being used as the 'bitch' of older boys, he'd sought help from – of all people – the Rev. J.L. Lyne, a brother of whom was at the school at the time. Lyne wrote to the headmaster, who wrote to Gatty's father, who had then promptly removed his son from the school. Indicative of the gravity with which the libel case was officially

---

* Charles Tindal Gatty (1851–1928), a Liverpool Art Museum curator turned Liberal candidate. Private secretary to the 3rd Marquess of Bute, editor of the *Western Chronicle*, and founder of the Irish Art Companions. Author of *George Wyndham: Recognita* (1917), a tribute to his friend, the Conservative M.P. and man of letters.
† Henry Richard Farquharson (1857–1895); Conservative M.P.; died at sea while returning from his tea plantations in Ceylon: "of acute dysentery," printed *The Times*, although it noted, he "had not been in ill health of late." [Obituary, *The Times*, 24 April 1895.]

viewed, the Lord Chief Justice presided. Forthrightly, he told the court: "everyone knew what went on at public schools, and any man with a spark of generosity would not have referred to it. Yet Mr. Gatty was dragged to the stake for what happened thirty years ago." Gatty won the case, and Farquharson was hit with a massive £5,000 in damages. On appeal, the sum was reduced to half that amount, but it had been an ugly affair.

In December 1893, while chasing a stag with Lord Rothschild's hounds, Cyril fell from his horse. While on the ground, he was trampled by another horse, injuring his back and ribs. While suffering great pain, no bones were broken, but for a time he was completely immobilised. It had been a close call. Cyril had been due to receive the freedom of the borough from Luton Town Council a few days hence, but the formal presentation was postponed. The celebration dinner, which could not be put off, went ahead without him; the toast to the Town and Corporation being made on his behalf by his radical supporter the Rev. Fillingham.

In early 1894, Constance sailed with her sister Annie on her steam yacht the Garland to Greece and the Adriatic, but Cyril travelled separately, wishing to explore Algeria instead. Nine years previously, the publication of Sir Richard Burton's translation of The Arabian Nights – *The Book Of The Thousand Nights And A Night*, with its enthusiastically explicit essay 'Social Conditions – Pæderasty' had sparked fresh interest in the region for many enterprising travellers,[*] and Bernard Fraser had likely spoken of it.

Passing through France in February, Cyril asked his valet John Compton to look out the window of their 'train du luxe' and tell him what station they were at. Compton replied: "I can't pronounce it, but it's spelt 'Hommes'." It was perhaps the appropriate answer.

From Algiers in February, Cyril wrote to Constance:

Not a cloud in the sky & the breeze as warm as a very warm day

---

[*] Perhaps Cyril had also dipped into the four-volume translation of the Biographical Dictionary of the 13th Century Islamic historian Ibn Khallikan, published between 1843 and 1871 by the Irish-French scholar William McGuckin, Baron de Slane. Those portions of the text deemed as having too pronounced a homosexual character were rendered in Latin, purely for the edification of gentlemen of the higher classes.

in June. The approach is fine & the city looks magnificent from the sea, terrace above terrace of white houses, with flat roofs & a fine range of hills behind and around it. I have an excellent room high up, with a delightful terrace in front of me, on which I am sitting looking over the harbour & the distant sea – & down upon a grove of palm trees, magnolias, bamboos & the whole port & long boulevards busy with myriads of men & women in every variety of dress, the arabs are excessively picturesque, their dirt adding to the 'local colour'.

He immediately befriended the Consul, Sir (Robert) Lambert Playfair, "a capital old fellow who has written the book in the Mediterranean…" This was a handbook to Algeria and Tunis published by Murray's, then the leading travel guides. Following Playfair's advice, Cyril set out to explore the land from top to toe. It was, he wrote, "an outlandish Country," but its magnificence was a revelation, and he penned rapturous descriptions of snowy mountains, fertile valleys, hedges of geraniums, and Arab markets:

orange groves laden with fruit, stone pine groves, shady roads with plane trees on either side high hills & all bordering the sea – which is intensely blue & reflecting a cloudless sky.

Utterly carried away, he further wrote:

I shall go on to the Desert! The Oasis! Biskra! …to Carthage & Dido's Palace & then set sail for Palermo.

It was travel in the grand manner. He telegraphed to the Garland to meet him at Tunis, and finally joined Constance at Capri.

In March that year, Cyril's friend Lord Rosebery achieved his ambition of becoming Prime Minister. The result was a short and disastrous premiership that ended in June the following year. Shortly after assuming office, Rosebery entertained at an intimate dinner the Archbishop of Canterbury (as head of the Church), the Dean of Christ Church (as the representative of Oxford), the Prince of Wales's equerry (representing the Crown), an admiral and captain (as representatives of the armed forces), and not least, Cyril and their mutual friend, the chronically effete, but always welcomed in the corridors of power, Alfred de Rothschild. According to the press, the latter two gentlemen were present because they represented Rosebery's marital relatives. However, it could equally be said they represented Rosebery's sexually sympathetic comrades.

While Cyril was away, the London evening newspaper *The Echo*, whose editor John Passmore Edwards was a champion of the working class, had published the latest in a series of satirical articles entitled 'Our New Nobility' which were wittily scathing of fresh inductions to the House of Lords. Its profile of Cyril was gleefully reprinted by Welsh newspapers and the *Bedfordshire Advertiser* – the new name of the *Luton Times* – Alfred Atkins having gone his grave earlier that year. However, Atkin's ghost could well have pushed the journalist's pen:

> The peerage of Battersea rests upon the couch of a fortunate marriage. The fortunate marriage has done much for the peerage and the ambitious politician. It may supply blood, and condone the absence the absence of great, or even reasonable, nobility. Mr. Disraeli's novels, indeed, pay tribute to the influence of a bride's dowry in politics. Their entire drift is towards riches, however acquired, and to ennoblement at any cost. In a word, it is the homage of social distinction which is the aim of statecraft...The new political peerage of Battersea was created in 1892. It was not exactly a gift to the gods, though it provided a safe place for the Apollo of the Commons. The title made our Old Nobility smile, for it is distinctly *bourgeois*. It is instinctively transpontine, with a flavour of Vauxall, and of the penny steamboats of that lively traveller 'Arry...The father of the peer resided in a mansion on Streatham-common, bearing the suggestive name of Furzedown. Clapham, in the early day of Mr. Philip Flower and of his father...was a dangerous suburb, infested with footpads and kindred vermin, and Streatham was almost an impenetrable waste...The dwellers there went armed, their wills ready made...The early life of the coming peer was passed at Streatham. He hardly admits it now...From Furzedown the beautiful Cyril was sent well labelled "With Care," if not with "This Side Up," to Harrow, and thence, with matured thews, he passed on to Trinity College, Cambridge...At one time Lord Battersea enjoyed the distinction of being regarded as the best-looking man in the House of Commons. He is certainly a *beau chevalier* of the Upper Chamber. His line of

beauty is artistic, and in his low collar, short brown beard, curling moustache, deep blue eyes, and waving hair he might in his Commons days have been mistaken for a successful contributor to the wall of Burlington House. One would instinctively number him, even to-day, with the Newlyn gang. But an Apollo at fifty is not as an Apollo at thirty, when the auburn locks gave back the challenge of the sun under

"Thy incomparable oil, Massar."

Still, Lord Battersea is a butterfly, a thing of gaudy texture, a device of sweetly tempered nature. Mr. Bobby Spencer is sometimes called a serious-minded butterfly, and no doubt that is an accurate description of Mr. Gladstone's polite Letter Writer to the Queen. But Lord Battersea is too beautiful to be serious. His gravity never takes any definite form, or, at any rate, he only relapses into the graver side of life when he has to contemplate himself, and then his admiration finds its true interpretation in silent homage to the Beautiful. Lord Battersea moves through life with a gay and easy swing. He looks the world proudly in the eye, and men stop and turn to see this picturesque being as he passes. He typifies the hero of the yellow-backed novel,* and might have sat as a model to the artist of the weekly number. Mr. Cyril Flower had the courage of some innovations as M.P. for Brecknock, and again of Luton. He introduced light tweeds into legislation, and the white waistcoat into the dress suit. Mr. Spencer has been equal to the white waistcoat, but to Lord Battersea belongs the undoubted distinction of being alone able to sustain a light drab, and look a gentleman still.

Apart from this sumptuary triumph, Lord Battersea has left behind but few of Common memories, except perhaps, a taste in neckties…His services to legislation were those rather of the silent philosopher. Upon *Hansard* he imposed few obligations. His speeches were by no means as numerous as his neckties. He was, however, a tireless Junior Whip, took his turn of sentry duty in the fascinating hours of the London Season with Spartan complacency, and made every stroller give an account of himself. The work was ill-paid at a thousand year; when measured by the

---

* The cheap popular novel. Developed in the 1840s to compete with 'penny dreadful' literature.

social sacrifices it entailed; but when it is remembered through the long grey autumn of Opposition, unrelieved by the solatium of that sum, one wonders that Lord Battersea really had the patience. But the reward was a peerage, and a life now passed upon beds amaranth and moly. In the summer evening, after the Wednesday rising, in the seven years of Radical famine, it became one of the gladsome sights of the Park to behold Mr. Cyril Flower, a short gentleman, mounted upon a very tall bay horse, and Mr. [Edward] Marjoribanks, a dark gentleman, astride a white nag, speckled like a spotted beagle.

Lord and Lady Battersea are fond of doing much social work south of the Thames, and Lord Battersea makes comforting speeches on Home Rule and the virtues of the present ministry. His business as a merchant keeps him in touch with commerce, and his company directorships answer the refrain, "What shall a nobleman find to do?" Lord Battersea dines with the party leaders while Lady receives the party items. The Eighty Club also owes his lordship much. But for all that Lord Battersea must often have asked himself, "Why was I made peer?"

The portrait was as devastating as any that Alfred Atkins had conjured in earlier years. And worse, it was half true. The mocking didn't end there. A few months later the article was partly reprinted and embellished by a Society weekly to coincide with his 50th birthday:

The 30th August half-a-century ago saw the advent into this vale of tears one of our most beautiful legislators, Cyril of Battersea… at Cambridge [he] became very chummy with that amiable Oriental, Leopold, Rothschild. It was the year of the voluptuaries at Cambridge, and everything was kisses, cream, and comforts. Then sweet Cyril studied law, which he never seriously practiced…The peerage came to this lovely being as sunlight to the rose; he merely expanded into the Upper Chamber.

In February 1895, at the Opening Of Parliament, Cyril and the bachelor civil servant Lord Welby* were selected to make the formal Address to the House of Lords on the Queen's Speech. A political reporter observed:

---

* Sir Reginald 'Reggie' Earle Welby, 1st Baron Welby, (1832–1915), Permanent Secretary to the Treasury for many years, and Liberal in the House of Lords.

They wore the gay Windsor uniform,* and they spoke for a Government which in this chamber at all events speaks and exists merely on sufferance…Lord Battersea, handsome, self-possessed, and with the House of Commons capacity of uttering the clearly-spoken word, drove home some excellently compacted sentences on Welsh Disestablishment, One Man One Vote, and the Liquor Bill. The House of Lords always seems to take a declaration of Progressive principles as a personal insult. But it listened to Lord Battersea with an elaborate tolerance which came with the consciousness that the speaker did not represent more than 30 votes.†

That spring, almost certainly on behalf of business opportunities, Cyril sailed to South Africa. It would be logical to assume his friendship with Reginald Brett had led to a meeting with Cecil Rhodes. In any case, the journey would soon pay dividends. The timing of Cyril's journey was also most fortuitous, and perhaps expeditiously arranged, as it occurred just as the first of the Oscar Wilde trials was causing sensation in London. Like the Cleveland Street Scandal of a few years prior, Wilde's overnight fall from international fame to infamy, and the hostility of the press and public, would have been dispiriting and stressful to every person of homosexual bent – impressing upon them anew that they lived on a knife edge. In the words of one sympathetic observer: "For all of them after this, there was neither law or justice in the land – only an unutterable hypocrisy, and another crucifixion."

The passage comes from *The Sphinx's Lawyer*, a 1906 novel that was in part a defence of Wilde. Its author was Julia Frankau, the daughter of a wealthy Jewish Maida Vale family. Given the relatively small London Jewish community, it's more than likely Frankau and Constance had met; they would certainly have been aware of each other. Frankau's novel includes an extraordinary one and a half-page dedication to her brother and fellow writer James Davis (known by his pen name of Owen Hall). It begins: "Because you 'hate and loathe' my book and its subject, I dedicate it to you. I have heard your argument; I know where I stand. It is at the foot of the Throne of Mercy." Homosexuality, even at a remove, had a way of splitting

* A court uniform of dark blue coat with scarlet collar and cuffs and gilt buttons.
† In the chamber.

families. Wilde's martyrdom gave license to press philistines and bullies. For Cyril, disenchantment with English society in its wake likely further encouraged his retreat to his seaside idyll.

In March 1896, the Eighty Club hosted a dinner at the Criterion restaurant in Piccadilly in honour of Lord Rosebery. Among the list of guests, who included Cyril and the Club's regular plethora of decorative young men, was a twenty-five-year-old soldier of good family. He was intellectual, rich, tanned (having recently returned from the tropics), and not least, randy. His name was Harold Boulton – the same 'Bolton' named at Fraser and Thorold's trial as one of the procurers who had bolted. We know this was he, because Bernard Fraser named him in his will as one of his executors. And so, Harold Boulton's line of fate, and that of Cyril's, converged.

The following year, Cyril accepted the post of chairman of the South African gold mining concern, A. Goerz and Company. He held the role until 1904, and remained a director of the company for the rest of his life. It had been founded by Adolf Goerz,[*] a German immigrant, who was to die of tuberculosis, while still young, in 1900. Glittering names were sought for the company's British board, which included Henry Strakosch,[†] a renowned global authority on finance and exchanges, and Carl Meyer,[‡] Chief Clerk of N.M. Rothschild & Sons, who also acted as private secretary to Cyril's friend Alfred de Rothschild, and also helped organise his London entertainments. Cyril's appointment, which placed him at the very heart of the South African mining boom that was rapidly creating massive 'Randlord' fortunes, further strengthened his already gilded financial connections.

At the opposite end of the financial spectrum, Cyril was also an honourary member of the miniscule South Bucks Friendly Society, whose meetings he presided over. Its members were mostly Aston Clinton villagers who were Rothschild servants and estate staff: their

---

[*] Adolf Goerz (1857–1900), German-South African mining engineer.
[†] Sir Henry Strakosch (1871–1943), knighted 1921; a bachelor until the age of seventy, when he married the widow of a shipowner.
[‡] Sir Carl Ferdinand Meyer, Bart. (1851-1922), Hamburg-born Jewish banker and diamond magnate. He worked for N.M. Rothschild from 1872 to 1897, including as private secretary to Alfred de Rothschild, and also for DeBeers, including as deputy chairman. Married Adèle Levis, and had issue. He donated £70,000 towards a national Shakespeare memorial, and was created a baronet in 1910.

investments fortuitously managed by Lord Rothschild.

In 1897, the Batterseas travelled to Spain and Tangier, and the following year to Italy, including Naples, where they visited the Rendels. Like other British tourists, they drove to the entrance gates of the Rosebery estate to peer in. They also visited the Riviera, and were the guests of its uncrowned queen, Alice de Rothschild.* This grand dame of the family was famed for having reprimanded Queen Victoria for stepping on the lawn at her magnificent estate, Villa Victoria at Grasse: thereafter the Queen referred to her as 'The All-Powerful One'. Constance told her mother that the place disconcerted her:

> It is a little too artificial here which mars the real enjoyment of what this is supposed to be – country life. I was warned by Alice never to put my foot upon the <u>grass</u> anywhere in her domain. Fancy, in a fit of abstraction, I did so, right under Alice's eyes, which sent her into a violent passion…I long for a little disorder. There is not one leaf or weed to be met with on the paths, and the worms are carefully picked up and taken away when they appear after rain.

Unsurprisingly, the reaction of her husband was decidedly different, as a fellow traveller recorded: "Cyril is in a state of unbounded ecstasy over the extraordinary beauty of this place and the genius of its owner." It was also noted that he'd "ordered an immense quantity of scents." The visit wouldn't have moderated his ambitions for The Pleasaunce either, likely inspiring him to even grander landscaping visions.

During these years, Constance's frustration with Cyril's chosen path, and her marriage, found regular expression in her diaries:

> Feel so disappointed about Cyril, he has entirely thrown his chances away, leads an idle cut up life & alas! I feel that I have been seriously to blame…

> I am not going to talk about myself for I do feel so acutely how I have failed & if I could but begin the last 20 years over again I

---

* Alice Charlotte von Rothschild (1847–1922).

think I might have made Cyril a happier man & therefore a better one. Alas! Too late now…

I do wish we had children. More for Cyril's sake than mine. They w[ou]ld have brought out all his great qualities. He would have been so successful for them. So loving, so brave…

I am not going to write about my feelings or intimate things – what is the use? It only makes me long for what is unobtainable. Cyril liked some of our guests & was barely with others, wh[ich] always vexes & terrifies me.

During The Season of 1897, the Batterseas hosted a glittering evening for the Eighty Club at Surrey House. Upwards of 1,500 invitations were issued, with a newspaper report capturing the mise-en-scène:

all the other Colonial Premiers, as well as several distinguished Indians, were on the list of guests. The Oriental costumes of these gentlemen struck the eye even in the richly furnished and decorated rooms of Surrey House…With the music of the white Hungarian band, the groups of flowers, the fumes of burning scent, and the brilliant toilettes a striking impression was made…Everybody…seemed in particularly good humour…Mr. Asquith, too, was jocular. When he reached Lord Battersea, that gentleman, with the expansive geniality which makes him so good a host, was talking with a lady. Mr. Asquith, a twinkle in his eye, stood close to him -- almost over him -- so that when Lord Battersea rose he almost rubbed his face against the ex-Home Secretary's. The latter then shook hands with him, as if that were his sole object in life.

Amongst the crowd of powerbrokers that evening were Lord Rosebery, Herbert Gladstone,* Sir Henry Campbell-Bannerman,† Arnold Morley, Henry Labouchère, and surprisingly given he was a High Tory, Sir Edward Lawson. *The Daily Telegraph's* toadying proprietor was one of Labouchère's *bête noires*: they had once come to fisticuffs, and Labby had "strained every nerve" to try and prevent

---

* Herbert John Gladstone, 1st Viscount Gladstone (1854–1930), Home Secretary Dec 1905–Feb 1910. Very good looking as a young man, at the age of 47 he married a baronet's daughter who was over twenty years his junior.
† Sir Henry Campbell-Bannerman (1836–1908), Prime Minister from 1905 to 1908.

him being granted his baronetcy.

In the summer of 1898, Cyril joined Lord Lorne and a distinguished audience at Mansion House, to give their support to the Lord Mayor for the expansion of Hampstead Heath, by the acquisition of the 36 acre Golders Hill estate of the late Sir Spencer Wells.* Lorne told the audience: "It was one of the few spots near the metropolis where one could get a whiff of Highland air."

At the close of that year, Ferdinand Rothschild died in empty splendour at Waddesdon after catching a cold. His health had never been good, and he expired in his valet's arms after a hot bath. As the Liberal M.P. for Rothschildian Aylesbury he'd been little more than a shy showpony. Yet with his obsessive collecting, adoration of panache, and secreted sexuality, he and Cyril had much in common – two spoilt boys with all the money in the world. "We had a very pleasant dinner at Ferdy's last night a mass of men!" one of Cyril's letters to Constance begins, "& the table all orchids!" Now he was gone, at the age of just fifty-nine.

Cyril was four years younger, but in appearance he was rapidly ageing, a development which surely contributed to his restlessness. The following year, Constance tallied his health problems, which included another fall from his horse while hunting:

> Accident in March – followed by prolonged severe gout. Ill all the spring. Influenza & feverish symptoms all May – massage ineffectual, he remained at Overstrand. Tiresome time. Oh dear. How wearying it all is. He has no occupations & plenty of time for endless complaint – never satisfied with anything. [A blacked out passage.] As for me I am nowhere.

In late 1899 the press reported "there has been quite an epidemic of blackmailing charges in London." For Cyril it was close to home in every respect. One victim was James Hyatt,† a poetical-faced

---

* Sir Thomas Spencer Wells, Bt., (1818–1897), Surgeon to the Queen's Household.
† James Hallet Lake Hyatt (1869–1955), son of Thaddeus Hyatt, a wealthy American manufacturer who invented street pavers with embedded translucent glass disks that brought light into basements. Married with issue. Some of Hyatt's photographs of Surrey House's interior are in the possession of Historic England. A Hyatt photograph of its conservatory, stuffed with topiary chrysanthemums, appears in: Priscilla Boniface, *The Garden Room*, Royal Commission On Historical Monuments England, 1982.

photographic engraver and possible friend, who'd captured several images of the interiors of Surrey House, including of Cyril's Bugatti bedroom. Hyatt received a letter stating:

> Unless you send me £10, I shall accuse you by means of post-cards of a certain indecent assault; also gross immorality, thereby insuring your ruin. I shall also forward to your wife a letter containing the accusations, stating both names, places, and times. Choose between 2 alternatives, ruin or sending £10 to the above address.

Hyatt's would-be extorter was an eighteen-year-old youth appropriately named Alexander 'Alec' Morgues, whom he'd previously employed for errands. Arrested, Morgues told the police "What's a fellow to do when he's out of work?" He admitted there was no truth in the allegations, but was already a veteran at the game, having twice been jailed for blackmailing gentlemen with the same accusation, including the manager of the Tivoli musical hall. Not even the deceased were safe from Morgues' attentions: another victim was the widow of actor and theatrical impresario Sir Augustus Harris,[*] who received the following letter from him:

> Madam — We are in possession of certain letters, etc., relating to the private and intimate life of the late Sir Augustus Harris, which, if published to the world, would place you in an unenviable position, the living having to suffer for the dead...our terms are, for remitting to you the letters, documents, etc. £40 in bank-notes, etc.[†]

When her ladyship failed to reply, Morgues wrote again, threatening to burn her house down. Cyril must have thanked himself that his procuring needs were in the trustworthy hands of the gentry.

In November, in a slew of similar appointments, the Queen made Cyril one of her Lieutenants in London; an unpaid representative sinecure which cast the light of royal regard upon him. As its fruity

---

[*] Sir Augustus Henry Glossop Harris (1852–1896); actor, impresario, dramatist. Married Florence Edgcumbe Rendle, and had a daughter.
[†] Harris was no random target for homosexual blackmail: at the Drury Lane theatre he had at one time a business partnership with the previously mentioned Alexander Meyrick Broadley. Like Broadley, Harris was a prominent freemason: his memorial fountain outside the Theatre Royal, Drury Lane is embellished with masonic square and compass symbols.

medieval wording put it: "Our right trusty and well-beloved Cyril, Lord Battersea." The appointment would be renewed by her successor.

The summer of 1900 saw Cyril undertaking a duty closer to his heart: opening a new pavilion at the Luton Golf Club. In a witty speech, he noted that in America judges considered the sport "a suitable subject for divorce".

The great issue of the day had become the Second Boer War. Given Cyril was chairman of a South African mining company he was in a sticky position, but like every other Randlord and investor in that moral sinkhole, including his wife's family, he wasn't prepared to champion the lives of anonymous young fighting men above the primacy of profit, nor place social regard or plutocratic friendships at risk. Amongst those was Rochfort Maguire,* one of Cecil Rhodes's closest friends, and later President of the British South Africa Company, who would be twice a guest at The Pleasaunce after the War.

In his public speeches Cyril took the position of deploring the War, but as it had begun, patriotically supporting it, in order it might be ended sooner, and the land better governed. The unstated implication was that this would be best under a British flag. It was devious political vapidness at its worst.†

In January 1901 came the news that Queen Victoria was ailing. A feeling of unease gripped the nation. When the inevitable occurred, a poet's cry summed up the prevailing bereavement: "We are all orphans, we are motherless!" Five days before her death, Cyril's first mentor Frederic Myers died in Rome, having gone there to recover from influenza that, together with Bright's disease, had debilitated him. Constance recorded:

---

* (James) Rochfort Maguire (1855–1925), Irish Nationalist M.P. Accompanied by his wife, he went through the Siege of Kimberley in the Boer War with Rhodes. He was one of the three men who signed the original concession on which was based the British South Africa Company, of which he was President, 1923–25.
† In sharp contrast, Sir William Harcourt's denunciations of the War were scathing. The previous November, *The Times* devoted three columns to a letter in which he contemptuously wrote: "Is there still no part of South Africa which has not been laid to waste? Are there no men or women of the Dutch race still alive?", and: "What has been the fatal feature of this unhappy war from the beginning to the present moment is the invincible ignorance of those responsible for it."[Guerilla War, *The Times*, 8 November 1901, p12.]

we heard that F Myers had at last been promoted (to use his own words)...what a strange man he was! Full of genius, animal passions, great spirituality, materialism – strange, strange! – an early friend of Cyril's then rather more a friend of mine.

For those who'd been even closer to him than Constance, Frederic Myers was to remain "a precious memory": as one wrote, "his friendship as one of the great privileges of my life." Another stated:

It was as much how a man listens as how he speaks that makes for charm, and Myers was a listener who drew one's best without crushing one's naturalness by superiority of manner; therein lay his fascinating personality, at least I thought so.

For Cyril, Myers' death was the end of an era in every respect. Besides being likely lovers in their youth, they were also true peers, born the same year. Their shared experience, together with Myers's magnetic vitality, would have ensured his death had a marked impact. The shades were now gathering over Cyril's own life, and an inevitable consciousness of shortening time may have spurred him to take greater risks in his sexual adventuring.

When, in the 1920s long after Cyril's death, Constance decided to publish her memoirs, the prospect alarmed Lord Rosebery. Likely worried for his own reputation as much as Cyril's, he begged her not to, warning that even a private printing for friends carried deep risk: "somebody dies to whom a copy has been given and his books are sold, and the book then becomes public...I think it is most dangerous." Princess Louise also considered it unwise. However the draft was gone over by George Russell, and rewritten several times, Constance necessarily exercising extreme tact and discretion. Passages referencing her husband's friends required all of it. Some of these associations she strongly disapproved of, and with delicate caution she painted a revealing picture of the tensions they caused within the marriage:

writers, often men and women of eminence, invariably spoke of my husband's genius for friendship and keen sense of what true hospitality should be. Indeed, I could not always keep pace with his views on the latter subject. At times I had to try and modify the warmth of his invitations, and to curtail, in as considerate a manner as was compatible with politeness, the length of a proposed visit that, beginning under a cloudless sky, threatened to end under a stormy one. I also felt, intuitively, that some of the very ardent and sudden likings he occasionally took to certain persons might lead to misplaced friendship, and that he might thus be preparing for himself hours and days of disappointment. But it was difficult to convince him of such possible pitfalls, and he went on trusting, caring, and taking endless pains in trying to help his friends, whenever they needed his help, to the very end.

Some of this help was altruistic – Cyril's generosity ran deep. However, hindsight does give the passage echoes of the immortal remark of one of the more innocent neighbours of the noted cabaret artist Douglas Byng*: "So kind! Not a night seems to pass when he doesn't give some homeless serviceman on leave a bed!"

While Cyril maintained close friendships with worshippers of boyhood such as Simeon Solomon, and Sir William Grantham's closing remarks in Fraser and Thorold's trial indicated it primarily or wholly involved boys, in the matter of age, boys is a loose term, that in age can extend to late youth. Apart from Josephine Butler's letter regarding Frederic Myers, no record of those with whom Cyril disported appears to have survived. That said, given the nature of the scandal, and the nature of homosexuality then, in which pederasty was inextricably entwined,† it's reasonable to assume Cyril's sexual tastes may have been similar. Lord Lorne's sister, the suffragette Lady Frances Balfour‡ also recalled:

> Where he [Cyril] was himself happiest was in the company of the little children, and no child but was happy with this careful guardian. Instinctively he knew the desire of the smallest heart,

---

* Douglas Coy Byng (1893–1987).
† Unlike pedophilia i.e. sexual involvement with pre-pubescents.
‡ Lady Frances Balfour, née Campbell (1858–1931); the high-minded daughter of the 8th Duke of Argyll, and women's suffrage leader. A staunch upholder of aristocratic privilege and paternalism, she was extremely pious, refusing to attend theatres: even Shakespeare was considered morally dubious. A childhood blighted by disease and parental strictness had left her deeply repressed, with a limp, constant pain, and a feeling of inferiority which she sought to counter through pugnaciousness and snobbery. According to her daughter Blanche: "She lived on her friendships…and by her letter writing killed them more than once." [William Knox *The Lives of Scottish Women: Women and Scottish Society 1800-1980*, Edinburgh University Press 2006, p98-105.]

and no fairy Prince fulfilled those dreams more wisely. He loved them with an unselfish affection, and he made even the children selfless in his presence.

Although a shadow of suspicion must, in the light of events, fall upon such an admiring recollection, such younger associations may have been entirely innocent. Violet Bonham Carter, daughter of Herbert and Helen Asquith, wrote that Cyril "adored my father and my mother (the word is not too strong) and their family became the children he had longed to have." As an eighteen-year-old guest at The Pleasaunce, Violet wrote to a friend about her host:

> he's an odd character[,] narrow & violent & personal in politics – intensely generous in private life; very rich and childless & fond of pictures & devoted to all of us whom he has known since we were born & still treats us as if we were 6 & 7. He has only just left off kissing Beb! [the twenty-four-year old Herbert junior*]...at meals Ly. B. shouts from one end of the table to the other "Cyril! Cyril! She's talking about Home Rule! Dear child! How clever she is!!" It makes me laugh too much to make me very angry..."

In February 1901, Cyril and Constance attended Edward VII's first Opening of Parliament. "The new peers were distinguishable by the brightness and newness of their robes," noted an observer. The most memorable figure of the day was Queen Alexandra, gowned in black with an enormous Indian necklace of pearls draped to her waist, and a rivulet of diamonds cascading to her feet. "The Queen was a vision of loveliness," wrote Constance, "every eye turned upon her & one felt that she held the assembly."

On the wedding anniversary of the Flowers in November that year, Constance was in Paris, but Cyril sent her an affectionate letter which, she told her diary, "did my heart good & cheered me up." However, in a crossed-out comment she also lamented: "Oh how I wish I could begin again & be a different wife."

At the beginning of the fateful year of 1902, Cyril's energies were directed to opposing new legislation proposed by Balfour's

---

* Herbert Dixon Asquith (1881–1947). Poet, novelist and lawyer. Second son of Herbert Asquith. Married Lady Cynthia Charteris.

Conservative Government. The Education Bill mandated the abolition of school administrative boards, handing over their duties to local councils – in theory, an efficient reform. However, it provoked a heated national dispute. Opposers argued that it meant Anglican and Catholic schools would now be subsidised by ratepayers, irrespective of their beliefs, and in remote regions, they could be forced to send their children to an Anglican or Catholic school if that were the only option in their area. Cyril was President of the National Education Association, which advocated for the principles of progressive state education, and in a public speech claimed the Government was thinking "less of the public interest than of private and sectarian interests."

In March, all London was startled by the elopement and marriage of Oscar Wilde's 'Bosie' – the increasingly deluded Lord Alfred Douglas. The not-so-lucky woman was Olive Custance, a poetry-loving heiress. Quipped Percy Wyndham,* "Anything short of murder in the Douglas family is a source of congratulation." †

That same month, Cecil Rhodes died in Cape Town. On his last visits to England, in 1899 and 1902, he'd been so ill from recurrent malaria and heart attacks, the "slightest exertion made him breathless." His rise to power had been unquestionably aided by a homosocial network,‡ which included Reginald Brett and Lewis Harcourt. The obituaries were respectful but qualified: "Mr. Rhodes represented the spirit of our age – adventurous, pushing, enterprising, full of resource, energy, and a perhaps too assertive materialism," noted *The Standard*, while *The Daily News* was blunter: "he had a false ideal. His aims were exclusively material, and his religion was 'the sensual idolatry of mere size.'" For *The Daily Telegraph*, he was naturally "a great Empire-maker and a great Englander," while *The St. James's Gazette* topped its conservative self with the reflection: "To-day one thought only springs to the mind of every Briton: 'Know yet not that there is a prince and a great man fallen this day in Israel.'"

---

* The Hon. Percy Wyndham (1835–1911), soldier, Conservative Party politician, collector and intellectual; one of the original members of The Souls, and a keen and early member of the Society for Psychical Research.

† By 1918, Douglas was proclaiming that Oscar Wilde was "the greatest force for evil that has appeared in Europe for the last 350 years," and that his works should be destroyed. [Billing Case, *The Westminster Gazette*, 1 June 1918, p6.]

‡ For a glimpse of it at work, see: Robert I. Rotberg; Miles F. Shore, *The Founder: Cecil Rhodes And The Pursuit Of Power*, Oxford University Press, 1988, pp280-281.

One Briton they'd not spoken to was W.M. Thompson, who offered his own spirited send off:

> The decay of the better spirit in England is shown in the attempt of some of the capitalistic and Jingo journals to glorify the man who made the theft of other people's territories the mission of his life.

When four years later, Rhodes's financier Alfred Beit* joined him in death, *Reynold's* reflected on his munificent bequests that matched those of his friend, the brevity of their existences, and the existential pointlessness of their "career of aggression", which for the highly strung, shy and kindly Beit, had been conducted far from the fields of its consequences:

> Newspapers, including Liberal journals, have been singing his praises on account of his charities. Money to such a man was nothing…his money oozed blood. Was it worth it? Rhodes died a comparatively young man. Barney Barnato committed suicide, and now, at the age of fifty-three, the Park-lane magnate goes out. How many happy days have these men had in their lives? Have they had one? Did they deserve one?†

However, England's imperialist military build-up continued. As part of a campaign for peace, W.T. Stead now published the first edition of a penny paper (it ran for twelve editions), *War Against War!* He reached out to women's associations, leading to predictable jibes that the campaign's meetings were full of old women. Stead also approached notables for their endorsements. Arthur Balfour replied,

---

* Alfred Beit (1853–1906), Anglo-German Jewish gold and diamond magnate. A bachelor who lived latterly in Park Lane with his secretary and cousin, Franz Gustav Voelklein. Like Alfred de Rothschild, he allegedly fathered an illegitimate daughter, but it has been long speculated that his brotherly friendship with Rhodes may have stemmed from the affinity of a shared sexuality. According to Rhodes: "all that Beit wanted was to be rich enough to give his mother £1,000 a year." He left one of the world's greatest fortunes of over £8 million. [Raleigh Trevelyan, *Grand Dukes And Diamonds: The Werners Of Luton Hoo*, Secker & Warburg, London 1991, p59; Henning Albrecht; Christopher Watson, Neil Munro (trans.), *Albert Beit: The Hamburg Diamond King*, Hamburgische Wissenschaftliche Stiftung, 2012, pp93,95; George Seymour Fort, *Alfred Beit: A Study of the Man and His Work*, Nicholson & Watson, London 1932, p58; Alfred Beit, UK Probate 1906.]

† Once been asked if he was happy, Rhodes had replied: "Happy? I, happy? Good God, no." [Ronald Hyam, *Empire And Sexuality: The British Experience*, Manchester University Press, 1990, p39.]

writing that he thought it "worthy of universal sympathy," while Cyril offered him his "whole sympathy". Lorne proved a wet blanket, responding that preventing war would require persuading nations to be content: "This is impossible: they all have their own ambitions, and some of them are most legitimate."

In April 1902, Cyril attended the annual display at the Gymnastic Teachers' Institute in Clerkenwell; in May, he headed a dinner for the Royal Hospital for Incurables at the Hotel Métropole; and in June presided over a provisional committee working to improve rural housing and sanitation. "In some villages in Buckinghamshire," he informed them, "the people actually preferred water which they said 'tasted of ducks'".

Since Easter, those who constituted the 'Upper Ten Thousand' had been streaming into London for The Season. Given it was also a Coronation year, it promised to be especially brilliant. The date of the Coronation was fixed for June 26th, but two days prior the King's illness was diagnosed, and to national shock the ceremony was postponed. Following his successful operation, the Coronation was rescheduled for August 9th.

Cyril was President of the Coronation Committee in Battersea, which was responsible for coordinating decorations and street parties. On the 12th of July he accompanied Princess Louise and Lorne – now Duke of Argyll,* to review a march past of 25,000 children in Battersea Park.

Five days later he was again busy with philanthropic business, at a meeting of the Recreative Evening Schools Association at Surrey House. On the 25th, he was in Wales, attending Speech Day at a girls' school, at which he spoke of his support for the advancement of women, including in politics, and of his admiration for Welsh audiences who "always overlooked his weaknesses and deficiencies by their kindness and intelligence."

As we have seen, Bernard Fraser was arrested on July 28th, and Arthur Thorold soon after. Cyril undoubtedly learned of the arrests through friends almost immediately. He would have certainly been all

---

* His father the 8th Duke having died in 1900.

too aware of the blind item that appeared in *Reynolds's Newspaper* that weekend concerning "a charge against a gentleman moving in aristocratic circles".* As the investigation continued, in the first week in August further evidence came to light which ensured that Fraser was refused bail. This was presumably the disturbing knowledge of the greater parties involved. Hunstanton, one of the locales where Fraser and Thorold had sailed with the boys, sits on the Norfolk coast to the west of Overstrand and The Pleasaunce, while the other location, Wroxham, lies to the south, a mere 19 miles away. Conveniently close. And by this time, uncomfortably so. Suspiciously so.

For parliamentarians in strife, their party's Whips Office is often the first port of call, given whips deal daily with personal troubles. Helping M.P.s cover up potential scandals was routine, not only to protect the reputation of the party, but because it provided leverage with which to coerce colleagues into obedience.† A later politician, Enoch Powell, would quip: "Parliament without whips would be like a city without sewers." Whips also sought to know about the lives of their members to identify any potential issues. To this end they maintained what were termed Black Books or Dirt Books. It's possible Cyril's proclivities had already found their way into such pages. Given he'd been a whip, Cyril was well-versed in the dark arts of the Whip's Office. And given he would have dispensed favours, now was surely the time to call in debts.

The Liberal Party's Chief Whip was then Herbert Gladstone, the youngest son of the former Prime Minister. For Cyril, he was more than a useful functionary: he was a friend who'd been a guest at Aston Clinton, and at Surrey House, where he'd once resided for an entire

---

* The reference was most likely to Bernard Fraser: if there was any charge at this time against Cyril, it was probably only verbal.
† Interviewed for a 1995 BBC documentary on the Government Whips Office, Tim Fortescue, who was a Conservative whip in 1970-73, spoke of matters requiring their assistance, and its benefits: "It might be debt, it might be, um…a scandal involving small boys…And we would do everything we can [to help] because we would store up brownie points…that sounds a pretty, pretty nasty reason, but it's one of the reasons because if we can get a chap out of trouble, then he will do as we ask forever more." While this urbanely-voiced candid admission caused no particular fuss at the time, a decade of child abuse coverups later it was brought to the attention of Parliament. Its claim of the abrogation of duty by Whips, both as politicians and human beings, to report criminal abuse, and to then cover it up, *and* engage in bribery and blackmail, all in pursuit of parliamentary advantage, was by then considered worthy of comment and examination. [*Westminster's Secret Service*, BBC TV, 1995; Ken Clarke: Tory Whips Did Not Bury Child Abuse Claims Against M.P.s, *Shropshire Star*, 15 March 2019.]

season. A letter to him from Cyril survives, written in 1895 from Waddesdon, after Herbert had faced a challenge to his candidature. Full of sympathy, Cyril wrote: "how thankful I am that you have won the day. I trembled for your fate."

The leader of the Liberal Party was then the future Prime Minister, Sir Henry Campbell-Bannerman. In a speech at the annual dinner of the Eighty Club the previous year, at which Cyril had presided, 'C.B.' called him "my old friend and comrade…of many happy and jovial days that we have passed together."

In addition to the Party Leader and Chief Whip on his side, Cyril had a wizard. This was his solicitor, Sir George Lewis. The saviour of elite black sheep, Lewis was a shaman of supernatural legal powers, and of less-legal clout, who could bend reality in the courtroom and beyond it. Frederick Cunliffe-Owen described him as "a white-haired and white-whiskered little man of most kindly and genial manner, whose very appearance invites confidence and inspires trust in his discretion." However, when it came to defending his wealthy clients, such as Lord Euston during the Cleveland Street Scandal, Lewis could be deviously cunning and coldly ruthless.

Even on hot days, Sir George sported a fur coat. As Cunliffe-Owen noted, he was:

> by far the most distinguished criminal lawyer of the present day in Great Britain. It is no exaggeration to assert that there has been no sensational case brought into court in the last five and thirty years in which Sir George has not figured, usually on the winning side, while as for the cases this shrewd and discreet knight has kept out of court, they are simply legion in number.

Given his illustrious career, Lewis was:

> popularly declared to know now enough to hang half a dozen of the biggest men in the city of London and to possess a sufficient number of dangerous secrets of people of rank to suffice, if they should ever be divulged, to shatter the entire social fabric of Great Britain.

While he appeared the summit of respectability, Lewis's very success rested on the fact he was prepared to play outside the rules to win – a lesson learnt early as a Semitic outsider. "He kept a central clearing-house for family scandals and skeletons, and could cancel one against the other with calculated precision." Lewis also maintained a famed network of contacts, including amongst London's low-life – what one source termed "a spider's web of narks and informers". For Cunliffe-Owen:

> One curious drawback to the celebrity of this extraordinary little Jew is the fact that his presence in court on behalf of a client is in nine cases of out of ten regarded as a kind of admission of the latter's guilt. For Sir George enjoys such fame for his ability to get his clients out of the most disgraceful situations that he is certain to be applied to for assistance whenever a man of any prominence finds himself in the mire…no matter how terrible the straits in which his client may have involved himself, Sir George can usually find a means of issue. If his client's guilt is sufficiently assured to admit no defence or excuse, Sir George usually possesses the knowledge of some skeleton in the cupboard of the other side of the case, and so brings about an abandonment of the prosecution.

The London office of Lewis and Lewis was located in Ely Place, a quiet backwater in Holborn, and was actually the house in which Sir George had been born. As another report described:

> It might be taken from its outward appearance as the Georgian residence of some city magnate, with its old-fashioned front door and certain air of dinginess. Inside all is quiet and formal. There is a sort of little wicket behind which stands an impressive looking man whose manner is as elegant as his frock coat. He is the major domo…There is no rush about the method of business. The visitor's name is written on a slip of paper, and a young man with an Oxford accent carries it upstairs. Presently you are ushered through a mysterious passage to a somewhat dingy waiting room, where another young man, with a Cambridge accent, gazes mildly at you over the bulwarks of a typewriter and says pleasant things while Sir George or Mr. George is dealing with another caller inside. A little bell tinkles and you are ushered within.

In that room Sir George has been in the habit of sitting morning after morning at a big Sheraton desk, with his fur coat, carefully folded, reposing on the back of his own particular armchair, his umbrella leaning on one arm of the chair and silk hat, brim upward, on the Turkish carpet. Then, with his finger tips pressed together, he would discuss the newcomer's case, invariably first taking the gloomiest side of the matter, pointing out its myriad flaws and pitfalls, until the client was prepared to give up utterly. Then, with a swing of the chair, he would utter a few illuminating phrases showing how these pitfalls and flaws could be vanquished, and five minutes later the client would be walking on air down Ely place.

Cyril's legal counseling may have taken a far cosier route. Conveniently, Sir George maintained an exquisite seaside home whose estate adjoined that of The Pleasaunce, and which could be accessed via a gate in its wall. Formerly the Danish pavilion at the 1900 Paris Exposition, it was rebuilt at Overstrand on four acres of gardens stretching to the cliff edge.* Whether Cyril visited Sir George's musty office or his ozonic drawing room, it's unlikely he'd felt very comforted upon departure. The situation he found himself in was far too grave.

When the Cleveland Street Scandal had arisen in 1889, several papers referred to it as 'The Nameless Scandal'. *The Star* newspaper informed its readers:

As we have said over and over again, we would rather have no light on this business…Some things are of the night and death, and we would rather keep them there. But as the light has come in, half-lights are worse than full light, and it is this which the public demands.

Night and death. It was no exaggeration. A stray or searching light falling upon desires such as Cyril's meant being cast forever into the utter darkness of social annihilation.

As he turned over the events in his mind, he must have wondered how his red carpet life had come to this. Only the previous year, a

---

* Both the house (which was damaged by a fire in 1951), and estate have been replaced by bungalows. A road, Danish House Gardens, marks the site.

magazine profile had cooed: "Lord Battersea touches life at many points, and contrives to find pleasure in all." And so he had. Fantastical yet practical, grand-gestured and generous, he'd sought to share his more private pleasures with a confederacy of friends. The ideal of a homosocial Whitmanesque brotherhood had likely infused his life. Whitman's own notebooks are littered with the scribbled names of working class men and youths, and notations of when he slept with them.* For Whitman, cruising the streets was democracy at its finest and most inspirational. Plutocratic procuring was something of a different order. But as always, Cyril was the host-with-the-most. Organising procurement through gentlemen of his own class had provided two protections: the first, against the waking nightmare of blackmailers, and the second, against what these friends would have believed was a deeply hypocritical society – one that knelt before the altar of Hellenism, while excoriating its sexuality.

Since childhood Cyril and his friends had been steeped in the Classics, and as adults, swooned in the vernal embraces of the Mediterranean. Daily they walked in the footsteps of the mentors of antiquity. Indeed, the busts of those who sanctified a mentoring pederasty lined the very walls of their schools, clubs and libraries. As the verses of *Don Leon* challenged:

> I love a youth; but Horace did the same;
> If he's absolv'd, say, why am I to blame?
> When young Alexis claimed a Virgil's sigh,
> He told the world his choice; and may not I?
>
> Shall every schoolman's pen his verse extol,
> And, sin in me, in him a weakness call?
> Then why was Socrates surnamed the sage,
> Not only in his own, but every age,
> If lips, whose accents strewed the path of truth,
> Could print their kisses on some favoured youth?

---

* e.g.: "Hugh Harrop boy 17 fresh Irish wool sorter…Robt Wolf, boy of 10 or 12 rough at the ferry lives cor 4th & Market…Wm Culver, boy in bath, aged 18 (gone to California '56)…Dan'l Spencer…somewhat feminine…slept with me Sept 3d…David Wilson – night of Oct. 11, '62, walking up from Middagh – slept with me…works in blacksmith shop…is about 19…Horace Ostrander…about 28 yr's of age…slept with him Dec. 4th '62." [Walt Whitman, William White (ed.) *The Collected Writings Of Walt Whitman: Volume I: Daybooks, 1876-November 1881*, pp2, 171; Walt Whitman, Edward F. Grier (ed.) *The Collected Writings Of Walt Whitman: Volume II: Washington*, New York University Press, 1984, pp481,487,496,497.]

Or why should Plato, in his Commonwealth
Score tenets up which I must note by stealth?

Undoubtedly the group saw themselves as the very embodiment of the enlightened elect – with the added blessings of golf. Like the pages of drawing room magazines that advertised gentleman's fur-lined astrakhan coats and other choice fancies for the discriminating, so a spiel for Cyril's circle might have read: 'Discreet introductions to lithe lads, facilitated by the gentry'. It was a parallel, upper class world: less lined with placid marble busts perhaps, than panting, tobacco-breathed, middle-aged geezers. But one that must have seemed to them a safe haven of sensual sanity.

And now suddenly, like the end of a dream, an awakening cry of 'Police!' had evaporated the pathway to this Elysium, replacing it with the gate-rattling moral demands of the modern Edwardian world. Cyril was now guilty of the only sin its high society really cared about — he had been found out.

Four years previously, a popular three-volume review of law enforcement had been published – *Mysteries Of Police And Crime: a general survey of wrongdoing and its pursuit*. Cyril's bookplate graces a surviving set; one that had possibly been idly contemplated by The Pleasaunce fireside. Now for its owner the subject matter was more than a mere hypothetical.

On August 9th, a warm day with some light showers, the Batterseas attended the Coronation in their new peers' robes. A studio photograph shows Cyril resembled a berobed pouter pigeon in silk breeches. Indeed, he was now sometimes mistaken for the King himself. As Edward's nickname, when out of earshot, was 'Tum-Tum', it would hardly have been elevating.

Being a new peer, and given his love of spectacle, attending the Coronation would normally have been a life pinnacle for Cyril. However, like Lord Henry Somerset seated nearby, his enjoyment of the day would have been poisoned by the dread that his entire world was about to collapse.

Unaware of the brewing storm, Constance blithely shared with her diary the events in the Abbey: "In spite of the long hours of waiting

I was neither tired nor exhausted…I fully enjoyed the day – to me it was inspiring as well as interesting". She also observed, "The King was at his best…He looked proud, touched, humble," before adding ruefully, perhaps thinking of her husband: "If only the monarch could remain at the very best, if only he never deviated from the high & lofty conception of what his life ought to be."

The magazine *Vanity Fair* observed: "It was quite curious to see the rush out of London the moment the Coronation was over." Belgravia and Mayfair once again became out-of-season ghost towns: "the blinds were down in most of the houses, and the humming streets were empty of all but luggage-laden cabs and omnibuses."

Two days later, the new Home Secretary, Aretas Akers-Douglas, kissed hands with the King and attended his first Privy Council meeting. In early September he was a guest at Balmoral for a week, attending another Privy Council, and spending a day with the King driving deer in Ballochbuie Forest. In December, he stayed at Sandringham, where the other guests included Cyril's friends, the Lords Esher and Rosebery. It's likely Cyril's situation was discussed at one or more of these occasions.

Thorold and Fraser's final court hearing was on August 16th. The following day, Lord Ronald Gower wrote in his diary:

> Weather fine & occasionally almost hot; the papers still full of the coronation & little else. I had an interesting letter from Lorne about it. Neither of us in good spirits – both have colds & both seem to feel the weariness of the world & its fardels.*

Like Julia Frankau's characters, they may have felt they were witnessing more crucifixions.

At The Pleasaunce the guests continued to arrive. In early August came Raymond Asquith (on his second visit for the year), Leopold de Rothschild and his wife Marie; Lady Dorothy Nevill, and Gerald Balfour. In late August there arrived Louise Creighton, the friend of Constance who was co-founder of the National Union of Women Workers, plus a clutch of bachelors who were Cyril's chums.

---

* Fardels: wearying burdens.

The first of these gentlemen was Lieutenant-Colonel Arthur Collins,* a courtier with a special link to both Cyril's dear friend Lorne, the Duke of Argyll, and his wife Princess Louise. Collins was Louise's Equerry and Comptroller, and as he'd been for Queen Victoria, also a Gentleman Usher to the King. Not least, he was a brother of Sir Robert Hawthorn Collins, who'd been an intimate friend of Frederic Myers, and who was Comptroller, and former tutor, to Prince Leopold. While Sir Robert had an expressed appreciation of young men, Arthur Collins was fond of boys: deeply concerned for their welfare, and keenly involved in philanthropic efforts that supported them. Pasted into his private scrapbook were sentimental poems hallowing them. When in 1899, Arthur had shown Cyril a handpainted Christmas card he'd received from the twelve year old artistic prodigy Brian Hatton,† with typical generosity, Cyril had promptly lent the boy his volume of reproductions of Windsor Castle's Rembrandt and Vandyke drawings.

Arthur Collins was also a director of that most dynamic startup – the District Messenger Company! With hundreds of England's most strapping and trustworthy lads on its payroll, for their admirers it must have seemed like the Niagara of wet dreams. One that was on tap via the mere press of a household electric call button. With such a covetable connection, and his own pleasing character, it's no wonder Arthur was popular. Whether he provided a private conduit to the Company's impressive personal resources is an unanswerable question. However, the mistranscription in one instance of Albert Collins's name on the indictment as 'Arthur Collins' may well be a Freudian Slip.

The Visitors Book shows that Arthur Collins stayed from August 23rd to the 28th. Mid-way through his visit, on the 25th, two other guests turned up for the day: the then Earl of Sandwich,‡ who maintained a home for disadvantaged boys, and an obscure Cambridge-educated preparatory schoolmaster. On a previous visit in 1897, this gentleman had penned his name in the Visitor's Book as F.A.H. Walsh,§ but he now wrote it more familiarly as Frank Walsh.

---

* Lieutenant-Colonel Arthur Collins (1845–1911).
† Brian Hatton (1887–1916). Col. Collins was a close friend and patron.
‡ Edward George Henry Montagu, 8th Earl of Sandwich (1839–1916), Conservative M.P.
§ Francis 'Frank' Alfred Hugh Walsh (1867–1950). His posts included Aysgarth School, North

Also arriving on the 25th and staying until September 1st was Augustus Hare. The author of *Cities Of Southern Italy and Sicily*, and other guidebooks and memoirs, Hare was a raconteur, and fastidious old maid, who was fond of fine living, travel, aristocrats, and not least young men, for whom his country house Holmhurst was, he believed, "the haven of their lives."

These guests of Cyril could well have been delegates to a youth welfare conference, and in a way, perhaps they were; although now in the light of circumstances, it would have been a fraught one.

On the 29th, Cyril and Constance hosted a charity fete: Constance's Coronation robe was on view for 3d admission, while amongst the fancy goods available in the stalls were photos of the hosts; a local paper noting: "some of his lordship in his Coronation robe finding a speedy sale." The following day, Cyril clocked up another birthday. Acknowledging his early career, the *Bucks Herald* printed:

> Mr. Cyril Flower, as he then was, sat in the House of Commons for a dozen years or more, and was reputed the handsomest man in that assemblage. He is still a strikingly good-looking one, and wears his nine-and-fifty years very lightly.

On the 11th of September, the Batterseas hosted a house party at Overstand that involved a two-day cricket match, and another fete. Typically, Constance's guests included one of her supporters on the National Union of Women Workers, while Cyril's guest list featured a famous golfing champion, Harry Vardon,[*] with whom he could tee off. Two other guests were Alfred and Charles Tennyson,[†] grandsons of the Poet Laureate, whose verse had resonated so deeply with Cyril and his circle those many years past.

In October, Cyril delivered two further speeches against the pending Education Bill. At the first, in Liverpool, he appealed for the Liberal Party to unite against the legislation and put its policy disputes aside,

---

Yorkshire, and Orley Farm School, Harrow. [UK Census 1911: Patrick Brompton and Newton le Willows; *The Schoolmasters' Yearbook & Educational Directory*, Vol 13, 1915, Year Book Press, p74.]

[*] Henry William Vardon (1870–1937). Married Jessie Bryant; no issue.

[†] Alfred Browning Stanley Tennyson, (1878–1952), poet and civil servant; Sir Charles Bruce Locker Tennyson (1879–1977), industrialist and scholar; sons of the Hon. Lionel and Emily Tennyson.

particularly "now that the war which was the cause of those divisions had come to an end." He added: "Wild horses will not drag from me whether I am a pro-Boer or an anti-Boer, whether I am a pro-War or an anti-War"...what he believed in was "the superiority of Liberal principles." His nemesis the *Luton Times* (now retitled the *Bedfordshire Advertiser*), pounced on this spineless reticence: "He refuses to reveal his opinions on the great question of the day, yet continues to pose as a leader of political thought."

Cyril's second speech on the Education Bill was given in his old constituency of Luton, and the paper was waiting for him, admitting in a subhead, 'Lord Battersea In Great Form'. Opening his speech, Cyril jested that: "When he came to Luton, the first thing he asked for was a copy of the *Luton Times*...He knew that paper of old (laughter); it was always spicey [*sic*]." He went on to accuse it of being restrained with the truth when it came to political opponents. To its credit the paper printed his comments, stating they had been received by the audience with "great merriment".

Cyril went on to say that the proposed Education Act: "did more to set up sectarian strife than any other Bill which could have been invented by the Evil One." It was reported this drew from an audience a collective "Oh" and laughter. The newspaper couldn't allow Cyril's performance to pass completely untarnished. It also featured a report captioned 'By One Who Was There', which laid on the snark with a trowel:

> On Tuesday night [at] Plait Hall the cork was drawn out of the Liberal ginger-beer bottle, and once more the fiz oozed away...What could have drawn the sweet Liberal women out in such force on Tuesday night? To hear the speeches? Fiddlesticks! The way in which they gazed on dear Lord Battersea all the night was most amusing; there was not a gesture, a movement, or a smile about his lordship which escaped their rapt gaze. But then 'dear Cyril' was always considered to be the Parliamentary Adonis, and never were his charms more deadly than when kissing the babies of his former constituents, and distributing £5 notes at chapel tea-meetings. And then, when the meeting was over dozens of these otherwise stern Liberal Women made a dash for the platform, tumbling over each other's toes in their haste to get into the serene presence of Lord Battersea, now that

the gas had evaporated. His lordship was fairly besieged, and must be pardoned if he immediately capitulated to their winning smiles and graceful courtesies that would have done credit to a French countess. There were handshakes and other little pleasantries, and when the noble-looking Battersea bowed or beamed his fair admirers all but became overpowered at the soothing influence of the South London nabob.

Despite intense opposition to the Education Bill, including that of Cyril's friend Lorne, the Duke of Argyll, who voted against it in the House of Lords, it was passed at the end of the year. This proved a political disaster for the Conservative Party who lost massively in the 1906 General Election. However, by standardising and upgrading the educational systems of England and Wales, it led to a rapid growth of secondary schools. It also ensured that denominational schools met mandated standards, and had the funds required to deliver them — albeit from local ratepayers.

The day following the Luton meeting, Cyril went to Aston Clinton. Constance noted in her diary on the subsequent days: "Cyril came down looking ill," "Cyril has cold," "Cyril left". The weather now became unsettled. London was wrapped in a pall described as "between a Scotch mist and Donegal downpour, accompanied by darkness Cimmerian in its intensity." This was primarily due to what was termed "the smoke nuisance".

In the middle of October the King returned to London, following a lengthy holiday and northern tour. Given the procession of the delayed Coronation had been "shorn of its amplitude of splendor," as befitting a King-Emperor, it was decided he would now make a grand progress through the streets with 30,000 troops and fresh decorations. These included triumphal arches, the most imposing of all being erected by the Freemasons. The unfettered imperial jingoism no doubt caused Labouchère's ill-fitting false teeth to be subject to a further round of grinding.

On the 13th of October, Constance and Cyril attended a protest meeting organised by the Women's Local Government Society to object to The Education Bill's discrimination against women. (Unlike the existing school boards, women could not be elected to the local councils the Bill mandated to henceforth administer schools.)

Constance delivered a speech and Cyril read "a letter of eloquent protest" from the rabbi of the West End Synagogue. Two days later, a popular Society magazine, *The Sketch*, featured an article on Aston Clinton, as part of a series 'Beautiful Homes And Their Owners'. It saluted the Batterseas for their endless generosity, stating:

> They are among those whom the nation should delight to honour, for they have done all in their power to make happier and better the many large circles of human beings with whom they are brought in contact.

On the 20th, two wealthy bachelors arrived at The Pleasaunce for a short visit. The first, Arnold Morley, Liberal M.P. and former fellow Whip, perhaps came with some Black Book advice, as well as sympathy. The second, Arthur Brown* hailed from a Quaker family of timber millers, and was a keen sportsman and motoring enthusiast. Perhaps the two men also came as worried suspects.

The Sportsman paper noted that Harry Vardon was also due to motor down to Overstrand in Cyril's car for another tee-off. With the trial of Thorold and Fraser set for October 31st, Cyril may have hoped that some swings of the clubs in the sea air would help clear his head. As well as being fearful for himself, he was surely wracked with guilt over their scapegoating. That the circumstances and options were chewed seems a certainty. If Cyril continued to manifest a placid lordly exterior, inwardly he was surely a roiling ocean of stress. The emotional storm precipitated a physical breakdown. It was influenza that took advantage of it.

During this time, Constance had been at Aston Clinton. However, she was now away in Edinburgh, at the annual conference of the National Union of Women Workers, of which she was President. One journalist noted: "Lady Battersea's priceless pearls, perfect sables and clouds of antique lace were not entirely lost upon the members". In her address to the assembled ladies, she cautioned them:

> women, because they become so desperately in earnest about their work and have less distractions in the way of recreation, society, physical exercise, and the like, than men, must bear being

---

* Arthur Brown (1871–1938), of timber millers Henry Brown & Sons.

occasionally called 'tiresome' by their male fellow workers. But this may be an unwilling tribute to the thoroughness and excellency of their work; perhaps when they have gained the sense of proportion, and also a keener sense of humour...they will add some of the larger views and lighter touches of the male workers to their own estimable qualities.

The Times noted that this sentiment was received with cheers. Two days later, Constance was re-elected President. The following day, the trial day of October 31st, a blacked out but still legible passage in her diary records: "On Friday, disconcerting news of Cyril, felt nervous, anxious, uncomfortable. Went foolishly to Dalmeny."

Dalmeny was Lord Rosebery's stately seat just west of Edinburgh on the Firth of Forth. He was due to give a major public speech to Liberal supporters on the Saturday, and Constance may have had a long-standing invitation to stay with him. However, it's possible the visit was a sudden one to seek advice and succour. In her diary, in a section titled 'Hasty Review of 1902', Constance writes of this day: "Dalmeny – A fiasco from beginning to end. Heard of Cyril's illness." As she'd already received the "disconcerting news of Cyril" before departing for Dalmeny, the earlier news surely concerned his arrest.

If the newspaper reports are accurate, immediately following the trial, the police had finally made their move, and following his arrest, Cyril was released on bail of £5,000. Given he was by then ailing, it would have been an even more gruelling experience.

During the Cleveland Street Scandal of 1889, the issuing of Lord Arthur Somerset's arrest warrant was delayed by an unequal tug of war between the Metropolitan Police and Department of Public Prosecutions on one side, who considered the arrest a straightforward application of the law, while the Prime Minister, the Prince of Wales and their facilitators, who held more exalted and self-righteous concerns, considered it deeply undesirable. It's very possible a similar delay occurred in bringing Cyril to account.

The prosecution timelines of both cases were certainly parallel: the initial discoveries were made in July; the committal hearings for the small fry took place in August, and it was not until late autumn that legal action was finally taken against the big fish of Lord Arthur, and thirteen years on, Cyril Flower.

Whatever unfolded behind the scenes with Cyril's and the police, the newspaper which printed: "steps were taken to prevent the matter coming to the knowledge of the Press," was dead on the mark. While the Government decided what to do with him, Cyril was left to stew.

On Saturday, the 1st of November,* Constance attended Rosebery's public speech, but told her diary: "disappointed probably because I was not in tune with surroundings." Cyril's condition, as she informed her diary, had also deteriorated: "News still more disconcerting, resolved to return that night." She set out for London on the evening mail train. The following morning, the Society physician Manley Sims joined her for the final leg of the journey to Overstrand. She now confessed to her diary: "Terrified." As she went on to detail, the scene that presented itself at Overstrand was indeed distressing:

> Cyril seriously ill, congestion of the lungs. [The following sentence blacked out but legible.] He never opened his eyes, spoke to me, or looked at me – still glad to be here. Two excellent nurses in attendance.

Perhaps he was sleeping. However, that Constance or one of her executors blacked out part of the passage may indicate that Cyril's non-response was thought to be less due to illness, than a shame that could not be voiced in the presence of staff. With Cyril's lungs congested, the following day Sims diagnosed bronchial pneumonia.

That Sunday of Constance's return, the faint smattering of stories alleging the arrest of a peer broke in the press. The news leak may have come from within the Metropolitan Police. During the Cleveland Street Scandal, the Prince of Wales's Comptroller and Treasurer, Sir Dighton Probyn, was incensed to discover that Scotland Yard inspectors had shared details of the case with Society gentlemen, and further, that the detective in charge of the case, Frederick Abberline – fed up with the obstruction of justice by higher powers – had gone to *The Pall Mall Gazette*. Perhaps Inspector Arrow

---

* A few newspapers later reported that Cyril was amongst the M.P.s present at a Liberal Party public meeting against the Education Bill held that afternoon. This was almost certainly a reporting error that relied on a list of attendees that had been issued prior to the event. [The Alexandra Palace Demonstration, *The Westminster Gazette*, 1 November 1902, p6.]

402

or his colleagues were motivated to offer a similar tip-off.

A statement on Cyril's illness was now provided to the Press Association. This could only have been issued with Constance's authorisation. Publicly announcing Cyril's illness seems like an attempt to dampen the rising scuttlebutt. If so, the ploy wasn't successful.

Five days later, with Cyril still very ill, another statement was issued, informing that: "Lord Battersea, acting under the doctor's advice, will be unable to fulfil any public engagement for some time to come." The Sunday weekly *The People* featured it on its front page. The reports fuelled false speculation that the illness was just a cover story for a hurried flight to the Continent, in the manner of so many previous miscreants.

On the 7th, Lord Ronald Gower recorded in his diary that "Lorne i.e. Argyll – had telegraphed early that he would come down [to Hammerfield, the country house of Gower and his adopted son and partner Frank Hird*] & and he appeared soon after 2". Lorne stayed the night. There was certainly much to discuss.

By the 7th of November the worst of Cyril's illness was over. However, his brother Lewis had died following a fall from a horse: a broken rib penetrating one of his lungs. The news had been kept from Cyril, but with his health improved he was now informed. Wrote Constance: "It was horrible – I felt knocked up afterwards – Cyril remained quiet by himself all the evening." Constance also noted that Dr. Sims had travelled down from London, "6 times in all, terrible extravagance". As physician to the Duke of Cambridge, Sims' charges were no doubt usurious, but a Rothschild daughter troubled by a doctor's bill seems bizarre, particularly when it concerned her husband's life.†

The 22nd of November was the Battersea's Silver Wedding Anniversary. The irony would have been deeply felt. Constance's diary records: "an extraordinary day, spent in an extraordinary manner...Lovely gifts...felt greatly touched by so much

---

* (Robert) Francis Hird, (1873–1937), journalist and author.
† Perhaps Constance never received the bill. Sims dropped dead of a heart attack the following month. [The Death Roll, *The St. James Gazette*, 10 December 1902, p17.]

kindness...Cyril was tired & could not enjoy it all." She also noted:

> Cyril is getting better – he is near convalescence, if not quite convalescent – His lungs are healing. He has been seriously ill, if not dangerously, but at any moment it might have become dangerous – I have had a very anxious time – And I have thrown myself into the force of events. I have looked the situation in the face, not only for the present but also for the future.

The 'situation' was more than just Cyril's illness: it was the state of their marriage.

That same November another grandee was brought down, with the death (allegedly from stroke, but possibly suicide) of the German steel magnate Friedrich Krupp, following reports by the Socialist paper *Vorwärts* of his liaisons with boys on Capri.* With Krupp's homes in Essen and Capri draped with black crepe, the Kaiser declared that Krupp was a man of "delicate and sensitive nature...who lived always only for others, and always had in view solely the welfare of the Fatherland, and, above all, of his own workmen." Despite this, he "had his honour assailed".

Refuting the allegations, the Kaiser summed them up as "nothing less than murder". In England, most newspapers treated the affair with propriety: referring only to slanders of 'gross immorality' and 'orgies', 'unnatural offences', or simply 'offences'. A notable exception to this was *Reynolds's Newspaper*, which quoted German and French newspaper reports, as it did on the 30th when it printed: "Whatever pity one might feel, explains the *Vorwärts*, for the victim of the mania *homosexualis*, this pity is mitigated when the vice is able to command millions for the purpose of its gratification." In London, Society would be distracted before Christmas by another messy divorce case: that of a baronet Sir Charles Cradock-Hartopp, who it was rumoured, had racked up a princely £30,000 in legal fees alone.

On the 9th of December it was reported that Lord Battersea was: "able to leave his bed for some hours each day. It will be some time before he can go out of doors". At the end of the month a more

---

* Norman Douglas considered the accusations false, but the evidence was damning. [Norman Douglas, *Looking Back : An Autobiographical Excursion*, Harcourt Brace, New York 1933, p157; William Manchester, *The Arms Of Krupp*, Little Brown & Company, Boston 1968, pp228-232.]

intimate report was published:

> A friend who is spending Christmas at Overstrand tells me that Lord Battersea is progressing satisfactorily. The bronchial symptoms, however, are still very pronounced, and he is troubled with a distressing cough... my friend, who saw him for a short time the other day, says the long illness has greatly pulled him down.

As Cyril gasped for breath, his illness gave those in authority additional time to consider his fate. Yet while social position, including being a member of Parliament, had never guaranteed immunity from prosecution for homosexual offences,* there was a constellation of reasons why, unlike like Fraser and Thorold, jail for Cyril Flower and his glittering friends was considered a step too far. And they went far beyond the concerns of Lord Halsbury and others for quarantining sordid narratives.

Aside from Cyril's political career, social prominence and wealth, there was his long commitment to philanthropy and improvements in education, housing and healthcare on behalf of the working classes. His looks, charm and bonhomie also ensured that Cyril was widely liked for himself, including on both sides of Parliament. He maintained friendships across Society, from King Edward and Queen Alexandra, and courtiers such as Sir Dighton Probyn, downwards. In short: he was ringfenced by power. The bastions of the Whip's Office and Sir George Lewis constituted the mere outer defences.

As for King Edward: he and Cyril were very different, yet strikingly similar. Both were cosmopolitan hedonists, with frustrated wives who deeply admired their husbands, but with whom they shared little in common. Both were born commanders and diplomatic pragmatists. Mutual respect to some degree there would have been. The King

---

* Possibly the most famous case involved M.P. William Bankes (1786–1855), who was committed to trial in 1833, charged with indecent behaviour with a soldier, James Flower, in a urinal outside Parliament – as the charge evocatively phrased it: "exciting each other to commit an unnatural offence." Bankes' denial of the charge and his excellent personal references enabled a judgement of innocence. However, in 1841, Bankes was again arrested with a guardsman, this time in Green Park. Forfeiting a £5,000 bond, he fled the country, retiring to Venice, from whence he shipped back art and antiques to enhance his country house, Kingston Lacy, for the sole benefit of his heirs. [Court Of King's Bench, *The Morning Chronicle*, 3 December 1833, p2.]

would also have been well-aware of Cyril's good works. Edward was patron of the Metropolitan Hospital in the East End, of which Cyril was, together with Leopold de Rothschild, a Treasurer. As Prince of Wales, Edward had been President of the South London Polytechnic Committee, and had laid the foundation stone of the Battersea Polytechnic Institute of which Cyril was a governor; Edward also opened the building upon its completion.

Equally important was Cyril's closeness to the Prime Minister, Arthur Balfour, with whom he shared so many sympathetic gentlemen friends in the Society for Psychical Research. He and Balfour had been Edmund Gurney's last dining companions. Indeed the closer one examines the Society, with its significant homosexual leadership, the more the sensitivity of the connection becomes apparent. As a former President of the Society, Balfour would have been politically vulnerable to any scandal that touched its members.

A further example of Cyril's social interconnections was the fact that, three years previously, Balfour had officially opened an additional hall of the Battersea Polytechnic Institute, which Cyril and Constance continued to fundraise for. Balfour's Private Secretary, Sir Bernard Mallet,* was a regular guest at The Pleasaunce with his wife.

Another bulwark of support for Cyril would have been his fellow liberal politician and friend Lord Suffield, who was also one of the King's closest friends, and a near neighbour at Gunton Park, Cromer. Cyril was also a stalwart of the powerful Eighty Club. Liberal Party pillar Herbert Asquith, whose career he'd fostered (and who, when Home Secretary, had authorised Oscar Wilde's arrest warrant), had been, with his family, a guest at Overstrand many times. There was also wide respect and sympathy for Constance, who was a role model of public duty in the service of temperance and assistance to 'fallen women'. What message would it send as to the efficacy of abstinence if her husband was revealed to be the ringleader of a homosexual procurement network?

Constance was a close friend of Princess Louise. First and foremost, she was also a Rothschild. Of course the latter connection, and the

---

* Sir Bernard Mallet (1859–1932), civil servant and Privy Counsellor. Married Marie Adeane. Son of Sir Louis Mallet, and brother of Sir Louis du Pan Mallet (see later Reginald Lister footnote.)

smothering of the case, plays perfectly for conspiracy theorists who view that family as great puppetmasters. Nonetheless, it was no small matter that the King was in debt to Constance's uncle Natty, Lord Rothschild, for the truly colossal sum of £160,000* – which was secured against the deeds of Sandringham no less: a deeply buried transaction with the weight of a state secret. Money talks, but vast wealth doesn't need to: its expectations are heeded.

It wasn't just the King whom the Rothschilds had in their pocket. One member of the family, Dorothy de Rothschild,† recalled: "As a child I thought Lord Rothschild *lived* at the Foreign Office, because from my classroom window I used to watch his carriage standing outside every afternoon – while of course he was closeted with Arthur Balfour."‡

Cyril's Rothschildian links extended beyond that of marriage. He was, for example, a director of the large insurance concern The Imperial Fire Office, whose chairman was again Lord Rothschild. There may have been legitimate concerns that exposing Cyril could smear the Anglo-Jewish community, and risk upsetting those within it, such as Edward's financial adviser Sir Ernest Cassel.

Lastly, there was the enormous risk such an outcome would damage the reputation of other gentlemen of consequence. In 1883, the Conservative M.P. Lord George Hamilton§ had concluded a public speech by half-jesting to his audience: "the effeminate men and the masculine women had all rushed into the Liberal Party."

As previously noted, during the Wilde trials the Liberal Government was bedevilled by the rumour that the Marquess of Queensberry would expose some of its most senior members as homosexual.**

---

* The equivalent of at least £16 million in 2018. [measuringworth.com]
† Dorothy Mathilde de Rothschild, née Pinto (1895–1988), philanthropist and activist for Jewish affairs; married her cousin James Armand de Rothschild.
‡ In December 1916, Balfour was appointed Foreign Secretary.
§ Lord George Hamilton (1845–1927), Conservative M.P., First Lord of the Admiralty and Secretary of State for India; son of the 1st Duke of Abercorn. Married Lady Maud Lascelles, and had issue.
** Lord Alfred Douglas wrote for a French magazine: "The fact is that the Liberal party then contained a large number of men whom I have referred to as the salt of the earth [i.e. homosexual]. The maniacs of virtue threatened a series of legal actions which would have created an unprecedented scandal in political circles. If Oscar Wilde was found guilty the matter would be hushed up." [H. Montgomery Hyde, *The Trials Of Oscar Wilde*, William Hoder

Indeed, the links between Liberal politics and homosexuality were as strong as those between the latter and High-Churchism.* Certainly, the likely suspects involved in the Battersea scandal suggest it was preeminently a scandal of the Liberal Party.

One such personage, whom it can be comfortably assumed was involved, was the M.P. Lewis 'Loulou' Harcourt. Possessing boundless charm and a caressing voice, his reputation as a sexual predator of the young of both genders was well-known to Society. Eton schoolboys were warned by their parents never to engage in solitary walks with either Harcourt or Reginald Brett (Lord Esher).

In February that year, Cyril and Constance, together with 800 other guests, attended an evening reception for members of the Eighty Club and Liberal supporters hosted by Harcourt and his wife. "The turquoises and diamonds, which Mrs. Lewis Harcourt wore at her Eighty Club party," noted a press report, "once formed part of the Crown jewels of France."

A series of undated letters from Cyril to Harcourt reveal how close their friendship was. In one, Cyril writes:

> When will you come back & see us…Visit was not a visit do come & bring any one you like male or female. I thought Smith† looked a real nice fellow bring him or any pal and get out of asphyxiating stinky London.‡

In another letter Cyril shares the news that he is off to Spain, and implores Harcourt to join him, writing, "I will keep a berth in the 'Garland' for you. Do come." A third letter, written from The

& Co. Ltd., London 1958, p364.]

* As demonstrated by the Oxford Movement and its followers.

† Possibly a Lionel Smith, whose signature appears in The Visitors Book of The Pleasaunce in early August 1902.

‡ The beginning of this letter penned on Aston Clinton letterhead, which only bears the date of 'November 24', and which is marked 'Very Private', hints at an unknown crisis involving Lewis's father, Sir William Harcourt, who died in 1904. Cyril writes: Dear Lulu 1st I hope you are fit again. 2nd I hope you meant that y[ou]r father w[oul]d like to meet Buckle [George Buckle, editor of The Times] after all it is not a tête-à-tête, read the enclosed & return it – If you approve of my answer post it. If not correct it. I have tried to get Etty [Ethel Grenfell, Baroness Desborough], Charlotte [de Rothschild], [Princess] Louise! to meet Sir W[illia]m all in vain who can I get we are in despair. If there is a man or woman he wants to talk to do like a good fellow lend me a line that we may try to get them." [MS. Harcourt 452, fol. 148, Bodleian Library.]

Pleasaunce, conveys the wish, "I long to show you my little 'ome here". Harcourt was also one of the friends who posed for Cyril for his photographic studies, as had Harcourt's confirmed-bachelor groomsman, Regie Lister.*

Another signature that appears twice in The Pleasaunce Visitor's Book, alongside that of his wife, is 'Portsmouth'. This was Newton Wallop,† who was a Liberal and Liberal Unionist member of Parliament before succeeding as 6th Earl of Portsmouth, and served as Under-Secretary of State for War in Sir Henry Campbell-Bannerman's government. When he died in 1917, George Ives noted in his diary: "He had the same tastes as Lord Battersea, but I don't know that he ever got into trouble as Lord B. did."

Besides sexuality and Liberal politics, the common threads in Cyril's male friendships included a fascination with psychical phenomena, and a passion for cricket and golf. Amongst the most regularly appearing signatures in The Pleasaunce Visitors Book are those of four bachelors who shared these enthusiasms, and are obviously amongst his closest friends.

The first name is that of Spencer Lyttelton, the brusque but kind-hearted former private secretary to Prime Minister Gladstone. A keen sportsman and music lover, in the fine close weave that constituted the British upper class, Arthur Balfour was his cousin. On one

---

* Sir Reginald Lister (1865–1912), diplomat; third son of the 3rd Baron Ribblesdale. (His nickname is occasionally spelt 'Reggie'.) Renowned for his irresistible charm and rollicking infectious enthusiasm for life, according to Maurice Baring: "I never saw anyone either before or after who could make such a difference to his surroundings and to the company he was with. He made everything effervesce." Possibly immune to his charm were children. One toddler bore a lifetime grudge against him after hearing him describe her as "a nice little thing a pity she dresses so badly". One of his lovers was likely E.F. Benson. He died at just forty-seven of malaria contracted at Venice. A memorial fountain in Sir Reginald Lister Square still survives at Tangier, his last diplomatic posting. He bequeathed the house he owned in Venice to fellow bachelor diplomat Sir Louis du Pan Mallet (1864–1936), who served as British ambassador to Constantinople in 1914, and after retirement, lived with the young homosexual magnate Sir Philip Sassoon. At his death, Mallet left a large legacy to his married manservant. [Maurice Baring, *The Puppet Show Of Memory*, William Heinemann, London 1922, p118-119; Annabel Goff, *Walled Gardens: Scenes from an Anglo-Irish Childhood*, Barrie & Jenkins, 1990, p149; E.F. Benson, *Our Family Affairs, 1867-1896*, Cassell and Company, London 1920, pp314-316 ;Sir Reginald Lister, *The Times*, 6 November 1912; Sir Reginald Lister's Bequests, *The Globe*, 7 May 1913, p6; Michael Bloch, *Closet Queens*, Little Brown, London 2015, p167; Headley: A Big Windfall, *Hampshire Telegraph*, 23 October 1936, p8; Archnet: Sir Reginald Lister Square: www.archnet.org/sites/18045]
† Newton Wallop, 6th Earl of Portsmouth (1856–1917). Married Beatrice Mary Pease; no issue.

occasion Spencer was asked if he'd ever kissed a woman. Came the reply: "Once. On the brow."

The second name is that of the renowned author, E.F. Benson. Fascinated by the supernatural, the Sidgwick brothers who helped found the Society for Psychical Research were his uncles. In addition to his many novels, Benson co-authored with Eustace Miles,* an athlete, college friend and possible lover, a series of exercise and sporting books, including one on golf. It was an obsession, he confessed, which occupied most of his day.

The third recurring signature in the Visitors Book is that of Cyril's motoring friend Arthur Brown. He formed a notably deep friendship with the champion golfer Harry Vardon, while his obituary would note he was "devoted to children".

Last in this quartet was Lieutenant-Colonel Arthur Collins. Besides his courtier position, and directorship of the District Messenger Company, Collins was also involved in Liberal politics – indeed, as Labby phrased it, "he was a Liberal of an advanced type". In the early November week that the Fraser and Thorold trial broke in the press, Collins was a guest at a dinner and reception for the Liberal League which M.P. Sir Edward Colebrooke and his wife held at their London palace, Stratford House. As a report of the event phrased it: "all the leading lights of the Liberal world were represented...the guest of the evening was, of course, Lord Rosebery, who was besieged by innumerable friends." Collins was also the keenest golfer: the magazine *Golf Illustrated* noted he was a frequent guest of the editor of the *Daily Telegraph*, Sir Edward Lawson, at Hall Barn, "where, perhaps, more golf is played than on any other private course in the kingdom."

There is another, almost annual signature in The Pleasaunce Visitors book: 'G.W. Balfour'. As previously mentioned, Cyril's friendship with the Prime Minister's brother was very close, and its very existence would have acted as yet another protective bulwark.

---

* Eustace Hamilton Miles (1868–1948), tennis player who competed in the 1908 Olympics, restaurateur, diet guru, and author of a string of books, including the euphonically-titled fitness book *A Boy's Control and Self Expression*. In 1906 he married the daughter of the rector of St Clement Danes, Hallie Killick, also an author. They ran a vegetarian restaurant and health food shops, and provided free food and clothing to the poor of London. He was later bankrupted.

While Cyril's friends were legion in number, there were at least five gentlemen who qualified for being, as Frederick Cunliffe-Owen put it when writing of the scandal: "Another still greater name, which must not be indicated...tinged by scandal" and "of wider than English reputation".

The first such name that must be considered is Cyril's companion on theatre first nights – and many other evenings as well – Alfred de Rothschild. 'Mr. Alfred' was a lavender-gloved fop of the first water, with an alleged illegitimate daughter, Almina.* Three years previously, he'd been forced to resign his directorship of the Bank of England, due to unethically checking the private account of an art dealer whom he believed had overcharged him.

Shielded by vast wealth, comprehensively destroyed personal papers, and family reticence, until recently Alfred's private life had remained, as it was then, mostly impenetrable. However, while he'd cultivated the beautiful women of the day for parties at his home in Mayfair, and his Buckinghamshire estate of Halton, in old age Almina told a godson† she'd been witness to "all male gatherings at Halton of the Oscar Wilde kind."

At the opening night of Wilde's *A Woman Of No Importance* in 1893, Alfred and Cyril had again shared a stage box. In that play, a Lady Hunstanton observes: "Bimetallism! Is that quite a nice subject? However, I know people discuss everything very freely nowadays."

Bimetallism – a monetary system based on both silver and gold, rather than merely the gold standard – was one of the financial talking points of the day. For the worldly, its expression of duality had also served to make it a slang term for bisexuality, and Alfred and Cyril would have richly appreciated Wilde's layered joke. In financial terms, Alfred proclaimed himself a "staunch supporter of Monometallism," but in his sexuality the case was plainly otherwise.

Tellingly, for the Duchess of Devonshire's celebrated costume ball of

---

* Almina Victoria Maria Alexandra Dennistoun, née Wombwell (1876–1969). Married George Edward Stanhope Molyneux Herbert, 5th Earl of Carnarvon, and had issue; and secondly, Guards officer, Ian Dennistoun.
† Anthony 'Tony' Leadbetter (1938–2019), godson and chaperone of Almina; son of Anne Leadbetter, her housekeeper from 1945 to 1969.

1897, of all the historical figures available to choose from, Alfred turned up dripping in pearls as Henri III of France,* a monarch who enjoyed mistresses, but is most renowned for *les mignons* – 'the cuties', his male favourites. While the ball was a highly exclusive event, it's difficult to see Alfred's choice of character to embody as anything other than an overt and brazen act by which he nailed his secret passions to the flagpole. A life of limitless entitlement had also made him quietly formidable in his demands. "Never say 'No' to Mr Alfred," a new assistant gardener was cautioned. "If he tells you to set up a ladder to the moon, at least go and fetch the ladder."

Another personage who bore a name 'wider than English reputation', and had been singed by scandal rather than merely tinged, was Henry Fitzroy, the Earl of Euston. While Frederick Cunliffe-Owen discounted him as being the ringleader, the possibility that Euston was involved in the case, even in a subsidiary role, wouldn't have been out of character. As George Ives recorded, the rumour was certainly out there. Although Euston looked every inch a nobleman, throughout his life he demonstrated a remarkable facility for self-indulgence and falling into trouble.

Only with the help of the best legal representation money could buy, and the discreet support of the Government, including possibly masonic sympathisers, had he succeeded in bluffing his way out of the Cleveland Street Scandal. Yet, he'd been as guilty as sin. The deposition of the thirty-two-year-old prostitute, John Saul, had bluntly stated Euston liked to 'spend' on his belly.

As mentioned, Euston was also a longstanding victim of blackmailer Robert Cliburn. Frederick Cunliffe-Owen's statement that a hint as to the greater name could not be given, may in fact have been the hint – Euston's fierce libel action in the Cleveland Street Scandal was a clear warning to journalists that they besmirched his noble name at their peril. However, in November 1902 Euston had considerably less financial means: he was now spending time in London's Bankruptcy Court.

Euston was a friend of both Cyril and Alfred de Rothschild. When the latter celebrated the visit of the Prince of Wales to his new country

---

* Henri III, King of France (1551–1589). Married Louise of Lorraine; no issue.

house of Halton in 1884, Euston was a guest of Cyril and Constance at nearby Aston Clinton, for the duration of Alfred's festivities.

The third greater name was an up-and-coming young man who'd just joined the Liberal Party – the dashing William Lygon, Lord Beauchamp. Like Cyril with whom he was connected, Beauchamp would champion the needs of working men, particularly through educational reform. A few years previously, at just twenty-six, he'd been catapulted into the role of Governor-General of New South Wales. His term was a series of missteps and misunderstandings that ended with his early resignation.

Beauchamp's background forged him into a model of strict outward observance of correct form, and private lasciviousness: he wore his Garter sash every night at dinner, and read prayers twice a day in the chapel at his seat of Madresfield Court, but job interviews for his admired retinue of male servants included evaluating hands slid over buttocks.

Even more than Cyril, Beauchamp's audaciousness and adoration of bohemia skated to the edge of the acceptable, while his marriage to Lady Lettice Grosvenor, a sister of the 2nd Duke of Westminster,* brought fresh financial abundance that kept the splendour afloat. Their wedding in July 1902 was one of the most brilliant social events of the year. Favoured invitees included Lord Ronald Gower, while the gift-givers included E.F. Benson, Lord Rosebery, and not least, Bernard Fraser. (Beauchamp was also a member of his club, the Bachelors'.) However, Bernard was possibly unable to attend the wedding due to pressing circumstances – his arrest warrant was issued the same day.

Beauchamp was a true connoisseur, with an educated eye and patrician panache: at Madresfield, he commissioned C.R. Ashbee and his team to craft the interiors of the chapel and library – in which resided the works of Whitman and Carpenter. On meeting his client for the second time, Ashbee recognised they shared an affinity beyond art and socialism, telling his diary:

My first impressions of Lord Beauchamp held good – but I

---

* Hugh Richard Arthur Grosvenor, 2nd Duke of Westminster (1879–1953); nicknamed 'Ben d'Or'. Four times married, with issue.

throw in a touch more of human tenderness, <u>that</u> comes I should say with the homogenic side of him... His lordship knows doubtless what a mighty solvent it is, & caste is caste. But I chuckle to myself when I look into the eyes of a man whom I know to feel as I do, & think how if I chose to put forth the power of the word I could make all the splendour & the pomp pass away like smoke, & leave only the bare soul of the man, naked as the Italian quattrocentrist* might have drawn it in its progress to heaven or hell.

The power of the word would be demonstrated in 1931 by his brother-in-law, the Duke. Madly jealous of Beauchamp, he attempted to destroy his life by insisting to the authorities they take action over his homosexuality: it resulted in Beauchamp's temporary exile from England, and Lettice filing for divorce.

The fourth of these illustrious suspects was, like Cyril, coincidentally also the bearer of a floral surname, and married to a Rothschild heiress – Archie Primrose, Lord Rosebery. He also had been well-touched by scandal. The suspected suicide of his young private secretary and protégé Francis Douglas, Viscount Drumlanrig, (the brother of Lord Alfred Douglas) in 1894; the baitings of the Marquess of Queensberry which followed; and perhaps worst of all, the involvement of his name during the Oscar Wilde trials, were only the most prominent incidents on the long trail of rumour that bedevilled him. And of course, Rosebery also knew, to some degree, Arthur Thorold. It may have been a mere passing acquaintance with a young man, but there had been so very many. It's logical to assume that Thorold and Fraser had mentioned to Cyril their sunny days at Naples, and Thorold had spoken of his failed application to manage Rosebery's villa. In which case, Cyril may have furthered the connection.

Rosebery and Cyril had been very close in their youth, and Constance was also his friend. The few letters that survive from Rosebery to Cyril are cordial, but not cosy. However, given Rosebery's secretive and withholding character, they cannot be held to be indicative of the nature of their friendship. After Hannah's death, and again when he suffered a breakdown in 1895 at the time of the Wilde trials, Cyril

---

* Of the Quattrocentro, the first phase of the Renaissance.

invited him to recover at The Pleasaunce.*

In early October 1902, as the Battersea scandal was rising to a white heat, Rosebery hosted a house party at his Scottish seat of Dalmeny. Two of the guests were the future Prime Ministers Herbert Asquith and Winston Churchill. Asquith wrote to his wife:

> I found R[osebery] in good form – rather distressed at RBH's [Richard Burdon Haldane's] unnecessary cordial benediction of the Ed[uca]tion Bill – but sensible. Winston was there for the night, & we had a good deal of fun chaffing him & drawing him on.

Given that Rosebery was highly sensitive, prone to depression, and at the time of the Wilde trials had been on the brink of mental collapse, his possible equanimity on this occasion is notable. That said, at a Liberal Club dinner in early November, a fellow diner observed, "Rosebery was evidently tired & he made a bad and pessimistic speech. He spoke of himself as having 'no following' & said he thought there was but little sign of a Liberal awakening…mercifully there were no reporters present." It's also worth noting that Rosebery was meeting regularly with the newspaper magnate Lord Northcliffe, who visited him twice in October, and again in November, when Rosebery hosted a lunch for the Kaiser at Dalmeny.

However, an entry in the diary of Violet Bonham Carter, written at The Pleasaunce three years later in 1905, casts a telling light on Cyril and Rosebery's relationship at this stage of their lives:

> our host is in splendid form[,] delighted with a laurel plantation on the cliff & with the New Government which for him has one paramount all-eclipsing virtue of not containing Rosebery. "A rotten turnip in a rotten furrow – that's what he is my dear!"

Cyril's disenchantment, obviously provoked by Rosebery's inept premiership and the way he'd strained Party loyalty, was widely shared by colleagues. Yet it always reduces the likelihood of his involvement in Cyril's troubles.

---

* Rosebery didn't take up the offers.

The final 'greater name' on the list of suspects must inevitably be that of Lorne, the 9th Duke of Argyll. During his lifetime rumours swirled around him, as they have ever since. His closest friends, including Cyril, Lord Ronald Gower, Lord Esher, and Lewis Harcourt were homosexual. He was also fascinated by psychical phenomena, an enthusiasm which Frederic Myers, and others of the friendship circle would have fostered.

Overwhelming evidence indicates that Lorne's marriage to Princess Louise was a shell: an occasionally affectionate companionship in which they lived the majority of their lives apart. In terms of names "of wider than English reputation," Lorne had been Governor General of Canada from 1878 to 1883. It was during this time reports of the rockiness of the couple's marriage arose, as well as gossip of his male friendships.

Yet it was not only this that made Lorne 'tinged by scandal'. The sensationally sordid 1886 divorce case of his brother Lord Colin Campbell,* who infected his wife with own venereal disease, was widely considered the 'Degradation of a Great British Family'. The officious phrasing of Cunliffe-Owen when referring to his inability to even hint at the name – "which must not be indicated"– typifies the language in which sensitive inferences to the Royal Family and their associations were couched by the press. The signatures of Lorne, his wife Princess Louise, and her Comptroller, Arthur Collins, all appear in The Pleasaunce's Visitors Book.

Lorne is therefore a particularly tantalising suspect as the 'greater name'. Even should he have been entirely innocent, as a homosexual married to the King's sister, he represented a major liability for the Government. Under prevailing Church and Government law, his very existence was an abomination. If Arthur Collins was implicated, it would have produced conniptions at Buckingham Palace, reviving nightmares of the Cleveland Street Scandal and another courtier – Lord Arthur Somerset, with his link to Prince Eddy.

Given the existing rumours about Lorne, it may have been assumed, not least by London's clubland, that Collins was his go-between in the

---

* Lord Colin Campbell (1853–1895), Scottish Liberal M.P.; son of the 8th Duke of Argyll. Married and divorced Gertrude Blood. See: Public Opinion On The Campbell Case, *Gloucestershire Echo*, 21 December 1886, p3.

matter. It's possible Frederick Cunliffe-Owen picked up just such a rumour. As with Prince Eddy, officials may not have known whether Lorne was guilty or innocent, but again that was almost irrelevant: the very rumour itself would have been disastrous had it got out. For the Government, Lorne's friendship with Cyril Flower, whatever its nature, was Bad News.

The middle of November 1902 witnessed the wedding of Blanche 'Baffy' Balfour,* who just happened to be the niece of both the Prime Minister and Lorne. Both were in attendance at the ceremony, together with Princess Louise and Lord Ronald Gower. Given what was going down, it would have been an interesting occasion.

> For a man of adventure 'tis balm to his soul
> To get himself happily into a hole...

So Lorne had written, in a poem about – what else? – golf. But the stakes in this affair were very different. The association of any member of the Royal Family, or those close to them, with scandal, however slight, provoked the greatest protective efforts for its suppression. This was to be again proven to the highest degree when, five years later, Lorne's homosexual friendships haplessly embroiled him in another scandal, creating a further crisis for the Government. In 1977, the great-nephew of a friend of Princess Louise, whose family held letters from her, told a researcher that "Lorne's proclivities, in the other direction, needed private 'handling' by Edward VII".

As with the Cleveland Street Scandal, the motivation to smother the Battersea case had, at bedrock, little to do with forbidden sexuality, and everything to do with power and its retention. What if the other gilded names involved were dragged into the legal maelstrom? If Cunliffe-Owen was correct there were at least thirty esteemed gentlemen. If even one in the glittering array was publicly implicated, like a line of dominos, they could all fall – further compromising the already threatened reputation of the ruling class. It was too horrible to contemplate. It could not be allowed to happen. And so almost inevitably, the social position, prestige, and connections of these gentlemen ensured that together they were inviolable.

---

* Blanche Elizabeth Campbell Dugdale, née Balfour (1880–1948), author and Zionist. She encouraged her husband, Edgar Dugdale, to translate the first English edition of *Mein Kampf*.

These privileges derived overwhelmingly from the possession of money – landed money, mercantile money, investment money. Collectively the group owned vaults of it: mines and factories that spewed it; mansions and palaces that were stuffed to the attics with its purchases; fields, lakes, and hillsides that breathed it; and yachts afloat on oceans of it. As the greatest aphrodisiac of all, enabling not merely possessions, but personal liberty, plus the purchase of position, power and influence, money stuck its gilded finger up the Law, and as since time immemorial, the Law went down on bended knee to do its bidding.

The high-level manoeuvring behind the scenes, and the outcome, was the Cleveland Street Scandal all over again. Thirteen years on, the privileged were not only still protected – but even more so. Unlike Lord Arthur Somerset, who was forced to live in exile for the rest of his days, the prominent guilty gentlemen in this case didn't even need to pack a lunchbox.

This state of affairs was all the more remarkable in regard to Cyril. Lord Arthur had been a mere boy-brothel client: Cyril had harnessed his chairmanship skills to become, from a legal standpoint, a criminal conspirator. What is more, while the minnows of Cleveland Street had received token sentences, this time they were the opposite of light. And to top it off, most of the 'Tricks With Justice' (to employ W.T. Stead's piquant phrase) that were embarked upon, would be completely hidden from the public.

There was another person besides Sir George Lewis whom Cyril may have consulted: the *éminence grise* of the Edwardian court, Reginald Brett. In 1899 he'd succeeded to the viscounty of his father and become Lord Esher. Cyril and Esher not only shared a sexuality and similar background, they were also good friends. A photograph exists of Esher posing for Cyril in his conservatory, looking every inch the cosmopolitan sophisticate. "He used to say," one of Esher's daughters recalled, "The only thing in life is not to be found out." Of a visit to Lord Rosebery, Esher confided to his son Maurice: "Our friends are the same, our interests are the same, and there is complete confidence and mutual help...But how difficult to explain to outsiders!" Assisting Cyril in his plight – or other friends like Lewis Harcourt, would have been instinctive.

Esher's actions during the Cleveland Street Scandal are proof of this. His desire to help his friend Lord Arthur Somerset and others involved in that case, and to shape events, led him to act as both a source of advice, and a discreet and important conduit of information. Employing his connections, he also attempted to suppress publication of the Scandal's details. When Lord Arthur's solicitor was prosecuted by the Crown for attempting to spirit some of the telegraph boys out of the country so they could not give evidence, Esher wrote to Labouchère: "Personally I think their [the Government's] behaviour scandalous. Had they stuck to their original intention to hush the thing up, I think they would have been right."

Esher had little faith in the common man. Some part of this may have stemmed from criticism by the press of the secretive and accountable-to-no-one role he'd forged for himself in government. His motives were rightly suspected. Wielding power at the top of the tree, influencing matters of state, and having the ear of the monarch delivered a daily adrenaline rush like no other, and Esher was addicted. The danger in being a member of the secret brotherhood of sexual outlaws would have added a complementary surge of testosterone to the thrill. Dampening such power-tripping thrills were pesky journalists and cynical citizens who would never know such exhilaration. In Esher's view:

> No one is more suspicious than the plebeian. He believes that he has been exploited for centuries by the wealthier classes, and he attributes the most sinister motives to the man who is not in his direct pay or employ...I speak from experience, for owing to circumstances, I have nearly all my life, with one pleasant interlude, held the disagreeable position of an unsalaried worker.

While Esher was a man of his time, in a book of essays published in 1916 on Crown and Government, in which he shared his thoughts about improving representation in government, he made equally apparent the deepest feelings of his heart on the matter – that he lacked faith in democracy, and England had been best governed by the enlightened aristocracy of the Whigs:*

---

* The British political faction and party that espoused moderate liberal ideals, and governed in opposition to the conservative Tories from 1688 until the mid-nineteenth century, when it evolved to become the Liberal Party.

419

When Englishmen were ruled and did not govern themselves, it seemed quite in accordance with the settled order of things that a select few should do the work of the many…In point of fact, we have lived splendidly and comfortably under an oligarchy…Great Britain thrived under this dispensation.

In short: the people's enlightened betters knew best. Including how to dispose of scandalous matters. However, in fairness to Esher – and a massive counterbalance in his favour it is, like Cyril Flower, he was the living embodiment of *noblesse oblige*. Both men's contributions on behalf of the nation had a positive impact on hundreds of thousands of lives – Esher through his unpaid work on behalf of army reform, and Cyril through his philanthropy.

As one might expect, Esher was a member of Brooks's, the gentlemen's club that had been a Whig bastion. It was renowned for its refined luxury, and its library and art, which had been enriched by the picture collection of the Society of Dilettanti. (One wit suggested the Club was "like dining in a Duke's house, with the Duke lying dead upstairs.") Other notable members included Spencer Lyttelton, Lord Rosebery, the King's private secretary Sir Francis Knollys, and not least, Cyril Flower.

Esher and the Prime Minister, Arthur Balfour, would also become very close. They first bonded over army reform, on which they shared the same views. Esher was drawn by Balfour's affability, and his talent for transacting the business of Prime Ministership with a patrician insouciance and the appearance of minimum effort. (Given how little Balfour achieved, it was no remarkable gift.) As their friendship developed, Esher would send him, as he did with the King, "notes of suggestions on every conceivable matter of topical importance." He often called on Balfour before breakfast; sitting on his bed to discuss the issues of the day. On one occasion Esher invited Balfour to lunch, at which the other guest was Teddie Seymour,* a beautiful golden-haired eighteen-year-old who'd been a paramour of Esher's for years.

Even more importantly, Esher was King Edward's most trusted advisor, meeting with him almost daily. As early as October 1902 the

* Major Sir Edward Seymour (1877–1948). Courtier, and veteran of the Nile Expedition and Boer War. Married Lady Blanche Frances Conyngham, and had issue.

King had appointed him chairman of a committee charged with deciding how to dispose of Osbourne House. Sir Lionel Cust, the Surveyor and Keeper of the King's Pictures, wrote that:

> the remarkable influence which Lord Esher exercised over King Edward VII in the early years of his reign was well-applied, of great assistance to the King at a critical moment in his life, and of benefit to the Nation at large.

George Ives and Frederick Cunliffe-Owen stated that royal intervention was required to forge the Battersea cover-up. No one in court circles would have doubted it. Edward was not only King, but "the Bismarck of London": the benevolent dictator of upper class society. Whatever the laxity of morals in private, not least his own, Edward demanded public decorum. As a contemporary wrote, "He was determined that in so far as his influence could secure it, even plutocratic society should present a decent front to the world."

Given Cyril and Constance's friendships with the Royal Family, the King's involvement in smoothing over the affair would seem entirely natural, especially as he was a born diplomat and mediator. He spent much of his life swatting down scandals, both his own, and those of the more wayward members of his circle. As an American newspaper put it:

> King Edward hates scandal of every kind, and his influence is constantly being exercised for the hushing up of unsavoury affairs, the publication of which would do infinitely more harm than good. In fact, there is no man living who has done more to prevent the public washing of dirty linen of aristocratic families in the courts of law than the British monarch.

Oliver Gwynne, a journalist of the period, would write after the King's death:

> That influence was one of King Edward's most remarkable acquirements. There are London editors to-day who could tell strange stories of invitations to call at Buckingham Palace, where, politely, but firmly, their delinquencies were pointed out to them, and suggestions made and proffers of assistance given.

Not for nothing did Lord Esher title his book of political essays *The Influence Of King Edward*. As sovereign, it was King Edward's right to be consulted, to encourage, and to warn his Government.* And throughout his reign, Edward pushed to the limits and beyond the royal prerogative. Just as with Cleveland Street, the "strong and subtle influence of royalty" was almost certainly brought to bear. While Sir Edward Clarke had referred to "unknightly and dishonouring deeds done by men of character," the King lamented to a friend, "The age of chivalry has, alas, passed, and one sees it daily, both in political and social life". It was entirely within his character to wish to do a favour for a friend. Lord Esher would write of him: "He talked over some very private affairs with me... he is certainly a great-hearted King". Lady Reid, the wife of the King's doctor, concurred: "King Edward had far more charm and real kindness of heart than any of the rest of the family." Wracked with illness in her old age, the courtesan Skittles confided to Wilfrid Blunt that, had it not been for the continued loyalty and support of the King, who sent his physicians to care for her, "you would not find me in this house still."

If the grant of immunity for Cyril and his friends required the wielding of royal influence, it wouldn't have mattered to Edward any more than it did his pushing for leniency on behalf of Lord Arthur Somerset. A scandal involving the sexual exploitation of vulnerable youths by a posse of privileged decadents would have been considered poisoning to fraternity between the classes.

Arthur Balfour had a condescending attitude to the King: in the words of a courtier, the Prime Minister treated him as "one of those irritating factors in general politics, which you cannot ignore, and which you must treat with dismal and fictitious solemnity." That Balfour would have discussed Cyril's predicament with the King is unquestionable, but it's unlikely much or any royal pressure would have been required to arrive at the final decision. Balfour was also a fellow grandee, and one who, while cultivating an affable exterior, lived by evasion. It would have been entirely in character for him to agree to the suppression. His own equally fraught romantic history, and the problematic issue of his past leadership of the Society for Psychical Research with its sexually wayward members, plus the close friendships of his family with Cyril Flower, predisposed him to cover-

---

* The rights and role of an English monarch as famously defined by Walter Bagehot.

up. However, in resolving the matter between Prime Minister and Sovereign, Lord Esher may well have acted as both glue and emollient.

Whatever advice the Lord Chancellor Lord Halsbury may have tended, it has not survived. However, his attitude to the handling of such cases was still the prevailing one in Establishment circles, and therefore unofficial government policy.

Of course it was outrageous, and unjust. In the long annals of British justice, and Establishment cover-ups for the purposes of self-protection, the decision stands as a particularly shaming example of brutal inequality and hypocrisy under the Law. It is the nature of institutions to look after themselves, and it is a truism that the British Establishment achieved a mastery of it. At the time of the Cleveland Street Scandal, the radical Australian magazine *The Bulletin* had printed:

> We all know what English 'justice' is. It is Caste justice; it is the high-handed administration of a Law, created in the interests of a ruthless and dominant caste by members of that caste…Every few years one of the same type [of scandal] breaks out, despite the superhuman efforts of 'everybody' to suppress them. And it is always the same class of people that is concerned in them. It is always 'the pick of the land'.…it is not for nothing that a Tory Government rules England today. 'What is the good of friends,' asked Disraeli, the prince of Tories, 'if they don't help you when you get into a scrape?'*

In *Truth* on the 6th of November, gentleman columnist Charles Edward Jerningham† cleverly aphorised:

---

* The actual quote is: "what is the use of friends if they do not help you in a scrape?", said by Lady Montfort in Disraeli's novel *Endymion*. W.M. Thompson was so impressed by *The Bulletin* article, he reprinted it in *Reynolds's Newspaper*. Writer and publisher Frank Harris had his own theory about the system: "The judges almost all come from the upper middle class and invariably, in my experience, toady to aristocratic sentiment. Every Judge's wife wants to be a Lady (with a capital, please, printer!), and her husband as a rule gets ennobled the quicker the more he contrives to please his superiors in the hierarchy" [Frank Harris, *My Life And Loves*, Vol 2, Privately Printed, Nice 1925, p337.]
† Charles Edward Aloysius Wynne Jerningham (1854–1921). A radical Catholic, and heir to the baronetcy of Jerningham, he wrote 3,000 'letters' in *Truth* under the pseudonym 'Marmaduke'. Unmarried, he adopted a daughter, Marie Louise Warr.

In England...for the poor, there are the Ten Commandments; for the rich, the Upper-Ten Commandments! The prominent men and women of the moment in this country – the upper-criminal class – are more notorious than famous. Many of them have done everything to make money; many of them are prepared to do anything to make money; the names of many others are associated with the Bankruptcy Court, the Divorce Court, or the Criminal Court; and scandal and suspicion hover over those of many more. There is no so sure a master as example! There are papers for the people now, and the "public" reads. "If you cannot desist, we must deceive;" that is the source of the present policy.

Yet as with Cleveland Street, it's unlikely any of the gentlemen involved in the final decision would have viewed the outcome as satisfactory. Rather, they would have viewed it as troubling, but demanded by prudent caution. They were urbane pragmatists charged with a higher responsibility – firstly, the protection of social order, which inherently meant ring-fencing the reputation of the governing class; and secondly, the protection of moral order, which included limiting the coarsest elements of the press from retailing degrading narratives. In short, they would have comforted themselves that they were acting for the greater good. Anything can be rationalised. And whoever holds the power, defines the reality. Promoting self-benefiting sophistries as rational and responsible, can be critical to maintaining power. As for the actual youths involved, and whether any had been traumatised by the experience – they were the very last consideration.

Had the case and its quashing become fully known there would have been public outrage – and not merely amongst the radical and disenfranchised. Nonetheless, a multitude of upright citizens such as Frederick Cunliffe-Owen might well have endorsed the suppression – including those living far beyond the realms of the Establishment. If preserving social harmony rather than risking turbulence requires a measure of injustice, it's a price regularly considered worth paying – in any era.

By virtue of his rank as a peer, one of the privileges Cyril held was the right to a private audience with the Sovereign.* However, given Cyril's illness, and that fact Sir George Lewis was also the King's personal solicitor and close friend, it would be logical to presume that Lewis acted as the intermediary for any plea. Edward's friendship with Lewis was so close, they annually holidayed together at the German spa towns of Homburg, Baden and Marienbad; Lewis on one occasion even used the pseudonym 'Duke of Lancaster', the name of the royal duchy.

Taking place behind closed doors, the resolution would have been an unwritten gentleman's agreement. Lord Esher noted that "far more than half the business transacted by the King was transacted orally, by personal interview...unlike Queen Victoria, he had his say verbally." In the words of the cockney aphorism of the King's favourite cook and hotelkeeper of secrets Rosa Lewis:† "No letters, no lawyers and kiss my baby's bottom." Following his death, Edward VII's personal papers were destroyed by his express wish.

Frederick Cunliffe-Owen would later allege that the plea employed on behalf of Cyril was that "he was not responsible for his actions". It's possible Sir George Lewis concocted just such a defence: a rift of madness beget by depression or stress. And after all: what greater risk factor for mental instability could there be than the heavy burdens of power and unlimited wealth? If in the heat of the proceedings, as Wilfrid Blunt had heard, it was suggested to Cyril that he should leave the country, such penance was never paid. King Edward's rages soon blew over, giving way to his good nature.

Extraordinarily, there was never a pause in Cyril's official invitations. Life appeared to go on as normal, with no apparent social exclusion, apart from what may have occurred on an individual level. Even the American ambassador, Joseph Choate,‡ who'd once been a guest at The Pleasaunce, now visited again with his wife. Gossip of the scandal certainly unsettled the Battersea's architect Edwin Lutyens, who had panicked. However, if any further underlining was necessary of the

---

* It is a privilege of the peerage which remains, although to what degree it is exercised is unknown. Other such privileges once included the right of peer to trial by his peers, and if hung, the dubious benefit of a silk rope, instead of one of hemp.
† Rosa Lewis (1867–1952) famed English chef and owner of The Cavendish Hotel in London, which was popular as a place of assignation due to its owner's deep discretion. She is reputed to have had an affair with Edward VII when Prince of Wales.
‡ Joseph Hodges Choate (1832–1917), U.S. ambassador to England 1889-1905.

cosiness of Cyril's links to power, in December he was elected Vice-President of the Golf Professional Association, whose President was none other than Arthur Balfour! As far as Cyril was concerned, the outcome of the scandal bore testimony to the lordly truth of the Latin motto on his coat of arms: *Flores Curat Deus* – God Cares for the Flowers.

Constance's journals, much excised and erased, give little clue as to what happened in those awful weeks, except with regard to the seachange in her attitude to her marriage. And it is not the one you might expect. In her diary summary for 1902, she wrote:

> This past year seems to stand out in my memory for 3 reasons, or rather events:
> 1. National
> 2. Individual
> 3. Conjugal.

The National event was the Coronation: "I fully enjoyed the day. To me it was inspiring as well as interesting." The Individual event was the annual convention of the National Union of Women Workers at Edinburgh, where she'd delivered her presidential speech:

> Very personal, individual, but also semi public! I enjoy the work, frankly I enjoy the position — I think my address was <u>good</u>, above the average — my lack of sympathy & great temper caused one or two awkward moments, but I fail in knowledge of business, in quickness of brainpower — I am not ready at framing resolutions, I do not always seize the point, I lack decisiveness. But I feel I am learning & I hope...

As for the third event, Conjugal – her explanation has been scissored out. Yet, despite the deep silence of absence, the jagged edge of the removed page like a white scar, another entry of the same period that was not removed, provides a key to at least some of what is now missing. In it, Constance states:

> I am determined to act up to my own presidential address. I have actually written it for my own edification — 'that difficult place our own fireside' 'the poor souls who have to live with us.' I am determined to get on at that difficult place — I will be good

426

friends with the poor souls.

Three and a half lines are blacked out and then "I want to be even far away from A[ston] C[linton] – away from all who really love me, appreciate me," followed by another two missing pages.

It seems to express something of a breakdown. However, what is clear is that the draft of her speech to the Women Workers constituted her private working out of what she believed was causing the rift in her marriage. Small wonder she called it: "Very personal, individual, but also semi public!" In her speech Constance spoke of the need for public and private life to be in harmony, and the chasm that sometimes existed between the two:

> Principles carefully enunciated from the platform may never have been brought to the test of private life…we may find it easier to treat with tolerance and open mindedness people whom we meet occasionally than those who are nearest to us…

Living with a crusader can be a living hell. Constance clearly felt her idealism had led her to become intolerant at home, and Cyril and other 'poor souls', and her marriage, had suffered because of it. At a house party in 1911, the Earl of Crawford* wryly noted that some of the ladies "with big neglected families, are engrossed in aggressive feminism," and that fellow guest Lady Battersea "gradually got worked up to a state of mental intoxication all about the progress of the sex – until she talked sorry nonsense." At least where her marriage was concerned, Constance now realised she needed to be more pragmatic, and square her idealism with domestic reality. As she put it: "Our public life must be the more conscious and active expression of our ideals, not always obtainable in home life."

As with many couples of their class, the Batterseas lived often separate lives, due to the possession of multiple homes, differing social engagements, and their pursuit of different interests. Including, in Cyril's case, his male friendships. Like many other wives in such a situation, Constance would have long ago made a mental accommodation which included turning a blind eye to the obvious. At the end of the day, it was still a marriage that needed to work. And

---

* David Alexander Edward Lindsay, 27th Earl of Crawford and 10th Earl of Balcarres, (1871–1940), Conservative politician and art connoisseur.

427

Constance still loved her Cyril. At the time, it was not uncommon to privately dismiss extra-marital affairs as 'a bit of nonsense'. It was a figure of speech suggesting they were mere trifling hijinks (boys will be boys), of no real consequence to the weft of a relationship, and thereby allowing their forgiveness.

After all her early years of biblical work, Constance's recollection in her speech of "the divine quality of pity," was ironic. Her diarised regrets blaming herself for the failings in her marriage and Cyril's loss of interest in his career, would have made pity and absolution easier. His sacrifice of the governorship, which had meant so much to him, would also have contributed. It seems likely Constance rationalised that her nagging and neglect had driven Cyril to seek refuge not only in gentlemanly company, but in a sensual 'act of madness'. She also well knew how her husband lived for Beauty in all its forms: perhaps in her mind, he'd also become a martyr to it.

Gathering her pride around her, and maintaining an insouciant exterior, it seems that Constance did follow through in her belief that it was she who needed to make concessions. From the grumblings that had bedevilled it for years, the marriage may have gently sailed into a placid late-life harbour of mutual understanding. If so, it was timely. Ever more empathy, love and support would be needed, because from hereon in, illness and pain would begin to shadow Cyril's formerly charmed life.

As to the public backdrop of the affair, at *Reynolds's Newspaper*, W.M. Thomson was sure of one thing at least:

> The muzzling of the Press under Imperialism continues. The Government, afraid of the exposure of their misdeeds in South Africa – crimes now being slowly admitted – placed a Russian censorship over the Press.

The prevailing feeling – that behind the flashy show of Edwardian power, great misdeeds were being covered up – had been crystallised by the events in Southern Africa, and also by the collapse of the London and Globe Finance Corporation.

The shares of this mining conglomerate had cratered in December 1900 following years of wildcat financial speculation and falsified balance sheets. However, the Government strangely declined to prosecute the gentleman who had run it, Whitaker Wright, nor the aristocratic directorate he'd bribed to provide a gloss of respectability. The long-simmering scandal of official inaction was finally addressed in the House of Commons in February 1903.

"The London and Globe Infamy! We can characterise it in no other fashion," exclaimed *The Investors' Review*, while *Reynolds's Newspaper* noted that the Balfour Government's "extraordinary attitude…has created a profound impression." On all sides its refusal to prosecute was criticised, and rightly or wrongly, it was believed this was due to Balfour and a member of the Royal Family, the Duke of Connaught,* holding shares in the company, and a desire to shield the exalted personages of its board, which included two former Governor-Generals. Other shareholders would eventually succeed in mounting a private prosecution of Wright, who was found guilty of fraud in January 1904, and sensationally suicided in the courthouse by downing cyanide.†

In January 1903 a number of newspapers, including Cyril's old nemesis the *Luton Times,* in its new guise as the *Bedfordshire Advertiser,* printed the news that: "Lord Battersea, whose health was reported to have given way some time ago, is travelling in Spain, and it is said he will most likely remain abroad for two or three years." It indicates that rumours of Cyril fleeing to the Continent were still current. The report provoked a terse and lordly published corrective that obviously came directly from an irritated inhabitant of The Pleasaunce:

> Several newspapers still persist in writing of Lord Battersea as if he were travelling abroad. He is still at his seat The Pleasaunce, Overstrand, recovering his strength after his recent serious illness, and will probably remain there for at least another month. He hopes, however, to come to London early in March, when

---

* Prince Arthur, Duke of Connaught and Strathearn (1850–1942), seventh child of Queen Victoria and Prince Albert; married Princess Louise Margaret of Prussia. Governor-General of Canada 1911-1916.
† A subterranean smoking room constructed under one of the artificial lakes of his estate, Lea Park (now Witley Park), Godalming, Surrey, survives to attest to his bravura. In 1912, Asquith's Liberal Government would be plagued by an insider-trading scandal involving the Marconi telegraph company. The affair contained the same elements of upper class privilege and government suppression of information, and served to further disillusion the British public about its masters.

the Princess of Wales* will open a bazaar in aid of a charity at his town residence, Surrey House...Meanwhile, his thoughts are bent on the building of a library wing at The Pleasaunce.

Yet the rumour of Cyril's flight persisted. As late as 1939, Lord Alfred Douglas would privately write that Cyril had "got into serious trouble for activities on the O.W. [Oscar Wilde] lines & had to leave the country hurriedly."

There was also news of other overseas travellers. The 'Secret History Of To-Day' – the column in *Reynolds's Newspaper* which broke the story of the Battersea case – also printed in January 1903:

> Lord Ronald Gower and his adopted son Mr. Frank Hird, have left Hammerfield, Penshurst, for Corsica and Sicily, and will remain abroad until the beginning of May, says the *Morning Post*. Is this of any importance?

It clearly and mischievously thought it was. However, given Ronnie's constant peregrinations, and the blanket absolution that had been granted to the guilty of the Battersea scandal, rather than a departure to escape the heat of scandal, it was probably just a desire for winter sun and southern flesh. In what reads like a teasing quote from Ronnie himself, *The Tatler* printed that it was his lordship's intention "to make some studies of the natives".

Six days later, Quintin Hogg,† the founder and great benefactor of the Regent Street Polytechnic, and its many branches, was found dead in his bath. An inquest would conclude asphyxiation from a gas heater, due to lack of ventilation. While that was the cause of death, it was not an accident, as George Ives told his diary:

> a Treasury official wrote to a distinguished friend of mine‡ saying

---

* Princess Mary – 'May', the future Queen Mary, consort of King George V.
† Quintin Hogg (1845–1903), philanthropist.
‡ Ives later added a postscript: "The person who told me this, was Sir James Agg Gardner." Sir James Tynte Agg-Gardner (1846–1928), was a brewery-owner, Conservative M.P. and close homosexual friend of Ives whom he met with regularly, including at the Junior Carlton Club, at meetings at the House of Commons for the Prison Reform League, and on trips to Portsmouth and Brussels. A biographer has written: "Agg-Gardner was another gently ineffectual man, who was one of the earliest Conservatives to support women's suffrage, and pioneered legislation on fire escapes. His homosexuality was of the discreet and sentimental kind – he lived much of his life in hotels, with their accommodating supply of lift-boys and

how sad it was that the day (or so) before, they had been obliged to issue a warrant for his arrest! on the complaint of the parents of one or more of the boys!... I never knew him, unfortunately. One day we met – I was a student there for First Aid work – and he looked over me as only the Greek-Souled people ever do. And I so wanted to speak with him, and we both hesitated. But he being older, and the president of the institution, I thought it was not my place to speak first. And so we never met. I had heard many things long before (The Order runs wide and deep sometimes) but did not know [till?] poor Q.H. really destroyed himself...I put these facts down for future knowledge for others who may make use of these Notes.

Even *Reynolds's Newspaper* didn't feel comfortable touching the story until the following year, when 'The Secret History Of To-day' printed:

A proposal is on foot for the erection of a statue in the West-end of a famous philanthropist who died last year. We strongly advise the promoters of the project to abandon it. The philanthropist in question died under very peculiar circumstances, although the evidence at the inquest revealed nothing sensational. Without committing ourselves to the statement that he died by his own hand, we are prepared to state that if he had lived another twenty-four hours he would have been arrested on a very grave charge.

However, Hogg's statue would go ahead. Cast in bronze, and featuring him reading a book to two lads, one clad in football attire, it was unveiled in 1906 by Lorne (the Duke of Argyll), in his position as both a friend and admirer of Hogg since their schooldays at Eton.* A recreation ground at Chiswick was created as a further memorial.

The tragedy would have hit several gentlemen doubly hard, not least Cyril. As with other distinguished personages so charged, Hogg had been graced with the standard twenty-four warning of the issue of an arrest warrant, to enable escape to the Continent. But like Wilde, he

waiters – and his preferences were never publicly surmised until his death." [George Cecil Ives diary, 7 June 1903, Harry Ransom Center, University of Texas; Richard Davenport-Hines, 'No Longer Outraged', *The Independent*, 15 November 1998.]
* The statue was relocated to Portland Place, in London. It now exists also as a memorial to Quintin's wife Alice, and members of the Regent Street Polytechnic killed in both world wars.

never boarded the boat. After a life of concentrated purpose, the prospect of spending the rest of his days shadowed by shame, drifting on the Riviera or Venetian Lido, just wasn't him. The stark difference in the official treatment of his case, and that of Cyril's, also again highlights the fact that, while class mattered, links to power mattered even more.

Several years later, George Ives wrote in his diary:

> The Polytechnic Magazine for Feb has a glowing – and well deserved – eulogy of the late Mr. Quintin Hogg whom I had seen, but never actually knew personally. There is a conspiracy of silence over the sad fact that he would have been arrested for inversion had he lived one day longer[.] Yet how much good the Homogenic spirit inspires can be seen at the Polytechnic. Of course from my point of view his Bible teaching was inconsistent & poisonous but as one of the boys said to me years ago, Mr. Studd* [[Hogg's successor] is very kind but he doesn't love us as Mr. Hogg did. And that love did great works.

From the vantage point of his connections and work on prison reform, George Ives perceived the simple truth: the wellspring for a significant degree of philanthropy, education, and educational and social reform lay in homosexual sympathy and eros. Beyond desire and love of persons, there could be a loving brotherhood of souls. So it was with Whitman, Carpenter, General Gordon, Quintin Hogg, Arthur Collins, Cyril Flower, and an unacknowledged multitude of others across the Empire and globe, in schools, churches, charitable institutions, and government. They sought to not only raise up boys and men out of poverty, but elevate them in mind, body, and above all, in spirit.† With Cyril, Quintin Hogg, the Rev. Nugée, and many

---

* Sir (John Edward) Kynaston Studd, 1st baronet (1958–1944), who succeeded Hogg as President of the Regent Street Polytechnic.
† A later champion of homoerotic socialism and "reckless comradeship" as a means of dissolving class boundaries and mentoring working class boys was William Anderson Paine (1865–1932). A former shop assistant, journalist, travel guide editor, and advertising agency employee, he was president of The Working Class Boys Athletic Club at the Passmore Edwards Settlement in London. In *Shop Slavery And Emancipation* (1912) he wrote: "My friend is my God. I know no other God…I find him everywhere, because once I found him in a single soul." Echoing John Gambril Nicolson's poem 'Your City Cousins', he continues, "He is the little apprentice who looks a momentary greeting to me across the counter…the little ink-stained clerk who moves nearer to me on the seat on the omnibus, he does not know why: he is the shy undergraduate whose eyes meet mine…" In *A New Aristocracy Of Comradeship*

more gentlemen, these goals also embraced girls and women.

Also in January 1903, the noted Socialist couple Sidney and Beatrice Webb* holidayed near the Pleasaunce, and were welcomed by at least one of its hosts. Beatrice was a cross between an austere Josephine Butler and a humourless Soviet commissar's wife, always insisting on purposeful conversation. It's likely Cyril considered the earnest pair even more wearisome than Constance's usual run of guests, and gave them short shrift: in this time of anguish and recovery from a deathly illness and scandal, they were the very last thing he needed. The sentiment was returned, Beatrice informing her diary:

> Half a dozen times we went in for a chat with our neighbours in their resplendent villa, or Lady Battersea came in to us. She is a good and true-natured woman and quite intelligent, though like all these 'Society Dames' quite incapable of anything but chit-chat, flying from point to point. He is distinctly objectionable, a man without either intellect or character, and I should imagine with many bad habits of body and mind – a middle-class Croesus, ex-Adonis, ennobled for party purposes, a most unpleasant type of functionless wealth. They live in a gorgeous villa overflowing with objects of virtue and art, with no individuality or taste. There are no children. He has no public spirit. They are both overfed. If it were not for her genuine kindness and good intention the household would be positively repulsive.

Beatrice surely wished the couple, and Constance's lapdogs, could be

---

(1920), he outlined a regime of physical, mental and spiritual instruction in order that lads may truly know themselves, their purpose in the world, and how to fulfil it 'nobly and worthily'. The adolescent boy, he wrote, "should have the feeling of being loved, and cherished, and cared for, and made to feel proud and happy at being alive." Paine's obituary recorded: "a wide circle of friends and acquaintances came under the spell of his exceptionally charming personality." One of them was polymath William Edward Arnold-Forster (1886–1951; husband of Rupert Brooke's lover Katherine 'Ka' Cox), who shared mutual interests, including the countryside, art, and in earlier life, youths, and to whom his latter treatise was dedicated. In both books Paine related an overwhelming romance he'd experienced with a flaxen-haired youth: a baronet's grandson nicknamed 'Ariel': "I had never read life before by the lamp of joy... He showed me joy absolute." [William Paine, *Shop Slavery And Emancipation*, P.S. King & Son, London 1912, pp107-109, 114-115; William Paine, *A New Aristocracy Of Comradeship*, Leonard Parsons, London 1920, pp31-36, 174; The Late Mr. W.A. Paine, *The Chronicle And Courier* (Sevenoaks Chronicle & Kentish Advertiser), 20 May 1932, p2.]

* Sidney James Webb, 1st Baron Passfield (1859–1947) and Martha Beatrice Webb, Baroness Passfield, née Potter (1858–1943), socialists, economists and reformers.

turned out to field labour, but her snubs over Cyril's intellect and public generosity showed just how ideologically myopic she could be.

True to his own press statement, under the guise of normality, in February, Cyril and Constance came up to London to attend the Opening Of Parliament. On its eve, a series of ministerial banquets were traditionally held by the owners of the great London houses. That year the dinner for Liberal peers was hosted by Lord Spencer at Spencer House. To this Cyril was invited. Given the intense discretion of the press over the scandal, if he had the belief Society gossip hadn't linked his name, he was to be quickly disillusioned. Lord Carrington told his diary: "Battersea appeared in public for the first time since 'the rumours'. He was not very well received."

Nevertheless, a report of the next day's parliamentary gathering noted that Cyril was "welcomed back on his recovery." If enthusiasm for his return was muted, a selection of portraits he sent to a photographic exhibition held in aid of charity, gained newspaper praise as "a most excellent series." The exhibition happened to be at Norwich: visits by serving prisoners to it were unfortunately not on the cards.

In March, Cyril was at the opening night of Sir Charles Wyndham's New Theatre, another occasion attended by the cream of society. As was common with his theatre-going, he was not accompanied by Constance. He also hosted the Royal Amateur Art Exhibition at Surrey House. The Princess of Wales was unable to attend, and they had to settle for one of Queen Victoria's granddaughters, Princess Marie Louise.* Given her marriage had been annulled three years previously due to the homosexuality of her husband, Prince Aribert of Anhalt, it possibly made her a more appropriate patroness. However, a reporter noted that visitors to the event tended to be distracted from the amateur efforts, such as Princess Victoria's flower panels, by the likes of Cyril's Botticelli and da Vinci hanging on the walls above them.

That same month, Major-General Sir Hector Macdonald,†

---

* Princess Marie Louise (1872–1956). Daughter of Prince Christian of Schleswig-Holstein and Princess Helena of the United Kingdom.
† Major-General Sir Hector Archibald MacDonald (1853–1903), known as 'Fighting Mac'. His triumphs on the battlefields of Egypt and the Sudan made him a household name. He

Commander-in-Chief of British forces in Ceylon, shot himself in the temple in a Paris hotel room. The death of this popular hero of the people wrought profound shock not only in Britain, but throughout the Empire. Near his body were found newspapers reporting that he was to be court-martialled on "very grave charges". The primness of the British press meant readers were initially left to assume the nature of these.

The story had broken when Sir West Ridgeway,[*] the Governor of Ceylon, admitted to it at a meeting of the Ceylon Legislative Council in reply to a question from a mercantile member.[†] Ridgeway privately informed his superiors in London that "some, indeed most, of his victims...are the sons of the best known men in the colony, English and Native." One of them was rumoured to be a son of Ridgeway. The suggestion of coercion likely concealed the more disconcerting reality of enthusiastic participation. The Sinhalese attitude to homosexuality was relatively relaxed, and its adoption by colonials was considered shocking.[‡] Macdonald had been discovered by a colonial planter in a railway carriage in Kandy, its blinds down, with four Singhalse boys.

"What a fine strong man he was," the hotel manager who'd seen the bullet hole told a reporter, adding that Macdonald looked younger than his age.[§] As *Reynolds's Newspaper* remarked, "had the person

contracted a secret marriage with a girl of seventeen, Christiana McDonald Duncan, with whom he never lived, but supported. Lady Macdonald was later granted a divorce. They had a son, Hector, an engineer and bachelor recluse, who died in 1951.

[*] Sir (Joseph) West Ridgeway (1844–1930), civil servant and colonial governor.

[†] The allegation that Macdonald was told by King Edward the best thing he could do was to shoot himself may be a fanciful slur on that tactful gentleman. Reports that Macdonald met the King in a special audience were denied the same day by "an authoritative source". The King had previously told Macdonald, "I am proud to have met you." [Sir Hector And The War Office Sunderland, *Daily Echo and Shipping Gazette*, Friday, March 27, 1903; Obiter Scripta, *St James's Gazette*, 13 April 1901, p5.]

[‡] As one historian has neatly put it: "Ceylon furnished MacDonald with a lethal combination of a military command which was inactive and uninteresting, and a community of boys who were interesting and very active". Unsurprisingly, important papers regarding the case have vanished. [Ronald Hyam, *Empire and Sexuality: The British Experience*, Manchester University Press 1990, p34.; Robert Aldrich, *Cultural Encounters and Homoeroticism in Sri Lanka: Sex and Serendipity*, Routledge, London 2014, p56.]

[§] Another permitted to view the corpse, as a good friend of MacDonald, was wealthy Irish J.P. George Moore-Browne. In a long letter to Winston Churchill congratulating him on winning the libel case brought by the Crown on his behalf against Lord Alfred Douglas, he poured out his loathing of sodomites, such as Douglas and "his boon companion" Lord Henry Somerset, before recalling the death of "Poor Mac. The War Office or whomever was to blame kept him too long in that beastly hot climate." [George Henry Moore-Browne to Winston Churchill, 14

charged been a lord, or even a lord's lackey," the public airing of the charges would never have occurred, but unlike his fellow officers, Macdonald's background was Scottish working class – he was a crofter's son.* *The Leeds And Yorkshire Mercury* stated:

> The belief prevails that he was hounded to his end by the irreversible hostility of certain of his superior officers, to whom names are given. Being merely a gallant soldier, and having neither the power of the purse, nor of social influence, he was unable to withstand the forces pitted against him.

The *Grantham Journal* noted "it is good to observe how for once judgement is suspended in favour of sympathy," but the Scottish were stunned and profoundly indignant at the way their hero had been treated.†

In his ongoing war against the ruling class, W.M. Thompson was prepared to advance the theory Macdonald had been set up. In a front page article in *Reynolds's Newspaper* titled 'The Strange Case Of Hector Macdonald' began:

> Over twelve months ago the writer of this article knew as a fact that certain grave charges had been made against Hector Macdonald. These allegations were laid before the Home Office – at any rate, in connection with the trial of the murderer Bennett.

This was Herbert John Bennett, a young man who'd been hanged in

---

December 1923; CHAR 2/127/42-43, The Churchill Archives Centre.]
* Of Macdonald's career, *Reynolds's Newspaper* sceptically commented: "Now, it is almost impossible, and practically unknown, that any man has risen from the ranks on his own merits exclusively. *Search we the springs, And backward trace the principle of things*, and we shall find that when soldiers are raised to the commissioned ranks there is generally a special cause – connections, birth, and so on. The British army, for the most part, is officered by boofy snobs and cads, who have a strong feminine attraction for male millinery. Like the Church, the fool of the family is generally sent into the army." It's very possible that together with his leadership skills and bravery, Macdonald's homosexuality was the third enabling factor in his ascendance. [Secret History Of To-Day, *Reynolds's Newspaper*, 29 March 1903, p1.]
† In the coarser antipodes, a Sydney paper took umbrage when a local preacher sermonised that Macdonald should be forgiven and that "had he lived centuries ago, he might have been a saint". In a story headlined "Horrid Homosexualist Hector…A Pederastic Pervert," it bluntly suggested the minister would have been better off preaching of "Moses' extermination of those who contracted the disgraceful disorder from the phallic worshippers of Baal". [Saint(!) Mucktonalt, *Truth* (Sydney), 14 June 1903, p5.]

1901 for the murder of his wife. Thompson continued:

> During the trial it was stated that Bennett had been to South Africa on a visit to an English officer of high rank, a point which was not accentuated by either the counsel for the prosecution, or the defence. But it must have been known to the Crown officers that Bennett was a well-known offender against the purity laws of this country, and that he had frequently acted as an agent for vices *non nominanda apud Christianos.**

To power his argument, Thompson most uncharacteristically cast a sympathetic light upon Macdonald's psyche:

> The well-informed in military circles knew that Hector Macdonald was a man of great physical passion. Exaggerated animalism is very often a characteristic of the successful soldier, whose moral centres are, by reason of his trade, less fine, less clean and less balanced than men in other spheres of activity. It was a matter of common talk that Bennett went to South Africa on account of some previous transaction. This was known to the general's peers and subordinates, and it is hard not to believe that his superiors had no knowledge of it. Thus we are left face to face with one of the most cruel acts that has disgraced a Government.
>
> Instead of calling on Macdonald to retire from the army and live without the borders of the Kingdom, the War Office, pretending ignorance of the matter, sent him to command one of the most important strategic points of the Empire. He had been wounded, was in ill-health, and without friends among his aristocratic colleagues. Fighting Mac, whose generalship saved Kitchener of Khartoum at Omdurman, had done his fighting, and there was no more for him in the immediate prospect...he was merely Major-General Sir Hector Macdonald, K.C.B., in command of a few nondescript troops in Ceylon.
>
> This, then, was the moment chosen by the little scions of an effete nobility to damn the strong man of the people who had outstripped them in their race for glory. They had been glad

---

* Not to be named among Christians. i.e. sodomy.

enough of his help in their hour of stress, but the moment their skins were safe, they turned on the lion who had helped them. So they whispered together – plotted the downfall which came to the brave man so terribly in an alien country.

In a further column, Thompson elaborated on the final scenario:

The charge for which Lieutenant-General Hector Macdonald committed suicide is a common vice among the well-to-do classes in London, both sexes of whom luxury, idleness and Imperialism have thoroughly corrupted...Quite a number of the members of the House of Lords – the body which governs England – are addicted to it. Nobody would have taken any notice of the matter had it not been that Macdonald was hustled, so well is the practice known in 'Society' circles.

The Government have had Macdonald's case under consideration for about a year...Macdonald came home to implore the authorities to save him. Their ultimatum, however, was – Court-martial, or cashiering. They advised him to go to Paris and think it over for a couple of days. The wretched man was at his wits end. On the day of his suicide he received a peremptory communication demanding an immediate answer. The revolver shot was the reply.

Thompson again pointed out the double-standard when it came to prosecuting the privileged for the offence, compared to a commoner:

We do not wish to appear in any way to be defenders of the practices with which Macdonald's name is mentioned, but we would bring it to our reader's memory that the law has moved very slowly against these offences on more than one occasion. Canon Eyton was "allowed to go," and is now said to have obtained a Colonial appointment; several officers we could name, offenders in this respect, have been allowed to travel eastward in search of military employment in Mohamedan countries;* furthermore, it is the secret history of the last few months that a prominent member of the Upper House and personal friend of royalty has been allowed, not to "go," but

---

* A reference to Lord Arthur Somerset of the Cleveland Street Scandal.

438

actually to stay in this country after the scandal which laid bare years of prurient conduct.

It was another guarded reference to Cyril. Thompson concluded by stating: "the Government have flashed out into the eyes of the world a sidelight in our moral being which it would have been better to dim with the screen of diplomacy."

In a blatant posthumous whitewash, an investigative commission found that there was "not the slightest particle of truth or foundation" in the accusations, and that "Sir Hector Macdonald was assassinated by vile and slanderous tongues." However, the widespread and vigorous discussion of Macdonald's fate would have been a chilling reminder to Cyril how things might have gone for him had he been born differently.

Despite this upset, Cyril's outward life found its old groove. No doubt pressed by Constance, in May he wrote to the Prime Minister requesting that, under the new Education Act, women be given some say in the administration of schools. In a dictated reply, Balfour stated: "Whether anything…can be done under the bill in the direction you desire, it is not so easy to say." It was a typically airy and noncommittal Balfourian response of the kind that must have driven many a head to bang against a wall.

Constance was away in Dublin to deliver a speech at a girl's school, but wrote to Annie: "Cyril seems to be very happy on yacht" – presumably the Garland. That same May, Cyril addressed the annual meeting of the Domestic Servants' Benevolent Institution, which managed a pension scheme, and of which he was President. In October, he gave an address to Liberal supporters in Luton. The *Bedfordshire Advertiser* was waiting for him. It dryly noted that he:

> had all his old after-dinner manner, which we know so well…of course, he was going to remain faithful to Luton for all time. But, as the autumn leaves began [to] fall, Cyril Flower, alas faded away too.

Cyril would further fade from the national stage. While he continued to engage in his charitable activities, including presiding over a meeting of the Shaftesbury Institute Mission, which aided the poor, since the shock of 1902 his health had continued to decline. In 1904 the cause was diagnosed: it was diabetes.

Before the discovery of insulin in 1921, this constituted a slow death sentence: its certainty could only be delayed by a modified diet, and the pain only eased by opium and other agents. "I know what it means, but do not say anything to frighten people," Cyril told a friend, "I am not afraid of death." He wrote in his diary: "Sono contento". ["I'm content".] However, the insidious encroachment of the disease upon all the body's systems was ghastly: the myriad symptoms included disrupted sleep, nerve pain, muscular cramps, and pulmonary fibrosis, making breathing ever more laboured. Constance confided in her own diary the seachange in him the disease wrought: "Three, no four years, getting steadily worse, wretchedly ill and suffering, depressed, low, oh, how changed..."

One new pleasure that distracted from the agony was motoring, which had rapidly become a popular pastime for the wealthy, including bachelors of means like Hugh Weguelin.* True to form, Cyril did it in style, clothing his chauffeur and attendant not in grey motoring uniforms, but coloured livery like coachmen. "Cyril enjoys his motor, his drivers," Constance wrote, "it makes him less restless and having as it were to lead a different life owing to his repeated & tiresome attacks of illness."

In 1904 he accompanied his bachelor friend Arthur Brown in his Napier car on a tour of the North of France. Constance was no particular fan of the young gentleman, informing her diary: "I miss the old intercourse with such as J. Morley, Haldane, Asquith – to have such down to a Brown is rather a bathos."

Cyril continued to play host to old and new friends. On the 1st of August, the aforesaid Arthur Brown arrived at The Pleasaunce, to be joined by Spencer Lyttelton, and the Lords Killanin† and Wolseley‡.

---

* Thomas Hugh Weguelin (1859–1923), stockbroker, man of the world, and patron of 19 Cleveland Street.
† Martin Henry FitzPatrick Morris, 2nd Baron Killanin (1867–1927), Irish Conservative M.P., barrister, and Privy Counsellor for Ireland.
‡ Field-Marshall Viscount Garnet Joseph Wolseley (1833–1913), military hero and administrator, author and bibliophile. Louisa, Viscountess Wolseley (1843–1920), was beautiful, cultivated, also a bibliophile, and considered to be one of the best dressed women in Europe.

Killanin was a cultivated bachelor Irish M.P. who split his time between Galway and Belgravia. Wolseley was a charming and vivacious military hero and author of great élan, who thrived on literary chat, and was totally at ease in such company. Henry James told Edmund Gosse* that Wolseley and his sophisticated and unconventional wife Louisa were "the best 'circus' one knows".

In 1904, a book titled *Society In The New Reign* caused a flutter. It was a lively and often catty study of some of the Kingdom's principal personalities, by an anonymous author who termed themselves 'A Foreign Resident'. The profile of Cyril, which mischaracterised him as Jewish, was both flattering and insinuating:

> Looking at his astonishingly well-preserved complexion and figure, one easily realizes that, in Harrow and Cambridge theatricals, he looked and dressed feminine parts to the life…for piquing himself on some personal resemblance to Alcibiades† ever since his school and college years, he has liked occasionally to play the Maecenas‡ …His villa on the Norfolk coast and his hunting-box in the Midlands…offer a healthy change of air to useful friends or to deserving *protégés*.

Alcibiades's name was then regularly employed to signify a handsome, wealthy and flamboyant public figure. There was usually no intention of suggesting licentiousness when making the analogy, although not always, and possibly not here. Many gentleman readers would have been aware of Alcibiades' admission in Plato's *Symposium* of attempting to seduce Socrates, and some would also have known of

---

* Sir Edmund Wilson Gosse (1849–1928), poet, author, critic. Although married, he struggled with homosexual desires. In a surreal episode, he spent the funeral of Robert Browning in Westminster Abbey, with George Meredith at his side, stealing glances at a photograph of a nude male that John Addington Symonds had gifted him. Symonds' granddaughter was incensed when Gosse informed her he had burnt Symonds' papers, entrusted to him, to protect his reputation. [Phyllis Grosskurth, *John Addington Symonds: A Biography*, Longmans, London 1964, p175; J. A. Symonds; *The Memoirs of John Addington Symonds: A Critical Edition*, Amber K. Regis (ed.) Palgrave Macmillan, London 2016, p27.]
† Alcibiades (c.450–404 BC). A brilliant and beloved Athenian politician, general, and wildchild of exceptional beauty. He used his celebrity and charm to achieve political power, and though brave in war, his recklessness led to ruin. It was said that as a boy he had drawn husbands away from their wives, and as a man, wives from their husbands. [Robert J. Littman, 'The Loves of Alcibiades', *Transactions and Proceedings of the American Philological Association*, Vol. 101, The Johns Hopkins University Press 1970, pp. 263-276.]
‡ Gaius Cilnius Maecenas (c.70 BC – 8 BC), a Roman legendary for his wealth and enlightened patronage of the arts.

his marriage to an heiress, and of her attempt to divorce him for infidelity.

That same year, Cyril was subject to an even more barbed attack when the popular and high-profile author Hilaire Belloc* published *Emmanuel Burden*. It was the first in a series of four novels satirising modern political and financial life, and were an expression of Belloc's belief in the negative influence of the Anglo-Jewish plutocracy. The narrative featured a crooked Jewish banker, the hooked-nosed and greasy-curled I.Z. Barnett, who by the end of the first novel has climbed to the House of Lords as Lord Lambeth – the name of the South London borough that adjoins Battersea.

While Cyril may have shrugged off the public slight – it was just one more in a lifetime of them – for Constance, as a proud Rothschild, the insinuations are likely to have been distressing, particularly as public attitudes to Jewish financiers hardened as the Edwardian period progressed.† When Belloc published the second novel in the series, his Semitic banker had risen in the peerage to become – even more cruelly – Duke of Battersea. However by then, Cyril had been six months dead.

In Cyril's latter years, the press continued to feature occasional paragraphs about him. In May 1904, a Welsh newspaper published:

> Lord Battersea has for some time lived a life of retirement. He was at one time among the busiest of men…He is a handsome

---

* Joseph Hilaire Pierre René Belloc (1870–1953) Anglo-French writer, historian, and Liberal politician.
† One of the many reasons, besides the belief that Jewish Randlords had instigated the 2nd Boer War, was the revelation of the high death rate of black workers in the Transvaal mines. The 2nd Baron Coleridge, who brought it to the attention of Parliament, and sought to warn of the 'tyranny' of international capital, and its neglect of the welfare of working people and their communities, referred to the "un-English nationality" of the mine owners. Elsewhere, including in the press, this became not a problem of unregulated labour and capital, but reductively, "the Jewish millionaires in Park Lane." Popular anti-semitic polemics, such as Arnold White's *The Modern Jew* (1899), also added to the concern. By 1913, a social column would casually print: "The authorities of the Opera have the hardest work in the world to prevent the Jews actually encroaching upon Their Majesties, and precautions are, therefore, taken of allotting the boxes adjoining the Royal ones only to persons nominated by the King…all around the Speyers, Beits, Ecksteins, Moss's, Zimmermanns and Duveens predominate." [Hansard, House of Lords Debate, 20 June 1904, vol 136 cc407-58; Honiton Division: Liberal Candidate Speaks At Cyst St. Mary, *The Western Times*, 26 February 1904, p3; The Royal Synagogue, *The Modern Man*, 3 May 1913, p2. See also: Lorenzo Kamel, *Middle East From Empire To Sealed Identities*, Edinburgh University Press, 2019, pp121-122.]

man, but at times affects costumes which would make him more at home in the pages of Ouida than in scenes of ordinary life.

In June, *Reynold's Newspaper* column 'The Secret History Of To-Day' suddenly expressed an interest in his welfare, printing: "Will anyone tell me what has become of Lord Battersea, as to whose movements there was something in this section of Reynolds's some months ago?"[*]

The gardens of The Pleasaunce were now opened to the public on Sunday afternoons in summer, the receipts being handed over to the local hospital. On one such occasion, to escape the hell of the crowds who "walked and talked and flirted and flaunted and read hymns and Psalms, and Spiritual songs," Cyril had been driven to Sheringham, and "sat among the fishermen on the beach," drinking whiskey and soda, and eating the remains of his dinner from the night before.

At such times of reflection, including in the deep of the night, his thoughts likely turned to Arthur Thorold and Bernard Fraser, rotting in their respective prisons for crimes he'd been a part of, and facilitated. He certainly didn't forget them. In August 1905, The Pleasaunce Visitors Book features the signatures of the prominent Anglican churchmen Basil and Ernest Wilberforce: they were guests for a day. Ernest was chairman of the Church of England Temperance Society, but it was Basil who was the more radical: even Queen Victoria condemned his teetotal excesses, and he'd been blocked from higher office because of them.

While it would have been Constance who knew the churchmen due to her temperance interests, Cyril may have encouraged her to invite them. For it seems likely it was he who asked Basil Wilberforce to intercede on Bernard Fraser's behalf, to request a reduction in his sentence. This strange intercession, detailed in a later chapter, proved unsuccessful. Arthur Thorold was released the following summer, but Bernard Fraser remained in prison until the autumn of 1908.

Cyril and Constance continued to participate in the social swim, but

---

[*] The reference is obscure. However, a recent item had revealed a further case of the law treating the upper class leniently: "Who, oh, who was the K.C. and Bencher of one of the Inns of Court who had an adventure in Hyde Park and pleaded 'Guilty,' along with the other person, and each was fined £3." [*Reynolds's Newspaper*, 10 January 1904, p1.]

time was catching up with them. At the beginning of The Season of 1906, Violet Bonham Carter wrote to a friend: "Ld. Battersea (Cyril) & 'Connie' are giving a dinner for a ball & beg me to bring as many young men as possible as they know none." It wasn't quite the truth.

As they had the previous year, that summer the Batterseas visited Karlsbad for the sake of Cyril's health. On June 9th, Constance told her diary: "Shocked at Cyril's appearance…and his low spirits." A few days later she added:

> Poor Cyril suffers awfully & is wonderfully good & patient. I couldn't bear to see him going thro' such a purgatory…Ice fomentations ordered provided some relief…Cyril suffers frightfully & is very miserable – sad days.

While they were away, Queen Alexandra made her first unannounced visit to The Pleasaunce, motoring over from Sandringham. Comic accounts of it later circulated: a version was told by E.F. Benson, who left it to the knowing to read between the lines. Apart from the servants, the royal party had found nobody at home except:

> a young man of dishevelled appearance who had just returned from playing golf in a high wind. So they made a private tour of the house, a species of exploration which the Queen much enjoyed, for her appetite for looking into other people's bedrooms and dressing-rooms and bathrooms was insatiable. Before she could be stopped, she plunged into a small useful apartment near the front door [i.e. a lavatory] and found there a large photograph of the beautiful Lady Dudley:* she thought this a very odd room in which to hang it. And in Lord Battersea's sitting-room was a photograph of his young valet in flannels with a cricket bat which instantly she pronounced to be a photograph of George Curzon.

Having a framed photograph of one's valet in one's bedroom, even a sporting photograph, was even more unusual than hanging an icy society beauty in the lavatory. But then, Cyril's relationship with John Compton was decidedly democratic at the least.

---

* Georgina, Countess of Dudley (1846–1929); second wife of the first Earl. A poised, retroussé-nosed fashionable beauty, her chaste countenance was endlessly reproduced on postcards, and in fashion illustrations.

In August, Hugh Godley,[*] a friend of Raymond Asquith, was a guest at The Pleasaunce, from whence he wrote to Violet Bonham Carter to share his own experience of the Overstrand fantasyland. Cyril's eyesight was now being impacted by his diabetes, but his spirits had rallied:

> Ld. Battersea is so different from what I imagined him, & he is very kind & playful but spends most of his time in Norwich having his eyes doctored & has to wear black goggles always. Lady B. trots me about, looking neither to right nor to left except to say from time to time "That is the water garden – pretty – is it not" and doesn't wait for an answer…The conversation at meals is on these lines: Ld B. "Where's my Raymond? I do wish he were here." Lady B. "Don't you think he's very clevah, Mr. Godley." I: "Yes very clever Lady Battersea." Ly B. "Yes. He ought to marry a clevah wife. Violet's so clevah too, don't you think?" I. "Yes, very clever." Ldy B. "Yes – dear Violet – I wish she were here too." …This morning they have both motored to the ends of the earth (different ends) & left me quite happy.

The year 1907 began for the Batterseas with their annual servants ball. More than forty couples danced in the new year at The Pleasaunce. Cyril and Constance continued to play host to a stream of guests. These included Princess Louise; Arthur Balfour's sister Alice;[†] entertainers, such as soprano Jessie Strathearn[‡] and pianist Alma Stenzel;[§] as well as Cyril's stalwart comrades: Spencer Lyttelton in February, Arthur Brown in March, and Arthur Collins in July. Another notable guest that month was one of Society's favourite dancing partners, the bachelor Bertie Stopford.[**]

However, the most important visitor for Cyril that spring was Karl Harko von Noorden, a leading German physician who founded the first clinic for the treatment of diabetes. Von Noorden had developed 'the oat cure', a depressing dietary mixture consisting of oatmeal,

---

[*] Hugh John Godley (1877–1950), 2nd Baron Kilbracken. Married with issue. Assistant parliamentary counsel to the Treasury.
[†] Alice Blanche Balfour (1850–1936), Scottish naturalist and geneticist.
[‡] Jessie Strathearn (1869–1932), soprano and gospel singer, committed to the welfare of the poor.
[§] Alma Stenzel (1887–1933), gifted American pianist from San Francisco.
[**] Albert 'Bertie' Henry Stopford (1860–1939), social figure, spy, hero.

butter and vegetable albumin that lowered blood sugar. It wasn't a genuine cure, but prolonged life; although for some Edwardian epicures a swift death may have been the preferable option.

June found Cyril motoring in Austria; in July he was amongst the guests at a State Ball held by King Edward at Buckingham Palace; while August found him again at The Pleasaunce to welcome another important guest. This was Octavius Rozenraad, a doctor based at the Homburg spa who specialised in thermotherapy – the use of heat and cold to treat the symptoms of chronic pain. He'd visited previously in 1901, which is indicative of how prolonged Cyril's decline had been.

As summer bled into autumn, The Pleasaunce saw still more visitors. Constance and her sister Annie stayed for just a few days; Lutyens overnighted – and no doubt departed with a commission for further 'improvements'; while not least, Cyril hosted a fetching young officer from the Argyll and Sutherland Highlanders, Edward Cuthbertson.*

Tall, moustachioed and handsome, Cuthbertson had served with distinction in the Boer War. He was also rich – the scion of a Scottish mercantile and manufacturing fortune built on wool and cotton. The patron of his regiment was Princess Louise, who had as keen an eye for the military as any of Lorne's friends, and through whom the acquaintance may have been made. Unlike Constance, Cutherbertson stayed at The Pleasaunce for almost three weeks in October. It would be later reported that he was "a young man in whom the late Lord Battersea took a great interest." In 1910, Cuthbertson would marry a widow very much his senior, as such gentlemen often seemed to do.

Lady Frances Balfour would write of Cyril:

> To the very last he lived the fullest life that was left to him. Always happy in the Garden of Eden that he had created out of the waste places by the sea, caring for the many interests and claims which he had made around him in his home by the white cliffs, he passed along, manfully bearing the burden of pain and disability which by degrees mastered the strong frame and brought the end.

---

* Edward Boustead Cuthbertson (1880–1942), later Brigadier-General and Equerry to Princess Beatrice. Married Constance Gertrude Cecily Clifton.

For some months Cyril had been experiencing heart trouble, and his friends feared his death might occur at any moment. This was compounded by breathlessness, due to the pulmonary fibrosis arising from his diabetes. With November fogs descending, he was advised by doctors to seek a change of air. He overnighted a Surrey House, where Constance recorded him as "looking wretchedly ill," before motoring on with a friend to the south coast, and then crossing to Isle of Wight.

On the Osborne estate he managed to tour the garden of Kent House, a residence of Princess Louise and Lorne. In a letter to Constance, Lorne later wrote: "as was his wont, he at once made friends with the old gardener there." However, by now pneumonia had Cyril in its grip. His condition worsened suddenly, and Constance hurried over. On the 27th of November, in the Royal Pier Hotel* at Ryde, he drew his last breaths. He was just sixty-four.

And so it was, in the first week of the final month of 1907, the press reported from Overstrand:

> in brilliant weather, and in the presence of a very large gathering from far and near, all that was mortal of Cyril Flower, first Baron Battersea, was laid to rest in the pretty churchyard of the village with which his name and fame will ever be associated. They came from the mansions of the rich, the cottages of the poor, the homes of the humble, and the dwellings of the great…None who stood around that open grave by the side of the old tower could feel other than how happy was the choice of such a resting place. Indeed, it seemed most fitting that he who in life delighted in all that was joyous in nature should now in death sleep near the gardens that he loved. It was through those lovely grounds, rich in their russet and their green, beneath the azure blue of a winter sky that knew no cloud, that the late lord of Overstrand was slowly borne to mother earth. Those who shared in that final, cherished task, were some forty in number, men who had known and worked for him.

They surely included some of those once-young Welshmen of Brecon.

---

* Long demolished.

The floral offerings were suitably profuse and splendid: showers of orchids, lilies, roses, and the choicest chrysanthemums. His motor car featured in the funeral procession, his seat within it covered with "a huge floral cushion in white and violet" featuring his crest, the letter 'B' and the words 'At Rest'. A magnificent wreath from Princess Louise was composed of flowers from her Isle of Wight garden that Cyril had admired only a few days before, while a wreath from Alfred de Rothschild featured the message "In memory of Cyril, a very, very dear friend."

Resting on the church's altar railing lay another wreath from Arthur Brown of Luton, with whom Cyril had shared motoring memories, while significantly placed in the very centre of the altar, lay a cross of violets from Edward Cuthbertson. Constance remained at The Pleasaunce with her sister. Memorial services were also held at Aston Clinton parish church, and at St. Marylebone in London, at which Archdeacon Basil Wilberforce assisted, and which was attended by, amongst others, Lorne and Spencer Lyttelton.

Cyril's obituary in *The Times* was judgementally short,* and its prose perfunctory, but it rightfully noted, "Lord and Lady Battersea have always done their best to fulfil the obligations of wealth". Naturally, it made no mention of the scandal.

Across the Atlantic, Frederick Frederick Cunliffe-Owen was under no such constraint. Having chronicled Cyril's fall under the guise of the 'Marquise de Fontenoy', he was not remiss in recording his passing. In 'her' column, the following appeared:

> Lord Battersea has for the last few years lived so entirely beyond the ken of society that the demise of this once so popular, handsome, and gifted man has attracted no attention beyond a quiet expression that his death was a happy release for the kindly and philanthropic woman who had taken his name and given him her fortune...Some years ago he became involved in a shocking scandal. He escaped by leaving England and remaining for a considerable time in a sanitarium, the plea being successfully advanced that he was not responsible for his

---

* When the member for Battersea, John Burns, died in 1943, his obituary in *The Times* was three times the length. [Obituary, *The Times*, 25 January 25, 1943, p6.]

actions...Lady Battersea charitably forbore from asking for any dissolution of her marriage, and since then has devoted most of her time, her energy, and much of her vast wealth to relieving the unhappy lot of the women convicts of England.

Like others, Frederick too had been misled by the rumours of Cyril's flight. More than this, he misjudged the Battersea union. While Constance was often desperately unhappy in her marriage, she had adored her Cyril. He'd been her priciest luxury purchase – one that delighted and frustrated in equal measure. Ten now-missing pages from Constance's diary for that November and December suggest the lengths to which further reflection on their marriage led her.

While her Rothschildian fortune had enabled Cyril's dreams, the marriage had not been a gilded sleigh ride for him either. Her skittish, cloying character would have taxed his easy-going nature and deep reserves of patience to the limit. With age, and his increasing illness, both became a good match in petulance. Social duties and personal interests provided them with a pressure valve. Their three palatial, lavishly-staffed residences also acted as escape spaces for them both, delivering nerve-soothing Rothschildian *luxe, calme et volupté.* Yet despite the balms of limitless wealth, the mutual accommodations they made of tolerance and understanding would have been, in the end, far more important to the marriage.

Obituaries elsewhere were more generous, recognising the breadth of Cyril's talents, kindnesses and contributions. *The Saturday Review* noted: "Ill-natured things have been said about him, but those who knew him well always had a very different account to give of him." Cyril's death also wrought a miracle – the *Bedfordshire Advertiser* (*Luton Times*) found some good words for him in its heart:

> His winning personality and bonhomie made him very popular in the Luton Division, where fond Radicals called him 'the people's Cyril.' His generosity at bazaars and stone-laying functions made a practical appeal to South Bed[fordshire] Radicals, who showed, after his elevation to the Second Chamber, how dearly they loved a lord. If local Unionists declined to regard him a serious politician, they always appreciated his genial disposition.

Cyril had what another theatrical life-giver and contemporary, Queen Marie of Romania, called the quality of "those who win". It is borne of a passionate love of life. For Lorne, Cyril "always seemed so full of life and geniality, that it is impossible to believe that we shall not see him again." An obituary written by Lady Frances Balfour strived to capture Cyril's uplifting "life-giving personality" which "always seemed to bring cheer and gladness," and his generosity of spirit:

> The lonely, the poor, and the old never felt their day was over when they had once become known to that host…Who shall attempt to say what were the number of errands of mercy he undertook, or the secret acts of thoughtful fondness which he rendered personally?…Very literally and beautifully was he all things to all men. He knew the lives of those who worked for him as he knew the lives of intimate friends. He was at home in all social spheres, and his tact and quick apprehension made him often the friend in need and the friend indeed.

A short obituary that appeared in *Truth* also made no mention of the scandal, but acknowledged that Cyril "made generous use of his wealth, and his house in town was a centre of practical philanthropy." However, Labouchère did take issue with the claim that Frederic Farrar had incorporated Cyril into *Eric, or Little By Little*, calling it "an insane invention".

In December, William Marcus Thompson, the barrister and editor of *Reynolds's Newspaper,* who'd spent his life campaigning against the injustices wielded by rank and privilege, and had hinted at Cyril's scandal as much as he dared, also succumbed to pneumonia.

At the dawn of King Edward's reign, when the imperial bombast that Labby and Thompson so loathed was in its ascendance, Cyril had given a magazine interview. The reporter recorded:

> As we brought to a close our talk with Lord Battersea we asked what was his message to his fellow countrymen of the present day. Without a moment's hesitation he replied:— "Unite! Unite! The true Imperialist is the man who works not for self and not for Party, but, sinking all prejudice and partiality, aims only at the good of the community at large; while the egotist, the man who thinks only of himself and his own advantage, is the smallest

'Little Englander' that the world has bred!"

Shortly before his own death in 1940, E.F. Benson wrote a final autobiography. He was keen to capture a pen portrait of Cyril because:

> Lord Battersea was of the type which Disraeli called 'the magnifico,' and he had a genial, careless consciousness of his own splendours that seldom left him. No one in the least like him exists now.*

Having enjoyed decades of Cyril's hospitality, Benson insightfully recalled:

> He saw himself in the eyes of others, masterful and opulent. He talked broad Norfolk dialect to the gnarled fisherman sunning themselves on the benches overlooking the sea, and as he went to play his morning round of golf, he talked to the children going to the beach with their spades and buckets with genuine *bonhomie* and the consciousness he was giving pleasure....There was an atmosphere of incense abroad and everybody chorused 'Good shot, my lord' on the smallest excuse...Though his wife sometimes overdid it, he loved the sense that the gnarled fishermen and the caddie and the gardeners admired and adored him. But he was a shrewd man, and he must have known what stuff and nonsense it all was, and I am sure that below this breezy swagger there was fear and perpetual apprehension, and that this magnificence was protection against that. He knew it was a sham, and when he died it was found that he had left nothing but a mountain of debts. His wife's devotion and loyalty were unshaken. "You can't judge dearest Cyril as you would judge anybody else," she said. "He was a genius."

Cyril left an estate of £186,747. However, as Benson wrote, it was indeed soon learnt he'd also left colossal debts. These Constance only cleared with the help of her mother and Alfred de Rothschild. Cyril's bequests included Burne-Jones' 'The Golden Stairs' to the National

---

* Another immensely wealthy and cultivated homosexual dilettante, the baronet Sir Philip Sassoon, had died in 1939. Like Cyril, he had been an M.P. (but Conservative), an art collector and society host, and maintained three palatial residences – including the fantasy house Port Lympne, plus a similar inner court of cultivated, ironical bachelors.

Gallery, and to the National Portrait Gallery the Frederick Sandys portraits of himself and Constance. He also gifted a hundred pounds each to his gardener and butler at Overstrand, while his handsome valet John Compton, who had no doubt witnessed much, was given a life annuity of £60 pounds.

Pining for Cyril, Constance told her diary how she did:

> long for his love. If only he could know it now. Does he? I cannot find his short one line diaries & he has left nothing of written importance. Oh if I could but have had one line.

Poignantly she recorded: "I found amongst his papers a number of favourite [biblical] texts, written in pencil, probably during his last illness." Her hunt continued, resulting in fresh discoveries: "Dear Cyril has kept every one of my letters from the first!" and "Have found all the diaries". Despite their brevity, what an interesting read they would have been for her – and for posterity. In 1873, Cory had written to a friend of Cyril's, "[Richard] Jebb has a great belief in his capacity and sets him down as one who ought to be the great novelist of the day." It was not to be.

As a memorial to Cyril, Constance began planning a botanical and horticultural library at The Pleasaunce, and even sought out a spiritualist medium in the hope of making contact: "he is absolutely happy," she was told.

In 1909, Constance gave up Surrey House, leasing as her London home 10 Connaught Place, a substantial Georgian terrace house. The former residence stood empty, except during The Season, when it was hired out for dances. A Society magazine lamented:

> To old friends of the House before its Doomsday, these re-visits of an evening are not without a certain melancholy, and not all the arts of the temporary decorator, nor the abundance of flowers that transforms otherwise empty rooms into bowers, can compensate for the treasures, once familiar, now lost from its walls.

However, Constance had finally warmed to The Pleasaunce. "Came to my sweet country home," she told her diary, "I LOVE IT. Never so quietly happy, so contented as I am here." In 1914, she entertained a very special guest at Overstrand – the now retired Lord Halsbury. Congratulating him on having reached his ninetieth birthday, Constance gifted him with a bouquet of ninety roses from the garden. Her flowers and hand of friendship were perhaps also a gesture of gratitude for whatever role he may have played as Cyril's saviour.

In private, Cyril's personal legend lingered on. That year, George Ives was a guest at Fairlawne, the country house of the wealthy Cazalet family. He wrote that the conversation amongst the guests, who included the Belgian ambassador and his wife,* included discussion of "the eccentricities of Prince A† and Lord B... I knew what they probably did not; but never said anything."

With the outbreak of war, Constance's life was upturned. She first put up Belgian refugees in one of the Overstrand cottages, and entertained them to an afternoon tea in the cloisters, informing Annie: "I stuffed in a little Temperance teaching, which they all took very well..." The Pleasaunce was given over to a recovery hospital for a score of wounded soldiers, while Aston Clinton was loaned to the command of an infantry division. Cyril would have revelled in it. Lord Rosebery wrote to her: "I see you cannot tear yourself from your barracks," dropping his guard to gush: "*Oh! que j'aime les militaires!*"‡

As well as providing for the needs of the nation's army, Constance faced the wearisome task of attending to her own. "I have tried not to neglect my duties in any of my three houses," she told her diary, "but find it difficult always to do as I feel I ought and as I should like." War-time stringencies decimated her battalion: Lester the butler was reduced to having not a single man-servant under him: all replaced by a lone parlour-maid.

Unlike her more down-to-earth and less-exciteable sister, fear of Zeppelin raids reduced Constance to a state of permanent anxiety and dread, and for a period she retreated to Aston Clinton. In the autumn of 1915, Lord Rosebery finally paid his first visit to The Pleasaunce in her absence, writing to her:

---

* Charles Maximilien, Count de Lalaing (1856–1919), Belgian diplomat, and Christine, Countess de Lalaing, née du Tour van Bellinchave (1886–1919).
† Likely Prince Alfred, Duke of Edinburgh, or Prince Albert Victor, Duke of Clarence.
‡ "Oh! how I love the military!"

On Friday after shooting, and greatly daring, I drove to…Overstrand…Here by anxious inquiry, we found your dominions, but where they began or where they ended I could never ascertain; they seemed as illimitable as they were gorgeous. Here was a lawn tennis party, there a cricket ground. I wandered timidly through a subway, came on a cloister and an azure bath and exclaimed 'I can trespass no more'…

By the following year, Constance had returned to Overstrand, but told Annie: "This is indeed a time of <u>terror</u> and tribulation; one thinks that one hears Zepps. at all hours of the evening and night, and there are constant explosions and gun-firing out to sea." When in London she slept in her pearls, with a fur cloak at the foot of the bed, ready to flee.

With the arrival of peace, and two years before his death in 1920, Wilfrid Blunt published his diaries. In what was printed, there was not the slightest allusion to Cyril's scandal. That same year Constance privately printed a slender, and regrettably insipid anthology, *Thoughts In Verse*. Its appearance was explained by an ode to her pen – "Who tends to make the hours less grey". Yet if Cyril had ever provoked her to poesy, there was not a word of him here.

In 1923, Constance's memoirs appeared: having begun them while recovering from diphtheria, she was able to record with satisfaction they were: "selling wonderfully…Dear Mother would have been delighted – Cyril less so." So proud was she of her first royalty cheque, that after cashing it she had it framed and hung in her bedroom. Browsing the signatures in her Visitors Books, she wrote:

> Beautiful women, clever men, kindly souls, affectionate friendly hearts, do you not all come trooping back when memory's cells are unlocked? Were you not at your best under the genial, sunny welcome of my parents, and was it not the case that "evil speaking, lying and slandering, vulgar gossip and malicious tittle-tattle, could not live in" the presence of my mother? At least, so wrote the late G.W.E. Russell, in some unforgettable words penned after her death.

Given the gossip Constance would have endured in 1902, or even the thought of it, George Russell's words of stainless days were obviously especially cherished. As the years went on, her diary marked the death of friends: "How the world is changing from me. I cannot bear to look forward. As we go on in life it is really walking thro' graveyards. But we must look upward & not think of them as lying there."

Her late husband remained a constant presence, and she dwelled on his virtues: "Cyril, so much with us. A man of sterling qualities, a...straight forward honest englishman. A very fine rider – a cheery bright companion, popular with everyone."

Now spending most of her time at The Pleasaunce, in 1923, Constance sold Aston Clinton for £15,000: it would be demolished in 1956. In London, Surrey House stood empty: a succession of polychromatic and gilded caverns of ghosts. During the War it had been a distribution centre for the Royal Flying Corps and British War Library, which provided reading material for serving men. In 1927 it was demolished and replaced by the Regal, a 2,400 seat cinema.* Noting the melancholy event, a journalist remembered Cyril as "the last of the 'exquisites'," adding, "He would probably turn in his grave if he knew what purpose the house on which he lavished so much care and money is to be put." Symptomatic of the changing times, Cyril's enormous statue of Sardanapalus was found impossible to dispose of, except as hewn marble. It was the stuff of a parable.

Cyril's spectre may yet have found delight in the decorative scheme of the picture palace's interior, which took its cue from a Roman temple. The auditorium side walls featured murals of glades flanked by columns, while across the ceiling stretched a grapevine-festooned pergola, through which could be seen the twinkling stars of an artificial sky. It was a pleasaunce for the masses.

Constance continued with her philanthropy, but as increasing age tightened its grip, her world contracted. The advent of the first Labour government in 1924 alarmed her, and after a long illness, her beloved sister Annie died in 1926. Constance confided to a friend: "I lead the quietest of lives and go nowhere." Like Charles Thorold and many other Victorians, the London of the 1920s seemed to her an "overwhelming metropolis...It seems so impossible ever to get to any

---

* The patrician reserve of the precinct was further extinguished in 1960–1963 by the widening of Park Lane for a dual carriageway.

destination in these crowded streets."

Having been gradually reduced to an invalid in a wheelchair, Constance died at The Pleasaunce on the 22nd of November 1931. It was the anniversary of her marriage. Mourned locally and nationally as an unstinting benefactress, despite Cyril's debts, she left an enormous estate of £244,515.

Having a fear of being buried alive, Constance left instructions that before being placed in her coffin, bells were to be tied to her wrists and ankles. She was interred in Willesden Jewish Cemetery. On quiet nights, perhaps old friends of her husband at the Society for Psychical Research heard her tinkling.*

In his own will, Cyril had stated with the greatest optimism it was his "earnest wish and desire" that the house, gardens, grounds and contents of Overstrand should always be kept up and maintained to the same order as in his lifetime. It was not to be. Constance bequeathed all her Norfolk property in trust to a young cousin twice removed, Rosemary de Rothschild;† her father Lionel Nathan de Rothschild acting as trustee.

In 1935 the contents of The Pleasaunce were auctioned, and the following year the property was subdivided. The majority of the magnificent gardens, upon which Cyril and a labouring army had expended their energies, and a fortune, were replaced by bungalows, many of a fairground shoddiness that would have appalled the former squire.‡

The house and immediate grounds of 2.5 hectares were sold to an Anglican foundation providing holiday accommodation. Due to the perceived risk of coastal erosion, the sale price was only a fraction of what Cyril had invested in the property. Its atmosphere and the

---

* Constance possibly shared her fear of live internment with her friend Francis Cobbe, whose will made the more sinewy request that a medical attendant "perform on my body the operation of completely and thoroughly severing the arteries of the neck and wind pipe, nearly severing the head altogether, so as to render any revival in the grave absolutely impossible." [Miss Francis Power Cobbe, *Reynolds's Newspaper*, 10 April 1904, p1.]
† Rosemary Leonara Ruth Seys, née de Rothschild (1913–2013). Married the Hon. Denis Gomer Berry, and secondly, John Antony Seys.
‡ Small portions of the former pleasure grounds, including the boathouse, survive within the subdivision. Paintings of the gardens by Beatrice Parsons, commissioned by the Batterseas, provide glimpses of the vanished fantasia.

portion of remaining gardens inexorably suffered. Today it is but a ghost of the dream that was. Yet the power of the great wealth that forged it is still obvious. On a fine day, with the house sun-washed and wrapped in a deep quiet broken only by birdsong, the faint spirit of what was once an earthly paradise lingers on.

In 1924, Constance had written to her sister Annie: "I am making a holocaust of my correspondence. I have found some queer old things amongst them, very precious best in the flames like the Gods in the Valkerie." Constance bequeathed her private papers to a cousin, Lucy Cohen, who used them to publish a biography of Constance's mother Louise, *Lady Rothschild And Her Daughters*. In its preface, Cohen wrote that despite Constance's disposal of papers, "a huge residue remained. And even the greater part of this was only fit for the same fate, or unsuitable for publication." She added:

> Lady Battersea, in her will, requested her cousin Mr. Leonard Montefiore, to cooperate with me. I wish to offer him my thanks for his help in the onerous task of the initial work of the destruction and selection of her papers.

The pair were exceedingly thorough in their task. Lucy, who died a spinster, handed over the residue to her bachelor nephew James Arthur Waley Cohen, who died in 1962. It would be rich irony if the censors of this fascinating history were homosexual themselves. In 1953, James bestowed one part of what remained of the papers, including Constance's occasionally-scissored and blacked-out diaries, to the British Library. The other portion went to N.M. Rothschild & Sons, where it ended up in the private Rothschild Archive.

Cyril's brief diaries were not included in the bequest. They are missing; presumed destroyed.* The diaries may have been burnt before Cohen and Montefiore assumed their executorship – a two-word quote from them that Cohen references in her book was actually drawn from Constance's diary. If Constance was responsible for their destruction, it may have been due to a desire to protect her husband's reputation – or an unresolved grudge to punish Cyril for his unfaithfulness, and lack of respect for her own literary and

---

* Dr. Alan Montefiore (b.1926), remembers Lucy Cohen, but is "virtually certain" the diaries do not reside with the Montefiore family. The Rothschild Archive also has no knowledge of them. [Dr. Montefiore and the Rothschild Archive to author.]

temperance endeavours. With her own *Reminiscences,* she was certainly determined to have the last word. Ironically, of the few letters of Cyril's to survive, one is to Walt Whitman, and another to the man who was possibly his first lover, Frederic Myers, informing him of his engagement.

There was further destruction. In 1910, following the death of Edward VII, Sir George Lewis, "the Napoleon of Lawyers" as he was dubbed, decided to retire. It was the end of an era. "George Lewis is the one man in England who should write his memoirs – and of course he never can," Edward had said. Lewis requested his clerk bring his office papers down to his home at Overstrand. There in the grounds of his estate they were burned, the smoke possibly wafting symbolically over The Pleasaunce. Given Lewis had been at the centre of the greatest scandals of the age, it was truly the bonfire of secrets to end them all.

By 1935, when Lucy Cohen published *Lady Rothschild And Her Daughters,* a reviewer referred to Cyril as "that rather tragic 'spoiled darling of fortune'," and wistfully reflected upon, "the pageant of the days of snug (and sometimes smug) security and permanence at the end of the Age of Privilege" comparing it to: "that new world of stark reality in which we have our being. Small wonder if we cast 'one longing, lingering look behind' to so much Ease, so much Grace, so much Security, so much velvet Luxury."

Sir Alfred Pease,* a Liberal M.P. who'd been both a friend and house-guest of Cyril's, had also published a memoir. In it he paid tribute to his former host, while admitting: "there were many people who were prejudiced against him. I knew him particularly well, and admired him very much…He is one who never had justice done to him, and who had shameless detractors."

Overlooking the sea at The Pleasaunce, Cyril had commissioned Edwin Lutyens to design a gazebo to provide an exquisite, light-flooded writing room and contemplation retreat for a deeply admired friend, the lesbian Irish novelist and poet Emily Lawless, who was asthmatic. "When Cyril cared for any one," Constance recalled, "he cared very much indeed, and to himself it was a delight to be in any

---

* Sir Alfred Edward Pease, 2nd Baronet (1857–1939), of a Quaker banking family. Married thrice, and had issue.

way helpful to his friend." Emily's days at Overstrand under the sheltering wing of its lordly hosts gave her, she told Constance, "the sense of the world as a happy and inspiring planet," and after Cyril's death, she composed *A Valediction*. It begins:

> Farewell again, truest, most helpful soul:
> This world is dearer to me for thy sake;
> No jot or tittle of its varying whole
> Is worth what love and loving friendship make.

15. THE ELUSIVE MISTER W

Given that the names of the two absconding procurers were not on the indictment, the press could only guess at their spellings. Boulton was also spelt as Bolton, while the name of the fourth man was printed as both Wiley and Willey.

No conclusive evidence has so far been uncovered as to the identity of this last gentleman. In which case, at least for the time being, one must rely upon circumstantial evidence.

There are so many further ways to spell the name: Wylie, Wyllie, Wyly, Wylly, Wily, Whiley, and Whyley. And in the British high society of the time, there were gentlemen answering to some of these variations.

However, there are *two* such persons whose associations and lives make strong claims for them to be regarded as suspects. What now follows could be considered evidence. The characters and lives of both gentlemen, each wholly different from the other, are in the best manner of journeys, wonderfully eye-opening...

I. Alexander Henry Wylie (1849–1911)

Travelling in America in the winter of 1877, Alexander Henry Wylie confided to friends, "the liberty of the press here is simply scandalous."

Alexander, or 'Alex', as his friends knew him, was accustomed to the good manners of the English press. As 'A.H. Wylie', London newspapers politely recorded his appearances as a man about town. Indicative of how well-connected he was, including through associations relevant to this story, can be gained from reports of the funeral of Reginald Brett's father, the 1st Lord Esher, which occurred in 1899. Newspapers placed Wylie's name upfront amongst those of the most distinguished guests:

> A special train left Waterloo yesterday morning for the convenience of those attending the funeral of the late Lord Esher at Esher. Among the passengers were Sir F. Knollys (representing the Prince of Wales), Colonel Arthur Collins (presenting the Marchioness of Lorne)...Mr. A.H. Wylie...Mr. Reginald Brett (who succeeds Lord Esher, his father, in the title).

Similarly, the following year when Gladstone's eldest son died, amongst the distinguished visitors who called at his Park Lane residence to express condolence and sympathy, and which the European edition of the *New York Herald* considered worthy of mention in a brief list, were the Marquess of Lorne, Mr. And Mrs. Cyril Flower, and A.H. Wylie.

Alex was the son of Alexander Henry Wylie senior,* and his wife, Elizabeth, née Crosbie. They were an Edinburgh family of means, and had been for a long time. There were similarities to Bernard Fraser's background, and indeed, both men had the same friends. When Viscount Castlereagh,† heir to the Marquess of Londonderry, married in 1899, the wedding gifts included, from Bernard, a gold pencil set with a turquoise, and from Alex, a miniature frame.

Alex's independent income was also the result of an enterprising father. At the age of twenty-one, Alex senior, like other young men of his station, had embarked on the Grand Tour through Europe to Italy. More unusually, that same year he'd also set off with his brother Macleod on a second journey to Havana, Cuba.

---

* Alexander Henry Wylie (1810-1869).
† Charles Vane-Tempest-Stewart, 7th Marquess of Londonderry (1878–1949). Married Lady Theresa Chetwynd-Talbot.

He then established himself as a merchant in Liverpool, importing cotton via a New Orleans partnership, and also exporting manufactured goods. He even published a pamphlet advocating the removal of trade restrictions.

Alex senior then went on, again like Bernard Fraser's father, to invest in the burgeoning railways. He was a prominent activist shareholder and auditor for the Midland Railway Company, and the York, Newcastle and Berwick Railway Company; and a director of the Dundee And Perth Railway Company. Thus are fortunes multiplied.

From Liverpool, Alex senior moved to Edinburgh: the family residences were a substantial terrace house at 19 Walker Street in that city, and a large marine villa, 'Eastfield', that faced the ocean at the Scottish seaside town of North Berwick.

Given his wealth, Alex senior's marriage in 1843 had involved a prenuptial contract, which established a trust for his future children. The Wylies had five sons and two daughters.* Named after his father, Alexander Henry Wylie junior was their third son. Born in their Edinburgh home on the 17 of May 1849, he only ever had one métier – Society.

When Alex junior was twenty, his industrious father died after a short illness. If Alex hadn't already come into his share of the family trust, he soon would. The following year, with his older brother George Crosbie, he was formally presented at Court to the Prince of Wales (representing the Queen), at a royal levee in London. Their introducer was the Earl of Camperdown,† a popular Liberal politician who was considered 'a good-egg'. Strongly community-minded, and greatly trusted, Camperdown was a confirmed bachelor with a 14,000-acre Scottish estate. Described as "an excellent, thoughtful host," he was

---

* Their first son, Henry Philip Miles Wylie, undertook a military career in the Royal Rifles, eventually becoming a colonel; the second son, George Crosbie Wylie, attended Oxford, and then became a captain in the Royal Perth regiment, a stockbroker, and Fellow of the Royal Horticultural Society. Their fourth son, Napier Macleod Wylie, was a sub-lieutenant in the Lancashire Artillery, before taking on the management of some farms, while their fifth son, Arthur Kinnaird, was also a stockbroker and a quartermaster in the Volunteer Medical Staff Corps. The daughters were Charlotte Ethel, a spinster, and a second who remains unidentified.
† Robert Adam Philips Haldane Haldane-Duncan, 3rd Earl of Camperdown (1841–1918), Liberal politician.

also "a shy retiring man, who cares not at all for Society," so making his favour to the two youths an even more special one.

In London, Alex lived with George at the premium address of 27 Beaufort Gardens in Knightsbridge. Although he'd already been 'out' in Society for a year, now Alex's social career really took off. Amongst the occasions he attended was a banquet thrown by the Lord Mayor at Mansion House, a grand ball at the same venue, and an embassy dinner. For a mere twenty-one-year-old it was a dazzling entrée into high life, but this was the norm for the sons and daughters of privilege entering the London Season.

In 1876, the day after his twenty-seventh birthday, Alex applied for a passport. He didn't depart immediately. There was the more important matter of the current London Season to complete. Amongst its visitors was the blind King of Hanover.* Sympathetic visitors who called at Claridges to pay their respects to His Majesty included, as the press reported, Alex.

In October, accompanied by a manservant, Alex embarked on a round-the-world tour. Upon his return the following year, encouraged by friends, he compiled (and no doubt polished) the letters he'd written whilst travelling, self-publishing them in bookform as *Chatty Letters From The East And West*. It was a handsome production; the leaves of premium paper were edged with gilt, and there was a fold-out map.

The material was slight, but entertaining: his letters of introduction had opened all doors. In Australia, he dined with the Governor of Victoria, and was a guest of William Clarke,† the richest man in the colonies, at his princely estate of Rupertswood.

As for New Zealand, Alex labelled it "the very Paradise of domestic servants," learning they were "highly paid and luxuriously fed." He also noted the amount of public drunkenness, and how intellectually incurious and insular the country was, finding the general conversation "inexpressibly wearisome". However, he acknowledged,

---

* George V, King of Hanover (1819–1878).
† Sir William John Clarke, 1st baronet (1831–1897); Australian businessman and philanthropist.

"The work of a new settlement cannot be done with kid gloves," and the antipodes were not a cossetting locale for dilettantes or "idle, self-indulgent scapegraces of good family".

Domestic reviews of the book in Britain were gently complimentary. "His letters are just such letters as a well-educated gentleman might be expected under these circumstances to write home to his own family circle," affirmed *The Daily News* of London. *The Scotsman* was also pleased: "Their very freedom from pretensions of any kind makes them exceedingly pleasant reading." However, it did express one caveat about the author: "Mr. Wylie is evidently a man of considerable taste and culture, though with a touch of insular exclusiveness in his composition." Nonetheless, "He records his impression of what he saw and heard on his long pleasure-trip with a quaint, dry humour."

More sober was *The Graphic*, which considered the work "may pass muster, if only for its airiness and vivacity…At all events the English reader will be satisfied with the final moral that there is no place like home." Then there was *The Morning Post*, which averred:

> He has a quick, observing eye, and sees everything that passes before him…and is so thoroughly good natured and genial in his observations that it would be difficult even for the New Yorkers, on whom he is exceptionally severe, to feel wrath with him.

Their confidence on that final point could not have been more misplaced. Alex's diverting but casually contemptuous observations of American manners and customs may have sat well with English prejudice: it was a very different thing elsewhere. The book provoked the *New York Herald's* London correspondent into a paroxysm of rage that found outlet in a long review titled 'A Literary Idiocy'. Its subhead was even more damning: "The trip of an English cad around the world – What he saw in the United States – News for Americans from a supercilious imbecile." Calling it "the most worthless volume in existence," and for good measure, "the most trivial and idiotic volume extant," it said of its author: "Mr. Wylie is apparently a person of an age equally as tender as his head, juvenility being the most charitable plea in extenuation of his offence." The reviewer liberally quoted some of the paragraphs less-flattering to his nation:

At a big hotel you certainly see American life...The waiters are all negroes, and they in no way hurry themselves in attending to your wants. The behaviour of the Americans at their meals has to be seen to be believed: they are far more like animals than human beings...The expressions in constant use by Americans sound strange to foreign ears...if you state any fact they are unaware of they always answer, "Is that so?"

Amongst other things, Alex had taken objection to the prevalence of spittoons. Of New York, he wrote that: "I was much surprised to find so grand a town," and that some of its stores were "far superior to anything we have". However:

all things in America are so very expensive that foreigners never think of buying anything they can possibly do without...The dress of the ladies is gorgeous, but very much over-done; in fact, in their attire, their houses, their carriages and horses, there is an outward show and display very repellant to our quiet ideas.

What particularly would have incensed American readers was the callow snobbism that followed:

With one exception I did not present any of my letters [of introduction]. I knew enough people already in New York, and it was quite clear to me that the society would not be to my taste...Foreigners must surely confess that well-bred Americans, as we understand the word, are few and far between. Could you see the display of diamonds, such as they are, you would be amused.

Once back in England, Alex concluded his letters with the further insulting reflection:

I am immensely glad, notwithstanding its atrocious climate, to find myself amongst cultivated human beings — a class one seldom meets abroad."

For *The New York Herald*, the fair author was "the worst type of a conceited, prejudiced, 'stuck-up' English cad," who'd paid the publishers "a liberal bonus, no doubt, for the sacrifice of reputation":

Assuredly no publishers would have taken his rubbishy 'Letters' for publication on their own account; hence the super excellent paper and type and the gorgeous binding which have been thrown away upon it.

Lavish self-publishing was just one of Alex's extravagances that needed to be paid for; he may already have been living beyond his trust income. An advantageous marriage can sometimes solve such difficulties, and in 1880, at the age of thirty-one, he proposed.

His fiancée, Louisa Lavinia Esther Evans Jennings was eminently respectable: the only child of the Venerable John Jennings, Archdeacon and Canon of Westminster. When her father died two years later, Louisa inherited the Twynersh estate in Surrey, whose then broad acres, unspoilt by today's noisome freeway and other blighting development, rolled in deep tranquillity from picturesque St Anne's Hill.

The couple married the following year in Westminster Abbey no less, *Vanity Fair* reporting the service was conducted, "With all the pomp and ecclesiastical ceremony befitting high dignitaries of the Church." One of the two canons assisting was Cyril Flower's admirer, the one and only Frederic Farrar, who was on his way to succeeding Jennings as Archdeacon. On the marriage registration form, under 'Rank or Profession', Alex wrote 'Gentleman'. The groomsmen were Alex's youngest brother, Arthur Kinnaird Wylie, and more curiously, the Lord Beaumont.

That this nobleman, one year older than Alex, was perhaps his closest male friend, gives serious pause. To appreciate why, a brief character sketch of this most colourful of peers is necessary.

Even at Eton, the 9th Baron Beaumont, Henry Stapleton, had been regarded as "somewhat peculiar". A journalist would later state: "The fact is that Lord Beaumont's idiosyncrasies amount almost, if not quite, to insanity, and his career proves this."

Beaumont's febrile imagination was seized by grandiose military ventures. In a loop of mutual lunacy, he was decorated with an Order of Military Merit by his hero, Ludwig II of Bavaria. He also shared with that monarch a mania for building.

In 1873, having converted to Catholicism, Beaumont dashed off to Spain to support a quixotic royal pretender, Don Carlos,* in the last Carlist War. He now dreamt of receiving Don Carlos at the Beaumont family seat of Carlton Hall, in the presence of all the Catholic bishops of Europe. However, for that residence to be worthy of such an occasion, he deemed a massive makeover would be required. For this he hired Edward Pugin, son of the architect of the Houses of Parliament, plus a further architect for the interiors, which would include a vast Venetian Room of shimmering gilt. The sober Carlton Hall was now transformed into the high gothic fantasia of Carlton Towers, with Pugin providing all the turrets, battlements, gargoyles, and heraldry that megalomania and money could buy – until it ran out.

By 1879, bankruptcy was looming. Having gone off to fight in the Zulu War, Beaumont was then obliged to live abroad. After an unfulfilling trawl in America for a suitable heiress, in 1888 he settled for Violet Isaacson. She was the conveniently lesbian daughter of a London Jewish silk merchant and Tory M.P., Frederick Wootton Isaacson, and his Court dressmaker wife, Elizabeth, née Jaeger, who went by the sobriquet of 'Madame Elise', and whose fortune had been built on the backs of sweated labour. At a time when a housemaid might earn 15 pounds a year, Madame charged upwards of 60 to 100 guineas for a single Court train. However, when one of her young seamstresses thoughtlessly dropped dead from overwork in the ill-ventilated workroom, it publicly exposed the fact that the standard shift in Madame's couture concentration camp was "fifteen hours a day, and twenty-four on very great emergencies". (In the event of hysteria, "chamomile and sienna" were administered by the housekeeper.) The breathtaking callousness of the couple led to one journal labelling them 'pachydermatous', and lamenting "No arguments and no remonstrances will tell with people of this sort."

Like mother, like daughter. While Violet was reported to be "exceedingly popular" in the parish, and "deadly with partridges," she was also something of a fright-bat. As her local church more delicately phrased it: "Her authoritative and somewhat high-handed manner

---

* Carlos María de los Dolores de Borbón y Austria-este, Duke de Madrid, byname Don Carlos (1848–1909), great-grandson of King Charles IV of Spain.

was not always popular with some estate tenants."* More particularly, she was unpopular with her husband. In 1889, Lord Beaumont filed for divorce on the grounds that the marriage had not been consummated, and revealed Violet's Sapphism, submitting as evidence her letters to female friends. These indicated that, as one foreign newspaper shared it, this "circle of ladies of fashion had been in the habit of practising some of the most revolting French vices." Given there was no charge of unfaithfulness, and thereby no co-respondent, the case could not be heard in the English courts, and so Beaumont sought an annulment in the House of Lords.

Although the petition was never reported by the British press, it was dropped, probably due to his father-in-law who, appalled by Society gossip, took out an injunction to stop him circulating the letters. However, later that same year the front page of *The New York Times* reported that Beaumont was a client of 19 Cleveland Street, and in the wake of the scandal, had fled to the Continent. There was never a dull moment at Carlton Towers, but again the British press remained silent about his tribulations.

In 1892, Lord Beaumont died of pneumonia at the age of 44. "His was a curiously romantic figure in these commonplace days, one that we could ill spare," mused the obituary writer of *The Graphic*. Such was the nature of Alex's best man.

Given what followed, it's painfully obvious Alex's marriage was also one of convenience – for him alone. The couple initially lived with Louisa's parents in London at Deans Yard, Westminster, and following her father's death, at Wilton Crescent and Twynersh. Almost from the outset, Alex continued the life he'd led as a bachelor, apparently presuming that marriage to an archdeacon's daughter would be no more burdening upon himself than the acquisition of an innocent pet. If he'd bet on Louisa's naivety and tolerance of ill-treatment, he was sadly correct.

In 1899 he made the first move to divorce, filing for restoration of conjugal rights. This was pure sham, as Louisa's countersuit revealed. It was Alex who'd deserted, a mere two years into the marriage, walking out of the the marital home at 24 Hans Place, Knightsbridge,

* In mitigation, in World War I she gained an O.B.E. for her support of nursing, and loaning her dower house for eighteen months as a hospital for 20 officers.

which had been leased for them by Louisa's mother. Louisa claimed Alex had treated her "with contempt, coldness, indifference, neglect and unkindness." The truth of her statements is made obvious by the lack of any serious attempt by Alex to substantiate the denials he sent to the court in response. Louisa's petition further stated:

> the said Alexander Henry Wylie is now an undischarged bankrupt, is a man of extravagant habits, and has habitually contracted debts which he has been unable to pay.

As early as 1883, Alex used the occasion of assisting friends of Louisa's family with a charity bazaar to misappropriate the funds and some of the goods. In what must have been an immensely embarrassing situation, to protect her good name, and save Alex from criminal proceedings, Louisa was forced to retrieve the merchandise with the help of friends.

Louisa further stated in her petition that Alex entertained guests unknown to her while refusing to allow her to be present; that he "represented himself as a bachelor," and also refused to take her out socially. Sure enough, in press reports of society functions, Alex's name always appears singularly. However, there was worse.

Following Alex's desertion, Louisa moved into her mother's house at 36 Cadogan Gardens. In 1891, with criminal cleverness Alex had his name inserted in social directories, such as the Blue Book, as the property's occupier. He then obtained an inventory of the house's contents. Scissoring off the name of Louisa's mother from the document, he applied his own coat-of-arms or monogram to it. Using this, and the false directory listings as identification of ownership, he then obtained a Bill Of Sale for the house's contents. With this as security, he was able to obtain large advances from both a bank, and money lender.

Before long, Louisa's mother was subject to visits by debt collectors. When the holder of the Bill of Sale learnt of the misrepresentation, he threatened to prosecute for fraud and perjury. Louisa alleged that Alex had threatened to commit suicide unless his debts were paid.

To save her daughter and Alex from disgrace, Louisa's mother was forced to borrow to pay back the advances. Over the years, Louisa estimated that her mother had outlaid more than £16,000 to meet Alex's debts. As her solicitor outlined it: "Petitioner has been for sixteen years in constant fear and dread...and she has constantly suffered in health from this cause."

While Alex was obviously charm itself amongst a wide circle of cultivated friends, the underlying stuck-up English cad that the *New York Herald* had fingered was far more than that. He was a monster of soul-destroying selfishness. In 1900, the couple were granted a judicial separation.

Alex's financial extortions may also have impacted on his brother George. In 1891, an engagement between George and Maud Trelawny, the artistic daughter of a wealthy landed family of Chester, was broken off. George's other social connections are also worthy of note. As well as being a freemason, he was highly sporting, being a member of the London Athletic Club, and a keen golfer, playing at many of the leading courses. He was one of the founders of the golf club on Hayling Island where Arthur Collins maintained a home, and also played in matches arranged with the House of Commons, and with Arthur Balfour. Such friendships made on the links may have proved especially useful if his brother had required sympathetic consideration by the State in later years.

In the meantime, with what seems not any pause for reflection, Alex continued his blithe socialising. That same year, at the height of the London Season, he attended a garden bazaar hosted by the Duchess of Sutherland in support of crofter homespun textiles and handicrafts. The venue was Stafford House,* the London palace of the Sutherlands and sometime home of Lord Ronnie Gower. Amongst other fashionable bachelors reported as in attendance were Alec Hood, Freddy Wallop,† Victor Bowring,‡ and not least, Bernard

---

* Now Lancaster House.
† The Hon. Frederick Henry Arthur Wallop (1870–1953). A son of the 5th Earl of Portsmouth, he collected miniatures, and was a trustee of the National Portrait Gallery.
‡ Victor Henry Bowring-Hanbury (1867–1943). A tall, conspicuous figure who sported brocaded waist-coats, orchid button-holes, and peered at the world through "a heavily jewelled gold lorgnette" that drew attention to fingers "covered with gems," his Belgrave Square home was a private museum, crammed with art. In 1904 he married wealthy widower Ellen Hanbury and added her surname to his own. Society gossiped that he'd murdered her first husband. His enthusiasms extended to guardsmen, wearing his wife's jewels in private, and living beyond his means. He was declared bankrupt in 1935, but discharged in 1938. [Rings On His Fingers, *The Daily Mirror*, 25 March 1936, p9; House A Private Museum, *Western Mail*, 18 July 1934,

Fraser.

Society did not completely dominate Alex's time. During his marriage, he had further dipped his toe into literature. In 1882, he published a Scottish short story, *The Braes o' Mar.* In marked contrast to the conflagration at his own hearth, as The *Liverpool Mercury* found, this was:

> a pleasantly told little story of family life, with sly hints at Scotch parish ministers, and the dull monotony at times of country house life. The author is most successful in his reproduction of the worthy old crones and their opinions on kirks and sermons.

However, the paper took offence to "the implied sneer in the allusions to the '*Sawbath*'* thus spelt and italicised." Apart from what may be this lone review, the slender volume made not a dent on literary life.

Alex also penned a trio of articles for a magazine appropriately titled *London Society.* One story was about a tour of the Scottish Highlands he'd undertaken; the second a recollection of the famous hostess Lady Holland,† whom he'd come to know as a neighbour at Twynersh; while the third article was titled 'Society In 1892'. Its purpose he outlined upfront: "to an on-looker who does not go to 'every lighted candle', the question naturally arises, What is now called 'society?'" To this most pressing of questions, Alex informed his breathless readers:

---

p13; £150,000 Surplus Disappeared, *Daily News*, (London) 3 June 1938, p3; Henry Channon, Simon Heffer (ed.), *Henry 'Chips' Channon: The Diaries 1943–57*, Huchinson Heinemann, London 2023, entry: 24 Dec 1943.]

* The Sabbath. The intensity of the grip of the evangelical revival is indicated by the other books the newspaper reviewed that day: *Old Faiths In A New Light* by the Rev. Newman Smyth; *Strictures On Religious Creeds and Religious Usages* by John Earp; *Dick the Newsboy* by the Rev. Thomas Keyworth (an improving work issued by the Scottish Temperance League); *Henry Wadsworth Longfellow* by the Rev. P Murphy; *Comfortable Words In The Time Of Sickness And Suffering* (an anonymously authored anthology of scriptural passages); and *How India Is Governed* by Alexander Mackenzie. [Literary Notices, *Liverpool Mercury*, 24 May 1882, p5.]

† Mary Augusta Fox, Lady Holland, née Coventry (1812–1889); daughter of the 8th Earl of Coventry; married the 4th Lord Holland. The Hollands lived in Italy for most of their lives, but she also became the venerable mistress of Holland House, Kensington, the Jacobean residence famous as a resort of cultivated Whig society, until its bombing in World War II. Beautiful, clever, eccentric and exhausting, "she exercised a natural authority over those around her." She also maintained a country seat, Ruxbury House, at St. Anne's Hill, Chertsey. [Death Of Lady Holland, *The St James's Gazette*, 24 September 1889, p12.]

I maintain 'society' of thirty years ago does not exist at the present day...A new word has cropped up in the last ten years: 'smart' society. Is it recruited from blood? assuredly not. Is it exemplary virtue? assuredly not. Is it exquisite wit? No, it is rich Jews, Americans and those who must be *en evidence*...Their ostentatious display would in itself prevent, and does prevent, many of the 'noble of the land' from ever encouraging their impertinent overtures to induce them to visit them or recognise them socially in any way.

In other words, it was more of the snobbery he'd dished up in *Chatty Letters*. The article went on to congratulate himself on knowing three 'distinguished ladies' of London who deigned not to receive the new arrivistes. Obviously thinking of Lady Holland, he bemoaned, "Where is the *grande dame* of only a few years ago?" He was clearly unaware that he himself had assumed the role and more – as a latter-day Lady Catherine de Burgh. He further pronounced:

What the *nouveaux riches* do not seem to understand, is that there is no true distinction in being rich, and that no *genuine* reverence is extended to them simply because of their wealth. One of the greatest signs of their vulgarity is the wanton and purposeless display of opulence by people who have no other possession in the whole world to recommend them.

Knowing that Alex was then burning through his mother-in-law's money on just such indulgence, shades such reflections with more than a tinge of irony. Indeed, the article was testament to Alex's skill in both self-delusion and maintaining a false appearance.

In 1901, newspapers recorded Alex and Bernard Fraser bestowing gifts upon on yet another fashionable nuptial: Alex giving the bride Indian embroidery, and Bernard, a fan. On the 19th of July 1902, nine days before Bernard's arrest, newspapers also noted Alex attending the marriage of the Countess De La Warr in London.

If Alex was the procurer who fled, where might he have gone? The answer is provided by *The Irish Times*. In December of 1902, Lady Dudley, the wife of the Lord-Lieutenant, fell ill. In a report that lists the eminent visitors who had called at the Vice-Regal Lodge in Dublin to make enquiries of her ladyship's health, sits the name 'A.H. Wylie'.

Alex's friendship with the couple may have been through her husband. Despite their seven children, and Lord Dudley's later second marriage to the queen of the music halls, Gertie Millar, *The New York Times* had also named him on its front page in 1889 as a patron of the famed house in Cleveland Street.* If the allegation was true, for Alex, the Dudleys must have almost felt like family.

The following year, there is another newspaper record for Alex crossing to Ireland again. However, if there was a shake-up in his life at this period, by the summer of 1904 things were back to normal, with the press recording his attendance at yet another London Society wedding. And so his purposeless life rolled on.

In May 1908, Alex inserted a classified advertisement in *The Morning Post*:

> Mr. A.H. Wylie can thoroughly recommend butler with footman; town or town and country; age 40; height 5ft 6in; abstainer and thoroughly understanding of all his duties; wages £65; would go temporarily for few months; disengaged when suited. – Butler, 24 Bryanston-square, Hyde Park W.

Advertisements recommending servants were mostly placed anonymously, using the terms 'a gentleman', 'a nobleman', etc. The fact Alex was prepared to use his own name suggests not only his pride, but that he considered his name still of social worth and its own recommendation. However, why he wished to dispense with servants at the beginning of the Season is curious, and may be indicative of his financial collapse.

On the 6th of December 1911, at the age of 62, Alex died in a rented cottage in Highland Perthshire. Its name was Cuil-aluinn ('the bonny nook'), and it sat on the north side of the Tay, a mile from Aberfeldy. With beautiful views across to the crags of Weem, it had previously been the beloved summer home of John Campbell Shairp, a former master of Rugby School, and Principal of St Andrews University, renowned for his spiritual and moral influence. Cuil-aluinn would

---

* In what seems like a sibling's vindictive grudge, his eldest son, the 3rd of Dudley, vigorously opposed decriminalisation of male homosexuality, informing Parliament: "They are the most disgusting people in the world." [*Hansard*, House of Lords, 16 June 1966, vol 275, c158.]

recently have seen little of that.

Alex died intestate. The executor documents baldly state: "left a Widow who has declined to accept office" (as executrix). As Alex's spinster sister Charlotte Ethel now resided in the old family villa at North Berwick, she was forced to step into the role. Again, the documents are coldly revealing of the bonny nook:

Cash in House – Nil.
Household furniture and personal effects in the deceased's house – Nil.

There was money due to the deceased, held by solicitors, which amounted to the grand sum of £64 and 2 shillings. It was also stated that he had "no fixed or known domicile except the same was in Scotland."

A life which began under the brightest auspices had come to this.

II.   Francis Robert Shaw Wyllie (1837–1907)

In 1886, Wilfrid Blunt, who would later record in his diary the doggerel recited about Cyril Flower in the London clubs, was furious at the rent-racking being conducted by unscrupulous English landlords on Irish farmers. Aching to be a 'tribune for the people', Blunt was eager to enter Parliament. The Prince of Wales wished it for him too, "because there is a want of gentlemen in the House". Blunt's lover, the famous courtesan Skittles, promised to arrange it for him through Cyril, one of whose brothers had been her lover.

Blunt would record the experience in his diary. Its entries are once again highly intriguing:

June 4 – Wyllie, the Liberal agent, writes inviting me to stand as a supporter of Mr. Gladstone's Irish policy...I shall accept...

June 6 – Cyril Flower writes to ask me to stand at the elections as a supporter of Gladstone's Irish policy. I have answered him and Wyllie that I should be disposed to do so on the simple issue of Home Rule…

June 16 – Met Cyril Flower in St James's Park, and he took me in by the garden door into Downing Street, where we talked over things connected with the elections. He and Artie Brand* [they were both Liberal Whips] are doing their best to find me a good constituency, but I doubt if I shall get one notwithstanding. There are two things against me, first my quarrel with Gladstone about Egypt, and second and more important, my Catholic status. This last is almost an absolute bar to Parliament just now, as the Irish quarrel has inflamed all Protestant minds, and Wyllie at the Liberal Office told me as much to-day. "We have a good many Catholic candidates on our lists," he said, "but the constituencies say 'Give us a Jew, if you like, but not a Catholic.'"

Wilfrid Blunt was eventually able to contest a parliamentary seat in the general election of July of that year, but in the backlash against Gladstone's attempt to introduce Home Rule for Ireland, he lost to the Tories. In any case, the closer Blunt got to the brutal coal face of politics, the more his interest had waned.

However in 1912, Blunt published an account of the Irish land war which incorporated these diary entries. The book's index listed the name of Wyllie as: "Mr. Wyllie, one of the Liberal Whips." This was inaccurate. As Blunt himself stated, Wyllie was the Liberal agent: more precisely, the Secretary of the Liberal Central Association, the office of which was also centrally situated, in Parliament Street.

The gentleman's full name was Francis (Frank) Shaw Wyllie. A bachelor, he was extremely well-connected, due to family and career associations, and his sociability and personableness. As party Whip, Cyril Flower would have been in constant contact with Frank Wyllie.

As previously noted, following the trial of Fraser and Thorold, an enterprising reporter managed to extract from the police the information that Harold Boulton had fled to Brussels. Yet the whereabouts of the fourth man was not shared. If he was indeed

---

* Arthur George Brand (1853–1917), Liberal politician; son of 1st Viscount Hampden.

Frank Wyllie, unlike the insignificant Boulton, for reporters his identity would have been like a Rosetta Stone, enabling them to deduce the possible connections. The past Secretary of the Liberal Central Association in hiding? The conjecture provoked would have been profoundly dangerous.

Born in India in 1837, Frank Wyllie was six years older than Lord Battersea, and a full thirty-four years older than Harold Boulton. He hailed from a family that, like the Frasers, had been associated with the military and naval history of England for centuries. Frank was the second son of the distinguished General Sir William Wyllie, and his wife Amelia. His father had been wounded at the battle of Miani, which secured for the East India Company a portion of the region now known as Pakistan.

In 1841, with his father absent on a campaign, his mother returned with their five children to England, presumably for their education. Sir William's subsequent glittering appointments included, in 1850, being given command of the Bombay Garrison. He returned to England in 1858.

Frank was schooled at Cheltenham College, before attending the East India College (later Haileybury), which was maintained by the East India Company to train young gentlemen to be future colonial administrators. Returning to India, he entered the Bombay Civil Service. However his health, always delicate, broke down, and he returned to England to recover.

His older brother, John William Shaw Wyllie, also suffered life-long impaired health from the effects of what was then called 'Gujarat fever' – "an object of horror all over Western India," as the journal *The Church Missionary Intelligencer*, informed its readers. "This subtle Gujarat fever, when once thoroughly in the system, asserts its power when any other illness comes on, and retards recovery," noted one missionary's wife. It was in fact malaria.

Having recovered, Francis again went to India, becoming Under-Secretary to the Governor of Bombay. His ability saw him appointed one of the trustees of the Bombay Port Trust, and a Fellow of Bombay University.

In 1867, John Wyllie, who was considered "one of the most brilliant and versatile men who have ever adorned the Indian Civil Service" was himself forced to return to England due to ill health. In 1868, he was elected to Parliament as a Liberal M.P., but the election was declared void after it was found a supporter (whom he didn't even know) had provided breakfast to prospective voters, which constituted 'treating' and was illegal. Aware of his precarious health, John was chasing time. On the 4th of March 1870, he wrote to Frank from Paris, where he was enjoying the social round during the last glory days of the Second Empire of Napoleon III:

> My health is infinitely better than it has been for years past; having now got rid of my chronic diarrhoea, I hope to keep clear of it during the London season...I have been to a ball at the Tuileries, and to some other entertainments...When I am not dining out, I generally go to the *table d'hôte* at the Grand Hôtel, where I always come across people I know, English or others. Then men friends from town are constantly passing through Paris...

Eleven days later he was dead. A bad cold, aggravated by his malaria, developed into severe inflammation. He told his nurse, "I should have liked to have gone to my mother, but it is too late now. Do not think I am afraid to die. I die in Christ." He was just 34. His death devastated the family, and was widely lamented both in England, and India. In John's memory, and for his elderly parents who lived through him, Frank arranged for John's admired political essays to be published in book form. Its preface stated:

> His was a life which only too faithfully represents the debt which India owes to England. There are many others who, devoured by their own restless energy, beat out their lives in unknown work on the burning plains or among the malaria-smitten jungles of Hindustan.

So it was with Frank. However in 1874, after prolonged ill-health, again almost certainly due to malaria, he too was obliged to resign from the Indian civil service, and return to England forever. Frank was only 37. *The Times* would later state, had he been able to remain, "There is no doubt that Mr. Wyllie's abilities might have assured him distinction in India." Frank wrote confidently to a friend:

I was fond of India, and proud of my service and the position I obtained in it. So I feel at times low-spirited at the severance from all that had occupied my time, hopes and interests for so many years.

In England's more equitable climate, Frank's health appears to have recovered somewhat. He was living with his parents at 2 Cleveland Row, St James's. Newspapers record his presence at entertainments during the London Season and beyond. In the 1870s, new mercantile money and flashy foreign investors had yet to make their assault on the capital: "London society was so much smaller then," remembered Lord Frederick Hamilton,*"it was a sort of enlarged family party". Frank went everywhere, and met everyone. From levees at Buckingham Palace, and the Duke of Devonshire's receptions at Devonshire House, to receptions at the Admiralty, and "select and fashionable" hunt balls in the counties, the social columns noted the presence of 'F.R.S. Wyllie'. He was also a member of the East India Association, and Treasurer of the National Indian Association, whose hopeful purpose was, "To extend a knowledge of India in England, and an interest in our Indian fellow-subjects."

In 1880, possibly with the help of the wealthy politician Sir William Hutt, who was his uncle, Frank obtained the post of Secretary to the Liberal Central Association. The new organisation acted as a national coordinating office for the Party, assisting regional associations, diffusing its opinions on the political questions of the day, and as with Wilfrid Blunt, selecting and assisting candidates – including for safe seats. When in the position, Frank was considered very influential, and was understandably courted. When in 1884 Gladstone, as Prime Minister, laid the foundation stone of the National Liberal Club building in Whitehall, Frank was there on the official platform with the dignitaries, including Lord Rosebery.

Following the General Election of 1886, and tired of the stressing jostle of politics, Frank accepted a more sedate role: Secretary of the Army Purchase Commission. This was a government department that

* Lord Frederick Spencer Hamilton,(1856–1928); diplomat, Conservative politician, journalist. Bachelor son of the 1st Duke of Abercorn, and author of three splendid memoirs: *The Days Before Yesterday*; *Here, There And Everywhere*; and *The Vanished Pomps Of Yesterday*.

was winding down. Until 1871, when the practice was abolished, aspiring Army officers were able to buy their commissions: no less than two-thirds of the officers in the British Army did so. However, it was an opportunity only available to the privileged classes: a letter to *Reynolds's Newspaper* rightly termed it: "the prescriptive monopoly of officering the army they and theirs had so long enjoyed." After 1871, the work of the Commission switched to making financial settlements with the thousands of officers who'd purchased commissions. However, even at the turn of the century, there had really been little change in the makeup of the officer class, as it still favoured those whose families could afford an expensive education, and had connections.

In 1886, Frank was proposed and granted membership of the gentlemen's club Brooks's, which appeared more to his liking than the National Liberal Club, of which he did not remain a member. Cyril Flower joined Brooks's the following year.

Also that year, Frank was executor to the will of Sir Maxwell Melvill, a handsome bachelor, and extremely popular pillar of the Bombay civil service, who had died at Poonah. Max, as he was affectionately known, was a paragon in every way, and his death was widely lamented. He left "my dear friend Francis" the then large bequest of £2,000. So attractive a personality was Max Melvill – the memory of whom is now lost in the dust with countless other colonial administrators of good heart and intentions, it's worth quoting a charming personal reminiscence of him:

> There was nothing didactic about him, and his cleverness was of an infectious sort that made the person he talked with feel on equal terms...He was always a centre of refinement and cheerfulness in all the minor troubles of life. And the wonder was that he could do all this with a fragile constitution...He was scarcely ever really well, and on two or three occasions at death's door from weakness...His hospitality was proverbial even in hospital in Bombay. He moved through life with a grace and tolerance that made him a favourite among a wide circle, and with a capacity for sincere and self-abnegating friendship that will long dwell in the memory of the few who knew the inner nature of the man.

Such was the person to whom Frank had meant much. Frank's own obituary in *The Times* would state:

> His singular amiability of character, a certain attractive sociability, his tact and sympathetic feeling in all relations of private life, attached to him many intimate and firm friends.

One such gentleman was John Henry Rivett-Carnac, who'd enjoyed a distinguished career in the Indian Civil Service, and was made an Aide-de-Camp by Queen Victoria. Upon retirement, he took up residence, with his wife Marie, in a picturesque stately pile, Schloss Rothberg (Château de Rougemont), in Vaud, Switzerland. Here Frank was to be a regular visitor for several years.

The late summer of 1890 found Frank again in the Swiss Alps. Another visitor that summer was the intrepid explorer – including into the realm of pederasty, Sir Richard Burton. He'd travelled to the mountains with his wife in the hope of recovering his own health. In the words of one who knew them, the Burtons were "a strange uncanny couple": with his "long beard and the cruel scar across his face", Burton was "a grim splendour of a man."

The Burtons first went to Davos, specifically to meet John Addington Symonds, who'd become a citizen of that town – the alpine air easing his tuberculosis. Immediately following their encounter, Symonds posted Burton a copy of his treatise on classical pederasty, *A Problem In Greek Ethics*. Greatly appreciative, Burton wrote back, "Will you kindly give me the name of the French (? German?) physicist who explains Le Vice by a third sex. It would correspond with my masculo-feminine temperament."

Next stop for the Burtons was Maloja. Here at the grand Hôtel Kursaal* they met up with other distinguished company, which an early biographer of Burton innocently catalogued: "Mr. Francis R.S. Wyllie, Mr. and Mrs. (Sir and Lady) Squire Bancroft, the Rev. Dr. Welldon and Mr. and Mrs. (Sir and Lady) Henry Stanley."

This mountain tableau provides a small window into Francis Wyllie's world that is worthy of a discursion. It was a group with much in

---

* Now known as the Maloja Palace.

common – not least in self-invention and sexual secrets.

The Bancrofts* were a renowned theatrical couple who'd transformed their art through naturalistic acting and technical innovations in the venues they managed. Progenitors of drawing-room comedy, they'd introduced matinees and abolished the rowdy 'pit' (a cluster of cheap bench seats next to the stage), so helping make theatre-going more respectable, whereas it had been previously looked upon as somewhat disreputable. She was the greater star of the two, and in line with theatrical tradition, had mothered two illegitimate children.

The Rev. Dr. James Welldon† was Head Master of Harrow, Honorary Chaplain to Queen Victoria, and also an author. A solidly built man, he ruled his domain with unquestioned authority like a Roman Emperor. Yet he also possessed an unconventional manner, with a ready awareness of "the absurdities of the human condition," and a mischievous wit and ability to mock himself. More popular with his students than his staff, in 1890, his youthful form was just beginning the bloat that inspired his Harrow nickname, 'The Porker'.

Although noted for his translations of Aristotle, in 1895 Welldon penned *Gerald Eversley's Friendship: a Study in Real Life*. This was a schoolboy romance so knee-slappingly naff, even E.F. Benson mocked it in a novel of his own.‡ In Welldon's narrative, Harrow is

---

* Sir Squire Bancroft (1841–1926) actor-manager; married Marie Effie née Wilton, Lady Bancroft (1839–1921); actor-manager, playwright, and novelist.
† James Edward Cowell Welldon (1854–1937), clergyman, scholar and author; headmaster of Harrow 1885–1898; Bishop of Calcutta 1898–1902; Canon of Westminster, Dean of Manchester and Durham, and member of the Society for Psychical Research. Noted for his translations of Aristotle. One of his students and greatest admirers was Sir Winston Churchill: they were friends for fifty years. [*Proceedings of the Society for Psychical Research*, Vol VII, Kegan Paul, Trench, Trübner & Co., London 1892, pp413-442; Fred Gluckstein, 'J. E. C. Welldon: Churchill's Head Master at Harrow', *Finest Hour*, International Churchill Society, 176, Spring 2017, p18.]
‡ The snark appears in Benson's university novel *The Babe, B.A.* (1897) – its title an obvious tease on William 'The Babe' Haynes-Smith, the partner of the wealthy author and host, Howard Overing Sturgis. However, the title character, "a cynical old gentleman of twenty years of age," was part-inspired by Jerome Pollitt, born Herbert Charles Pollitt (1871–1942), a wealthy golden youth who was the son of the proprietor of the *Westmorland Gazette*. Pollitt collected Aesthetic and Decadent art, including as a patron of Aubrey Beardsley. He had a fling with Aleister 'The Beast' Crowley, and gained a reputation at Cambridge for female impersonation. During World War I, Pollitt served in the Royal Army Medical Corps, achieving the rank of lance-corporal. In 1923, in a series of dramatic trials of a gay circle in Cumbria, he was imprisoned for two years for 'tampering' (as the Judge phrased it) with young men. [Richard Kaczynski, *Perdurabo: The Life of Aleister Crowley* (Revised ed.), North Atlantic Books, Berkeley 2010, p37; The Kendal Immorality Cases, *The Penrith Observer*, 5 June 1923,

thinly disguised as 'St Anselm's'. With startling frankness, he writes:

> A public school is the home of the commonplace. It is there that mediocrity sits upon her throne. There the spirit which conforms to custom is lauded to the skies. There the spirit which is independent is apt to be crushed.

As for the masters, Welldon squarely observed:

> They take their tone from the boys, as well as the boys from them. Sometimes they admire the boys whom the boys themselves admire; they ignore those whom the boys ignore. It is only here and there that a master has the courage and self-denial to leave the popular, pleasant, responsive boys to themselves and seek those who are destitute and out of the way.

In the novel, Welldon went on to fashion a passionate tale of the bespectacled, weedy Gerald, the son of a poor clergyman, and a peer's son, the Hon. Harry Vennicker, who is described as "a splendid animal, healthy, vigorous, proud, elate":

> whose bright complexion and soft blue eyes were passports to favour, even without the radiant smile that played now and again, like a wandering sunbeam, on his mobile features...No being, perchance, is so distinct, none so beautiful or attractive, as a noble English boy. He is open-hearted, open-handed; there is not a cloud upon his brow: he looks the world in the face; for him all life is, as it were, sunshine without rain.

On his first night at school, Gerald is found sobbing in his bed by Harry, who lays a hand upon his shoulder, saying, "Don't cry any more. I'll be your friend, I said I would, whatever happens for ever." To which incident, Welldon adds, "the pale moon, throned in heaven, was the sole arbitress." A latter-day historian of Harrow would write in wonderment: "This, from a Head Master of a public school, writing under his own name and title, in the year of Oscar Wilde's trials is remarkable".*

---

p3.]
* According to John Addington Symonds, Harrow's greatest headmaster, Charles John Vaughan (1816–1897), conducted a discreet affair with an older student. See: Christopher Tyerman, *A History of Harrow School, 1324-1991*, Oxford University Press, 2000, pp278-280.

Welldon left the School in 1898 to become Bishop of Calcutta. By the time of the Battersea scandal he was Canon of Westminster, and would stride on in fruity glory to become Dean of Manchester, and latterly of Durham. Welldon was gathered into the Lord's arms at his residence, 'The Dell' at Sevenoaks, having never recovered from the death, the year prior, of his companion of fifty years (and to whom his entire estate had been bequeathed) his 'manservant' Edward Hudson Perkins. In his autobiography, Welldon termed friendship "that abiding benediction of human life". Undoubtedly, Perkins was also with the party in Switzerland.

The most famous member of this alpine group, the explorer Henry Morton Stanley,* was on his honeymoon. His thirty-five-year-old bride was Dorothy Tennant, from the noted family whose wealth derived from an ancestor's invention of bleaching power. She was also the sister of Frederic Myers' wife. Frank knew the Stanleys through Dorothy's mother, Gertrude Tennant, a prominent Society figure. (In her widowhood, Gertrude hosted a Parisian-style salon at her mansion in Whitehall which was frequented by artists, writers, and Liberal members, as she doted on Mr. Gladstone.)

Following Dorothy's engagement, Frank wrote to her:

> I remember so well your talking to me of W. Stanley and showing me his portrait. If you are to disappear and become the Queen of Africa as the *Pall Mall* [*Gazette*] suggests we shall all miss you in London very much.

It would have been an appropriate appellation. Prior to the wedding, Frederic Myers, whose friendship with Stanley was one of mutual admiration, warned him that Dorothy had been, "somewhat over-

---

* Sir Henry Morton Stanley, born John Rowlands (1841–1904), explorer, Liberal Unionist M.P., journalist, and national icon. After finding fame as a journalist in the American West, he was sent to Africa to find the famous Scottish missionary Dr. Livingstone. After a second mission charting Africa, he then explored the Congo as an agent for King Leopold II, thereby helping him to claim it, before leading an expedition to the Sudan to rescue a governor, Mehmed Emin Pasha. Lecture tours, consultancies, books and honours followed. One contrarian in the face of this brouhaha was the Rev. Fillingham, whose diary for 1889 records: "Monday, November 25. It was a cold, dull day, I was tired, and did not wake till nearly 11...I had my b[rea]kfast in bed, reading the paper, w[hic]h was full of accounts of the doings in Africa of some uninteresting person named Stanley: whereof I did not read a word." [25 November 1889, Rev. R.C. Fillingham diary, p405; Merton College Library.]

indulged in life, and that has left her too impetuous…beneath is a power of steady devotion"

Like many an idle heiress, Dorothy's letters convey a bored, needy, actressy personality, who thrived on the thrill of intoxicating herself with high emotion. After toying with other suitors, she set her sights on the naive-in-feminine-wiles Stanley, who wrote to her: "I am only rich in love with you, filled with admiration for your royal beauty."

Right down to his self-chosen name, Henry Morton Stanley was a mythomane of the first order, which perfectly suited his artistic and calculating bride, who had her own grand designs, as the gracious partner of a national icon. Their wedding in London was an event of enormous public interest: so great were the crowds, as one newspaper noted, "it was not until some hours later that Whitehall had resumed its normal appearance."

Not everyone was a fan. John Burns denounced him as a "buccaneer", and *Reynolds's Newspaper* called him "unscrupulous", stating that the "cruelty and rapacity" of his treatment of African natives was "only equalled by the credulity, stupidity, and hypocrisy of his countrymen."

The wedding almost had to be postponed: Stanley was suffering from the gastritis that had plagued him during his travels: he only made it up the aisle with the aid of a walking stick, and spent much of the ceremony in an armchair. Accompanying him was, "the black boy who has been Mr. Stanley's constant attendant in his travels." It was frankly a showbiz wedding as bizarre as any.

Frank gave the couple two silver basins, and Lord Lorne and Princess Louise two silver vases, possibly to match. The high-camp Alick Yorke furnished a large oriental bowl, and typical of his generous nature, Hamilton Aïdé bestowed on the bride a clutch of diamond jewellery. Within months of the marriage, the couple were quarrelling over Dorothy's cloyingness. Nevertheless, their sexual relations comforted Stanley, as did the domestic cosiness and stability. He wrote to Dorothy: "To me you are more beautiful and precious each day." Before their marriage, the future bride had coolly tallied her fiancée's attractions:

He is thickly, strongly built, with a deep broad chest and thick

484

short arms...His look has something intense and penetrating...The eye shines out clear, with the observancy of some clear-eyed bird, who is watching you, listening to you rather with the eye than with the ear...He has in common with all great men, a great simplicity, shall I call it a kind of innocence?...He has, shall I say, a rich vein of tenderness underlying the surface of will and masterfulness.

Photos taken of Stanley as both a young and older man, posing in a succession of tropical outfits, certainly convey an intense, self-aware personality, and a crafting of image as premeditated as that of Walt Whitman. In short (and he was indeed short), Henry Morton Stanley was a Welsh Napoleon: a magnetic man who attracted admirers as any self-invented demagogue. He was also primarily homosexual, but so mentally scarred by a lonely, hard childhood, much of it spent in a workhouse, as well as by prevailing social attitudes (which taught those attracted to their own gender to hate themselves), that it would have been a miracle if he wasn't deeply conflicted. When a friend took him to a brothel, he fled after the women entered. In his notebook he summed up his thoughts:

> To me who to tell the truth never was a great admirer of women, who looked upon them as natural enemies to mankind, idlers of valuable time, pretty excuses for man's universality, toys to while slow time, heirs to a man's fame, to me who regarded them with that special concern a man should look upon moveable talkable trifling human beings.

In contrast, Stanley was the keenest admirer of what he termed, "fine manliness". On holiday in Norfolk in 1893, he had particularly appreciated the fishermen at Yarmouth:

> The seed of the old Vikings and Anglian invaders of Britain were all around me...I saw some splendid specimens of manhood among them...It was far better than going to a theatre to watch the healthy fellows swinging up their crates of salted herrings.

Throughout his earlier life, Stanley's companions were men or youths, including a ship-boy, the fifteen-year-old Lewis Noe, whom he convinced to desert and travel with him, and two strapping adolescents. These were Kalulu, the black boy at his wedding, a former slave presented to him by an Arab merchant (and after whom he named Kalulu Falls), and Selim, one of his interpreters or bearers, who was possibly a Christian Palestinian. In what seems wish-fulfilment, Stanley reimagined them both in a novel he wrote: *My Kalulu: Prince, King and Slave* (1873). The fictional Kalulu is the son of a tribal chief, and is rapturously described as: "a perfect youthful Apollo in form. The muscles of his arms stood out like balls, and the muscles of legs were as firm as iron." The fictional Selim, whose friendship with Kalulu is consecrated in blood-brotherhood, is a youth:

> whose appearance at once challenged attention from his frank, ingenuous, honest face, his clear complexion, his beautiful eyes, and the promise which his well-formed graceful figure gave of a perfect manhood in the future.

Unlike butch Kalulu, a character remarks of his friend: "Truly Selim, thou appearest to me like a little girl whose mother bathes her in new milk every day to preserve her complexion."

In the preface, Stanley wrote: "This book has been written for...clever, bright-eyed, intelligent boys, of all classes, who have begun to be interested in romantic literature, with whom educated fathers may talk without fear of misapprehension." Indeed.

Given the novel bears no little resemblance in spirit to *Gerald Eversley's Friendship*, it's easy to imagine Stanley and the Rev. Welldon's mutual appreciation. Quite possibly they swapped literary notes while strolling in the alpine meadows. Certainly, in 1892, Welldon wrote to Dorothy to ask if Stanley could deliver a lecture at Harrow.

Frank Wyllie's presence at the Stanley's honeymoon hotel may have been by prior arrangement. Frank was a member of the Royal Geographical Society, and Dorothy had parliamentary ambitions for her husband. Stanley asked his friend, the charming, handsome and open-hearted Arthur Jephson,* to join them on the honeymoon.

---

* Arthur Jermy Mounteney Jephson (1859–1908), merchant seaman, army officer and Queen's Messenger. His aunt, Helene, Comtesse de Noailles, was his patron. The worldly American heiress and art collector Isabella Stewart Gardner (1840–1924), who delighted in the company of sophisticated homosexuals, adored him, and he her. His long frank letters to her share encounters with cowboys and grand dames, and reveal he was introduced to "the 'under-side' of New York," including a particular Turkish Bath, by the social figure Henry 'Harry' Le Grand

Jephson was as short and physically well-made as Stanley, and not least, of the same sexual complexion: they were certainly two peas from a pod.* Kalulu may have also have accompanied the Stanleys.

Not least amongst this happy alpine group was Oscar Browning! Browning and Welldon were childhood friends, and longtime travelling companions.† Browning summered at the hotel for several years, and became responsible for keeping other guests entertained. The Bancrofts christened him 'The Wicked Monk,'; Squire writing: "I never felt quite certain how much of him was 'Jekyll' and how little there was of 'Hyde.'"

When Sir Richard Burton died the following year, Frank Wyllie and Oscar Browning attended the funeral. Topping off these homosocial connections, Dorothy would ask Frank Hird, Lord Ronald Gower's partner, to write Stanley's official biography.

Cannon (1858–1895). When Cannon became engaged, Jephson told Gardner: "He asks me to go & stay with him & his wife, & then travel with them on their honeymoon to Constantinople. How simple & naive, is it not? Do you not think I should enjoy it?" Gardner also gave Jephson refuge at her estate in Maine; he later writing of it: "your enchanted island, where we were out of doors the whole day long, & you read Walt Whitman to me, and his 'Song of Joys.' Till the shadow that was over me lifted a little, & I seemed to feel quieter & better." In 1901, Bernard Berenson wrote to Gardner about a later incident: "Poor dear Jephson. The scandal about him was to the effect that he had come to Florence to have improper relationships with men." Gardner replied: "don't advise Jephson to marry. He wouldn't be happy." However, Jephson did find a measure of comfort in the last four years of his life in a marriage to Anna Head of San Francisco, with whom he had a son. [Jephson to Gardner, 30 January 1890, ARC.002240; 15 May 1891, ARC.002242; 8 February 1901, ARC.002257, Isabella Gardner Museum; Douglass Shand-Tucci, *The Art Of Scandal: the life and times of Isabella Stewart Gardner*, HarperCollins, New York 1997, pp100-102; Luther Munday *A Chronicle of Friendships*, Frederick A. Stokes, New York, p103.]

* Encountering Stanley's young male entourage in a railway carriage, a journalist was struck by the difference between celebrity myth and reality, writing: "Can this effeminate little man who sits there twisting his moustache be the Jephson who fought and intrigued with [Mehmed] Emin [Ali Pasha]? And that slim and delicate young Apollo with the open countenance, be the plucky [Dr. Thomas Heazle] Parke we have heard so much of as the man who saved Stanley's life? What a contrast these innocent young gentlemen present to that foxy old Ulysses." [*Poor Stanley's Ride To London*, *The Pall Mall Gazette*, 28 April 1890, p6.]

† It has been incorrectly written of this occasion: "Unknown to Stanley and to the virtuous Welldon, Oscar Browning, who walking with them had been clandestinely dismissed as an Eton housemaster for molesting the boys in his charge." Firstly, there were several factors in Browning's dismissal: the *suspicion* of molestation being but one of them. Secondly, given Welldon's close friendship with Browning, as well as his connections to academic and homosexual networks, and the fact the dismissal was addressed in the national press, he would have been fully aware of the circumstances. The matter may also have been discussed with Stanley. [Tim Jeal, *Stanley: The Impossible Life of Africa's Greatest Explorer*, Faber & Faber, London 2007; Ian Anstruther, *Oscar Browing: A Biography*, John Murray, London 1983, pp45-66.]

Frank Wyllie's work with the Army Purchase Commission lasted until its dissolution in 1892. That summer he took up an invitation to cruise the Norwegian fiords on the magnificent steam yacht of a friend, Valentine Smith, the heir to a brewing fortune. However, from this period until his death, he was, according to *The Times*, "disabled by recurrent attacks of illness from further active public employ, although he continued to take part in the administration of two important Indian railways."

In the summer of 1899, Frank wrote to Dorothy Stanley to congratulate her husband on his knighthood, stating, "It is long since I have had the pleasure of seeing you but bad health drove me from London a year ago." He was now sixty-two, and winter ailments, intensified by his probable malaria and the city's suffocating smogs, had likely been taking their toll. Frank chose to settle in that ozonic community ever-popular with bachelors – Brighton.* His new home, at 6 Montpelier Villas, was an attractive semi-detached Regency villa that was a mere pleasant stroll away from the foreshore.

At the time of the Battersea scandal, Frank still maintained a London *pied-a-terre*. The 1903 edition of *Boyle's Fashionable Court & Country Guide, and Town Visiting Directory*, which was published in January of that year, records the address as 35 Duke Street, St. James's. When the arrests occurred, if Frank was indeed the fourth procurer, he may well have taken a sudden Swiss vacation with his friends the Rivett-Carnacs.

Whatever unfolded, by March 1904, Frank was back in London, attending the opening of the new premises of the Northbrook Society, a foundation established by the Earl of Northbrook for the education in Europe of 'native gentlemen from the East'. Two years later, Frank was residing at 11 Southwick Street, Cambridge Square.

By this time there was a further deterioration in his health, and he now hired a nurse. On the 6th of February 1907, an overcast day in which, as one weather report had it, "there was a raw cold feeling in the air," Frank died. He was in his seventieth year. He left an estate of £21,160 – at the very least, equating to £2.1 million today. The amount is striking, as Frank didn't inherit any significant sum. When

---

* The town had drawn bachelors ever since enormous numbers of soldiers were garrisoned there during the Napoleonic Wars.

his older brother John died in 1869, he had left just under £200; their father, Sir William, left only £3,860 in 1891, while at his death in 1909, Frank's younger brother, Sir William Hutt Curzon Wyllie, (known as Sir Curzon) left less than half what he had: £10,073.

Frank's civil service work and prominent secretaryships would have been well remunerated, but even so, he was also a spender, living at prominent addresses, travelling regularly to the Continent, and was apparently a soft touch: one of the first statements in his Will is, "I forgive all persons any sums of money owing to me at the time of my death". In the absence of further evidence, it's likely the money derived from his directorship of the Great Indian Peninsula Railway Company. A vitally important line, it extended to 2,388 kilometres, helping connect Bombay with Calcutta.

The year before his death, Frank made a new will. He bequeathed £500 to his nurse, and a later codicil doubled the sum. Aside from that, his bequests were all to family members, with his unmarried sister Florence bequeathed the majority of his estate. To Sir Curzon, he left their father's orders and decorations and "all my oil paintings, and the pictures of the battle of Meeanee and the storming of Khelat."

Sir Curzon, who after a distinguished career in the Indian civil service was appointed Aide-to-Camp to the Secretary of State for India in London, did not have long to enjoy such a gladsome artistic legacy. In 1909, while leaving an evening function at the Imperial Institute, he was shot dead by an Indian student revolutionary.

The assassination caused enormous shock in Britain and India. Besides leaving a broken widow, Sir Curzon was widely respected by Indians for his sympathy and work for the country, and his philanthropy. The assassin had selected his target merely because he knew him – having pleaded for his help with entering an engineering college. Curzon, who was acquainted with his wealthy family, and had previously helped his brother, agreed to assist him. Death was the thanks he received. The student was hanged.*

The lengthy obituaries of Sir Curzon also mentioned Frank, who was

---

* As a sweet talker for Indian independence, the assassin is now portrayed in India not as a despicable, egocentric murderer, but as an heroic patriot. A statue of him has even been erected in his home city.

489

recalled as being "universally loved and respected." In his memory, his sister Florence used his bequest to establish The Francis Wyllie Scholarship at his alma mater of Cheltenham College. It was for boys who were the sons of officers of the Army or Indian civil service.

16. A SWORDSMAN OF HIS HOLINESS

Those acquainted with London's more colourful history might have assumed the procurer Bolton/Boulton who absconded to have been Ernest Boulton.

Ernest was the stockbroker's son known as 'Stella', whom together with Frederick Park, a barrister's son known as 'Fanny', were the cross-dressing stars (the only appropriate word) of a sensational London trial of 1871, which acquitted them of the charge of buggery. The case for the defence had been handled by none other than George Lewis.

Lord Arthur Clinton,* a Liberal party politician, who had lived with Stella as husband, reportedly died after receiving his subpoena for the trial, possibly by suicide, although there is circumstantial evidence he may have fled and lived in exile. However, the 'He-She Ladies' (as Boulton and Park were dubbed), would have been considered far too camp and outré for the gentlemen of Lord Battersea's circle. Lord Battersea's Mr. Boulton was someone eminently more respectable. His full name was Harold Edward Baker Boulton.

Born in 1871, Harold was the second son of Joseph Boulton, a Dorset landowner, shareholder and county magistrate, and his wife Alicia. The family resided in Iwerne Minster, a village of 665 persons on the edge of the Blackmore Vale in North Dorset. The family home of West Lodge, which featured an indoor staff of six, was and still is an excessively picturesque neo-classical country house. Originally a royal

---

* Lord Arthur Pelham-Clinton (1840–1870), a son of the 5th Duke of Newcastle.

hunting lodge, it was remodelled in the nineteenth century as a central pavilion with flanking wings. Surrounded by formal and walled gardens, it was set within an estate of cottages, ancient parkland, farmland, and dramatic wooded valleys. In short: an English paradise.

In 1874, when Harold was only three, his father died. Seeking renewal, his mother moved to the Riviera with the family, who included his older brother Thomas Leonard Lees, and sisters Helen Josephine and Emily Mary. In 1882, a children's magazine *Little Folks* listed "Harold E.B. Boulton, Nice (France)" as a member of its 'Humane Society'.

A few years later the Boultons returned to London, residing at 52 Elm Park Gardens in Chelsea with five servants; Harold attending St Paul's School. In 1889 he went up to Cambridge where he fully participated in university life, including becoming a member of its famous debating society. Upon his election to membership, its first topic just happened to be: "That this house deeply deplores the depraved condition into which politics have fallen in this country."

After Cambridge, Harold followed Thomas into the Royal Artillery Volunteer Corps, the part-time citizens army division. In 1894, his family was again been struck by tragedy when Thomas, by then a captain, died on the Isle of Wight at the age of just twenty-seven, leaving a widow.

The following year, Harold was garrisoned in Jamaica where, for intellectual stimulus, he became a member of the high-brow Institute Of Jamaica. It mounted lectures for English residents on topics such as 'Herodotus the Father Of History' and 'Fielding and the English Novel'.

In August, Harold visited New York, and by early 1896, was back in England. He was twenty-five, wealthy, and with the glow of a tropic tan: a most decorative and eligible young man ripe for the plucking. And so it happened. On the 3rd of March, he was a guest at a dinner of the Eighty Club. The invitation – a prestigious one for an unknown young soldier – was likely extended by the Club's stalwart Lord Battersea, but may also have come from the guest of honour himself – Lord Rosebery.

Still smarting from the crushing electoral defeat of the previous year,

Rosebery was in a querulous mood. However, in his after dinner speech he paid tribute to the Club's members, saying: "You gather up the budding youth and energies of our party." It was certainly true that night. It might even have been a joking insinuation for the knowing.

The following summer, London was *en fête*: packed with visitors for the celebrations of Queen Victoria's Diamond Jubilee. In April, Harold had been promoted to a Second Lieutenant, the most junior rank of officer. This was apparently the culmination of his career desires, for in August he resigned his commission. Of course, there is always the possibility he'd got himself into a spot of trouble. Whatever the situation, he now embarked on that most demanding of careers: that of a gentleman of leisure.

Like Lord Battersea, Arthur Brown, and Hugh Weguelin, who perhaps encouraged him, in 1901 Harold took up the new hobby of the wealthy, and joined the Royal Automobile Club, becoming a keen early motorist.

In 1901 and early 1902, he again visited America. Following the arrests of Bernard Fraser and Arthur Thorold in late July, he absconded to Brussels until the scandal blew over. In 1905 his sister Helen, who'd married Edward H.C. Thurston of Thornbury, died at just thirty-four. She bequeathed Harold a tranche of shares in the Great Western Railway Company. It recorded his address in its register of shareholders as 35 Chester Terrace, SW,* a grand street just off Eaton Square. However, it appears he'd deemed it not yet safe to return to England, as the address is crossed out and replaced with a pencil notation: "C/o National Prov[incial] Bank of England Ltd, South Kensington Branch". One of the social registers also confirms that he wasn't living there in 1903.

In December 1905, Harold was at Dax, near Biarritz, writing from the Hôtel de Thermes to the editor of the magazine *Mercure de France*, to provide his own contribution to a question that, in an on-going correspondence, had been troubling its cultivated readers: the origin of the word 'bitter' in English with regard to alcoholic beverages. Harold informed them:

---

* Now Chester Row. Renamed in 1939 to eliminate confusion with other 'Chester Terrace' which faces Regents Park.

In the plural, 'Bitters', noun, never has any other meaning than that of the aperitif, such as Angostura, which is sometimes poured, according to English custom, a few drops in a glass of sherry wine, taken before meals.

It was a world away from the then highly bitter existence of Fraser and Thorold. While arrest warrants for felonies don't have expiration dates, they can be subject to unofficial exhaustion in the pursuit of the quarry, due to restraints on budget and manpower. Or they can be put to bed through access to power. Influential contacts were certainly something Harold had no shortage of. By the time of the First World War – and possibly well before, he was remarkably confident of not being arrested.

This can be said because during the War, Harold volunteered to work – in of all places, given the scandal – the Admiralty itself! He became a member of its civil staff, "appointed or lent for temporary service during the War". Unlike Bernard and Arthur, he didn't even feel the need to alter his name. Those influential contacts were clearly gold-plated.

Following on the heels of nineteenth century Oxford Movement devotees, Harold joined the queue of interwar ex-public schoolboys – mostly bisexual or homosexual – who rejected the muscular Christianity of their schooldays for the more byzantine theology and grander theatre of Vatican vaudeville. In 1920, he was received into the Catholic Church at Quarr Abbey on the Isle of Wight, while the Sacrament of Confirmation was performed in Rome itself. Given that Harold's father, brother and sister had met premature deaths, this may have been driven by a search for answers, for meaning, and for redemption from an apparently vindictive god. However, the stimulus may equally have been a desire for novelty, bachelor company, intellectual stimulation, and campery to high heaven from the institution that did it best. Fellow travellers included Evelyn Waugh[*] and Tom Driburg.[†]

By 1926, Harold had been appointed to the decorative sinecure of

---

[*] Arthur Evelyn St. John Waugh (1903–1966), novelist, biographer, and journalist.
[†] Thomas Edward Neil Driberg, 1st Baron Bradwell (1905–1976) journalist, politician, and Soviet spy.

Private Chamberlain of Sword and Cape to Pope Pius XI. His application was supported by William Cotter, Bishop of Portsmouth, and Sir Odo Russell,* Minister to the British Legation of the Holy See, who wrote to the Vatican: "Mr Harold Boulton has been known for many years by this Legation and also by myself personally."

Papal Privy Chamberlains (now abolished and replaced by the less-picturesque Gentlemen of His Holiness) were officials, both clerics and laymen, who assisted in various duties in and about the papal apartments. They wore a variety of attractive liveries, of which, in the view of one reverend author, "the black 16th–century court dress of 'sword and cape' is the most becoming." It featured a black velvet doublet with puffed sleeves edged wide with lace, a short cape, high ruff, gold chains, high boots, a velvet beret pinned with a jewel of individual taste, and a silver-hilted sword. It was all very gallant – or as a camp spectator in a Gore Vidal novel termed the Vatican Easter service —"absolutely yummy!"

The appointment also constituted a holy elevation for Harold so swift that it can only have been enabled by the kindly eye which Vatican insiders have always cast upon the yearnings of cosmopolitan bachelors.† Indeed, the previous Privy Chamberlain of Cape and Sword to Pius XI and Benedict XV had been the notorious Evan Morgan, Viscount Tredegar.‡ He was caricatured by Ronald Firbank in his novel *The Flower Beneath The Foot* as the Hon. 'Eddie' Monteith, an eccentric Englishman from Wales who joins an archaeological expedition to Sodom. Tredegar was one of the intimate gentlemen friends of Giovanni Battista Montini, the future Pope Paul VI,§ and

---

* The Hon. Sir Odo William Theophilus Russell (1870–1951) diplomat. Married Countess Marie Louise Rex, and had issue.

† A previous English stalwart at the Vatican had been the theatrically-named Hartwell de la Garde Grissell (1839–1907). Chamberlain of Honour to no less than three popes, he was dubbed by Oscar Wilde: "the withered eunuch of the Vatican Latrines". In 1900, Wilde turned up in Rome on Easter Day. As he wrote to Robert Ross, "to the terror of Grissell and all the Papal Court, I appeared in the front rank of the pilgrims in the Vatican, and got the blessing of the Holy Father – a blessing they would have denied me."[Oscar Wilde; Merlin Holland, Rupert Hart-Davis, (eds.) *The Complete Letters Of Oscar Wilde*, Henry Holt & Co, New York, 2000, pp1191, 1179.]

‡ Evan Morgan, 2nd Viscount Tredegar (1893–1949). Married actress Lois Ina Sturt, and secondly, Princess Olga Sergeivna Dolgorouky. No issue.

§ Montini was blackmailed over his homosexuality. His boyfriend of younger days was actor Paolo Carlini. There was also a rumoured association with the later much-married actor Edmund Purdom. [Dino Martirano, 'Dossier su un tentato ricatto a Paolo VI', *Corriere Della Sera*, 27 January 2006, p20; Gerald Posner, *God's Bankers: A History of Money and Power at the Vatican*, Simon and Schuster, New York, 2015, p174; private information from an aristocratic

was once glimpsed running down Victoria Station in papal uniform trying to delay the Golden Arrow train with the cry: "Secret papers for the Holy Father!" More troublingly, in association with Aleister 'The Beast' Crowley,* Tredegar had a passion for the occult: his black masses in Rome's Protestant cemetery proved an invocation too far for Pope Pius, and Tredegar was forced to return to Wales.

Harold's appointment also enabled him to join the Pontifical Court Club, an elite social group that met for dinners in London. Its members included baronets from old Catholic families, and confirmed bachelors seeking theology and theatre, who'd converted. One notable figure was George Shanks,† the first translator of the *Protocols of the Elders of Zion*, and a friend of the courtier Sir Alexander Hood.

In the early 1920s, Harold is recorded as living at 12 Southgate Street, Winchester, a substantial Georgian brick residence on a high street. In 1923, after vacationing at – where else – Naples, he embarked on the cruiser liner Ormuz, sailing 1st Class to Australia. His profession on the shipping register is described as 'nil'. He arrived in Brisbane in June. It was obviously a visit to his old friend Arthur Thorold, who was by then living under his second name of Charles. The reunion was evidently a happy one, as in 1927 Harold again sailed to Australia.

The following year, the official diary of the Venerable English College in Rome, a seminary dedicated to the training of young priests for England and Wales, recorded Harold as a solo dinner guest. Catholicism was indeed the gift that just kept on giving. Harold also continued to mix high religion with high society: earlier in February, the *International Herald Tribune* had noted him amongst the illustrious names at a tea dance at the Hotel du Palais. He was a guest there with another notable name: the Honourable Gerald Agar-Robartes, the future Viscount Clifden,‡ who was then forty-eight. By this time, the two men had become very close friends, and possibly lovers.

Roman source.]

*Aleister Crowley, born Edward Alexander Crowley (1875–1947), occultist, poet, painter, novelist, and mountaineer.

† George Shanks (1896–1957). A Russian-born Englishman of the renowned 'Magasin Anglais' Moscow outfitters Shanks & Co., and civil servant, Royal Naval Air Service officer, and founder of Radio Normandy.

‡ (Francis) Gerald Agar-Robartes, 7th Viscount Clifden, commonly known as Gerald Clifden and Gerald Robartes, (1883–1966).

Gerald's father,* a Liberal politician, had been well-known to Cyril Flower: besides their political association, they'd worked together on behalf of the Domestic Servants Benevolent Institution. Despite their immense wealth, the High-Anglican Clifdens were, like the Boultons, a scarred family. Gerald's older brother Thomas,† known as 'Tommy', had died at just thirty-five, of wounds sustained at the battle of Loos. Another brother, Alexander, an awarded officer of the grenadier guards, experienced a nervous breakdown, and suicided at thirty-seven by leaping from a third-floor window of the family's Grosvenor Square terrace. Two other brothers and a sister would also die young.

Harold's friendship with Gerald may well have developed from an acquaintance or friendship with the older Tommy. He'd been a prominent dandy and playboy, who came of age in 1902, the same year as the Battersea scandal. Tommy remained a bachelor despite being "known in Paris and Monte Carlo as in London," and "greatly but unsuccessfully courted by matchmaking mammas." Tommy's mentor was Lord Rosebery, to whom "he was almost like another son." Under this lordly guidance, Tommy had been elected as Liberal M.P. for Bodmin in 1906, but was disqualified on account of bribery and treating. He was elected again in 1908 for Mid-Cornwall, and held the seat until his death. While he voted against the People's Budget of 1909, Tommy held the same political views as Gerald, who later wrote: "The hereditary principle was absolutely indefensible...the will of the people should prevail over the privileges of the Peers."

Tommy's best friend, for whom he would be best man at his wedding a few months before his own death, was Rosebery's son Neil, a fellow Liberal M.P., who was also to die of battle wounds. A parliamentary writer observed: "Being quite young men they both keep to the old-fashioned custom of always wearing their hats in the House." Together with James de Rothschild,‡ they were known as 'The Inseparables'. Another report stated:

> Mr. Primrose and Mr. Agar-Robartes are unmarried. Their

---

* Thomas Charles Agar-Robartes, 6th Viscount Clifden (1844–1930). He married Mary Dickinson, and had ten children.
† The Hon. Thomas Charles Reginald Agar-Robartes (1880-1915).
‡ James 'Jimmy' Armand Edmond de Rothschild (1878–1957), Liberal politician and Zionist. He married Dorothy Mathilde Pinto, and inherited the Waddesdon Manor estate.

invitations to dances are three deep every night. Mr. Primrose is, I believe, the favourite son of his father. He is very like Lord Rosebery in feature, in manner, and peculiarity of speech. He has the rich, soft tone of voice which so distinguishes the head of the house of Primrose. Mr. Agar-Robartes is serious, but he does not look it. He likes the theatre, he has a weakness for first-class restaurants, he dines out every night, he invariably has a flower in his button-hole, and he wears his hat at the back of his head. If you met him coming down the Haymarket you would think he was one of the 'boys'. Both these young men like to be called democrats, and when you look into the Chamber and see one of them you may be certain the other is close by.

It was entitled toffery at its most gilded. After Tommy's death, a journalist wrote of him with all the delicacy of loaded phrasing an obituarist can muster:

> He was too rich a man to have need to devote himself to politics with that entire concentration which is necessary to a man who would reach Ministerial rank, and he had tastes and pursuits other than political. Until the call of war came to him he was a connoisseur in the arts of life rather than a man of action, a lover of society, and the refined pleasures of existence rather than the gratification of ambition. Yet he made his mark in the House...His speeches suggested that there was far more ability in him than one would have suspected from his rather dandified appearance. Mr. 'Lulu' Harcourt in the glory of his youth was never more scrupulously dressed than Mr. Agar-Robartes, or his close companion Mr. Neil Primrose.

When the War came, Tommy was at pains to ensure he was sent to the Front to shoulder the risks alongside men such as the workers of his family estates. He acquitted himself admirably; his mortal wounds were sustained shortly after rescuing a comrade in the face of machine-gun fire.

As a young man, Gerald shared a house in Chesham Place, London with the composer Lord Berners.* He embarked on a diplomatic

---

* Gerald Hugh Tyrwhitt-Wilson, 14th Baron Berners (1883–1950); composer, novelist, painter and aesthete. The inspiration for the character Lord Merlin in Nancy Mitford's novel *The Pursuit Of Love*. Berners' partner in later life was Robert Heber-Percy, who bore the wholly

career, before resigning in 1930 following the death of his father. The death of Tommy made Gerald the family heir, and along with the viscounty, he inherited two great country houses: Lanhydrock in Cornwall, and Wimpole Hall in Cambridgeshire, both set within vast estates.

During the Second World War, Gerald served as a government whip in the House of Lords. While in middle age he assumed the blimpish appearance of a stereotypical upper class British civil servant of the period, Gerald was a man of taste, and scholarly connoisseur. He was also highly public-spirited, acting as president, chairman, director and patron of a string of charities. Appointed a Knight Commander of the Royal Victorian Order by George VI, he eventually donated Lanhydrock (where he lived with two of his sisters) to the National Trust, plus a considerable portion of his fortune to enable its upkeep.

Harold's own philanthropy was more limited: together with the great and good he joined the National Art Collections Fund, a charity (now the Art Fund) which raises monies for the acquisition of artworks for the nation.

The year 1931 found Harold visiting Bath, to which he would soon relocate. For those seeking a more gracious world, the city's Georgian vistas have ever since been a sanctuary and balm, and Gerald, who for years had partaken of its then still-thriving social Season, likely supported the move. Harold's terrace home at 15 Somerset Place, on a grand crescent, was blessed with a large garden. At the end of it lay a small orchard of apple and pear trees underplanted with narcissi, which gave him great pleasure.

It's fortunate that aristocrats are born hoarders, as a number of letters survive from Harold to the wife of the 8th Baron Berwick.* Teresa, Lady Berwick† was described by National Trust representative James Lees-Milne as a proud but lonely woman; her kindness chilled by an intimidating *grande dame* manner. Although Harold stayed with the couple at their stately home Attingham Park in Shropshire, in his letters he never addresses her as anything less than 'Lady Berwick'. Her intensely shy older husband, with "his little fluffy dog Muffet,"

---

appropriate nickname of 'Mad Boy'.
* Thomas Henry Noel-Hill, 8th Baron Berwick (1877–1947).
† Edith Teresa Noel-Hill, née Hulton, Baroness Berwick (1890–1972).

was recalled by Lees-Milne as "one of the most endearing men I have ever met – feckless, helpless, courteous". Whether Harold's initial friendship was with Teresa or her husband is unknown. Both the Berwicks were connoisseurs: Teresa was the daughter of a painter and had been raised in Italy, and their mutual appreciation of that country no doubt encouraged their affinity.

As a presentable bachelor of means, Harold's life was a round of parties, interspersed with travel. In 1933, he wrote to Teresa from Somerset Place:

> I do not know what to tell you about Bath, for, as you know from experience, nothing very much happens. Mr. & Mrs. Knight gave a theatrical entertainment at their new home in Marlborough Buildings last week of a very modern kind with a Greek chorus & megaphones & other oddities of that kind.

Of his predecessor at the Vatican, he wrote: "Evan Morgan came to Bath for a month to do a cure, and I saw a great deal of him, but I can never make him out really, and conclude he is slightly mad like most of his family."

Despite his claim of the town's quietude, the climate of gossip appears to have rivalled that of the provincial ladies of E.F. Benson's *Mapp and Lucia* novels: "Mrs. Thynnes' tea-party of 50 or more people, with a sumptuous tea from Fortt's* made some talk, as she was accused of frivolity and extravagance."

It's entirely possible Harold knew Benson through Lord Battersea, and perhaps even provided him with material. Another author certainly attracted his attention. As he told Teresa: "I have lately read a novel called *Paradise City* by Henry Channon, that young American who goes about a lot in smart society, 'Chips' Channon,† you probably know him." The homosexual Channon was then carving a swathe through London society, which was accelerated the following year by

---

* Fortt's Restaurant: a renowned Bath establishment.
† Sir Henry 'Chips' Channon (1897–1958), American-born British Conservative M.P. and author, famed for his diaries, in which he wrote: "I am rivetted by lust, furniture, glamour and society and jewels." Elliott Templeton, the crashing snob in Somerset Maugham's novel *The Razor's Edge*, is a portrait. [Rhodes James, Robert, *Chips: The Diaries of Sir Henry Channon*, Weidenfeld & Nicolson, London 1967, p12; Peter Burton, 'W. Somerset Maugham', *Gay News*, Issue 39, 31 January-13 February 1974, p10-11.]

his marriage into 'the beerage', to heiress Lady Honor Guinness. Inevitably, Harold was curious about one of the characters in the novel, the sensitive 'Daniel Springer' who finds Venice agreeable to his temperament and collects *objets d'art*: "I rather wonder if he is founded on a real person, & if so who he was." The character was, in fact, Channon's alter-ego.

In 1933 Harold wrote to Teresa: "I have not been to Rome for 3 years, & am glad to go again. I am to do a week's duty at the Vatican". It was a stint that included the Opening of the Holy Door ceremonies. He also stayed in Florence, whose large English expatriate community had become, after the Wilde trials, another refuge for those seeking a more sympathetic clime. As artist Mina Loy* phrased it: "they gathered round them a scattering of expatriated bachelors deeply attached to their furniture" where "he who treads tactfully may keep one foot in society and one in Fairyland". Two such Florentine social fixtures, who were also friends of Lady Berwick, were the artist Reggie Temple,† and the director of the British Institute, Arthur Spender.‡ In his letter to Lady Berwick, Harold informs her, "I saw as much as I could of the De Robecks§ and Arthur Spender."

In 1932, Harold spent Holy Week and Easter at the Benedictine abbey of St. Maurice and St. Maurus in Luxembourg, before meeting up with Gerald at the Hotel Gallia in Paris for more worldly pleasures. In September of that year he wrote to Teresa from his favourite Biarritz

---

* Mina Gertrude Loy, née Löwy (1882–1966), British artist, novelist, poet, playwright, and feminist.
† Reginald Willock Temple (1868–1954), artist and social arbiter. A friend of Oscar Wilde's, his diminutive stature had thwarted his acting ambitions. Despite a sensitive appearance – he was described by Mabel Dodge Luhan as a "soft, round little thing, so blond and so neat, always showing lavender and mauve in his exquisite handkerchiefs as they edged his pale gray shirts," his tongue could be anything but. He also had a taste for the macabre. According to Harold Acton, "Tea was his dominant meal: he seemed to live on buttered toast and nightmares." [Mabel Dodge Luhan, *Intimate Memories: European Experiences*, Harcourt, Brace and Company, 1935, p246; Harold Acton, *More Memoirs Of An Aesthete*, Methuen & Co, London, 1970 pp63-64.]
‡ Arthur Francis Spender (1869–1947). One of the "hoary lions" of Anglo-Florentine and Venetian society, he was "a very thin, delicate and sensitive man," who once fell into a pool while staring at the moon. [Harold Acton, *Memoirs Of An Aesthete*, Viking, New York 1971, p 46; Molly Berkeley (Countess of Berkeley), *Winking At The Brim*, Houghton Mifflin, Boston 1967, p166.]
§ Eleanor de Robeck, née Okeden, Australian wife of Major Charles de Robeck, and their daughter Nesta Mary Emily de Robeck (1886–1983), Renaissance and Franciscan historian best known for her biography of Francis Of Assisi; buried at La Foce, the estate of Iris Origo, Marchesa di Val d'Orcia whose friend she was.

nest, the Hotel Du Palais:

> Gerald and I have been together in Paris & here but he left yesterday for Vichy to begin his cure, & I shall rejoin him there later...till yesterday it has been quite lovely with blue skies & hot sunshine, & the sea-bathing delightful...Almost all the women here go about in trousers, so much so that skirts have quite an eccentric air...

Subsequent letters record stays at Gerald's London house in Grosvenor Square. In such an idyllic life of cultured leisure, Harold also had time for time itself. In 1934, ostensibly as an experiment, the B.B.C. began listing its programme timings using the 24-hour clock system. Not surprisingly, the shires erupted. The Corporation received over 3,000 written protests; of written appreciations there were but 400. One of the latter was from Harold, and it was gratefully published by the BBC's own magazine, the *Radio Times*:

> I earnestly hope that the B.B.C. is in no way discouraged by the inept and thoughtless criticism of the 24-hour clock system, which has appeared in the Press. This is the deplorable way, unfortunately, in which ideas new to this country are generally received, and it does us no credit. I trust that you will continue to use and advocate the 24-hour clock system with all your power and influence. H.E.B. Boulton, Bath.

Regrettably for Harold, in the wake of the criticism, the experiment was abandoned. Despite championing this innovation, the fact was, Harold was easing into old dufferdom; the *Week-end Review* and *New Statesman* recorded his wins of their crossword puzzles. At the outbreak of the Second World War he was again living in London, in a spanking new mansion flat in a smart block, at 44 Richmond Hill Court, Richmond, that overlooked a stretch of Thames-side gardens.

By this time Harold had also become a regular attendee of funerals, including that of Rudyard Kipling. He also attended Requiem Mass for a friend, Lieutenant Arthur Bevan, whose obituary in the *Chronicle of the King's Royal Rifle Corps* is sweetly revealing:

> Before the days of the Great War our ideas of good military material were perhaps prejudiced, but most of us would have

smiled at the thought of Arthur Bevan in the Army. Four years of a nation in arms made us realise what different types could, for one reason or another, be useful to their country or their Regiment...Physically he was never strong. He loathed taking the initiative, but he was utterly courageous, truthful and honest. But those were not the qualities which made for his peculiar success. He had an absorbing interest and love of people and a capacity to find and bring out the best in those around him. He was friend and confessor to every man in his platoon.

In his last years, Harold relocated yet again to that ultimate retirement locale of Tunbridge Wells, at 46 Claremont Road, a large semi-detached Edwardian villa. His surviving sister Emily, who'd married a George Frederic Campbell Mackenzie and had three children, died in 1953, and on the 14th of August 1958, at the age of 87, Harold died.

Apart from a certain exciting incident in 1902, Harold lived what appears to have been a quiet, cultured, very pleasurable, and well-managed life of society and travel, which was still typical of the (increasingly unlanded) gentry. The need to keep this lifestyle afloat, and post-War inflation, meant he left a modest estate of £1,533. All his personal chattels were bequeathed to his two nieces, and the entire remainder of his estate and property to a Royal Air Force officer, Howard Ford.

A Welshman born in 1905 in Hawarden, Howard was affectionately known as 'Bunny'. A Cambridge scholar and outstanding athlete, he excelled at snow skiing and the shot put. In 1928, Howard represented Great Britain in the decathlon at the Olympic Games at Amsterdam, and at the Empire Games of 1930 and 1934, where he won medals. In 1936 he married, and went on to a distinguished career in the Royal Air Force. Photographs show him to have been a handsome, strongly built man with a friendly open face.

Retiring in 1962 as an Air Vice-Marshall, Howard Ford died a childless widower in 1986 at his apartment in Duke Street, St James's. As for the private history between himself and Harold E.B. Boulton, Private Chamberlain of Sword and Cape, it appears they took it to their graves.

17. AN IDEAL ENGLISH GENTLEMAN

Arthur Thorold was as much a product of his background as the oak pews that sat in the churches of his father, the Reverend Algernon.* For it was the Church of England that was the natural calling of the Thorolds. For centuries they'd been its pillars, supplying endless priests and functionaries. Stretching back to the Plantagenets could also be found upstanding Thorold parliamentarians, knights, seamen, sheriffs and squires: a prominent and proud family that were part of the very fabric of England.

The Reverend Algernon Thorold had married a gentleman's daughter, Edith Clay,† and served in a string of parishes in Sussex, Kent and Essex, before finally becoming, like Thorolds before him, rector of Hougham-cum-Marston, two small adjoining villages in Lincolnshire that had been consolidated into a single parish. Both lay along the River Witham, and were each blessed with fine churches: so close were they, that the only thing separating All Saints at Hougham, from St Mary's at Marston, was a pleasant stroll.

This was Thorold country, and the family were surrounded by relations. The Rev. Algernon's patron was his second cousin, Sir John Thorold, twelfth holder of the Thorold of Marston baronetcy. His stately seat, Syston Hall, stood on a low yet commanding eminence some three miles to the south-east. To him belonged estates stretching to 12,000 acres, which included the parish and the gift of the rectorship and its living. This came with the rectory itself, a

---

* Rev. Algernon Charles Edward Thorold (1850–1922).
† Edith Mary Thorold, née Clay (1845–1909).

substantial three-storied red brick manor at Hougham, that was set within several acres of gardens, plus the farmed acres of a glebe that provided the income. In total, the land amounted to 389 acres.* Together with the Rev. Algernon's family connections, it ensured that, like other Thorolds, he was considered gentry, a status he was highly conscious of. His arrogance and pomposity made him unpopular in the parish, a fellow minister confiding to the Bishop of Lincoln:

> if he could only change his nature from one of self-importance and self-will to one of fine brotherly charity for his people he would then find no difficulty – until he does there is nothing to look forward to but feuds.

The Rev. Algernon's hubris is suggested by the fact he was twice convicted and fined in the court of petty sessions for keeping a dog without a licence; then a notable offence: he contending it was a shepherd dog. However, it was out-of-character behaviour for a clergyman.

Arthur Thorold, christened Arthur Charles Campbell Thorold, was born on 13 September 1873; the second of what were to be five children: three sons and two daughters.† When Arthur was twelve the family finally settled at Hougham rectory.

The rural, staunchly manorial Lincolnshire Arthur knew could well have been, on first appearances, of a hundred years earlier – or two hundred. Surrounded by the deep stillness of broad flat fields, only the whistle of a passing train at tiny Hougham Station broke the silence, and served to remind that this was the time of Queen Victoria, rather than that of the Tudors.

Yet this sense of sleepy permanence was an illusion. The railway had reached Hougham in 1855. With the sudden jerk of a piston, life had

---

* In the 1830s the Thorold rector was also the recipient of toll income from the local turnpike gate, before its removal. [Edward Mogg, *Paterson's Roads*, Longman, Rees, Orme, etc., London 1832, p226.]

† The children were: Rev. Algernon Herbert (1872–1931) Vicar of Gwennap, Cornwall and Honorary Priest-Vicar of Truro Cathedral, married with issue; Arthur Charles Campbell (1873–1939); Violet Hilda (1874–1935), assistant secretary, unmarried; Rev. Dr. Ernest Hayford (1879–1940), Chaplain General to Forces and to King George V, and married with issue; and Edith Muriel (1881–1967), nurse, unmarried.

speeded up and the world had got much smaller. Coaching inns and turnpikes, and a whole way of existence, receded swiftly into memory. Before then the parish had lived, like others across the kingdom, with a sense of time and geographical consciousness that hadn't much changed since pre-history.

Arthur was also born on the eve of an agricultural depression that would slowly but inexorably change England forever. The advent of reliable steamships and refrigeration enabled the importation of grain and meat from America's prairies, squeezing the incomes of English tenant farmer and landlord alike. By the 1890s, the additional pincher of rising income tax accelerated the breakup of estates, rural depopulation, and the ebbing of aristocratic power. Lady Bracknell's aspersion regarding land – "It gives one position and prevents one from keeping it up," became very often true. The breakup was further enabled by the Settled Lands Acts of 1881-2, which loosened the bonds of strict settlements by which estates had been preserved within families for generations.

When Reverend Algernon's family arrived in Hougham, this erosion of the old order, while still largely inconceivable, was quietly underway. By the time of Queen Victoria's Diamond Jubilee in 1897, it had become a massive undertow, and one that the ruling class was all too aware of.

A bulwark against the uncertainty and doubt created by change was the Christian faith. It is difficult to underestimate how deeply religion permeated everyday Victorian life. The 1870s further witnessed an evangelical revival that swept the United Kingdom. As one author observed in 1878:

> The minds of men everywhere are agitated at present by religious questions. There is not a periodical or even a newspaper in which these do not occupy a prominent place.

In addition to being eminently respectable, the Thorolds were naturally deeply pious, and Arthur's religious upbringing soaked deep into his bones. "Over and above Truth, Courage and Manners was his Catalyst of Religion," one of his former pupils recollected. "He practised his religion with intensity and kept the Christian Calendar thoroughly."

506

Arthur was taught first by a governess, and then sent to a preparatory boarding school, Cambridge House School in Tunbridge Wells. At fourteen he went on, again as a boarder, to the famous Marlborough College in Wiltshire. The school had been specifically established to educate the sons of clergymen.* Here Arthur was immersed in an alternative world of boys from devout and privileged families such as his. Marlborough provided its pupils with the typical spartan character-building regime of the period: lessons heavily weighted on the Classics, plus rugby and cricket, plain food, fascist prefects, bitter cold, adolescent crushes, and endless summoning bells. Most essentially, it built loyalty, dependability, and self-reliance, and inculcated the code of honour that so distinguished, and brought respect to a gentleman of Her Majesty's realms. Arthur would later write with lip-smacking relish of the virtues of the prefectorial system:

> Observe that fancy waistcoat, those flowery socks, that gorgeous tie – it is a great chief, a blood. He is a prefect, a man under authority having many under him. He says to this one, Go, and he goeth and to another, Come and he cometh, and to his fag, Do this, and he doeth it….these schoolboys, young as they are…are accustomed to govern and be governed, frame their own laws and administer their own Commonwealth… [it] is what prepares them for life, its struggles and its responsibilities.

The passage's theatrical echoing of the *New Testament*'s words of the centurion to Jesus no doubt resonated with its audience: Arthur wasn't a rector's son for nothing. However, it also smacks of the unconscious campery, so ubiquitous at the time, of those whose happiest days had been lived in a school blazer.

In October 1892, Arthur went up to Worcester College, Oxford,† to further study the Classics.‡ The university was then still imbued with the spiritual and monastic traditions of centuries past, but reinvigorated by a reformed secular curriculum. However, even the *Oxford And Cambridge Undergraduate's Journal* – the same organ that had carried the correspondence on *Boy-Worship*, contained page after page

---

* It is now co-educational.
† The academic year at Oxford begins in October and ends in June. The year is divided into three terms: Michaelmas (autumn), Hilary (spring), and Trinity (summer).
‡ The undergraduate course known as Literae Humaniores: nicknamed the Greats.

of the full text of sermons by leading ecclesiastical figures. For young men drawn to philosophical reflection as they sought to piece together their characters and place in the world, these preachings were not considered dusty harangues, but rather, intellectually rigorous and challenging discourses of pressing immediacy.

Like others of his class, Arthur had spent almost his entire life up to this point in exclusively male societies, and Oxford was a continuation of it. Young ladies were usually met socially under highly artificial chaperoned circumstances; their unexpected presence oft viewed as an embarrassment and intrusion. Walter Woodgate,* an Oxford man considered "the finest oarsman of his generation," once suffered the frightful shock of a lady unknown to him wilfully boarding the smoking carriage of a train in which he was seated. As he recalled:

> In terror I hailed the guard, and bade him shift my kit to another coach: he demurred – as the train was due to start. I insisted: out came my gun, birds, and the like, I murmuring "Sooner have a mad dog than a single woman in the carriage."

At Cambridge, the sexually repressed Arthur Benson viewed a dinner with rapt fascination:

> The public fondling and caressing of each other, friends and lovers sitting with arms enlaced, cheeks even touching, struck me as curious, beautiful in a way, but rather dangerous.

These homosocial environments fostered a Platonic eros, and yearning friendships that often tipped into romance, or simply met more pressing needs.

At Oxford, Arthur may have encountered the fellow student and boyfriend of Oscar Wilde, Lord Alfred Douglas, who was already gaining a reputation, including as owner-editor of the student magazine *Spirit Lamp*, for which he eagerly solicited contributions from prominent homosexual authors, including Wilde, Symonds and Kains Jackson. In May 1893 the Dean of Divinity of Magdalen stumbled upon Lord Alfred:

---

* Walter Bradford Woodgate (1841–1920), oarsman, barrister, author, and bachelor.

lying in the middle of the road, sunning himself with very little on, but covered over like a babe in the wood, with masses of lilac. Truly aesthetic!

Arthur Thorold was the very opposite of a willowy, pre-Raphaelite vision. Highly masculine, he'd grown into a tall and solidly-built young man. His natural muscularity was enhanced by competitive running – he won the One Mile Handicap in 1893, as well as rowing. Although the captain of Worcester College's Boat Club minuted of him: "Rows with half a blade [,] very slow with hands, on the whole not much use," Arthur persevered, later writing: "Rowing was my forte at Oxford." Perhaps it was another of his personal myths, and the truth lay elsewhere.

Many rowers in those years made their way to Parson's Pleasure: a secluded male-only nude swimming and sunbathing enclave on the bank of the river Cherwell. On long summer afternoons it was popular with both students and dons, and bore a discreet notoriety. Now long abolished due to prudery, it was to be recalled with deep nostalgia; in the words of one student "the most enchanting spot in Oxford".*

Arthur threw himself wholeheartedly into university life. Given students were under an evening curfew, campus clubs played an important part in social activities, and he was a member of a string of them, including as acting Treasurer of the Debating Society, and Honorary President of the De Quincey Society – an essay club named after Worcester College's famous former student.†

Most of all, Arthur loved performing: it took him out of himself. He gained a reputation for entertaining in his room, where popular songs were the order of the day. There was also the Oxford University Dramatic Society, but apart from possibly participating in its country-house theatricals or pastoral plays, he was never a member. Arthur much preferred melodrama, musicals, and the music hall: The Empire theatre, south of Magdalen Bridge, was very likely his opium.

---

* According to a Mr Cox who managed it: "We never could trace that anyone of the name of Parsons had it, and we believe it is called 'Parsons Pleasure' because so many of the University men who came here intended to be parsons." [Ralph Thomas, *Swimming*, Sampson Low, Marston & Company, London 1904, p352.]
† Thomas De Quincey (1785–1859), essayist. Most noted for *Confessions of an English Opium Eater*.

In 1895, the sensational newspaper reports of the trials and imprisonment of Oscar Wilde were followed as avidly at Oxford as they were elsewhere in the nation, and the gravity of the charges and universal opprobrium would have impressed itself upon Arthur. Undoubtedly he would have felt some sense of self-recognition, and also fear. However, the seductive distractions of those halcyon days were many. As a former student wrote:

> oysters and champagne were the order of the day, both at College feasts and at lodgings...At Oxford, as at Florence, everyone who was not revelling seemed pleased to make a flowery way for the revellers.

It was easy for a young man from a stuffy provincial family to be swept away, and swept away Arthur was. Although in his second year of studies he achieved 2nd Class Honours, in his third year, social distractions – including being on the planning committee of his college's triennial ball, led him astray, and he failed to graduate. Students having to repeat studies was hardly unusual in a time when Oxford was solely for the sons of privilege, but for Arthur's parents it would have been profoundly troubling. The Rev. Algernon Thorold's management of the glebe had only proven he was no farmer, and his income had been seriously compromised. With the expense of providing three sons with premium educations, he was now under financial stress.

When Arthur returned to Oxford for the first term of his fourth year, he didn't live in College. He also submitted a request for leave of absence, which was granted. This was likely due to his father's difficulties. Arthur was absent for second term, only returning for the third.* Yet, when the end of the academic year arrived, he *still* didn't have his degree. It was now June 1896.

---

* A later Registrar at Oxford believed the pattern in Thorold's studies suggested he'd been rusticated (suspended). However, a thorough review of Worcester College records by its current Archivist reveals no such sanction. The then Provost at Worcester College, the Rev. William Inge (1829–1903), was a Marlborough Old Boy, while the Headmaster of Marlborough, George Charles Bell (1832–1913), was a Worcester alumni, who'd progressed to a fellowship around the same time. Bell likely recommended Worcester to Thorold, and it's possible this connection led Provost Inge to treat any infractions by Thorold, if there were such, more benevolently.

Given the state of his father's finances, Arthur needed to support himself. While waiting for something more promising to turn up, it was not uncommon for students to seek tutoring jobs. Normally such arrangements were finalised through college dons or a scholastic agency. Which is probably how Arthur secured the temporary position at Naples, as tutor-cum-secretary for the illustrious George Rendel. After enduring the family's disappointment over his academic performance, the engagement must have seemed a gift from Heaven. The Rendel's Villa Maraval was certainly very near to it.

In his spare time away from his duties at the Villa, the warm embrace of Naples surely caused Arthur's blood to surge and rush like so many English travellers to the city before him. The heady feeling would have flooded him with the confidence to fulfil his desires. Dangerously so. Because the Oxford he needed to return to was not Naples, and England was never Italy.

While university would have immersed Arthur in a milieu of well-connected, sophisticated, and wealthy young men, his introduction at Naples to the cosmopolitan Bernard Fraser opened grander doors, and opportunities for greater dissipations. It's apparent Bernard's social status and family money had endowed him with a sense of entitlement and self-assurance that tipped into arrogance. But then, all the world, including the parallel homosocial world, awaited his pleasure.

For Arthur, being in such breezy, swaggering, monied company, with its patrician outlook that knew no boundaries, would have been both exhilarating and liberating. If he had any remaining provincial inhibitions or religious hesitations, it's likely Bernard and the outgoing boys of Naples soon put them to bed. As popular bachelors about town, Bernard Fraser and Harold Boulton knew a wide circle, while their friend Cyril Flower, Lord Battersea, knew simply everyone. While Lord Rosebery quashed Arthur's hopes of a salubrious Neapolitan life as the managing agent of his villa, another secret life had opened out.

Returning to Oxford, in December 1899, Arthur finally graduated with a Bachelor of Arts degree. Then it was a homecoming to Hougham once more. Like something from the deeply provincial life portrayed in Mrs. Gaskell's *Chronicles of Cranford*, the local newspaper recorded:

> A Social Evening was held on Friday, January 13th at the School, arranged by the ladies of Hougham, in aid of the Church fund. Unfortunately, the weather was wet and stormy, and a good many people were unable to attend who would otherwise have been present, but about sixty persons assembled…a number of songs and quartettes were given during the evening by Mr. Arthur Thorold, Mr. Ernest Thorold, the Misses Thorold, and Mrs. Glover, which were very much appreciated by the audience. The profits of the entertainment amounted to rather less than £2.

Little wonder Arthur pined for Naples! It was possibly during this time he indulged in his theatrical ambitions and toured with some theatre companies: years later he would speak of such experience, although no record of these engagements has been found. However, unlike his wealthier friends, he now needed permanent gainful employment. In September 1900, he finally secured a position as junior assistant master at the Anglican High Church boys school, St. Edward's at Oxford. Then twenty seven years old, Arthur was described by a member of his form as "young, smartly dressed".

At St. Edward's there was another smartly dressed bachelor master with whom Arthur possibly found affinity: the majestically named Wilfred Hammerton Antrobus Cowell.* Sporting an upturned collar and trim pointed beard, the handsome Cowell also had theatrical leanings, and was the indefatigable director of its annual Shakespearean play, as well as the school librarian, editor of its newspaper, and more. A definite character, he spent his entire life at the School, becoming a beloved local legend, and ultimately expiring there at the age of eighty-one.

The School's other stalwart was made of sterner stuff: John Millington Sing† was the Warden, and an ardent imperialist. He possessed a "fanatical devotion to the sanities of mind and body; his insistence upon perfection, the Spartan streak in him." This included compulsory nude bathing in icy water, rigorous fagging,‡ and

---

* Wilfred Hammerton Antrobus Cowell (1956–1937).
† John Millington Sing (1863-1947).
‡ A system whereby younger students acted as personal servants to those in higher forms.

birchings that involved a solemn ritual of drawn curtains, locked doors, and a matron standing by with an iodine-soaked pad. It was the very stuff that forged Empire-builders, and the school archives feature many a letter of condolence from Sing to the families of Old Boys who were slaughtered in the Great War.

In January 1901, Queen Victoria died. Even at the time, it was recognised as the end of an era. The School mourning included black tie for all pupils. It looked very dapper: so much so, that it subsequently found its way into the school uniform for many decades.

By this time Arthur's friendship with Bernard Fraser had developed to the point where, despite his position of trust, Arthur introduced him to some of his students. Perhaps it was done in gratitude, or in complicity, or Bernard simply pressed him to. A comment in Fraser's criminal file states that he "corrupted" them.

In October 1901, Arthur was best man at the wedding of his eldest brother Algernon (junior), who'd joined the family calling, and was by then a curate. The following year his brother Ernest also became a curate.

In January 1902 a local paper recorded that, in aid of funds for the Hougham Sunday School, Arthur's father gave a lantern exhibition on "the recent Royal voyage around the world in the Ophir."* The second part of the entertainment involved "humorous songs and recitations by Mr. Arthur Thorold who accompanied himself on the pianoforte," together with his brother Ernest and sisters. It was all so wholesome and innocent. Arthur's arrest at the end of July 1902 would have hit his family with the force of a bomb.

His father's mental and physical health was already in a precarious state due to financial stress. He was now two years in arrears on his mortgage. What is more, his character had ensured his continued unpopularity. The Rev. T.J. Crossfield, a minister from the Diocese who was sent to Hougham by the Bishop of Lincoln, reported to him

---

Duties of a fag could include running errands, cooking breakfast and supper, polishing boots, and occasionally more *outré* tasks, such as body-warming the fagmaster's toilet seat in winter.
* The Empire tour of the Duke and Duchess of Cornwall (the future King George V and Queen Mary), which included the opening of the first parliament of the Commonwealth of Australia.

in a letter: "There is an evil feeling in this parish against Mr. Thorold…he has made no end of enemies." The Rev. Algernon's anguish was compounded by neuralgia, sciatica, and insomnia. The destruction of false pride can do that. His doctor wrote:

> Serious family trouble coming upon him in his weak state has reduced him to a condition of great nervous debility… I am of the opinion that a prolonged absence from Hougham is essential for his recovery.

Arthur's mother also felt she could no longer live in the parish. It's easy to imagine the gossip and stares. Rev. Thorold was granted leave of absence from the diocese. Presumably accompanied by his wife, he departed on a sea voyage for his health. In July 1903, Rev. Crossfield breathlessly communicated to the Bishop of Lincoln the further troubling news we already know:

> Since I came to Grantham this morning I learnt that the 'bride' I married the other day was the sister of the boy with whom Mr. Thorold's son committed so grievous a Sin."

The innocent yet attainted young lady was Benjamin Brumfield's older sister Anna Louisa.

By this time it was observed, "the Rectory grounds and house having been so long unoccupied have become most unhealthy and malarious". It was the manifestation of a complete family breakdown. In October 1904, an advertisement appeared in the local newspaper, *The Grantham Journal*:

> A RECTORY HOUSE with Stabling for Nine Horses, to be LET, for the Hunting Season. – Rev. A. Thorold, Hougham, Grantham.

The Rector's absences from the parish would become a steady occurrence up until his death in January 1922.

At St. Edward's School the story was put about that Arthur had left to take up a position elsewhere. Given the police enquiries, the school authorities would have known the truth. While the story broke in newspapers in August, with the first court hearings, the July edition of St. Edward's school magazine bravely stated that, together with another teacher, the Rev. C. Stocks, who was departing for parish work, Mr. Thorold was leaving:

> for the Lower Sixth Form Mastership at Bancroft's School, Woodford. One and all of us will be very sorry indeed to say good-bye to them and we wish them every success, while hoping that they will find it possible to get away from their work sometimes and visit us here.

Unfortunately for Arthur's pining pupils, taking a happy respite from prison wasn't on the cards. There is no way to underestimate the life-changing experience that lay ahead of him. Those found guilty of serious offences usually served the first nine months of their sentence in solitary confinement at a metropolitan prison. They were then removed to one of the convict prisons. Here the intention of the regime was to break the hardened criminal will. The most dreaded was Dartmoor, set on a high windswept wilderness that seemed the very embodiment of human desolation. After initially being confined in Chelmsford Prison, it was to Dartmoor that Arthur was sent.

The prison uniform was a short loose jacket and vest, and baggy knickerbockers. These were emblazoned with the broad arrow symbol of classic convicthood. The boots were exhaustingly heavy: weighing as much as 6kg (14lbs) they were the next best thing to a ball and chain. On the prisoner' left breast pocket, in metal numerals, was their number. Arthur's was c505. From the moment it was allotted, he no longer had a name. Another patch bore his wing, floor and cell number.

The standard cells at Dartmoor were seven feet by four; the walls corrugated iron, the floor of slate. The one hundred and sixty-eight cells were stacked in four tiers within a hall. The only ventilation came from a two or three inch gap at the bottom of each door, the air itself only originating from the hall. Consequently, the atmosphere was foul, and in summer, almost suffocating. The only natural light emanated from a high small window that was rarely cleaned; at Dartmoor these were internal windows into the hall, not external ones; so like the air, the light was also second hand. Even had it been an external window it would have made little difference. At Reading Gaol, in which Oscar Wilde was imprisoned, he recalled:

Outside, the day may be blue and gold but the light that creeps down through the thickly-muffled glass…is grey…It is always twilight in one's cell, as it is always midnight in one's heart.

Even more memorable was the cold. One former prisoner wrote:

It was not so much the intensity of the cold, for probably the cold was not so intense, as the abominable feeling of always waking cold and the hopeless and helpless feeling that there was no prospect of going to sleep again, and no possible way of getting warm till the bell rang and you were allowed to get up and put on your clothes.

Prisoners were woken by a bell at 6.20 a.m. Their daily activity included meals, chapel, school instruction and, of course, work. Of meals, Michael Davitt, an Irish Republican Brotherhood prisoner recalled:

The food in Dartmoor prison I found to be the very worst in quality and the filthiest in cooking of any of the other places I had been in…from about November till May it is simply execrable…To find black beetles in soup, 'skilly', bread, and tea, was quite a common occurrence.

Hard labour in penal servitude accounted for between six and ten hours each day. Due to Dartmoor's trying climate, which included wet snow and freezing fogs, being assigned to an outside work gang was feared; the very worst labour being reclamation of bog-land. As one prisoner wrote: "the intense cold experienced on the upper moorland, made the task a Herculean one."

Michael Davitt wrote:

The labour I was first put to was stone-breaking, that being considered suitable work for non-able-bodied prisoners. I was put to this employment in a large shed, along with some eighty or ninety more prisoners…my hand becoming blistered by the action of the hammer after I had broken stones for a week…during the winter I was compelled to work outside in the cold and damp foggy weather. I was left at this work until spring,

516

and was then removed to a task from the effects of which I believe I will never completely recover.

The new task was 'cart labour', which involved dragging large carts of stones, coals, manure and rubbish by a harness attached to a chain.

In drawing the cart along, each prisoner has to bend forward and pull with all his strength, or the warder who is 'driving' will threaten to 'run him in', or report him for idleness.

Those incapable of ordinary prison labour were put to 'bone-breaking', which involved pounding into dust the bones from the prison's meat supply which had "often lain putrefying for weeks."

It was common for convicts to consider themselves the living dead, existing outside of time and the human world. Those who endured it were scarred forever: for Arthur it would have been a deep wound within himself that he possibly never shared with another living soul.

And so the long years passed. With nine months of his sentence reduced for good behaviour, on the 31st of July 1906, prisoner c505 was finally released.

Arthur Thorold was now thirty-two. To return to Hougham permanently was unthinkable. In any case, everything there had changed. With his youngest sister Muriel working as a nurse in London, only his sister Hilda was still living at home, shouldering the burden with their mother. Given the state of their father, it is likely to have been a grim trapped existence for a spinster. Arthur's youngest brother Ernest had joined the forces as a chaplain. Notably, between 1904 and 1906 he'd served as curate of Battersea! Whether Cyril had exercised his influence to enable the appointment, in guilt and gratitude for Arthur's sacrifice on his behalf, makes for an interesting speculation.

Benjamin Brumfield was now no longer a boy or youth, but a nineteen-year-old man, helping to support his widowed mother and younger siblings. In 1905, his father had fallen from a ladder while nailing a plum tree to a wall, and after then undertaking a ten-hour work stint, had lapsed into an unconsciousness from which he never woke. Whether Arthur dared pay Benjamin a call, or wrote to him, is unknown.

With the depression in agriculture lingering, like so many other farm workers in those years, Benjamin decided to leave the land and seek fresh opportunities. In 1908 he joined the Lincolnshire police force. In this story of many ironies, it is one of the richest. Benjamin may have warmed to the career choice due to his close encounter with law procedure. However, having to give testimony in such a case in a public court, in front of his parents, would have been a profoundly shaming experience. If he'd been tortured with guilt over his involvement with Thorold, joining the force may have been spiked by the desire to seize back control of his life, and also save and prosecute others.

On Arthur Thorold's Scotland Yard criminal register, his address at the time is given as the "Birmingham Church Army". This evangelistic organisation, an Anglican variation of the Salvation Army, had been founded in 1882, and sent its representatives into slums and prisons to work with social outcasts and criminals, such as Arthur. As there was now no place for him in England as a gentleman – and certainly not as a schoolmaster, immigration appeared the only solution. In Australia lived friends of his father. For his reputation's sake, it was as far away as possible – indeed, the bottom of the world. The transportation of British convicts to the country had only ceased thirty-eight years before.

In September 1906, Arthur departed England on the steamship Runic as a steerage passenger. Not only was it a wrench from the England that was part of his soul; he would never see his parents again. On the ship's register he stated his profession as 'actor'. Given he had to reinvent himself, the thought of pursuing such a career in the antipodes held great appeal. He'd always enjoyed performing at local functions, and dabbling in the theatre had only increased his desire for more of the same. His father would almost certainly have frowned upon such a path as frivolous and disreputable, but having burned his bridges so thoroughly, what was there to lose? As a precaution against exposure, he would also no longer be Arthur: his first name was shed like a tree dropping a decayed branch. Henceforth he would call himself Charles Thorold, or C.C. Thorold for Charles Campbell Thorold. It was, in every way, a new beginning.

After 40 days sailing, Charles arrived in Melbourne on October 10th. Unlike raffish Sydney which had originally been a convict settlement, 'Marvellous Melbourne' as it was then nicknamed, was founded by free settlers. The wealth of mid-century gold rushes had transformed it into one of the great boom cities of the Victorian era. Lord Rosebery, who travelled widely in Australia in 1883, was charmed by Sydney, considering its harbour "next to Naples the finest thing I have seen," but admitted of Melbourne: "This is what is called a noble city – great wide streets like Edinburgh New Town or St. Petersburg."

For Charles, the surroundings would have felt different yet reassuringly familiar. With a cool-temperate climate and magnificent architecture set amidst the broad elm-lined streets, and superb parks and gardens, it was a careful recreation of an English provincial city in the very best sense. It was also then the seat of the federal government, and the business, intellectual and cultural capital of Australia. The city fathers prided themselves on Melbourne's graciousness and deep conservatism: the bluestone granite foundations which marked so many of the city's buildings were considered a symbol of its steadfast Christian integrity. Importantly for Charles's intended new career, the city also had a small but vibrant theatre district.

The replication of English life included an Italianate Government House that echoed Victoria and Albert's Osborne House, and an annual river regatta called Henley on the Yarra. There was fox hunting, Parma violets and primroses, and even a Melbourne version of the popular British humour magazine *Punch*. As in England, the occasional stipulation in advertisements for servants – 'No Irish need apply', had broadly disappeared, but a strict immigration policy maintained the homogeneity of Australia's Anglo-Saxon populous. When Charles arrived the city was still recovering from a spectacular banking crash of 1891 that led to a series of recessions, but the population was rapidly growing beyond half a million persons.

Amongst those persons were, as the headline of an Austral tabloid phrased it, "Masculine Messalinas And Their Mashes". The newspaper went on to warn that "Oscar Wildeism" or "pæderastic practices" of "ancient origin" were:

becoming alarmingly prominent in the capital cities of the

Commonwealth…as things are now in Melbourne, public resorts are defiled by the loathsome presence of shameless creatures who slink there for the vilest of purposes. The large gardens adjacent to Melbourne have become glaringly conspicuous in this respect and, although the police make an occasional arrest – hushed up carefully by the very respectable press – the evil shows no sign of diminution, but rather the reverse.

Detailed in both word and sketch were some of the most notable male streetwalkers, under their nicknames, Miladi, Nana, The Princess, and Little Peach. When the latter was arrested, found in his pocket was a letter from an 'Oscar', which was published: "Dear Little Peach – When am I to see you and be with you again to press your plump —? I dream of you sleeping and waking…" The report continued:

They are noted for their flowing butterfly ties, and have secret signs, known to their seekers, which they interchange by a movement of the tongue, a certain style of buttoning the coat, flowers, and other devices.

The nickname of The Princess was derived from his favoured loitering locale, Princes Bridge, on the city's main boulevard. It was a highly prominent position that would have drawn attention from even a casual observer.

The newspaper calling attention to this local colour was *Truth* – yet another purloined English masthead, but unlike Labouchère's paper, it was principally a 'scandal sheet' targeted at the working and lower-middle class, and anyone who lived for sensation. At its helm was an equally brilliant and unpredictable owner-editor and parliamentarian, John Norton.* Unlike Labby, Norton was no gentleman; but rather, a bull-headed bullying alcoholic who accumulated libel suits like bottle-tops. Far more aggressively muckraking, he lived for a good newspaper fight: "a monarch of alliterative abuse," he dished up derision of authority figures, which delighted readers and swelled the paper's enormous circulation. Within its pages, Queen Victoria was "semi-senile…podgy-fingered, sulky-faced…fat and flatulent," while her heir was a "turf-swindling, card-sharping, wife-debauching, boozing rowdy."† *Truth* was published in several state editions, but it

---

* John Norton (1858–1916), English-born Australian newspaper-proprietor and politician.
† Norton characterised the handsome General Hector Macdonald for readers as "a sexual

and Norton were appropriately quartered in larrikin* Sydney.

Australia was also not unfamiliar with the prostitution of justice by privilege. A notorious example occurred in 1894, when a case of gross indecency with schoolboys against a gentleman who'd secured a lucrative civil service post in Western Australia, and was a distant relative of a Postmaster General of England, was abruptly dropped. According to one newspaper:

> It was said at the time that his trial would implicate too many of the sons of an ancient aristocracy, and that he was smuggled out of the country with the knowledge of the police.

Opined another: "One law for the rich, another for the poor, and none at all for gentlemen with English letters of introduction." †

Waiting in Melbourne to greet Charles was an infinitely more respectable couple: a friend of his father, the Reverend Thomas Holyoake Rust, who'd emigrated some years previously, and Ethel, his Australian wife.‡ They were childless, and became parental figures to Charles: he would eventually call them 'Pater' and 'Mater'.

The Rev. T.H. Rust had begun his career in Australia as a master at Melbourne's Church of England Grammar School, and it was likely due to his persuasion that Charles abandoned his ambitions for the Australasian stage. A Thorold an *actor*? The idea would have been considered more than *déclassé*: it was unseemly. Marguerite Cunliffe-Owen's opinion of the profession — "Actors! I wouldn't give them Christian burial any more than the Church did in old times," was a sentiment still shared by many.

The day after his arrival, Charles's attention was directed to an

---

pervert...indicated by his prognathous jaw, his protruding hin, elephantine, fly-flapping ears, gleaming sea-green eyes, morose mood and manners, and St. Vitus-like motions...damned from his birth as a degenerate...little better than a fighting savage — splendid, but savage." [One Of Britain's Bravest Soldiers Blows His Brains Out In A Paris Pub, *Truth* (Qld.), 29 March 1903, p5.]

* An Australianism for a raffish person who has no regard for convention.

† The privileged personage was Gerald Raikes (1851–?), Sub-Collector of Customs, Western Australia.

‡ The Reverend Thomas Holyoake Rust (1852–1935), and Ethel Dagmar Rust, née Hopkins (1863–1940).

employment advertisement that appeared in a morning newspaper:

MASTERS (resident) WANTED. February, £200, £176, £130, £120, and several Juniors. S. Atchison, M.A., University Agency, 237 Collins St.

He immediately contacted the agency regarding a position, and also sought registration as a teacher. Such applications naturally called for a detailed curriculum vitae, supported with solid references. To disguise the problematic period from July 1902 to July 1906 would require some delicate cosmetic surgery on his résumé.

The alibi Charles concocted, with the help of a loving brother, was that he'd been a master during those years at Hartford House School, in Wintney, Hampshire. This was a genuine small preparatory school run by a Mr. Edward and Mrs. Eleanor Lloyd. The couple were recalled as a "dear little man who did everything his wife wanted"; Mrs. Lloyd "ruled the family with a rod of iron."* The parish of Wintney was where Charles's eldest brother Algernon had been a curate since 1899. Algernon had obviously mentioned the school and the Lloyds to Charles, and perhaps even introduced them – Mr. Lloyd was also an old Marlborough College boy.

In far-off Melbourne, Charles wasted no time in flagging his need to Algernon for a false reference. Perhaps over a glass of sherry, accompanied by a good deal of flattery of Mrs. Lloyd, and maybe a reference to the Good Samaritan, the dear little man was encouraged to assist an Old Marlboroughian. Edward Lloyd put pen to paper and wrote a testimonial dated the 28th of November, which included the reassurance that Charles:

> was an <u>excellent</u> teacher, and never had any difficulties in the matter of discipline. He is fully qualified to teach Classics, English, French, and Elementary Mathematics.

Mr. Lloyd may have comforted his conscience with the thought that the reference was merely for the antipodes, which in some English minds were not exactly in the front rank of civilisation. Charles also eliminated from his resume any gap in his Oxford studies, and only

---

* She reigned until 1960, dying at 106.

claimed to have worked as a tutor to the Rendels following his graduation.

Charles's Oxford background carried its own imprimatur: at the time, the thought of moral obliquity in 'an Oxford man' was almost inconceivable. And this was no mere false belief. The rounding of character and understanding of rectitude were considered amongst the principal "graces and benedictions" an Oxford education bestowed.

The application to the employment agency with its massaged c.v. and false reference came good with an offer of a £180 per year mastership at the Southport High School in subtropical Queensland.* Known today simply as The Southport School, it is one of Australia's finest private academies: its noble tower, gothic chapel, and splendid teaching and sporting facilities summon a vision of a subtropical Eton. Yet it lies only a few kilometres from the heart of the skyscraper-strewn beachside glitterstrip of Surfers Paradise.

In 1906, Surfers Paradise did not even exist on the map. That area, mostly allotments of scrub filled with plum pines, lilly pilly and ferns, plus a former sugar plantation, was officially designated Elston, but known colloquially as Main Beach, and was only accessible by boat. The nearby sandy village of Southport had therefore become the summer resort for the state capital of Brisbane. The local council encouraged tree planting, sideshow amusements, donkey rides, and that municipal construction which no decent seaside could then exist without – a pier. There was a hotel, some weatherboard English-style guesthouses scented of salt, sweat and sausages, and a building housing the Pacific Cable Station, which linked Australia and North America via a copper cable running across the ocean floor. Electricity for domestic use wouldn't arrive until near the end of the Great War; until then lighting was by acetylene gas and kerosene. Apart from the holiday weeks of Christmas and Easter, Southport quietly drowsed in the subtropical heat.

The Southport High School was barely four years old. It too was a very different place then. The school had been the dream of a young Anglican clergyman, the Reverend Horace Dixon,† who'd been

---

* 1064 miles (1,712 kilometres) north of Melbourne.
† Right Reverend Horace Henry Dixon (1869–1964), schoolmaster and bishop.

consigned from England in 1899 to serve the parish. This extended to over 2,000 square miles, from the hinterland to the New South Wales border. To meet with his parishioners Dixon was forced to spend many hours in the saddle. One day it struck him that what the vastly-distanced community of 1,000 souls needed most was a good boys' school, and he conceived the idea of establishing one based on the great English public schools.

For this he would first require a schoolhouse, and his eyes alighted upon the estate of 'Summerplace'. This was graced with a rambling timber mansion with an adjoining tower and other out buildings. It had once been the summer residence of the state governors, but was then unoccupied, and in a tumbledown state. Featuring broad and deep verandahs in the gracious subtropical style, its position was unrivalled, being gloriously situated on a pretty knoll overlooking the Pacific. The picturesque grounds amounted to 120 acres. They rolled down to the banks of the wide Nerang River that flowed along the entire frontage, before debouching into the ocean. With endless white beaches within a rifle shot, even on the hottest day the area received cooling breezes. For bathing, boating and fishing, let alone as a place to shape boys into men, it presented a paradise.

With financial support from two parishioners, Dixon negotiated for the use of the residence, and was offered the buildings and the land around it rent-free, if he would undertake repairs, with the option after three years of purchasing the buildings and land for £1,000, which he duly took advantage of. Having made the place habitable, the school opened its doors in 1902. It was an almost immediate success, and in 1907 would be formally recognised by the Church as a Diocesan school for boys. *The Brisbane Courier* proclaimed:

> It has been favoured with surroundings so auspicious that it could not have been otherwise. There is the climatic advantage which it enjoys, the picturesqueness of its locale, the unfaltering energy of its principal, the Rev. H.H. Dixon...No prettier spot exists along the whole of the South Coast.

A week later, a reporter from the same paper visited the new school and again described it in glowing terms:

> The atmosphere of pure boy, sunburned lively boy, was

refreshing; but there was discipline apparent. One motto above others might be written over the porch – there are a good many porches – and that is 'Public spirit'.

The boys' nickname for Horace Dixon was 'Jimmy', after Jimmy Governor, an Australian outlaw. Dixon would eventually become the world's oldest active Anglican Prelate, living until 1964. He could be both stern and full of fun, and enjoyed a practical joke. Hardworking and a visionary, he described things as they ought to be rather than as they were, and possessed an impressive voice and dramatic manner, with "an infinite capacity for clothing the humblest incident with a cloak of the utmost grandeur." This would appeal to Charles Thorold's own sense of theatre, and was something he increasingly emulated.

In December 1906, Charles bid farewell to the Reverend and Mrs. Rust to take up his Queensland post. Upon his arrival at the port of Brisbane, reaching Southport then involved a three-hour train journey. The enervating hours in the rattling wooden carriage took him through an unfamiliar landscape – a mostly grey-green scrub of eucalyptus trees, broken occasionally by a rough-hewn homestead and plantations of pineapples, bananas, sugar-cane and millet. The tiny fly-blown stops alternated between English and native names, suggesting the inhabitants of this country were still slightly estranged from it – Yatla, Stapylton, Pimpama, Coomera, Helensvale, Coombabah, Ernest Junction. On and on the stations rolled, the hot summer breeze rushing through the open window. Until at last, he was there.

Alighting on the platform of the small station with his luggage, Charles Thorold might well have pondered what he was doing in this sandy nowheresville, far from all he knew and cherished. In sunlight so diamond-bright it made one squint, he may have felt even more exposed under the carapace of his reconstructed persona. However, there would have been little time for such thoughts, as Rev. Dixon was waiting to greet him at the station. The welcome would have been warmer than the one Dixon received when he had emigrated in 1899. His ship was delayed, and on arrival at the Brisbane dock the exasperated local Bishop greeted him with, "Oh dammit! I've wasted the day." "What a strange place," the stunned Dixon wrote to his wife, "even the Bishop swears!"

The strongly-built and smartly-dressed Charles made an excellent impression. Dixon recalled that he was "at once attracted by his charming and courtly manner". He seemed the very embodiment of Christian virtue. Dixon observed that Charles had "strength of character and common sense, combined with the utmost tact and courtesy," later stating: "no Headmaster ever had a more trustworthy and delightful colleague". He was also pleased to note that Charles was a "devoted and earnest churchman (who) entered fully into the religious life of the School" saying that "many a boy has cause to be thankful for his manly Christian influence". One student later wrote: "no one could be for long in association with him without absorbing many of his ideals."

Others would remember Charles as "a perfectly groomed, clean, unfoppish, beautifully spoken, handsome English gentleman, in all the best meaning of the word 'gentleman'." However, some of the earthier parents of students, including those with a chippy, defensive attitude, looked upon his English dress and manner, his reticence, and upper class Oxford drawl, as affected and snobbish.

While a land of broad horizons, Australian boundaries of acceptable male behaviour were exceptionally narrow. The writer Jack Lindsay recalled the oppressive conformity demanded in his youth in 1920s Brisbane, where even "the slightest oddity of dress," such as a coloured bow tie, could incite not just comment or suspicion, but was "liable to bring about assault and battery".*

That such an apparent paragon as Charles Thorold had ended up in Southport also encouraged the quietly spoken belief that he was a 'remittance man' – the disparaging term given to inconvenient English gentlemen exiled to the colonies by their families for one reason or another, and regularly sent money to ensure they remained there.

Although Charles had a great sense of fair play, the Southport boys

---

* Charles's dapper appearance would have drawn glances for another reason. As an Australian visitor to London in 1898 remarked, what struck her was "the dowdiness of the women and the spruceness of the men. Now, it is just the opposite in our cities, where the ladies are always well dressed, while the men have a reach-me-down appearance." [An Australian Girl In London, *The Argus* (Melbourne), 19 Nov 1898, p14.]

were to cheekily dub him 'Squeery', after Wackford Squeers, the cruel headmaster in Dickens' *Nicholas Nickleby*. The nickname later evolved to 'Squarey'.

Charles arrived during the School's long summer break, but his appointment had been earlier announced during the Speech Day which closed the School Year. Parroting unawares Charles's false resume, Dixon proclaimed that:

> Mr. Thorold, besides being related to the famous Bishop of Winchester of that name, possessed the highest credentials. He was a member of Worcester College, Oxford, and took there an honour classical degree, besides which he had eight years' experience in teaching.

Dixon also added: "It would tell much in his favour with the boys that he was a good tennis player and oarsman, and competent at both cricket and football." And at stone-breaking too.

At the close of his first day at the School, Charles might well have wandered down to the banks of the Nerang River to take in the view from his new home. Here he would have gazed across to the junction of the river with the Pacific, and the scattered rooftops of Southport above the scrub of eucalyptus. Directly below on the bank sat a picturesque boathouse, and to the left a slow-winding streamlet which drifted into shadows of rock and foliage. Here the boys would, as a newspaper reporter phrased it, "gather in undress on the banks to plan the details of 'the great swimming sports.'"

Charles's thoughts might well have reflected some of the verses of *The Rhyme of the Remittance Man*, by the British-Canadian poet Robert W. Service:

> Now I've had my lazy supper, and the level sun is gleaming
> On the water where the silver salmon play;
> And I light my little corn-cob,* and I linger, softly dreaming,
> In the twilight, of a land that's far away.
> Far away, so faint and far, is flaming London, fevered Paris,
> That I fancy I have gained another star;

---

* A form of pipe.

Far away the din and hurry, far away the sin and worry,
Far away — God knows they cannot be too far.

Like the great English 'public schools', the curriculum of Southport High School was based on the classical tradition as laid down in the early nineteenth century by the famous reforming headmaster, Thomas Arnold. The writings of the great Greeks and Romans (or at least, those deemed suitable), and in their original languages, were inculcated – not only for literary reasons, but as a means of instilling intellectual discipline and moral rigour. This was combined with plenty of sport, and a prefect system, to produce well-rounded, phlegmatic individuals with a fund of common sense, who could ably assist in the administration of Australia, and that vast British Empire that lay so pink across the atlas.

Bringing with him all the most desirable hallmarks of an English public school and Oxford education, Charles was to dramatically contribute to the School's development, and its goal of turning out Australian gentlemen.

When the new academic year began, his impact was immediate. Dixon's initial impressions were borne out: the new young master was methodical, tactful, "intensely practical," had a "keen sense of humour," a concern for excellence, and was committed wholeheartedly to the life of the School. After years of soul-crushing convicthood, Charles could now channel his virile energy into a true calling, and his enthusiasm gushed out like a force of nature.

In addition to encouraging in students his love of literature and of rowing, Charles organised cross-country races, staged school concerts, established and trained its choir, acted as secretary of its debating society, and changed the school colours and its blazer to a copy of those of his alma mater Marlborough College. For the first time in an Australian school, he also introduced the English public school tradition of the house system. This divided the pupils into separate named 'houses'; the principal aim being to promote a healthy rivalry in sport. Not least, Charles founded and edited a bi-annual school magazine, *The Southportonian*. It was of a high literary standard, and included contributions from notable public figures, as well as essays from Charles himself. He was most concerned it should exhibit a "bright and healthy vitality" and humour.

When the Governor of Queensland, Lord Chelmsford, visited the School on Speech Day in 1907, Charles was careful to cultivate him. As Chelmsford was an Oxford man and almost same age, Charles certainly had far more in common with him than the blustering Dixon. For Speech Day, Charles went so far as to compose an ode in Latin in honour of Lady Chelmsford: such honeyed words resulted in the Chelmsfords sending their eldest son to the School for a year, a vice-regal seal of approval that did no end of good for School enrolments.

Charles was to play another crucial role in the School's development. It so happened he'd arrived at an opportune time: Dixon was short on capital. So impressed was the headmaster by the practical contributions his new hire was making to the school, that the following year he offered him the first of two deals that proved both advantageous for the School, and the deal of a lifetime for Charles.

The offer made was that Charles would build a much-needed boarding house for not less than £300, in return for receiving all its students' payments for boarding and tuition. Charles agreed, and a timber boardinghouse bearing his name was constructed. As a consequence, between January 1908 and July 1910 he earned £1,236 – an extraordinary investment return for just 30 months. The money, plus a loan from the Rusts, enabled him in 1910 to take up a second offer from Dixon to purchase a one-third partnership in the School.

The School's entire land and chattels were valued at £6,000. When in 1913 the Diocese purchased the School, Charles received £2,200 cash, plus guaranteed employment for three years at £465 per annum. (The Diocese had requested the sale price be set "at the lowest figure," and as the senior partner with his eye on a future bishopry, Dixon wasn't about to quibble.)

The payout for Charles constituted a small fortune. While it wouldn't have funded his 1902 bail, he surely comforted himself on his financial progression and social rehabilitation. Yet, it would have been a nervous comfort. The higher his public profile became, so too the risk of possible exposure increased. All it could have taken was the memory of one mouthy immigrant from the Old Country to be jogged by a name. The record shows that at least one prominent

Brisbane figure knew, and likely several others. The more success Charles gained, the more there was to lose. As the years went on, like the pages of old newspapers that told of things unspoken, the fear no doubt faded, but it would have been always in the background. Living on a knife's edge, only a whisper away from having one's life plunge into a chasm, can be a terrible psychological burden.

One of the pupils in Charles's boardinghouse was a son of wealthy graziers, the McConnels. No doubt viewing Charles as an eligible young man, in early 1908 the McConnels invited him to spend part of the long summer break at their pastoral estate of Cressbrook, north of Brisbane. In October of that year, the McConnels suddenly announced Charles's engagement to their daughter Elspeth.*

By any measure, Elspeth was a glittering catch – one of the most eligible girls in the entire state! The family owned vast tracts of central Queensland, and had also operated the first condensed milk factory in Australia, which for a time pushed Nestlé out of the country. What would have added further lustre to her appeal for suitors, was for Charles problematic – the McConnnels were also highly well-connected. At Cressbrook, and at their grand and gabled riverside villa, Shafston House at Kangaroo Point in Brisbane, their guests included the State Governors from England.

Elspeth's father James Henry McConnel was President of The Queensland Club, the premier gentleman's club. Further to this, the McConnels maintained exceptionally close links with the home country. James had studied at Cambridge, and the McConnels sent their children back to England to complete their studies. There was also their extended English family. The McConnels weren't just one of the first families of Queensland: they had been one of the first families of the Industrial Revolution. In the 1830s, McConnel & Co. had been the largest privately owned company in the United Kingdom; the English branch would retain the landmark Cressbrook Mill cotton spinning complex in Derbyshire until 1925.

As a prominent family, the Queensland newspapers recorded the movements and associations of the McConnels, including the visit of Elspeth and her brother to England and Scotland. 'Daphne', the

---

* (Mary) Elspeth McConnel (1882–1956), daughter of J.H. and Madge McConnel. Married Bevis Gerald White, later mayor of Murrurundi, Queensland.

indefatigable scribbler of the social column 'L'Eternel Feminin', which graced the pages of the weekly *Queensland Figaro,* ensured her readers were kept abreast of essential McConnel titbits, such as Elspeth's attendance at a Highland shooting party. Other social columns keenly noted Elspeth's 'London frocks'. If Charles had assumed the grand McConnels were living in an isolated colonial bubble, far from the world of his past, he was very much mistaken.

To celebrate the engagement, in November 1908 the Rev. Dixon and his wife hosted a dance at the school, with Elspeth and her parents staying at the Grand Hotel in Southport. However the following month, while out riding on the Cressbrook estate, Elspeth's horse shied and threw her, kicking and slightly fracturing her skull. The McConnels chartered a special train to convey her to a private hospital in Brisbane. She soon made a recovery, but Charles' visit to Cresswork in April the following year would be his last. By that time the McConnel's high-level connections had almost certainly informed them as to the true history of their daughter's fiancé. The engagement was quietly called off. That August Elspeth left on a visit to England where she joined her father and sister.

The very idea that a former convict bearing a notable name, and little more than two years out of Dartmoor Prison, could have married an heiress from a wealthy and highly connected family, while retaining the secret of his past, is more like something out of a Victorian potboiler than reality. It again highlights Charles's audaciousness. This was a man who lived by the motto *carpe diem*. That he could have inserted himself into a prominent school was remarkable enough. Perhaps he'd not seen the newspaper articles of his trial when in prison. Perhaps distant rural Queensland made him feel safe. Yet since 1872, when Port Darwin was connected to Java by submarine cable, Australia had been but a telegram away from the beating heart of London. Only by sheer chance had the Austral press in 1902 (unlike its New Zealand counterparts) not carried articles on the scandal. Charles's proposal to Elspeth McConnel was not to be the last of his vaulting social ambitions.

Even if Charles had quelled his pederastic yearnings, his enjoyment in taking a youth sailing was undiminished. And in dramatic circumstances, it would now almost bring his new life to an end – and that of his companion. This time the lad was another pupil from the

Thorold boardinghouse: Arthur Andersen, the seventeen-year-old son of a sawmill owner of Danish origin.*

In the late afternoon of the 4th of September 1909, a clerk manning the local post office by sheer chance spotted their boat in the Southport Broadwater, the estuary of the Nerang River. However, it wasn't sailing – it was capsized, with Thorold and Andersen clinging desperately to the hull. Worse, a strong ebb-tide was drawing the vessel out to sea, and directly into the path of mountainous breakers at the River's sandbar.

The clerk immediately leapt on his bicycle and pedalled hard to the jetty. At the time there were only two motor boats that could have made the rescue in the entire district: again as luck would have it, the owner of one of them, Jack Tuesley, had just returned from a fishing trip. As an account of the event captured it:

> He [Jack] could see that it was touch and go, and every second was precious, so without waiting to take petrol he raced at top speed for the bar. The sea was very rough even inside the bar and it was with the greatest difficulty and risk that he picked up the exhausted men. Even then they were not out of the danger zone as the spray of the breakers was splashing over the launch, but they edged clear and reached land safely.

For his bravery, Tuesley was awarded the Silver Medal of the Royal Humane Society; the ceremony taking place at Southport School, but likely privately. The school magazine made no mention of the capsizing, and the local press abstained from printing the names of the two persons rescued for over forty years, which suggests no little discretion. The almost-drowning of a schoolmaster and pupil whilst sailing alone would have been an uncomfortable story for any school. It would also have alarmed those aware of Charles's true backstory.

Nine days after his almost-drowning, Charles held a fancy dress party, at The Retreat, a rented cottage he maintained overlooking the ocean. While the Thorold boardinghouse included a masters quarters, he likely desired the peace and privacy the cottage offered. *Queensland Figaro* did not neglect to record the entertainment:

---

* Arthur Dunlop Andersen (1892–1926). The following year, while his father was overseas, Arthur managed the three family sawmills. [Obituary, *The Brisbane Courier*, 21 July 1926, p6.]

The Retreat seemed suddenly to become a part of the East. The whole place was illuminated with Chinese lanterns, and the verandahs and reception rooms quaintly and prettily decorated with Chinese draperies. Beautiful flowers were placed in every possible nook, the host's school-house colour pink taking a leading part,* while the upper tables sported the cardinal, navy, and white, the High School colours. Mr. Thorold received his guests seated on a couch robed as an Eastern prince. Mr. Bere acted as his wife, and wore a robe in princess style. Some of the High School boys were arrayed as royal attendants, and a huge Chinese gong was sounded as each guest made his or her obeisance to the royal pair.

Mrs. Dixon turned up as the Duchess of Southport, and the wife of the aforementioned Mr. Bere, as another aristocrat.

Despite such provincial gaieties, for anyone of ambition and culture, not even Southport's beauty, or a near-death experience, could save it from being numbingly dull. The following year, Charles applied for the position of Registrar at the University of Melbourne. One of the testimonials he submitted was from the Anglican Archbishop of Brisbane, St. Clair Donaldson.† A bachelor of arresting presence, who was a friend of Arthur Benson, Donaldson was both convivial and reserved, being most at ease in high society. The Rev. Ernest Thorold's father-in-law later privately wrote:

> the Archbishop says he has known Mr. Thorold during <u>the whole period</u> of his residence in Australia from 1907, to the present time. I am informed that he also knows all the circumstances which resulted in his going to Australia.

Luckily for Charles, the intensely religious Donaldson believed in salvation. Possibly he also shared his sexuality. In any case, Donaldson's testimonial on Charles's behalf was glowing: "By his education and experience no less than by his natural ability he is well

---

* As delightful as it would have been, as far as The Southport School Archives are aware, the Thorold house colours were only ever black and gold. The mistake is curious.
† Right Reverend St Clair George Alfred Donaldson (1863–1935), later Bishop of Salisbury. Arthur Benson termed him "a very fine, simple-minded, robust, sensible prelate". [Percy Lubbock (ed.), *The Diary Of Arthur Christopher Benson*, Hutchinson, London 1926, p300.]

qualified for an office of this kind. He is a man of tact and address," and of Southport School, "his presence and work there has been of the greatest value." Yet it was not enough. Charles's application was unsuccessful. Southport would have him a little longer.

Aside from Charles's work at the School, he was also active in the life of the local parish in all manner of increasingly important roles, including as a lay reader at the local church, and holding services when its Rector was elsewhere.

In his leisure time, just as at Parsons Pleasure, he bathed in a stream that ran through the school grounds, which the boys nicknamed 'Pong Creek', teasing that he was responsible for its smell. He also travelled regularly to the capital Brisbane for a few days at a time, to take in cinema and theatre performances. Although the city then only had a population of 143,000, it possessed a small but flourishing homosexual subculture, including coffee shops* and soliciting precincts. Whether these visits enabled Charles to indulge in a double life, or he'd brought the shutters down on such desires, can again be only speculated. The common rooms of schoolteachers are forever a hotbed of gossip, latent jealousies, and suspicions, and these visits of his to Brisbane, then a journey not undertaken lightly, aroused talk amongst them, and speculations as to whom he was mixing with there.

Behind his formal, beautifully spoken exterior, with its buttoned-up Edwardian suits and Greek and Latin quotations, he remained a man who, as his family were to recall, had a "bohemian, somewhat improvident, approach to life." He relished the pleasures of Englishness, including imported cigarettes and recordings of musical hall songs, and biscuits, coffee, and the London *Daily Mail*. The scraps of life lived in the grand manner, that he'd picked up from relations, and the Rendels, Bernard Fraser, Lord Battersea and others, stayed with him forever.

In addition to his reading of the *Daily Mail*, Charles surely followed – and somewhat more keenly than other citizens – the coverage of certain vice cases in the local press. While the 'serious' newspapers covered these in a thin-lipped manner that eschewed salaciousness,

---

* A beverage then rarely imbibed in Australia.

John Norton's paper *Truth*, which was published in a Queensland edition, was lavish in prurient detail. Its local editor carefully adhered to his boss's fondness for alliteration and extended headlines. A February 1910 criminal case was summarised as:

> Guilty of Gross Indecency.
> Beastly Behaviour to Boys.
> Shocking Conduct of Brisbane Business Man.
> Lads Lewdly and Lasciviously Handled.

The accused in this particular 1910 case was a shop manager by the name of Arthur Hatton. When interrogated by the police over the fondling of boys under his employ, he had breezily confessed: "I did do so, in fact, I often did it. I used to do it to brighten them up, and encourage them in their work."

One of the lads was a former cadet bugler called Jack Fogarty who suffered from 'weak eyes'. Jack told the court that he "had never had any quarrel or disagreement with the accused, either before or since". Although Jack had resigned his position, this wasn't due to being brightened up manually, but rather, being brightened up naturally. He informed the court that he'd been adversely affected by the subtropical Brisbane sun, and further, that the electric light in the office had given him headaches. Indeed, he'd later returned to request a job reference from Mr. Hatton. This all led to Hatton's defence arguing that, if anything, the fourteen-year-old was an accomplice.

Hatton was sentenced to 12 months' imprisonment with hard labour. However, given his good reputation in the community, shining references, and being a 'first offender', the sentence was suspended on his surety of £100 to be of good behaviour. The judge remarked that:

> he could not understand why the community was so full of unmarried men...He thought it would be better for the morals of the community if all young men were married.

Later that same year there was another sensational Brisbane case which, given Charles's High Church upbringing, is likely to have particularly engaged his attention. As *Truth* lyrically proclaimed it in caps and lowercase:

535

"REV. ROBERT WESLEY BALLANTINE.
BESTIAL BEHAVIOUR TO A BUGGY BOY.
Pinched Pulpit Pounder's Putrid Practices.
Lascivious Lay of a Lecherous Lay Preacher.
QUEST OF QUARRY IN A QUARRY.

The accused* was a Methodist missionary charged with gross indecency and attempted sodomy, who had penned many a love letter to lads. One read to the court included the sentiments:

> You will find a tip-top mate in me...You stick to me and I'll stick to you...I have something good to give you...I love you already...Try hard, there's a good chap...Don't let anyone see this letter.

To this cheery missive four X's were appended.

It was at a "Joyful News open-air mission meeting" that Ballantine's eyes had lit upon the lad on whom the case rested: a sixteen-year-old buggy boy (carriage assistant) by the name of Ulverston Vincent Williamson – more felicitously known as Victor. *Truth* detailed (with caps) their subsequent evening assignation:

> Going on to speak of the subject of salvation raised by the boy, Ballantine said one must go to A QUIET PLACE to discuss such matters and asked the boy if he knew of such a place.

The prosecutor asked Ballantine:

> Why didn't you take him home to pray?
> — He suggested the quarries!

These were the Leichhardt Street quarries: a discreet location with an "evil reputation" – a haven of amatory unorthodoxy. As Victor was nervous, on the way there the Reverend took him to a chemist where he purchased a shilling bottle of Phosferine – the favoured tonic of authoress Rita, and whose advertisements promised was just the thing if one was "living on your nerves," "jaded and run down," or suffering

---

* His name was printed in some reports as Ballantyne.

from "brain fog".

According to *Truth's* court reporter, in a "well-secluded nook" of the quarries, the following exchange occurred:

> "Have you ever been out with a girl, Victor?" said the soul-seeker.
> "No sir," replied the lad.
> "That's right, Victor: don't have anything to do with the girls," and then started to stroke a portion of the boy's body.

Resonant courtroom testimony then illuminated Ballantine's ministry of salvation-via-sodomy:

> "You swear the boy never lay on his back in the quarries?
> — "Yes, we knelt down, and I impressed on him the necessity for repentance..."

> "Why did you tell him he would have to strip to be saved?"
> — "I was quoting the plan of salvation as described in *Revelations* xi: 'You must come poor, wretched, miserable, blind, and naked...' "

Seeking further contrition, Reverend Ballantine broached the subject of penetration. At which point Victor experienced some form of enlightenment, and fled.[*]

So much for the life of the spirit. In January 1913, Charles travelled to Melbourne on another bold venture. It was for his marriage to an Englishwoman, Kathleen Jeffery,[†] the twenty-eight-year-old daughter of a travelling salesman. Tall and very good-looking, with blue eyes and dark hair, Kathleen was also charming. Three bridesmaids had been rustled up from Melbourne Society, presumably by the Rusts, while Thorold had a handsome and eligible groomsman in Harold Bartram, from a family who were the state's leading farming

---

[*] The quarry appears to have been the Queensland equivalent of Lourdes. In a 1914 prosecution of a similar case that had occurred there, the defendant claimed to suffer from paralysis, informing the court he'd only engaged in what his youthful male partners termed 'stuffing' in order to manipulate his back. [Clive Moore, *Sunshine And Rainbows*, University of Queensland Press, Brisbane, 2001, p102.]
[†] Kathleen May Jeffery (1885–1922), only daughter of Frederick and Ada Jane Jeffery, of Russell Square, Bloomsbury.

machinery suppliers. They'd possibly met through Elspeth McConnel.

The Reverend Rust was the marriage celebrant. The previous week Charles had been in hospital for a scheduled operation on his tongue, and Kathleen only arrived in Australia two days before the service. How Charles met her isn't known, although given his love of the theatre, she may have been a chorus girl – then considered part of the demi-monde, and not what previously would have been considered suitable marriage material for a Thorold. Like actresses the world over, she also wiped four years from her age in the marriage register, and elevated her father's profession to that of a solicitor.

Of course, the question that begs to be asked is whether Kathleen knew of Charles's imprisonment. Even if they had only first met following his release in 1906, and courted in those fleeting few weeks before he sailed to Australia, it seems likely he would have made some form of confession – if perhaps misrepresenting the reasons for his incarceration. Regardless, they had obviously maintained a correspondence.

Kathleen's sunny disposition disguised a dreadful tragedy. It was actually not her first time in Australia. When she was just two years old, her parents had emigrated, arriving in Melbourne in 1887, together with her younger brother and a servant. The following year her father Frederick had displayed his wares at the city's Centennial Exhibition, one newspaper noting: "Mr. F. Jeffery, of London and Manchester, contributes quite a bewitching array of lingerie". Two years later, Frederick was dead at just thirty-one. The cause of death was recorded as 'phthisis' – tuberculosis, otherwise known as consumption, and 'The White Death'. His estate amounted to no more than £500. His widow Ada and her two young children returned to England. Two years later, Ada also died at just thirty-one. Given its communicable nature, tuberculosis could run in families for two or even three generations. The seven-year-old Kathleen, together with her brother Hugh, was now an orphan. It was a terrible introduction to the brevity of life.

By the time she met Charles, Kathleen also knew her time on earth would be short. From 1908 to 1912 she'd received respite care for tuberculosis in a sanatorium at Mundesley in Norfolk. Indeed, the date of Charles's engagement to Elspeth coincided with the date of Kathleen's admittance.

Until the discovery of the antibiotics streptomycin in 1944, and isoniazid in 1952, tuberculosis was an extended death sentence: a chronic illness with intermittent periods of lung destruction that slowly but relentlessly increased in their debilitation. Extended stays in sanatoria offered temporary relief: for patients who'd previously lain in shuttered rooms, terrified of chills, their regimes of copious fresh air (even in the depth of winter), plenty of rest, abundant food, and gentle exercise invariably helped. Yet even then the prognosis was grim: a follow-up of patients admitted to the King Edward VII Sanatorium in Sussex between 1907 and 1914 revealed that 44% had died by 1916.

Residing in a climate that was bracing alpine, ozonic, or balmy was also thought to be beneficial, although there was no consensus as to which was optimal. However, given Southport ticked two of these options, Charles likely encouraged Kathleen's migration because of them. He'd originally intended to visit the U.K. in 1912 to marry her there, but a suitable substitute master could not be found at the time.

Charles would come to emotionally rely on Kathleen very deeply. She was remembered as "capable and energetic and very popular with the boys," and the couple were "devoted to each other". Despite her ill health, she keenly supported Charles in all his endeavours. It was indeed a love match. Yet behind the facade of normality was a wife living with a death sentence, and a husband with a deathly secret that could have ruined both their lives. It was possibly a pact of the damned – a wish to overcome suffering, renew themselves, and seize life. At least while it lasted.

Just two months after his marriage, Charles would again find himself in court, and in the press. It involved a spat with a Lieutenant-Colonel William Lather. A respected local identity, Lather was a district pioneer, the former Chairman of the local council, the town clerk, and owner of 'Newholm', a Southport residence set within a private park. As a newspaper reported:

> the land lies on the town side of the high school, between the school and Mr. Thorold's house. Mr. Lather complained that Mr.

Thorold and the scholars were continually crossing the land going to and from the school. He had put up a notice board, warning trespassers, and had placed two men on duty, to take the names of persons crossing the land, and require them to desist. On 22nd February, one of the men spoke to Mr. Thorold, and said that he had been engaged by the owner to take the names of trespassers. Mr. Thorold said, "You will have to take mine six times a day," and then walked away.

Lather was not a man to be trifled with, especially by any smug pommy blow-in, and immediately took legal action. For Charles, re-entering a courtroom would have been a sickening occasion. And made even worse by the fact the case was heard in the Supreme Court of Queensland by the Chief Justice, Sir Pope Cooper no less. Lather was granted a restraining order at the first hearing, and the following week a perpetual injunction, with Charles agreeing to refrain from any future trespassing. Lather waived any claim to damages, but Sir Pope ordered Charles to pay costs, remarking that he was "very lucky to have settled the matter in the way he had done." Had Charles's past intruded, additional expense would have been the least of it.

In May there was a happier event, when Charles was visited by his younger brother, the Rev. Ernest Thorold, who'd taken leave from serving as chaplain to the British forces in South Africa. Their mother had since died, so this would have been an especially affecting meeting. Clearly the scandal had not damaged the family ties, and as his later actions suggest, Ernest had few doubts about his brother's suitability for his position: like their older brother, Algernon, he was also complicit in keeping Charles's secret. Wise, scholarly, and very handsome, but a man of heavy silences, by 1926 Ernest would be chaplain to King George V.

The first year of her marriage was to be a gruelling one for Kathleen. Almost immediately becoming pregnant, she was struck down by rheumatic fever. Having recovered, she gave birth in October to a son, John Jeffery.* Given the baby was at least five weeks premature, and the abilities of medical practice in 1913, it was only by good fortune he survived. However, soon after the birth Kathleen contracted pneumonia, accompanied by rheumatism and erysipelas, a

---

* (John) Jeffery de Buckenhold Thorold (1913–1982). School principal. Married Nancy Thomas; no issue.

bacterial skin infection. The combination of maladies nearly killed her, but the trauma possibly drew the couple even closer. In 1916, their second son Patrick* was born.

In distant Lincolnshire there'd also been developments. In the summer of 1914, Benjamin Brumfield, still with the Lincolnshire police force, again also found himself in court, as the defendant in a breach of promise case. He'd broken off the engagement when, after telling his fiancée he needed to spend his next leave with his mother, she allegedly spat out that he thought more of his home than he did of her, and she didn't care if he visited again; ending with: "That's straight; I mean it."

The plaintiff, Maud Mary Dickinson of Hull, told the court she'd knitted Constable Brumfield's socks for two and a half years, and had hoped to knit them for the rest of her life. She had also gifted him a hand-worked waistcoat, a silver matchbox, gold signet ring, walking stick, and a gold toothpick. For his part, Benjamin was characterised as "a man of honourable character" who'd been supporting his aged mother, while providing Maud with ten shillings a month, plus occasional presents. Despite Benjamin bluntly telling the young woman that "if he married her he would lead her a life of misery," it was alleged she threatened suicide. Observed the judge: "most breach of promise actions seemed to be after the nature of a comedy, but this appeared to be rather the nature of a tragedy." The court was told: "Those three years had passed for ever, and left her three years older." Maud was awarded £40 damages. Several papers covered the case: *The Daily Mail* of Hull devoted over two and a quarter columns to it – a far greater length than any paper had seen fit to report the trial of Fraser and Thorold. The following year, Benjamin Brumfield married a local lass, Florence Blakey, and was promoted to police sergeant.

Back in Australia, a new religious immigrant may have drawn the attention of Charles Thorold. The charismatic Theosophy† leader Charles Leadbeater‡ had relocated to Sydney in 1914, and two years

---

* Patrick Hayford Thorold (1916–2009). Professional golfer; lessee of Ivanhoe Golf Club. Married Dorrit Wilhelmina Charles, and secondly, Maureen Margaret Mason, with issue from both marriages.
† A religion founded in the late nineteenth century by a Russian-American Helena Blavasky, promising mystical insight into the nature of the Divine and the soul.
‡ Charles Webster Leadbeater (1854–1934), Anglican clergyman, leading Theosophist, Bishop of the Liberal Catholic Church, and prolific esoteric author.

later John Norton's *Truth* published a scandalous two-part profile of him. Australia was a major outpost of the movement, and Leadbeater further helped popularise its beliefs. He found his adopted nation entirely congenial, and having decided its inhabitants represented a thrillingly new Aryan sub-race, delivered lectures to that effect. However, the local Theosophical community was experiencing ructions due to Leadbeater's enthusiasm for higher teachings. These involved hands-on instruction with boys in how to masturbate, with the promise of enhanced manhood, and occult insights – Leadbeater advocated 'psychic orgasm' to obtain 'buddhic consciousness'. Two of his letters to a boy – "Glad sensation is so pleasant. Thousand kisses." – had caused a similar upset in America upon their discovery, and attempts to drum him out of the movement had been made on both sides of the Atlantic.

Leadbeater's erotic trainings provided him with unlimited access to pliant acolytes. However, while eternally randy, he was not a cynical charlatan, believing what he shared was to their benefit. This was in accord with other Uranians of the time and their Neo-Hellenic ethos, in which the relationship between teacher and pupil, and its spiritual and erotic possibilities, was exalted. As with most matters occult, the local press rigorously eschewed sharing the Theosophical Society's endless drama, with the notable exception of *Truth*, for whom it was bread and butter.

In 1921, *Truth* shone its spotlight again on Leadbeater, publishing a circulated letter from his Sydney host, a wealthy stockbroker and eminent Theosophist Thomas Martyn, who'd become intensely unhappy about Leadbeater being in his house: "Naked boys were seen in his bed." A police investigation had already been undertaken and gone nowhere, and now a second was embarked upon with the same result. The belief that the authorities dropped the case because they believed the intense devotion of the boys to Leadbeater would make it difficult to prove any charge in court has merit; yet equally, the influence that came with Leadbeater's position as Administrator General of the Co-Masonic Order* in Australia, cannot be ignored.

He'd been inducted into the Order by James Wedgwood,† a member

---

* A branch of Freemasonry that offered mixed-sex lodges.
† James Ingall Wedgwood (1883–1951), first Presiding Bishop of the Liberal Catholic Church, and Grand Secretary of the Order of Universal CoMasonry. In his pastoral work he was

of the ceramics family who was a fellow Theosophist, homosexual, and founder-Bishop of a rackety but lavishly costumed order, the Liberal Catholic Church. At this heavenly level of high camp and preposterousness, any thought of restraint might as well have been the argument of an ant, and Wedgwood made Leadbeater a fellow bishop. In the pages of *Truth*, Norton could only splutter helplessly: "Leadbeater rigs himself out like the Archbishop of Canterbury…surrounded by his ever-present galaxy of boys." And so the pantomime continued, until Leadbeater's elevation from the mortal plane in 1934.

By 1917, Charles Thorold had been at Southport for over a decade and had accomplished more than even he could have reasonably expected. Yet he hadn't progressed in his career — Horace Dixon remained headmaster. Given Charles's leadership skills and drive, it wouldn't have been surprising if he was by then chafing in his position, and feeling stale. That year an advertisement appeared in the press for the joint position of Headmaster of The Hutchins School and Warden of Christ's College (a university college) in Hobart, Tasmania. Hutchins was both a primary and secondary school, but unlike Southport, only a portion of its boys were boarders.

The Hobart role was a choice one: Hutchins was one of Australia's oldest and most prestigious private boys' schools. Its administrators were seeking a man of high character, educational experience and organisational ability, and also, given the new headmaster had to manage a boarding house, previous experience with such. In Southport, Charles's name actually resided on one. Given summer temperatures at Southport could sometimes climb to 38C (100F), Charles perhaps also believed that the more temperate clime of Tasmania would be better for his wife's delicate condition.

He wrote off and applied for the double Hobart role. As with his application to The Southport High School, and as a glibly fluent master of the English language, he once again crafted a resume that was a compelling confection of truth and fiction. Of his journey to Australia he blithely wrote: "I came out to take up a position as Senior Classical Master". This was patently untrue. (Biographies of him in

---

tireless: a Sydney detective logged him visiting "eighteen public toilets in a period of two hours". Tertiary syphilis delivered him into the Lord's arms. [Gregory Tillett, *The Elder Brother: A Biography of Charles Webster Leadbeater*, Routledge, Abingdon 2016, pp196, 312n2.]

school histories would later innocently accept this artifice.) His time with the Rendels had now expanded to "nearly two years on the Continent". He was also able to include a testimonial from Henry Frewen Le Fanu,* a warm aristocratic Irishman who was then Coadjutor Bishop of Brisbane. He'd attended Oxford with Charles's brother Algernon, and was one of a number of influential churchmen Charles met through his lay preaching. He was also a guest of Charles at The Retreat.

There were twenty-six applications for the Hutchins role, but after an interview by Hutchins' selection board, Charles was successful. Dixon later wrote, "I felt it to be my duty to advise him to accept" but "I knew it would be a sad day for Southport which he had loved so much and served so well." So it was that Charles and Kathleen sailed to Tasmania in January 1918 to take up his new post.

There was just one problem. As Warden of Christ College, in order to take his seat on the University Council, Charles was expected to obtain a Master of Arts degree from Oxford, which the University of Tasmania would then mirror by granting him its own M.A. degree.† Obtaining an M.A. from Oxford for a graduate is usually a mere formality.‡ In his application to Hutchins, Charles wrote that he'd intended to obtain it in 1912, as part of the abandoned plan to marry Kathleen in England. While it was the truth, it was a half-truth.

What he conveniently left out is revealed in a letter written by Francis John Lys, who was at the time Fellow and Bursar of Charles's Oxford college of Worcester, and would soon become its Provost. Lys stated: "I knew A.C.C. Thorold well, and also know what happened in 1902." He explained that Charles had submitted an application for the M.A., but the Vice-Chancellor had objected, and it had gone no further.

---

* Rt. Rev. Henry Frewen Le Fanu (1870-1946), Archbishop of Perth, Western Australia.
† A *ad eundem* degree: i.e. 'of the same rank'. The process is often known as incorporation.
‡ Unlike most other universities, a Master of Arts at the universities of Oxford, Cambridge, and Dublin is an academic rank, available on application after six or seven years to those holding a Bachelors of Arts – not a postgraduate qualification requiring further study or achievement. As a contemporary observer put it: "Were it not that England is permanently a land of anomalies, a land where anomalies are held in worship and veneration rather than considered as evils and absurdities which should be removed, the fact that at the Universities of Cambridge and Oxford, the higher degrees are so much easier to get than the lower ones would cause much surprise." [The M.A. Degree, *Oxford And Cambridge Undergraduate's Journal*, 29 April 1880, pp370-371.]

Now desperate to obtain the degree, Charles wrote to his youngest brother, the Rev. Ernest Thorold, for help. The good clergyman, then assisting the Chaplain-General at the War Office, came up trumps with a big lever. It took the form of Huth Jackson,[*] an Oxford graduate (and once keen member of its Amateur Dramatic Society), who was a wealthy and prominent merchant banker, and a director of the Bank of England. Jackson also just happened to be a member of the University's Board of Finance. It was a considerably more gentlemanly approach than putting the Vice-Chancellor in a headlock, but just as effective. Given Oxbridge's cardinal life lesson has forever been 'it isn't what you know that matters, but who', it was also fitting.

In the same month Charles sailed to Hutchins, Jackson submitted an appeal to Worcester College on his behalf. Lys responded with the letter quoted from above, which detailed the circumstances of the previous application in 1912. However, in the same letter, Lys went on to inform Jackson that the opinion of Worcester regarding Charles Thorold had now – surprise! – considerably mellowed:

> I think myself that after so many years of good work we ought to do anything we can to help a complete rehabilitation. I have seen the Provost, and all the Fellows of my College and find that they are all agreed in this view. I have also seen the Vice-Chancellor who thinks that such a question is one for the College to decide and will not raise any objection.

Huth Jackson having exercised his clout with a mere ask, all that was now required for the M.A. were the standard fee payments and forwarding of testimonials. The task of dealing with the paperwork fell to the Rev. Ernest Thorold and his father-in-law, Edward Herbert, whom the clergyman and his wife were then living with. Herbert was a partner in the family sharebroking firm of G.S. Herbert & Sons, and had most likely provided the introduction to Jackson. A string of letters from him to Francis Lys indicates his diligence on Charles's behalf. In February 1918, he told Lys:

> I have only once seen A.C.C. Thorold a good many years ago,

---

[*] Frederick Huth Jackson (1863–1921), a partner in the merchant bank Frederick Huth & Co., was founded by his great-grandfather. His wife, Annabel, an author, poet and society hostess, was painted by Sargent.

but I heard years ago, after the miserable event that he was quite regenerate, and events seem to have proved it. His brother whom I have known intimately I have a high opinion of.

Putting things into perspective, he added:

One of my boys was at Balliol 1898/1901 but alas the Germans killed him in September last. The second I have lost in this wretched war – and I have 2 more out there now.

Four days later he wrote to Lys again with a delicious *quid pro quo*:

I am going to spend tomorrow at the request of Mr. Huth Jackson in reviewing the stock movements of your University & preparing a little report on them, which may come before you in due time as I see you are one of the Curators of the Varsity Chest. I only hope it may be of some little use to you.

The following May, he informed Lys:

We were to send you some of the original testimonials of which you saw copies. We are not quite sure some have not been sent to the bottom of the sea by a torpedo…May I beg your kind efforts to complete the matter, which is of such enormous importance to Mr. Thorold. By the way you will see that he is called <u>Charles</u>. He dropped the use of his first name Arthur in the other hemisphere.

The testimonials were from the Coadjutor Bishop of Brisbane, Henry Frewen le Fanu; Archbishop Donaldson of Brisbane (Edward Herbert twice informing Lys "I believe he knows the history" – thereby making Donaldson's testimony the more impressive), and not least, from Horace Dixon. The first, written in 1910, affirmed:

His character is beyond reproach…as a Churchman and Communicant he is most earnest, and endeavours in every way to set the boys the example of a practical Christian life.

The second, penned in 1917, added:

Personally, I can only say how very highly I esteem the whole of his work and how very grateful I am for his unswerving loyalty…the high moral tone and principles which he has always inculcated have left a permanent mark upon the school.

By the close of 1919, Thorold finally had his essential M.A. A decade later, Herbert again wrote to Lys, enclosing a clipping from a Hobart paper about Charles at the Hutchins School. He added:

You may remember you kindly helped me when C. Thorold wanted to get his M.A. degree, and I just want you to see that he does not seem to have let you down…

It was true. At Hutchins, Charles fully came into his own. The official history of the school states: "He has been widely acclaimed as the greatest of the early headmasters of Hutchins," and one of the greatest in Australian educational history. Subsequent headmasters at Hutchins were judged against him, with few measuring up. He was lauded for his "high ideals and keen enthusiasm," devotion and sense of mission, and the far-reaching changes he instituted that made a permanent impact.

For both masters and students at Hutchins, Charles was an imposing figure: "a tall, well-built good-looking man with a ready smile and one who always carried an air of authority". It did not need an announcement to know who was the Headmaster: Charles commanded and warranted attention wherever he went. Recalled one former student:

He had an 'aura'. I can't recall any boy of my age group up to 1926 or 1927 having anything but feelings of profound respect, not unmixed with awe, for him.

In his inaugural address, Charles outlined the goals that would underpin his actions at Hutchins: the development of the School's public spirit; the importance of inherited tradition, including its Old Boys' Association; and most importantly, the development of the character of its students and the moral tone of the School, in which all played their part.

In his daily sermons to the boys, Charles constantly reiterated the need for truthfulness, moral courage and manners. It was hammered home that these simple precepts were what mattered in judging a man's standing amongst his fellows. His absolute insistence upon them firmly set in place the high tone of the School. As another Old Boy remembered, when Charles commanded "Own up the boy who did that" – they did. He added:

> We had William of Wykeham* in many a morning address, certainly no hands in pockets or shuffling of feet...when addressed by a master. Stand immediately for V.I.P.s and ladies. Caps off the head to ladies, staff, etc.; not a touch of fingers to the peak. Stand up and look well. Subordinate one's self to the ease and comfort of others. Think.

Charles created a hierarchical system of prefects held to the high standards he laid out, thereby giving other boys gentlemanly examples to emulate. To reinforce what he aimed to develop, Charles introduced a prize that was awarded on the same moral lines as the Rhodes Scholarship. At his installation, he urged his students to remember Lord Tennyson's words: "Self-reverence, self-knowledge, self-control, these three alone lead life to sovereign power". In his Annual Report for 1925, Charles stated his goal for each boy as:

> the development of a great harmonious personality...to turn out Christian gentlemen, grounded in sound Christian principles, ready to think and act for themselves according to these principles, sufficiently conscious of their own ignorance to be willing to go on learning day by day.

It was later said that you could always pick Old Boys from Thorold's time at Hutchins, so strong was their common bond; something that only a headmaster of greatness could have created.

To further build the school spirit, as at Southport Charles introduced the English public school house system. This immediately improved competition in team games. He also enhanced the quality of life for the boys by encouraging the formation of school clubs and societies for drama, photography, boxing, shooting, nature studies, scouting, wireless, debating, dancing and literary studies. Like the instructive entertainments his father had hosted for his parishioners in far-off

---

* The medieval Bishop of Winchester famed for his motto 'Manners makyth man'.

Hougham, Charles introduced Saturday evening entertainments for the boys, which were hosted by Kathleen. Highly popular, they included lantern-slide lectures, musical performances, and recitations.

While firmly basing the School's curriculum on the classical tradition, Charles also widened it to include modern aspects, and strongly supported the teaching of science. The scholastic results during his time were outstanding. Not least, he introduced "regular and judicious" physical training under a drill instructor, and annual trophies for physical culture and athletics.

Such was his impact, the school began attracting pupils from far beyond its normal catchment. Recalled one Old Boy: "My father met Thorold one day and had me enrolled the next".

A photograph of Charles reviewing scouts, accompanied by the State Governor, and captioned "Rev. Charles Thorold" appeared in the Hobart press. A family friend of the future 15th Thorold baronet mailed it to him with the intention of provoking wonder or bemusement, which it likely did.

Charles's addresses on Hutchins Speech Days were regularly quoted by the local press. As one paper printed:

> One could not find a better definition of the modern object of education than that given by Mr. Thorold: to cultivate and encourage the better qualities which make for good citizenship.

With the syncopated tremors of the Jazz Age having reached even Tasmania, Charles was led to quote Kipling's words: "Teach us to delight in simple things," while adding that he himself:

> was not opposed to having a good time, but held strongly that it should be the good time of a real boy, and not that of a blasé youth. There is an unfortunate tendency by the youth of the present day to regard jazzing as the only pleasure worthwhile.

Charles also drew attention to the fact Australians were developing unlovely habits of speech, including a broad accent:

> The trouble mainly is that in this, and in the matter of formal

courtesy, Australian boys sometimes get the idea that it is unmanly to speak with a pure accent, and to be careful about the little courtesies…Let us not forget in our anxiety to be men that to be gentlemen is a greater thing.

In 1926, one of Charles's end-of-year speeches on modern youth made the national press:

We must recognise, of course, that last century's repression of youth has gone for ever, but the unrestricted freedom which so many boys claim nowadays, and get, is going to make it very hard for them when they come into contact with a world which makes no allowances.

Clearly speaking from his heart, Charles went on to say:

Boys are the most wonderful creatures to study, and because the future lies with them, the most desirable creatures to know. Not that one ever does really know them. Boys are like golf – one can never attain perfection in understanding them.

It was a sentiment that Cyril Flower might have ringingly endorsed. Someone who certainly endorsed it was Lawrence Arthur Adamson,* a bachelor and Oxford alumnus whom Charles met the previous December at an inter-school teachers' conference. This is because Adamson had spoken the same sentences, word-for-word, three days prior in a speech of his own, as headmaster of Wesley College in Melbourne – one of Australia's most esteemed private schools. In 1932, Adamson restated them for posterity (preserved on gramophone disc), including the golf reference, in a farewell address after thirty years as headmaster. Either Charles pinched them without attribution, or more intriguingly, he and Adamson had already shared the passages in private.

Like Charles at Hutchins, Adamson remains a legendary figure at Wesley, where he also exercised a powerful influence over generations of boys, in his desire they embody the very highest standards of gentlemanly chivalry and achievement. It was written: "every boy was

---

* Lawrence Arthur Adamson (1860–1932). For a frank and perceptive account of his remarkable life, see: Andrew Lemon, *A Great Australian School: Wesley College Examined*, Helicon Press, Wahroonga 2004, pp91, 198-210.

an honourable man to Adamson, and this was perhaps the secret of the love his boys bore him." Another account simply put it: "They adore him…At heart he is a boy himself." When Adamson temporarily went abroad, and his beloved dog "drooped and died," hundreds of boys treated the canine to a grand funeral and subscribed to a tombstone.

Known to one and all as 'Dicky', Adamson was rich through inheritance. He'd been the first person in Australia to import their own aeroplane, and it was his promise to "accept full financial responsibility for the satisfactory growth of the College" that actually led to his appointment. Adamson Hall at Wesley College today bears his name. A school history records his taste for "songs, purple dressing gowns, young male athletes, and the great Victorian virtue of success." Adamson also had favourites, and post-canings in his cigarette-scented study could devolve into intimate chats that included warnings of the evils of self-abuse. One pupil subjected to deserved canings later asserted there had also been brief backside fondlings in the aftermath – "I didn't know what it was about, naturally." Perhaps not for the purpose of softening the sting.

"'Queer card that Adamson,' you will hear in circles not educational," Melbourne's version of *Punch* magazine ventured, referring to milder idiosyncrasies. Yet it said of him: "There is no more ideal type of the public school teacher." It also observed: "He is barely tolerant of female society – endures it with evident difficulty," and not least: "Since he arrived here his career has been plain to all; but there is an insatiable curiosity as to his life before that."

Adamson had turned up in Australia in 1885, having just joined the Bar. By his own account this sudden relocation was due to his need for a warmer clime following a bout of pleurisy. However, it was heat that Adamson was escaping from, rather than seeking. The Rev. R.C. Fillingham, Lord Battersea's sometime electoral advocate, learnt the true story from a friend, Melville Lee.* In February 1886, while an undergraduate at Oxford, Fillingham informed his diary:

He told me a queer thing about Adamson, which throws a light

---

* Major (William Lauriston) Melville Lee (1865–1955). After a career in the British Army, in 1916 he briefly joined MI5 as a sectional head. Author of *A History of the Police in England* (1901). Married Winifred Acton Barter; one son.

on his departure to Australia:– he was staying at Windsor in the Vac.[ation], with another man, and they kept having a number of Eton boys over, to breakfast and dinner, & continually committed unnatural offences with them (two of them being sons of Lord Rosslyn.)* This, through the continual absences of the boys, got to the ear of the headmaster: enquiries were made: the visitors from London of course disappeared from the hotel: & then a detective was employed. Hence, I suppose, Adamson's departure.

Wealth and clout, and the desire to protect the reputation of a noble earl's teenage sons, including from having to give testimony in a public court, (a benevolence not accorded to Benjamin Brumfield or Albert Collins), ensured the scandal was thoroughly suppressed: perhaps Charles Thorold also learned of it.

By his late forties, Charles's thwarted acting ambitions, further inspired by Horace Dixon's oratorical flights, had developed his own staginess. They included all the familiar rhetorical tics of headmasters – especially the pregnant pause. Prefects were appointed and scholarships awarded with hushed drama. On one occasion a special assembly was called to publicly expel two boys for theft, at which Charles theatrically ripped off their cap badges, like shamed hussars. His religious convictions had also deepened, and like his father, he'd become sanctimonious. He established the practice of holding services in the School on saints' days, during which his sermons frequently extended beyond half-an-hour; trying not only the patience of his youthful congregation, but also that of his staff, who rued the

---

* Robert Francis St. Clair-Erskine, 4th Earl of Rosslyn (1833–1890). The boys were his heir, the sixteen-year-old Harry, Lord Loughborough (1869–1939), and his brother, the fifteen-year-old Alexander Fitzroy St. Clair-Erskin (1870–1914). As 5th Earl, Harry was bankrupted at twenty-nine with stupendous debts of £166,622 from gambling and high living. "Yet in appearance 'tis harmless enough," observed an American paper: "Satyr, thin, delicate, spindle shanked, with a very slight mustache as the only facial evidence of manliness." Priding himself on female impersonations in amateur theatricals, to the further horror of his relations, under the name James Erskine, he took to the professional stage. Marrying three times and fathering five children, he became Private Secretary to the Secretary of State of Scotland, and a war correspondent for the *Daily Mail*, fighting in both the Boer and First World Wars. In later life he handed Nancy Mitford £1, saying: "I know you keep my son…If you can earn £1,000 a year you may marry him." Harry's brother Alexander was bankrupted in 1894. He married a widow and died without issue, six months before the outbreak of World War I. [Earl Of Rosslyn's Affairs, *Falkirk Herald*, 18 June 1898, p2; Noble Earl In Ballet, *The Kansas City Journal*, 23 January 1898, p20; Selina Hastings, *Nancy Mitford*, Vintage, London 2002, p76; Meeting Of Creditors, *The Globe*, 5 January 1894, p2.]

loss of teaching time.

An eleven-year-old pupil upon whom such cant was completely lost was the future Hollywood star Errol Flynn, who'd been enrolled at Hutchins in 1918 and was to remain for over a year. One of his school friends recalled:

> He was Robin Hood even then…"Fuck the old school and their tie, too," he would comment…He didn't give a damn for the dear old school, although the then headmaster, Mr. C. C. Thorold M.A. Oxon, bashed our ears every morning in assembly about tradition. Errol showed his feelings about the subject one morning by letting off a resounding fart in the middle of one of the old man's tedious orations.

It was not by chance that Charles chose a hymn which, recited daily and sung on Saints' days at Hutchins, included the verses:

> May faith, deep rooted in the soul,
> Subdue our flesh, our minds control;
> May guile depart and discord cease
> And all within be truth and peace.

Another former Hutchins boy recalled that Charles was:

> a despotic bigot on certain offences which would now be par for the course. Any reference to sex almost warranted expulsion, yet he could tolerate smoking and drinking by his seniors provided it was hidden from the juniors.

Charles's view of "the sinful desires of the flesh" needing to be quenched and subdued, was very much in keeping with the thinking of his times. Hypocritical he was, but he may have deeply regretted his earlier facilitation of carnality. He was certainly all too aware of the potential to morally fall – of 'The Beast that lurked within' – and would have hoped that his pupils did not succumb to the punishment and ostracism he'd endured. In this, he was not entirely successful. A taunting ditty recited by students of other Hobart schools, especially on the sporting field, lilted: "Get a woman, get a woman, get a woman if you can; If you can't get a woman get a Hutchins man."*

The subdued flesh may have been stirred in its memories by an encounter Charles had with Englishman, Herbert Gilbert E.S. Bellamy, who was then working as a hydraulic engineer in Australia. Bellamy was the son of the former stationmaster of Grantham, the town six miles to the east of Charles's home village. In a letter of reminiscences published in the local paper, Bellamy recalled that in his youth he had been a choirboy, and more recently, "In Tasmania I met a Mr. C. C. Thorold, M.A. (Oxon), who was related to the Syston family." Left unsaid was whether it was their first meeting, or a reunion. It certainly has an echo of a certain railway signalman's son at Hougham.

In January 1922, Charles's father died. Four days later, his beloved wife Kathleen succumbed to heart failure at just 37. It was almost nine years to the day of her arrival in Australia to marry him. Her death left Charles bereft. For an intensely private man who may have shared his inner life with no one else, the loss was irreparable. At the end of 1922, Charles's sister Muriel arrived from England to assist with his sons, Jeffery then nine, and Patrick, who was just six. She would stay for two years.†

Reticence is a Thorold family trait, and Charles further withdrew into himself. In the words of one school historian, "The charm and urbanity remained, but they simply masked his lonely isolation." From being a constant presence at the School, he now increasingly retreated into the seclusion of his study.

While in his study, Charles's thoughts are likely to have dwelled on a

---

* A derivation of the first lines of the bawdy song *Do Your Balls Hang Low?*, which in one version began: "Ting-a-ling, God damn, find a woman if you can; If you can't find a woman, find a clean old man." On hearing it sung by a troop in World War I, General Haig was reported to have informed their commander, "I like the *tune*, but you must know that in any circumstances those words are inexcusable!" In Sydney, the same taunt was directed at a prestigious Bellevue Hill school as 'Tiddlywinks old man, get a woman if you can; If you can't get a woman, get a Cranbrook man.' [*The Jack Horntip Collection:* www.horntip.com; Lyn MacDonald, *Somme*, Michael Joseph, London 1983, pp. 200-203; Dugald Jellie: High Society, *Sydney Morning Herald*, 7 December 2010.]

† As with Bernard Fraser's sisters, Charles's two sisters remained spinsters: the war, the shortage of men of marrying age in its aftermath, the stigma of the scandal, and the family breakdown and managing their father inevitably damaged their marriage prospects. [J.H. Day, *Charles Thorold Gentleman Emigrant*, University Of Queensland 1989, unpublished thesis, p182 n.24.]

sensational 1923 Tasmanian criminal case that had striking parallels to his own. It involved another Anglican minister's son named Arthur Charles, who was also a twenty-eight-year-old schoolmaster arrested for the buggery of a thirteen-year-old boy.* The accused, whose full name was Arthur Charles Pennefather Elrick, was also a keen churchman.

The previous year, a letter writer to the Hobart morning newspaper had objected to the attempt by a new Anglican church "to thrust High Church teaching down their parishioners' throats." In response, Elrick penned a letter in defence of "the ritualistic practices". In a time when letters to the editors of newspapers were keenly read, the exchange would have drawn Charles's attention. Elrick wrote his letter from Selma, a large estate in central Tasmania that was the seat of a gentry family, the McCraes. He was probably there as a tutor, which he'd previously been at Hobart.

The knowledge Elrick expressed in the letter of the church involved – St Michael and All Angels, suggests his close association with it. Hobart was a small town, the Anglican community even smaller: given the church hall was not far from Hutchins, it's probable Charles had attended its dedication service two years previously. It is equally likely, during this or on another occasion, that he was introduced to Elrick, given they were both the sons of ministers. Elrick may have even applied for a position at Hutchins.

While Elrick was out on bail, he absconded, leaving letters to his solicitor, his bondsman, and the Commissioner of Police. These were published in both the Tasmanian and mainland press. One stated:

> It seems to be of no use my facing this out. You see I am on my own, yet even then should not fear, only that the other side, Mrs. — and the boy, are distorting the facts so, and that on top of my admission. So as I do not want further intolerable disgrace to my family and friends, I am seeking the more honourable way out of the difficulty. If I had no folk and it was in a state where I was quite unknown, things would be different. I think you will understand.
>
> Yours truly, A. C. Pennefather Elrich[*sic*]

---

* Ironically named Arthur George Liberty.

P.S. My deposit, I suppose, carries me to Tuesday.

To the Commissioner, he added: "I do not want any sensations or enquiries with pressmen. I am simply going into the mountains, which I have always loved, and there I shall end my life quietly and painlessly."

Elrick never committed suicide – on the contrary, he fled to Melbourne. There he was arrested, but absconded again, this time to Sydney, where he re-arrested and returned to Hobart for trial. The one blessing was that his father, the Rev. Charles Elrick, was not alive to witness it, having accidentally fallen from a train three years previously. In court, Elrick's sister made an impassioned plea on his behalf, while his counsel argued:

> the nature of the offence had been much exaggerated. It was the case of a single lapse of a sober, honest, cultivated, and industrious gentleman, the whole of whose family were of a very high respectability, were held in high regard, and who had done much good in the world.

He also read to the court, "several strongly worded testimonials in the accused's favour, showing that until now he had filled high positions in the teaching world and borne himself with the highest credit."

The judge admitted the pleas impressed him, but like Sir William Grantham twenty-one years before, stated he "had a duty to perform." However, he agreed that "the man was to be pitied almost as much as to be blamed." He sentenced Elrick to a reformatory prison to be detained at the Governor's pleasure, until such time as he showed reformation.*

The extended case, and the public shaming of this other Arthur Charles, would surely have been psychologically troubling for Charles

---

* Elrick was discharged 20 months later in December 1924. In 1933, he turned up at his father's old parish of Myrtleford in north-eastern Victoria. Printed the regional paper: "After an absence of 30 years, Arthur Elrick, who will be remembered by old residents, spent a few days here last week. He journeyed on a push bike from Melbourne, via the Alps." Having possibly changed his name, he then disappears from the record. [Elrick-Pennefather, Arthur Charles, Prisoners Record Books, p75, GD63/1/6, Archive Office of Tasmania; Myrtleford, *Albury Banner and Wodonga Express*, 17 February 1933, p44.]

Thorold, reinforcing once again that he lived but a stray whisper away from damning scandal. Without the calming presence and companionship of Kathleen, his desolation caused a breakdown in his health, and in 1925 he was hospitalised, resulting in him taking leave for an entire school term.

On the last day of that year, Charles remarried. His new wife, Jessie Were,* was a forty-three-year-old spinster, from a wealthy family that was a pillar of the Melbourne Establishment. Her father Francis (Frank) Wellington Were was the senior partner in J.P Were Ltd., then Australia's leading stockbrokers. For Charles it was the status marriage that the breaking of the McConnel engagement had denied him. In theory, re-marriage might have been a wise move. This turned out not to be the case.

Considered "plain and ungainly" by her family, Jessie possessed a generous and hard-working disposition, but she was also stubborn. Despite Jessie having been 'on the shelf', the marriage was opposed by her father, and their union was sealed in what the press termed a "very quiet wedding". Whether this opposition was because it meant her separation from the family home or, like the McConnels, Frank Were had made enquiries into Charles's backstory, is unknown.

Jessie was not a success in the role of headmaster's wife at Hutchins. Unfavourable comparisons were drawn with the beautiful, younger and vivacious Kathleen. It was also said that she nagged Charles, including insisting on a change of residence. This apparently led to a loss of confidence in him by the School authorities. The formerly strong authoritarian, whose word had been law, was now someone vacillating and ill.

The Were family held a different opinion. They believed Charles mistreated Jessie in private. Certainly, she too had frequent illnesses. Whatever the truth, the marriage of this martinet to a deeply reserved and troubled man was a disaster, both personally and for Hutchins.

In 1926, Charles took another long leave of absence, returning to England with Jessie. The couple motored widely, including to Lincolnshire and Oxford. He may have caught up with Harold

---

* Jessie Isabel Marjory Were (1882–1954), daughter of Francis (Frank) Wellington Were and Anne Isabella Were, née McVean.

Boulton, who although then living in Winchester, was soon to move to Bath. That summer, Charles may also have read in the press of the arrest of a distant relation, the Rev. A.R. Thorold Winckley, who was sentenced in November at the Lincolnshire Assizes for gross indecency with youths.*

Charles later wrote an essay for the school magazine about the holiday, calling it 'The Wonderful Visit'. Arriving in London after an absence of twenty years, he observed: "what a change!…Gone were the quiet hansoms and the growlers; gone were the horse-drawn omnibuses." After the quiet of Hobart, the new pace and "almost intolerable" din of London's motor traffic came as a shock. However, he noticed fashionable gentlemen still wore spats. Most especially, seeing the English countryside again wrenched his heart: "there is one thing in England that never changes, and that is the glorious, unbelievable greenness of the countryside in early springtime". He mused whether he had:

> ever seen anything so beautiful – the hedgerows covered with

---

* Rev. Alfred Reginald Thorold Winckley (1865–1951). He held several incumbencies, including British chaplain at Aix-la-Chapelle. In 1900 it was reported he'd "done much excellent work in Buxton, especially amongst the young people." It was while serving as vicar of Cadney-cum-Howsham in Lincolnshire in 1926, at the age of sixty-one, that he pleaded guilty to eight charges of gross indecency, and was sentenced to six months imprisonment. The press recorded: "The offences related to youths, mostly farm labourers who said that the Vicar invited boys to the Vicarage, where he was in the habit of kissing them, and where the offences took place." Promises of presents had been made to one lad while committing the offence, which was confirmed to the court by a letter Winckley had written to him: "Dear Tom, I have not forgotten my promise, but I have not yet been to London. I am going on Monday next for a few days." Another indiscretion allegedly involved goosing a schoolboy bent over a comic paper at a railway bookstall. Winckley would bequeath his extensive collection of documents, prints, maps, press cuttings and books to the Wealdstone Library. "Mr Winckley was obviously a very methodical man," remarked the local Harrow paper, "and at the library is a chest filled with cuttings on local personalities and subjects which took his fancy." At least one volume from his collection of Uranian books survived – the poetic anthology *Men & Boys*, which found its way to the Library of the British Museum with a letter to Winckley from its compiler and publisher, who enthused: "It is printed on imported 100% rag paper with generous margins". [Preferment Of A Buxton Curate, *Derby Daily Telegraph*, 6 November 1990, p3; A Vicar's Downfall, *The Citizen*, 9 November 1926, p8; £200 Bail For Vicar, *The Leeds Mercury*, 4 August 1926, p6; Timothy d'Arch Smith (Intro), *The Quorum: A Magazine Of Friendship*, reprint, Asphodel Editions 2001, p6, n17; Books And Records Of Old Harrow, *The Observer And Gazette* (Harrow), 11 December 1952, p7; Donald Mader, 'The Greek Mirror: The Uranians and Their Use of Greece', in: Beerte C. Verstraete, Vernon L. Provencal (eds.) *Same-Sex Desire and Love in Greco-Roman Antiquity and in the Classical Tradition Of The West*, Routledge, Abingdon 2013, p381; Edward Mark Slocum; Donald H. Mader, Timothy D'Arch Smith (intro), *Men & Boys*, Coltsfoot Press reprint, New York 1978.]

hawthorn white and pink, the embankments studded with primroses and bluebells, and the trees clad in their prettiest garb of green.

He claimed that: "My visit to England was eminently worthwhile...I have come back with restored health, with wider vision, and renewed inspiration."

If so, it didn't last. Having settled back into Hobart, the incompatibilities of Charles's new marriage continued to manifest themselves. While the couple were away, there had been another death that may have deeply affected Charles: that of Arthur Andersen, the Southport youth who'd almost drowned with him. Andersen had subsequently fought in the War, and was wounded in the Battle of the Somme, and again at Ypres. He'd become managing director of his family's sawmilling business; married and begun a family; and then that July, had suddenly sickened and died. He was just thirty-four.

In 1927, Charles and a student teacher were fined for riding their bicycles through a public park. It was a trivial offence, but seeing their headmaster's name featured in the press under 'Police Court News' would not have warmed the hearts of Hutchins' governors.

As the 1920s progressed the School's finances worsened: a problem compounded when in 1926 its affiliation with Christ College came to an end. Charles struggled to increase endowments, but the debts and expectations of the School Board bore down on him. "His sensitive nature did not cope well with criticism." Hutchins had flourished under his leadership, but it was now felt his impetus was spent. The Board encouraged him to resign. Charles tendered his resignation in March 1929. The Board announced that it "accepted with regret" the news, but it was not sorry to see him go. Nonetheless, in the words of one member of the Board: "I later believed strongly that Thorold was our great Headmaster...I always sought another."

During his 11 years in Tasmania, Charles had also served as deputy-chairman of the Soldiers' Children Education Board, which administered a Federal Government scheme for educating and training the children of deceased and incapacitated soldiers. On his departure he was thanked for his devotion to the work, and in a speech referred to the "many very, pleasant evenings passed at the

Repatriation Department."

A prominent Anglican school in Sydney, Barker College, was now advertising for a replacement for its retiring headmaster. Charles applied, and made so favourable an impression at his interview that his appointment was confirmed unanimously by the School's Council. Barker was a smaller school, but the salary of £300 per annum was higher than that of Hutchins. It was also in every sense a fresh start. His commencement was scheduled for June 1929.

However, Charles's tenure was compromised from the very beginning. Jessie was reluctant to relocate to Sydney. Their two boys would be enrolled at the school, but other than that, Charles initially had to go it alone. He told the School Board his wife was ill. Given Jessie had been expected to look after the boy boarders and undertake some housekeeping, Charles hired a local woman, a Mrs Hallings, in her place, with the woman's husband acting as his secretary. This arrangement displeased the School Board. Yet an infinitely worse event now occurred. On the 29th of October 1929, Wall Street crashed, heralding the Great Depression.

In an attempt to raise School spirits, and as a step up from the Saturday evening lantern slide shows he'd staged at Hutchins, Charles purchased a movie projector using school profits, including those from the tuck shop. He then obtained as a gift two further 35mm projectors. These were installed in the old gymnasium, with his sons placed in charge. The boys erected curtains, coloured lights, and a sign lettered "Talkies". Newsreels, travelogues, and cartoons were screened, and there were 'song slides' for community singing. It could be described as a sort of early audiovisual facility. While a modern innovation of sorts, in the grim economic climate the School Council considered it a frivolous distraction, and it became a focus of criticism. In the jaundiced opinion of one staff member, the school had been reduced to "a picture show with teaching attached." When at considerable expense Charles also engaged a physical education instructor, the pattern of his actions were considered to exhibit "a total lack of discretion and balance".

Jessie only visited him at the School: when she saw the accommodation on offer, she caused "an enormous rumpus". In 1932, Charles wrote somewhat pathetically to the unhappy School

Council that "My wife's health is so very much improved now that she will be able to stand by me and help me in every way possible." It reads like the reworded demands of a private argument. The fact was, in Hobart Jessie had left him several times.

As the Depression deepened, by 1933 Barker's student enrolments plummeted from 206 pupils to just 83. There was a real possibility the School would be forced to close. Salaries were cut, and staff sacked. With his deep reserve, the headmaster's manner informing staff of their termination was, as one later recalled, a perfect recipe for paranoia:

> Thorold's method of conveying the 'glad tidings' was to sneak down in the [staff] Common Room late at night and deposit letters containing 'the order of the boot' in the letter rack.

The School Council was in despair. The previous headmaster William Carter, who'd owned the school before selling it to the Anglican Church, believed the School's problems lay with Charles. Carter used his prestige to undermine his successor's authority and credibility with the Council and Old Boys.

Charles came under enormous pressure. As in his later years at Hutchins, it drove him to physically retreat, and created a mental paralysis. Gone was the acuteness of his early years: Barker's School historian notes "His vagueness became proverbial." It was said he was uninterested in the normal activities of the school, undertook no teaching until forced to take Latin classes due to the reduced staff, and even then, needed to resort to a translation guide.

Alone and besieged, "surrounded by a sea of hostile faces" he blocked out the pain by blocking out reality. It was likely a survival response he'd developed at Dartmoor, but it led to a spiral downwards into mismanagement and neglect.

The reiterated insistence on 'the tone of school', which had so marked his dynamic and successful early years at Hutchins, was absent. His loss of drive, resolution and leadership resulted in school discipline being the worst for many years. Together with his deep reticence when confronted by failure, it further alienated the pupils, staff, parents, and the School Council. As the School's financial position and morale deteriorated, encouraged by Carter, the Old Boys Union stepped in and added its voice to the mounting criticism.

It has been suggested the School Council's management was amateurish, and Charles was made the scapegoat for an impossible economic situation. However, it's clear his personality and marital circumstances rendered him incapable of meeting a challenge of the scale Barker now presented. The last straw for the School authorities was widespread gossip that Charles was conducting an affair with Mrs Hallings: the placement of washing on her clothesline was, it was said, the signal to him that the coast was clear.

In March 1932 the School Council requested Charles's resignation. As his contract was until May 1933, he was able to negotiate a financial settlement. Jessie's indifferent health enabled a convenient public reason for his departure. When Thorold left the staff Common Room after announcing he'd resigned there were shouts of 'Hoo-ray'. Wrote one member "We had long since lost all liking and respect for him, and I am afraid to say we showed it." Charles was quite simply exhausted.

It was a surrender borne of deep unhappiness, and another scarring experience. Charles returned to Melbourne to recover. He was now fifty eight years old, in a troubled marriage, with two teenage sons. Yet once again fate threw out what seemed like a lifeline. In September, the small Melbourne school of Mentone Grammar advertised for a new headmaster. Due to the Depression, it too was in a parlous financial state, with enrolments having fallen below fifty. The employment offer included the lease of the School for twelve months for £104, with the option to purchase at the end of the period. In exchange, the appointed headmaster would agree to the expenditure of £50 repair costs prior to opening, and the payment of all running costs.

With no other employment offers on the horizon, Charles considered it a risk worth taking, and successfully applied. For the School Council, his application was also providential.

After the debacle of Barker College, Mentone would have felt just what Charles's spirit needed. The School lay fourteen miles (twenty-one kilometres) from Melbourne's city centre, on a low rise overlooking Port Phillip Bay, just a short walk from a beach. The bracing ozone and open prospects are likely to have reminded Charles of the bright years at Southport. Even the locality's street names – Naples Road, Palermo Street – there was even a Cromer Road – were redolent of sunny shores and happier times. The School advertised its charms in the press as: "an ideal boarding school for boys from the hotter parts of Australia," and provided a comprehensive curriculum from kindergarten to Leaving.

Charles commenced in the new year. As he'd done elsewhere, he immediately set about putting the School in order. For the beleaguered School Council, his arrival was like "a breath of Spring". Once again, his sense of purpose and flair for occasion lifted the spirits of his staff.

Despite this, the Depression was still pervasive, and by September 1933 the School Council could no longer service its debts. However, it was so impressed by the impact Charles was making, that it opened negotiations for the sale of the School to him earlier than planned. The Council had no other options, and Charles was the only interested purchaser. He must have seemed like a godsend. In this buyer's market, he was able to make the purchase for £2,900 – one-third of its book value. Even so, the financing was only possible through the auspices of Jessie's father, Frank Were.

Ownership suited Jessie: unlike at Hutchins and Barker, she now fully committed herself to the venture, and supporting Charles to make it a success. One of her nieces observed that Jessie:

> worked so hard, scrubbing the kitchen floors, cleaning the boarders' bedrooms and bathrooms, washing all the blankets (by hand) every holidays; coping with parents, always making do without staff; doing the cooking, mending and ironing. She was just like a mother to all of them.

Her change of attitude restored the marital relationship to some degree. A colleague of Charles observed that he "seemed to admire Mrs. C.C. with an extraordinary degree of humour and tolerance – and perhaps patronage." Jessie was a personage requiring a significant degree of forbearance.

Both Charles's sons were now also assisting with the School: Jeffery monitoring the boarders, as his father "used to retire into his shell after the evening meal". Jeffery had also become a trainee accountant working in grandfather Were's company during the day.

A staff member insightfully recalled of Charles during this time:

> His smile was generally there – there was a secret in his very being that he did not share. I don't know if Jeff knew him. I am sure that Mrs. T.[horold] did not.

Together with assorted municipal notaries, Charles was now invited with Jessie to the annual Government House garden party. On these days he encouraged the pupils to inspect him in his morning suit and top hat, before setting off.

One pupil who was enrolled at Mentone Grammar after being educated elsewhere, noted: "a distinct change of atmosphere...you were taught to be a gentleman...This was because of Mr. Thorold." A staff member recalled: "He seemed to cause good manners by just being there. A reprimand was always a firm suggestion, not a humiliating experience." It was a mental discipline of personal appearance, right conduct, and respect for the feelings of others that stuck for life. Also recalled was Charles's warm humanity that, in the words of the School's historian, "gave some boys their first feelings of self-respect in the presence of an adult." His impact on shaping character was profound. It was the same with his teaching. As a former pupil put it simply: "he was a gorgeous teacher – the best English teacher I ever came across". Lessons were voyages of discovery. Charles believed strongly in the mental discipline of language studies, another pupil recalling:

> He made Latin more interesting to those capable of responding to his methods, not by interesting us in Roman society...but by somehow making the structure and articulation of the language intellectually interesting (to boys under twelve!).

Yet despite the Thorold family's best efforts for the School, the economic mood remained pessimistic, and enrolments continued to be dire. Adding to the stress, after years of drought that had reduced Melbourne to water restrictions, the summer of 1938–39 had begun exhaustingly hot. In early January came a succession of suffocating days of temperatures over 40C, sometimes accompanied by a fearsome dry wind that felt like standing next to an open blast furnace, and which old settlers called 'The Scavenger'. Folk belief had it that even microbes perished in its wake. It meant that despite the punishing heat, windows could not be opened, and in an era before air-conditioning, homes and offices soon became ovens.

Far worse, the drought had stripped fields and forest floors of moisture. On Friday the 13th, the thermometer reached a record 45°C (114°F). Nature exploded. Several bushfires had broken out days before, but now, accelerated by the scorching wind, they combined into massive fire fronts. Across the State, millions of acres burned, whole townships were obliterated in minutes, and scores of citizens lost their lives. Even the Governor's summer residence at the hill station of Mount Macedon was burnt to cinders. Apocalyptic amounts of smoke and ash were produced, covering Melbourne and reaching as far as New Zealand. Given the School's prospects seemed almost hopeless, the oppressive red skies, and smoke-filled burning air must have felt like an omen.

In desperation, Charles reduced the School's fees, and opened it up to girls; a kindergarten class was established, and evening education classes offered. It was all to naught: by the third term of 1939 enrolments had declined to just thirty-two pupils. Adding to Charles's plight, their parents were often tardy in paying the fees.

Yet there are circumstances even worse than economic depression and bushfire. On the 3rd of September 1939, Australians tuned in their radio sets to hear the Prime Minister, Robert Menzies, announce that the Commonwealth of Australia had joined the Mother Country in the war against Germany.

Given this news, and no doubt pressured by Jessie and her father to whom he was debtor, Charles crumbled and agreed the venture needed to be wound up. Just three days after the declaration of war, subdivision estimates for the School grounds were undertaken.

Charles had lived for the School. Now there was to be nothing. Only war, death, and ashes. It's likely the embers of his relationship with Jessie had also died. Not only was he alone, but he would also have been feeling Time's hand. In 1931 his eldest brother Algernon had died, and in 1935 his eldest sister Hilda.

On the brink, and clearly done with this world, on the 25th of September 1939, Charles wrote his will. It has the signs of something undertaken in wretchedness and haste. Penned on both sides of a single foolscap sheet of thin lined paper torn from a school exercise book, it was witnessed by two teachers at Mentone. For a gentleman who was so particular, its scrubby quality was out of character, and further evidence Charles was in a dark place. In the testament, he thanked "my beloved wife for her devoted love and care of me". Amongst its bequests were his gold watch and signet ring to his eldest son Jeffery, and his black oak cabinet with its blue china to Patrick. Like Cyril Flower, whose own collection he may have seen, Charles too had caught the blue china mania.

A mere three weeks later, on the evening of October 16th, Charles C. Thorold, headmaster of Mentone Boys Grammar School, unexpectedly succumbed at the age of sixty-six to what was reported to be "a severe heart attack". The following day, as a mark of respect, the School remained closed. Yet as the mourners gathered, a troubling rumour circulated. Contrary to what the family and press stated, it was whispered that Charles's death was not due to any coronary event.

In those days, a feature of Mentone beach was a long, deepwater pier.* Originally constructed to allow steamers to call, the dark green depths glimpsed between the wide gaps of its planks frightened nervous children as they progressed along it. On one side, there was a waist-high wooden railing, but on the other, and at its extremity, there was no barrier at all. Just infinity.

Within the district, the sight of Charles Thorold riding his English Humber bicycle had been a regular one. And it was said that on the evening of the 16th he had ridden it hard to the very end of the pier and beyond. Despite his years of rowing and sailing, Charles could not swim. For the sake of appearances, both for the School and his wife's eminent family, a coverup was allegedly arranged. The rumour has the strangeness of truth, and within the family, was one that lingered.

---

* Demolished 1964.

Back in 1895, when the nascent Charles was at Oxford, and his world was young and full of promise, one of the argued topics of the Debating Society, of which he was Treasurer, had been: "The establishment of a Suicide Club." Had the young man then called Arthur advocated for it, those many years ago?

Under Catholic and Anglican canon law, suicide was viewed as a crime against God, and those who died by their own hand were not accorded full funeral rites,* nor were their coffins permitted to lie within a church. This may explain why Charles's funeral was not held at St. Matthews, the church adjoining the School. Rather, it took place in the chapel of an undertakers in Caulfield: a suburb more noted for its Jewish community than as an Anglican heartland.

At his death, Charles owed £2,500 to F.W. Were, and £548 to his wife, Jessie. Astonishingly, he also still owed £750 to the widow of the Rev. T. H. Rust, being the balance of the loan the Rusts had provided some thirty years earlier. Charles's will made allowances for this to be repaid. Despite the fact he was seen by the Rusts as something of an adopted son, it suggests a cavalier attitude to debt. Clearly, obligations to others could be put on hold while living the good life. Charles's assets consisted of Mentone Grammar School, a property at Hornsby in Sydney, shares worth £450, and cash and bank deposits totalling £4,750. The following February his young brother the Rev. Ernest Thorold died at Marston. Ernest's will, which hadn't been updated, bequeathed Charles £50.

As executor of Charles's estate, Jeffery Thorold was told by Frank Were: "Let the school go. I consider it dead. My opinion is to sell the property on the best price and terms available." Jeffery indeed put it up for sale, but in the wartime climate, there were no takers. Ultimately, Jeffery decided to try and keep the School running. The official school historian records the miracle that then occurred:

> By 1939, C.C. Thorold's Grammar School was practically a lost cause…Yet, within a year of Jeffery Thorold's management, a nation at war transformed the situation. The opportunity to offer low-cost accommodation to families wishing to board out their

---

* The Anglican Church abolished the sanction in 2015.

sons proved irresistible. The School became part of the War effort.

Due to Jeffery's determined efforts to maintain his father's legacy, Mentone Grammar would grow and thrive, to eventually become one of the nation's greatest private schools.

Charles Thorold's own achievements had been remarkable. He had been headmaster of three schools, in three different Australian states, including as the owner of one, and part owner of another. His contributions to each, and to the betterment of the lives of their pupils, were immeasurable. Not least, to have commenced this academic career in the southern hemisphere a mere half year after breaking stones on Dartmoor as a convict, is an academic employment record that may be unique – and one not likely to be repeated.

Charles's legacy lives on at Southport School, where generations of boys have passed through Thorold House. In 1960, his memory was honoured at Hutchins when it also named a house after him.

The year before Charles' death, Benjamin Brumfield retired from the Lincolnshire police force after thirty years of upstanding service, lastly as a superintendent. The willowy lad of Hougham who'd been up for forbidden adventure had long vanished: replaced by a more ossified personage. When still policing in 1935, Brumfield had informed local magistrates that "he was strongly opposed to Continental programmes being broadcast in licensed premises on Sundays," and that if licenses to permit radio music in such premises were granted, they should be "for British programmes only". Aside from the provincial priggery, this respect for the Sabbath suggests he may have had more in common with Charles Thorold than just a love of sailing. Residing with his wife in the northern seaside resort of Cleethorpes, Brumfield died at the age of seventy-eight in 1965.

In 1982, the then headmaster of The Southport School, John Henry Day, began researching Charles Thorold's life for his PhD, having felt that Thorold had been somewhat written out of the existing school history. The resulting thesis, titled *Charles Thorold, Gentleman Emigrant: A Study Of The Transmission of the Gentleman Ideal To Australia*, took Day seven years to write and research, in both Australia and England. It outlined how Charles established the philosophies and internal structures of the English public school system in the Australian schools he both led and owned, with the goal of imprinting the ideology of gentlemanliness under antipodean skies.

John Day was fortunate in uncovering a cache of Charles's personal papers in the School's archives, and received assistance from archivists at the other schools Charles had mastered at. A goodly number of the elderly Southportians whom Day interviewed recalled that Charles was thought to be 'a remittance man'. Having expected to write a straightforward biography, to his surprise Day was increasingly presented with an enigma. Disentangling the real person from the fog of history was not going to be easy. Day soon learned of the suicide rumour, but given it was only hearsay – albeit from an informed source, felt it could not be included in the thesis, particularly given Jeffery Thorold had only just died, Patrick Thorold was still living, and the family's close connections with Mentone Grammar. However, Day also uncovered the factual discrepancies in Thorold's curriculum vitae. He eventually wrote:

> Thorold kept his private life, especially his past, very much to himself. Indeed, he wrote very little about himself. Furthermore, as a master of the English language, his written references to the past were couched in such a way as to veil the full truth from the reader unless he or she was already in possession of it. For example, Thorold's letter of application for the position of Warden of Christ College and Headmaster of The Hutchins School, embroiders the truth in such a way as to mislead the reader. At the very least, Thorold rearranged the events of 1899 to 1906 to suit his purpose and glossed over details with the outcome that school histories, using this source, paint a fairly distorted picture of his background.

Day's researches also revealed that in 1902 there had been a family crisis of some kind. In the records of the Diocese of Lincoln, an assistant researcher uncovered the letter from the Rev. T.J. Crossfield to the Bishop with its stunning sentence: "Since I came to Grantham this morning I learnt that the 'bride' I married the other day was the sister of the boy with whom Mr. Thorold's son committed so grievous a Sin." That the reference was to homosexual fornication was the most obvious deduction, but it could also have referred to

569

some other mortal sin. With nothing else to go on, it seemed like a dead end, and Day inserted the quote in an extended note.

In May 1987, having left The Southport School, Day travelled to England to complete his research, journeying to Marston to meet with the son of Charles's younger brother, Ernest. This was the Wodehousian bachelor the Reverend Henry Thorold, the self-appointed custodian of the family history, at his seven-hundred-year-old manor.[*]

With his unforgettable voice of "sonorous, modulated tones," Henry was "a marvellous raconteur, with a masterly use of the pause." That pause included a bone-deep aversion to sharing the more delicate portions of Thoroldian history with outsiders, however gentlemanly. Despite the fact the 13th Thorold baronet, who died in 1951, had junked much of the family's Lincolnshire patrimony, demolishing the grand family seat of Syston Hall and moving to sunnier Devon, Henry had not the slightest intention of elucidating the reason why. This being that in a time when homosexuality was criminalised, the esteemed bachelor Major Sir John Thorold Bt. J.P., preferred not to be the resident squire of a parish where he was on first name terms with the policeman.

Henry's discretion over family matters extended even further back – at least eighty years back to be precise. Tootling through Hougham-cum-Marston in his ancient Bentley with Day, and acknowledging villagers like a grand seigneur, Henry shared not the slightest particle of information regarding the family shame that had engulfed Arthur Charles Campbell Thorold – or whatever he may have called himself in the distant antipodes. Day became increasingly conscious that he was being subjected to a very odd, stage-managed encounter: one that included the private lunch at the Thorold Arms that had been purged of the village regulars. It was a perfectly polite snow job. Henry's reasons for keeping the secret likely went beyond the desire to protect his ancient family's reputation. The Thorolds were still the pillar of the parish, and quite simply, Henry had to face the villagers every day.

---

[*] For an amusing account of Henry's recherché existence, see: Michael Hodges, 'The Revd. Henry Coryland Thorold – An Ordinate Priest ahead of his time?', *Friends Of The Ordinariate*, Summer 2021, London, pp11-12;
https://web.archive.org/web/20221231025615/http://friendsoftheordinariate.org.uk/wp-content/uploads/2021/06/GADS1541-Ordinariate-Newsletter-Spring-Summer-2021-DRAFT-7-WEB_compressed-2.pdf

His principal concern, expressed to Day, was that the thesis should contain no element of 'gossip'.

Henry's brother, the Rev. John Thorold[*] could only suggest in a letter to Day: "I have heard it said...that the reason why my uncle...emigrated to Australia was because the girl whom he subsequently married was the daughter of a pawnbroker." As previously noted, Kathleen's father had been a travelling salesman. In any case, as someone who surely knew the truth, the Rev. John's response was a feline half-truth.

Back in Australia, Charles Thorold's two sons were equally courteous to Day, but no more forthcoming. In the Introduction of his thesis, Day admitted his frustration, writing diplomatically: "As the research developed, the author became aware of a reticence on the part of the Thorold family, especially the English branch, to supply the details being sought."

Day's research at the offices of the local paper, *The Grantham Journal*, was also mostly fruitless because it had never reported Arthur's trial. This was no casual oversight. In 1897, when a Grantham tradesman's daughter and distant relation, Mary Sophia Thorold, took out a breach of promise suit and was awarded £125 by a London court for her troubles, *The Grantham Journal* devoted one-third of a page to reporting the case. The paper's studious avoidance of the scandal that embroiled Arthur Thorold, and his imprisonment, was unquestionably in deference to the squire and his kinsmen.

Dr. Day's research was nevertheless commendable. It corrected many unwitting errors in the histories of the schools Thorold had helped shape, and detailed his own influences, and the breadth of his contributions. In 1989 the thesis was submitted to Queensland University. In documenting the development of an important phenomenon in the history of Australian education, it was more than worthy of the doctorate it attained. Yet at the very core of the deeply reserved, twice-married Thorold there was an obvious lingering

---

[*] Rev. John Robert Hayford Thorold (1916–2010); son of the Rev. Dr. Ernest Hayford Thorold. Also a bachelor, he had a housekeeper, a Mrs. Wills, of whom it was said: "you wouldn't pick a fight with."

mystery that Day admitted he had not been able to crack. He mused: "no one will ever know for sure why Charles Thorold emigrated to Australia".

When Day laid down his pen, the digitisation of newspapers had yet to commence, and the World Wide Web and search engines were non-existent. The access and filtered search of historical documents which can make obscured life stories suddenly less opaque, was then a dream. The revelation of the ultimate truth, made here, would have to wait almost another three decades.

Maintaining Arthur Thorold's ruse would seem almost impossible today. It also begs the question: was it ultimately more beneficial for society that it lay unrevealed? The evidence strongly suggests so. That aligns with the policy, now enshrined in dubious law in the European Union, of 'the right to be forgotten,' which seeks to ensure that, after a period of time, a living person is not stigmatised as a consequence of a past action, and gives them the right to have information about their crime hidden from the public record. However, such privilege does not extend to convicted pederasts seeking employment in the teaching profession. Hence the conundrum.

This is a story that is still unfolding. In May 2017, Mentone Grammar inaugurated a large building on its campus for the performance, visual, and scientific arts. It includes the 450-seat Thorold Theatre, named in honour of Charles's son, Jeffery. As someone who loved the theatre; whose life *was* theatre; and who was devoted to the inculcation of learning, Arthur Charles Campbell Thorold would have loved it.

18. A LAIRD MOST RICH AND POWERFUL

When Justice Grantham, in his summing up at their trial, intoned that Fraser and Thorold bore names "honoured in the field and the forum, and in every branch of life," it was painfully true. If the Thorolds were a pillar of the English religious establishment, and a power in Lincolnshire, the mighty clan of the Frasers also stretched across the nation's public life. The army was their favoured field, but they were everywhere influence could be wielded.

Head of the Fraser clan were the Lords Lovat of Beaufort Castle in Inverness-shire, who held sway over 500 square miles of the Highlands. Bernard Fraser hailed from a lesser branch, the Frasers of Gortuleg near Loch Ness.

While Bernard Fraser's family, like the Thorolds, constituted gentry, the stream of their history had divided. Unlike the Reverend Thorold struggling with his acres in Lincolnshire, Bernard's father had succeeded in riding the wave of new urban wealth. They were an 'old family' with pots of freshly minted money – the best of all possible worlds. It enabled Bernard to enjoy a swaggering level of privilege and cosmopolitan pleasure that Arthur Thorold could only dream of.

Bernard's father, John Fraser, born in 1820, was the third of six sons. Had he been born a generation earlier John might have remained on the land, or gone into the military. However, the 1840s witnessed a subsistence crisis in the Highlands, which caused a collapse of the old social structure. Meanwhile, the Industrial Revolution, which began the redistribution of power from the landowning class to the financial

573

and mercantile sector, required a new desk-bound infrastructure of support services – including accountants, actuaries, bankers and lawyers. Scotland's educational system, which was supported and expanded by the 'muscular Christianity' of its Free Church, assisted the rise of this middle class. Edinburgh became what San Francisco is for Silicon Valley – a services hub for these new industries.

Pursuing opportunity, John Fraser became an accountant in Edinburgh, and so was perfectly positioned to take advantage of this seachange. Much of the work of the city's accountants involved dealing with bankruptcy and sequestration, as the economy transitioned from a rural to an industrial one.

The Industrial Revolution also accelerated the need for the professional management of risk. The advent of the railways, for example, introduced a host of new dangers. Insurance became an area of Scottish expertise. John moved from being an accountant to an actuary, and joined one of the insurance companies, the Life Association of Scotland, as its manager. He was just twenty-five, and would head the association for 30 years. As well as life policies it provided securities for debts, loans, and provisions under marriage settlements.

It's easy to think of John as being both prudent and cautious: not till 1862, at the age of forty-two, did he commit to marriage. His wife was Susan Foulis Webster, the daughter of a landed gentleman, Major General Thomas Webster. They would have five sons, and three daughters. Together with seven servants (two nurses, a house-maid, sewing-maid, laundry-maid, table-maid, and a cook), the Frasers eventually resided in one of the imposing stone terraces of Moray Place. It was not only the grandest street in Edinburgh's New Town – the suburb for the affluent, but in all of Scotland.

Born on the 27th of January 1866, Bernard Fraser (christened John Bernard) was the couple's third son. Following in the Fraser tradition, three of his brothers, Thomas Oliver (known by his second name), Henry Francis, and Robert Webster achieved distinguished service in the military. Henry's awards included the C.M.G. (Companion of the Order of St Michael & St George), D.S.O. (Distinguished Service Order), and the French Legion of Honour. The eldest son, Alexander Edmund (also known by his second name), became a barrister, before joining the diplomatic service, where he forged an impressive career in Africa, Egypt and Europe. A homosexual bachelor, Edmund cared enough about status to have his own coat of arms drawn up (mottoes: *Je suis prest* – I am ready and *Tout bien ou rien* – All or nothing). He was also a member of the King's Bodyguard (Royal Archers) in Scotland, and a knight and the librarian of the charitable chivalric Order of St John of Jerusalem.

Bernard's three sisters were Ada Susan, Helen Agnes (called Nellie), and Florence Margaret. Unusually, only two of the children, Henry and Robert, ever married. The girls were reasonably attractive: while one or more may not have married due to inclination, and the family's wealth alleviated them from the need to contract advantageous alliances, it is very possible the public stain of Bernard's scandal scared off eligible suitors. The succeeding blow of the Great War thinned the ranks of those who remained, leaving a generation of spinsters in its wake.

The thriving Edinburgh that Bernard Fraser grew up in was still deeply hierarchical, and ravishingly picturesque. When Queen Victoria visited in 1842 she recorded in her diary:

> The view of Edinburgh from the road before you enter Leith is quite enchanting; it is, as Albert said, 'fairy-like', and what you would only imagine as a thing to dream of, or to see in a picture. There was that beautiful large town, all of stone (no mingled colours of brick to mar it), with the bold Castle on one side, and the Carlton Hill on the other, with those high sharp hills of Arthur's Seat and Salisbury Crags towering above all, and making the finest, boldest background imaginable. Albert said he felt sure the Acropolis could not be finer, and I hear they sometimes call Edinburgh "the modern Athens".

Bernard was sent to Leamington College, as a boarder in the household of the headmaster. In January 1885, when he was nineteen, his father died from influenza. John Fraser left a fortune of over £71,000, which at the very least approximates to £7 million in 2021.

Until recent times Scotland was a relatively poor country, and even as late as the 1960s less than half of its people left testamentary evidence of any sort. However, John Fraser's will stretches over many pages: it is indicative of his substance, and the wide-ranging investment perspective of the upper class. It features several life insurance policies, and stocks in the Life Association of Scotland, a string of Scottish and Indian banks, as well as railway companies (English, Canadian and Indian, such as the Great Indian Peninsula Railway Company), and The Newfoundland Land Company. Not least, it includes a tranche of shares in the Life Association of Scotland, held in trust for his sons. It was a huge legacy that offered them the promise of blessed lives.

In the Census of 1891, Bernard is recorded as still living in the family home at Moray Place, and giving his profession as that of wine merchant – the perfect hobby job for a rich man's son. It was the only time in his life he would trouble himself with any kind of employment. For a year he'd been a partner in a vineyard in Algeria, with the previously mentioned Vicomte Joseph de Kergariou.

Joseph hailed from Brittany, but through his maternal grandmother was related to the Pirie family: wealthy paper manufacturers of Aberdeenshire. He regularly holidayed with them, and it was possibly on one of these occasions he first met Bernard. Both were keen hunters.

Photographs of Joseph show him to have been quite good-looking: bald, but blessed with large pellucid eyes, and under a sweeping moustache, a sensual mouth. In 1890 he'd sold his farms in Brittany and rented for six years an estate at Cherchill, on the northern Algerian coast, planting vineyards there. From the nearby Villa Claudins, he wrote to a cousin:

> In January we will change our residence to settle in our castle of Closville. A real candy box on which we have built our cellar and from where we have the prettiest view of sea and land that we can dream of.

The dream didn't last long. For reasons unknown, in 1893 Joseph and Bernard dissolved the business partnership. However, Bernard gave his share of the assets to the nobleman. It is not the only evidence of their closeness. The two men remained friends for life.

That year, Bernard spent time in Canada. However, three years on, there was a harbinger that his life might not be all effortless sailing. He and his brother Henry featured in an unpleasant story in the press, which headlined it: 'A New Sport For Perthshire Gentlemen'. While out rabbit hunting together, Bernard had shot and wounded a dog belonging to a shepherd, whom he believed was a poacher. As it was only a grazing wound to the animal's leg, it was probably intended as a warning shot. Both Bernard and Henry pleaded not guilty, but the prosecuting sheriff believed the circumstances formed sufficient basis for a charge of 'malicious mischief', and inflicted a fine of 7s 6d, with the option of twenty-four hours' imprisonment.

While poaching there may have been, the story suggests a tetchy assumption of class superiority on Bernard's part. Family photographs suggest he possessed an air of self-assurance. Tall and slim, with dark brown hair, ice-blue eyes, and a neatly-clipped moustache, Bernard clearly revelled in the world laid out for a gentleman of his class in that glorious age. His name now appeared regularly in newspaper social columns, such as the Park Lane party of Countess Lützow,* where in a series of tableaux from Wagner's operas, he appeared as Lohengrin. As we have seen, in the winter of 1897 he visited Naples. He returned again in the spring of 1901, *The Times* dutifully recording: "Mr. Bernard Fraser has left town for the Riviera and Italy".

Presumably for the society, including the hope of presenting her daughters to more prospective partners, Bernard's widowed mother Susan now relocated the family to London, renting a six-storey terrace at 14 Chester Street, Belgravia. The 1901 census reveals she was living there with Bernard, Henry, and her three daughters Ada, Florence and Nellie. London's West End was then still quiet and deeply aristocratic; as a guide to the capital phrased it, "there is an indefinable something in the very atmosphere that makes humble but sensitive folk wish they were elsewhere". Until the *London Streets (Removal of Gates) Act* of 1890, the roads and squares of its great estates had even been protected by gates manned by liveried keepers in cockaded hats.

In the parlance of the period, Bernard was now well into his career as

---

* Anna Gustava, Countess von Lützow, née von Bornemann (1853–1932). She and her Bohemian (Czech) husband Franz 'Francis' (1849–1916), a champion of Bohemian independence from the Austro-Hungarian Empire, were a socially prominent couple before World War I. Their many friends included Frederic Myers and Oscar Browning.

a 'swell' – an elegant dandy who resided in London's West End. He was a member of one of the smartest and exclusive London clubs, the Bachelors', and popular in Society. Such was his social profile, that *Boyle's Fashionable Court & Guide, and Town Visiting Directory* listed him and his mother as residing at 14 Chester St, but no other members of the family!

In January 1901, the press announced the forthcoming marriage, which would "take place quietly" of Vicomte Joseph de Kergariou to Margaret Ellen Barrow, the daughter of a London wine merchant. Later the same month, there was another press notice: "Owing to the illness of the bridegroom, the marriage arranged to take place... is unavoidably postponed." It was, in fact, postponed forever: later that year the young lady would marry another gentleman, her father dying soon after. Whatever had occurred between Joseph and his intended, is unknown. He would go on to seek adventure and success (the latter in vain) in Kenya and elsewhere.

In March 1902, Bernard attended a levée held by the King at Buckingham Palace. Amongst the hundreds of other guests were a smattering of the confirmed bachelors later to feature in this story, as well as Sir Paynton Pigott, the Chief Constable Of Norfolk who would attend his trial. Bernard was also a stalwart of the annual Royal Caledonian Ball, where amongst the other gentry and aristocrats he was assured of meeting a phalanx of Frasers. Only days before his arrest he was dancing Highland reels at the Hôtel Métropole. As with Arthur Thorold, it is almost impossible to conceive the shock, horror and immense shame that his arrest and the resulting scandal inflicted upon his family.

Following his sentencing, Bernard initially served his time at Portland Prison on the Isle of Portland in Dorset. For someone who until then had lived an indulged life, and unlike Arthur Thorold, was no longer young, its impact would have been devastating. Soon after, Bernard began suffering toothache, and petitioned that he might receive the services of a dentist at his own expense. His request was granted, but not before someone attached to his criminal file a newspaper clipping about his trial, with the paragraphs most scathing of him underlined.

After 1903, Bernard was transferred to Parkhurst Convict Prison on the Isle of Wight. Set within a hollow of undulating green upland,

Parkhurst was the most select of all prisons: to it were sent the higher class of criminals, such as bankers, military officers and gentry, as well as invalids, the mentality damaged, and Jews – the only synagogue in the prison system being most advantageously placed there. As one inmate wrote, "The chain of Destiny, I soon found, is not allowed to chafe too closely in this goal." Bernard's labours there may have included sewing mailbags and naval hammocks.

Bernard's transfer to the cushiest prison in the system suggests powerful connections at work. Certainly, following the release of Thorold in July 1906, Bernard's family and friends made efforts to mitigate his sentence. The prominent Anglican churchman Basil Wilberforce,* a grandson of the slavery abolitionist William Wilberforce, was approached.

Archdeacon Wilberforce is not the first name one might consider to intercede on behalf of a convicted pederast. Not only was Wilberforce a leader in the temperance movement, from the pulpit of Westminster Abbey he had denounced Sarah Bernhardt for bringing her illegitimate son to England and "flaunting her skirts in the very face of royalty". However, as previously noted, in 1905 he and his elder brother Ernest, Bishop of Chichester, were the guests of the Batterseas at Overstrand. That such a high-level church figure could have become interested in Bernard Fraser's case is more likely due to a request by Cyril Flower, than Arthur Thorold's father. It certainly shows a high card being played. It resulted in Wilberforce pleading to the trial judge Sir William Grantham that imprisonment had caused a breakdown in Fraser's health. Although some of Grantham's capricious sentencing could be feudally severe, he was kind-hearted in private, and "intensely religious".† The plea of such a figure as Wilberforce, erratic but saintly, worked a treat.

Early in 1907, Grantham wrote to the Home Secretary, then Herbert Gladstone, to request a reduction in Bernard's sentence by one year due to his ill-health. Given that Gladstone was a friend of Cyril's, what his private thoughts on the matter were can only be guessed.

---

* Albert Basil Orme Wilberforce (1841–1916), Chaplain to the Speaker of the House of Commons and Archdeacon of Westminster.
† True to form, Grantham only had time for the state religion. He upset the Irish, and received a rebuke from the *Law Journal*, for stating from the bench that "he disliked the Roman Catholic faith as much as anybody". [*Exeter and Plymouth Gazette*, 2 May 1903, p6.]

However, there then ensued a chain of correspondence that engaged the time and mental energy of some of the highest individuals On His Majesty's Service in the Home Office, which managed the Prerogative of Mercy.

When letters were received at the Home Office, they were circulated to select civil servants who wrote their observations and opinions on an attached Minutes sheet to enable the composition of a suitable response. By the Edwardian period any handwritten letters received were typed up, prior to internal circulation, to enable easier reading. Bernard's criminal file includes original letters to the department, the typed copy, and the corresponding departmental Minutes.

However, Grantham's original letter, its typed copy, and the corresponding Minutes are missing, as is the Home Office's reply to him. They may have gone astray, but almost certainly they were deliberately destroyed by a later censor. It's possible that in framing his plea Grantham touched on the suppressed details of the case a little too frankly for posterity.

That Grantham wrote and received a reply is clear because he wrote again to the Home Secretary from the Carlton Club on the 11th of April that year, and this letter, its typed copy, and the department Minutes do survive. As the letter makes apparent, in response to his plea, Grantham had been forwarded a medical officer's report* on Bernard's alleged illness, which showed him to be in good health. Perhaps the illness had been temporary. Grantham writes:

> The Prison report as to the prisoner's illness I am afraid negatives [*sic*: negates] most of the ground claimed for a reduction of sentence claimed by Canon Wilberforce, and as the suggested illness was the reason for asking me to acquiesce in a reduction, I feel much difficulty in approving. Still, as I believe there was a reduction made in the other prisoner's case [i.e. Thorold], and as I perceive the severe sentences that I felt bound to give in these and other kindred cases about the same time have very materially diminished the crime, I should be inclined to reduce it by one year.
>
> Faithfully yours,

---

* Now also missing from the file.

The departmental Minutes provide an unfiltered view of the internal response to the letter. Grantham's oddly repeated request for a remission, despite being told of Bernard's good health, did not go down well. Nor did the suggestion that his sentencing had markedly reduced forbidden pastimes throughout the kingdom. The withering comments of Home Office mandarins, with their appended signatures, included:

> it is impossible to say whether such a crime as sodomy has or has not become less common since 1902. Anyway the sentences passed by Judge in that year are not likely to have the slightest effect except in so far as they restricted & are restraining individual criminals from repeating their offences. Fraser's case was a very bad one...The Judge said it was 'without exception the worst he had ever heard of'. If the indictment for felony had been proceeded with, defendant might have got PS [prison sentence] for life. He appears to have no particular claim for clemency of the Crown.
>
> HBS 29.4.7

The initials were those of Harry Butler Simpson, Assistant Secretary of the Home Office. Bernard was never going to get sympathy from that quarter. Simpson considered the rise in crime was due to "a marked growth in compassion for the criminal": one that was encouraged by the press and popular novels, and which led to soft prison conditions, that failed to act as a strong deterrent.

Simpson's colleague Ernley Blackwell,* Assistant Secretary for the Home Office, who was later to be involved in the prosecution of Roger Casement, also delivered short shrift:

> It is a great pity that this man cannot be kept in prison for the rest of his life. I doubt whether this class of crime has diminished of late years. At any rate Fraser should not be let loose upon society one day before he is entitled to be released in the ordinary course.

---

* Sir Ernley Robertson Hay Blackwell (1868–1941), Assistant Secretary at the Home Office, 1906 to 1913, then Legal Assistant Under-Secretary of State.

Inform Judge Grantham that Thorold's sentence was not reduced but that he was released on licence in the ordinary course after he had completed three-fourths of his 5 years sentence and that Fraser, subject to any loss of marks owing to misconduct, will be entitled to be released on licence when he has served a like proportion of his 10 years term.

Having regard to the importance of maintaining the deterrent effect of the sentences passed in these cases, upon which stress is laid in his lordship's letter, S. of S. [Secretary of State] regrets that he does not feel justified in advising any exercise of the Prerogative of Mercy.

Inform Archdeacon Wilberforce of the purport of the M.O. [Medical Officer's] report and say that S. of S. regrets that having regard to the shocking nature of the offences of which Fraser was guilty he cannot find sufficient grounds for advising any interference in this case.

E.B. 30.4.07

Sir Mackenzie Chalmers,* a judge who was then serving as Permanent Under Secretary of State in the Home Office, added his view:

This was a most shocking case in which men of good position used their position to corrupt young lads. According to the police this class of crime is by no means diminishing. As proposed by Mr. Blackwell.

M.C. 2/5/7

Lastly, the Home Secretary, Herbert Gladstone, stated his judgement:

I agree. Express regret to the Archdeacon that I am unable to interfere. H.G. 4/5/07 Should any fresh considerations arise later on, like any change in the prisoner's mental or physical condition, the Judge's suggestion no doubt will be considered.

As per the Minutes, on the 10th of May, Sir Mackenzie Chalmers replied to Grantham on behalf of the Home Secretary. He informed

* Sir Mackenzie Dalzell Edwin Stewart Chalmers (1847–1927), Permanent Under Secretary of State of the Home Office from 1903 to 1908.

him that Gladstone had:

> given very careful consideration to the circumstances of the case. He agrees with your Lordship that it is of the utmost importance to maintain the deterrent effect of sentences passed in such cases as this and therefore regrets that he is unable consistently with his public duty to advise the exercise the Prerogative of Mercy in favour of Fraser. I am to add that there was no reduction of the sentence of Fraser's accomplice, Thorold: he was released on licence in ordinary course.

However, the matter didn't end there. Justice Grantham was evidently being strongly leaned on. Given Bernard's eldest brother Edmund was a diplomat and had been a barrister, and Bernard's other three brothers, Oliver, Henry and Robert, were loyally serving in His Majesty's Armed Forces, a plea that called in notional owed favours due their national service and status, may also have been made. That said, it's questionable whether even the Frasers had the clout to make an impact. Bernard's influential friends, or possibly one in particular at Overstrand, again surely played their part. It worked. Like a blowfly that can't be shown the door, on the 17th of June Grantham again wrote to Herbert Gladstone:

> Dear Home Secretary,
>
> The Fraser Case.
>
> Since we corresponded about this case as to a reduction of his sentence in consequence of the sentence of Thorold having been much less than the sentence on Fraser, Mr. Gill, the counsel for Fraser, has been to see me to know if I would see him and Mr. Elliott, the counsel for Thorold, as the latter wished to make a statement to me as to his conduct at the trial. I have accordingly seen them, and Mr. Elliott tells me that he found out after the trial that he was not justified in making the statement to me on behalf of Thorold for the purpose of getting his sentence as light as possible, viz. that he was younger and innocent until he came into contact with Fraser and was entirely led into it by him. He says he made his statement on the authority of Thorold's father, who came to him the night before the trial and he then believed the statements to be true.

After the trial he heard that Thorold was very indignant that he had received such a lighter sentence than Fraser at the expense of Fraser as the statements were not true except as to age, and as to that there was not such difference as I was led to believe.

He agreed with Mr. Gill that though Thorold was the younger slightly, yet Fraser was a weaker man physically and mentally and was not likely to lead Thorold but much more likely to be led by him.

Under these circumstances I think it is a case in which you would be justified in remitting part of Fraser's imprisonment and I would suggest that (at) the end of the present year his sentence might be remitted.

Faithfully Yours
Wm. Grantham

Once again, the Minutes sheet indicates that Grantham's fresh plea received an icy reception:

Whether [Thorold was the more guilty party]…it affords no ground for regarding Fraser's sentence as excessive considering the long list of crimes to which he pleaded guilty…

HBS 19.6.7 [Harry Butler Simpson]

I agree. Thorold undoubtedly got off lightly owing to untrue statements made at the trial. The fact that Fraser did not corrupt the schoolmaster should make no difference whatever in his case – he had corrupted so many others including some of Thorold's pupils. There could not be a worse case of this kind. Fraser deserved every day of the maximum sentence and in the interests of the public should be kept in prison as long as possible.

E.B. 19.6.07 [Ernley Blackwell]

It was a ghastly case. But because these 2 ruffians have nice relations in a good position, people have forgotten the original crime. Hence all these attempts to get remission.

On the 29th of June, Edward Troup,[*] a Home Office mandarin who was elevated to Permanent Secretary of the Department in December, penned a memo to Gladstone, on whether to accept the judge's recommendations for a reduced sentence. It was less than flattering to Grantham:

> Home Office,
> Whitehall,
> S.W.
>
> I agree with the general principle. The Secretary of State must give great weight to a judge's recommendation in favour of reduction of sentence – but the decision is the S. of S.'s and must exercise his own judgement.
>
> Where a good judge, acting independently & without pressure from the prisoner's friends, makes a recommendation and supports it on any reasonable ground it is practically conclusive – But here there are strong reasons against accepting implicitly the judge's guidance.
>
> (a) Grantham J's judgement is not to be trusted.
>
> (b) He has clearly been got at by the prisoner's friends. It is clear would appear that the case has been engineered so as to get Thorold a light sentence and, when he had served the light sentence, to use it to get Fraser's reduced. If Thorold & his friends were shocked at the statements made by Counsel which exculpated Thorold at Fraser's expense, why did they not say so at once? Of course Mr. Elliott was misled; but, as the case is now being worked out, this misrepresentation is to result in benefit to <u>both</u> prisoners.
>
> (c) The case of Fraser ought in the circ[umstances] to be considered altogether apart from Thorold – as it might have been considered if (say) Thorold had fled the country. If that view point of view is taken I think it is clear that in view of considering

---

[*] Sir Charles Edward Troup (1857–1941).

his systematic crime, & his corruption of innocent boys, ten years is none too much.

C.T. 29.6.07

Troup's statement that "the case has been engineered" could not have been truer, but of course, in a far greater manner than of what he wrote. Having absorbed all this advice, on the 1st of July, Herbert Gladstone wrote a more considered memo for the Permanent Under-Secretary, Sir Mackenzie Chalmers:

The Judge's letter appears to me to raise a question of principle. To what extent, if at all, should the S. of S. accept the recommendation of a Judge that a sentence passed by him should be reduced? I have discussed this question in the abstract with the L.C.J. [Lord Chief Justice – then Lord Alverstone, the former Sir Richard Webster], and, briefly, with Mr. Asquith [the former Prime Minister, in office at the time of trial]. The L.C.J. considers, speaking generally, that the recommendation should only be accepted if the S. of S. concurs with the argument; and provided that nothing against the prisoner has arisen since conviction. He agreed however that there might be reason to follow the opinion of the Judge, if he showed that he passed a sentence under a misapprehension. Mr. Asquith considered that it would be a serious matter to ignore any deliberate recommendation of the Judge who had presided at the trial.

It is obvious that no general rule can be laid down. S. of S. should be free to act on his own judgement and responsibility. If he was bound to accept the recommendation of a Judge for remission, he would be bound to accept it when it was against interference.

Again a Judge from age or infirmity may yield too much to sentiment – perhaps from a natural wish to be at peace with the world. Every case therefore, as it appears to me, has to be considered on its own merits, but I agree that it is a serious matter to ignore the deliberately expressed and reasoned view of a Judge in favour of remission. The S. of S. has to administer the Prerogative of Mercy. He is not a Judge in the case, nor can he be in the best position for declaring what sentence should be passed. He may have his opinion, but it is a strong measure to assert his opinion against that of the responsible Judge who advises the exercise of the Prerogative on the ground that he, the Judge, under a misapprehension, passed an unduly severe sentence.

It may be that 10 years p.s. [prison sentence] is not an excessive sentence having regard to Fraser's foul offences. But the degree of punishment is for the Judge, and the S. of S. only interferes on grounds of mercy. When a Judge declares virtually that he made a mistake, that had he known what he now says he knows he would not have given 10 years, and now asks for remission, it appears to me a serious matter to say in effect "though you were originally wrong in your judicial diagnosis, you are now wrong in your estimate of what the sentence should have been, and your recommendation therefore cannot be entertained."

Thorold served 3 years 9 months, and Fraser has now served 4 years 8 months, and under ordinary circumstances he would have to serve 2 years 10 months more. The Judge proposes release on December 31 this year, making 5 years 2 months. I see no reason for so much remission. Thank the Judge for his letter and say that on his recommendation for remission I have directed that the case shall come up for consideration in December next year.

H.G. 1/7/07

On the 5th of July, Chalmers drafted a brief letter to Sir William Grantham that precisely enunciated Gladstone's decision. Perhaps he also crossed himself in the hope that it would finally achieve peace with this oddly chastened terror of the Bench.

As suggested by Gladstone's order, two days before Christmas 1908 Bernard Fraser finally stepped out of Parkhurst Prison into freedom, after serving six years and two months of his ten year sentence. His esteemed and scot-free client, Lord Battersea, had been dead for a year.

It's doubtful Bernard felt any particular guilt for his past actions – more likely, he felt hard done by. Just as he'd thought little of popping off a shot at a poacher's dog, Bernard's sense of entitlement extended into the sexual sphere. The adolescent boys he'd procured may have been deeply affected – possibly for life. However, it's equally possible the only trauma they felt had been from the police enquiries and fallout, and they'd been knowing, hormonally eager for pleasure, and perhaps some extra pocket money.

Bernard presumably spent Christmas with the family: it must have been a happy, but melancholic and awkward occasion. Whether he returned to the family home for any length of time is unknown, but given there would have been questions that couldn't be asked or answered, and consequently some heavy silences, it's debatable. Nonetheless, later evidence suggests the family remained close.[*]

The Post Office London Directory for 1910 lists 'Mrs. Fraser' at 14 Chester Street, but the Census of 1911 records the occupants of the house as being a seventy-five-year-old Kings Counsel, John Stafford Dugdale, his sister-in-law, and their six servants. It notes this as his temporary address. Bernard's mother Susan, his three sisters, and brother Henry later returned to the house, so either it was sublet or loaned out for a period. Neither the English or Scottish Census records of 1911 contain the family's names, so they may have gone abroad for a time to escape the gossip and stares.

For Bernard to return to his previous social life was impossible. Like Arthur Thorold, he also adjusted his name to throw off those who might scent a lingering prison stench. He now called himself Bernard Fraser-Ross – Ross having been the maiden name of his maternal grandmother Agnes Ross. He also sometimes used his other Christian name of John, and during the War, would resort to Ian.

While Bernard was still only 42, incarceration would have been both ageing, and soul-scarring. Oscar Wilde had endured only two years imprisonment, yet it broke him. Bernard suffered more than three times that sentence. In such circumstances, an ocean cruise can do wonders for personal renewal. Undoubtedly unsettled and seeking new horizons, in 1909 Bernard sailed to Buenos Aires, and the following year to New York, travelling of course First Class.

Of all places, it was in a village of just over twelve hundred souls in

---

[*] The probated Will of Susan Fraser records Bernard, his brother Robert, and sisters Ada, Florence and Helen declining to be executors in favour of their brothers Oliver and Henry. [Fraser, Susan Foulis, 1925, Wills and Testaments: SC70/4/588, SC70/1/730), National Records of Scotland.]

the far west of Austria that he eventually chose to settle – during its summers at least. Sandwiched between Germany, Switzerland and Lichtenstein, where the alps give way to lush hills that eventually slope down to Lake Constance, Au in the Bregenz Forest offered soul-healing alpine scenery to wake up to. Perhaps when he had gazed up at the grey light from his prison cell window, Bernard had envisioned living in such a postcard Eden. Not just a solace, it may have acted as a personal vindication that he was not some loathsome creature, but worthy of all the beauty the world could offer. And if he was unworthy, then he could at least damn well afford to buy it. And so he did, with the purchase of a chalet – what he called his 'shooting box'. The region was renowned for its hunting. Indeed, alpine serenity may have been in short supply as Bernard vented six years of frustration on the local wildlife.*

His idyll was short lived. While the clouds of war had been rumbling in the early months of 1914, its sudden outbreak created a special chaos for travellers and foreign residents who, with a stroke of a pen, were transformed into 'enemy aliens'. They found themselves at the mercy of angry crowds who shouted insults and even threw stones. Far away in his secluded village, Bernard left his escape too late and was trapped. The worry for his mother and family began all over again.

Unlike Germany, where enemy aliens tended to be interned behind barbed wire in prison camps, the Austro-Hungarian government chose to confine the majority of foreign civilians to a number of villages in Lower Austria. Here they were permitted to reside in privately-rented rooms and houses, and while subject to curfews, were still able to enjoy a limited freedom of movement. Bernard was initially interned in Baden. Bucolic it wasn't. In the words of one outraged Englishwoman:

> We were exploited in every way…most of the houses were only peasant houses – and an Austrian peasant's house can only be described as a hole…The village shops have two distinct charges – one for the inhabitants – one for the interned.

---

* In the 1930s, Austria's elite Sports and Shooting Club would come under the gaze of the Nazi police due to its membership of rich homosexuals and other State enemies. [Charles Higham, *Wallis: Secret Lives of the Duchess of Windsor*, Sidgwick & Jackson, London, 1988, pp197-198.]

At least they were more fortunate than the military captives. Austria-Hungary and Germany were utterly unprepared to cope with the massive numbers of prisoners of war from the eastern front. The conditions of their internment in the winter-spring of 1914-15 were abysmal: some soldiers were forced to sleep in open muddy fields without blankets.

However, like the military prisoners, the civilian captives also endured problems with insufficient clothing, food shortages, delayed posts, but most of all boredom – and trepidation of what was to come. Time for them stood still. While a few took advantage of the opportunity for creative activity and self-discovery, for Bernard, whose life had already been halted by years of prison, it would have been even more frustrating. In 1914 there was talk of the War being over in weeks. The one positive element for the prisoners was that they had no conception of how many long years of conflict and confinement lay ahead.

As a diplomat, Bernard's eldest brother Edmund was the natural choice to take charge of the family's attempts to repatriate him. In 1915, Edmund submitted a request through the Foreign Office that 'Ian Fraser-Ross' be exchanged for an Austrian, Eugen Malcher, interned at Pietermaritzburg, South Africa. Bernard's altered name was likely due to doubts that a plea made on behalf of an ex-prisoner of his record would be kindly looked upon. As it happened, the exchange offer was unsuccessful.

Prisoners who were fortunate enough to have private means found that their resources, even when supplemented with food parcels, quickly began to erode, particularly as wartime inflation rose. The following year, still in Baden, Bernard appealed for relief funds.

Edmund managed to get some parcels to Bernard via the American Embassy in Vienna, where Bernard had friends. However, by November 1916, Bernard was writing that he needed clothes and boots, and that he hadn't seen white bread, butter or cheese for some months, and could only get milk with a doctor's order. By that period in the War it was hardly an uncommon complaint.

One of Bernard's sisters visited an American Express office in

London, but was told that sending any packet to a British subject in enemy countries required a permit from the Foreign Office. Edmund therefore wrote to Lord Newton,* the Secretary of the Prisoners of War Department, whom he apparently knew. Newton informed him that he couldn't help: it was settled government policy, administered by the Postal Censor, that parcels were only permitted to be sent to military and civilian prisoners of war. Bernard was classed as a mere confinee – still permitted to wander within a restricted distance of his allotted residence. His dairy produce was not forthcoming.

Later in 1916, the British Government made another exchange offer for Bernard. This time the suggested person to be traded was Lieutenant Guido von Georgevits, an Austro-Hungarian subject who'd had the bad luck of being arrested on the Orkney Islands – possibly while admiring puffins. One would think the Austro-Hungarian Government would have jumped at the opportunity to exchange a lieutenant for an ageing Society roué, but not since the declaration of war, or even before it, had it been thinking rationally. This tempting offer was also turned down.

In January 1917, Edmund Fraser again wrote from 14 Chester Street to Lord Newton. Addressing him as "Dear Newton," he stated that he'd received a postcard from Bernard saying he'd been moved from Baden to the village of Kautzen, and that the Austrian government had accepted a British proposal to exchange civilians over the age of 51. "Please let me have a line as to whether this arrangement is now complete." Edmund also complained that the Austrians were withholding Bernard's correspondence:

> I believe it must be on account of the lying publication about British ill-treatment of civilian & other Prisoners of War, by that dirty little squirt Albert Mendsdorf.†

Edmund received a reply on behalf of Newton, who presented his compliments, and stated of Bernard's present situation:

> Kautzen is not an internment camp but a confinement station. The confinees have to report twice daily to the police, but have

---

* Thomas Wodehouse Legh, 2nd Baron Newton (1857–1942) of Lyme Park, Cheshire.
† Count Albert von Mensdorff-Pouilly-Dietrichstein (1861–1945), Austrian diplomat and former ambassador to Great Britain.

the liberty within the limits of the village and for a distance of 2 kilometres from the village on any road. They are also free to use the restaurants and public-houses at stated times in the day.

Compared to other Prisoner of War hardship cases the Department was dealing with, this no doubt seemed to them an idyllic circumstance of little pressing urgency. However, the letter stated:

> it is hoped that an agreement for the repatriation of Austrian and British civilians over 51 years of age may be concluded at no very distant date.

In May 1917, Harry Brittain,* the Director of Intelligence of the National Service Department, also wrote to the Prisoners of War Department in the hope of expediting Bernard's repatriation, stating that a postcard had been received from 'Mr. Fraser Ross' reading as follows:

> I am still a prisoner of War in Austria, as our English Government will not trouble to make any arrangement about exchange of civil prisoners – all the Frenchmen of my age have long ago left. I have been for nearly two years in Baden, near Vienna, but have now been sent to this little place as I am not allowed to live in my own shooting-box, as the Tryol is in the War-zone. Herr Jan Fraser Ross [presumably a mistranscription of Ian]

Brittain added "I do not know Mr. Fraser-Ross personally, but made the enquiry on behalf of a mutual friend."

The same month Edmund wrote again to Lord Newton requesting an update on the negotiations, and complained once more of Austria delaying Bernard's correspondence. With regard to German submarine warfare in the English Channel supposedly suspending repatriations, in a rather dictatorial manner Edmund wrote:

> I would remind you that in the case of my brother…the shipping arrangements would not concern his individual case, because he

---

* Sir Harry Ernest Brittain (1873–1974), journalist and Conservative M.P. Married Alida Luisa Harvey, and secondly, Muriel Leslie Dixon.

only wants to get as far as Switzerland.

On behalf of Lord Newton, the Prisoners of War Department replied to the letters of both Brittain and Edmund stating that "the Austrian government have not replied to our last proposals…In the meantime, I am afraid there is nothing which we can do to help him." This was far from the truth, as an internal memo detailed:

> I am afraid that Lord Newton's reply to Mr. Ross is not quite accurate. The position is that we have been waiting for about 5 weeks to get an answer out of the HO [Home Office] on which to base our reply to the Austrians.

This information irritated the operational head of the Department, Robert Vansittart,* who sat under Lord Newton. He wrote internally:

> It is annoying that an inaccurate letter sh[ou]d have gone out from this Dept. I think we had better let well alone & not correct it now to Mr Brittain. (I signed the one to Mr. B[rittain] & Lord Newton the one to Mr. Fraser & both are inaccurate.)

However, Vansittart had second thoughts, and wrote again to Brittain and Edmund Fraser apologising for the previous inaccuracy, and that:

> The position is that we have recently replied to certain enquiries made by the Austrian Government on points of detail, and I hope that the agreement will be concluded at an early date.

It was still a fudged answer. In late September, Edmund's family were informed that the Germans had sent Bernard back to Gmunden. Edmund fired off a four page letter to Lord Newton, stating:

> it seems rather hard on my brother, who does not want to cross the Channel at all…that he should be personally held back, merely because other individuals cannot cross the Channel.

Edmund suggested that the Department should be expediting the freeing of prisoners who merely wanted to cross the border. No one

---

* Robert Gilbert Vansittart, 1st Baron Vansittart (1881–1957), known as Sir Robert Vansittart between 1929 and 1941; diplomat, civil servant, poet, novelist and playwright. Married Gladys Robinson-Duff Heppenheimer, and secondly, Sarita Enriqueta Ward.

likes being told how to do their job, and Edmund's suggestions did not go down well in Whitehall. An internal memo stated: "Say we are not prepared to make special arrangements". Newton, who had a reputation for disparagement and had clearly had enough of Edmund's badgering, replied: "Please have a letter written to him accordingly. He is a disagreeable brat."

"The Secretary of the Prisoners of War Department presents his compliments to Mr. Edmund Fraser..." began the subsequent anodyne letter, which diplomatically apprised him of the information that:

> Lord Newton does not, to his regret, think it possible to make arrangements for the earlier repatriation of any special persons from Austria in advance of that of the main body of British civilians.

It was a classic insincere Civil Service brush-off. Only with the cessation of hostilities in 1918 was Bernard able to travel to Switzerland. Whatever the level of discomfort he'd endured, the length of internment would have been debilitating, and further impacted on his physical and mental health. Like the interned soldiers, some civilians also experienced mental breakdowns due to what was termed 'barbed wire disease'.

Bernard was now in his fifties, and English and certainly Austrian winters had become too chilling for even his Scottish bones. He now sought a locale that would not just warm them, but renew his battered soul. Like others of his kind, he found his nirvana in Algeria – temptingly exotic, but with its large colonial population, reassuringly civilised and familiar. He knew the country well, having jointly owned the winery there with de Kergariou. There were also strong familial links. A maternal uncle, Robert Farquhar Webster, was a Major-General in the Bengal Army who'd retired to Algiers, and died there in 1889. A maternal aunt, Agnes Ranken Webster, was the wife of Colonel Sir Lambert Playfair, Consul-General for Algeria, whom Cyril befriended in 1894. In addition to Murray's handbook to Algiers & Tunis, Playfair authored *The Scourge of Christendom*, a rollicking account of the Barbary pirates of Algiers.

However, of books about Algeria, none was more read than Ouida's* romantic novel *Under Two Flags* (1867). Its beautiful dandified hero, the Hon. Bertie Cecil, who is forced into exile in Algiers, and whom Bernard perhaps identified with, is described as "languid, nonchalant, with a certain latent recklessness," and "more luxuriously accommodated than a young Duchess". Ouida also described, "the Mediterranean so softly lashing with its violet waves the feet of the white, sloping town." Less romantically, a Thomas Cook guidebook of the period pronounced in a brigadier manner that brooked no contradiction:

> Algiers is not only a healthy resort for the consumptive and for the dyspeptic, but there is not a healthier, brighter place between the Gut of Gibraltar and the Dardanelles.

Henry Spencer Ashbee, the likely author of the Victorian pornographic classic *My Secret Life*, who visited in 1885, was equally impressed, describing it as a "pleasant, picturesque, & well-ordered town" under its French administration. This was in contrast to the Arabs, whom he considered "inherently stupid," fanatical, uncivilised and decadent, and whose cruelty to animals appalled him.

On their annual spring cruise in 1905, King Edward and Queen Alexandra had dropped anchor in its waters, it being reported that: "The very considerable English colony of Algiers was assembled near the quay, and raised hearty cheers as their Majesties landed." Other distinguished visitors to Algiers included Queen Victoria's daughter Princess Beatrice and her son Prince Leopold who, as a haemophiliac, had been advised by doctors to avoid the rigours of an English winter until he had at least passed the age of twenty-one.

An enthusiastic promoter of the health-preserving virtues of Algiers was Dr. Alfred S. Gubb, who detailed its delights in 1909. Of Mustapha Superieur, the hillside where the English colony tightly clustered, he wrote:

> It consists of a number of hotels distributed among residential villas, more or less spacious buildings of Moorish architecture,

---

* Maria Louise Ramé – 'Ouida' (1839–1908), popular English romantic novelist. Even Queen Victoria was a fan.

each standing in its own grounds and half buried in verdure, orange trees laden with their luscious fruit, pepper trees with their graceful trailing branches...Roses clamber up the walls mid-winter and various flowering shrubs contribute their splashes of vivid colour...Mustapha is most comfortably reached in an open carriage. Its slow progress up the hill enables the visitor to appreciate the unrivalled panoramas that unfold themselves as one proceeds upwards. At every turn of the road – and they are many – the view sweeps over the bay and the picturesque harbour, resting at length on distant snow-clad mountains that close in the horizon. Anon a Moorish villa is seen from its embowerment of trees...The sun beats down on the toiling horses, and bathes the whole landscape in summer sheen, the azure sky above being reflected in the Mediterranean, making a blaze of colour difficult to match anywhere.

On an adjoining slope of looping streets named for nut and fruit trees, was the Rue des Bananiers.* Here Bernard acquired a villa, one of the modest but spectacularly situated homes which, in the words of one resident, felt like "a kind of balloon-gondola suspended in the brilliant sky over the motley dance of the world". Every autumn Bernard exchanged the pure mountain air of the Bregenzerwald for the sensual zephyrs of North Africa.

The English expatriates of Algiers tended to keep to their own, rather than mingling with the teeming population, which as Dr. Gubb described, consisted of:

> half-a-dozen races and innumerable subdivisions thereof, each with its distinctive attire. The stately Arab with tawny skin, the veiled woman with bolster like legs and ample white investments, the Nubian porter, and heterogeneous collection Moorish Jews, Italians, Maltese and Spanish...The tourist naturally prefers to remain in the vicinity of the native town, the Kasbah, which provides an inexhaustible field of investigation in its narrow, tortuous, steep streets, through which a constant stream strange figures make their way to and fro. Crowds of impish children with swarthy skin and bright eyes dart hither and thither.

---

* Now the unrecognisable Rue Bouchareb Tayeb, a continuation of Rue des Oliviers.

Bernard also spent time in Blida,* the small town at the foot of the Atlas Mountains, south of Algiers, whose scenery and moderate climate made it an enticing destination for monied European travellers and invalids; the barracks of three thousand soldiers further adding to its pleasures for some. In his guidebook, Sir Lambert Playfair extolled its springtime virtues:

> the air for miles round is perfumed with the scent of orange blossoms…the environs are a succession of the most exquisite gardens, the roads are well shaded with trees, and there are charming promenades in every direction.

Here Bernard befriended Belotte, the owner or a servant of the coffee house 'Chalgo', where presumably he whiled away many happy hours. Bernard also dabbled in painting, and for the purposes of a studio purchased a five bedroom house with stable and sheds that sat on 28 acres at Cherchell,† a coastal town renowned for its ancient ruins, on what was then colloquially known as the Algerian Riviera.

Even if his British compatriots were unaware of his past, evidence suggests Bernard held a dim view of most of them. That said, it's difficult to imagine that anyone so previously sociable and popular in London, completely eschewed their company. As one visitor recorded, "The English afternoon tea and tennis receptions are delightful, in gardens luxuriant". Yet Bernard would have been rightly cautious. The less they knew of him, the better – especially in an expatriate colony where everyone tended to know everyone else's business.

He was far from alone in seeking to be discreet: Algeria played host to a stream of distinguished-looking gentlemen drawn by a reputation beyond that of scenery and a cosy climate. Like all the regions of the Mediterranean, Algeria was noted for the ready availability of its boys. For the sexually transgressive, it was a Mecca.‡

ÆElgeria! Sweet creation of some heart

---

* Then spelt: Blidah.
† Then spelt: Cherchel.
‡ For a history of homosexuality, and particularly pederasty, in the Middle East and its impact on the West, see: Joseph Allen Boone, *The Homoerotics Of Orientalism*, Columbia University Press, 2014.

Which found no mortal resting place so fair
As thine ideal breast

So proclaimed *Childe Harold's Pilgrimage*, Lord Byron's epic poem in which a disillusioned outcast seeks distraction in foreign lands. As the carefully coded correspondence of Byron and his Cambridge friends John Cam Hobhouse and Charles Skinner Matthews makes clear, it was the private shared dream of illicit sodomitical adventure on Mediterranean shores that occupied their fantasies.*

The feminist Frenchwoman Hubertine Auclert, who spent four years in Algeria between 1882 to 1892, blamed its widespread homosexuality on polygamy, writing:

> These primitive beings should not be accused like ultra-civilised people who look to pederasty as a refinement of debauchery. If they resort to unnatural means of satisfying their amorous instincts, it is because the polygamists make a clean sweep and cause a dearth of women.

Somewhat more romantically, in the explicit essay 'Social Conditions –Pæderasty' that appended his 1885 translation of *The Arabian Nights*, Sir Richard Burton had propounded the existence of what he termed a 'Sotadic Zone' which stretched across the globe:

> bounded westwards by the Northern shores of the Mediterranean (N.Lat.43°) and by the Southern (N.Lat.30°)…Within it the Vice is popular and endemic…[and] prevails through all the old regencies of Algiers, Tunis and Tripoli, and all the cities of the Southern Mediterranean

---

* On the eve of Lord Byron's first departure from England, he more openly wrote to a friend who was a master at Harrow: "I have laid down my pen, but have promised to contribute a chapter on the state of morals, and a further treatise on the same to entituled [sic] 'Sodomy simplified or Pederasty proved to be praiseworthy from ancient authors and modern practice.'" This was a joking allusion to a notorious pamphlet of homosexual advocacy *Ancient and Modern Pæderasty Investigated and Exemplify'd*, written in 1749 by Thomas Cannon, a son of the Dean of Lincoln. Given his intense interest in its subject, Byron was clearly fully aware of the publication. It forthrightly stated: "Unnatural Desire is a Contradiction in Terms; downright Nonsense. Desire is an amatory Impulse of the inmost human Parts: Are not they, however constructed, and consequently impelling, Nature?" [Louis Crompton, *Byron and Greek Love*, Faber & Faber, 1985, p127; Thomas Cannon, Hal Gladfelder (ed.), 'The Indictment of John Purser, Containing Thomas Cannon's Ancient and Modern Paederasty Investigated and Exemplify'd', *Eighteenth-Century Life*, Duke University Press 2007, Vol 31, No. 1, pp39–61.]

seaboard.

There was definitely something in the warm and fragrant Arabian air that was liberating to the senses. General Lamoricière, one of the conquerors of Algeria, is quoted as having stated: "There [in Africa] we were all pederasts."

The popular and widely circulated North African photographs of photographers such as Rudolf Lehnert and Ernest Landrock, which featured romantic landscapes, peoples, and erotic female and male nudes (often posed in a manner more to appeal to European fantasies than reflect cultural realities), captured imaginations and drew new travellers to the region, eager to taste its delights.

Touring Algeria in 1895 with Lord Alfred Douglas, Oscar Wilde wrote flippantly to Robert Ross: "The beggars here have profiles, so the problem of poverty is easily solved." By the time Wilde arrived in Algiers, some of its youths had become well-rehearsed experts in propositioning European men for their own advantage, as writer and trader John Stuart-Young[*] recalled: "I have sat in the blazing sunshine at Algiers while cupids in bronze, dressed in nondescript garments of yellowing gauze, have shamelessly offered themselves *pour l'amour au rebours.'*[†]

Another traveller was André Gide,[‡] who was both shocked and thrilled to see Oscar Wilde's name in a hotel guestbook. They had met before in Paris. Wilde was contemptuous of the young Gide's bourgeois moral rigour and conformity, and sensing his repressed homosexuality, was keen to use it as a means of ripping open his straightjacket. Gide was equally aware and terrified of Wilde's intentions, describing him to his mother as "the most dangerous product of modern civilisation". And so it came to pass one evening that Wilde lured Gide to a café in the casbah of Algiers. Recalled Gide in his autobiography:

> in the half-open doorway there suddenly appeared a marvellous

---

[*] John Moray Stuart-Young, born John James Young (1881–1939), poet, memoirist, novelist and wealthy palm oil trader. [See: Timothy d'Arch Smith, *Love In Earnest*, Routledge & Kegan Paul, London 1970, pp202-219; Stephanie Newell, *The Forger's Tale: The Search for Odeziaku*, Ohio University Press, 2006.]

[†] For love in reverse, i.e. buggery.

[‡] André Paul Guillaume Gide (1869–1951), French author.

youth. He stood there for a time, leaning with his raised elbow against the door-jamb, and outlined on the dark background of the night.

The youth joined them; his name was Mohammed; he had a reed flute and began to play.

> The song of the flute flowed on through an extraordinary stillness, like a limpid steady stream of water, and you forgot the time and the place, and who you were and all the troubles of this world.

Wilde took Gide outside and asked him what would prove a transformative question: "Dear, would you like the little musician?". After a moment, Gide managed a strangled "Oui". Laughing all the way back to the hotel, Wilde arranged the assignation that broke the dam of Gide's desire.

Edith Wharton,* who also enjoyed unbuttoning straightlaced young gentlemen, knew exactly the place to take Henry James's acolyte Percy Lubbock,† whisking him to Algiers in 1914. In no time at all, Percy had mailed to a friend a postcard (sealed in an envelope) of nude Arab boys with the inscription, "The disconsolate are beginning to enjoy the distractions of travel."

In February 1919, Bernard Fraser's mother Susan died at the family home in London. She left an estate of £4,455, but as was obvious from Bernard's spending, her children had already been well provided for. Susan had endured the public shaming of her son, and of the family name, but that pain had not altered her love for Bernard. She had known she was dying, but her will, made eleven days before her death and witnessed by her maid and a nurse, makes her unchanged affections expressly clear in the fair division of her assets to her children:

> The contents of the smaller silver plate chest to be divided equally among my 4 sons Edmund, Oliver, Henry and Robert,

---

* Edith Wharton (1862–1937), wealthy American novelist and short story writer. One of the many lovers of Morton Fullerton.
† Percy Lubbock (1879–1965), essayist, critic and biographer. Contracted a marriage of convenience with a daughter of the 5th Earl of Desart.

my son John Bernard to receive £200 pounds instead.

Perhaps Bernard hadn't wanted it. In any case, she requested that all the other silver plate, and non-specified pictures and portraits were to be divided equally amongst her eight children, and of special bequests, Bernard was to receive four silver salt cellars. The furniture and linen were bequeathed to her daughters; her books to the antiquarian Edmund; and of additional monies, £1,000 to Robert, "who has had less than the rest."

With his mother's death it would be understandable if Bernard felt the hand of time. It may have spurred him to make one more bold grab at life. In that same year or thereabouts, Bernard Fraser had his own fateful meeting with a flute-playing boy named Mohamed. His full name was Mohamed Ben Saïd Iguerbouchène, and in Algeria he would eventually become its most lauded and fabled composer. His exotic Berber surname would be spelt in many permutations.* What is immutable is that the boy's encounter with Bernard had extraordinary consequences.

In the 1930s, an Algerian journalist and film director André Sarrouy published three interviews with Iguerbouchène, who was by then an emerging talent. The articles appeared in a local magazine, *L'Afrique du Nord Illustrée*. Together with a newspaper interview conducted in the 1950s by another Algerian journalist, Kamel Bendisari, they have provided what has been, until now, almost the only information about Iguerbouchène's early life, and have formed the foundation of his cultural myth. Sarrouy wrote lyrically, even romantically, of the young artist:

> It would be difficult to sketch the profile of this grand adolescent who has retained in the intonations of his voice a spontaneous candour and a delicious naivety. He ignores the coquetry, the preciousness, and flattering attitudes which are the essential trait of second-rate artists. He talks about himself without exaggeration, with a frankness never concealed. His whole personality is entirely dominated by his gaze, which is both dreamy and bright, and dark and nostalgic as an autumn

---

*Including Iguerbouchen, Igherbouchène, Iquerbouchen, Igarbouchen, Igerbucen, Ygerbouchen, Ygerbuchen, Yguerbuchen, and Yguerbouchen. The prevailing spelling here is what is now most commonly used.

landscape…I would add his smile, so full of gentle kindness and childlike grace.

Iguerbouchène confessed to Sarrouy: "When I write music, I am in such a state of excitement that I have fever. Sometimes I cry too…it might be better not to say it!"

The truth of Iguerbouchène's early life and relationship with Bernard Fraser has been garbled, embroidered, and whitewashed, both unintentionally and intentionally, including by Iguerbouchène himself. The "spontaneous candour" and "frankness never concealed" that so impressed Sarrouy may have existed in private. What Iguerbouchène shared with the public was another matter. Several of the repeated 'facts' about his early life fall apart under even the slightest scrutiny. Yet this falsified history has been accepted at face value by Algerian writers. One such journalist admitted:

> To evoke his name and the work he has left for posterity generally provokes shaking of the head and raising of the eyes to heaven. And for good reason! Of Mohamed Iguerbouchène we know very little.

In Algeria, rumour, suspicion, and irrationalism are a part of everyday life. An expatriate memorably phrased it to this author as: "The moment a window is opened, Truth flies out." Supporters of Iguerbouchène's legacy often make preposterous claims, adding to the dissembling that Iguerbouchène himself engaged in. Ever present in his consciousness would have been the paramount precept of his culture: family honour, and the horror of bringing shame upon it. As the protégé of a formerly imprisoned pederastic procurer, Iguerbouchène had every good reason to disguise the story of his youth. "The life of Iguerbouchène is a fairy tale," one Berber official has been quoted as saying, "if you follow his path, you will be fixed on his exceptional destiny." What follows is a necessary disentangling of the truth from that fairy tale. The real story is a far more interesting and human one.

Of at least one previously retailed fact we can be certain: Iguerbouchène was born on the 13th of November 1907 in northern Algeria, the eldest of eleven children. He told Sarrouy:

The day I was born, it was snowing. Kabylia, where I come from, was all white. It is, moreover, in this stirring landscape of vast biblical solitudes, I spent all my childhood. I still remember being wrapped in my little 'burnouss' [a hooded cloak] of wool, running after the lost sheep of the herd and playing folk tunes on a reed flute in the shade of the fig trees.

The Kabyles are an ethnic sub-group of the Berber people. Life in Kabylia was mostly one of austerity and poverty. The modest home of the Iguerbouchène family overlooked a rugged valley. Almost destitute they may have been, but in addition to their own traditions, culture, and language – an identity they were fiercely proud of, Kabyles held a singular advantage. Under the French colonial administration they represented an indigenous elite. In the same manner as the European colonists, they were deliberately favoured over Arabs in education and employment as part of a 'divide and rule' policy. It was believed the measure of European blood they carried made a positive difference in character so profound, the policy was also necessary if the country was not to stagnate. As Sir Lambert Playfair phrased it in 1890:

> In almost all their essential characteristics the Kabyles are the very opposite of the Arabs…the Kabyle character lends itself more readily to social progress than that of the Arab: he is less distrustful, more industrious, and less disposed to that life of lazy indifference which is characteristic of the latter.

Seeking better prospects, Iguerbouchène's parents[*] relocated to Algiers, and the bright, vibrant city made him hungry to learn – as he put it: "to closely know this beautiful and generous French civilisation". It was here that Iguerbouchène acquired his taste for music. Algiers had a thriving musical culture: it was proud of its opera and home-grown minor composers like Raoul de Galland and Eugène Hovelacque, whose delicate and romantic melodies captivated its French citizenry. Mohamed could not afford a seat at a theatre, but was able to enjoy the summer orchestral concerts then held in the city's Square Bresson.[†] There, three times a week in front of the picturesque bandstand, he lived what he called:

---

[*] Saïd ben Ali and Sik Fatma bent Areski. (Occasionally spelt 'Arezki'.)
[†] Now Square Port Saïd, and a shadow of its former colonial self.

the most beautiful dream...I loved music. I will say more. I understood her. But I would never have dedicated my life to it, if I had not had the opportunity to meet on my way Mr. Bernard Ross.

He went on to explain:

Mr. Ross was a Scottish seigneur who regularly came to Algeria every year to shelter his fragile old age from the cold and the northern mists.

While Iguerbouchène referred to Bernard as both a plain monsieur and a seigneur – no doubt in reference to the Frasers being lairds, like Chinese Whispers, Bernard metamorphosed in later Algerian and French accounts (including Algerian Government publications) into "a rich and powerful lord" who was called Lord Fraser Ross, Earl Ross, Count Ross, or even 'Roth'. In one account he is a commander; in another, he is gifted with a wife. Adding to the confusion, the leading French-language Algerian newspaper *El Watan*, would inform its readers that "Count Roth...was a rich and noble Englishman who met the young Iguerbouchen with the painter Ross."

Iguerbouchène briefly detailed to Sarrouy the circumstances of their first meeting:

He noticed me during an audition given by the young natives of the English school which was then located in Algiers, in the Rue du Croissant, which I attended assiduously. Immediately, he took me under his tutelage.

Another account has it that, while they met at the school audition where Bernard "detected the seed of the artist," the Scotsman maintained a painting studio in the Casbah, close to the Iguerbouchène family home. If true, he may have been aware of the boy before then. Whatever the case, according to Iguerbouchen, Monsieur Ross was:

A great lover of music, a personal friend of Professor Livinson of London, he soon proposed to my parents to take me with him to England. My father – as you might imagine – welcomed this request with a scepticism comparable to that of the French bourgeoisie of the last century, but he eventually accepted, seduced as he was by the distinction and the tone of sincerity of my future protector.

In an earlier 1931 interview with Sarrouy, Iguerbouchène was more circumspect, stating only that:

One day – I had just reached my fifteenth birthday – a London family, to whom I am immensely grateful, proposed to take me to England. I accepted.

While Iguerbouchène specifically states they met when he was fifteen, which would make the year 1922, and he told Kamel Bendisari he left Algeria in 1923, other Algerian accounts claim that Fraser adopted him as 'his spiritual son' when Iguerbouchène was just twelve, in 1919. Like any young man keen to make a good impression, under questioning Iguerbouchène may well have ratcheted up his age due to a reluctance to reveal that when taken to London he'd been a mere boy. This would also account for the dissembling in the 1931 interview, with its suggestion that the patronage derived from a family, rather than a lone bachelor.

In wooing Iguerbouchène's parents to agree to his proposal, Bernard dined several times at their home: a family memory remains of him stating it was the best couscous he ever ate. Of course it was! His desire to remove the gazelle-eyed Berber boy with chestnut hair from his home and family, and take him back to England for the sake of his musical schooling was also a most generous offer. Although perhaps not entirely surprising coming from someone who'd spent six years and two months incarcerated at His Majesty's pleasure for pederastic acts and procuring. Whether Iguerbouchène was a warm Berber replacement for Albert Collins and the Boss, or the offer was entirely altruistic, is unknown. The description of their meeting has the markings of a *coup de foudre* on Bernard's part. Certainly, without infatuated patrons the history of the arts would be far shorter.*

---

* A similar example is the minor poet and novelist Frederic Manning (1882–1935), who in 1898, at the age of fifteen, was taken from Australia to England by his tutor, the Rev. Arthur Galton (1851–1921), a fussy bachelor from the gentry, with whom he lived for two years. An ex-Catholic priest and scholar-aesthete, Galton was a friend of such homosexual luminaries as Lionel Johnson, Walter Pater, and John Addington Symonds. [See: *Frederick Manning: An Unfinished Life* (1989), and Vera Coleman, *The Last Exquisite: A Portrait Of Frederic Manning*, Melbourne University Press, 1990.]

As well as being musically precocious, Iguerbouchène may have been, like some of the boys of Algiers, streetwise beyond his years. Writing half a century later, the writer Tony Duvert* marvelled at the precocity and independence of the uncoddled boys of North Africa who roamed the streets at all hours: "Tough and cheerful...they owe their flourishing to others lack of concern...Playing the role of stray cats." Victor, Lord Churchill,† who was partly raised in Algeria, later wrote: "it was there my sex education was accomplished...the [notorious] street of the Ouled Naïl had turned out to be an unexpected gold mine for a kid who was blond and looked Anglo-Saxon."‡

For an Algerian newspaper in 1951, Sarrouy penned yet another version of the pivotal encounter, beginning with: "The history of Mohamed-Georges Iguerbouchen [sic] is both a miracle and a legend." According to this narrative, in Algiers the boy had led:

> a rather unexpected life: during the day, he went to school in the rue Montpensier; the evening, he sold newspapers in the street and, twice a week, he assiduously attended the lessons of a professor of music theory!

As to the moment of their meeting, Bernard was:

> on the spot, very deeply impressed by his lively intelligence. The Honorable Ian Bernard Ross, having no family, wasted no time in making a proposal to the father of Iguerbouchen, that of adopting, in a way, his son and taking him with him to England.

A surviving photograph of an elderly Bernard, posing in a kilt with a silver-topped cane, shows him to be strikingly thin. In 1919 he was

---

* Tony Duvert (1945–2008) French novelist and philosopher, defender of pedophilia, and critic of modern child-rearing.
† Major Victor 'Peter' Alexander Spencer Churchill, 2nd Viscount Churchill (1890–1973), journalist, soldier, socialist activist, actor, scriptwriter, and cowboy; twice married, the first time, at his mother's pressing, to a widow and spiritualist medium who was her lover. He spent much of his latter life in Morocco. [See: Viscount Churchill, *All My Sins Remembered*, Heinemann, London 1964; Robin Bryans, *The Dust Has Never Settled*, Honeyford Press, London 1992; also: Bryans, *Let the Petals Fall* (1993) and *Blackmail & Whitewash* (1996).]
‡ Churchill claimed to have earned pocket money acting as a tout for the 'Dancing Girl' prostitutes, so why his own looks mattered begs a question. Former male lovers complained his autobiography, *All My Sins Remembered*, was markedly forgetful. [e.g. see: David Herbert, *Second Son: An Autobiography*, Peter Owen, London 1972, p43.]

only fifty-three, but the double blow of prison and wartime confinement had prematurely aged him, and Iguerbouchène suggests he was in precarious health. Nevertheless, given Bernard's dominating personality, the relationship would have had a strong instructional basis, platonic or otherwise.

Perhaps Bernard had dipped into a novel then circulating in the homosexual demi-monde, *The Romance Of A Choir-Boy*. Its author was the schoolmaster-poet John Gambril Nicholson. The book's story details the passionate obsession of a young Anglican curate – the author's alter-ego – for a twelve-year-old country boy who possesses a beautiful singing voice, and whose life prospects he opens up through his sponsorship. Nicholson chose to close the story with a quotation from *Sister Teresa*, the novel by George Moore. It reads:

> physical intimacies are but surface emotions, forgotten as soon as they are satisfied; whereas spiritual intimacies live in the heart, they are part of our eternal life, and reach beyond the stars.

It was a sentiment the Rev. E.E. Bradford, ever-fructful, had also shared in his 1913 anthology *Passing the Love of Women*:

> Sweet trance will wake to sweeter truth,
> And lover yield to lifelong friend.

If Bernard's patronage was shaded more by earthly passion than transmuted desire, its legacy might be considered his redemption. For Iguerbouchène was to prove a prodigy. Without Bernard, that fire may never have been kindled.

So the little Berber arrived in England. It doesn't appear that either Bernard or Iguerbouchène resided in the family house in Belgravia. The 1921 Census only records Bernard's three unmarried sisters still resident there with a cook and maidservant. Similarly, the *Royal Blue Book: Fashionable Directory and Parliamentary Guide*, which annually catalogued the occupants of residences in the more fashionable precincts of the metropolis, only lists the 'Misses Fraser' throughout the nineteen-twenties. Iguerbouchène told Sarrouy:

> I then went to Norton College, London, where, without giving up music theory, I studied English, literature, Latin, and

philosophy. Having obtained after six months my diploma of music theory, my benefactors made me learn piano with the celebrated professor Livinson. I worked more than eight hours a day, under the direction of Mr. Livinson himself, successively deciphering the sonatas of Clementi, the sonatas of Mozart, of Beethoven and of Chopin.

Unfortunately for his account, despite determined searching by this author and archivists, no record of a Norton College for boys in London during the nineteen-twenties, or in the entire United Kingdom, has been found.* While many schools of the time were ephemeral in character, Iguerbouchène's claim is false. So why would he make it, and what was the truth?

Had Iguerbouchène been placed in a school, it would have exposed Bernard – with his notorious public profile and jail record – to the grave risk that questions might be raised over his relationship with the boy. And adolescents are never particularly good at maintaining cover stories. Private tutoring, particularly if the tutor or tutors were friends of Bernard's, would have been the far safer option. As Iguerbouchène was not only precocious, but something of a musical savant, it would have made this educational option easier, and given the evidence, it seems the more logical course of events. Also, if there was one thing about Bernard, he was controlling: keeping Iguerbouchène close to home under his eye, even if he wasn't under his sheets, would have been his preference. Iguerbouchène's college fib may have been a young man's boastful exaggeration, but it was more likely a deliberate cover story to blur the sticky truth of having been a Berber boy shacked up in London with a rich, predatory bachelor.

The music teacher whom Iguerbouchène claimed was a friend of Bernard, "the celebrated Professor Livinson," has hitherto also remained elusive in identification. Sarrouy mentions that Iguerbouchène had "a very pronounced accent," and the Kamel

---

* There was a school by that name operated by a Mrs. Laura Norton in Upper Kennington Lane, SE11, but it was for girls. A Norton College once existed in Luton in the nineteenth century, but it closed and the buildings and land were sold off in 1902. The current Norton College in Yorkshire was founded in 1963, and that in Worcester in 2010. A recent biography of Iguerbouchène published in Algeria even claimed that Norton College is now the Royal Academy of Music! However, the latter has only ever been known by that name since George IV granted its Royal Charter. Period sources consulted included the Post Office London Directory, the Public Schools Yearbook, and London trade directories.

Bendisari interview prints the name as 'Livingston'. A check of London trade directories of the 1920s reveals no record of music teachers bearing the name of Livinson (or Levinson), but a music professor and piano teacher with the name of Livingstone *did* exist.

The bachelor Alfred Livingstone Hirst (1874–1940) – he favoured his second name, was a church organist, pianist, composer, tenor, choirmaster, and author of several slender booklets, including *Counterpoint...For Beginners* (1897) and *Harmony in Eight Pages* (1911).* A heavily moustachioed Yorkshireman who sported a pinz-nez, he was a freemason, and organist for the Middlesex Grand Lodge.

This energetic multifaceted career provided Hirst with considerable means. He travelled extensively, visiting Iceland, Morocco and Jamaica, and resided at premium addresses, including 'Llandysilio' in Montpelier Road (now Row), Twickenham, one of finest Georgian streets in Greater London. During the First World War he lodged an appeal against undertaking military service on the grounds that the national interest would be better served by his current occupations, and it would cause hardship to his business obligations. Crushing the Kaiser with melody was certainly a novel hope, and Hirst seems to tick several boxes as the kind of wealthy, cultivated bachelor who would have been a friend of Bernard's.†

Famous he may not have been, but Hirst was an assiduous advertiser of his works and talents in the musical periodicals, where he was not above quoting his own reviews: e.g. "Mr. A. Livingstone Hirst sang the part of Death very effectively, infusing into his voice a tone fitted to the character" – *Richmond Times*." Not everyone was a fan. A review in *The Daily Telegraph* of three of Hirst's dance compositions was withering: "This composer does not, perhaps, write for the pianoforte as if to the manner born," while *Musical News* dismissed his suite, *Pampas Grass*, stating that it featured "some attractive ideas imperfectly expressed. The free use of semitones and weird

---

* Hirst may have maintained a teaching studio in Poets Rd., Fulham: the 1910 Post Office London Directory has a listing under the business partnership name of 'Livingstone & Cook, pianofte.mas'. Given his publishing ventures, there may also have been a share in a printing business, as another listing records 'Cook Alfred Livingston, printer' in Finsbury. [*Post Office London Directory 1910*, pp540; 618.]

† Hirst left his estate to a brother, and the spinster daughter of his housekeeper. While there is no evidence, it's possible she was his illegitimate daughter. [Hirst, Alfred Livingston: Probate Calendar, 1940.]

accidentals does not, *ipso facto*, spell modernism in writing."
Nonetheless, gentle praise for some of his other fancies for the piano
was forthcoming. The same periodical praised a piece for its
"delightfully barbaric flavour," while another review of *Pampas Grass*
noted that it was of a "florid character," but considered, "The
somewhat unusual chords and modulations which occur here and
there add to the pleasing effect." This employment of bold and
eclectic musical effects is notable in that it mirrors Iguerbouchène's
own later enthusiasms.

As a music lover, Bernard may also have known Isidore Pavia,* "a
Jewish Dr. Johnson," as his friend the theatre critic James Agate
described him. A child prodigy and polymath, Pavia made his début
as a pianist in London in 1890, and became, like Hirst, a minor
composer and author of a book on piano technique. Between 1909-
11 he also published a six-part article, *Male Homosexuality in England
with Special Consideration of London* for the German homosexual rights
organisation, The Scientific-Humanitarian Committee
(Wissenschaftlich-humanitäres Komitee), and together with the
Austrian barrister and homosexual rights activist Baron Hermann von
Teschenberg,† was responsible for German translations of the works
of Oscar Wilde.

It is commonly claimed, depending on which profile of
Iguerbouchène one reads, that he went on to study at London's Royal
Academy of Music, the Royal College of Music, or even one of the
predecessors of the Royal Northern College of Music.‡ However, no
Algerian writer has ever troubled themselves to enquire if such claims
were actually true. None of the archives of these institutions have any
record of him as a pupil – neither under his own name in any of its
derivations, or that of Fraser/Fraser-Ross. Such tales possibly began
with Kamel Bendisari quoting Iguerbouchène referring to "Professor
Livingston, of the Royal Academy of Music" – phrasing that could be
taken to imply it was the teacher's alma mater. However, given what
followed in the interviews, Iguerbouchène more likely meant to
deceive that it was his own. Sarrouy further recorded him as stating:

---

* Isidore Leo Pavia (1875–1945).
† Baron Hermann von Teschenberg (1866–1911).
‡ The Royal Northern College of Music incorporates the Northern School of Music (known
in the 1920s as the Matthay School of Music), and the Royal Manchester College of Music.
Enrolment records for the former survive, but only from the late 1940s for the latter. Earlier
examination papers do survive, and were also checked.

I left London after a stay of three years to make a long study trip to France, Italy, Switzerland and Germany... In possession of this important experience, I presented myself at the Austrian National Conservatory of Vienna.

Like Sarrouy, Bendisari then quotes him saying:

I continued my studies of harmony and counterpoint, and piano technique with Robert Fischof [*sic*] and Alfred Grunfeld,[*] both professors at the Vienna Conservatory.

However, the composer Alfred Grünfeld (1852–1924) taught piano not at the state academy, but at a private music school, the New Viennese Conservatory.[†] The pianist and composer Robert Fischhof (1856–1918) *did* teach at the State Academy,[‡] but only from 1884 until 1903. Moreover, he died when Iguerbouchène was only eleven.

If Iguerbouchène had been fifteen when Fraser took him to London, as he claimed, by the time he arrived in Vienna three years later, Alfred Grünfeld too would have been in his grave. It is only possible Iguerbouchène could have been taught by Grünfeld if he left Algeria at twelve. However, that Iguerbouchène could lie so boldly about Fischhof, does not encourage belief about Grünfeld.

After allegedly studying in Vienna, Iguerbouchène claimed to have travelled successively to Budapest, Berlin, Munich, Milan, Rome and Barcelona, "studying the great German Classics and Italian and the Spanish school." Wherever he did visit, it was certainly on Bernard's wallet.[§]

---

[*] In many Algerian publications, this has metamorphosed into 'Alfred Kronfeld'.

[†] Neues Wiener Konservatorium. Also known as the Neues Konservatorium für Musik. (Until 1931 the names were unofficial; the Ministry of Education objecting that they could lead to public confusion with the state Akademie.) The school closed in 1938. Its successor today is the Music and Arts University of the City of Vienna – Musik und Kunst Privatuniversität der Stadt Wien.

[‡] Originally called the Conservatory of the Society of Music Friends – Konservatorium der Gesellschaft der Musikfreunde. The common moniker of 'conservatory' would have lingered in common speech. After 1909 it became the Imperial Academy of Music and Performing Arts (k.k. Akademie für Musik und darstellende Kunst), and after 1919 the State Academy (Staatsakademie). Its successor today is the University of Music and Performing Arts, Vienna (Universität für Musik und darstellende Kunst, Wien).

[§] One aspiring composer Iguerbouchène may have encountered in Weimar Berlin's cosmopolitan society, who held similar interests in folkloric music, was Hans Helfritz (1902–

It has been stated by Iguerbouchène's biographers and supporters that his first public success was at a "grand concert" in Bregenz, Austria in June 1925. Here he supposedly presented two of his rhapsodies inspired by Algeria. At the time of the alleged concert, Iguerbouchène was just over seventeen-and-a-half years old, yet he would later tell Sarrouy: "At the age of 19, I wrote my first work: an Arabian rhapsody." Clearly, he was never good with dates.

As the story goes, the concert seduced music lovers and placed him on a public pedestal. However, any report of the said concert is absent from the cultural pages of the regional newspapers of the period, the *Vorarlberger Tagblatt* and *Vorarlberger Volksblatt*. Yet column space was found to report two calves falling into Lake Constance, and to complain about Jewish tourists "advancing to the last villages in the Bregenzerwald". The Landesarchiv Bregenz (City Archive) also has no record of such an event.* Iguerbouchène may have played the piano in Bregenz that month, but if so, the evidence suggests it was either at a private function, or a public one so insignificant it was not considered worth reporting.

In 1928, at the age of twenty-one, Iguerbouchène returned to Algiers to attend a family funeral. He stayed on, and was commissioned to write the music scores for a number of early sound dramatic films and documentaries, including some directed by André Sarrouy. In the same street that Bernard resided when in Algiers, he took a villa 'Mon Repos' – described by Sarrouy as a little Moorish house in the upper town which "so beautifully evokes the best canvases of Utrillo". Less serene was Iguerbouchène's relationship with his father, who entered into a legal fight with his son over extending the period of his guardianship. Whether it was due to reservations over Mohamed's maturity, money, or his friendships, is unknown.

On the 25th of August 1929, a worn out Bernard Fraser, ill beyond even the healing warmth of Algeria, died at the age of just sixty-three, at Northlands House in Southampton, a red brick country house that

1995). Like fellow composer Walter Spies (1895–1942), who left Europe in 1923 and became a painter and legend in Bali, Helfritz was a free-spirited homosexual, and was the first to record Bedouin songs in Yemen, as an explorer, travel writer and photographer.
* The authoritative reference *Musik in Bregenz: einst und jetzt* by Erich Schneider (Bregenz, 1993), also makes no mention of the performance.

had recently been converted into a nursing home. He may have become ill en route from Algiers: ironically, it was the same port city from where he'd attempted to flee England so many years before. Bernard was buried in Dean Cemetery – Edinburgh's most fashionable, in the Fraser family plot that is marked by a massive Celtic cross of granite.

The previous year, a wealthy Anglo-American scholar-philanthropist Edward Perry Warren* had privately published, in an edition of 50 copies, the third volume of *A Defence of Uranian Love*: a half-vellum and gilt-stamped magnum opus that championed the nobility of Athenian pederasty as one of the corporeal and spiritual graces of life. "There is now no heaven to shine over boy-lovers," Warren opined, "we are good citizens of a bad state." Bernard might well have wished the words chiselled for his epitaph.

Bernard's estate, valued at £9,650 gross (equivalent to well over half a million pounds today), was probated the following year. His will is worth quoting at length, not only for being his last testament, but because it is intensely personal – a gem of idiosyncrasy. Its demanding, pernickety instructions offer a clear view of Bernard's crotchety, indulged and forceful personality.

Witnessed in Austria on 21 December 1926, the will immediately suggests the testator may have had a somewhat chequered past. While signing himself as 'Ian Fraser Ross', it additionally records Bernard as "John Bernard Fraser-Ross otherwise Ian Fraser-Ross otherwise 'John (Ian) Bernard Fraser-Ross rue des Bananiers Algiers." His bequests begin:

---

* Edward 'Ned' Perry Warren (1860–1928), antiquities collector, poet and philosopher. A Boston Brahmin, Warren's contributions to scholarship (the Warren Cup in the British Museum takes its name from him) were for a long period ignored due to bigotry, but he was "the most important American collector and connoisseur of Greek art" of his time; "*the* leading philanthropic gentleman scholar," who laid the foundation for some of the great American public collections of Greek antiquities. Warren lived not far from E.F. Benson at Lewes House, East Sussex, with his partner John Marshall who, to Warren's distress, later married a Warren cousin. Although the Warren and Marshall Papers (previously held at the Sackler Library and now in the custody of the Ashmolean) were re-discovered in 1972, almost half a century passed before a proper indexing was undertaken. [Michael Matthew Kaylor (ed.), *The Collected Works & Commissioned Biography of Edward Perry Warren*, Masaryk University Press, Brno 2013, pviii; private information. See: David Sox, *Bachelors of Art: Edward Perry Warren and the Lewes House Brotherhood*, Fourth Estate, London 1991.]

> To Mohamed Ben Saïd Iquerbouchen of 'Mon Repos' rue des Bananiers Algiers and of No 57 Rampe Valle Algiers all my property in Algeria whether in house property or otherwise.

Bernard bequeathed Iguerbouchène a further £1,500 conditionally on his not marrying "a woman or girl of European birth whom I consider would only make him a bad wife and render him unhappy". He states that this was also the wish of his parents, who desired he marry a Muslim, blithely adding: "whether she become a christian will not matter provided her parents were mohamedans [*sic*]" However, he also reassures: "I do not wish to force this Mohamed Iquerbouchen to marry unless he wishes".

Bernard expresses the hope he will:

> gain a good position as an arab in the Bureau Arabe of Algeria or the Bureau Renseignement [Intelligence Service] in Morocco, and that he should now continue his studies in music (piano) and in Arabic, and if possible, become a Christian without losing his superior position as a respectable arab i.e. one that does not drink strong drinks and should Mohamed Iquerbouchen become an honest Caid or even Cadi [senior official or local governor] under the French government, I consider that better than being what most europeans are.

The scornful language suggests Bernard's scars remained raw, and that he harboured a deep resentment for the way his countrymen, and the Austrians and Germans, had treated him. He'd certainly had a gutful of their justice. In this vein he continued:

> I hope every encouragement will be given Mohamed Iquerbouchen to become a great musician, if only he will agree and understand the enormous advantage he would have with a British or French public if he would continually wear the dress of his country instead of our hideous European dress, and I hope that at no future time he will live in either Austria, Germany or German Switzerland.

Given the succession of swanky Parisian addresses Mohamed resided at, it's likely Bernard had already provided him with additional financial means. Bernard's will then details provisions for his own family. To his brother Henry he bequeathed the chalet in Austria plus its contents, or if Bernard had sold it prior to his death, £400 instead. His brother Oliver is gifted £300; brother Robert £100, plus the interest on half the residue of the estate. The capital of this half was to be divided: a quarter going to Mohamed, and a quarter to Bernard's nephew Alisdair "Ian Hugh" [*sic:* Hew Iain] Fraser, who was also bequeathed £100, Bernard's signet ring, and "rifles with telescopes, fishing rods, etc." Bernard's last family bequest is to his three spinster sisters Ada, Nellie and Florence, on whom he bestowed the other half of his residuary estate, equally divided. Whether the sisters bore Bernard some resentment for damaging their marital prospects, or were they resigned to their fate, was a secret they took to their graves.

Obsessively thought out, the will features one striking omission: it contains no mention or provision for Bernard's eldest brother, the bachelor diplomat Edmund Fraser. And this is despite Edmund's efforts on his behalf to expatriate him during the War, and the possible efforts he made, as a former barrister, during Bernard's imprisonment in England. Perhaps Bernard felt Edmund hadn't tried hard enough. Or maybe he believed that Edmund, with his specially commissioned personal crest and prestigious diplomatic career, considered him a dilettante (even a depraved one) who'd degraded the family name. Bernard may also have been jealous or contemptuous of Edmund for living what, on the surface, looks like a productive, if fussily cautious life. Alternatively, Bernard may have considered that, with a generous Foreign Office pension to look forward to, Edmund simply didn't need his support.

Even so, the fact the will didn't mention Edmund, or offer even the smallest bequest, suggests some degree of bad blood had developed between them. Perhaps it had grown out of the knowledge and mutual suspicion of sharing what was then a criminal sexuality. Edmund would live on until 1937, dying of a heart attack in The Grand Hotel, Vienna. For someone so meticulous in other matters, Edmund left no will, suggesting there was no one surviving outside the family he deeply cared for. His estate amounted to a very significant £26,186 for his executors and surviving heirs, those being his brother Oliver and sister Ada.

Bernard also made two small bequests to Algerians: one of £50 "to my friend Saïd ben Ali Iquerbouchen of 25 rue Bruce, Algiers" – who was Mohamed's father, and another of £50 to "Mohamed ben Kaurt, called Belotte, of the Cafe maure Chalgo, rue Coulouglie Blida, Algeria". Bernard also expressed the hope that Mohamed will ensure Belotte "is not destitute".

The gentleman whom Bernard describes as "my old friend the Vicomte Joseph de Kergariou," was also remembered. Then residing near Dinan in Brittany, Joseph had married during the War at the age of fifty-six; his bride, a fifty-year-old widower. Bernard bequeathed him £200 plus, most intimately, "my crystal toilet set of nine pieces with silver tops bearing initial 'K'. The question arises as to why someone as fastidious as Bernard was using a toiletry set engraved with an initial other than his own. It obviously suggests he was returning what had been a very intimate gift.

Lastly, there is another eccentrically phrased bequest of £100 to a "Gilbert Marie Jumean whose last address was at Hotel de la Post a Avignon (rue des Chevaliers)". Bernard asks if the Vicomte will "try to find an employ for said Gilbert, perhaps as gardener and cook, and try to prevent this said Gilbert from his weakness for strong drink which is the sole cause of his wifes[*sic*] having left him, her last address being Griste Jumean nee Ricard of the Cottage Les Andelys Eure." To a jaundiced eye, Gilbert smacks of ageing rough trade – a once florescent Gallic Boss.

Bernard requested his brother Henry (by then a retired colonel, who was living at the family home in 14 Chester Street, Belgravia), and the Vicomte Joseph, to be his executors and trustees, and failing either, "my friend Harold E.B. Boulton of the St James Club, London" – thereby calling in a very old favour. As the will makes clear, he was particularly concerned that his instructions with regard to Mohamed were followed through on. The probate record notes Bernard's address as "Villa André rue des Bananiers, Algiers, North Africa, formerly of Au, Bregenzerwald."

When the will was probated in 1930, journalists were tipped off to its peculiarities, and once again, for the last time, Bernard Fraser's name appeared in the press. Under headlines such as 'An Arab Protégé', newspapers in Britain, and as far away as Australia, published titillating reports regarding this bequest of "a fortune" to a young Arab by a gentleman, and the "curious instructions" pertaining to it.

In London's *The Sphere* magazine, Lady Drummond-Hay,[*] who penned 'An Intimate Causerie On Matters Of International Import' was compelled to observe: "Stranger than the vagaries of fiction-created eccentrics, are some of the provisions in recent wills."

Undoubtedly the reports raised eyebrows, possibly a few sniggers, and even perhaps some memories – including, if he ever saw the articles, with the then still-living Charles Thorold. Like Bernard, he too had travelled a long, long way to erase the past and forge a new life.

According to André Sarrouy, in the aftermath of Bernard's death Iguerbouchène "experienced immense grief" and "a period of depression which brought him back to Algiers." When it came to marriage, he met Bernard's desires halfway: his bride Louise Gomez[†] was Algerian-born, but a French national. Whether Iguerbouchène received any marital payment as specified in Bernard's will is unknown. However, Bernard's money certainly enabled the young composer to live the carefree life of a dilettante, as an artist friend Jean Berger-Buchy[‡] recalled:

> at that time, where we met as often at Lyon's Corner[§] of Piccadilly Circus as on the terraces of the boulevards, it seemed

[*] Grace Marguerite, Lady Hay Drummond-Hay, née Lethbridge, (1895–1946), intrepid journalist. At twenty-five she married diplomat and widower Sir Robert Hay Drummond-Hay, who was half-a-century older.
[†] Louise Melle Gomez (1913–?), born at Blida. It has been claimed Iguerbouchène's wife was Swedish, but no name or factual support has been furnished to support the claim. Louise may have been politically active, and met Mohamed through such activities. A 1938 report in the Oran newspaper of the Parti Populaire Français (PPF) records a Louise Gomez soliciting comrades for its youth wing. Founded in 1936, the PPF was fascist and antisemitic, and the most collaborationist party in France. After the malaise and disruption of the Depression, the shiny, brave new world of fascism, with its promise of order and certainties, appealed to those ready to ignore its brutalities, or view them as a necessary means to an end. Given Iguerbouchène's later political activities, it would have been a meeting of minds. However, the newspaper report possibly refers to another Louise Gomez (1909–1992), who was born at Oran, and at nineteen married Joseph (Jose) Dura, who was a despot, but only a domestic one. After the death in 1929 of their second child, a son, she left him, and a daughter, was raised by another woman. [Report: Iguerbouchen, Mohamed, Direction Générale de la Sûreté Nationale, 20 May 1946: 20100166/3: dossier n° 9091, Archives Nationales, Pierrefitte-sur-Seine; Mohamed Iguerbouchen dossier: n° 77W1751-104355: Les Archives De La Préfecture De Police, Paris; Relizane, *L'Oranie Populaire*, 4 June 1938; private information from Janet Martinez.]
[‡] Jean Berger-Buchy (1901–1976), newspaper cartoonist, journalist, painter, treasurer of the right-wing charity and recruitment organisation Algérie Française, and collaborator. [Joshua Cole, *Lethal Provocation: The Constantine Murders and the Politics of French Algeria*, Cornell University Press, Ithica 2019, pp218-219, 303,n21.]
[§] One of a chain of popular teashops.

that any desire for work overwhelmed him. The thought alone threw him into an unspeakable despondency. He immediately planned either a long trip to Vienna, or a few months of vacation, at home in Algiers. But he eventually gave it up, Montparnasse attracting him anyway, still preferring work to any idea of immigration.

As the years went on, Iguerbouchène gradually became an intensely prolific artist. The free-flowing form of the rhapsody, suggestive of improvisation, and often inspired by regional themes and folk music, was tailored to his eclectic musical passions, and one he excelled at. Music was also opening up to new global rhythms, including from America and Latin America, and possessed of an inexhaustible thirst for knowledge, he was influenced by them all. The result was musical compositions exhibiting a very modern melodic fusion of African, Arabic and western influences. Iguerbouchène also collaborated with a plethora of Algerian, North African, and Cuban artists whose careers he helped advance.

Bernard's faith in the little Berber had not been misplaced: Iguerbouchène's eventual commitment to his vocation more than realised the promise of his gift. He was now his own man. This included, as with many North Africans keen to advance themselves in *La France*, frenchifying his name. He now called himself 'Georges M. Iguerbouchen'. Despite this necessity, Iguerbouchène was deeply attached to his homeland of Kabylia, and its culture, including its folkloric melodies.

The popularity of 'Oriental cabarets' in Paris in the 1930s led Iguerbouchène to become the co-proprietor of a bar-restaurant and cabaret, 'El Djazaïr' ('Algiers' in Arabic), on the rue de la Huchette in the Latin Quarter. To gain the confidence of his backer, Aziz Chaldi, Iguerbouchène lied to him that Bernard's house at Cherchell, which he'd inherited, was worth more than seven times its true value. Twice in the 1930s the property was to be subject to expropriation sales. In 1935 it was listed at the starting price of 25,000 francs; in 1939 at 45,000 francs. Operating a nightclub can be a precarious business, but Iguerbouchène's financial difficulties may have been due to another reason. A French police intelligence report states that his father was a partner in the venture, and had Mohamed banned by the Algerian authorities due to his extravagance.

El Djazaïr would showcase many of the stars of the Arab world. Its regular singer was Salim Halali,* a pretty Algerian Jewish youth who was openly homosexual, and known as "the boy with a giant's voice". Iguerbouchène composed many songs for him, and his name appears on all the discs of Halali's early recordings.

Iguerbouchène was also active on Algerian radio. A program listing for 1936 notes: "During the concert, 'Considerations on the Origins of Oriental Music', by M. Mohammed Iguerbouchen."

In 1937, Iguerbouchène's work on film scores led to him being asked to provide Arabian-themed music for the French feature film *Pépé Le Moko*, to supplement its Western score of Vincent Scotto. This was a film noir about a jewel thief, played by Jean Gabin, who hides in Algier's Casbah. Mohamed's was the sole Arab name in the credits, where he was billed as 'Mohamed Yguerbouchen'. Writing in the magazine *Modern Music*, Paul Bowles characterised Scotto's contribution as "indescribably cheap symphonic interludes," but said Mohamed had saved the film score:

> It is certainly due to him that we have the exquisite background for the streets of Algiers' Casbah: a great brouhaha of native horns, Kabyle flutes and drums, together with sad lost wisps of *bal musette* tunes on the accordion…life in the Casbah *is* one long soundtrack like this.

The film was a smash hit, and the following year was remade in Hollywood (apart from some exteriors) as *Algiers*, starring Charles Boyer and Hedy Lamarr. The music score was reused and he was credited as 'Mohammed Igarbouchen'. He would go on to score other films. The soundtracks again demonstrate his ability to synthesise the rhythms and melodies of his country with those of Europe and elsewhere, and reinterpret them in a modern way.†

The year 1939 was a significant one for Iguerbouchène. In March he

---

* Salim (born: Simon) Halali, also Hilali and Hallali (1920–2005), French-Algerian singer.
† Iguerbouchène received an offer in 1937, from a Parisian impresario Arnold Meckel, to go to Hollywood. However, it was on the *proviso Pépé Le Moko's* director, Jean Duvivier, shot the remake there. Duvivier never got the job, and Meckel died suddenly a few months later. [Le Cinema, *L'Afrique Du Nord Illustree*, 1 December 1937, p16.]

made his performing début in Algiers as part of a grand gala. He also provided the background music for a Parisian-produced play – *South*, a story of gun smuggling set in Tangier. The Parisian periodical *Le Journal* thought the drama excellent, and wryly noted: "all the characters are men, and none of these men is even a pederast."

Even more significantly for Iguerbouchène's career, in June, BBC Radio played one of his Moorish Rhapsodies for the first time. He'd first approached the BBC the previous year, writing from a flatlet in Bayswater to request "an opportunity to present myself" while in London for a few days. In August 1938, the BBC wrote to invite him to a meeting, asked him to bring a few scores. An internal BBC memo from a music department employee states that he met with Iguerbouchène, and advises that his music is suitable for broadcasting; he also mentions that he attended a screening of *Pépé de Moko* to hear the score.

Following this introduction, in March 1939 the BBC Director of Music wrote to inform him that they would like to include a Moorish Rhapsody in a BBC program. Further letters from the Director, sent to his apartment at 10 Rue Saint Didier, a chic Art Deco block in Paris's wealthy 16th arrondissement, advise of the subsequent broadcast and express the hope he had heard it. (Contrary to claims published in Algeria, Iguerbouchène did not conduct the performance, nor was he invited to.) It has been said that some BBC listeners thought they had heard the work of a Russian composer, leading to further confusing bastardisations of his name, and that he was known as Igwer Bouchen, Igar Bouchen, and even Igor Bouchen.

On the 3rd of September 1939, Britain and France declared war on Germany. Eight years previously, Iguerbouchène had spoken to Sarrouy of "this beautiful and generous French civilisation". Since then, his time in France amongst expatriate Algerians had modified his opinions. As a relatively wealthy young man who mixed with a marginalised immigrant community, it was almost inevitable he would be courted by Algerian nationalists. Possessing a sensitive and high-strung artistic nature made him especially susceptible to bold and crusading opinions. Before long he was authoring anti-French songs. More than this, he became an ardent member of the nascent Algerian nationalist party, Parti du Peuple Algérien – the PPA, which, following outbreak of the War, was shut down by the French

Government due to subversion. It then became a clandestine group.

Algeria had unofficially become two nations with separate economies. The first belonged to the increasing number of French settlers who owned the finest agricultural land. The second nation was a subsistence one: that of the dispossessed and discriminated against Arab population. The infant mortality of the latter had been dramatically reduced by French medicine, but this had resulted in a massive population increase which its farms could not sustain. The pressure was partly offset by Arab immigration to France, but the growing hunger and resentment could not be bottled up forever. Algiers, where by 1931, settlers formed 69% of the population, was – apart from the casbah – its own enclave, but beginning in 1937, a succession of famines ravaged the countryside.

It may have been a series of articles Albert Camus wrote in the communist-supporting newspaper *Alger Républicain* about the starvation in Iguerbouchène's homeland of Kabylia that contributed to altering his attitudes to colonialism. The succession of riots between Jews and Muslims in the Algerian city of Constantine in 1934, and interventions by the French police, provided additional ferment for Algerian nationalists.

Some PPA members saw collaboration with the Germans as a means of furthering the cause of Algerian independence, and formed a breakaway group, the Comité d'Action Révolutionnaire Nord-Africain (CARNA), which included many Kabyles. They were not alone. Like the Grand Mufti of Jerusalem, large numbers of Muslims in France would collaborate with the Nazis. The reasons for this included the French colonial yoke, including the detested Code de l'Indigénat laws which accorded inferior legal status to the natives of colonies; the belief the Germans would provide self-determination in Algeria and Morocco; the British management of Palestine; and not least, sympathy with National Socialist ideology and its anti-semitism.* The sentiment was very much: the enemy of my enemy is my friend.†

---

* Even in the 1890s, a visitor to Algeria noted, "The hatred that exists between Arab and Jew is very marked". [Frederick Arthur Bridgeman, *Winters In Algeria*, New York, Harper & Brothers,1890, p43.]
† Because the Third Reich needed allies such as Egypt and Turkey, it was forced to split hairs and peddle the official line that its Aryan racial policy – the Nuremburg Laws – only applied to Jews, although in reality, men from those countries consorting with German women in Nazi Germany were imprisoned or deported. Iguerbouchène may have been more protected

Not all radicalised native Algerians agreed. When PPA leader Messali Hadj[*] learned of CARNA's Nazi collaboration he denounced its leaders and expelled them from the association. He also repeatedly refused invitations to collaborate. Such rectitude earned him a sentence of 16 years hard labour courtesy of a Vichy court. Risking their own lives, personnel of the Grand Mosque of Paris would also hide a number of Jews.

Mohamed Iguerbouchène had no such reservations. In fact, so enthused was he by the opportunities provided by the German invasion of France, that in late 1940 the Paris police opened a dossier on him. It reveals that even at this early stage of the War, he'd insinuated himself into the heart of the Nazi regime, and was residing in the plush comfort of the grand Hotel Lutetia on the Left Bank. The beautiful Art Nouveau establishment had been requisitioned by the Abwehr, the German military intelligence service, and was being used to house, feed, and entertain the officers in command of the Occupation.

Out on the streets, the lethal glamour and Teutonic virility of the conquerors was mesmerising other Parisians, more than they would later care to admit. Confessed one:

> What adolescent of my generation did not dream, even if only briefly and shamefully, of being a young, twenty-year-old SS soldier leaning on his tank, spreading butter on his bread with his dagger. Ten or so of us would just hang around to watch him and look intensely at the death heads on his uniform.

A December 1940 report in Iguerbouchène's file informs that then lodging with him was a close friend and comrade from the P.P.A., Abderrahmane Yassine.[†] It was likely he who secured their plush quarters. A Tunisian, Yassine was one of a number of educated North Africans who'd been selected by the Nazis to receive ideological training in Germany, in order that they might serve as propagandists

---

because one of the principal ideologues of Nazi racial policy, Alfred Rosenberg, considered Berbers to be Aryan – part of "the prehistoric Atlantic Nordic human wave". [Jeffrey Herf, *Nazi Propaganda For The Arab World*, Yale University Press, New Haven 2009. pp15-35, 151; Alfred Rosenberg, *The Myth of the Twentieth Century* (1930), Historical Review Press, 2004, p.7]
[*] Ahmed Ben Messali Hadj (1898–1974).
[†] Belhadj 'Yassine' Abderrahmane, alias 'Dr. Mourar', alias 'Quo Vardis' (1910–?).

for their home countries. By late 1939 he was already making broadcasts from Berlin. When the German troops marched into Paris in June 1940, like a happy bacillus, Yassine returned. Iguerbouchène's police file states that the two were engaged in "active propaganda...both in Paris and in North Africa" through other militants from the former PPA. Mohamed also had meetings with Messali Hadji, and received German soldiers at his home.

To further exploit Muslim discontent, and strengthen their support, the Germans established a large propaganda organisation for the Maghreb countries. Yassine was placed in charge, and to manage the Algerian division, he recruited Belkacem Radjef, a former PPA leader disavowed in 1939 by Messali Hadji, following his expression of pro-German opinions. Radio broadcasts targeting North Africa, in both Arabic and the Amazigh (Berber) language, were established, and Yassine recruited Iguerbouchène to manage the musical direction. Iguerbouchène also participated in various broadcast talks, and was reported to have engaged in surveillance of Muslim milieux. An October 1941 report in Iguerbouchène's police file states that there had been an apparently temporary moderation in his activities, "for fear, it seems, of later reprisals."

The Germans paid their puppets well. However, the double game the Algerians were playing – undermining colonialism and promoting nationalist interests while also serving the Nazi agenda, was a fractured ethical nightmare of opportunistic idealism. It was also dangerous. Although not as dangerous as being a Jew like Salim Halali, for whom Iguerbouchène had composed so many songs, and who was now enduring the War sequestered in Paris's Grand Mosque, passing as a Muslim.* As one Franco-Algerian psychoanalyst has written: "We are entitled to ask ourselves about the society that was going to be built by people ready to ally themselves with Nazis to achieve their ends."

By 1941, Iguerbouchène and his wife Louise had separated. A year later he was living with a woman he'd met at a radio show in Berlin, Yvonne Vom Dorp.† Born in a Prussian region of Belgium, her own

---

* Other Jewish North African musicians stranded in France, such as Gaston Bsiri (1882–1942), who died in Auschwitz, would not be so lucky.
† Iwane Irmgard 'Yvonne' Vom Dorp (1919–1995), née Axmacher. Born in Malmedy, Belgium, she married Karl Vom Dorp. The Eupen-Malmedy region was originally part of

marriage to a German had also broken down. Twelve years younger than Iguerbouchène, she was now working as a cashier at 'El Djazaïr', which had become a favoured meeting place for Algerian nationalists and the Germans. His police dossier fragrantly states: "Iguerbouchène and his concubine are domiciled in the Rue Saint Didier (16th arrondissement)." Like his previous addresses, it was one of Paris's best.

It has been alleged that years later, when in private, Yvonne Vom Dorp would talk of her and Iguerbouchène's visits to Germany, saying that they had been regular guests of the Führer, as he admired Iguerbouchène's music; but adding that she couldn't bear the situation, as when Iguerbouchène was absent on tour, Hitler flirted with her. This claim cannot be substantiated. No Nazi documentation of Iguerbouchène's activities in Berlin appears to have survived, but his name and that of Vom Dorp are absent from surviving documents and guestbooks for the Berghof, and Obersalzberg generally. In any case, his music was utterly contrary to what is known of Hitler's musical tastes.*

However, the Berlin gramophone disc label Bedaphone did feature Iguerbouchène's work, and with the Reich compromising its own racial ideology to butter up the peoples of the Maghreb in aid of the War effort, even those previously regarded as Untermensch were rubbing their shoes on the Reich Chancellery welcome mat. In National Socialism's finely graded racial hierarchies, the European stream in the Kabyle bloodline also counted for much. Given Iguerbouchène had made himself right at home at the Hotel Lutetia, swanning in Nazi Berlin perhaps felt like warm revenge on the France that had ignored him.

Germany, but annexed by Belgium in 1919 under the Versailles Treaty; in 1940 it was reintegrated into the German Reich, but was returned to Belgium in 1945.

* One of the more outlandish claims is that Iguerbouchène became the favourite pianist of Hitler. However, Hitler was more of an opera fan – as is well known, of Wagner. That said, pet pianist of the Fuhrer was a much-coveted accolade, for which others have far more claim, including Walter Gieseking, Wilhelm Backhaus, Wilhelm Kempff, and his press-chief Ernst 'Putzi' Hanfstaengl, who used to pound out Wagner for him in the early days. Pianist Elly Ney would dearly have wished to play for him, but possibly never realised her dream. Searches for Iguerbouchène in the Bundesarchiv proved fruitless. [For the claim, see: Bari Stambouli: Des lapins dans le bureau du compositeur, *Le Temps d'Algeria*, Algiers, 22 November 2009. For substantiated histories, see: Michael H. Kater, *The Twisted Muse : Musicians and Their Music in the Third Reich*, Oxford University Press, 1997; Peter Conradi, *Hitler's Piano Player*, Duckworth, London, 2005.]

In 1943, Iguerbouchène was embroiled in a major metal smuggling affair with the purchasing departments of the German occupying authorities. He had acted as an intermediary for Henri Farman,* of an Anglo-French family of aviators and industrialists. Remarkably, there was no judicial follow-up due to "the relocation of the prosecution witness," suggesting the case was suppressed.

The following year, a three-hundred-strong brigade of Arabs and Berbers joined the German fight against the French Resistance. However, as the War progressed, many Muslims came to oppose the Vichy government, in part due to Charles de Gaulle's efforts in Algeria to unite French Resistance movements, and institute legal reforms to the benefit of Muslims. The result was the participation of Muslim members of the Resistance in the battles of Paris in 1944. Between 200,000 and 250,000 Muslims also served in the French armies.

A few weeks before Allied troops rolled into Paris in August 1944, Iguerbouchène's old friend and fellow collaborator Jean Berger-Buchy† chanced upon him "casually strolling on the Champs-Elysées." They retired to a café to recall "happy and heroic" old times. As Berger-Buchy discovered, steady employment at the radio station had energised him:

> The good old days, where he could gently drag his African laziness around, are over. Work overwhelms him more than ever, he even seems to have taken refuge there with a sort of frenzy... We can only recognise him by his kindness and his usual courtesy.

> So a rehearsal for Radio-Mondial brought us to rue Christophe-Colomb and ended our meeting. I left him to his musicians. There, Isa Kyprianna,‡ for whom he is developing the music for a Hindu ballet, entitled *La Danse Devant La Mort*, was waiting for him, installed on a pile of record binders, slightly impatient and worried at the memory of his famous delays!

---

* Henri Farman (1874–1958), Anglo-French aviator and aircraft designer.
† Jean Berger-Buchy (1901–1976), French painter and press illustrator.
‡ A Russian dancer and actress.

Given the darkening situation for collaborators, Iguerbouchène's desire to bury himself in work is understandable. Upon the liberation of Paris, he took refuge in the apartment of a friend, Anne-Laure Sarreluis,* at 99 Boulevard Haussmann. When Sarreluis was arrested by the American military police, he fled the capital.

Wartime collaboration in France was vast, and following the Liberation came retribution. Most of the 38,000 individuals given prison sentences were released under a partial amnesty in 1947. Nonetheless, 6,763 persons (3,910 in absentia) were sentenced to death for treason and related offences, although only 791 of those sentences were carried out. A further 49,723 persons were sanctioned. In total, 350,000 persons were marked, but the lives and careers of the majority were not significantly affected. No one was punished for genocidal crime: that was imputed to the Germans alone.

Mohamed's alleged friend Edith Piaf,† herself half-Berber, was one of the many who now felt the sting of being branded a traitor. In December 1944, the directorate of the National Police was ordered to actively seek Iguerbouchène out. His dossier records he was the subject of many reports: "Speaking several foreign languages, he has made many trips abroad and especially in Germany," and was "a notorious collaborator and anti-French." Incriminating correspondence and photographs were also in police possession.

Yet despite the Court of Justice of the Seine being briefed on Iguerbouchène's violations, his case was eventually closed. A police intelligence file of 1946, with photographs of Iguerbouchène at various events attended by senior German officers, explained why. He "had benefited, during the Liberation, from the protection of a high official," and a hearing of his case was "likely to have repercussions of a very delicate character: this is the reason why new instructions are necessary."

Iguerbouchène's contacts included a strong defender in the form of André Meradji,‡ an Algerian-born lawyer at the Paris Court of Appeal

---

* Unidentified. Possibly Sarrelouis or Saarlouis.
† Édith Piaf, born Édith Giovanna Gassion (1915–1963), French singer-songwriter, cabaret performer and film actress.
‡ Arezki 'André' Meradji (1914–?), lawyer and Muslim advocate. Vice-President of the Circle of Education or 'Nadi Ettahdib', a group established in 1936 with the aim of continuing the intellectual, moral and social education of North African Muslims resident in France.

with militant North African clients. Characterised in intelligence reports as "a muslim fanatic," with a "pan-Islamic tendency," Meradji advocated on behalf of militants, and was in contact with PPA members and German officers. At the urging of Meradji, Iguerbouchène returned to Paris. According to another intelligence report, he then relied on his connections in the police and 'American circles'.

That Iguerbouchène had acted as an occasional informant for the Directorate General of Indigenous Affairs in Algeria, and as an agent of the Service des Renseignements de l'Artillerie – the SRA: a military intelligence service – may also have worked in his favour. Another who may have advocated on his behalf as a valued artist was Si Kaddour Benghabrit,* the rector of the Grand Mosque, who'd already saved the lives of hundreds of Jews like Salim Halali, as well as those of many resistance fighters.

Even Belkacem Radjef (so he later claimed) was not questioned by the police. (Only after the outbreak of the Algerian War would his collaboration be used to justify his arrest.) This indicates the power of connections, but also some nervousness on the part of the French authorities, in the unsettled post-War climate, about generating further hostility in the immigrant community. There were so many collaborationists, French nationals may have been the principal focus for the application of justice.†

By 1946, Iguerbouchène had commenced divorce proceedings, but allegedly Louise did not wish it, due to her desire for an annuity.

---

* Abdelkader Ben Ghabrit, commonly Si Kaddour Benghabrit (1868–1954), Algerian religious leader and first rector of the Great Mosque of Paris.

† The subject of collaboration with the Nazi regime remains a radioactive one in France and Algeria, and is rife with lies and dissembling. Some Algerian writers have erroneously claimed that Iguerbouchène was jailed by the French in 1944 for activism on behalf of Algerian independence. [e.g. Mohand Akli Haddadou, *Les Berbères Célèbres*, Berti editions, Algiers 2003, p165.] While also believing he'd been incarcerated, at least one Algerian scholar slapped down this revisionism, by writing: "Mohamed Iguerbouchene was not sentenced, towards the end of the Second World War, for "nationalist activity", as *El Watan* notes (16 November 2006), but for collaboration with Nazi propaganda." [Abdellali Merdaci, *Auteurs Algériens De Langue Française De La Période Colonial: Dictionnaire Biographique*, L'Harmattan, Paris 2010, p15, n12.] It has also been claimed that if it hadn't been for Iguerbouchène's status as a British subject, and the admiration in which his talent was held by many, he would have been executed. [Karim Kherbouche, 'Mohamed Iguerbouchen: une légende, une œuvre aux racines multiples', *Kabyle.com*, 21 October 2005.] However, Iguerbouchène didn't hold British citizenship (his name is absent from UK naturalisation records), and Bernard Fraser's distaste for his homeland's authorities would not have encouraged it.

Given his subsequent actions, any fears she entertained that financial support might dry up would have been legitimate. With Vom Dorp, Iguerbouchène went on to have five illegitimate children – two sons and three daughters. While indicative of his haute bohemian sensibility, even for the conditions of wartime and after, such a de facto relationship was then highly unconventional.

In 1947, Iguerbouchène decided to call it quits with 'El Djazaïr', and sold his share. His backer Aziz Chaldi had submitted a complaint about him to the licensing authorities, but the new owner was also forced to drag him before the law. After making several failed appeals, Iguerbouchène was ordered by a Paris employment tribunal to pay the outstanding wages of the cook – with interest.

Iguerbouchène remained financially comfortable, living in Paris with his growing family in an apartment at 6 Avenue des Gobelins, in the 5th arrondissement. However, despite his boundless musical talent and experience, the taint of wartime collaboration and his Algerian background ensured his compositions and conducting remained mostly confined to Arabic and Kabyle language radio broadcasts. Notable exceptions were the scores for two French films set in Algeria: the 1951 *Bim*, about two boys and a donkey, and the following year, *Heart Of The Casbah*, which returned to the world of *Pépé le Moko*. He also scored a documentary short on bodybuilders – *The Most Beautiful Man In The World*.

On the 1st of November 1954, guerrillas of the National Liberation Front, the FLN, attacked military and civilian targets throughout Algeria. It was the beginning of the War of Independence that would last for over seven years. Hoping to improve his prospects, in June 1957 Iguerbouchène returned to Algeria: he later claimed it was at the request of the country's future president Ferhat Abbas. Yvonne Vom Dorp and their children accompanied him.

As he had in Paris, in Algiers, Iguerbouchène composed, conducted, and presented radio programs of Arab and Berber music. At Beau Fraisier, a picturesque historic quarter* on the heights of Algiers, which had always been popular with artists for its glorious views, he purchased a villa. Here he entertained a wide circle, and it is claimed,

---

* Now part of the municipality of Bouzaréah.

628

also harboured political activists.

However, home life was not happy. Although Yvonne lived a relatively privileged existence, as both a German and a woman 'living in sin', she was not accepted in Algiers, and her reserve led Iguerbouchène's extended family to consider her haughty. Without friends or relatives, her only company during the long days were her young children and 'Galland', her German Shepherd. Adding to her isolation and loneliness, it is claimed that, just as Iguerbouchène had allegedly previously bedded Edith Piaf,* and fellow singer Dalida,† he now made a mistress of the family's housekeeper. It was too much. In December 1957, Yvonne took the children and returned to their Paris apartment.

Iguerbouchène adored his children: the separation brought him anguish, and marked the beginning of his descent into chronic illness. For at least one relation, who regretfully calls Iguerbouchène "selfish", he'd reaped what he had sown. Iguerbouchène had also distanced himself from his Algerian relations, who were living in near-destitution. Though he regularly visited his mother, it is suggested she also continued to live in semi-poverty.

In the wake of attacks on police officers by the FLN, in May 1960 Iguerbouchène's Paris apartment was raided by the police, looking for weapons, documents, and other incriminating evidence. Nothing was found except a locked safe in the children's bedroom, to which, claimed Yvonne, only Iguerbouchène had the key. After a safecracker was summoned, it was found to contain a pistol and its ammunition. Yvonne provided the police with a statement saying she recalled he'd been given it by a friend in 1946, but as far as she was aware, he'd never used it. She also told them she was "in legal proceedings to request alimony." Her situation was not good: with five children aged between four and thirteen to provide for, she'd been forced to take work as a seamstress, and sublet a room of the apartment to an African student. He had subsequently begged her to allow another African student, a friend who'd been evicted, to inhabit a second room.

---

* Iguerbouchène's name is absent from Piaf's personal papers and correspondence. [Private information from biographer Carolyn Burke – *No Regrets: The Life Of Edith Piaf* (2012).]
† Iolanda Cristina Gigliotti (1933–1987), professionally known as Dalida; French singer and actress, born in Egypt to Italian parents. She won the Miss Egypt beauty contest in 1954.

In Algeria, the situation was also deteriorating. As the War progressed, the cosmopolitan and civilised Algiers that Bernard Fraser had known was transformed into a shabby and dangerous battleground. Eventually, in March 1962 the signing of the Évian Accords formally ended hostilities. Approximately 24,614 French soldiers were dead, and of Algerians, at least twelve times that number. Many more pro-French Algerians would be murdered by the FLN in post-war reprisals. Both sides had perpetrated unspeakable atrocities, and almost a million European-Algerians had fled forever. But the country was now independent. For Iguerbouchène, it might have been a case of 'be careful of what you wish for'. The adage of the royalist journalist Jacques Mallet du Pan — "the Revolution devours its children", could also have been hung above his bed.

For a time, Mohamed's work for Algerian radio continued; in 1961-62 he also composed and conducted for the orchestra of the Opera of Algiers; the following year wrote his last cinema score: it was for a French documentary short on the wild horses of the Camargue. However, in reaction to French cultural imperialism, the new Algerian dictatorship committed itself to the complete Arabisation and Islamisation of the country's culture. For many of the educated elite who'd grown up under the colonial administration, it represented a cultural coarsening.

Whatever his commitment to the Revolution, as a previously favoured Kabyle, Iguerbouchène had a strike against him. But to have been a prominent artist who'd worked half his life in the country of the enemy, as a 'westernised' man, was infinitely worse. He now woke up to find he lived in a nation whose new administration had turned its back on him. His achievements were irrelevant: nothing that had gone before mattered. Disowned and marginalised, he was now unofficially a non-person. Frustrated and embittered, in private Iguerbouchène would, like many Kabyles before him, damn greater Algeria as a land of "vauriens" – scoundrels.

Suffering from high blood pressure and diabetes, on the 21st of August 1966, Georges Mohamed Iguerbouchène died in anonymity in Algiers at the age of fifty-eight. In the years that followed, the erasure of French-Algerian culture slowly proceeded, like the fall of Constantinople or Mao's Cultural Revolution on slow burn.

Iguerbouchène was forgotten, his works unplayed. When one of his best friends visited his villa at Beau Fraisier in the 1970s, they discovered his study was being used to raise rabbits. A quarter of a century of deep obscurity passed.

However, as the new millennium approached, the nostalgia of the old, and the curiosity of the young, wrought glimmerings of lament for the lost culture of that sunken Atlantis of French-Algeria, and a desire to recover some of its treasures. In 1989, the First Secretary of the Algerian Embassy in Germany submitted to the journal of the International Association of Music Libraries, Archives and Documentation Centres what they termed a "somewhat difficult request". It was stated that the life and work of Iguerbouchène were now to be the subject of "significant commemorative events" organised by the municipal government of Algiers:

> Nevertheless, the responsible Algerian authorities find it difficult to reconstruct the life of our artist, because certain stages of his life are still in the dark…The information we have is extremely vague.

Repeating the slender and incorrect details furnished by the Sarrouy articles, it went on to request:

> We would be very grateful if you could assist us, as far as possible, with the reconstruction of the life and work of the artist Mohamed Iguerbouchène. If you do not have any documents, then we ask you to give us a guide for our further research.

Nothing of import was received, as the inaccuracies and downright fantasies continued to be retailed.

The rise of Kabyle nationalism further pressed Iguerbouchène's case. In 1992, an association was established by his admirers, with the aim of rehabilitating him, and highlighting his musical contributions. However, in the 1990s, Algeria was again reduced to a slaughterhouse as civil war broke out between Islamists and the FLN government. It was to rage for most of the decade, and with Islamists assassinating artists, rehabilitating a Franco-Algerian composer, even of Arabic music, was not something to be aggressively pursued, even though he was safely dead.

With the arrival of the new Millennium, and the war finally extinguished, a smattering of articles on the maestro appeared in the press, and in 2003 a 12-part wildly romanticised television drama series based on his mostly-imagined life. The scenes of Bernard as the lordly Fraser Ross, accompanied by a supposed wife, and performed by Arabic-looking actors portraying upper class Scottish Edwardians, carried a whiff of Monty Python.

Since then, a television documentary, and small conferences and exhibitions on Iguerbouchène have eventuated, including to celebrate the centenary of his birth in 2007. An Iguerbouchène Prize has also been founded to recognise young musical talent. Another small step in his reclamation was the publishing in 2015 of a musical appreciation that included a brief biography. It regrettably repeated the myths, and contained nothing of his private life or problematic wartime activities. At his former villa at Beau Fraisier, now in the ownership of nephews, a member of the Iguerbouchène cultural association was able to rescue for posterity yellowing musical scores and other personal records from its cellar.

It has been claimed that Iguerbouchène's works amount to nearly 600, and that they range across all musical forms, including rhapsody, symphony, symphonic poem, and concerto. However, Iguerbouchène's success in the West has also been wildly overstated in Algeria. This springs from an ardent but regrettable patriotic desire (especially in Kabylia, which has adopted him as a cultural hero), to exaggerate the success of native artists beyond Algerian shores.

While North Africans constituted the largest immigrant community in France, like his fellow Algerian artists, Iguerbouchène's career in France existed almost solely within a marginalised culture that barely entered mainstream French consciousness – one that was mostly confined to immigrant nightclubs and colonial radio broadcasts. Composer Ned Rorem,[*] who lived in Paris from 1949 until 1957, and knew *le tout Paris* as well as bohemian Paris, including leading artistic figures such as Poulenc, Boulez, Dali, and Cocteau, diplomatically states that he "does not recall" Iguerbouchène. Even allowing for a lapse of memory, the reality of Franco-Algerian cultural apartheid at

---

[*] Ned Rorem (1923–2022) American composer and diarist.

the time is painfully obvious from the slender French newspaper record for even stars such as Salim Halali. The fame of the half-Berber Piaf is no exception at all, as she was wholly francophile. After the rendition of one of his Moorish rhapsodies in 1939, the BBC never played Iguerbouchène's music again during his lifetime.

In Algeria, the myths continue to be embroidered. Published claims that Iguerbouchène conquered all Vienna with his rhapsodies, and that Metro-Goldwyn-Mayer clamoured for his talent, would have been news to both.[*] Iguerbouchène's personal achievement is substantial enough on its own terms without needing the support of lazy falsehoods.

There have been efforts to have the ruins of Iguerbouchène's family home at Aït Ouchène given a heritage classification, and his association succeeded in raising a memorial to him in the village. It features a cameo plaque, an image from a score of a slow waltz he composed, and a brief, partially inaccurate, biography.[†]

Despite Iguerbouchène's treason, in 2021 the French Government announced he would be one of 318 "heroes of diversity" to have streets and public buildings named after them; one more historically awkward figure appropriated to assuage the belated needs of modern tokenism. In recent years, events honouring Iguerbouchène have also been held at the House of Culture at Tizi-Ouzou, in Kabylia. On one such occasion, its foyer displayed photographs of him, copies of his music scores, and explanatory texts in an assortment of faux-gilt frames. One proclaimed: "Le Comte Roth, riche et puissant lord…"

Bernard Fraser would surely have been greatly amused. And proud of his little Berber boy, out of whom the music had flowed like a living spirit. Unlike Iguerbouchène's conflicted mortal self, it was pure and noble, with an enduring life of its own.

---

[*] Only one reference to Iguerbouchène has been identified in any Austrian press of the period – as Yguerbuchen in a 1937 film magazine in a listing of *Pépé Le Moko*. [ANNO: Historische österreichische Zeitungen und Zeitschriften.]
[†] "After brilliant studies at the Royal Academy of Music in London and at the Conservatory in Vienna…"

19. JEWELS

Five years after the Battersea case, the United Kingdom witnessed another scandal of national consequence. The affair could almost serve as a coda for Lord Battersea's case, for it was also homosexual in character, and again embroiled friends of his – the Duke of Argyll (Lorne) and Lord Ronald Gower.

Whatever their innocence or otherwise in 1902, Lorne and Ronnie were dragged into this scandal unwittingly. Once more the British Government would aggressively suppress it, but a Cleveland Street-style welter of official lies was required for its smothering. The consequences of exposure of the truth were so grave, the lying would stretch across decades.

It all began on the 6th of July 1907, when a cleaning woman at Dublin Castle, the seat of the British Government in Ireland, found the door of its strong room ajar. Within the room was a safe holding the regalia of the Order of St. Patrick.* Ceremonially worn by the Lord Lieutenant of Ireland (the British governor), it was colloquially known as the Irish Crown Jewels. A few hours later, the door of the safe was found to be unlocked, and its treasure missing.

The regalia – a massive star of diamonds, emeralds and rubies, plus badge and chain, as well as three gold collars, were never recovered. It was an inside job, involving a coterie of homosexual officials. Lord

---

* An order of chivalry, limited at any time to 22 men – its knights, and bestowed upon those who held high office in Ireland.

Haddo,* the son of the Lord Lieutenant, Lord Aberdeen,† was just one of those rumoured to have participated in orgies at the Castle. The investigation of the theft was compromised to avoid a far greater scandal that could have further torn Ireland apart.

The robbery occurred only days before a royal visit. King Edward took it as a personal insult: his alleged table-thumping rant to Lord Aberdeen upon learning of the theft – "I will have no scandals! I will never come to Ireland again! I will give nothing!"‡ – has passed into royal legend.

The anecdote was first shared in a biography of the King published in 1913 by veteran journalist Edward Legge.§ He went on to state:

> I regard this episode as one of the leading events of the nine years reign. I am sure the King so considered it; I am equally certain, from the information which has been placed at my disposal by knowledgeable Irish friends, that this ugly business caused the Sovereign the utmost exasperation and dismay…It

---

* George Hamilton-Gordon, 2nd Marquess of Aberdeen and Temair (1879–1965), styled Lord Haddo until 1916 and Earl of Haddo from 1916 to 1934; politician. Due to his parents fearing his epilepsy would be inherited, they forbade him to have children and pushed him into a marriage with a widow as old as his mother, Mary Florence Clixby. After her death, he married Anna Orrok Stronach Sheila Forbes. No issue. [John Cafferky, Kevin Hannafin, *Scandal & Betrayal*, The Collins Press, Cork 2002, pp64-67.]

† John Campbell Hamilton-Gordon, 1st Marquess of Aberdeen and Temair (1847–1934), Earl of Aberdeen from 1870 to 1916; Liberal M.P., Lord Lieutenant of Ireland, and a Governor General of Canada. Possibly homosexual, he and his suffragist wife Ishbel were highly active reformists and philanthropists. "They looked an incongruous pair: she was large and matronly, he slight and dapper." Lady Violet Bonham Carter described them as: "he fidgety with a high falsetto voice always jumping & twitching & jerking out one anecdote after another, she heavy & heifer-like with an odd hesitating delivery & I should think no sense of humour…To her Life offers two vocations[:] suffering – & ministering thereto." The marked contrast was a gift to gossip. [John Cafferky, Kevin Hannafin, *Scandal & Betrayal*, The Collins Press, Cork 2002, pp63,68; Padraig Yeates, *Lockout: Dublin 1913*, Gill & MacMillan, New York 2013, p126.; Mark Bonham Carter, Mark Pottle (eds.), *Lantern Slides: The Diaries & Letters Of Violet Bonham Carter 1904–1914*, Weidenfeld & Nicholson 1996, p96.]

‡ i.e. No honours.

§ Edward Legge (1843–1927). Beginning on the staff of *The Morning Post*, in 1876 he founded the political and social paper *The Whitehall Review*. Considered "violently Conservative in politics," it achieved a number of 'scoops'. In an odd comedown, he then became editor of the *Fish Trade Gazette*, and was declared bankrupt in 1885, after a failed libel action. He then edited a series of short-lived Society papers, *Travel and Talk*, and *Piccadilly*, before again finding some success with a series of royal biographies. No admirer of Oscar Wilde, he considered the Marquess of Queensberry had done a "great public service." [Joseph Hatton, *Journalistic London*, S. Low, Marston, Searle, & Rivington, London 1882, p92; Edward Legge, *Fifty Years Of London Society*, 1870-1920, Brentano's, New York 1920, p158.]

was not merely the material loss of the jewels which provoked the anger of one who was ordinarily so self-possessed; environing circumstances, the nature of which I am not disposed to describe explicitly for reasons of public policy, added fuel to the flame. I believe this story of a crime has not its parallel.

It was those 'environing circumstances' that were everything.

Two years earlier, Sir Arthur Vicars,* who was Registrar and Knight Attendant of the Order of St Patrick, had been appointed Ulster King of Alms. This made him responsible for the heraldic affairs of Ireland, and custodian of the regalia. Vicars was a kindly but foolish man, who although homosexual, later married. He appointed friends to part-time ceremonial roles associated with his new position. A step-nephew of Irish landed gentry, Peirce Gun O'Mahony,† he made Cork Herald. Francis (Frank) Shackleton,‡ the younger brother of the Antarctic explorer Sir Ernest Shackleton, was appointed a Gold Staff Officer, and then Dublin Herald.

Keenly interested in genealogy, Frank Shackleton had previously spent two years working as an unpaid assistant to Vicars, and was possibly either a sometime boyfriend, or household pet. He then gained a commission in the Royal Irish Fusiliers, and fought in the Boer War. Invalided home, he was granted a Queen's Medal and disability pension, but may have been forced to resign his commission for suppressed reasons. Behind his facade of boyish handsomeness, and large, innocent-looking blue eyes, lurked another person entirely: a calculating criminal psychopath straight out of the textbooks, who was completely devoid of human empathy — as Vicars and others would in time discover.

---

* Sir Arthur Vicars (1862–1921), genealogist and heraldic expert. In 1917 he married Gertrude Wright. No issue. After the scandal he retreated to the family seat of Kilmorna House in County Kerry, only to be shot dead by the IRA in 1921 as an alleged (but innocent) British informer. Lady Vicars escaped. The house, like nearly 300 other historic homes in Ireland between 1919 and 1923, was mindlessly burnt to the ground.
† Peirce Gun O'Mahony (1878–1914). Married Ethel Tindall Wright; no issue. At the age of thirty-six he lived up to his second name, being shot through the heart, allegedly due to his shotgun discharging while he was climbing a fence. Suicide or murder seem more likely possibilities. He was the eldest son of Peirce Charles de Lacy O'Mahony, half-brother of Sir Arthur Vicars. n.b. Accounts differ on the spelling of 'Peirce': a majority preferring 'Pierce'. *A Genealogical And Heraldic History Of The Landed Gentry Of Ireland* (1912), and two authoritative studies of the theft, *Vicious Circle* (1967) and *Scandal & Betrayal* (2002), give the former.
‡ Francis 'Frank' Richard Shackleton (1876–1941).

The honorary roles of the Office of Arms demanded at most two months presence in Dublin annually, enabling Shackleton to pursue a dodgy business career in London. Vicars assisted him with introductions to men of influence. However, it was Shackleton's brother Sir Ernest who was responsible for another fateful encounter. At a luncheon party given in his honour, he introduced Frank to Lord Ronald Gower. Ronnie was more than charmed, and through him, Frank Shackleton soon met Ronnie's nephew, Lorne.

A third appointee of Arthur Vicars was the wealthy Francis Bennett-Goldney,* who was already Mayor of Canterbury. Although lugubrious in character, through masonic connections Bennett-Goldney had managed to enter Gower's circle, where he met Vicars, and pestered him until he was made Athlone Pursuivant. This was another post of medieval mummery, whose duty it was, apart from appearing scenic in heraldic livery, to announce the approach of the monarch. As Edward VII only made two visits to Ireland during his reign, it was not exactly an onerous role. None of them were.

When Bennett-Goldney died in 1919 in a motoring accident, it was discovered he'd been a chronic thief – his home an Aladdin's Cave of stolen treasures, including a painting belonging to the Duke of Bedford. When the Corporation of Canterbury sought to retrieve some of its more valuable possessions that he'd looted, its barrister delicately suggested to a courtroom that the deceased, "was unable to distinguish between his own property and the property of other persons."

Joining this rum circle at the Office of Arms for evening drinking parties and much more, was Captain Richard Gorges,† an utterly

---

* Major Francis Bennett-Goldney (1865–1918), antiquary, Mayor and Member of Parliament for Canterbury, and thief.
† Captain Richard William Howard Gorges (1876–1944). His later life was rackety to say the least. In 1925, he shot dead one of a pair of detectives who visited his Hampstead home after a local vicar reported him for soliciting young men. Although Gorges had fired at point-blank range, he was so drunk, only a twelve year sentence for manslaughter was handed down. Upon release, he later served a brief sentence for cheque fraud. By the age of sixty-nine he was registered as blind, and having pitched forward, or thrown himself from a crowded London tube station platform, he died after both his legs were severed by a train. In late life, he boasted about his role in the theft to family members. [Jan Bondeson, *Murder Houses of Greater London*, Matador, Kibworth Beauchamp 2015, p23; John Cafferky, Kevin Hannafin, *Scandal & Betrayal*, The Collins Press, Cork 2002, p198.]

fearless veteran of the Boer War, "with a face like Mephistopheles in *Faust,* and the manners that a duke might envy." Frank Shackleton had befriended him in South Africa, possibly as a bum chum in its fullest sense. A scion of Irish landed gentry, Gorges had been (literally) kicked out of the mounted infantry after being caught having sex with a drummer boy. However, he succeeded in joining another mounted regiment, and back in Dublin, probably through the efforts of his influential family, obtained a captaincy, and the position of musketry instructor in the Royal Irish Regiment.

A year before the theft of the jewels, during an evening drinking party at the Castle, Lord Haddo had removed the regalia from their safe as a prank, but promptly returned them the following morning when sober. However, it enabled Shackleton to see how easily this could be accomplished. On another party evening in July 1907, he and Gorges plied Vicars with enough whiskey for him to pass out, before removing the keys to the safe from his pocket. Shackleton reportedly pawned the jewels in Amsterdam for £20,000, a quarter of their value. Also looted from the safe were the jewels of Vicars' late mother.

A newspaper publisher, J. A. Jennings,* was told by the chauffeur of an American millionaire (probably John Pierpont Morgan, who was a guest of Bennett-Goldney in the autumn of 1907), that a larger petrol tank had been fitted to Bennett-Goldney's car, thereby potentially explaining how the jewels were spirited away.

The Royal Irish Constabulary conducted an investigation, with the assistance of Scotland Yard, and a Chief Inspector John Kane was assigned to the case. Arthur Vicars told a friend: "Kane admits he [Shackleton] is very clever & at first entirely threw them off the scent by his cool manner." However, they succeeded in unravelling the mystery within a few days. Indeed, they found out too much. As would be written: "To find out more than is wanted is a very bad thing for a detective to do in a case of this sort."

The Scotland Yard detectives returned home, Kane's report was suppressed, and he was dismissed from the case by the Irish administration. The case files have also disappeared. The report possibly mistakenly identified Lord Haddo as one of the culprits, and

---

* John Adolphus Jennings (1850–1938), proprietor from 1902 of the *Kent Herald* and *Kentish Chronicle.*

Haddo's father, the Lord Lieutenant Lord Aberdeen, instigated Kane's removal.

Three weeks after Kane's dismissal, King Edward's Private Secretary Lord Knollys wrote to Lord Aberdeen to convey the monarch's displeasure with the tardiness of the Dublin police in capturing the culprits, and commanded that Vicars be punished for his carelessness. In September, Knollys wrote again to press the issue, requesting that Aberdeen deliver a report to the King in person at Balmoral.

Lord Aberdeen was concerned that dismissing Vicars might open a Pandora's box of scandal, particularly with regard to his own son. He sought the advice of the Under-Secretary for Ireland, Sir Anthony MacDonnell, who agreed to write the report.

By this time, thanks to Kane's report, the Anglo-Irish administration was not only aware of Lord Haddo's partying with the group, but had concluded Frank Shackleton played a major role in the theft. They were also aware of his association, through Lord Ronald Gower and his circle, with the Duke of Argyll, husband of H.R.H. Princess Louise. MacDonnell's report would have acquainted King Edward with these sobering facts. It altered everything. For the King, what mattered most now was suppressing any mention of his brother-in-law in regard to the case, or the son of the Lord Lieutenant of Ireland.

Under pressure from the King, Vicars was finally dismissed from his post, but he refused to resign. Taking the enormous risk that his homosexuality might be formally exposed, he asked the Knights of St Patrick to petition the monarch for a proper inquiry. This they did. The Home Secretary Herbert Gladstone informed Augustine Birrell,[*] the Chief Secretary for Ireland (i.e. the government minister responsible for its administration), that: "Knollys writes that H.M. 'insists' on publicity". In blunt contradiction, one of the Knights, the Earl of Iveagh, wrote: "I happen to have been told by Lord Knollys that the presentation of this petition would be distasteful to the King."

Indeed, King Edward refused to sanction a Royal Commission. However, with the scandal growing, he was forced to agree to a Vice-

---

[*] Augustine Birrell (1850–1933), British Liberal M.P.

Regal Commission of Inquiry, where the terms of reference could be restricted to guard against the risk of any airing of the 'graver charge' – as the issue of homosexuality in the case was referred to by officials. Meanwhile, just as with the Cleveland Street Scandal, the press was fed the suggestion that the King was committed to full exposure of the affair.

The Inquiry was a preposterous whitewash: more concerned with scapegoating Vicars than establishing the true facts of the case. Its hobbled scope of investigation was simply to determine the general circumstances of the theft, and whether Vicars had been vigilant in his role as custodian of the Jewels. As one of the Commissioners stated: "We are not here to find out who the thief was. That is a job for the police."

The Inquiry's chief finding was that Vicars had been negligent. Which, with regard to his staff appointments, he had been – grossly so. However, as the witnesses were not sworn, and could not be cross-examined on oath, Vicars had walked out at the start of the Inquiry, refusing to have anything more to do with it. His barrister told the Commissioners that for the previous three months, Vicars had been "opportuning the Lord Lieutenant for a public judicial inquiry." His clerk and a secretary also declined to give evidence, both giving as their reason that they believed the Inquiry did not give fair play to their chief.

Amongst the farcical testimony provided was that of a detective-sergeant who revealed that he and Vicars had groped around for the jewels in two Irish churchyards, following a séance with a clairvoyant that Vicars held at his London home. Shackleton had sought her out at an exhibition.

Most dubiously, the Inquiry exonerated Shackleton. Despite the fact it was not a criminal investigation, and any evidence it took could not be for the purpose of ascertaining the thief, its report stated: "the name of Mr. Francis Richard Shackleton was more than once named as that of the probable or possible author of this great crime". Because of this, the Commissioners believed:

> it only due to that gentleman to say that he came from San Remo at great inconvenience to give evidence before us, that he

appeared to us to be a perfectly truthful and candid witness, and that there was no evidence whatever before us which would support the suggestion that he was the person who stole the Jewels.

In his appearance before the Inquiry, Shackleton admitted that at a Society lunch in July 1907, when the conversation had turned to Sir Arthur Vicars and his fussiness, he'd casually remarked of the Jewels: "I should never be surprised to hear that they were stolen some day," adding for the benefit of the Inquiry, "I never considered they were safe." He was asked where he'd been on various dates that month, including on the weekend following the theft's discovery. He replied that he'd been staying with "my friend Lord Ronald Sutherland Gower" in Kent. This was Hammerfield, the country house of Ronnie and his partner Frank Hird. Without prompting, Shackleton added: "I think on one week end before that the Duke of Argyll was there also. I remember coming up [to London] certainly with the Duke of Argyll one Monday in July."

Given that Lorne was Gower's close friend, his presence would not have been unexpected: he was a regular visitor. But Shackleton's seemingly oh-so-casual mention of the fact that the King's brother-in-law was part of his circle, was artfully cunning. A short time earlier, Shackleton had been reminded that his evidence was "being taken down by the short-hand writer; it will be printed; and it may be published". The story wasn't simply a matter of Shackleton being on a train with the Duke of Argyll "one Monday in July". As Shackleton damn well knew, it was the very morning the news of the theft of the jewels broke in the press – while sitting in the carriage Lorne had read out the report to him from *The Times*. (Given Shackleton's unstoppable greed, it's not unlikely Lorne had also been subject to the full force of his snake-like charm.) Poor Lorne: a quiet weekend in the country – but the wrong place, at the wrong time, and in the wrong company – suddenly made him, perhaps for a second time, a national liability.

At a later stage in the proceedings, Shackleton further stated with regard to the jewels, "I know perfectly well that I am accused of aiding Lord Haddo in taking them away," whereupon the Solicitor General replied: "You need not mention that."

Shackleton's evidence served to put officials on notice not only of whom he associated with, but his readiness to sing like a canary about them if necessary. It was golden self-protection. Just as with the mouthy Cleveland Street rentboy John Saul, the thought of what Shackleton might publicly say if backed into a corner was the stuff of Government nightmares. It's possible officials hadn't even wanted him to testify at the Inquiry: whether due to intent or incompetence, he only received a summons to appear on the day it began its proceedings, at which time he was, as stated, in Italy – in the company of Lord Ronnie and Frank Hird, no less.

As Shackleton was leaving the Inquiry, he was called aside by a detective and led to another part of the Castle, where William Harrel, the Assistant Commissioner of the Dublin Metropolitan Police, was holding another inquiry – a secret one. It would be later reported:

> Here Shackleton's whole private life was turned inside out – evidence of his disgusting conduct was dragged to light and after having been cross-examined by the detectives at great length he was let go with the admonition to leave the country as quickly as possible.

The King's Private Secretary, Lord Knollys, wrote that after authorising the Inquiry, Edward "washed his hands of the whole affair". Only the naïve believed him. The stakes were simply too high. The affair took place while all Europe watched aghast as the German Imperial Court was rent apart by a succession of homosexual scandals involving the Kaiser's favourite, Philipp, Prince zu Eulenburg-Hertefeld, and other high officials. As if the lessons of Cleveland Street and the 1885 Dublin Castle homosexual scandal weren't enough, the humdinger of a media circus unfolding in Germany provided a daily reminder to the British Establishment that the less the public knew of their betters – homosexual and otherwise – the better.

After discussing the Irish scandal over lunch with the newspaper editor Wilfrid Meynell, Wilfrid Blunt wrote in his diary:

> This, Meynell explains, is a case very much like that which made so much scandal at Berlin, and is being hushed up, as it is considered that a full revelation would make the Government of

Ireland impossible.

It was barely governable as it was. In December 1907, the Attorney-General for Ireland, echoing the analogy of Lord Salisbury, compared the lawlessness in parts of the country as worse than amongst the savages of West Africa. With much of the country still battered due to the evils committed during the Great Famine, the British were fully right to be fearful for their grip on power.[*]

A society commentator aptly referred to "the studied darkness in which the late Commission left the affair." Sir Arthur Vicars was under no illusions. He confided to a friend:

> Shackleton, when he was suspected, worked the alleged scandal for all he was worth & even blackened his own character! threatening to produce a social scandal & involve high persons.

Years later, Vicars also wrote:

> Shackleton's wicked threats of a scandal (which were & are all bunkum & lies) were utilised to frighten the late King & make him hush it up. S. was the thief & shields himself by threatening blackmail. I can't move or get at him & am powerless.

Augustine Birrell had travelled to Ireland for the Inquiry, and the shenanigans surrounding it, and Vicars' stubbornness, maddened him. In January 1908 he wrote to Herbert Gladstone:

> You do not & cannot appreciate the situation which exists <u>here</u> in Dublin. The man ought to have been <u>dismissed</u> long ago, peremptorily...Nothing will satisfy 'the other side' as you call it but a General Inquiry of a <u>police</u> character as to the stories and rumours affecting a number of persons more or less closely

---

[*] The Great Famine of 1845 to 1852 irrevocably altered Ireland. Although created by the potato blight, it was infinitely worsened by absentee landlordism, the continuing export of food (including at escorting troop gunpoint), and the failure of the British administration to undertake proper relieving measures – due to *laissez-faire* economics, and a belief the crisis was a reflection of flaws in the moral character of the Irish beyond their *perfervidum ingenium* – very ardent disposition. An estimated million citizens died, tens of thousands were evicted from their homes, and over two million emigrated; the Irish language was destroyed; and an undying generational contempt for British government further instilled, with a burning drive for freedom and justice. [Ciarán Ó Murchadha, *The Great Famine: Ireland's Agony 1845-1852*, Bloomsbury Publishing, London 2011, *passim*.]

associated with Vicars.

Birrell was a philosophical intellectual. Like Herbert Gladstone he was also a friend of the Batterseas, and wholly aware of what was at stake. Gladstone's own opinion of Vicars may have been further blighted by the petitions on behalf of Bernard Fraser he'd had to deal with: here he was again having to fuss over a fancy man who lacked self-governance. There was also the plague of gossip: as one Irish newspaper sketched it, "the consequences are already most disagreeable, for everyone in the clubs, at dinner parties, in the streets, wherever people congregate and quid nuncs* abound, has a different version of the affair."

On the 20th of January, under the title 'The Dublin Star Chamber', *The Globe*, a popular London mainstream newspaper, published the following editorial:

> There can be no doubt that the feeling on this side of the Channel about the extraordinary conduct of the Irish Government in regard to what is popularly known as the "Mystery of the Crown Jewels" is growing stronger by the day. And so long as the Government refuse to take the country into their confidence, and to offer some explanation, that feeling will continue to grow.
>
> So soon as it was announced that the proceedings of the Commission were to be secret, and Sir Arthur Vicars…and Mr Healy, had refused, in consequence, to take part in the inquiry, we pointed out that a public investigation became an absolute necessity. The view has since been endorsed by the entire Press, by the Knights of St Patrick, by many distinguished men of various shades of political creed – and, finally, by public opinion.
>
> We have no hesitation in saying that the view of the man in the street at the present moment is that there is something behind it all – that the secrecy of the proceedings was intended to shield somebody – that the Government know more about the loss of the jewels than they care to admit; and that the endeavour to keep things hushed up is not for the purpose of aiding the law,

---

* Busy bodies.

but to avoid a scandal.

We do not say that this is so; but we do say that the Government have nobody but themselves to thank if, by the egregious mismanagement of the whole affair, they have created such an impression in the minds of men. The method they have adopted to get rid of the Ulster King of Arms, whatever might be their justification for doing so, is an absolute scandal, and the position is a false one which cannot be allowed to continue. It is entirely opposed to public polity, to public justice, and to the dignity of the Ministers themselves, that no step should be taken to put an end to a situation which has become scandalous in the extreme.

Given this public pressure, on the last day of January 1908, the Inquiry report was, as one paper phrased it, "reluctantly published", with an appendix containing the full testimony. Sir Arthur Vicar's appointment as Ulster King-Of-Arms was also formally revoked.

However, Peirce O'Mahony senior,* Vicars' half-brother, and father of the Cork Herald, was determined to expose the Government's scapegoating of Vicars, and the shielding of Shackleton. He forwarded to the Dublin press his lengthy private correspondence Lord Aberdeen and other members of the Anglo-Irish Government regarding Vicars' dismissal. These exchanges were also printed by the English press.

They revealed that in October 1907, Vicars met with Augustine Birrell and Lord Aberdeen, and Birrell had "read out from a typed document trivial charges of negligence". Soon afterwards, O'Mahony senior learnt that behind the Government's accusation of carelessness lay another charge that Birrell was privately sharing. In November, Birrell told him what it was: that Vicars had associated with a man of "undesirable character". The press reports omitted Shackleton's name, but anyone who'd read the Inquiry's report would have known whom was meant – and how at odds this characterisation was with the Inquiry's exoneration of him.

---

* Peirce Charles de Lacy O'Mahony, from 1912 self-styled The O'Mahony of Kerry (1850–1912); Irish nationalist M.P., land commissioner and magistrate. Married married Helen Louise Collis, and secondly, Alice Jane Johnstone, and had issue, including eldest son, Peirce Gun O'Mahony.

It was further reported Birrell told O'Mahony senior that if Vicars pressed for a public inquiry it couldn't be refused, but he was warned "in an inquiry of this kind, involving character, no matter how innocent a man might be, a certain amount of dirt would stick." By such understated phrasing does the English Establishment voice its threats.

In reply, O'Mahony sharply informed Birrell that his half-brother "had believed this man to be a man of good character, and that I presumed this man's other friends, including Lord Ronald Gower, the Duke of Argyll, and the Bishop of Peterborough,* believed the same." The appearance of the Duke's name in the press reports of this conversation was precisely what the authorities had wished to avoid.

O'Mahony went on to state that, "owing to the incontinence of official tongues, scandalous matters are being gossiped about in Dublin to my brother's detriment." Seeking to discredit Vicars, the administration had leaked rumours of his homosexuality.

There was more. On behalf of Lord Aberdeen, the Under-Secretary for Ireland, Sir Anthony MacDonnell, had ticked off O'Mahony for expressing in a letter his determination "to bring the true state of affairs under the notice of His Majesty". MacDonnell informed him that the decision to dismiss his half-brother had been made by the Irish Government, "and therefore the introduction of the King's name into your letter is out of place and improper." Having received this, O'Mahony promptly banged off a reply to Lord Aberdeen, bluntly reminding him that at the private meeting at which Vicars had been accused, "Mr. Birrell was the first to introduce the King's name into the matter," and adding "I am convinced that my brother is being sacrificed in order to shield others really culpable." This exchange O'Mahony also provided to the press, which for the Crown and Government, would have been additionally embarrassing and infuriating.

Sometimes it takes the unscrupulous to do the work of the righteous. Moreton Mandeville† was a financier and swindler, who published a

---

* Rt. Rev. Edward Carr Glyn (1843–1928), Bishop of Peterborough from 1896 to 1916. A younger son of the 1st Baron Wolverton, he married Lady Mary Emma, a daughter of the 8th Duke of Argyll.
† (Alexis) Moreton Mandeville (1869–1952). For a brief period he enjoyed a reputation as one

popular news and literary magazine, *London Opinion*. (Contributors included T.P. O'Connor and Hillaire Belloc.) On the last day of February 1908, it published a banner two-page emotive article about the case that ratcheted up public disquiet. Provocatively titled 'Thieves Of Honour', its author was none other than the famous Marie Corelli. Infuriated by the handling of the case, she poured out her caustic contempt for the Establishment's deceit and hubris:

> Everything can be done, and is done, for money, and we are just now proving that even the robbers of our own national property can be screened from their proper discovery and punishment when there is enough Cash and Influence behind them. Cash and Influence are the modern terms for Law and Justice...

Corelli then went on to quote a paragraph that had appeared in the *Daily Mail* the previous fortnight:

> *There is no prospect, unless new evidence is obtained, that a fresh inquiry will be opened into the loss of the jewels. No further search is being made by Scotland Yard. It is understood that an intimation has been given that the matter should be allowed to drop, and no notice be taken of the demand for a public inquiry from any quarter whatsoever. The police believe that the regalia are still intact.*

Corelli treated the announcement with the derision it deserved:

> This is a high and mighty ruling! But the people of this country have the right to ask who it is that has given this "intimation"...Such an order, no matter from whom it emanates, is mere cowardly despotism.

As she told readers, the Government's refusal to undertake further investigation implied "knowledge of the thief and complicity" in enabling them to evade the consequences of their actions:

> No attempt would be made to 'hush up' such a robbery had it

---

of London's brainiest and most enterprising share brokers. Such fizz collapsed in a sticky mess in 1926 when he was exposed as a psychopathic swindler, and sent to prison for fraud, together with his brothers Walter and Henry. In a thirty-year run of ponzi schemes, they generated only massive investor losses. [See: Frank Dilnot, *Getting Rich Quick*, Geoffrey Bles, London 1935, pp217-220.]

been committed by one of the so-called 'lower' classes. But every effort is put forth to shield a possible criminal among the degenerate 'great' of family...

As for Sir Arthur Vicars, he must have been what is called 'a figure of fun' indeed...It may be taken for granted, however, that Scotland Yard knows who the thief is, and remains simply inactive because forbidden to act. And here is again the crucial point of the whole mystery. Who is it that forbids the law to proceed on its proper course? Who presumes to 'intimate' that the proper inquiry into a theft of national property should be 'allowed to drop', simply because it may turn out that persons of name and family connection are concerned in the robbery?...Rank injustice such as has been so openly and scandalously displayed in the matter of the Dublin Crown Jewels inquiry, is something quite new to Britain and Britons...That someone in governmental power is protecting the thief, is equally clear.

The people of this country are witnessing strange things in our later-day 'society', and many stranger things are yet to come. Not the least strange of all is the fact that they must no longer rely on the British press for the open and honest discussion of a public question, no matter whether it be as purely of national interest as the theft of a country's crown jewels. For since it was 'intimated' that the matter "should be allowed to drop," every allusion to this shameless robbery has been carefully eliminated from every newspaper. Hence we must conclude that there is now apparently a Censorship of the press in 'free' Britain as in enslaved Russia...And yet what do we sing? "Britons never, never, never shall be slaves!" Yes! – that is all very well; but till we have the courage to drag forth our Thieves of Honour from their 'society' holes and corners, the song is out of place!

In March, *London Opinion* underlined Corelli's inference that King Edward was behind the suppression of the case, printing: "The secret Commission appointed to inquire into the matter was worthy of the best days of Russian despotism." Echoing *The Globe*, and calling it a mere Star Chamber for the excoriation of Sir Arthur Vicars, it asked why the English Press had suddenly dropped the story:

Was it because the highest in the land declared with warmth that he would have no Berlin scandal in his dominions, he having discovered that some of the chief actors in the matter were mixed up with personages in London, and throughout England whose social status is high, but whose crimes would disgrace the lowest of the costermongers in the East End?

In *Truth*, Charles Jerningham was prompted to muse that the changing circumstances of the upper class were driving them to be even more determined that their scandals be hidden:

> There are three circumstances to be considered in the governing of a country which has the monarchical system, and they are, in their order, the interests of the dynasty, those of Party, and those of the community. The dynastic considerations include the interests of the class which is most directly dependent upon the continuation of the system. In these days the influence of this class is undoubtedly decreasing in England; it is impoverished, and the Liberal spirit of the country is opposed to its domination. It is, therefore, of enormous importance in the opinion of those who rule here – of the executive, which is still mostly composed of men of the class – that most scandals which discredit that element should be suppressed. This causes the condition which is now so often deplored, that amongst those of considerable social position misconduct is hushed up which would not be tolerated in others of less importance. It follows that as the members of the class become still more impoverished by the circumstances of the time, and as their behaviour is concealed and is unpunished to protect State interests, they become more and more reckless in their misconduct. The article written by Miss Marie Corelli on "The Thieves Of Honour," which is attracting general attention, attacks this concealment so courageously that it should lead the authorities to reconsider their policy in this direction. It is justice *à la carte* for the prominent, the set forms for the poor.

Further fuelling this furnace was a letter Sir Arthur Vicars now wrote to the Press:

> It is intolerable that in the twentieth century a public servant can be summarily dismissed without trial under circumstances which

649

suggest the gravest possible reflection of his character, and that in the full blaze of the present century His Majesty's Irish Government can put the Magna Carta in the waste-paper basket without the voice of the public being raised in protest.

I appeal to the public to make their voice heard, and insist that I may receive the privilege which the meanest criminal is entitled to – a public inquiry.

Desperate diseases require desperate remedies, and should the voice of the public be unheard, I feel I cannot be blamed for forcing to come out into the open, even by desperate devices, those who are sheltering themselves behind the entrenchments of title, dignity, privilege, and brief authority.

Possibly badgered by Peirce O'Mahony senior, a few days later in Parliament, Irish M.P. William Redmond* demanded that Augustine Birrell inform the House whether there was truth in the newspaper reports:

that the police authorities, in their investigation into the loss of the Dublin Crown jewels, discovered the existence of a most grave and criminal scandal affecting a number of officials of Dublin Castle; and whether the Government will order a full and public inquiry into the whole matter.

Smooth as silk, Birrell replied:

I am glad the honourable Member has asked this Question. The statements that have appeared in certain London newspapers are a parcel of lies of a particularly cruel and offensive kind. No grave or criminal scandal affecting officials in Dublin Castle has been discovered. No person or persons are being shielded from prosecution, whether for the theft or for any other crime. The police are busily engaged in prosecuting their inquiries. Criminal proceedings will at once be taken when any evidence justifying prosecution is forthcoming. A full and public inquiry at present would not be of any use, and would probably interfere with the course of justice.

---

* William Hoey Kearney Redmond (1861–1917), Irish nationalist politician, lawyer and soldier.

When Birrell was questioned as to whether the private inquiry had proved useful, he admitted, "it has served some purpose," but when asked "What purpose?" *Hansard* records: "No answer was returned".

The following month in the House of Commons, Birrell replied to another M.P.'s enquiry to indignantly contradict the widespread and published rumour of Lord Haddo's involvement with the theft, stating that he'd been in Scotland at the time; adding that Lord Aberdeen was "most anxious that there should be the fullest possible inquiry into all the circumstances attending the loss of the Crown Jewels."

Another M.P. asked why no proceedings had been commenced for criminal libel over such claims. Birrell replied: "That is a very proper question. I can only say that legal advice has been taken on the matter, and action, or rather inaction, has been adopted in accordance with that advice." Of course it had.

While the British press printed speculative articles about the theft, in April 1908 an American newspaper, *The Sunday Star* of Washington D.C., published a full background analysis of the scandal. The anonymous article, which is bylined "Special Correspondence of The Star" is almost without doubt the handiwork of Frederick Cunliffe-Owen, exhibiting as it does his keen insight into the workings of the British press and Establishment. As a voracious reader, he'd clearly been reflecting on the contributions of Corelli, Jerningham, and others. The points he made on the state of the press are pertinent not only to the jewel theft, but also the Battersea Scandal. The article is therefore worth quoting almost in its entirety:

> England is trembling on the brink of a social earthquake. At least, so declare the people who claim to know. The scandal in connection with the theft of the Dublin crown jewels is to blame. The friends of Sir Arthur Vicars, the deposed Ulster King-At-Arms, say they are determined to vindicate his honour by making public the whole story. They declare that the publication "cannot be prevented by all the power of England, and within a short time the world will be familiar with a blot on English society that will shock the world." Readers are, of course, familiar with most of the points in the crown jewel theft and inquiry. For weeks the

cables have carried the story. But it is strange to Americans that the British press has not, ere this, solved the entire mystery. For weeks the daily papers in this country carried news paragraphs and articles always asking the question: "Who stole the crown jewels?" There was never the suspicion of a definite answer. In the United States in a few days the press would have pointed its all-powerful finger and declared, "There is the man."

It is little wonder that Marie Corelli emerged from her retreat in Stratford-on-Avon as she did a week or two ago and through the medium of a weekly paper, scorched English society and the British government. Miss Corelli declares that the press of England is censored as it is in slave-driven Russia. It is true that the press has been strangely silent of late and that only two or three minor weeklies have dared discuss the present condition of affairs.

The *Daily Mail* several weeks ago contained a paragraph given as official. It contained this passage: "An intimation has been given that the matter should be allowed to drop and no notice be taken of the demand for public inquiry from any quarter whatsoever." For a few following weeks there was the silence of death. Then Sir Arthur Vicars in an appealing letter to the press asked the public to demand an inquiry. This has been followed by other letters and articles and questions in the House of Commons by Irish members, notably by the brother of the leader of the Irish party, William Redmond. But the government has turned a deaf ear to all entreaties. It is declared that by order of no less a personage than King Edward a public inquiry has been forbidden.

And so it remains for the friends of the discredited Sir Arthur Vicars to make public the scandals involved in their own way. They are even now looking out for a Herr Harden* courageous enough to take his chances of imprisonment and are engaged in

---

* Maximilian Harden, the German journalist and editor who generated the Eulenburg Scandal. He later admitted to sexual researcher Magnus Hirschfeld that removing the moderating influence of the gay Eulenburg circle from the Kaiser's court, which set Germany on its war course, was the biggest political mistake of his life. [James D. Steakley, *Iconography Of A Scandal; Political Cartoons And The Eulenburg Affair In Wilhelmin Germany*, in, Martin Duberman, Martha Vicinus, George Chauncey Jr. (eds.) *Hidden From History: Reclaiming The Gay And Lesbian Past*, New American Library, New York 1989, p246.]

raising a fund to fight the law cases which would ensue.

It is strange that the libel law in England, the boasted most free country on the face of the earth, is such that a paper may not publish anything derogatory about any person, even if absolutely true, until a court of law has first found that person guilty.

But it is going to be very hard work to find an English Herr Harden. The German may be called phlegmatic and slow. But the Englishman is far slower, colder and more difficult to rouse. A German is easily excited. In fact, a native of any part of continental Europe can be worked up to hysteria in short order. In England, it is only the socialists and the suffragettes who appear to get at all excited over national affairs. To rouse the Englishman one must tread on his personal and individual corn. Then only would he chance jail by attacking you.

The great editors of Britain do not number a Harden among them. George Buckle of *The Times* has his own troubles and must now be wondering what is going to become of his paper under the newly reorganised company.* C. Arthur Pearson† also has his own worries. Harmsworth, or as he is titled, Lord Northcliffe, is making too much money and is too strong a friend of the powers-that-be to dream of mixing up in any unsavoury boiling-pot as this great scandal. The editor-owners of the other big papers of Britain are far too respectable and calculating to associate themselves with any scandal. They are also too busy looking after political questions such as the navy, the church and education, the liquor license act and the suffragettes.

To find a Harden it will be necessary to go to the editors of weekly papers. Labouchère of *Truth*, the boldest pen in England, has practically retired from the arena. He is very old and the strongest thing his paper has said of the Dublin scandal is contained in one sentence: "It is justice *a la carte* for the prominent, the set forms for the poor."

A. Moreton Mandeville, of *London Opinion,* the journal that

---

* Lord Northcliffe purchased the paper in 1908, and instituted modernisation measures which Buckle, as editor, had long resisted. Buckle was forced to resign.
† Sir Cyril Arthur Pearson, 1st baronet (1866–1921); founder of the *Daily Express*.

originated the Limerick competition, is head of the London and Paris Exchange, a big financial corporation, which also issues a financial paper called *The Daily Report*. He is perhaps too prosperous to touch the scandal except with a pair of tongs. In such manner has he been handling it for the past few issues of his weekly.

There is, as a possible last resort, Horatio Bottomley of *John Bull*. He calls his paper the Penny Truth. Mr. Bottomley has appeared in the law courts and knows what they are like. He has been before the bankruptcy court and has been charged with running a lottery in connection with his paper. He has financial interests in the city. He owns race horses and is a member of Parliament. He has a vitriolic pen and is outspoken enough in his paper generally. But Mr. Bottomley knows English law. He knows that the government is all powerful. By becoming in this case the Harden of England he would be the man of the hour. His paper might have a furious circulation for the time being. But the position of people's champion against the all-powerful government, against certain sections of society and titled aristocracy, and even against the King's august majesty, would be fraught with danger, not alone involving imprisonment and a stupendous expenditure of money, but the loss of position as [a] member of parliament and many other important privileges.

Sir Arthur Vicars, or his half-brother, Peirce O'Mahony [senior], may soon write out a full and detailed account of the scandals, and if no paper will publish it, will endeavour to make it public in pamphlet form as was done in similar cases a century ago. I have here a statement by Peirce O'Mahony, which is about as strong as it would be without mentioning names. Here it is, written and signed by the half-brother of the man who claims he has been wronged:

"The robbery of the crown jewels was discovered July 6. But it was not until October that charges were brought against my brother. From that day to this I have never ceased to work for the vindication of my brother's character from the stain sought to be cast upon it by a minister of the crown, Mr. Birrell, chief secretary for Ireland."

"I have openly accused the chief secretary of conduct unworthy of a gentleman. I have brought this accusation before the speaker of the House of Commons, once called the finest club in Europe; I have brought it under the notice of His Majesty the King. The Rt. Hon. Augustine has taken it lying down because he knows that if he challenges me in public court I will drive this accusation home, vindicate the honour to the full of my brother and expose the corruption and rottenness of Dublin castle officialdom, over which he presides."

"I have accused the police of wilfully withholding evidence in their possession that is in favour of my brother. I now go further and I state deliberately that the government does not wish to find the thief because one suspected man and one of his associates, also suspected, are known to the police as men of unclean lives and have threatened to involve society in an unsavoury scandal."

"And so, in this twentieth century, under the enlightened rule of the most constitutional monarchy in the world, an official of hitherto unblemished character and name is to be dismissed and ruined and denied the opportunity of meeting his accusers in the open – a right accorded to the meanest criminal – because a few titled members of what, are falsely called 'the upper ten', and who circle round the throne, possess characters so absolutely rotten and degraded that they fear to face the threats of two men whom Mr. Birrell knows and whom he had described as 'abandoned ruffians.' [Shackleton and Gorges] My brother's honour is of no account to them – titled corruption must be shielded from the public gaze. Not thus, however, can they stem the fetid tide. We will leave no stone unturned until we have justice." *

The whole affair has been a sad blow to the Aberdeens. Both Lord and Lady Aberdeen are known all over the English-speaking world. They are interested in religion, in philanthropy and in numberless good works for the plain people, which has brought, them on occasions dangerously near the line of Socialism. In Canada, when Lord Aberdeen was Governor General, he and his wife were very popular and did much good.

---

* A longer, slightly different version of the statement was published by *London Opinion* on 7 March 1908 under the title 'Traducers Of Honour' – echoing Corelli's earlier article.

They had many American friends, entertained largely and frequently visited the United States.

Lord Aberdeen's oldest, son, Lord Haddo, is twenty nine years old. It is always given out that the family is disturbed because of his health. He was quietly married a couple of years ago to a most estimable lady, the widow of a Manchester and Liverpool cotton factor. She possessed some means, but the Aberdeens do not want for money. The strange part of the affair is that the lady is old enough to be her husband's mother...He is a very earnest young man, and has lately been elected an elder in the Scotch Presbyterian church.

In connection with the crown jewels no official mention of his name has been made. One or two papers have suggested that a 'noble lord' figures in the case, and one illustrated weekly, after advertising the week ahead 'The True Story of the Dublin Crown Jewels' printed a page of old facts without mentioning a nobleman, yet in the centre of the page it published Lord Haddo's photograph, with the innocent line beneath it: 'Lord Haddo, who has just been elected an elder in the Scotch church.'

In commenting on the case *John Bull* has referred to the nobleman by saying: "Lord Haddo's name has been mentioned." Beyond this the British press has not gone, and dares not go. What will be the result can hardly be foretold. That the Earl of Aberdeen will in the next six months resign, is almost a certainty."

Frederick Cunliffe-Owen's article concluded by reporting there was speculation Lord Aberdeen's successor would be Lord Beauchamp. Given Beauchamp was a deluxe amalgam of liberal politics, high-churchism, aestheticism, aristocratic panache, impishness, and not least homosexuality – very possibly being one of the unnamed gentlemen in the Battersea affair, it would have been an entertaining appointment, but was not to be. However, the article was exceptional journalism. There was one other brave editor who might have pursued the case, but William Marcus Thompson of *Reynolds's Newspaper* had died in 1907.

In September, in an article boldly titled 'King Edward VII: Wire-

Puller', *Pearson's Weekly* in London allowed itself to print:

> That His Majesty intervened with success in a recent scandal in Ireland is one of those open secrets that never get into the papers. Things were beginning to leak out, and several reputations were tottering. The King decided that this was not for the good of the public service, so he put his almost irresistible influence to the task of smoothing matters over before it was too late. Again, in Parliament some members showed a disposition to ask questions, but in the end it was allowed to fizzle out. One of those mysterious "hints from high quarters" reached the leaders of the Opposition — and that was an end of it.

In April 1909, another Irish nationalist M.P., Laurence Ginnell,[*] took up in Parliament the matter of the theft. He asked Augustine Birrell whether he was:

> aware of the existence of reports – if he has not read them – implicating, as principal and accomplices in theft, and also as principals in sodomy and other beastly crimes, of F. R. Shackleton and Captain Gorges –

Such frankness was not to be borne. Before Ginnell could state a third name the Speaker called "Order!", and rebuked him, claiming he had "no right to bring in the names of gentlemen in connection with matters of that sort without submitting his question to me" – i.e. in writing: "I will say whether it is a proper one to ask."

Ginnell wasn't to be put off, and further asked Birrell:

> Is it not a fact that the only practical steps taken by the Irish Government to recover the stolen jewels and to get others in their stead was to shower honours by way of bribes upon a Belfast millionaire?[†] (Laughter and cries of "Oh!")

To which Birrell replied: "No, Sir." (Laughter.)

Meanwhile in Ireland, a young leading member of the secret Irish

---

[*] Laurence Ginnell (1852–1923) Irish Parliamentary Party M.P.
[†] The reference remains obscure.

Republican Brotherhood, Bulmer Hobson,* had done his own digging into the theft. He now constructed an article that went further than any in solving the mystery. Its general accuracy would later be confirmed to him by Richard Gorges, who also told him of Haddo's Christmas prank. However, as Hobson wrote in his memoirs:

> Having got this story, mainly from Peirce O'Mahony,† supplemented by one or two pieces I managed to pick up, I found it impossible to use it. No papers in Ireland dared print it, and would have been sued for criminal libel if they had.

Frustrated, Hobson sent the article to a Irish nationalist newspaper in New York for which he was already contributing articles, *The Gaelic American*. Its highly radical editor, John Devoy,‡ made his own alterations, but it finally appeared in July 1908, anonymously-authored, under the headline: 'Abominations Of Dublin Castle Exposed'. The extended sub-head said it all:

> Mystery of the Theft of the Crown Jewels Brought to Light – Gang of Aristocratic Degenerates Carried on Their Orgies in the Citadel of British Rule and the Thieves Were Among Them – Sir Arthur Vicars Made a Scapegoat to Screen Lord Haddo, Son of Lord Aberdeen, and the Duke of Argyll, King Edward's Brother-in-Law...

Of Frank Shackleton, it stated:

> Mr. Shacklton was...a man well known to the police. Around his name had gathered a lot of very unsavoury rumours. Some of his associates, titled and untitled, were men suspected of unspeakable and disgusting offences.

> After his arrival rumours began to circulate in Dublin that there were nightly orgies at the Castle, in which several prominent Government officials were mixed up. The names of Mr.

---

* (John) Bulmer Hobson (1883–1969), Irish nationalist and journalist.
† He doesn't say whether it was Peirce O'Mahony junior or senior, but given his aggressive defence of his half-brother, it was almost certainly the latter.
‡ John Devoy (1842–1928), Irish republican rebel and journalist. *The Times* labelled him: "the most bitter and persistant, as well as the most dangerous, enemy of this country which Ireland has produced since Wolfe Tone." [Obituary, *The Times*, 1 October 1928, p19.]

Shackleton, the 'Dublin Herald'. Mr. John Mills Goldsmith,[*] I.S.O.,[†] the head of the English secret police in Ireland; Lord Haddo, the son of Lord Aberdeen; Lord Liverpool,[‡] and some others were mentioned…Rumour said that again Dublin Castle had become a nest of unnatural vice, and rumour was right.

The only name disguised in the article was that of Richard Gorges, described as "a man of absolutely depraved character," but called "Captain Gaudeons". (Given Gorges was so dangerously unstable, this was a wise measure: when he eventually read the article, unaware that Hobson was responsible, he told him: "If I knew who wrote that I would murder him!")

The one point the article got wrong, due to Hobson being misled by Vicars' champion Peirce O'Mahony, was in painting Vicars as a totally innocent man, when in fact he would have been fully aware of the sexual proclivities of his colleagues.

However, on the right track the article continued: "So things went on till one fine day it was discovered that the Jewels were gone. Who stole them we can surmise." It then pointed the finger directly at Shackleton and Gaudeons (Gorges). It also explained how Shackleton had been a guest of Lord Aberdeen, and associated with the Duke of Argyll, who it characterised as:

> a man of very bad reputation to say the least of it, and it is to shield such abandoned aristocratic ruffians that a public inquiry was refused, and the men who stole the Jewels were allowed by the police to escape…Now *The Gaelic American* will see to it that the public know these facts as well…This time, however, the conspiracy of silence has been defeated and the truth published

---

[*] John Mills Goldsmith (1845–1912), officially: Secretary and Accountant to the Dublin Metropolitan Police; unofficially: as described above. Married, and had issue.

[†] Imperial Service Order: a now-defunct award for long and meritorious service in the Civil Service, established by Edward VII.

[‡] Arthur William de Brito Savile Foljambe, 2nd Earl of Liverpool (1870–1941). State Steward and Chamberlain to the Irish Vice-Regal Court as Viscount Hawksbury, before succeeding as to the earldom in March 1907, and from 1908 as Comptroller. Later Governor and Governor-General of New Zealand. Married the Hon. Annette Louise Monck; no issue. On his tour of New Zealand in 1920, Edward, Prince of Wales in a letter to his then-mistress, Freda Dudley Ward, complained: "he's a liar & a cheat at any games, cards, golf & everything. And he's too pricelessly pompous for words." [Gavin McLean, *The Governors: New Zealand's Governors and Governors-General*, Otago University Press, Dunedin 2006, p182.]

to the world.

Unfortunately, fellow editors responded to the libellous article with deep silence: not least, the cowered press of the realms of His Majesty King Edward VII. However, the simmering scandal would be brought to the boil again through extraordinary circumstances. In early 1911, Lord Ronald Gower was declared bankrupt. In a late-life infatuation, Gower had granted Frank Shackleton power of attorney over his investments. In short order, Shackleton set himself up in a mansion in Park Lane, and with the aid of a criminal accountant, drained Gower's fortune. Lord Ronald only became aware of his predicament when a firm of stockbrokers sued him for non-payment of a tranch of shares that Shackleton had purchased in his name. Shackleton's own speculative investments also saw him declared bankrupt a few months later, with liabilities worthy of a plutocrat.

Yet despite the fraud being exposed when the stockbrokers' case came to court, and also at Gower's bankruptcy hearing – Lord Ronald's defence counsel openly calling Shackleton "a thief"– the authorities took no immediate action, and Shackleton skipped the country. Once again, the British press played dumb. However, in plain-speaking America, a newspaper posed the obvious question:

> Why Shackleton was not prosecuted criminally at the time was one of those mysteries for which no adequate explanation is forthcoming. It was stated that one reason was that any proceedings against him would inevitably involve more highly placed persons, and that great influence was brought to bear on the authorities to turn the blind eye to the revelations of the bankruptcy court.

Finally, in late 1912 the Director of Public Prosecutions acted, and a warrant was issued. Shackleton was promptly arrested in Angola and brought back to England. Its press was prepared to state the case had "been agitating officials in the Home Office for some time." And how! Edward VII had gone to his grave in 1910, but preventing the stirring up of Ireland was a constant concern. So nervous was the Government of the Gower-Argyll royal connection that the warrant only charged Shackleton for fraudulently converting to his own use the proceeds of a cheque of Josephine Browne, a spinster friend of Lord Ronald's. Only later were additional charges laid for the greater frauds against Gower and Frank Hird.

Across the Atlantic, the American press was again eager to inform the public of what was really at stake. In a report also quoted by some colonial newspapers, it was stated:

> The trial of Frank Shackleton, who recently lived in New York, and who was arrested in Portugese East Africa… is expected to be the most sensational of the year, and possibly of many years. The prosecution intends to revive the smouldering scandal of the Dublin crown jewels, and will make some remarkable allegations regarding Shackleton's share in that mysterious robbery.

Not a bit of it! All the arts of legal camouflage were brought to bear, and Shackleton and his accomplice were ultimately only convicted on the frauds perpetrated against Josephine Browne, due to a suspiciously convenient claim by the Crown Prosecutor that Lord Ronald was too ill to give testimony. Shackleton was sentenced to a mere fifteen months.

However, the long proceedings against Shackleton, and his continued shielding with regard to the Crown Jewels case, galvanised others. In what became a personal crusade, between 1912 and 1913, Laurence Ginnell again repeatedly attempted to get to the truth of the matter. The Cleveland Street Scandal had shown that all it took to tear open a Potemkin facade was one determined hothead with an amplified voice who was pissed off at Establishment injustice. However, the British Government had absolutely no intention of allowing Ginnell to become another Ernest Parke. This would lead to some of the nation's most respected figures resorting to desperate behaviour.

News of Shackleton's arrest in Africa broke in the first week of November 1912. Ginnell again raised the issue of the Jewels in Parliament on the 28th of that month. He asked Augustine Birrell, as Chief Secretary of Ireland, whether the Director of Public Prosecutions had been given a full list of those persons who, at the time of the theft, had official access or had been admitted to the room where the Jewels were kept. Dodging the question, Birrell replied:

> All available information has been long since in the hands of the police, who are ready to take advantage of any opportunity of

discovering the guilty persons. Until they are detected no question of prosecution can arise.

Ginnell demanded Birrell answer what he'd been asked; receiving the reply: "No, Sir, I do not think they have." To this Ginnell replied, "Why not?" before stating he would bring the matter to the attention of the House the following day.

At the next parliamentary sitting when Birrell stood to address the House, Birrell, together with some fellow ministers, picketed the doors of the Chamber. They persuaded M.P.s not to enter, with the result that the required quorum of forty members could not be secured, and Ginnell was forced to stop speaking.

He complained to the Speaker of the House about their actions, but was informed there was no way to stop it. Ginnell then appealed to the Prime Minister, Herbert Asquith, for an opportunity to discuss the Dublin crime, but was dismissed with a lordly, "I am afraid I am not in a position to do so."

In 1908, Birrell had written to Herbert Gladstone of the case: "I don't think anybody need be frightened of a debate in the House of Commons. I certainly shall not be." Now the cockiness had been replaced by literal scrambling desperation. It was an ugly and degrading state of affairs.

Two days later in the House, Ginnell asked the Attorney-General whether the Director of Public Prosecutions would now obtain a list of all persons who'd had access to the Jewels at the time of the theft. He received the reply: "The powers of the Director of Public Prosecutions are confined to offences which are alleged to have been committed in England and Wales, and do not extend to Ireland." Ginnell was fast learning how curiously hamstrung the British Government could be when effective action was against its interests.

On the 6th of December 1912, Ginnell again stood up the House, to say: "I ask to be allowed to deal with the subject I am about to raise without interruption." Reading the riot act, he stated:

> We often hear and read idle platitudes about the purity of public life. I am going to test whether anything practical can be done

towards that end by grappling with a concrete case of grave impunity and crime.

Ginnell bluntly called the Vice-Regal Commission of Inquiry a sham, and charged that the theft was connected with:

> criminal debauchery and sodomy being committed in the castle by officials, Army officers, and a couple of nondescripts of such position that their conviction and exposure would have led to an upheaval from which the Chief Secretary shrank. In order to prevent that he suspended the operation of the Criminal Law, and appointed a whitewashing commission with the result for which it was appointed.

He again threatened to name the criminals in Parliament because he was unable to do so in the Press:

> One of the most powerful means for fostering crime in high places is the boycott placed upon its exposure by the legitimate Press. Any crime among the poor is paraded and magnified, but the character of the wealthy and official class is treated as sacrosanct and any word impeaching it is rigorously suppressed.

His speech was again stopped, and a head count demanded. The required quorum again not being met, the House was adjoined. One press report stated:

> It was evident that members had no desire to have scandal raked up, and as Mr. Ginnell has no political friends, a count out soon took place. He made the process easier by his prolixity.

Never underestimate the stubbornness of the Irish. Six days later in the House, when in answer to the question of another member, Birrell denied knowing where the jewels might be, Ginnell interjected: "The Chief Secretary is able if he likes to lay them on the Table."

A fortnight later, Ginnell yet again raised the matter in the House, stating:

> The Chief Secretary's evasive answers on this subject render it necessary for me to disregard form and logic and sequence and

deal with the crime in Dublin Castle in any way I can.

In the traditional manner of the British ministers when called upon to spout half-truths and lies, Augustine Birrell manifested a smugly avuncular attitude. Like other Irish politicians so patronised, it incensed Ginnell, who told the Commons: "A jaunty air of blank ignorance has served the Chief Secretary very well." True to his earlier promise, as he had in 1909, Ginnell again named Gorges and Shackleton as being the likely culprits, describing the former as:

> the greatest scoundrel then in South Africa. He was well known in the Army to be a reckless bully, a robber, a murderer, a bugger, and a sod. I believe that the exploit for which he was court-martialled, I think, in 1906, was robbery of the Buluwayo-Salisbury mail coach, but the crime for which some years later he was kicked out of Thorneycroft's Horse Regiment was sodomy...He came to Ireland, and, as if nothing had happened, was given a commission in the Third Battalion of the Royal Irish Regiment. Finding robbery of mail coaches not feasible in Ireland, he practised his other accomplishments there, and got congenial spirits in Dublin Castle to admit him to their society. He awaited his opportunity, and availed of it when it came, to steal, in conjunction with others, the Crown Jewels.

Moving on to Shackleton, Ginnell stated he was a lieutenant in the Royal Irish Fusiliers who'd been "a participant in the debauchery".

In its Parliamentary report the following day, *The Times* proved Ginnell's charge regarding the failings of the mainstream press. It studiously avoided even the suggestion that he'd named anyone in connection with the matter. Nor did it report Ginnell's echoing of the allegations of Vicars with regard to Shackleton. However, *Hansard* records Ginnell telling the Chamber that:

> This person [Shackleton] threatened what is called the Irish Government that if they attempted to put him on trial he would make a full disclosure of worse crimes and of everybody connected with them...so notorious was that person's connection with crimes and criminals, that no one wishing to avoid exposure would venture to accuse him. It was a pretty state of things when a criminal so bad knew his environment to be so

bad that he could safely flout a thing calling itself a Government.

Prolix he was, but Ginnell's words were ringing apt. He went on to allege that the Inquiry had been an 'imposture', and "a greater crime than the theft of the jewels":

> To conceal criminals, with a knowledge of their guilt, is to become an accomplice and conpounder [*sic:* compounder] of felony, and the more closely the criminals are connected with the Government, the graver the crime of shielding them. With what object but shielding the crime and the criminals was the Viceregal Commission set up?

Rising to speak, the holier-than-thou Birrell informed the House he did not intend to "adopt a tone of virtuous indignation," and professed ignorance of what Ginnell claimed, stating:

> I do not know of any person whom I am shielding at the present time. I do not know of any criminal…All I know is the police assure me that during the course of their inquiries into the robbery of these jewels they did not come across the names of any persons to whom they could depose, and they were not put upon the track of any crime of any sort, horrible, or the reverse.

In a series of sharp exchanges, Ginnell asked him: "Didn't I give you the names of Gorges and Shackleton?"

Birrell answered that Ginnell could:

> communicate with the War Office and ascertain the circumstances under which those officers resigned their positions in the Army. I am not here to say a word in defence of either of these gentlemen whose names have just been given. Their names have been known to the police, and if the police were in possession or have any information which would lead to their detection, not necessarily as stealers of the jewels, but as having been guilty of odious crimes, every effort will be made to bring them to justice. Does the hon. Member suggest that I am in collusion?

Ginnell replied: "Will you not accept a sworn inquiry?"

665

Birrell offered the fudged reply: "That is not the way to ascertain whether people have been guilty of odious crimes. You do not have a sworn inquiry before you arrest a person. You proceed upon evidence..." He went on to again claim: "I want to discover who stole these jewels," and that "every effort I can make will be made in that direction." Lastly, he took issue with Ginnell having called the commissioners of the previous Inquiry his "creatures", stating that one such judge had since gone to his grave: "Will the hon. Member dare to get up, and say that that man, one of the most honourable and upright who ever lived in Ireland, was a 'creature of mine'?"

Ginnell shot back: "He got his reward within twelve months."

The coarse response was just what Birrell needed to divert the argument and reinforce his assumption of sanctity. He replied:

> I leave the House to judge whether a person capable of making a remark of that sort is likely to be of use to me in the further conduct of this inquiry. I assure him that I shall totally disregard what he says in the future.

Ginnell's final question, "Will you put these men on their trial?" was smugly ignored.

On the first day of 1913, the relentless Ginnell renewed his attack in Parliament, asking the Attorney General, Sir Rufus Isaacs:* "How is it that it is only in this particular case that the administrators of the criminal law have no information, refuse to seek it, and refuse to take it when given?" Ginnell again received the reply that the matters, including a sworn investigation, were not within the jurisdiction of the Director of Public Prosecutions.

The following week Ginnell asked that the Home Secretary, Reginald McKenna,† table a copy in the House of Inspector Kane's police report on the case. When the request was denied, and a request for an

---

* Rufus Daniel Isaacs, later 1st Marquess of Reading (1860–1935), Liberal M.P. and judge; Attorney General, Lord Chief Justice of England, Viceroy of India, and Foreign Secretary. Only the second Jewish member of cabinet, he was involved in the Marconi scandal. Married Alice Edith Cohen, and had issue.
† Reginald McKenna (1863–1943); banker and Liberal M.P. Married Pamela Jekyll, and had issue.

independent examination of the report was also turned down, Ginnell asked "if Kane's report did not contain the names of Lord Haddo, Lord Ronald Gower and Lord —"

At this point there was uproar with loud cries of 'Order!' The Speaker immediately once more rebuked Ginnell, stating: "The honourable Member has no right to use his position in the House to make such charges." This brought cries of 'Hear, hear!' Tellingly, *Hansard* didn't record any of the names, nor did any British newspaper dare. Even *The Labour Leader* only published of Ginnell: "He horrified the Speaker by suddenly calling out the names of three well-known men as those persons who were implicated." However, *The New York Herald* published the exchange, as featured here, although if its reporter had heard the name of the third nobleman, the paper's editor baulked at printing it. Given the mention of Gower, it was surely Lord Lorne (though by then he was Duke of Argyll); yet Lord Liverpool or Lord Aberdeen were also possibilities.

Every week of that January, Ginnell continued to lob questions about the theft, and a no-doubt weary Birrell, aided by McKenna, dutifully batted them away. When February rolled around, Birrell again faced his accuser to state, as he'd been doing since 1908:

> Nothing whatever has been discovered to throw any new light on the mystery of the theft of the Crown Jewels; nor is there any evidence whatever in existence at the present moment which would justify the arrest or prosecution of any person. The story, which someone must have invented out of spite, that anyone is being shielded from prosecution is simply a lie and I am sorry to have to add that it has lately been revived in connection with the name of Lord Haddo. The introduction of his lordship's name into the matter is a particularly cruel outrage, for, as already stated, he was not in Ireland for months before or after the robbery; he had no connection with the Office of Arms, and was only inside that office once in his life.

This time Ginnell asked him: "Will the right honourable gentleman say why Lord Haddo was not produced before the Commission?" Tellingly, no answer was given. In his final baiting of Birrell, Ginnell enquired: "Can the right honourable gentleman inform the House why, during the last five years, he has not been able to get anybody in

Ireland to believe his version of the story?" Again, no answer was given.

It would be nice to think that Augustine Birrell had actually believed what he'd been briefed about the case. But the picketing of the Chamber was the visible manifestation of the Government's lies, and proof that its priority was to bury the matter at all costs. In the face of Government stonewalling, and the claimed lack of evidence, those who sought the truth were helpless.

In 1911, a magazine published: "The true facts of the theft are known to a good many people," but reiterated that had the truth come out, a Eulenburg-style scandal would have been the result. "The thieves are safe, because they have it in their power to blast the honour of more than one great family."*

Cynicism over the Government's actions ran deep. When in 1912, private and state correspondence of George III and IV was discovered hidden behind a wall in the cellars of Apsley House, the London palace of the Duke of Wellington (a trustee of George IV), there were official denials. However as an American newspaper quipped, these were "no more sincere than the official assertions concerning the Dublin crown jewels."

In 1913, a journalist in *Truth* recorded: "To the Club, and all talking of this question of Ginnell's in the Commons yesterday concerning the Irish Crown Jewels, whose disappearance is still, after near 5 years, as great a mystery as ever." They considered it did "look as though these long persistent rumours that the Government be shielding someone have good foundation. But who it be is a matter of entire incertitude." By that date this seems less like puzzlement than blatant dissembling.

That summer, a libel case Arthur Vicars had taken out against the London *Daily Mail*, came to court. Following Shackleton's arrest, it had published a baseless story alleging a woman had stolen the Jewels

---

* Less believably the writer also claimed: "the jewels are in existence, intact, and the authorities still hope to recover them without a scandal…Some time ago a wealthy Irish peer offered to ransom the jewels on condition of being made Lord Lieutenant of Ireland when Lord Aberdeen retires. The offer was refused, chiefly because its acceptance would have led to serious trouble with the Irish nobility, with whom the peer in question is unpopular." [The Crown Jewels Mystery by W.F., *The Modern Man*, 8 April 1911, p3.]

using a copy of the safe's key. The newspaper's editor, by then the notorious Moreton Mandeville, believed her to be Vicars' mistress. Vicars and Lord and Lady Haddo testified in court to the falsehood of the claims, and Vicars was awarded a substantial £5,000 in damages – ten years his salary as Ulster King Of Alms.

As late as 1914 an Irish peer, Lord Winterton,* asked Birrell in the Commons whether he would order a judicial inquiry into the theft of the Jewels. Birrell replied that he didn't have the power to do so, even should he consider the circumstances warranted it. While technically correct, it was a conveniently misleading answer, implying that the Chief Secretary for Ireland had no influence on the path of justice there.

A government memorandum of 1927, that was only released in the mid-1970s, recorded the then President of the Irish Free State, W.T. Cosgrave, believed "that the Castle jewels are for sale and that they could be got for £2,000 or £3,000." There is no record of any action being taken.

Beyond the Kane dossier, files on the theft have been destroyed with a thoroughness that further points to malfeasance, and that this was no ordinary crime, but one of lofty connections. Even in the 1960s, when Viola Bankes and Francis Bamford began investigating the case for their book *Vicious Circle*, the cover-up was still in force. They would write:

> Our efforts to unravel the tangled yarns of evidence and narrative were, almost from the beginning, made more difficult by that enveloping cloak of silence with which, for his own mistaken reasons, King Edward the Seventh sought to shroud the whole affair...Even now, after more than fifty years, the mere mention of the case retains the power of afflicting reputedly intelligent persons with a kind of mass amnesia, rending them unable to remember anything of events in which they themselves, or their close relatives, were personally involved.

The impact of homosexuality in shaping social, political and artistic

---

* Edward Turnour, 6th Earl Winterton (1883–1962), Conservative M.P. Married the Hon. Cecilia Monica Wilson; no issue.

history continues to be far less known and appreciated than it should be. Suppressed, ignored, and depreciated, both at the time, and by historians subsequently, as part of the constant reassessment of the past, its significance is slowly being reclaimed, enabling a richer and truer historical perspective.

The late Victorian and Edwardian eras in Britain played host to a succession of major homosexual scandals, of which four have been known:

- the Dublin Castle Scandal of 1883-85
- the Cleveland Street Scandal of 1889-90
- the Trials of Oscar Wilde in 1895
- the Irish Crown Jewels Theft of 1907.

Now the Battersea Scandal can be added to this infamous roster. At least two of these cases, that of Cleveland Street and the Irish Crown Jewel Theft, had the potential to develop into constitutional crises. The interventions of officials, Prime Ministers, and not least Edward, as Prince of Wales and King, remain sobering case studies in the compromising of British law. Only with the Battersea Scandal was suppression almost completely successful, which is why it remained almost unknown. Until now.

One hundred and twenty years on, what was possibly the Edwardian era's biggest buried scandal has been disinterred, the dirt blown off, and its brassy exterior polished. All that's left is to speculate about the concealed names of all the distinguished participants. While the identities of some of these gentlemen are surely not a total mystery, at least for the present, this gallery of ghostly suspects will continue to pose intriguing questions.

ENVOI

In 1926, the famous detective Charles Arrow, who brought Bernard Fraser and Arthur Thorold to heel and unravelled Lord Battersea's procurement ring, published his memoirs, *Rogues and Others*. It was said of Arrow: "The most interesting things which he could write about if he chose are those which will not be dealt with in print."

Charles Arrow *was* prepared to write in discreet terms about the blackmailers with their decoy youths who haunted Piccadilly and Pall Mall. Yet of his most sensational case there was not a word. Given it was still highly radioactive, he was understandably not at liberty to discuss it, and would take its details to his grave.

Writing this book has also been a detective story: one with many twists, turns, and startling revelations. Indeed, another volume could have been written about writing it. For myself, as its author, the adventure began in late 2016. The *Chicago Tribune* had just digitised its archives, and while the project was in beta mode, it offered free access, inviting readers around the world to explore them.

Taking advantage of the opportunity, I was delighted to discover the vigour of nineteenth-century American journalism. Nor did the newspaper miss an opportunity to highlight the shortcomings of the Old World. News stories which reflected adversely upon it found an eager outlet in Chicago. This included matters that the British press, in its good manners, declined to publish. I also became acquainted with the syndicated gossip columns of the 'Marquis de Fontenoy', and wondered at the acerbic personality behind them.

So it was that one night while browsing the *Tribune* Archive, I came across the story from 1902 bearing the hyperbolic headline 'Britain Bows In Shame'. It stopped my screen scrolling in its tracks. Being late in the evening I was tired, and it was only some minutes after reading the article's broad hint as to the identity of the leading figure in the scandal —'the most handsome man in Parliament' — that I recalled this was the term regularly employed for Lord Battersea.

I knew Battersea had been involved in a homosexual scandal, the details of which were unknown. This was it! As the names of Fraser and Thorold were also given, I opened another browser window to Google, and typed in 'Arthur Thorold'. As it was the less common surname, it seemed a more promising search prospect. In my haste, I didn't enclose the name in inverted commas. Making a less defined search was actually fortuitous, because the very first item in the search results that came up was a document from The Southport School appropriately titled "Did You Know". It began:

> Arthur Charles Campbell 'Squarey' Thorold was born in Sussex, England in 1873. He attended colleges at Cambridge, Oxford and Marlborough and later became assistant housemaster at St. Edward's, Oxford. In 1906 he arrived in Australia and accepted a teaching position at The Southport School.

In a split second, the power of advanced digital search had made the connection between *that* Arthur and *this* Charles to reveal the truth — the deathly secret he'd been able to keep all his life. And which eluded even the assiduous Dr. Day in the 1980s.

However, at that moment my natural response was that The Southport School article couldn't possibly be referring to the same man. It was only after some hours of further research that the extraordinary truth of it began to seep in. By this time, dawn was breaking. But I was gripped. A few days later, an enquiry to the archivist of the School brought the reply: "We hold a copy of an unpublished thesis on Charles Thorold by a former headmaster. Would that be of interest?"

Bernard Fraser was initially harder to crack. Frederick Cunliffe-Owen's error that he was the son of a General led me down many blind alleys. Frasers had bred like rabbits, and with the military being their stomping ground, there were several General Frasers. I also came across newspaper references to the bizarre will of a Bernard Fraser Ross, with bequests to a 'Mohamedian'. Surely this too was someone different.

In one of those indexing quirks that bedevil archives, an online search of the UK National Archives catalogue for 'Bernard Fraser' brought up nothing relevant. However, when another search was undertaken without his name in inverted commas, or the name was reversed as 'Fraser, Bernard', a listing for his criminal file appeared in the results. As the days, weeks, months, and eventually years passed, the story slowly revealed itself; each new discovery making it ever more quietly thrilling. It begged to be told.

One surreal experience was visiting the Victorian Archives Centre in Melbourne, to view Charles Thorold's last testament. The Reading Room of the Archives is a modern and pristine subterranean bunker, which contributes to a sense of a liminal space where time itself feels anomalous, and the past and present meet. Removing the document from its protective clear plastic envelope, which shone under the bright halogen lighting, felt like examining forensic evidence. The thin sheet of school exercise book paper, with its hastily composed bequests, was more like a suicide note than a will.

Similarly, to stand under the low coved ceiling of the holding cell of the Norwich Criminal Court, where Fraser and Thorold had awaited their trial, was a sobering experience. At Norwich railway station, the original police office, where prisoners would have awaited transfer, also still existed.

In St. James's I was fortunate enough to take tea with the semi-mythical author, bibliophile, and fin de siècle expert Timothy d'Arch Smith. Sitting in the Cavendish Hotel with this charming godson of Princess Beatrice (the first one), felt a wonderful link with the past. His confession that he'd never heard of the Battersea scandal confirmed to me how well it had been smothered. "Was it to do with those chaps at the Society of Psychical Research?" he enquired in his soft voice – a speculation which made me laugh out loud at its percipience. I replied to him that it was possible some members were involved, but that a greater link was Liberal politics and golf – which made things seem rather pedestrian. However, as we have seen, it ultimately lead to circumstances that read like fiction. One professor suggested I investigate the circle around Henry James at Rye, due to it being, in his amusingly fogeyish words, "some kind of homosexual coven".

Visiting The Pleasaunce was another remarkable experience. Its dreamy privilege could still be felt in the deep silence broken by birdsong, and the vast lawn that stretched out to the blue haze of the sea. Lutyens' sun-washed kitchen suggested its staff were also blessed. However, reading Lady Battersea's diaries the following day in the British Library revealed the saga of servant trouble that provided off-stage grumbling in Paradise. Visits to seats of power, including Inveraray Castle, with its fairytale lichen-draped forest, and the palatial Lancaster (Sutherland) House in London, gave insight into the breathtaking other-worlds of the Dukes of Argyll and Lord Ronald Gower. In such environs, to believe oneself a god-like person, not bound by earthly constraints, including legal ones, would have been the easiest thing in the world. Particularly given that, in terms of entitlement, it was the truth.

Conducting interviews with elderly sources, and rescuing recollections from the brink of memory that stretched back to the Victorians, was a humbling experience. John Day also amused with deadly impressions of the high-pitched and strangled upper class voices of elderly dons and other relics, that were still to be encountered on his visit to England in 1987. My biggest outtake: how deeply privilege, family connections, and the gentlemanly code of honour had mattered.

That air of privilege lingers. In the preface to *Vicious Circle*, their 1965 book on the Dublin Crown Jewels theft, Viola Bankes and Francis Bamford wrote of the wall of "courteous evasion" they struck. Bankes was a daughter of the wealthy landed gentry family of the famed Kingston Lacy estate, while Bamford was a former Major in the Gordon Highlanders who became librarian to the 7th Duke of Wellington. Even with *their* backgrounds, they found prising open half-a-century-old Establishment secrets tough going.

In a similar experience, polite enquiries of my own to a few aristocratic families went unanswered. If it wasn't for the reassurance of *Debrett's*, one might have thought them extinct. America and the former colonies have something to teach of simple courtesy. A once-grand family played the game of polite inertia, where the doors seem wide open, but gracious apologies over poverty of time always precluded the goal. One descendant informed in a measured silvery tone: "If you do find out what happened – I don't. want. to. know." Fair enough. Happily, there were others that couldn't have been more helpful, sharing in the fun of discovery. Amusingly, one banker was so tickled to learn they possessed a disreputable predecessor, I had to beg for their pre-publication silence.

As the research progressed, and I reached out to scholars, I also became aware of the otherworld that lurks behind the pages of British historical and biographical scholarship. Due to the fact many documents of its historical ruling class are still held by them, the intrepid must tiptoe carefully. I was the grateful recipient of unprinted facts, collegiate gossip, and tips about more touchy descendants. It was reassuring to be told by a prominent historian that only a fraction of his own research enquiries elicit a response. One bizarre situation involved a clutch of privately-owned royal letters I sought, which had been loaned out to a biographer, and allegedly not returned. Another biographer cautioned: "One thing I learned in applying to private archives is avoid mentioning the 'H' word, and making suggestions of any sex scandal. These sensitivities suck of course, but best to play the innocent fool, and be the serpent under it." Too late for that!

When our lives on earth are but fleeting, the desire to hide century old family secrets would seem the last word in hubris. How many death beds does a person have to be present at before they wake up to such pointlessness: only their own?

Unfortunately, money and status not only swell pride, but warp everything. It's also a truism that the pride of formerly grand families sometimes expands in inverse proportion to their submergence into the middle class. Yet no coronet or bulging bank vault saves us from becoming dust. Sharing our humanity, in all its strange richness, can help make our own brief lives more comprehensible and meaningful. Hopefully, after reading the book, anyone who'd been concerned it would be an exercise in simple muckraking, will be grateful that the wayfarer who chanced upon the story within was as sympathetic as he has been.

Research in the Royal Archives proved fruitless, but if it hadn't been made so difficult, may have been more rewarding. The Archive is housed in Windsor Castle's Round Tower – never have I mounted two hundred stone steps to be confronted with so restricted a view. Despite its archivists having catalogues and finding aids (some of which appear to be digitised), at the time of writing, researchers are flatly denied access to them. Instead, they're expected to play a tiresome, time-wasting, and patronising question-and-answer guessing game to establish what might be there. As one historian aptly put it, it's "like going to a restaurant where there's no menu." That such preening opaqueness by a publicly-funded* institution has been indulged for so long is a wondrous testament to past deference, and the many authors – but not all – who have bitten their tongues over this farce for fear of losing access. However, with modern accountability rapping even on royal doors, for years a public online catalogue has supposedly been in the works.†

After assisting with some straightforward queries, The Rothschild Archive also disappointed with pointless obstructive officiousness that felt both bewildering and *plus royal que le Roi*. A brief biography of the Batterseas on the Archive's website states (in 2022): "Lord Battersea favoured the company of men, and he rumoured [*sic*] to have been involved in an 'indiscretion' in 1902." That's one word for it. In a Catch-22 situation, access to the Archive itself requires membership of an online Rothschild research forum: the first was denied me, making the latter impossible. Even a request for a mere catalogue list of the letters of Constance Battersea they hold was refused. "The Archive encourages research into every aspect of Rothschild history," so it has been printed. Clearly not.

Attempting a more direct connection with the family in the hope there might be some generational memories of the Batterseas, I was

---

* Partly through admission fees to publicly-owned royal residences.
† For Royal Archives suppression, see: Ben Macintyre, 'Royal Family Are More Secretive Than MI5', *The Times*, 29 October 2016; 'History And The Royal Family's "Secret" Archives', Letters To The Editor, *The Times*, 2 November 2016; and 'Author's Note' in Julia Baird, *Victoria the Queen*, Harper Collins, London 2016. For an historical perspective, see Yvonne M. Ward, *Censoring Queen Victoria: How Two Gentlemen Edited a Queen and Created an Icon*, Oneworld Publications, London 2014, *passim*; and Jane Ridley's 'Afterword: 'Bertie And The Biographers' in *Bertie: A Life of Edward VII*, Chatto & Windus, London 2012.

strung along for months by a representative, even receiving an apology for their being "dilatory about this". Eventually, silence reigned. (In glaring contrast, a nonagenarian relation responded within twenty minutes with a frank and helpful email.) The evasive politeness, which felt like trying to wade across a moat of pink marshmallow, I put down to plutocratic protectiveness and paranoia, but it also served to make me doubly appreciative of the unfussed help and interest I'd received from others.

One historian who *did* receive help from Rothschild family members was Derek Wilson, for his 1988 study *Rothschild: A Story of Wealth and Power*. However, after cataloguing Alfred de Rothchild's eccentricities, Wilson felt compelled to write:

> all these traits together are not sufficient to explain why the familiar smoke screen of Rothschild secrecy blows across the path leading to the *real* Alfred de Rothschild. Why, for instance, is access denied to the Halton* visitors book, which would tell us much more about his circle of close friends? And did he, or did he not, sire an illegitimate daughter? It seems there was something so shocking about Alfred's sex life that his relatives and even some of his more liberal-minded descendants have kept the facts to themselves.

In late 2021 there appeared *The Women Of Rothschild* – a multiple biography extensively featuring the Batterseas. The research timeline roughly parallelled my own, but that's where the similarities ended: married to a billionaire, the author was a highly connected Jewish and women's history scholar who enjoyed the support of Rothschild family members. Suddenly all seemed a little more understandable: when dealing with the history of a fraught family alliance, who would not welcome a rich fragrant friend over a snooping stranger?

Happily, the book was well researched and written, bringing to the biographical forefront the women behind the men, and proved helpful to this work. That said, in dealing with the Batterseas it omitted less attractive aspects of Constance's character and behaviour, and even allowing for the work's focus, shortchanged Cyril. Beatrice Webb's snap judgement that he had no public spirit

---

* Alfred's Buckinghamshire estate.

was quoted, but seemed to be taken at face value. While Constance's philanthropy was extensively outlined, there was not a word of her husband's own generosity. The scandal was referred to, but in the absence of details, the author even pondered whether his illness was "emphasised both by Cyril and Constance in her diaries, to diminish what had happened," or that his sudden withdrawal from social activities due to the illness resulted in the belief he was embroiled in a scandal that may have only involved others. George Ives' diary entry stating that the King had quashed the scandal was quoted, but there was striking incuriosity as to how the law could be so readily overturned, or why, had Cyril been guilty, he escaped any form of punishment or ostracism. Writing from a position of privilege isn't always a plus. Being an outsider sometimes serves very well.

Despite the occasional roadblocks I encountered, the research terrain could have been far worse. It could have been Algeria. Enquiries regarding Iguerbouchène needed to be directed to that sunny but shadowed land, where they struck a wall of unhelpfulness from institutions, businesses and individuals that, with rare exception, ranged from indifference to rebuffs. And that was just when email accounts and phone numbers actually worked. (As one visitor quipped: "Nothing works here except the sun.") Turning to an embassy for help, even they couldn't raise a response. The impression delivered was that the national characteristic is suspicion, and anything achieved is only accomplished by stubbornness, subterfuge, or pure accident. It was a sobering glimpse into the profound attitudinal problems the country faces in building a better future.

On a brighter note, there was heartening assistance and wisdom from a great many people I never met. Including an archivist at London's Guildhall who answered a discreet written query about Bernard Fraser with a fascinating reply of over a thousand words, that began with the explanation: "I became intrigued by this man!" Dr. John Day responded ever-graciously to waves of questions.

The identity of the fourth procurer was pursued down many blind alleys – and even glens: the 9th Duke of Argyll's Chamberlain at Inveraray being one of the many who bore the name Wyllie. Like some other suspects, this seemed too unlikely a prospect. I finally became resigned to the fact that the true Mr. W would remain an enigma. Then one evening I encountered the name again, but this time a mere few words away from Cyril Flower's, quietly staring back at me in Wilfrid Blunt's published diary.

That was not the end of it. After eliminating further Wylliesque candidates who'd cropped up in the research,* I spied the name 'A.H. Wiley' sitting near Bernard Fraser's, in a newspaper article on Lord Beauchamp's wedding which listed the gift-givers. Searches to find further mentions of 'A.H. Wiley' proved frustrating failures. Backtracking, I looked for further reports of the wedding. Luckily, there was another which also featured the names of gift-givers. However, it spelt the crucial name 'A.H. Wylie'. Bingo! This variation brought up a host of appearances at Society events. All I had to do, as with everyone else, was to find out who he was. Unless even more likely suspects are uncovered, one must presume the fourth man is either Frank or Alex.

While I had incorporated into the narrative *The Times* obituary of Arthur Collins, which references his concern for the welfare of District Messenger boys, it was only much later when rechecking facts that I learnt he'd been a director of the company! It was a sobering reminder that one can never review sources enough.

An email exchange with a kindly, politically conservative historian proved helpful in clarifying the narrative. Having shared aspects of the book with him, but not the text which was still in draft, he remarked: "I'm sorry you should take the view that all those gay toffs deserved imprisonment for buggery rather than being given the chance to flee to the Continent". I replied that he'd misunderstood me: the crux of the matter wasn't whether one believed they deserved it, in either an historical or modern context, but rather, that of class injustice: the hypocrisy of allowing the high-born, rich, and celebrated to escape or be granted legal immunity, while punishing the middle class for the same offences, and even more brutally the working class. And all for the reason the British Government believed it was necessary if respect for the ruling class was to be preserved, and thereby, effective government and social order.

Then in March 2020 the pandemic from Wuhan arrived. Shutting

---

* Dismissed candidates included Sir Francis James Wylie (1865–1952), a tutor to Lord Rosebery's sons, who went on to become first secretary of The Rhodes Trust; and Alexander Wylie (1839–1921), Conservative M.P. for Dumbartonshire from 1895 to 1906.

down archives and libraries, it created the quiet time to go over the entire book and make additions and improvements. Early in the research I had come across accounts of Francis Widdows. When the scholar of gay history Rictor Norton wrote to say that, that as part of his online project of transcribing trial reports, he was uploading those of Widdows, I was prompted to look more closely at the ex-monk's chequered career. This lead in turn to the Rev. J.L. Lyne, Aelred Carlyle, and others. While I'd mentioned Anglican notables in the draft, I realised these colourful renegades needed to be incorporated. After all, the oppression of homosexual people was justified, and rested upon the foundation of the State religion and its superstition, which they and the army of more compliant homosexual priests represented. Fortunately, new studies are now filling in the gaps in this homo-religious sphere that was previously overlooked, and whose importance and influence on Victorian and Edwardian society can't be underestimated.

The memo by Falconer Madan in the Beinecke Library's copy of *Boy-Worship* revealed the suppression of the Rev. Huth Walters scandal. It was while researching this that I also came across the later scandal of the Rev. John Edwards. Who would think that a note in the back of a pederastic tract, printed by a university student in 1880, would contain clues to matters of national consequence? It was again proof that even seemingly trivial sources can sometimes prove hugely important, especially when context is taken into account. Now I had three further examples of Lord Salisbury's 'tricks with justice'. Intensely religious himself, he sincerely believed in suppressing these incidents for a higher good.

It was while investigating these clergymen's cases that I also came across the Rev. R.C. Fillingham, and his links to Lord Battersea. A newspaper report of his will mentioned his diaries, bequeathed to Merton College. A simple email enquiry produced the astonishing reply that they amounted to 186 volumes. All unpublished. And unread. Except apparently by a previous librarian, when they were being catalogued.

I had been stymied by the deaths of those who might have known Mohamed Iguerbouchène during his time in Paris, but a faint-hearted query to the archives of the Paris police uncovered a revealing dossier bearing his name. At the end of 2015, the French government finally made available the police and legal archives of the Vichy regime. A query to the Ministry of the Interior subsequently uncovered another crucial intelligence dossier. As it contained recent material, and was still closed, gaining access required submitting a further special request.

Attempts to make contact with those close to Iguerbouchène also ultimately paid off when two sources cautiously responded. It had literally taken years, and required all the delicacy of walking on broken glass. One of the sources, while admiring Iguerbouchène's artistic achievement, was bitterly disappointed in the man.

Mindful of the sentiment "good writing never comes from the display of virtue,"* with a few exceptions I have been conscious that moral judgements are best left to readers. Obviously, desire lay deep at the heart of the concern for the welfare of boys and youths manifested by such figures as Lieutenant-Colonel Arthur Collins with the Gordon Boy's Home; Lord Euston and The Royal Masonic Institution for Boys; Quintin Hogg and his Ragged School and Polytechnic; and Charles Thorold who lived to shape his students into well-rounded gentlemen. With characters like Kitchener, Rhodes and Baden-Powell in the Edwardian driving seats, one could be forgiven for thinking the British Empire ran on sublimated lad lust.† Those who acted on their desires may have been the exception – although perhaps a larger exception than previously believed. Reading the diaries and letters of the cabinet ministers of the period is to sense that, however sophisticated they might be, at heart they remained public schoolboys.

Reading what I could of the voluminous diaries of the Rev. Fillingham – a fascinating, sobering, and occasionally unintentionally comic experience – I could only conclude that his own relationships with youths had been nearly or wholly platonic. Even the lyrically unleashed Reverend E.E. Bradford cautioned his readers regarding "checking the wayward will", and in the blank pages of the personal copies of his published works he recorded the praise of admirers for,

---

* "the most beautiful and important truths are found where the glare of certainty can't reach." George Packer, 'The Enemies of Writing', *The Atlantic*, 23 January 2020; https://www.theatlantic.com/ideas/archive/2020/01/packer-hitchens/605365/]
† For an analysis, see: Ronald Hyam, *Empire and Sexuality: The British Experience*, Manchester University Press, 1990; Robert Aldrich, *Colonialism and Homosexuality*, Routledge, 2002.

as one put it, "your glorious crusade for winning over the plain man to an understanding of Platonic Love."

In our own cynical and highly sexualised age, scarred by endless exposures of abuse, and where public admiration of youthful beauty is now often frowned upon, the very notion of platonic pederasty, however philanthropic, pedagogic, or chivalric, is likely to be considered by many as self-delusion, and as unsettling as its sexualised form. Yet transmuted desire is a thing the Victorians understood very well: it was a marker of the age. However, the changing boundaries of acceptability currently now serve to make even Henry Scott Tuke's canvases 'challenging' – as the monograph* of a recent Tuke exhibition addressed. That depictions of youthful naked beauty now cause unease, and are felt to need disclaimers, is a sadness that would have bewildered many Victorians, and may cause wonder in future generations.

Personally enlightening to me was how important Walt Whitman's poetry had been in the lives of many of these men:† how his alchemy of eros and liberty had left them feeling lightning-stuck; how homosexual desire and a longing for fellowship with working men played an important role in British life and Liberal and Labour politics; and how Cyril Flower, with his wealth and influence, was one of those who took it to the next level. Including through his work on behalf of polytechnics and adult education. It was an enormous contribution to the public good. It also serves as a reminder that most homosexual history is not a niche history: it exists within the greater world of its time, which shapes it, but which it equally impacts upon.‡

The historiography of Whitman scholarship mirrors that of most

---

* Cicely Robinson, et al, *Henry Scott Tuke*, Yale University Press, 2021, pp14-16.
† In 1887, when the poet's financial situation was precarious, Lord Ronald Gower was one of three gentlemen who discreetly forwarded Whitman the New Year's present of £80. The two others were the handsome and discreetly bohemian diplomat Sir Edward Baldwin Malet (1837–1908), who was married to an eccentric daughter of the 9th Duke of Bedford, and built a magnificent Beaux-Arts villa near Monaco; and Arnold Gerstenberg (1864–1887), the son a Jewish financier, graduate of Trinity College, Cambridge, and lieutenant in the Hussars, who committed suicide. Under the terms of his will, a scholarship was founded for the study of moral philosophy and metaphysics. [Henry Norman to Walt Whitman, 3 February 1887, The Charles E. Feinberg Collection of the Papers of Walt Whitman, Library of Congress; Whitman Archive ID: loc.00720.]
‡ For a discussion of the influence of Whitman and Carpenter on British colleges, guilds, socialist clubs, and alternative religion, see: H.G. Cocks, *Nameless Offences: Homosexual Desire In The Nineteenth Century*, I.B. Tauris, London, 2003, pp157-198.

other historical gay figures, beginning with wilful evasion, obtuseness, and scholarly bullying worthy of the Thought Police. Incredibly, even as late as the 1970s, academic studies were still either straight-washing him or anomalising his sexuality, presenting it as something obsessive or abnormal. It's an erasure which blithely continues across other historical figures, and which it would be remiss not to note.

In 1902, Lord Ronald Gower replied to a letter from his friend Hugh Lane: "With much travail I have been able partially to read your cryptogram my dear Hugh and arrive at a gleaning of the meaning of your hooks & grappling wires." Gower was likely referring to the idiosyncrasies of Lane's handwriting, but written and verbal disguise was also once a basic means of daily survival for those whose sexuality contradicted law. Yet when some historians and biographers can still be so tone-deaf, dumb and blind to nuance, let alone to social associations, a mature and balanced treatment of other sexualities can occasionally still seem a distant prospect. Edward Carpenter's literary executor called it "a failure of the heterosexual imagination". It's more than that. It's a failure of the imagination period – and of basic human empathy.* If there's one thing I've learnt from writing this book, it's never to assume *anything* about anybody. A richer and more rewarding history will be the result. At the opposite extreme, I was also keen to avoid forcing my characters into the airless, self-admiring mirror-maze of 'Queer Theory', whose ideologies and works are often untenable, irrelevant, and worse, unreadable.

Another thing that struck me while writing the book was how brief the majority of these lives had been – most of the gentlemen were

---

* The litmus test might well be Shakespeare's sonnets, for which tortuous evasions of the meaning of most explicit and obvious lines to the Fair Youth (e.g. Sonnet 52) continue to be peddled. Historical studies encountered during the writing of this book included a biography of Bret Harte penned by an editor of the journal *American Literary Scholarship*, which reproved a prior biography of Harte by Axel Nissen, for being "marred by its search for evidence of homoeroticism in Harte's life and writing." (Scharnhorst, *Bret Harte*, 2000, p238.) What a warning for any enterprising scholar! There was also a 2018 BBC documentary on Sir Thomas Lipton, which succeeded in omitting any reference to his private life. A journalist who wrote an accompanying article informed this author: "If his sexuality had been relevant, I'd have mentioned it. It wasn't." In response, the question was posed: "If Lipton had lived with a woman for 30 years [rather than William Love], and there was not a particle of other evidence about her, would she be mentioned?" This elicited the response: "Fair point...I'll bear it in mind." One would bloody like to hope! What could be more formative to a life than existing, and succeeding, in a society which virulently condemned one's true self? What could be more illuminating of character than the masks and ruses adopted for self-protection, the personal sacrifices made, and the outsider perspective bestowed?

dead by their mid-sixties.* I was also impressed by how self-reinventing they were. You really *can* be whoever you wish to be. And, you really *can* will into reality your wildest fantasy – from a pleasaunce to an abbey. It's a very gay thing.

Just as fresh information on the Cleveland Street Scandal has come to light, the passage of time will surely reveal more information about the Battersea Scandal. Somewhere in a castle, country house or archive, the truth awaits. At least one attic close to the story holds a hoard of family correspondence stretching back centuries, that may reveal more.

One hope had lain at Palermo. There, the grand Villa Malfitano had been a virtual international crash pad for cosmopolitan confirmed bachelors, whose hostess, Caterina ('Tina') Whitaker, delighted in them. Her guests had included Lord Ronnie Gower, and other friends of Cyril who may have been involved in the scandal. The Villa with its contents, including Tina's hefty correspondence, was bequeathed to a foundation. However, Sicily being Sicily, according to one account, for a time following the death of Tina and her daughter, the Villa was "extensively raided by jackals and regional traffickers" who made it their domain, before proper management was asserted. There were allegedly other troubling issues. Whatever occurred, with the exception of some letters from author Robert Hichens, the archive now holds no correspondence, if it ever did, from any of Tina's wayward friends.†

Amongst the people who kindly answered my requests for help was John Montagu, the 11th Earl of Sandwich. He is a collateral descendant of Edward, 8th Earl, who'd visited The Pleasaunce that

---

* Obviously partly due to smoking, and London's air, of which an American journalist wrote: "The smoke and the coal-dust, the sulphate of ammonia, produced in the atmosphere by burning enormous quantities of coal, and the sulphurous acid, are at first intensely disagreeable to the stranger. If a window be left slightly open, books, writing paper, fine linens, and silks are found soiled and besmirched with the black particles which hover in to do their unpleasant work; and a wristband, immaculate at nine o'clock, must be changed at noon. One soon discovers why it is that the Londoner is perpetually washing his hands..." [Edward King, *Descriptive Portraiture Of Europe In Storm And Calm*, C.A. Nichols & Company, Springfield, Mass. 1886, p620.]

† Fortunately, a month before the death of her daughter Delia in 1971, Raleigh Trevelyan (1923–2014) had with her support completed his biography of the family, *Princes Under The Volcano*. The erudite, cosmopolitan, and homosexual Trevelyn was the perfect authorial match for the material.

fatal August of 1902, with Colonel Collins and Frank Walsh. Following a morning rummage in the 8th Earl's papers, in a somewhat surprised and apologetic email, the current Earl replied to me: "unfortunately it seems there is a gap in our archive. I found no letters from close personal friends." Amongst the papers he did turn up was some general correspondence with members of the Royal Family, and with a nephew, but nothing else of the period. It was not an unusual circumstance. As I had come to learn, curious absences abounded in the records of Lord Battersea's circle of friends.

The private papers of Reginald, Viscount Esher, now principally held at Cambridge, are voluminous. He made Charles 'Chat' Williamson, a schoolfriend who lived in Venice with a gondolier, his executor, instructing him: "all my papers, letters, etc. are to be examined personally by you – rubbish etc. destroyed and the rest sealed up and handed over to Nellie for Oliver [his wife and older son] to see later on." Amongst the sensitive files Williamson boldly preserved for posterity is a volume labelled 'The Case Of Lord Arthur Somerset'. It contains the letters exchanged during the Cleveland Street Scandal between Esher, Lord Arthur, his solicitor Arthur Newton, and friends, and makes plain the interventions Esher made on Somerset's behalf.

In the 1930s, Esher's younger son Maurice edited his father's diaries and letters for publication, at which time typescripts were made, and the manuscript diaries apparently destroyed. The only original diaries now known to exist are from 1872 to 1890, with a gap from June to November 1890, that is explained by an entry dated November 5:

> From June 1889 onwards, certain events in connection with a great sorrow to a personal friend* and his unfortunate family, occupied nearly all my time. They ended disastrously for all concerned in the closing months of last year. The worry of them was maintained through the first half of the present year.

The typescripts of the diaries, bound in 21 volumes, run from 1870 to 1922. Yet the entries for the years 1895 to 1907, when Esher was at the peak of his influence, fill but a single volume. Only two entries exist for 1902. While he was certainly very busy during this period,

---

* i.e. Lord Arthur Somerset.

the highly suspicious gaps suggest substantial expurgation. Whether Esher's desires led him to greater involvement in the Battersea case, beyond possibly providing discreet assistance to the guilty, remains an enigma. At least for now.

Lewis, Viscount Harcourt's papers are held at Oxford. His appointment diaries between 1899 and 1907 are missing, and there are even larger gaps in the run of his political journals. The surviving papers of the Earl of Halsbury in the British Library also contain nothing touching on the Battersea Scandal. It is not surprising. For the Victorians and Edwardians, destroying discreditable and sensitive private papers was second nature.* In 1910, Aretas Akers-Douglas casually informed a friend that he was reviewing his correspondence, and had destroyed fifty-three letters from Queen Victoria and over sixty from Lord Salisbury. For Akers-Douglas to preserve any paper from his time as Home Secretary which indicated he'd facilitated a miscarriage of justice on behalf of Lord Battersea, was never going to be on the cards.

Cyril's friend Edward Marjoribanks, Lord Tweedmouth, was equally discreet. His sister wrote:

> Lord Tweedmouth made it a rule never to keep any notes or journal of any kind, and he made it a point of honour to destroy all confidential communications between himself and Mr. Gladstone and many other politicians and public men with whom he corresponded.

At the time of the Eulenburg scandal, a German newspaper, the *Leipziger Volkszeitung,* alleged that Tweedmouth had recently been

---

* The truism that truth can take a long time to surface is even truer where grand families and homosexuality are concerned. For example, it took almost three-quarters of a century for the knowledge that Lewis Harcourt's death was a suicide to become known outside the small Establishment circle. When in 1995 *The Times* political columnist Matthew Parris, in his book *Great Parliamentary Scandals,* shared the further titbit that Lord Esher had cleansed Harcourt's home of his collection of youthful porn following the event, a *third generation* descendant banged off an aggrieved letter to biographer James Lees-Milne, from whence the information had originally come. Adding to this wry comedy, the rebuked Lees-Milne – a conflicted homosexual married to a lesbian, then wrote in his diary of the gay Parris: "I don't like these flaunting homosexuals with their pleased-with-themselves attitude, as though they were deprived and stood for a noble cause. It isn't a noble cause. It is a mistake." [*The Milk Of Paradise: James Lees-Milne Diaries, 1993-1997,* Michael Bloch (ed.), John Murray, London 2005, p196.]

accused of the new-fangled *homosexualität*. However, given the then-as-now overwrought character of some of that nation's press, the claim must be treated with caution.

The 9th Duke of Argyll – 'Lorne', and Princess Louise, may possibly have destroyed correspondence with the industriousness of Constance Battersea's executors. Louise was as outspoken on paper as she was in conversation. When her remaining papers arrived at Windsor Castle following her death in 1939, the file was purged to within an inch of its life – or "dispersed", as the Royal Librarian of the time, Sir Owen Morshead, unctuously phrased it. At Windsor, there is no correspondence from either Cyril, Constance or Ronnie Gower, which given the closeness of their friendships, is its own statement. I was informed the Princess's file had been "generally closed for research" as late as 2014, which given the mostly mundane contents that survived, is telling. Although it has been denied, it's bleedingly obvious a miasma of custodial nervousness lingered over Louise and Lorne's legacy for decades.

At Inveraray Castle, only a fraction of Lorne's diaries survive, as "literally odd pages torn from their original binding". What remains contains no mention of Cyril Flower. No letters to Lorne from Lord Ronnie exist either, despite the fact he sometimes wrote to him daily. Possibly the main person responsible for this loss was the 11th Duke of Argyll. An indolent, abusive alcoholic and chronic gambler, who is only really known for his sensational 1963 divorce case against Margaret, his third Duchess, he apparently funnelled frustration at his own failures into suppressing those of others. An envelope in Inveraray's archive containing letters from Lorne to his brother Lord Archibald Campbell, bears the Duke's initial, and the words: "Weeded 10.1.72". Most of Princess Louise's letters also appear to have been destroyed.

Elsewhere the story is the same. What remains of Alfred de Rothschild's personal papers, now at the Rothschild Archive, has been thoroughly sanitised. Amongst the boxes of domestic receipts, his hypochondriacal medical bills live on. As for the secretive Earl of Rosebery: the National Library of Scotland holds many of his private papers, but others remain at Dalmeny which have only very rarely been made available to scholars. This author was not one of them. However, anything compromising that was not destroyed by

Rosebery is unlikely to have lasted long. Following his death, his papers, which "were in a terrible muddle," were gone through by his youngest daughter, Lady Margaret ('Peggy'). She married Robert Crewe-Milnes, 1st Marquess of Crewe, who wrote the official biography of Rosebery, published in 1931.

What is perhaps even more remarkable are the omissions from the published record. John Morley's memoirs aren't the only ones in which Cyril Flower is curiously absent. Despite their friendship and mutual interests, Cyril scores not a single mention in George Moore's three-volume autobiography. He is similarly absent from the memoirs of Herbert Asquith, which stretched to four volumes. Yet Cyril had championed Asquith's entry into politics: as Constance recalled, "he took the greatest pleasure in offering Mr. Asquith all the opportunities that lay in his power of meeting such men as would appreciate him and be useful to him in his career." Asquith had also met his second wife Margot at a dinner given by Cyril, and was so close a friend, they'd gone on a walking tour in Switzerland together. Cyril Flower's absence from Asquith's memoirs therefore seems less a casual omission, than a conscious decision to write him out of his own problematic personal history. Perhaps it was too painful and close to home. After all, Herbert Gladstone had sought Asquith's advice on Bernard Fraser's case. And there were Asquith's own foibles: aside from his drinking, which earned him the nickname of 'Squiff', he carried a reputation as an 'inveterate groper', who would take a lady's hand as she sat with him on a sofa and make her feel his erection.

The mostly unpublished diaries of another prominent Liberal figure Lord Carrington (later Lord Lincolnshire), are obviously written with an eye for posterity, rather than as a private confessional. He later indexed them, and glued blank slips of paper over at least two entries, for the 22nd and 24th of July 1902.* These possibly dealt with the King. Despite Carrington being near the heart of events of the Battersea affair, he committed nothing to his diary regarding it until Cyril's public return, when he made the discreet entry, earlier quoted. Yet Carrington had holidayed at Cromer that September, when he dined with Cyril's neighbours Lord and Lady Suffield, and dined tête-

---

* The diaries were photographed for the Bodleian in 1972. There are missing pages on its copy of the 1902 diary, for 21 September–2 October and 11–12 October. While this might be assumed to be further bowdlerisation, the pages are in fact blank in the original diary. [The 7th Baron Carrington to author, August 2022.]

à-tête with Rosebery in November.

Carrington had a wife and family, and while a political radical, was as solidly an Establishment a figure as any man could be, including in the matter of discretion. However, he had a double emotional life: as also previously noted, his name was logged by a Scotland Yard detective for engaging in homosexual activity. Like Cyril and Lord Beauchamp, this secret was very possibly the seed crystal that drew him beyond the bubble of privilege and politically radicalised him. (Carrington was a confidant of the King: it was he who encouraged and accompanied him, as Prince of Wales, to make his incognito tour of the East End slums in the 1880s.) While Carrington was no particular friend of Cyril's, the danger, including psychological, that the scandal represented for certain gentlemen even at arm's-length, apparently led him to consider it unmentionable.

In 1976, when the first study of the Cleveland Street Scandal was published, a book reviewer in *The New York Times* was struck by the eternal dilemma its prosecutors faced:

> how vigorously to proceed against big names...This predicament has a very modern ring. Title, wealth and class position are still very heavy thumbs on the scale of justice.

How much has really changed since then in the governing of Britain makes for an interesting debate. Half a century after men first walked on the moon, the head of state still retains purposely vague high powers due to sheer luck of birth. In the House of Lords, like a feudal gathering, sit the life peers, alongside 92 hereditary peers – dukes, marquesses, earls, viscounts, and barons, plus 26 Church of England bishops: all of them unelected, but shaping the legislation under which tens of millions live.*

Other troubling aspects of Britain's governance also remain

---

* On the positive side: in 2021, the 9th Duke of Wellington tabled a proposal in the House of Lords to hold the country's gimcrack water companies to account for releasing sewage effluent. It was voted down by Tories in the Commons, but following public protests, which caught the Government unawares, an amendment by the Duke was accepted. That it took a nobleman to remind a lower chamber of their duty to provide the people with clean rivers and seas, and stand against what critics termed a Government of 'spivs, chancers and conmen,' would have warmed the hearts of Walter Bagot and Arnold White. [Duke of Wellington battles for sewage U-turn, *Evening Standard*, 27 October 2021.]

unchanged. Its media remains shackled by punitive libel law, and with a weakened Freedom Of Information Act,* the nation remains very much a secret state, where information is locked down and duplicity reigns. "The British are, in large part, a deferential people" historian Ian Cobain wrote with magnificent understatement in his study of national secrecy *The History Thieves*.

All this occurs in the service of the Crown, which has always been far more than the symbolic and ceremonial entity most of the British public take it for. It exists as an amorphous supra-governmental entity. One that is served by a self-perpetuating civil service priesthood, who are adept in the dark arts of obscurantism in overriding democratic purpose and Parliament. The Crown provides a handy umbrella for Governments to implement and disguise acts that might wither under public scrutiny. As the State is pushed and shaped by modern pressures, technologies, and attitudes to assume ever more Orwellian a form, so the Crown and what is perpetrated in its name becomes more ominous and oppressive.

In 1995, a former editor of *The Times*, Lord Rees-Mogg,† wrote that "Moral relativism is...the spongiform creed of the British Establishment, of modern government, of modern education, of modern broadcasting...of the whole moral consciousness of present-day Britain." This is true. However, he sought to cast its adoption by the Establishment as a recent development – an appealing fogeyish fantasy, but a fatuous one. As another writer put it: "British national conceit and history books are replete with double standards and moral relativism."

It was a matter of simple pragmatism. As we have seen, 'whatever it takes' has always been the Establishment's prevailing ethic. The very flexibility of its morality, its ready willingness to compromise, has been its greatest survival tactic. What *has* evolved and fractured is the Establishment itself: there is no longer a unifying, governing interest at work. Once cohesive – Anglo-Saxon, male, and public school – it is now unstable and riven by self-interested opportunists.‡

---

* A fortune in public money is wasted annually by UK Government departments in legal challenges to FOI disclosure. Documents are also withheld by deploying the diabolical ruse that they are Crown copyright.
† William Rees-Mogg, Baron Rees-Mogg (1928–2012).
‡ See: Aeron Davis, *Reckless Opportunists: Elites at the End of the Establishment*, Manchester University Press, 2019.

Despite socialist additions, most notably the National Health System and inheritance tax, Britain remains a country rigged for the rich. The descendants of those who once administered Britain's Empire now oversee a vast financial services industry that has made London, the money laundering capital of the world, and penetrated government to shape its laws for their own interests. This is all made possible by ludicrously weak financial legislation and policing. It includes offshore tax avoidance on behalf of elites and multinational corporations, for whom sweetened closed-door tax deals with the government are also arranged. Other rorts include the extortionate private financing of public infrastructure. This legal looting of the public purse erodes the ability of government to look after the interests of ordinary people. The situation has become so outrageous that even the vast neoclassical Custom House that fronts the Thames, which is an office building tenanted by the tax authority, Her Majesty's Revenue and Customs, is offshore-owned to avoid tax!

The most marked change in national life is the degree of public cynicism, due to a greater awareness of the lies and manipulations of government, corporations, and powerful individuals. New forces that corrode moral leadership have also arisen: the most dangerous being the influence of foreign dictatorships, criminal regimes, and their cronies. The pernicious influence of China within British universities – now eager to prostitute themselves as its regional service centres, has drawn alarm, while a Parliamentary report published in 2020 confirmed that Russian interference in British politics was pervasive. Three years previously, a news investigation revealed Israel seeking to do the same.

The infiltration of Russian and former Soviet state black money, corruption, and soft power into the highest reaches of British society has become another cancer, which the Government's delayed and feeble response to Vladimir Putin's invasion of Ukraine in 2022 only underlined. However, the attack also served as a wake-up call to Government, and some tightening of financial legislation has consequently occurred. Yet the lack of transparency in the administration of Britain's financial sector is inextricably tied to the culture of secrecy which infects the nation's governance as a whole.

In a global trend, free speech, free media, and free inquiry are also increasingly under attack, supported by a new generation of ideologues and self-appointed censorship brigades, who demand arbitrary mob justice. Blind to history, and intolerant of nuance and ambiguity, their closed minds, and violent resentment of divergent ideas and opinions they view as undebatable heresy, represent an increasing danger to enlightened democracy. Subjected to public shaming, or the mere threat of it, those who disagree are driven to silence themselves.*

Like other Western democracies, Britain is also facing popular movements driven by race, gender, and other ideological concerns, that seek to relativise objective truth, and substitute it with subjective perspectives and feelings. Government and public bodies are acceding to these demands, threatening an era of 'post-truth'. Hearteningly, intelligent debate and resistance is manifesting in these culture wars.

Nonetheless, national unity is dissolving, setting the stage for the rise of showboating demagogues. The growth of tribalism is amplifying this, yet public acknowledgement of it is frowned upon. Disraeli's 'two nations' have become many. Widely felt, but dared not spoken, is a belief that profound demographic change is breeding an intemperateness that the British – or at least the English – once frowned upon as a foreign failing. A corresponding decline in national serenity and contentment is noticeable.

As well as these deficiencies, there is revived concern in policing quarters over the felonious underclass – The Mob. Not only has it multiplied, but it is also more alien and alienated than ever. Given the nihilistic inner city riots of August 2011, which produced the greatest civil unrest in Britain since the Gordon Riots, including an assault on the then Prince of Wales and his wife, such anxiety is not undue.

Reflecting the political malaise, the edifice of the State appears ramshackle; shored up by increasing constrictions on civil liberties, and the surveillance and policing of thought. Perhaps it was ever so. As in most jurisdictions, the belief within Whitehall that 'nobs know better than plebs' – that the proletariat should not be privy to the

---

* The closing lines of the Tennyson poem which Cyril Flower quoted in his speech at Luton in 1885 seem timely: "Should banded unions persecute/Opinion, and induce a time/When single thought is civil crime/And individual freedom mute;/…I seek a warmer sky."

innermost workings of their governments, as it is not in the best interests of either – remains the prevailing one. Its facilitation of the crucifixion of Julian Assange, for his humiliating exposure of imperialist misdeeds, is simply a vindictively ugly public demonstration of this creed.

In 2019, *The Mountbattens*,[*] a biography of Earl Mountbatten and his wife by historian Andrew Lownie, was published. It catalogued how, for half a century, British Governments and the Establishment allowed a charming, but imperious incompetent[†] to run rampant merely because he was royalty. While others were checked and punished, covering up Louis Mountbatten's failures and sexual criminality was unceasing; the red carpet not only rolled out before him, but also behind him in protective memory.[‡] A costly multi-year legal battle by Lownie with the Government to release Mountbatten's private papers, that had been purchased with public money, became a landmark freedom of information case. In a witness statement, the Orwellian-titled head of 'knowledge and information management' at the Cabinet Office suggested that, if released, the material could impact the 'dignity' of the Sovereign. It was the same justification that had been used to smother any number of scandals with royal connections, from Cleveland Street to Maundy Gregory. The vigour

---

[*] Andrew Lownie, *The Mountbattens: Their Lives & Loves*, Blink Publishing, London 2019.

[†] Noted historian Andrew Roberts dubbed Mountbatten "a mendacious, intellectually limited hustler…promoted wildly above his abilities, with consistently disastrous consequences." [Andrew Roberts, *Eminent Churchillians*, Weidenfeld & Nicholson, London 1994. For a discussion of Mountbatten's biographical reputation, see: Adrian Smith, *Mountbatten: Apprentice War Lord*, Bloomsbury, London 2010, Introduction.]

[‡] This includes suppressing an alleged association with the infamous Kincora Boys Home of Belfast. This scandalous level of censorship is actually the standard for matters dealing with that surreal entity, the monarchy. As another scholar has detailed, the manuscripts of Harold Macmillan's diaries, held by the Bodleian Library at Oxford, have been "quite heavily censored by the Cabinet Office, which redacted most references to Macmillan's audiences with the Queen." Additionally, the published version of the diaries printed only the most anodyne material of what survived. "The Palace has been extremely active in recent years in lobbying for ever greater restrictions on the public's access to records relating to the Royal Family, and successive governments have largely surrendered to this pressure. As a result it is becoming increasingly difficult to conduct serious historical research into the role of the British monarchy, even in relation to events that took place half a century ago." [Clive Irving, 'Lord Mountbatten's Diaries May Finally Reveal the Truth About the Royal Family and the Nazis,' *The Daily Beast*, 24, July 2021; https://www.thedailybeast.com/lord-mountbattens-diaries-may-finally-reveal-the-truth-about-the-royal-family-and-the-nazis]; Letters (Philip Murphy), *London Review Of Books*, Vol 33, No18, 22 September 2011. See also: Peter Jukes, Hardeep Matharu, 'The History Racket', *Byline Times*, 2 September 2021, [https://bylinetimes.com/2021/09/02/the-history-racket-blowing-the-whistle-on-the-official-versions-and-perversions-of-the-past/]

of the Government's fight only served to underline the gravity of its fears, and the lengths it was prepared to go to hide truth.

Seeking to make the costs of the case prohibitive for Lownie, the Crown engaged in the familiar dirty tactics of delay and constantly changing the grounds of defence. While denounced by a former Foreign Secretary as "a grotesque abuse of public money," official bodies and prominent fellow historians were almost wholly silent. British rectitude and justice are as readily sodomised by power and privilege as they were a hundred years ago, and fear of rocking the boat, and the hope of honours and entitlements, remain a powerful means of ensuring conformity. Legislation is desperately needed to throttle the innately defensive ethos of Britain's civil service, and its tradition of burning embarrassing archival documents on the altar of chummery.

Meanwhile, other members of the Royal Family had been delivering sterling public service in demonstrating what happens when the privileged are issued a free pass for any behaviour, and knowledge of transgressions, and their sanctioning, is blocked by lickspittlers.

The implosion of the career of one of the family's gifts to republicanism, Prince Andrew, over his alleged embroilment in under-age sex trafficking in the Jeffrey Epstein* scandal, was less remarkable, despite the prominence accorded it by the media, than his flagrant betrayal of the public's trust in even grosser matters. For a decade he'd cultivated financially advantageous friendships with wildly corrupt despots, and other heinous figures; acting as a paid fixer, and working to legitimise them with the hallowed light of royal approval. Unforgivably, he even lobbied on behalf of a Luxembourg private bank that reportedly sought to service the very worst of the globally shady. His participation was explainable only in terms of the baroque levels of entitlement, greed and idiocy that he and his unshameable ex-wife manifested. However, the greater scandal was that despite the press cataloguing these moral outrages for over a decade, successive British Governments turned a blind eye.

A cynic could argue that the Prince – who reportedly made clear to palace officials that he "didn't have to answer to anyone" with the

---

* Jeffrey Edward Epstein (1953–2019), an American financier who supplied under-age girls to men of wealth and influence.

exception of the monarch – was the ideal ambassador for the modern, corrupted British state. After all, for dictators, oligarchs and their families enriched through kleptocracy, it provides a green and blessed home away from home, where they are welcome to wash their dirty money, and buy influence, respect, and honours via political donations, carefully targeted philanthropy, bribery, and other exchanges.* In America, they risk being called out by indignant individuals backed by the freest press on Earth; but in Britain, their dirty arses are gratefully licked by national institutions, Governments, and even the Crown. British courts and oppressive libel laws are abused to protect them, and further shore up the looting regimes that enabled them.

The fiasco of a televised interview in which Andrew sought to exonerate himself of the sex charges offered a banquet for forensic psychologists and body language experts, but also provoked visceral public anger and loathing.† It was not merely the brazen lies: the entitlement and emotional stuntedness on display made him seem the very embodiment of privileged impunity. And that was just the man: never had the institution he represented appeared so hollow. When the Crown, the symbol of moral authority, and dispenser of honour and justice, appears more focused on self-protection, the goodwill from decades of collective royal good deeds can evaporate overnight. What happens if the national bedrock is seen to be a tinselled mirage?

In a maxim for the unillusioned new times, the evening after the interview's screening, a character in the seminal television hacker drama *Mr Robot* offered up the dictum: "Power is just an arsehole stuffed with money." When integrity and empathy are absent, so it is.

---

* In 2022 it was revealed a donation of £250,000 to Conservative Party funds bought membership of a secret government advisory and lobby group with access to the Prime Minister and highest levels of government. The rum bunch of tycoons included the wife of Vladimir Putin's former deputy finance minister; an Iranian who'd gained his fortune from tobacco distribution; and an identity accused in Parliament of ill-gotten wealth and the intimidation of an M.P. The trade in honours is also as nakedly cynical as it has ever been. A donation of £3 million to the Tories – mere chump change for today's Horace Farquhars – buys a life peerage. [Gabriel Pogrund, Henry Zeffman, 'The Tory donors with access to Boris Johnson's top team', *The Sunday Times*, 19 February 2022; Jonathan Calvert, George Arbuthnott, Tom Calver, 'New Tory Sleaze Row As Donors Who Pay £3m Get Seats In House Of Lords', *The Sunday Times*, 6 November 2021.]

† A journalist for leading conservative newspaper *The Daily Telegraph* confessed that when the Prince raised the issue of his "mental health" during the interview, he'd wished "to put a bullet in the TV". [Tim Stanley, 'Prince Andrew's Pathetic Excuses Make Me Spit', *The Daily Telegraph*, 17 November 2019.]

The royal circus of dissembling, stonewalling, and finally silencing of His Royal Highness's accuser via a multi-million-pound payoff,* was an unedifying display of the impunity of wealth and privilege. The entire Epstein scandal, aspects of which continue to remain buried, has strong parallels with the Battersea case. It serves as a reminder – as if one was ever needed – that power (and especially unearned power) must always be questioned and held to account. Personal accountability is *everything*.

The former colonies have witnessed their own gamut of sordid exposures. In Australia, a Royal Commission into 'Institutional Responses to Child Sexual Abuse' in 2014-15 revealed widespread abuse at The Hutchins School during the 1960s and 70s. The School board had forced the headmaster of the time to resign, but there were allegations it also attempted to whitewash what had occurred. One of the affected pupils sought an apology from the School, which was refused for two decades. When the Commission announced it would hold a public hearing on the School's response, it was magically forthcoming. Subsequently, claims of historical child abuse at Barker College and The Southport School also emerged. Possibly emboldened by the allegations, in 2018 the Anglican Church Diocese of Sydney sent a letter to the Prime Minister of Australia, signed by thirty-four Principals of its schools (including Barker College), requesting the retention of legislation that enabled gay teachers to be sacked, and gay students to be expelled. When it comes to breathtaking hypocrisy, religious bigotry can be hard to beat, and the astonishing missive caused a furore amongst current and former students.

Given such narratives, it will be interesting to see whether the names of Charles Thorold and Lawrence Adamson remain honoured in the schools where they made such great and lasting contributions. Forgiveness and redemption lies at the heart of Christianity, and Oxford University and Archbishop Donaldson at least believed that Thorold was due his rehabilitation. However, in the current social climate, where hasty bows to emotive groups are considered more important than reflective judgements, anything is possible. Only one

---

* It led to a report Buckingham Palace staff were reciting a revised nursery rhyme: "The grand old Duke of York, he had 12 million quid. He gave it to someone he'd never met, for something he never did." [Roya Nikkhah, 'Behind the scenes at Buckingham Palace during a week that shook the monarchy,' *The Sunday Times*, 19 February 2022.]

thing is certain: unlike the ancient Athens of Uranian dreams, the imperative of modern life to protect vulnerable youths from not only the desires of men, but also from their own nascent desires and curiosity, will remain an irresolvable societal problem.[*]

As for Iguerbouchène: supporters of his legacy worry that it continues to remain largely unknown by the public: his recordings are almost never programmed in Algeria; some of his music is plagiarised; and his strong Kabyle identity underplayed to flatter Algeria's Arab nationalism. While his Nazi collaboration has long been known, almost nothing has been known of his patron. In Muslim counties, private life is still viewed as a protected area, even in biographies. More than this, in modern Algeria homosexuality remains criminalised, with censorship and punishment of any publication that might smile upon it. Outside of artistic and bohemian circles it is still widely considered a scourge and curse: a government minister who recently stated such people were "dangerous pests that threaten the national fabric," has endless mental bedfellows.

Rare is the artist without a multi-faceted and often messy personal history. It is such aspects that often drive and shape their artistry. However, when the fame of an individual sees them co-opted into being a national icon, as the persona of Iguerbouchène is evolving to become in Algeria (particularly for those seeking to promote Kabyle cultural identity and politics), this becomes even more of a problem when anodyne myth, and a sense of ownership of a persona, collides with the revealed truth of the actual life.

One only has to consider some of the distortions of the past perpetrated in the First World with regard to historical figures who are considered emblematic of their countries, such as Abraham Lincoln and Walt Whitman in America, or Frederick the Great and Alexander von Humboldt in Germany. Late 2020 witnessed a farcical kerfuffle in Poland over national icon Frédéric Chopin, when a Swiss radio documentary pointed out the aggressive suppression of his homosexuality.

Most countries prefer their emotionally complex and sexually

---

[*] e.g. For a singular personal account, see: Andrew Goldman, 'In Conversation: Joel Schumacher', *Vulture*, 28 August 2019. [https://www.vulture.com/2019/08/joel-schumacher-in-conversation.html].

wayward national icons to be reforged into heterosexual or asexual Christ-like figures. How much greater then the problem in Third World countries poisoned by religious superstition, hate, and violence. It's been almost three decades since the Algerian government begged for information on the life of Iguerbouchène. Better late than never – here it is. It will be interesting to see what they make of it. Possibly, like most homosexual history, it will be wilfully ignored.

Beyond Algeria, Iguerbouchène's collaboration with Nazism at the highest level is unlikely to favour uptake of his music anytime soon. This is particularly so given the culture wars, exported from America to the world, that arose in the last years of Queen Elizabeth II's reign. Besides questioning and seeking to diminish the entire heritage and values of Western civilisation, they introduced the new secular religion and tyranny of 'Wokeism'. Its dogma went far beyond the time-worn debate of whether art should be separated from the artist. It sought to make human beings answerable for every moment of their lives; considered the work of artists and their lives as not only one and the same, but equally accountable; and demanded both be damned should any aspect of the individual's character, ideas, or actions be deemed unacceptable at any time. It also insisted that history and its inhabitants be viewed and judged through the moral lens of today.

Like other fashions and anxieties which time eventually renders to be of no consequence, this fatuousness too will pass; leaving later observers to wonder, as of other such foolery, how it ever found such an investment of passion. Such are the tides of history. It is reassuring to remember that, in the Western world, common sense generally asserts itself in the end – although it can take an achingly long time to get there.

When John Day set out to discover the life of Charles Thorold, a local historian wrote to remind him:

> He came of a family and lived in an age when the code of gentlemanly reticence was strongly held. He would have been accepted on his family name and even close friends would have never asked or thought to ask anything about his private life... even if the whole College had been aware of every salacious

698

detail of an escapade, no gentleman would have uttered a word outside.

I was reminded of these mores when interviewing an elderly long-standing friend and co-author of the Rev. Henry Thorold. Near the end of our conversation I delicately asked if he thought Henry might have been gay.* The response was quiet umbrage: he claimed to have had no knowledge of Henry's private life, or of any partner, of either gender, and that the thought to pose the question had never crossed his mind.†

The Hellenism of the British public school and university curriculms of the late Victorian and Edwardian eras, and their exclusively male cultures, were at strange odds with the self-restraint demanded of the budding gentlemen they raised. More than one scholar has noted "the sheer fragility of the boundary," and its social effects.‡ An Old Boy of one of the great public schools once confessed to me that, for an entire term, he and a handsome fellow pupil were tasked with hoisting the flag before morning assembly. The tower of the school building, on which the flagpole stood, was a quiet retreat; the rolls of various flags lying there, as softly enticing as bedding. Irrepressible teenage hormones did the rest. Before the flag was raised each day, youthful

---

* When Henry died in 2000, his executors were his brother, the Rev. John Thorold; a married Lancing College schoolmaster, John Fancourt Bell, (1932–2019); and John Peter Barratt (1936–2009), a bachelor schoolmaster and connoisseur, who was the son of chemist Sir Sydney Barratt, who helped to secure the development of the bouncing bomb. Peter Barratt lived at Crowe Hall, one of Bath's most palatial Regency villas, filled with art and antiques, and set in thirty acres of formal gardens, parkland and woods. An obituary penned by a former pupil recalled him as "a boyish, sandy-haired, totally unpretentious, likeable figure with the affable directness of the perfectly well-bred…He taught history as if it had just happened yesterday, the pre-modern way, full of incidents and characters, peasants and royals and popes. He hated what modernism had wrought. He believed that, everywhere, the pre-World War I *ancien régime* was the last moment of near-happiness the world had known." In 1974, Barratt privately published *Through Lightest Africa*, an account of his treks across that continent. The ex-pupil also took him on a trek through New York's West Village, then a gay ghetto, prompting Barratt to remark it was: "just like a moment in the Middle Ages…when they substituted sex for religion but kept all the garb and ritual and theatre." The eulogist concluded: "If I had to distil J.B.'s life into a code, I'd say: Put not thy faith in ['isms and 'ologies]…Whatever is self-evidently beautiful will show you the way." [Melik Kaylan, 'Requiem for an English Gentleman', *Forbes*, 10 February 2009.]

† For period English attitudes regarding the exposure of homosexuality, see the interviews with contemporary figures that accompany the dramatisation of the Peter Wildblood-Lord Montagu scandal of 1954 in: Patrick Reams, *A Very British Sex Scandal*, 2007, Blast! Films, via Channel 4.

‡ David Vincent, *The Culture of Secrecy: Britain, 1832-1998*, Oxford University Press, 1998, p131.

limbs intertwined in passionate release. From a tower window, the two boys would then watch as the assembled pupils on the parade ground below saluted the flag – flapping increasingly stained and stiffer as the school term progressed. "It gave me a quiet thrill," recalled the gentleman, "to see all the pupils and teachers standing there, right arms across their hearts as they recited the school oath, unknowingly honouring the symbol of our boyish passion."

Years later, he ran into his fellow-flag-raiser, now accompanied by a wife and children, at a social function. A warm and urbane conversation took place. "Of course," he said, "neither of us mentioned that particular shared history, but the silent acknowledgement of it floated delicately in the air!" In polite English society, silent acknowledgements of all kinds are a currency, but those of similar schooldays pasts must once have been legion. Hopefully they remain so.

I have trespassed upon the deepest secret of Lord Battersea and his closest friends. However, like the government which hid it, I believe it will be for the greater good. The fear that lay behind Lord Rosebery's caution to Lady Battersea with regard to publishing her memoirs – "I think it is most dangerous," has hopefully long passed.

Several of the individuals in this book, including the gentleman of its title, lived rich, complex, and generous lives, and were – despite their personal failings – gallant and noble in every sense of the word. Although the scandal has served here to illuminate them, hopefully it will not be seen as defining them. Whatever unfolds, *A Secret Between Gentlemen* has a far wider bearing than just the smothering of scandal, sexual or otherwise. Early in the writing of the book a friend bluntly asked: "What is its point?" – always a good question for focusing authorial intentions. My answer is: to hold up a distant mirror.

In 1887, when the Home Secretary requested a blanket court ruling to suppress the publication of divorce evidence, *The Pall Mall Gazette* responded in a front page editorial which called it: "simply a euphemism for a proposal to hush up scandals in high life. It is the thin end of the wedge." The *Gazette* went on to state:

700

The Macaulay* of the future will find more valuable material for painting his picture of English society at the close of the Victorian era in the reports of the Dilke and Colin Campbell divorce cases than in any of the other publications of recent years, and that altogether irrespective of the question of immorality.

The same surely applies to the Battersea case. First to last this is a story about power, and how it can distort not just the law, media, and public opinion, but reality itself. Despite its great glories, the United Kingdom of 1902 was also a kingdom of lies – the falsehoods perpetrated for good, and for bad. Like every nation, it remains so today. In this time of information wars, when governments, corporations and individuals seek to control public narratives; when calls for reckonings over abuses of wealth and privilege are widespread; and truth is under assault as never before, this story of its suppression by the powerful seems more relevant than ever.

The second volume in the *A Secret Between Gentlemen* trilogy, *Suspects, Strays & Guests,* profiles a group of intriguing gentlemen friends of Lord Battersea who can be considered suspects in his scandal. It also features additional material uncovered during the research that was unable to be included here due to reasons of space. The third volume, *Faith & Desire,* further explores the idiosyncrasies of religious belief and sexuality in their vanished world.

I hope you enjoyed the journey.

---

* Thomas Babington Macaulay (1800–1859), historian; author of *The History Of England.*

Appendices

BATTERSEA CASE TIMELINE

- Early 1902 – Interception of letters. The Lords of the Admiralty contact the Metropolitan Police (Scotland Yard).
- 23 June 1902 – Case referred to the DPP.
- Middle of July 1902 – Statement taken from Albert Collins.
- 22 July 1902 – Albert Collins discharged from the Navy.
- 26 July 1902 – Charles Arrow lays the information at Norwich.
- 28 July 1902 – Fraser arrested.
- 30 July 1902 – Fraser received into custody at Norwich; Thorold arrested.
- 1 August 1902 –Thorold received into custody at Norwich.
- 2 August 1902 – 1st Court Hearing of Fraser and Thorold.
- 3 August 1902 – Blind item appears in *Reynolds's Newspaper.*
- 3-7 August 1902 – Further evidence comes to light of why bail must not be granted to Fraser.
- 8 August 1902 – 2nd Court Hearing.
- 14 August 1902 – 3rd Court Hearing.
- 16 August 1902 – 4th Court Hearing.
- 31 October 1902 – Trial and imprisonment of Fraser and Thorold.
- 31 October 1902 – Arrest of Lord Battersea?
- 3 November 1902 – Lord Battersea's illness announced in the press, and stories of the arrest and flight of a peer break widely.
- 31 July 1906 – Thorold released from gaol. (Full term was until 28 October 1907).
- 27 November 1907 – Death of Lord Battersea.
- 23 December 1908 – Fraser released from gaol (Full term was until 28 October 1912).
- 1915 – Benjamin Brumfield marries.
- 1929 – Death of Bernard Fraser.
- 1939 – Death of Arthur Charles Thorold
- 1965 – Death of Benjamin Brumfield.

SELECT BIBLIOGRAPHY

Robert, Aldrich *Colonialism and Homosexuality*, Routledge, Abingdon 2003.

Robert Aldrich *Cultural Encounters and Homoeroticism in Sri Lanka: Sex and Serendipity*, Routledge, Abingdon 2014.

Aldrich, Robert *The Seduction of the Mediterranean: Writing, Art and Homosexual Fantasy*, Routledge, Abingdon 1993.

Allfrey, Anthony *Edward VII And His Jewish Court*, Thistle Publishing, London 2013.

Anstruther, Ian *Oscar Browning: A Biography*, John Murray, London 1983.

Aronson, Theo *Prince Eddy And The Homosexual Underworld*, John Murray, London, 1994.

Backhouse, Sir Edmund; Hoeppli, Reinhard (ed.); Jordaan, Peter (ed.) *The Dead Past*, 4th Edition, Alchemie Books, 2023.

Bankes, Viola; Bamford, Francis *Vicious Circle: The Case Of The Missing Irish Crown Jewels*, Max Parrish and Co. Ltd., London,1965.

Battersea, Constance *Reminiscences*, Macmillan and Company, London, 1922.

Benson, E.F. *Final Edition: Informal Autobiography*, Longmans Green & Co, 1940.

Bloch, Michael *Closet Queens: Some 20th Century British Politicians*, Little Brown, London 2015.

Cafferky, John; Hannafin, Kevin *Scandal & Betrayal: Shackleton And The Irish Crown Jewels*, The Collins Press, Cork, 2002.

Chandler, Glenn *The Sins Of Jack Saul* 2nd Edition, Grosvenor House Publishing, Guildford, Surrey, 2017.

Chester, Lewis; Leitch, David; Simpson, Colin *The Cleveland Street Affair*, Weidenfeld & Nicolson, London, 1976.

Cohen, Lucy *Lady de Rothschild And Her Daughters 1821-1931*, John Murray, London 1935.

Cook, Matthew *London and the Culture of Homosexuality, 1885-1914*, Cambridge University Press, 2003.

Crook, J. Mordaunt *The Rise Of The Nouveaux Riches*, John Murray, London, 1999.

Day, John H. *Charles Thorold Gentleman Emigrant: A Study Of The Transmission Of The Gentleman Ideal To Australia*, Thesis, University Of Queensland 1989, Unpublished.

Ferguson, Niall *The World's Banker: The House Of Rothschild, Weidenfeld & Nicholson*, London 1998.

Gower, Lord Ronald *My Reminiscences*, Kegan Paul, Trench & Co, 1883.

Gower, Lord Ronald *Old Diaries*, John Murray, London, 1902.

Hawksley, Lucinda *The Mystery Of Princess Louise*, Chatto & Windus, London 2014.

Hyam, Ronald *Empire And Sexuality: The British Experience*, Manchester University, 1990.

Hyam, Ronald *Understanding The British Empire*, Cambridge University Press, 2010.

Hyde, H. Montgomery *The Cleveland Street Scandal*, W.H. Allen, London 1976.

Kaplan, Morris B. *Sodom on the Thames: Sex, Love, and Scandal in Wilde Times*, Cornell University Press; Ithica, New York; 2012.

Katz, Ethan B. *The Burdens of Brotherhood: Jews and Muslims from North African to France*, Harvard University Press, Harvard, 2015.

Lees-Milne, James *The Enigmatic Edwardian: The Life of Reginald, 2nd

Viscount Esher, Sidgwick & Jackson, London, 1986.

Legge, Edward *More About King Edward*, Eveleigh Nash, London, 1913.

Livingstone, Natalie *The Women Of Rothschild*, John Murray, London 2021.

Longford, Elizabeth (ed.) *Dearest Loosy: Letters to Princess Louise, 1856-1939*, George Weidenfeld & Nicolson, London 1991.

McKenna, Neil *The Secret Life Of Oscar Wilde*, Century, London 2003.

McKinstry, Leo *Rosebery: Statesman In Turmoil*, John Murray, London 2005.

Mainwaring, Marion *Mysteries Of Paris*, University Press of New England, Hanover, N.H. 2001.

Pearsall, Ronald *The Worm In The Bud*, Weidenfeld & Nicolson, London 1969.

Pearson, Michael *The Age Of Consent: Victorian Prostitution And Its Enemies*, David and Charles, Newton Abbot 1972.

Pope-Hennessy, James; Vickers, Hugo (ed.) *The Quest for Queen Mary*, Zuleika, London 2018.

Ridley, Jane *Bertie: A Life of Edward VII*, Chatto & Windus, London, 2012.

Smith, Timothy d'Arch *Love in Earnest: Some Notes On The Lives and Writings of English 'Uranian' Poets from 1880-1930*, Routledge & Kegan Paul, London, 1970.

Symonds, John Addington; Regis, Amber K. (ed.) *The Memoirs of John Addington Symonds: A Critical Edition*, Palgrave Macmillan, London 2017.

Thomas, Kate *Postal Pleasures: Sex, Scandal, and Victorian Letters*, Oxford University Press, 2012.

Trevelyan, Raleigh *Princes Under The Volcano*, Macmillan, London 1972.

Wingfield-Stratford, Esmé *The Victorian Aftermath*, Routledge & Sons, London, 1933.

IMAGE CREDITS

Front & Back Cover

Lord Battersea by Frederick Sandys. © Norwich Castle Museum & Art Gallery.
The Palace of Westminster: Author's collection.
Criminal File of Bernard Fraser. HO144/710/108656, National Archives, UK.
The Pleasaunce, aerial view. Postcard, Author's collection.
Charles Thorold at Southport High School. The Southport School Archives.
The Fraser family. Susan and David Boag.

Between pages 204 and 205

Bookplate of Cyril Flower. Author's collection.
Furze Down House, Streatham, 1872. Charles Flower collection.
Cyril Flower in costume as Victor Hugo's Ruy Blas. Charles Flower collection.
Cyril Flower as Mrs Sebright, Cambridge A.D.C. Paul Frecker collection.
Lord Ronald as Mrs Rabbits, Cambridge A.D.C. Paul Frecker collection.
'The great world' in Rotten Row, Hyde Park. Postcard, Author's collection.
Cyril Flower by Frederick Sandys, 1872. Private collection.
Cyril Flower's copy of *Leaves of Grass*. Michael DiRuggiero, Manhattan Rare Book Company.
Cyril Flower. Constance, Lady Battersea, *My Reminiscences*, Macmillan and Company, London 1923.
Constance Flower photographed by Cyril Flower. © National Portrait Gallery, London.
Lord Battersea as Lord Hunsdon, the Duchess of Devonshire's Ball, 1897. *Devonshire House Fancy Dress Ball: July 2nd 1897*, Privately Printed, London 1899.
Lord & Lady Battersea in later life. Constance, Lady Battersea, *My Reminiscences*, Macmillan and Company, London 1923.
The Pleasaunce. Postcard, Author's collection.
The Pleasaunce, aerial view. Postcard, Author's collection.
A Snuggery, The Pleasaunce. Cromer Museum.
The Grass Walk and Dovecote, The Pleasaunce. Cromer Museum.
Pergola Walk, The Pleasaunce. Postcard, Author's collection.
The Pleasaunce, The Cloisters today. Author's photo.
Lord Battersea's bedroom by Carlo Bugatti, Surrey House. Prof. James Stevens Curl
1st Floor, Surrey House. BB78/04803, © Historic England Archive.
Sardanapalus statue advertisement. *The Connoisseur*, Volume 86, Issue 348, Hearst Corporation, 1930, plxv.
William Cory. Francis Warre Cornish (ed.), *Cory: Extracts From The Letters And Journals Of William Cory*, Oxford University Press, 1897.
Frederic Myers. © National Portrait Gallery, London.
The Marquess of Lorne, later Duke of Argyll. Carte-de-visite, Author's collection.
Reginald Brett, later Lord Esher, photographed by Cyril Flower. © National Portrait Gallery, London.
Lord Rosebery, 1890s: Postcard, Author's collection.

Alfred de Rothschild as Henri III, the Duchess of Devonshire's Ball, 1897.
Devonshire House Fancy Dress Ball: July 2nd 1897, Privately Printed, London 1899.
Lord Euston. *The Sphere*, 18 May 1912.
Lord Harcourt. Cigarette card, Henry Welfare & Co.
Lord Beauchamp, 1902. *The Sketch*, 23 July 1902.
Lord Ronald Gower. Lord Ronald Gower, *Old Diaries 1881-1901*, John Murray, London 1902.
Frank Shackleton. *Daily Mirror*, 25 October 1913.
Arthur Brown on his Gordon Bennett Napier. *The Car*, No 16, 10 September 1902.
Princess Louise in Canada, 1880. RCIN 2903560, Royal Collection Trust, © Her Majesty Queen Elizabeth II.

Between pages 284 and 285

A District Messenger. Postcard, Author's collection.
Detective Inspector Charles Arrow. *El Diluvio* (Barcelona), 27 July 1907.
Sir George Lewis, 1903. *The Tatler*, 11 February 1903.
A cartoon published during the Tranby-Croft Scandal. *The Entr'acte*, 28 February 1891.
Sir William Grantham. *The Tatler*, 6 December 1911.
Scandal headlines. Another Sensation In Modern Sodom, *The Salt Lake Herald*, 3 November 1902; Deserve The Lash, *Williston Graphic*, 6 November 1902; Depraved Society Dudes, *Albuquerque Daily Citizen*, 3 November 1902; It is Horrible, *Belding Banner*, 13 November 1902; Wieder ein Skandal in London, *Der Deutsche Correspondent* (Baltimore), 4 November 1902, Grave Society Scandal, *Lancashire Evening Post*, 11 December 1902; Flight Of A Peer, *The Minneapolis Journal*, 3 November 1902.
Dartmoor Prison quarry. *The Sphere*, 20 December 1927.
Arthur Charles Thorold, Commemoration Ball, Oxford, 1895. Worcester College Library. (Relocated to Archives.)
Charles Thorold at Southport High School, 1907. The Southport School Archives.
Charles Thorold's wedding to Kathleen Jeffery, 1913. *Punch* (Melbourne), 23 January 1913.
Charles, Kathleen and Jeffery Thorold, Southport, 1913. The Southport School Archives.
Charles Thorold reviewing scouts. Sir Oliver Thorold.
Jeffery Thorold. Mentone School Archives.
The Fraser family. Susan and David Boag.
The Fraser brothers: Edmund, Henry and Bernard. Susan and David Boag.
Bernard Fraser. Susan and David Boag.
Vicomte Joseph de Kergariou. Hubert Cottin.
Bernard Fraser's criminal file. HO 144/710/108656, National Archives, UK.
Bernard Fraser Ross in old age. Author's collection.
Mohamed Iguerbouchène, c.1931. *L'Afrique Du Nord Illustrée*, 14 Feb 1931.
Mohamed Iguerbouchène's French intelligence service file. Direction Générale de la Sûreté Nationale, 20100166/3: dossier n° 9091, Archives Nationales, Pierrefitte-sur-Seine.
The last of Cyril. *The Daily Mail*, 28 November 1907
Lord Battersea's bookplate. Author's collection.

PREFACE

"A great many people": Henry M. Stanley, *My Kalulu: Prince, King and Slave*, Simpson Low, Marston, Low, And Searle, London 1873, ppvii.

PROLOGUE

It was May 1987: The events in this chapter are reconstructed from the author's interviews with Dr. John Day, and from his thesis: John H. Day, *Charles Thorold Gentleman Emigrant: a study of the transmission of the 'gentleman ideal' to Australia'*, University of Queensland, 1989, Unpublished.

Behind the garage, though much altered: Christopher Cox and Nigel Surry: The Archaeology of Turnpike Roads, *Industrial Archaeology: The Journal of the History of Industry and Technology*, Volume 2, 1965, p38.

"Marston – a place seldom patronised": The Belvoir Hunt, *The Grantham Journal*, 25 March 1876, p4.

"a profile like George III's": James Lees-Milne, *A Mingled Measure*, John Murray, 1994, p276.

"an amazing spectacle": James Lees-Milne, Michael Bloch (ed.), *Diaries, 1984-1997*, John Murray, London 2008, p287.

"resounding, melodic": Hugh Massingberd, A Great Reader Of The Ruins, *The Daily Telegraph* (London), 24 July 1993, p69.

"once heard...never forgotten": Much Like A Squarson, *The Spectator*, 21 March 1992.

"a splendid, indeed unrivalled": Hugh Massingberd, A Great Reader Of The Ruins, *The Daily Telegraph* (London), 24 July 1993, p69.

"Don't you ask me about the Church": Harry Reid, *The Soul of Scotland: Celebrating Scotland's Spiritual Richness*, Saint Andrew Press, Edinburgh 2016, p3.

"declamatory style of preaching": The Rev. Henry Thorold, *The Times*, 8 February 2000, p23.

"I don't *like* duties.": Jeremy Paxman, *Friends in High Places: Who Runs Britain?* Michael Joseph, 1990, p198.

"He believed you could learn": Reid *The Soul of Scotland*, p4.

from which he had been dismissed: Christopher R. Campling, *I Was Glad: The Memoirs of Christopher Campling*, Janus Publishing Company, London 2005, pp213-226.

Change was one of Henry's: Campling, *I Was Glad*, p216.

the coldest house in Europe: The Rev. Henry Thorold, *The Times*, 8 February 2000, p23.

Henry's close friend Sir Giles Isham: James Lees-Milne, *A Mingled Measure*, John Murray, London 1994, p276.

However, with the help of another friend: Much Like A Squarson, *The Spectator*, 21 March 1992.

The heavy embossed wallpaper: Paxman, *Friends in High Places*, p199.

The visitor noted there appeared to be no television: Paxman, *Friends in High Places*, p198.

It was wholly in keeping that Henry dedicated: Reid *The Soul of Scotland*, p4.

"as if God himself had arrived": Private information from John Day.

"We are not the oldest family": Day, *Charles Thorold Gentleman Emigrant*, p42.

"very much a member of the family": Day, *Charles Thorold Gentleman Emigrant*, p36.

"spent most of his undergraduate life": Day, *Charles Thorold Gentleman Emigrant*, p75.

"as a cautionary tale": Interview with the Rev. Henry Thorold, Day, *Charles Thorold Gentleman Emigrant*, p75.

"on account of certain great family troubles": Day, *Charles Thorold Gentleman Emigrant*, pp18-19.

"Since I came to Grantham this morning": Day, *Charles Thorold Gentleman Emigrant*, p181, n16.

charming conversationalist: Campling, *I Was Glad*, p216.

"In the face of cold north-easterly winds": Coronation Festivities At Grantham. Dinner To The Aged Poor, *The Grantham Journal*, 8 August 1902, p4.

1. THE NEW REIGN

"the jewels, almost lost in the afternoon gloom": 'God Save The King', *The Daily News* (London), 11 August 1902, p5.

"There was a somewhat theatrical touch": The Coronation, *Falkirk Herald*, 16 August 1902, p3.

a photograph that escaped: Leslie Field, *The Queen's Jewels*, Weidenfeld & Nicolson, London 1987, p108.

Into the latter a discreet hole: Our London Letter, *The Argus* (Melbourne), 30 September 1902, p9.

"made one rub one's eyes": Elizabeth Longford (ed.), *Louisa, Lady In Waiting*, Jonathan Cape, London 1979, p97.

Alexandra was loving: Jane Ridley, *Bertie: A Life of Edward VII*, Chatto Windus, London 2012, p477.

"an arch vulgarian": Leon Edel, *Henry James: The Master, 1901-1916*, Lippincott, New York, 1953, p88.

"Like a sort of cement-mixer": Bruce Robinson, *They All Love Jack*, Harper, New York 2015, p42.

"the most extensively quoted": Reynolds's Newspaper, *Reynolds's Newspaper*, 14 December 1902, p1.

"but for its violent politics": Charles Mitchell, *The Newspaper Press Directory*, London 1857, p30.

one of the paper's keenest: The Secret History Of To-Day, *Reynolds's Newspaper*, 8 May 1910, p1.

and of newspapers generally: David Newsome, *On The Edge of Paradise: A.C. Benson Diarist*, John Murray, London 1980, p327.

"The Rich Men's Government is so busy": The Lamp, *Reynolds's Newspaper*, 7 December 1902, p1.

"the very incarnation of advanced Radicalism": W.M. Thompson, *The Daily News* (London), 30 December 1907 p6.

"The House of Landlords": Our Aristocratic Rulers, *Reynolds's Newspaper*, 3 August 1902, p1.

"the loathsome snobs and toadies": Reynolds And Royalty, *Reynolds's Newspaper*, 3 May 1896, p1.

"He is affable, good-natured, kind-hearted": Reynolds And Royalty, *Reynolds's Newspaper*, 3 May 1896, p1.

"the universal uncle": Esmé Wingfield-Stratford, *The Victorian Aftermath*, William Morrow, New York, 1934, p42

"the King, if he stood for the best time": Wingfield-Stratford, *The Victorian Aftermath*, pp. 45, 41.

"I'm not sure that he could": Lord Fisher, *Memories*, Hodder And Stoughton, London 1919, p12.

"He would see both sides": Ridley, *Bertie*, p242.

Longtime courtiers: James Lees-Milne, *The Enigmatic Edwardian*, Sidgwick & Jackson, London, 1986, p131; Sir Frederick Ponsonby, *Recollections Of Three Reigns*, Eyre & Spottiswoode, London 1951, p124.

In 1928, almost two decades after his death: Ridley, *Bertie*, p490.

"the one discordant note": Longford, *Louisa, Lady In Waiting*, p97.

"For now the suspense was over": The 'Recess', *The Daily News* (London), 11 August 1902, p5.

"Mille Baisers ": Ros Black, *A Talent for Humanity: The Life and Work of Lady Henry Somerset*, Antony Rowe Publishing, 2010 Eastbourne, p26.

"Oh, Thou, who on my empty": Lord Henry Somerset, *Songs of Adieu*, Chatto & Windus, London, 1889, pp vii, 5.

having been fed a false story: Nigel Burwood (ed.), *The Last Weeks: Urania From The Collection Of Donald Weeks*, Callum James Books, Portsmouth 2014, p26.

Unfortunately, he hadn't reckoned: Timothy D'Arch Smith, *Love In Earnest*, Routledge & Kegan Paul, London, 1970, p27.

From page 34 –

"those she-devils": Burwood (ed.), *The Last Weeks,* p26.

"found humour in everything": E.F. Benson, *Final Edition: Informal Autobiography*, Longmans, Green & Co, London 1940, p28.

"her heart failed her": Smith, *Love In Earnest*, p27.

A quarter of London: Charles Booth *Life and Labour of the People in London*, Vol1, Williams and Norgate, London 1889, p156 & passim.

Booth estimated they amounted: [General (William) Booth, *In Darkest England and the Way Out*, International Headquarters Of The Salvation Army, London 1890, pp22-23.]

out of every thousand persons: Robert Blatchford, *Britain For The British*, Clarion Press, London 1902, p15.

There was further concern: Bernard Gainer, *The Alien Invasion: The Origins of the Aliens Act of 1905*, Heinemann, London, 1972, *passim*.

"a set of miscreants, whose purpose": Saturday's Post, *Jackson's Oxford Journal*, 10 June 1780, p3.

fifteen thousand troops sent in: London June 8, *Jackson's Oxford Journal*, 10 June 1780, p2.

"the choicest manuscripts ever known": Thursday's Post, *Jackson's Oxford Journal*, 10 June 1780, p2.

"History cannot parallel a convulsion": Saturday's Post, *Jackson's Oxford Journal*, 10 June 1780, p3.

The official death count: Charles Reith, *The Police Idea, Its History and Evolution in England in the Eighteenth Century and After*, Oxford University Press, 1938, p74.

A decade later during: John Barrell, *Spirit of Despotism: Invasions of Privacy in the 1790s*, Oxford University Press, 2006, pp28, 34.

"of the lowest and most abandoned": David Goodway, *London Chartism*, Cambridge University Press, 1982, p120.

"The Queen, her progeny, the present Government": Goodway, *London Chartism*, p120.

"the vilest scum of the metropolis": The Reform Meeting In Hyde-Park, *The Morning Post*, 24 July 1866, p5.

"never, in the memory of the oldest inhabitant": The Reform Meeting In Hyde-Park, *The Morning Post*, 24 July 1866, p5.

"a gentleman of strikingly handsome appearance": The Reform Meeting In Hyde-Park, *The Morning Post*, 24 July 1866, p5.

"He was the son a peer, his son-in-law was a peer": The Reform Meeting In Hyde-Park, *The Morning Post*, 24 July 1866, p5.

"three cheers for the Queen were proposed": The Reform Meeting In Hyde-Park, *The Morning Post*, 24 July 1866, p5

"I presume the police had instructions": The Hyde Park Mobs, *The Scotsman*, 27 July 1866, p2.

"I dearly loved what is called 'a row'": Lord Ronald Gower, *My Reminiscences*, Vol I, Kegan Paul, Trench & Co., London 1883, p250-251.

"On reaching the Marble Arch": Gower, *My Reminiscences*, p250-251.

"Nobody makes me feel more the happiness": Gower, *My Reminiscences*, p170.

Given his connections, perhaps it's not surprising: Diary of Lord Ronald Gower, 1867 *passim*; D6578/15/21, Staffordshire Record Office.

"there was more mischief than malice": D. G. Wright, *Popular Radicalism: The Working Class Experience 1780-1880*, Routledge, Abingdon 2013, p177.

played any meaningful part in bringing about: Wright, *Popular Radicalism*, pp176-177.

265 police were injured: Hansard, House of Lords, 3 August 1866: vol 184, c1988.

"I do not think Mr Beales and his followers": The Hyde Park Mobs, *The Scotsman*, 27 July 1866, p2.

By the close of the demonstration an estimated: London's Grand Demonstration In Favour Of County Franchise,*The Penny Illustrated Paper*, 26 July 1884, p52-54.

Edward had opposed reform in 1866: Ridley, *Bertie*, p241.

had to be dissuaded from voting for the Bill: Ridley, *Bertie*, p241.

When a group of processionists: London's Grand Demonstration In Favour Of County Franchise, *The Penny Illustrated Paper*, 26 July 1884, p52-54.

"In a word, the West-End": Yesterday's Riot And The Unemployed, *The Times*, 9 February 1886, p9.

"jewels ripped from the necks": The Rioting In The West End, *The Times*, 10 February 1886, p5.

In Grosvenor Square, volleys of stones: Jehanne Wake, *Princess Louise: Queen Victoria's Unconventional Daughter*, Collins, London 1988, p281.

In November, they would finally be cleared: John Burnett, *Idle Hands: The Experience Of Unemployment, 1790-1990*, Routledge, London 1994, pp 145-146.

In one room they came across: Ridley, *Bertie*, p237.

"My experience of the way": Montagu Williams, *Later Leaves: being the further reminiscences of Montagu Williams, Q.C.*, Macmillan And Co, London 1891, p163.

Armies of working-class children: Robert Harborough Sherard, *The Child-Slaves Of Britain*, Hurst and Blackett, London 1905, pp8,10.

While the average lifespan in 1902: Robert Blatchford, *Britain For The British*, Clarion Press, London 1902, p15.

"Hoxton was a poor slum": Sonia Keppel, *Edwardian Daughter*, Hamish Hamilton, London 1958, p29.

"especially on Saturdays and Sundays": Princess Mary Adelaide to Aretas Akers-Douglas, 6 April

1897; C513/4, *Letters and papers of 1st Viscount Chilston*, Kent History and Library Centre.

"The streets were filled will sullen faces": Christopher Hibbert, *Edward VII, A Portrait,* Allen Lane, London 1976, p260; Ridley, *Bertie,* p242.

Although Edward later made light of the event: Ridley, *Bertie,* p242.

"Seldom has West London": F.A. McKenzie, *Famishing London: a study of the unemployed and unemployable*, Hodder & Stoughton, London, 1903, pp9-10.

"there exists, side by side": Williams, *Later Leaves,* p255.

"Not for many a long year": London Week By Week, *Reynolds's Newspaper*, 23 November 1902, p1.

From page 45 –

"The spacious days": Alexander Claude Forster Boulton, *Adventures, Travels And Politics*, Heath Granton Limited, London 1939, p223.

"Riches were still respectable": Osbert Sitwell, 'The Machine Breaks Down', *The Best British Short Stories Of 1923*, Small, Maynard & Co., Boston 1293, p281.

"every day it is proved that money alone": Walter Bagehot, *The English Constitution*, No. V. The House of Lords, *The Fortnightly Review*, No XVIII, February 1866, p658.

"the Stock Exchange was in full swing": Osbert Sitwell, *The Scarlet Tree*, Macmillan And Co, London 1948, pp289.

"Mammon underlay": Sitwell, *The Scarlet Tree*, pp289-90.

"Many drawing rooms in the West End": *The Daily Mail*, 3 June 1913.

"it was the duty": Maude M.C. ffoulkes, *My Own Past*, Cassell And Company, London, 1915, p228.

"Where are the manners": Cotsford Dick, *The Ways Of The World: Vers De Sociéte*, George Redway, London 1896, p15.

"I hate London at this time!": Hamilton Aïdé to Mrs Lord, undated; private collection, Benjamin Chubb.

"she intended to have her portrait": Social Gossip From Home, *The Argus* (Melbourne), 13 November 1886, p4.

"they behave as well": George William Erskine Russell, *Collections and Recollections*, Harper & Brothers, New York & London, 1903, p315.

Whereas, only a generation previously: J. Mordaunt Crook, *The Rise of the Nouveau Riches*, John Murray, London 1999, p12.

"The King's mind": John Juxon, *Lewis And Lewis: The Life And Times Of A Victorian Solicitor*, Ticknor & Fields, New York 1984, p302.

By the 1880s, he had been in desperate financial straits: Ridley, *Bertie*, pp269-70.

"The most sensational figure": Social Gossip From Home, *The Argus* (Melbourne, Australia), 23 August 1890.

Society might have been: Anthony Allfrey, *Edward VII And His Jewish Court*, Thistle Publishing, London 2013, p62.

When Hirsch died: Ridley, *Bertie,* p334.

"Very pretty stuff": Peter Thorold, *The London Rich*, Viking, London 1999, p310.

Edward's friendship with the world-weary: E.F. Benson, *As We Are*, Longmans, Green And Co., London 1932, pp236-247.

However, the King's social approval: Allfrey, *Edward VII and his Jewish Court*, pxxix.

"Fair play is the pith and fibre of the Empire": Shane Leslie, *The End Of A Chapter*, Constable, London 1916, pp148, 166, 186.

This was given greater focus: Ridley, *Bertie,* pp321,301.

Edward had a keen interest: Richard Davenport-Hines, *Edward VII: The Cosmopolitan King*, Penguin, London 2016, p60.

One example of his practical efforts: Brian Connell, *Manifest Destiny*, Cassel And Company, London 1953, p72-73.

It was Cassel who furnished: Connell, *Manifest Destiny*, p72-73.

"I have had everything in the world": Allfrey, *Edward VII And His Jewish Court*, p318.

Having no interests outside of finance: Allfrey, *Edward VII And His Jewish Court*, p142.

"the race for amusement": Lady (Violet) Greville, *The Gentlewoman in Society*, Henry and Company, London 1892, p99.

a few even sported striped awnings: Arthur Warren, *London Days*, T. Fisher Unwin, London 1921, p157.

"Quite a lot of my 'pals'": Taximeter Cabs Triumph, *The Lowestoft Journal*, 6 July 1907, p2.

"Every male above the age and status": Warren, *London Days*, p15.

"Everybody rushes now.": Warren, *London Days*, p14.

"Are you working here, mate?": Pall Mall Gazette Office, *The Pall Mall Gazette*, 27 November 1902, p7.

Although not without precedent: A Baronet In A Workhouse, *Essex Newsman*, 21 February 1903, p4.

"What a comment is that single fact": Literature, Illustrated London News, 25 May 1901, p17.

"The inhabitant of a large town": Max Nordau, *Degeneration*, William Heinemann, London 1895, p35.

"one of the deities to whom": Nordau, *Degeneration*, p230.

"a pathological aberration": Nordau, *Degeneration*, p318.

The latter he argued was a public evil: Men And Things, *Sheffield Independent*, 5 October 1899, p4.

'kakocrats': Arnold White, *Efficiency and Empire*, Methuen & Co., London 1901, p73.

"aristocracy is nothing more": White, *Efficiency and Empire*, p23.

"Labby's mind long ago": Vanity Fair by J.M.D., *The Argus* (Melbourne, Australia), 13 January 1894, p13.

"the most brilliant talker": Wilfrid Scawen Blunt, *My Diaries: Part Two*, Martin Secker, London 1920, p30.

"As far as a man can be": Labby by Hesketh Pearson, *Truth*, 4 January 1952, pp10-11.

"absolutely no reverence": Labby by Hesketh Pearson, *Truth*, 4 January 1952, pp10-11.

"he used to go about London": Mr Labouchere, *The Brisbane Courier* (Australia), 23 March 1912, p14.

was once glimpsed: Mr Labouchere, *The Brisbane Courier* (Australia), 23 March 1912, p14.

From page 53 –

"one of the most extraordinary things": Horace Voules, *The Herald* (Melbourne, Australia), 24 June 1909, p3.

An admiration for King Edward: Anon (Robert Augustus Bennett), The Real Labouchère, *Truth*, 24 & 31 January 1912.

"a man of the world": Scrutator: The King, *Truth*, 3 July 1902, p21.

"The policy of the party": Neurotic Degeneration In Politics, *Truth*, 21 August 1902, p444.

"the Imperialism inculcated": Scrutator: The King, *Truth*, 3 July 1902, p21.

"the desire for shows": Entre Nous, *Truth*, 24 July 1902, p185.

"the most famous living engine driver": Vanity Fair by J.M.D., *The Argus* (Melbourne), 25 November 1899, p4.

Patriots even took to sporting: Cockneyisms, *Reynolds's Newspaper*, 29 May 1904, p10.

"There was scarcely a single": Vanity Fair by J.M.D., *The Argus* (Melbourne), 25 November 1899, p4.

"Our very crassness of blood": King And Country, *The Review of Reviews*, Vol. 26, Iss. 156, Dec 1902, p618.

an alien tribal conspiracy: Anthony Julius, *Trials of the Diaspora: A History of Anti-Semitism in England*, Oxford University Press, 2010, pp268-276; Claire Hirshfield, The British Left and the 'Jewish Conspiracy': A Case Study of Modern Antisemitism, *Jewish Social Studies*, Vol. 43, No. 2 (Spring, 1981), pp. 95-112.

"the Anglo-Jewish financiers who are the masters": Cockneyisms, *Reynolds's Newspaper*, 5 April 1903, p5.

"We have no objection": Cockneyisms, *Reynolds's Newspaper*, 5 April 1903, p5.

"The practical reason for the further acquisition": Some Rhodes Reminiscences, *Daily Mail*, 14 August 1899, p4.

Indeed, the consulting engineer of the Consolidated: H.J. Ogden (ed.), *The War against the Dutch Republics in South Africa*, National Reform Union, Manchester 1901, p77.

"Imperialism is only another name": Edward B. Rose, *The Truth About The Transvaal: A Record of Facts Based Upon Twelve Years' Residence in the Country*, E.B. Rose, London 1902, pp133.

"Plenty of honest people supported the late war": The Lamp, *Reynolds's Newspaper*, 12 October 1902, p1.

"Getting the Transvaal under English": The New Enemies Of Mankind, *Reynolds's Newspaper*, 24 August 1902, p1.

Its first edition alone sold: Sandra Kemp; Charlotte Mitchell; David Trotter, *Edwardian Fiction: An Oxford Companion*, Oxford University Press, 1997, p385.

"In her own time": Marie Corelli - A Contrast, *Morecambe Guardian*, 7 June 1924, p11.

"the prophet of all the simple souls": Marie Corelli, *The Guardian* (Manchester), 22 April 1924, p8.

"Everywhere strong signs of discontent": Marie Corelli, *Temporal Power: A Study In Supremacy*, Grosset & Dunlap, New York, 1906 Edition, 'Special Preface' p iii.

Or to quote his title in full: *The London Gazette*, No. 26323, 6 September 1892, p 5090.

"It was touching & stirring.": Lady Battersea diary, Summary of 1902: Battersea Papers, Add MS 47943, Vol XXXV; British Library.

2. THE WAY OF THE WORLD

"Never was the Lobby of the House": Small Talk Of The Week: The Lobby, *The Sketch*, 19 June 1901, p331.

"the outsider who happens": Outis, The Great Democratic Joke, *The New Review*, Vol 12, Issue 69, February 1895.

"a fugitive who is in danger": Andrew Roberts, *Victorian Titan*, Orion, London 1999, p546.

"English morality is inscrutable": Shane Leslie, *The End Of A Chapter*, Charles Scribner's Sons, New York 1916, p180-181.

"a tin kettle tied to a dog's tail": De Fonblanque, Edward Barrington, *Lives of the Lords Strangford: With Their Ancestors and Contemporaries Through Ten Generations*, Cassell, Petter & Galpin, London 1877, p253.

"Deeply embedded in English nature": Princess (Eleanor Calhoun) Lazarovich-Hrebelianovich, *Pleasures And Palaces*, The Century Company, New York 1915, p31.

"It seemed to me": Lazarovich-Hrebelianovich, *Pleasures And Palaces*, pp21,27.

"petty robbery": Edward Carpenter, The Parish And The Duke, *The Salisbury Times And Southern Wilts Gazette*, 13 July 1889, p6.

As late as 1890, the radical: Perpetual Pensions By Mr Bradlaugh, *Northampton Mercury*, 1 August 1890, p6.

"divinely instituted for the good": Paula Bartley, *Queen Victoria*, Routledge, London, 2016, p108.

"Sifting an unearned": A.A. Gill, *The Golden Door: Letters to America*, Weidenfeld & Nicolson, London 2012, p1.

"The office of an order": Walter Bagehot, *The English Constitution*, No. V. The House of Lords, *The Fortnightly Review*, No XVIII, 1 February 1866, p657.

"A great part of 'the best'": Walter Bagehot, *The English Constitution*, No. V. The House of Lords, *The Fortnightly Review*, No XVIII, 1 February 1866, p659.

Its goal was to instil: Ministering Childrens League, *Belfast News-Letter*, 29 October 1900, p6.

The Sacrifice of the Peerage: The Sacrifice Of The Peerage, *The Times*, 15 February 1916, p.8.

"the noblest possible answer": A Noble Vindication, *Preston Herald*, 23 February 1916, p6.

"Monty Guest was *persona gratissima*": Fine Arts, *The Athenaeum*, Issue 4358, May 6, 1911, p515.

"the most imposing specimen of *dégagé* swelldom": A Foreign Resident (Thomas Hay Sweet Escott or George Washburn Smalley), *Society In The New Reign*, T Fisher Unwin, London 1904, pp148-149.

jammed with expensive *bric-à-brac*: In Town And Out, *The Tatler*, 17 November 1909.

"she gave to *bric-à-brac*": Fine Arts, *The Athenaeum*, Issue 4358, May 6, 1911, p515.

"a selfish creature": Lady Gregory, James Pethica (ed.), *Lady Gregory's Diaries, 1892-1902*, Colin Smythe, Buckinghamshire 1996, p89.

"dear old Monty": Princess Daisy of Pless, *From My Private Diary*, John Murray, London 1931, 253p

whom he looked down upon: In Town And Out, *The Tatler*, 17 November 1909.

"the Government of Britain is still": Outis, The Great Democratic Joke, *The New Review*, Vol 12, Issue 69, February 1895.

"Only those who have come into contact": The Moral Of South Bedfordshire, *The Speaker: The Liberal Review*, London, 8 October 1892, p425.

As far back as 1848: Imperial Parliament, *The Nation* (Dublin), 1 April 1848, p215.

In 1893, a National League: The Abolition of the House of Lords, *Reynolds's Newspaper*, 1 October 1893, p5.

According to one press report: Peers And People, *Portsmouth Evening News*, 27 August 1894, p2.

but the majority of the press: Hyde Park And The Lords, *Cheltenham Chronicle*, 1 September 1894, p7.

From page 67 –

"Mr. Henry Labouchère, who is at": Personal, *Illustrated London News*, 1 September 1894, p6.
"rotten to the core": Mail Mems, *Hull Daily Mail*, 7 June 1895, p3.
"the indiscriminate and untempered heredity": *The Eighty Club 1895*, London 1895, p22.
"One of the chief causes of our catastrophes": Mesopotamia, *The Saturday Review*, Vol. 124, Iss. 3220, London 14 July 1917, p27.
"A secret prerogative": Walter Bagehot, *The English Constitution*, Chapman & Hall, London, 1867, pp85-86.
"Our Constitution withholds power": Viscount Esher, *The Influence Of King Edward*, John Murray, London 1915, pp41-42, p44.
"chiefly not waste": Christopher Hibbert, *Edward VII: The Last Victorian King*, Palgrave Macmillan, London, 2007, p110.
For courtiers like Esher with an inside: Reginald (Viscount) Esher; Maurice Brett, (ed.) *Journals and Letters of Reginald, Viscount Esher:* Volume II, Ivor Nicholson & Watson, 1934, Page 105.
At Edward's instigation: Brian Connell, *Manifest Destiny*, Cassel And Company, London 1953, p75-76.
"The editors of newspapers are really very glad": Sir Philip Magnus, Montefiore *King Edward the Seventh*, John Murray, London 1964, p389.
"The power of the press": Susan Ratcliffe, *Oxford Treasury of Sayings and Quotations*, Oxford University Press, 2011, p242.
"The millionaire's quickest and surest route": A Foreign Resident, *Society in the New Reign*, p114.
"I am sure that the country": Giles St.Aubyn, *Edward VII: Prince And King*, Collins, London, 1979, p162.
"Mr. Gladstone, who was the Prime Minister": Ridley, *Bertie,* p158.
"to the famous affair of the Diamond Necklace": Shane Leslie, *Men Were Different*, Michael Joseph, London 1937, p138.
"There is a strong and subtle": Sir William Gordon-Cumming, *Gordon Gordon-Cumming V. Wilson and Others: Speeches for the Plaintiff Delivered by Sir Edward Clarke*, Stevens & Haynes, London, 1891, p71.
"To The King/Queen and the Craft": The Prince Of Wales And Freemasory, *The Times*, 29 November 1893, p10.
Masonic membership ranged down: Robinson, *They All Love Jack*, pp56, 60.
"fraternal and philanthropic instincts": Sir Sidney Lee, *King Edward VII, Vol II*, Macmillan And Co, London 1925, p568.

From page 74 –

"We both belong to one brotherhood": The Dramatic Arsenic Case, *The Sketch*, 20 March 1912, p6.
The fraternity was also of no use to Oscar Wilde: Joseph Pearce, *The Unmasking Of Oscar Wilde*, HarperCollins, London 2000, p 52.
Democracy he considered: Andrew Roberts, *Salisbury: Victorian Titan*, Orion, London 1999, pp10-11.
In this he was simply following: William Coxe, *Memoirs of the Life and Administration of Sir Robert Walpole, Earl of Orford*, Vol 3, London 1800, p343.
"Whatever happens will be for the worse": Roberts, *Salisbury,* p328.
In his youth in the 1850s: e.g. H.J Leech, (ed.) *The Public Letters Of John Bright*, Sampson Low, Marston, Searle and Rivington, 1885, p223-4; What Is Parliament Doing, *The Grantham Journal*, 9 February 1856; The Borough Election, *Huddersfield Chronicle*, 10 July 1852.
"English policy is to float lazily": Lady Gwendolen Cecil, *Life of Robert, Marquess Of Salisbury, Volume 2*, Hodder and Stoughton, 1921, p130.
"The gusts of mass suggestion": Esmé Wingfield-Stratford, *The Victorian Aftermath*, William Morrow, New York, 1934, p21.
"A lounging, rather effeminate": *The New House Of Commons, 1892*, Pall Mall Gazette Office, 1892, p91.
"as a bored semi-invalid": Balfour a Leader for Half a Century, *The New York Times*, 20 March 1930, p18.

"That Lord Salisbury should assign": A Parliamentary Hand, *Woman At Home*, quoted in Mr Arthur Balfour, *The Northern Whig* (Belfast), 22 May 1895, p6.

"supercilious indifference to abuse": *The New House Of Commons, 1892*, Pall Mall Gazette Office, 1892, p91.

the press dubbed him: *The World*, via Society Gossip, *The Liverpool Weekly Courier*, 19 July 1890, p2.

Correspondence suggests Balfour conducted: R. J.Q. Adams, *Balfour: The Last Grandee*, John Murray, London 2007, pp46-48.

"His conversation is noted for its": *The New House Of Commons, 1892*, Pall Mall Gazette Office, 1892, p91.

"Mr. Balfour's lack of sympathy": Edward T. Raymond, *Uncensored Celebrities*, T. Fisher Unwin, London 1919, p67.

"I would rather be known": Balfour a Leader for Half a Century, *The New York Times*, March 20, 1930, p18.

"Nothing matters very much": Lady Clodgah Anson, *Book: Discreet Memoirs*, G.B. Blackshaw, London 1931, p139.

"If you wanted nothing": George Allardice Riddell, Baron Riddell *Lord Riddell's Intimate Diary of the Peace Conference and After, 1918-1923*, Reynal & Hitchcock, London 1934, p325.

"in many matters": Davenport-Hines, *Edward VII: The Cosmopolitan King*, Penguin, London 2016.

To most of the British people: Balfour A Leader For Half A Century, *The New York Times*, 20 March 1930, p18.

3. NOBLE DECADENCE

"How comes it": Sex-Mania, *Reynolds's Newspaper*, 21 April 1895, p1.

"an overshadowing inhibition": Esmé Wingfield-Stratford, *The Victorian Aftermath*, William Morrow, New York, 1934, p41.

"Our society is honeycombed": W.MT., 'Public And Social Letters', *Reynolds's Newspaper*, 1 December 1889, p2.

"filthy, covered in vermin": Richard Davenport-Hines, *Sex, Death And Punishment : attitudes to sex and sexuality in Britain since the Renaissance*, Collins, London 1990, p172.

"a slave class of women": Josephine E. Butler, *Personal Reminiscences Of A Great Crusade*, Horace Marshall & Son, London 1910, p42.

"I wish she would keep to her welfare work": Richard Deacon, *The Private Life Of Mr. Gladstone*, Frederick Muller Limited, London 1965, p107.

Contrary to the accusation of purity campaigners: *Hansard*, House of Commons, 20 July 1870, vol 203, cc589-590.

Official statistics also indicated the Acts: *Hansard*, House of Commons, 20 July 1870, vol 203, cc595-600.

"Not only in Plymouth": *Hansard*, House of Commons, 27 July 1885, vol 300, c154.

including in what was termed 'unripe fruit': Ronald Pearsall, *The Worm In The Bud: The World Of Victorian Sexuality*, Macmillan, London 1969, p316.

girls as young as ten years: L. Hay-Cooper, *Josephine Butler and Her Work for Social Purity*, Society for Promoting Christian Knowledge, 1922, p103.

one house in every sixty: Michael Pearson, *The Age Of Consent : Victorian Prostitution And Its Enemies*, David and Charles, Newton Abbot 1972, p25.

"From three o'clock in the afternoon": Pearson, *The Age Of Consent*, p23.

More concerning still was testimony: Pearson, *The Age Of Consent*, 25.

"The traffic in children for infamous purposes": Ronald Pearsall, *The Worm In The Bud*, Weidenfeld and Nicolson, London 1969, p290.

The London Society for the Protection of Young Females recorded: Pearsall, *The Worm In The Bud*, p290.

whom they dubbed 'an Empress of Vice': Pearsall, *The Worm In The Bud*, p100.

"did business with persons in the highest ranks": The Foreign Traffic In English Girls, *The Sentinel*, Dyer Brothers London, May 1885, pp415-417.

"brothels for the nobility": The Jeffries Case And Mr Minahan, *The Pall Mall Gazette*, 3 August 1885, p9.

"highly improper": The Jeffries Case And Mr Minahan, *The Pall Mall Gazette*, 3 August 1885, p9.

When the Committee first applied: *The Purity Crusade : Its Conflicts & Triumphs*, Morgan & Scott, London 1886, p48.

Despite the magistrate at a preliminary hearing: Pearson, *The Age Of Consent*, p109.

her coachman let drop: The Foreign Traffic In English Girls, *The Sentinel*, Dyer Brothers London, May 1885, pp415-417.

"The inferences from the evidence": Notes On Current Topics, *The Sentinel*, London Issue 73, May 1885, 413-414.

"one could not help pondering": The Foreign Traffic In English Girls, *The Sentinel*, Dyer Brothers London, May 1885, pp415-417.

Williams had been one of the leading: Vanity Fair by J.M.D., *The Argus* (Melbourne) 10 June 1899, p4.

The previous year, he'd defended: The Folkestone Abduction Case, *The Bury Free Press*, 24 May 1884, p6.

A former servant of Jeffries: Titled Criminals And Their Protegee, *The Sentinel*, Dyer Brothers, London Issue 74, June 1885, pp425-427.

the Committee's counsel considered her an unreliable: Giles Playfair, *Six Studies In Hypocrisy*, Secker & Warburg, London 1969, p97.

However, *The Sentinel* alleged that Williams: Notes On Current Topics, *The Sentinel*, Dyer Brothers, London, February 1886, Volume 7 Issue 2, p23.

Jeffries was then fined a token sum: Titled Criminals And Their Protegee, *The Sentinel*, Dyer Brothers, London, Issue 74, June 1885, pp425-427.

"a little, mean, drunken aristocrat": Paul McHugh, *Prostitution and Victorian Social Reform*, Routledge, Abingdon 2013, p205.

named in the police statement: Glenn Chandler, *The Sins of Jack Saul,* 2nd Edition, Grosvenor House Publishing, Guildford 2016, p214.

he was suspicious and contemptuous: A.G. Gardiner, *The Life Of Sir William Harcourt, Vol. I* Constable, London 1923, p607.

"a just and holy vengeance": A Christian Woman's Appeal, *Gloucestershire Chronicle*, 20 June 1885, p2.

"Where they come from or to what place": The Naming Of Some Of The High-Placed Accomplices Of Mrs Jeffries, *The Sentinel*, Dyer Brothers, London, June 1885, pp427-428.

Wookey then proceeded to name some of her clients: The Naming Of Some Of The High-Placed Accomplices Of Mrs Jeffries, *The Sentinel*, Dyer Brothers, London, June 1885, pp427-428.

He and other purity agitators spread: *Hansard*, House of Commons Debate, 27 July 1885, vol 300, cc162-163.

"a reigning sovereign, four nobleman": Extraordinary Revelations Of Alleged High-Life Profligacy, *Reynolds's Newspaper*, 31 May 1885, p3.

"If the statements made are true": Social, *The Bulletin (Sydney)*, 25 July 1885, p16.

Distributors W.H. Smith promptly: Edward J. Bristow, *Vice And Vigilance: Purity Movements in Britain since 1700*, Gill And Macmillan, Dublin 1977, p107.

In May 1885, Benjamin Scott approached: Gretchen Soderlund, *Sex Trafficking, Scandal, And The Transformation Of Journalism, 1885-1917*, University Of Chicago, Press, 2013, pp29-30.

From page 88 –

"Like many journalists, he was": Dominic Sandbrook, Fleet Street's Crusading Villain, *The Sunday Times*, 13 May 2012, pp40-42.

'The Devil's Chapel': Pearson, *The Age Of Consent*, p118.

"That may account for his numerous": Secret History Of To-Day, *Reynolds's Newspaper*, 16 October 1904, p1.

"he exudes semen through the skin": Grant Richards, *Memories Of A Misspent Youth*, 1872-1896, Harper & Brothers, p307.

"Nothing has happened to Britain since 1880": Victor Pierce Jones, *Saint Or Sensationalist: The Story Of W.T. Stead*, Gooday Publishers, Wittering East Sussex, 1988, p17.

"He is wild and odd as ever": Reginald Baliol Brett; Maurice Brett (ed.), *Journals And Letters Of Viscount Esher Vol I*, Ivor Nicholson & Watson, London 1934, p229.

were also convinced the soliciting of girls: Pearson, *The Age Of Consent*, pp94-97.

"I. The sale and purchase and violation": The Maiden Tribute of Modern Babylon I: the Report of our Secret Commission, *The Pall Mall Gazette*, 6 July 1885, p2.

The fifth part, which included homosexuality: Ex-Attaché (Frederick Cunliffe-Owen), Europe Hushes Up Crimes Of Upper Classes In Order To Protect Morals Of The People, *The Chicago Sunday Tribune*, 3 November 1907.

"in dealing with this subject": We Bid You Be Of Hope, *The Pall Mall Gazette*, 6 July 1885, p1.

"'In my house,' said a most respectable": The Maiden Tribute of Modern Babylon I: The Report of Our Secret Commission', *The Pall Mall Gazette*, 6 July 1885, p.5.

"sexual immorality, however evil it may be": The Maiden Tribute Of Modern Babylon - I, *The Pall Mall Gazette*, 6 July 1885, p2.

"gross violation of public decency": Obscene Prints, *The St James's Gazette*, 16 July 1885, p9.

eleven news-boys were charged: Indecent Literature, *The St James's Gazette*, 9 July 1885, p11.

"We knew we had forged a thunderbolt": A Flame Which Shall Never Be Extinguished, *The Pall Mall Gazette*, 8 July 1885, p1]

While the Archbishops of Canterbury and York: The Prelates And the 'New Apocalypse Of Evil', *The St. James's Gazette*, 5 August 1885, p2.

"carnival of filth": The New Apocalypse Of Evil, *John Bull*, 8 August 1885, pp513-514.

"new apocalypse of evil": The New Apocalypse of Evil, *The St. James's Gazette*, 8 August 1885, p11.

"our distinct opinion is that four-fifths": A Little Too Bad, *The St James's Gazette*, 7 July 1885, p3.

"these good women, in the depth of their zeal": The New Apocalypse of Evil, *The St. James's Gazette*, 8 August 1885, p11.

"We venture to say that no other capital": Opinions Of The Press, *The Pall Mall Gazette*, 17 July 1885, p11.

"The battle is already won": Opinions Of The Press, *The Pall Mall Gazette*, 17 July 1885, p11.

In July 1885, a monster petition demanding: *The Purity Crusade : Its Conflicts & Triumphs*, Morgan & Scott, London 1886, p48.

(For boys, the age of criminal responsibility: Louise A. Jackson, *Child Sexual Abuse in Victorian England*, Routledge, Abingdon, Oxon 2000, pp13-14.

Stead had sent him a report: *Hansard*, House Of Commons, 28 February 1890, vol 341, cc1534-1535.

The evidence presented in court suggested: Pearson, *The Age Of Consent*, pp180-181, 188, 201-211.

"An irreparable injury": [Editorial], November 11, 1885, *The Times*, 11 November 1885, p9.

"a disgrace to journalism": [Editorial], November 11, 1885, *The Times*, 11 November 1885, p9.

by Royal Command, Stead was allowed: Sir Henry S.L. Lund, *Chapters From My Life*, Cassell And Company, London 1918, p138; Mr Stead Made A First Class Misdemeanant, *Aberdeen Evening Express*, 14 November 1885, p2.

"the little ones, oh! not too hard": Edmond de Goncourt , Jules de Goncourt, *Journal Des Goncourt, Vol II 1862-1865*, Bibiothèque-Charpentier, Paris 1894, p27.

"Probably I have had to give evidence": The 'New Apocalypse Of Evil', *The St James's Gazette*, 10 September 1885, p8.

"set class against class": Esher diary, 15 July 1885, quoted in: Morris B. Kaplan, *Sodom On The Thames: Sex, Love & Scandal In Wilde Times*, Cornell University Press, Ithaca & London, 2005, p174.

The 'New Woman'": Sex-Mania, *Reynolds's Newspaper*, 21 April 1898, p1.

"All that we ask of the average woman": Notes & Comments, *The Methodist* (Sydney), 10 August 1895.

"there is nobody now": Vanity Fair by J.M.D., *The Argus* (Melbourne), 29 July 1893.

"It is time that a healthier": Sex-Mania, *Reynolds's Newspaper*, 21 April 1898, p1.

"Lord Kitchener is supposed": Club Window, *East & South Devon Advertiser*, 15 May 1909, p8.

"The 'man of ice and iron'": Kitchener Is Getting Into Trouble, *Dundee Evening Post*, 10 November 1902, p6.

"the woman-hater is generally": Beware Of Womanhaters, *Dundee Evening Post*, 30 March 1901, p6.

"Morocco is a paradise": Moorish Memories, *The Cornhill Magazine*, London Vol. 9, Issue 49, (July 1900), p80.

From page 96 –

"A feature of a low state": W.M.T., 'Public And Social Letters', *Reynolds's Newspaper*, 1 December

1889, p2.

"The sins of Sodom and Gomorrah": Minor Mention", *Sacramento Daily Record-Union*, 20 April 1889.

"Dorian Gray with his "finely-curved": Mr Oscar Wilde's "Dorian Gray", *The Pall Mall Gazette*, 26 June 1890, p3.

"it is poisonous if you like": 'Mr Punch' On 'Dorian Gray', *St James's Gazette*, 16 July 1890, p7.

"The plot is the most powerful": Magazines, *The Graphic*, 12 July 1890, p17.

"Pleasure there is none": From Our London Correspondent, *Lancashire Evening Post*, 22 July 1890, p2.

While sales of the magazine: Art And Artists, *The Sunday Times*, July 13, 1890, p2.

its British distributor W.H. Smith: Nicholas Frankel (ed.), Oscar Wilde, *The Picture of Dorian Gray: An Annotated, Uncensored Edition*, Belknap Press, Cambridge, Massachusetts, 2011, pp7-8.

the defence would read to the court: Trial Of Lord Queensberry, *The Standard*, 4 April 1895, p6.

"madcap dissipation": George Augustus Sala, *Things I Have Seen And People I Have Known*, Vol II, Cassell and Co., London, 1894, pp71-73.

"Not for years, ere I met ": Peter Blake, *George Augustus Sala and the Nineteenth-Century Periodical Press*, Ashgate Publishing, Farnham 2015, pp227,254.

A significant factor in encouraging the belief: George Robb; Nancy Erber (Eds.) *Disorder in the Court: Trials and Sexual Conflict at the Turn of the Century*, New York University Press, 1999, pp1-2.

"The English aristocracy is cutting": A Very Bad Lot, *Reynolds's Newspaper*, 5 January 1890, p4.

New halfpenny evening papers retailing: Merry-Go-Round, *The Entr'acte* (London), 4 January 1890, p4.

"An eminent author once wrote": Society Scandals, *Dundee Evening Post*, 17 December 1902, p2.

"For a body so limited in numbers": W.M.T., 'Public And Social Letters', *Reynolds's Newspaper*, 6 October 1889, p7. Repeated in: Sex-Mania, *Reynolds's Newspaper*, 21 April 1895, p1.

"united in the indissoluable bands": Oswald Mosley, *My Life*, Nelson, London 1968, p19.

"Lady Cardigan oversteps not only": Lady Cardigan's Recollections, *Irish Times*, 1 October 1909, p9.

"Let us drink to the health": Raleigh Trevelyan, *Princes Under The Volcano*, William Morrow, New York 1973, p352.

"more and more the landed gentry": George W.E. Russell, Is Society On The Down-Grade?, *The Daily News* (London), 18 April 1902, p12.

"the increasing luxury of the age": Sex-Mania, *Reynolds's Newspaper*, 21 April 1898, p1.

"History teaches us that moral corruption": Sex-Mania, *Reynolds's Newspaper*, 21 April 1898, p1.

"It sounds very sweeping": *The Week-End*, quoted in The Peoples Press, *The Labour Leader*, 29 March 1902, p8.

"Scarcely a week passes but some high name": Rita, *Souls: A Comedy Of Intentions*, Hutchinson & Co., London 1903, ppvii-ix.

"Their hypocrisies of friendship": The Sin & Scandal Of The Smart Set, *The Gentlewoman*, 31 October 1903, p601 (p35).

Such was reader demand, ten thousand: The Sin And Scandal Of The Smart Set, *The Gentlewoman*, 7 July 1906, p34 (p62).

"neither a Juvenal": Our Bookshelf, *The Graphic*, 18 April 1903, p28.

'The Bungalow, Swanage': A Celebrated Authoress, *Northern Daily Telegraph*, 5 January 1904, p7.

"retired from the polluting contact": 'Rita' And 'The Smart Set' by Ella Hepworth Dixon, *Daily Mirror*, 2 November 1903, p10.

"absurdly exaggerated, highly coloured": White And Gold, *The Referee*, 1 November 1903, p7.

"I have great pleasure in stating": A Celebrated Authoress, *Northern Daily Telegraph*, 5 January 1904, p7.

"men and women drawn from the humbler ranks": To Reform The 'Smart Set', *London Daily News*, 18 December 1902, p3.

"weekly meetings will be held": To Reform The 'Smart Set', *London Daily News*, 18 December 1902, p3.

Not to left out, a celebrity Jesuit priest: The Sin And Scandal Of The Smart Set, *The Gentlewoman*, 7 July 1906, p34 (p62).

"very little British blood, or British bullion": Mustard And Cress, *The Referee*, 1 July 1906, p11.

"What of the titled youth who turns his castle": The Sin & Scandal Of The Smart Set, *The Gentlewoman*, 5 December 1903, p788 (p30).

Tall, elegant, perfumed: Gardner, Viv: Would you trust this man with your fortune?, *The Guardian*,

10 October 2007.

"Just how I could not tell you": Marquess of Anglesey, *Weekly Mail* (Cardiff), 2 July 1904, p10.

"The Marquess of Anglesey has throughout": Gossip of the Day, *Yorkshire Evening Post*, 16 November 1901, p2.

"sick of world and its vanities": Lord Anglesey May Become A Monk, *Portsmouth Evening News*, 24 January 1905, p4.

"much regret": Spendthrift Marquess, *Evening Express* (Cardiff), 14 March 1905, p2.

With the organ already playing: The Yarmouth Wedding, *Weekly Times* (Melbourne) 25 Jul 1903, p2.

Five years later the marriage: Countess Gets Divorce From Earl, *Los Angeles Herald*, 6 February 1908, p1.

He lost: An Earl And His Heiress, *The Daily Telegraph* (Sydney), 11 Jun 1910, p13.

and the following year: Our Splendid Paupers, *Maryborough Chronicle* (Qld), 21 October 1911, p7.

"the hope and the despair": Our Skirted Dancer, *Leader* (Melbourne) 1 Oct 1898, p28.

"for the good of his health": Clive Moore, *Sunshine And Rainbows*, University of Queensland Press, Brisbane, 2001, p47.

"when the Earl of Yarmouth appeared": An Earl On The Stage, *The Australian Star*, 24 November 1894, p8.

There his dance 'The Moth And The Candle': Woman's World, *The Brisbane Courier*, 6 February 1895, p7.

"At the close of the performance": The Earl Of Yarmouth, *The Tasmanian*, 16 February 1895, p6.

"his general appearance suggested a scraggy": Sundry Shows, *The Bulletin*, 9 February 1895, p8.

Appropriately, he also made an appearance: The Theatre, *Mackay Mercury*, 1 August 1896, p3.

It was said that the locals: Moore, *Sunshine And Rainbows*, pp46-48.

"Empty pockets and a supreme contempt": Notes And Notices, *Morning Post* (Cairns), 16 June 1897, p2.

He left in 1897: Moore, *Sunshine And Rainbows*, p47; Our Skirt Dancer, *Leader* (Melbourne) 1 Oct 1898.

"he gathers no Mosscockle": Untitled item, *The Sporting Times*, 12 July 1913, p1.

"the wedding day should be a joyful one": The New Pepys, *Truth*, 14 May 1913, p1218.

"the lady...means to fight": Lord Dunlo, *The Cumberland Argus and Fruitgrowers Advocate* (Parramatta, Australia), 12 Jul 1890, p3.

"She was ambitious of the title": Lord Dunlo's Divorce Case, *The Daily News* (London), 26 July 1890, p6.

the astounding sum of £50,000 pounds: Touching Passages, *The Pall Mall Gazette*, 2 July 1913, p1.

'divorce muck': Ex-Attache (Frederick Cunliffe-Owen): Movement To Suppress Publication Of Divorce Muck, *New York Daily-Tribune*, 13 February 1910, p5.

put pressure on the President of the Divorce: Should Scandals In High Life Be Hushed-Up?, *The Pall Mall Gazette*, 4 February 1887, p1.

"The Divorce Court has so laid bare": Humbug And Hypocrisy, *Reynolds's Newspaper*, 19 December 1886, p4.

"There are newspapers of enormous": The Duke Was Our Friend, *The World* (New York), 12 December 1886, p10.

"One doesn't care what the press": Jilly Cooper, *Class*, Mandarin, London 1979, p25.

"I 'ave always lived with the best families": Cosmo Gordon-Lennox, *The Marriage Of Kitty*, Samuel French Ltd., London 1909, p33.

4. THE OTHER WORLD

"There is no doubt": *Hansard*, House of Commons, 28 February 1890, vol 341 c1523.

"nervous collapse in the face of feverish": John Clarke, *The Practitioner's Handbook: Hysteria and Neurasthenia*, London: Bodley Head, London 1905, p.176.

Homosexual desire was then: D. H. Mader and Gert Hekma, 'Same Sex, Different Ages: On Pederasty in Gay History', in Thomas K. Hubbard and Beert C. Verstraete (eds), *Censoring Sex Research: The Debate over Male Intergenerational Relations*, Left Coast Press, Walnut Creek 2013, p 161.

"Without offending the ears": Central Criminal Court, *The Bell's New Weekly Messenger*, Vol 4 . No 197, October 1835, p635.

At a dinner in London: Fun, Facts, And Fancies, *Northern Scot and Moray & Nairn Express*, 10 April 1897, p3.

"I thought so much of my darling": John Gore, King George V, John Murray, London 1941, pp58-9.

after his death his son discovered: Ben Pimlott, Hugh Dalton, Jonathan Cape, London 1985, p198.

"abnormally dormant condition": Kenneth Rose, *King George V*, Weidenfeld & Nicolson, London 1983, p8.

Upon reaching middle age: Theo Aronson, *Prince Eddy and the Homosexual Underworld*, John Murray, London 1994, p78-9.

On an autumn evening in 1884: Serious Charge Against A Dean, *Reynolds's Newspaper*, 30 November 1884, p8.

Officials undertook the usual jobbery: Serious Charge Against A Parson, *Evening News* (Sydney), 14 January 1885, p4.

Herbert was released on £300 bail, but: Serious Charge Against A Dean, *Reynolds's Newspaper*, 30 November 1884, p8.

"after long investigation": The Charge Against The Dean Of Hereford, *St James's Gazette*,16 December 1884, p12.

the deliberation had been brief: Central Criminal Court, *Reynolds's Newspaper*, 21 December 1884, p6.

"an indignant protest": The Dean Of Hereford, *Worcestershire Chronicle*, 13 December 1884, p7.

"been at some pains to ascertain": The Society Papers, *Faringdon Advertiser and Vale of the White Horse Gazette*, 10 January 1885, p7.

"It is said of the Dean of Hereford": Lewis Harcourt Harcourt (Viscount), Patrick Jackson (ed.), *Loulou: Selected Extracts from the Journals of Lewis Harcourt (1880-1895)*, Fairleigh Dickinson University Press, 2006, p73.

presented with an illuminated address: The Dean Of Hereford, *The Daily Telegraph* (London), 20 December 1884, p2.

"In all that school, there is an element": Charles Kingsley, Frances Kingsley (ed); *Charles Kingsley: His Letters and Memories of his Life*, C. Kegan Paul and Co., 1881, Vol I, p201.

Critics also dismissed its congregations: David Hilliard, 'Unenglish and Unmanly: Anglo-Catholicism and Homosexuality', *Victorian Studies*, University of Indiana, Winter 1982.

"foremost, perhaps, among the devotees": Ritualism, *The Times*, 27 August 1866, p.8.

One such young man drawn: Philip Magnus, *Kitchener: Portrait Of An Imperialist*, John Murray, London 1958, p8.

The histories of these orders were punctuated: David Hilliard, 'Unenglish and Unmanly: Anglo-Catholicism and Homosexuality', *Victorian Studies*, University of Indiana, Winter 1982.

"Ritualist of the most advanced order": To-Day, *Portsmouth Evening News*, 8 October 1892, p2.

he devoted his life and fortune: Father Nugee's Life Work, *The South London Press*, 8 August 1891, p2.

"There were many sides to Fr Nugée's": Peter F. Anson; A.W. Campbell (ed.), *The Call Of The Cloister: religious communities and kindred bodies in the Anglican Communion*, S.P.C.K, London 1964, p101.

"a 'Monkery' of rich men": Thomas Wright, *The Life Of Walter Pater*, Vol II, Everett & Co, London 1907, p32

Its deluxe interiors: The Lecture Room, St Austins, Wright, *The Life Of Walter Pater*, Vol II, Plate 8.

"The services at St Austin's": Wright, *The Life Of Walter Pater*, Vol II, p37.

"high alters banked with flowers": Wright, *The Life Of Walter Pater*, Vol II, p28.

"I am interested in the Christian religion": *Wright, The Life Of Walter Pater*, Vol II, p38.

"the fetchingly-faced": Brother A. Becket, Wright, *The Life Of Walter Pater*, Vol II, Plate 10.

"Come, gentle Saviour": Wright, *The Life Of Walter Pater*, Vol II, p33

but not before it witnessed the induction: Anson, Campbell (ed.), *The Call Of The Cloister*, p103

"a paradise…If Caldey did not belong": Rene M. Kollar, 'Anglo-Catholicism in the Church of England, 1895-1913: Abbot Aelred Carlyle and the Monks of Caldey Island', *The Harvard Theological Review*, Vol. 76, No. 2 (Apr., 1983), p218.

"fabulous and gorgeous dream": Peter Anson, *Abbot Extraordinary: Memoirs Of Aelred Carlyle*, Faith Press, Leighton-Buzzard 1958, p8.

"a smart private yacht": Anson, *Abbot Extraordinary*, p8.

"religious life without starch": Dominic Janes, *Visions of Queer Martyrdom from John Henry Newman to Derek Jarman*, University of Chicago Press, Chicago 2105, p84.

made their nude bathing: Janes, Visions of Queer Martyrdom, p86.

he was inclined to favouritism: Anson, *Abbot Extraordinary*, pp124-126.

From page 118 –

Elizabeth, Queen of Bohemia: Anecdotal Photographs: Father Ignatius, *Truth*, 23 September 1880, p391.

"performed religious rites of a highly original": A Brace Of Pious Imposters, *The North-Eastern Daily Gazette* (Middlesbrough) 14 April 1888, p3.

including monastic kisses and floggings: Fr. Ignatius, *Leonard Morris, or The Benedictine Novice*, Richard Bentley, London 1871, p146-147.

"If I may say so": Police Intelligence, *Daily Telegraph*, 18 February 1869, p2.

"almost too monstrous": Baroness Beatrice de Bertouch, *The Life Of Father Ignatius, O.S.B., the Monk of Llanthony*, Methuen, London 1904, pp430-432.

"If Brother Osmund [Widdows]": de Bertouch, *The Life Of Father Ignatius,* pp430-431.

When Widdows' trial again came: A Brace Of Pious Imposters, *The North-Eastern Daily Gazette* (Middlesbrough), 14 April 1888, p3.

Born illegitimate, and raised in: Popery—Mongers, *The Catholic Telegraph* (Canada), 26 April 1888, p5; Information From Mr Long Respecting Widdows, *The Dundee Advertiser*, 13 May 1879, p5.

"those localities where fanaticism": A Brace Of Pious Imposters, *The North-Eastern Daily Gazette* (Middlesbrough), 14 April 1888, p3.

"a peculiar and incongruous combination": A Brace Of Pious Imposters, *The North-Eastern Daily Gazette* (Middlesbrough), 14 April 1888, p3.

saw him jailed thrice: Chris Ferguson, Firebrand preacher Francis George Widdows was the darling of the Orange Order in Dundee, *The Courier* (Dundee), 13 May 2019.

"Widdow's true history": Hansard, House of Commons Debate, 27 February 1902, vol 103, c1284.

"I will show you your God": Frater Aloysius In Dundee, *Dundee Advertiser*, 8 April 1879, p7.

"In a few days he converted": A Brace Of Pious Imposters, *The North-Eastern Daily Gazette* (Middlesbrough), 14 April 1888, p3.

To maintain order: The Roman Catholic Disturbances In Dundee, *The Dundee Courier And Argus*, 19 April 1879, p3.

"the priests of the Church of Rome": Mr Widdows Visit, *The Dundee Courier And Argus*, 29 April 1879, **p2.**

"now took on the high rank": The Press On The Widdows Long Affair (From The Evening Citizen), *The Dundee Courier And Argus*, 29 April 1879, p5.

"SODOMY; FIVE MONTHS": Extraordinary Antecedents The 'Rev. F.G. Widdows,' *Prater Aloysius, The Dundee Advertiser*, 23 April 1879, p5.

"There is no doubt the terrible charge": Mr Long, Of Glasgow, Interviewed, *The Dundee Advertiser*, 24 April 1879, p7.

"A large proportion of the audience": The Conviction Of Mr Widdows, *The Dundee Advertiser*, 24 April 1879, p7.

"I write this in bed": Sentence On Ex-Monk Widdows, *The Dundee Courier And Argus*, 2 May 1888, p3.

"recommended to me for a place": Entres Nous, *Truth*, 4 June 1896, p1425.

"unspeakable" and "a disreputable scoundrel": Entres Nous, *Truth*, 2 March 1910, p490.

"Thank you for your notice": Entre Nous, *Truth*, 9 March 1910, p555.

"I tell them, they've got to pay": Seraphim (William Henry Hugo) Newman-Norton, *The Terrible Tale of Ex-Monk Widdows*, The Seraphic Press, London 2006, p91.

until released by senility and death: Newman-Norton, *The Terrible Tale of Ex-Monk Widdows*, p114.

From Queen Victoria downwards: Hope Dyson; Charles Tennyson (eds.) *Dear and Honoured Lady: The Correspondence Between Queen Victoria and Alfred Tennyson*, Macmillan, London, 1969 p67.

"he said I could not believe": Hallam Tennyson, *Alfred Tennyson, A Memoir*, Macmillan and Co., London 1899, p800.

"To this conclusion we must": Anonymous, *Don Leon*, Printed For The Booksellers (William Dugdale), London, 1866, pp12-13.

"the most brilliant Eton tutor": James Lees-Milne, *The Enigmatic Edwardian: The Life of Reginald, 2nd Viscount Esher*, Sidgwick & Jackson, London 1986, p8.

"William Cory…was a sower": Reginald, Viscount Esher, *Ionicus*, John Murray, London 1923, p14.

"His love of literature, his knowledge": Esher, *Ionicus*, pp25-26.

"I have seen young lovers": Lees-Milne, *The Enigmatic Edwardian*, p14.

"I envy you being kissed": Lees-Milne, *The Enigmatic Edwardian*, p12.

"a wondrous sympathy": An Eton Master, *The National Review*, Volume 30, W.H. Allen, London 1898, p871.

"the art of awakening": William Cory, Arthur C. Benson (Intro) *Ionica*, George Allen, London 1905, pxix.

"Oh, lost and unforgotten friend": William Cory, *Ionica*, Smith Elder And Co, 1858, pp1-2.

The inspiration of the poem: Esher, *Ionicus*, p250.

After decades of service: Henry S. Salt, *Memories of Bygone Eton*, Hutchinson & Company, London 1928, p119; William C. Lubenow, *The Cambridge Apostles, 1820-1914*, Cambridge University Press, 1998, pp287-288.

"reveals the extraordinary quality of his mind": Cory, Benson, *Ionica*, pxxx.

The volume's 23 subscribers: William Cory, Francis Warre Cornish (ed.) *Extracts From The Letters And Journals Of William Cory*, Horace Hart, Oxford 1897, subscriber list.

"who at Eton learnt the elements": Esher, *Ionicus*, p5.

"as a Hampstead neighbour and intimate": J.A. Spender, Cyril Asquith, *Life Of Herbert Henry Asquith, Lord Oxford and Asquith*, Vol1. Hutchinson & Co., London 1932, p33.

"Be unworldly; don't worship celebrities": Esher, *Ionicus*, p27.

"Every boy of good looks": J.A. Symonds, *The Memoirs of John Addington Symonds: A Critical Edition*, Amber K. Regis, (ed.) Palgrave Macmillan, London 2016, p147.

At Eton, the prettiest boy: James Lees-Milne, *Holy Dread: Diaries 1982-1984*, John Murray 2001, p115.

"harangued us for twenty minutes": Raymond Asquith, John Jolliffe, (ed.) *Raymond Asquith Life and Letters*, Collins, London 1980, p24.

"The mind of the average schoolboy": Correspondence, *Oxford And Cambridge Undergraduate's Journal*, No 311, 29 April 1880, p372.

"On many a man boys exercise": Correspondence, *Oxford And Cambridge Undergraduate's Journal*, No 311, 29 April 1880, p372.

"There is no doubt that a boy": Correspondence, *Oxford And Cambridge Undergraduate's Journal*, No 312, 6 May 1880, p387.

"It is acknowledged by all that the evil": (Editorial), *Oxford And Cambridge Undergraduate's Journal*, No 312, 6 May 1880, p388.

"The youth…was one of the miserable": Thomas Hughes ('By An Old Boy'), *Tom Brown's Schooldays*, Macmillan & Co., Cambridge 1857, p257.

"You know how to do it properly": Anonymous *The Memoirs of a Voluptuary: The Secret Life Of An English Boarding School*, New Orleans [Paris], Privately Printed, 1905.

"fair slim boys": Oscar Wilde; Karl Beckson, Bobby Fong (eds.) "Wasted Days" in *The Complete Works of Oscar Wilde*, Vol1, Oxford University Press, 2000, p42.

From page 130 –

"Turn away from the wench": Rev. E.E. Bradford, *The New Chivalry*, Kegan Paul, London 1918, p5.

"Desire itself is no more": Rev. E.E. Bradford, 'My Casus Belli 'in *Lays of love and life*, Kegan Paul, Trench, Trubner, London 1916, p11.

"Arseholes are cheap today": Anon, *Count Palmiro Vicarion's Book of Bawd Ballads*, The Olympia Press, Paris,1956, No45.

"Hot as summer": John Gambril Nicholson, Webb, Paul (ed.) Youth And Desire, *In The Dreamy Afternoon*, The Gay Men's Press, London 1989, p14.

"As I go down the street": John Gambril Nicholson: Your City Cousins, *A Garland of Ladslove*, Privately Printed, 1911. p27.

"Have you ever been to the Trocadero": Paul Levy (ed.), *The Letters of Lytton Strachey*, Viking, London 2005, p130.

"Edward Bruce was": Christopher Carr (pseud.) *Memoirs of Arthur Hamilton, B.A., Of Trinity College, Cambridge*, p155-156.

"if we give boys Greek books": Laurel Brake, *Subjugated Knowledges: Journalism, Gender, and Literature in the 19th Century*, New York University Press, New York 1994, p201.

"discovered the true *liber amoris*": John Addington Symonds, Phyllis Grosskurth, (ed.) *The Memoirs Of John Addington Symonds*, Hutchinson, London 1984, p99.

"Being physically below the average": John Addington Symonds *Walt Whitman: A Study*, London 1893, p157.

"'Prick to prick'": John Addington Symonds, Regis Symonds, (ed.) *The Memoirs Of John Addington Symonds,* p307.

"In the autumn of that year": John Addington Symonds, *Walt Whitman: A Study*, London, 1893, p157-158.

"I will make divine": Walt Whitman: For You O Democracy, *Leaves of Grass*, William E. Chapman & Co., New York 1867, p125.

"I mind how once we lay": Walt Whitman: Song Of Myself *Leaves of Grass*, DoubleDay Page & Co, 1902, p72.

"Of a crowd of workmen": Walt Whitman: A Glimpse, *Leaves of Grass*, William E. Chapman & Co., New York 1867, pp138-9.

"If the strong, full grown working man": Edward Dowden: The Poetry Of Democracy, *Westminster Review*, 96, July 1871, pp33-68.

"It is quite indispensible": Michael Robertson, *Worshipping Walt: The Whitman Disciples*, Princeton University Press, 2010, p141.

***Leaves of Grass* became Symond's**: Sarah J. Heidt: Let JAS words stand: Publishing John Addington Symonds's Desires.", *Victorian Studies*, Autumn 2003, Vol. 46 Issue 1, p7-31.

"Ah, but the fragrance": John Addington Symonds, *The Memoirs Of John Addington Symonds*, p400.

"Symonds is as tall": Horace Traubel, *With Walt Whitman In Camden*, Vol 2, Mitchell Kennerley, New York 1915, p277.

"I have pored for continuous hours": Robertson, *Worshipping Walt,* p142.

"I think [Whitman] was afraid": Robertson, *Worshipping Walt*, p165.

"concealed, studiously concealed": Edward Carpenter, *Days with Walt Whitman: With Some Notes on His Life and Work*, George Allen, London 1906, p43.

"How well I remember": Edward Carpenter, *My Days and Dreams*, Allen & Unwin Ltd, London, 1916, p49.

"one of the Fellows of Trinity Hall": Carpenter, *My Days and Dreams*, p64.

"From that time forward": Carpenter, *My Days and Dreams*, p64.

"the insuperable feeling of falsity": Carpenter, *My Days and Dreams*, pp57-9.

Despite this, Carpenter was more: Colm Tóibín: Urning, *London Review of Books*, Vol. 31 No. 2, January 2009.

"Because you have, as it were": Traubel, *With Walt Whitman In Camden*, Vol 2, p160.

"I am yours.": Sheila Rowbotham, *Edward Carpenter: A Life Of Liberty And Love*, Verso, London 2008, p44.

"The thick-thighed": Edward Carpenter, *Towards Democracy*, 2nd Edition, J. Heywood, London 1885, pp73,76-77.

For many young socialists it became: Chushichi Tsuzuki, *Edward Carpenter 1844-1929: Prophet of Human Fellowship*, Cambridge University Press, 1980, p150.

"An Eastern saint": George Cecil Ives diary, 29 January 1929, Harry Ransom Center, University of Texas.

Equally overwhelmed by Whitman: Neil McKenna, *The Secret Life Of Oscar Wilde*, Century, 2003, p31; Meredith Hindley: When Bram Met Walt, *Humanities*, November/December 2012 | Volume 33, Number 6.

"If you are the man": David J. Skal, *Something In The Blood: The True Story Of Bram Stoker*, Liveright, 2016, p92-97.

"he seeks strong fellows": Bart Schultz, *Henry Sidgwick - Eye of the Universe: An Intellectual Biography*, Cambridge University Press, 2004, p778, n142.

"No pleasure he has enjoyed": Havlock Ellis, John Addington Symonds, *Sexual Inversion*, Wilson & Macmillan, London 1897, pp62-3.

"He was not merely a democrat": Edward Carpenter, *The Australian Worker* (Sydney), 16 September 1920, p13.

"Carpenter's personal charm was the result": Edward Carpenter, *The Derbyshire Times*, 28 June 1930, p10.

"His head and features were of extraordinary": Chushichi Tsuzuki, *Edward Carpenter 1844-1929: Prophet of Human Fellowship*, Cambridge University Press, 1980, p151.

"We exchanged a few words": Rowbotham, *Edward Carpenter*, p179.

"All night long in love": Edward Carpenter, *Towards Democracy,* T. Fisher Unwin, London 1892, p274.

Writing such a general series: Rowbotham, *Edward Carpenter*, p189-190.

"as the ordinary love": Edward Carpenter, *Homogenic Love and its place in a free society*, Labour Press Society, Manchester, 1894, p43.

Carpenter himself fulfilled: Rowbotham, *Edward Carpenter*, p230.

When the wife of C.R. Ashbee: Fiona MacCarthy, *The Simple Life: C.R. Ashbee in the Cotswolds*, University of California Press, Berkley 1981, p67.

To further his spiritual studies: Edward Carpenter, 'On the Connection Between Homosexuality And Divination, and the Importance of the Intermediate Sexes Generally In Early Civilisations', *The American Journal of Religious Psychology and Education*, Volume 4 (1911), p219.

"About vice I never care to argue": *To-Day*, 29 December 1894, p241.

"Between thine arms I find my only bliss": To A Sicilian Boy, *The Artist And Journal Of Home Culture*, 1 August 1893.

he envisioned a natural aristocracy: See: Donald Mader, 'The Greek Mirror: The Uranians and Their Use of Greece', in Beerte C. Verstraete, Vernon L. Provencal (eds.) *Same-Sex Desire And Love In Greco-Roman Antiquity And The Classical Tradition In The West*, Routledge, Abingdon 2014.

"to the highest point, freely, in every direction": Grant Allen, The New Hedonism, *The Fortnightly Review*, Vol 55, Issue 327, 1 March 1894, pp377-392.

"will rest content with beauty": Charles Kains Jackson: The New Chivalry, *The Artist and Journal of Home Culture*, 2 April 1894.

The owners of the magazine were less: Laurel Brake, Marysa Demoor (eds.), *Dictionary of Nineteenth-century Journalism in Great Britain and Ireland*, Academic Press & British Library, London 2009, p25.

"for women we have ceased": Rev. E.E. Bradford, *The New Chivalry And Other Poems*, Kegan Paul, Trench, Trubner, London 1918, p26.

From page 146 –

"We are within measurable distance": The Oscar Wilde Episode, *Table Talk* (Melbourne, Australia), 12 April 1895.

"A cheap spick-and-spandy": Cuff Comments, *The Sketch*, 26 October 1910, p8.

"Y is the Youth": Dick, *The Ways Of The World*, p13.

"Behold him mincing": Dick, *The Ways Of The World*, p88.

Havelock Ellis then rewrote: John Addington Symonds, Havelock Ellis, Ivan Crozier (ed.) *Sexual Inversion: A Critical Edition*, Palgrave Macmillan, Basingstoke, 2008, pp1-86 passim; Brady, Sean *John Addington Symonds (1840-1893) and Homosexuality: A Critical Edition of Sources*, Palgrave Macmillan, Basingstoke, 2012, pp31-32 passim.

"a person of a wicked": Bedborough Case-Collapse, *Reynolds's Newspaper*, 6 November 1898.

"If this thing called 'comrade love'": To The Editor, *Sheffield Daily Telegraph*,13 April 1909, p9.

"a few scientific friends": To The Editor, *Sheffield Daily Telegraph*, 17 April 1909, p10.

"It would be a pleasure": Rowbotham, *Edward Carpenter*, p285.

"discreet watch": Indecent Publications, Homogenic Love: Home Office, Registered Papers, Supplementary: HO144/1043/183473, National Archives.

This was due to the couple: Helen Smith, *Masculine And Same-Sex Desire In Industrial England, 1895-1957*, Palgrave, Basingstoke 2015, pp74-80.

"Dealing with the more refined phases": The Scarlet Man In Melbourne, *Truth* (Brisbane), 13 April 1902, p5.

"They were dandies too": Arthur Warren, *London Days*, T. Fisher Unwin, London 1921, p17.

"without lawful purpose": Matt Cook, *London and the Culture of Homosexuality*, Cambridge University Press, 2003, pp25-26.

"Lord Roberts and General Baden-Powell": Another Oscar Wilde Case, *The Modern Man: A Weekly Journal Of Masculine Interest*, 11 December 1909, p1.

"The best known is now closed": Anonymous *The Sins Of The Cities Of The Plain*, Vol1, Privately Printed, London 1881, p90.

"He was a very nice fellow": Symonds, Regis (ed.), *The Memoirs of John Addington Symonds*, pp489-490.

"They were more than willing": *Gay Life*, London Weekend Television, 1981.

"The straightforward, pagan coarseness": John Lehmann, *In The Purely Pagan Sense*, Blond & Briggs, London 1976, p51.

"They went with men like myself": Lehmann, *In The Purely Pagan Sense*, p52.

"Police could be intimidated actually": *Gay Life*, London Weekend Television, 1981.

"Why is your friendship": Oscar Wilde; Nicholas Frankel (ed.) *The Picture of Dorian Gray*, Harvard University Press, 2011.

"The word 'Immorality'": Anonymous *Shams*, Greening & Co., London 1899, Preface, px.

"Knowing as I do, thousands": Edward Carpenter, *George Merrill: a true history, & study in psychology*, MSS 363/17, Edward Carpenter Papers, Sheffield Archive.

"one day I was at the station there": Carpenter, *George Merrill*.

"Eros is a great leveller": Edward Carpenter *The Intermediate Sex*, Swan Sonnschein & Co., London, 1908, pp114-115.

"Two rows of foolish faces": Horatio Brown: Bored: At A London Music, *Drift*, Grant Richards, London 1900.

"It is noticeable how often": Carpenter *The Intermediate Sex*, pp114-115.

"Providentially the cowardice": William O'Brien, *Evening Memories*, Maunsel & Co. Ltd, Dublin & London, p21

"a criminal confederacy": O'Brien, *Evening Memories*, p22.

"In the interest of public morality": Ireland, *The Times*, 7 August 1884, p5.

"In doing so he will have the hearty": Ireland, *The Times*, 7 August 1884, p5.

"imaginative reports will be furnished": Ireland, *The Times*, 7 August 1884, p5.

Given the details were considered: Harford Montgomery Hyde, *The Other Love: an historical and contemporary survey of homosexuality in Britain*, Heinemann, London 1970, p132.

between 1872 and 1885 it reported: Sean Brady, *Masculinity and Male Homosexuality in Britain, 1861-1913*, Palgrave Macmillan, Basingstoke 2005, p53-54.

A corporal of the Scots Guards: Police, *The Times*, 9 July 1881, p14.

"his suspicions being aroused, he put a detective": The Charge Against A Bournemouth Magistrate, *Bournemouth Guardian*, 27 July 1895, p7.

"arm in arm together down the street": The Charge Against A Bournemouth Magistrate, *Bournemouth Guardian*, 27 July 1895, p7.

"was enclosed with a book of prayer.": The Charge Against A Bournemouth Magistrate, *Bournemouth Guardian*, 27 July 1895, p7.

"chairman of the Bournemouth Magisterial Bench": Summary, *The Manchester Courier*, 23 November 1895, p6.

his spouse a leading light: Presentation To Mrs. R. Stephens At Bournemouth, *Blandford And Sturminster Weekly News*, 18 December 1890, p1.

He'd also helped found a cottage hospital: Bournemouth, *Dorset County Express and Agricultural Gazette*, 8 February 1859, p4; Bournemouth, *The Salisbury and Winchester Journal*, 15 January 1868, p7.

Stocks had become acquainted: Hants Assizes And General Gaol Delivery: The Charge Against A Bournemouth Magistrate, *Hampshire Chronicle*, 23 November 1895, p3.

"It means over the wall for me": Hants Magistrate, *The Evening News* (Portsmouth), 1 August 1895, p2.

"Good God, Sir, have mercy on me.": Serious Charge Against A Magistrate, *The Westminster Gazette*, 31 July 1895, p5.

Richard Stephens was arrested at his hilltop mansion: Magistrate And Constable, *Weekly Dispatch* (London), 28 July 1895. p2.

However, radicals in the borough: The Grave Charge Against A Magistrate, *The Westminster Gazette*, 25 July 1895, p8.

More damning letters: Hants Magistrate, *The Evening News* (Portsmouth), 1 August 1895, p2.

The men were charged with both: Hants Magistrate, *Portsmouth Evening News*, 1 August 1895, p2.

Early there was a crowd round the Guildhall: Bournemouth Magistrate, *The Southern Echo*, 25 July 1895, p3.

"this hideous conspiracy of foulness and filth": Charge Against A County Magistrate, *Hants And Berks Gazette*, 30 November 1895, p3.

"every fragment of the correspondence": The Charge Against A Bournemouth Magistrate, *The Southern Echo*, 16 November 1895, p3.

"absolutely incredible": The Charge Against A Bournemouth Magistrate, *The Southern Echo*, 16 November 1895, p3.

Nonetheless, the Jury threw out: The Charge Against A Bournemouth Magistrate, *The Southern Echo*, 16 November 1895, p3.

"A cruel wrong had been done": The Charges Against A Magistrate And Ex-Constable, *The* (Weymouth) *Telegram*, 26 November 1895, p2.

"by offers of assistance, by presents": Charge Against A County Magistrate, *Hants And Berks Gazette*, 30 November 1895, p3.

"senile madness": The Charges Against A Magistrate And Ex-Constable, *The* (Weymouth) *Telegram*, 26 November 1895, p2.

"no doubt his mind was in a disordered": The Charges Against A Magistrate And Ex-Constable, *The* (Weymouth) *Telegram*, 26 November 1895, p2.

"I cannot believe for an instant": Hants Assizes And General Gaol Delivery: The Charge Against A Bournemouth Magistrate, *Hampshire Chronicle*, 23 November 1895, p3.

"in a very feeble condition": Hants Assizes And General Gaol Delivery: The Charge Against A Bournemouth Magistrate, *Hampshire Chronicle*, 23 November 1895, p3.

"it is a matter with which I have no concern": Hants Assizes And General Goal Delivery: The Charge Against A Bournemouth Magistrate, *Hampshire Chronicle*, 3 November 1895, p3.

"Oh my God": Hants Assizes And General Goal Delivery: The Charge Against A Bournemouth Magistrate, *Hampshire Chronicle*, 23 November 1895, p3.

"you are a man apparently of good character": Charge Against A County Magistrate, *Hants And Berks Gazette*, 30 November 1895, p3.

"most beautiful poetry and expressions": Serious Charge Against A Magistrate, *The Westminster Gazette*, 31 July 1895, p5.

5. THEM AND US

The reporter persisted: Extraordinary Scene In London, *Liverpool Mercury*, 27 May 1889, p5; Alleged Assault By The Duke Of Cambridge, *Reynolds's Newspaper*, 2 June 1889, p3.

"When will a law be passed": The Secret History Of To-Day, *Reynolds's Newspaper*, 31 August 1902, p4.

"a high position under the War Office": London Correspondence, *Birmingham Daily Post*, 29 May 1889, p4.

"a charge which cannot here be particularised": London Correspondence, *Birmingham Daily Post*, 28 May 1889, p5.

"when the whole matter is made public": An Alleged Scandal, *St James's Gazette*, 28 May 1889, p8.

"What are you to do with it?": The Serious Charge against the Earl of Galloway, *Western Daily Press* (Yeovil) , 15 October 1889.

"if I knew who he was": Last Week's Latest News, *Reynolds's Newspaper*, 6 October 1889, p3.

While Galloway had been: Social Gossip From Home, *The Argus*, 1 March 1890, p13.

The police had handed: Last Week's Latest News, *Reynolds's Newspaper*, 6 October 1889, p3.

"We are constantly assured": Our Old Nobility, *North London Press*, 28 September 1889.

"There is another fallacy": Our Old Nobility, *North London Press*, 28 September 1889.

"It is only to be regretted": Reynolds And Royalty, *Reynolds's Newspaper*, 3 May 1896, p1.

His defence argued: The Earl of Galloway Acquitted, *Derby Daily Telegraph*, 15 October 1889, p4.

"very fond of children": The Serious Charge against the Earl of Galloway, *Western Daily Press* (Bristol), 15 October 1889, p8.

"A more ridiculous accusation": Vanities, *Vanity Fair*, 19 October 1889.

Despite several witnesses": Charge Against The Earl of Galloway, *Glasgow Herald*, 24 January 1890, p9.

"The Earl of Galloway, who has made": The Earl of Galloway, *Edinburgh Evening News*, 24 January 1890, p2.

"People are fast losing faith": General Snobbishness and Servility, *Reynolds's Newspaper*, July 28, 1889, p4.

In early July 1889: H. Montgomery Hyde, *The Cleveland Street Scandal*, W.H. Allen, 1976, p20.

"I thought he was acted": Charge of Libelling Lord Euston, *The Daily Telegraph* (London), 16 January 1890, p3.

"I wonder if it is really a fact": Hyde, *The Cleveland Street Scandal*, p126.

While a slow developer: Richard Alleyne, History of royal scandals, *The Daily Telegraph* (London), 28 October 2007.

intractable gonorrhea: Euan Mclelland, Jack The Ripper suspect Prince Albert Victor is revealed to have been suffering from gonorrhoea – most likely caught from a prostitute, *Daily Mail Online*, 26 February 2016.

and possibly syphilis: James Pope-Hennessy, Hugo Vickers (ed.) *The Quest For Queen Mary*, Zuleika, London 2018, p191.

He stated that he'd only informed Probyn: Hyde, *The Cleveland Street Scandal*, pp94-95.

"Probyn played me an ugly trick": Ridley, *Bertie,* p539n84.

"he said quite enough to induce Lord Arthur Somerset": Mr. Labouchere's Suspension, The London and China Express, 7 March 1890, p5.

"The Convention of Silence": What We Think, *The Star*, 25 November 1889, p1. Reprinted in: The West End Scandals, *Reynolds's Newspaper*, 1 December 1889, p5.

in the hour and a half that followed: Hyde, The Cleveland Street Scandal, p223.

"Of all the occasions": *Hansard,* House of Commons, 28 February 1890, vol 341, c1550.

"moral dynamite sufficient to wreck": The West End Scandal, *North London Press*, 23 November 1889.

"a British standard": Matthew Parris, Kevin MacGuire, *Great Parliamentary Scandals: Five Centuries of Calumny, Smear and Innuendo,* Chrysalis Books, London 2005, p89.

"His cheeks were as round": Lord Halsbury The Tireless Octogenarian, *Oamaru Mail*, (New Zealand), 17 June 1910, p1.

"the 'true blue' of the Old Tories": Lord Halsbury The Tireless Octogenarian, *Oamaru Mail*, (New Zealand), 17 June 1910, p1.

"a deathless reputation": Up To Date, *Reynolds's Newspaper* , 2 January 1898, p8.

"If the Attorney-General had had to select": Mr. Labouchere And Lord George Hamilton, *Daily News* (London), 3 March 1890, p3.

"a perennial spring": A Parliamentary Hurricane, *The Pall Mall Gazette*, 17 October 1902, p9.

"As long as the Marquess": A Parliamentary Hurricane, *The Pall Mall Gazette*, 17 October 1902, p9.

In the constitutional crisis: Charles Petrie, *Walter Long and His Times*, Hutchinson & Co, London 1936, p147.

Not least, the Prince: The Prince Of Wales And Freemasory, *The Times*, 29 November 1893, p10.

"really ought to have been": From The Radical Benches, *Reynolds's Newspaper*, 9 March 1890, p3.

"a popular evil": Ex-Attaché: Movement To Suppress Publication Of Divorce Muck, *New-York Tribune*, 13 February 1910, Page 5.

Officials were leery: H.G. Cocks, *Nameless Offences: Homosexual Desire In The Nineteenth Century*, I.B. Tauris, London, 2003, pp50-51.

"on grounds of public policy": Cocks, *Nameless Offences*, p147. (Stephenson , 20 July 1889, DPP 1/95/1, National Archives.)

"Mr Poland is of opinion": *Hansard*, House of Commons, 28 February 1890, vol 341, c1556.

From page 174 –

"within the last two or three": *Hansard*, House of Lords, 20 March 1896, vol 28, c1449.

"The reason why the publication": *Hansard*, House of Lords, 20 March 1896, vol 38, c1445.

"great discrimination was shown": *Hansard*, House of Lords, 20 March 1896, vol 38, c1441.

"You are going to legislate": *Hansard*, House of Lords, 20 March 1896, vol 38, c1447.

"likely to provoke the 'imitation'": *Hansard*, House of Lords, 20 March 1896, vol 38, c1446.

Given Rosebery was one of the nation's foremost collectors: Harford Montgomery Hyde, *A History of Pornography*, Heinemann, London 1964, p180.

"Do you think I'm going to shake": Who Are They?, *Justice* (Social Democratic Federation newspaper), 7 December 1889, p1.

"The whole nation is upbraided": The Horrible National Scandal, *Reynolds's Newspaper*, 26 January 1890, p4. Colonial source is: Tooraloorl!, *The Bulletin* (Sydney), 14 December, 1889, p4.

"We are so accustomed to speak": Editorial, *The Timaru Herald*, 5 February 1885, p2.

Walters was also a staunch supporter: Great Conservative Demonstration At Oxford, *Jackson's Oxford Journal*, 7 February 1880, p6.

In 1884, as a result of complaints: Falconer Madan, memorandum in *Boy-Worship*, Beinecke Rare Book And Manuscripts Library.

"In this position he": Special Cables, *Toronto Daily Mail*, 21 July 1892, p1.

"Hertford (County). For committing": *The Police Gazette*, quoted in: A Hatfield Scandal, *The Salisbury Times*, 22 July 1892, p8.

"The rich, the privileged": Editorial, *The Star*, 17 January 1888, p1.

"Mr. Edwards…became exceedingly popular": *The Star* quoted in: A Hatfield Scandal, *The Salisbury Times*, 22 July 1892, p8.

"*The Star* is the only paper": Special Cables *Toronto Daily Mail*, 22 July 1892, p1.

"The horrible scandal which has": Special Cables, *Toronto Daily Mail*, 21 July 1892, p1.

"It transpires that Lord Salisbury": Special Cables *Toronto Daily Mail*, 22 July 1892, p1.

collapsed with enormous liabilities: Heavy Failure Of Solicitors, *The Morning Post* (London), 29 October 1891, p5.

not only bankrupted, but jailed: The Serious Charges Against A Solicitor, *The Thanet Advertiser*, 25 November 1893, p3.

who alleged Gwendolen had had: Alleged Libel, *Herts Advertiser*, 18 August 1906, p4; The Cecil Plot, *Evening Express And Evening Mail* (Cardiff), 18 September 1906, p3.

"The probability is": The Society Libel Case, *Leeds Mercury*, 12 September 1906, p5.

"a perfect farce": Lady Gwendolen Cecil to Lady Selborne, 21 September 1906; Hatfield House Archives.

"the ludicrous absurdity": Lady Gwendolen Cecil to Lady Selborne, 21 September 1906; Hatfield House Archives.

"I have no doubt they all genuinely": Lady Gwendolen Cecil to Lady Selborne, 16 September 1906; Hatfield House Archives.

Salisbury was personally informed: *Account of Events leading to the Resignation of the Revd Robert Eyton M.A., Canon of Westminster, Rector of St. Margarets, Westminster and Sub Almoner to the Queen (Also documents relating to such Resignation), January 1899*: Chapter Office, Westminster Abbey.

"In such cases, where the evidence": Preacher Takes His Leave, *Omaha Daily Bee* (syndicated from *The World,* New York), 22 January 1899, p1.

6. THE AGE OF BLACKMAIL

"There is no security now": Marmaduke (Charles Edward Aloysius Wynne Jerningham), 'Letter From The Linkman', *Truth*, 30 January 1907, p267 (p25).

"A journalist friend of mine": Sir Melville L. Macnaghten, *Days of My Years*, Edward Arnold, London 1915, p127.

"at Drawing Rooms, Levées, &c.": Blackmailing, *Reynolds's Newspaper*, 18 December, 1898, p8.

Like a Fagan: John Stokes, *Oscar Wilde: Myths, Miracles and Imitations*, Cambridge University Press, 1996, p42, p44.

Tall with dark brown hair: The Metropolitan Police Register of Habitual Criminals 1881-1925, via Digital Panopticon: https://www.digitalpanopticon.org

"a beautiful but dangerous": Neil McKenna, *Secret Life Of Oscar Wilde*, Century, London 2003, p310.

"a bold, scheming": Oscar Wilde, Ian Small, (ed.) *The Complete Works of Oscar Wilde Vol 2*, Oxford University Press, 2005, p275 Note 22.

"a beautiful but mad face": Jeremy Reed, *Dilly: A History of Piccadilly Rent Boys*, Peter Owen, London 2014, p31.

"Clibborn *(sic)* and Atkins were wonderful": Oscar Wilde, *De Profundis* in Holland, Merlin (ed.) *The Complete Works of Oscar Wilde*, Harper Collins, London 2003, p1042.

Another victim was: Theo Aronson, *Prince Eddy And The Homosexual Underworld*, John Murray, London, 1994, p160.

"wrought most terrible havoc": Alleged London Blackmailing Gang, *Edinburgh Evening News*, 8 April 1897, p3.

"Mr Wallis": Blackmailing Gangs, *Reynolds's Newspaper*, 13 March 1898, p5; Robert Cliburn: Theft, 7th March 1898, Old Bailey Online: Ref No: t18980307-243.

"Ah! wherefore must I": Cotsford Dick: *Forget, Forgive*, W.N. Swett & Co. Publishers, New York, 1883.

"a venerable looking": The Oxford Scandal, *The Penny Illustrated Paper*, 27 February 1892, pp2-3.

731

Morland perpetrated his terror: The Blackmailing Of Peers, *Manchester Courier and Lancashire General Advertiser*,12 March 1892, p9; The Morland Case, *The Mercury* (Hobart, Tasmania), 1 March 1892; Maitland Francis Morland, *The Proceedings of the Old Bailey*, 7 March 1892.

cut a further peephole: The Serious Charge Against An Austrian Prince, *The Illustrated Police News*, 26 July 1902, p8.

Having witnessed the royal: Charge Against A Prince, *Dundee Evening Telegraph*, 10 July 1902, p3.

"Come on, get up": The Prince In The Dock, *The Evening Post* (Dundee), 18 July 1902, p2.

"I will take the blame": Charge Against A Prince, *Dundee Evening Telegraph*, 10 July 1902, p3.

"I cannot help it": Charge Against A Prince, *Dundee Evening Telegraph*, 10 July 1902, p3.

"The names of the prisoners": Blackmailing A Prince, *Manchester Courier and Lancashire General Advertiser*, 28 June 1902, p2.

Before the prisoners were brought: A Royal Prince In A Blackmail Case, Edinburgh Evening News , June 27, 1902, p3.

"did not interfere": Mysterious Police Case, *The Evening Telegraph* (Dundee), 3 July 1902, p3.

"The Prince was dressed": Charge Against A Prince, *Dundee Evening Telegraph*, 10 July 1902, p3.

"although the four defendants": Serious Charge Against A Prince, *The Dundee Courier And Argus*, 13 September 1902.

Gerry, whom the Judge: Central Criminal Court, *The Times*, 13 September 1902.

in early 1903 he departed, or was: A Wayward Prince, *Museums Of History New South Wales*; https://web.archive.org/web/20230323215817/https://mhnsw.au/stories/general/wayward-prince/;

Summoned back to Europe: Departure Of Count F. De Neiva, *Referee* (Sydney), 23 September 1903, p9.

he was placed under curatel: Prinzen Franz Josef von Braganza unter Curatel, *Neues Wiener Journal*, 24 September 1902; Marquise de Fontenoy, *Chicago Tribune*, 21 October 1902

Nonetheless, by 1909 he succeeded: Die Wechiel des Prinzen von Braganza, *Berliner Tageblatt*, 14 April 1910, p5; Marquise de Fontenoy, *Chicago Tribune*, 13 July 1916.

While a prisoner of war: Death of Prince Francis Joseph of Braganza, *Aberdeen Journal*, June 23, 1919, p5.

"a respectably-dressed man": The Charge Against A Prince, *Sheffield Evening Telegraph*, 24 July 1902, p9.

"in the exuberance of youth": A Statesman Blackmailed, *John Bull*, 20 August 1927, p22.

"No semi-savage bred in the gutter": A Statesman Blackmailed, *John Bull*, 20 August 1927, p22.

"The loss of income sent him": A Statesman Blackmailed, *John Bull*, 20 August 1927, p22.

"That boy is the worst blackguard": Letter from Lord Alfred Douglas to Maurice Schwabe, 5&9 March 1893; Safe 1/2c, State Library of New South Wales.

7. NAPLES 1897

"The past eight years": E Neville-Rolfe, *Naples In The Nineties*, Adam and Charles Black, London 1897, p1.

"Naples has been truly": Augustus J.C. Hare, *Cities Of Southern Italy and Sicily*, George Allen, London 1891, p84.

"the horrible condiment": Augustus J.C. Hare, *Cities Of Southern Italy and Sicily*, George Allen, London 1891, p85.

"(1) boatmen, (2) cab-drivers": Eustace A. Reynolds-Ball, *Mediterranean Winter Resorts*, 3rd Edition, Kegan Paul, Trench & Co., London 1896, pp196-197.

"the time is coming when a Neapolitan": Neville-Rolfe, *Naples In The Nineties*, p25.

"so much of the local colour": Neville-Rolfe, *Naples In The Nineties*, p2.

"the most beautiful shore": John Arthos, *Milton And The Italian Cities*, Bowes & Bowes, London 1968, p106, n1.

"a delightful winter residence": John Pemble, *The Mediterranean Passion: Victorians and Edwardians in the South*, Clarendon Press, Oxford 1987, p100.

"A few weeks stay in this lively city": Reynolds-Ball, Mediterranean Winter Resorts, p188.

"the vast and motley crowds": Hamilton Geale, *Notes Of A Two Years Residence In Italy*, William S. Orr & Co., London 1849, p232-233. (The book was shamelessly plagiarised by U.S. Senator and newspaper editor James Walter Wall for his own 1856 travelogue *Foreign Etchings*.)

"the most over-rated place": Lord Ronald Gower, *My Reminiscences,* Vol II, Kegan Paul, Trench & Co, London 1883, p282.

"A more deformed, bestial-looking": Lord Ronald Sutherland Gower, *Old Diaries 1881-1901*, John Murray, London, 1902, p231.

"During my stay in Naples": James Boswell, John Wain (ed.) *The Journals of James Boswell, 1762-1795*, Yale University Press, 1991, p143.

"the prettiest thing at Sorrento": Lord Ronald Gower, My Reminiscences, Vol II, Kegan Paul, Trench & Co., London 1883, p284

"we are all of us God": Toby Hammond, Paidikion: A Paiderastic Manuscript, *International Journal Of Greek Love*, Oliver Layton Press, New York 1966, Vol1, No2, p35.

"A male prostitute whom I once": H.M. Schueller, R.L. Peters (eds.) *The Letters of John Addington Symonds* Vol3, Detroit 1969, p755.

"here in Naples love between men": Robert Aldrich, *The Seduction of the Mediterranean: Writing, Art and Homosexual Fantasy*, Routledge, Abingdon 1993, p65.

"the boy fell in love with me": Norman Douglas, *Looking Back: An Autobiographical Excursion*, Harcourt, Brace and Company, New York 1933, p202.

In southern Italy, adolescent homosexual experience: Mario Bolognari, 'Taormina and the Strange Case of Baron Von Gloeden,' in *Homosexuality in Italian Literature, Society, and Culture, 1789–1919*, Lorenzo Benadusi, Paolo L. Bernardini, Elisa Bianco, and Paola Guazzo (eds.), Cambridge Scholars Publishing, Newcastle, 2017, pp159-160, p178.

the city was notorious for the number: Rachel Hope Cleves, *Unspeakable: A Life Beyond Sexual Morality*, The University Of Chicago Press, 2020, p51n15.

"I certainly do not feel to care": The Marquess of Crewe, *Lord Rosebery*, Harper & Brothers, London 1931, p32.

"when the Prince of Wales went up": Leo McKinstry, *Rosebery: Statesman In Turmoil*, John Murray, London 2005, p1.

From page 196 –

"firm, grave, sleek, plump as a church cat": Frederick Rolfe, (Baron Corvo) *The Desire And Pursuit of the Whole*, Cassell & Co., London 1934, p232.

"Snob Queers": Matthew Parris, Kevin MacGuire, *Great Parliamentary Scandals: Five Centuries of Calumny, Smear and Innuendo*, Robson Books, London, 1995, p69.

It was rumoured Queensberry: H. Montgomery Hyde, *The Trials Of Oscar Wilde*, William Hoder & Co. Ltd., London 1958, p364.

Not least, letters from Queensberry: Montgomery-Hyde, *The Trials Of Oscar Wilde*, pp41-42.

"I saw him once at Lord Rothschild's": George Ives diaries, 21 May 1929, Harry Ransom Center, University of Texas at Austin.

"as if it were a well-known fact": Paul B. Remmey, Jr., 'Lord Spencer's Recollections of Balfour, Curzon, Rosebery, and George V', *Research Studies*, Volume 38 (4), December 1970, Washington State University, p312–318.

Eustace Neville-Rolfe had been Rosebery's fag-master: Arthur Lambton, *My Story*, Hurst & Blackett, London 1925, p79.

"the flâneur resident": Lord Rosebery to E. Neville Rolfe, 6 January 1901, GUN 71: Vol. IV, Norfolk Record Office.

"I breakfast at noon": Lord Rosebery to E. Neville Rolfe 16 February 1897, GUN 71: Vol. IV, Norfolk Record Office.

"Descend from your heights": Lord Rosebery to E. Neville Rolfe, 18 February 1897, GUN 71: Vol. IV, Norfolk Record Office.

"Shall we take a prowl" : Lord Rosebery to E. Neville Rolfe, 22 February 1897, GUN 71: Vol. IV, Norfolk Record Office.

Rosebery lunched with Nathaniel Rothschild: Lord Rosebery to E. Neville Rolfe, 26 January 1897, GUN 71: Vol. IV, Norfolk Record Office.

"to surpass even Vanderbilt": *The Album: A Journal of Photographs of Men, Women, and Events of the Day*, Vol 2, Ingram Brothers, London 1895, p166.

who was infatuated with Rosebery: Niall Ferguson, *The World's Banker: The History Of The House Of Rothschild*, Weidenfeld & Nicholson, London 1998, p751.

"My dear Rolfe, Ought we": Lord Rosebery to E. Neville Rolfe, 11 February 1897, GUN 71: Vol. IV,

Norfolk Record Office.

"army of retainers.": Josiah Clement Wedgwood, *Memoirs Of A Fighting Life*, Hutchinson & Co.; London 1940, p27.

a temporary secretary: Day, *Charles Thorold Gentleman Emigrant*, pp120-123.

Almost six feet tall, with dark brown: Arthur Thorold alias Arthur Charles Campbell Thorold c505, p224; Metropolitan Police: Criminal Record Office, Habitual Criminal Registers and Miscellaneous Papers, MEPO6/017/00282, National Archives UK.

a passion for rowing: Day, *Charles Thorold Gentleman Emigrant,* pp69-70.

At a corner of his lower lip: Arthur Thorold alias Arthur Charles Campbell Thorold c505, p224; Metropolitan Police: Criminal Record Office, Habitual Criminal Registers and Miscellaneous Papers, MEPO6/017/00282, National Archives UK.

A surviving photograph of a seated: See Images in this volume. Archives, The Southport School.

Arthur was also keenly interested: Day, *Charles Thorold Gentleman Emigrant,* pp16,75.

"No country so much as Italy": Douglas Ainslie, *Adventures Social and Literary*, Fisher Unwin, London 1922, p283.

"I had a divine expedition": Lord Rosebery to E. Neville Rolfe, 20 February 1897, GUN 71: Vol. IV, Norfolk Record Office.

"the most stately and courteous": Josiah Clement Wedgwood, *Memoirs Of A Fighting Life*, Hutchinson & Co.; London 1940, p27.

"amiable young men": Harford Montgomery Hyde, *The Other Love*, Heinemann, London 1970, p147.

a tall, thin, dark-haired and moustachioed: Bernard Fraser, c504, p393; Metropolitan Police: Criminal Record Office, Habitual Criminal Registers and Miscellaneous Papers, MEPO6/019/00457, National Archives UK; Photographs, David Boag collection.

known to family and friends as 'Boom': Evelyn Waugh, Mark Armory, (ed.) *The Letters Of Evelyn Waugh*, Weidenfeld and Nicolson, London 1980, p89,n1.

Accompanied by his sister, he was: Pall Mall Gazette Office, *The Pall Mall Gazette*, 9 February 1897, p8.

Whatever happened, it was during these months: Norwich and Norfolk Assizes, *Norwich Mercury*, 1 November 1902, p4.

A further wealthy gentleman: Untitled Item, *The [Evening] Standard*, 8 February 1897, p5; Personal Items, *Leamington Courier*, 6 February 1897, p4.

for a £16,000 fortune: Robert Rhodes James, *Rosebery*, Weidenfeld & Nicolson, London 1964, p398.

"has been the dream": Crewe, *Lord Rosebery*, p446.

"was amazed and stupefied": James, *Rosebery*, p398.

Maintained by thirty gardeners: The Villa Rosebery, *Truth*, 25 May 1932, (p808) p6.

"The view from the windows": Cosy Corner Chat, *The Gentlewoman and Modern Life*, 9 July 1904, Vol. 29, Issue 731 p. 51.

"There are many 'house-proud' women": Cosy Corner Chat, *The Gentlewoman and Modern Life*, 9 July 1904, Vol. 29, Issue 731 p. 51.

"P.S. Thorold (late of Villa Maraval)": Lord Rosebery to E. Neville Rolfe, 23 November 1897, GUN 71: Vol. IV, Norfolk Record Office.

"I only told you of Thorold's application": Lord Rosebery to E. Neville Rolfe, 10 December 1897, GUN 71: Vol. IV, Norfolk Record Office.

"makes me fear that the villa": Lord Rosebery to E. Neville Rolfe,, 26 December 1897, GUN 71: Vol. IV, Norfolk Record Office.

"He and Lord Alfred Douglas": E. Neville Rolfe to Lord Rosebery, 30 December 1897, 5th Earl of Rosebery Papers, Box 75, MS 10110, f249-50, National Library of Scotland. For background see: Joseph.O. Baylen; Robert L. McBath Jr, A Note On Oscar Wilde, Alfred Douglas, And Lord Rosebery, *English Language Notes*, Duke University Press, Vol XXIII, No1, September 1985. n.b. The article incorrectly ascribes, in Note 11, two quotes concerning homosexuality to Robert Rhodes James's biography of Rosebery.

"The papers a little while ago": E. Neville Rolfe to Lord Rosebery, 30 December 1897, 5th Earl of Rosebery Papers, Box 75, MS 10110, f249-50, National Library of Scotland.

"It is not for pleasure that I come here": Oscar Wilde, Rupert Hart-Davis (ed.), The Letters of Oscar Wilde, London 1962, Letter to Carlos Blacker, p647.

"Lord Rosebery has a villa": The Secret History Of To-Day, *Reynolds's Newspaper*, 25 May 1902, p1.

"unrivaled all the western world": Lucas Malet, *The History of Sir Richard Calmady: A Romance*,

Methuen & Co., London 1901, p377.

"One eminent personage": Xavier Mayne, (pseud. Edward Prime-Stevenson) *The Intersexes*, Privately Printed, Naples (?) 1908, p237.

"a love for Italy and for all things": Day, *Charles Thorold Gentleman Emigrant*, p122.

Bernard Fraser would return: Court And Society, *The Sunday Times*, 31 March 1901, p2.

8. CARELESS PASSION

Here in 1902: Our Naval Training Ships To Be Dispensed With, *Western Morning News*, 15 November 1902.

The minimum entrance age: Hardisworth, Alfred C.: What Shall I Be, *Our Young Folk's Weekly Budget*, 26 February 1887; The Bluejackets and Marines Of The Royal Navy, *Fraser's Magazine*, Volume 12, August 1875.

although privately operated: Naval And Military News, *Portsmouth Evening News*, 27 June 1891.

When he became a First Class boy: Hardisworth, Alfred C.: What Shall I Be, *Our Young Folk's Weekly Budget*, 26 February 1887; The Bluejackets and Marines Of The Royal Navy, *Fraser's Magazine*, Volume 12, August 1875.

"unspeakable value": The Gordon Camp Penny Memorial, *Southhampton Herald*, 9 May 1885.

The fifteen-month training: Naval Cadets and Their Training, *Glasgow Herald*, 18 December 1897.

On board the Impregnable: The Devonport Training Ships, *Portsmouth Evening News*, 10 February 1894.

and at one stage: The Devonport Training Ships, *Western Morning News*, 31 October 1892.

Epidemics of fever: The Devonport Training Ships, *Western Morning News*, 31 October 1892.

but in November 1902: Our Naval Training Ships To Be Dispensed With, *Western Morning News*, 15 November 1902.

Although the Government denied it: Letter to the Editor, *Peterhead Sentinel and General Advertiser for Buchan District*, 4 February 1905.

In one month alone: An Inducement To Learn Swimming, *The St James's Gazette*, 27 July 1904.

The zealous commander: Naval and Military Intelligence, *Morning Post* (London), 4 August 1900.

"Great zeal": John de Mestre Hutchinson: Royal Navy officer service record, National Archives: ADM 196/42/111 & ADM 196/88/5.

When Hutchinson died: Untitled item, *Hull Daily Mail*, 11 October 1932.

"Soon after four o'clock": Forestreet To The Royal Yacht, *Western Morning News*, 8 March 1902.

It may have been during: The Society Scandal, *Nottingham Journal*, 7 November 1902.

a sixteen-year-old: Serious Charges At Norwich, *The Eastern Daily Press* (Norwich), 4 August 1902, p6.

Collins's service record states: Collins, Albert: Official Number: 214870, Admiralty: Royal Navy Registers of Seamen's Services, National Archives: ADM 188/376/214870.

Epistolary flirtations: Kate Thomas, *Postal Pleasures: Sex, Scandal, and Victorian Letters*, Oxford University Press, 2012, *passim.*

As a result of Hutchinson's: The Society Scandal, *Nottingham Journal*, 7 November 1902.

Its contents were indicative: Serious Charges At Norwich, *The Eastern Daily Press* (Norwich), 4 August 1902, p6.

While some worldly: Theo Aronson, *Prince Eddy And The Homosexual Underworld*, John Murray, London 1996, p57; Rick Jolly, *Jackspeak: A Guide To British Naval Slang & Usage*, Bloomsbury, London 2014, p71.

a dire threat: Admiral Sir Louis Le Bailly, Rum, bum & the lash: Some thoughts on the problems of homosexuality in the Royal Navy, *RUSI (Royal United Services Institute) Journal*, Volume 141, 1996 - Issue 1, pp 54-58.

Homosexuality was a court-martial: Arthur Gilbert, Buggery and the British Navy, 1700-1861, *Journal of Social History*, Vol 10, 1976, pp78-98.

Nevertheless, in the Navy's: Leonard Charles Williams, *Gone A Long Journey*, Hillmead Publications, 2002, p141.

The expression 'chuff'": Jon Pertwee, *Moon Boots and Dinner Suits*, David & Charles, 1985, p147.

while The Golden Rivet: Rick Jolly, 'Jackspeak: A Guide To British Naval Slang & Usage', Bloomsbury, London 2014, p201; Eric Partridge, *A Dictionary of Catch Phrases*, Routledge, 2003, p500.

"Backside rules": Wayne R Dynes (ed.) *Encyclopaedia of Homosexuality*, Vol 2, Garland Publications, 1990, p1173.

"they were after": Interview with John Beardmore: *It's Not Unusual*, Episode 1, BBC TV 1977.

There was reluctance: Christopher McKee, *Sober Men and True: Sailor Lives in the Royal Navy 1900-1945*, Harvard University Press, 2002, pp192-203.

However, the lower deck: McKee, pp192-203.

Letters were discovered in the same hand: The Serious Charges At Wroxham, *The Eastern Daily Press*, 15 August 1902, p6.

The content was more than just a matter: A Scandalous Case', *The New Zealand Herald* (Auckland, New Zealand), 20 December 1902.

and was considered so serious: Serious Charges At Norwich, *The Eastern Daily Press* (Norwich), 4 August 1902, p6. Unlike the newspaper report, the published minutes of the Board Of The Admiralty (ADM 167/35, National Archives) are very minimal, and unsurprisingly, make no reference to the matter.

After reviewing the matter: Serious Charges At Norwich, *The Eastern Daily Press* (Norwich), 4 August 1902.

Energetic but sanguine: Plots against a Famous Detective, *Nottingham Evening Post*, 21 August 1907.

When the young Albert Collins next: The Society Scandal, *Nottingham Journal*, 7 November 1902.

Before joining the Navy: Collins, Albert: Official Number: 214870, Admiralty: Royal Navy Registers of Seamen's Services, National Archives: ADM 188/376/214870.

and as a messenger boy: The Serious Charges At Wroxham', *The Eastern Daily Press* (Norwich), 9 August 1902, p6.

Clients paid one guinea: The Post Office and Messenger Companies, *The Standard* (London), 6 August 1900, p6.

Its hero, Tommy Bang: 'The Messenger Boy At The Gaiety, *Bury and Norwich Post*, 25 September 1900, p6.

These were an early: Unveiled: World's oldest pair of roller skates [sic] – as worn by the big wheels of Victorian business, *Daily Mail*, 23 April 2010.

"merrily dodging along": A London Novelty, Road Skate Messengers, *Evening Post* (Wellington, New Zealand), 6 November 1897, p11.

Nonetheless the days were long: 'Jaggers': District Messengers' Mendicity, *John Bull*, 14 June 1913, p851 (p15).

"In consequence of the infinite": A London Novelty, Road Skate Messengers, *Evening Post* (Wellington, New Zealand), 6 November 1897, p11.

"Few men, indeed, are proof": Anon, *Boy-Worship*, 1880, p9.

the author of the incriminating letters: His name is rendered "John Bernard Frazer" by both *The Eastern Daily Press* and *Norwich Mercury* when covering the hearings, but correctly as "John Bernard Fraser" when covering the trial. Their recording of his address as "Chester Street, Grosvenor Square"(Serious Charges At Norwich, *The Eastern Daily Press*, 4 August 1902.), accords with his mother's address listed on his appeal files as "14 Chester Street, Belgrave Square" (National Archives: Home Office, Registered Papers, Supplementary: HO/144/710/108656/), and the 14 Chester Street address of the Fraser family in the 1901 Census. (1901 Census; Public Record Office Reference: RG 13/84; Administrative County: London; Civil Parish: S. George Hanover Square; Page 2). It should be noted there was another Bernard Fraser in Society during the period: Bernard Norman Fraser (1862–1955), a married gentleman with several children, who was a son of Alexander Casper Fraser of Mongewell Park, Wallingford, Oxfordshire.

From page 214 –

The lad subsequently travelled: Serious Charges At Norwich, *The Eastern Daily Press* (Norwich), 4 August 1902, p6.

When in London, Bernard Fraser: 1901 Census; Public Record Office Reference: RG 13/84; Administrative County: London; Civil Parish: S. George Hanover Square; Page 2.

Now twenty-eight years old, Arthur: Serious Charges At Norwich, *The Eastern Daily Press* (Norwich), 4 August 1902, p6; Day, *Charles Thorold Gentleman Emigrant*, p87.

"The sunny afternoon": John Gambril Nicholson, Paul Webb (ed.) *In The Dreamy Afternoon*, Gay Mens Press, London 1989, p74.

At Wroxham in Norfolk: The Serious Charges At Wroxham, *The Eastern Daily Press* (Norwich), 9 August 1902, p6.

Arthur Thorold brought another lad: Brumfield, Benjamin: Lincolnshire Baptisms & 1939 Register, FindMyPast.com. His surname is rendered as 'Bromfield' on the Calendar of Prisons record of indictment. (Calendar of Prisons, Home Office: Series HO140:TNA-CCC-HO140-219-158/TNA-CCC-HO140-219-159, National Archives.) However it is rendered as 'Brumfield' in all the newspaper reports of both Norwich papers which covered the hearings and trial, *The Eastern Daily Press* and *Norwich Mercury*. The fact that a Benjamin Brumfield lived in Thorold's village of Hougham (Census of 1901 and 1911); that its population in 1890 was just 271; (Day, *Charles Thorold Gentleman Emigrant*, p99n53), and that Detective-Inspector Arrow "went down into Lincolnshire and saw Brumfield"(The Serious Charges at Wroxham, *The Eastern Daily Press*, 9 August 1902), confirms the identification beyond doubt.

one of the eleven children: Sad Death Of A Hougham Signalman, *The Grantham Journal*, 18 February 1905, p3.

A later resident: Recollections of Peter Stonebridge:
www.hougham.info/peter/Peter_Stonebridge.htm

Born in 1887: 1901 UK Census: Public Record Office Ref: RG 13/3201; Administrative County: Lincoln; Civil Parish: Hougham; p2.

Both the minimum school leaving age: Paul Close, *Child Labour in Global Society (Sociological Studies of Children and Youth: Volume 17),* Emerald Books, Bingley UK, 2014, p99.

"Of living light": On A Picture By H.S. Tuke, *The Artist and Journal of Home Culture*, 1 May 1889.

"Two nations": Benjamin Disraeli, *Sybil, or The Two Nations*, Henry Colburn Publisher, London 1845.

"It was like feasting": Oscar Wilde, Ian Small (ed.) *The Complete Works of Oscar Wilde,* Vol 2, Oxford University Press, 2005, p130.

However, the record of later charges shows: Calendar of Prisons, Home Office: HO 140: TNA-CCC-HO140-219-158 / TNA-CCC-HO140-219-159, National Archives.

In September the group yachted: Calendar of Prisons, Home Office: HO 140: TNA-CCC-HO140-219-158 / TNA-CCC-HO140-219-159, National Archives.

Bernard sought out fresh company: The Serious Charges At Wroxham, *The Eastern Daily Press,* 9 August 1902, p6.

It would have been an intimidating: The Serious Charges At Wroxham, *The Eastern Daily Press,* 9 August 1902, p6.

The official reason listed for his discharge: Albert Collins: Official Number: 214870, Admiralty: Royal Navy Registers of Seamen's Services, ADM 188/376/214870, National Archives.

He claimed to have taken: Serious Charges at Norwich, *The Eastern Daily Press* (Norwich), 4 August 1902, p6.

In it, he again attempted: Serious Charges at Norwich, *The Eastern Daily Press* (Norwich), 4 August 1902, p6.

On July 26th, Detective-Inspector: The Serious Charges At Wroxham, *Eastern Daily Press*, 9 August 1902, p6.

Two days later, accompanied by: The Serious Charges At Wroxham, *Eastern Daily Press*, 9 August 1902, p6.

Mr Clarke – for that was the name: Serious Charges at Norwich, *The Eastern Daily Press* (Norwich), 4 August 1902, p6.

There was a cool fresh breeze: Today's Weather Forecasts, *Western Daily Press*, 28 July 1902.

"I believe you are Mr. Bernard Fraser": The Serious Charges At Wroxham, *The Eastern Daily Press*, 9 August 1902, p6.

The latter had immediately: Wreck Report: No 6368, Cambrian Princess And Alma (S.S.), London Board Of Trade, 1902.

"sumptuously appointed": Railways, Pleasure Trips, &c., *The Standard* (London), 3 July 1895, p4.

And life, like the lives: Wreck Report: No 6368, Cambrian Princess And Alma (S.S.), London Board Of Trade, 1902.

Bernard Fraser was not so: Bernard Fraser, Calendar Of Prisons, HO140-219-158, National Archives.

at Oxford, where he had begun teaching: Day, John H. *Charles Thorold Gentleman Emigrant: a study of the transmission of the 'gentleman ideal' to Australia*, Unpublished thesis, University of Queensland, 1989, p124.

Arthur was received into custody: Arthur Thorold, Calendar Of Prisons, HO140-219-159, National Archives.

9. A SERIOUS QUESTION OF PUBLIC POLICY

"it is asserted that": A Public Scandal, *Daily Express*, 5 November 1902, p5.

As Detective-Inspector Arrow's: London Shocked By Scandal, *The Sun* (New York), 9 November 1902, p9.

"well known country houses": London Shocked By Scandal, *The Sun* (New York), 9 November 1902, p9.

"a regular campaign": London Wrought Up, *Evening Star* (Washington, DC), 3 November 1902, p9.

"involves names of wider": London Shocked By Scandal, *The Sun* (New York), 9 November 1902, p9.

The leader of the group: London Shocked By Scandal, *The Sun* (New York), 9 November 1902, p9.

"Another still greater name": London Shocked By Scandal, *The Sun* (New York), 9 November 1902, p9.

"Since the Cleveland Street scandal": Swell Thieves – Amazing Revelations, *John Bull*, 21 April 1923, p16.

With the Battersea Case, this occurred: Case No: 223; List of all Cases in which the Conduct of the Prosecution was undertaken by the Director of Prosecutions, *Prosecution of Offences Acts, 1879 and 1884*, Parliamentary Paper, No. 154, Session of 1902; House of Commons and Command; Vol 56, London 1903; p64.

"Hand Cuff": Social Gossip, *The Australasian* (Melbourne) 17 August 1901.

Akers-Douglas was also a member: The Prince Of Wales And Freemasonry, *The Times*, 29 November 1893.

"tucked away in the drawers": Sir Harold Scott, *Your Obedient Servant*, Andre Deutsch, London 1959, p62.

Originally held at the Home Office: Home Office: Registered Papers Supplementary, HO 144/710/108656, National Archives.

10. FEARSOME CHARGES

The police also held: Norfolk Assizes, *Evening Star*, 1 November 1902.

Some charges could have: Louise A. Jackson, *Child Sexual Abuse in Victorian England*, Routledge, Abingdon, Oxon 2000, p14.

As for attempted buggery: Public General Acts 44 and 45 Vict. (London: 1861), p833, sec. 61 & 62.

It rated the crime: Public General Acts 48-49 Vict. (London: 1885), p6, sec.11.

While homosexual acts committed: H.G. Cocks, *Nameless Offences: Homosexual Desire In The Nineteenth Century*, I.B. Tauris, London 2003, p31.

The prohibition would remain: Alan Turing (Statutory Pardon) Bill, *Hansard,* House of Lords, 19 July 2013, c1006.

It was not uncommon: Edward William Cox (ed.), *Reports of Cases in Criminal Law Argued and Determined in All the Courts in England and Ireland, Vol XII 1871-1874*, Law Times Office, 1875, p88.

The indictment read: Calendar of Prisons, Home Office: Series HO 140: TNA-CCC-HO140-219-158 / TNA-CCC-HO140-219-159, National Archives.

"Fraser had for a long while": Heavy Sentences, *Rhyl Record And Advertiser*, 8 November 1902.

11. THE WORST OFFENCES KNOWN TO LAW

It was then codified: Cosmas Moisidis, *Criminal Discovery: From Truth to Proof and Back Again*, Institute of Criminology Press, 2008, p19.

On Saturday the 2nd of August: Serious Charges At Norwich, *Eastern Daily Press*, 4 August 1902, p5; Serious Charges At Norwich, *Norwich Mercury*, 9 August 1902, p11.

Yet the courtroom's high windows: Mark Shields, Norwich's historic Shirehall courtroom reopened to the public, *Eastern Daily Press* (Norwich), 12 September 2013.

"worst offences known": Norfolk Assizes, *The Evening Star* (Ipswich), 1 November 1902, p2.

the highly exacting: Sir Archibald Henry Bodkin, *Oxford Dictionary of National Biography*, Oxford University Press, 2004.

The hearing was opened: Serious Charges At Norwich, *Eastern Daily Press*, 4 August 1902, p5; *Serious Charges At Norwich*, Norwich Mercury, 9 August 1902, p11.

An application for bail: Serious Charges At Norwich, *Eastern Daily Press*, 4 August 1902, p6.

The second hearing: The Serious Charges At Wroxham, *Eastern Daily Press*, 9 August 1902, p6; Magisterial Proceedings: Norwich, *Norwich Mercury*, 13 August 1902, p3.

"Brilliant. Formidable.": John Juxon, *Lewis & Lewis; The Life and Times of a Victorian Solicitor*, William Collins Sons & Co., Glasgow 1983, p15.

However, another of Sir George's: Information from Sara Flower.

A lifelong bachelor: Sir Henry Chartres Biron, *Without Prejudice: Impressions of Life and Law*, Faber and Faber, London 1936.

"not one word": Novel Condemned As Obscene, *The Times*, 17 November 1928, p5.

"he hoped his friend Biron": The Serious Charges At Wroxham, *Eastern Daily Press*, 9 August 1902, p6.

Once again, Fraser: The Serious Charges At Wroxham, *Eastern Daily Press*, 9 August 1902, p6; *Magisterial Proceedings*, Norwich Mercury, 13 August 1902, p3.

Salutes were fired: Coronation Day At Norwich, *Norwich Mercury*, 13 August 1902, p1.

On the following Thursday: The Serious Charges At Wroxham, *Eastern Daily Press*, 15 August 1902, p6.

Two days later on Saturday: The Serious Charges At Wroxham, *Eastern Daily Press*, 18 August 1902, p6.

"as regards the charge of felony": The Serious Charges At Wroxham, *Eastern Daily Press*, 18 August 1902, p6.

In respect of Thorold: The Serious Charges At Wroxham, *Eastern Daily Press*, 18 August 1902, p6.

At his death twenty years: Day, *Charles Thorold Gentleman Emigrant*, p182, n24.

He was granted bail at £20: Worcester City Police, Worcestershire Chronicle, 22 November 1902

The record is silent: HM.P. 1/17; Prison Registers, Norfolk Record Office.

"the ball was kept merrily rolling": Honington, *The Grantham Journal*, 11 October 1902, p3.

12. A MOST PAINFUL CASE

As the *Norwich Mercury* reported: Norwich and Norfolk Assizes, *Norwich Mercury*, 1 November 1902, p4.

"His Lordship was at once": Norwich and Norfolk Assizes, *Norwich Mercury*, 1 November 1902, p4.

"the picture of an English squire": Death Of Mr. Justice Grantham, *The Times*, 1 December 1911, p11.

"the public were warned": Death Of Mr. Justice Grantham, *The Times*, 1 December 1911, p11.

"Her Majesty would rather": Robert Standish Sievier, *The Autobiography of Robert Standish Sievier*, The Winning Post, London 1906, p271.

"He was never much": Up To Date, *Reynolds's Newspaper*, 4 February 1900, p1.

A still vigorous 72: Sir William Grantham, *Oxford Dictionary of National Biography*.

"with him, as with some others": Death Of Mr. Justice Grantham, *The Times*, 1 December 1911, p11.

"a notorious Tory political wirepuller": Trafalgar Square, *Justice*, 7 July 1888, p1.

"Mr Justice Grantham, like necessity": E.T. Raymond, *Portraits Of The Nineties*, T Fisher Unwin, London 1921, p281.

"I know which was the winner": When Wig And Gown Are Doffed, *The Bystander*, 22 April 1908, p173.

"This may account for": Robert Standish Sievier, *The Autobiography of Robert Standish Sievier*, The Winning Post, London 1906, p262.

"the series of charges": Norwich and Norfolk Assizes, *Norwich Mercury*, 1 November 1902, p4.

"Thank you, your Honour": Norwich and Norfolk Assizes, *Norwich Mercury*, 1 November 1902, p4

Appearing for the prosecution: The Assizes, Eastern Daily Press (Norwich), 1 November 1902, p8.

Avory was an austere: Bernard O'Donnell, *The Trials Of Mr Justice Avory*, Rich & Cowan, 1935, Preface.

Although no great lawyer: Ambrose Hoopington, 'Mr. Justice Avory', *The Spectator*, 4 October 1935, p26.

"Like most judges he was at his best": Ambrose Hoopington, 'Mr. Justice Avory', *The Spectator*, 4 October 1935, p26.

Appearing for Bernard Fraser: A Great Advocate, *The Times*, February 23, 1923, p15.

George Elliot: The Assizes, Eastern Daily Press (Norwich), 1 November 1902, p8.

Grantham's son: The Assizes, Eastern Daily Press (Norwich), 1 November 1902, p8.

When the charges were read out: The Assizes, Eastern Daily Press (Norwich), 1 November 1902, p8.; Norwich and Norfolk Assizes, *Norwich Mercury*, 1 November 1902, p4; Norfolk Assizes, *The Evening Star* (Ipswich), 1 November 1902, p2.

Some of the press: Corruptors Of Youth In The Toils, *New York Tribune*, 4 November 1902, p12.

There was a strong feeling: Society Sensation, *Daily Express*, 4 November 1902, p5.

"influenced by the fact": The Assizes, *Eastern Daily Press* (Norwich), 1 November 1902, p8.

"I think you have exercised": The Assizes, *Eastern Daily Press* (Norwich), 1 November 1902, p8.

Nicknamed 'Slim': Roy T. Matthews, Peter Mellini, *In Vanity Fair*, University of California Press, 1982, p116.

"one of the very worst": The Assizes, *Eastern Daily Press* (Norwich), 1 November 1902, p8.

"The shocking story": Norfolk Assizes, *The Evening Star* (Ipswich), 1 November 1902, p2.

It would have left: A Public Scandal, *Bradford Daily Telegraph*, 5 November 1902, p6.

"his habit of removing": A Great Advocate, *The Times*, February 23, 1923, p15.

"having considered the documents": The Assizes, Eastern Daily Press (Norwich), 1 November 1902, p8.

"a fact which carried its own": Norwich and Norfolk Assizes, *Norwich Mercury*, 1 November 1902, p4.

"He suggested it was a case": Norfolk Assizes, *The Evening Star* (Ipswich), 1 November 1902, p2.

He was considered an astute: Mr. George Elliott, K.C., *The Daily Telegraph* (London), 28 October 1916, p10; Death of Mr George Elliott, K.C., *The Times*, 28 October 1916, p11.

"Until 1897, when he": Norwich and Norfolk Assizes, *Norwich Mercury*, 1 November 1902, p4.

"it was impossible to deny": Norfolk Assizes, *The Evening Star* (Ipswich), 1 November 1902, p2.

Unbeknownst to him: Sir William Grantham to Home Secretary, 17 June 1907, Registered Papers, Supplementary: HO 144/710/108656, National Archives.

"showers of sparks": Death Of Mr. Justice Grantham, *The Times*, 1 December 1911, p11.

"it was one of the most painful": Grantham's summation speech is reconstructed from three reports of 1 November 1902: The Assizes, *Eastern Daily Press* (Norwich); Norwich and Norfolk Assizes, *Norwich Mercury*; and Norfolk Assizes, *The Evening Star* (Ipswich). Where what he said appears to have been paraphrased, truncated, or missed by a reporter, one of the two other reports has been used. (e.g. His remark regarding boys "being reduced to the condition of those of whom they read in ancient history" only appears in the *Norwich Mercury*.) As is common for the period, no court transcripts of the case are known to survive.

Twelve days later: The Assizes, *The Times*, 12 November 1902, p10; The Assizes, *The Times,* 12 December 1902, p9.

"He shrank from such innovations": Death Of Mr. Justice Grantham, *The Times*, 1 December 1911, p11.

"Personally he was": E.T. Raymond, *Portraits Of The Nineties*, T Fisher Unwin, London 1921, p281-282.

In 1902, the DPP prosecuted 454 cases: List of all Cases in which the Conduct of the Prosecution was undertaken by the Director of Prosecutions, *Prosecution of Offences Acts, 1879 and 1884*, Parliamentary Paper, No. 154, Session of 1902; House of Commons and Command; Vol 56, London 1903; pp51-78.

13. THE AIR IS ELECTRIC

"Do not fear circumstances": Religious Truths, *Richmond Planet*, (Richmond, Virginia) 1 November 1902, p7.

The most detailed accounts: *Eastern Daily Press*: 4, 9, 15, 18 August & 1 November 1902; *Norwich Mercury*: 6, 9, 13, 23 August & 1 November 1902; *The Evening Star* (Ipswich), 1 November 1902.

"a series of felonies and misdemeanours": Abominable Crimes – Heavy Sentences, *Norwich Mercury*, 1 November 1902, p4.

"committing and inciting to commit": The Assizes, *Eastern Daily Press* (Norwich), 1 November 1902, p8.

"one of the most discreditable offences": A Scandalous Case, *The Daily Telegraph* (London), 4 November 1902, p10.

"Fraser had been engaged in a regular system": Norfolk And Norwich Assizes, *The Norfolk Chronicle*, 8 November 1902, p12.

"I understand that a serious matter": The Secret History Of To-Day, *Reynolds's Newspaper*, 3

August 1902, p8.

"A week or two ago we intimated": Serious Charges, *Reynolds's Newspaper*, 31 August 1902, p6.

"An ugly rumour was in circulation": The Secret History Of To-Day, *Reynolds's Newspaper*, 2 November 1902, p8.

"has set everyone talking": Untitled item, *Worcestershire Chronicle*, 8 November 1902, p3.

"There are persistent rumours": *Sunday Special* quoted in: Rumoured Society Scandal, *Northern Whig* (Belfast), 3 November 1902, p12.

"Speculation is rife": Today's London Letter, *Edinburgh Evening News*, 3 November 1902, p2.

"A most sensational story": Reported Scandal In London, *Sunderland Daily Echo and Shipping Gazette*, (Tyne and Wear), 3 November 1902, p6.

"A tremendous sensation": Another Scandal Agitates London, *New-York Tribune*, 3 November 1902, p2.

"According to one account, he was arrested": English Peer A Fugitive, *The Sun* (New York), 3 November 1902, p1.

"The excitement yesterday": London Wrought Up, *The Evening Star* (Washington D.C.), 3 November 1902, p1.

By Tuesday, *The New York Times*: London Society Scandal, *The New York Times*, 4 November 1902, p5; Sentenced For Depravity, *The Waxahachie Daily Light* (Texas), 4 November 1902, p3.

"Another of those painful scandals": *To-Day* quoted in: A Painful Scandal, *Sheffield Evening Telegraph*, 5 November 1902, p7.

"Considerable feeling has been aroused": Society Sensation, *Daily Express*, 4 November 1902, p5.

"The case of the men Fraser and Thorold": A Public Scandal, *Daily Express*, 5 November 1902, p5.

while at least one provincial paper: A Public Scandal, *Bradford Daily Telegraph*, 5 November 1902, p6.

five days later *The Weekly Dispatch*: Ten Years For Debauchery, *The Weekly Dispatch* (London), 9 November 1902, p17.

"The recent notorious case at Norwich": Who Are They?, *Daily Express*, 6 November 1902, p5.

"It would be idle to attempt": Happenings In London: Can It Be True?, *Wigan Observer and District Advertiser*, 5 November 1902, p5.

"Considerable feeling has been aroused": A Society Sensation, *Weston Mercury* (Weston-super-Mare, Somerset), 8 November 1902, p7.

"The last few days it has been said": George Ives diary, 5 November 1902: Harry Ransom Center, The University of Austen at Texas.

"We regret that Lord Battersea": Lord Battersea's Illness, *Eastern Evening News*, 3 November 1902, p3.

"Lord Battersea is very much better": News In Brief, *Daily Express*, 7 November 1902, p5.

"Sodomism in London": *Daily Dispatch*, 13 November 1902.

"These riddles again": Sporting Notes, *The Sporting Times*, 15 November 1902, p1.

"They are cackling a great deal": Cockney Cackle, *The Scottish Referee*, 17 November 1902, p2.

"Meynell was full of a new scandal": Wilfrid Blunt diary, 22 November 1902; MS 6-1975, The Fitzwilliam Museum, Cambridge.

"The air is electric": George Ives diary, 27 November 1902: Harry Ransom Center, The University of Austen at Texas.

From page 263 –

"he's looking very robust": George Ives diary, 25 October 1902; Harry Ransom Center, The University of Austen at Texas.

"I am engaged in cricket fixtures": George Ives to Oscar Browning, undated 'Friday late' [c. 1901-03], Oscar Browning Papers, OB/1/858, Archive Centre, King's College, Cambridge.

"I cannot imagine what good I can do": George Ives to Oscar Browning, undated 'Sunday' [c. 1901-03], Oscar Browning Papers, OB/1/858, Archive Centre, King's College, Cambridge.

"It probably was [Lord Battersea].": George Ives diary, postscript on page opposite entry 5 November 1902: Harry Ransom Center, The University of Austen at Texas.

"Two fashionable individuals": The Secret History Of To-Day, *Reynolds's Newspaper*, 16 November 1902 p8.

"It is not generally known": The Secret History Of To-Day, *Reynolds's Newspaper*, 23 November 1902, p8.

"We are glad to be able": Lord and Lady Battersea's Silver Wedding, *Bucks Herald*, 29 November 1902, p8.

"A highly unpleasant story": London Letter, *Birmingham Daily Gazette*, 11 December 1902, p4.

"Grave Society Scandal": Grave Society Scandal, *Lancashire Evening Post*, 11 December 1902, p2.

"Lord Battersea, it is said": Politics and Parliament, *Lancashire Evening Post*, 13 November 1902, p2.

"Motor car was the feature": Sporting Notes, *The Sporting Times*, 10 January 1903, p1.

However, they readily combined: A Peer In Disgrace, *The Wanganui Chronicle* (Wanganui, New Zealand), 8 December 1902, p2; *A Scandalous Case*, New Zealand Herald, 20 December 1902, p2.

The appointment diary: Aretas Akers-Douglas, 1st Viscount Chilston *Engagement Diary*, 1902, U564/F30, Kent Archives.

O'Connor's assistant editor: A Great Journalist, *Cairns Post* (Australia), 24 Nov 1924, p5.

"An amiable but politically obscure": Eleusis Club Dinner, *Reynolds's Newspaper*, 27 November 1892, p5.

"who is a fool. He must have paid": Renowned French journalist Pierre Mille (1864–1941), who lived in London from 1890 to 1893 and knew Labouchère, gives two different versions of the story, published eight years apart: in the first, Labby gives Marjoribanks a spoken reply; in the later version, Labby provides Gladstone with a written reply, which Mille claims to have seen. — Pierre Mille, 'Notre Époque', *La Dépêche* (Toulouse), 18 February 1914, p1; Pierre Mille, 'Excelsior', *Excelsior* (Paris), 10 July 1922, p2.

"If you were to take them": Wilfrid Scawen Blunt *My Diaries: Part Two*, Martin Secker, London 1920, p16.

"Who was Prime Minister": Three Questions For Mr Labouchère To Answer, *The Globe*, 3 March 1890, p4.

During his time in prison: Lewis Chester, David Leitch, Colin Simpson, *The Cleveland Street Affair*, Weidenfeld and Nicolson, London 1976, p227-8.

As for the mainstream press: Society Gossip, *Shepton Mallet Journal*, 20 December 1901, p3.

"terribly disappointed at not": Marquess of Lincolnshire diaries, 7 December 1902; MS. Film 1104, Bodleian Library.

"full of ability, novelty": Matthew Arnold, Up To Easter, *The Nineteenth Century*, May 1887, p638.

"The time of editors as preachers": E.T. Raymond, *Portraits Of The Nineties*, T. Fisher Unwin, London 1921, pp297-305.

"So great is the tacit and ignorant boycott": The Secret History Of To-Day, *Reynolds's Newspaper*, 11 October 1903, p1.

"An array of prominent": Prison For Society Men, *The Evening World* (New York, NY) 3 November 1902, p3.

A number of reports: English Society Scandal: Two Men Connected with Well-Known Families Receive Heavy Sentences, *The New York Times*, 4 November 1902, p5.

"The government determined": A London Scandal, *The Times* (Richmond, Virginia) 9 November 1902, p7.

"A scandal involving peers": News Of The World, *The Intermountain Catholic*, (Salt Lake City) 15 November 1902; News Of The World, *Iowa County Democrat*, 20 November 1902.

"posh dirty pigs": Schöne Geschichten, *Der Deutsche Correspondent* (Baltimore), 4 November 1902, p1.

"While such conditions prevail": Wochenplauderei, *Der Deutsche Correspondent* (Baltimore), 7 November 1902, p2.

"Last Sunday we picked up": (Untitled Editorial), *The Appeal. A National Afro-American Newspaper*, (Saint Paul, Mn.), 15 November 1902, p2.

"London Shocked By Scandal": London Shocked By Scandal, *The Sun* (New York), 9 November 1902, p9.

"Britain Bows In Shame": Britain Bows In Shame, *Chicago Tribune*, 9 November 1902, p2.

"Straws showed him how": Edward Forrester Holden Sutton, *The Princess Au Revoir*, (Unpublished manuscript), Sutton and Cunliffe-Owen Collection, C0487, Princeton University Library, pp162.

In British newspaper offices: Sutton, *The Princess Au Revoir*, pp161-3.

Lord Ronald Gower had assisted: Exhibition medallion gifted to Lord Ronald Gower, Dunrobin Castle.

At the unveiling: Unveiling Of The Shakespeare Monument at Stratford-on-Avon, *Leamington Spa Courier*, 13 October 1888, p9.

Sir Philip and Gower: The Royal Windsor Tapestry Manufactory, *Illustrated London News*, 29 April 1882, p18.

Intriguingly, Princess Louise: Princess Louise's Cheque, *Bradford Daily Telegraph*, 10 June 1899, p2.

"Perhaps it is a mere coincidence": London Shocked By Scandal, *The Sun* (New York), 9 November 1902, p9.

"are the police of Richmond": The Secret History Of To-Day, *Reynolds's Newspaper*, 2 November 1902, p8]

a search of London residential directories: His surname is absent from the London social directories *Royal Blue Book: Court and Parliamentary Guide* for 1890-1902, and *Webster's Royal Red Book; or Court and Fashionable Register* for 1892, 1895, 1897 or 1899. Nor does it feature in directories for 1890-1902 covering Richmond, Kew, Twickenham, St Margaret's, Petersham, Mortlake, Sheen and Teddington. The Court section of London suburban directories for 1892 (southern suburbs), 1894 (northern and southern suburbs), 1896 (northern suburbs) and 1900 (northern and southern suburbs) were also checked without result.

"Scandal Stirs Britain": Scandal Stirs Britain, *Chicago Tribune*, 16 November 1902, p4.; Too Prominent To Punish, *The Evening Herald* (Syracruse, N.Y.), 17 November 1902, p8.

"it may safely be taken for granted": Hushing It Up by Ex-Attaché (Frederick Cunliffe-Owen), *New York Tribune*, 17 January 1897, p3

"whereas on this side of the Atlantic": *Europe Hushes Up Crimes Of Upper Classes In Order To Protect Morals Of The People*, by Ex-Attache, The Chicago Sunday Tribune, 3 November 1907, p16.

"Never before did peers and plutocrats": Twenty-First Birthday Of The S.D.F., *Justice*, 17 January 1903, p2.

14. THE MOST HANDSOME MAN IN PARLIAMENT

"Lord Battersea's love of bright colour": Lord Battersea, (By M.A.P.), *South Wales Daily News*, 6 December 1898, p3.

"the keenest sense of humour": Maud Nathan, *Once Upon A Time And Today*, G. P. Putnam's sons, 1933, p155.

"always very genial": Walter Crane, *An Artist's Reminiscences*, The Macmillan Company, New York 1907, p212.

"Mr. Cyril Flower is all smiles": *The New House Of Commons, 1892*, Pall Mall Gazette Office, 1892, p36.

"If you met Mr. Cyril Flower": London Correspondence, *Sheffield Daily Telegraph*, 6 September 1904, p6.

"a touching belief in his powers": Leo McKinstry, *Rosebery: Statesman in Turmoil*, John Murray, London 2005 (Thomas Gilmour diary, 12 February 1885, Acc 8989/3, National Library of Scotland).

"The Flower of the Flock": *Punch, or The London Charivari*, 9 March 1895, p115.

"a funny little man": Private information from Sara Flower.

It became the largest enterprise: Horace Flower, *Australian Dictionary of Biography*, Volume 4, Melbourne University Press, 1972; Severin Kanute Salting, *Australian Dictionary of Biography*, Volume 2, Melbourne University Press, 1967; Martin J. Daunton, *State and Market in Victorian Britain: War, Welfare and Capitalism*, The Boydell Press, Woodbridge 2008, p168.

He also became a director: Edwin Green, Stuart Muirhead, *Crisis Banking in the East: The History of the Chartered Mercantile*, Ashgate Publishing, 1996.

This was perhaps fortunate: Hyde, H. Montgomery *The Other Love*, Granada, London 1972, p131.

whose central character was: Constance Battersea, *Reminiscences*, Macmillan and Company, London 1922, p167.

"May every schoolboy": Farrar W. Frederic, *Eric Or Little By Little*, Adam And Charles Black, Edinburgh, 1858, p102.

"everything is served up": Eric; Or Little By Little, *The Saturday Review*, 6 November 1858, p453-4.

The granting of favours: Christopher Tyerman, *A History of Harrow School, 1324-1991*, Oxford University Press, 2000, p477; Selina Hastings, *The Red Earl*, Bloomsbury Continuum, London, 2014, p24; Valerie Grove, *A Voyage Round John Mortimer*, Viking Books, London 2008, p28.

"his mind seemed cast": Farrar, *Eric Or Little By Little*, p3.

The fair face was further sanctified: William Callow, H.M. Cundall (ed.), *An Autobiography*, Adam And Charles Black, London 1908, p118.

"Christ is a healthy, beautiful boy": Anon (Frederic George Stephens), *William Holman Hunt and His*

Works: A Memoir Of the Artists Life, James Nisbet & Co., London 1861, pp86, 91, 111.

"he was simply 'too handsome'": Vanity Fair by J.M.D., *The Argus* (Melbourne, Australia), 8 October 1892, p4.

"our long and unclouded": Battersea, *Reminiscences*, p176.

In his novel: Leon Edel, *Henry James:The Middle Years, 1882-1895*, Lippincott, Philadelphia 1962, p254.

"a lean, strong, clear-faced": Henry James, *The Tragic Muse*, Richard Clay & Sons, London 1890, p6.

"The more I see of Flower" : Battersea, *Reminiscences,* p167-168.

'Flowery-Bowery': Reginald, Viscount Esher, *Cloud-Capp'd Towers*, John Murray, London, 1927, p40.

"He is a nice fellow": Esher, *Ionicus*, p61.

"He is the only man": Battersea, *Reminiscences*, p167-168.

"No doubt the most remarkable": W.G. Elliot (ed.), *Amateur Clubs & Actors*, Edward Arnold, London 1898, p73.

Also in the play: Oscar Wilde, Nicholas Frankel (ed.), *The Picture of Dorian Gray: An Annotated, Uncensored Edition*, The Belknap Press of Harvard University Press, 2011, p68.

A handsome blond: A. H. Marshall, The Cambridge 'A.D.C.', *The Pall Mall Magazine*, London August 1896.

He and his brother Lord Archibald: Battersea, *Reminiscences*, p380.

Letters indicate that the closeness: Ferguson, *The World's Banker*, pp1202-3, n39.

"He was far too beautiful": Miriam Rothschild*, Dear Lord Rothschild: Birds, Butterflies and History*, Balaban, London 1983, p16.

"In 1863, just before my degree": Trevor Hamilton, *Immortal Longings: FWH Myers and the Victorian Search for Life After Death*, Imprint Academic, Exeter, 2009, p23.

Strong, good-looking: Hamilton, *Immortal Longings*, pp1-22.

Prior to meeting Cyril: Phyllis Grosskurth, *John Addington Symonds: A Biography*, Longmans, London, 1964: p114-15; Bart Schultz, *Henry Sidgwick - Eye of the Universe: An Intellectual Biography*, Cambridge University Press, 2004, p336.

"I consider the tone": Herbert M. Schueller, Robert Peters, *The letters of John Addington Symonds*, Volume 1", Wayne State University Press, 1969, p666.

"I am he who long ago": F.W.H. Myers, Evelyn Myers (ed.) *Collected Poems*, Macmillan, London 1921, pp325-6.

"Yes, I have heard also as you have": Hamilton *Immortal Longings*, p23. [Josephine Butler to Stanley Butler, 24 Apr 1895: 3JBL/34/20, The Women's Library, The London School Of Economics & Political Science.]

"They drew from me": Myers, Myers (ed.), *Collected Poems*, p9.

"this upholsterous and hypnotic world": William Cory, Francis Warre Cornish (ed.), *Extracts From The Letters And Journals Of William Cory*, Oxford, 1897, p559, p543.

However, Cyril got there even earlier: Walt Whitman, William White (ed.), *Daybooks and Notebooks Vol. 1*, New York University Press, 2007, p24 Note51.

"Whitman is a cowboy, a New York tough": Burwood, *The Last Weeks*, p16.

According to Carpenter: Winston Leyland (ed.) *Gay Sunshine Interviews*, Volume 1, Gay Sunshine Press, San Francisco, 1978, pp126-128; Martin Murray: *Walt Whitman, Edward Carpenter, Gavin Arthur, and The Circle of Sex* in *Walt Whitman Quarterly Review*, 2005, Volume 22, Number 4.

"give any idea of the extraordinary": Richard Maurice Bucke, *Cosmic Consciousness: A Study in the Evolution of the Human Mind*, Innes & Sons, Philadelphia 1905, p180.

Cyril met the poet at his workplace: Cyril Flower to Walt Whitman, 23 April 1871; MSS18630, Box 9; Charles E. Feinberg Collection, Library of Congress.

Whitman gifted him a signed edition of *Leaves of Grass*:
https://web.archive.org/web/20210202154716/https://www.manhattanrarebooks.com/pictures/2299.jpg
https://web.archive.org/web/20210202154946/https://www.manhattanrarebooks.com/pictures/2299_3.jpg
https://web.archive.org/web/20210202160307/https://www.manhattanrarebooks.com/pictures/2299_5.jpg

plus some of his works: Thomas Donaldson, *Walt Whitman The Man*, Francis P. Harper, New York 1896, p223.

"I have often wished": Horace Traubel, *With Walt Whitman In Camden*, Vol 2, p461-463.

"Many a soldier's kiss": Walt Whitman: The Wound Dresser, *Leaves of Grass*, James R. Osgood and

Company, 1881-82, p241-243.

"The Prussian soldiers": Horace Traubel, *With Walt Whitman In Camden*, Vol 2, pp461-463.

"You may think yourself neglected": Traubel, *With Walt Whitman In Camden,* Vol 2, pp461-463.

"I have an admiration": Harold Blodgett, *Walt Whitman In England*, Cornell University Press, 1934, p151.

"He is the grandest man": Oscar Wilde, *Boston Herald*, 29 January 1882.

"as Victor Hugo says: we are all": Walter Pater, *Studies in the History of the Renaissance*, Macmillan, London 1873, pp212-213.

"To burn always with this hard, gemlike": Pater, *Studies in the History of the Renaissance*, p210.

"quickened, multiplied consciousness": Pater, *Studies in the History of the Renaissance*, pp212-213.

"duty, responsibility and reason": Patrick J. Quinn, *The Femme Fatale and the New Woman in American Literature and Culture, 1870-1920*, Cambridge Scholars Publishing, Newcastle 2015, p30.

"We must seriously dissent": New Books, *The Illustrated London News*, 19 April 1873, p375.

From page 300 –

"If the moral and intellectual": New Books, *The Illustrated London News*, 19 April 1873, p375.

"it might possibly mislead": Walter Pater, *The Renaissance : studies in art and poetry*, Macmillan, London 1902, p233, n1.

"in those of an artistic or aesthetic temperament": Anon, *Boy-Worship*, 1880, pp7-8.

"Owners of more than 800": The Liberal Candidate For Brecon, *The Cardiff Times*, 2 August 1879, p3.

"the superior class of workingmen": The Liberal Candidate For Brecon, *The Cardiff Times*, 2 August 1879, p3.

Cyril and his estate architect: Keith Alan, *The metamorphosis of Battersea, 1800-1914: a building history*, Phd Thesis: The Open University,1995, p195; oro.open.ac.uk/18803/

As well as funding and fundraising: The Liberal Candidate For Brecon, *The Cardiff Times*, 2 August 1879, p3.

Despite these commitments: Frederick Feild Whitehurst, *Hark Away: Sketches of Hunting, Coaching, Fishing, Etc., Etc*, Tinsley Brothers, London 1879, p48.

His vague instructions: Priscilla Metcalf, *The Park Town Estate and the Battersea Tangle*, London Topographical Society, 1978, pp39-41.

In another, Sandys: Thomas Tuoby, *Frederick Sandys* in *The British Art Journal*, Vol III, No2, pp82-83. (The current whereabouts of the painting is unknown.)

He was a fearless horseman: The Liberal Candidate For Brecon, *The Cardiff Times*, 2 August 1879, p3.

"He hoped little and believed little": T. Wemyss Reid, *The Life, Letters, And Friendships Of Richard Monckton Milnes*, First Lord Houghton, Vol II Cassell & Company, London 1890, p491.

"Yes, I live for Pleasure": Reid, *The Life, Letters, And Friendships Of Richard Monckton Milnes*, p496.

"As years advanced he became": George W. E. Russell, *Collections & Recollections*, Thomas Nelson & Sons, London 1903, p58.

Houghton was also an admirer: James Pope-Hennessy, *Monkton-Milnes: The Flight Of Youth*, Constable, London 1951, pp175, 244.

and added to it by pseudononymously authoring: James G. Nelson, *Publisher to the Decadents: Leonard Smithers in the Careers of Beardsley, Wilde, Dowson*, Pennsylvania University Press, 2000, p10n11.

Its text was hand-corrected for him: John R. Godsall, *The Tangled Web: A Life Of Sir Richard Burton*, Matador; Leicester 2008, p193.

the supplier of erotica to them both: Nelson, *Publisher to the Decadents*, p10.

Together with Houghton, Swinburne: Silvia Antosa, 'Cannibal London: Racial Discourses, Pornography, and Male-Male Desire in Late-Victorian Britain', in: Simon Avery, Katherine M. Graham (eds.), *Sex, Time and Place: Queer Histories of London, c.1850 to the Present*, Bloomsbury, London 2018, pp153-156.

After leaving Yorkshire, Cyril joined: Simon Reynolds, *The Vision Of Simeon Solomon*, Catalpa Press, Stroud 1984, p15.

Swinburne and other friends, distanced themselves: John Y. LeBourgeois, Swinburne and Simeon Solomon, *Notes And Queries*, Oxford University Press, March 1973, p94.

However Cyril, who'd become a patron: Carolyn Conroy, *He Hath Mingled With The Ungodly: The*

Life Of Simeon Solomon After 1873, With A Survey Of The Extant Works, Vol I, Thesis, University Of York 2009, p143-144.

A fussy febrile dilettante: Michael Hall, *Waddesdon Manor: The Heritage of a Rothschild House*, Scala Publishers Ltd, London 2009, *passim*.

"I can remember that we were much struck": Battersea *Reminiscences*, p166.

"buying everything he could lay": Lucy Cohen, *Lady de Rothschild And Her Daughters 1821-1931*, John Murray, London 1935, pp165-166.

This booty Cyril installed at: Bruce Elliot Tapper, Mary Kay Zuravleff (eds.) *The Peacock Room: A Cultural Biography*, Yale University Press, New Haven 1998, p191.

"Cyril Flower was a superb, golden-bearded": Maud Howe Elliott, *Three Generations*, Little Brown And Company, Boston 1923, p149.

"heavenly morning": Lady Battersea diary, 29 August 1874: Battersea Papers, Add MS 47929, Vol XXI, British Library.

"took me in his arms and kissed me": Lady Battersea diary, 23 August 1874: Battersea Papers, Add MS 47929, Vol XXI, British Library.

As for Constance: since adolescence: Richard Davis, *The English Rothschilds*, University of North Carolina Press, Chapel Hill 1983, p162.

In her teenage years there were: Lady Battersea diary, 6&14 September 1858, Add MS 47913, Vol V; 26 June 1861, Add MS 47914, Vol VI, British Library.

and in her twenties she was tempestuously: Lady Battersea diary, 21 March & 1 June 1865, Add MS 47915, Vol VII, British Library.

until lectured to by Ferdinand: Lady Battersea diary, 29 May 1865, Add MS 47915, Vol VII, British Library.

She rejected a wealthy suitor: Lady Battersea diary, 2&3 August 1865 Add MS 47915, Add MS 47915, Vol VII, British Library.

"I was a little fool": Davis, *The English Rothschilds*, p162.

In a surreal situation, during a visit: Lady Biddulph of Ledbury, *Charles Philip Yorke, Fourth Earl Of Hardwicke, Vice-Admiral. R.N. A Memoir.*, Smith Elder & Co., London 1910, p300.

The tragedy drew the Yorke and Rothschild: Biddulph, *Charles Philip Yorke,* p300-301.

"I wish I could be a Christian": Davis, *The English Rothschilds*, p162.

"Eliot came, sat down, cried": Davis, *The English Rothschilds*, p162.

upset the Jewish community: Elliott, *Three Generations*, p148.

He left her £300,000: Davis, *The English Rothschilds*, p148.

"I am the happiest man": Cyril Flower to F.W.H. Myers, Undated; MYER/1/58, Trinity College Library.

"You are indeed a lucky man": Cohen, *Lady de Rothschild And Her Daughters*, p171.

"I seem to know you so well": Lord Houghton to Cyril Flower, 21 September 1877: Houghton 8/182, Trinity College Library Cambridge.

"You and I belong to a race": Battersea, *Reminiscences*, p232.

"the only present I can think of": Lord Houghton to Cyril Flower (Tatton Park, undated): tipped-in letter within presentation copy of *The Poetical Works of Richard Monckton Milnes*; Item H2506, Common Crow Books, Pittsburg, 2019.
[https://web.archive.org/web/20191013061607/https://www.commoncrowbooks.com/pages/book s/H2506/richard-monckton-milnes-lord-houghton/the-poetical-works-of-richard-monckton-milnes-lord-broughton-2-volumes-1876-presentation-copy-to/]

"You could not have sent me a present": Cyril Flower to Lord Houghton, undated: Houghton 8/183, Trinity College Library Cambridge.

To top things off, the wedding ceremony: Battersea, *Reminiscences*, p170.

"I am radiantly happy": Lady Battersea diary, 15 September 1877: Battersea Papers, MS 47932, Vol XXIV; British Library.

Cyril loved the Bible: Battersea, *Reminiscences*, p175.

"intensely cross and irritable": Lady Battersea diary, 18 November 1881: Battersea Papers, Add MS 47935, Vol XXVII; British Library.

While *The Jewish Chronicle*: Davis, *The English Rothschilds*, p167.

the couple readily attended: Maud Nathan, *Once Upon A Time And Today*, G. P. Putnam's sons, 1933, p156.

"a 'true Briton'": Lord Battersea, *The Argus* (Melbourne, Australia), 11 October 1892, p3.

"always interested by any form": Cohen, *Lady de Rothschild And Her Daughters,* p182.

Before her marriage: Personal, *Leader* (Melbourne, Australia), 22 November 1902, p31.

Constance had published: C. & A. de Rothschild, *The History and Literature of the Israelites According To The Old Testament And the Apocrypha*, Longmans, Green, Reader, and Dyer, London, 1870.

"They resembled, indeed, in not a few": Constance de Rothschild, 'The Hebrew Woman', *New Quarterly Magazine*, Ward, Lock & Tyler, January 1876, pp390, 408. Reprinted in booklet form by Hazell, Watson and Viney, London & Aylesbury c.1876.

"He never encouraged me": Cohen, *Lady de Rothschild And Her Daughters*, p332.

"my husband...would often tell me": Battersea *Reminiscences*, p171.

"I trust that on the whole": Cohen, *Lady de Rothschild And Her Daughters*, p170.

"She had a boundless fund": E.F. Benson, *Final Edition*, p50.

From page 311 –

"When he [Cyril] was present": Benson, *Final Edition*, p51.

"He dines in pomegranate velvet": Mark Bonham Carter, Mark Pottle (eds.), *Lantern Slides: The Diaries & Letters Of Violet Bonham Carter 1904–1914*, Weidenfeld & Nicholson, London 1996, p94.

"deep-seated streak": Rothschild, *Dear Lord Rothschild*, p16.

"Cyril brought two young men": Lady Battersea diary, 30 March 1881: Battersea Papers, Add MS 47934, Vol XXVI; British Library.

The next day, he took: Lady Battersea diary, 31 March 1881: Battersea Papers, Add MS 47934, Vol XXVI; British Library.

"as usual rough & unkind": Lady Battersea diary, 1 June 1881: Battersea Papers, Add MS 47934, Vol XXVI; British Library.

"in such a cold halfhearted way": Lady Battersea diary, 1 January 1882: Battersea Papers, Add MS 47935, Vol XXVII; British Library.

"He will never love me": Lady Battersea diary, 20 January 1882: Battersea Papers, Add MS 47935, Vol XXVII; British Library.

"At the beginning of my married life": Battersea, *Reminiscences*, p172.

"Constance had made it a condition": John Davis,*Constance Flower*, Oxford Dictionary of National Biography, Oxford University Press, 2004.

"The Flowers seem to me aloft": Henry James to Lady Wolsely, July 1884: Henry James, Michael Anesko (ed.), Greg W. Zacharias (ed.) *The Complete Letters of Henry James, 1883–1884*, Vol 2, University of Nebraska Press, 2019, p176.

"it is a stopping-point": Small Talk, *The Sketch*, 3 June 1896, p227.

"Entering from the noisy thoroughfare": S.E. Thomas (ed.), *Celebrities Of The Day, British and Foreign*, Vol 1, W.Poole, London 1881, p200.

Cyril had the hall: Cohen, *Lady de Rothschild And Her Daughters*, p172.

"like angelic visitants": Thomas (ed.), *Celebrities Of The Day, British and Foreign*, Vol 1, p200.

in a prominent position in the dining room: Lord Battersea at Home, *The Harmsworth Magazine*, vol 6, Feb-July 1901, p554.

"the space at the back": Battersea, *Reminiscences*, pp172-173.

A further scenic acquisition: Chaim Bermant, *The Cousinhood*, The Macmillan Company, New York 1971, p148.

The cult for beauty was unlike: Elliott, *Three Generations*, p147.

"Very different in character": Bermant, *The Cousinhood*, p199.

One diarist records: James Laver, *Vulgar society: the romantic career of James Tissot, 1836-1902*, Constable & Co, 1936, p35.

Studiously unmentioned: Herbert Vivian to James Whistler, 16 May 1890, MS Whistler V78, Glasgow University Library.

"Julian Sturgis...entered with zest": Battersea, *Reminiscences*, p205.

"one of the first-rate minds": Ralph Barton Perry, *The Thought and Character of William James, as Revealed in Unpublished Correspondence and Notes*, Vol 1, Little Brown, New York 1935, pp596,609.

"had been much struck": Battersea, *Reminiscences*, p205.

However, according to James' sister: Alice James, Ruth Bernard Yeazell (ed.), *The Death And Letters Of Alice James: Selected Correspondence*, University of California Press, Berkeley 1983, pp145-146.

Myer's close friendship with Edmund Gurney: Hamilton, *Immortal Longings*, p164.

On an evening back in 1868: Bart Schultz, *Henry Sidgwick – Eye of the Universe: An Intellectual*

Biography, Cambridge University Press, 2004, p93.

"handsome, feminine in manner": Phyllis Grosskurth, *The Woeful Victorian: a biography of John Addington Symonds*, Holt, Rinehart and Winston, New York 1965, p119.

In 1894, the Society gained: Max Egremont, *Balfour: a life of Arthur James Balfour*, Collins, London, 1980, p50.

Other distinguished members included: Obituary Notice, *Journal of the Society for Psychical Research*, Trübner & Co., London 1886, p92.

registered under Constance's name: *Proceedings of the Society for Psychical Research*, Vol VII, Kegan Paul, Tench, Trübner & Co., London 1892, pp413-442.

honorary members included: Janet Oppenheim, *The Other World: Spiritualism and Psychical Research in England, 1850-1914*, Cambridge University Press, 1985, p135.

Not a member, but also enraptured: Charles Warr, *The Glimmering Landscape*, Hodder & Stoughton, London, 1960, p36-37.

Yorke was an amateur medium: Michaela Reid, *Ask Sir James*, Hodder & Stoughton, London, 1987, p55.

a very close, sexually sympathetic friend: R. H. Collins to F.W.H. Myers, 12 June 18?; MYER/1/139; R.H. Collins to F.W.H. Myers, Undated; MYER/1/168, Trinity College Library, Cambridge University.

"Mr. Podmore's young men": Trevor H. Hall, *The Strange Case Of Edmund Gurney*, Duckworth, London, 1980, p173.

Eros and yearning: Jeffrey J. Kripnal, *Authors of the Impossible: The Paranormal and the Sacred*, University of Chicago Press, 2010, p88.

"Lord Rosebery, one of our most": The Liberal Candidate For Brecon, *The Cardiff Times*, 2 August 1879, p3.

It had hitherto: *The Late Mr Gwynne Holford,*The Brecon County Times Neath Gazette and General Advertiser,10 February 1916, p5; *Memorial Service At Aston Clinton*, Buckinghamshire Herald, 7 December 1907.

"my first impression of the Brecon Borough": Battersea, *Reminiscences*, p186.

"the moist atmosphere": Battersea, *Reminiscences*, p189.

He claimed to have met: Cyril Flower, *Oxford Dictionary of National Biography*, 2004.

"He came, he saw": Memorial Service At Aston Clinton, *Buckinghamshire Herald*, 7 December 1907, p7.

"Cyril made way very quickly": Battersea, *Reminiscences*, p187.

"He is a first-rate canvasser": The Liberal Candidate For Brecon, *The Cardiff Times*, 2 August 1879, p3.

"As a striking instance": The Liberal Candidate For Brecon, *The Cardiff Times*, 2 August 1879, p3.

"Cyril took infinite trouble": Battersea, *Reminiscences*, p190.

In her assessment: Battersea, *Reminiscences*, p190.

"orders of admission to the very best": Mr. Cyril Flower, M.P., *The Brecon County Times*, 23 October 1885, p9.

"anonymous and threatening letters": Battersea, *Reminiscences*, p184.

"the very attempt to intimidate": Election Incidents At Brecon.*The Cardiff Times*, 3 April 1880, p6

"Cyril felt very unwell": Lady Battersea diary, 2 June 1879: Battersea Papers, MS 47933, Vol XXV, British Library.

With 5 ballot papers spoiled: Liberal Victory At Brecon, *The Cardiff Times*, 3 April 1880, p8.

A Welsh-language Liberal newspaper: Buddugoliaeth Y Rhyddfrydwyr Yn Aberhonddu, *Baner ac Amserau Cymru*, 7 April 1880, p7.

"Gladstone is very marked": Our New Nobility, *The Echo*, 27 February 1894, p1.

From page 323 –

"From his entry into": Our New Nobility, *The Echo*, 27 February 1894, p1.

Gladstone privately held substantial: Ferguson, *The World's Banker*, pp839-40.

In 1889, when Gladstone: Mr. Gladstone's Visit, *Torquay Times*, and South Devon Advertiser, 14 June 1889.

Gladstone would spend Easter: Untitled Item, *Dundee Advertiser*, 26 March 1890, p6.

Britain had no right to aggrandise itself: United Railways Employees' Dinner At Brecon, *The Brecon County Times*, 25 September 1880, p10.

"a blot in the history of England": Borough Election, *The Brecon County Times*, 20 March 1880, p7.

Between 1880 and 1885: Charles Higham, *Dark Lady: Winston Churchill's Mother and Her World*, Da Capo Press, Cambridge, Massc. 2006, p80-81.

The Fourth Party opposed: Higham, *Dark Lady*, p79.

For older gentleman: *The Eighty Club 1895*, The Eighty Club, London 1895, p5.

The Club's more colourful: *The Eighty Club 1895*, pp16-34.

"the Eighty Club is entirely composed": The Eighty Club, *Reynolds's Newspaper*,11 March 1894.

One such young man: Lucy Cohen, *Arthur Cohen: a memoir*, Bickers & Son, London, 1919, p115.

"to my utter amazement": Cohen, *Lady de Rothschild And Her Daughters*, p196.

"Eat, drink, indulge thy lust": William W. Goodwin, *Plutarch's Morals*, Vol 1, Boston 1874, p82.

"The sculptor has represented this effeminate": Mary Elizabeth Phillips, *Reminiscences Of William Wetmore Story,* Rand, McNally & Company, Chicago & New York, 1897, p112/212.

The statue was eventually: Cohen, *Lady de Rothschild And Her Daughters*, p196.

amidst topiaried chrysanthemums: Priscilla Boniface, *The Garden Room*, Royal Commission on Historical Monuments, London 1982, Plate 41.

"the Hotel Flower": J.M. Whistler to Cyril Flower, September 1874/July 1875?, MS Whistler F553, Glasgow University Library.

"Go round one morning": Cohen, *Lady de Rothschild And Her Daughters,* p198.

the Café Royal, where Cyril was: The Genesis Of This Number, *The Artist And Journal Of Home Culture*, Volumes 17-18, 1896, p651

All the men he 'don't know': G.W., Ballade Of A Man Of The Period, *The Artist And Journal Of Home Culture*, Vol 14, 1 March 1893, p67.

"September 23rd. Fast Day.": Cohen, *Lady de Rothschild And Her Daughters*, p201.

"Have lost James from drink": Lady Battersea diary, 1 January 1892: Battersea Papers, Add MS 47940, Vol XXXII, British Library.

"Of course it is secret": Jane Ridley, Clayre Percy (eds.) *The letters of Edwin Lutyens to his wife Lady Emily*, Collins, 1985, p180.

"No home life can be perfect": Lady (Constance) Battersea, *Waifs & Strays*, Arthur L. Humphreys, London, 1921, pp290,298.

"Have started a Home": Cohen, *Lady de Rothschild And Her Daughters*, p205.

This particular initiative: Cathy Hartley, *A Historical Dictionary of British Women*, Europa Publications Limited, London 2003, pp352-353.

Constance's other activities on behalf: Battersea, *Reminiscences*, p417.

"She dresses herself": Cohen, *Lady de Rothschild And Her Daughters*, p124.

"To Connie's despair": Cohen, *Lady de Rothschild And Her Daughters,* p121.

"all my life long": Cohen, *Lady de Rothschild And Her Daughters,* pp152-3.

"a tone of the trousers": Cohen, *Lady de Rothschild And Her Daughters*, pp256.

"dear precious Cobby": Cohen, *Lady de Rothschild And Her Daughters,* p225.

"devoted to Miss Cobbe": Sally Mitchell, *Frances Power Cobbe: Victorian Feminist, Journalist, Reformer*, University of Virginia Press, 2014, pp142,140.

In 1885, two charities: Battersea, *Reminiscences*, pp433-438.

"Christian charity is invoked": Arnold White, *Efficiency and Empire*, Methuen & Co. London 1901, p97.

National student numbers: Lord Battersea At Home, *The London Magazine*, Vol 6, July 1901, p554.

Cyril voted five times: United Railways Employees' Dinner At Brecon, *The Brecon County Times*, 25 September 1880, p10.

"we do not believe in the whole Parliamentary": Mr. Cyril Flower, *The Brecon County Times*, 30 August 1889, p5.

"if his Liberal principles": Mr. Cyril Flower M.P. In Luton, *Luton Reporter*, 17 October 1885, p5.

"Let him stay and learn": Mr. Cyril Flower M.P. In Luton, *Luton Reporter*, 17 October 1885, p5.

"One after another their ideals": Mr. Cyril Flower M.P. In Luton, *Luton Reporter*, 17 October 1885, p5.

"The interests of the landlord": Mr. Cyril Flower M.P. In Luton, *Luton Reporter*, 17 October 1885, p5.

"There was a great wave": Mr. Cyril Flower M.P. In Luton, *Luton Reporter*, 17 October 1885, p5.

"he had not the slightest objection": Mr. Cyril Flower M.P. In Luton, *Luton Reporter*, 17 October 1885, p5.

"A land, where girt with friends": Mr. Cyril Flower M.P. In Luton, *Luton Reporter*, 17 October 1885, p5.; Alfred Tennyson, You Ask Me Why, *Poems*, Vo1, Edward Moxon, London 1845, p219.

749

"genial, kindly soul": J. Stock, In Memoriam, *Bedfordshire Advertiser*, 9 March 1894, p4.

"pleasantly tickled his supporters": Witticisms Of Mr. Cyril Flower, *Luton Times and Advertiser*, 6 February 1885, p4.

"The Devil was dressed": Mr. Flower, M.P. At Dunstable, *Luton Times and Advertiser*, January 30 1885, p8.

"the uneasy memory of a farcical": Witticisms Of Mr. Cyril Flower, *Luton Times and Advertiser*, 6 February 1885, p4.

"indicative of Mr Flower's mingled": Witticisms Of Mr. Cyril Flower, *Luton Times and Advertiser*, 6 February 1885, p4.

"had amused him more than": Mr. Cyril Flower M.P. In Luton, *Luton Reporter*, 17 October 1885, p5.

"Let us consider for a moment": Rival Candidates, *Luton Times and Advertiser*, 27 March 1885, p5.

"Mr. Cyril Flower is a gaudy": Rival Candidates, *Luton Times and Advertiser*, 27 March 1885, p5.

"he attunes his utterances": Luton Politics, *Luton Times and Advertiser*, 16 January 1885, p4.

"Mr. Cyril Flower attained great fame": Mr. Sydney Gedge At High Town, *Luton Times and Advertiser*, 27 February 1885, p6.

"the labourer's revolt": South Bedfordshire Election, *Luton Times and Advertiser*, 4 December 1885, p5.

From page 335 –

"whether he [Dilke] has done": Kali Israel, *Names and Stories: Emilia Dilke and Victorian Culture*, Oxford University Press, 1999, p214, n107.

"All was going pleasantly": Our Domestic Circle, *The Manchester Courier*, 20 March 1886, p9.

"Rather stormy discussions": Diary of Louisa, Lady de Rothschild, 22 February 1886: Add MS 47957, British Library.

"Mrs. Cyril Flower then addressed the meeting": Aston Clinton: The Temperance Society, *Bucks Herald*, 13 December 1890, p6.

While Cyril chaired temperance: Mr Cyril Flower, M.P., *The Brecon County Times*, 3 September 1886, p11.

As was common, in compensation: T. Baker, *The Insidious 'Red Tape' System of Government in England*, Watson Brothers, 1870 p28.

"self-government, but which is really": Lord Salisbury's Alternative To Home Rule, *The Pall Mall Gazette*, 17 May 1886, p11.

"cleverly contrived to make a heroic-looking bust": The Royal Academy, *John Bull*, 3 July 1886, p11.

The decorations in one West End: The Jubilee Illuminations, *Pall Mall Gazette*, 21 June 1887, p10.

Cyril's arrangement of coloured: The Celebration Of The Jubilee, *Bucks Herald*, 25 June 1887, p5.

In Frederick Sargent's panoramic painting: The Garden Party at Buckingham Palace, 20 June 1887, RCIN 407255, Royal Collection Trust.

The problem was so overwhelming: The London Unemployed, *The Standard* (London), 2 February 1888.

The evening before his death: Hamilton *Immortal Longings*, p167.

"I hope Myers has got a fright": Hamilton *Immortal Longings*, p23. [Josephine Butler to Stanley Butler, 24 Apr 1895, 3JBL/34/20, The Women's Library, The London School Of Economics & Political Science.]

"Edmund Gurney was one": Battersea *Reminiscences*, p206.

George Eliot simply called him: Gordon Epperson, *The Mind of Edmund Gurney*, Associated University Presses, Cranbury, New Jersey, 1997, p149.

Constance had on one occasion: Battersea, *Reminiscences*, p174.

"It is difficult to convey": The East Coast And Summer Visitors, *Essex Standard*, 1 September 1883, p7.

Capitalising on the demand: Simon Appleyard, *Poppyland* in *This England*, Autumn, pp10-15, 1987; Bel Bailey, *Whatever happened to Poppyland?* in *The Countryman*, v105. No. 2. 116-119, 2000.

Following Constance's approval: The Pleasaunce, *Gardeners Chronicle & New Horticulturist*, 7 October 1911, Page 260.

"I do wish the Battersea house": Jane Ridley, *The Architect And His Wife: a life of Edwin Lutyens*, Chatto & Windus, 2002, pp102-3.

In the beginning, the house: The Pleasaunce Visitors Book, Sara Flower.

On wind-swept dunes surrounding: Viscount Templewood, *The Unbroken Thread*, Collins, London

1949, pp139-140.

With the advice of one: Cohen, *Arthur Cohen*, p118.

"all for outside show": London Letter, *Manchester Evening News*, 29 November 1907, p7.

"dozens of gardeners": Benson, *Final Edition*, p52.

"Lord Battersea set himself": Holiday Haunts, *Bedfordshire Mercury*, 27 August 1909.

"the Garden of Dreams": Ellen Thornycroft Fowler, *Ten Degrees Backward*, George H. Doran Co., New York 1915, p202-203.

"paved with coral and amethyst": Fowler, *Ten Degrees Backward*, pp203-204

To create the deception: Gossip Of The Day, *The Evening News*, 24 September 1898, p1.

"weak grow strong and the old feel young again": Fowler, *Ten Degrees Backward*, p198

Lutyens considered Cyril a thwarted: Jane Brown, *Lutyens And The Edwardians*, Viking, London 1996, p97.

The dream of an Arcadia: Byrne R.S. Fone: *This other Eden: Arcadia and the Homosexual Imagination* in *Journal of Homosexuality*, Vol 8, Nos 3/4, Spring/Summer 1983, pp13-34.

"The joys of the palaestra": Charles Kains Jackson, *The New Chivalry* in *The Artist and Journal of Home Culture*, 2 April 1894.

"brinily radiant": George Meredith, William Maxse Meredith (ed.) *Letters*, C.Scribner's & Son, 1913, p498.

It was a holistic vision: St. Paul's Gymnasium, *Globe* (London), 1 December 1892, p3; St James's Athletic Club, *Sporting Life*, 21 December 1894, p4.

In 1899, he played host to Olof Rudbeck: The Pleasaunce Visitors Book, Sara Flower.

his signature appears in the Visitors Book: The Pleasaunce Visitors Book, Sara Flower.

Parsons was a confirmed bachelor who lived: Henry James; Michael Anesko, Greg W. Zacharias (eds.), *The Complete Letters of Henry James, 1883-1884, Volume 1*, University of Nebraska Press, 2018, pxlv.

the 'fidus achates' of "dear little Abbey": James; Anesko, Zacharias (eds.) *The Complete Letters of Henry James, 1883-1884*, p278.

or equally by Princess Louise, who was: Nicole Milette, *Landscape-Painter As Landscape-Gardener: The Case Of Alfred Parsons, Vol 1*, unpublished thesis, The University Of York, 1997, p119,n198,n200, p213.

"At Overstrand everything is as simple": Metropolitan Notes, *Nottingham Evening Post*, 6 September 1889, p2.

"Cyril has been buying": Cohen, *Lady de Rothschild And Her Daughters*, p214.

"an extraordinary mixture": Benson, *Final Edition*, p49.

"The house is warm & dark": Carter, Pottle (eds.), *Lantern Slides*, p95.

These were gazed upon by: *The Pleasaunce, Overstrand, Norfolk* (Catalogue of Contents Sale), Mackintosh, A.D. & Company, 1935; CRRMU: 1981.80.1616, Cromer Museum; author's visit.

"Little cottage quite lovely": Cohen, *Lady de Rothschild And Her Daughters*, p221.

"Overstrand, August 28th": Cohen, *Lady de Rothschild And Her Daughters*, p221.

"Cyril tells me that we are spending": Lady Battersea diary, January 1891: Battersea Papers, Add MS 47940, Vol XXXII, British Library.

Construction of The Pleasaunce: Our Village: Sir Edwin Lutyens: Overstrand Parish Council [https://www.overstrandparishcouncil.org.uk/our-village/sir-edwin-lutyens/]

"Overstrand, August 14th": Cohen, *Lady de Rothschild And Her Daughters*, p222.

"I rather look upon life": Anon (William Hurrell Mallock), *The New Republic, or, Culture, faith, and philosophy in an English country house*, Chatto And Windus, London 1877, Vol1, p41.

"There above the sea, and overlooking it": Anon (Mallock), *The New Republic*, Vol1, p8,n1.

"seeks retirement from the caresses": Anon (Mallock), *The New Republic*, Vol1, p9.

"This singular retreat was the work": Anon (Mallock), *The New Republic*, Vol1, p8.

"my soul, if I have one": Anon (Mallock), *The New Republic*, Vol1, p6.

"so many proud monarchs": Anon (Mallock), *The New Republic*, Vol1, pp5-6.

Attracted by the presence of the Flowers: Jamie Champlin, *The Rise of the Plutocrats: Wealth and Power in Edwardian England*, Constable & Robinson Limited, 1978, p256.

From page 347 –

and was less-charitably nicknamed: George W. Liebmann, *The Fall of the House of Speyer: The Story of a Banking Dynasty,* I.B. Taurus, London 2015, p62.

While Cyril and Constance lived: A Norfolk Nook, *The Queen: The Lady's Newspaper*, 22 September 1894, p54.

Cyril also opposed another development: London's New Street, *The Daily Telegraph* (London), 2 May 1899, p4.

"a picturesque former 'inn'": Michael Harrison, *The London of Sherlock Holmes*, Drake Publishers, London, p143.

"that queer, old-fashioned abode": William Le Queux, *Strange Tales Of A Nihilist,* Cassell, New York 1892, p158.

Wych Street housed several brothels: Matthew Green, 'The Secret History of Holywell Street', *The Public Domain Review*, 30 June 2016 [https://publicdomainreview.org/essay/the-secret-history-of-holywell-street-home-to-victorian-london-s-dirty-book-trade]

The Flowers and/or Rothschilds: Andrew Saint (ed.) *Survey of London, Vol 49: Battersea*, Yale University Press for English Heritage, 2014, Ch3.

"no case has been so infinitely sad": Local Chit-Chat, *The Western Chronicle*, 1 May 1891, p8.

"Fyffe had been charged with": Alleged Offence By A Reputed M.A., *The Croydon Times*, 25 April 1891, p6; The Charge Against Mr. Fyffe, *Croydon Advertiser and Surrey County Reporter*, 18 July 1891, p8.

Despite being devotedly nursed: Sad End To A Distinguished Career, *The Yorkshire Evening Post*, 23 February 1892, p2.

Earlier in the year, the Paris police: The Paris Scandal, *Sheffield Daily Telegraph*, 11 April 1891, p6.

including a wealthy American: Of Interest To Poughkeepsians, Poughkeepsie Daily Eagle, 30 April 1891, p8.

early reports that over half: The Paris Scandal, *South Wales Echo*, 24 April 1891, p3.

George Paston Cooper, a baronet's son: The Paris Scandal – Sentences, *The Pall Mall Gazette*, 4 May 1891, p6. For further reports, see: Michael D. Sibalis, 'Defining Masculinity in Fin-de-Siécle France: Sexual Anxiety and the Emergence of the Homosexual', *Proceedings Of The Western Society For French History*, Vol 25, New Mexico State University Press 1995.

alleged to have been implicated in the Cleveland Street: The Paris Scandal, *Sheffield Daily Telegraph*, 11 April 1891, p6.

During his campaigning: Mr Cyril Flower M.P. and Mr Arnold White, *Leighton Buzzard Observer and Linslade Gazette*, 7 June 1892.

"the most prominent, uncompromising": The "Radical Person", *Hastings and St Leonards Observer*, 12 January 1907, p4.

"he would have been hanged": The "Radical Person", *Hastings and St Leonards Observer*, 12 January 1907, p4.

"hero of religious and political": The "Radical Person", *Hastings and St Leonards Observer*, 12 January 1907, p4.

While still a student at Oxford: Revolting Charges, *The People*, 20 June 1886 p15; The Revolting Charges, *The People*, 27 June 1886, p14; A Shocking Charge, *The People*, 8 August 1886, p11; To The Editor Of The Evening Standard, *The [Evening] Standard*, 6 August 1886, p2.

Moffatt was sentenced to eighteen: Central Criminal Court, *The Morning Post*, 6 August 1886, p3.

"a violent Tory": Entre Nous, *Truth*, 11 August 1892, p18.

To laughter and cheering: Mr Flower's Candidature, *The Luton Reporter*, 2 July 1892, p5.

"six years of useless legislation": Mr Flower's Candidature, *The Luton Reporter*, 2 July 1892, p5.

"when you can get tea": Mr Flower's Candidature, *The Luton Reporter*, 2 July 1892, p5.

"They didn't want to weaken": Mr Flower's Candidature, *The Luton Reporter*, 2 July 1892, p5.

"although he was a Radical parson": Mr Flower's Candidature, *The Luton Reporter*, 2 July 1892, p5.

"We will sweep this Government": Mr Flower's Candidature, *The Luton Reporter*, 2 July 1892, p5.

A week later at another: Mr Flower's Candidature, *The Luton Reporter*, 9 July 1902, p5.

"He was especially happy": 6 July 1892, Rev. R.C. Fillingham diary, Merton College Library.

"the *beau ideal* of the best kind": *The New House Of Commons, 1892*, Pall Mall Gazette Office, 1892, p36.

"as Mr. Cyril Flower...we none": Wobble, Bubble And Boggle, *Bedfordshire Advertiser*, 20 April 1894.

"if the Member for Luton is not given": The Representation Of The Luton Division: The Liberal Candidate, *The Luton Reporter*, 18 June 1892, p5.

The Battersea Polytechnic Institute: Untitled Item, *Bedfordshire Advertiser*, 15 July 1897, p2.

"great on polytechnics": Lord Battersea At Home, *The London Magazine,* Vol 6, July 1901, p554.

"immense quantity of beautiful orchids": 'At Home' At Surrey House, *The Gentlewoman*, 25 June 1892, p872 (p44).

As usual he was holding large receptions: Lady Battersea diary, Dec 1892: Battersea Papers, Add MS 47940, Vol XXXII, British Library.

He was also rummaging: Battersea, Constance *Reminiscences*, p197.

"grown rather stout": Vanity Fair by J.M.D., *The Argus* (Melbourne, Australia), 8 October 1892.

the next House will be as rum: Stephen Gwynn, Gertrude M. Tuckwell, *The Life of the Rt. Hon. Sir Charles W. Dilke, Vol. 2*, John Murray, London 1917, p282-283.

which tainted the political and social worlds: Battersea, *Reminiscences*, p193.

"The Liberal Whips have recently": Gossip of the Day, *Yorkshire Evening Post*, 31 May 1892.

Bartering political services for honours: H.J. Hanham: *The Sale of Honours in Late Victorian England* in *Victorian Studies*, Indiana University Press, Vol. 3, No. 3.

"Cyril Flower wanted a Peerage": Sir Algernon West, Horace G. Hutchinson (ed.) *Private Diaries Of The Rt. Hon. Sir Algernon West*, John Murray, London 1922, p46.

"because he married a Rothschild": *Vanity Fair: A Weekly Show of Political, Social, and Literary Wares*, London, Vol 36, 1886, p14.

"Mr Cyril Flower mainly owes his peerage": *Figaro*, quoted in: Comic And Gossip Papers, *Bucks Herald*, 3 September 1892, p3.

While it became known in political: London Letter, *Sheffield Daily Telegraph*, 8 September 1892.

The press had fun with it: Lord Battersea Blesses the House of Lords, *Leighton Buzzard Observer and Linslade Gazette*, 25 February 1902.

'Squirrel Flower': How Britain Votes, *Chicago Tribune*, 6 November 1898.

"Mr. Labouchère the sworn enemy": Summary Of Today's News, *Western Morning News*, (Plymouth), 16 December 1892.

Being anointed 'Baron Battersea': *The London Gazette*, No. 26323, 6 September 1892, p 5090.

"Mr Flower's is a *bourgeois*": Gossip of the Day, *Yorkshire Evening Post*, 14 June 14, 1892, p2.

The old nobility even smirked: Lord Battersea, *Bedfordshire Advertiser*, 2 March 1894, p6

"part of the racket": Niall Ferguson, *The House of Rothschild: The World's Banker 1849-1998*, Viking Penguin, New York 1998, pxxv. (The quote only appears in the two-volume U.S. edition of *The World's Banker*.)

"I was not pleased": Cohen, *Lady de Rothschild And Her Daughters*, p236.

"Letters from home": Cohen, *Lady de Rothschild And Her Daughters*, p236.

"I think Cyril is doing right.": Herbert Asquith to Lady Battersea, 1892; Battersea Papers, Battersea Papers, Add MS 47911, f115, British Library.

"I feel that I was foolish": Lady Battersea diary, 22 August 1892: Battersea Papers, Add MS 47940, Vol XXXII, British Library.

"I may here put into words": Battersea, *Reminiscences*, p194.

"I tried to be pleased": Cohen, *Lady de Rothschild And Her Daughters*, p237.

"Cyril minds it less.": Cohen, *Lady de Rothschild And Her Daughters*, p237.

"Everyone in the clubs is laughing": London Correspondence, *Dublin Daily Express*, 16 December 1892, p5.

From page 358 –

"not very 'bien vu'... he ought never": Richard Davenport-Hines, 'A Radical Lord Chamberlain at a Tory Court: Lord Carrington, 1892–95', *The Court Historian*, Taylor & Francis, 2011, Volume 16, Issue 2, p207.

"Mr. Cyril Flower had a speech": Reading Primrose League Festival, *Berkshire Chronicle*, 27 April 1895.

"Lord Battersea is already beginning to shed": From Our London Correspondent, *Dundee Advertiser*, 16 December 1892, p5.

"find looking after a lot of sheep": Lord Alfred Douglas to Alphonse James Albert Symons, 14 March 1939; MS.Douglas, D733L S988, William Andrews Clark Memorial Library.

the remark was meant innocently: Lord Alfred Douglas to Alphonse James Albert Symons, 16 March 1939, MS.Douglas, D733L S988, William Andrews Clark Memorial Library.

In contrast, her husband had the issue: Auction Lot 247, Christie's, London, 30 November 2005.

While at Felbrigg, Oscar and Lord Alfred: Laura Lee, *Oscar's Ghost*, Amberley Publishing, Stroud 2017, pp39-40.

"early, reckless, improvident": The Democratic World, *Reynolds's Newspaper*, 22 January 1893, p3.

"not a whit too strong": Occasional Notes, *The Luton Reporter*, 7 January 1893, p5.

"a slander": The Democratic World, *Reynolds's Newspaper*, 22 January 1893, p3.

"My correspondent affirms": The Democratic World, *Reynolds's Newspaper*, 22 January 1893, p3.

"Cyril came home at 6.30": Lady Battersea diary, 1 February 1893: Battersea Papers, Add MS 47940, Vol XXXII, British Library.

The Jewish half of Sydney: The Wild-Cat Column, *The Bulletin* (Australia), 11 February 1893, p9.

"for so long a term of years": Battersea, *Reminiscences*, p325.

"I went almost mad": Lady Battersea diary, 2 February 1893: Battersea Papers, Add MS 47940, Vol XXXII, British Library.

and a chronic hypochondriac: Bermant, *The Cousinhood*, p149.

"Constance behaved splendidly": Bermant, *The Cousinhood*, p239.

"Cyril performed one of the greatest": Battersea, *Reminiscences*, p326.

"had it been otherwise": Cohen, *Lady de Rothschild And Her Daughters*, p224.

"I am full of loving gratitude": Lady Battersea to Lord Battersea, 9 February 1893: Battersea Papers, Add MS 47910, f147, British Library.

"blighted my dear Cyril's": Ferguson, *The World's Banker,* p765.

"Were I to live again": Battersea, *Reminiscences*, p326.

"He was ambitious": Benson, *Final Edition*, p47.

Here he could marshal his army: Estate Dinner At Overstrand, *Norfolk News*, 11 January 1902, p3.

"a gentle Westerly breeze": Cohen, *Lady de Rothschild And Her Daughters,* p218.

Cyril's increasingly idle: John Davis, *Constance Flower* in *Oxford Dictionary of National Biography*, 2016.

"My husband was never tired": Battersea, *Reminiscences*, p332.

Nonetheless, when Lutyens: Battersea, *Reminiscences*, p333.

"a distant portion was made accessible": London Letter, *Manchester Evening News*, 29 November 1907, p7.

"were amused by stories of secret": Email from Sara Flower to author, 8 September 2017.

"that a secret passage led to cottages": Email from Sara Flower to author, 12 February 2021.

"I expected to find": John Jolliffe (ed.) *Raymond Asquith Life and Letters*, Collins, 1980, p42.

"there are throngs of people": Cohen, *Lady de Rothschild And Her Daughters*, p264.

"that precious possession": Battersea, *Reminiscences,* p378.

Its signatures include: *The Pleasaunce Visitors Book*, Sara Flower.

While wearied by her petulance: Natalie Livingstone, *The Women Of Rothschild*, John Murray, London 2021, eBook p299.

who was a former pupil and friend of Oscar Browning: Alfred Clayton Cole to Oscar Browning, Oscar Browning Papers; OB/1/367/C, Archive Centre, King's College, Cambridge.

"as original, interesting, and delightful": Battersea, *Reminiscences*, p218.

"Lady Betty told me to make use of Gerald": Peter Lord, *Between Two Worlds: The Diary of Winifred Coombe Tennant 1909-1924*, National Library of Wales, Aberystwyth 2011.

were convinced their bastard: Lord, *Between Two Worlds*.

"He was extremely handsome": Battersea, *Reminiscences*, pp401-402.

At Eton, Gerald had been one of: Ian Anstruther, *Oscar Browning: A Biography*, John Murray, London 1983, pp43-44, 57, 59.

One of his private passions: Crown Prince Crochets, *The Shetland Times*, 19 August 1905, p4.

"I wish there were more earnest people": Richard Haldane to Cyril Flower, 28 Jan 1891; GB 186 MSA/1/62, Newcastle University Special Collections and Archives.

"the happiest days of my life": Battersea, *Reminiscences,* p173.

"Chat with Cyril F.": John Morley, *Recollections*, Macmillian, New York, 1917, Vo1, p280.

"Autobiography is the literature": John H. Morgan, *John, Viscount Morley: An Appreciation And Some Reminiscences*, Houghton Mifflin Company, Boston 1924, p160.

Cyril was President of the Overstrand: Overstrand Cricket Club, *Eastern Evening News*, 22 March 1905.

"It is the people who don't play": The Golfer, *The Sporting Gazette*, 2 December 1899, p12.

"Lord Battersea is a typical example": *Golf Illustrated*, Volume 2 1902, page 115.

"to show, perhaps," sniffed one: Notes From Cromer, *Sheffield Daily Telegraph*, 8 October 1901.

The Club boasted an illustrious membership: History of Royal Cromer Golf Club Established 1888, Royal Cromer Golf Club, royalcromergolfclub.com

"as blackberries in September": The Boy Caddie, *London Evening Standard*, 30 December 1908.

"Finer links are seldom": Holiday Haunts, *Bedfordshire Mercury*, 27 August 1909.

"was no doubt a healthy": Trunch District Horticultural Society Annual Show, *Norwich Mercury*, 15 August 1896.

"The volume called *In The Key*": A Chat About Books, *The Queen*, 4 March 1893, p336 (p30).

"He made my life one living spring": John Addington Symonds, *In The Key Of Blue*, Elkin Mathews & John Lane, London 1893, p168.

"Against the golden gaslight; grapes": Symonds, *In The Key Of Blue*, pp6,15.

"in every club in London": Alleged Libel On A Parliamentary Candidate, *The Aberdeen Journal*, 17 June 1893, p5.

He also alleged that, more recently: Political Libel Action, *The Evening Standard*, 19 June 1893, p1; The Law Courts: Queen's Bench Division, *The Evening Standard*, 20 June 1893, p6.

"Removed, Impudicitice Causa": West Dorset Election, *The Bristol Mercury*, 20 Jun 1893, p8.

"everyone knew what went on": Political Libel Case, *Reynolds's Newspaper*, 25 June 1893, p3.

Farquharson was hit with a massive: Obituary, *The Times*, 24 April 1895.

While on the ground, he was trampled: Lord Battersea And Luton, *Leighton Buzzard Observer and Linslade Gazette*, 26 December 1893, p8.

the toast to the Town and Corporation: Lord Battersea And Luton, *Leighton Buzzard Observer and Linslade Gazette*, 26 December 1893, p8.

"I can't pronounce it": Baron Battersea to Baroness Battersea, 5 Feb 1894, Battersea Papers, MS 47910, Vol II, f12 British Library.

"Not a cloud in the sky": Baron Battersea to Baroness Battersea, 9 Feb 1894, Battersea Papers, MS 47910, Vol II, f12; British Library

"a capital old fellow": Baron Battersea to Baroness Battersea, 10 Feb 1894; Battersea Papers, MS 47910, Vol II, f13; British Library.

"an outlandish Country": Baron Battersea to Baroness Battersea, ? Feb 1894; Battersea Papers, MS 47910, Vol II, f14; British Library.

"orange groves laden": Baron Battersea to Baroness Battersea, 10 Feb 1894; Battersea Papers, MS 47910, Vol II, f13; British Library.

"I shall go on to the Desert!": Baron Battersea to Baroness Battersea, Feb 1894; Battersea Papers, MS 47910, Vol II, f14; British Library.

Rosebery entertained at an intimate dinner: Politics And Persons, *The St James's Gazette*, 28 May 1894.

"The peerage of Battersea": Our New Nobility, *The Echo*, 27 February 1894, p1.

"The 30th August half-a-century ago": Lord Battersea's Biography, *The Luton Reporter And Beds. And Herts. News*, 8 September 1894, p5. (Originally published in *Modern Society*.)

From page 376 –

"They wore the gay Windsor uniform": The Opening Of Parliament, *The Norwich Mercury*, 9 February 1895, p2.

That spring, almost certainly: West of England News, *Western Morning News*, 26 March 1895, p5.

"For all of them after this": Julia Frankau, *The Sphinx's Lawyer*, William Heinemann, London, 1906, p111.

"Because you 'hate and loathe'": Frankau, *The Sphinx's Lawyer*, Dedication; see also: Timothy d'Arch Smith, *The Frankaus: Prejudice & Principles within a London Literary Family*; Michael Russell, London, 2015.

Wilde's martyrdom give license: Davenport-Hines, *Sex, Death And Punishment*, pp139-142.

In March 1896: *Year Book: The Eighty Club*, London, 1897, p3.

The following year, Cyril accepted: City Notes, *The Sketch*, 19 August 1903.

and Carl Meyer: Our City Article, *The Tatler*, 5 July 1905, pp37-38.

and also helped organise his London: Private information from Dr Tessa Murdoch.

At the opposite end of the financial: Club Feasts And Athletic Sports, *Bucks Herald*, 6 June 1896, p5.

and the following year to Italy: Lady Battersea diary, April 1898: Battersea Papers, Vol XXXIV; Add MS 47942; British Library.

"It is a little too artificial": Cohen, *Lady de Rothschild And Her Daughters*, p259.

"Cyril is in a state": Cohen, *Lady de Rothschild And Her Daughters*, p260-261.

"Feel so disappointed": Lady Battersea diary, [No day date: final entry for year] December 1893:

Battersea Papers, Add MS 47941,Vol XXXIII, British Library.

"I am not going to talk about myself": Lady Battersea diary, 1 January 1898: Battersea Papers, Add MS 47941,Vol XXXIV, British Library.

"I do wish we had children": Lady Battersea diary, 22 November 1898: Battersea Papers, Add MS 47941,Vol XXXIV, British Library.

"I am not going to write about my feelings": Lady Battersea diary, 22 December 1898: Battersea Papers, Add MS 47941,Vol XXXIV, British Library.

all the other Colonial Premiers: The Eighty Club At Lord Battersea's, *The Daily News* (London), 8 July 1897, p6.

Upwards of 1,500 invitations: Brilliant Reception At Surrey House, *Leicester Daily Post*, 8 July 1897, p5.

"strained every nerve": Gossip, *The Ardrossan And Saltcoats Herald*, 2 September 1892, p2.

"It was one of the few spots": London Day By Day, *Daily Telegraph & Courier*, 20 July 1898, p9.

His health had never been good: Death Of Baron Ferdinand De Rothschild, *Reynolds's Newspaper*, 18 December 1898, p8.

"We had a very pleasant dinner": Lord Battersea to Lady Battersea, 4 Feb 1886: Battersea Papers, MS47910, f6; British Library.

"Accident in March": Lady Battersea diary, 25 December 1899: Battersea Papers, Add MS 47943, Vol XXXV, British Library.

"there has been quite an epidemic": Gossip Of The Day, *Sheffield Weekly Telegraph*, 3 October 1896, p9.

the poetical-faced son: James Hallett Hyatt, Ancestry.com [https://web.archive.org/web/20210114085857if_/https://www.ancestry.com/search/?name=James+Hallett_Hyatt&types=p]

several images of the interior of Surrey House: Ref: BB78/04801, BB78/04803, BB78/04807, Historic England: historicengland.org.uk

"Unless you send me £10": Scandalous Menaces In A Letter, *The People*, 16 July 1899, p11.

"What's a fellow to do": Scandalous Menaces In A Letter, *The People*, 16 July 1899, p11.

He admitted there was no truth: Heavy Sentence For Blackmailing, *Dublin Evening Telegraph*, 27 July 1899, p4.

"Madam – We are in possession": The Late Sir Augustus Harris, *Sheffield Daily Telegraph*, 22 September 1896, p9.

"Our right trusty": *The London Gazette*, No 27149, 29 December 1899, pp8654-8655.

The appointment would be renewed: *The London Gazette*, No 27399, 21 January 1902, pp447-448.

"a suitable subject for divorce": Luton Golf Club, *The Luton Times and Bedfordshire Advertiser*, 15 June 1900, p6.

who would be twice guest with his wife and children: The Pleasaunce Visitors Book, Sara Flower.

In his public speeches: Lord Battersea On The War, *The Derry Journal*, 1 December 1899, p8; Lord Battersea On The War, *Eastern Evening News*, 26 April 1900, p4.

"We are all orphans": Sir John Alexander Hammerton (ed.), *The Passing Of Victoria; the poets' tribute,* Horace Marshall & Son, London 1901, pp80-81.

Myers had journeyed: The Top Of The Morning, *The Pall Mall Gazette*, 19 January 1901.

Two years previously he'd also: Jeffrey J. Kripal, *Authors of the Impossible: The Paranormal and the Sacred*, University of Chicago Press, 2010, p48.

"we heard that F Myers": Lady Battersea diary, 1 January 1901: Battersea Papers, Add MS 47943, Vol XXXV, British Library.

"I esteem his friendship": Luther Munday, *A Chronicle of Friendships*, Frederick A. Stokes, New York, p146.

"It was as much how a man listens": Munday, *A Chronicle of Friendships*, p147.

"somebody dies to whom a copy": Cohen *Lady de Rothschild And Her Daughters*, p329.

Princess Louise also considered it: Princess Louise to Lady Battersea, 12 June 1921: MS 47909, f101, British Library.

However the draft was rewritten: Cohen *Lady de Rothschild And Her Daughters*, p327.

"writers, often men and women": Battersea *Reminiscences*, p178.

"So kind! Not a night": Francis King, Henry *Yesterday came suddenly: an autobiography*, Constable, London, 1993, p265.

"Where he [Cyril] was himself": Lord Battersea By An Old Friend (Lady Frances Balfour), *Buckinghamshire Herald*, 7 December 1907.

756

"adored my father and my mother": Carter, Pottle (eds.), *Lantern Slides*, p427.

"he's an odd character": Carter, Pottle (eds.), *Lantern Slides*, p94.

"The new peers were distinguishable": The Opening Of Parliament, *The Queen: The Lady's Newspaper*, 23 February 1901, p26

"The Queen was a vision": Lady Battersea diary, February 1901: Battersea Papers, Add MS 47943, Vol XXXV, British Library.

"did my heart good": Lady Battersea diary, 22 November 1901: Battersea Papers, Add MS 47943, Vol XXXV, British Library.

"less of the public interest": Real Education, *Shipley Times and Express*, 14 February 1902.

"Anything short of murder": Elizabeth Longford, *A Pilgrimage of Passion: The Life of Wilfrid Scawen Blunt*, Weidenfeld and Nicolson, London 1979, p373.

"slightest exertion made him breathless": Robert I. Rotberg, Miles F. Shore*, The Founder: Cecil Rhodes And The Pursuit Of Power*, Oxford University Press, 1988, p670.

"Mr. Rhodes represented the spirit"; "he had a false ideal"; "a great Empire-maker": London Press Opinions, *The St. James's Gazette*, 27 March 1902, p11.

"To-day one thought only": A Prince In Israel, *The St. James's Gazette*, 27 March 1902, p3.

"The decay of the better spirit": A Millionaire's Will, *Reynolds's Newspaper*, 13 April 1902, p4.

"Newspapers, including Liberal journals": Topics Of The Week, *Reynolds's Newspaper*, 22 July 1906, p6.

leading to predictable jibes: London Letter, *Bucks Herald*, 11 March 1899, p8.

From page 388 –

"worthy of universal sympathy": Views From Many Standpoints, *War Against War! A Chronicle of the International Crusade of Peace,* Issue 1, 13 January 1899, p1.

"whole sympathy": More Benedictions, *War Against War! A Chronicle of the International Crusade of Peace*, Issue 2, 20 January 1899, p2.

"This is impossible": Views From Many Standpoints, *War Against War! A Chronicle of the International Crusade of Peace*, Issue 1, 13 January 1899, p1.

In April, Cyril attended: Lord Battersea On Physical Culture, *The Sunday Times*, 27 April 1902.

in May, he headed a dinner: News, *The Times*, 23 May 1902.

"In some villages in Buckinghamshire": The Rural Housing Problem, *Buckingham Advertiser and Free Press*, 21 June 1902, p8.

Five days later he was again: Lord Battersea and Evening Schools, *Bedfordshire Advertiser*,18 July 1902.

"always overlooked his weaknesses": Speech Day At Howell's School, *Denbighshire Free Press*, 26 July 1902.

"Parliament without Whips would be": Westminster's Secret Service, *The Spectator*, 20 May 1995, p11.

maintained what were termed Black Books: Westminster's Secret Service, *The Spectator*, 20 May 1995, p11.

He was a guest Cyril and Constance: Battersea, *Reminiscences*, p207.

"how thankful I am that you have won": Herbert, Viscount Gladstone Papers, British Library, MS46056, f138.

"my old friend and comrade": Liberals And The War, *The Daily News*, 4 March 1901, p7.

his solicitor, Sir George Lewis: Private information from Sara Flower.

"a white-haired and white-whiskered": Hushing It Up by Ex-Attaché (Frederick Cunliffe-Owen), *New York Tribune*, 17 January 1897, p3.

Even on hot days: John Juxon, *Lewis and Lewis: The Life and Times of a Victorian Solicitor*, Collins, London 1983, p11.

"by far the most distinguished": Hushing It Up by Ex-Attaché (Frederick Cunliffe-Owen), *New York Tribune*, 17 January 1897, p3.

"He kept a central clearing-house": Shane Leslie, *The End Of A Chapter*, Constable, London 1916, p174.

"a spider's web": Juxon, *Lewis and Lewis*, p62.

"One curious drawback": Hushing It Up by Ex-Attaché (Frederick Cunliffe-Owen), *New York Tribune*, 17 January 1897, p3.

"It might be taken": Confidant Of Society To Remain Silent, *New York Herald*, 24 January 1910.

"The Nameless Scandal": The Nameless Scandal, *Gloucester Journal*, 21 December 1889, p2.

"As we have said over": *The Star* quoted in: The West End Scandals, *Reynolds's Newspaper*, 22 December 1889, p8.

"Lord Battersea touches life": Lord Battersea At Home, *The London Magazine,* Vol 6, July 1901, p554.

Whitman's own notebooks: Charley Shively, *Calamus Lovers*, Gay Sunshine Press, San Francisco 1987, *passim*.

"I love a youth": Anonymous, *Don Leon*, Printed For The Booksellers (William Dugdale), London, 1866, p10.

Cyril's bookplate graces a surviving set: Arthur Griffiths, *Mysteries Of Police And Crime*, Cassell and Co., London 1898: Harry Ransom Center, University of Texas at Austin, OCLC number 22999279.

A studio photograph: Lafayette Archive, ID 1000LF0040, Victoria & Albert Museum.

To what was surely his consternation: London by Day & Night, *Western Times* (Exeter), 1 August 1904.

"In spite of the long hours": Lady Battersea diary, Summary of 1902: Battersea Papers, Add MS 47943, Vol XXXV, British Library.

"It was quite curious": In Society, *Vanity Fair: A Weekly Show of Political, Social, and Literary Wares,* London, 28 August 1902.

Two days later, the new Home Secretary: Aretas Akers-Douglas, 1st Viscount Chilston, *Engagement Diary* for 1902, U564/F30, Kent Archives.

"Weather fine & occasionally": Lord Ronald Gower diary, 17 August 1902; D6578/15/57, Staffordshire Record Office.

At The Pleasaunce the guests continued to arrive: The Pleasaunce Visitors Book, Sara Flower.

Pasted into his private scrapbook: Axel Nissen, *Bret Harte: Prince and Pauper*, University Press of Mississippi, Jackson 2000, p241.

When in 1899, Collins had shown Cyril: Celia Davies, *Brian Hatton: A Biography Of The Artist (1887–1916),* Terrence Dalton Ltd, London 1978, p28.

Arthur Collins was also a director: Interesting Will, *Reynolds's Newspaper,* 24 December 1911, p3.

"the haven of their lives": Augustus Hare, *The Story of My Life*, Vol 6, London, George Allen 1900, p530.

"some of his lordship in his Coronation robe": Village News: Overstrand, *Norfolk Chronicle*, 30 August 1902, p10.

"Mr Cyril Flower, as he then was": Tring, *Bucks Herald*, 6 September 1902, p6.

Typically, Constance's guests: Tring, *Bucks Herald*, 6 September 1902, p6.

while Cyril's guests included: Rank and Fashion, *The St James's Gazette*, 3 September 1902.

Two other guests were: The Pleasaunce Visitors Book, Sara Flower.

"now that the war which was the cause": Now Or Never Separate Or Unite, *Westminster Gazette*, 4 October 1902, p6.

"Wild horses will not drag": A Reticent Radical, *Bedfordshire Advertiser*, 10 October 1902, p5.

"the superiority of Liberal principles": Now Or Never Separate Or Unite, *Westminster Gazette*, 4 October 1902, p6.

"He refuses reveal his opinions": A Reticent Radical, *Bedfordshire Advertiser*, 10 October 1902, p5.

"When he came to Luton": Luton Radicals and the Education Bill, *Bedfordshire Advertiser*, 17 October 1902, p8.

"did more to set up sectarian": Luton Radicals and the Education Bill, *Bedfordshire Advertiser*, 17 October 1902, p8.

"On Tuesday night [at] Plait": Lord Battersea At The Plait Hall, *Bedfordshire Advertiser*, 17 October 1902, p5.

Despite intense opposition: The Education Bill, *Sunderland Daily Echo and Shipping Gazette*, 8 December 1902, p6.

"Cyril came down": Lady Battersea diary, 'Hasty Review of 1902': Battersea Papers, Add MS 47943, Vol XXXV, British Library.

"between a Scotch mist": Remarkable Weather, *The Pall Mall Gazette*, 11 October 1902, p7.

"the smoke nuisance": The Smoke Nuisance In London, *The Pall Mall Gazette*, 11 October 1902, p8.

"shorn of its amplitude": Throned In Our Hearts, *The Pall Mall Gazette*, 25 October 1902, p1.

These included triumphal arches: The Royal Progress, *The Pall Mall Gazette*, 13 October 1902, p5.

"a letter of eloquent protest": Women's Share In Education, *The Queen: The Lady's Newspaper*, 18 October 1902, p48.

"They are among those": Beautiful Homes And Their Owners: XIV Aston Clinton, *The Sketch*, 15 October 1902, p508.

On the twentieth, the bachelor: The Pleasaunce Visitors Book; Sara Flower.

The Sportsman paper: Golf, *The Sportsman*, 27 October 1902.

"Lady Battersea's priceless pearls": London Society Airs Scandal At The Restaurant, *Herald Democrat*, November 25, 1902.

"women, because they become": Battersea, *Lady Waifs and Strays*, p302.

"The Times noted that this sentiment": The National Union Of Women Workers, *The Times*, 31 October 1902.

"On Friday, disconcerting news of Cyril": Lady Battersea diary, Undated [November 1902]; Battersea Papers, Vol XXXV; Add MS 47943; British Library.

"Dalmeny – A fiasco": Lady Battersea diary, Undated [December 1902]: Battersea Papers, Add MS 47943, Vol XXXV, British Library.

From page 402 –

"steps were taken to prevent": London Letter, *Birmingham Daily Gazette*, 11 December 1902, p4.

"disappointed probably because": Lady Battersea diary, Undated [November 1902]: Battersea Papers, Add MS 47943, Vol XXXV, British Library.

"News still more disconcerting": Lady Battersea diary, Undated [November 1902]: Battersea Papers, Add MS 47943, Vol XXXV, British Library.

"Terrified.": Lady Battersea diary, 2 November 1902: Battersea Papers, Add MS 47943, Vol XXXV, British Library.

"Cyril seriously ill": Lady Battersea diary, 2 November 1902: Battersea Papers, Add MS 47943, Vol XXXV, British Library.

During the Cleveland Street Scandal: Hyde, Hartford Montgomery *The Cleveland Street Scandal*, W.H. Allen, London 1976, p89.

A statement on Cyril's illness: Lord Battersea's Illness, *Eastern Evening News*, 3 November 1902, p3.

"Lord Battersea, acting under": Lord Battersea, *Shields Daily News*, 8 November 1902; Lord Battersea, *The People*, 9 November 1902 p1.

"Lorne i.e. Argyll – had telegraphed": Lord Ronald Gower diary, 7 Nov 1902: D6578/15/57, Staffordshire Record Office.

"It was horrible": Lady Battersea diary, Undated [15? November 1902]: Battersea Papers, Add MS 47943, Vol XXXV, British Library.

"6 times in all" : Lady Battersea diary, Undated [15? November 1902]: Battersea Papers, Add MS 47943, Vol XXXV, British Library.

"an extraordinary day": Lady Battersea diary, 22 November 1902: Battersea Papers, Add MS 47943, Vol XXXV, British Library.

"delicate and sensitive nature": The Death of Herr Krupp, *London Evening Standard*, 27 November 1902, p7.

'gross immorality': Krupp's Tragic End, *The Echo*, 24 November 1902; The Slanders Against The Late Herr Krupp, *Sheffield Daily Telegraph*, 29 November 1902; The Charges Against Herr Krupp, *The St James's Gazette*, 29 November 1902.

"Whatever pity one might feel": The Secret History Of To-Day, *Reynolds's Newspaper*, 30 November 1902, p1.

London Society would be distracted: Sir Edward Walter Hamilton Diary, 7 & 10 December 1902; MS ADD 48680, British Library.

"able to leave his bed": Untitled, *The Evening Star* (Ipswich), 9 December 1902, p2.

"A friend who is spending": From Our London Correspondent, *Lancashire Evening Post*, 24 December 1902.

including on both sides of Parliament: The Representation Of The Luton Division, *The Luton Reporter,* 18 June 1892, p5.

As Prince of Wales, Edward had been President: Prince and Princess of Wales, *Lancaster Gazetter*, 28 February 1894, p4.

A further example of Cyril's: Mr. Balfour On Technical Education, *The Times*, 4 February 1899, p.12.

Balfour's Private Secretary, Sir Bernard Malet: The Pleasaunce Visitors Book, Sara Flower.

Another bulwark: Lord Battersea and Cromer, *Bedfordshire Advertiser*, 5 September 1902.

Nonetheless, it was no small matter: Allfrey, *Edward VII And His Jewish Court*, p191.

"As a child I thought Lord Rothschild": Rothschild, *Dear Lord Rothschild,* p38.

He was, for example, a director: The Imperial Fire Office (advertisement), *The Straits Times* (Singapore), 11 November 1902, p7; *Derbyshire Advertiser And Journal,* 7 April 1905, p1.

"the effeminate men and the masculine women": Political Speeches, *The Globe,* 15 November 1883, p6.

His reputation a sexual predator: Lees-Milne, *The Enigmatic Edwardian,* p338.

In February that year: Liberal Reunion At The Grafton Galleries, *Derby Daily Telegraph,* 6 February 1902.

"The turquoises and diamonds": News, *Yorkshire Evening Post,* 7 February 1902, p3.

"When will you come": Lord Battersea to Lord Harcourt: Papers of Lewis, 1st Viscount Harcourt; MS. Harcourt 452, f148, Bodleian Library.

"I will keep a berth": Lord Battersea to Lord Harcourt: Papers of Lewis, 1st Viscount Harcourt; MS. Harcourt 452, f146, Bodleian Library.

"I long to show you": Lord Battersea to Lord Harcourt: Papers of Lewis, 1st Viscount Harcourt; MS. Harcourt 452, f144, Bodleian Library.

"He had the same tastes": George Ives diary, 5 December 1917; Harry Ransom Center, University of Texas at Austin.

Amongst the most regularly: The Pleasaunce Visitors Book, Sara Flower.

"Once. On the brow": Benson, *Final Edition,* p56.

In addition to his many novels: J. Braid, J.A.T. Bramston, H.G. Hutchinson, E.F Benson, (ed); E.H. Miles, *A Book Of Golf,* Dutton, E.P. New York, 1903.

It was an obsession he confessed: Benson *Final Edition,* p56.

"devoted to children": Death Of Mr Arthur Brown, *Bucks Herald,* 19 August 1938.

"he was a Liberal of an advanced type": Entres Nous, *Truth,* 29 November 1911, p5.

"all the leading lights of the Liberal world": Social Side Of Politics, *Daily Express,* 7 November 1902, p5.

"where, perhaps, more golf": Col. Arthur Collins, C.B., *Golf Illustrated,* Vol. 3, 30 March, London 1900, p. 280.

There is another, almost annual signature: The Pleasaunce Visitors Book, Sara Flower.

"Another still greater name": London Shocked By Scandal, *The Sun* (New York), 9 November 1902, p9.

"all male gatherings at Halton": William Cross, *Lies, Damned Lies and the Carnarvons,* William P. Cross, Newport, Gwent 2022, Ch3, p6.

at the opening night: Franny Moyle, *The Tragic and Scandalous Life of Mrs Oscar Wilde,* 2012, Pegasus Books, London, p223.

"Bimetallism! Is that quite": Oscar Wilde, *Complete Works of Oscar Wilde,* William Collins Sons & Co., London 1966, p463.

its expression of duality had made it: William C. Carter, *Marcel Proust: A Life,* Yale University Press, New Haven 2013, p589.

"staunch supporter of Monometallism": Ferguson, *The World's Banker,* p874.

"Never say 'No' to Mr Alfred": Derek Wilson, *Rothschild: A Story Of Wealth And Power,* André Deutsch, London 1988, p258.

"The deposition of the thirty-two-year-old prostitute" Glenn Chandler, *The Sins Of Jack Saul,* Grosvenor House Publishing; Guildford, Surrey 2016, p216.

When the latter celebrated the visit: Visit Of The Prince Of Wales To Mr Alfred De Rothschild, *Bucks Advertiser & Aylesbury News,* 19 January 1884, pp4-5.

he wore his Garter sash every night: Leslie Field, Bendor: *The Golden Duke Of Westminster,* Weidenfeld & Nicholson, London 1983, p244.

but job interviews for his admired retinue: Paula Byne, *Mad World: Evelyn Waugh And The Secrets Of Brideshead,* HarperCollins, London 2011, p131.

while the gift-givers included: The Presents, *Worcestershire Chronicle,* 2 August 1902, p6.

Beauchamp was a member of his club: Gossip Of The Hour, *The Tatler,* 28 May 1902, p4.

in which resided the works: Jane Mulvagh, *Madresfield: The Real Brideshead,* Doubleday, London 2008, pp294, 387.

"My first impressions of Lord Beauchamp": C.R. Ashbee diary, [no day date] March 1902; GB 272 CRA/1/11, Archive Centre, King's College, Cambridge.

After Hannah's death: Lord Rosebery to Lord Battersea, 4 August 1891: Battersea Papers, Add MS 47909, f145, British Library.

Cyril invited him to recover: Lord Rosebery's Illness, *The Eastern Weekly Leader* (Norfolk), 23 March 1895, p7.

I found R[osebery] in good form: H.H. Asquith to Margot Asquith, 4 October 1902, MS. Eng. c.6689, fols. 183-184, Bodleian Library.

"Rosebery was evidently tired": Marquess of Lincolnshire diaries, 5 November 1902; MS. Film 1104, Bodleian Library.

It is also worth noting: Diary of Lord Northcliffe, 1902; MS62390, British Library.

"our host is in splendid form": Carter, Pottle (eds.), *Lantern Slides*, p94.

was widely shared by colleagues: Marquess of Lincolnshire diaries, 25 November 1902; MS. Film 1104, Bodleian Library.

His closest friends: Elizabeth Longford, *Darling Loosy: Letters to Princess Louise 1856-1939*, Weidenfeld & Nicolson, London 1991, p52.

He was also fascinated: Charles Warr, *The Glimmering Landscape*, Hodder & Stoughton, London, 1960, p36-37.

'Degradation of a Great British Family': The Colin Campbell Case, *Morning Despatch* (Auburn, New York), 11 December 1886.

The middle of November saw the wedding: Wedding, *The Globe*, 19 November 1902, p2; Our English Letter, The Queenslander (Brisbane), 3 June 1903, p55.

"For a man of adventure": Duke Of Argyll, *The Westminster Gazette*, 4 May 1914, p11.

"Lorne's proclivities": Lucinda Hawksley, *The Mystery Of Princess Louise*, Chatto & Windus, London, 2013, p125.

"He used to say": Sean Hignett, *Brett: From Bloomsbury to New Mexico – A Biography*, Hodder & Stoughton, London 1983, p32.

"Our friends are the same": Maurice V. Brett, *Journals And Letters Of Reginald, Viscount Esher*, Vol I, Ivor Nicholson & Watson, London 1934, p228

Employing his powerful connections: Hartford Montgomery Hyde, *The Cleveland Street Scandal*, W.H. Allen, London 1976, p46 and *passim*.

"Personally I think their": Hyde, *The Cleveland Street Scandal*, p199.

"No one is more suspicious": Viscount Esher, *The Influence Of King Edward*, John Murray, London 1915, pp118-119.

"When Englishmen were ruled": Esher, *The Influence Of King Edward*, p166-117.

"like dining in a Duke's house": Brooks's Club, *Memorials Of Brooks's*, Ballantyne & Co. Limited, London 1907, pxiii.

Other notable members: Brooks's Club, *Memorials Of Brooks's*, pp198, 214, 218, 228, 230.

They had first bonded: Lees-Milne, *The Enigmatic Edwardian*, p146.

"notes of suggestions": Lees-Milne, *The Enigmatic Edwardian*, p156.

He often called on Balfour: Michael Bloch, *Closet Queens: Some 20th Century British Politicians*, Little Brown, London 2015, p50.

On one occasion Esher invited: Lees-Milne, *The Enigmatic Edwardian*, p94.

Even more importantly, Esher: Walter Reid, *Architect of Victory: Douglas Haig*, Birlinn Ltd, Edinburgh 2006, p129.

As early as October 1902: Sir Edward Walter Hamilton Diary, 27 October 1902; MS ADD 48680, British Library.

From page 421 –

"the remarkable influence": Lionel Cust, Lady Sybil Lyttelton Cust, *King Edward VII and His Court: Some Reminiscences,* John Murray, London 1930, p 145.

Frederick Cunliffe-Owen stated: London Shocked By Scandal, *The Sun* (New York) 9 November 1902, p9.

"the Bismarck of London": George William Erskine Russell, *One Look Back*, W. Gardner, Darton & Co, 1911, p126.

"He was determined": Esmé Wingfield-Stratford, *The Victorian Aftermath*, William Morrow, New York, 1934, p45.

"King Edward hates scandal": Gossip Of The Courts Of Europe, *Buffalo Evening News*, 2 January 1902.

"That influence was one": Oliver Gwynne, *Sunday Chronicle* (Manchester), 6 October 1912, quoted in Legge, Edward *More About King Edward*, Eveleigh Nash, London 1913, ppxiv-xv.

"The age of chivalry": Sir Sidney Lee, *King Edward VII*, Vol II, Macmillan And Co, London 1925, p567.

"He talked over some": Lees-Milne, *The Enigmatic Edwardian*, p131.

"King Edward had far more": James Pope-Hennessy, Hugo Vickers (ed.), *The Quest For Queen Mary*, Zuleika, London 2018, p152.

"you would not find me": Katie Hickman, *Courtesans*, William Morrow, New York 2003, p327.

"one of those irritating factors": Hugh Evelyn Wortham, *The Delightful Profession: Edward VII, a Study in Kingship*, Jonathan Cape, London, 1931, p304.

"We all know what English 'justice'": In Moral And Merrie England, *The Bulletin* (Sydney, Australia), 25 January 1890, p5.

"In England... for the poor": Letter From The Linkman, *Truth*, 6 November 1902, p1122.

Edward's friendship with Lewis: Juxon, *Lewis And Lewis*, p304.

"far more than half the business": Esher, *The Influence Of King Edward*, p43.

"No letters, no lawyers": Ridley, *Bertie*, p133.

"he was not responsible": Marquise de Fontenoy, *Chicago Tribune*, 4 December 1907.

The American ambassador, Joseph Choate: The Pleasaunce Visitors Book, Sara Flower.

Gossip of the scandal: Ridley, *The Architect And His Wife,* p102.

However, if any further underlining: Town Notes, *Bedfordshire Advertiser*, 26 December 1902, p5.

The entire affair lived up: Presentation To Mr Cyril Flower, M.P., *South Wales Daily News* 19 October 1885, p3.

"This past year seems to stand out": Lady Battersea diary, 'Hasty Review of 1902': Battersea Papers, Add MS 47943, Vol XXXV, British Library.

"I am determined to act up": Lady Battersea diary, 'Hasty Review of 1902': Battersea Papers, Add MS 47943, Vol XXXV, British Library.

"Principles carefully enunciated": Battersea, *Waifs & Strays*, p296-297.

"gradually got worked up": David Lindsay, Earl of Crawford; John Vincent (ed.), *The Crawford Papers*, Manchester University Press, Manchester, 1984, p231.

"Our public life must be": Battersea, *Waifs & Strays*, p298.

"a bit of nonsense": Information from Timothy d'Arch Smith.

"The muzzling of the Press under Imperialism": Secret History Of To-Day, *Reynolds's Newspaper*, 11 January 1903, p1.

"The London and Globe Infamy!": *The Investors' Review* quoted in: Secret History Of To-Day, *Reynolds's Newspaper*, 11 January 1903, p1.

"extraordinary attitude...has created": The Secret History of To-Day, *Reynolds's Newspaper*, 24 May 1903, p1.

"Lord Battersea, whose health": Luton, *Bedfordshire Advertiser*, 30 January 1903, p5.

"Several newspapers still persist": Our London Letter, *Gloucester Citizen*, 31 January 1903, p3.

"got into serious trouble for activities": Lord Alfred Douglas to Alphonse James Albert Symons, 16 March 1939, William Andrews Clark Memorial Library, MS.Douglas, D733L S988.

"Lord Ronald Gower and his adopted son": Secret History Of To-Day, *Reynolds's Newspaper*, 11 January 1903, p1.

"to make some studies of the natives": Society Gossip, *The Tatler*, 4 February 1903, p20.

An inquest would conclude: Ethel M. Hogg, *Quintin Hogg: A Biography*, Archibald Constable, London 1904, p369.

"a Treasury official wrote to a": George Ives diary, 7 June 1903, Harry Ransom Centre.

A proposal is on foot for the erection: Secret History Of To-Day, *Reynolds's Newspaper*, 12 June 1904, p10.

and was unveiled in 1906 by Lorne: Mr Quintin Hogg, *London Daily News*, 26 November 1906, p9.

as a friend since their schooldays: The Late Mr Quintin Hogg, *The Globe*, 26 January 1903, p5.

"The Polytechnic Magazine for Feb": George Ives diary, 10 February 1913, Harry Ransom Centre.

"Half a dozen times we went in for a chat": Beatrice Webb, Norman Ian MacKenzie, Jeanne MacKenzie, *The Diary of Beatrice Webb*, Vol 2, Harvard University Press, 1982, p267.

Cyril was invited to that held: Ministerial Banquets, *The Daily Telegraph*, 17 February 1903, p11.

"Battersea appeared in public": Marquess of Lincolnshire diaries, 16 February 1903; MS. Film 1104, Bodleian Library.

"welcomed back on his recovery": Politics and Parliament, *Lancashire Evening Post*, 18 February 1903, p2.

"a most excellent series": Photographic Exhibition At Norwich, *Norfolk News*, 28 February 1903, p12.

In March, Cyril was at the opening night: The New Theatre, *Manchester Courier and Lancashire General Advertiser*, 13 March 1903, p6.

The Princess of Wales was unable: Women's Sphere, *The Sphere*, 28 March 1903.

However a reporter noted: Art Notes, *Truth*, 26 March 1903, p52.

Near his body were found newspapers: Sir Hector Macdonald, *The Daily Telegraph* (London), 27 March 1903, p9.

"very grave charges": Charges Against Hector Macdonald, *The Times*, 25 March 1903, p5.

"some, indeed most, of his victims": Ronald Hyam, *Empire And Sexuality: The British Experience*, Manchester University Press, 1990, p35.

Macdonald had been discovered: Hyam, *Empire And Sexuality*, p34.

"What a fine strong man he was": Sir Hector Macdonald, *The Daily Telegraph* (London), 27 March 1903, p9.

"had the person charged been a lord": Hector Macdonald, *Reynolds's Newspaper*, 5 April 1903, p1.

"The belief prevails that he": London Letter, *The Leeds And Yorkshire Mercury*, 30 March 1903, p4.

"it is good to observe how for once": The Suicide Of Sir Hector Macdonald, *The Grantham Journal*, 28 March 1903, p7.

the Scottish were stunned and profoundly indignant: Hector Macdonald, *Reynolds's Newspaper*, 5 April 1903, p1.

"Over twelve months ago the writer": The Strange Case Of Hector Macdonald', *Reynolds's Newspaper*, 29 March 1903, p1.

"The charge for which Lieutenant-General Hector Macdonald": Secret History Of To-Day, *Reynolds's Newspaper*, 29 March 1903, p1.

"We do not wish to appear in any way": The Strange Case Of Hector Macdonald', *Reynolds's Newspaper*, 29 March 1903, p1.

"the Government have flashed out": The Strange Case Of Hector Macdonald', *Reynolds's Newspaper*, 29 March 1903, p1.

"not the slightest particle of truth": McDonald's Vindication, *The Washington Times*, October 19, 1903.

"Whether anything...can be done": Arthur James Balfour to Lord Battersea, 18 May 1903: Battersea Papers, MS 47912, British Library.

"Cyril seems to be very happy": Constance, Lady Battersea to Hon. Mrs Annie Yorke, 10 May 1903: Battersea Papers, Add MS 47963, f189, British Library.

That same month, Cyril spoke: Domestic Servants' Pensions, *Nottingham Evening Post*, Wednesday 13 May 1903, p3.

"had all his old after-dinner": Town Notes, *Bedfordshire Advertiser,* 23 October 1903, p5.

While he continued to engage: Lord Battersea On Slum Work In West London, *Eastern Daily Press*, 28 June 1904, p8.

From page 440 –

"I know what it means": Cohen, *Lady de Rothschild And Her Daughters,* p284.

"Three, no four years": Cohen, *Lady de Rothschild And Her Daughters,* p284.

True to form, Cyril: A School for Chauffeurs, *Strand Magazine*, October 1903.

"Cyril enjoys his motor": Lady Battersea diary, 1 June 1905: Battersea Papers, Add MS 47944, Vol XXXVI, British Library.

In 1904 he accompanied: Town Notes, *Bedfordshire Advertiser*, 10 June 1904, p5.

"I miss the old intercourse": Lady Battersea diary, 4 Jan 1905: Battersea Papers, Add MS 47944, Vol XXXVI, British Library.

On the 1st of August, the aforesaid Arthur Brown: The Pleasaunce Visitors Book, Sara Flower.

"the best 'circus' one knows": Robert L. Gale, *A Henry James Encyclopedia*, Greenwood Press, New York 1989, p735.

Looking at his astonishingly well-preserved complexion: A Foreign Resident, *Society In The New Reign*, pp90-91.

While Cyril may have shrugged off: Ranald Michie, *Jewish Financiers In The City Of London* in Carmen Hofmann, Martin L. Müller (eds.) *History of Financial Institutions: Essays On The History Of European Finance 1800-1950*, Routledge; Abingdon, Oxon 2017, p50.

"Lord Battersea has for some time": Personal Pars, *The Weekly Mail* (Cardiff), 21 May 1904, p4.

"Will anyone tell me what": Secret History Of To-Day, *Reynolds's Newspaper*, 19 June 1904, p10.

In Cyril's latter years: Overstrand, *Norfolk Chronicle*, 5 October 1907.

"walked and talked and flirted": Cohen *Lady de Rothschild And Her Daughters,* p219

In August 1905, The Pleasaunce: The Pleasaunce Visitors Book, Sara Flower.

Ernest was chairman: Jack S. Blocker, David M. Fahey, Ian R. Tyrrell, *Alcohol and Temperance in Modern History: An International Encyclopedia,* Vo1, ABC Clio, Santa Barbara, 2003, p660.

"Ld. Battersea (Cyril) & 'Connie' are giving": Carter, Pottle (eds.), *Lantern Slides,* p104.

"Poor Cyril suffers awfully": Lady Battersea diary, 9–29 June 1906: Battersea Papers, Add MS 47944, Vol XXXVI, British Library.

While they were away: Social And Personal, *The Daily News* (London), 23 June 1906, p6.

"a young man of dishevelled": Benson *Final Edition,* pp 49-50.

"Ld. Battersea is so different": Carter, Pottle (eds.), *Lantern Slides,* p109.

More than forty couples: Ball At Overstrand, *Eastern Daily Press,* 2 January 1907, p8.

They included entertainers: The Pleasaunce Visitors Book, Sara Flower.

The leading German physician: The Pleasaunce Visitors Book, Sara Flower.

Von Noorden had developed: James B. Herrick, The Oatmeal Diet In The Treatment Of Diabetes Mellitus, *Journal Of The American Medical Association,* 14 March 1908.

June found Cyril motoring: Fremden-Liste, *Grazer Volksblatt,* 14 June 1907, p8.

in July he was amongst the guests: Their Majesties' State Ball, *Morning Post,* 20 July 1907, p5.

while August found him again: The Pleasaunce Visitors Book, Sara Flower.

a doctor based at the Homburg spa: Friedrich Lotz , Heinz Grosche, *Geschichte der Stadt Bad Homburg vor der Höhe,* Vol 3, Waldemar Kramer, Frankfurt am Main 1964, p201.

Tall, mustachioed and handsome: Susan's Family History Pages, Image: E. B. Cuthbertson; [https://web.archive.org/web/20190622084938/http://www.wauchopecottage.co.uk/susan/Cuthbertson/Cuthbertson%20Indirect%20Ancestors/Edward%20Cuthbertson.jpg]

Unlike Constance, Cuthbertson stayed: The Pleasaunce Visitors Book, Sara Flower.

Not least he was rich: Cutbertson, Edward Boustead, 1942, ProbateSearch UK.

"a young man in whom": Funeral At Overstrand, *The Norfolk News,* 7 December 1907, p5.

"To the very last": Lord Battersea By An Old Friend [Lady Frances Balfour], *Buckinghamshire Herald,* 7 December 1907, p7.

For some months Cyril: Personal Gossip, *St Andrews Citizen,* 7 December 1907, p2.

"looking wretchedly ill": Lady Battersea diary, 10 November 1907: Battersea Papers, Add MS 47944, Vol XXXVI, British Library.

"as was his wont": Duke of Argyll to Lady Battersea, 28 November 1907: Battersea Papers, Add MS 47909, f76; British Library.

In the Royal Pier Hotel: Death Of Lord Battersea, *Bucks Herald,* 30 November 1907, p7.

"in brilliant weather": Funeral At Overstrand, *The Norfolk News,* 7 December 1907, p5.

The floral offerings: Funeral At Overstrand, *The Norfolk News,* 7 December 1907, p5.

"a huge floral cushion": The Late Lord Battersea, *The Bucks Herald,* 7 December 1907, p7.

"Lord and Lady Battersea have always": Lord Battersea, *The Times,* November 28, 1907, p8.

"Lord Battersea has for the last few": Marquise de Fontenony, *Chicago Tribune,* 4 December 1907, p8.

"Ill-natured things have been": *The Saturday Review of Politics, Literature, Science and Art,* John W. Parker and Son, London 1907, Volume 104, p656.

"His winning personality": Luton Jottings, *Bedfordshire Advertiser,* 29 November 1907, p5.

"those who win": Queen Marie Roumania, *Story Of My Life,* Vol 2, Cassell & Company, 1934, p67.

"always seemed so full of life": Duke of Argyll to Lady Battersea, 28 November 1907: Battersea Papers, Add MS 47909, f76; British Library.

"his life-giving personality": Lord Battersea By An Old Friend, [Lady Frances Balfour], *Westminster Gazette,* reprinted *Buckinghamshire Herald,* 7 December 1907, p7.

"made generous use of his wealth": Entre Nous, *Truth,* 4 December 1907, Vol 62, p1344.

"As we brought to a close our talk": Lord Battersea At Home, *The London Magazine,* Vol 6, July 1901, p557.

From page 451 –

"Lord Battersea was of the type": Benson, *Final Edition,* p47.

"He saw himself in the eyes": Benson, *Final Edition,* p52-53.

Cyril left an estate: Will of Cyril, Baron Battersea, 1908; probatesearch.gov.uk

These Constance only cleared: Cohen *Lady de Rothschild And Her Daughters*, p285.

He also gifted: Will of Cyril, Baron Battersea, 1908; probatesearch.gov.uk

"long for his love": Lady Battersea diary, April(?) 1908: Battersea Papers, Add MS 47944, Vol XXXVI, British Library.

"I found amongst his papers": Battersea *Reminiscences*, p175.

"Have found all the diaries": Cohen, *Lady Rothschild And Her Daughters*, p287.

"Jebb has a great belief in his capacity": Esher, *Ionicus*, p61.

As a memorial to Cyril: Lady Battersea diary, 23 July 1908: Battersea Papers, Add MS 47944, Vol XXXVI, British Library.

"he is absolutely happy": Livingstone, *The Women Of Rothschild*, p328.

"To old friends of the House": Small Talk, *The Sketch*, 19 June 1912, p8.

"Came to my sweet country": Cohen, *Lady Rothschild And Her Daughters*, p285.

In 1914, she entertained: Battersea *Reminiscences*, p403.

"the eccentricities of Prince A": George Ives diary, 26 & 27 December 1914; Harry Ransom Center, University of Texas at Austin.

She first put up Belgian refugees: Cohen, *Lady De Rothschild And Her Daughters*, p303.

"I stuffed in a little Temperance teaching": Cohen, *Lady De Rothschild And Her Daughters*, p306.

The Pleasaunce was given over: Cohen, *Lady De Rothschild And Her Daughters*, pp303, 307, 312.

"I see you cannot tear yourself": Cohen, *Lady De Rothschild And Her Daughters*, p303.

"I have tried not to neglect": Cohen, *Lady De Rothschild And Her Daughters*, p313.

War-time stringencies manifested: Cohen, *Lady De Rothschild And Her Daughters*, p313.

"On Friday after shooting": Cohen, *Lady De Rothschild And Her Daughters*, p310.

"This is indeed a time of terror" Cohen, *Lady De Rothschild And Her Daughters*, p312.

When in London, she slept in her pearls: Cohen, *Lady De Rothschild And Her Daughters*, p308.

having begun them while recovering: Cohen, *Lady Rothschild And Her Daughters,* p319-320.

"Who tends to make the hours", Lady Battersea, *Thoughts In Verse*, Goose And Son, Norwich 1921, p33.

"selling wonderfully": Cohen, *Lady Rothschild And Her Daughters,* p332.

So proud was she of her first: Cohen, *Lady Rothschild And Her Daughters,* p335.

"Beautiful women, clever men": Battersea *Reminiscences*, p224.

"How the world is changing": Lady Battersea diary, 5 December 1913: Battersea Papers, Add MS 47945, Vol XXXVII, British Library.

"Cyril, so much with us": Lady Battersea diary, 1 January 1912: Battersea Papers, Add MS 47945, Vol XXXVII, British Library.

During the War it had been: Exhibitions Of Women's Work, *The Sphere*, 27 May 1916, p196 (p16); The Pen To The Rescue Of The Sword, *The Graphic*, 21 August 1915, p242 (p20).

"the last of the 'exquisites'": Men And Women Of Today: Time's Changes, *The Courier And Advertiser* (Dundee), 16 April 1927, p10.

Symptomatic of the changing times: Cohen, *Lady de Rothschild And Her Daughters,* p196.

The advent of the first Labour government: Cohen, *Lady de Rothschild And Her Daughters,* p336,n1.

"I lead the quietest of lives": Constance, Lady Battersea to Lady Elizabeth Babington Smith, 14 June (1924?): MYER/HBS 92/79, Trinity College Library, Cambridge.

"overwhelming metropolis": Lady Battersea to Lady Elizabeth Babington Smith, 10 June (1926?): MYER/HBS 92/76, Trinity College Library, Cambridge.

Having been gradually reduced to an invalid: Cohen, *Lady de Rothschild And Her Daughters,* p342.

Having a fear of being buried alive: Rothschild, *Dear Lord Rothschild*, p15.

"earnest wish and desire": Will of Cyril, Baron Battersea, 1908; probatesearch.gov.uk

Constance bequeathed all her Norfolk property: Lady Battersea's Estate, *Bucks Herald*, 18 December 1931, p12.

her father Lionel Nathan: Email of Michael Hall, curator of Exbury House to Meghan Gray, Curatorial Associate, Nelson-Atkins Museum of Art, 22 October 22 2018; https://art.nelson-atkins.org/objects/9914/

Due to the perceived risk: historicengland.org.uk/listing/the-list/list-entry/1001013

"I am making a holocaust": Cohen, *Lady de Rothschild And Her Daughters*, pxvi

"a huge residue remained": Cohen, *Lady de Rothschild And Her Daughters*, pxvi

"Lady Battersea, in her will": Cohen, *Lady de Rothschild And Her Daughters*, pxiii.

"the Napoleon of Lawyers": Sir George Lewis, *Newry Reporter*, 18 January 1910.

"George Lewis is the one man": John Juxon, *Lewis and Lewis: The Life and Times of a Victorian*

Solicitor, Collins, London, 1983, p12.

There, in the grounds: Richard Batson, Story of the Overstrand house that crossed the channel, and hosted a bonfire of secrets, *The Eastern Daily Press* (Norwich), 15 February 2013.

"that rather tragic spoiled darling": Lady de Rothschild And Her Daughters, *The Sphere*, 18 May 1935, p8.

"there were many people who were prejudiced": Sir Alfred Edward Pease, *Elections And Recollections*, John Murray, London 1932, p254-255.

"When Cyril cared for any one": Battersea *Reminiscences*, p268.

"the sense of the world as a happy": Battersea *Reminiscences*, p177.

"Farewell again, truest": Battersea *Reminiscences*, p390.

15. THE ELUSIVE MISTER W
I. Alexander Henry Wylie

"the liberty of the press": A.H. Wylie, *Chatty Letters From The East And West*, Sampson Low, Marston, Searle & Rivington, London 1879, p217.]

"A special train left": Funeral Of Lord Esher, *The Standard*, 30 May 1899, p2.

"Similarly, the following year when Gladstone's": Mr Gladstone's Bereavement, *The New York Herald* (European Edition: Paris), 6 July 1891, p1.

When Viscount Castlereagh: Marriage Of Viscount Castlereagh, *The Yorkshire Herald*, 29 November 1899, p6.

At the age of twenty-one: Alexander Henry Wylie diary, Ms. Codex 1796, University of Pennsylvania.

He then established himself: *Reports From Committees: Commercial Distress*, Vol VIII, Part III, The House of Commons, London 1848, p227.

He was a prominent activist: Railway Intelligence, *Leeds Mercury*, 21 February 1866, p4; York, Newcastle And Berwick Railway Company, *Newcastle Courant*, 30 August 1850, p3; Dundee And Perth Railway, *Edinburgh Evening Courant*, 1 March 1862, p7.

the family residences: Will of Alexander Henry Wylie, National Records Of Scotland; Deaths, *The Scotsman*, 8 December 1911, p12.

a prenuptial contract: *The Scottish Law Reporter*, Vol XLIII, John Baxter & Sons, Edinburgh1906, p383-385.

Their first son: Obituary, *Army and Navy Gazette*, 30 December 1905, p17.

the second son: Militia, *The Broad Arrow*, 13 January 1877, p27; Partnerships Dissolved, *Manchester Courier and Lancashire General Advertiser*, 27 April 1876, p7; George Crosbie Wylie England and Wales Census, 1901; Notes & Gleanings, *The Journal Of Horticulture*, Cottage Gardener And Home Farmer, Vol VIII. Third Series, London 1884, p382.

their fourth son: *The Broad Arrow*, 6 May 1876, p25; Highland And Agricultural Society, *Aberdeen Press and Journal*, 20 June 1885, p3.

Alexander Henry Wylie, the junior: Deaths, *The Scotsman*, 8 December 1911, p12.

Born in the Edinburgh family: Births, *Edinburgh Evening Post and Scottish Standard*, 23 May 1849, p3.

The following year, with his brother: The Levee, *The Morning Advertiser*, 27 February 1871, p5.

"an excellent, thoughtful host": Statesman No649, The Earl Of Camperdown, *Vanity Fair*, 24 March 1895.

In 1876, the day after: Index To Register Of Passport Applications 1851-1903, Great Britain, FindMyPast.com

Sympathetic visitors who called: The King Of Hanover, *Morning Post*, 17 June 1876, p5.

"the very Paradise": Wylie, *Chatty Letters From The East And West*, p120.

"His letters are just such letters": Current Literature, *Daily News* (London), 13 May 1879,p3

"Their very freedom from pretensions": Literature, *The Scotsman*, 11 March 1879, p3.

"may pass muster, if only": The Reader, *The Graphic*, March 22, 1879, p19.

"He has a quick, observing eye": Chatty Letters From The East And West, *Morning Post*, 20 March 1879, p3.

'A Literary Idiocy': A Literary Idiocy, *New York Herald*, 14 April 1879 - Triple Sheet, p5.

"I am immensely glad": Wylie, *Chatty Letters From The East And West*, p224.

"the worst type of a conceited": A Literary Idiocy, *New York Herald*, 14 April 1879 - Triple Sheet, p5.

"whose then broad acres": St Anne's Hill Trees, *Surrey Advertiser*, 1 April 1944, p7.

"With all the pomp": *Vanity Fair*, Volume 25, 1881, p80.

On the marriage registration: Wylie vs Wylie: J 77/671/416; J 77/669/349; UK National Archives.

"somewhat peculiar": London In And Out Of Season, *Otago Daily Times* (New Zealand), 22 June 1889.

"The fact is that Lord Beaumont's idiosyncrasies": **"**: London In And Out Of Season, *Otago Daily Times* (New Zealand), 22 June 1889.

In a loop of mutual lunacy: Hugh Montgomery-Massingberd, Christopher Simon Sykes, *Great Houses of England & Wales* , Laurence King Publishing, London 1994, p401.

From page 467 –

He now dreamt of receiving: Montgomery-Massingberd, Sykes, *Great Houses of England & Wales*, p401.

By 1879, bankruptcy was looming: Montgomery-Massingberd, Sykes, *Great Houses of England & Wales*, p405.

"No arguments and no remonstrances": The Regent Street Tragedy, *The Saturday Review*, June 27 1863, p822.

"exceedingly popular": Obituary, *The Yorkshire Herald*, 25 January 1892, p5.

"deadly with partridges": Country House Parties - Past And Present, *The Tatler*, 7 October 1908, p12.

"Her authoritative and somewhat high-handed": Violet, Lady Beaumont: St Mary's Church, Slindon; 02/2015; http://www.stmarysslindon.co.uk/obituaries/

"circle of ladies of fashion": A Society Scandal, *New Zealand Herald*, 4 May 1889, p10.

Although the petition: Shocking English Scandal, *The Observer* (New Zealand), 11 May 1889, p8.

Lord Beaumont had fled: Swindling The Emigrants, *The New York Times*, 17 November 1889, p1.

"His was a curiously romantic": Obituary, *The Graphic*, 30 January 1892, p7.

"with contempt, coldness, indifference": Wylie vs Wylie: J 77/671/416; J 77/669/349; UK National Archives.

"the said Alexander Henry Wylie is now an undischarged": Wylie vs Wylie: J 77/671/416; J 77/669/349; UK National Archives.

"Petitioner has been for sixteen years": Wylie vs Wylie: J 77/671/416; J 77/669/349; UK National Archives.

In 1900, the couple were granted: Wylie vs Wylie: J 77/671/416; J 77/669/349; UK National Archives.

In 1891, an engagement between: Society, *John Bull*, 3 January 1891, p13.

a member of the London Athletic: Highland Gathering In London, *Inverness Courier*, 12 May 1896, p5.

He was one of the founders: Hayling Golf, *Portsmouth Evening News*, 27 October 1892, p3.

also played in matches arranged: Golf, *West London Observer*, 24 March 1899, p2.

also with Arthur Balfour: Mr. Balfour At Ranelagh, *The Sportsman*, 11 April 1908, p3.

Amongst the other fashionable bachelors: An Active Peer, *Dundee Evening Post*, 11 July 1900, p2; Scottish Homecraft Industries, *The Daily Telegraph* (London), 10 July 1900, p7.

"a pleasantly told little story": Literary Notices, *Liverpool Mercury*, 24 May 1882, p5.

"I maintain 'society' of thirty years ago": Alexander Henry Wylie, Society In 1892, *London Society*, F.V. White & Co.; July 1892, Vol 62, Issue 367, p611.

In 1901, newspapers record: Fashionable Scotch Marriage In London, *Aberdeen Press and Journal* , 7 June 1901, p6.

On the 19th of July 1902: Marriage Of Constance Countess De La Warr And The Rev. Paul Williams Wyatt, *The Sussex Express Surrey Standard & Weald Of Kent Mail*, 19 July 1902, p7.

In a report that lists the eminent visitors: Countess of Dudley's Illness, *The Irish Times*, 13 December 1902, p5.

in 1889 *The New York Times*: Swindling The Emigrants, *The New York Times*, 17 November 1889, p1.

The following year, there is another newspaper: Cross-Channel Steamers, *Dublin Daily Express*, 14 November 1903, p7.

with the press recording: Marriage Of Capt. Skeffington Smyth And The Hon. Violet Monckton, *The Morning Post*, 8 July 1904, p6.

"Mr A.H.Wylie can thoroughly recommend": Married Couples And Menservants, *The Morning Post*, 8 May 1908, p13.

With beautiful views across to the crags: Knight, William Angus *Principal Shairp And His Friends*, John Murray, London 1888, *passim*.

"Cash in House – Nil": Alexander Henry Wylie, 1912; Wills & Testaments SC70/1/526/Edinburgh Sheriff Court Inventories, National Records Of Scotland.

II. Francis Robert Shaw Wyllie

"because there is a want of gentlemen": Elizabeth Longford, *A Pilgrimage of Passion: The Life of Wilfrid Scawen Blunt*, Tauris Park, New York 2007 p232.

Blunt's lover, the famous courtesan: Wilfrid Scawen Blunt, *The Land War In Ireland*, S. Swift & Co, London 1912, pp139, 141,151.

"June 4. – Wyllie, the Liberal agent": Blunt *The Land War In Ireland*, p510.

In 1841, with his father absent: J.W.S. Wyllie, W.W. Hunter (ed.) *Essays On The External Policy Of India*, Smith, Elder & Co., London 1875, pviii.

He would return to England: R.H. Vetch, revised by Roger T Stern: Sir William Wyllie, *Oxford Dictionary of National Biography*.

Frank was schooled: Wyllie, Hunter (ed.) *Essays On The External Policy Of India*, pix.

However, his health, always delicate: Obituary, *The Times*, 9 February 1907.

His older brother: R.H. Vetch, revised by Roger T Stern: Sir William Wyllie, *Oxford Dictionary of National Biography*.

"an object of horror": Missionary Proceedings In The Bombay Presidency, *Church Missionary Intelligencer*, Church Missionary Society, London 1864, p167.

"This subtle Gujarat fever": Mrs. George T. Rea, *A Broken Journey: Memoir of Mrs. Beatty, Wife of Rev.William Beatty, Indian Missionary*, Nisbet 1894, p106.

His ability saw him become one of the trustees: Obituary, *The Times*, 9 February 1907.

From page 477 –

"one of the most brilliant and versatile": Francis Henry Skrine, *Life of Sir William Wilson Hunter*, Longmans, Green, and Co., London 1901, p233.

but the election was declared void: Hunter Wyllie (ed.), *Essays On The External Policy Of India*, pxxiv-xxv.

"My health is infinitely better": Hunter Wyllie (ed.), *Essays On The External Policy Of India*, pxxviii.

"I should have liked to have gone": Hunter Wyllie (ed.), *Essays On The External Policy Of India*, ppxxviii-xxix.

In John's memory: Skrine, *Life of Sir William Wilson Hunter*, p233.

His was a life which only too faithfully: Wyllie, Hunter (ed.) *Essays On The External Policy Of India*, ppxxx.

"There is no doubt that Mr. Wyllie's abilities": Obituary, *The Times*, 9 February 1907.

"I was fond of India": Skrine, Francis Henry *Life of Sir William Wilson Hunter*, Longmans, Green, and Co., London 1901, p249 n1.

He was living with his parents: Will of Sir William Wyllie, 1891, Probate Search, UK; Will of Sir Maxwell Melvill, 1887, ProbateSearch, UK.

"London society was so much smaller": Lord Frederic Hamilton, *The Days Before Yesterday*, Hodder And Stoughton, London 1920, p195.

From levees at Buckingham Palace: The Queen's Levee, *Morning Post* (London), 1 June 1886; Devonshire House, *Morning Post* (London) 11 July 1878 and 17 June 1880; Fashionable Entertainments, *Morning Post* (London), 22 May 1879; Fife Hunt Ball, *Fife Herald*, 2 November 1876.

He was also a member of the East India: *Journal of the East India Association*, Volume 10, London, Volume 10, 1877, p162

"To extend a knowledge of India": *Journal of the East India Association*, Volume 10, London, Volume 10, 1877,, p60.

The new organisation acted: The Liberal Central Association And The General Election, *Daily News* (London), 13 April 1880.

Frank was considered very influential: R.P. Masani, *Dadabhai Naoroji: The Grand Old Man Of India*, George Allen & Unwin, London 1919, pp 230, 248.

Frank was there on the official: The National Liberal Club, *The Daily News*, 5 November 1884.

no less than two-thirds of the officers: Richard Holmes, *The Soldier's Trade in a Changing World*,

History Trails: War and Conflict, BBC, 28 February 2005: bbc.co.uk/history/trail/wars_conflict/
"the prescriptive monopoly of officering": Gracchus: The Privileges Of The Privileged, *Reynolds's Newspaper*, 21 May 1871, p3.
After 1871, the work of the Commission: The Story Of The Abolition Of Purchase, *The Times*, 1 November 1892.
it favoured those whose families: Local Topics, *Bedfordshire Times and Independent*, 9 February 1900.
In 1886, Frank was proposed and granted: Brooks's Club *Memorials Of Brooks's*, Ballantyne & Co. Limited, London 1907, pp228, 230; Michael Meadowcroft, National Liberal Club Archives to author.
In 1887, Frank was executor: The Late Sir Maxwell Melvill, *The Illustrated London News*, 22 October 1887.
"my dear friend Francis": Will of Maxwell Melvill, 1887 Probate Search UK.
"There was nothing didactic": *Bombay 1885 To 1890: A Study In Indian Administration*, Henry Frowde, London 1892, pp65-67.
"His singular amiability": Obituary, *The Times*, 9 February 1907.
Here Frank was to be a regular visitor: J.H. Rivett-Carnac, *Many Memories Of Life In India At Home And Abroad*, William Blackwood And Sons, Edinburgh and London 1910, p15.
"a strange uncanny couple": Gibson, *The Erotomaniac*, p104.
"a grim splendour of a man": Gibson, *The Erotomaniac*, p104.
The Burtons first went to Davos: John R. Godsall, *The Tangled Web: A Life Of Sir Richard Burton*, Matador; Leicester 2008, p405.
"Will you kindly give me the name": Richard Burton to J.A. Symonds 18 August 1890: Problem In Greek Ethics. With: Two Autograph Letters Signed; Item 114073, Bauman Rare Books, New York 2019. [https://web.archive.org/web/20191013054524/https://www.baumanrarebooks.com/rare-books/symonds-john-addington-burton-richard-f/problem-in-greek-ethics-with-two-autograph-letters-signed/114073.aspx]
Here at the grand Hôtel Kursaal: Thomas Wright, *The Life of Sir Richard Burton*, 1906, Everett & Co, London 1906, p228.
A solidly built man, he ruled: Christopher Tyerman, *A History of Harrow School, 1324-1991*, Oxford University Press, 2000, pp364-367; James Edward Cowell Welldon, National Portrait Gallery, NPG Ax5444, NPG Ax38365, NPG x123188.
"A public school is the home": James Edward Cowell Welldon, *Gerald Eversley's Friendship: A Study in Real Life*, Smith, Elder, & Company, London 1895, p77.
"They take their tone": Welldon, *Gerald Eversley's Friendship,* p78.
"whose bright complexion": Welldon, *Gerald Eversley's Friendship,* p33.
"Don't cry any more": Welldon, *Gerald Eversley's Friendship,* pp24-25.
"This, from a Head Master": Tyerman, *A History of Harrow School,* p368.

From page 483 –

his companion of 50 years: J.W.S. Tomlin, M.C. Curthoys: James Edward Cowell Welldon, *Oxford Dictionary of National Biography*, Oxford University Press, 2004.; George MacDonald Fraser (Intro) *The World Of The Public School,* St Martins Press, New York 1977, p149.
"that abiding benediction": J. E. C. Welldon, *Forty Years On: Lights And Shadows*, Nicholson and Watson, London 1935, p50.
In her widowhood: Princess (Eleanor Calhoun) Lazarovich-Hrebelianovich, *Pleasures And Palaces*, The Century Company, New York 1915, p169; Francis Wyllie to Dorothy Tennant, 17 August 1892, Stanley Archive, SA6598, Musée Royal De L'Afrique Centrale, Tervuren.
"I remember so well": Francis Wyllie to Dorothy Tennant, May 1890: Stanley Archive, 6075, Musée Royal De L'Afrique Centrale, Tervuren.
"somewhat over-indulged": Tim Jeal, *Stanley: The Impossible Life Of Africa's Greatest Explorer*, Yale University Press, 2007, p398-399.
Like many an idle heiress: Jeal, *Stanley*, p398-399.
"I am only rich in love": Jeal, *Stanley*, p310.
who had her own grand designs: Jeal, *Stanley*, p398-399.
"it was not until some hours later": Marriage Of Mr. H.M. Stanley And Miss D.Tennant, *Western Mail*, 14 July 1890.
"cruelty and rapacity": Scraps From Various Journals, *Reynolds's Newspaper*, 9 March 1890.

"the black boy who has been": The Marriage Of Mr. Stanley, *The Times*, 14 July 1890.

The high-camp Alick Yorke: Marriage of H.M. Stanley And Miss D. Tennant, *Western Mail* (Cardiff), 14 July 1890.

"To me you are more beautiful": Jeal, *Stanley*,p404.

"He is thickly, strongly built": Jeal, *Stanley*, p307.

"To me who to tell the truth": Aldrich, *Colonialism and Homosexuality*, p44.

"The seed of the old Vikings": Sir Henry Morton Stanley, Lady Dorothy Stanley (ed.), *The Autobiography Of Sir Henry Morton Stanley*, Houghton Mifflin Company, Boston 1909, p451.

Throughout his earlier life: Aldrich, *Colonialism and Homosexuality*, pp36-54.

"a perfect youthful Apollo in form": Henry M. Stanley, *My Kalulu: Prince, King and Slave*, Simpson Low, Marston, Low, And Searle, London 1873, p137,p5,p11.

"This book has been written": Stanley, *My Kalulu*, ppv-vi.

Certainly, in 1892, Welldon: Rev Welldon to Dorothy Stanley, 12 September 1892; 3849, Stanley Archives, Musée Royal De L'Afrique Centrale, Tervuren.

Frank was a member of the Royal: *Proceedings Of The Royal Geographical Society*, Vol X, Edward Stanford, London 1880, p66.

Stanley definitely asked his friend: Maurice Denham Jephson, Dorothy Middleton (ed), *The Diary of A J Mounteney Jephson: Emin Pasha Relief Expedition 1887-1889*, Cambridge University Press, 1969. p416.

Not least amongst this happy group: Jeal, *Stanley*, p405.

Browning and Welldon were childhood: Oscar Browning, *Memories Of Later Years*, D. Appleton & Co, New York 1923, p206.

Browning would summer at the hotel: Browning, *Memories Of Later Years*, pp34-37.

"I never felt quite certain": Squire Bancroft, *Empty Chairs*, John Murray, London 1925, p142.

When Sir Richard Burton died: The Late Sir Richard Burton, *North Devon Gazette*, 23 June 1891.

That summer he took up an invitation: Francis Wyllie to Dorothy Stanley, 17 Aug 1892; SA6598, Stanley Archives, Musée Royal De L'Afrique Centrale, Tervuren; Ownership: Dobhran, 73703, Caledonian Maritime Research Trust; www.clydeships.co.uk

"disabled by recurrent attacks": Obituary, *The Times*, 9 February 1907.

"It is long since I": Francis Wyllie to Dorothy Stanley, 2 June 1899: Stanley Archive, 6089; Musée Royal De L'Afrique Centrale, Tervuren.

"His new home, at 6 Montpelier": Will of F.R.S. Wyllie, 1907, Probate Search UK.

At the time of the Battersea scandal: *Boyle's Fashionable Court & Country Guide, And Town Visiting Directory*, London 1903, p 934.

the Northbrook Society: Untitled item, *The Homeward Mail*, 12 March 1904, p2.

By this time there was a further deterioration: Will of F.R.S. Wyllie, 1907, Probate Search UK.

"there was a raw cold feeling": The Weather, *Morning Post*, 7 February 1907.

equating to £2.1 million: Measuringworth.com

When his older brother John: Will of J.W.S. Wyllie, 1869, Probate Search UK.

their father, Sir William: Will of Sir William Wyllie, 1891, Probate Search UK.

Sir William Hutt Curzon Wyllie: Will of Sir William Hutt Curzon Wyllie, 1909, Probate Search UK.

"I forgive all persons": Will of F.R.S. Wyllie, 1907, Probate Search UK.

his directorship of the Great Indian Peninsula: *The Universal Directory of Railway Officials 1896*, Directory Publishing Company, Limited, London 1896, p131.

"all my oil paintings": Will of F.R.S. Wyllie, 1907, Probate Search UK.

The assassin had selected his target: The Murder of Sir W.C. Wyllie, *Leominster News and North West Herefordshire & Radnorshire Advertiser*, 9 July 1909; A Political Crime, *The Times*, 4 July 1909.

"universally loved and respected": Interviews With Prominent Men, *Aberdeen Press and Journal*, 3 July 1909.

The Francis Wyllie Scholarship: *Cheltenham College Register 1841-1910*, G.Bell And Sons, London 1911, p706.

16. A SWORDSMAN OF HIS HOLINESS

However, the 'He-She Ladies': Neil McKenna, *Fanny & Stella: The Young Men Who Shocked Victoria England*, Faber and Faber, London, 2013, *passim*.

Born in 1871: 1871 Census, RG10/1969, Parish of Iwerne Minster.

With its indoor staff of six: 1871 Census, RG10/1969, Parish of Iwerne Minster.

an English paradise: J. Newman, N. Pevsner, *The Buildings of England: Dorset*, 1972, p.240; The farmland market is booming, *Country Life*, July 22, 2010.

In 1874: John Venn, J.A. Venn (eds.) *Alumni Cantabrigienses: A Biographical List of All Known Students*, Volume 2, Cambridge University Press, 1940, p333.

"Harold E.B. Boulton, Nice": The 'Little Folks' Humane Society, *Little Folks, A Magazine For The Young*, Cassell Petter Galpin & Co.,1882, p50.

52 Elm Park Gardens: 1891 Census: Civil Parish: Chelsea; p42; GBC/1891/0058/0307.

In 1889 he went up to Cambridge: Venn, Venn (eds.) *Alumni Cantabrigienses,* p333.

becoming a member of its famous: Charles Leslie Ferguson, *A history of the Magpie and stump debating society, 1866-1926*, W. Heffer & sons ltd., 1931, p33.

"That this house deeply deplores": Trinity, *The Cambridge Review*, 27 November 1890, p121.

After Cambridge, Harold: *The London Gazette*, 1897, Page 1885.

In 1894, his family was again struck: Royal Artillery Officers 1883-1942 1716-1899, p122A, Find My Past; Calendar of Probate 1894, Boulton, Thomas Leonard Lees.

he became a member of the high-brow: *Journal of the Institute Of Jamaica*, Vol II, No 11, April 1895, p82.

In August, Harold visited New York: Guests At Leading Hotels, *New York Daily Tribune*, 13 August 1895.

On the 3rd of March, he was a guest: *Year Book: The Eighty Club*, London, 1897, p3.

"You gather up the budding youth": Lord Rosebery On The Situation, *The Times*, 4 March 1896, Lord Rosebery At The Eighty Club, *The Economist*, 7 March 1890.

This was apparently the culmination: *The London Gazette*, Issue 26838, 3 April 1897, Page 1885; Issue 26879, 3 August 1897, p4348.

in 1901 Harold took up the hobby: *Year Book: Royal Automobile Club*, London, 1912, p59.

In 1901 and early 1902, Harold again: *London American*, Volume 10, 1901, p9; Hotel Arrivals, *Evening Star* (Washington D.C.), 11 March 1902.

Following the arrests: The Society Scandal, *Nottingham Journal*, 07 November 1902.

In 1905 his sister Helen: thornburyroots.co.uk/families/thurston-arabella-henry-neville/

"C/o National Prov[incial] Bank": *Great British Railway Shareholders*: 1835-1932; GWR/PB/100/157; 28 August 1905, Harold Edward Baker Boulton.

One of the social registers: *Boyle's Fashionable Court & Guide, and Town Visiting Directory*, London, Court Guide Office, 1903, p60-61.

"In the plural, 'Bitters', noun": *Mercure de France*, 1 January 1906, Volume 59, p159.

"appointed or lent for temporary": Viscount Jellicoe, *The Crisis Of The Naval War*, George H. Doran Company, New York, 1920, p281.

In 1920, Harold was received into: Sir Francis Cowley Burnand, *The Catholic Who's Who And Yearbook*, Volume 34, Burns & Oates, 1924, p41.

the Sacrament of Confirmation performed: *The Tablet*, 20 November 1920, Page 678.

Harold was part of an interwar: Paul Chigwiddenm, *Peripeteia: The Somersault Divine and England's Interwar Converts to Catholicism and Communism*, Thesis, Charles Sturt University, 2015, p193.

By 1926 Harold had been appointed: Herman Joseph Heuser, *The American Ecclesiastical Review: A Monthly Publication for the Clergy*, Volume 75, 1926, p68.

"Mr Harold Boulton has been known": Palazzo Ap., Titoli 98, fasc. 20, ff. 412r-414r, Archivio Apostolico Vaticano.

"the black 16th–century court dress": Rev. Fr. Donald Attwater (ed.) *A Catholic Dictionary*, Macmillan, London 1958.

"absolutely yummy!": Gore Vidal, *The City And The Pillar*, Dutton, New York 1965, p176.

He was caricatured by Ronald Firbank: Steven Moore, *Ronald Firbank: An Annotated Bibliography of Secondary Materials, 1905-1995*, Dalkey Archive Press; Normal, Illinois 1996, p57.

From page 496 –

"Secret papers for the Holy Father!": Robin Bryans, *The Dust Has Never Settled*, Honeyford, London 1992, pp75-76.

More troublingly, in association with Aleister: Hugh Montgomery-Massingberd, Christopher Simon Sykes, *Great Houses of England & Wales*, Laurence King Publishing, London 1994, p209.

his black masses in Rome's Protestant cemetery: Bryans, *The Dust Has Never Settled*, p129.

In the early 1920s: Burnand, *The Catholic Who's Who And Yearbook,* Volume 34, p41.

Harold's appointment also enabled him to join: Pontifical Court Club, *The Tablet*, 14 February 1931, p207.

a friend of the courtier Sir Alexander: Sir Alexander Hood, 5th Duke of Bronte, *Recollections*, July 1920; unpublished: Collection of the 4th Viscount Bridport, 7th Duke of Bronte.

In 1923, after vacationing: Mr Harold E.B Boulton, 1923, 1927; UK Passenger Lists 1878-1960, Ancestry.com.

the official diary of the Venerable English College: *The Venerable*, Vol IV, No1, October 1928, Salesian Printing School, Rome, p97.

Earlier in February, *the International*: Smart Gatherings Feature Week Among Society Folk at Biarritz, *International Herald Tribune*, 28 February 1928, p10.

Another guest at the hotel: Liste Des Étrangers, *La Côte Basque: revue illustrée de l'Euzkalierra*, 26 February 1928, p181.

they'd worked together on behalf of the Domestic Servants: London Day By Day, *The Daily Telegraph* (London), 26 May 1898, p9.

another brother, Alexander: Peer's Son Killed By Fall From Window, *Western Daily Press* (Yeovil), 17 February 1930; Lord Clifden, *The Times*, 21 July 1930.

"known in Paris and Monte Carlo": *London Opinion*, 10 October 1915.

Tommy's mentor had been Lord Rosebery: Paul Holden, A Very English Gentleman: The Honourable Thomas Charles Reginald Agar-Robartes M.P. (1880-1915), *Journal Of Liberal History*, Issue 66, Spring 2010, pp8-18.

"he was almost like another son": Mr Agar-Robartes, M.P., *Leeds Mercury*, 4 October 1915, p2.

"The hereditary principle was absolutely": Holden, A Very English Gentleman, pp8-18.

"Being quite young men they both": John Foster-Fraser, Peeps In Parliament, *The Looker-On*, 11 April 1914, p8.

known as 'The Inseparables': Personalia, *West Briton and Cornwall Advertiser*, 8 April 1915, p4.

"Mr Primrose and Mr Agar-Robartes are unmarried": John Foster Fraser, Peeps In Parliament, *Hull Daily Mail*, 29 April 1911, p6.

"He was too rich a man to have need": Mr Agar-Robartes, *Birmingham Daily Post*, 4 October 1915, p6.

at pains to ensure he was sent to the Front: Holden, A Very English Gentleman, pp8-18.

He acquitted himself admirably: Holden, A Very English Gentleman, pp8-18.

As a young man, Gerald: Peter Dickenson, *Lord Berners: Composer, Writer, Painter*, The Boydell Press (Woodbridge), 2008, p57.

he was a man of taste: Alfred Leslie Rowse, *Friends and Contemporaries*, Methuen, London 1989, p55.

He was also highly public spirited: Viscount Clifden, *The Times*, 18 July 1966.

together with the great and good: *National Art Collections Fund: Twenty Fifth Annual Report*, 1929, London, 1930, p68.

The year 1931 found Harold visiting: Bath Visitors List, *Bath Chronicle and Weekly Gazette*, 7 February 1931.

At the end of it: Boulton to Lady Berwick, 11 May 1932, Attingham Papers, 112/22/9/292/5, Shropshire Archives.

"one of the most endearing men": James Lees-Milne, *People and Places: Country House Donors and the National Trust*, John Murray, London 1992, pp53-67.

"I do not know what to tell you": Harold Boulton to Lady Berwick, 18 January 1933; 112/22/9/306/9, Attingham Papers, Shropshire Archives.

"Evan Morgan came to Bath": Harold Boulton to Lady Berwick, 31 March 1932; 112/22/9/288/6, Attingham Papers, Shropshire Archives.

"Mrs Thynne's tea-party": Harold Boulton to Lady Berwick, 31 March 1932; 112/22/9/288/6, Attingham Papers, Shropshire Archives.

"I have lately read a novel": Harold Boulton to Lady Berwick, 31 March 1932; 112/22/9/288/6, Attingham Papers, Shropshire Archives.

"I have not been to Rome": Harold Boulton to Lady Berwick, 18 January 1933; 112/22/9/306/9, Attingham Papers, Shropshire Archives.

"they gathered round them": Carolyn Burke, *Becoming Modern: The Life of Mina Loy*, Farrar Straus & Giroux, New York, 1996, p108-109.

Two such Florentine social fixtures: Photograph: Edith Teresa, Lady Berwick, Reggie Temple and Arthur Spender in the Picture Gallery at Attingham Hall, 1922, National Trust Collections.

In 1932 he spent Holy Week: Harold Boulton to Lady Berwick, 31 March 1932; 112/22/9/288/6, Attingham Papers, Shropshire Archives.

"Gerald and I have been together": Harold Boulton to Lady Berwick; September 10, 1932, 112/22/9/298/7; Attingham Papers, Shropshire Archives.

The Corporation received: Pete Boardman, *Counting Time: A brief history of the 24-hour clock*, Pete Boardman, 2011, p84.

"I earnestly hope that the B.B.C.": *Radio Times*, 11 May 1934.

By 1939 he was back living: *The Week-end Review*, Volume 6, Issues 121-147, 1932, p 61; *New Statesman*, Volume 18, 1939, p503.

including that of Rudyard Kipling: Court Circular, *The Times*, 24 January 1936.

He also attended Requiem Mass for a friend: Deaths, *The Times*, 11 August 1938.

"Before the days of the Great War": Lieutenant A.F.J. Bevan, *The King's Royal Rifle Corps Chronicle*, Warren and Son Limited, 1939, p179.

The need to keep this lifestyle afloat: Harold Edward Baker Boulton, 1958; Last Will and Testament, UK Probate.

affectionately known as 'Bunny': In Memoriam, *The Times*, 3 April 1986.

Photographs show him: Howard Ford, 1959, Howard Ford, 1959, NPG x74849; NPG x74850; National Portrait Gallery; Oliver Stewart, 'Air Eddies', *The Tatler*, 26 January 1938, p180.

Retiring in 1962: Obituaries, *The Times*, London, 17 April 1986.

17. AN IDEAL ENGLISH GENTLEMAN

"if he could only change": Day, *Charles Thorold Gentleman Emigrant,* p119.

His presumption is hinted: News Items, *Liverpool Echo*, 8 March 1898, p4.

When Arthur was twelve: Day, *Charles Thorold Gentleman Emigrant*, pp38-46.

"It gives one position": Oscar Wilde, *The Importance of Being Earnest*, 1895.

The breakup was further: John Morley, *Recollections*, Vol 2, Macmillan & Co, London 1917, p357; B. Afton, J. V. Beckett, M. E. Turner, *Agricultural Rent in England, 1690-1914*, Cambridge University Press, 1997, p112; T. W. Fletcher: The Great Depression of English Agriculture 1873-1896, in P. J. Perry, (ed.), *British Agriculture 1875-1914*, Methuen, London 1973, pp. 30-55; Anthony Taylor, *Lords of Misrule: Hostility to Aristocracy in Late Nineteenth and Early Twentieth Century*, Palgrave McMillan, Hampshire 2004, p10.

By the time of Queen: H.J. Hanham, The Sale of Honours in Late Victorian England, *Victorian Studies*, Vol. 3, No. 3 (March 1960), Indiana University Press, pp. 277-289.

"The minds of men": Gavin Carlyle, *The Battle of Unbelief*, Hodder & Stoughton, London 1878, pV.

"He practised his religion": Day, *Charles Thorold Gentleman Emigrant*, p35.

At fourteen he went: Day, *Charles Thorold Gentleman Emigrant*, p47.

"Observe that fancy waistcoat": *The Wonderful Visit*, The Hutchins School Magazine, December 1926, p10.

Young ladies were usually: Vincent O'Sullivan, *Long Journey to the Border: A Life of John Mulgan*, Bridget Williams Books, Wellington, New Zealand 2011, p117.

"the finest oarsman of his generation": Joseph Mordaunt Crook, *Brasenose: The Biography of an Oxford College*, Oxford University Press, 2008, p255.

"Sooner have a mad dog": Walter B. Woodgate, *Reminiscences Of An Old Sportsman*, Eveleigh Nash, London 1909, p444.

The public fondling: Simon Goldhill, *A Very Queer Family Indeed: Sex, Religion, and the Bensons in Victorian Britain*, University of Chicago Press, 2016, p139.

lying in the middle: David Lindsay, Earl of Crawford; John Vincent (ed.), *The Crawford Papers*, Manchester University Press, Manchester 1984, p22.

he won the One Mile Handicap: Athletics At Oxford University, *The Sporting Life*, 30 November 1893, p4.

"Rows with half a blade": Worcester College Boat Club minute book, 1893, Worcester College Archives.

"Rowing was my forte": Day, *Charles Thorold Gentleman Emigrant*, pp70, 85

"the most enchanting spot": Anthony Gibbs, *In My Time*, Peter Davies, London 1969, p29.

Treasurer of the Debating Society: Worcester, *The Oxford Magazine*, 30 January 1895, p187.

Honorary President of the De Quincey: Worcester, *The Oxford Magazine*, 6 March 1895, p279.

He gained a reputation for entertaining: Information from John Day, via local historian Christine Cowham.

apart from possibly participating: Day, *Charles Thorold Gentleman Emigrant*, pp83-84,111n217.

Arthur much preferred: Day, *Charles Thorold Gentleman Emigrant*, pp84,112n225.

"oysters and champagne": Ainslie, *Adventures Social and Literary*, pp84-85, 90-91.

Although in his second year: University Intelligence, *The Morning Post*, 13 April 1894, p3.

including being on the planning committee: Commemoration Ball, *The Oxfordshire Weekly News*, 3 July 1895, p3.

The Rev. Algernon Thorold's management: Day, *Charles Thorold Gentleman Emigrant*, p116.

When Arthur returned to Oxford: Abstract Ledgers, WOR/BUR 1/53/3, Worcester College Archives.

He also submitted a request: Minutes of College meeting held 27 November 1895, WOR/GOV 3/3/6, Worcester College Archives.

Arthur was absent for second term: Buttery Book, WOR/BUR 3/3/8, Worcester College Archives.

a tutor-cum-secretary to the illustrious George Rendel: Dr. Day wrote: "No records exist of Thorold's involvement with the Rendel family other than his assertion that this was so." Follow up research by two members of the Rendel family, Rosemary Rendel and Thomas Dunne, appeared to indicate Thorold had been employed as a tutor cum private secretary for a short while in 1900. (Day, *Charles Thorold Gentleman Emigrant*, pp-14-15.) However, Rosebery's letter to Neville-Rolfe confirms that Thorold took the position with the Rendels in 1897 during his suspension from Oxford, *not* after his graduation in 1899. That he was in Naples in 1897 is also confirmed by the court evidence regarding his introduction to Fraser. Arrivals in the city were recorded by the Anglo-French newspaper, *The Universal Tourist/The Naples Echo*. Unfortunately, holdings of the paper at the Bibliothèque Nationale de France and the Biblioteca Nazionale Centrale di Firenze, do not include 1897.

A Social Evening was held: Hougham And Marston, *The Grantham Journal*, 21 January 1899, p6.

years later he would speak of such: Day, *Charles Thorold Gentleman Emigrant*, pp84-85.

"young, smartly dressed": Day, *Charles Thorold Gentleman Emigrant*, pp121-124.

Sporting an upturned: *St Edward's Chronicle* 2011-12,Vol XXXIII, St Edward's Oxford, p91-94.

The School's other stalwart: J.A. Mangan, *The Games Ethic and Imperialism: Aspects of the Diffusion of an Ideal*, Frank Cass, London 1986, p23.

"fanatical devotion": Richard Desmond Hill, *A History of St Edward's School, 1863 – 1963*, Oxford: The St. Edward's School Society, 1962, p123.

Happily enabling the Spartan streak: Malcolm Oxley, *A New History of St Edward's School 1863-2013*, St Edwards School, 2015, *passim*.

It was the very stuff: Anthony Seldon, David Walsh, *Public Schools and The Great War*, Pen And Sword Military, Barnsley 2013, p131.

so much so, that it subsequently found: *St Edward's Chronicle* 2011-12,Vol XXXIII, St Edward's Oxford, p89.

A comment in Fraser's: Home Office: Registered Papers Supplementary, HO 144/710/108656, UK National Archives, Petition 108656.

In October 1901: Marriage of the Rev. Algernon Herbert Thorold and Miss Inez Theodora Beer, *The Grantham Journal*, 12 October 1901, p4.

"humorous songs and recitations": Hougham and Marston, *The Grantham Journal*, 18 January 1902, p2.

"He was now two years in arrears": Day, *Charles Thorold Gentleman Emigrant*, p117.

From page 514 –

"There is an evil feeling": Day, *Charles Thorold Gentleman Emigrant*, p119.

"Serious family trouble": Day, *Charles Thorold Gentleman Emigrant*, p118.

Arthur's mother also felt: Day, *Charles Thorold Gentleman Emigrant*, p119.

"Since I came to Grantham": Day, *Charles Thorold*, 181, n16: Rev. T. J. Crossfield, Letter to Bishop of Lincoln, 1 July 1903, *Bishop's Correspondence*, Diocese of Lincoln Records, B7/1/H45/14,3.

The innocent yet attainted: Anna Louisa Brumfield: Baptism Register, p52-53, (1876) Kirkby la Thorpe, Lincolnshire Archives; Marriages registered April, May June 1903, p48, Anna Louisa Brumfield, Newark, Nottinghamshire, Find My Past.

"the Rectory grounds": Day, *Charles Thorold Gentleman Emigrant*, p117.

"A Rectory House": To Be Let, *The Grantham Journal*, 1 October 1904.

The Rector's absences: Day, *Charles Thorold Gentleman Emigrant*, p181.

"for the Lower Sixth Form Mastership": *St Edward's School Chronicle*, No239, Vol IX, July 1902, p234.

After initially being confined: Arthur Thorold, Prison Register: HM.P. 17, Norfolk Record Office.

it was to Dartmoor: Arthur Thorold, alias Arthur Charles Campbell Thorold, C505 Parkhurst, p224; Metropolitan Police: Criminal Record Office, *Habitual Criminal Registers and Miscellaneous Papers*, MEPO6/017/00282, National Archives UK.

It was c505: Arthur Thorold, alias Arthur Charles Campbell Thorold, C505 Parkhurst, p224; Metropolitan Police: Criminal Record Office, *Habitual Criminal Registers and Miscellaneous Papers*, MEPO6/017/00282, National Archives UK.

Another patch bore: Neil R. Storey, *Prisons and Prisoners in Victorian Britain*, The History Press, Stroud 2010, p54.

The standard cells at Dartmoor: Michael Davitt, *The Prison Life Of Michael Davitt*, J.J. Lalor, Dublin 1882, p15.

"Outside, the day may be": Oscar Wilde, Isobel Murray (ed.) *The Soul of Man, and Prison Writings*, Oxford University Press, 2000, p83.

"It was not so much the intensity": Jeremiah O'Donovan Rossa, *O'Donovan Rossa's Prison Life: Six Years in Six English Prisons*, The American News Company, New York, 1874, p86.

"The food in Dartmoor": Davitt, *The Prison Life Of Michael Davitt*, p17.

"the intense cold experienced": The Gates Of Doom: Part II, *Buchan Observer and East Aberdeenshire Advertiser*, 17 February 1903, p3.

"The labour I was first put": Davitt, *The Prison Life Of Michael Davitt*, pp18-19.

"In drawing the cart along": Davitt, *The Prison Life Of Michael Davitt*, p18.

Those incapable of ordinary prison labour: Davitt, *The Prison Life Of Michael Davitt*, p19.

Little wonder then: Alyson Brown, *English Society and the Prison: Time, Culture, and Politics in the Development of the Modern Prison, 1850-1920*, Boydell Press, (Suffolk) 2003, p20.

With nine months of his sentence: Arthur Thorold, alias Arthur Charles Campbell Thorold, C505 Parkhurst, p224; Metropolitan Police: Criminal Record Office, *Habitual Criminal Registers and Miscellaneous Papers*, MEPO6/017/00282, National Archives UK.

Given the state of their father: Day, *Charles Thorold Gentleman Emigrant*, p120.

Arthur's youngest brother Ernest: Thorold, Ernest – Spent most of his life as Army chaplain, *Grantham Matters*: granthammatters.co.uk

In 1905 Benjamin's father: Sad Death Of A Hougham Signalman, *The Grantham Journal*, 18 February 1905, p3.

in 1908 he joined the Lincolnshire police force: Constabulary Promotions, *Lincolnshire Echo*, 28 January 1938, p6.

On Arthur Thorold's Scotland Yard criminal register: Arthur Thorold, alias Arthur Charles Campbell Thorold, C505 Parkhurst, p224; Metropolitan Police: Criminal Record Office, *Habitual Criminal Registers and Miscellaneous Papers*, MEPO6/017/00282, National Archives UK.

In September 1906: Day, *Charles Thorold Gentleman Emigrant*, p371.

"next to Naples the finest": The Marquess Of Crewe, *Lord Rosebery*, Vol1, John Murray, London 1935, p177.

As in England, the occasional: No Irish Need Apply, *The North Eastern Ensign* (Benalla, Victoria), 2 February 1902, p3.

"Masculine Messalinas": The Scarlet Man In Melbourne, *Truth* (Brisbane), 13 April 1902, p5.

"a monarch of alliterative": Writers' World by Maurice Dunlevy, *The Canberra Times*, 1 September 1973, p12.

"semi-senile...podgy-fingered": God Save The Queen, *Truth* (Sydney) 27 September 1896, p4.

"It was said at the time": Unnatural Vice, *Truth* (Perth, W.A.), 12 December 1903, p4.

"One law for the rich": The Convict Brand Of Justice, *The Bulletin,* 7 September 1895, p7. See also: Supreme Court – Civil Sittings: Wilson v. Faulkner, *The Western Australian*, 12 July 1895, pp2,6.

who had emigrated some years previously: Obituary: Rev T.H.Rust, *The Age* (Melbourne), 22 Aug 1935, p9.

his Australian wife: Ethel Dagmar Rust, Warringal Cemetery, Victoria, Australia: [https://www.findagrave.com/memorial/219428308/ethel-dagmar-rust]

Thomas Rust had begun: Obituary: Rev T.H.Rust, *The Age* (Melbourne), 22 Aug 1935, p9.

"Actors! I wouldn't give them": Edward Forrester Holden Sutton, *The Princess Au Revoir*,

(Unpublished manuscript), Sutton and Cunliffe-Owen Collection, C0487, Princeton University Library, p99.

"Masters (resident)": Tutors, Clerks, &c.", *The Argus* (Melbourne), 11 October 1906.

Algernon had obviously: Day, *Charles Thorold Gentleman Emigrant,* p125, p184.

was an *excellent* teacher: Day, *Charles Thorold Gentleman Emigrant,* p128, p185.

Charles also eliminated: Day, *Charles Thorold Gentleman Emigrant,* p120, p182.

"graces and benedictions": George William Erskine Russell, *One Look Back,* W. Gardner, Darton & Co, 1911, pp100-105.

The application: Day, *Charles Thorold Gentleman Emigrant,* p190 n116.

That area, mostly allotments: Reminiscences Of Early Southport, *The South Coast Bulletin,* 9 April 1947, pp13-18; Robert Longhurst, *75 Years Of Saving Lives,* Southport Surf Lifesaving Club, Main Beach 1999, pp2-3.

With endless white beaches: Southport High School, *The Brisbane Courier,* 10 Jan 1902, p4.

It was an almost immediate success: Orbilius: The Southport School, *The Brisbane Courier,* 22 October 1932, p19; Day p153.

It has been favoured: Southport High School, Speech Day, *The Brisbane Courier,* 12 December 1906, p2.

The atmosphere of pure boy: The Southport High School, *The Brisbane Courier,* 16 Dec 1905, p15.

"an infinite capacity for clothing": C.G. Pearce, The Right Reverend Horace Henry Dixon C.B.E., M.A. (CANTAB.), Th.D. (1869-1964), and the genesis of a public school, *Journal of the Royal Historical Society of Queensland,* Vol 10 Issue 1, 1976.

In December 1906: Day, *Charles Thorold Gentleman Emigrant,* p151; Shipping, *The Telegraph* (Brisbane), 7 December 1906, p8.

Upon his arrival: Southport Timetable, *The Week* (Brisbane), 12 January 1889, p26.

an unfamiliar landscape: H.M.Vaughan, *An Australasian Wander-Year,* Martin Secker, London 1914, p286.

However, there would have been little time: Information from John Day.

"Oh dammit! I've wasted the day": C.G. Pearce, The Right Reverend Horace Henry Dixon C.B.E., M.A. (CANTAB.), Th.D. (1869-1964), and the genesis of a public school, *Journal of the Royal Historical Society of Queensland,* Vol 10 Issue 1, 1976.

"at once attracted by": Day, *Charles Thorold Gentleman Emigrant,* pp154-156.

"no one could be for long in association": Day, *Charles Thorold Gentleman Emigrant,* p156.

"a perfectly groomed": Margaret Mason-Cox, *Character Unbound: A History Of The Hutchins School,* The Hutchins School, Hobart, 2013, p28.

However, some of the earthier: Day, *Charles Thorold Gentleman Emigrant,* p349.

upper class Oxford drawl: Day, *Charles Thorold Gentleman Emigrant,* p90.

"the slightest oddity": Jack Lindsay, *Life Rarely Tells,* Penguin, Melbourne, 1982, p225.

That such an apparent paragon: Information from John Day who was told it by a number of elderly pupils, and Cecil G. Pearce, Master of the Junior School (1931-36; 1941-50) and Head Master (1951-71).

From page 527 –

The nickname: C.G. Pearce, 'The Right Reverend Horace Henry Dixon C.B.E., M.A. (CANTAB.), Th.D. (1869-1964), and the genesis of a public school', *Journal of the Royal Historical Society of Queensland,* Vol 10 Issue 1, 1976.

"Mr. Thorold, besides being related": Southport High School, *The Brisbane Courier,* 12 Dec 1906.

"gather in undress on the banks": The Southport High School, *The Brisbane Courier,* 16 Dec 1905, p15.

"Now I've had my lazy": Service, Robert *The Spell Of The Yukon,* Dodd, Mead & Company, New York, 1907, pp81-82.

This was of a high literary: Day, 161-171; Orbilius: The Southport School, *The Brisbane Courier,* 22 October 1932, p19.

"bright and healthy vitality": Day, *Charles Thorold Gentleman Emigrant,* p175.

For Speech Day Charles went so far: Day, *Charles Thorold Gentleman Emigrant,* p158.

The money, plus a loan: Day, *Charles Thorold Gentleman Emigrant,* p196-197.

The Diocese had requested: Day, *Charles Thorold Gentleman Emigrant,* p159-162.

No doubt viewing Charles: Social, *The Brisbane Courier,* 3 Feb 1908, p7.

In October of that year: Le Beau Monde, *Darling Downs Gazette*, 7 Oct 1908, p8; Day 181.

Further to this, the McConnels: Information from Caitlan McConnel.

'Daphne', the indefatigable: L'Eternel Feminin, *Queensland Figaro*, 24 September 1903, p6.

In celebration of the engagement: Southport, *The Brisbane Courier*, 24 Nov 1908, p7.

The McConnels chartered a special train: Serious Accident, *Queensland Times, Ipswich Herald and General Advertiser*, 21 Dec 1908, p5.

She soon made a recovery: Social, *The Brisbane Courier*, 28 Dec 1908, p7.

Charles' visit to Cresswork in April: Our Neighbours, *The Queenslander*, 1 May 1909, p13.

That August Elspeth left: Social and Personal, *The Telegraph* (Brisbane), 18 August 1909, p8.

And in dramatic circumstances: Southport's 'Old Man Of The Sea', *The South Coast Express* (Surfers Paradise), 12 April 1950, p5.

This time the lad was another pupil: Southport School Archives.

a clerk manning the local post office: For Bravery, *Queensland Times* (Ipswich), 26 August 1910, p6.

"He [Jack] could see that it was touch and go": Eventful Life Of Mr. Jack Tuesley, Southport Identity, *The Telegraph* (Brisbane), 25 March 1940, p7.

the ceremony taking place: Southport's 'Old Man Of The Sea', *The South Coast Express* (Surfers Paradise), 12 April 1950, p5.

The Retreat, a rented cottage: Houses, Land, Etc., *The Brisbane Courier*, 15 February 1904, p2.

The Retreat seemed suddenly to become: Party At Southport, *Queensland Figaro* (Brisbane),16 September 1909, p10.

A bachelor of arresting presence: Donaldson, St Clair George Alfred by Betty Crouchley, *Australian Dictionary of Biography, Vol 8*, Melbourne University Press, 1981.

"the Archbishop says he has known": Edward Herbert to Francis John Lys, 18 May 1919; A.C.C. Thorold file, Worcester College Archive, Oxford University.

"By his education and experience": Testimonial of St Clair Donaldson, 28 April 1910; A.C.C. Thorold file, Worcester College Archive, Oxford University.

Aside from Charles's work: Day, *Charles Thorold Gentleman Emigrant,* 194.

In his leisure time: History Tour, *Band of Brothers* (The Southport School magazine), Issue 18, December 2018, p67.

He also travelled: Day, *Charles Thorold Gentleman Emigrant,* p20, 112-113.

Although the city then: Rosamond Siemon, *The Mayne Inheritance*, Queensland University Press, Brisbane 2003, p146; Clive Moore, *Sunshine And Rainbows*, University of Queensland Press, Brisbane, 2001, p88.

aroused talk amongst them: Information from John Day, who learned of it from Cecil G. Pearce, a former Master and Headmaster of The Southport School who lived for gossip, and had heard it from predecessors.

"bohemian, somewhat improvident": Day, *Charles Thorold Gentleman Emigrant,* p163.

"Guilty of Gross": Guilty of Gross Indecency, *Truth* (Brisbane), 6 February 1910, p5.

"I did do so, in fact": Guilty of Gross Indecency, *Truth* (Brisbane), 6 February 1910, p5.

This all led to Hatton's: Guilty of Gross Indecency, *Truth* (Brisbane), 6 February 1910, p5.

"he could not understand": 'Handler' Hatton, *Truth* (Brisbane), 6 February 1910, p6.

"REV. ROBERT WESLEY": 'Rev' Robert Wesley Ballantine, *Truth* (Brisbane), 31 Jul 1910, p5.

"You will find a tip-top": 'Rev' Robert Wesley Ballantine, *Truth* (Brisbane), 31 Jul 1910, p5.

"Going on to speak": 'Rev' Robert Wesley Ballantine, *Truth* (Brisbane), 31 Jul 1910, p5; Methodist Missioner, *Truth* (Brisbane) 19 June 1910, p6; Findmypast.com: Victor Williamson Ulverston, 1894-1972.

Tall and very good-looking: Day *Charles Thorold Gentleman Emigrant*, p164.

a handsome and eligible groomsman: Scientifically Arranged Dairy Farm, *Goulburn Valley Stock and Property Journal*, 29 April 1925, p3.

The Reverend Rust was the marriage: Day, *Charles Thorold Gentleman Emigrant,* p149.

Kathleen had only arrived: Day, *Charles Thorold Gentleman Emigrant,* pp185, 373.

When she was just two: Shipping: Arrived: March 10, *The Australasian* (Melbourne), 12 March 1887, p31.

"Mr. F. Jeffery": Great Britain: Lancashire; Exhibition Supplement, *The Argus* (Melbourne), 16 October 1888.

Two years later, Frederick: Deaths, The Argus (Melbourne), 23 December 1890, p1; Grave of Frederick Jeffery, Melbourne General Cemetery, Church of England, Section M, Grave 742; Death Certificate: No2579, Registered 1891; Frederik Jeffery: Probate and Administration Files, VPRS

28/PO unit 621, item 49/112, Public Record Office Victoria.
Two years later, Ada: Probate: Jeffery, Ada Jane; 1916 :probatesearch.service.gov.uk.
From 1908 to 1912: Day, *Charles Thorold Gentleman Emigrant*, p185.
In fact, the date: Day, *Charles Thorold Gentleman Emigrant*, p198.
Yet even then the prognosis: O.R. McCarthy, The key to the sanatoria, *Journal Of The Royal Society Of Medicine*, Vol 94(8), August 2001, pp413–7.
He had originally intended: Day, *Charles Thorold Gentleman Emigrant*, p198.
"capable and energetic": Day, *Charles Thorold Gentleman Emigrant*, p232.
"the land lies on the town side": Restraining Order, *The Telegraph* (Brisbane), 6 March 1913, p4.
"very lucky to have settled": In Civil Jurisdiction, *The Brisbane Courier*, 13 March 1913, p4.
Charles was visited by his younger brother: Social, *The Brisbane Courier*, 31 May 1910, p7.
Wise, scholarly, and very handsome: Thorold, Ernest – Spent most of his life as Army chaplain, Grantham Matters: granthammatters.co.uk
but a man of heavy silences: Served Western Command, *Chester Chronicle*, 17 February 1940, p8.
The combination of maladies: Day, *Charles Thorold Gentleman Emigrant*, p198.

From page 541 –

In 1916, their second son: Day, *Charles Thorold Gentleman Emigrant*, p299.
"That's straight; I mean it.": Hull Breach Of Promise, *The Daily Mail (Hull Packet And East Yorkshire And Lincolnshire Courier)*, 11 July 1914, p6.
She had also gifted him a hand-worked: P.C. To Pay £40, *Liverpool Echo*, 11 July 1914, p4.
"a man of honourable character": Hull Breach Of Promise, *The Daily Mail* (Hull), 11 July 1914, p6.
"if he married her he would": Hull Breach Of Promise, *The Daily Mail* (Hull), 11 July 1914, p6.
"most breach of promise actions": Policeman's Romance, *Daily Gazette for Middlesbrough*, 10 July 1914, p8.
"Those three years had passed": Hull Breach Of Promise, *The Daily Mail* (Hull), 11 July 1914, p6.
The following year, Benjamin Brumfield: England Marriages 1538-1973, FindMyPast.com; Lincolnshire Day by Day, *Lincolnshire Echo*, 07 April 1932, p4; Constabulary Promotions, *Lincolnshire Echo*, 28 January 1938, p6.
published a scandalous two-part profile: 'Luminous Leadbeater', *Truth* (Brisbane), 25 Jun 1916, p10; 2 Jul 1916, p9.
having decided its inhabitants: C.W. Leadbeater, *Australia And New Zealand As The Home Of A New Sub-Race*, Theosophical Society Of Australia, Sydney 1915, *passim*.
he advocated 'psychic orgasm': Gregory Tillett, *The Elder Brother: A Biography of Charles Webster Leadbeater*, Routledge, Abingdon 2016, pp190, 281-282.
"Glad sensation is so pleasant.": Tillett, *The Elder Brother*, p83.
attempts to drum him out: Teacher Of Filth, *John Bull*, 6 February 1909, p141.
in accord with other Uranians: Tillett, *The Elder Brother*, p282.
"Naked boys were seen": Theosophical Scandal, *Truth* (Sydney) 21 May 1922, p7.
The belief that the police dropped: Tillett, *The Elder Brother*, p200.
Administrator General of the Co-Masonic Order: Tillett, *The Elder Brother*, p168.
a fellow Theosophist, homosexual: Tillett, *The Elder Brother*, p189.
"Leadbeater rigs himself out": Theosophical Scandal, *Truth* (Sydney) 21 May 1922, p7.
"I came out to take up": Day, *Charles Thorold Gentleman Emigrant*, p147.
In their biographies: Day, *Charles Thorold Gentleman Emigrant*, p11.
"nearly two years on the Continent": Day, *Charles Thorold Gentleman Emigrant*, p120.
He was also able to include: Day, *Charles Thorold Gentleman Emigrant*, p158.
He'd also been Charles' guest: Our Neighbours, *The Queenslander* (Brisbane) 20 May 1911, p15.
"I felt it to be my duty": Day, *Charles Thorold Gentleman Emigrant*, p177.
In his application to Hutchins, Charles: Day, Charles Thorold *Gentleman Emigrant*, p198, n181.
"I knew A.C.C. Thorold well, and also know": Francis John Lys to Frederick Huth Jackson, 21 January 1918, A.C.C. Thorold alumni file, Worcester College Archive, Oxford University.
and once keen member of its: Oxford And The Drama, *Oxford Chronicle and Reading Gazette*, 14 July 1905, p7; Alan McKinnon, *The Oxford Amateurs: A Short History of Theatricals at the University*, Chapman And Hall, London 1910, p85.
Jackson also happened to be: Reform At Oxford, *The Pall Mall Gazette*, 2 August 1912, p7.
"I think myself that after so many years": Francis John Lys to Frederick Huth Jackson, 21 January

1918, A.C.C. Thorold alumni file, Worcester College Archive, Oxford University.

"I have only once seen A.C.C. Thorold": Edward Herbert to Francis John Lys, 4 February 1918, A.C.C. Thorold alumni file, Worcester College Archive, Oxford University

"One of my boys was at Balliol": Edward Herbert to Francis John Lys, 4 February 1918, A.C.C. Thorold alumni file, Worcester College Archive, Oxford University.

"I am going to spend tomorrow": Edward Herbert to Francis John Lys, 8 February 1918, A.C.C. Thorold alumni file, Worcester College Archive, Oxford University.

"We were to send you some of the original": Edward Herbert to Francis John Lys, 18 May 1919, A.C.C. Thorold alumni file, Worcester College Archive, Oxford University.

"I believe he knows the history": Edward Herbert to Francis Lys, 29 January 1918; A.C.C. Thorold alumni file, Worcester College, Oxford University.

"His character is beyond reproach": Testimonial of Horace H. Dixon, 24 May 1910, A.C.C. Thorold alumni ile, Worcester College Archive, Oxford University.

"Personally, I can only say how": Testimonial of Horace H. Dixon, 20 August 1917, A.C.C. Thorold alumni ile, Worcester College Archive, Oxford University.

"You may remember you kindly helped": Edward Herbert to Francis John Lys, 8 April 1929, A.C.C. Thorold alumni file, Worcester College Archive, Oxford University.

"He has been widely acclaimed": Mason-Cox, *Character Unbound*, p53.

one of the greatest in Australia's history: Day, *Charles Thorold Gentleman Emigrant*, p293.

It has been claimed that: Day, *Charles Thorold Gentleman Emigrant*, p293.

"high ideals and keen": Mason-Cox, *Character Unbound*, p53.

"a tall, well-built": Day, *Charles Thorold Gentleman Emigrant*, p208.

It did not need an announcement: Mason-Cox, *Character Unbound*, p27.

He had an 'aura': Day, *Charles Thorold Gentleman Emigrant*, p209.

In his inaugural address: Day, *Charles Thorold Gentleman Emigrant*, p210.

His absolute insistence: Day, *Charles Thorold Gentleman Emigrant*, p212.

As one Old Boy: Day, *Charles Thorold Gentleman Emigrant*, p211.

At his installation: Day, *Charles Thorold Gentleman Emigrant*, p212.

"the development of a great": Day, *Charles Thorold Gentleman Emigrant*, p213.

It was later said: Day, *Charles Thorold Gentleman Emigrant*, p231.

He also enhanced: Day, *Charles Thorold Gentleman Emigrant*, pp221-222.

Highly popular: Day, *Charles Thorold Gentleman Emigrant*, p225.

The scholastic results: Mason-Cox, *Character*, p51.

Not least, he introduced: Mason-Cox, *Character Unbound*, p56.

"My father met Thorold": Mason-Cox, *Character Unbound*, p60.

A family friend mailed: Information from Sir Oliver Thorold.

"One could not find a better definition": Jazzing Youth, *The News* (Hobart) 17 December 1925, p4.

"was not opposed to having a good": Jazzing Youth, *The News* (Hobart) 17 December 1925, p4.

"The trouble mainly is that": Habit Of Speech, *The Examiner* (Launceston), 11 December 1928, p7.

"We must recognise that last century's": Youth Of To-Day, *The Mercury* (Hobart), 14 December 1926, p6.

"Boys are the most wonderful": Youth Of To-Day, *The Mercury* (Hobart), 14 December 1926, p6.

whom Charles had met the previous December: Teachers' Conference, *The Mercury* (Hobart), 1 December 1925, p6.

Adamson had voiced the sentiments: Wesley College, *The Herald* (Melbourne), 12 December 1925, p10.

In 1932, Adamson restated them: L. A. Adamson: For The Class of 2004; https://web.archive.org/web/20210307002308/https://martynsmith.info/wesley/adamson.htm

"every boy was an honourable man": Felix Meyer (ed.), *Adamson Of Wesley : the story of a great headmaster*, Robertson and Mullens, Melbourne 1932, p15.

From page 551 —

"They adore him": People We Know, *Punch* (Melbourne), 8 July 1909, p6.

"drooped and died": Prattle About People, *Punch* (Melbourne), 8 July 1909, p6.

"accept full financial responsibility": Lawrence Arthur Adamson, *Australian Dictionary of Biography*, Vol VII, Melbourne University Press, 1979.

"songs, purple dressing gowns": Geoffrey Blainey, James Morrissey, S. E. K. Hulme, *Wesley College:*

The First Hundred Years, Wesley College & Robertson and Mullens, Melbourne 1967, p103.

Adamson also had favourites: Andrew Lemon, *A Great Australian School: Wesley College Examined*, Helicon Press, Wahroonga 2004, p202.

"I didn't know what it was about": Lemon, *A Great Australian School*, p207

"Queer card that Adamson": People We Know, *Punch* (Melbourne), 29 March 1917, p6.

"There is no more ideal type": People We Know, *Punch* (Melbourne), 8 July 1909, p6.

"He is barely tolerant of female": People We Know, *Punch* (Melbourne), 8 July 1909, p6.

"By his own account this was due": Meyer (ed.), *Adamson Of Wesley*, p35.

"He told me a queer thing about Adamson": 4 February 1886, Rev. R.C. Fillingham diary, pp111-112; Merton College Library.

perhaps Charles Thorold also learned of it: Generalised rumours of Adamson's past lingered at Wesley amongst teachers who'd been students under his headship even in the early 1970s. Former housemaster Martyn Smith email to author, April 2022.

On one occasion: Geoffrey Stephens, *The Hutchins School Macquarie Street Years 1846-1965*, Hobart:The Hutchins School, 1979, p243.

He established the practice: Mason-Cox, *Character Unbound*, p54.

"He was Robin Hood": Charles Higham, *Errol Flynn: The Untold Story*, Doubleday, New York, 1980, p13-17.

"May faith, deep rooted": Day, *Charles Thorold Gentleman Emigrant*, p41.

"a despotic bigot": Stephens, *The Hutchins School Macquarie Street Years 1846-1965*, pp243-244.

"Get a woman": Mason-Cox, *Character Unbound*, p95.

"In Tasmania I met": Interesting Reminiscences Of Grantham, *The Grantham Journal*, 9 July 1927, p6.

Reticence was a Thorold: Day, *Charles Thorold Gentleman Emigrant,* p240.

Charles further withdrew into himself.: Mason-Cox, *Character Unbound*, p60.

"The charm and urbanity": Stuart Braga, *Barker College: A History*, John Ferguson in association with the Council of Barker College, Sydney 1978, p188.

It involved another gentleman: New South Wales Police Gazette and Weekly Record of Crime, 14 February 1923 (Issue No.7) p 90.

and was also the twenty-eight-year-old schoolmaster son: Pennefather Elrick, Arthur Charles, Army Service Record, T8896, National Archives Of Australia.

"to thrust High Church teaching": Knocklofty: Church Controversy, *The Mercury* (Hobart), 20 July 1922, p10.

"the ritualistic practices": A.C. Pennefather: Confession, *The Mercury*, 27 July 1922, p2.

He was probably there as a tutor: Recruiting, *The Mercury*, 20 August 1918, p3.

"It seems to be of no use": Would Not Face Disgrace, *The Examiner* (Launceston), 21 February 1923, p5.; A Strange Letter, *The Observer* (Adelaide) 24 February 1923, p38 (The latter report incorporates a passage omitted from the former report.)

"I do not want any sensations": Would Not Face Disgrace, *The Examiner* (Launceston), 21 February 1923, p5.; A Strange Letter, *The Observer* (Adelaide) 24 February 1923, p38.

The one blessing was that: Personal, *The Argus* (Melbourne), 23 April 1919, p8.

"the nature of the offence had been much exaggerated": Sent To A Reformatory Prison, *The Mercury* (Hobart),12 May 1923, p8.

"several strongly worded testimonials": I Sent To A Reformatory Prison, *The Mercury* (Hobart),12 May 1923, p8.

"had a duty to perform": Sent To A Reformatory Prison, *The Mercury* (Hobart),12 May 1923, p8.

Considered "plain and ungainly": Day, *Charles Thorold Gentleman Emigrant,* pp308-9.

Despite her having been: Day, *Charles Thorold Gentleman Emigrant,* p238.

"very quiet wedding": Social Notes, *The Australasian* (Melbourne), 9 Jan 1926, p98.

They believed Charles: Day, *Charles Thorold Gentleman Emigrant,* p237-238.

Charles later wrote an essay: Day, *Charles Thorold Gentleman Emigrant,* p385.

"what a change!...Gone were the": The Wonderful Visit, *The Hutchins School Magazine*, December 1926, p7.

"there is one thing": The Wonderful Visit, *The Hutchins School Magazine*, December 1926, pp6-7.

Andersen had subsequently: Obituary, *The Brisbane Courier*, 21 July 1926, p6.

In 1927, Charles and a student teacher: Police Court News, *The Mercury*, 17 March 1927, p11; *The State Schools*, Advocate (Burnie), 25 July 1927, p6.

"His sensitive nature": Mason-Cox, *Character Unbound*, p60.

The Board encouraged: Mason-Cox, *Character Unbound,* p60.

"I later believed strongly": Mason-Cox, *Character Unbound,* p137.

"many very pleasant evenings": Soldiers' Children Education Board, *The Mercury* (Hobart), 17 May 1929, p12.

Barker was a smaller: Day, *Charles Thorold Gentleman Emigrant,* p243.

This arrangement displeased: Braga, *Barker College,* p191.

"a picture show with teaching attached": Braga, *Barker College,* p190.

"a total lack of discretion": Braga, *Barker College,* p191.

"an enormous rumpus": Day, *Charles Thorold Gentleman Emigrant,* p260.

"My wife's health": Day, *Charles Thorold Gentleman Emigrant,* p260.

Thorold's method of conveying: Day, *Charles Thorold Gentleman Emigrant,* p263.

Carter used his prestige: Day, *Charles Thorold Gentleman Emigrant,* p252.

"His vagueness became proverbial": Braga, *Barker College,* p199.

It was said he was uninterested: Braga, *Barker College,* p191.

"surrounded by a sea": Braga, *Barker College,* p199.

As the School's financial position: Braga, *Barker College,* p196.

It has been suggested: Braga, *Barker College,* p199.

For the School authorities the last straw: Day, *Charles Thorold Gentleman Emigrant,*p319, n238.

Jessie's indifferent health: Day, *Charles Thorold Gentleman Emigrant,* pp260-267.

"We had long since lost": Braga, *Barker College,* p198.

It was a surrender: Day, *Charles Thorold Gentleman Emigrant,* p268.

In exchange, the appointed: Day, *Charles Thorold Gentleman Emigrant,* p272.

"an ideal boarding school": James H. Rundle, *Against All Odds: a history of Mentone Grammar School*, Mentone Grammar School, Melbourne, 1991, p81.

"a breath of Spring": Rundle, *Against All Odds,* p115.

Once again, his sense of purpose: Rundle, *Against All Odds,* p83.

Even so, the financing: Day, *Charles Thorold Gentleman Emigrant,* p274.

"worked so hard, scrubbing": Day, *Charles Thorold Gentleman Emigrant,* p275,276.

"seemed to admire Mrs. C.C.": Day, *Charles Thorold Gentleman Emigrant,* p276.

"used to retire into his shell": Day, *Charles Thorold Gentleman Emigrant,* p277

"His smile was generally": Day, *Charles Thorold Gentleman Emigrant,* p298.

On these days: Rundle, *Against All Odds,* p115.

"a distinct change": Rundle, *Against All Odds,* p105.

"He seemed to cause": Day, *Charles Thorold,* 290.

"gave some boys": Rundle, *Against All Odds,* p115.

"he was a gorgeous": Janet McCalman, *Journeyings: The Biography of a Middle-Class Generation 1920-1990*, Melbourne University Press, 1993, p117.

"He made Latin": Rundle, *Against All Odds,* p89.

'The Scavenger': Henry Jones Thaddeus, *Recollections Of A Court Painter*, John Lane, The Bodley Head", London 1912, pp270-271.

Even worse, their parents: Day, *Charles Thorold Gentleman Emigrant,* p278-81.

Just three days after: Day, *Charles Thorold Gentleman Emigrant,* p288.

Like Cyril Flower: Will of Charles C. Thorold: VPRS 7591/P2 unit 1104, item 313/266, Public Record Office Victoria, Australia.

"a severe heart attack": Mr. C. C. Thorold, *The Age* (Melbourne) 18 Oct 1939, p12.

The following day: Mr. C. C. Thorold, *The Age* (Melbourne) 18 Oct 1939, p12.

On one side: Leo Gamble, The Rise and Fall of Mentone Pier, *City of Kingston Historical Website*: localhistory.kingston.vic.gov.au

And it was said that on the 16th: Information from John Day who learned it from an early archivist at Mentone Grammar.

and within the family, was one that lingered: Information from Ruth Dunn.

"The establishment of a Suicide Club": Worcester, *The Oxford Magazine*, 30 January 1895, p187.

Rather, it took place in the chapel: Mr. C. C. Thorold, *The Age* (Melbourne) 18 Oct 1939, p12.

At his death, Charles owed : Day, *Charles Thorold Gentleman Emigrant,* p327.

The following February his young: King's Chaplain, *Nottingham Evening Post*, 30 May 1940, p6.

"Let the school go": Rundle, *Against All Odds,* p100.

"By 1939, C.C. Thorold's": Rundle, *Against All Odds,* p166.

In 1960, his memory: Mason-Cox, *Character Unbound,* p84.

The year before Charles' death: Constabulary Promotions, *Lincolnshire Echo*, 28 January 1938, p6.
"he was strongly opposed to Continental": Continental Music, *Leeds Mercury*, 22 April 1936, p9.
Benjamin Brumfield died in 1965: England and Wales Death Index, FindMyPast.com
A goodly number of elderly Southportians: Information from John Day.
"Thorold kept his private": Day, *Charles Thorold Gentleman Emigrant*, p11.
Day's researches also revealed: Day, *Charles Thorold Gentleman Emigrant*, p15.
"Since I came to Grantham": Day, *Charles Thorold Gentleman Emigrant*, 181, n16.
 "sonorous, modulated tones": Much Like A Squarson, *The Spectator*, 21 March 1992.
This being that in a time: Information from Sir Oliver Thorold.
His principal concern: Information from John Day.
"I have heard it said": Rev. John Thorold to John Day, 13 October 1986; Day, *Charles Thorold Gentleman Emigrant*, p128.
"As the research developed": Day, *Charles Thorold Gentleman Emigrant*, p10.
In 1897, when a Grantham tradesman's: Breach Of Promise Of Marriage, *The Grantham Journal*, 13 November 1897, p3.
"no one will ever know": Day, *Charles Thorold Gentleman Emigrant*, p145.

18. A LAIRD MOST RICH AND POWERFUL

Bernard Fraser hailed: Alexander Mackenzie, *History of the Frasers of Lovat*, A. & W. Mackenzie, London 1896, p577-8.
Scotland's educational system: Thomas Alexander Lee, *Seekers of Truth: The Scottish Founders of Modern Public Accountancy*, Studies in the Development of Accounting Thought Volume 9., JAI Press, Elsevier, Oxford, UK, 2006, p4.
Much of the work: Michael Fry, *A New Race Of Men: Scotland 1815-1914*, Birlinn Ltd, Edinburgh 2013, Part 1: Economy, *passim.*
He was just twenty-five: The Late Mr John Fraser, *Edinburgh Evening News*, 2 February 1885, p2.
His wife was Susan Foulis: Alexander Mackenzie, *History of the Frasers of Lovat*, A. & W. Mackenzie, 1896, p577-8.
the Frasers eventually resided: 13 Moray Place, New Town: 1871 Census.
Born on the 27th of January: Ancestry.com
It was not only the grandest: *The Secret History of Our Streets: Moray Place Edinburgh Moray Feu*, BBC TV, 2014.
A homosexual bachelor: Private information from Susan Boag.
He was also a member: Arthur Charles Fox-Davies, *Armorial families: a directory of gentlemen of coat-armour 1871-1928*, Hurst And Blackett, London, 1905, p516.
"The view of Edinburgh": Queen Victoria, *Leaves from the Journal of Our Life in the Highlands, from 1841 to 1848*, Smith, Elder and Co, London, 1868, p8.
Bernard was sent to Leamington: UK Census 1881.
In January 1885: The Late Mr John Fraser, *Edinburgh Evening News*, 2 February 1885, p2.
John Fraser left a fortune: Wills and Bequests, *Belfast Newsletter*, 9 May 1885.
which at the very least: measuringworth.com
even as late as the 1960s: Wills and Testaments", National Records of Scotland: nrscotland.gov.uk/research/guides/wills-and-testaments
It was a huge legacy: John Fraser, 1885 (Wills And Testaments Regiment: SC70/1/239), National Records of Scotland.
It was the only time: 1891 Census: 685/1 7/8: 13 Moray Place, New Town, Edinburgh; National Records of Scotland.
For a year he'd been a partner: Comtesse (Rosalie Alexandrine) Isaure de Las Cases to daughter Napoléone de Las Cases, 7-8 March 1890; family archives, via Goulven de Kergariou; Dissolution De Société, *Le Tell : Journal Politique Et Des Interêts Coloniaux* (Blida), 18 March 1893, p4.
Joseph hailed from Brittany: Geneanet: Joseph de Kergariou
[https://gw.geneanet.org/hubertcottin?lang=en&n=de+kergariou&oc=0&p=joseph]
through his maternal grandmother: Geneanet: Sophie Tyrrell
[https://gw.geneanet.org/hubertcottin?lang=en&pz=hubert+regis&nz=cottin&p=sophie&n=tyrrell]; Private information from Hubert Cottin.
He regularly holidayed: Private information from Hubert Cottin. Two later visits he made to Alexander Charles Pirie were reported: The Rejoicings At Dunecht, *Aberdeen Press And Journal*, 31

August 1899, p6; Improvements At Dunecht, *Aberdeen Press and Journal*, 4 July 1900, p5.
Both were keen hunters: Private information from Hubert Cottin and Goulven de Kergariou.
Photographs of Joseph: Joseph de Kergariou: Geneanet.org
[https://gw.geneanet.org/hubertcottin?lang=en&n=de+kergariou&oc=0&p=joseph]; and Hubert
Cottin collection.
In 1890 he'd sold his farms in Brittany: Comtesse (Rosalie Alexandrine) Isaure de Las Cases to
Napoléone de Las Cases, 7-8 March 1890: family archives, via Goulven de Kergariou.
"In January we will change our residence": Vicomte Joseph de Kergariou to Comtesse (Rosalie
Alexandrine) Isaure de Las Cases, quoted by her in a letter to daughter Napoléone de Las Cases, 27
September 1890: family archives, via Goulven de Kergariou.
However, Bernard gave his share of the assets: Dissolution De Société, *Le Tell : Journal Politique Et
Des Interêts Coloniaux* (Blida), 18 March 1893, p4.
That year, Bernard spent time: Passenger Lists Leaving UK 1890-1960: FindMyPast.com.
'A New Sport For Perthshire': A New Sport For Perthshire Gentlemen, *The Dundee Courier And
Argus*, 23 December 1895, p4.
Tall and slim, with dark brown: Bernard Fraser C504 Parkhurst, p393; Metropolitan Police: Criminal
Record Office, *Habitual Criminal Registers and Miscellaneous Papers*, MEPO6/019/00457, National
Archives UK; family photos of Susan Boag.
such as the Park Lane party: Wagner Tableaux At The Countess Lützows, *The Pall Mall Gazette*, 24
June 1889, p6.
"Mr Bernard Fraser has left": Court And Society, *The Sunday Times*, 31 March 1901, p2.
The 1901 census reveals she: 1901 Census: RG 13/84; Administrative County: London, Page 29.
"there is an indefinable": Anon, *Round London*, George Newnes Ltd, 1896, p42.
a 'swell': Anonymous, *Slang and Its Analogues Past and Present*, John S Farmer & WE Henley,
London, 1909.
He was a member: Britain Bows In Shame, *Chicago Tribune*, 9 November 1902, p2.
His social profile was such that: *Boyle's Fashionable Court & Guide, and Town Visiting Directory
1903*, London, Court Guide Office, 1903, p60.
"take place quietly": Untitled Item, *The Morning Post*, 7 January 1901, p5.
"Owing to the illness of the bridegroom": Notices, *The Morning Post*, 25 January 1901, p4.
later that year the lady would marry: Margaret Ellen Barrow and George Larkins, Marriages
Registered July-September 1901; Emily Margaret Barrow (mother), bequest to Margaret Ellen
Larkins: 1909, Probate UK.
her father dying soon after: Robert Philipson Barrow, 1901: Probate UK.
He would go on to seek adventure: Private information from Hubert Cottin and Goulven de
Kergariou.
In March 1902 he attended a levée: The King's Levee, *The Times*, 7 March 1902, pp9-10.
Only days before: Eightsome Reels in London, *The Evening Telegraph* (Dundee), 9 July 1902.
Following his sentencing: Home Office: Registered Papers Supplementary, HO 144/710/108656,
National Archives, UK.
His request was granted: Home Office: Registered Papers Supplementary, HO 144/710/108656,
Petition 108656, National Archives UK.
After 1903, Bernard was transferred: Bernard Fraser C504, p393; Metropolitan Police: Criminal
Record Office, Habitual Criminal Registers and Miscellaneous Papers, MEPO6/019/00457, National
Archives UK.

From page 579 –

"The chain of Destiny": The Gates Of Doom: V, *Buchan Observer and East Aberdeenshire Advertiser*,
17 March 1903, p3.
The prominent Anglican churchman: William Grantham to Home Secretary, 11 April 1907; Home
Office: Registered Papers Supplementary, HO 144/710/108656, National Archives UK.
"flaunting her skirts": Patricia Marks, *Sarah Bernhardt's First American Theatrical Tour, 1880-1881*,
McFarland, Jefferson, N.C., 2003. p137.
"intensely religious": E.T. Raymond, *Portraits Of The Nineties*, T Fisher Unwin, London 1921, p281.
"The Prison report as to the": Home Office: Registered Papers Supplementary, HO
144/710/108656, National Archives UK.
"a marked growth in compassion": The Crank, The Criminal And The Increase Of Crime, *The*

Graphic, 11 February 1911; H.B. Simpson, 'Crime And Punishment': *Contemporary Review*, July 1896.

"It is a great pity": Home Office: Registered Papers Supplementary, HO 144/710/108656, National Archives UK.

"given very careful consideration": Home Office: Registered Papers Supplementary, HO 144/710/108656, National Archives UK.

"Dear Home Secretary": Home Office: Registered Papers Supplementary, HO 144/710/108656, National Archives UK.

"I agree with the general principle": Home Office: Registered Papers Supplementary, HO 144/710/108656, National Archives UK.

"The Judge's letter": Home Office: Registered Papers Supplementary, HO 144/710/108656, National Archives UK.

As suggested by Gladstone's: Bernard Fraser C504 Parkhurst, p393; Metropolitan Police: Criminal Record Office, Habitual Criminal Registers and Miscellaneous Papers, MEPO6/019/00457, National Archives UK.

It notes this as his temporary: 14 Chester Street, London: Census of England & Wales 1911.

He also sometimes used: Will of Fraser-Ross, John Bernard.

Undoubtedly unsettled: Passenger Lists Leaving The UK 1890-1960, FindMyPast.com.

Of all places: Will of Fraser-Ross, John Bernard.

Here they were permitted: Matthew Stibbe (ed.) *Captivity, Forced Labour and Forced Migration in Europe During the First World War*, Routledge 2009, Oxon, pp57-60.

Bernard was initially interned: Foreign Office files: 1915, British Prisoners: FO 383/3; National Archives UK.

"We were exploited": Stibbe (ed.) *Captivity, Forced Labour and Forced Migration in Europe During the First World War*, pp57-60.

The conditions of their internment: Stibbe (ed.) *Captivity, Forced Labour and Forced Migration in Europe During the First World War*,, p22.

In 1915, Edmund submitted a request: Foreign Office files: 1915, British Prisoners: FO 383/3; National Archives UK.

Prisoners who were fortunate: Stibbe, pp57-60.

The following year, still in Baden: Foreign Office files: 1916, British Prisoners: FO 383/113; National Archives UK.

Bernard was merely a confinee: Foreign Office files: 1916, British Prisoners: FO 383/113; National Archives UK.

This time the suggested trade: Foreign Office files: 1916, British Prisoners: FO 383/113; National Archives UK.

"Dear Newton": Foreign Office files: 1917, British Prisoners: FO 383/249; National Archives UK.

"I believe it must be on account": Foreign Office files: 1917, British Prisoners: FO 383/249; National Archives UK.

"Kautzen is not an internment": Foreign Office files: 1917, British Prisoners: FO 383/249; National Archives UK.

"it is hoped that an agreement": Foreign Office files: 1917, British Prisoners: FO 383/249; National Archives UK.

"I am still a prisoner of War": Foreign Office files: 1917, British Prisoners: FO 383/249; National Archives UK.

"I would remind you": Foreign Office files: 1917, British Prisoners: FO 383/249; National Archives UK.

"It is annoying": Foreign Office files: 1917, British Prisoners: FO 383/249; National Archives UK.

"the Austrian government": Foreign Office files: 1917, British Prisoners: FO 383/249; National Archives UK.

"a disagreeable brat": Foreign Office files: 1917, British Prisoners: FO 383/249; National Archives UK. (On Lord Newton's trying manners, see: Isherwood, Christopher *Kathleen and Frank*, Vintage Books, 2013, p267-268.)

"Lord Newton does not": Foreign Office files: 1917, British Prisoners: FO 383/249; National Archives UK.

In addition to Murray's handbook: Lieut-Colonel R.L Playfair, *The Scourge of Christendom: Annals of British relations with Algiers prior to the French Conquest.*, Smith, Elder, & Co., London 1884, p5.

"languid, nonchalant, with a certain latent": Ouida *Under Two Flags*, Chapman And Hall (London, 1867), Vol1, pp3-4,296.

"Algiers is not only a healthy resort": *Cook's Practical Guide to Algeria and Tunisia*, Thomas Cook & Son Ltd, London 1908, p75.

"inherently stupid": Ian Gibson, *The Erotomaniac*, Faber, London 2001, p96, p111.

"The very considerable English colony": News From Abroad, *The Grantham Journal*, 22 April 1905, p3.

Other distinguished visitors: Our Ladies Letter, *Dundee Evening Telegraph*, 30 December 1907, p6.

"It consists of a number": Alfred S. Gubb, A Winter In Algiers, *Manchester Courier and Lancashire General Advertiser*, 28 January 1905.

"a kind of balloon-gondola": Alice Kaplan, *Looking for The Stranger: Albert Camus and the Life of a Literary Classic*, University of Chicago Press, 2016, pp23-24.

"half-a-dozen races": Alfred S. Gubb, A Winter In Algiers, *Manchester Courier and Lancashire General Advertiser*, 28 January 1905.

"the air for miles round": Lieut.-Col. R.L. Playfair, *Handbook for Travellers in Algeria and Tunis*, 2nd Edition, John Murray, London 1878, p169.

for the purposes of a studio: Private information from source 'G.'

a five bedroom house with stable: Expropriation: Iguerbouchen, *L'Echo d'Algier*, 10 October 1939.

Here Bernard befriended Belotte: Will of John Bernard Fraser-Ross, ProbateSearch, UK.

a dim view of most: An Arab Protégé, *The Sunday Times,* 25 May 1930, p17.

"The English afternoon tea": Frederick Arthur Bridgeman, *Winters In Algeria*, Harper & Brothers, New York 1890, p13.

"Ælgeria! Sweet creation": Lord Byron, *Childe Harolde's Pilgrimage*, John Murray, London, 1814, Stanza CXV.

"These primitive beings": Hubertine Auclert, Jacqueline Grenez Brovender, (trans.*) Arab Women in Algeria*, De Gruyter 2014, p18.

"bounded westwards by the Northern": Richard F. Burton (trans.), *The Book Of The Thousand Nights And A Night*, Vol X, Terminal Essay Part IV/D, Burton Club, London 1885.

From page 599 –

"There [in Africa] we were all": Jeffrey Merrick, Michael Sibalis (eds.) *Homosexuality in French History and Culture*, Haworth Press, Philadelphia, 2012, p208.

"The beggars here have profiles": Oscar Wilde; Rupert Hart-Davis, Merlin Holland (eds.) *The Complete Letters Of Oscar Wilde*, Fourth Estate, London 2000, p629.

By the time Wilde: Robert Aldrich, *Colonialism and Homosexuality*, Routledge, London 2002, p338.

"I have sat in the blazing sunshine": Stephanie Newell, *The Forger's Tale: The Search for Odeziaku*, Ohio University Press, Athens, OH 2006, p77.

"the most dangerous product": Alan Sheridan, *André Gide: A Life in the Present*, Harvard University Press, Harvard, 1999, p116.

"in the half-open doorway": André Gide; Dorothy Bussy (trans.) *If It Die*, Vintage, New York, 2011, p203-6.

"The disconsolate are beginning": Michael Anesko, *Monopolizing The Master: Henry James And The Politics Of Modern Literary Scholarship*, Stanford University Press, 2012, pp85-86.

"The contents of the smaller": Susan Foulis Fraser, 1925 (Wills and testaments Regiments: SC70/4/588, SC70/1/730), National Records of Scotland.

"It would be difficult to sketch": André Sarrouy, La Magnifique Vocation De G. Iguerbouchen, *L'Afrique du Nord Illustrée*, 14 February 1931, p6.

Together with another interview conducted in the 1950s: Kamel Bendisari, 'Kabylie Foklore: Sur Deux Nots Mohamed Iguerbouchen Compositeur De Plus de 200 Mélodies Kabyles': unidentified newspaper clipping, circa 1950s, Archives of SACEM (Société des Auteurs, Compositeurs et Éditeurs de Musique): https://musee.sacem.fr

"When I write music": André Sarrouy, La Magnifique Vocation De G. Iguerbouchen, *L'Afrique du Nord Illustrée*, 14 February 1931, p6.

"Evoking his name": Hamid Tahri, Mohamed Iguerbouchen (Ariste, scénariste, musicologue universaliste) : Le berger des Aghribs devenu maestro, *El Watan*, 16 October 2008.

In modern Algeria, rumour: John Pierre Entelis, *Culture and Counterculture in Moroccan Politics*, University Press of American 1996, p32.

"The life of Iguerbouchen": Hamid Tahri, "Le berger des Aghribs devenu maestro", *El Watan*, 16 October 2008.

"The day I was born": Le Cinema, *L'Afrique du Nord Illustrée*, 1 December 1937, p18.

The modest Iguerbouchène family: Mouloud Ounnoughene, *Mohamed Iguerbouchène: Un Oeuvre Intemporelle*, Dar Khettab, Algiers, 2015, p53.

Under the French colonial: *Algeria: A Country Study*, American University, Foreign Area Studies, 1994, p88.

"In almost all their essential characteristics": Sir Robert Lambert Playfair, *Handbook for Travellers in Algeria and Tunis*, John Murray, London 1890, p8.

"to closely know this beautiful": André Sarrouy, La Magnifique Vocation De G. Iguerbouchen, *L'Afrique du Nord Illustrée*, 14 February 1931, p6.

Algiers had a thriving: L'Humanitaire, *La Pensée Libre*, Algiers, 2 April 1905.

"the most beautiful dream": Le Cinema, *L'Afrique du Nord Illustrée*, 1 December 1937, p18.

"Mr. Ross was a Scottish seigneur": Le Cinema, *L'Afrique du Nord Illustrée*, 1 December 1937, p18.

like Chinese Whispers, Bernard metamorphosed: e.g. Abdellali Merdaci, Auteurs algériens de langue française de la période coloniale: Dictionnaire Biographique, *L'Harmattan*, 2010, Paris, pp146-147; Karim Kherbouche, Mohamed Iguerbouchen : une légende, une œuvre aux racines multiples, *Kabyle.com*, 21 October 2005; Bari Stambouli, Des lapins dans le bureau du compositeur, *Le Temps d'Algeria*, Algiers, 22 November 2009; Mohamed Iguerbouchen, Un Musicologue Universaliste, *Le Courrier d'Algérie,* 20 Novembre 2009. Given that few aristocracies are so rigorously documented as that of Britain, such nonsense could have been nipped in the bud with a mere glance at Debrett or Burke.

"Count Roth...was a rich and noble": Hamid Tahri, Mohamed Iguerbouchen (Ariste, scénariste, musicologue universaliste) : Le berger des Aghribs devenu maestro, *El Watan*, 16 October 2008.

"He noticed me": Le Cinema, *L'Afrique du Nord Illustrée*, 1 December 1937, p18.

Another account has it: Mohamed Iguerbouchen, Un Musicologue Universaliste, *Le Courrier d'Algérie*, 20 November 2009.

"A great lover of music": Le Cinema, *L'Afrique du Nord Illustrée*, 1 December 1937, p18.

"One day – I had just reached": André Sarrouy, La Magnifique Vocation De G. Iguerbouchen, *L'Afrique du Nord illustrée*, 14 February 1931, p6.

other Algerian accounts: Mohamed Iguerbouchen, Un Musicologue Universaliste, *Le Courrier d'Algérie*, 20 November 2009; *Association Culturelle Mohand Iguerbouchene*, Facebook, 17 September 2015.

a family memory remains: Private information from source 'G'.

From page 606 –

"Tough and cheerful": Tony Duvert, *Diary Of An Innocent*, Semiotext(e), Los Angeles, 2010, p231-2.

"it was there my sex education": Viscount Churchill, *All My Sins Remembered*, Heinemann, London 1964, p63.

"The history of Mohamed-Georges Iguerbouchen": A.S., 'L'Algérie Se Distingue', *L'Echo D'Alger*, 13 July 1951, p3

"physical intimacies are": George Moore, *Sister Teresa*, T. Fisher Unwin, 1901, p36.

"Sweet trance will wake": E.E. Bradford, *Passing the Love of Women; and Other Poems*, Kegan Paul, London 1913, p19.

The 1921 Census only records: 1921 Census, GBC_1921_RO12_00459_0767: FindMyPast.com

The *Royal Blue Book*: Royal Blue Book: Fashionable Directory and Parliamentary Guide (B W Gardiner & Son, London, 1920-30.

"I then went to Norton College": André Sarrouy, *La Magnifique Vocation De G. Iguerbouchen*, L'Afrique du Nord illustrée, 14 February 1931, p6.

While many schools of the time: Donald Leinster-Mackay, Old School Ties: some nineteenth and early twentieth century links between public and preparatory schools, *British Journal of Educational Studies*, XXXII, No1, 1984, pp78-79.

"a very pronounced accent": André Sarrouy, La Magnifique Vocation De G. Iguerbouchen, *L'Afrique du Nord Illustrée*, 14 February 1931, p6.

The bachelor Alfred Livingstone Hirst: John Henderson, *A Directory of Composers for the Organ*, J. Henderson, 2005; Maggie Humphreys, Robert Evans, *Dictionary of Composers for the Church in Great Britain and Ireland*, Mansell Publishing, London, 1997, p164; Census of England and Wales, 1911: 316 Richmond Road, East Twickenham. Hirst's occupations are listed in the Census as "Organist, pianist, vocalist, teacher of music".

A heavily moustachioed: Portraits Of The Year II, *The Surrey Comet*, 22 December 1909, p26.

he was a freemason: Freemasonry, *The Daily Telegraph* (London), 2 June 1911, p21.

considerable means: Census of England And Wales, 1911: 316 Richmond Road, East Twickenham.

He travelled extensively: John Henderson, *A Directory of Composers for the Organ*, J. Henderson, 2005; UK, Outward Passenger Lists, 1890-1960, Ancestry.com.

resided at premium addresses: *Musical News*, Vol 13, 1897, p563.

During the First World War: Ministry of Health files, MH 47/51/7, Case Number: M5611. Alfred Livingston Hirst, National Archives UK.

Famous he may not: e.g. *Musical News & Herald*, Volume 30, 1906, pp215, 263, 325.

"Mr A. Livingstone Hirst sang": *The Musical Times*, Musical Times Publications, December 1905, p772.

"This composer does not": New Music, *The Daily Telegraph* (London), 17 October 1899.

"some attractive ideas imperfectly": *Musical News and Herald*, Volumes 64-65, 1923, p318.

"delightfully barbaric flavour": *Musical News*, Volume 34, 1908, p562.

"The somewhat unusual chords": New Music, *Western Morning News* (Devon), 12 March 1923.

"a Jewish Dr Johnson": James Agate, *A Shorter Ego: The Autobiography of James Agate*, Vol 1, Readers Union, London 1946, p65.

"I left London after a stay": André Sarrouy, La Magnifique Vocation De G. Iguerbouchen, *L'Afrique du Nord Illustrée*, 14 February 1931, p6.

"I continued my studies of harmony": Kamel Bendisari, 'Kabylie Foklore: Sur Deux Nots Mohamed Iguerbouchen Compositeur De Plus de 200 Mélodies Kabyles': unidentified newspaper clipping, circa 1950s, Archives of SACEM (Société des Auteurs, Compositeurs et Éditeurs de Musique): https://musee.sacem.fr

Sarrouy was told the same: Le Cinema, *L'Afrique du Nord Illustrée*, 1 December 1937, p18.

"studying the great German Classics": Le Cinema, *L'Afrique du Nord Illustrée*, 1 December 1937, p18.

"At the age of 19": André Sarrouy, La Magnifique Vocation De G. Iguerbouchen, *L'Afrique du Nord illustrée*, 14 February 1931, p6.

As the story goes: Facebook post: 23 September 2015, *Association Culturelle Mohand Iguerbouchene*; Ounnoughene, p58; Mohamed Iguerbouchen, Un Musicologue Unisersaliste, *Le Courrier d'Algérie*, 20 novembre 2009 ; Arezki Ibersiene, Concours de musique classique Mohamed Iguerbouchene, *Liberte*, Algiers, 14 November 2011.

"advancing to the last villages": Aus Vorarlberg, *Vorarlberger Tagblatt*, 13 June 1925, p4.

In 1928, at the age of twenty-one: Bari Stambouli, Des Lapins Dans Le Bureau Du Compositeur, *Le Temps d'Algeria*, Algiers, 22 November 2009.

While there, he was commissioned: Une intelligente propagande en faveur de l'Algérie, *L'Echo d'Alger : journal républicain du matin*, 24 December 1937; Matthew Bernstein, Gaylyn Studlar (eds.) *Visions of the East: Orientalism in Film*, I.B. Tauris & Co. Ltd, London, 1997, p227 n12.

In the same street in Algiers: Will of John Bernard Fraser-Ross: ProbateSearch, UK.

He stayed on, and was commissioned: André Sarrouy, 'La Magnifique vocation of G. Iguerbouchen', *L'Afrique Du Nord Illustree*, 14 February 1931, p6; A.S. 'Ombres Sur Sur Le Riff', *L'Afrique Du Nord Illustree*, 14 October 1933, pp28-29; La Leçon de Dzaïr, *L'Afrique Du Nord Illustrée*, 7 December 1935, p26; Le Cinema, *L'Afrique Du Nord Illustree*, 20 February 1937, p13; Le Cinema, *L'Afrique Du Nord Illustree*, 20 December 1937, p18.

"so beautifully evokes the best canvases": André Sarrouy, Un Berbère En Espagne, *L'Afrique du Nord Illustrée*, 3 March 1934, p3.

Less serene was Iguerbouchène's relationship: Petit Announces Classées: Avis Divers, *La Dépêche Algérienne*, 19 September 1928, p4.

Northlands House in Southampton: Will of John Bernard Fraser-Ross: ProbateSearch, UK. Northlands House was demolished in 2004 and replaced by an aged care facility of the same name. See: M.P. Smith, A.D. Russel, Nortlands House 1882-2004: The Last Country House In Southampton, *Proceedings of the Hampshire Field Club Archaeological Society 59*,2004, pp210-218, in Hampshire Studies 2004.

Bernard was buried: gravestonephotos.com

in an edition of 50 copies: Michael Kaylor (ed.), *The Collected Works & Commissioned Biography of Edward Perry Warren*, Vol I, Masaryk University Press, Brno 2013, pcxviii.

"There is now no heaven": Arthur Lyon Raile (Edward Perry Warren), *A Defence of Uranian Love*, Vol3, Privately Printed, London 1928, p79.

equivalent to well over: measuringworth.com

"To Mohamed Ben Saïd Iquerbouchen": Will of John Bernard Fraser-Ross: ProbateSearch, UK.

Edmund would live on: Mr Edmund Fraser, *The Scotsman*, 24 July 1937, p13.

His estate amounted to a very significant: Alexander Edmund Fraser, 1938, probatesearch.service.gov.uk.

Bernard also made two small bequests: Will of John Bernard Fraser-Ross: ProbateSearch, UK.

Joseph had married during the War: Geneanet: Joseph Charles Marie Tugdual de Kergariou, Henriette Marie Lainé Darvel [https://gw.geneanet.org]

"An Arab Protégé": An Arab Protégé, *The Sunday Times*, 25 May 1930, p17.

"Stranger than the vagaries": Lady Drummond-Hay Writes On World Affairs, *The Sphere*, 8 November 1930, p266 (p24).

"experienced immense grief": A.S., 'L'Algérie Se Distingue', *L'Echo D'Algier*, 13 July 1951, p3.

his bride Louise Gomez: Report: Iguerbouchen, Mohamed; Direction Générale de la Sûreté Nationale, 20 May 1946: 20100166/3: dossier n° 9091, Archives Nationales, Pierrefitte-sur-Seine; Mohamed Iguerbouchen dossier: n° 77W1751-104355: Les Archives De La Préfecture De Police, Paris.

"at that time, where we met": J. Berger-Buchy, "Paris-Paris: Iguerbouchen", *L'Union Français* (Lyon), 2 August 1944, p3.

The result was musical compositions: Karim Kherbouche, Mohamed Iguerbouchen : une légende, une œuvre aux racines multiples, *Kabyle.com*, (Lyon, France), 21 October 2005.

He now called himself: André Sarrouy, La Magnifique Vocation De G. Iguerbouchen, *L'Afrique du Nord Illustrée*, 14 February 1931, p6.

was worth more than seven times: Report: Iguerbouchen, Mohamed; Direction Générale de la Sûreté Nationale, 20 May 1946: 20100166/3: dossier n° 9091, Archives Nationales, Pierrefitte-sur-Seine.

Twice in the 1930s the property: Expropriation, L'Echo d'Alger, 9 June 1935; Expropriation: Iguerbouchen, *L'Echo d'Algier*, 10 October 1939.

A French police intelligence report: Report: Iguerbouchen, Mohamed; Direction Générale de la Sûreté Nationale, 20 May 1946: 20100166/3: dossier n° 9091, Archives Nationales, Pierrefitte-sur-Seine.

From page 619 –

"the boy with a giant's voice": Hisham Aidi, *Rebel Music: Race, Empire, and the New Muslim Youth Culture*, Pantheon, New York, 2014, pp263, 322.

Iguerbouchène composed many songs: Ethan B. Katz, *The Burdens of Brotherhood: Jews and Muslims from North African to France*, Harvard University Press, Harvard, 2015, p77; Ofer Aderet, The Great Mosque of Paris That Saved Jews During the Holocaust, *Haaretz*, Tel Aviv, 23 March 2012.

"During the concert": T.S.F., *L'Echo d'Alger : journal républicain du matin*, 23 May 1936.

"It is certainly due to him": Paul Bowles, On The Film Front, *Modern Music: A Quarterly Review*, Volumes 17-18, 1939, p195.

he was credited as: Roy Armes, *African Filmmaking: North and South of the Sahara*, Indiana University Press, 2006, p23-24.

In March he made his performing début: Mahieddine Bachetarzi, *Memoires 1919-1939*, Editions Nationales Algériennes, 1968, p95.

"all the characters are men": Sud au Théâtre de l'Étoile, *Le Journal* (Paris), 4 March 1939.

Even more significantly: *Radio Times*, Issue 818, 2 June 1939, p62: via genome.ch.bbc.co.uk.

"an opportunity to present myself": Iguerbouchène to BBC, Undated letter; BBC to Iguerbouchène, Letter 22 August 1938; BBC memo, G. Willoughby, 31 August 1939; BBC Director of Music to Iguerbouchène, Letters 1 March 1939, 1 May 1939, 30 June 1939: Iguerbouchène file, BBC Archives.

It has been said that some BBC: Faten Hayed, Mouloud Ounnoughène: Neurochirurgien et auteur du livre Mohamed Iguerbouchène, une œuvre intemporelle, *El Watan*, Algiers, 21 July 2015.

"this beautiful and generous French": André Sarrouy, La Magnifique Vocation De G. Iguerbouchen, *L'Afrique du Nord Illustrée*, 14 February 1931, p6.

Before long he was authoring anti-French songs: Paul Dominique Crevaux, *Yves Chataigneau, Fossoyeur Général de l'Algérie*, Éditions Nationales, Algiers, 1948, p66.

It may have been a series of articles: Martin Evans, John Phillips, *Algeria: Anger of the Dispossessed*, Yale University Press, New Haven, 2007, pp37-40.

The succession of riots: Katz, *The Burdens of Brotherhood*, p89.

Some PPA members saw collaboration: Rabah Aissaoui, *African Political Movements in Post-Colonial France*, Tauris Academic Studies (London, 2009), pp125-6.

The sentiment was very much: Katz, *The Burdens of Brotherhood*, p127.

Such rectitude earned him: Katz, *The Burdens of Brotherhood*, p145.

Risking their own lives: Katz, *The Burdens of Brotherhood*, p122.

In fact, so enthused: Mohamed Iguerbouchen dossier: n° 77W1751-104355: Les Archives De La Préfecture De Police, Paris.

"What adolescent of my generation": Ronald Rosbottom, *When Paris Went Dark: The City of Light Under German Occupation, 1940-44*, Back Bay Books, 2015, p146.

A Tunisian, Yassine: Badra Lahouel, Germany's Psychological War Against France (1939-1945), *Revue Français d'Histoire d'Outre-Mers*, 306, Paris 1995, p67.

By late 1939 he was already: *Revue d'Histoire de la Deuxième Guerre Mondiale*, Volumes 28-29, Presses Universitaires de France, 1978, p112.

When the German troops marched: Daniel Brückenhaus, *Policing Transnational Protest: Liberal Imperialism and the Surveillance of Anticolonists in Europe*, Oxford University Press, 2017, p198.

"active propaganda…both in Paris": Mohamed Iguerbouchen dossier: n° 77W1751-104355: Les Archives De La Préfecture De Police, Paris.

German soldiers at his home: Report: Iguerbouchen, Mohamed; Direction Générale de la Sûreté Nationale, 20 May 1946: 20100166/3: dossier n° 9091, Archives Nationales, Pierrefitte-sur-Seine.

Yassine recruited Iguerbouchène to manage: Jacques Cantier, *Algérie Sous Le Régime de Vichy*, Odile Jacob, Paris, 2002, p114.

Iguerbouchène also participated in various: Mohamed Iguerbouchen dossier: n° 77W1751-104355: Les Archives De La Préfecture De Police, Paris.

and was reported to have engaged in surveillance: Katz, *The Burdens of Brotherhood*, p127.

"for fear, it seems, of later reprisals": Mohamed Iguerbouchen dossier: n° 77W1751-104355: Les Archives De La Préfecture De Police, Paris.

The Germans paid their puppets well: Badra Lahouel, 'Germany's Psychological War Against France (1939-1945)', *Revue Français d'Histoire d'Outre-Mers*, No 306, Paris 1995, p68.

"We are entitled to ask ourselves": Saïd Bellakhdar, 'Des Arabes Chez Les Nazis', *Le Temps Du Non*, Paris 1988.

By 1941, Mohamed and his wife: Report: Iguerbouchen, Mohamed; Direction Générale de la Sûreté Nationale, 20 May 1946: 20100166/3: dossier n° 9091, Archives Nationales, Pierrefitte-sur-Seine.

a woman he'd met at a radio show: Private information from source 'G'.

From page 624 –

which had become a favoured: Report: Iguerbouchen, Mohamed; Direction Générale de la Sûreté Nationale, 20 May 1946: 20100166/3: dossier n° 9091, Archives Nationales, Pierrefitte-sur-Seine.

"Iguerbouchène and his concubine": Mohamed Iguerbouchen dossier: n° 77W1751-104355: Les Archives De La Préfecture De Police, Paris. The police dossier incorrectly gives her surname as 'Vandorf'.

It has been alleged that years later: Private information from source 'G'.

No Nazi documentation: Michael Schelter, Bundesarchive to author: December 2019, October 2020.

absent from surviving documents and guestbooks: Christina Kunkel, Institut für Zeitgeschichte, Munich to author, November 2020.

However, the Berlin record: Report: Iguerbouchen, Mohamed; Direction Générale de la Sûreté Nationale, 20 May 1946: 20100166/3: dossier n° 9091, Archives Nationales, Pierrefitte-sur-Seine.

"the relocation of the prosecution witness": Report: Iguerbouchen, Mohamed; Direction Générale de la Sûreté Nationale, 20 May 1946: 20100166/3: dossier n° 9091, Archives Nationales, Pierrefitte-sur-Seine.

The following year, a three hundred-strong: Daniel Brückenhaus, *Policing Transnational Protest: Liberal Imperialism and the Surveillance of Anticolonists in Europe*, Oxford University Press, 2017, p198.

Between 200,000 and: Katz, p145-148.

"casually strolling on the Champs-Elysées.": Paris-Paris: Iguerbouchen, *L'Union Français* (Lyon), 2

August 1944, p3.

"The good old days, where he": Paris-Paris: Iguerbouchen, *L'Union Français* (Lyon), 2 August 1944, p3.

Upon the liberation of Paris, he: Report: Iguerbouchen, Mohamed; Direction Générale de la Sûreté Nationale, 20 May 1946: 20100166/3: dossier n° 9091, Archives Nationales, Pierrefitte-sur-Seine.

Wartime collaboration in France: Tony Judt, *Postwar: A History of Europe Since 1945*, Pimlico, London, 2007, p46.

In December 1944, the directorate of the National Police: Report: Iguerbouchen, Mohamed; Direction Générale de la Sûreté Nationale, 20 May 1946: 20100166/3: dossier n° 9091, Archives Nationales, Pierrefitte-sur-Seine.

"Speaking several foreign languages": Mohamed Iguerbouchen dossier: n° 77W1751-104355: Les Archives De La Préfecture De Police, Paris.

"had benefited, during the Liberation": Commissariat de police, service de la memoire et des archives, Archives des Renseignements generaux, 23 May 1946: quoted in Mohammed Aïssaoui, *L'Etoile Jaune Et Le Croissant*, Gallimard, Paris 2012, p72. (The current author has not been able to trace this dossier.)

"likely to have repercussions": Aïssaoui, *L'Etoile Jaune Et Le Croissant*, p72.

"a muslim fanatic": Report: A.S. de Meradji Arezki; Secrétaire d 'Etat à l'Intérieur, 7 January 1941: 20100166/3: dossier n° 9091, Archives Nationales, Pierrefitte-sur-Seine.

At the urging of Meradji: Report: Iguerbouchen, Mohamed; Direction Générale de la Sûreté Nationale, 20 May 1946: 20100166/3: dossier n° 9091, Archives Nationales, Pierrefitte-sur-Seine.

According to another intelligence report: Report: Iguerbouchen, Mohamed; Direction Générale de la Sûreté Nationale, 20 May 1946: 20100166/3: dossier n° 9091, Archives Nationales, Pierrefitte-sur-Seine.

That Iguerbouchène had acted: Report: Iguerbouchen, Mohamed; Direction Générale de la Sûreté Nationale, 20 May 1946: 20100166/3: dossier n° 9091, Archives Nationales, Pierrefitte-sur-Seine.

Another who may have advocated: Aïssaoui, *L'Etoile Jaune Et Le Croissant*, pp71-73.

Even Belkacem Radjef: Private information from source 'T'.

By 1946, Iguerbouchène had commenced divorce: Report: Iguerbouchen, Mohamed; Direction Générale de la Sûreté Nationale, 20 May 1946: 20100166/3: dossier n° 9091, Archives Nationales, Pierrefitte-sur-Seine.

allegedly Louise did not wish it: Private information from source 'G'.

In 1947, Mohamed decided: Mohamed Iguerbouchen dossier: n° 77W1751-104355: Les Archives De La Préfecture De Police, Paris.

His backer Aziz Chaldi had: Report: Iguerbouchen, Mohamed; Direction Générale de la Sûreté Nationale, 20 May 1946: 20100166/3: dossier n° 9091, Archives Nationales, Pierrefitte-sur-Seine.

After making several failed appeals: Le Droit Ouvrier, *Confédération Générale du Travail*, Issues 2-9, 1948, p491-492.

at 6 Avenue des Gobelins: Yvonne Vom Dorp dossier: HD 30-519 760 (1960); Archives de la Préfecture de Police, Paris; Post by Iguerbouchene's daughter Kerima Vom Dorp (1959–1981) on Algeria - Thamazighth - History and Culture, 12 Jun 2006. [http://hardeur48.over-blog.fr/article-35617848.html]

in June 1957 Iguerbouchène returned: Mohamed Iguerbouchen dossier: n° 77W1751-104355: Les Archives De La Préfecture De Police, Paris.

he later claimed it was at the request: Bari Stambouli, Mohamed Iguerbouchène: Une Institution Devrait Porter Son Nom, *Le Temps d'Algerie*, 23 August 2017.

and it is claimed, also harboured: Bari Stambouli, Des Lapins Dans Le Bureau Du Compositeur, *Le Temps d'Algeria*, Algiers, 22 November 2009.

Yvonne lived a relatively privileged existence: Private information from source 'F'.

she was not accepted: Private information from sources and 'G' and 'F'.

Adding to her isolation: Private information from source 'G'.

In December 1957, Yvonne: Yvonne Vom Dorp dossier: HD 30-519 760 (1960); Archives de la Préfecture de Police, Paris.

For at least one relation: Private information from source 'F'.

In the wake of attacks: Information from the Département Patrimonial, Préfecture de Police, Paris.

Nothing was found except: Yvonne Vom Dorp dossier: HD 30-519 760 (1960); Archives de la Préfecture de Police, Paris.

"in legal proceedings to request alimony": Yvonne Vom Dorp dossier: HD 30-519 760 (1960);

Archives de la Préfecture de Police, Paris.

Approximately 24,614 French soldiers: Alistair Horne, A Savage War of Peace, *New York Review Books*, New York, 2006, p538.

In 1960-61, he also composed: Ounnoughene, *Mohamed Iguerbouchène*, p73.

Frustrated and embittered, in private: Private information from source 'G'.

Suffering from high blood pressure and: Private information from source 'F'.

When one of his best friends: Bari Stambouli, Des Lapins Dans Le Bureau Du Compositeur, *Le Temps d'Algeria*, 22 November 2009.

"somewhat difficult request": Information, *Fontes Artis Musicae*, IAML, Volume 36, 1989, p330.

a 12-part wildly romanticised: *Mohamed Iguerbouchene*, ENTV, 2003; Belloula, Nassira: Coup d'envoi d'un feuilleton télévisé : 12 épisodes sur la vie d'Iguerbouchène, *Kabyle.com* (Lyon, France,), 4 September 2003.

At his former villa at Beau Fraisier: Ali Boudjelil, Iguerbouchen ou l'œuvre enterré, *Le Dépêche de Kabylie: Le journal des homes libres*, 7 September 2016.

It has been claimed that Iguerbouchène's: Arezki Ibersiene, Concours de musique classique Mohamed Iguerbouch, *Liberte*, Algiers, 14 November 2011.

"does not recall" Iguerbouchène: Ned Rorem to author, January 2018.

the BBC never played his music: genome.ch.bbc.co.uk

Published claims that Iguerbouchène conquered: Rachid Lourdjane, "L'histoire fascinante de la rue Tanger", *L'Expression* (Algiers), 7 October 2015.

Despite Iguerbouchene's treason, in 2021: Samia Lokmane Khelil, "Des Figures Algériennes Disparues Honorées Par Macron", *Liberte*, 13 March 2021.

"Le Comte Roth, riche et puissant lord": Hommage à Iguerbouchène à Tizi-ouzou, Kabylie News Télévision BRTV, December 2013: youtube.com/watch?v=E1Csl3oZQ0k, Accessed 2017.

19. JEWELS

Lord Haddo, the son of the Lord Lieutenant: Tomás O' Riordan, 'The Theft of the Irish Crown Jewels, 1907', *History Ireland*, Vol 9, Issue 4 (Winter 2001).

"I will have no scandals": Edward Legge, *More About King Edward*, Eveleigh Nash, London, 1913, p55.

"I regard this episode": Legge, *More About King Edward*, ppxiv-xv.

Vicars was a kindly but foolish: John Cafferky, Kevin Hannafin, *Scandal & Betrayal: Shackleton and the Irish Crown Jewels*, The Collins Press, Cork 2002, p28, p69.

At a luncheon party: The Late Lord Ronald Sutherland Gower, *The Kent & Sussex Courier*, 17 March 1916, p3; Sued By Stockbrokers, *Hartlepool Northern Daily Mail*, 16 February 1911, p6.

Although he was lugubrious: Cafferky, Hannafin, *Scandal & Betrayal*, p73.

Following Bennett-Goldney's death: Audrey Bateman, *The Magpie Tendency*, A. Bateman, Whitstable 1999, pp82-83, 85.

"was unable to distinguish": Historical Documents, *Dover Express*, 21 January 1921.

"with a face like Mephistopheles": Bulmer Hobson, *Ireland Yesterday and Tomorrow*, Anvil Books, Tralee 1968, p88.

and back in Dublin: *The London Gazette*, 5 December 1902, p8443; *The London Gazette*, 22 May 1904, p2586.

A year before the theft: Hobson, *Ireland Yesterday and Tomorrow*, pp86-88.

Also looted from the safe: Susan Hood, *Royal Roots, Republican Inheritance: The Survival of the Office of Arms*, Woodfield Press, Dublin 2002, p53.

A newspaper publisher: Sean J. Murphy, *A Centenary Report on the Theft of the Irish Crown Jewels in 1907*, Centre for Irish Genealogical and Historical Studies, Windgates, County Wicklow 2008, p13.

The Royal Irish Constabulary conducted: *The Theft of the Irish ' Crown Jewels'* , Digital resources: Exhibitions, 2007, National Archives Of Ireland.

"Kane admits he [Shackleton]": Viola Bankes, Francis Bamford,*Vicious Circle: The Case of the Missing Irish Crown Jewels*, Max Parrish and Co. Ltd., London,1965, p164.

"To find out more than is wanted": Abominations of Dublin Castle Exposed, *The Gaelic American*, 4 July 1908, p1.

The report possibly mistakenly identified: Cafferky, Hannafin, *Scandal & Betrayal*, p95.

Three weeks after Kane's dismissal: Cafferky, Hannafin, *Scandal & Betrayal*, p108.

In September Knollys wrote again: Mark Bence-Jones *Twilight Of The Ascendancy*, Constable,

London 1987, p125.

Lord Aberdeen was concerned that dismissing: Cafferky, Hannafin, *Scandal & Betrayal*, pp109-111.
By this time, the Anglo-Irish administration: Cafferky, Hannafin, *Scandal & Betrayal*, p285 n3; p287 n4.
For the King, what mattered most: Bankes, Bamford, *Vicious Circle*, p94.
"Knollys writes that H.M. 'insists' ": Cafferky, Hannafin, *Scandal & Betrayal*, p162.
"I happen to have been told by Lord Knollys": Cafferky, Hannafin, *Scandal & Betrayal*, p127.
the 'graver charge': Cafferky, Hannafin, *Scandal & Betrayal*, p127.
"We are not here to find out": Cafferky, Hannafin, *Scandal & Betrayal*, p158.
"opportuning the Lord Lieutenant": *Appendix to the Report of the Viceregal Commission, Commission Appointed to Investigate the Circumstances of the Loss of the Regalia of the Order of St Patrick*, His Majesty's Stationery Office,1908., p3.
His clerk and a secretary: *Appendix to the Report of the Viceregal Commission*, pp35,79.
"the name of Mr. Francis Richard Shackleton": *Report of the Viceregal Commission Appointed to Investigate the Circumstances of the Loss of the Regalia of the Order of St Patrick*, His Majesty's Stationery Office,1908., p xi.
"it only due to that gentleman": *Report of the Viceregal Commission*, p xi.

From page 641 –

"I should never be surprised": *Appendix to the Report of the Viceregal Commission*, p71.
"my friend Lord Ronald": *Appendix to the Report of the Viceregal Commission*, p73.
"being taken down by the short-hand": *Appendix to the Report of the Viceregal Commission*, p69.
while sitting in the carriage: Bankes, Bamford, *Vicious Circle*, p53.
"I know perfectly well": *Appendix to the Report of the Viceregal Commission*, p77.
he only received a summons: Cafferky, Hannafin, *Scandal & Betrayal*, p305.
in the company of Ronnie Gower: Bankes, Bamford, *Vicious Circle*, p135.
"Here Shackleton's whole private life": Abominations of Dublin Castle Exposed, *The Gaelic American*, 4 July 1908, p1.
"washed his hands": Sir Sydney Lee, King *Edward VII: A Biography*, Macmillan & Co., London 1927, Vol II, p474.
"This, Meynell explains": Wilfrid Blunt Diaries, 24 January 1908, MS 8-1975, The Fitzwilliam Museum, Cambridge.
worse than amongst the savages: The Condition Of Ireland, *Northern Scot and Moray & Nairn Express*, 14 December 1907, p4.
"the studied darkness": The World's Pageant, *The Bystander*, 22 February 1911, p368 (p6).
"Shackleton, when he was suspected": Bankes, Bamford, *Vicious Circle*, p185.
"Shackleton's wicked threats": Bankes, Bamford, *Vicious Circle*, p189.
"You do not & cannot appreciate": to Birrell to Gladstone, 14 Jan 1908, MS46065, ff187-197, Herbert, Viscount Gladstone Papers, British Library.
Birrell, a philosophical intellectual who: Battersea, *Reminiscences*, p310.
"the consequences are already most disagreeable": Kleptomania Alleged, *Northern Whig*, 23 January 1908, p7.
"There can be no doubt": The Dublin Star Chamber', *The Globe*, 20 January 1908, p1.
"reluctantly published": Strange Story Of The "Dublin Herald", *The Irish Weekly and Ulster Examiner*, 22 February 1908, p8.
"read out from a typed document": Ireland, *The Times*, 3 February 1908, p12.
a man of "undesirable character": Ireland, *The Times*, 3 February 1908, p12.
"in an inquiry of this kind, involving character": Ireland, *The Times*, 3 February 1908, p12.
"had believed this man to be": Ireland, *The Times*, 3 February 1908, p12.
"owing to the incontinence": Ireland, *The Times*, 3 February 1908, p12.
Seeking to discredit Vicars: Cafferky, Hannafin, *Scandal & Betrayal*, p285,n5.
"to bring the true state of affairs": Ireland, *The Times*, 3 February 1908, p12.
"and therefore the introduction": Ireland, *The Times*, 3 February 1908, p12.
"Mr. Birrell was the first to introduce": Ireland, *The Times*, 3 February 1908, p12.
"Everything can be done, and is done": Marie Corelli, 'Thieves Of Honour', *London Opinion*, 29 February 1908, pp392-393.
"The secret Commission appointed to inquire": *London Opinion*, March 1908 quoted in: An Irish

Dreyfus, *Kerry News*, 20 March 1908, p3.

"There are three circumstances": 'Marmaduke' (C.E. Jerningham), Letter From The Linkman, *Truth*, 26 February 1908, p27.

"It is intolerable that in the twentieth century": Dublin Jewel Robbery, *The Courier* (Dundee) 4 March 1908, p4.

"that the police authorities, in their investigation": *Hansard*, House of Commons , 11 March 1908, vol 185, c1533.

"most anxious that there should be": *Hansard*, House of Commons Debate, 1 April 1908 vol 187 cc509-10509.

"That is a very proper question": *Hansard*, House of Commons Debate, 1 April 1908 vol 187 cc509-10509.

"England is trembling on the brink": Aim To Expose Dublin Crown Jewels Scandal, *The Evening Star: Sunday Star* (Washington), 12 April 1908.

"That His Majesty intervened": King Edward VII: Wire-Puller, *Pearson's Weekly*, 24 September 1908, p254.

"aware of the existence of reports": *Hansard*, House of Commons Debate, 27 April 1909 vol 4 cc180-2180.

"Having got this story": Bulmer Hobson, *Ireland Yesterday and Tomorrow*, Anvil Books, Tralee 1968, p87.

"Mystery of the Theft of the Crown Jewels": Abominations of Dublin Castle Exposed, *The Gaelic American*, 4 July 1908, p1.

"If I knew who wrote that I": Hobson, *Ireland Yesterday and Tomorrow*, p88.

"So things went on till": Abominations of Dublin Castle Exposed, *The Gaelic American*, 4 July 1908, p1.

"a man of very bad reputation": Abominations of Dublin Castle Exposed, *The Gaelic American*, 4 July 1908, p1.

"a thief": £10,000 Lawsuit, *Reynolds's Newspaper*, 19 February 1911, p9.

"Why Shackleton was not prosecuted": Irish Crown Jewel Mystery Revived by F.X. Cullen, *The Age-Herald*, (Birmingham, Alabama) 29 December 1912, p6.

"been agitating officials in the Home Office": F.R. Shackleton Arrested, *Daily News & Leader* (London) 2 November 1912, p1

So nervous was the Government: F.R. Shackleton At Bow-Street, *Daily News*, 11 January 1913, p3

From page 661 –

"The trial of Frank Shackleton": U.S. press report quoted in: Personagraphs, *The Sun* (Kalgoolie, Western Australia), 29 December 1912, p15.

Shackleton and his accomplice: Prison For F.R. Shackleton, *The Pall Mall Gazette*, 24 October 1913, p5.

"All available information has been": House of Commons Debate, *Hansard*, 28 November 1912, vol 44 cc1475-61475.

At the next parliamentary sitting: House of Commons Debate, *Hansard*, 29 November 1912, vol 44 c1840; Our London Letter, *Belfast News-Letter*, 3 December 1912, p7.

"I am afraid I am not": House of Commons Debate, *Hansard*, 2 December 1912, vol 44, c1909.

"I don't think anybody need be frightened": Cafferky, Hannafin, *Scandal & Betrayal*, p166

"The powers of the Director": House of Commons Debate, *Hansard*, 4 December 1912, vol 44 cc2309.

"I ask to be allowed to deal": *Hansard*, House of Commons, 6 December 1912, vol 44, c2751.

"We often hear and read idle": *Hansard*, House of Commons, 6 December 1912, vol 44, c2751.

"criminal debauchery and sodomy": *Hansard*, House of Commons, 6 December 1912, vol 44, c2751.

"One of the most powerful means": *Hansard*, House of Commons, 6 December 1912, vol 44, c2751.

"It was evident that members": Parliament In Session, *The Scotsman*, 7 December 1912.

"The Chief Secretary is able": *Hansard*, House of Commons, 12 December 1912, vol 45 cc747.

"The Chief Secretary's evasive": *Hansard*, House of Commons, 20 December 1912 vol 45, c1955.

"A jaunty air of blank ignorance": *Hansard*, House of Commons, 20 December 1912 vol 45, c1955.

"the greatest scoundrel": *Hansard*, House of Commons, 20 December 1912 vol 45, c1955.

"This person [Shackleton] threatened": *Hansard*, House of Commons, 20 December 1912 vol 45, c1955.

"To conceal criminals": *Hansard*, House of Commons, 20 December 1912, vol 45, c1955.

"I do not know of any person": *Hansard*, House of Commons, 20 December 1912 vol 45, c1955.

"Didn't I give you the names": *Hansard*, House of Commons, 20 December 1912 vol 45, c1955.

"I want to discover who stole": *Hansard*, House of Commons, 20 December 1912 vol 45, c1955.

"How is it that it is only in this particular case": *Hansard*, House of Commons, 1 January 1913, vol 46 cc368-70368.

"if Kane's report did not contain": Renews Crown Jewels Charge In Commons, *The New York Herald* (N.Y. edition only), 8 January 1913, p11.

"The hon. Member has no right": Crown Jewels Mystery, *Dublin Daily Express*, 8 January 1913, p10.

Hansard didn't record any of the: *Hansard*, House of Commons, 7 January 1913, vol 46, c1004.

"He horrified the Speaker": Parliament Day By Day, *The Labour Leader*, 9 January 1913, p3.

"Every week of that January": *Hansard*, House of Commons, 7 January 1913, vol 46 cc1004-51004; 13 January 1913, vol 46 cc1659-601659; 16 January 1913, vol 46 cc2237-82237; 23 January 1913, vol 47 cc589-90589; 28 January 1913, vol 47 cc1189-901189.

"Nothing whatever has been discovered": *Hansard*, House of Commons, 13 February 1913, vol 48, c1159.

"why, during the last five years": *Hansard*, House of Commons, 13 February 1913, vol 48, c1159.

"The true facts of the theft": The Crown Jewels Mystery by W.F., *The Modern Man*, 8 April 1911, p3.

"no more sincere than the official assertions": Recovery Of Royal Secrets, *Evening Star* (Washington), 18 January 1913.

"To the Club, and all talking": The New Pepys, *Truth*, 15 January 1913, p24.

Following Shackleton's arrest, it had published: Cafferky, Hannafin, *Scandal & Betrayal*, pp210-211.

He replied that he did not have: *Hansard*, House of Commons, 19 February 1914, vol 58, c1113.

"that the Castle jewels are for sale": 1 June 1927, S 3926A, National Archives, Ireland.

"Our efforts to unravel the tangled yarns": Bankes, Bamford, *Vicious Circle,* pix-x.

ENVOI

"The most interesting things": Charles Arrow, *Rogues and Others*, Duckworth, London 1926, p9.

Arthur Charles Campbell 'Squarey' Thorold: Did You Know: http://philanthropy.tss.qld.edu.au/wp-content/uploads/2016/03/Did-You-Know-Charles-Thorold.pdf

"like going to a restaurant": Peter Jukes, Hardeep Matharu, 'The History Racket', *Byline Times*, 2 September 2021, [https://bylinetimes.com/2021/09/02/the-history-racket-blowing-the-whistle-on-the-official-versions-and-perversions-of-the-past/]

"Lord Battersea favoured the company": Constance (Connie) de Rothschild), The Rothschild Archive:https://web.archive.org/web/20220705210940/https://family.rothschildarchive.org/people/64-constance-connie-de-rothschild-1843-1931

"The Archive encourages research": Jonathan Fishburn, 'Family Treasure Trove', *Jewish Quarterly*, Vol 51, No2, p30.

all these traits together are not: Derek Wilson, *Rothschild : A Story Of Wealth And Power*, André Deutsch, London 1988, p260.

"emphasised both by Cyril and Constance": Livingstone, *The Women Of Rothschild*, p570,n10.

except it appears by a previous librarian: Merton College Library to author, August 2020.

"checking the wayward will": Rev. E.E. Bradford, 'The Touchstone Of Love', *The New Chivalry*, Kegan Paul, London 1918, pp76-77.

"your glorious crusade for winning": Timothy d'arch Smith, *Bradford's Own Copies*, undated sale monograph. (The six copies are now held by Exeter College Library.)

"With much travail": Lord Ronald Gower to Hugh Lane, 17 June 1902; MS 13,071/3/15/11, National Library Of Ireland.

"a failure of the heterosexual": Jonathan Cutbill, 'The Truth Untold', *The New Statesman*, 16 January 1987.

"extensively raided by jackals": Private information from a close source.

Whatever occurred, with the exception of: Beatrice Palmigiano Gozzo, *I Whitaker di Villa Malfitano L'Archivio*, Fondazione Giuseppe Whitaker, Palermo 2003.

From page 685 –

"unfortunately it seems there is a gap": The 11th Earl of Sandwich to author, May 2020.

"all my papers, letters, etc are to be examined": Kaplan, *Sodom On The Thames*, p165.

From June 1889 onwards: 5 November 1890, Esher Diary: ESHR 1/3, Churchill Archives Centre.

In 1910, Aretas Akers-Douglas casually: David Lindsay, Earl of Crawford; John Vincent, (ed.) *The Crawford Papers,* Manchester University Press, 1984, pp151-152.

"Lord Tweedmouth made it a rule": *Edward Marjoribanks, Lord Tweedsmouth K.T, 1849–1909. Notes and Recollections*, Constable And Company, London 1909, pp v-vi.

At the time of the Eulenburg scandal: Wieder Einer, *Leipziger Volkszeitung*, 5 June 1908. Referenced in: Norman Domeier, Deborah Lucas Schneider (trans.), *The Eulenburg Affair: A Cultural History of Politics in the German Empire*, Camden House, Rochester N.Y, 2015, p219.

"dispersed": Elizabeth Longford, *Darling Loosy: Letters to Princess Louise 1856-1939*, Weidenfeld & Nicolson, London 1991, p1.

At Windsor, there is no: Royal Archives to author, 2017/2018.

"generally closed for research": Royal Archives to author, 11 December 2017.

"literally odd pages torn": Alison Diamond, Inveraray Archivist to author.

despite the fact he sometimes wrote: Diary of Lord Ronald Gower, 17 August 1902; D6578/15, Staffordshire Record Office.

An indolent, abusive alcoholic: Lyndsy Spence, *The Grit In The Pearl: The Scandalous Life Of Margaret, Duchess of Argyll*, The History Press, London 2019, *passim*.

"Weeded 10.1.72": The Marquess of Lorne to his brother Lord Archibald Campbell, 1209/3687, Inveraray Castle Archive.

What remains of Alfred de Rothschild's: Information from William P. Cross.

"were in a terrible muddle": Paul B. Remmey, Jr., 'Lord Spencer's Recollections of Balfour, Curzon, Rosebery, and George V', *Research Studies*, Volume 38 (4), December 1970, Washington State University, p312-318.

"he took the greatest pleasure": Battersea, *Reminiscences*, p268.

Asquith had also met: Margot Asquith, *The Autobiography of Margot Asquith*, Thornton Butterworth, London 1922, p261.

they had gone on a walking tour: London Letter, *The Bucks Herald*, 25 August 1888, p8.

which earned him the nickname: Margot Asquith; Michael & Eleanor Brock (eds.), *Margot Asquith's Great War Diary 1914–1916*, Oxford University Press, 2014, p285.

'inveterate groper': Colin Clifford, *The Asquiths*, John Murray, London 2002, p207.

"how vigorously to proceed": Alden Whitman, Books of The Times, *The New York Times*, 30 August 1976, p20.

"Moral relativism is… the spongiform": William Rees-Mogg, The Headmaster's Lesson For Us All, *The Times*, 11 December 1995, p16.

"British national conceit": Finian Cunningham, 'Disregarding Its Own Bloody Colonial history, Britain Still Pontificates On Syria And Iran', *Stop The War Coalition*, 12 May 2013; www.stopwar.org.uk.

The descendants of those who once administered: Michael Oswald, *The Spider's Web: Britain's Second Empire*, Queuepolitely Films, 2017; Nicholas Shaxson, *Treasure Islands: Tax Havens and the Men who Stole the World*, Bodley Head, London 2011, *passim*; Nicholas Shaxson, The Finance Curse: How Global Finance Is Making Us All Poorer, Bodley Head, London 2018, *passim*; Tom Buris, 'Will 'Global Britain' clamp down on money laundering?', *Financial Times*, 28 April 2021.

The situation has become so outrageous: Jon Ungoed-Thomas, Dipesh Gadher, 'Tax haven firm owns HMRC London office', *The Times*, 8 May 2016.

The pernicious influence of China: Ewan Somerville, 'Universities 'should declare Chinese funding' amid spying concerns', *The Telegraph*, 9 June 2022

a Parliamentary report published in 2020: *Intelligence and Security Committee of Parliament: Russia*, HC632, Her Majesty's Stationery Office, London 2020

Victoria Ward: 'Cabinet Office accused of lying to MPs to keep Mountbatten papers private', *The Telegraph*, 15 November 2021: https://www.telegraph.co.uk/royal-family/2021/11/15/cabinet-office-accused-lying-mps-keep-mountbatten-papers-private/

Three-years previously, a news investigation: Ian Cobain, Ewen MacAskill, 'Israeli official who plotted to 'take down' British MPs resigns', *The Guardian*, 12 January 2017; Al Jazeera Investigative Unit, 'Exclusive: Israel lobby infiltrates UK student movement', aljazeera.com, 11 Jan 2017, https://www.aljazeera.com/news/2017/1/11/exclusive-israel-lobby-infiltrates-uk-student-movement

Seeking to make the costs of the case: Andrew Lownie, 'David And Goliath Battle Over The

Mounbatten Papers', *Daily Express*, 9 December 2021, pp26-27.

"a grotesque abuse of public money": Jon Ungoed-Thomas, 'Anger over 'grotesque abuse' of £600,000 case to keep Mountbatten papers secret,' *The Observer*, 7 November 2021.

Meanwhile, other members of the Royal Family: See: J. A. McGrath, 'Carlton House is jewel in the crown after Dante triumph', *The Daily Telegraph*, 12 May 2011; J. A. McGrath, 'Carlton House is jewel in the crown after Dante triumph', *The Daily Telegraph*, 12 May 2011; David Brown, Rob Wright, Dominic Kennedy, 'It's royal gifts as usual amid the mystery of the sheikh's missing daughters', *The Times*, 1 March 2021; Catherine Philp, 'Dubai Sheikh's friendship with Queen is one of many ties that bind', *The Times*, 17 February 2021; Sean O'Neill, 'Oligarch's donation drags Prince Charles into 'Troika Laundromat' scandal', *The Times*, 5 March 2019; Gabriel Pogrund, Valentine Low, 'Prince Charles 'backed citizenship for Saudi donor', *The Times*, 6 September 2021; Dipesh Gadher, Gabriel Pogrund, 'Regulators investigate Prince Charles's 'doctored' charity letter', *The Times*, 19 September 2021; David Leppard, 'Secret cash funnelled to pauper prince', *The Sunday Times*, 13 May 2012; Jonathan Calvert, George Arbuthnott, Tom Calver, 'Prince Michael of Kent 'selling access' to the Putinistas', *The Sunday Times*, 8 May 2021.

For a decade he'd cultivated: See: 'Norman Baker, ...*And What Do You Do?: What The Royal Family Don't Want You To Know*, Biteback Publishing, London 2019; Nigel Rosser, 'Andrew's Fixer', *The Evening Standard*, 22 January 2001, p10; Isabel Oakeshott, Mark Hookham: 'Exposed: Andrew's Deals With Tax Haven Tycoons', *The Mail On Sunday*, 1 December 2019, pp1,2-10.; Ben Glaze, Christopher Bucktin, 'Prince Andrew 'plugged private bank for millionaire who paid Fergie's debts'', *Daily Mirror*, 1 December 2019. [https://www.mirror.co.uk/news/uk-news/prince-andrew-plugged-private-bank-21006573]; Gavin Finch, Harry Wilson, 'Prince Andrew Helped a Secretive Luxembourg Bank Woo Sketchy Clients', *Bloomberg*, November 19, 2020; Guy Adams, 'Andrew and 'a £4m kickback', *The Daily Mail*, 21 May 2016; [https://www.dailymail.co.uk/news/article-3601690/Andrew-4-million-kickback-Duke-brokered-385m-deal-Greek-firm-corrupt-regime-acting-British-trade-envoy.html]; Richard Kerbaj, Daniel Foggo, 'Revealed: Andrew And The £20,000 Diamond Necklace', *The Sunday Times*, 27 March 2011, p1; Robert Booth, 'Prince Andrew row intensifies as he lobbies for Azerbaijan' *The Guardian*, 9 March 2011 [https://www.theguardian.com/uk/2011/mar/09/prince-andrew-lobbies-azerbaijan].

Lawrie Holmes, 'Simon: Why did Prince Andrew visit Gaddafi in Libya with 'shady' Tory?', *Mail On Sunday*, 20 March 2011; [https://www.dailymail.co.uk/news/article-1368001/Why-did-Prince-Andrew-visit-Gaddafi-Libya-shady-Tory.html]

"didn't have to answer to anyone": Nick Enoch, Nick Fagge, Andrew 'could be asked to stop using Duke of York title', *Daily Mail*, 2 January 2022 [https://www.dailymail.co.uk/news/article-10361451/Prince-Andrew-asked-stop-using-Duke-York-title-loses-Giuffre-lawsuit.html]

British courts and oppressive libel laws: Andrew Higgins, Jane Bradley, Isobel Koshiw,Franz Wild,' The Power of Money: How Autocrats Use London to Strike Foes Worldwide', *The New York Times*, 18 June 2021.

forensic psychologists and body language experts: The Psychology of Prince Andrew, JCS - Criminal Psychology [https://www.youtube.com/watch?v=q-y2g9Ot5GA]; Prince Andrew & Epstein Interview Body Language Analyzed: www.thebehaviorpanel.com [https://www.youtube.com/watch?v=HC40bgA2wKA; http://www.youtube.com/watch?v=PFYTBMfVqr0]

"Power is just an arsehole [asshole]": Sam Esmail, *Mr Robot*, Series 4, Episode 7, Anonymous Content & Esmail Corp.

One of the affected pupils: Report Of Case Study No.20, *Royal Commission into Institutional Responses to Child Abuse*, November 2015.

Subsequently, claims of historical child abuse: Olivia Lambert, 'Sascha Chandler tells story of child abuse ahead of Child Protection Week', *News.com.au*, 3 September 2017; Revealed: Million dollar payouts from elite Coast school for abuse, *Gold Coast Bulletin*, 6 November 2020; The Southport School: payouts to TSS students after abuse, *The Gold Coast Bulletin*, 9 November 2020;

in 2018, the Anglican Church Diocese: Naaman Zhou, 'Leaders of two Anglican schools back away from letter on sacking gay teachers', *The Guardian*, 6 November 2018.

As for Iguerbouchène: Bari Stambouli, 'Mohamed Iguerbouchène: Une Institution Devrait Porter Son Nom', *Le Temps d'Algerie*, 23 August 2017.

"He came of a family and lived in an age": Day, *Charles Thorold*, p14.

"simply a euphemism for a proposal": Should Scandals In High Life Be Hushed-Up?, *The Pall Mall Gazette*, 4 February 1887, p1.

INDEX

Abbas, Ferhat, 628

Abberline, Frederick, 402

Abderrahmane, Belhadj ('Yassine'), 622

Abdul (servant), 314, 327

Aberdeen, George, 2nd Marquess of, 635&n, 638-639, 641, 651, 656, 658-659, 666-667

Aberdeen, Ishbel, Marchioness of, 635&n, 655

Aberdeen, John, 1st Marquess of, 635&n, 638-639, 645-646, 651, 655-656, 658-659, 667

Adamson, Lawrence Arthur, 550&n-552, 696

Adare, Viscount, 316n

Agar-Robartes, Alexander, 497

Agar-Robartes, Gerald (see: Clifden, Gerald, 7th Viscount)

Agar-Robartes, Thomas (see: Clifden, 6th Viscount)

Agar-Robartes, Thomas, 497-498

Agg-Gardner, Sir James 430n

Aïdé, Hamilton, 46&n, 345n, 365, 484

Ainger, Arthur Campbell, 126

Akers-Douglas, Aretas (see: Chilston, 1st Viscount)

Albert Victor, Prince, 30&n, 112, 138n, 167, 175, 221, 223, 416-417, 453n

Albert, Prince, 37n, 277n

Alcibiades, 441&n

Alexandra, Queen, 29-30, 43, 45, 161, 209, 364, 385, 405, 444, 595

Alfred, Prince, Duke of Edinburgh, 306n, 453n

Alington, 2nd Baron, 42-43

Allen, Grant, 145&n

Allen, William, 182

Alverstone, 1st Viscount, 167&n, 169, 170, 172-173&n, 175, 586

Andersen, Arthur, 532&n, 559

Anderson, Wherry, 202n

Andrew, Prince, Duke of York, 694-696

Anglesey, 5th Marquess of, 103-104

Antrim, Louisa, Countess of, 30, 32

Argyll, 11th Duke of, 687

Argyll, 8th Duke of, 292, 384n, 416n, 646n

Argyll, 9th Duke of ('Lorne'), 277&n-278, 292, 318, 329, 364, 380, 384, 388, 395-396, 399, 403, 416-417, 431, 446-448, 450, 461, 484, 634, 637, 641, 667, 687

Aribert, Prince of Anhalt, 434

Armstrong, Eliza, 89, 92

Arnold, Matthew, 270&n

Arnold-Forster, William, 433n

Arrow, Det. Inspector Charles, 211, 216-218, 220, 234-236, 258, 402-403, 671, 705

Arthur, Prince, Duke of Connaught, 429&n

Ashbee, Charles Robert, 139&n, 142, 413-414

Ashbee, Henry Spencer, 98n, 595

Ashbee, Janet Elizabeth, 142,

Ashton, 1st Baron, 355n

Asquith, Herbert (see: Oxford and Asquith, 1st Earl of)

Asquith, Raymond, 127&n, 363, 395, 445

Asquith, Violet, Baroness, 311&n, 385, 415, 445

Balfour, Alice, 445&n

Balfour, Arthur, 1st Earl of Balfour, 61&n, 71, 76-77, 126, 222-223, 316&n, 318, 338, 366, 386, 388, 406-407&n, 409, 420, 422, 426, 429, 439, 470

Balfour, Lady Francis, 384&n, 446, 450

Balfour, Gerald, 2nd Earl of Balour, 311, 365&n-366, 395, 410

Balfour, John Blair (see: Kinross, 1st

Baron)
Ballantine, Rev. Robert, 536-537
Ballin, Robert, 69
Bamford, Francis, 669, 674
Bancroft, Sir Squire & Lady, 480-
  481&n, 487
Bankes, Viola, 669, 674
Bankes, William, 405n
Baring, Maurice, 409n
Barnato, Barney, 48&n, 387
Bartram, Harold, 537-538
Bastard, Lieut. Reginald, 238
Battenberg, Prince Maurice, 65n
Battersea, Constance, Baroness, 58,
  221, 304-316, 318-322, 325-330,
  334-336, 338-341&n, 343-345, 347,
  350, 353-367, 371-372, 376, 378,
  380, 382-383, 385, 394-395, 397,
  399-404, 406-408, 412, 414, 421,
  426-428, 433-434, 439-440, 442-
  449, 451-458, 676-678, 687-688
Battersea, Cyril, 1st Baron, 57-58, 165,
  190, 207, 221, 223-224, 233, 260-
  275, 287-459, 461, 466, 474-475,
  476, 479, 491-493, 500, 511, 517,
  534, 550-551, 566, 579, 587, 594,
  634, 644, 671-674, 676-680, 685-
  686, 699, 705
Beaconsfield, 1st Earl of, 39&n, 49,
  215, 308, 320, 322-323, 373,
  423&n, 451, 692
Beales, Edmund, 37&n, 40
Beatrice, Princess, 65n, 446n, 595, 673
Beauchamp, Lettice, Countess, 199n,
  413-414
Beauchamp, William, 7th Earl,
  199&n-200, 413-414, 656, 679, 689
Beauchamp, Lady Violet, 252n
Bell, John Fancourt, 699n
Bellamy, Herbert, 5t54
Belloc, Hilaire, 442&n, 647
Bennett, Herbert John, 436-437
Bennett-Goldney, Francis, 637&n-638
Benson, Arthur Christopher, 126&n,
  132-133&n, 508, 533&n
Benson, Edward Frederic, 34&n, 56n,
  100, 126n, 233n, 310-311, 340, 343,
  347n, 362, 409n-410, 413, 444, 451,
  481&n, 500, 613n
Benson, Most Rev. Edward,
  Archbishop of Canterbury, 29, 132,
  372, 543
Bentham, Jeremy, 62n

Bentinck, Lord George, 95n
Bentinck, Lord Henry, 95n
Bere, Mr. & Mrs., 533
Berlyn, Annie, 346&n
Berners, 14th Baron, 498&n
Bernhardt, Sarah, 579
Bertouch, Baroness Beatrice de,
  119&n
Berwick, 8th Baron, 499&n-500
Berwick, Theresa, Baroness, 499&n-
  501
Bessborough, Louisa, Countess of,
  328
Betjeman, John, 20n, 130n
Bevan, Lieutenant Arthur, 502-503
Bey, Ali Kamel Fahmy, 73n
Bilton, Belle (see: Clancarty, 5th Earl
  & Belle, Countess of)
Biron, Henry Chartres, 233&n-236,
  243
Birrell, Augustine, 639&n, 643-646,
  650-651, 654-655, 655, 657, 661-
  669
Blackwell, Sir Ernley, 581&n-582, 584
Bloxam, Rev. John 'Jack', 143&n
Blunt, Wilfrid, 52&n, 262, 268, 422,
  425, 454, 474-475, 478, 642, 679
Bodkin, Sir Archibald, 231&n-232,
  235-236, 242
Bonham Carter, Lady Violet (see:
  Asquith, Violet, Baroness)
Booth, Bramwell, 88&n
Booth, William, 34, 88
'Boss' (Fraser's boy), 216, 218-219,
  604
Bottomley, Horatio, 256&n-257, 654
Boulton, Alicia, 491-492
Boulton, Emily, 492
Boulton, Harold Edward Baker, 244,
  253-254, 259, 377, 475-476,
  491-503, 511, 557-558, 616
Boulton, Helen (see: Thurston, Helen)
Boulton, Joseph, 491-492
Boulton, Thomas, 492
Boulez, Pierre, 632
Bower, Major-General Sir Hamilton,
  95n
Bowles, Paul, 619
Bowles, Thomas, 269
Boyer, Charles, 619
Bradford, Rev Edwin Emmanuel,
  130&n, 145&n, 607, 681
Bradwell, 1st Baron, 494&n

Braganza, Prince Francis Joseph of (see Francis Joseph, Prince)
Brett, Reginald (see Esher, Reginald, 2nd Viscount)
Brittain, Harry, 592&n-593
Broadley, Alexander Meyrick, 74&n, 381n
Brooke, Rupert, 317n, 433n
Brown, Arthur, 400&n, 410, 440, 445, 448, 493
Brown, Horatio, 147&n, 153-154, 195&n
Browning, Oscar, 133n, 263&n, 303, 324, 365, 486, 576
Brumfield, Anna Louisa, 514
Brumfield, Benjamin, 215-217, 226-229, 232, 234, 236-237, 514, 516-517, 541, 552, 568, 705
Brumfield, Florence, 541
Brunner, Sir John, 354
Bucke, Dr Richard Maurice, 143&n
Buckle, George, 253&n, 408n, 653&n
Bugatti, Carlo, 314&n, 381
Burdett, Sir Henry, 48&n
Burne-Jones, Sir Edward, 314, 451
Burnham, 1st Baron, 269&n, 379, 410
Burns, John, 352&n, 356, 448n, 484
Burton, Peter, 20n
Burton, Sir Richard, 303, 342n, 366n, 371, 480, 487, 598
Bush, Alonzo, 137n
Butler, Josephine, 80&n, 88, 294&n, 338, 341, 384, 433
Buxton, Sir Thomas Foxwell, 239
Byng, Douglas, 384&n
Byron, 6th Baron, 123, 294, 326, 598
Cambridge, Duke of (see George Prince, Duke of Cambridge)
Campbell, Lord Archibald, 292&n, 687
Campbell, Lord Colin, 416&n
Campbell-Bannerman, Sir Henry, 379&n, 390, 409
Camperdown, 4th Earl of, 461&n
Camus, Albert, 621
Cannon, Henry 'Harry' Le Grand, 486-487n
Cannon, Thomas, 598n
Cardigan, Adeline, Countess of, 45, 99&n
Carlini, Paolo, 495n
Carlos, Don, 467&n
Carlyle, Rev. Benjamin, Abbot Aelred, 117&n, 120, 680
Carrington, Baron (see: Lincolnshire, Marquess of)
Carpenter, Edward, 61&n, 112, 136-143, 148-149, 152-155, 295-296, 413, 432, 683
Carter, William, 561
Carter, Violet-Bonham (see: Asquith, Violet, Baroness)
Casement, Roger, 231n, 581
Cassel, Sir Ernest, 47&n, 49, 69, 70, 76, 323, 407
Cavendish-Bentinck, George, 85&n
Cazalet, William Marshall, 453
Cecil, Lady Gwendolen, 179-180
Cecil, Rev. Lord William, 177
Chaldi, Aziz, 618, 628
Chalmers, Sir Mackenzie, 582&n-587
Chamberlain, Joseph, 46
Chandler, Henry, 185, 187
Channon, Sir Henry 'Chips', 500-501
Charles III, King, 48
Chelmsford, 1st Viscount & Viscountess, 529
Chilston, 1st Viscount, 223&n, 266, 395, 686
Choate, Joseph, 425&n
Chopin, Frédéric, 608, 697
Churchill, Lord Randolph, 98, 323
Churchill, 2nd Viscount, 606&n
Churchill, Sir Winston, 49, 77, 415, 435n, 481n
Clancarty, 5th Earl & Belle, Countess of, 106-107
Clarke, Sir Edward, 72&n, 422
Clarke, Sir William, 463&n
Clementi, Muzio, 608
Cliburn, Robert Henry, 183-184, 412
Clifden, Thomas, 6th Viscount, 497
Clifden, Gerald, 7th Viscount, 496-499, 501-502
Clifford, Charles, 37-38
Cobbe, Frances Power, 329&n, 456n
Cockburn, Sir Alexander, 71
Cocteau, Jean, 632
Cohen, Alfred J., 96n
Cohen, James Arthur Waley, 457
Cohen, Lucy, 457&n-458
Cole, Alfred, 365
Colebrooke, Sir Edward & Lady, 410
Coleridge, 2nd Baron, 442n
Collins, Albert, 209-217, 226-229, 232, 234, 236, 396, 552, 605, 705

Collins, Charles Glen, 364&n
Collins, Lieut-Col. Arthur, 396&, 410,
    416, 432, 445, 461, 470, 679, 681
Collins, Sir Robert, 318&n, 396
Colman, Jeremiah James, 354
Compton, John, 367-368, 371, 444,
    452
Condor, Claude, 114&n
Connaught, Duke of, 429&n
Cooper, Sir Pope, 540
Corelli, Marie, 56&n-57, 647-649, 651-
    652
Corvo, Baron (see:
    Rolfe, Frederick)
Cory, William, 124-126, 143, 292, 294,
    315n, 342, 452
Cottam, Rev. Samuel Elsworth, 130n
Courtenay, William (see
    Devon, 9th Earl of)
Cradock-Hartopp, Sir Charles, 404
Crane, Walter, 288&n
Crawford, 27th Earl of, 427&n
Creighton, Louise, 364&n, 395
Crossfield, Rev. T.J., 513-514, 569
Crowley, Aleister, 481n, 496&n
Cubitt, Frank Astley, 231, 232, 237
Cunliffe-Owen, Frederick, 276&n-
    277, 279-282, 390-391, 411-412,
    416-417, 421, 424-425, 448, 651-
    656, 672
Cunliffe-Owen, Marguerite, 276-277,
    278, 521
Cunliffe-Owen, Sir Philip, 277
Curzon, George, 1st Marquess,
    364&n, 444
Cust, Sir Lionel, 421
Cuthbertson, Edward, 446, 448
Dale, Alan (see Cohen, Alfred J.)
Dalton, Canon John, 112
Davies, Rev. Llewelyn, 90&n
Davitt, Michael, 516-517
Day, Dr. John Henry, 568-572, 672,
    674, 678, 698
De Cobain, Edward, 348n
de Galland, Raoul, 603
de Gaulle, Charles, 625
De La Warr, Countess, 472
Dennistoun, Almina, 411&n
De Quincey, Thomas, 509&n
De Robeck, Major Charles & Eleanor,
    501&n
Derby, 14th Earl of, 39
Desart, 5th Earl of, 222&n-223, 243,

281
Desborough, Baroness, 408n
Devon, 9th Earl of, 149n
Devonshire, 7th Duke of, 268n
Devonshire, 8th Duke of, 337&n
Dick, Cotsford, 45&n-46, 146, 184
Dickens, Charles, 52, 80n, 527
Dickinson, Goldsworthy Lowes,
    139&n
Dickinson, Maud Mary, 541
Dilke, Sir Charles, 33n, 69&n, 334-
    335, 354, 700
Dilke, Emilia, Lady, 69, 335
Dixon, Ella Hepworth, 101&n
Dixon, Rt. Rev. Horace, 523&n-529,
    531, 543-544, 546, 552
Donaldson, Rt. Rev. St Clair, 533&n-
    534, 546, 696
Douglas, Lady Alfred, 386
Douglas, Lord Alfred, 138n, 143,
    154n, 189, 196, 201, 222, 233n,
    324n, 359, 368, 386, 414, 430,
    435n, 508-509, 599
Douglas, Norman, 191n, 1947n, 195n,
    202, 404n
Doyle, Peter, 135n, 295n
Doyle, Sir Arthur Conan, 112&n,
    270n
Drumlanrig, Viscount (see: Kelhead,
    1st Baron)
Dudley, 1st Earl of, 99, 444n
Dudley, 2nd Earl of, 162&n, 471-472
Dudley, Georgina, Countess of,
    444&n
Dugdale, Blanche, 417n
Dugdale, John Stafford, 588
Duke, Colonel, 352
Duncan, Isadora, 299
Dunlo, Viscount & Viscountess (see
    Clancarty, 5th Earl & Belle,
    Countess of)
Dunraven, 3rd Earl of, 316n
Duvert, Tony, 606&n
Dyer, Alfred, 81&n-83, 87, 93
Edmunds, Dr James, 93&n
Edward VII, King, 29-32, 40-41, 43,
    46-50, 53, 57, 61, 68-74, 87n, 155,
    161, 209, 263, 269, 307, 385, 394,
    405-407, 416, 420-422, 424-425,
    435n, 446, 450, 457-458, 595, 635-
    636, 639-640, 642, 646-648, 652,
    655, 656-658, 660, 669-670
Edward VIII, King, 18n

Edwards, John Passmore, 373
Edwards, Rev. Edward John, 176&n-180, 680
Eliot, George, 293n, 294, 339
Elliott, George, 243&n, 245-246
Ellis, Havelock, 140, 146-147, 193
Elrick, Arthur Pennefather, 555-556
Elrick, Rev. Charles, 556
Ernst Ludwig, Grand Duke of Hesse, 139n
Esher, Eleanor, Viscountess, 32&n
Esher, William, 1st Viscount, 418, 461
Esher, Reginald, 2nd Viscount, 32&n, 68-69, 88, 93, 124-126&n, 155,167, 282, 324&n, 376, 386, 395, 408, 416, 418-423, 461, 685-686
Eugénie, Empress, 200
Eulenburg-Hertefeld, Philip, Prince zu, 110n, 197n, 282&n, 336n, 642, 652n, 668, 686
Euston, Earl of, 165&n-167, 184, 262, 269, 275, 390, 412, 681
Eyton, Rev. Robert, 180&n-181, 438
Fahmy, Marie Marguerite, 72n
Farman, Henri, 625&n
Farquhar, Horace, 1st Earl, 282n, 695n
Farquharson, Henry, 370-371
Farrar, Rev. Frederic, 289&n-290, 308, 450, 466
ffoulkes, Maude, 99n
Fife, Lord & 1st Duke of, 87&n, 368
Fillingham, Rev. Robert, 155n, 264n, 349&n-351, 371, 551-552, 680
Finlay, 1st Viscount, 223
Firbank, Ronald, 495
Fischof, Robert, 611
Fisher, Admiral, 1st Baron, 32, 50n,
Fitzpatrick, Douglas Graham Persse, 347n
Flower, Constance (see: Battersea, Constance Flower, Baroness)
Flower, Cyril (see: Battersea, Cyril Flower, 1st Baron)
Flower, James, 405
Flower, Lewis 'Peter', 261&n, 403
Flower, Philip William, 288-289, 301, 309, 373
Flynn, Errol, 553
Fogarty, Jack, 535
Ford, Howard, 503
Fortescue, Tim, 389n
Fowler, Ellen Thornycroft, 340-341

Fox-Pitt, St. George Lane, 324&n
Francis Joseph, Prince of Braganza, 185&n-188
Frankau, Julia, 376, 395
Fraser, (Alexander) Edmund, 574-575, 583, 590-594, 600-601, 615
Fraser, Ada Susan, 575
Fraser, Alisdair Hew Iain, 615
Fraser, Bernard, (see: Fraser-Ross, Bernard)
Fraser, John (father of Bernard), 573-576
Fraser, Susan Foulis (mother of Bernard) 217, 574, 577, 588&n, 600-601
Fraser-Ross, (John) Bernard, 199-200, 203, 213-214, 216-220, 224-239, 241-251, 253-259, 271-275, 279, 371, 377, 384, 388-389, 395, 400, 405, 410, 413-414, 443, 461-462, 470-472, 475, 493-494, 511, 513, 534, 541, 573-633, 644, 671-673, 678-679, 688, 705
Frederick II, the Great, 697
Frederick III, Kaiser, 276
Fremantle, Very Rev. William Henry Dean, 119&n
Fry, Oliver Armstrong, 269&n
Fullerton, Morton, 600n
Fyffe, Charles Alan, 348
Gabin, Jean, 619
Galloway, 10th Earl of, 162&n-165
Galton, Rev. Arthur, 605n
Gardner, Isabella Stewart, 486-487n
Gaskell, Mrs., 511
Gatty, Charles, 370-371
George III, King, 19, 35, 43n, 161, 302, 354, 668
George IV, King, 19, 608n, 668
George V, King, 18n, 43n, 112, 138n, 154n, 429n, 540
George VI, King, 18n, 499
George V, King of Hanover, 463
George, Prince, Duke of Cambridge, 161&n-162, 403
George, Prince, Duke of Kent, 324n
Georgevits, Lieutenant Guido von, 591
Gerry, William, 185-186
Gerstenberg, Arnold, 682n
Gide, André, 599-600
Gieseking, Walter, 624n
Gigliotti, Iolanda Cristina, 629&n

Gilbert, Sir Alfred, 111n, 337
Gill, Adrian Anthony, 63&n
Gill, Sir Charles, 243&n-245
Gillett, George, 82&n, 93
Gilmour, Thomas, 288&n
Ginnell, Laurence, 657&n, 661-668
Gladstone, Herbert, 1st Viscount,
    379&n, 389, 579, 582-583, 585-
    587, 639, 643-644, 662, 688
Gladstone, William Ewart, 32&n, 39,
    71, 80, 154, 267-268, 275, 294, 314,
    318, 319, 322-324, 334, 336-337,
    355, 357, 374, 409, 461, 474-475,
    478, 483, 686
Glyn, Rt. Rev. Edward Carr, 646&n
Godley, Hugh, 445
Goerz, Adolf, 377&n
Gomez, Louise (see: Iguerbouchène,
    Louise)
Goncourt, Edmond & Jules, 93&n
Gordon, Major-General Charles,
    88&n, 329, 432
Gordon-Cumming, Sir William, 71-72
Gordon-Lennox, Lord Henry, 80-81
Gorges, Captain Richard, 637&n-638,
    655, 657-659, 664-665
Gorst, John, 324n
Goss, Sir Edmund, 336n, 441&n
Gottsberger, William S., 96n
Gower, Lord Ronald, 33n, 38&n-
    39&n, 192-193, 277, 292, 318, 395,
    403, 413, 416, 417, 430, 470, 487,
    634, 637, 639, 641, 646, 660, 666-
    667, 674, 683-684, 687
Grafton, 7th Duke of, 165&n-167
Grantham, Sir William, 234, 239&n-
    250, 253, 257-258, 274, 384, 578-
    586
Grantham, William Wilson, 234, 243
Granville, 2nd Earl, 82&n
Gregory, Lady, 65
Grimston, Lady Waechter de, 21n
Grissell, Hartwell de la Garde, 495n
Grünfeld, Alfred, 611
Guest, Montague, 65&n-66, 213n
Gull, William, 71
Gurney, Edmund, 315&n-319, 338-
    339, 406
Gurney, Richard, 347
Gwynne, Oliver, 421
Gwynne-Holford, James, 320, 322,
    353
Haddo, Lord (see: Aberdeen, George,

2nd Marquess of)
Hadj, Messali, 622&n
Halali, Salim, 619&n, 623, 627, 633
Haldane, 1st Viscount, 366&n, 415,
    440
Hall, Radclyffe, 233
Hallam, Arthur, 123&n
Hallings, Mrs, 560, 562
Halsbury, Earl of, 73, 170&n-175,
    222-223, 405, 423, 452, 686
Hamilton, Lord Frederick, 478
Hamilton, Lord George, 407&n
Hammond, Charles, 166n, 167&n-168
Hanfstaengl, Ernst, 624n
Hankey, Frederick, 93&n, 303
Harcourt, Lewis, 1st Viscount, 85n,
    113&n-114, 386, 408&n-409, 416,
    418, 498, 686&n
Harcourt, Sir William, 85&n, 382n,
    408n
Harden, Maximillan, 652&n-653
Hardie, Keir, 50, 352
Hare, Augustus, 191&n, 365, 397
Harmsworth, Alfred (see: Northcliffe,
    1st Viscount)
Harmsworth, Sir Arthur Geoffrey,
    70n
Harrel, William, 642
Harris, Frank, 423n
Harris, Sir Augustus, 381&n
Harrison, Mary St Leger, 202n
Harte, Bret, 683n
Hatton, Arthur, 535
Hatton, Brian, 396&n
Haynes-Smith, William, 126n, 481n
Helena, Princess, Duchess of Albany,
    318n
Helfritz, Hans, 611n
Herbert, Edward, 545
Herbert, Very Rev. George, Dean of
    Hereford, 113-114
Herschell, Baron, 338&n
Hertford, 7th Marquess 104&n-106
Hichens, Robert, 684
Hillingdon, Baron, 347&n
Hird, Francis (Frank), 403&n, 430,
    487, 641-642, 660
Hirsch, Baron Maurice de, 47&n
Hirst, Alfred Livingstone, 609&n-610
Hobhouse, John Cam, 598
Hobson, Bulmer, 657&n-659
Hogg, Quintin, 430&n-432, 681
Holland, Baroness, 471&n-472

Holman, William, 234
Home, Daniel Dunglas, 316n
Hood, Sir Alexander, Duke of Bronte, 154&n, 345n, 470, 496
Hopkins, Gerald Manley, 123n
Hopkins, Manley, 123n
Houghton, 1st Baron, 302&n-303, 307- 308, 318
Hovelacque, Eugène, 603
Hughes, James Barrett, 118
Hughes, Thomas, 129
Humboldt, Alexander von, 697
Humphreys, Eliza Margaret (Mrs. Desmond), 100&n-104, 536
Hunt, Margaret Raine, 152n
Hunt, William Holman, 290&n
Hurst, Brian Desmond, 151n
Huskisson, William, 154n
Hutchinson, Rev. Charles Edward, 128n
Hutchinson, Capt. John de Mestre, 208-211, 217, 232, 236, 249
Hutt, Sir William, 478
Hyatt, James Hallet Lake, 380&n-381
Hyndman, Henry Mayers, 283&n
Iguerbouchène, Louise, 617&n, 623, 627-628
Iguerbouchène, Mohamad, 601-614, 617-633, 678, 680-681
Iguerbouchène, Saïd ben Ali & Sik Fatma bent Areski, 603&n, 605, 615, 618
Illingworth, Alfred, 354
Inge, Rev. William, 510n
Ingram, Edward, 21n
Irving, Laurence & Mabel, 96n
Isaacs, Sir Rufus (see: Reading, 1st Marquess of)
Isaacson, Elizabeth, 467
Isaacson, Frederick, 467
Isaacson, Violet (see: Beaumont, Violet, Baroness)
Isham, Sir Gyles, 21&n
Ives, George, 138&n-139, 144n, 145n, 183, 196, 260, 262, 265, 267, 409, 412, 421, 430-432, 453, 678
Jackson, Charles Kains, 144&n-145, 215, 296, 342, 508
Jackson, Huth, 544&n-545
Jackson, Richard Charles, Brother à Becket, 116&n-117
James, Henry, 30&n, 126, 291, 313, 315, 343, 441, 600, 674

Jebb, Sir Richard, 291&n-292, 452
Jeffery, Ada, 538
Jeffery, Frederick, 538
Jeffery, Hugh, 538
Jeffery, Kathleen (see Thorold, Kathleen),
Jeffries, Mary, 83&n-87, 167
Jenkins, Mrs, 93
Jennings, John Adolphus, 638&n
Jennings, The Ven. John, 466
Jennings, Louisa (see: Wylie, Louisa)
Jennings, Mrs. (mother of Louisa Wylie), 469-470
Jephson, Arthur, 486&n-487
Jerome, Jerome K., 143-144
Johnson, Dr. Samuel, 193, 610
Johnson, Ernlé, 324&n
Johnson, Francis, 21&n
Jowett, Benjamin, 119&n, 127, 133n
Jumean, Gilbert Marie, 616
Kane, Inspector John, 638-639, 666
Kaurt, Mohamed ben ('Belotte'), 597, 615-616
Kelhead, 1st Baron, 154&n, 196, 414
Kempff, Wilhelm, 624n
Keppel, Alice, 32, 42, 69, 70n
Keppel, Sonia, 42
Kergariou, Vicomte Joseph de, 279&n, 576, 578, 594, 616
Kertbeny, Karl-Maria, 110n
Killanin, 2nd Baron, 440&n-441
King, Rt. Rev. Edward, Bishop of Lincoln, 505, 513-514
Kingsley, Charles, 114
Kinross, 1st Baron, 164&n
Kinsey, Alfred, 195n
Kipling, Rudyard, 502, 549
Kitchener, 1st Earl, 95&n, 114&n, 437, 681
Knight, Mr. & Mrs., 500
Knollys, Sir Francis, Lord, 38&n, 69, 71, 168n, 420, 461, 639, 642
Knowles, Charles, 348&n
Krupp, Friedrich, 404&n
Labouchère, Emily (see: Thorold, Emily)
Labouchère, Henry, 52&n-54, 67, 92, 110, 117, 122, 168&n-171, 182, 226, 267-269&n, 350, 356, 379- 380, 399, 419, 450, 520, 653
Lalaing, Count Charles & Countess de, 453&n
Lamarr, Hedy, 619

Lamoricière, General, 599
Landrock, Ernest, 599
Lane, Sir Hugh, 683
Lather, Lieutenant-Colonel William, 539-540
Lawless, Emily, 329n, 458-459
Lawson, Sir Edward (see: Burnham, 1st Baron)
Lazarovich-Hrebelianovich, Princess, 61&n
Le Fanu, Rt. Rev. Henry Frewen, 544&n, 546
Leadbeater, Charles Webster, 541&n-543
Lees-Milne, James, 499-500, 686n
Leeves, Edward, 154n
Legge, Edward, 635&n
Lehmann, John, 151&n
Lehnert, Rudolf, 599
Lennox, Lord Henry (see Gordon-Lennox, Lord Henry)
Leopold II, King of Belgium, 83&n, 86, 483n
Leopold, Prince, Duke of Albany, 318, 396, 594
Leslie, Sir Shane, 48&n-49, 60, 72
Levy, Joseph Moses, 269n
Lewis, Elizabeth, Lady, 233
Lewis, Sir George, 233, 281-282, 367, 390, 405, 418, 425, 458, 491
Lewis, Rosa, 425&n
Lincoln, Abraham, 697
Lincoln, Bishop of (see King, Rt. Rev. Edward)
Lincolnshire, Marquess of, 358&n, 434, 688-689
Lindsay, Jack, 526
Linton, Lynn, 88&n
Lipton, Sir Thomas, 76n, 683n
Lister, Sir Reginald, 406n, 409&n
Llandaff, 1st Viscount, 107&n, 171-172, 175
Lloyd, Mary, 329
London, Bishop of (see Winnington Ingram, Rt. Rev. A.F.)
Londonderry, 7th Marquess of, 461
Louise, Princess, Duchess of Argyll, 277&n-278, 329-330, 335, 343, 364, 383, 388, 396, 406, 416-417, 445-448, 484, 639, 687
Lovat, Baron, 573
Love, William, 683n
Lownie, Andrew, 693&n-694

Loy, Mina, 501&n
Loynes, John, 214, 234
Lubbock, Percy, 600&n
Ludwig II, King of Bavaria, 466
Luhan, Mabel Dodge, 501n
Lurgan, Baron, 162&n
Lutyens, Sir Edwin, 327&n, 339-341, 343-345, 363, 425, 446, 458, 674
Lützow, Anna, Countess von, 577&n
Luxmoore, Henry Elford, 126
Lynar, Count Guido zu, 156&n
Lynch, Archbishop John Joseph, 121n
Lyne, Rev. Joseph Leycester, Father Ignatius, 117&n-120, 370, 680
Lynn, Detective-Sergeant, 217-218
Lys, Francis, 544-547
Lyttelton, Spencer, 154&n, 409, 420, 440, 445, 448
Lytton, 1st Earl of, 75, 365
Macdonald, Sir Hector Archibald, 434&n-438
Mackenzie, James, 47
Macnaghten, Sir Melville, 182, 196&n
Madan, Falconer, 176n, 680
Maecenas, Gaius Cilnius, 441&n
Magnay, Frederick William, 231-232, 237
Maguire, Rochfort, 382&n
Malet, Sir Edward Baldwin, 682n
Mallet, Sir Bernard, 406&n
Mallet, Sir Louis, 406&n
Mallet, Sir Louis du Pan, 406n, 409n
Mallock, William, 345&n-346
Mandeville, Alexis Moreton, 646&n, 653
Manning, Cardinal Henry Edward, 338&n
Manning, Frederic, 605n
Marguerite, Comtesse du Planty (see: Cunliffe-Owen, Marguerite)
Marie, Dowager Empress of Russia, 364
Marie, Queen of Romania, 450
Marie Louise, Princess, of Schleswig-Holstein, 434&n
Marjoribanks, Edward (see: Tweedmouth, 2nd Baron)
Markham, Daisy, 107
Marshall, John, 613
Martyn, Thomas, 542
Mary Adelaide, Princess, Duchess of Teck, 43&n
Mary, Queen, 43n, 105, 429&n,

513&n
Massingham, Henry William, 178&n, 267
Matsell, Arthur Harry, 236
Matthews, Charles Skinner, 598
Matthews, Henry (see: Llandaff, 1st Viscount)
Mayne, William, 39
McCarthy, Justin, 324n
McConnel, Elspeth, 530&n-531, 538, 557
McKenna, Reginald, 666&n-667
Meath, Earl & Countess of, 64&n-65
Melvill, Sir Maxwell, 479-480
Mendl, Ella ('Elsie'), Lady, 324n
Mendl, Sir Charles, 324&n
Mensdorff, Count Albert, 591&n
Menzies, Sir Robert, 565
Meradji, Arezki ('André'), 626&n-627
Meredith, George, 364&n, 441n
Merrill, George, 141&n-143, 148-149, 152-153
Meyer, Carl, 377&n
Meynell, Wilfrid, 262&n, 642
Michelangelo, 134, 294
Michelham, 1st Baron, 70n
Miles, Eustace, 410&n
Mill, John Stuart, 61
Millet, Frank, 343
Milnes, Richard Monckton (see Houghton, 1st Baron)
Minahan, Jeremiah, 83&n
Moffatt, Rev. Henry, 350
Molique, Anna, 329n
Montefiore, Alan, 457&n
Montefiore, Leonard, 456-457
Moor, Norman, 128n, 133n, 136
Moore, George, 329&n, 342&n, 607, 688
Moore-Browne, George, 435
Mordaunt, Sir Charles & Lady, 70-71
Morgan, Evan (see: Tredegar, 2nd Viscount)
Morgues, Alexander 'Alec', 381
Morland, Maitland Francis, 184-185
Morley, Arnold, 336&n, 354, 379, 400
Morley, John, 1st Viscount, 366&n-367, 440, 688
Morris, William, 139n
Morshead, Sir Owen, 687
Mosscockle, Harriet, 106&n
Mountbatten, 1st Earl, 693&n-694
Mozart, Wolfgang Amadeus, 608

Mundella, Anthony, 85
Myers, Eveleen, 365
Myers, Frederic, 134&n, 137, 293-295, 307, 315-319, 338, 365, 382-384, 396, 416, 458, 576, 483-484
Nathan, Maud, 287&n
Nevill, Lady Dorothy, 364&n, 395
Neville-Rolfe, Eustace, 191&n-192, 197, 200-201
Newcastle, 4th Duke of, 36
Newman, Cardinal John Henry, 114
Newton, 2nd Baron, 591&n-594
Newton, Arthur, 166&n-167, 184, 223, 231-232, 234-235, 237, 685
Ney, Elly, 624
Nicholson, John Gambril, 131&n, 143, 214, 607
Noailles, Helene, Comtesse de, 486
Nobbs, George (see: Widdows, Francis)
Noe, Lewis, 485
Noel, Roden, 317&n-318
Nollekens, Joseph, 314
Noorden, Karl Harko von, 445-446
Nordau, Max, 50&n-51&n
Northampton, 6th Marquess of, 107
Northbrook, 1st Earl of, 488
Northcliffe, 1st Viscount, 69-70, 271, 276, 415, 653
Northcote, 1st Baron, 126
Northumberland, 6th Duke of, 337
Norton, Henry, 317n
Norton, John, 520&n, 535, 542
Norton, Laura, 608n
Norton, Rictor, 680
Nugée, Rev. George, 115&n-117, 432
O'Brien, William, 155
O'Brien, Manuel Donatus, 148&n-149&n
O'Connor, Thomas Power, 170&n, 178, 267, 269, 287, 647
Origo, Iris; d'Orci, Marchesa di Val, 501n
Ouida (see: Ramé, Maria Louise)
Oxford and Asquith, 1st Earl of, 126&n-127, 147, 250, 268, 311, 325, 357, 379, 385, 406, 415, 429n, 440, 586, 662, 688
Oxford and Asquith, Margot, Countess of, 126n, 195&n, 680
Paine, William, 432n
Park, Frederick, 491
Parke, Ernest, 163&n, 166-167, 170,

175, 269, 661
Parris, Matthew, 686n
Parsons, Alfred, 343&n
Parsons, Beatrice, 456n
Pasha, Ahmad Arabi, 323-324
Paston-Cooper, George, 349&n
Pater, Walter, 116&n, 128, 299-
    300&n, 605n
Paton, Rev. Dr. John, 329&n-330
Paul, Pope VI, 495&n
Pavia, Isidore Leo, 620&n
Pearson, Sir Arthur, 270&n, 653&n
Pease, Sir Alfred, 458&n
Pelham-Clinton, Lord Arthur, 491&n
Pembroke, 14th Earl of, 126
Percival, John, 133n
Perkins, Edward Hudson, 483
Peterborough, Bishop of (see
    Glyn, Rt. Rev. Edward)
Piaf, Edith, 626&n, 629&n, 633
Pickering, Neville, 55n
Pigott, Sir Paynton, 231&n, 578
Piper, John, 20
Pius, Pope XI, 495-496
Platen, Count von, 194&n
Plato, 90n, 119&n, 124, 133, 134, 136,
    142, 201&n, 294, 394, 441
Playfair, Sir Lambert, 372, 594, 597,
    603
Pless, Princess Daisy of, 65
Podmore, Frank, 317&n-319
Poland, Sir Harry, 173&n
Pollitt, Jerome, 481n
Ponsonby, Sir Frederick (see: Sysonby,
    1st Baron)
Portland, 3rd Duke, 85n
Portland, 5th Duke of, 95n
Portsmouth, 6th Earl of, 409&n
Poulenc, Francis, 632
Powell, Enoch, 389
Pratt, James, 111
Prime-Stevenson, Edward, 202&n-203
Primrose, Neil, 497-498
Probyn, Sir Dighton, 168&n, 307, 402,
    405
Professor Livinson, 604, 608
Puleston, John, 81&n
Purdom, Edmund, 495
Queensberry, 9th Marquess of, 74&n,
    97, 154n, 196, 324n, 407, 414, 635n
Quennell, Sir Peter, 194n
Radjef, Belkacem, 623, 627
Raikes, Gerald, 521&n

Ramé, Maria Louise, 443, 595&n
Reading, 1st Marquess of, 666&n
Reddie, James Campbell, 98&n, 303
Redmond, William, 650&n, 652
Rees-Mogg, William, Baron, 690&n
Regina, Duke della, 197&n
Reid, Susan, Lady, 422
Rendel, George, 198-199, 354, 378,
    511, 523, 534, 544
Rendel, Stuart, 354
Rentoul, James, 358
Reynolds-Ball, Eustace, 192
Rhodes, Cecil, 55&n-56, 95, 376,
    382&n, 386-387&n, 681
Rice, Rev. John Morland, 126
Ridgeway, Sir West, 435
Robinson, Fletcher, 270&n
Rogers, James, 121
Rolfe, Frederick, 195&n
Rorem, Ned, 632&n
Rose, Sir Charles, 265-266&n
Rosebery, 5th Earl of, 41n, 67&n, 74,
    126, 153-155, 174, 195-203, 222,
    268, 288, 304&n, 307, 319, 322,
    343, 355, 367&n, 368, 372-373,
    377-379, 383, 395, 401-402, 410,
    413-415, 418, 420, 453, 478, 492-
    493, 497-498, 511, 519, 687-689,
    700
Rosebery, Hannah, Countess of, 197,
    200, 307, 312n, 414
Rosenberg, Alfred, 622n
Ross, Robert, 495n, 599
Rossetti, William Michael, 137&n
Rothschild, Alfred de, 292&n, 372-
    373, 377, 411-413, 448, 451, 671
Rothschild, Alice de, 378&n
Rothschild, Anselm von & Charlotte,
    197n, 304
Rothschild, Sir Anthony de, 304&n,
    307
Rothschild, Dorothy de, 407&n
Rothschild, Emma, Lady, 47n, 328&n
Rothschild, Ferdinand, Baron de,
    197&n, 304, 306, 380
Rothschild, James de, 497&n
Rothschild, Leopold de, 292&n, 304-
    305, 375, 395, 406
Rothschild, Baron Lionel and
    Baroness Charlotte de, 292&n
Rothschild, Louise, Lady de, 304&n-
    305, 307, 310, 335, 360-361, 457
Rothschild, Baron Mayer Amschel &

Baroness Juliana de, 307
Rothschild, Nathaniel 'Natty' Mayer, 1st Baron de, 47&n, 197, 328n, 323, 378, 407
Rothschild, Nathaniel 'Puggy' Mayer von, 197n
Rozenraad, Octave, 446
Rudbeck, Olof, Baron, 343
Ruskin, John, 139n, 294&n, 318
Russell, 2nd Earl, 184&n-185, 324
Russell, Sir Charles, 268
Russell, George, 99, 319&n, 333, 338, 383, 454-455
Russell, Sir Odo, 495&n
Rust, Rev. Thomas and Ethel 521&n, 525, 529, 537-538, 567
Sala, George Augustus, 97&n-98
Salisbury, 3rd Marquess of, 60&n, 66-67, 71, 74-76, 163, 168&n, 170-172&n
Salisbury, 4th Marquess of, 172n
Saltoun, 19th Baron, 62n
Sandwich, 8th Earl of, 396&n, 684-685
Sandwich, 11th Earl of, 684-685
Sandys, Frederick, 302&n, 452
Sardanapalus, 325-326, 455
Sargent, Frederick, 338
Sargent, John Singer, 233n, 343
Sarreluis, Anne-Laure, 626
Sarrouy, André, 601-608, 610-612, 617, 620, 631
Sassoon, Sir Philip, 409n, 451n
Saul, John ('Jack'), 85&n, 167, 222, 412, 642
Scott, Benjamin, 82-83, 87, 88
Scott, Clement, 339&n, 347
Scotto, Vincent, 619
Searight, Arthur Kenneth, 193&n
Seddon, Frederick, 73
Selborne, 2nd Earl of, 211
Selim, 486
Service, Robert W., 527-528
Seymour, Major Sir Edward ('Teddie'), 420&n
Seys, Rosemary, 456&n
Shackleton, Francis ('Frank'), 636&n-643, 645, 655, 657-661, 664-665
Shackleton, Sir Ernest, 636
Shaftesbury, 7th Earl of, 111, 207
Shairp, John, 473
Shakespeare, William, 33n, 40n, 277, 294, 321, 377n, 384, 512, 683n

Shaw, George Bernard, 147
Sherbrooke, 1st Viscount, 78&n
Sherman, Charles, 185, 187
Sidgwick, Arthur, 317&n
Sidgwick, Henry, 316&n-317
Simpson, Henry ('Harry') Butler, 224&n, 581, 584
Sims, Francis, 231-232
Sims, Manley, 402-403&n
Sing, John Millington, 512&n-513
Sitwell, Sir Osbert, 45&n
Skinner, Gifford, 150&n-151
Skittles (see: Walters, Catherine)
Slane, Baron de, 371n
Smith, George Albert, 319&n, 338
Smith, Thomas Eustace, 33n, 335n
Smith, Timothy D'Arch, 673
Socrates, 124, 201, 316, 393, 441
Solomon, Simeon, 114n, 303&n-304, 384
Somerset, Lord Arthur, 165&n-168, 172, 223, 268, 401, 416-419, 438n, 685n
Somerset, Lady Henry, 33&n, 94-96, 308n, 335, 364
Somerset, Lord Henry, 33&n-34, 335&n, 394, 435n
Spencer, 5th Earl, 434
Spencer, 6th Earl, 336&n
Spencer, 7th Earl, 196&n
Spencer, Lady Sarah, 329
Spender, Arthur, 500
Speyer, Sir Edgar, 346&n-347, 367, 442n
Spies, Walter, 612n
Sprowston, Vicar of, 239
Stanley, Dorothy, Lady, 483-484, 486-488
Stanley, Henry Morton, 14, 483-487
Stanley, Lavinia, 180&n
Stead, William Thomas, 48&n, 87-93, 109, 170, 266, 335, 387, 418
Stenzel, Alma, 445&n
Stephenson, Sir Augustus, 173&n, 281
Stocks, Rev. C., 515
Stoker, Bram, 139&n, 295-296
Stonor, Sir Harry, 154&n
Stopford, Albert (Bertie), 445&n
Stracey, Gilbert Hardinge, 231-232, 235, 237
Strachey, Lytton, 132&n
Straight, Sir Douglas, 266&n
Strakosch, Sir Henry, 377&n

Strangford, 8th Viscount, 60
Strathearn, Jessie, 445&n
Stuart-Young, John Moray, 599&n
Studd, Sir Kynaston, 432&n
Sturgis, Howard, 126&n, 481n
Sturgis, Julian, 315&n
Suffield, Baron, 347, 406
Sutherland, Millicent, Duchess of, 67n, 470
Swanson, Donald, 358n
Swinburne, Algernon, 302n, 303&n-304, 366n
Symonds, John Addington, 127&n-128, 133&n-136, 138-142, 146-147, 150, 193-194, 293, 295-296, 300&n, 317&n-318, 346n, 369, 441n, 480, 482n, 508
Sysonby, 1st Baron, 32&n
Telfer, Charles, 113-114
Temple, Reginald ('Reggie'), 501&n
Tennant, Gertrude, 483
Tennant, Winifred, 365
Tennyson, Alfred, 1st Baron, 122&n-123&n, 134, 287n, 294-296, 302n, 306, 318, 331, 397, 548
Tennyson, Alfred (jnr), 397&n
Tennyson, Charles, 397&n
Teschenberg, Baron Hermann von, 610&n
Tewfik, Khedive, 323
Thaw, Alice Cornelia, 104
Thompson, Edward Roffe, 77&n, 189, 240
Thompson, William Marcus, 30&n-31, 53, 55-56, 79, 94, 96, 98-100, 107, 162-164, 169-170, 175, 202, 266, 268, 280, 319n, 387, 423n, 436-439, 450, 656
Thorold, Algar Labouchère, 269n
Thorold, Rev. Algernon Charles (father of Arthur), 23, 237-238, 246, 504&n-506, 510, 513-514, 554
Thorold, Rev. Algernon Herbert, 505n, 513, 522, 540, 544, 566
Thorold, Rt. Rev. Anthony, 252&n, 269, 274
Thorold, Arthur Charles, 20-25, 198&n-201, 203, 214-216, 119-220, 223-259, 266, 271-274, 377, 384, 388-389, 395, 400, 405, 410, 414, 443, 455, 475, 493-494, 496, 504-573, 578-578-580, 582-588, 617, 671-673, 681, 696-699, 705

Thorold, Edith Mary (mother of Arthur), 504&n, 503, 514, 517, 540
Thorold, (Edith) Muriel, 505n, 512, 517, 554
Thorold, Emily, 268
Thorold, Rev. Dr. Ernest Hayford, 18, 505n, 512, 513, 533, 540, 545, 567, 570,
Thorold, Dame Eugenia, 21
Thorold, Rev. Henry Croyland, 18&n-25, 570-571, 699
Thorold, Jessie, 557&n, 560-565, 567
Thorold, Sir John Henry, 12th Baronet, 18
Thorold, Major Sir John George, 13th Baronet, 19, 570
Thorold, Rev. John Robert, 571&n, 699n
Thorold, Jeffery, 540, 554, 564, 566-569, 571-572
Thorold, Rev. John Robert, 559, 680
Thorold, Kathleen, 537&n-541, 544, 549, 554, 557, 571
Thorold, Mary Sophia, 571
Thorold, Montague George, 238
Thorold, Patrick, 541&n, 554, 566, 569, 571
Thorold, (Violet) Hilda, 505n, 512, 517, 564, 566
Thurston, Helen, 492-493
Tilly, Vesta, 66&n
Tissot, James, 315
Tredegar, 2nd Viscount, 495&n-496
Tree, Sir Herbert Beerbolm, 367&n
Trelawny, Maud, 470
Trevelyan, Raleigh, 684n
Troubetzkoy, Prince Paolo, 344
Troup, Sir Charles Edward, 585&n-586
Truman, Mrs, 150
Tuesley, Jack, 532
Tuke, Henry Scott, 214&n-215, 296, 682&n
Tweedmouth, 2nd Baron, 267, 336&n, 686
Tyrwhitt-Wilson, Harry, 87&n
Ulrichs, Karl Heinrich, 142&n
Upcher, (Henry) Thomas Simpson, 347n
Upward, Allen, 202n
Valdemar, Prince of Denmark, 221n
Vansittart, Robert, 1st Baron, 593&n
Vardon, Henry 'Harry', 397&n, 400,

808

410

Vaughan, Fred, 135n, 295n
Vaughan, Rev. Bernard, 102&n
Verney, Captain Edmund, 348&n
Vicars, Sir Arthur, 636&n-641, 643-
    646, 641, 643-646, 648-649, 651-
    652, 654, 658-659, 664
Victoria, Princess, 209, 434
Victoria, Queen, 32, 37, 41&n, 43, 62,
    65, 79, 92, 95, 105, 112, 122, 133,
    277, 318&n, 337, 342, 355, 358,
    378, 382, 396, 425, 429n, 434, 443,
    480, 481, 493, 505, 506, 513, 520,
    575, 595&n, 686
Vidal, Gore, 495
Virgil, 293n, 342&n, 393
Vladimir, Grand Duchess (see:
    Maria Pavlovna)
Voelklein, Franz Gustav, 387n
Vom Dorp, Iwane Irmgard
    ('Yvonne'), 623&n-624, 628-629
Vom Dorp, Karl, 623n
Wade, John, 62n
Wallop, Frederick, 470&n
Walpole, Sir Robert, 75&n
Walsh, Francis ('Frank'), 396&n, 685
Walters, Catherine ('Skittles'), 99&n,
    422, 474
Walters, Rev. Huth, 176&n, 680
Wandsworth, 1st Baron, 355n
Warren, Edward Perry, 613&n
Warren, Sir Charles, 73
Warwick, Daisy, Countess of, 32&n,
    48, 67n, 168n
Waugh, Evelyn, 494&n
Webb, Sidney & Beatrice, 433&n-434
Webster, Richard (see: Alverstone, 1st
Viscount)
Wedgwood, James, 542&n-543
Weguelin, Hugh, 440&n, 493
Welby, 1st Baron, 375&n-376
Welldon, Rt. Rev. Dr. James, 481&n-
    483, 486-487&n
Wells, Sir Spencer, 380&n
Wemyss, Mary, Countess of, 76
Were, Anne Isabella, 557n
Were, Frank, 557&n, 563, 567
West, Sir Algernon, 355&n
Westminster, 2nd Duke of, 413&n
Weyer, Eleanor van der (see:
    Esher, Eleanor, Viscountess)
Wharton, Edith, 126n, 600&n
Whewell, William, 291

Whistler, James, 314315, 326
Whitaker, Caterina ('Tina'), 684
White, Arnold, 51&n, 261, 280, 329,
    338, 349, 442n, 689n
White, Joseph William Gleeson,
    326&n
Whitman, Walt, 51, 132n, 134-139,
    142-143&n, 155, 295&n-299, 301-
    303, 309, 312, 342&n, 362&n, 369,
    393&n, 413, 432, 458, 485, 487n,
    682&n-683, 697
Widdows, Francis, 118&n-122, 680
Wilberforce, Rt. Rev. Ernest, 443
Wilberforce, Rev. (Albert) Basil, 443,
    448, 579&n-580, 582
Wilberforce, William, 579
Wilde, Oscar, 51-52, 74, 94, 96-97,
    101, 129, 139, 143&n-144, 146,
    151-152, 157, 159, 173, 183-184,
    189, 196, 201-202, 216, 222-223,
    233&n, 243, 250, 255-256, 271,
    277, 292, 294-295, 298&n, 300,
    312, 315, 318, 324, 338, 359, 370,
    376-377, 386&n, 406-407&n, 411-
    415, 430-431, 482, 495n, 501&n,
    508, 510, 515, 519, 588, 599-600,
    610, 635n, 669
Williams, Montagu, 42, 44, 84-85
Williamson, Charles, 685
Williamson, 'Victor' Ulverston
    Vincent, 536-537
Winckley, Rev. Alfred Reginald,
    558&n
Winterton, 6th Earl, 668&n
Winnington Ingram, Rt. Rev. A.F.,
    Bishop of London, 49, 90, 130n
Wolfe de, Elsie (see: Mendl, Ella
    ('Elsie'), Lady)
Wolff, Henry Drummond, 324n
Wolseley, Garnet, Field-Marshall 1st
    Viscount 440&n-441
Wolseley, Louisa, Viscountess,
    440&n-441
Wolton, Eric, 194n
Wood, Alfred, 189-190, 233n
Woodgate, Walter Bradford, 508&n
Wookey, James, 86&n-87
Woolf, Leonard, 132&n
Wratislaw, Theodore, 144&n
Wright, Whitaker, 428
Wykeham, William of, 548&n
Wylie, Alexander Henry, 460-474, 679
Wylie, Arthur Kinnaird, 462n, 466

Wylie, Charlotte Ethel, 462n, 474
Wylie, George Crosbie, 462&n-463, 470
Wylie, Henry Philip, 462n
Wylie, Louisa, 466, 468-470
Wylie, Napier Macleod, 462n
Wylie, Sir Francis James, 679n
Wyllie, Amelia, Lady, 476
Wyllie, Francis ('Frank') Robert Shaw, 474-490, 679
Wyllie, General Sir William, 476

Wyllie, Sir Curzon, 489
Wyndham, Hon. Percy, 386&n
York, Archbishop of, 30
Yorke, Alexander ('Alick'), 154-155&n, 306, 318, 484
Yorke, Annie, 305&n-306, 308-309&n, 320, 323, 328, 356, 360-361, 371, 439, 446, 453-455, 457
Yorke, Eliot, 306&n
Yorke, Victor, 306&n
Younger, 1st Viscount, 70n

Milton Keynes UK
Ingram Content Group UK Ltd.
UKHW011353030823
426278UK00016B/141/J